CONTENTS

PART III: THE MUʿTAZILITES AND SHĪʿITES

COMMANDING RIGHT AND FORBIDDING WRONG IN ISLAMIC THOUGHT

What kind of duty do we have to try to stop other people doing wrong? The question is intelligible in just about any culture, but few of them seek to answer it in a rigorous fashion. The most striking exception is found in the Islamic tradition, where 'commanding right and forbidding wrong' is a central moral tenet already mentioned in the Koran. As a historian of Islam whose research has ranged widely over space and time, Michael Cook is well placed to interpret this complex yet fascinating subject. His book, which represents the first sustained attempt to map the history of Islamic reflection on this obligation, covers the origins of Muslim thinking about 'forbidding wrong', the relevant doctrinal developments over the centuries in all the major Islamic sects and schools, and its significance in Sunnī and Shīʿite thought today. In this way, the book contributes to the understanding of contemporary Islamic politics and ideology and raises fundamental questions for the comparative study of ethics.

MICHAEL COOK is Cleveland E. Dodge Professor of Near Eastern Studies in the Department of Near Eastern Studies, Princeton University. His publications include *Population Pressure in Rural Anatolia, 1450–1600* (1972), *Early Muslim Dogma* (1981) and most recently *The Koran: A Very Short Introduction* (2000).

COMMANDING RIGHT AND FORBIDDING WRONG IN ISLAMIC THOUGHT

MICHAEL COOK

PRINCETON UNIVERSITY

CAMBRIDGE
UNIVERSITY PRESS

CAMBRIDGE UNIVERSITY PRESS
Cambridge, New York, Melbourne, Madrid, Cape Town, Singapore,
São Paulo, Delhi, Dubai, Tokyo

Cambridge University Press
The Edinburgh Building, Cambridge CB2 8RU, UK

Published in the United States of America by Cambridge University Press, New York

www.cambridge.org
Information on this title: www.cambridge.org/9780521130936

First published 2000
Fourth printing with corrections 2006
This digitally printed version 2010

A catalogue record for this publication is available from the British Library

Library of Congress Cataloguing in Publication data

Cook, M. A.
Commanding right and forbidding wrong in Islamic thought / Michael Cook.
p. cm.
Includes bibliographical references and index.
ISBN 0 521 66174 9
1. Islamic ethics. 2. Religious life – Shīʿah. 3. Religious life – Islam.
4. Islam – Doctrines. I. Title.
BJ1291.C66 2000 297.5–dc21 99-054807

ISBN 978-0-521-66174-4 Hardback
ISBN 978-0-521-13093-6 Paperback

PART IV: OTHER SECTS AND SCHOOLS

PREFACE

In the early evening of Thursday 22 September 1988, a woman was raped at a local train station in Chicago in the presence of several people.

A brief account of the incident appeared that Sunday in the *New York Times*, based on what the police had said on the Friday.[1] The salient feature of the incident in this account was that nobody had moved to help the victim, and her cries had gone unheeded – for all that the rape took place during the rush hour. As Detective Daisy Martin put it: 'Several people were looking and she asked them for help, and no one would help.'

A longer account which likewise appeared on the Sunday in the *Chicago Tribune*[2] placed the matter in a very different light. Quoting what the police had said on the Saturday, the article began by stating that six bystanders were to be recommended for citizen's awards for their work in helping the police arrest and identify the suspect. The account that followed emphasised two features of the situation which did not emerge from the notice in the *Times*. The first was that the rape took place in a part of the station to which access was blocked by an exit-only turnstile. The second was that the bystanders were confused in their understanding of what was going on: the rapist had ordered his victim to smile, which she did. Although at one point she reportedly mouthed the word 'help', it was only after her assailant had run off that she screamed. Initially, at least, the bystanders took the woman to be engaged in voluntary sex. But one young bystander, Randy Kyles, took a second look and thought, 'Man, this is strange.' Something seemed not to be right, so he did not get on his train when it came in. (Others on the platform, by contrast, remarked that what was happening was weird, but nevertheless boarded the train.) When the victim ran up the steps screaming that she had been raped, Kyles chased

[1] *The New York Times*, 25 September 1988, 33.

[2] *The Chicago Tribune*, 25 September 1988, Section 2, 1. All further information on the incident is taken from this account.

after the rapist, eventually flagging down a police car and getting him arrested. Kyles later explained his action as follows: 'I had to do something to help that woman. It just wasn't right. It could have been my mother, my aunt, one of my mother's friends.'[3]

It is clear from these accounts that neither paper considered a rape at a local station in Chicago to be newsworthy in itself. The focus of journalistic attention – and the anticipated focus of the reader's interest – was the conduct of the bystanders. The account given in the *Times*, which went back to Detective Daisy Martin's statements on the Friday, placed their behaviour in a most unflattering light: though they greatly outnumbered the lone rapist, they had simply stood by and let it happen. The implication was that their conduct was shameful, and the reader reacts with appropriate indignation. How differently we would have behaved had we been there! Or at least, we hope we would have.[4]

The account given in the *Tribune*, by contrast, suggests that at least some of the bystanders, and Kyles in particular, behaved commendably. They had two good excuses for not intervening during the rape itself – the physical layout of the station, and the appearance of consent created by the coerced smiles of the woman, even if these did not look quite right. Kyles himself behaved with energy and courage when the situation became clear. He felt that he had to do something to help the woman, just as we would have felt had we been there; and we hope that we would have acted as well as he did in the distinctly confusing circumstances of the case.

Underlying these two accounts, and the remarks of Martin and Kyles, is a broad moral consensus.[5] One cannot just stand by and watch a

[3] I leave aside the roles of the other bystanders commended by the police; the part they played is in fact somewhat obscure in the account.

[4] But then again, what if the rapist had turned out to have a gun? There is no indication that he did, although he had a record of criminal violence. He had been in jail since February after robbing a young woman and breaking her nose with a bottle, and had only been released the previous week through a clerical error. During the rape he likewise threatened his victim with a bottle. But confronting a man with an apparently unbroken bottle is significantly less dangerous than confronting a man with a gun.

[5] Just how widely this consensus is in fact shared by the American population at large is not a question that need be taken up here. There are certainly cases where, as represented in the *New York Times* version of our incident, bystanders look on and do nothing, and such behaviour can easily be read as a product of callous indifference. A notorious example of such inaction is the murder of Kitty Genovese in Queens in 1964, in the course of a series of stabbings witnessed by thirty-eight people (see M. Hunt, *The compassionate beast: what science is discovering about the humane side of humankind*, New York 1990, 128f.; someone did shout 'Let that girl alone!', but took no further action). However, the research of social psychologists suggests that such inaction is more likely to be a product of what has been dubbed 'the bystander effect': the very fact that a number of people are present socially inhibits each one of them from stepping forward (*ibid.*, 132–5; I am

woman, even a complete stranger, being raped in a public place.[6] Either one must do something about it; or one must have good and specific reasons for not doing anything. In other words, we have a clear conception that we have some kind of duty not just to behave decently ourselves, but to prevent others from doing things to their fellow humans which are outrageously wrong.[7] Yet in everyday life we lack a name for the duty, still less a general formulation of the situations to which it applies and the circumstances that dispense us from it. The value is there, but it is not one that our culture has developed and systematised. 'It just wasn't right' is the bottom line in Kyles's explanation of what he did; the 'just' signals that, had he been pressed to explain himself further, he would have had nothing to say. We either understand or we don't. In fact, of course, we understand perfectly well, and some of us can on occasion wax quite eloquent on the subject; but our culture provides us with no ready-made articulation of our understanding. It is true that lawyers and philosophers carry on a discussion of the conditions under which we have a duty of 'rescue'.[8] But this discussion is too arcane to be described as a possession of our culture at large. Randy Kyles had clearly not heard of it; nor, for that matter, had I, until I became aware of it as a by-product of my research on Islam.

Islam, by contrast, provides both a name and a doctrine for a broad moral duty of this kind. The name – *al-amr bi'l-ma'rūf wa'l-nahy 'an al-munkar* – is somewhat unwieldy, as is its literal translation, 'commanding right and forbidding wrong'. For simplicity, therefore, I shall usually shorten the Arabic to *al-amr bi'l-ma'rūf* in my notes, which in any case are intended mainly for the erudite and the intrepid. In my text, where I try as far as possible to avoid inflicting naked Arabic on the reader, I will normally refer to

indebted to Rhoda Howard for referring me to this very readable survey of research on altruism). If we sought to establish the extent of an American consensus, the key question would not be whether people act in such situations, but rather whether they feel ashamed when they do nothing.

[6] On the other hand the bystanders, though 'shocked and amazed', do not seem to have had a problem with standing by while a couple had sex in a public place, provided the element of coercion was absent; and there is no indication that subsequent commentators felt differently. Not all cultures would take this view.

[7] I have deliberately left blurred at this point a subtle but significant distinction brought to my attention by Margaret Gilbert. Does the duty arise from the fact that the rapist is doing wrong, or from the fact that the victim is being wronged? Kyles himself is not very clear about this. He felt he had to do something to help that woman; yet what he actually did was not to help her in any material sense, but rather to bring the wrongdoer to justice. I shall return to this distinction (see below, ch. 20, section 2).

[8] See, for example, J. Feinberg, *The moral limits of the criminal law*, New York and Oxford 1984–8, vol. 1, ch. 4; T. C. Grey, *The legal enforcement of morality*, New York 1983, ch. 4.

the duty as 'forbidding wrong'; this sounds less awkward in English than 'commanding right'.[9] The existence and general character of the duty is well known to Islamicists. It has received passing attention in one connection or another from a good many scholars, and is the subject of a concise but informative encyclopaedia article.[10] It is the purpose of this book to build on this by providing a full monographic treatment of forbidding wrong.[11] I should make it clear from the start that my interest here is in the duty of individual believers; this book is only tangentially concerned with the place of rulers in forbidding wrong, or with the officially appointed censor (*muḥtasib*) and his administrative role (*ḥisba*).

The first objective of the book is to set out an intelligible account of the duty as it appears in the scholastic literature of Islam. In one way this

[9] Occasionally a distinction is insisted on between *al-amr bi'l-ma'rūf* and *al-nahy 'an al-munkar*, but this is the exception rather than the rule. The Persian exegete Maybudī (writing in 520/1126) quotes an anonymous saying to the effect that *al-nahy 'an al-munkar* is a weightier duty than *al-amr bi'l-ma'rūf* (*Kashf al-asrār*, Tehran 1331–9 sh., 2:234.9 (to Q3:104); for this work, see below, ch. 2, note 23); the Ḥanbalite Abū Ya'lā ibn al-Farrā' (d. 458/1066) makes a distinction between the two (see below, ch. 6, note 127); likewise some accounts of the duty separate the two for purposes of exposition, or treat only one of them (see, for example, below, ch. 9, note 121, and ch. 11, note 69). On the other hand, the Imāmī exegete Ṭabrisī (d. 548/1153) remarks à propos of Q9:112 that *al-amr bi'l-ma'rūf* includes *al-nahy 'an al-munkar*, and that it is as though they are one thing (*ka-annahumā shay' wāḥid*) (*Majma' al-bayān fī tafsīr al-Qur'ān*, Qumm 1403, 3:76.4; cf. also the Shāfi'ite Kamāl al-Dīn ibn al-Zamlakānī (d. 727/1326f.) in a philological analysis of Q9:112 *apud* Tāj al-Dīn al-Subkī (d. 771/1370), *Ṭabaqāt al-Shāfi'iyya al-kubrā*, ed. M. M. al-Ṭanāḥī and 'A. M. al-Ḥulw, Cairo 1964–76, 9:203.2; the Imāmī Karakī (d. 940/1534) (*Fawā'id al-Sharā'i'*, ms. Princeton, Arabic Manuscripts, New Series 695, f. 138a.15; for this manuscript, see R. Mach and E. L. Ormsby, *Handlist of Arabic manuscripts (New Series) in the Princeton University Library*, Princeton 1987, 300 no. 1332); the Ḥanafī 'Alī al-Qārī (d. 1014/1606) (*Sharḥ 'Ayn al-'ilm*, Cairo 1351–3, 1:433.27); and the view of Ibn Taymiyya cited below, ch. 7, note 69). For a late scholastic dispute over the question whether the term *al-nahy 'an al-munkar* can be held to be redundant alongside *al-amr bi'l-ma'rūf* on the ground that 'commanding something is forbidding its opposite', see 'Abd al-Bāqī al-Zurqānī (d. 1099/1688), *Sharḥ*, Cairo 1307, 3:109.9, and Bannānī (d. 1163/1750), *Ḥāshiya*, in the margin of Zurqānī, *Sharḥ*, 3:109.1; the argument goes back to the omission of 'forbidding wrong' in Khalīl ibn Isḥāq (d. 767/1365), *Mukhtaṣar*, ed. Ṭ. A. al-Zāwī, Cairo n.d., 111.5. See also the anecdote quoted below, ch. 4, 71, where a traditionist attempts to get out of trouble by making a distinction.

[10] *Encyclopaedia Iranica*, London 1982–, art. 'Amr be ma'rūf' (W. Madelung). There is no article on *al-amr bi'l-ma'rūf* in the first or second editions of the *Encyclopaedia of Islam*, or their supplements to date.

[11] In principle, I am interested in all Islamic manifestations of this moral value, irrespective of how they are expressed. In practice I have traded heavily on the salience of the phrase *al-amr bi'l-ma'rūf* in this context: treatments are readily located in works that devote a chapter to it, and the phrase is easy to scan for in those that do not. I have not deliberately discriminated against material that employs the term *ghayyara* (cf. below, ch. 3, 34), but this usage is a lot harder to spot in a page of Arabic text. I have given scant attention at best to material that does not employ one or other of these usages. In other words, my principled conceptual aspirations may not always have been well served by my pragmatic lexical methods.

prosaic task is simple enough. A typical account of the duty in this literature will run to no more than a few pages, and these will rarely be characterised by the baffling abstraction of discussions of divine attributes, or the excruciating technicality of the law of inheritance. What makes the research time-consuming and its presentation complicated is the fact that there are very many such accounts, and that the doctrine they present is far from uniform. It varies with time and place, from sect to sect, from school to school, and from scholar to scholar. As a glance at the table of contents will show, I have chosen to present the bulk of the material by schools and sects; within them, the organisation is largely chronological. Not all readers will want to read all of this material; but those that do will find that, while some of it is tedious, most of it is reasonably accessible.

The book has further objectives which go beyond the modest aim of describing a scholastic tradition. As a historian of ideas, I naturally aspire to explain why Islam came to have such a doctrine, and why this doctrine varied as it did from one milieu to another. As a historian of society, I would like to know how this intellectual tradition was related to the society in which it flourished, and what difference it made to life on the street. It will not surprise anyone that my achievement in these respects is a much more limited one. The limitations are sometimes those of my own knowledge. For example, I would never have completed this book had I not in many cases confined my reading of a work to its chapter on forbidding wrong; this undoubtedly means that I have on occasion missed other relevant features of an author's thought. Sometimes the limitations are those of the sources. For example, it is notorious that we tend to know too much about scholars in the pre-modern Islamic world and too little about anyone else – apart from rulers.[12] Moreover, 'practice' in this book almost invariably means practice as described in Islamic literary sources. And sometimes the limitations we are up against arise from the inherent murkiness of historical causality, even where information is vastly more abundant than it is for most of Islamic history.

The overall structure of the book should be seen against this background. Part I is intended to lay the descriptive foundations; its core is the analysis of the normative material found in the Koran, Koranic exegesis, tradition and biographical literature about early Muslims. Part II is devoted to the Ḥanbalites; the reason for this lengthy treatment is not any intellectual sophistication in Ḥanbalite doctrine, but rather the relative abundance of

[12] It should thus come as no surprise that much of the discussion in this book turns on the relationship between scholars and rulers.

material which can be used to relate the doctrine to practice. Part III, by contrast, is concerned with the groups that offer the richest documentation for the intellectual history of the duty – the Muʿtazilites and their Zaydī and Imāmī heirs. Part IV collects the remaining sects and schools, and ends with a chapter pulling together the discussion of classical Islam. Part V is more ambitious. It starts by surveying the place of forbidding wrong in modern Islam; the scope of the survey is limited, however, by the fact that the only Islamic languages I read in some fashion, other than Arabic and English, are Persian and Turkish. In the last two chapters I take up the question of the pre-Islamic antecedents of the duty, and offer some comparisons with non-Islamic cultures, including that of the modern West.

The structure of the book is perhaps less in need of apology than its dimensions. In the decade since I began serious work on the project, I have watched the growth of the typescript with increasing alarm, and my attempts to cut it back in the final stages of editing have met with only limited success. The result of my labours is not, I think, the largest book on forbidding wrong ever written; for this, the prize still goes to the Damascene Zayn al-Dīn al-Ṣāliḥī (d. 856/1452).[13] But mine may well retain for some considerable time the distinction of being the largest in a Western language.[14] If it is any consolation to my colleagues, I have no intention of writing a book of this length again.

Some remarks on conventions of transcription and citation can be found at the beginning of the bibliography. Where a passage from a primary source has already been adduced by a previous scholar in a relevant context, I have generally (but not invariably) acknowledged this.[15] When I give a cross-reference to a footnote, it may in fact refer to the text immediately preceding the note-indicator in question.

Finally, a word on technology. The passage of time will make it increasingly obvious that this book is the product of an era when Islamic texts were not yet available in significant numbers on CD-ROMs.

[13] See below, ch. 7, 161. The work runs to 854 pages in the Riyāḍ edition.

[14] A contemporary work in Arabic on a large scale is that of Dr ʿAbd al-ʿAzīz Aḥmad al-Masʿūd (see below, ch. 18, note 1); but to my knowledge his promised second volume has yet to appear.

[15] But note that when I say that a passage was cited by a previous scholar, this does not necessarily mean that he cited it from the edition to which I refer.

ACKNOWLEDGEMENTS

The research on which this book is based was begun while I held a position in the History Department of the School of Oriental and African Studies in the University of London. The bulk of it, however, was carried out after I joined the Department of Near Eastern Studies at Princeton in 1986, mostly during semesters of leave. During this phase of the work, I received from the University Committee on Research in the Humanities and Social Sciences several small but strategic grants which funded particular aspects of my research. For one semester of full-time leave in the spring of 1990 I was supported by a generous grant from the Guggenheim Foundation, and in 1995 I was the recipient of a National Endowment for the Humanities Summer Stipend.

Like any scholar working in such a field, I have depended on a number of research libraries in a variety of countries, both for printed works and for microfilms of manuscripts (a good many of them since published). For the latter I am grateful in particular to the British Library, Leiden University Library, the Staatsbibliothek zu Berlin, the Vatican Library, the Süleymaniye Library, Istanbul, and the Maktabat al-Asad, Damascus. I also benefited considerably from access to the relevant files of the İslâm Araştırmaları Merkezi, Üsküdar, and would like to thank Tufan Buzpınar and Ayhan Aykut of the Centre for their help in this and other connections. But the foundation of my research has been the superb Islamic collection of the Firestone Library at Princeton and the helpfulness of its staff (I am particularly indebted to Azar Ashraf for first aid in Persian matters).

I owe my earliest sense of the significance of forbidding wrong in Islamic thought to conversations with Fritz Zimmermann, and my first opportunity to put some ideas together on the subject to Roy Mottahedeh, who in the spring of 1985 organised a conference at Princeton on 'Justice and Injustice in Islamic Political Thought'. Over the years I have used much of the material in the book for talks and lectures delivered in various academic contexts. In particular, a draft of chapter 5 was presented in written form to the fifth colloquium on the theme 'From Jahiliyya to Islam' held in Jerusalem in July 1990,[1] and a draft of chapter 14 to a conference on 'Saber religioso y poder político en el Islam' held at the Escuela de Estudios Árabes in Granada in October 1991. I am grateful to the respective organisers for the opportunity to discuss the material with specialist audiences.

Numerous scholars have helped me by giving me references and answering my queries, and I have done my best to acknowledge them in their proper places. I owe one of my first references to Basim Musallam, and a quite disproportionate number of them to Nurit Tsafrir and Maribel Fierro. I have incurred a special debt to my colleague Şükrü Hanioğlu for material that would otherwise have been inaccessible to me. A number of colleagues read parts of this work at various stages of drafting, and gave me their suggestions and comments. The first attempt I made to put together a substantial paper on forbidding wrong was read and thoroughly criticised by Ella Landau-Tasseron. A draft of chapter 2 was read by Etan Kohlberg and Uri Rubin. A first, primitive, version of chapter 5 was read by Emmanuel Sivan. Drafts of the chapters on the Ḥanbalites were read by Nimrod Hurvitz, Frank Stewart, Sarah Stroumsa and Nurit Tsafrir. A draft of chapter 8 was read by Fred de Jong, one of chapter 12 by Şükrü Hanioğlu , one of chapter 14 by Maribel Fierro, and one of chapter 18 by Houchang Chehabi. Drafts of the preface and chapter 19 benefited from the sharp philosophical eye of Margaret Gilbert. Patricia Crone, Gerald Hawting, Etan Kohlberg and Everett Rowson read and commented extensively on a draft of the entire study.

So also did my colleague Hossein Modarressi, to whom I owe a special debt for numerous references and much material not separately acknowledged, for extensive help with queries of all kinds, and for enabling me to understand countless things that would otherwise have remained opaque to me. Without all this, the book would have been immeasurably poorer.

In the course of writing the book, I have received much good advice from many sides. I know that I have not always followed it. Particularly towards the end of the process, I have become almost as disinclined to make drastic revisions to what I have written as Pontius Pilate. If I have persevered in error, the responsibility is mine alone.

In very practical terms, I owe an enormous debt to my wife, Kim. Without her help in numerous connections, the book would have taken

[1] A summary of the material and a few of the ideas presented in this draft appear with acknowledgement in C. Gilliot, 'Islam et pouvoir: la commanderie du bien et l'interdiction du mal', *Communio*, 16 (1991).

twice as long to write, or alternatively have ended up half the size (an outcome she would have been the last to regret).

Last but not least, I would like to express my appreciation to Lennart Sundelin for his courage in undertaking the indexing of so large a book, and to my department for a generous contribution towards the expenses of its publication.

PART I

INTRODUCTORY

CHAPTER 1

THE GOLDSMITH OF MARW

In the year 131/748f. the rebellion which was to overthrow the Umayyad dynasty had already been launched. The ʿAbbāsid army was advancing on Iraq, while the architect of the revolution, Abū Muslim (d. 137/755), remained in Marw, effectively ruling Khurāsān. His exercise of his power was nevertheless challenged – if only morally – by a local goldsmith (*ṣāʾigh*), one Abū Isḥāq Ibrāhīm ibn Maymūn.[1] This goldsmith went into the presence of Abū Muslim and addressed him in these words: 'I see nothing more meritorious I can undertake in God's behalf than to wage holy war against you. Since I lack the strength to do it with my hand, I will do it with my tongue. But God will see me, and in Him I hate you.' Abū Muslim killed him.[2] Centuries later, his tomb was still known and visited in the 'inner city' of Marw.[3]

[1] This incident, and its significance, were first discussed in W. Madelung, 'The early Murjiʾa in Khurāsān and Transoxania and the spread of Ḥanafism', *Der Islam*, 59 (1982), 35f. Madelung based his account on the entry on Ibrāhīm ibn Maymūn in Ibn Abī ʾl-Wafāʾ (d. 775/1373), *al-Jawāhir al-muḍiyya fī ṭabaqāt al-Ḥanafiyya*, Hyderabad 1332, 1:49.11, citing also Ṭabarī (d. 310/923), *Taʾrīkh al-rusul waʾl-mulūk*, ed. M. J. de Goeje *et al.*, Leiden 1879–1901, series II, 1919.1. In the addenda to the reprint of his article in his *Religious schools and sects in medieval Islam*, London 1985 (item III, 39a), he added a reference to the entry in Ibn Saʿd (d. 230/845), *al-Ṭabaqāt al-kabīr*, ed. E. Sachau *et al.*, Leiden 1904–21, 7:2:103.6. In what follows, I have extended this documentation; however, my findings lead me to modify Madelung's conclusions only on one point (see below, note 19). The goldsmith was first mentioned by Halm, who however stated erroneously that he was *qāḍī* of Marw (H. Halm, *Die Ausbreitung der šāfiʿitischen Rechtsschule von den Anfängen bis zum 8./14. Jahrhundert*, Wiesbaden 1974, 88). More recently van Ess has discussed him in his monumental history of early Islamic theology (J. van Ess, *Theologie und Gesellschaft im 2. und 3. Jahrhundert Hidschra*, Berlin and New York 1991–7, 2:548f.), with some further references of which the more significant will be noted below. See also M. Q. Zaman, *Religion and politics under the early ʿAbbāsids*, Leiden 1997, 71 n. 6, 72 n. 7.

[2] See Madelung, 'The early Murjiʾa', 35, citing Ibn Abī ʾl-Wafāʾ, *Jawāhir*, 1:50.7.

[3] Samʿānī (d. 562/1166), *Ansāb*, ed. ʿA. al-Muʿallimī al-Yamānī, Hyderabad 1962–82, 8:267.9; for the 'inner city' of Marw, see G. Le Strange, *The lands of the eastern caliphate*, Cambridge 1905, 398f. It should be noted that Samʿānī's *tarjama* of the goldsmith comes to us in two very different recensions. There is a short form, for which Samʿānī borrowed the entry in Ibn Ḥibbān (d. 354/965), *Thiqāt*, Hyderabad 1973–83, 6:19.7, adding an

We do not need to concern ourselves with the origins or historicity of this story.[4] It suffices that Abū Muslim killed the goldsmith, or had him killed,[5] and that it was the religio-political stance of the goldsmith that brought this upon him.[6] Nor need we concern ourselves with Abū Muslim's side of the story, except to note that a certain irritation on his part is understandable – this was, we are told, the third such visit he had

Footnote 3 (*cont.*)
explanation of the *nisba* and the detail about the grave; this is found in the British Library manuscript of the *Ansāb* published in facsimile by D. S. Margoliouth (Leiden and London 1912, f. 348b.15). Secondly, there is a long form marked by the insertion (very likely by Samʿānī himself) of much extra material (but without the detail about the grave); this long recension is that of the Istanbul manuscript used by Muʿallimī as the basis of his edition (see his introduction to the first volume of his edition, 33).

4 The account given by Ibn Abī 'l-Wafā' appears already in Jaṣṣāṣ (d. 370/981), *Aḥkām al-Qur'ān*, Istanbul 1335–8, 2:33.18, with a full *isnād* (and cf. *ibid.*, 1:70.22, drawn to my attention by Patricia Crone). The key figure in this *isnād* is one 'Aḥmad ibn ʿAṭiyya al-Kūfī', an alias of Aḥmad ibn Muḥammad ibn al-Ṣalt al-Ḥimmānī (d. 308/921) (for his biography, see E. Dickinson, 'Aḥmad b. al-Ṣalt and his biography of Abū Ḥanīfa', *Journal of the American Oriental Society*, 116 (1996), 409f., and for the alias, *ibid.*, 415). Traditionist circles had a low opinion of his probity as a scholar, particularly in connection with his transmissions on the virtues of Abū Ḥanīfa (d. 150/767f.) (*ibid.*, 412, 414f.). A *faṣl fī manāqib Abī Ḥanīfa* in a Cairo manuscript has been ascribed to him (*ibid.*, 413 n. 34; F. Sezgin, *Geschichte des arabischen Schrifttums*, Leiden 1967–, 1:410, 438 no. 16), but I owe to Adam Sabra the information that it does not contain our anecdote. There is a parallel version from ʿAlī ibn Ḥarmala, a Kūfan pupil of Abū Ḥanīfa, in Ibn Ḥamdūn (d. 562/1166), *Tadhkira*, ed. I. and B. ʿAbbās, Beirut 1996, 9:279f. no. 529 (I owe this reference to Patricia Crone; for ʿAlī ibn Ḥarmala, see al-Khaṭīb al-Baghdādī (d. 463/1071), *Ta'rīkh Baghdād*, Cairo 1931, 11:415.6). The story does not seem to have caught the attention of the historians; Ṭabarī mentions the goldsmith only in an earlier, and unrelated, historical context (see above, note 1), and occasionally as a narrator.

5 In addition to the works cited above, see particularly Bukhārī (d. 256/870), *al-Ta'rīkh al-kabīr*, Hyderabad 1360–78, 1:1:325.6 no. 1016 (whence Mizzī (d. 742/1341), *Tahdhīb al-Kamāl*, ed. B. ʿA. Maʿrūf, Beirut 1985–92, 2:224.6, and Ibn Ḥajar al-ʿAsqalānī (d. 852/1449), *Tahdhīb al-Tahdhīb*, Hyderabad 1325–7, 1:173.3); Fasawī (d. 277/890), *al-Maʿrifa wa'l-ta'rīkh*, ed. A. Ḍ. al-ʿUmarī, Baghdad 1974–6, 3:350.8 (noted by van Ess); Ibn Ḥibbān (d. 354/965), *Mashāhīr ʿulamā' al-amṣār*, ed. M. Fleischhammer, Cairo 1959, 195 no. 1565; Abū Nuʿaym al-Iṣbahānī (d. 430/1038), *Dhikr akhbār Iṣbahān*, ed. S. Dedering, Leiden 1931–4, 1:171.24 (noted by van Ess). Ibn Saʿd knows an account similar to that given above (*Ṭabaqāt*, 7:2:103.12), but gives pride of place to one in which the goldsmith is a friend of Abū Muslim. When Abū Muslim brings the ʿAbbāsid cause out into the open, he sends an agent to ascertain the goldsmith's reaction, which is that Abū Muslim should be killed; Abū Muslim reacts by having the goldsmith killed (*ibid.*, 103.7). According to a report preserved by Abū Ḥayyān al-Tawḥīdī (d. 414/1023f.), he was beaten to death (*al-Baṣā'ir wa'l-dhakhā'ir*, ed. W. al-Qāḍī, Beirut 1988, 6:213 no. 756).

6 Our sources indicate that the goldsmith's dislike of Abū Muslim did not arise from affection for the Umayyads. He indicates that his allegiance to the Umayyad governor Naṣr ibn Sayyār had not been voluntary (Taqī al-Dīn al-Tamīmī (d. 1010/1601), *al-Ṭabaqāt al-saniyya fī tarājim al-Ḥanafiyya*, ed. ʿA. M. al-Ḥulw, Cairo 1970–, 1:285.17); and an account transmitted from Aḥmad ibn Sayyār al-Marwazī (d. 268/881) suggests that he was a disappointed revolutionary who had initially believed in Abū Muslim's promises of just rule (*ibid.*, 286.3). Jaṣṣāṣ states that the goldsmith rebuked Abū Muslim for his oppression (*ẓulm*) and wrongful bloodshed (*Aḥkām*, 1:70.27; similarly Ibn Ḥibbān (d. 354/965), *Kitāb al-majrūḥīn*, ed. M. I. Zāyid, Aleppo 1395–6, 1:157.12, cited in Zaman, *Religion and politics*, 72 n. 7).

received from the goldsmith. The image of Ibrāhīm ibn Maymūn as he appears in our sources is, however, worth some attention. A man of Marw,[7] he was, in the first instance, a child of Islam.[8] When asked his descent, his reply was that his mother had been a client of the tribe of Hamdān, and his father a Persian;[9] he himself was a client (*mawlā*) of God and His Prophet.[10] He was also that familiar figure of the sociology of religion, a craftsman of uncompromising piety and integrity.[11] He would throw his hammer behind him when he heard the call to prayer.[12] While in Iraq he was too scrupulous to eat the food which Abū Ḥanīfa (d. 150/767f.) offered him without first questioning him about it, and even then he was not always satisfied with Abū Ḥanīfa's replies.[13] His politics were of a piece with this. His temperament was not receptive to counsels of prudence, as his discussions with Abū Ḥanīfa will shortly underline. Indeed, his death was little short of a verbal suicide mission – in one account he appeared before Abū Muslim already dressed and perfumed for his own funeral.[14] The goldsmith was a man of principle, in life as in death, and it is his principles that concern us here.

The principle that informed his last act, in the eyes of posterity and perhaps his own, was the duty of commanding right and forbidding

[7] A variant tradition has him originally from Iṣbahān (Abū ʾl-Shaykh (d. 369/979), *Ṭabaqāt al-muḥaddithīn bi-Iṣbahān*, ed. ʿA. ʿA. al-Balūshī, Beirut 1987–92, 1:449.2, whence Abū Nuʿaym, *Dhikr akhbār Iṣbahān*, 1:171.24, 172.3, whence in turn Mizzī, *Tahdhīb*, 2:224.8). Van Ess, who notes two of these references in a footnote (*Theologie*, 2:549 n. 15), states in the text that the goldsmith came from Kūfa, citing a Kūfan Ibrāhīm ibn Maymūn, a client of the family of the Companion Samura ibn Jundab (d. 59/679), mentioned in an *isnād* quoted by Fasawī (*Maʿrifa*, 3:237.1). This latter is, however, a Kūfan tailor (see, for example, Bukhārī, *Kabīr*, 1:1:325f. no. 1018), and there is no reason to identify him with our Marwazī goldsmith (*ibid.*, no. 1016).

[8] Cf. his name and *kunya*: Abū Isḥāq Ibrāhīm. Khalīfa ibn Khayyāṭ (d. 240/854f.), however, has the *kunya* Abū ʾl-Munāzil (*Ṭabaqāt*, ed. S. Zakkār, Beirut 1993, 596 no. 3,120).

[9] Elsewhere we learn that his father was a slave (Samʿānī, *Ansāb*, 8:266.13), as the name Maymūn suggests.

[10] Ibn Ḥanbal (d. 241/855), *al-ʿIlal wa-maʿrifat al-rijāl*, ed. W. M. ʿAbbās, Beirut and Riyāḍ 1988, 2:379 no. 2,693. This is why Bukhārī (d. 256/870) describes him as *mawlā ʾl-nabī* (*Kabīr*, 1:1:325.4; Bukhārī, *al-Taʾrīkh al-ṣaghīr*, ed. M. I. Zāyid, Aleppo and Cairo 1976–7, 2:27.1).

[11] Samʿānī tells us that he modelled his life on that of the Successors he had met (*Ansāb*, 8:266.9).

[12] *Ibid.*, 266.10; cf. al-Khaṭīb al-Baghdādī (d. 463/1071), *Mūḍiḥ awhām al-jamʿ waʾl-tafrīq*, Hyderabad 1959–60, 1:375.11, and Ibn Ḥajar, *Tahdhīb*, 1:173.5.

[13] Jaṣṣāṣ, *Aḥkām*, 2:33.8; Ibn Abī ʾl-Wafāʾ, *Jawāhir*, 1:49.16. Such conduct on the part of a guest was not approved by the Ḥanafī jurists unless there was at least specific reason for doubt (see Shaybānī (d. 189/805), *Āthār*, ed. M. Tēgh Bahādur, Lucknow n.d., 155.4 (*bāb al-daʿwa*), mentioning the concurrence of Abū Ḥanīfa). It is not clear whether the questions related to the provenance of the food itself or to that of the money that paid for it.

[14] Ibn Saʿd, *Ṭabaqāt*, 7:2:103.13 (*taḥannaṭa . . . wa-takaffana*). In this account his body is thrown into a well.

wrong.[15] The goldsmith was known as a devotee of commanding right,[16] and it was one of the topics he had brought up in his discussions with Abū Ḥanīfa.[17] More specifically, we can see him in death as having lived up to a Prophetic tradition which states: 'The finest form of holy war (*jihād*) is speaking out (***kalimat ḥaqq***) in the presence of an unjust ruler (*sulṭān jā'ir*), and getting killed for it (*yuqtal 'alayhā*).' This tradition is attested in a variety of forms, usually without the final reference to the death of the speaker, in the canonical and other collections.[18] But we also find it trans-

[15] As pointed out by Madelung ('The early Murji'a', 35f.). An account of the goldsmith's death preserved by Tamīmī has him go in to Abū Muslim and 'command and forbid' him (*fa-amarahu wa-nahāhu*) (Tamīmī, *Ṭabaqāt*, 1:285.11, and cf. *ibid.*, 286.3); likewise al-Khaṭīb al-Baghdādī states that he was killed in performing the duty (***Mūḍiḥ***, 1:375.8).

[16] Thus Ibn Ḥibbān describes him as ***min al-ammārīn bi'l-ma'rūf*** (*Thiqāt*, 6:19:10; see also Ibn Ḥibbān, *Mashāhīr*, 195 no. 1565). Aḥmad ibn Sayyār remarks on his devotion to *al-amr bi'l-ma'rūf* (*apud* Tamīmī, *Ṭabaqāt*, 1:286.12; and cf. Tamīmī's own summing-up, *ibid.*, 287.5).

[17] Madelung, 'The early Murji'a', 35, citing Ibn Abī 'l-Wafā', *Jawāhir*, 1:49.17; Jaṣṣāṣ, *Aḥkām*, 2:33.9.

[18] For the classical collections, see Ibn Ḥanbal (d. 241/855), ***Musnad***, Būlāq 1313, 3:19.16, 61.24, 4:314.28, 315.2, 5:251.8, 256.18; Ibn Māja (d. 273/887), ***Sunan***, ed. M. F. 'Abd al-Bāqī, Cairo 1972, 1329 no. 4,011, 1330 no. 4,012; Abū Dāwūd al-Sijistānī (d. 275/889), ***Sunan***, ed. 'I. 'U al-Da''ās and 'A. al-Sayyid, Ḥimṣ 1969–74, 4:514 no. 4,344 (whence Jaṣṣāṣ, ***Aḥkām***, 2:34.15); Tirmidhī (d. 279/892), *Ṣaḥīḥ*, ed. 'I. 'U. al-Da''ās, Ḥimṣ 1965–8, 6:338f. no. 2,175; Nasā'ī (d. 303/915), ***Sunan***, ed. Ḥ. M. al-Mas'ūdī, Cairo n.d., 7:161.7. (Neither Bukhārī nor Muslim include the tradition.) For other collections, see Ḥumaydī (d. 219/834f.), *Musnad*, ed. Ḥ. al-A'ẓamī, Cairo and Beirut n.d., 331f. no. 752; Ṭabarānī (d. 360/971), ***al-Mu'jam al-kabīr***, ed. Ḥ. 'A. al-Salafī, n.p. *c.* 1984–6, 8:281f. no. 8,081, and cf. no. 8,080 (I owe these references to Etan Kohlberg); al-Ḥākim al-Naysābūrī (d. 405/1014), ***Mustadrak***, Hyderabad 1334–42, 4:506.7; Quḍā'ī (d. 454/1062), ***Musnad al-shihāb***, ed. Ḥ. 'A. al-Salafī, Beirut 1985, 2:247f. nos. 1286–8; Bayhaqī (d. 458/1066), ***Shu'ab al-īmān***, ed. M. B. Zaghlūl, Beirut 1990, 6:93 nos. 7,581f., and cf. Bayhaqī, ***al-Sunan al-kubrā***, Hyderabad 1344–55, 10:91.3. The tradition is transmitted from several Companions with a variety of Kūfan and Baṣran *isnāds*. For entries on the tradition (without *isnāds*) in post-classical guides to the *ḥadīth* collections, see Majd al-Dīn ibn al-Athīr (d. 606/1210), *Jāmi' al-uṣūl*, ed. 'A. al-Arnā'ūṭ, Cairo 1969–73, 1:333 nos. 116f.; Haythamī (d. 807/1405), *Majma' al-zawā'id*, Cairo 1352–3, 7:272.2; Suyūṭī (d. 911/1505), ***al-Jāmi' al-ṣaghīr***, Cairo 1954, 1:49.20; Suyūṭī, *Jam' al-jawāmi'*, n.p. 1970–, 1:1155–7 nos. 3,724, 3,728f., 3,734; al-Muttaqī al-Hindī (d. 975/1567), *Kanz al-'ummāl*, ed. Ṣ. al-Saqqā *et al.*, Aleppo 1969–77, 3:66f. nos. 5,510–12, 5,514, 3:80 no. 5,576. In none of these cases does the tradition include the final reference to the death of the speaker (a fact pointed out to me with regard to the classical collections by Keith Lewinstein). However, such a version appears in a Syrian tradition found in the ***Musnad*** of Bazzār (d. 292/904f.) (*al-Baḥr al-zakhkhār al-ma'rūf bi-Musnad al-Bazzār*, ed. M. Zayn Allāh, Medina and Beirut 1988–, 4:110.3 no. 1285); and cf. Ghazzālī (d. 505/1111), *Iḥyā' 'ulūm al-dīn*, Beirut n.d., 2:284.25, 284.27. Moreover, the Mu'tazilite exegete Rummānī (d. 384/994) in his commentary to Q3:21 seems to have adduced a version transmitted by Ḥasan (sc. al-Baṣrī) which included this ending (see Abū Ja'far al-Ṭūsī (d. 460/1067), *al-Tibyān fī tafsīr al-Qur'ān*, Najaf 1957–63, 2:422.17, and Ṭabrisī, *Majma'*, 1:423.32 (both to Q3:21)), and the same form of the tradition appears in the Koran commentary of the Mu'tazilite al-Ḥākim al-Jishumī (d. 494/1101) (see the quotation in 'A. Zarzūr, *al-Ḥākim al-Jushamī wa-manhajuhu fī tafsīr al-Qur'ān*, n.p. n.d., 195.3). The *ḥadīth* is not a Shī'ite one, although there is an Imāmī tradition in which it is quoted to Ja'far al-Ṣādiq (d. 148/765), who seeks to tone

mitted by our goldsmith – complete with the reference to the speaker's death – from Abū Ḥanīfa.[19] A variant version likewise transmitted to the goldsmith by Abū Ḥanīfa makes explicit the link between this form of holy war and the principle of forbidding wrong, and one source relates this to his death.[20]

As mentioned, the goldsmith had discussed this duty with Abū Ḥanīfa.[21] They had agreed that it was a divinely imposed duty (*farīḍa min Allāh*). The goldsmith then gave to this theoretical discussion an alarmingly practical twist: he proposed then and there that in pursuance of this duty he should give his allegiance (*bay'a*) to Abū Ḥanīfa – in other words, that they should embark on a rebellion. The latter, as might be expected, would have nothing to do with this proposal. He did not deny that the goldsmith had called upon him to carry out a duty he owed to God (*ḥaqq min ḥuqūq Allāh*). But he counselled prudence. One man acting on his own would merely get himself killed, and achieve nothing for others; the right leader, with a sufficient following of good men, might be able to achieve something.[22] During subsequent visits, the goldsmith kept returning to this question, and Abū Ḥanīfa would repeat his view that this duty (unlike others) was not one that a man could undertake alone. Anyone who did so would be throwing his own blood away and asking to be killed. Indeed, it

down its implications (Kulaynī (d. 329/941), *Kāfī*, ed. 'A. A. al-Ghaffārī, Tehran 1375–7, 5:60.7 no. 16; Ṭūsī (d. 460/1067), *Tahdhīb al-aḥkām*, ed. Ḥ. M. al-Kharsān, Najaf 1958–62, 6:178.6 no. 9); cf. also al-Ḥurr al-'Āmilī (d. 1104/1693), *Wasā'il al-Shī'a*, ed. 'A. al-Rabbānī and M. al-Rāzī, Tehran 1376–89, 6:1:406.8 no. 9. It is, however, known to the Ibāḍīs (Rabī' ibn Ḥabīb (d. 170/786f?) (attrib.), *al-Jāmi' al-ṣaḥīḥ*, n.p. n.d., 2:17 no. 455). The link between the tradition and *al-amr bi'l-ma'rūf* is made explicit by the commentators to Suyūṭī's *al-Jāmi' al-ṣaghīr* (see Munāwī (d. 1031/1622), *Taysīr*, Būlāq 1286, 1:182.6; 'Azīzī (d. 1070/1659f.), *al-Sirāj al-munīr*, Cairo 1357, 1:260.20).

[19] Sam'ānī, *Ansāb*, 8:267.1, with a typically Ḥanafī *isnād* (and cf. Abū Ḥanīfa (d. 150/767f.), *Musnad*, Beirut 1985, 370.6, without *yuqtal 'alayhā*). This tradition, Sam'ānī tells us, is the only one the goldsmith transmitted from Abū Ḥanīfa. If we set this detail alongside his idiosyncratic reservations about Abū Ḥanīfa's food, and the way in which they argue on equal terms, we cannot confidently classify the goldsmith as a disciple of Abū Ḥanīfa; this in turn means that we have no compelling ground for classifying him as a Murji'ite (contrast Madelung, 'The early Murji'a', 35, and van Ess, *Theologie*, 2:548f.).

[20] Abū Ḥanīfa relates that he had transmitted to the goldsmith the Prophetic tradition: 'The lord of the martyrs (*sayyid al-shuhadā'*) is Ḥamza ibn 'Abd al-Muṭṭalib and a man who stands up to an unjust ruler, commanding and forbidding, and is killed by him' (Jaṣṣāṣ, *Aḥkām*, 2:34.17, and similarly 1:70.24; see also Ibn Abī 'l-Wafā', *Jawāhir*, 1:193.3, and Tamīmī, *Ṭabaqāt*, 1:285.13). (This tradition appears also in Ḥākim, *Mustadrak*, 3:195.7; Khaṭīb, *Mūḍiḥ*, 1:371.20; Haythamī, *Zawā'id*, 7:266.3, 272.4; and cf. *ibid.*, 272.6.) The Kūfan A'mash (d. 148/765) states that this tradition motivated the goldsmith's death (Ibn Ḥibbān, *Majrūḥīn*, 1:157.13, cited in Zaman, *Religion and politics*, 72 n. 7). There is even a version of this tradition that makes a veiled reference to the goldsmith (Ibn Ḥamdūn, *Tadhkira*, 9:280 no. 530; I owe this reference to Patricia Crone).

[21] In what follows I cite the text of Jaṣṣāṣ, for the most part leaving aside that of Ibn Abī 'l-Wafā'.

[22] Jaṣṣāṣ has *l' yḥwl*. Ibn Abī 'l-Wafā' omits the phrase.

was to be feared that he would become an accomplice in his own death. The effect of his action would be to dishearten others. So one should wait; God is wise, and knows what we do not know.[23] In due course the news of the goldsmith's death reached Abū Ḥanīfa. He was beside himself with grief, but he was not surprised.

Abū Ḥanīfa, to judge from his relations with the goldsmith, was not a political activist. His cautious attitude to the political implications of forbidding wrong finds expression in rather similar terms in an apparently early Ḥanafī text.[24] This work begins with a doctrinal statement of which forbidding wrong is the second article.[25] Then, at a later point, Abū Ḥanīfa is confronted with the question: 'How do you regard someone who commands right and forbids wrong, acquires a following on this basis, and rebels against the community (*jamāʿa*)? Do you approve of this?' He answers that he does not. But why, when God and His Prophet have imposed on us the duty of forbidding wrong? He concedes that this is true enough, but counters that in the event the good such rebels can achieve will be outweighed by the evil they bring about.[26] The objection he makes here is more far-reaching than that with which he deflected the dangerous proposal of the goldsmith: it is not just that setting the world to rights is not a one-man job; it is not even to be undertaken by many. The imputation of such quietism to Abū Ḥanīfa may or may not be historically accurate.[27] There are also widespread reports that he looked with favour on the

[23] Abū Ḥanīfa cites Q2:30, where the angels protest at God's declared intention of placing a *khalīfa* on earth, on the ground that he will act unjustly, and are silenced with the retort that He knows what they do not know.

[24] Abū Ḥanīfa (d. 150/767f.) (attrib.), *al-Fiqh al-absaṭ*, ed. M. Z. al-Kawtharī, in a collection of which the first item is Abū Ḥanīfa (attrib.), *al-ʿĀlim wa'l-mutaʿallim*, Cairo 1368, 44.10.

[25] Abū Ḥanīfa, *al-Fiqh al-absaṭ*, 40.10; and see Māturīdī (d. *c.* 333/944) (attrib.), *Sharḥ al-Fiqh al-akbar*, Hyderabad 1321, 4.1, and A. J. Wensinck, *The Muslim creed*, Cambridge 1932, 103f., art. 2. For an elegant analysis of the relationship between these three texts, showing Wensinck's 'Fiqh Akbar I' to be something of a ghost, see J. van Ess, 'Kritisches zum *Fiqh akbar*', *Revue des Etudes Islamiques*, 54 (1986), especially 331f.; for his commentary on the second article, see *ibid.*, 336f. (For a briefer treatment, see his *Theologie*, 1:207–11.) A possibility van Ess does not quite consider ('Kritisches', 334) is that articles 1–5 may represent an interpolation into the text of *al-Fiqh al-absaṭ*: Abū Ḥanīfa's distinction between *al-fiqh fī 'l-dīn* and *al-fiqh fī 'l-aḥkām*, of which the former is the more excellent (*ibid.*, 40.14, immediately following the passage), looks suspiciously like the answer to the disciple's request to be told about 'the greater *fiqh*' (*al-fiqh al-akbar*, *ibid.*, 40.8, immediately preceding the passage). The commentary ascribed to Māturīdī mentioned above has now been critically edited by H. Daiber, who argues that its author was Abū 'l-Layth al-Samarqandī (d. 373/983) (see below, ch. 12, note 22, and, for our passage, note 24). [26] Abū Ḥanīfa, *al-Fiqh al-absaṭ*, 44.10.

[27] In the same text Abū Ḥanīfa states that, if commanding and forbidding are of no avail, we should fight with the *fiʾa ʿādila* against the *fiʾa bāghiya* (cf. Q49:9), even if the ruler (*imām*) is unjust (*ibid.*, 44.16; see also *ibid.*, 48.2, where the term used is *sulṭān*). Van

use of the sword[28] and sympathised with ʿAlid rebels,[29] and an activist disposition would not be out of line with the Murjiʾite background of Ḥanafism.[30] But even if Abū Ḥanīfa was not a political activist, what is significant for us in the texts under discussion is not what he in practice denies, but what he in principle concedes: he agrees with both the goldsmith and his questioner in the early Ḥanafī text that forbidding wrong is a divinely imposed obligation, and one whose political implications cannot be categorically denied. The goldsmith, for all that he is mistaken, retains the moral high ground.

What we see here is the presence, within the mainstream of Islamic thought, of a strikingly – not to say inconveniently – radical value: the principle that an executive power of the law of God is vested in each and every Muslim. Under this conception the individual believer as such has not only the right, but also the duty, to issue orders pursuant to God's law, and to do what he can to see that they are obeyed. What is more, he may be issuing

Ess is inclined to ascribe the relative quietism of this text to Abū Muṭīʿ al-Balkhī (d. 199/814), the disciple who transmits Abū Ḥanīfa's answers to his questions ('Kritisches', 336f.; *Theologie*, 1:210). This may be right, but it should be noted that early Ḥanafism in Balkh, and perhaps north-eastern Iran in general, was marked by a sullen, and sometimes truculent, hostility towards the authorities of the day (see Madelung, 'The early Murjiʾa', 37f.).

28 ʿAbdallāh ibn Aḥmad ibn Ḥanbal (d. 290/903), *Sunna*, ed. M. S. S. al-Qaḥṭānī, Dammām 1986, 181f. no. 233, 182 no. 234, 207 no. 325, 213 no. 348, 218 no. 368, 222 no. 382 (and cf. 217 no. 363); Fasawī, *Maʿrifa*, 2:788.13; Abū Zurʿa al-Dimashqī (d. 281/894), *Taʾrīkh*, ed. S. N. al-Qawjānī, Damascus n.d., 506 no. 1331; Jaṣṣāṣ, *Aḥkām*, 1:70.19 (I owe this reference to Patricia Crone); Abū Tammām (*fl.* first half of the fourth/tenth century), *Shajara*, *apud* W. Madelung and P. E. Walker, *An Ismaili heresiography*, Leiden 1998, 85.3 = 82, and cf. 85.19 = 83 on the followers of Abū Ḥanīfa (this material is likely to derive from the heresiography of Abū ʾl-Qāsim al-Balkhī (d. 319/931), see 10–12 of Walker's introduction; these and other passages of Abū Tammām's work were drawn to my attention by Patricia Crone); Khaṭīb, *Taʾrīkh Baghdād*, 13:384.6, 384.11, 384.17, 384.20, 385.19, 386.1, 386.6. In this last tradition, as in ʿAbdallāh ibn Aḥmad's second, Abū Yūsuf (d. 182/798) dissociates himself from his teacher's attitude; compare the half-dozen quietist traditions he cites in his treatise on fiscal law (*Kharāj*, Cairo 1352, 9f.), including that which enjoins obedience even to a maimed Abyssinian slave if he is set in authority (*ibid.*, 9.12).

29 See, for example, C. van Arendonk, *Les débuts de l'imamat zaidite au Yémen*, Leiden 1960, 307, 315; van Ess, 'Kritisches', 337; K. Athamina, 'The early Murjiʾa: some notes', *Journal of Semitic Studies*, 35 (1990), 109 n. 1.

30 See M. Cook, *Early Muslim dogma: a source-critical study*, Cambridge 1981, ch. 6, and cf. my review of the first volume of van Ess's *Theologie* in *Bibliotheca Orientalis*, 50 (1993), col. 271, to 174. For a rather different view of the politics of the early Murjiʾa, see Madelung, 'The early Murjiʾa', 32 (but cf. his position in *The Encyclopaedia of Islam*, second edition, Leiden and London 1960– (hereafter *EI*²), art. 'Murdjiʾa', 606a). The question has also been discussed by Athamina with considerable erudition (see his 'The early Murjiʾa', 115–30); however, he does not take into consideration the testimony of the *Sīrat Sālim ibn Dhakwān*, and his evidence does not seem to support his conclusion that there existed a quietist stream among the early Murjiʾites alongside an activist one (*ibid.*, 129f.). See also below, ch. 12, note 5.

these orders to people who conspicuously outrank him in the prevailing hierarchy of social and political power. Only Abū Ḥanīfa's prudence stood between this value and the goldsmith's proposal for political revolution, and in the absence of prudence, the execution of the duty could easily end, as it did for the goldsmith, in a martyr's death. Small wonder that Abū Ḥanīfa should have squirmed when his interlocutors sought to draw out the implications of the value.

There were others, however, who were less willing to concede a martyr's crown to the likes of the goldsmith. Zubayr ibn Bakkār (d. 256/870) preserves a remarkable account of a confrontation between the caliph al-Maʾmūn (r. 198–218/813–33) and an unnamed zealot.[31] The caliph was on one of his campaigns against the infidel, presumbly in Anatolia, and was walking alone with one of his generals.[32] A man appeared, shrouded and perfumed,[33] and made for al-Maʾmūn. He refused to greet the caliph, charging that he had corrupted the army (*ghuzāt*) in three ways. First, he was allowing the sale of wine in the camp. Second, he was responsible for the visible presence there of slave-girls in litters (*ʿammāriyyāt*) with their hair uncovered. Third, he had banned forbidding wrong.[34] To this last charge al-Maʾmūn responded immediately that his ban was directed only at those who turned commanding right into wrongdoing; by contrast, he positively encouraged those who knew what they were doing (*alladhī yaʾmur biʾl-maʿrūf biʾl-maʿrifa*) to undertake it. In due course al-Maʾmūn went over the other charges levelled at him by the zealot. The alleged wine turned out to be nothing of the kind, prompting the caliph to observe that forbidding the likes of this man to command right was an act of piety.[35] The exposure of the slave-girls was intended to prevent the enemy's spies from thinking that the Muslims had anything so precious as their daughters and sisters with them. Thus in attempting to command right, the man had himself committed a wrong.[36]

The caliph then went onto the attack. What, he asked the man, would he do if he came upon a young couple talking amorously with each other here in this mountain pass?

[31] Zubayr ibn Bakkār (d. 256/870), *al-Akhbār al-Muwaffaqiyyāt*, ed. S. M. al-ʿĀnī, Baghdad 1972, 51–7. The passage is quoted in full in F. Jadʿān, *al-Miḥna*, Amman 1989, 256–60, whence my knowledge of it. There is a parallel in Ibn ʿAsākir (d. 571/1176), *Taʾrīkh madīnat Dimashq*, ed. ʿA. Shīrī, Beirut 1995–8, 33:302–5 (I owe this reference to Michael Cooperson). I shall return to this narrative (see below, ch. 17, 497f.).

[32] The presence of ʿUjayf ibn ʿAnbasa makes the Anatolian campaign of 215/830 a plausible setting for the story (see Ṭabarī, *Taʾrīkh*, series III, 1103.12).

[33] For *mutakhabbiṭ mutakaffin* read *mutaḥanniṭ mutakaffin*, as in Ibn ʿAsākir's parallel (and cf. above, note 14). [34] Zubayr, *Akhbār*, 52.15. [35] *Ibid.*, 54.13.

[36] *Ibid.*, 55.9.

THE ZEALOT: I would ask them who they were.

THE CALIPH: You'd ask the man, and he'd tell you she was his wife. And you'd ask the woman, and she'd say he was her husband. So what would you do with them?

THE ZEALOT: I'd separate them and imprison them.

THE CALIPH: Till when?

THE ZEALOT: Till I'd asked about them.

THE CALIPH: And who would you ask?

THE ZEALOT: [First] I'd ask them where they were from.

THE CALIPH: Fine. You've asked the man where he's from, and he says he's from Asfījāb.[37] The woman too says she's from Asfījāb – that he's her cousin, they got married and came here. Well, are you going to keep them in prison on the basis of your vile suspicion and false imaginings until your messenger comes back from Asfījāb? Say the messenger dies, or they die before he gets back?

THE ZEALOT: I would ask here in your camp.

THE CALIPH: What if you could only find one or two people from Asfījāb in my camp, and they told you they didn't know them? Is that what you've put on your shroud for?

The caliph concluded that he must have to do with a man who had deluded himself by misinterpreting the tradition according to which the finest form of holy war is to speak out in the presence of an unjust ruler.[38] In fact, he observed, it was his antagonist who was guilty of injustice. In a final gesture of contempt, he declined to flog the zealot, and contented himself with having his general rip up his pretentious shroud. The caliph's tone throughout the narrative is one of controlled fury and icy contempt: it is he, and not the would-be martyr, who occupies the moral high ground.

That the political implications of forbidding wrong would give rise to controversy is exactly what we would expect. And yet the strategy adopted by al-Ma'mūn is not to expose the zealot as a subversive. Rather, his charge is that the man has made the duty into a vehicle of ignorance and prejudice. The effect is enhanced when the caliph goes onto the attack. By the answers he gives to the hypothetical questions put to him by al-Ma'mūn, the zealot reveals himself not as a heroic enemy of tyrants, but rather as a blundering intruder into the private affairs of ordinary Muslims. With men like him around, no happily married couple can go for a stroll in a mountain pass without exposing themselves to harassment on the part of boorish zealots.

The contrasting moral fates of the goldsmith of Marw and the nameless zealot can help us mark out the territory within which the doctrine of the

[37] Asfījāb was located far away on the frontiers of Transoxania.

[38] *Ibid.*, 56.12. For the tradition, see above, note 18.

duty must operate. At one edge of this territory, a thin line separates forbidding wrong from culpable subversion. At the other edge, the frontier between forbidding wrong and the invasion of privacy is no thicker. Away from these tense borders we shall encounter few stories as dramatic as those of the goldmith and the zealot, and the bulk of this book will be taken up with the description and analysis of scholastic arguments and distinctions. But subversion and intrusion are themes that will often recur in the course of this study. Though not quite the Scylla and Charybdis of forbidding wrong, they represent significant ways in which the virtuous performance of the duty can degenerate into vice, and they are accordingly major foci of the scholastic thought we shall be examining.

As we shall see, scholasticism comes into its own within the framework of the sects and schools of classical Islam; it is here that systematic doctrines of the duty are eventually to be found. However, many of the ideas elaborated in this scholastic literature appear already in earlier contexts. The following chapters will accordingly consider, in turn, the Koran and its exegesis, traditions from the Prophet and his Companions, and biographical literature about early Muslims.

CHAPTER 2

KORAN AND KORANIC EXEGESIS

1. THE KORAN WITHOUT THE EXEGETES

In the course of a call for unity among the believers, God addresses them as follows: 'Let there be one community of you (*wa-l-takun minkum ummatun*), calling to good, and commanding right and forbidding wrong (*wa-ya'murūna bi'l-ma'rūfi wa-yanhawna 'ani 'l-munkar*); those are the prosperers' (Q3:104).[1] This conjunction of 'commanding right' and 'forbidding wrong' is found in seven further Koranic verses (Q3:110, Q3:114, Q7:157, Q9:71, Q9:112, Q22:41, Q31:17);[2] the two phrases scarcely appear in isolation from each other.[3] It is clear, then, that the phrase 'commanding right and forbidding wrong' is firmly rooted in Koranic diction. But what, on the basis of the Koranic material, can we say about the actual character of the duty? Who performs it, who is its target, and what is it about?

It is reasonably clear who performs it in Q3:104. The context of the verse is an appeal for the unity of the community of believers, with contrasting reference to earlier communities;[4] the believers, according to this verse, are to be (or at least include) a community (*umma*) which commands right and forbids wrong. Some of the other passages referring to the duty invite

[1] All Koranic quotations follow the Egyptian text; my translations are based on those of Arberry, but frequently depart from them (A. J. Arberry, *The Koran interpreted*, London 1964). Throughout, I use 'right' to translate *ma'rūf* and 'wrong' to translate *munkar*. For a discussion of some of the questions addressed in this chapter, see A. A. Roest Crollius, 'Mission and morality', *Studia Missionalia*, 27 (1978), 258–73 (drawn to my attention by Noha Bakr).

[2] We also find in Q9:67 the transposition 'commanding wrong' and 'forbidding right'; the reference is to the hypocrites (*munāfiqūn*), in contrast to the believers of Q9:71.

[3] A possible reference to 'commanding right' is found in Q4:114: *man amara bi-ṣadaqatin aw ma'rūfin aw iṣlāḥin bayna 'l-nās*. Here Arberry translates *ma'rūf* as 'honour', which is his standard rendering of the term. There are two references to 'forbidding indecency (*al-faḥshā'*) and wrong' (Q16:90, Q29:45; and cf. Q24:21). Q5:79 (*kānū lā yatanāhawna 'an munkarin fa'alūhu*) will be discussed below, notes 11f.

[4] Q3:105, and cf. Q3:100.

a similar interpretation (Q3:110, Q3:114, Q9:71); in other words, the obligation seems here to be one discharged by the collectivity of the believers.[5] There are, however, two verses (Q9:112 and Q22:41) where the context suggests that those who perform the duty are the believers who engage in holy war (and therefore not all believers?). The first is syntactically problematic; but the believers have been mentioned in the previous verse for their commitment to holy war.[6] The second verse seems to pick up an earlier reference to 'those who fight because they were wronged' (Q22:39).[7] There are also two verses in which the duty appears as one performed by individuals: in Q7:157 it is the gentile prophet (*al-rasūl al-nabī al-ummī*) who executes it, and in Q31:17 Luqmān tells his son to perform it.

Who is the target of the duty? The only verse that specifies this is Q7:157, where the gentile prophet commands and forbids those who follow him. In no case does the duty appear as something done to an individual, or to particular individuals. In general we are left in the dark.

What is the duty about? In none of the verses we have considered is there any further indication as to what concrete activities are subsumed under the rubric of commanding right and forbidding wrong. We might suspect from this that we have to do with a general duty of ethical affirmation to the community, or to the world at large, but this is by no means clear.

[5] In Q3:110, God tells the believers that they, as opposed to the people of the Book, were (*kuntum*) the 'best community' that has come forth, commanding right and forbidding wrong; while in Q3:114, He concedes that among the people of the Book there exists an 'upstanding community' which commands right and forbids wrong. Whereas in Q9:67 the hypocrites 'are as one another', commanding wrong and forbidding right, in Q9:71 the believers 'are friends one of the other', commanding right and forbidding wrong. In Q22:41, the believers are those who, if established in the land, will command right and forbid wrong.

[6] The verse speaks, in a string of present participles in the nominative case, of 'those who repent, those who serve, those who pray, . . . those who command right and forbid wrong (*al-āmirūna bi'l-ma'rūfi wa'l-nāhūna 'an al-munkari*), those who keep God's bounds'. There is no obvious predicate, so that it is natural to see the participles as in apposition to a previously mentioned subject; and the previous verse appropriately offers 'the believers' – but in the genitive case ('God has bought from the believers (*al-mu'minīna*) their selves and their possessions against the gift of Paradise; they fight in the way of God; they kill, and are killed' (Q9:111)). The syntactic problem is resolved in a textual variant in which the participles appear in the genitive. This variant is quoted from Ibn Mas'ūd (d. 32/652f.), Ubayy ibn Ka'b (d. 22/642f.), and A'mash (d. 148/765) (see A. Jeffery, *Materials for the history of the text of the Qur'ān*, Leiden 1937, 45, 134, 319; the attribution to Ibn Mas'ūd appears already in Farrā' (d. 207/822f.), *Ma'ānī al-Qur'ān*, ed. A. Y. Najātī and M. 'A. al-Najjār, Cairo 1980–, 1:453.8). Imāmī sources also ascribe this variant to Muḥammad al-Bāqir (d. *c.* 118/736) and Ja'far al-Ṣādiq (d. 148/765) (Ṭabrisī, *Majma'*, 3:74.12; Ṭabrisī, *Jawāmi' al-jāmi'*, Beirut 1985, 1:633.16; and see 'Ayyāshī (early fourth/tenth century), *Tafsīr*, Qumm n.d., 2:112f. no. 140).

[7] Or, just possibly, 'those who believe' in Q22:38. What binds the passage together syntactically is the series of relative pronouns in verses 38, 39, 40 and 41.

We can seek to shed a little more light on the Koranic conception of commanding right and forbidding wrong by looking at some related material from the Koran.

First, the term 'right' (*ma'rūf*) often appears elsewhere in the Koran, usually but not always in legal contexts (Q2:178, 180, 228, 229, etc.).[8] There is, however, no indication that it is itself a technical, or even a legal term. Rather, it seems to refer to performing a legal or other action in a decent and honourable fashion; this finds some confirmation in the synonymy with 'kindliness' (*iḥsān*) which is suggested by certain verses (Q2:178, 229 and cf. 236). Just what constitutes such conduct is never spelled out. Thus it seems that we have to do with the kind of ethical term that passes the buck to specific standards of behaviour already known and established.

Secondly, there are locutions elsewhere in the Koran of the form 'commanding X' and 'forbidding Y', where X and Y are similarly broad-spectrum ethical terms.[9] These parallels reinforce the impression that the Koranic conception of forbidding wrong is a vague and general one.

Thirdly, it is worth noting the kinds of themes that appear in conjunction with commanding right: performing prayer (Q9:71, Q9:112, Q22:41, Q31:17); paying alms (Q9:71, Q22:41); believing in God (Q3:110, Q3:114), obeying Him and His Prophet (Q9:71), keeping His bounds (Q9:112), reciting His signs (Q3:113); calling to good (Q3:104), vying with each other in good works (Q3:114); enduring what befalls one (Q31:17).[10] Here again, there is nothing to narrow the concept of the duty.

Finally, there are two passages that are worth particular attention.

One is Q5:79. Having stated that those of the Children of Israel who disbelieved were cursed by David and Jesus for their sins, God continues: ***kānū lā yatanāhawna 'an munkarin fa'alūhu***. This is the only Koranic occurrence of the verb *tanāhā*. If we care to interpret it etymologically in

[8] Normally it appears as a substantive, occasionally as an adjective modifying *qawl* (e.g. Q2:235, 263; Q4:5, 8) or *ṭā'a* (Q24:53). The term *munkar* is rarer (Q22:72, Q29:29, Q58:2). For an introduction to both terms, see T. Izutsu, *Ethico-religious concepts in the Qur'ān*, Montreal 1966, 213–17.

[9] Thus X may be *birr* (Q2:44), *qisṭ* (Q3:21, and cf. Q7:29), *'urf* (Q7:199), *'adl* (Q16:76), *'adl* and *iḥsān* (Q16:90), *taqwā* (Q96:12) or, with reversal, *sū'* (Q12:53) and *faḥshā'* (Q24:21); Y may be *sū'* (Q7:165), *fasād* (Q11:116), *faḥshā'* (Q29:45), *faḥshā'* and *baghy* (Q16:90), or *hawā* (Q79:40). The only one of these verses in which 'commanding X' and 'forbidding Y' are conjoined is Q16:90. The only cases where the verbs have an object are Q2:44 (*al-nās*) and Q79:40 (*al-nafs*).

[10] I leave aside the rather different themes that appear in Q7:157 (where it is the Prophet who commands right) and Q9:67 (where the hypocrites command wrong).

a reciprocal sense, the meaning might be that the Children of Israel 'forbade not one another any wrong that they committed'; in this case we would have here a Koranic basis for the conception of forbidding wrong as something that individual believers do to each other. But there seems to be no independent attestation of such a sense of the verb.[11] In the Arabic of ordinary mortals, *tanāhā* is usually synonymous with *intahā*, itself a common Koranic verb with the sense of 'refrain' or 'desist' (as in Q2:275 and Q8:38). In this case the sense would merely be 'they did not desist from any wrong that they committed'; and in fact this understanding of the verse is explicit in a variant reading with *yantahūna* for *yatanāhawna*.[12] If we either read *yantahūna*, or understand *yatanāhawna* in the same sense, then the verse is of no further interest to us.[13]

The other passage is Q7:163–6. These verses tell a story of the divine punishment of the people of an (Israelite) town by the sea who fished on the Sabbath. We have to understand from the context that a part of this community had reproved the Sabbath-breakers; another part (*ummatun*) then asked the reprovers why they bothered to admonish people whom God was going to punish anyway. In due course God saved those who forbade evil, and punished those who acted wrongly. Here again, we have a conception of a duty of forbidding evil as one performed by members of a community towards each other; and here, for the first time, we have a concrete example of the performance of such a duty.

Yet neither case is unambiguously connected with our duty of 'commanding right and forbidding wrong'. Neither verse makes any reference

[11] Wensinck's concordance of *ḥadīth* literature contains six entries for the sixth form of the root *nhy* (A. J. Wensinck *et al.*, *Concordance et indices de la tradition musulmane*, Leiden 1936–88, 7:13b.51); none of these would bear a sense of 'forbid one another'. The concordance omits a well-known Prophetic tradition in which *tanāhaw* clearly does mean 'forbid one another'; but in this case the context makes it clear that the diction is Koranic (see below, note 68, and ch. 3, note 40). See also Ibn Abī 'l-Dunyā (d. 281/894), *al-Amr bi'l-ma'rūf wa'l-nahy 'an al-munkar*, ed. Ṣ. 'A. al-Shalāḥī, Medina 1997, 61 no. 18, for a tradition in which *tanāhaw* is clearly used in the sense of 'refrain from' (and cf. the use of the verb *intahā* in the parallels in Jaṣṣāṣ, *Aḥkām*, 2:33.27, and Bayhaqī, *Shu'ab*, 6:89 no. 7,570). I am grateful to Avraham Hakim for sending me a copy of Ibn Abī 'l-Dunyā's *Amr*. The Concordance of Pre-Islamic and Umayyad Poetry of the Hebrew University of Jerusalem contains some dozens of entries for the sixth form of the root; but here again, I can find no example of *tanāhā* used in a sense of 'forbid one another'. I am much indebted to Etan Kohlberg for transcribing these entries for me, and to Albert Arazi and Andras Hamori for further assistance.

[12] This reading is ascribed to Ibn Mas'ūd (Jeffery, *Materials*, 40), to Ubayy ibn Ka'b (*ibid.*, 129), and to Zayd ibn 'Alī (d. 122/740) (A. Jeffery, 'The Qur'ān readings of Zaid b. 'Alī', *Rivista degli Studi Orientali*, 16 (1937), 258).

[13] For the sake of completeness it should be added that Q65:6 offers an eighth form of *amara* with *ma'rūf*: *wa-'tamirū baynakum bi-ma'rūfin*. The context is reasonable conduct in divorce where the ex-wife suckles the ex-husband's child. Arberry's plausible translation is 'and consult together honourably'; there is nothing here to suggest *al-amr bi'l-ma'rūf*.

to 'commanding right'. Whether Q5:79 refers to 'forbidding wrong' turns on the sense of the verb *tanāhā* (not to mention the variant reading); and Q7:165 speaks of 'forbidding evil' (*sū'*) rather than 'forbidding wrong' (*munkar*). The precision that these verses might bring to our conception of the duty is thus qualified by the uncertainty as to whether they actually refer to it at all. In short, scripture on its own has relatively little to tell us about the duty of forbidding wrong – apart, that is, from its name.

2. KORANIC EXEGESIS

What does Koranic exegesis have to tell us about the meaning of these verses? As will appear in the course of this book, the exegetes are often more concerned to set out the school doctrines on forbidding wrong to which they happen to subscribe than they are to elucidate what is there in scripture. Abū Ḥayyān al-Gharnāṭī (d. 745/1344) in his commentary to Q3:104 is a refreshing exception to this trend: he observes that the verse says nothing about the conditions of obligation and other such matters, and refers the reader to the appropriate literature on these questions.[14] I shall take my cue from him, and defer consideration of all such material – including the strongly sectarian variety of Imāmī exegesis – to later chapters. Much exegesis, again, is concerned with points of difficulty which, for all that they arise from the relevant Koranic verses, have little or no bearing on forbidding wrong; such material will not be considered at all. What answers, then, do the exegetes provide to the questions raised by our examination of the Koranic data in the previous section?

With regard to the question who performs the duty, the focus of exegetical attention is an ambiguity in Q3:104: does the 'of' (*min*) in 'of you' impose the duty on all believers, or only on some of them?[15] Some exegetes held the first view: as the philologist Zajjāj (d. 311/923) put it, 'Let there be one community of you' meant 'Let all of you (*kullukum*) be a community'.[16] This,

[14] Abū Ḥayyān al-Gharnāṭī (745/1344), *al-Baḥr al-muḥīṭ*, Cairo 1328, 3:21.4.

[15] Or, in the technical language of the exegetes, is its function *tabyīn* (specification) or *tabʿīḍ* (partition)? (See, for example, Zamakhsharī (d. 538/1144), *Kashshāf*, Beirut 1947, 1:396.8, 397.1; Ṭabrisī, *Majmaʿ*, 1:483.23, 483.25; Fakhr al-Dīn al-Rāzī (d. 606/1210), *al-Tafsīr al-kabīr*, Cairo *c.* 1934–62, 8:177.14, 177.19; Bayḍāwī (d. *c.* 710/1310), *Anwār al-tanzīl*, Cairo n.d., 2:35.7, 35.11.)

[16] Zajjāj (d. 311/923), *Maʿānī al-Qurʾān wa-iʿrābuhu*, ed. ʿA. ʿA. Shalabī, Beirut and Sidon 1973–4, 1:462.5. In support of this view, Zajjāj adduces the *min* of Q22:30: *fa-'jtanibū 'l-rijsa min al-awthāni* – which is not, he points out, an order to avoid some idols rather than others. He then quotes a verse of the pre-Islamic poet Aʿshā Bāhila (for which see R. Geyer (ed.), *Gedichte von 'Abû Baṣîr Maimûn ibn Qais al-'Aʿšâ nebst Sammlungen von Stücken anderer Dichter des gleichen Beinamens*, London 1928, 267, verse 17), in which the *min* refers to a single individual, and therefore cannot have the function of partition. Finally, he finds confirmation in Q3:110.

however, was a minority view.[17] The more common view was that God was requiring only that there be a group (a *firqa*, as Zajjāj put it) among the believers performing the duty.[18] This looks like a major disagreement, and one arising directly out of the understanding of the verse: the second view would seem to lay a foundation for a partition of the community which would restrict the duty to a specially qualified elite. There are in fact three types of restriction which come into play in these arguments. First, supporters of the majority view emphasise the corollary (or at least closely related view) that the duty is a 'collective' one (*farḍ ʿalā ʾl-kifāya*), in the technical sense that when one member of the community discharges it, others are thereby dispensed from it.[19] Secondly, they are occasionally quoted as pointing out that some people are incapable of performing the duty – such as women and invalids.[20] Thirdly, they stress that not all are qualified to perform it. In particular, it

[17] It was nevertheless adopted by the celebrated Imāmī scholar Abū Jaʿfar al-Ṭūsī (*Tibyān*, 2:548.5, setting out the two views, and *ibid.*, 549.9, making clear his adoption of the minority view; see further below, ch. 11, notes 156–61). Ṭūsī also mentions the Muʿtazilite Jubbāʾī (presumably Abū ʿAlī, d. 303/915f.) as a proponent of this view (*ibid.*, 548.14; but see below, ch. 9, note 33). To these we can add Māturīdī (d. *c.* 333/944), Wāḥidī (d. 468/1076), and Baghawī (d. 516/1122) (Māturīdī, *Taʾwīlāt al-Qurʾān*, ms. British Library, Or. 9,432, f. 44b.15 (where both views are stated but only one is supported with proof-texts); Wāḥidī, *al-Wajīz fī tafsīr al-kitāb al-ʿazīz*, ed. Ṣ. ʿA. Dāwūdī, Damascus and Beirut 1995, 226 to Q3:104; Wāḥidī, *Tafsīr al-basīṭ*, ms. Istanbul, Nuru Osmaniye 240, I, f. 432a.2 (I owe all references to this manuscript to the kindness of Michael Bonner) (and cf. Wāḥidī, *al-Wasīṭ fī tafsīr al-Qurʾān al-majīd*, ed. ʿA. A. ʿAbd al-Mawjūd *et al.*, Beirut 1994, 1:474.16); Baghawī, *Maʿālim al-tanzīl*, ed. M. ʿA. al-Namir *et al.*, Riyāḍ 1993, 2:84.22).

[18] Zajjāj, *Maʿānī*, 1:463.3; Zamakhsharī, *Kashshāf*, 1:396.8 (adding a brief mention of the alternative view at 397.1); Qurṭubī (d. 671/1273), *al-Jāmiʿ li-aḥkām al-Qurʾān*, Cairo 1967, 4:165.11; Abū Ḥayyān, *Baḥr*, 3:20.6; Ibn Kathīr (d. 774/1373), *Tafsīr*, Beirut 1966, 2:86.17; Muḥsin al-Fayḍ (d. 1091/1680), *Tafsīr al-ṣāfī*, Mashhad 1982, 1:338.21. Ṭabarī's position is unclear, unless we are to infer his acceptance of the majority view from his glossing of *umma* as *jamāʿa* (Ṭabarī (d. 310/923), *Tafsīr*, ed. M. M. and A. M. Shākir, Cairo n.d., 7:90.4; cf. Abū Ḥayyān, *Baḥr*, 3:20.6, where Ṭabarī is cited as a proponent of this view); indeed his commentary to Q3:104 is so brief as to suggest that the text as we have it may be defective. Muqātil ibn Sulaymān (d. 150/767f.) does no more than gloss *umma* as *ʿuṣba* (*Tafsīr*, ed. ʿA. M. Shiḥāta, Cairo 1979–89, 1:293.18). Fakhr al-Dīn al-Rāzī offers an elaborate account of the competing views (*Tafsīr*, 8:177.14), but concludes only that God knows best (*ibid.*, 178.12). Bayḍāwī merely states the alternatives (*Anwār*, 2:35.7).

[19] Zamakhsharī, *Kashshāf*, 1:396.8; Fakhr al-Dīn al-Rāzī, *Tafsīr*, 8:178.10; Qurṭubī, *Jāmiʿ*, 4:165.14; Bayḍāwī, *Anwār*, 2:35.7; Abū Ḥayyān, *Baḥr*, 3:20.13; and for Rummānī, see below, ch. 9, note 38. Cf. also the reporting of this view in Wāḥidī, *Basīṭ*, I, f. 432a.8, Ṭūsī, *Tibyān*, 2:548.7, and Ṭabrisī, *Majmaʿ*, 1:483.23.

[20] See Thaʿlabī (d. 427/1035), *al-Kashf waʾl-bayān fī tafsīr āy al-Qurʾān*, ms. British Library, Add. 19,926, f. 67a.3; Fakhr al-Dīn al-Rāzī, *Tafsīr*, 8:178.2; Niẓām al-Dīn al-Naysābūrī (*fl.* early eighth/fourteenth century), *Gharāʾib al-Qurʾān*, ed. I. ʿA. ʿIwaḍ, Cairo 1962–71, 4:28.10. The placing of women in this category may seem surprising, since God explicitly includes the female believers (*al-muʾmināt*) among those who command right in Q9:71 (on the question of women forbidding wrong, see below, ch. 17, 482–6).

requires (or may in some instances require) knowledge that not everyone possesses; an ignorant performer may make all sorts of mistakes.[21] From here it is but a short step to speaking of the duty as one for scholars to perform,[22] or even to seeing it as something like a prerogative of the scholarly estate.[23] This last view suggests a strongly elitist construction of the duty, but it is a

[21] Zamakhsharī, *Kashshāf*, 1:396.9; Ṭabrisī, *Jawāmiʿ*, 1:230.20 (a passage not found in his *Majmaʿ* and clearly borrowed from the *Kashshāf*, cf. *Jawāmiʿ*, 1:12.1); Fakhr al-Dīn al-Rāzī, *Tafsīr*, 8:178.3; Bayḍāwī, *Anwār*, 2:35.8; Abū Ḥayyān, *Baḥr*, 3:20.7; also Abū 'l-Layth al-Samarqandī (d. 373/983), *Tafsīr*, ed. ʿA. M. Muʿawwaḍ *et al.*, Beirut 1993, 1:289.19. A rather similar argument is advanced by Zajjāj in presenting this side of the question: since the verse speaks of those who 'call to good' (*yadʿūna ilā 'l-khayr*), it refers to propagandists for the faith (*al-duʿāt ilā 'l-īmān*), who need to be learned (*ʿulamāʾ*) in that which they are propagating, as not everyone is (*Maʿānī*, 1:463.3). But note that exegetes who advance this argument can still speak of the obligation as universal (see Bayḍāwī, *Anwār*, 2:35.10; Zamakhsharī, *Kashshāf*, 1:398.3, noting that anyone is qualified to rebuke someone who fails to pray).

[22] Such language is used by Fakhr al-Dīn al-Rāzī in the passage just cited (which does not necessarily represent his own view): the obligation would be restricted to the scholars (*mukhtaṣṣ biʾl-ʿulamāʾ*) (*Tafsīr*, 8:178.3). Similarly Qurṭubī says that those who command right must be scholars (*ʿulamāʾ*) (*Jāmiʿ*, 4:165.12). Ibn Qutayba (d. 276/889) glosses *umma* in Q3:104 as 'the community of scholars' (*jamāʿat al-ʿulamāʾ*) (*Taʾwīl mushkil al-Qurʾān*, ed. A. Ṣaqr, Cairo 1954, 345.13). The Imāmī Miqdād al-Suyūrī (d. 826/1423) describes 'commanding and forbidding' as 'one of the duties (*waẓāʾif*) of scholars' (*Kanz al-ʿirfān*, ed. M. B. al-Bihbūdī, Tehran 1384–5, 1:407.3 (to Q3:104), followed by Fatḥ Allāh Kāshānī (d. 988/1580f.), *Manhaj al-ṣādiqīn* (in Persian), Tehran 1336–7 sh., 2:294.23 (likewise to Q3:104)). Cf. also the reporting of such a view in Wāḥidī, *Basīṭ*, I, f. 432a.7 (to Q3:104, speaking of *takhṣīṣ al-ʿulamāʾ waʾl-umarāʾ waʾlladhīna hum aʿlam fī 'l-amr biʾl-maʿrūf*). The restrictive overtones of such statements are perhaps not to be taken too seriously. Thus Qurṭubī has already laid down (in his commentary to Q3:21) that commanding right is incumbent on everyone (*ʿāmm fī jamīʿ al-nās*) (*Jāmiʿ*, 4:47.19); and it is generally possible to take *ʿulamāʾ* in the sense of 'those who know', who need not in every case be professional scholars. It is by no means the case that Koranic exegesis at large restricts the performance of the duty to scholars (contrast Athamina, 'The early Murjiʾa', 122f.).

[23] Thus Ibn ʿAṭiyya (d. 541/1146) (in setting out one view) and Thaʿālibī (d. 873/1468f.) (without qualification) interpret the verse as a divine command that there should be scholars in the community, and that the rest of the community should follow them, in view of the extensive learning required by the duty (Ibn ʿAṭiyya, *al-Muḥarrar al-wajīz*, Rabat 1975–, 3:186.18 (I am grateful to Maribel Fierro for supplying me with copies from volumes of this work which were inaccessible to me); Thaʿālibī, *al-Jawāhir al-ḥisān*, ed. ʿA. al-Ṭālibī, Algiers 1985, 1:354.13); and cf. the view they proceed to develop about the distinctive roles of scholars, rulers and others (Ibn ʿAṭiyya, *Muḥarrar*, 3:188.4, and Thaʿālibī, *Jawāhir*, 1:355.9; both limit this division of labour to cases of persistent wrong). A Persian exegete writing in 520/1126 holds similar views on this last point (Maybudī, *Kashf*, 2:234.16); and he quotes the view that those who command right are the scholars (*ʿulamāʾ*) and counsellors (*naṣīḥat-kunandagān*), while those who forbid wrong are the warriors (*ghāzīyān*), the scholars, and the just ruler (*sulṭān-i ʿādil*) (*ibid.*, 235.4; on this work, see G. Lazard, *La langue des plus anciens monuments de la prose persane*, Paris 1963, 110, and 119 no. 54). On the roles of scholars, rulers and others, see also below, ch. 6, note 166. But note that even Thaʿālibī does not in the end attempt to confine the duty to scholars (or rulers) (*Jawāhir*, 1:355.12). For an explicit rejection of the view that the duty is restricted to the scholars by an Ibāḍī exegete, see Aṭfayyish (d. 1332/1914), *Hīmyān al-zād*, ed. ʿA. Shalabī, Oman 1980–, 4:203.18 (the author's name is given on the title-page as Muḥammad ibn Yūsuf . . . al-Muṣʿabī).

relatively uncommon one. Whatever their understanding of the verse, the commentators at large show little interest in interpreting it in a substantively restrictive sense.

The exegesis of other verses has less to offer on this question. Thus in Q3:110, the exegetes discuss a number of views as to whom God is addressing when He says: 'You were the best community brought forth.'[24] One of these views, ascribed to Ḍaḥḥāk ibn Muzāḥim (d. 105/723f.), is that the addressees are the Companions in their roles as the transmitters (*ruwāt*) and propagandists (*duʿāt*) to whom God has enjoined obedience;[25] another, ascribed to Qatāda ibn Diʿāma (d. 117/735f.), identifies the addressees as those who wage holy war, bringing people to Islam by fighting them.[26] On the other hand, prominent exegetes stress that the verse applies to the members of the community at large.[27] Yet these differences are never related to the question who should or should not forbid wrong. Moving on to Q9:112, the commentators entertain a variety of ingenious hypotheses with regard to its syntax,[28] and tend to the view that 'those who command right and forbid wrong' are to be identified with the believers who commit themselves to holy war in the previous verse.[29] But

[24] See, for example, Ṭabarī, *Tafsīr*, 7:100.16; Ibn Abī Ḥātim al-Rāzī (d. 327/938), *Tafsīr al-Qurʾān al-ʿaẓīm*, ed. A. ʿA. al-ʿAmmārī al-Zahrānī and Ḥ. B. Yāsīn, Medina 1408, 2:469–74 nos. 1156–71; Ṭūsī, *Tibyān*, 2:557.16; Ṭabrisī, *Majmaʿ*, 1:486.18; Abū Ḥayyān, *Baḥr*, 3:27.33; Khāzin (d. 741/1341), *Lubāb al-taʾwīl*, Cairo 1328, 1:288.6. The problem arises in part from the puzzling use of the past tense in the verse (*kuntum khayra ummatin* . . .); on this see, for example, Zajjāj, *Maʿānī*, 1:466.17; Ṭabarī, *Tafsīr*, 7:106.1; Ṭūsī, *Tibyān*, 2:557.2; Ibn ʿAṭiyya, *Muḥarrar*, 3:194.15; Bayḍāwī, *Anwār*, 2:36.15; Abū Ḥayyān, *Baḥr*, 3:28.9; Fakhr al-Dīn al-Rāzī, *Tafsīr*, 8:189.13. The view that the tense of the verb has no temporal connotation here is nicely reflected in one translator's rendering of *kuntum* as *būdīd-u shudīd-u hastīd* (Najm al-Dīn al-Nasafī (d. 537/1142), *Tafsīr* (in Persian), ed. ʿA. Juwaynī, n.p. 1353–4 sh., 1:95.5).

[25] Ṭabarī, *Tafsīr*, 7:102 no. 7,613; Khāzin, *Lubāb*, 1:288.10; Abū ʾl-Futūḥ-i Rāzī (first half of sixth/twelfth century), *Rawḍ al-janān* (in Persian), ed. ʿA. A. Ghaffārī, Tehran 1382–7, 3:148.6 (on the author, see the editor's introduction, esp. 7–10; also Lazard, *Langue*, 120 no. 57); Abū ʾl-Maḥāsin al-Jurjānī (ninth or tenth/fifteenth or sixteenth century?), *Jilāʾ al-adhhān* (in Persian), n.p. 1378, 2:102.9; and cf. Wāḥidī, *Basīṭ*, I, f. 433b.4. (The two Imāmī authors find here an invitation to identify the addressees with the imams.) A similar interpretation of Q3:104 is likewise attributed to Ḍaḥḥāk (Ṭabarī, *Tafsīr*, 7:92 no. 7,597; see also Ibn ʿAṭiyya, *Muḥarrar*, 3:186.14; Ibn Kathīr, *Tafsīr*, 2:86.14 (with the explanation 'this means those who wage *jihād* and the *ʿulamāʾ*'); Suyūṭī (d. 911/1505), *al-Durr al-manthūr*, Cairo 1314, 2:62.10; and cf. Fakhr al-Dīn al-Rāzī, *Tafsīr*, 8:178.13).

[26] Abū ʾl-Futūḥ-i Rāzī, *Rawḍ*, 3:150.14; and cf. Abū ʾl-Layth al-Samarqandī, *Tafsīr*, 1:291.11.

[27] Zajjāj, *Maʿānī*, 1:467.1 (reporting this view); Fakhr al-Dīn al-Rāzī, *Tafsīr*, 8:191.1 (quoting the view as that of Zajjāj); Abū Ḥayyān, *Baḥr*, 3:28.7; Ibn Kathīr, *Tafsīr*, 2:89.9. Cf. also Wāḥidī, *Basīṭ*, I, f. 433b.5.

[28] For a neat presentation of these views, see Ibn al-Samīn al-Ḥalabī (d. 756/1355), *al-Durr al-maṣūn*, ed. A. M. al-Kharrāṭ, Damascus 1986–7, 6:129.4. Most major commentaries mention several of them.

[29] See Farrāʾ, *Maʿānī*, 1:453.7; Ṭabarī, *Tafsīr*, 14:500.8; Fakhr al-Dīn al-Rāzī, *Tafsīr*, 16:202.8. Maybudī holds the unusual view that the verse refers back to 'the believers' of Q9:71 (*Kashf*, 4:220.8).

they do not consider (and would doubtless have rejected) any suggestion that the duty is restricted to those engaged in holy war. In the case of Q22:41, the exegetes again offer several views as to the identity of the performers: the community at large,[30] the Companions of the Prophet,[31] the Muhājirūn,[32] the Orthodox caliphs,[33] rulers (*wulāt*).[34] But again, there is no attempt to restrict the duty on this basis.[35] It may be noted in passing that the activities of the officially appointed censor of morals and commercial practice (*muḥtasib*) are almost universally ignored by the exegetes.[36]

As to who is the target of the duty, the exegetes have almost as little to tell us as do the verses themselves. Occasionally they supply the vague object 'people' (*al-nās*) for the verb 'command'.[37]

30 Wāḥidī, *Wasīṭ*, 3:274.8 (citing Ḥasan (al-Baṣri) (d. 110/728) and ʿIkrima (d. 107/725f.); Qurṭubī, *Jāmiʿ*, 12:73.3, citing ʿIkrima, Ḥasan al-Baṣrī and Abū ʾl-ʿĀliya (d. 90/708f.). Wāḥidī adds that the conjunction of forbidding wrong with prayer and the alms-tax in this verse shows it to be obligatory.

31 *Ibid.* (citing Qatāda); Ṭabarī (d. 310/923), *Jāmiʿ al-bayān*, Cairo 1323–9, 17:126.24; Wāḥidī, *Wasīṭ*, 3:274.7 (also citing Qatāda); Hūd ibn Muḥakkam al-Hawwārī (third/ninth century), *Tafsīr*, ed. B. S. Sharīfī, Beirut 1990, 3:120.16 (for this work and its author, see J. van Ess, 'Untersuchungen zu einigen ibāḍitischen Handschriften', *Zeitschrift der Deutschen Morgenländischen Gesellschaft*, 126 (1976), 42f. no. 5; for its heavy dependence on the *Tafsīr* of Yaḥyā ibn Sallām (d. 200/815), see 23f. of Sharīfī's introduction; also M. Muranyi, 'Neue Materialien zur *tafsīr*-Forschung in der Moscheebibliothek von Qairawān', in S. Wild (ed.), *The Qurʾan as text*, Leiden 1996, 228). 32 Fakhr al-Dīn al-Rāzī, *Tafsīr*, 23:41.21; and cf. Ṭūsī, *Tibyān*, 7:322.16.

33 Fakhr al-Dīn al-Rāzī, *Tafsīr*, 23:41.24; Qurṭubī, *Jāmiʿ*, 12:73.1; Maybudī, *Kashf*, 6:380.18; and the early Persian commentary (second half of the fourth/tenth or first half of the fifth/eleventh century) preserved in Cambridge (anon., *Tafsīr-i Qurʾān-i majīd*, ed. J. Matīnī, n.p. 1349 sh., 1:162.17) (for this text, see Lazard, *Langue*, 56–8 no. 9).

34 Qurṭubī, *Jāmiʿ*, 12:73.5, and Abū Ḥayyān, *Baḥr*, 6:376.11 (both citing Ibn Abī Najīḥ (d. 131/748f.), and adding a saying of Ḍaḥḥāk's); Naḥḥās (d. 338/950), *Maʿānī ʾl-Qurʾān al-karīm*, ed. M. ʿA. al-Ṣābūnī, Mecca 1988–, 4:420.1 (citing Ibn Abī Najīḥ). Another Persian commentary mentions a view that the reference is to the Orthodox caliphs and just rulers (*amīrān-i ʿādil*) (anon. (fourth/tenth or first half of fifth/eleventh century), *Tafsīrī bar ʿushrī az Qurʾān-i majīd*, ed. J. Matīnī, Tehran 1352 sh., 263.4; for the dating, see the editor's introduction, xxii). An exegesis transmitted by Kalbī (d. 146/763f.) refers the verse to the Banū Hāshim (sc. the ʿAbbāsids), past and future (Khaṭīb, *Taʾrīkh Baghdād*, 14:69.3; I owe this reference to Nurit Tsafrir).

35 Qurṭubī, however, invokes the verse in discussing the restriction of the duty to the scholars in his commentary to Q3:104 (*Jāmiʿ*, 4:165.15; as this passage confirms, *yumakkan* is to be read for *yakun*, *ibid.*, 12:73.2).

36 I know only one exception: Niẓām al-Dīn al-Naysābūrī, who devotes a large part of his commentary on Q3:104 to the role of the official *muḥtasib* (*Gharāʾib*, 4:28.17). Where other exegetes use the term *iḥtisāb*, the reference is simply to *al-amr biʾl-maʿrūf* in general (Bayḍāwī makes occasional use of the term, see *Anwār*, 2:35.9 (to Q3:104), 38.9 (to Q3:114); whence Abū ʾl-Suʿūd al-ʿImādī (d. 982/1574), *Irshād al-ʿaql al-salīm*, Riyāḍ n.d., 1:528.14 (to Q3:104); Fayḍ, *Ṣāfī*, 1:344.4 (to Q3:114); Kāshānī, *Manhaj*, 2:305.23 (to Q3:114)). This usage is borrowed from Ghazzālī (d. 505/1111), see below, ch. 16, 428f.

37 So Muqātil to Q3:110 (*Tafsīr*, 1:295.5), Ṭabarī to Q3:104 (*Tafsīr*, 7:91.1), and Abū ʾl-Suʿūd to Q3:104 (*Irshād*, 1:529.4); in the case of Q3:110 this echoes the occurrence of the word earlier in the verse. Ibn ʿAṭiyya, in his analysis of the view that Q3:104 is addressed to the community at large, states that in this view the verse would be a command for the community to call the whole world (*jamīʿ al-ʿālam*) to good – the unbelievers to Islam, the sinners to obedience (Ibn ʿAṭiyya, *Muḥarrar*, 3:187.12). Abū ʾl-Fatḥ

With regard to the question of the scope of the obligation, the most interesting phenomenon in the exegetical literature is an early approach which tends to present the duty as simply one of enjoining belief in God and His Prophet.[38] This approach is first firmly attested in the works of Muqātil ibn Sulaymān (d. 150/767f.), especially in one on the meanings (*wujūh*) of Koranic terms. According to this work, 'commanding right' in Q3:110, Q9:112 and Q31:17 means enjoining belief in the unity of God (*tawḥīd*), while 'forbidding wrong' in these verses means forbidding polytheism (*shirk*); at the same time, in Q3:114 and Q9:71, 'commanding right' refers to following (*ittibāʿ*) and affirming belief (*taṣdīq*) in the Prophet, and 'wrong' refers to denying (*takdhīb*) him.[39] This analysis is repeated in later works of the same genre.[40] There are also examples of this type of thinking in the mouths of even earlier authorities. There is a sweeping view ascribed to Abū 'l-ʿĀliya (d. 90/708f.) according to which, in all Koranic references to 'commanding right' and 'forbidding wrong', the former refers to calling people from polytheism to Islam, and the latter to forbidding the worship

Footnote 37 (*cont.*)
al-Jurjānī (d. 976/1568f.) in his paraphrase of Q3:110 speaks of the believers commanding and forbidding each other (*Tafsīr-i shāhī*, ed. W. al-Ishrāqī, Tabrīz 1380, 2:102.6; cf. Miqdād, *Kanz*, 1:405.15). Q66:6 tells the believers to 'guard yourselves and your families' from hellfire; Ṭūsī remarks that this verse requires that the duty be performed in the first instance towards those closest to us (*lil-aqrab fa'l-aqrab*) (*Tibyān*, 10:50.9).

38 On the rare occasions when we encounter this approach outside exegetical and related literature, it tends to remain tied to the relevant Koranic verses. A case in point is the treatment of Q9:67 and Q9:71 by Wāqidī (d. 207/823) in his chapter on scripture revealed during the Tabūk expedition of the year 9/630 (*Maghāzī*, ed. M. Jones, London 1966, 1067.12, 1068.6). For an exception, see below, ch. 8, note 96. This exegetical trend is perceptively noted by van Ess (*Theologie*, 2:389).

39 Muqātil ibn Sulaymān (d. 150/767f.), *al-Ashbāh wa'l-naẓā'ir*, ed. ʿA. M. Shiḥāta, Cairo 1975, 113f. no. 13 (cited in van Ess, *Theologie*, 2:389 n. 23; on the work and the genre in general, see *ibid.*, 524–7). (There is no reference here to Q3:104, Q7:157, Q9:67, or Q22:41.) The exegeses of Q3:114, Q9:71, Q9:112 and Q31:17 also appear in his *Tafsīr* (1:296.12, 2:181.13, 199.2, 3:435.8 (where for *al-sharr* read *al-shirk*)). The exegesis of Q31:17 appears further in Muqātil's *Tafsīr al-khams mi'at āya*, ed. I. Goldfeld, Shfaram 1980, 278.15 (also cited in van Ess, *Theologie*, 2:389 n. 23). However, at Q3:110 Muqātil in his *Tafsīr* glosses *maʿrūf* as *īmān*, and *munkar*, it seems, as *ẓulm* (*Tafsīr*, 1:295.5). Turning to the exegeses given in the *Tafsīr* for verses ignored in the *Ashbāh*, Q3:104 is unglossed (*Tafsīr*, 1:293.18); to Q7:157 we are offered the glosses *īmān* and *shirk* (*Tafsīr*, 2:67.9); Q9:67 is glossed similarly to Q3:114 and Q9:71 (*ibid.*, 180.9); and Q22:41 is glossed similarly to Q3:110, Q9:112 and Q31:17 (*ibid.*, 3:130.7). I am grateful to Uri Rubin for giving me access to many of these passages through his copy of the manuscript of Muqātil's *Tafsīr*; this was in the days before Shiḥāta's full publication had become available.

40 It appears, with little change, in works of Yaḥyā ibn Sallām (d. 200/815), Ḥusayn ibn Muḥammad al-Dāmaghānī (fifth/eleventh century?), Ibn al-Jawzī (d. 597/1201), and Ibn al-ʿImād (d. 887/1482) (Yaḥyā ibn Sallām, *Taṣārīf*, ed. H. Shalabī, Tunis 1979, 203 no. 42; Dāmaghānī, *al-Wujūh wa'l-naẓā'ir*, ed. A. Bihrūz, Tabrīz 1366 sh., 113.3 (on this work and its author, see E. Kohlberg, *A medieval Muslim scholar at work: Ibn Ṭāwūs and his library*, Leiden 1992, 387f. no. 658); Ibn al-Jawzī, *Nuzhat al-aʿyun*, ed. M. ʿA. K. al-Rāḍī, Beirut 1984, 544 no. 270, 574 no. 286; Ibn al-ʿImād, *Kashf al-sarā'ir*, ed. F. ʿA. Aḥmad and M. S. Dāwūd, Alexandria n.d., 145 no. 38).

of idols and devils.[41] Similar views are attributed to other early authorities, such as Saʿīd ibn Jubayr (d. 95/714) (regarding Q9:112 and Q31:17)[42] and Ḥasan al-Baṣrī (d. 110/728) (regarding Q9:112).[43]

This approach is adopted from time to time by the classical exegetes, though never, to my knowledge, consistently;[44] and as might be expected,

41 Ṭabarī, *Tafsīr*, 14:348 no. 16,938 (to Q9:71); *ibid.*, 507 no. 17,317 (to Q9:112); Ibn Abī Ḥātim, *Tafsīr*, 2:460 nos. 1128, 1130 (to Q3:104), and cf. *ibid.*, 475 no. 1173 (to Q3:110). For similar traditions from Abū ʾl-ʿĀliya, see Ṭabarī, *Jāmiʿ al-bayān*, 17:126.32 (to Q22:41), and Mujāhid ibn Jabr (d. 104/722f.), *Tafsīr*, ed. ʿA. Ṭ. M. al-Sūratī, n.p. n.d., 505.1 (to Q31:17; for this work see F. Leemhuis, 'MS. 1075 Tafsīr of the Cairene Dār al-Kutub and Muǧāhid's *Tafsīr*', in R. Peters (ed.), *Proceedings of the Ninth Congress of the Union Européenne des Arabisants et Islamisants*, Leiden 1981; and F. Leemhuis, 'Origins and early development of the *tafsīr* tradition', in A. Rippin (ed.), *Approaches to the history of the interpretation of the Qurʾān*, Oxford 1988, 19–25). The common link in these transmissions is the second/eighth-century traditionist Abū Jaʿfar al-Rāzī. For citations without *isnāds*, see Wāḥidī, *Basīṭ*, II, f. 579b.8 (to Q9:71); Abū Ḥayyān, *Baḥr*, 3:29.32 (to Q3:110), 5:70.33 (to Q9:71); Abū ʾl-Futūḥ-i Rāzī, *Rawḍ*, 6:68.10 (to Q9:71); Suyūṭī, *Durr*, 2:62.6 (to Q3:104), 3:255.15 (to Q9:67).

42 Māwardī (d. 450/1058), *al-Nukat waʾl-ʿuyūn*, ed. S. ʿA. ʿAbd al-Raḥīm, Beirut 1992, 2:407.20, 408.3 (to Q9:112); Suyūṭī, *Durr*, 5:166.19 (to Q31:17).

43 Ṭabarī, *Tafsīr*, 14:506 no. 17,315 (to Q9:112); and cf. Hūd ibn Muḥakkam, *Tafsīr*, 2:151.1 (to Q9:71). A similar view is ascribed to Ibn ʿAbbās (d. 68/687f.) in one tradition (Suyūṭī, *Durr*, 3:282.9 (to Q9:112); and cf. Ṭabarānī (d. 360/971), *Duʿāʾ*, ed. M. ʿA. ʿAṭā, Beirut 1993, 447 no. 1543 (re Q3:110; I owe this reference to Mona Zaki); Wāḥidī, *Basīṭ*, I, f. 436b.18 (to Q3:114), II, f. 578a.7 (to Q9:67), II, f. 579b.7 (to Q9:71); Fakhr al-Dīn al-Rāzī, *Tafsīr*, 8:202.25 (to Q3:114), and Abū Ḥayyān, *Baḥr*, 3:29.32 (to Q3:110); cf. below, note 47. See also Mujāhid, *Tafsīr*, 133.8 (to Q3:110).

44 Hūd ibn Muḥakkam sometimes adopts it (as he does to Q3:110, *Tafsīr*, 1:306.13), but sometimes explains *maʿrūf* as that which people know to be justice (*ʿadl*) and *munkar* as that which they know to be injustice (*jawr*) (as to Q9:112, *ibid.*, 2:171.1), and sometimes offers both as alternatives (as to Q9:67, *ibid.*, 149.5). Zajjāj adopts it in his commentaries to Q9:67 (*Maʿānī*, 2:509.15), Q9:112 (*ibid.*, 523.17), and in part Q3:114 (*ibid.*, 1:471.10); but in the case of Q9:112, he offers as an alternative the view that the reference may be to 'all *maʿrūf*' and 'all *munkar*' (*ibid.*, 2:524.1). Māturīdī cites both these views to Q3:114 without making a choice (*Taʾwīlāt*, f. 47b.25). Abū ʾl-Layth al-Samarqandī regularly speaks of *tawḥīd* or *ittibāʿ Muḥammad* on the one hand and of *shirk* on the other (*Tafsīr*, 1:291.15 (to Q3:110), 292.25 (to Q3:114), 574.8 (to Q7:157), 2:61.15 (to Q9:71), 76.6 (to Q9:112), 397.17 (to Q22:41), and cf. *ibid.*, 1:289.16 (to Q3:104, citing Kalbī), 589.26 (to Q7:199), 2:60.10 (to Q9:67), 3:22.21 (to Q31:17)). This is likely to reflect his marked dependence on Muqātil (see the remarks of ʿA. A. al-Zaqqa in his introduction to his partial edition of the *Tafsīr* of Abū ʾl-Layth, Baghdad 1985–6, 1:136f.; nevertheless Abū ʾl-Layth usually adds wordings which widen the meaning). Wāḥidī sometimes does likewise, as in his commentaries to Q9:67 and Q9:71 (*Wajīz*, 471, 472; *Wasīṭ*, 2:508.15, 509.21); but in his commentaries to Q9:112, for example, he adopts or adds a mainstream view (*Wajīz*, 483; *Wasīṭ*, 2:527.6; *Basīṭ*, II, f. 601b.10). Another example is Ṭabrisī in his commentary to Q3:114 (*Majmaʿ*, 1:489.30), but contrast his glossing of *maʿrūf* as *ṭāʿāt* and of *munkar* as *maʿāṣī* in his commentary to Q3:110 (*ibid.*, 1:486.21). Maybudī follows the same approach in his commentary to Q3:114 (*Kashf*, 2:248.17), but contrast below, note 49. The Khāzin confines himself to this approach in his commentary to Q3:110 (*Lubāb*, 1:289.14), but elsewhere tends to give alternatives (see the following note). The Zaydī imam al-Nāṣir Abū ʾl-Fatḥ al-Daylamī (d. 444/1052f.) offers such glosses to Q9:112 (*al-Burhān fī tafsīr al-Qurʾān*, in a manuscript copied in 1046/1637 of which I possess a xerox but am not certain of the location, f. 85b.17, and cf. *ibid.*, f. 155a.25, to Q29:45) (for this imam, see W. Madelung, *Der Imam al-Qāsim ibn Ibrāhīm und die Glaubenslehre der Zaiditen*, Berlin 1965, 205).

they not infrequently mention it among competing views.[45] But Ṭabarī (d. 310/923) in his commentary to Q9:112 explicitly states his disagreement, observing that 'commanding right' refers to *all* that God and His Prophet have commanded, and 'forbidding wrong' to *all* that they have forbidden.[46] Elsewhere his formulations tend to take up the terms of Muqātil's exegesis, but to indicate in one way or another that the duty has a wider range.[47] Other commentators rarely take as strong a stand as Ṭabarī,[48] but likewise tend to indicate the broad scope of the duty, even when giving pride of place to Muqātil's terms.[49] This, of course, goes well with the generalised character of 'right' and 'wrong' (*maʿrūf* and *munkar*) as ethical terms elsewhere in the Koran.

As Ṭabarī clearly perceived, if the scope of the duty is restricted to enjoining belief in God and His Prophet, then it has nothing to do with reproving other Muslims for drinking, wenching and making music. Yet the implication that was obvious to Ṭabarī is never spelled out by the early exegetes themselves when they propound their view. This silence is doubtless related to the fact that the whole approach, though widely attested in Koranic exegesis, is virtually unknown elsewhere.

[45] Thus some commentators to Q7:157 mention the equation of *maʿrūf* with *īmān* and of *munkar* with *shirk* among other interpretations of the terms (Abū Ḥayyān, *Baḥr*, 4:403.31, citing Muqātil; Abū 'l-Futūḥ-i Rāzī, *Rawḍ*, 5:306.12; Khāzin, *Lubāb*, 2:147.27, giving this view pride of place, as he also does in his commentary to Q9:112, *ibid.*, 2:285.16). See also Ibn ʿAṭiyya, *Muḥarrar*, 3:188.17 (to Q3:104, spelling out the implication that the verse would then refer to *jihād*); Khāzin, *Lubāb*, 1:291.9 (to Q3:114); Abū 'l-Fatḥ al-Daylamī, *Burhān*, f. 83a.24 (to Q9:67); Aṭfayyish, *Hīmyān*, 4:229.20 (to Q3:114).

[46] Ṭabarī, *Tafsīr*, 14:507.8. Cf. also his generalising exegesis of the injunction *wa-'mur bi'l-ʿurf* in Q7:199 (*ibid.*, 13:331.13).

[47] *Ibid.*, 7:105.4 (to Q3:110), 130.8 (to Q3:114), 13:165.12 (to Q7:157), 14:338.2 (to Q9:67), 347.7 (to Q9:71), 506.8 (to Q9:112); Ṭabarī, *Jāmiʿ al-bayān*, 17:126.26 (to Q22:41)). A view he quotes from Ibn ʿAbbās makes the point nicely: affirmation of the unity of God is the highest good (*aʿẓam al-maʿrūf*), and its denial (*takdhīb*) is the worst evil (*ankar al-munkar*) (*Tafsīr*, 7:105 no. 7,624 (to Q3:110); similarly Ibn Abī Ḥātim, *Tafsīr*, 2:474f. nos. 1172, 1174 (to Q3:110); Māturīdī, *Taʾwīlāt*, f. 46a.26 (to Q3:110); Ṭabarānī, *Duʿāʾ*, 447 no. 1543 (re Q3:110); Suyūṭī, *Durr*, 2:64.18 (to Q3:110), 3:255.13 (to Q9:67); Fakhr al-Dīn al-Rāzī, *Tafsīr*, 8:192.4 (to Q3:110)).

[48] One exception is Fakhr al-Dīn al-Rāzī in his commentary to Q3:114, where he emphasises that the terms *maʿrūf* and *munkar* must be taken without restriction, and comprehend all *maʿrūf* and all *munkar* (*Tafsīr*, 8:202.26). See also Abū Ḥayyān, *Baḥr*, 3:20.33 (to Q3:104), for a less forcible statement to the same effect.

[49] See, for example, Wāḥidī, *Basīṭ*, II, f. 449b.6 (to Q7:157), citing Kalbī; Ibn ʿAṭiyya, *Muḥarrar*, 3:189.2 (to Q3:104), 8:287.2 (to Q9:112); Maybudī, *Kashf*, 3:760.17 (to Q7:157), 4:220.21 (to Q9:112); Fakhr al-Dīn al-Rāzī, *Tafsīr*, 15:24.15 (to Q7:157), 16:126.11 (to Q9:67), 204.26 (to Q9:112); Bayḍāwī, *Anwār*, 2:298.16 (to Q9:112); Abū Ḥayyān, *Baḥr*, 3:29.31 (to Q3:110); Najm al-Dīn al-Nasafī, *Tafsīr*, 1:95.6 (to Q3:110); Ḥusayn Wāʿiẓ Kāshifī (d. 910/1504f.), *Mawāhib-i ʿaliyya*, Tehran 1317–29 sh., 1:174.17 (to Q3:114); Kāshānī, *Manhaj*, 2:305.19 (to Q3:114). Cf. also such translations of *maʿrūf* as *kārhā-yi pasandīda* (to Q3:110) (Muʿīn al-Dīn Nīshāpūrī (sixth/twelfth century), *Tafsīr-i baṣāyir-i yamīnī*, n.p. 1359– sh., 1:364.4), *shāyast-hā wa bāyast-hā* (to Q3:114) (*ibid.*, 366.3), *kārhā-yi nīk* (to Q3:104) (Najm al-Dīn al-Nasafī, *Tafsīr*, 1:94.7).

What do the commentators have to say about the more significant elements in the peripheral Koranic material we looked at above?

The glossing of the term 'right' (*maʿrūf*) in the numerous Koranic passages in which it occurs has relatively little to offer us. Such explications tend to vary widely with the context,[50] yielding a proliferation of meanings formally recognised in the literature on the meanings of Koranic terms.[51] But as might be expected, 'right' and 'wrong' (*munkar*) also attract attempts at more formal definition. Many of these definitions make reference to both revelation and reason; thus for Rāghib al-Iṣbahānī (*fl.* later fourth/tenth century), right can be defined as 'any action the goodness (*ḥusn*) of which is known by reason (*ʿaql*) or revelation (*sharʿ*)'.[52] Still more of them refer only to revelation; thus for Zajjāj, right means 'everything recognised (*ʿurifa*) by revelation (*sharʿ*)'.[53] A few definitions refer only to reason (*ʿaql*).[54] This variation, whatever its

[50] An indication of the ways in which Muqātil deals with occurrences of the term in his commentary to the first four Sūras will suffice here. He offers as synonyms *rifq* (*Tafsīr*, 1:158.7 (to Q2:178)) and *iḥsān* (*ibid.*, 194.20 (to Q2:229), 196.9 (to Q2:231), 364.18 (to Q4:19)). He glosses *qawl maʿrūf* as *ʿida ḥasana* (*ibid.*, 199.11 (to Q2:235), 358.2 (to Q4:5), 359.14 (to Q4:8)) or *qawl ḥasan* (*ibid.*, 220.1 (to Q2:263)). Elsewhere he repeats the term *maʿrūf* in his exegesis (as at *ibid.*, 159.10 (to Q2:180)), ignores it (as at 194.15 (to Q2:228)), or gives it a behavioural specification appropriate to the context (as at *ibid.*, 197.9 (to Q2:232), *ibid.*, 358.9 (to Q4:6), *ibid.*, 406.16 (to Q4:114)).

[51] Muqātil, *Ashbāh*, 114f. no. 14 (where *qarḍ* is to be read for *farḍ*); Yaḥyā ibn Sallām, *Taṣārīf*, 204f. no. 43; Dāmaghānī, *Wujūh*, 766f.; Ḥubaysh ibn Ibrāhīm al-Tiflīsī (writing 558/1163), *Wujūh-i Qurʾān*, ed. M. Muḥaqqiq, Tehran 1340 sh., 272f.; Ibn al-Jawzī, *Nuzha*, 574f.; Ibn al-ʿImād, *Kashf al-sarāʾir*, 146f. no. 39 (again read *qarḍ* for *farḍ*).

[52] See al-Rāghib al-Iṣbahānī (*fl.* later fourth/tenth century), *al-Mufradāt fī gharīb al-Qurʾān*, ed. M. A. Khalaf Allāh, n.p. 1970, 2:496b.4. See also Ṭūsī, *Tibyān*, 5:299.10 (to Q9:71), 8:279.17 (to Q31:17, defining *munkar*); Ṭabrisī, *Majmaʿ*, 3:50.3 (to Q9:71), 4:319.16 (to Q31:17); Abū ʾl-Futūḥ-i Rāzī, *Rawḍ*, 5:306.15 (to Q7:157); Muʿīn al-Dīn Nīshāpūrī, *Baṣāyir*, 1:362.8 (to Q3:104); Khāzin, *Lubāb*, 1:285.22 (to Q3:104, but contrast the following note); Abū ʾl-Fatḥ al-Daylamī, *Burhān*, f. 155a.25 (to Q29:45, defining *munkar*, but cf. below, note 54). Ṭūsī has a different definition in his commentary to Q3:104 (*Tibyān*, 2:549.3; similarly Abū ʾl-Futūḥ-i Rāzī, *Rawḍ*, 3:141.3).

[53] *Apud* Abū Ḥayyān, *Baḥr*, 4:403.31 (to Q7:157). See also Ṭabarī, *Tafsīr*, 7:105.12 (to Q3:110), 9:201.14 (to Q4:114); Wāḥidī, *Basīṭ*, II, f. 449b.8 (to Q7:157, citing Kalbī's definition of *munkar* as what is not recognised in *sharīʿa* or *sunna*); Ibn ʿAṭiyya, *Muḥarrar*, 7:179.17 (to Q7:157, subsuming *murūʾa* under *sharʿ*); Abū ʾl-Futūḥ-i Rāzī, *Rawḍ*, 6:68.10 (to Q9:71, defining *munkar*); Khāzin, *Lubāb*, 2:147.28 (to Q7:157, mentioning rather than adopting the definition), 2:260.4 (to Q9:71, with a definition of *munkar* which refers also to *ṭabʿ*); Thaʿālibī, *Jawāhir*, 2:77.20 (to Q7:157, following Ibn ʿAṭiyya); Kāshifī, *Mawāhib*, 1:171.15 (to Q3:104); Kāshānī, *Manhaj*, 2:299.7 (to Q3:110).

[54] Such formulations appear in Jaṣṣāṣ, *Aḥkām*, 3:38.10 (*al-maʿrūf huwa mā ḥasuna fī ʾl-ʿaql fiʿluhu*), Ṭūsī, *Tibyān*, 3:596.10 (to Q5:79, defining *munkar*), 4:594.6 (to Q7:157), Abū ʾl-Fatḥ al-Daylamī, *Burhān*, f. 83a.24 (to Q9:67, defining *munkar*), and Ṭabrisī, *Majmaʿ*, 2:231.29 (to Q5:79, defining *munkar*), 487.29 (to Q7:157); and cf. Ibn al-Jawzī (d. 597/1201), *Zād al-masīr*, Damascus and Beirut 1964–8, 3:272.20 (to Q7:157), and Māwardī, *Nukat*, 2:268.20 (to Q7:157), 379.11 (to Q9:67). Māturīdī presents both views within a framework of three possible interpretations (*wujūh*), without expressing a preference (*Taʾwīlāt*, f. 46a.22, to Q3:110). Abū ʾl-Layth al-Samarqandī cites both views anonymously, and offers no comment (*Tafsīr*, 1:289.17 (to Q3:104)). Cf. also below, ch. 7, notes 69, 108, and ch. 15, note 59.

doctrinal significance,[55] has no real implications for the character of the duty, and the upshot is to confirm 'commanding right' and 'forbidding wrong' as second-order duties which have no determinate content in themselves.[56]

With regard to the Koranic expressions 'commanding X' and 'forbidding Y', the tendency of the exegetes is to assimilate them to 'commanding right' and 'forbidding wrong' with little if any reflection. Thus Ṭabarī has no difficulty equating the term *ʿurf* in Q7:199 with 'right' (*maʿrūf*),[57] while Qurṭubī (d. 671/1273) goes so far as to pin his main discussion of forbidding wrong to the reference to 'those who command justice (*qisṭ*)' in Q3:21.[58] Commentators to Q7:165 regularly assume that the whole passage to which it belongs is concerned with the duty,[59] but they rarely bother to comment specifically on the locution 'forbid evil (*sūʾ*)'.[60]

We come now to the two verses that, despite their lack of unambiguous reference to the duty, alone give support to the idea that it is to be performed by members of the community to each other.

With regard to the *yatanāhawna* of Q5:79, the commentators ignore the variant reading *yantahūna*, and favour the interpretation of *yatanāhawna* as 'forbid each other', rather than 'desist'. Thus Fakhr al-Dīn al-Rāzī

[55] It does not seem to be very great, despite the disagreement between Muʿtazilites and Ashʿarites as to whether good and evil are so by nature or by divine fiat (see M. J. McDermott, *The theology of al-Shaikh al-Mufīd*, Beirut 1978, 62f.). Ṭabrisī in his commentary to Q3:104 quotes alternative definitions, one appealing to revelation alone, and the other to revelation and reason; he comments that there is no real difference in meaning (*maʿnā*) between them (*Majmaʿ*, 1:483.30 (to Q3:104); and cf. Abū ʾl-Barakāt al-Nasafī (d. 701/1301), *Madārik al-tanzīl*, Cairo 1936–42, 1:240 nn. 1f. (to Q3:104)).

[56] As one Ashʿarite scholar puts it, the details of the duty are tantamount to the entire law of Islam (*tafāṣīluhā al-sharʿ min muftataḥihi ilā mukhtatamihi*) (Juwaynī (d. 478/1085), *al-Irshād ilā qawāṭiʿ al-adilla fī uṣūl al-iʿtiqād*, ed. M. Y. Mūsā and ʿA. ʿA. ʿAbd al-Ḥamīd, Cairo 1950, 370.9).

[57] Ṭabarī, *Tafsīr*, 13:331.8 (despite some inhomogeneity in the views of earlier exegetes, see *ibid.*, 330f. nos. 15,547–51); and see ʿAbd al-Razzāq ibn Hammām al-Ṣanʿānī (d. 211/827), *Tafsīr al-Qurʾān*, ed. M. M. Muḥammad, Riyāḍ 1989, 1:245.15.

[58] Qurṭubī, *Jāmiʿ*, 4:47–9. His precursor Ibn al-ʿArabī (d. 543/1148) had already taken the verse as an invitation to plunge straight into a major discussion of *al-amr biʾl-maʿrūf* (*Aḥkām al-Qurʾān*, ed. ʿA. M. al-Bajāwī, Cairo 1957–8, 266.5). Ṭūsī states explicitly that the verse refers to 'those who command right and forbid wrong' (*Tibyān*, 2:423.13; cf. also Abū ʾl-Futūḥ-i Rāzī, *Rawḍ*, 2:483.9; Abū ʾl-Layth al-Samarqandī, *Tafsīr*, 1:256.1; Māwardī, *Nukat*, 1:381.17). The equation of commanding justice with commanding right is already implicit in the Prophetic tradition quoted by the commentators from Abū ʿUbayda ibn al-Jarrāḥ (d. 18/639) (*ibid.*, 381.18; Qurṭubī, *Jāmiʿ*, 4:46.17; Ṭūsī, *Tibyān*, 2:422.10; Ṭabrisī, *Majmaʿ*, 1:423.16; Abū ʾl-Futūḥ-i Rāzī, *Rawḍ*, 2:483.12; Fakhr al-Dīn al-Rāzī, *Tafsīr*, 7:229.13; Suyūṭī, *Durr*, 2:13.24).

[59] See below, note 69.

[60] Muqātil glosses *sūʾ* with *maʿāṣī* (*Tafsīr*, 2:71.2). Ibn ʿAṭiyya comments that *sūʾ* is a general term for all sins, though in this context referring specifically to fishing (on the Sabbath) (*Muḥarrar*, 7:189.14); this is repeated by Abū Ḥayyān (*Baḥr*, 4:412.21) and Thaʿālibī (*Jawāhir*, 2:82.12).

(d. 606/1210) notes both interpretations, but describes the first as that of the mainstream (*jumhūr*).[61] Of other commentators who refer to both, a few give no indication of preference,[62] or even combine the two meanings;[63] but most in one way or another relegate 'desist' to a secondary position.[64] Commentators who confine themselves to only one interpretation almost always choose 'forbid each other';[65] the only significant exception is Wāḥidī (d. 468/1076) in one of his works.[66] At the same time, several commentators treat the verse as an invitation to rail against laxity in the performance of the duty.[67] It is clear, then, that Koranic exegesis has put most of its weight behind the interpretation of Q5:79 as a reference to the mutual forbidding of wrongs committed within the community.[68]

61 Fakhr al-Dīn al-Rāzī, *Tafsīr*, 12:64.12; so already Wāḥidī, *Basīṭ*, II, f. 221a.19, 221b.11.

62 So Bayḍāwī and Muḥsin al-Fayḍ (Bayḍāwī, *Anwār*, 2:164.8; Fayḍ, *Ṣāfī*, 2:75.7).

63 So Ṭabarī, Abū 'l-Layth al-Samarqandī, Ṭūsī, and Ṭabrisī in his major commentary (Ṭabarī, *Tafsīr*, 10:496.4; Abū 'l-Layth al-Samarqandī, *Tafsīr*, 1:453.5; Ṭūsī, *Tibyān*, 3:595.21; Ṭabrisī, *Majmaʿ*, 2:231.25 (and cf. 231.5)). Ṭabarī's commentary to this verse is again surprisingly brief – a few lines and a single short tradition.

64 So Zamakhsharī, Ṭabrisī in his minor commentary, the Khāzin, and Abū Ḥayyān (Zamakhsharī, *Kashshāf*, 1:667.3, 667.11; Ṭabrisī, *Jawāmiʿ*, 1:397.1; Khāzin, *Lubāb*, 1:516.22; Abū Ḥayyān, *Baḥr*, 3:540.14, 540.26). Ibn Manẓūr (d. 711/1311f.) follows this line in his lexicon (*Lisān al-ʿArab*, Beirut 1968, 15:344a.5).

65 This seems to be the view taken by Muqātil (*Tafsīr*, 1:496.14), and is unambiguously that adopted by Tujībī (d. 419/1028), Thaʿlabī, Wāḥidī in his *Wasīṭ*, Baghawī, Ibn al-Jawzī, Qurṭubī, Ibn Kathīr, Biqāʿī (d. 885/1480), and the two Jalāl al-Dīns, Maḥallī (d. 864/1459) and Suyūṭī (Tujībī, *Mukhtaṣar min Tafsīr al-imām al-Ṭabarī*, Cairo 1970–1, 1:152.7; Thaʿlabī, *Kashf*, f. 204b.23; Wāḥidī, *Wasīṭ*, 2:215.12; Baghawī, *Maʿālim*, 3:84.10; Ibn al-Jawzī, *Zād al-masīr*, 2:406.9; Qurṭubī, *Jāmiʿ*, 6:253.7; Ibn Kathīr, *Tafsīr*, 2:618.15; Biqāʿī, *Naẓm al-durar*, Hyderabad 1969–84, 6:265.10; Maḥallī and Suyūṭī, *Tafsīr al-Qur'ān al-karīm* (= *Tafsīr al-Jalālayn*), Cairo 1966, 121.2). The Persian exegetes follow suit, as in the translations of the (fourth/tenth century?) *Qur'ān-i Quds*, Najm al-Dīn al-Nasafī and Ḥusayn Wāʿiẓ Kāshifī, and the commentaries of Abū 'l-Futūḥ-i Rāzī, Abū 'l-Maḥāsin Jurjānī, and Fatḥ Allāh Kāshānī (anon., *Qur'ān-i Quds: kuhantarīn bargardān-i Qur'ān bah Fārsī?*, ed. ʿA. Riwāqī, Tehran 1364 sh., 60; Najm al-Dīn al-Nasafī, *Tafsīr*, 1:171.5; Kāshifī, *Mawāhib*, 1:345.20; Abū 'l-Futūḥ-i Rāzī, *Rawḍ*, 4:301.15; Jurjānī, *Jila' al-adhhān*, 2:417.12; Kāshānī, *Manhaj*, 3:300.12).

66 Wāḥidī, *Wajīz*, 331 (*lā yantahūn*). Cf. also the anonymous *Tarjuma-i Tafsīr-i Ṭabarī* (third quarter of the fourth/tenth century), ed. Ḥ. Yaghmā'ī, Tehran 1339– sh., 421.9 (*nah bāz īstādand az zishtī*) (for this text, see Lazard, *Langue*, 41–5 no. 3).

67 Zamakhsharī is particularly eloquent on this theme (*Kashshāf*, 1:667.5); see also Maybudī, *Kashf*, 3:197.4 (and cf. *ibid.*, 2:234.10 to Q3:104); Kāshifī, *Mawāhib*, 1:345.22; Kāshānī, *Manhaj*, 3:300.17. Ibn Kathīr takes the verse as an occasion to introduce a long series of *ḥadīth*s regarding *al-amr bi'l-maʿrūf* in general (*Tafsīr*, 2:619.28–622.9).

68 Compare the tendentiousness of Ṭabarī's understanding of *wa-'tamirū baynakum bi-maʿrūfin* in Q65:6 (see above, note 13) as 'accept from one another, oh people, that right which you command each other (*mā amarakum baʿḍukum bihi baʿḍan min maʿrūf*)' (Ṭabarī, *Jāmiʿ al-bayān*, 28:96.4; similarly Ṭūsī, *Tibyān*, 10:37.15; Wāḥidī, *Wajīz*, 1108; Zamakhsharī, *Kashshāf*, 4:559.10; Ṭabrisī, *Jawāmiʿ*, 2:708.15; Fakhr al-Dīn al-Rāzī, *Tafsīr*, 30:37.10 (quoting Mubarrad (d. 286/900)); Qurṭubī, *Jāmiʿ*, 18:169.3; Bayḍāwī, *Anwār*, 4:207.26; Khāzin, *Lubāb*, 7:94.19; Abū Ḥayyān, *Baḥr*, 8:285.20; Maybudī, *Kashf*, 10:145.20; Abū 'l-Futūḥ-i Rāzī, *Rawḍ*, 11:188.7; and cf. Rāghib al-Iṣbahānī, *Mufradāt*, 1:30a.19). These interpretations of Q5:79 and Q65:6 are neatly brought

Turning to the Sabbath-breakers of Q7:163–6, the exegetes seem to have had no doubts that the reproof of the Sabbath-breakers was an instance of 'commanding right and forbidding wrong'.[69] What troubled them was rather an apparent discrepancy of divine accounting.[70] There appear to be three distinct groups involved in the story: the Sabbath-breakers themselves, those who reproved them, and those who could see no point in such reproof. Yet God specifies only two fates: the reprovers (*alladhīna yanhawna ʿani ʾl-sūʾ*) were saved, and the evil-doers (*alladhīna ẓalamū*) were damned. What then became of the third group? Were they too among the evil-doers by virtue of their failure to reprove the Sabbath-breakers? Or could deft exegesis extricate them from this fate? We need not examine the responses of the exegetes to this dilemma, except to note that a considerable confusion prevailed. For example, we have discordant traditions from Ibn ʿAbbās (d. 68/687f.) to the effect that the third group were damned, that they were saved, and that he did not know their fate.[71]

It will be instructive to end by looking at what the exegetes have to say about some verses which bear (or are seen by them to bear) on the high-risk performance of the duty, and the adverse consequences that are likely to afflict those who engage in it.

In Q31:17 the sage Luqmān is said to have admonished his son as follows: 'O my son, perform the prayer, and command right and forbid wrong, and bear patiently whatever may befall thee (*wa-ʾṣbir ʿalā mā aṣābaka*).' The exegetes have two interpretations of Luqmān's injunction

Footnote 68 (*cont.*)
together in the wording of a Prophetic tradition which urges on the believers that they mutually command right and forbid wrong: *iʾtamirū biʾl-maʿrūf wa-tanāhaw ʿani ʾl-munkar* (for references, see below, ch. 3, note 40). The phrase *al-iʾtimār biʾl-maʿrūf waʾl-nahy ʿan al-munkar* occurs in a Syrian tradition (Ibn Ḥanbal, *Musnad*, 3:187.5).

69 See, for example, the following commentaries to Q7:164: Zajjāj, *Maʿānī*, 2:426.11; Ṭabarī, *Tafsīr*, 13:185.3; Wāḥidī, *Wajīz*, 418, and *Wasīṭ*, 2:420.11; Zamakhsharī, *Kashshāf*, 2:171.18; Ṭabrisī, *Majmaʿ*, 2:492.7; Ibn Kathīr, *Tafsīr*, 3:239.10.

70 For a succinct account, see Zajjāj, *Maʿānī*, 2:427.3.

71 Ṭabarī, *Tafsīr*, 13:194.9 no. 15,278, 187 no. 15,269, 194 no. 15,279. All three are transmitted by ʿIkrima, the *mawlā* of Ibn ʿAbbās. (In another tradition, Ibn ʿAbbās labels the reprovers the 'rightists' (*aymanūn*) and those who saw no point in reproof the 'leftists' (*aysarūn*) (*ibid.*, 189.5 no. 15,272; cf. also Qummī (alive in 307/919), *Tafsīr*, ed. Ṭ. M. al-Jazāʾirī, Najaf 1386–7, 1:244.20).) Ṭabarī gives no statement of his own view in the text of his commentary as we have it (*Tafsīr*, 13:186–98), though this could be defective (at *ibid.*, 193–8, it is noteworthy that nos. 15,279–82, and still more nos. 15,283–6, do not speak to the rubric at *ibid.*, 193.15). An unusual view quoted at length from Kalbī in an Ibāḍī source has it that only two groups were involved, namely the sinners and the reprovers, it being the former who address the latter in Q7:164 (Hūd ibn Muḥakkam, *Tafsīr*, 2:54.8, as part of a long citation; Kalbī's view is cited in a short form in ʿAbd al-Razzāq, *Tafsīr*, 1:239.10, in Ṭabarī, *Tafsīr*, 13:195.5 no. 15,280, in Ṭūsī, *Tibyān*, 5:16.17, and elsewhere, while Hūd also knows the usual view that there were three groups: *Tafsīr*, 2:54.16, 55.6).

to fortitude: it may pertain to life's afflictions in general, or it may refer more particularly to unpleasant reactions met with in the course of forbidding wrong. The weight of exegetical opinion inclines strongly to the second. Some commentators mention both;[72] but the majority refer only to one, and this is always the interpretation linking fortitude to commanding right.[73] In a similar vein, there is a variant reading to Q3:104 which adds after 'forbidding wrong' the words 'and they seek God's help against whatever may befall them (*wa-yastaʿīnūna ʾllāha/biʾllāhi ʿalā mā aṣābahum*)';[74] some exegetes are not above drawing the same moral from this textual variant, even while rejecting it.[75] There are also a couple of verses which, though they make no mention of forbidding wrong, are often interpreted to refer to incurring death in the course of it. One is Q2:207. Here, in a contrast between sincere and insincere adherents of the Prophet (Q2:204–7), the sincere follower is described as one 'who sells himself desiring God's good pleasure (*man yashrī nafsahu ʾbtighāʾa marḍāti ʾllāhi*)'.[76] Among the traditions that are quoted regarding the circumstances in which this verse was revealed, there is one from ʿUmar (d. 23/644) according to which it referred to a man who engaged in commanding right

[72] Bayḍāwī combines them, with emphasis on the second (*Anwār*, 4:31.10). Māwardī, Zamakhsharī, Qurṭubī and Abū Ḥayyān mention both without indicating a preference (Māwardī, *Nukat*, 4:338.12; Zamakhsharī, *Kashshāf*, 3:496.13; Qurṭubī, *Jāmiʿ*, 14:68.17; Abū Ḥayyān, *Baḥr*, 7:188.11). Ṭabrisī and Maybudī give precedence to the second (Ṭabrisī, *Majmaʿ*, 4:319.17; Maybudī, *Kashf*, 7:493.19).

[73] Muqātil, *Tafsīr*, 3:435.9; Muqātil, *Khams miʾa*, 278.16; Ṭabarī, *Jāmiʿ al-bayān*, 21:47.12 (and the tradition to the same effect from Ibn Jurayj (d. 150/767), *ibid.*, 47.16); Jaṣṣāṣ, *Aḥkām*, 2:486.6; Abū ʾl-Layth al-Samarqandī, *Tafsīr*, 3:22.23; Ṭūsī, *Tibyān*, 8:279.17; Wāḥidī, *Wasīṭ*, 3:444.1; Ṭabrisī, *Jawāmiʿ*, 2:295.22; Fakhr al-Dīn al-Rāzī, *Tafsīr*, 25:149.11; Ibn Kathīr, *Tafsīr*, 5:385.11; Thaʿālibī, *Jawāhir*, 3:326.16; Suyūṭī, *Durr*, 5:166.20 (from Saʿīd ibn Jubayr); also Sūrābādī (d. 494/1101), *Tafsīr-i Qurʾān-i karīm*, n.p. 1345 sh., 269.15 (for this Karrāmī text, see Lazard, *Langue*, 91–4 no. 29, and J. van Ess, *Ungenützte Texte zur Karrāmīya*, Heidelberg 1980, 73f.). For an anecdote that assumes this interpretation of the verse, see below, ch. 4, note 190. Cf. also Ibn ʿAṭiyya, *Muḥarrar*, 3:188.13 (to Q3:104).

[74] Jeffery, *Materials*, 34 (Ibn Masʿūd), 227 (Ibn al-Zubayr (d. 73/692)); Ibn Abī Dāwūd (d. 316/929), *Maṣāḥif*, ed. Jeffery in his *Materials*, 39.3 ('Uthmān (d. 35/656)), 82.18 (Ibn al-Zubayr); Ṭabarī, *Tafsīr*, 7:91 no. 7,595 ('Uthmān), 91f. no. 7,596 (Ibn al-Zubayr); anon. (writing 425/1034), *al-Mabānī li-naẓm al-maʿānī*, in A. Jeffery (ed.), *Two Muqaddimas to the Qurʾanic sciences*, Cairo 1954, 102.3 (Ibn al-Zubayr), 102.9 ('Uthmān); Qurṭubī, *Jāmiʿ*, 4:165.16 (Ibn al-Zubayr), 165.20 ('Uthmān); Suyūṭī, *Durr*, 2:62.1 (Ibn al-Zubayr). This reading was among those that earned Ibn Shanabūdh (d. 328/939) a flogging (see Ibn al-Nadīm (d. 380/990), *Fihrist*, Beirut 1978, 48.7, and, for the incident, *EI*^{2}, art. 'Ibn Shanabūdh' (R. Paret)).

[75] Ibn ʿAṭiyya, *Muḥarrar*, 3:188.9; Abū Ḥayyān, *Baḥr*, 3:21.6; Thaʿālibī, *Jawāhir*, 1:355.14 (read *yastaʿīnūna* for *yastaʿīdhūna*).

[76] The insincere adherent, by contrast, does not accept reproof (Q2:206); it is thanks to this, no doubt, that Q2:207 has attracted exegesis in terms of forbidding wrong. The relevance of this verse, and Ṭabarī's commentary on it, were drawn to my attention by Etan Kohlberg.

and forbidding wrong, and was killed.[77] Ṭabarī takes the wider view that the scope of the verse includes both commanding right and holy war.[78] The other verse is Q3:21, which refers to those who 'slay those who command justice (*al-qisṭ*)'; this again is taken to refer to death incurred through commanding right and forbidding wrong.[79] Thus the exegetes display a fairly consistent tendency to enhance the standing of forbidding wrong by relating it to Koranic material which does not require such an interpretation.

As might be expected from all this, the exegetes are much concerned with the apparent negation of the duty in Q5:105: 'O believers, look after your own souls (*ʿalaykum anfusakum*). He who is astray cannot hurt you, if you are rightly guided.'[80] Their tendency here is in one way or another to minimise the erosion of the duty that this verse might suggest to the unwary Muslim. Thus Ṭabarī presents two main views. The first is that the verse refers to some future time when forbidding wrong will cease to be effective, so that the duty will lapse;[81] in other words, the verse has no application in the present. The second view does not deny the relevance of the verse to our own times, but sees a catch in the clause 'if you are rightly guided': those who fail to forbid wrong are *ipso facto* not rightly guided.[82] Ṭabarī himself opts for the second view.[83] Elsewhere we even encounter talk of abrogation within Q5:105.[84] Overall, the sources abound in vague references to men of straw who misconstrue the verse in a sense antithetical to

[77] Ṭabarī, *Tafsīr*, 4:250 no. 4,007; Wāḥidī (d. 468/1076), *Asbāb nuzūl al-Qurʾān*, ed. A. Ṣaqr, Cairo 1969, 59.7; Ibn al-ʿArabī, *Aḥkām*, 144.21; Qurṭubī, *Jāmiʿ*, 3:21.5; Suyūṭī, *Durr*, 1:241.15. The Imāmī exegetes, who cannot bring themselves to quote ʿUmar, allude to other traditions to the same effect from ʿAlī (d. 40/661) and Ibn ʿAbbās (see, for example, Ṭūsī, *Tibyān*, 2:183.19); such traditions are also known to the Sunnīs and Zaydīs (see, for example, Qurṭubī, *Jāmiʿ*, 3:21.2, and Māwardī, *Nukat*, 1:267.3; Abū ʾl-Fatḥ al-Daylamī, *Burhān*, f. 24a.14).

[78] Ṭabarī, *Tafsīr*, 4:251.1 (but cf. *ibid.*, 250.7); compare the view of Ḥasan (al-Baṣrī) quoted by Ṭūsī (*Tibyān*, 2:183.20). Ṭabrisī seems to take the view that the reference is exclusively to *al-amr biʾl-maʿrūf* (*Majmaʿ*, 1:301.26). For Ibn al-ʿArabī, the verse tends to support the view that it is good to risk one's life in forbidding wrong (*Aḥkām*, 145.14).

[79] Qurṭubī sees the verse as a proof of the permissibility of commanding right even when one risks getting killed (*Jāmiʿ*, 4:48.19; and cf. Ibn al-ʿArabī, *Aḥkām*, 266.5). Fakhr al-Dīn al-Rāzī quotes from Ḥasan (al-Baṣrī) the view that the verse highly commends performance of the duty in the face of risk (*Tafsīr*, 7:230.13). Ṭūsī likewise quotes a view to the effect that the verse permits commanding right even at the risk of one's life, but he goes on to refute it (*Tibyān*, 2:422.16; similarly Ṭabrisī, *Majmaʿ*, 1:423.31).

[80] For an extended account of the problem, see Ṭabarī, *Tafsīr*, 11:138–53.

[81] *Ibid.*, 138–46 nos. 12,848–63.

[82] *Ibid.*, 148–51, supported by Ṭabarī with nos. 12,869–78, although only nos. 12,869f. do so explicitly. [83] *Ibid.*, 152.15.

[84] See Abū ʿUbayd al-Qāsim ibn Sallām (d. 224/838f.), *al-Nāsikh waʾl-mansūkh*, ed. J. Burton, Cambridge 1987, 98.11; Hibatallāh ibn Salāma (d. 410/1019), *al-Nāsikh waʾl-mansūkh*, Cairo 1960, 42.4; Ibn al-ʿArabī (d. 543/1148), *ʿĀriḍat al-aḥwadhī bi-sharḥ Ṣaḥīḥ al-Tirmidhī*, Cairo n.d., 9:13.18). Jaṣṣāṣ reports that some consider the verse to abrogate or limit the duty (*Aḥkām*, 2:486.17), and proceeds to refute this view.

forbidding wrong, but it is extremely rare to find an author who actually adopts such a position.[85]

The general conclusion from this account of the activity of the exegetes is that their detailed understanding of the verses and their wider conception of the duty do not have very much to do with each other. As we have seen repeatedly, their reading of scripture tends to be informed by an understanding of forbidding wrong which cannot be derived directly from the verses themselves. They understand the duty primarily as one to be performed by individual believers to each other, and not, say, by the community as a whole towards the world at large; and they see its scope as in the first instance response to specific misdeeds, rather than vague and general ethical affirmation.[86] This perspective is by and large one that they simply assume; they do not generally expend much energy in forcing it on an unwilling scripture. The overall effect is to insert the duty into the daily life of the community in a far more concrete way than the Koran, read as naked scripture, would seem to require. It is this concrete understanding of forbidding wrong that will be the central concern of this book.

85 The verse is invoked to play down the duty by Jāḥiẓ (d. 255/868f.) (*Kitmān al-sirr wa-ḥifẓ al-lisān*, in ʿA. M. Hārūn (ed.), *Rasāʾil al-Jāḥiẓ*, Cairo 1964–79, 1:163.6), and again by Ibn ʿAbd al-Barr, (d. 463/1071) (*Tamhīd*, ed. M. A. al-ʿAlawī *et al.*, Rabat etc. 1967–, 16:161.12; Ibn ʿAbd al-Barr, *Istidhkār*, Damascus and Beirut 1993, 6:363f. nos. 9,388, 9,393). I owe these references to Larry Conrad, Etan Kohlberg and Maribel Fierro respectively.

86 The narrow view of the scope of forbidding wrong discussed above, 22–4, is an interesting exception; but as we have seen, as a theory of the duty it was stillborn.

CHAPTER 3

TRADITION

1. THE 'THREE MODES' TRADITION

There are numerous Prophetic and other traditions on the subject of forbidding wrong,[1] several of them well known; but one, a Kūfan tradition, is far more prominent in our sources than any of the others. For reasons that will appear, I shall call it the 'three modes' tradition. It is encountered in two main forms. Either the Prophetic core of the tradition occurs on its own, or it is found within the framework of an anecdote relating to a later period. We can best begin with the anecdote.[2]

[1] This abundance is explicitly noted by some Koranic exegetes (Qurṭubī, *Jāmiʿ*, 4:48.6 (to Q3:21, quoting Ibn ʿAbd al-Barr (d. 463/1071)); Ibn Kathīr, *Tafsīr*, 2:87.2 (to Q3:104); *ibid.*, 619.28 (to Q5:79)).

[2] Abū Dāwūd al-Ṭayālisī (d. 204/819), *Musnad*, Hyderabad 1321, 292 no. 2,196 (whence Jaṣṣāṣ, *Aḥkām*, 2:30.7); ʿAbd al-Razzāq ibn Hammām al-Ṣanʿānī (d. 211/827), *Muṣannaf*, ed. Ḥ. al-Aʿẓamī, Beirut 1970–2, 3:285 no. 5,649; Ibn Abī Shayba (d. 235/849), *Muṣannaf*, ed. K. Y. al-Ḥūt, Beirut 1989, 1:492f. nos. 5,686f. (both lacking the Prophetic tradition); Ibn Ḥanbal, *Musnad*, 3:10.12, 20.8, 49.10, 52.29, 54.23, 92.22; ʿAbd ibn Ḥumayd (d. 249/863f.), *Musnad*, in the *Muntakhab* of his pupil Ibrāhīm ibn Khuzaym al-Shāshī, ed. Ṣ. al-Badrī al-Sāmarrāʾī and M. M. K. al-Ṣaʿīdī, Beirut 1988, 284 no. 906; Muslim ibn al-Ḥajjāj (d. 261/875), *Ṣaḥīḥ*, ed. M. F. ʿAbd al-Bāqī, Cairo 1955–6, 69 no. 49; Ibn Māja, *Sunan*, 406 no. 1275, 1330 no. 4,013; Abū Dāwūd, *Sunan*, 1:677f. no. 1140; Tirmidhī, *Ṣaḥīḥ*, 6:337 no. 2,173; Ibn Abī ʾl-Dunyā, *Amr*, 115 no. 78; Ibn Ḥibbān (d. 354/965), *Ṣaḥīḥ*, in the arrangement of ʿAlāʾ al-Dīn al-Fārisī (d. 739/1339), ed. ʿA. M. ʿUthmān, Medina 1970–, 1:311f. nos. 301f.; Bayhaqī, *Shuʿab*, 6:85f. no. 7,559; and cf. Ibn al-Athīr, *Jāmiʿ*, 1:324f. no. 107 (without *isnād*). The tradition is partly paraphrased and partly translated in Wensinck, *The Muslim creed*, 106f. The *isnād*s of these versions (together with those referred to below, note 6) point strongly to a Kūfan provenance for the tradition. One group of *isnād*s, characterised by the presence of Ismāʿīl ibn Rajāʾ al-Zubaydī (*fl.* first half of the second/eighth century), remains solidly Kūfan into the late second/eighth century (see, for example, Ibn Ḥanbal, *Musnad*, 3:52.29). The other, marked by the presence of Qays ibn Muslim al-Jadalī (d. 120/737f.), is mainly Kūfan into the mid-second/eighth century (of four transmitters of this vintage, the only non-Kūfan is the Baṣran Shuʿba ibn al-Ḥajjāj (d. 160/776)); thereafter non-Kūfan transmitters (all Iraqi, and mostly Baṣran) become more prominent (see, for example, *ibid.*, 3:54.23; Abū Dāwūd al-Ṭayālisī, *Musnad*, 292 no. 2,196; Ibn Abī ʾl-Dunyā's *isnād* is defective).

The scene is set on a feast-day in Medina during the governorship of the future Umayyad caliph Marwān ibn al-Ḥakam (r. 64–5/684–5).[3] Marwān, presiding over the congregation in his role of governor, commits two ritual improprieties: he brings out the pulpit (*minbar*) on a feast-day, and he begins with the sermon (*khuṭba*) before the prayer (*ṣalāt*).[4] A man then arises and rebukes him: 'Marwān, you've gone against the proper custom (*sunna*)! You've brought out the pulpit on a feast-day, when it used not to be, and you've started with the sermon before the prayer!' At this point the Companion Abū Saʿīd al-Khudrī (d. 74/693) intervenes: he inquires the identity of the author of the rebuke, and pronounces that the man has done his duty. Here, then, we have a concrete example of the practice of rebuke within the community. Somebody had done something wrong – something quite specific – and someone else thereupon took it upon himself to upbraid him for it.

The Prophetic tradition that Abū Saʿīd then proceeds to relate provides a succinct theory of this practice. 'Whoever sees a wrong (*munkar*)', says the Prophet, 'and is able to put it right with his hand (*an yughayyirahu bi-yadihi*), let him do so; if he can't, then with his tongue (*bi-lisānihi*); if he can't, then with [or in] his heart (*bi-qalbihi*),[5] which is the bare minimum of faith.'[6] This tradition is referred to, quoted and commented upon with great frequency in subsequent literature.[7] It owes this distinction to the fact

[3] That Marwān is governor in Medina, not caliph in Syria, is clear from the presence of the Companion Abū Saʿīd al-Khudrī (d. 74/693), and explicit in a related tradition (Bukhārī (d. 256/870), *Ṣaḥīḥ*, ed. L. Krehl, Leiden 1862–1908, 1:244.2; Bayhaqī, *Sunan*, 3:280.9). Marwān was twice governor of Medina, once in the 40s/660s and once in the 50s/670s (see *EI*², art. 'Marwān I', 621b (C. E. Bosworth)).

[4] For the ritual issues, see *EI*², art. 'Khuṭba' (A. J. Wensinck). The details of Marwān's innovations vary slightly in some versions; in these and other particulars, I follow Abū Dāwūd's version.

[5] The problematic character of the idea of putting something right with (or in) the heart was clearly seen by Nawawī (d. 676/1277) in his commentaries on the tradition (see his *Sharḥ Ṣaḥīḥ Muslim*, Beirut 1987, 1:384.25, and his commentary on his own selection of forty traditions published as *Sharḥ matn al-Arbaʿīn al-Nawawiyya*, Damascus 1966, 92.7).

[6] For versions of the tradition that include the frame-story, see above, note 2 (but note that Ibn Abī 'l-Dunyā's version is defective). For versions in which the Prophetic tradition appears on its own, see Abū Dāwūd, *Sunan*, 4:511 no. 4,340 (whence Jaṣṣāṣ, *Aḥkām*, 2:486.12); Ibn Abī 'l-Dunyā, *Amr*, 51 no. 10; Nasāʾī, *Sunan*, 8:111.6, 112.3; Bayhaqī, *Sunan*, 6:95.1, 10:90.13; and, for versions without *isnād*s, Muttaqī, *Kanz*, 3:68 no. 5,524, 75 no. 5,556; Muḥammad ibn ʿAbd al-Wahhāb (d. 1206/1792), *Naṣīḥat al-muslimīn bi-aḥādīth khātam al-mursalīn*, Cairo n.d., 65.2. Later writers felt free to omit the frame-story. Thus an unframed version quoted by Jaṣṣāṣ (*Aḥkām*, 2:30.14) derives from Abū Dāwūd's framed version (for which see above, note 2); and Nawawī, in adopting the tradition from Muslim for his selection of forty traditions (see the following note), likewise left the frame-story aside. For the hierarchy of hand, tongue and heart, compare, for example, Muslim, *Ṣaḥīḥ*, 70.5 no. 50.

[7] See, for example, below, ch. 5, note 76; ch. 6, note 125; ch. 7, note 60; ch. 8, 173, and notes 32, 101. The tradition also owes some of its celebrity to Nawawī's inclusion of it

that it provided later generations with a fundamental building-block for their scholastic doctrines of forbidding wrong. Whereas the Koranic diction of 'commanding' and 'forbidding' suggests a purely verbal duty, this Prophetic tradition spells out a hierarchy of modes of response to wrong: deed, word and thought.

There is, however, one thing about this tradition that is unsettling. At no point does the Prophet – or anyone else – refer explicitly to 'commanding right' or 'forbidding wrong'. What the diction of the tradition and the Koran have in common is the term 'wrong' (*munkar*). Yet in speaking of what is to be done about the wrong, our tradition uses a term of its own, namely to 'put right' (*ghayyara*).[8] The literal meaning of this verb is to 'change', whether for better or for worse.[9] But in the usage that doubtless lies behind that of the tradition, it seems rather to have the sense of putting things to rights in the context of a personal injury.[10] The upshot is that

Footnote 7 (*cont.*)
in his popular selection of forty traditions (published as *Matn al-Arbaʿīn al-Nawawiyya*, Beirut 1977, 76 no. 34 (from Muslim)), whence its discussion in the numerous commentaries on this little work, starting with his own (*Sharḥ matn al-Arbaʿīn,* 91f. no. 34; Ibn Daqīq al-ʿĪd (d. 702/1302), *Sharḥ al-Arbaʿīn ḥadīthan al-Nawawiyya*, Cairo n.d., 55–7 no. 34; Taftazānī (d. 793/1390), *Sharḥ ḥadīth al-Arbaʿīn al-Nawawī* (*sic*), Istanbul 1316, 105 no. 34; Ibn Rajab (d. 795/1393), *Jāmiʿ al-ʿulūm waʾl-ḥikam*, Beirut 1987, 346–52 no. 34; Ibn Ḥajar al-Haytamī (d. 974/1567), *Fatḥ al-mubīn li-sharḥ al-Arbaʿīn*, Cairo 1352, 244–8 no. 34; ʿAlī al-Qārī (d. 1014/1606), *al-Mubīn al-muʿīn li-fahm al-Arbaʿīn*, Cairo 1910, 188–94 no. 34; Ismāʿīl Ḥaqqī Brūsevī (d. 1137/1725), *Sharḥ al-Arbaʿīn ḥadīthan* (in Turkish), Istanbul 1253, 336–41 no. 34; and many others).

8 A few versions of the tradition use *ankara* in place of *ghayyara* (Abū Dāwūd al-Ṭayālisī, *Musnad*, 292 no. 2,196; Ibn Ḥanbal, *Musnad*, 3:92.22; Tirmidhī, *Ṣaḥīḥ*, 6:337 no. 2,173; Bayhaqī, *Shuʿab*, 6:85f. no. 7,559); the distribution of this variant does not correlate with the lines of transmission. The verb *ghayyara* appears frequently in other traditions (see, for example, below, notes 16, 18, 54, 60).

9 The Koran uses *ghayyara* only where the change is for the worse (see Q4:119, Q8:53, Q13:11, and cf. Q47:15). The lexicographers, however, report usages referring to the easing or repairing (the verb employed is *aṣlaḥa*) of camel-saddles, where the change is clearly for the better, and they illustrate these usages from poetry (E. W. Lane, *An Arabic–English lexicon*, London 1863–93, 2,315a; Azharī (d. 370/980), *Tahdhīb al-lugha*, ed. ʿA. M. Hārūn *et al.*, Cairo 1964–7, 8:189b.16, 190a.1; Ibn Manẓūr, *Lisān*, 5:40a.26, 40b.3, 42b.1; Murtaḍā al-Zabīdī (d. 1205/1791), *Tāj al-ʿarūs*, ed. ʿA. A. Farrāj *et al.*, Kuwait 1965–, 13:289.13, 289.18).

10 Note, for example, the verse of the pre-Islamic Ṭāʾī poet Qays ibn Jurwa (for whom see W. Caskel, *Ǧamharat an-nasab: Das genealogische Werk des Hišām ibn Muḥammad al-Kalbī*, Leiden 1966, index, *s.n.*) in which he makes a dire threat should his enemy not put right some of what his tribe have done: *la-in lam tughayyir baʿḍa mā qad faʿaltum* (*apud* A. A. Bevan (ed.), *The Naḳāʾiḍ of Jarīr and al-Farazdaḳ*, Leiden 1905–12, 1082.13, appendix XI; and see Abū Zayd al-Anṣārī (d. 215/830f.), *al-Nawādir fī ʾl-lugha*, ed. M. ʿA. Aḥmad, Beirut and Cairo 1981, 266.6; Ḥātim al-Ṭāʾī, *Dīwān*, ed. ʿA. S. Jamāl, Cairo n.d., 170 no. 16, line 4; Mubarrad (d. 286/900), *Kāmil*, ed. W. Wright, Leipzig 1864–92, 564.8; I owe these references to the Concordance of Pre-Islamic and Umayyad Poetry of the Hebrew University of Jerusalem). When ʿAbdallāh ibn Ubayy interceded for the Jewish Banū Qaynuqāʿ in the events leading to their expulsion in the year 2/624, he was slightly wounded in the face; his Jewish confederates then protested that they would

without the unthinking unanimity of the scholastic tradition, we would not know for sure that the Prophet and Abū Saʿīd were talking about 'forbidding wrong'.[11]

2. OTHER TRADITIONS OF POSITIVE TENDENCY

We can deal more briefly with the rest of the traditions on forbidding wrong transmitted from the Prophet, since these have much less to offer in doctrinal terms.

The largest group consists, predictably, of sayings which in one way or another exhort believers to perform the duty. A widely quoted example is a further Kūfan tradition with a structure similar to the 'three modes' tradition.[12] In the frame-story, the caliph Abū Bakr (r. 11–13/632–4) quotes Q5:105, with its suggestion that the righteous believer need not concern himself with the misdeeds of others;[13] implicitly or explicitly, he tells the community that this is a misinterpretation. He makes his point by quoting a saying of the Prophet (although there are other versions in which it is ascribed to Abū Bakr himself).[14] This saying threatens people with collec-

not reside in a place where their protector had suffered this injury without their being able to put things right (*lā naqdir an nughayyirahu, la nastaṭīʿ lahu ghiyaran*, Wāqidī, *Maghāzī*, 178.10). The crucified Māhān al-Ḥanafī (d. 83/701f.) rebukes ʿAmmār al-Duhnī (d. 133/750f.) for watching the scene and doing nothing about it (*wa-lā tughayyir*, Fasawī, *Maʿrifa*, 2:615.4).

[11] Compare the cases of Q5:79 and Q7:165 (see above, ch. 2, 15–17, for the verses themselves, and 26–8 for their exegesis).

[12] This tradition has pride of place in Ibn Ḥanbal (d. 241/855), *Musnad*, ed. A. M. Shākir, Cairo 1949–58, 1:153 no. 1; also 163 no. 16, 168f. nos. 29f., 176 no. 53; Abū ʿUbayd, *Nāsikh*, 99.21; Ibn Abī Shayba, *Muṣannaf*, 7:504f. no. 37,583; Ibn Māja, *Sunan*, 1327 no. 4,005; Abū Dāwūd, *Sunan*, 4:509f. no. 4,338 (whence Jaṣṣāṣ, *Aḥkām*, 2:31.6); Tirmidhī, *Ṣaḥīḥ*, 6:335f. no. 2,169, 8:221 no. 3,059; Ibn Abī ʾl-Dunyā, *Amr*, 37 no. 1; Abū Yūsuf, *Kharāj*, 10.18; Ḥumaydī, *Musnad*, 3f. no. 3; Abū Bakr al-Marwazī (d. 292/905), *Musnad Abī Bakr al-Ṣiddīq*, ed. S. al-Arnāʾūṭ, Beirut n.d., 154–6 no. 86; Ṭabarī, *Tafsīr*, 11:150f. nos. 12,876, 12,878 (to Q5:105); Ibn Ḥibbān, *Ṣaḥīḥ*, in the arrangement of Fārisī, 1:310f. no. 300; Jaṣṣāṣ, *Aḥkām*, 2:486.25; Bayhaqī, *Sunan*, 10:91.21; Bayhaqī, *Shuʿab*, 6:82 no. 7,550 (where the text is corrupt, cf. Abū Dāwūd's version); for versions without *isnād*s, see Ibn al-Athīr, *Jāmiʿ*, 1:330f. no. 111; Ibn ʿAbd al-Wahhāb, *Naṣīḥa*, 65.22. The common link of most of these versions is the Kūfan Ismāʿīl ibn Abī Khālid (d. 145/762f.); the transmitters from Ismāʿīl are a mixture of Kūfans and others from lower Iraq. That the provenance of the tradition is Kūfan finds confirmation in the *isnād*s of the non-Prophetic versions cited below, note 14. At the same time, two brief traditions adduced by Ṭabarī to the same effect have Kūfan *isnād*s (*Tafsīr*, 11:148 nos. 12,869f.; in the first, the authority quoted is the Medinese Saʿīd ibn al-Musayyab (d. 94/712f.), while in the second, it is the Kūfan Companion Ḥudhayfa ibn al-Yamān (d. 36/656f.). There is also a parallel in a letter of ʿUmar ibn ʿAbd al-ʿAzīz (r. 99–101/717–20) in which he makes no mention of Abū Bakr or any other early authority (ʿAbdallāh ibn ʿAbd al-Ḥakam (d. 214/829), *Sīrat ʿUmar ibn ʿAbd al-ʿAzīz*, ed. A. ʿUbayd, Damascus 1964, 162.11).

[13] See above, ch. 2, note 80.

[14] These other versions are to be found in Ṭabarī, *Tafsīr*, 11:148–51 (nos. 12,871f., 12,874f.,

tive punishment from on high if they do not take action to right wrongs – according to one version, if they see a wrongdoer (*ẓālim*) and do not restrain him;[15] according to another, which more directly concerns us, if they see a wrong (*munkar*) and fail to put it right (*ghayyara*).[16] Thus the same disparity appears here between the wording of the tradition and the Koranic terminology of commanding and forbidding.[17] This time, as it happens, neither version of the saying of the Prophet seems to appear independently of the frame-story, though a somewhat similar saying is transmitted by another Companion.[18]

Another much-quoted example of such exhortatory traditions urges the believers to perform the duty (usually with the wording *la-ta'murunna bi'l-maʿrūf wa-la-tanhawunna ʿan al-munkar*) or be visited with unpleasant consequences.[19] Just what these consequences will be varies in the different

Footnote 14 (*cont.*)
12,877); cf. also Ibn Ḥanbal, *Musnad*, 1:168 no. 29, and Tirmidhī's comments to both his versions. The common link of all but one of Ṭabarī's versions is the Kūfan Qays ibn Abī Ḥāzim (d. 97/715f.). (He in turn is the transmitter from whom Ismāʿīl ibn Abī Khālid relates most of the Prophetic versions cited above, note 12.) The *isnād*s remain predominantly Kūfan into the later second/eighth century.

15 So, for example, Tirmidhī's versions.

16 So, for example, the versions of Ibn Māja and Abū Yūsuf; cf. also Muttaqī, *Kanz*, 3:67 no. 5,517, and 83 no. 5,595, both lacking the frame-story. It should be noted that none of the non-Prophetic versions is of this type. Another variant (Ibn Ḥanbal, *Musnad*, 1:176 no. 53) uses *ankara* in place of *ghayyara*.

17 By contrast, in two of the non-Prophetic versions quoted by Ṭabarī (see above, note 14), Abū Bakr enjoins: 'By God, you will command right and forbid wrong . . .' (nos. 12,874, 12,877).

18 See, for example, Abū Dāwūd al-Ṭayālisī, *Musnad*, 92 no. 663; ʿAbd al-Razzāq, *Muṣannaf*, 11:348 no. 20,723; Ibn Ḥanbal, *Musnad*, 4:361.4, 363.8, 364.15, 366.4; Ibn Māja, *Sunan*, 1329 no. 4,009; Abū Dāwūd, *Sunan*, 4:510f. no. 4,339; Ibn Abī 'l-Dunyā, *Amr*, 47 no. 6; Ibn Ḥibbān, *Ṣaḥīḥ*, in the arrangement of Fārisī, 1:308f. nos. 296, 298; Bayhaqī, *Sunan*, 10:91.31. All versions use the term *ghayyara*; some (as that of Abū Dāwūd al-Ṭayālisī) speak of collective punishment. The Companion who transmits the tradition is the Kūfan Jarīr ibn ʿAbdallāh al-Bajalī (d. 51/671f.); the common link of the *isnād*s is the Kūfan Abū Isḥāq al-Sabīʿī (d. 127/744f.), and subsequent transmitters are mostly Kūfans or Baṣrans. Compare also Haythamī, *Zawā'id*, 7:269.13, and Muttaqī, *Kanz*, 3:85 no. 5,601 (from the Syrian Companion Abū Umāma al-Bāhilī (d. 86/705)).

19 Abū ʿUbayd, *Nāsikh*, 100.14; Ibn Ḥanbal, *Musnad*, 5:388.28, 390.1, 391.18; Tirmidhī, *Ṣaḥīḥ*, 6:336 no. 2,170; Ibn Abī Shayba, *Muṣannaf*, 7:460 no. 37,221; Ibn Abī 'l-Dunyā, *Amr*, 54 no. 12; Jaṣṣāṣ, *Aḥkām*, 2:488.32; Bayhaqī, *Sunan*, 10:93.22; Bayhaqī, *Shuʿab*, 6:84 no. 7,558; and for versions without *isnād*s, see Ibn al-Athīr, *Jāmiʿ*, 1:332 no. 113; Muttaqī, *Kanz*, 3:70 no. 5,529, 76 no. 5,562; Ibn ʿAbd al-Wahhāb, *Naṣīḥa*, 65.16. All these versions are transmitted by the Companion Ḥudhayfa (except that in Ibn Abī 'l-Dunyā's version, the saying appears as Ḥudhayfa's own); the *isnād*s, where given, are Medinese or Kūfan. Other versions are transmitted by ʿĀ'isha (d. 58/678) (Ibn Ḥanbal, *Musnad*, 6:159.3; Ibn Māja, *Sunan*, 1327 no. 4,004; Ibn Abī 'l-Dunyā, *Amr*, 48 no. 7; Bayhaqī, *Sunan*, 10:93.26), ʿAlī (d. 40/661) (Ibn Abī Shayba, *Muṣannaf*, 7:504 no. 37,576), Ḥasan ibn ʿAlī (d. 49/669f.) (Nuʿaym ibn Ḥammād (d. 228/843), *Fitan*, ed. S. Zakkār, Mecca n.d., 141.22, whence Muttaqī, *Kanz*, 3:77 no. 5,563), Abū Bakr (see the references given above, note 17), and others (see, for example, Ibn Abī 'l-Dunyā, *Amr*, 49

versions of the tradition. One formulation is that God will bestow power on the worst of them and then ignore the prayers of the best of them;[20] a more colourful one is that He will send the Persians (*ʿAjam*) against them to smite their necks and eat their spoils (*fay*ʾ).[21] This tradition, or at least its opening injunction, can also appear as a component of more complex traditions.[22] Unlike the other traditions we have considered so far, the injunction is also at home among the Shīʿites, who transmit it from their own authorities.[23]

It would be unprofitable to attempt to cover all traditions that in one way or another make favourable reference to forbidding wrong. What follows should give a fair idea of the character of the remaining material in this category.

no. 8; Haythamī, *Zawāʾid*, 7:266.15, 266.19). Overall, the *isnād*s are Medinese or Kūfan. For Zaydī versions, see below, ch. 10, note 9.

[20] So Ibn Ḥanbal, *Musnad*, 5:390.1.

[21] So Nuʿaym ibn Ḥammād's version. The Zaydī ʿAbdallāh ibn al-Ḥusayn ibn al-Qāsim (*fl.* later third/ninth century), brother of the imam al-Hādī ilā ʾl-Ḥaqq (d. 298/911), quotes a version (without *isnād*) in which the threat runs: 'or you will assuredly turn into miserable peasants' (*aw la-takūnunna ashqiyāʾ zarrāʿīn*) (*al-Nāsikh waʾl-mansūkh*, ms. Berlin, Glaser 128, f. 45b.7; for this manuscript, see W. Ahlwardt, *Verzeichniss der arabischen Handschriften der Königlichen Bibliothek zu Berlin*, Berlin 1887–99, 9:574 no. 10,226). For the reference to miserable peasants, compare the activist tradition quoted in Abū Bakr al-Khallāl (d. 311/923), *al-Musnad min masāʾil Abī ʿAbdillāh Aḥmad ibn Muḥammad ibn Ḥanbal*, ed. Z. Ahmed, Dacca 1975, 18.18.

[22] For one case see above, note 17. In another case the initial injunction appears in some versions of a Kūfan tradition describing the misdeeds of the Israelites, in particular their habit of socialising with offenders whom they had previously rebuked, a practice which led to their being cursed in the manner described in Q5:78–81 (Abū Dāwūd, *Sunan*, 4:508f. no. 4,336; Ibn Abī ʾl-Dunyā, *Amr*, 45 no. 4; Muḥammad ibn Waḍḍāḥ (d. 287/900), *Kitāb al-bidaʿ*, ed. and trans. M. I. Fierro, Madrid 1988, 230 = 359f. no. 58; Ṭabarī, *Tafsīr*, 10:491 no. 12,306; Bayhaqī, *Sunan*, 10:93.5; Bayhaqī, *Shuʿab*, 6:80 no. 7,545; and for versions without *isnād*s, see Ibn al-Athīr, *Jāmiʿ*, 1:327–9 no. 109; Haythamī, *Zawāʾid*, 7:269.17; Muttaqī, *Kanz*, 3:69 no. 5,527, 79 no. 5,573). This tradition is more widely attested without the injunction (see for example Ibn Ḥanbal, *Musnad*, 5:268 no. 3,713; Ibn Māja, *Sunan*, 1327f. no. 4,006; Tirmidhī, *Ṣaḥīḥ*, 8:215f. nos. 3,050f.; Ibn Waḍḍāḥ, *Bidaʿ*, 229 = 359 no. 57; Ṭabarī, *Tafsīr*, 10:492–4 nos. 12,307–9, 12,311; Bayhaqī, *Shuʿab*, 6:79f. no. 7,544); it is generally transmitted by the Kūfan Companion Ibn Masʿūd (d. 32/652f.).

[23] For the Imāmīs, see Kulaynī, *Kāfī*, 5:56 no. 3, and Ṭūsī, *Tahdhīb*, 6:176 no. 1. The tradition is here a saying of Abū ʾl-Ḥasan, who is presumably ʿAlī al-Riḍā (d. 203/818). (The transmitter is listed among the latter's companions, see Ṭūsī (d. 460/1067), *Rijāl*, ed. M. Ṣ. Āl Baḥr al-ʿUlūm, Najaf 1961, 388.2, and cf. the editor's footnote thereto; cf. also the *isnād* of Kulaynī, *Kāfī*, 5:59 no. 13, and Ṭūsī, *Tahdhīb*, 6:177 no. 7.) For the Zaydīs, see Zayd ibn ʿAlī (d. 122/740) (attrib.), *Majmūʿ al-fiqh*, ed. E. Griffini, Milan 1919, 294 no. 995 (where the saying is ascribed to ʿAlī); Abū Ṭālib al-Nāṭiq (d. 424/1032f.), *Amālī* (in the recension of Jaʿfar ibn Muḥammad ibn ʿAbd al-Salām (d. 573/1177f.), *Taysīr al-maṭālib fī Amālī al-imām Abī Ṭālib*), ed. Y. ʿA. al-Faḍīl, Beirut 1975, 293.15 (from the Prophet). In this chapter, I make reference to Shīʿite traditions only to indicate parallels to Sunnī traditions; I cite Imāmī parallels only from Kulaynī's *Kāfī* and Ṭūsī's *Tahdhīb*, and leave aside versions found in Zaydī sources with mainstream Sunnī *isnād*s.

The high standing of the duty in Islam is emphasised. Commanding right and forbidding wrong are two religious obligations (*farīḍatān*) which God has inscribed in His book;[24] they are two of the shares that, taken together, make up Islam.[25] The most pious (*atqā 'l-nās*) are those most zealous in performing the duty (*āmaruhum bi'l-ma'rūf*) and most loyal to their kinsfolk;[26] he who commands right and forbids wrong is God's deputy on earth (*khalīfat Allāh fī 'l-arḍ*), and the deputy of His book and of His Prophet.[27] Conversely, 'a dead man among the living' is explained as one who fails to perform the duty;[28] one who abandons it is no believer.[29]

At the same time an activist tone is often in evidence. The Prophet tells his followers that victory and conquest lie ahead; if they live to see them, they should fear God, command right and forbid wrong.[30] The duty may be explicitly linked to holy war. According to one saying of 'Alī (d. 40/661), the finest form of holy war is commanding right;[31] another of his sayings has it that the duty comprises two of the four parts of holy war.[32] As

[24] So Ḍaḥḥāk ibn Muzāḥim (d. 105/723f.) (Abū 'Ubayd, *Nāsikh*, 101.4; Jaṣṣāṣ, *Aḥkām*, 2:489.5; the transmitter from Ḍaḥḥāk is Kūfan).

[25] So 'Umar (d. 23/644) (Abū 'Ubayd, *Nāsikh*, 100.29; Jaṣṣāṣ, *Aḥkām*, 2:489.2; the *isnād* is Baṣran or Kūfan). Cf. also the saying of Ḥudhayfa referred to below, ch. 5, note 173.

[26] So the Prophet (Ibn Abī Shayba, *Muṣannaf*, 7:504 no. 37,580; Ibn Ḥanbal, *Musnad*, 6:432.4; Ibn Abī 'l-Dunyā, *Amr*, 65 no. 21; Haythamī, *Zawā'id*, 7:263.17). The *isnād* is Kūfan.

[27] P. Crone and M. Hinds, *God's caliph*, Cambridge 1986, 98, citing Nu'aym ibn Ḥammād, *Fitan*, 57.10 (from anonymous authorities); also Ibn 'Adī (d. 365/976), *Kāmil*, Beirut 1984, 2,104.5; Shīrawayh ibn Shahradār al-Daylamī (d. 509/1115), *al-Firdaws bi-ma'thūr al-khiṭāb*, Beirut 1986, 3:586 no. 5,834, whence Muttaqī, *Kanz*, 3:77 no. 5,564; Najm al-Dīn al-Nasafī (d. 537/1142), *al-Qand fī dhikr 'ulamā' Samarqand*, ed. N. M. al-Fāryābī, Saudi Arabia 1991, 233.18; 'Abd al-Ghanī al-Maqdisī (d. 600/1203), *al-Amr bi'l-ma'rūf wa'l-nahy 'an al-munkar*, ed. S. A. al-Zuhayrī, Riyāḍ 1995, 42 no. 53, 56 no. 80. Apart from Nu'aym's version, all are from the Prophet. The provenance seems to be Syrian or Egyptian. For a Zaydī version, see below, ch. 10, note 43.

[28] So Ḥudhayfa (Bayhaqī, *Shu'ab*, 6:96 no. 7,590; contrast the version given with the same Kūfan *isnād* in Ibn Abī Shayba, *Muṣannaf*, 7:504 no. 37,577, where it is all a matter of the heart). The Imāmīs transmit a similar saying from 'Alī (Ṭūsī, *Tahdhīb*, 6:181 no. 23).

[29] Ibn al-Jawzī (d. 597/1201), *al-'Ilal al-mutanāhiya*, Beirut 1983, 791f. no. 1,322; Muttaqī, *Kanz*, 3:67 no. 5,516 (Kūfan?). Ibn al-Jawzī is citing this Prophetic tradition to condemn it as inauthentic.

[30] Ibn Ḥanbal, *Musnad*, 5:257 no. 3,694, 305f. no. 3,801; 6:96 no. 4,156; Tirmidhī, *Ṣaḥīḥ*, 7:37 no. 2,258; Bayhaqī, *Sunan*, 10:94.19; Bayhaqī, *Shu'ab*, 6:84 no. 7,557; Ibn al-Athīr, *Jāmi'*, 1:332 no. 114. The tradition is Kūfan.

[31] Zamakhsharī, *Kashshāf*, 1:397.6; Maybudī, *Kashf*, 2:234.6; Abū 'l-Futūḥ-i Rāzī, *Rawḍ*, 3:142.6; Fakhr al-Dīn al-Rāzī, *Tafsīr*, 8:179.13; Abū 'l-Barakāt al-Nasafī, *Madārik*, 1:240 no. 3; Niẓām al-Dīn al-Naysābūrī, *Gharā'ib*, 4:29.24; Abū 'l-Su'ūd, *Irshād*, 1:529.20; Aṭfayyish, *Himyān*, 4:204.3 (all to Q3:104). I have not seen this saying outside the literature of *tafsīr*, where it is quoted without *isnāds*.

[32] 'Abd al-Ghanī al-Maqdisī, *Amr*, 51 no. 68; Muttaqī, *Kanz*, 3:66 no. 5,513. Cf. also Ṭabarī, *Tafsīr*, 7:91.3 (to Q3:104); Haythamī, *Zawā'id*, 7:275.22; and, for the Zaydīs, Zayd ibn 'Alī, *Majmū'*, 235f. no. 851, 273 no. 942.

we have seen, the Prophet declares that the finest form of holy war is speaking out in the presence of an unjust ruler[33] – and, in some versions, being killed for it.[34] He likewise urges that respect of persons – or more precisely, fear of them (*haybat al-nās*) – should not inhibit anyone from taking action when he sees something wrong.[35] No community, he warns, can be deemed holy which fails to secure the rights of the weak against the strong.[36]

3. TRADITIONS OF NEGATIVE TENDENCY

Against the considerable body of traditions that urge the performance of the duty there is a smaller number that tend to downplay it. These, of course, are more interesting, since they go against the rhetorical grain. We can best approach them through the eschatology of forbidding wrong. At first sight this might seem a strange place to look. Traditions linking forbidding wrong to eschatology are nevertheless quite common – sufficiently so to account for the choice made by the compilers of three of the classical collections and one major pre-classical collection to place their traditions on forbidding wrong among those concerned with eschatology.[37]

What concerns us in these traditions is the bad times that lie ahead, not the good ones. As might be expected, those will not be propitious times

[33] See above, ch. 1, note 18, and cf. also Haythamī, *Zawāʾid*, 7:265.15.

[34] See above, ch. 1, notes 18–20.

[35] Ibn ʿAbd al-Wahhāb, *Naṣīḥa*, 66.19; and cf. Ibn Ḥanbal, *Musnad*, 3:5.29, 19.15, 53.13, 71.14; Ibn Māja, *Sunan*, 1328 no. 4,007; Tirmidhī, *Ṣaḥīḥ*, 6:351 no. 2,192 (all versions with Baṣran *isnāds*). The transmitter, Abū Saʿīd al-Khudrī, laments that the opposite has been the case.

[36] Ibn Māja, *Sunan*, 810 no. 2,426, 1329 no. 4,010; Ibn Waḍḍāḥ, *Bidaʿ*, 234 = 365 no. 81; Bayhaqī, *Sunan*, 6:95.8, 10:93.30, 94.7, 94.9, and cf. 94.1; Bayhaqī, *Shuʿab*, 6:81f. no. 7,549; Muttaqī, *Kanz*, 3:74 nos. 5,544–9. The tradition does not refer explicitly to *al-amr biʾl-maʿrūf*, but, as these references show, it is associated with it by the collectors. The *isnāds* are Meccan, Kūfan or mixed. The tradition is also current among the Shīʿites. Imāmī sources sometimes ascribe it to Jaʿfar al-Ṣādiq (d. 148/765) (Kulaynī, *Kāfī*, 5:56 no. 2; Ṭūsī, *Tahdhīb*, 6:180 no. 20). The Zaydīs know a variant form (with explicit mention of *al-amr biʾl-maʿrūf*) as a Prophetic tradition (Zayd ibn ʿAlī, *Majmūʿ*, 294 no. 996).

[37] Thus Abū Dāwūd's *bāb al-amr waʾl-nahy* (*Sunan*, 4:508–15 nos. 4,336–47) falls in his *kitāb al-malāḥim*; the relevant chapters of Tirmidhī (*Ṣaḥīḥ*, 6:335–9 nos. 2,169–75) are to be found in his *kitāb al-fitan*, as are those of Ibn Māja (*Sunan*, 1327–32 nos. 4,004–17). Ibn Abī Shayba devotes no chapter to *al-amr biʾl-maʿrūf*, but includes a series of traditions about it in his *kitāb al-fitan* (*Muṣannaf*, 7:504f. nos. 37,575–83). Muslim, by contrast, places his versions of the 'three modes' tradition (*Ṣaḥīḥ*, 69f. nos. 49f.) in his *kitāb al-īmān*; Nasāʾī devotes no chapter to *al-amr biʾl-maʿrūf*, but similarly includes his versions of the 'three modes' tradition in his *kitāb al-īmān wa-sharāʾiʿihi* (*Sunan*, 8:111f.). Here the concern is clearly with the implication of the phrase *aḍʿaf al-īmān* for the concept of faith. Bukhārī, Dārimī (d. 255/869), and ʿAbd al-Razzāq neglect the subject altogether. Overall, these facts strongly suggest that the collectors were not much interested in *al-amr biʾl-maʿrūf* as such.

for the duty. Thus the Companion Ibn Masʿūd (d. 32/652f.) foretells that the Hour will come when people are at their worst, neither commanding right nor forbidding wrong.[38] This disarray may be presented as a shortcoming of the believers, to be visited with divine displeasure; thus another Companion, ʿAbdallāh ibn ʿUmar (d. 73/693), holds that the eschatological beast which God will bring forth from the earth (Q27:82) will emerge when people no longer practise forbidding wrong.[39] But these conditions may also be seen as a context in which it will be appropriate for the believers to desist from performing the duty at all.

There are several examples of this trend. One is a well-known Syrian tradition in which the Prophet is asked about the implications of Q5:105, with its advice to the believers to look to their own souls.[40] In response he enjoins them to command right and forbid wrong until they find themselves confronted with the utter corruption of values;[41] they should then look to themselves and forget the populace at large.[42] Likewise the Companion Ibn Masʿūd is present during a dispute as to whether Q5:105

[38] Nuʿaym ibn Ḥammād, *Fitan*, 395.6 (Kūfan); I owe this reference to Nurit Tsafrir. For further predictions of the decay of *al-amr biʾl-maʿrūf*, see Ibn Abī Shayba, *Muṣannaf*, 7:475 no. 37,349 (also Kūfan, from Ḥudhayfa); Ibn Waḍḍāḥ, *Bidaʿ*, 203 = 327 no. 5 (Egyptian, *mursal*), 211 = 337f. no. 38 (Baṣran, *mursal*); Bayhaqī, *Shuʿab*, 6:94 no. 7,584 *bis* (also Kūfan, from Ibn Masʿūd); Ibn Abī ʾl-Dunyā, *Amr*, 69 no. 25 (= 128 no. 96), 74 no. 29 (similarly 122 no. 87), 77 no. 33, 121 no. 86; Haythamī, *Zawāʾid*, 7:270.23, 280.9, 280.19; Muttaqī, *Kanz*, 3:68 no. 5,519. For a prediction shared by Sunnī and Imāmī sources, see Ibn Abī ʾl-Dunyā, *Amr*, 76 no. 31; Haythamī, *Zawāʾid*, 7:280.22; Kulaynī, *Kāfī*, 5:59 no. 14; Ṭūsī, *Tahdhīb*, 6:177 no. 8.

[39] Nuʿaym ibn Ḥammād, *Fitan*, 402.8, 404.8 (in the first, a *ʿan* has dropped out before *Ibn ʿUmar*, and in the second, the *wāw* which the editor has appended to *ʿUmar* belongs in the Koranic quotation that follows; I owe these references to Nurit Tsafrir); Ibn Abī Shayba, *Muṣannaf*, 7:504 no. 37,575; Ibn Abī ʾl-Dunyā, *Amr*, 75 no. 30; Ṭabarī, *Jāmiʿ*, 20:10.4, and the two traditions there following; cf. also *ibid.*, 10.10. The *isnāds* are Kūfan. In an Imāmī tradition, Muḥammad al-Bāqir (d. *c.* 118/736) foretells that in the last days (*fī ākhir al-zamān*) there will be those who regard *al-amr biʾl-maʿrūf* as obligatory only if it will cost them nothing, and invoke excuses of all kinds for not performing it; God will punish them collectively (Kulaynī, *Kāfī*, 5:55f. no. 1; Ṭūsī, *Tahdhīb*, 6:180f. no. 21; see further below, ch. 11, 256). On the other hand, those who do practise *al-amr biʾl-maʿrūf* under eschatological conditions may earn a greatly increased reward (Haythamī, *Zawāʾid*, 7:261.23, 271.6).

[40] Abū ʿUbayd, *Nāsikh*, 98.20; Ibn Māja, *Sunan*, 1330f. no. 4014; Abū Dāwūd, *Sunan*, 4:512 no. 4,341 (whence Jaṣṣāṣ, *Aḥkām*, 2:31.13, 487.10); Tirmidhī, *Ṣaḥīḥ*, 8:221f. no. 3,060; Ibn Abī ʾl-Dunyā, *Amr*, 41 no. 2; Ibn Waḍḍāḥ, *Bidaʿ*, 218f. = 345 no. 11; Ṭabarī, *Tafsīr*, 11:145f. nos. 12,862f. (to Q5:105); Bayhaqī, *Sunan*, 10:92.5; Bayhaqī, *Shuʿab*, 6:83f. nos. 7,553f.; and, for versions without *isnāds*, Muttaqī, *Kanz*, 3:71 no. 5,531 (and cf. 3:75f. no. 5,557); Ibn ʿAbd al-Wahhāb, *Naṣīḥa*, 66.10. The tradition is transmitted with a Syrian *isnād* from the Companion Abū Thaʿlaba al-Khushanī (d. 75/694f.). On the wording, cf. also above, ch. 2, note 68; for Q5:105, cf. above, ch. 2, note 80.

[41] In Abū Dāwūd's version: *ḥattā idhā raʾayta shuḥḥan muṭāʿan wa-hawan muttabaʿan wa-dunyā muʾtharatan wa-iʿjāba kulli dhī raʾyin bi-raʾyihi*; compare Ṭabarī, *Tafsīr*, 11:143.2 no. 12,858.

[42] In Abū Dāwūd's version: *fa-ʿalayka – yaʿnī bi-nafsika – wa-daʿ ʿanka ʾl-ʿawāmm.*

overrides the duty of commanding right. He intervenes to insist that the conditions of moral disorder to which the verse refers have not yet come, and accordingly instructs his hearers that until that time they should continue to perform the duty.[43] Similar interpretations of the verse are ascribed to other authorities.[44] Thus the young Syrian Jubayr ibn Nufayr (d. 80/699f.) finds himself in a gathering of Companions and others in which forbidding wrong is under discussion. He foolishly quotes Q5:105, and is reproved by those present, who afterwards tell him that, since he is so young, he may in fact live into the time to which the verse refers.[45] Kaʿb al-Aḥbār (d. 34/654f.) holds that the verse will only apply when (among other things) the church of Damascus has been demolished and replaced with a mosque; the Damascene transmitter Abū Mushir (d. 218/833) identifies this building activity with the works carried out by the caliph Walīd ibn ʿAbd al-Malik (r. 86–96/705–15).[46] In yet another Syrian tradition, the Prophet is asked when forbidding wrong is to be abandoned; he answers in different terms, but to similar effect.[47] Even more striking is an Egyptian tradition transmitted by Ibn Lahīʿa (d. 174/790), in which the

[43] Ṭabarī, *Tafsīr*, 11:143f. nos. 12,859f.; Abū ʿUbayd, *Nāsikh*, 99.8; Jaṣṣāṣ, *Aḥkām*, 2:488.13; Bayhaqī, *Sunan*, 10:92.11; Bayhaqī, *Shuʿab*, 6:82f. no. 7,552. Although Ibn Masʿūd is a Kūfan Companion, the *isnād*s are not Kūfan; their common link is Abū Jaʿfar al-Rāzī, a traditionist of the second/eighth century. In another transmission, Ibn Masʿūd similarly states that the verse does not refer to the present, and that the duty is to be performed as long as those against whom it is directed are receptive to it (Ṭabarī, *Tafsīr*, 11:138–41 nos. 12,848–50, 12,855, of which the last is the most explicit; cf. also Naḥḥās, *Maʿānī ʾl-Qurʾān*, 2:374.3; Abū ʿUbayd, *Nāsikh*, 99.18; and Jaṣṣāṣ, *Aḥkām*, 2:488.26). This time, the *isnād*s are Baṣran, with Ḥasan al-Baṣrī (d. 110/728) as the common link.

[44] Ibn ʿUmar states that it applies neither to himself nor to his companions, but to people (*aqwām*) who will come after (Ṭabarī, *Tafsīr*, 11:139 no. 12,851; contrast *ibid.*, 140f. no. 12,854). In a Baṣran transmission from Qatāda (d. 117/735f.) an anonymous Companion or Companions again take the view that the verse refers to a future time (*ibid.*, 140–2 nos. 12,852f., 12,856f. (where the time is referred to as *ākhir al-zamān*)). Another such view is reported from an anonymous Companion by Ḥasan al-Baṣrī (*ibid.*, 144f. no. 12,861). See also Ibn Waḍḍāḥ, *Bidaʿ*, 218 = 344f. nos. 9f. None of this material has Kūfan *isnād*s.

[45] Ṭabarī, *Tafsīr*, 11:142f. no. 12,858. The *isnād* indicates a Syrian provenance (for the identity of the 'Ibn Faḍāla' who appears in the *isnād*, see M. I. Fierro, 'Muʿāwiya b. Ṣāliḥ al-Ḥaḍramī al-Ḥimṣī: historia y leyenda', in M. Marín (ed.), *Estudios onomástico-biográficos de al-Andalus*, vol. 1, Madrid 1988, 346).

[46] Abū ʿUbayd, *Nāsikh*, 98.26; Jaṣṣāṣ, *Aḥkām*, 2:487.22; as might be expected, the *isnād* is Syrian. For Walīd's building works, see K. A. C. Creswell, *Early Muslim architecture: Umayyads*, Oxford 1969, esp. 188–91.

[47] Ibn Ḥanbal, *Musnad*, 3:187.5; Ibn Māja, *Sunan*, 1331 no. 4,015; Ibn Waḍḍāḥ, *Bidaʿ*, 213 = 339 no. 43; Bayhaqī, *Shuʿab*, 6:84 nos. 7,555f.; and the parallel cited in van Ess, *Theologie*, 1:81 n. 13. In what seems to be a Syrian tradition, the Prophet predicts a time of troubles (*fitna*) in which the believer will be unable to perform the duty by hand or tongue; but this will not detract from his faith more than the smallest leak from a waterskin (Ibn Rajab, *Jāmiʿ al-ʿulūm waʾl-ḥikam*, 347.10; Haythamī, *Zawāʾid*, 7:275.6; Muttaqī, *Kanz*, 3:78 no. 5,571).

Prophet tells his followers to cease forbidding wrong at the beginning of (the year) 200/815f.[48]

For those who transmitted such traditions (not to mention those who may have put them into circulation by placing them in the mouths of earlier authorities), the bad times could readily be understood to have begun already. These traditions thus lend themselves to the unusual view that the duty has lapsed. Such an attitude, which is scarcely represented in the doctrines of the legal and theological schools, can best be seen as an expression of the quietist tendencies often found among the traditionists (*ahl al-ḥadīth*). We will encounter examples of this kind of thinking in the following chapter,[49] and a similar tone is in evidence in the thought of Aḥmad ibn Ḥanbal (d. 241/855).[50]

There are also non-eschatological traditions which can be seen as expressions of the same tendency to draw the teeth of the duty, though the picture they present is far less coherent and consistent.

Some traditions suggest that failure to forbid wrong need not be damning. In one, Ibn Masʿūd is confronted with the view that one who does not command right and forbid wrong is damned (*halaka*); he replies that this is rather the fate of one who fails to approve of right and disapprove of wrong in his heart.[51] The Prophet describes how, on the day of the Resurrection, God will ask a man what had prevented him from righting the wrongs he had seen; the answer 'I relied on you and was afraid of people' apparently suffices to exculpate him.[52]

Other traditions seek to discourage tendencies to heroism. There is a Prophetic tradition that the believer should not court humiliation by exposing himself to an ordeal he cannot endure,[53] and this is adduced in

[48] Abū Bakr al-Mālikī (fifth/eleventh century), *Riyāḍ al-nufūs*, ed. H. Monés, Cairo 1951–, 1:74.11; Abū Zayd al-Dabbāgh (d. 696/1296f.), *Maʿālim al-īmān fī maʿrifat ahl al-Qayrawān*, in the recension of Ibn Nājī (d. 839/1436), ed. I. Shabbūḥ *et al.*, Cairo and Tunis 1968–, 1:212.8. Unfortunately the transmitter from Ibn Lahīʿa is not mentioned. I owe my knowledge of this tradition to Nurit Tsafrir. [49] See below, ch. 4, 76f.

[50] See below, ch. 5, notes 184f.

[51] Nuʿaym ibn Ḥammād, *Fitan*, 89.14 (the fullest version); Ibn Abī Shayba, *Muṣannaf*, 7:504 no. 37,581; Ṭabarī, *Jāmiʿ al-bayān*, 27:132.4 (to Q57:16; I owe this reference to Etan Kohlberg); Bayhaqī, *Shuʿab*, 6:95 no. 7,588; Haythamī, *Zawāʾid*, 7:275.19; and cf. Muqātil, *Khams miʾa*, 279.16; Ibn Waḍḍāḥ, *Bidaʿ*, 230 = 360 no. 62; and Abū Bakr al-Khallāl (d. 311/923), *al-Amr biʾl-maʿrūf waʾl-nahy ʿan al-munkar*, ed. ʿA. A. ʿAṭā, Cairo 1975, 87 no. 12. The *isnād* is Kūfan.

[52] Ḥumaydī, *Musnad*, 324 no. 739 (I owe this reference to Nurit Tsafrir); Ibn Ḥanbal, *Musnad*, 3:27.8, 29.23, 77.25; Ibn Māja, *Sunan*, 1332 no. 4,017; Ibn Abī ʾl-Dunyā, *Amr*, 53 no. 11; Bayhaqī, *Sunan*, 10:90.27; Bayhaqī, *Shuʿab*, 6:90f. nos. 7,574f.; and for versions without *isnāds*, see Muttaqī, *Kanz*, 3:73 no. 5,542, 78 no. 5,569. The Companion who transmits the tradition is Abū Saʿīd al-Khudrī; the *isnāds* are Ḥijāzī.

[53] Ibn Ḥanbal, *Musnad*, 5:405.22; Ibn Māja, *Sunan*, 1332 no. 4,016; Tirmidhī, *Ṣaḥīḥ*, 7:35 no. 2,255; Ibn Abī ʾl-Dunyā, *Amr*, 131 no. 100 (all from Ḥudhayfa); Ibn Waḍḍāḥ, *Bidaʿ*,

the context of forbidding wrong.[54] Cold water is poured on the idea that it is necessarily a fine thing to speak out in the presence of an unjust, or any, ruler.[55] Thus Ibn ʿAbbās (d. 68/687f.) takes the view that one should not command and forbid those in authority if there is a risk of getting killed for it.[56]

Finally, there are traditions that – perhaps quite innocently – dwell on the ifs and buts of the duty. One ought to start by putting oneself to rights before venturing to command and forbid others.[57] One should likewise take no action if one fears bringing upon oneself a calamity worse than the evil one is forbidding.[58] In any event, one has to be suitably qualified. Thus the Prophet states that one should not forbid wrong unless one possesses 'three qualities': civility, knowledge and probity.[59] At the same time one must respect privacy.[60] One should not seek to expose people: a well-

233 = 364 no. 77; and cf. Haythamī, *Zawāʾid*, 7:274.20 (from Ibn ʿUmar), 275.2 (from ʿAlī). The *isnād* is Baṣran. The tradition is also ascribed by the Imāmīs to Jaʿfar al-Ṣādiq (Ṭūsī, *Tahdhīb*, 6:180 nos. 17f.).

54 Haythamī's version from Ibn ʿUmar is framed in an anecdote in which the latter disapproves of something Ḥajjāj has said, and wishes to do something about it (*an ughayyir*); he then remembers this saying of the Prophet, and thinks better of it. Ibn Māja's version appears in his chapter on the duty. Later authors likewise cite the tradition in the context of *al-amr bi'l-maʿrūf* (see, for example, below, ch. 6, note 141, but contrast ch. 5, note 125).

55 Compare the Imāmī tradition from Jaʿfar al-Ṣādiq that there is no reward for suffering incurred through exposing oneself to (the anger of) an unjust ruler (Kulaynī, *Kāfī*, 5:60f. no. 3; Ṭūsī, *Tahdhīb*, 6:178 no. 12); contrast the tradition cited above, ch. 1, note 18.

56 See below, ch. 4, note 52. There is also a tradition transmitted by Ibn ʿAbbās in which a man comes to the Prophet proposing that he should engage in *al-amr bi'l-maʿrūf*, only to be told that this is not for him, rather for the ruler (Abū Yaʿlā ibn al-Farrāʾ (d. 458/1066), *al-Amr bi'l-maʿrūf wa'l-nahy ʿan al-munkar*, ms. Damascus, Ẓāhiriyya, Majmūʿ no. 3,779 = Majāmīʿ 42, item 7, f. 104a.22, without *isnād*; for this work, see below, ch. 6, note 116).

57 So Ibn ʿAbbās (Bayhaqī, *Shuʿab*, 6:88f. no. 7,569; the *isnād* is problematic). A Prophetic tradition describes the grim punishment meted out in hell to those who commanded right while themselves acting wrongfully (see, for example, Ibn Ḥanbal, *Musnad*, 5:205.13, 207.7, 209.13; Bukhārī, *Ṣaḥīḥ*, 2:319.10; Muslim, *Ṣaḥīḥ*, 2,290f. no. 2,989; Bayhaqī, *Sunan*, 10:95.2; Bayhaqī, *Shuʿab*, 6:88 no. 7,568; and cf. Ḥumaydī, *Musnad*, 250 no. 547; the *isnād*s are Kūfan). Yet another Prophetic tradition urges that one should command right even if one's own conduct is not fully righteous (see, for example, Ibn Waḍḍāḥ, *Bidaʿ*, 234 = 365 no. 83; Jaṣṣāṣ, *Aḥkām*, 2:33.27; Bayhaqī, *Shuʿab*, 6:89 no. 7,570; also Haythamī, *Zawāʾid*, 7:277.4; the *isnād*s would seem to be Meccan or Syrian).

58 Ibn Waḍḍāḥ, *Bidaʿ*, 230 = 360 no. 59; Muttaqī, *Kanz*, 3:76 no. 5,559.

59 Daylamī, *Firdaws*, 5:137f. no. 7,741; Muttaqī, *Kanz*, 3:76 no. 5,561. The transmitter is the Baṣran Companion Anas ibn Mālik (d. 91/709f.), who in turn transmits to the Baṣran Abān (ibn Abī ʿAyyāsh) (d. 138/755). This saying is well known, though it is rarely attested, as here, as a Prophetic tradition (cf. below, ch. 5, note 74; ch. 6, note 126; ch. 8, note 102). Another tradition states that one should not command right until one is knowledgeable (*ʿālim*), and knows what one is commanding (Muttaqī, *Kanz*, 3:76 no. 5,560).

60 See, for example, the Kūfan tradition from Ibn Masʿūd cited below, ch. 4, note 261, with implicit reference to the Koranic prohibition of spying on people (Q49:12). A Prophetic tradition avers that a hidden sin harms only the sinner, whereas one that is public knowledge, and is not put right (*lam tughayyar*), harms people at large (Ibn Abī 'l-Dunyā (d. 281/894),

known Prophetic tradition states that he who keeps concealed something that would dishonour a Muslim (*man satara Musliman* or the like) will receive the same consideration from God.[61] All in all, if one cannot perform the duty, then one cannot, and it is enough that God should know that one disapproves in one's heart.[62]

On the other hand, just as in Koranic exegesis, there is little attempt to confine the duty to an elite.[63] The one tradition that bears directly on this question states that God will not punish people at large (*al-ʿāmma*) for the sins of the elite (*al-khāṣṣa*), until the point is reached at which they see wrongs all around them which they are in a position to put right; at that point, if they fail to act, He will punish the lot of them.[64]

4. CONCLUSION

Two things are worth attention in conclusion. The first is the geographical provenance of the material. In presenting the traditions, I have attempted where possible to indicate where they come from, and we can now review this evidence. As might be expected, relevant traditions reach us from all the major centres of traditionist activity: Kūfa, Baṣra, Syria and

Footnote 60 (*cont.*)
ʿUqūbāt, ed. M. K. R. Yūsuf, Beirut 1996, 43 no. 40, and the editor's references thereto; Muttaqī, *Kanz*, 3:73 no. 5,539, 81 no. 5,582). Neither of these traditions refers explicitly to *al-amr biʾl-maʿrūf*, but both are found in pages devoted to the duty.

61 Ibn Ḥanbal, *Musnad*, 8:46 no. 5,646, 13:161 no. 7,421, 15:86 no. 7,929; 2:514.26, 522.3, 4:62.20, 104.3, 104.7, 5:375.17; Bukhārī, *Ṣaḥīḥ*, 2:98.13; Muslim, *Ṣaḥīḥ*, 1996 no. 2,580, 2,074 no. 2,699; Ibn Māja, *Sunan*, 82 no. 225, 850 nos. 2,544, 2,546; Abū Dāwūd, *Sunan*, 5:234f. no. 4,946; Tirmidhī, *Ṣaḥīḥ*, 5:113–15 nos. 1425f., 6:175 no. 1931; Ibn ʿAbd al-Ḥakam (d. 257/871), *Futūḥ Miṣr wa-akhbāruhā*, ed. C. C. Torrey, New Haven 1922, 275.8; and cf. Ḥumaydī, *Musnad*, 189f. no. 384; Ibn Ḥanbal, *Musnad*, 2:389.1, 404.30, 500.20, 4:159.7; Muslim, *Ṣaḥīḥ*, 2002 no. 2,590. In a striking variant, one who covers the shame of a believer (*man satara muʾminan*) is as one who brings to life a buried infant (*mawʾūda*) from her grave (cf. Q81:8) (Ibn Ḥanbal, *Musnad*, 4:147.26; and cf. *ibid.*, 147.29, 153.26, 158.14; Abū Dāwūd, *Sunan*, 5:200f. no. 4,891). All major centres of transmission are represented in the *isnād*s. Again, these traditions make no mention of *al-amr biʾl-maʿrūf*, but their relevance is clear, and they are quoted in this context (see below, ch. 5, note 135; ch. 6, notes 152f.).

62 Ibn Abī Shayba, *Muṣannaf*, 7:504 no. 37,582; Bukhārī, *Kabīr*, 2:1:278 no. 951; Ibn Waḍḍāḥ, *Bidaʿ*, 232 = 362 no. 70; Ibn Abī ʾl-Dunyā, *Amr*, 136 no. 105; Haythamī, *Zawāʾid*, 7:275.14; Muttaqī, *Kanz*, 3:75 no. 5,553. The tradition is Kūfan.

63 For Koranic exegesis, see above, ch. 2, 18–20.

64 Nuʿaym ibn Ḥammād, *Fitan*, 378.20 (I owe this reference to Nurit Tsafrir); Ibn Ḥanbal, *Musnad*, 4:192.13; Ibn Abī ʾl-Dunyā, *Amr*, 101 no. 62; Haythamī, *Zawāʾid*, 7:267.9, 268.10; Muttaqī, *Kanz*, 3:67 no. 5,515; Ibn ʿAbd al-Wahhāb, *Naṣīḥa*, 67.15. This tradition is also attested as a saying of ʿUmar ibn ʿAbd al-ʿAzīz (d. 101/720) (so Abū Yūsuf, *Kharāj*, 11.2, and Ibn Saʿd, *Ṭabaqāt*, 5:282.13), or as an anonymous saying transmitted by him (so Mālik (d. 179/795), *Muwaṭṭaʾ*, ed. M. F. ʿAbd al-Bāqī, Cairo 1951, 991 no. 23, and Ibn Abī ʾl-Dunyā, *Amr*, 102 no. 63). The *isnād*s are Ḥijāzī.

the Ḥijāz. There are, however, a couple of features of the geographical distribution of our traditions which are striking. One is the disproportionate role of Kūfa in the provenance of those traditions (the majority) that do not attempt to play down the duty: Kūfa is the source of about twice as much of this material as all other centres put together.[65] The other feature is the relative prominence of Syria in the provenance of the traditions that work to play down the duty: here Syria is as productive as all other centres taken together.[66] Such a contrast between the roles of the Kūfan and Syrian traditionists must surely be a reflection of the political geography of Umayyad times, with Kūfa as the leading centre of provincial opposition and Syria as the focus of metropolitan government. This in turn suggests that the material is often implicitly political even when not explicitly so.

The second aspect of the material that merits attention is its nature. It does not share the vague and general character of the Koranic references to the duty, but neither does it do much to elaborate a precise code of conduct. Most of the traditions are concerned to encourage believers to forbid wrong, or alternatively to discourage them from it; in other words, their purpose is to convey a mood, and the primary means through which they seek to achieve this is rhetoric. Here and there, however, we encounter potential building-blocks for later scholastic doctrines. The prime instance of this is, of course, the 'three modes' tradition, with its triad of deed, word and thought.[67] A few other traditions are couched in what might be described as a proto-scholastic idiom, though none achieved the same success; an example is the tradition according to which one should refrain from forbidding wrong if one fears subjecting oneself to something worse than the wrong itself.[68] A final point worth emphasising is that, just as in the context of Koranic exegesis, it is the consensus of the later scholarly tradition that establishes that we are talking about forbidding wrong even when this is not evident from the wording of the traditions themselves.

[65] Note particularly the Kūfan provenance of the 'three modes' tradition (see above, note 2), and the role of Kūfans in the transmission of all other major traditions in this category (see above, ch. 1, note 18, and above, notes 12, 19). By contrast, Kūfa plays only a limited role in the transmission of traditions of negative tendency (for two clear cases, see above, notes 51, 62; cf. also notes 57, 60). At the same time, Kūfa is the source of some predictions of the decay of *al-amr bi'l-ma'rūf* (see above, notes 38f.).

[66] Note particularly the Syrian provenance of Abū Tha'laba's tradition (see above, note 40), and cf. the Syrian role in the transmission of minor traditions of this eschatological type (above, notes 45–7). By contrast, Syria plays little role in the propagation of traditions of positive tendency (but cf. above, notes 27, 57).

[67] See above, section 1.

[68] See above, note 58.

CHAPTER 4

BIOGRAPHICAL LITERATURE ABOUT EARLY MUSLIMS

1. INTRODUCTION

Islamic biographical literature is varied, and often rich, in its genres. It offers collections of biographies of traditionists, judges, poets, grammarians, Koran reciters, exegetes, women and others. Yet before modern times the idea does not seem to have occurred to anyone to collect into a single work biographical material on those who commanded right and forbade wrong.[1] This is a pity, since the existence of such a collection would have made the writing of this chapter much easier. Nevertheless, the broad range of biographical literature is our main source for the practice of the duty of forbidding wrong by individual Muslims, and it also provides incidental statements of their opinions on the subject.[2] The material is uneven and often threadbare; on occasion a writer may tell us no more than that the subject of a biography was assiduous in performing the duty.[3] But fortunately most references are not as bald as this, and the anecdotal detail we are sometimes given can be colourful and significant.

Although this body of material does not lend itself to systematic presentation, I shall attempt in this chapter to identify its more striking features. By way of introduction, I shall look briefly at what the Muslim sources have to say about pre-Islamic figures, followed by the Prophet himself. But the bulk of the chapter will be devoted to individual Muslims of the first two centuries of Islam, with some forays into the third. My coverage is subject to two major limitations. The first is imposed by the sources: given the fact that the traditionists are the biographers of early Islam *par excellence*, the

[1] Cf. the little work of Ṣalāḥ al-Dīn al-Munajjid entitled *al-Āmirūn bi'l-maʿrūf fī 'l-Islām*, Beirut 1979.

[2] The bulk of the material used in this chapter is drawn from this biographical literature, but I have freely added relevant information from non-biographical sources. Some material regarding the views of Companions of the Prophet has already been covered in ch. 3.

[3] See below, note 19.

material collected here relates disproportionately to traditionists and other figures in the major centres of learning who came to be accepted as religious authorities in Sunnī retrospect. The other limitation is a matter of convenience: I shall defer consideration of figures identifiable as members of the classical sects and schools until the chapters devoted to those communities.

We begin, then, with what might be called the prehistory of forbidding wrong. It was a matter of general agreement that the value, and indeed the duty, antedated the Islamic revelation. This view had support from the Koran, particularly as it was understood by the commentators. Q3:114 refers to a group of the 'People of the Book' who command right and forbid wrong.[4] If we follow the mainstream of the commentarial tradition, Q5:79 condemns certain Israelites for failing to forbid each other wrong.[5] Q7:163–6 describe an incident in which some Israelites forbade 'evil' (*sūʾ*) and others did not, and the commentators again understand this in terms of forbidding wrong.[6] In Q31:17 the pre-Islamic sage Luqmān tells his son to command right and forbid wrong.[7] Thus it is no surprise that Qurṭubī (d. 671/1273) should hold that the duty had been incumbent on earlier communities (*al-umam al-mutaqaddima*),[8] and that we find numerous references in the sources to its performance or neglect among the ancient Israelites.[9] Nevertheless, instances in which the duty is performed by a named individual are not particularly common. One example is Noah: there was, we are told, no one among the people of those days who forbade wrongs (*yanhā ʿan munkar*), so God sent Noah to them.[10]

[4] See above, ch. 2, note 5.
[5] See above, ch. 2, 15f. (for the verse) and 26f. (for the commentators).
[6] See above, ch. 2, 16 (for the passage) and notes 60, 69 (for the commentators).
[7] See above, ch. 2, 28f.
[8] Qurṭubī, *Jāmiʿ*, 4:47.4; he draws this inference from Q3:21 (cf. above, ch. 2, note 58).
[9] One example is a tradition describing a slaughter of forbidders of wrong in the context of the killing of prophets referred to in Q3:21 (*ibid.*, 4:46.17; Fakhr al-Dīn al-Rāzī, *Tafsīr*, 7:229.15; Ṭabarī, *Tafsīr*, 6:285f. no. 6,780, and Bazzār, *Musnad*, 4:110.8 (no. 1285), with a Syrian *isnād*). Another is a tradition about Jesus passing by a ruined village, and learning that its inhabitants had failed to forbid wrong (ʿAbd al-Malik ibn Ḥabīb (d. 238/853), *Wasf al-firdaws*, Beirut 1987, 128 no. 317; I owe this reference to Maribel Fierro). See also below, notes 55, 224. Cf. the passage ascribed to the Torah by Kaʿb al-Aḥbār (d. 34/654f.) in the tradition quoted in Ghazzālī, *Iḥyāʾ*, 2:285.13, 306.9 (and for an equally apocryphal citation from the Gospel, see Ibn Aʿtham al-Kūfī (writing 204/819f.), *Futūḥ*, Hyderabad 1968–75, 1:127.10). Note, however, that according to an Ibāḍī source, Khaḍir is not obligated to forbid wrong (Warjlānī (d. 570/1174f.), *Dalīl*, Cairo 1306, 3:163.10); I have not seen other statements on this point.
[10] Ibn Saʿd, *Ṭabaqāt*, 1:1:16.24. Other such instances are found in Kisāʾī's accounts of Idrīs's confrontation with the musical and sexual depravities of the descendants of Cain (Kisāʾī (uncertain date), *Qiṣaṣ al-anbiyāʾ*, ed. I. Eisenberg, Leiden 1922–3, 82.11) and of Lot's embarrassment at the sexual orientation of his people (*ibid.*, 148.15).

Moving on to Islamic times, it goes without saying that the Prophet commanded right and forbade wrong. He is described as doing so in Q7:157,[11] a verse traditionally considered to go back to the Meccan period of his career.[12] Here and there, we accordingly encounter references to his activity in such terms. Thus a prophecy regarding the Prophet placed in the mouth of the pre-Islamic Yemeni king Sayf ibn Dhī Yazan (*fl. c.* AD 570) mentions that he will forbid wrong.[13] An account of the conversion of Abū Dharr al-Ghifārī (d. 32/652f.) has it that he sent his brother to Mecca to find out more about the self-proclaimed prophet who had recently appeared; on his return his brother reported to him that the man was commanding right and forbidding wrong.[14] An Ibāḍī scholar speaks of the hostility with which people reacted when the Prophet counselled them, commanded them right and forbade them wrong.[15] Yet the fact of the matter is that references to the duty are infrequent in accounts of the life of the Prophet. Thus there is almost nothing to be found in the biographical works of Ibn Isḥāq (d. 150/767f.)[16] or Wāqidī (d. 207/823).[17] The only significant qualification is that a few accounts of the form of words by

[11] See above, ch. 2, 14.

[12] As were Q7:199 and Q31:17 (but cf. T. Nöldeke *et al.*, *Geschichte des Qorāns*, Leipzig 1909–39, 1:157, 159f.). Shāṭibī (d. 790/1388) adduces Q31:17 to show that *al-amr bi'l-ma'rūf* was already established in the Meccan period (*al-Muwāfaqāt fī uṣūl al-sharī'a*, ed. 'A. Darrāz, Cairo n.d., 3:50.6).

[13] Muḥammad ibn Ḥabīb (d. 245/860), *Munammaq*, Hyderabad 1964, 544.1 (in a narrative which is not from Ibn Ḥabīb himself, see *ibid.*, 538.6).

[14] Ibn Sa'd, *Ṭabaqāt*, 4:1:165.5.

[15] Bisyawī (fourth or fifth/tenth or eleventh century), *Jāmi'*, Ruwī 1984, 4:190.11. See also 'Abdallāh ibn Buluqqīn (writing *c.* 487/1094), *Tibyān*, ed. A. T. al-Ṭībī, Rabat 1995, 50.1 (I owe this reference to Maribel Fierro).

[16] In his account of the revelation which gave the Prophet permission to fight his enemies, Ibn Isḥāq quotes Q22:39–41, which includes a reference to forbidding wrong, and then proceeds to paraphrase it (Ibn Hishām (d. 218/833), *al-Sīra al-nabawiyya*, ed. M. al-Saqqā *et al.*, Cairo 1955, 1–2:467.20, 468.2). Q3:114 is likewise quoted (*ibid.*, 558.3). The wording *amartuka bi . . . 'l-ma'rūfi* appears in a poem (see below, ch. 19, note 37). I also noted the use of the verb *ankara* in reference to protests against a misdeed of Khālid ibn al-Walīd (d. 21/641f.) (*ibid.*, 3–4:429.22, not from Ibn Isḥāq); this might be construed as a case of forbidding wrong. I did not attempt to examine recensions of Ibn Isḥāq's work other than Ibn Hishām's.

[17] Here too the verb *ankara* occurs in the sense of to 'object to' (Wāqidī, *Maghāzī*, 908.19, 960.18). Wāqidī also relates that when the caliph Mu'āwiya (r. 41–60/661–80) instituted some earthworks which disturbed the graves of the martyrs slain at the battle of Uḥud in the year 3/625, their bodies were found to be perfectly preserved (for this see E. Kohlberg, 'Medieval Muslim views on martyrdom', in Koninklijke Nederlandse Akademie van Wetenschappen, *Mededelingen*, Afdeling Letterkunde, 60 (1997), 292f.); the Companion Abū Sa'īd al-Khudrī (d. 74/693), whose own father was among those who had fallen at the battle, remarked cryptically: 'No wrong will ever be denounced after this' (*lā yunkar ba'da hādhā munkar abadan*, Wāqidī, *Maghāzī*, 268.1; for the death at Uḥud of Mālik ibn Sinān, the father of Abū Sa'īd, see *ibid.*, 302.10). But this is long after the Prophet's death.

which the Medinese gave their allegiance to the Prophet at the second meeting at ʿAqaba include a reference to forbidding wrong.[18]

With the Companions of the Prophet and those who came after them, the number of figures for whom biographical information is available increases enormously. But only a relatively small proportion of them have anything relevant to offer us. All in all, the total number of such persons caught in my net for the period with which we are concerned in this chapter is around sixty. Each of these said or did something that relates to forbidding wrong, though the claims of some to inclusion in the group are rather marginal, and the information we are given may be minimal.[19]

Before we plunge into this material, it is worth drawing out the implications of a couple of general points. The first is that we owe the literature on which this chapter is based to the Sunnī traditionists. As we have seen, this is a group among whom we find a certain tendency to downplay the duty.[20] Even the hostile reports of the categorical denial of the obligatoriness of forbidding wrong among the 'Ḥashwiyya'[21] – a rude term for anthropomorphist traditionists – have some basis in historical fact.[22] The traditionists, of course, did not generally care to see things this way. Thus Ibrāhīm ibn Mūsā al-Rāzī (d. *c.* 230/844) was asked: 'Who are "those who command right and forbid wrong"?' He responded that the people referred to (sc. in Q9:112) were none other than the traditionists (*naḥnu*

[18] Ibn Ḥanbal, *Musnad*, 3:322.27, 340.1, 5:325.11; Ibn Ḥibbān, *Thiqāt*, 1:109.13 (without *isnād*); Ḥākim, *Mustadrak*, 2:625.6; Bayhaqī (d. 458/1066), *Dalāʾil al-nubuwwa*, ed. ʿA. Qalʿajī, Beirut 1985, 2:443.6, 452.2. Leaving aside Ibn Ḥibbān's account, there are essentially two traditions here, albeit with a common link: the Meccan ʿAbdallāh ibn ʿUthmān ibn Khuthaym (d. 132/749f.). The Baghdādī Abū ʾl-ʿAbbās al-Abbār (d. 290/903) had a dream in which he saw the Prophet and did allegiance to him with such a formula (Khaṭīb, *Taʾrīkh Baghdād*, 4:306.19; I owe this reference to Nurit Tsafrir).

[19] Thus the Wāsiṭī Khālid ibn ʿAbdallāh al-Ṭaḥḥān (d. 179/795) is said to have commanded right (Dhahabī (d. 748/1348), *Tadhkirat al-ḥuffāẓ*, Hyderabad 1968–70, 260.7, drawn to my attention by Nurit Tsafrir); but this is all we are told. Things are not much better in the case of the pious Wāsiṭī traditionist Yazīd ibn Hārūn (d. 206/821), who according to a statement widely quoted in the sources 'was counted among those who command right and forbid wrong' (Khaṭīb, *Taʾrīkh Baghdād*, 14:346.16; Dhahabī (d. 748/1348), *Siyar aʿlām al-nubalāʾ*, ed. S. al-Arnaʾūṭ *et al.*, Beirut 1981–8, 9:361.15 (I owe this reference to Nurit Tsafrir); Dhahabī, *Taʾrīkh al-Islām*, ed. ʿU. ʿA. Tadmurī, Beirut 1987–, years 201–10, 457.15; Ibn Ḥajar, *Tahdhīb*, 11:369.5; the source of the statement is Yaʿqūb ibn Shayba (d. 262/875f.)). Possibly the reference is to an incident in which he intervened in the building of a mosque (see van Ess, *Theologie*, 2:431, citing Baḥshal (d. 292/904f.), *Taʾrīkh Wāsiṭ*, ed. K. ʿAwwād, Baghdad 1967, 158.17, 158.19). Abū ʾl-ʿĀliya (d. 90/708f.) refers to Ḥasan al-Baṣrī (d. 110/728) rather dismissively as 'a Muslim man who commands right and forbids wrong' (Fasawī, *Maʿrifa*, 2:52.7; Abū Isḥāq al-Shīrāzī (d. 476/1083), *Ṭabaqāt al-fuqahāʾ*, Baghdad 1356, 70.17); in context, the implication seems to be that he felt no need to take notice of Ḥasan as a scholar.

[20] See above, ch. 3, section 3.

[21] See below, ch. 9, notes 40, 160; and cf. note 7 and 224, and Abū Hayyān, *Baḥr*, 3:20.19.

[22] Cf. below, ch. 5, 106.

hum), since it is they who transmit the commands and prohibitions of the Prophet.[23] But it has also been observed that forbidding wrong hardly figures in traditionist creeds.[24] In short, there is some reason to expect that the interest of the Sunnī biographers in forbidding wrong should be limited; the value carried overtones of an uncongenial political activism.

This expectation, however, is balanced by the other general point to be made here. Our authors, or their sources, were biographers. As such, they were engaged in, among other things, the great early Islamic pastime of entertaining their audiences.[25] Forbidding wrong was a theme that lent itself to this purpose. It is typically an individual performance, and as such fits well into a biography: unlike a participant in holy war, someone who undertakes this duty is normally on his own. He is, moreover, embarking on an enterprise with an open outcome. This is an agonistic activity; it takes courage, skill, nerve, and judgement – not to mention luck – to pull it off. It is quite unlike prayer or fasting, duties that any normal person can adequately fulfil just by keeping at them. It also differs from them in that the conditions under which it is undertaken, and the eventual outcome, can be very varied indeed. Superior performances in forbidding wrong are thus likely to be dramatic and distinctive – highly eligible material for biographers, irrespective of their religious preoccupations. The importance of this factor will be evident in what follows.

2. CONFRONTING THE STATE

The single most prominent theme in the biographical material is confrontation with the authorities, typically the caliphs and their governors. The hero goes in to someone in power and reproves him for his wrongdoing in the manner of the goldsmith of Marw;[26] the consequences, however, are often less dire. Such encounters are regularly reported in a tone of approval – the negative image of the zealot who sought to get himself killed by the caliph al-Maʾmūn (r. 198–218/813–33) is unusual.[27] As we have seen, this confrontational theme is also present in tradition,[28] but it is by no means so prominent there. If we accept this robust attitude towards reproving rulers as mainstream, we can go on to define two contrasting trends of thought as extreme in relation to it, though by no means entirely beyond

[23] See al-Khaṭīb al-Baghdādī (d. 463/1071), *Sharaf aṣḥāb al-ḥadīth*, ed. M. S. Hatîboğlu, Ankara 1972, 46 no. 91. [24] Madelung, *Qāsim*, 17.

[25] The later institutionalisation of Islamic scholarship in the *madrasa* must have significantly reduced the pressure on scholars to be interesting. This may help to account for the dry character of much of the biographical literature of later centuries, a character which makes it much less rewarding for the study of forbidding wrong. [26] Cf. above, ch. 1, 3–7.

[27] Cf. above, ch. 1, 10f. [28] See above, ch. 3, 39, and cf. above, ch. 2, 29f.

the pale. One is an activist trend which is prepared to go beyond verbal confrontation with unjust rulers, and to risk armed insurrection against them. The other is a quietist trend which regards even verbal confrontation with the authorities with deep misgivings. Let us begin with the extremes.

We have already encountered one early Muslim for whom forbidding wrong entailed rebellion, namely the goldsmith of Marw.[29] As we saw, his view caused great consternation to Abū Ḥanīfa (d. 150/767f.), whom Ibrāhīm was casting in the role of prospective leader of his rebellion. This did not, however, impel Abū Ḥanīfa to break with him; he responded rather with counsels of prudence. Another such activist is the well-known Kūfan Shīʿite Ḥasan ibn Ṣāliḥ ibn Ḥayy (d. 167/783f.).[30] When Ṭabarī (d. 310/923) describes him as holding with action against wrong (*inkār al-munkar*) by any available means,[31] what he has in mind is doubtless Ḥasan's notorious espousal of the sword, that is to say of armed rebellion against unjust rule.[32] 'This Ibn Ḥayy', as one of his contemporaries observed, 'has been asking to be crucified for a long time, but we can't find anyone to do it for him.'[33] Yet the greatly respected Shāfiʿite Ibn Ḥajar al-ʿAsqalānī (d. 852/1449) did not find it difficult to enter a defence on behalf of Ḥasan: his belief in such recourse to the sword was a well-known persuasion among the early Muslims, for all that it was later abandoned in the light of its results – and in any case, Ḥasan did not actually rebel against anyone.[34] In the same way ʿAbdallāh ibn Farrūkh (d. 175/791), a Persian Ḥanafī who migrated to Ifrīqiya, associated commanding right with rebellion against unjust rule – though he never launched or joined an insurrection either.[35] Someone who came closer to this was Aḥmad ibn Naṣr al-Khuzāʿī (d. 231/846), grandson of one of the leaders of the movement that brought the ʿAbbāsids to power. He is described in the sources as given to commanding right and speaking out boldly (*ammāran bi'l-maʿrūf qawwālan bi'l-ḥaqq*).[36] This

[29] See above, ch. 1, 7. Compare the way in which Ibrāhīm tells Abū Muslim (d. 137/755) that he is attacking him verbally only because he lacks the strength to do so physically (see above, ch. 1, 3). [30] On whom see van Ess, *Theologie*, 1:246–51.

[31] Ṭabarī, *Ta'rīkh*, series III, 2,516.14 (I owe this reference to Nurit Tsafrir). The phrase *inkār al-munkar* is used synonymously with forbidding wrong; it has some basis in tradition (see above, ch. 3, notes 8, 16).

[32] See, for example, Mizzī, *Tahdhīb*, 6:181.12, 181.15, 181.17, 182.4, 182.16, 184.6, 185.14.

[33] *Ibid.*, 184.2, from Zā'ida ibn Qudāma (d. 161/777); and cf. Dhahabī (d. 748/1348), *Mīzān al-iʿtidāl*, ed. ʿA. M. al-Bajāwī, Cairo 1963–5, 1:498.12.

[34] Ibn Ḥajar, *Tahdhīb*, 2:288.6. For similar views expressed by later Shāfiʿites, see K. Abou El Fadl, 'The Islamic law of rebellion', Princeton Ph.D. 1999, 278 n. 841.

[35] See below, ch. 14, 385.

[36] Khaṭīb, *Ta'rīkh Baghdād*, 5:174.8; Samʿānī, *Ansāb*, 5:116.12; Mizzī, *Tahdhīb*, 1:506.9; Dhahabī, *Siyar*, 11:166.13; Dhahabī, *Ta'rīkh al-Islām*, years 231–40, 55.7; and cf. Ibn al-Jawzī (d. 597/1201), *Muntaẓam*, ed. M. ʿA. and M. ʿA. ʿAṭā, Beirut 1992–3, 11:165.8.

characterisation is undoubtedly based on two episodes in his life, both involving political activities verging on rebellion which our sources associate with commanding right and forbidding wrong. The first episode was in 201/817, when Aḥmad was one of the leaders who arose in Baghdad under conditions of anarchy and sought to restore some kind of order in the streets.[37] The second was in 231/846, when he plotted rebellion against the caliph al-Wāthiq (r. 227–32/842–7) and his imposition of the doctrine of the created Koran; the plot was divulged and he was executed.[38] Men such as these represent the relatively faint echo among the Sunnīs of a theme that is fully audible in more activist quarters: among the Khārijites, the Zaydīs, and perhaps the Muʿtazilites.[39]

This flirtation with rebellion as a means of forbidding wrong is explicitly condemned by some distinguished authorities. A man came to the Companion Ḥudhayfa ibn al-Yamān (d. 36/656f.) and asked him: 'Don't you command right and forbid wrong?' To this Ḥudhayfa replied: 'Commanding right and forbidding wrong is indeed a fine thing, but it is no part of the normative custom (*sunna*) to take up arms against your ruler (*imām*).'[40] Another Companion, ʿAbdallāh ibn ʿUmar (d. 73/693), drew a firm line between, on the one hand, commanding and forbidding those in power and, on the other, armed subversion against them.[41] For Ḥasan al-Baṣrī (d. 110/728) there is likewise no question of resorting to arms in performing the duty. He rejects the suggestion that he should rebel in order to right wrongs (*a-lā takhruj fa-tughayyir?*), replying that God himself rights wrongs through repentance, not the sword.[42] Told of a Khārijite who had rebelled in Ḥīra, he comments that the man had seen a wrong and objected to it (*ankarahu*), but in seeking to right it had fallen into a worse

[37] For references, see below, ch. 5, notes 189f.

[38] For references, see below, ch. 5, note 194.

[39] For the Khārijites, see below, ch. 15, 393–5, 395f.; for the Zaydīs, see below, ch. 10, section 3; for the Muʿtazila, see below, ch. 9, 196–8, 204. A couple of sayings of ʿAlī (d. 40/661) link forbidding wrong to *jihād* (see above, ch. 3, notes 31f., and Ghazzālī, *Iḥyāʾ*, 2:285.19); this is doubtless a resonance of the early Shīʿite political activism strongly reflected in Zaydī sources (for the role of ʿAlī in Zaydī tradition, see above, ch. 3, note 23, and below, ch. 10, notes 5, 8f., 11), and present also in Imāmī ones (for the (rather limited) role of ʿAlī in Imāmī tradition, see above, ch. 3, note 28; below, ch. 11, notes 11 (items (4), (10), (11)), 12, 20, 21f., 40, 41, 43, 45, 49, and cf. 57; there is an activist tone in evidence in much of this material, and Imāmī quietism is conspicuously absent from it).

[40] Ḥanbal ibn Isḥāq (d. 273/886), *Dhikr miḥnat al-imām Aḥmad ibn Ḥanbal*, Cairo 1977, 99.3; similarly Nuʿaym ibn Ḥammād, *Fitan*, 85.11; Ibn Abī Shayba, *Muṣannaf*, 7:508 no. 37,613; Ibn Abī Ḥātim al-Rāzī (d. 327/938), *Taqdimat al-maʿrifa*, ed. ʿA. al-Muʿallimī al-Yamānī, Hyderabad 1952, 270.10 (drawn to my attention by Nimrod Hurvitz).

[41] Nuʿaym ibn Ḥammād, *Fitan*, 92.10; also *ibid.*, 89.8 (defective?).

[42] Ibn Saʿd, *Ṭabaqāt*, 7:1:125.14 (cited in H. H. Schaeder, 'Ḥasan al-Baṣrī: Studien zur Frühgeschichte des Islam', *Der Islam*, 14 (1925), 57, and H. Ritter, 'Studien zur Geschichte des islamischen Frömmigkeit: I. Ḥasan al-Baṣrī', *Der Islam*, 21 (1933), 52).

one.[43] The Kūfan ʿAbdallāh ibn Shubruma (d. 144/761f.) replies in verse to a letter from the Muʿtazilite ʿAmr ibn ʿUbayd (d. 144/761), in which ʿAmr has encouraged him to perform the duty, or reproached him for not doing so. One point made by Ibn Shubruma in his response is that commanding (right) is not to be carried out by unsheathing the sword against rulers.[44] We have already met Abū Ḥanīfa's rejection of rebellion in terms of its adverse consequences.[45] These condemnations suggest that the association of forbidding wrong with rebellion was widespread. But it can hardly have been the norm: in general, it is simply taken for granted in our sources that rebellion is not an option for those who would forbid wrong.

At the other extreme there are those who, far from contemplating rebellion against unjust rulers, are against even verbal admonition of them. The true commander and forbidder, says ʿAbdallāh ibn al-Mubārak (d. 181/797), is not someone who goes into the presence of rulers to command and forbid them, but rather someone who avoids contact with them altogether (*iʿtazalahum*).[46] This attitude too is commonly justified in terms of the likely consequences of such action. When asked why he did not go to the ruler (*sulṭān*) and command him, Sufyān al-Thawrī (d. 161/778) replies: 'When the sea overflows, who can dam it up?'[47] Ḥasan al-Baṣrī is against going in to rulers to command and forbid them;[48] he explains that it is not for a believer to humiliate himself,[49] and that the

[43] Ibn al-Jawzī (d. 597/1201), *al-Ḥasan al-Baṣrī*, ed. Ḥ. al-Sandūbī, Cairo 1931, 34.12 (cited in Ritter, 'Studien', 52).

[44] For references, see below, note 226. The terms used are *al-aʾimma* (so Khallāl) and *al-khalīfa* (so Ibn Abī 'l-Dunyā, but corrupted in the text of Wakīʿ to *al-khalīqa*).

[45] See above, ch. 1, 7–9.

[46] Ibn Rajab (d. 795/1393) *apud* Ibn ʿAbd al-Barr (d. 463/1071), *Jāmiʿ bayān al-ʿilm*, Cairo n.d., 1:179.1, in a text inserted by the editor. In the separate edition of this little work published by Ḥallāq, a line has been omitted by haplography at this point (Ibn Rajab, *Sharḥ wa-bayān li-ḥadīth Mā dhiʾbān jāʾiʿān*, ed. M. Ṣ. Ḥ. Ḥallāq, Beirut 1992, 65.2). For Ibn al-Mubārak, see van Ess, *Theologie*, 2:551–5.

[47] Khallāl, *Amr*, 90 no. 20, and cf. below, ch. 5, note 154; for Sufyān, see van Ess, *Theologie*, 1:221–8. A more nuanced view is quoted from Sufyān by Ibn ʿAbd al-Barr (d. 463/1071): it used to be the case that it was the best people who confronted those in power and commanded them, while those who stayed at home were held of no account; but now those who go and command them are the worst people, and the best are those who stay at home (*Jāmiʿ bayān al-ʿilm*, ed. A. al-Zuhayrī, Dammām 1994, 640 no. 1107). Compare the remark of the Companion Abū Hurayra (d. 58/677f.) that it is no longer possible to speak out in the presence of rulers (*inna 'l-sulṭān lā yukallam al-yawm*); this, as the transmitter points out, was in the time of Muʿāwiya (Nuʿaym ibn Ḥammād, *Fitan*, 89.13; the implication is that things must be far worse today). The term *sulṭān* in these texts is used for a caliph or a governor without distinction.

[48] Hūd ibn Muḥakkam, *Tafsīr*, 1:305.9, and cf. Qurṭubī, *Jāmiʿ*, 4:48.8 (both to Q3:104); Ibn Saʿd, *Ṭabaqāt*, 7:1:128.18; Ibn al-Jawzī, *al-Ḥasan al-Baṣrī*, 32.7.

[49] This saying is often met with as a Prophetic tradition transmitted by Ḥasan (see above, ch. 3, note 53).

swords of the rulers are mightier than our tongues.[50] Likewise the well-known ascetic Fuḍayl ibn ʿIyāḍ (d. 187/803) enjoins that you should command only someone who will accept it from you; reproving a ruler may spell disaster for yourself, your family and your neighbours.[51]

The rejection of such activity tends, however, to be somewhat less categorical than in the case of rebellion. For example, when the Companion ʿAbdallāh ibn al-ʿAbbās (d. 68/687f.) is asked about the idea of reproving those in authority by Saʿīd ibn Jubayr (d. 95/714), he tells him that if he fears being killed for it, he should not upbraid the imam.[52] Presumably, then, there is no objection provided the attempt is risk-free; and it is doubtless for this reason that Ibn ʿAbbās goes on to tell Saʿīd that, if he must engage in such conduct, he should do it by speaking to the ruler in private.[53] Scholars in this camp also consider the possibility that, even if there is serious risk, the protagonist might perhaps be strong enough to endure the consequences. Thus Fuḍayl is greatly concerned that, through engaging in commanding and forbidding, people will subject themselves to ordeals they cannot endure and become infidels;[54] yet he makes an exception in favour of someone of unusual fortitude.[55] The Kūfan ascetic Dāwūd ibn Nuṣayr al-Ṭāʾī (d. 165/781f.), however, does not make even this concession. Asked about a man who goes in to rulers to command and forbid them, he replies that he fears that such a man would be whipped. But what if he can endure that? Then he fears he would be killed. And if he can endure that too? Then

50 So Ibn Saʿd's version. Schaeder seeks to set this testimony aside as incompatible with Ḥasan's whole persona ('Ḥasan al-Baṣrī', 57f.); but see below, note 224.

51 Ibn Abī ʾl-Dunyā, *Amr*, 94 no. 50. In another account, Fuḍayl is asked whether one should forbid a *shurṭī*, an armed man, or a *sulṭān* who is wronging someone; he answers that one should if one can, but goes on to stress that one should not endanger oneself, one's family, one's neighbours, or any Muslim (*ibid.*, 133 no. 101). There are stories in which Fuḍayl meets the caliph Hārūn al-Rashīd (r. 170–93/786–809) and counsels him; but his counsels tend to be mild, and in the most widespread version it is made very clear that the meeting was forced on Fuḍayl against his will (for this version see J. Chabbi, 'Fuḍayl b. ʿIyāḍ, un précurseur du Hanbalisme', *Bulletin d'Etudes Orientales*, 30 (1978), 344 (second anecdote), citing Abū Nuʿaym al-Iṣbahānī (d. 430/1038), *Ḥilyat al-awliyāʾ*, ed. M. A. al-Khānjī, Cairo 1932–8, 8:105.16; also Mizzī, *Tahdhīb*, 23:293.15; Dhahabī, *Siyar*, 8:378.10).

52 Ḥanbal, *Miḥna*, 99.8 (for *taghtab* read *taʿtab*, and for *muqīman* read *fa-fī-mā*); similarly Ibn Abī Shayba, *Muṣannaf*, 7:470 no. 37,307; Ibn Abī ʾl-Dunyā, *Amr*, 113 no. 76; Bayhaqī, *Shuʿab*, 6:96 nos. 7,591f. The *isnād* is Kūfan.

53 Cf. below, 79f.

54 Ibn Abī ʾl-Dunyā, *Amr*, 134 no. 102; Ghazzālī, *Iḥyāʾ*, 2:285.24.

55 Ibn Abī ʾl-Dunyā, *Amr*, 92 no. 47, with a story about a courageous Israelite who rebuked an unjust king and endured the consequences without breaking. Compare Sufyān al-Thawrī: 'I don't forbid you to command and forbid, it's just that I fear for you that you may subject yourself to an ordeal you cannot endure' (Isḥāq ibn Ibrāhīm ibn Sulaymān ibn Wahb al-Kātib (writing after 334/946), *al-Burhān fī wujūh al-bayān*, ed. A. Maṭlūb and K. al-Ḥadīthī, Baghdad 1967, 277.16; I shall cite this author hereafter as Isḥāq ibn Wahb).

he fears that he would fall into the sin of self-conceit (*ʿujb*).[56] There is also the danger that when one actually finds oneself in the presence of the ruler, one will not have the nerve to go through with the intended reproof, and will instead fall into complicity with the wicked ways of the court. Maymūn ibn Mihrān al-Raqqī (d. 117/735f.) warns against putting oneself to the test by entering into the presence of someone in authority (*sulṭān*), even when one tells oneself that one will command him to obey God.[57] Ibn ʿAbbās is perhaps making the same point when he discourages a man from going to reprove a ruler on the ground that it would put him in the way of temptation (*fitna*).[58] The assumption is clearly that, were it not for these pitfalls, rebuking unjust rulers would be a virtuous act.

All in all, there are a good many scholars who pour cold water on the idea of commanding and forbidding rulers;[59] but their reservations, though far-reaching, tend to fall short of unqualified rejection. We are told that Ibn ʿUmar on one occasion had it in mind to rebuke Ḥajjāj (d. 95/714), but then thought better of it when he recalled the Prophetic tradition that a believer should not humiliate himself.[60] Despite his second

[56] Abū Nuʿaym, *Ḥilya*, 7:358.14; Ibn al-Jawzī (d. 597/1201), *Ṣifat al-ṣafwa*, ed. M. Fākhūrī, Aleppo 1389–93, 3:142.8 (I owe this reference to Nurit Tsafrir); Dhahabī, *Taʾrīkh al-Islām*, years 161–70, 181.4; R. Gramlich, *Alte Vorbilder des Sufitums*, Wiesbaden 1995–6, 1:303.

[57] Ṣāliḥ ibn Aḥmad ibn Ḥanbal (d. 266/880), *Sīrat al-imām Aḥmad ibn Ḥanbal*, ed. F. ʿA. Aḥmad, Alexandria 1981, 51.7. For Maymūn, see *EI*², art. 'Maymūn b. Mihrān' (F. M. Donner). He had himself held office under the pious caliph ʿUmar ibn ʿAbd al-ʿAzīz (r. 99–101/717–20) and others, to his subsequent regret (Dhahabī, *Tadhkira*, 99.11; Mizzī, *Tahdhīb*, 29:218.16). Compare the observation made by Ibn Rajab after quoting the saying of Ibn al-Mubārak cited above, note 46: people readily entertain fantasies about confronting rulers with tough talk when they are still far away from them, but they feel differently about it once they get there.

[58] ʿAbd al-Razzāq, *Muṣannaf*, 11:348 no. 20,722, whence Bayhaqī, *Shuʿab*, 6:96f. no. 7,593; Ibn Abī ʾl-Dunyā, *Amr*, 128 no. 97. The *isnād* is Yemeni.

[59] For further examples, see below, ch. 5, 101f., on Ibn Ḥanbal (d. 241/855) and Bishr al-Ḥāfī (d. 227/841f.); ch. 11, 257, on Jaʿfar al-Ṣādiq (d. 148/765); and cf. ch. 14, note 16.

[60] See above, ch. 3, notes 53f. The sources offer a range of indications of Ibn ʿUmar's attitudes towards rebuking rulers. We hear that at a certain point he stopped going in to see governors; his explanation was that if he were to speak out he risked having his motives misunderstood, while if he were to remain silent he risked falling into sin (Ibn Abī ʾl-Dunyā, *Amr*, 137 no. 108; Ghazzālī, *Iḥyāʾ*, 2:285.16). That forbidding wrong is the right activity to be engaged in when in the presence of a governor is implied in a question he asks about some people who appear in the mosque, after he is told that they have come fresh from the governor's presence: '[Does that mean that] if they saw a wrong, they took a stand against it (*ankarūhu*), and if they saw a right, they commanded it?' On being informed that their practice was rather to praise the governor to his face and damn him behind his back, he in effect brands this as hypocrisy (*nifāq*) (Dhahabī, *Siyar*, 11:435.2; I owe this reference to Nurit Tsafrir). Like any self-respecting contemporary of Ḥajjāj, he finds occasion to dress him down (Ibn Saʿd, *Ṭabaqāt*, 4:1:135.26; Ibn ʿAbd al-Barr (d. 463/1071), *al-Istīʿāb fī maʿrifat al-aṣḥāb*, ed. ʿA. M. al-Bajāwī, Cairo n.d., 952.11; Dhahabī, *Tadhkira*, 37.10, 39.15).

thoughts, the anecdote does not suggest that the idea of rebuking Ḥajjāj was unthinkable for him.

With the extremes disposed of, we come to the mainstream of the biographical material on confronting rulers: the cases of men who command and forbid those in power, and are generally felt to be doing the right thing, and doing it well. For convenience I shall arrange a substantial part of the material around two distinct types. One is the notable who, however pious, owes a substantial part of his authority to his social standing. The other is the zealot who comes from nowhere, and whose authority reflects an achieved piety rather than an ascribed social status. It is not that those who forbid wrong fall neatly into one or other of these two categories; but a good many of them can usefully be seen either as instances of these types, or as departures from them.

A good example of the notable type is Ibn Abī Dhiʾb (d. 159/775f.), a Medinese traditionist of good family. Despite a youthful infatuation with love-poetry, he had a reputation for piety.[61] The sources characterise him as a man endowed with a strong personality and the courage to speak out.[62] It is therefore not surprising that they describe him in general terms as given to forbidding wrong.[63] As often in such cases, what they have in mind here would seem to be his way of speaking out in the presence of the authorities. In this respect he is favourably contrasted with Mālik (d. 179/795): Ibn Abī Dhiʾb would speak out while Mālik remained silent.[64] But while the sources imply that this was habitual behaviour on his part, the concrete details they offer relate overwhelmingly to a particular context: his courageous, not to say brazen, conduct in one or more audiences with the caliph al-Manṣūr (r. 136–58/754–75).[65]

[61] His biography is examined by van Ess in *Theologie*, 2:681–7. Van Ess (*ibid.*, 687) understands *kāna yansib fī ḥadāthatihi* (Khaṭīb, *Taʾrīkh Baghdād*, 2:302.4) to mean that he was a genealogist in his youth, but the parallels have *yatashabbab* for *yansib* (Ibn Saʿd (d. 230/845), *al-Ṭabaqāt al-kubrā: al-qism al-mutammim li-tābiʿī ahl al-Madīna wa-man baʿdahum*, ed. Z. M. Manṣūr, Medina 1983, 414.4; Mizzī, *Tahdhīb*, 25:637.9; Dhahabī, *Siyar*, 7:148.5); it seems the better reading.

[62] See, for example, Ibn Saʿd, *Ṭabaqāt, al-qism al-mutammim*, 414.4: *wa-kāna min rijāl al-nās ṣarāmatan wa-qawlan biʾl-ḥaqq.*

[63] Van Ess, *Theologie*, 2:684, citing Muṣʿab al-Zubayrī (d. 236/851), *Nasab Quraysh*, ed. E. Lévi-Provençal, Cairo 1976, 423.9; Khaṭīb, *Taʾrīkh Baghdād*, 2:296.20, 297.8, 298.3; Mizzī, *Tahdhīb*, 25:635.1. It is said that he and Saʿd ibn Ibrāhīm were *aṣḥāb amr wa-nahy* (Fasawī, *Maʿrifa*, 1:686.18; Ibn Abī Yaʿlā (d. 526/1131), *Ṭabaqāt al-Ḥanābila*, ed. M. Ḥ. al-Fiqī, Cairo 1952, 1:251.20; Mizzī, *Tahdhīb*, 25:638.11); I take it that the reference is to the Saʿd ibn Ibrāhīm who was *qāḍī* of Medina and died in 126/743f., rather than to his grandson who became *qāḍī* of Wāsiṭ and died in 201/816f. (*ibid.*, 10:240–7 and 238–40 respectively).

[64] See below, ch. 14, note 190.

[65] For an analysis of the material, see van Ess, *Theologie*, 2:682f. (and note also Ibn Ḥibbān, *Thiqāt*, 7:390.9, where the caliph in the text as we have it is Hārūn al-Rashīd, who began to rule only in 170/786!). A version is quoted by Ghazzālī (*Iḥyāʾ*, 2:318.13). There is also

A plausible example of the same type from Transoxania is the Murji'ite Abū Muṭīʿ al-Balkhī (d. 199/814), who held the office of judge in Balkh.[66] Abū Dāwūd (d. 275/889) is unkind enough to stigmatise him as a Jahmī,[67] but nevertheless adds that he had heard that he was outstanding in forbidding wrong (*min kibār al-āmirīn bi'l-maʿrūf wa'l-nāhīn ʿan al-munkar*).[68] He offers no examples, but the biographers of Abū Muṭīʿ tell the story of his public protest (for which he had procured the tacit support of the governor of the city) against a letter received from the central government in which a Koranic quotation was misapplied for political ends.[69] Another possible instance of the type is Salm ibn Sālim al-Balkhī (d. 194/810), who was likewise involved in this protest; he arrived girt with his sword.[70] He too is said to have forbidden wrong, though again we are given no details of this.[71] As with Abū Muṭīʿ, it may be connected to his relations with the ʿAbbāsid authorities: though he is not depicted as actively subversive, his attitude was sullen and threatening, and this led to his imprisonment by the caliph Hārūn al-Rashīd (r. 170–93/786–809).[72] However, it is not clear from what we are told that Salm was jailed on account of his forbidding wrong, and other sources indicate that the problem was what he said *about* the authorities, not what he said *to* them.[73]

We can find a final example of the notable type among the Abnā', the descendants of the Khurāsānīs who brought the ʿAbbāsid dynasty to power

a story about his refusal to rise to his feet when the caliph al-Mahdī (r. 158–69/775–85) entered the Prophet's mosque in Medina (van Ess, *Theologie*, 2:683, and the sources there cited; also Mizzī, *Tahdhīb*, 25:642.3). Told to stand for the Commander of the Faithful, he retorted that one stands only for the Lord of the Worlds. But he does not *address* the caliph on this occasion. [66] On whom see van Ess, *Theologie*, 2:536–40.

[67] For the accusation of Jahmism, cf. *ibid.*, 538 n. 30.

[68] Dhahabī (d. 748/1348), *ʿIbar*, ed. Ṣ. al-Munajjid and F. Sayyid, Kuwait 1960–6, 1:330.5 (drawn to my attention by Nurit Tsafrir); U. Rudolf, *Al-Māturīdī und die sunnitische Theologie in Samarkand*, Leiden 1997, 58.

[69] Madelung, 'The early Murji'a', 38 n. 25, and van Ess, *Theologie*, 2:536, with the sources there cited; Dhahabī, *Ta'rīkh al-Islām*, years 191–200, 159.9; Ibn Abī 'l-Wafā', *Jawāhir*, 2:266.5.

[70] Khaṭīb, *Ta'rīkh Baghdād*, 8:224.12. On Salm, see W. Madelung, *Religious trends in early Islamic Iran*, Albany 1988, 21; van Ess, *Theologie*, 2:540f.

[71] Ibn Saʿd, *Ṭabaqāt*, 7:2:106.5. Ibn Saʿd's statement is quoted in later sources (Khaṭīb, *Ta'rīkh Baghdād*, 9:141.20; Dhahabī, *Siyar*, 9:321.9; Dhahabī, *Ta'rīkh al-Islām*, years 191–200, 208.7).

[72] Ṣafī al-Dīn Wāʿiẓ-i Balkhī (writing 610/1213f.), *Faḍā'il-i Balkh*, ed. ʿA. Ḥabībī, Tehran 1350 sh., 156.9, 157.10; Khaṭīb, *Ta'rīkh Baghdād*, 9:141.14, 142.15; Dhahabī, *Siyar*, 9:322.1, 322.5; Dhahabī, *Ta'rīkh al-Islām*, years 191–200, 208.14, 209.2; and cf. Ibn Saʿd, *Ṭabaqāt*, 7:2:106.5. Van Ess aptly remarks on Salm's 'Staatsverdrossenheit' (*Theologie*, 2:541), but does not bring out the full menace of his remark about Hārūn: Salm's boast was not that the caliph had earned himself a beating (*ibid.*, 540), but that he – Salm – could, if he so wished, raise 100,000 swords against him.

[73] Contrast Athamina, 'The early Murji'a', 124.

and subsequently settled in Baghdad. Hāshim ibn al-Qāsim al-Kinānī (d. 207/823), known as 'Qayṣar', belonged to this milieu.[74] Ibn Ḥanbal (d. 241/855) used to describe him as one of those who command right and forbid wrong.[75] The transmitter of this remark, Ḥārith ibn Abī Usāma (d. 282/896), also passes on an anecdote that explains how Hāshim came by his nickname. One day Hārūn al-Rashīd's police-chief went into the baths, leaving instructions not to start the afternoon prayer until he came out. Hāshim, however, took it upon himself to countermand this order. When the chief of police reappeared and was told what had happened, he observed, 'This is not Hāshim, this is Qayṣar', likening him to the Byzantine ruler.[76] Though not the best joke in Islamic history, this remark may have helped to defuse a potentially ugly confrontation.

Most notables were doubtless too enmeshed in local politics, and not sufficiently pious, to make a name for themselves in forbidding wrong. One who perhaps just made the grade was Hishām ibn ʿAbdallāh al-Makhzūmī, a successful Medinese notable and close associate of Hishām ibn ʿUrwa (d. 145/762f.), who was appointed judge of the city thanks to the excellent impression he made on Hārūn al-Rashīd.[77] Ibn Saʿd states that he commanded right.[78] No further details are given; at his meeting with Hārūn he did, among other things, admonish him (*waʿaẓahu*),[79] but the tone of the occasion was far from abrasive.

A more interesting group are members of notable families who embrace piety in a style that significantly distances them from their social background. One example is ʿAbdallāh ibn ʿAbd al-ʿAzīz al-ʿUmarī (d. 184/800f.), a descendant of ʿUmar ibn al-Khaṭṭāb (r. 13–23/634–44) who resided in Medina until – characteristically – he left the city in disgust when his worldly brother became governor.[80] He stood out among his family as the ascetic (*al-ʿābid*).[81] We are told that he used to command right, and in this connection would confront caliphs, who would put up with him.[82] The reference is to accounts of how he admonished Hārūn

[74] Ibn Saʿd, *Ṭabaqāt*, 7:2:77.16; Khaṭīb, *Taʾrīkh Baghdād*, 14:65.15.

[75] *Ibid.*, 64.14; Mizzī, *Tahdhīb*, 30:133.18; Dhahabī, *Tadhkira*, 359.8; Dhahabī, *Siyar*, 9:547.11; Dhahabī, *Taʾrīkh al-Islām*, years 201–10, 418.8; Ibn Ḥajar, *Tahdhīb*, 11:19.6; and cf. Samʿānī, *Ansāb*, 11:153.5.

[76] Khaṭīb, *Taʾrīkh Baghdād*, 14:64.7; Mizzī, *Tahdhīb*, 30:133.9; Dhahabī, *Siyar*, 9:547.2; Dhahabī, *Taʾrīkh al-Islām*, years 201–10, 418.1. The chief of police is named as Naṣr ibn Mālik, which is impossible, since Naṣr had died in 161/777f. (Ṭabarī, *Taʾrīkh*, series III, 491.20).

[77] Ibn Saʿd, *Ṭabaqāt*, 5:312f.

[78] *Ibid.*, 313.1.

[79] *Ibid.*, 313.6.

[80] Ibn Ḥibbān, *Mashāhīr*, 129 no. 1009. In the same style he wrote to Mālik and Ibn Abī Dhiʾb to tell them they were worldlings (Dhahabī, *Siyar*, 8:332.13; Ibn Abī Dhiʾb responded with reciprocal rudeness, Mālik in the manner of a scholar).

[81] Ibn Saʿd, *Ṭabaqāt*, *al-qism al-mutammim*, 221.3, 222.1.

[82] Muṣʿab al-Zubayrī, *Nasab Quraysh*, 359.2 (this passage was drawn to my attention by

al-Rashīd;[83] the hapless caliph would respond, 'Yes, uncle.'[84] Some opinions transmitted from him about forbidding wrong in general fit well with his uncompromising attitudes. He is in favour of commanding even someone who will not accept it from one, since it serves as a justification (*maʿdhira*), sc. before God.[85] He likewise condemns failure to command and forbid that is motivated by fear of anyone but God.[86]

Another such case is Shuʿayb ibn Ḥarb (d. 196/811f.), who like Qayṣar stemmed from the Abnāʾ.[87] Despite his background, his lifestyle was very much that of a pietist.[88] We are told by al-Khaṭīb al-Baghdādī (d. 463/1071) that he was remembered, among other things, for forbidding wrong.[89] Why he was so remembered is explained by an anecdote which the Khaṭīb goes on to quote.[90] On the road to Mecca he saw the caliph Hārūn al-Rashīd. He then engaged in a little dialogue with his soul. He told it: 'It's your duty (*wajaba ʿalayki*) to command and forbid.' His soul replied: 'Don't do it! This man is a tyrant, and when you command him, he'll chop off your head!' But he told it: 'There's no choice (*lā budda min dhālika*).' So when the caliph was close by, he shouted out: 'Hey Hārūn! You've worn down the community (*umma*), and worn down the beasts (*bahāʾim*)!' Thereupon Hārūn had him seized, and questioned him as to who he was and how he had the temerity to address the caliph by name. Shuʿayb, in a moment of inspiration, pointed out that he likewise addressed God by name, and was released.

As a final example of this phenomenon we can take the Companion Hishām ibn Ḥakīm ibn Ḥizām (d. 36/656?).[91] Although a rather minor figure, he is the only Companion in whose biography forbidding wrong

Amikam Elad). Cf. Dhahabī, *Siyar*, 8:332.4, describing him as *qawwāl biʾl-ḥaqq, ammār biʾl-ʿurf.* [83] Dhahabī, *Siyar*, 8:332.11, 332.17, and cf. 333.3. [84] *Ibid.*, 332.17.

[85] Ibn Abī ʾl-Dunyā, *Amr*, 119 no. 84, whence Zayn al-Dīn al-Ṣāliḥī (d. 856/1452), *al-Kanz al-akbar fī ʾl-amr biʾl-maʿrūf waʾl-nahy ʿan al-munkar*, Riyāḍ and Mecca 1997, 128.18 (with implied reference to *maʿdhiratan* in Q7:164); Suyūṭī, *Durr*, 3:139.3 (to Q7:164). For the theme of rebuking only someone who will accept it, see below, 77f.

[86] Ibn Abī ʾl-Dunyā, *Amr*, 57 no. 14; Ibn Abī ʾl-Dunyā, *ʿUqūbāt*, 41f. no. 38 (drawn to my attention by Mona Zaki); Abū Nuʿaym, *Ḥilya*, 8:284.19; ʿAbd al-Ghanī al-Maqdisī, *Amr*, 41 no. 50; Dhahabī, *Siyar*, 8:333.15; and cf. the stirring Prophetic tradition he transmits, Abū Nuʿaym, *Ḥilya*, 8:287.11. For the view that fear is a respectable motive for not proceeding, see below, 77. [87] Ibn Saʿd, *Ṭabaqāt*, 7:2:66.15.

[88] See M. Jarrar, 'Bišr al-Ḥāfī und die Barfüssigkeit im Islam', *Der Islam*, 71 (1994), 223 no. 1.

[89] Khaṭīb, *Taʾrīkh Baghdād*, 9:239.15 (I owe this and the next reference to this source to Patricia Crone). This statement is repeated in later biographies (Samʿānī, *Ansāb*, 12:145.14; Mizzī, *Tahdhīb*, 12:511.5; cf. also Dhahabī, *Taʾrīkh al-Islām*, years 191–200, 225.6).

[90] Khaṭīb, *Taʾrīkh Baghdād*, 9:239.18.

[91] Ibn Ḥazm (d. 456/1064) states that he was killed at the Battle of the Camel (*Jamharat ansāb al-ʿArab*, ed. ʿA. M. Hārūn, Cairo 1982, 121.16); Ibn Qutayba (d. 276/889), however, says this of his brother ʿAbdallāh (*Maʿārif*, ed. T. ʿUkāsha, Cairo 1981, 219.19).

is a central theme. Given his background, this is surprising. His father, Ḥakīm ibn Ḥizām (d. 54/673f.), was a Qurashī notable who converted only at the time of the conquest of Mecca in 8/630, though his conversion is said to have been sincere.[92] Hishām himself became a Muslim at the same time as his father.[93] He does not, however, seem to have taken advantage of the opportunities available to someone of such a background: we are told that he had no family,[94] and there is no indication of his holding office.

His biographers regularly state that Hishām forbade wrong.[95] He had a reputation for this – we are told that when ʿUmar ibn al-Khaṭṭāb saw a wrong, he would declare that it would not stand so long as he and Hishām remained alive.[96] The sources further describe how he used to forbid wrong with a group of Syrians: no one had authority over them, and they would wander around selflessly putting things to rights and giving counsel.[97] Yet when we are given actual examples of his forbidding wrong, he acts alone in the usual fashion.

In each such case, his target is the authorities. One anecdote has him visit a governor in Syria who intends to do something objectionable; he threatens to denounce him to the caliph.[98] Much more widespread in the sources are the stories that provide the context in which Hishām transmits a Prophetic tradition to the effect that those who torture people in this world

[92] Ibn ʿAbd al-Barr, *Istīʿāb*, 362f. no. 535; Ibn Hishām, *Sīra*, 3–4:493.1. He was one of the *muʾallafa qulūbuhum* (cf. Q9:60). [93] Ibn ʿAbd al-Barr, *Istīʿāb*, 1538.15 (no. 2,681).

[94] Mālik likened him to a vagrant (*sāʾiḥ*), without a wife or children (*ibid.*, 1539.3; Mizzī, *Tahdhīb*, 30:195.12); Ibn Qutayba likewise says he had no offspring (*Maʿārif*, 219.18). On the other hand, Mizzī quotes a report according to which he had eight children (*Tahdhīb*, 30:196.2).

[95] Zubayr ibn Bakkār (d. 256/870), *Jamharat nasab Quraysh wa-akhbārihā*, ed. M. M. Shākir, Cairo 1381, 377f. no. 661 (I owe this reference, which first drew my attention to Hishām, to Amikam Elad); Ibn ʿAbd al-Barr, *Istīʿāb*, 1538.15; Ibn ʿAsākir (d. 571/1176), *Taʾrīkh madīnat Dimashq*, *apud* Ibn Manẓūr (d. 711/1311f.), *Mukhtaṣar Taʾrīkh Dimashq li-Ibn ʿAsākir*, ed. R. al-Naḥḥās *et al.*, Damascus 1984–90, 27:84.16; ʿIzz al-Dīn Ibn al-Athīr (d. 630/1233), *Usd al-ghāba*, Cairo 1280–6, 5:61.12; Mizzī, *Tahdhīb*, 30:196.2, 196.8; Dhahabī, *Siyar*, 3:52.3.

[96] Zubayr ibn Bakkār, *Jamhara*, 378 no. 662; Ibn ʿAbd al-Barr, *Istīʿāb*, 1538.16; Ibn ʿAsākir, *Taʾrīkh*, in the *Mukhtaṣar* of Ibn Manẓūr, 27:84.17; Ibn al-Athīr, *Usd al-ghāba*, 5:61.13; Mizzī, *Tahdhīb*, 30:195.10, 195.13; Dhahabī, *Siyar*, 3:52.3.

[97] Mālik quotes Ibn Shihāb (al-Zuhrī) (d. 124/742) as saying: *kāna Hishām ibn Ḥakīm fī nafar min ahl al-Shām yaʾmurūn biʾl-maʿrūf wa-yanhawn ʿan al-munkar laysa li-aḥad ʿalayhim imāra*; Mālik then adds: *kānū yamshūn fī ʾl-arḍ biʾl-iṣlāḥ waʾl-naṣīḥa yaḥtasibūn* (Ibn ʿAbd al-Barr, *Istīʿāb*, 1538.18). For parallels, see Ibn ʿAsākir, *Taʾrīkh*, in the *Mukhtaṣar* of Ibn Manẓūr, 27:85.3; Mizzī, *Tahdhīb*, 30:195.9, 195.18; Ibn Ḥajar al-ʿAsqalānī (d. 852/1449), *al-Iṣāba fī tamyīz al-ṣaḥāba*, ed. ʿA. M. al-Bajāwī, Cairo 1970–2, 6:539.3 (no. 8,969); Ibn Ḥajar, *Tahdhīb*, 11:37.10. Mālik is the source of much of our information on Hishām.

[98] Ibn ʿAsākir, *Taʾrīkh*, in the *Mukhtaṣar* of Ibn Manẓūr, 27:85.1 (corrupt); Mizzī, *Tahdhīb*, 195.15.

will be tortured by God in the next.[99] In the standard version, some natives (who may be Nabateans or Copts) are being pressured (usually by being denied shade) to pay their taxes (commonly the poll-tax) somewhere in Syria (be it Ḥimṣ or Palestine); the villain of the story is the local governor, who may be ʿUmayr ibn Saʿd or ʿIyāḍ ibn Ghanm (d. 20/640f.), and the hero is of course Hishām, who steps in and quotes his tradition from the Prophet.[100]

Another version, however, offers an intriguing twist that would have warmed the heart of al-Maʾmūn. Here the victim is a prominent non-Muslim who is flogged at the time of the conquest of Dārā in Mesopotamia by the Muslim commander, the same ʿIyāḍ ibn Ghanm. Hishām is very rude to ʿIyāḍ about this, causing a break between the two men. Later Hishām goes to ʿIyāḍ and excuses himself, but repeats his objection by quoting his Prophetic tradition. ʿIyāḍ then responds by quoting a Prophetic tradition of his own, to the effect that anyone rebuking a person in authority (*sulṭān*) should do so in private. He goes on to reproach Hishām for his recklessness in going up against someone established in authority by God (*sulṭān Allāh*), and thereby courting death at his hands.[101] It is significant that in this version it is ʿIyāḍ who has the last word; he represents the misgivings of those who are against rebuking those in power, but at the same time ascribes to that power an uncompromising religious legitimacy. Hishām, like the shrouded figure who accosted al-Maʾmūn, has been put in his place.

Despite their background, well-born dropouts such as Hishām have much in common with the second category of my typology, those whose burning religious zeal is not supported by elite social standing. We have

[99] The tradition also appears without the cover story (Ibn Qāniʿ (d. 351/962), *Muʿjam al-ṣaḥāba*, ed. Ṣ. S. al-Miṣrātī, Medina 1997, 3:193 no. 1169).

[100] Abū Yūsuf, *Kharāj*, 125.10; Abū ʿUbayd al-Qāsim ibn Sallām (d. 224/838f.), *Amwāl*, ed. M. K. Harrās, Cairo 1981, 45 no. 110; Ibn Ḥanbal, *Musnad*, 3:403.20, 403.24, 403.26, 404.7, 404.11, 468.23; Ibn Zanjawayh (d. 251/865f.), *Amwāl*, ed. S. D. Fayyāḍ, Riyāḍ 1986, 164 no. 169; Muslim, *Ṣaḥīḥ*, 2,017f. nos. 117–19; Abū Dāwūd, *Sunan*, 3:433f. no. 3,045; Bayhaqī, *Sunan*, 9:205.19; Ibn ʿAsākir, *Taʾrīkh*, in the *Mukhtaṣar* of Ibn Manẓūr, 27:84.4, 84.9; Ibn al-Athīr, *Usd al-ghāba*, 5:62.6; Mizzī, *Tahdhīb*, 30:197.5, 197.16; Ibn Qayyim al-Jawziyya (d. 751/1350), *Aḥkām ahl al-dhimma*, ed. Ṣ. al-Ṣāliḥ, Beirut 1983, 34.13. See also M. R. Cohen, *Under crescent and cross: the Jews in the Middle Ages*, Princeton 1994, 69f. The *isnād*s are initially Medinese, but then branch out to Kūfa, Yemen, Egypt and Ḥimṣ.

[101] Ibn Ḥanbal, *Musnad*, 3:403.29 (for *dār* read *Dārā*), whence Ibn al-Athīr, *Usd al-ghāba*, 4:165.4. ʿIyāḍ's reproof, but not the earlier part of the story, appears in Abū ʿUbayd, *Amwāl*, 46 no. 113; Ibn ʿAsākir in his entry on Hishām as epitomised by Ibn Manẓūr has only the beginning of the story (*Mukhtaṣar*, 27:84.12), but there are complete versions in his entry on ʿIyāḍ (Ibn ʿAsākir, *Taʾrīkh*, 47:265.18, 266.12, 266.23). ʿIyāḍ took Dārā in the year 19/640 (Ṭabarī, *Taʾrīkh*, series I, 2,505.16, 2,506.3).

already met an example of this type in the goldsmith who met his death through his repeated verbal assaults on Abū Muslim.[102] A similar figure is his contemporary Yazīd ibn Abī Saʿīd al-Naḥwī (d. 131/748f.), likewise a non-Arab from Marw who was killed by Abū Muslim;[103] according to one source, he met this fate because he commanded him right (*li-amrihi iyyāhu bi'l-maʿrūf*).[104]

An earlier example of this type is the Companion Abū Dharr al-Ghifārī (d. 32/652f.), who stemmed from a rather insignificant Ḥijāzī tribe.[105] Late in life he clashed with Muʿāwiya (d. 60/680), then governor of Syria on behalf of ʿUthmān (r. 23–35/644–56), and as a result was sent back to Medina; from there he went on to the village of Rabadha, where he died virtually alone.[106] He appears in accounts of these events as a surly critic of the patrimonial tendencies of the proto-Umayyad state. In this role he can readily be seen as forbidding wrong; thus in his isolation in Rabadha, he tells a visitor that forbidding wrong has left him without a friend.[107]

A final example of this type is the Medinese Muḥammad ibn ʿAjlān (d. 148/765f.). He was a non-Arab, a scholar, a pietist, and a slightly ridiculous figure who got himself into trouble by joining the rising of Muḥammad al-Nafs al-Zakiyya in 145/762.[108] Shāfiʿī (d. 204/820) tells us that he used to command right and forbid wrong; what he has in mind is shown by the anecdote he proceeds to relate.[109] The governor of Medina

[102] See above, ch. 1, 3–5.

[103] Mizzī, *Tahdhīb*, 32:143f.; Madelung, 'The early Murjiʾa', 34f.; van Ess, *Theologie*, 2:548f.

[104] Ibn Ḥibbān, *Thiqāt*, 7:622.10, whence Mizzī, *Tahdhīb*, 32:144.9, and Ibn Ḥajar, *Tahdhīb*, 11:332.14, the latter quoted in Madelung, 'The early Murjiʾa', 35.

[105] See *EI*[2], art. 'Ghifār' (J. W. Fück).

[106] For an account of these events, see Ṭabarī, *Taʾrīkh*, series I, 2,858–62, 2,895–7; also K. ʿAthāmina, ''Uqūbat al-nafy fī ṣadr al-Islām wa'l-dawla al-Umawiyya', *al-Karmil*, 5 (1984), 70–3.

[107] Ibn Saʿd, *Ṭabaqāt*, 4:1:174.7; cf. the saying of his quoted in Samʿānī, *Ansāb*, 10:65.12. As might be expected, such invocations of the duty are also to be found in Shīʿite accounts of Abū Dharr. In an exchange with ʿUthmān, he cites forbidding wrong as his justification for his outspokenness (Majlisī (d. 1110/1699), *Biḥār al-anwār*, Tehran 1376–92, 22:417.15). Similarly Mālik al-Ashtar (d. 37/657f.), in an oration at the grave of Abū Dharr, describes him as someone who saw a wrong, and took a stand against it (*ghayyarahu*) with his tongue and his heart; as a result he died in lonely exile (Kashshī (*fl.* first half of the fourth/tenth century), *Rijāl*, ed. Ḥ. al-Muṣṭafawī, Mashhad 1348 sh., 66.2 (no. 118), whence Majlisī, *Biḥār*, 22:400.3).

[108] Van Ess, *Theologie*, 2:678–81. For his pretensions to archery during the rebellion, see Abū 'l-Faraj al-Iṣbahānī (d. 356/967), *Maqātil al-Ṭālibiyyīn*, ed. A. Ṣaqr, Cairo 1949, 281.13; Ṭabarī, *Taʾrīkh*, series III, 251.18. For his piety, see Mizzī, *Tahdhīb*, 26:102.2.

[109] Ibn Abī Ḥātim al-Rāzī (d. 327/938), *Ādāb al-Shāfiʿī wa-manāqibuhu*, ed. ʿA. ʿAbd al-Khāliq, Cairo 1953, 48.5, cited in van Ess, *Theologie*, 2:681 n. 43, together with the parallel to the anecdote in Abū 'l-ʿArab al-Tamīmī (d. 333/945), *Miḥan*, ed. ʿU. S. al-ʿUqaylī, Riyāḍ 1984, 422.13.

was once somewhat prolix in his Friday sermon. When he came down from the pulpit, Ibn ʿAjlān shouted out: 'Hey you! You should fear God! No long robes and long words on the pulpit of the Prophet!'[110] The governor responded by having him jailed. When Ibn Abī Dhiʾb came to hear of this, he went to see the governor about it. The latter complained bitterly that Ibn ʿAjlān could have rebuked him in private, in which case he would have been glad to comply; but instead he had gone out of his way to humiliate him by shouting at him in front of everyone. Ibn Abī Dhiʾb then secured Ibn ʿAjlān's release, telling the governor that the man was a complete idiot: 'He sees you eating and wearing things that are forbidden, and all he can criticise you for is your long robes and long words on the pulpit of the Prophet!' It is evident here that we are among Sunnīs, not Zaydīs: what earns Ibn ʿAjlān a reputation for forbidding wrong is telling off a governor for prolixity, not rebelling against the state.[111]

Lack of social standing might, of course, seem a sensible reason for not venturing too far into the dangerous game of forbidding wrong to those in power. It is not hard to find people from relatively disadvantaged backgrounds whose behaviour seems much more restrained than that of the zealots we have just considered. Among the Companions, Anas ibn Mālik (d. 91/709f.) is perhaps an example. Anas was an Anṣārī, but his low status is indicated by the fact that he had been a servant of the Prophet; he settled in Baṣra and lived to a very old age.[112] Two anecdotes about him bear on the question of speaking out in the presence of the authorities. In one, he is at the headquarters of Ḥajjāj in Wāsiṭ, and is accosted there by a young member of a delegation which has arrived from Anbār to complain about an injustice perpetrated by their governor. Anas encourages the youth by telling him that he had heard the Prophet say: 'Command right and forbid wrong as far as you can (*mā ʾstaṭaʿta*)'[113] – hardly an electrifying tradition. The other anecdote is set at the time of the rebellion of Ibn al-Ashʿath in 81–2/701. Ḥajjāj insults Anas as an inveterate subversive; Anas leaves without responding to the charge, but subsequently remarks on the fine speech he would have made on this occasion had he not been so concerned about the interests of his offspring after his death.[114] This was not a trivial consideration: his children and grandchildren numbered some one hundred.[115]

[110] I follow van Ess in reading *thiyāb* for *bayān*, as in the briefer parallel given by Abū ʾl-ʿArab.
[111] Cf. below, ch. 10, section 3.
[112] *EI*², art. 'Anas b. Mālik' (A. J. Wensinck and J. Robson).
[113] Khaṭīb, *Taʾrīkh Baghdād*, 8:259.5, and cf. *ibid.*, 258.9, 258.16 (I owe these references to Nurit Tsafrir). [114] Mizzī, *Tahdhīb*, 3:373.6. [115] *Ibid.*, 364.14.

Two somewhat later examples are Ḥasan al-Baṣrī and Awzāʿī (d. 157/773). Ḥasan was a non-Arab and a bureaucrat.[116] We are told that he visited rulers and would criticise them (*yaʿībuhum*), whereas his contemporary Muḥammad ibn Sīrīn (d. 110/729) did neither.[117] But despite a dramatic clash with Ḥajjāj,[118] the tone of his criticism has been described as by and large not too aggressive.[119] Awzāʿī is a similar case. He made his reputation as a scholar, specifically a jurist – he was the founder of a law-school.[120] The obscurity of his origins,[121] his orphanhood[122] and his secretarial profession[123] indicate that he had no other claim to social standing. We have it on divine authority that he practised the duty: he is said to have had a dream in which two angels took him up to heaven and stood him in front of God, who asked him: 'Are you my servant ʿAbd al-Raḥmān who commands right and forbids wrong?' Awzāʿī answered politely, and was returned to earth.[124] What God had in mind, if it was not simply Awzāʿī's activity as a jurist, was doubtless the tenser moments in his dealings with the authorities. Here pride of place must go to his audience with ʿAbdallāh ibn ʿAlī (d. 147/764f.), the ʿAbbāsid who conquered Syria, and then proceeded to massacre the Umayyads in unedifying circumstances. Putting the jurist on the spot, ʿAbdallāh demanded to hear Awzāʿī's opinion as to the legality of this massacre. The terrified Awzāʿī, for all that he had no wish to get himself killed, called to mind his standing in front of God (sc. at the

116 For his life, see *EI*², art. 'Ḥasan al-Baṣrī' (H. Ritter), and van Ess, *Theologie*, 2:41–5. In one anecdote he is disparagingly referred to by some Arabs as *hādhā 'l-ʿilj* (Ibn Saʿd, *Ṭabaqāt*, 7:1:119.14, translated in Schaeder, 'Ḥasan al-Baṣrī', 56).

117 Fasawī, *Maʿrifa*, 2:64.15 (from the Baṣran Rajāʾ (ibn Ṣubayḥ al-Ḥarashī)). It is unclear whether we are to take it that he criticised rulers to their faces. Cf. also Ibn Saʿd, *Ṭabaqāt*, 7:1:118.19.

118 Schaeder, 'Ḥasan al-Baṣrī', 58–62; Ritter, 'Studien', 53f., 55; van Ess, *Theologie*, 2:43. The sources do not usually portray the clash as one sought by Ḥasan; for an exception, see Schaeder, 'Ḥasan al-Baṣrī', 60, citing Tanūkhī (d. 384/994), *al-Faraj baʿd al-shidda*, Cairo 1955, 48.6.

119 Ritter, 'Studien', 50.

120 See *EI*², art. 'Awzāʿī' (J. Schacht).

121 Is the Awzāʿ after which he is known to be understood to refer to a place (so, for example, Abū Zurʿa al-Dimashqī (d. 281/894) in Mizzī, *Tahdhīb*, 17:313.3, and Ibn Ḥibbān, *Mashāhīr*, 180 no. 1425), or to a Yemeni tribal group? If the latter, was he one of them (so Ibn Saʿd, *Ṭabaqāt*, 7:2:185.3), or was it just that he settled among them (so Bukhārī, *Kabīr*, 3:1:326 no. 1035, and Ibn Ḥazm, *Jamhara*, 437.9)? Or was he in fact of Indian war-captive stock (so Abū Zurʿa in Mizzī, *Tahdhīb*, 17:313.3)?

122 Dhahabī, *Tadhkira*, 178.19.

123 Mizzī, *Tahdhīb*, 17:313.5; Dhahabī, *Tadhkira*, 178.17, 183.2.

124 Abū Nuʿaym, *Ḥilya*, 6:142.17; Dhahabī, *Tadhkira*, 179.16; Dhahabī, *Siyar*, 7:118.13 (all from the Damascene ʿAmr ibn Abī Salama al-Tinnīsī (d. 213/828f.)); also Abū Nuʿaym, *Ḥilya*, 6:142.23 (a variant in which no immediate transmitter from Awzāʿī is given). I owe these references to Nurit Tsafrir. The anecdote does not seem to have been widely transmitted: Ibn ʿAsākir, who unlike Dhahabī tells us where he gets his material, knows the story only from Abū Nuʿaym (Ibn ʿAsākir, *Taʾrīkh*, 35:192.19, 193.3).

resurrection), and declared ʿAbdallāh's action illegal. This predictably infuriated the ʿAbbāsid, who had Awzāʿī removed from his presence – but sent after him with a gift.[125] In this anecdote Awzāʿī does not speak out on his own initiative; he simply replies to a question he cannot evade.

There are, of course, cases that are hard to place in terms of the categories I have deployed, and some of these involve people who matter. One is the Kūfan Sufyān al-Thawrī.[126] As a celebrated traditionist and the founder of a law-school, he enjoyed great respect from posterity.[127] He was an Arab with a genealogy which our sources are pleased to recount,[128] and his father is described as a highly respectable person (*aḥsab al-nās*);[129] so it seems likely that he enjoyed an elite social status independent of his scholarship, and this may have carried relatively more weight for his contemporaries than it did for posterity. Be this as it may, Sufyān is presented to us as a compulsive forbidder of wrong.[130] Nearly all the material concerns his relations with the caliphs;[131] usually his antagonist is al-Mahdī (r. 158–69/775–85), though occasionally it is his predecessor, al-Manṣūr.[132] The standard theme in accounts of his confrontation with al-Mahdī is the caliph's luxurious style of pilgrimage, so unlike the frugal practice of ʿUmar ibn al-Khaṭṭāb.[133] Sometimes Sufyān can be very rude indeed. One account has him present himself at court and tell al-Manṣūr's chamberlain, 'Shut up, Hāmān!'; he goes on to compare the caliph's viziers unfavourably to Pharaoh's.[134] Small wonder that Dhahabī (d. 748/1348) describes him as someone who spoke out with the truth and was zealous in condemning wrong.[135]

[125] See, for example, Dhahabī, *Tadhkira*, 180.17; and cf. Dhahabī, *Siyar*, 7:123.4 (with Dhahabī's wholehearted approval, *ibid.*, 125.6); Ibn Abī Ḥātim, *Taqdima*, 212.16.

[126] On whom see van Ess, *Theologie*, 1:221–8.

[127] The sources transmit one opinion from him which is very much a jurist's: if someone does something about the legality of which there is disagreement among the scholars (*ikhtilāf*), and you happen to hold a view different from his, you are not entitled to forbid him (Ṣāliḥī, *Kanz*, 231.8, where *al-Nawawī* should, of course, be *al-Thawrī*; Abū 'l-Layth, *Tafsīr*, 1:289.18).

[128] Van Ess, *Theologie*, 1:222, with references.

[129] Ibn Ḥazm, *Jamhara*, 201.6.

[130] Ibn Abī Ḥātim, *Taqdima*, 124.12; Abū Nuʿaym, *Ḥilya*, 7:15.1; Dhahabī, *Siyar*, 7:243.7, 259.16.

[131] For exceptions, see below, notes 151, 165.

[132] As at Ibn Abī Ḥātim, *Taqdima*, 106.1, 113.10; Abū Nuʿaym, *Ḥilya*, 7:43.2; Dhahabī, *Siyar*, 7:262.19; and Abū 'l-ʿArab, *Miḥan*, 433.4.

[133] Ibn Abī Ḥātim, *Taqdima*, 108.3, 110.20; Abū Nuʿaym, *Ḥilya*, 6:377.8, and the three further versions there following; *ibid.*, 7:44.24; Khaṭīb, *Ta'rīkh Baghdād*, 9:160.2; Dhahabī, *Tadhkira*, 205.19; Dhahabī, *Siyar*, 7:264.15, 265.15 (I owe these references to Nurit Tsafrir). Cf. also Ghazzālī, *Iḥyā'*, 2:290.24.

[134] Abū 'l-ʿArab, *Miḥan*, 433.15, 434.1. The tone of this account is set when Sufyān's associates refer to the authorities as 'these damnable people (*ashqiyā'*) into whose hands the affairs of Muḥammad's nation have fallen' (*ibid.*, 433.6).

[135] Dhahabī, *Tadhkira*, 206.9 (*kāna qawwālan bi'l-ḥaqq shadīd al-inkār*).

Abū Isḥāq al-Fazārī (d. 186/802) is another such figure. Likewise an Arab, he was born in Wāsiṭ, grew up in Kūfa, and settled in Mopsuestia in the Arab–Byzantine frontier area; we know that his family at one time enjoyed high status in Kūfa.[136] We can thus plausibly think of him as a notable, though not as one operating in his home environment. He seems nevertheless to have made a considerable impact on frontier society. ʿIjlī (d. 261/874f.) tells us that it was he who educated (*addaba*) the frontiersmen (*ahl al-thaghr*); he taught them the normative custom (*sunna*), and used to command and forbid them. Once, he adds, he commanded and forbade someone in authority (*sulṭān*); he received a hundred lashes for this, but Awzāʿī interceded on his behalf.[137] This information is often repeated in the sources, but never elaborated on.[138] The rest of the evidence regarding his relations with the rulers of his day is mixed. One source tells us that during his visit to Damascus, those excluded from his circle included anyone who had been frequenting the rulers.[139] But against this there are several indications that he did not himself adhere to such a standard.[140] One report describes a reasonably civil exchange with the caliph Hārūn al-Rashīd on an occasion when Abū Isḥāq went to see him;[141] on another such occasion, Abū Isḥāq is polite and most anxious to deny a rumour that he had forbidden the wearing of black,[142] the colour of the ʿAbbāsids. The tone of these interactions lacks the harshness that characterises Sufyān al-Thawrī's remorseless jousts with the caliphs.

In the course of this discussion of the attitudes and practices of early Muslims regarding confrontation with the authorities, the reader may have noticed a curious paradox. Where we have both words and deeds for the same figure, we may find that his bite is worse than his bark. A flagrant

[136] See M. Muranyi, 'Das *Kitāb al-Siyar* von Abū Isḥāq al-Fazārī', *Jerusalem Studies in Arabic and Islam*, 6 (1985), 67–70; for the standing of his great-grandfather, see *ibid.*, 67 n. 13.

[137] ʿIjlī (d. 261/874f.), *Ta'rīkh al-thiqāt*, in the rearrangement of Haythamī (d. 807/1405), ed. ʿA. Qalʿajī, Beirut 1984, 54 no. 37.

[138] Abū 'l-ʿArab, *Miḥan*, 379.5; Ibn ʿAsākir, *Ta'rīkh*, 7:126.13; Mizzī, *Tahdhīb*, 2:169.9; Dhahabī, *Siyar*, 8:474.25; Dhahabī, *Ta'rīkh al-Islām*, years 181–90, 56.15; and see M. Bonner, *Aristocratic violence and holy war: studies in the Jihad and the Arab–Byzantine frontier*, New Haven 1996, 112f. In the wording of these quotations it is not specified whom Abū Isḥāq commanded and forbade while teaching the frontiersmen the *sunna*, and the number of lashes inflicted on him rises to 200.

[139] Dhahabī, *Tadhkira*, 273.10.

[140] See, in addition to the sources cited in the following notes, Muranyi, 'Das *Kitāb al-Siyar*', 69f.

[141] Ibn ʿAsākir, *Ta'rīkh*, 7:129.4; Dhahabī, *Tadhkira*, 274.5; Dhahabī, *Siyar*, 8:476.13.

[142] Ibn ʿAsākir, *Ta'rīkh*, 7:130.1; he accepts a substantial sum of money from Hārūn, but subsequently gives it away in alms. We are told that he used to accept money from the state for the benefit of the people of Tarsus (*ibid.*, 129.11).

instance of this is Sufyān al-Thawrī. On the one hand, when asked why he does not go in to rebuke those in power, he responds with a graphic metaphor about the futility of trying to dam up the sea;[143] yet on the other hand, he himself goes in to the caliph and as good as tells him that he is Pharaoh.[144] Another example is Shuʿayb ibn Ḥarb. We encountered him on the road to Mecca, insulting Hārūn al-Rashīd in a quite gratuitous manner – there is no reference in the anecdote to any present or particular wrong, and the situation was hardly one in which silence implied consent to the wider iniquities of Hārūn's rule, whatever they might be.[145] And yet the same Shuʿayb responds in these words to a questioner who asks him about forbidding wrong: 'But for the sword, the whip, and things of that ilk, we would command and forbid. If you are up to it (*in qawīta*), go ahead.'[146] Shuʿayb, we are given to understand here, was not himself robust enough to engage in such activity.

These discrepancies raise the question of what we are to believe: the words, the deeds, both, or neither. Any attempt to answer this question in absolute terms would take us into historiographical issues which are at once too profound and too indeterminate to be worth discussing here. But it may be ventured that, relatively speaking, stirring deeds are more likely to be fictitious than prudent words. Those who live prudently may live longer than the reckless, but they do not generate the kind of events with which a biographer can enthral an audience. The temptation to have Sufyān al-Thawrī confront the caliph face to face and treat him like Pharaoh may well have been irresistible.[147]

3. CONFRONTING SOCIETY

Let us now leave the world of caliphs and governors, and descend to less exalted wrongdoers. Here the variety of wrongs to forbid is somewhat greater, though much of it reduces to three themes that will become very familiar in the course of this book: wine, women and song.

Liquor is of course a widespread wrong. An unnamed Companion of the Prophet who had taken to drink in Syria is rebuked by ʿUmar ibn

[143] See above, note 47.

[144] See above, note 134. An intermediate position is expressed in a variant of the saying of Sufyān's quoted below, note 242: in this version, he sets out the three qualities – among which is civility – as prerequisites for commanding right to a *ruler* (Abū Nuʿaym, *Ḥilya*, 6:379.7). [145] See above, 59. [146] Khallāl, *Amr*, 86 no. 9.

[147] I have not attempted to examine the accounts of these confrontations closely, but it is striking that Ibn Saʿd, an early source, has a couple of detailed narratives of Sufyān's life in hiding – the period relevant for our purposes – which make no reference to any such encounters (*Ṭabaqāt*, 6:258–60).

al-Khaṭṭāb.[148] A jug of wine (*nabīdh*) forms part of a scene of revelry in Kūfa which draws the attention of the Companion ʿAbdallāh ibn Masʿūd (d. 32/652f.).[149] In Egypt the neighbours of Dukhayn al-Ḥajrī (d. 100/718f.) are persistent wine-drinkers.[150] Back in Kūfa, the druggists would seem to be in the business of marketing a certain alcoholic drink, and are forbidden to do so by Sufyān al-Thawrī.[151]

Wrongs related to women include cases in which men engage them in conversation. Such men are rebuked by the Medinese Muḥammad ibn al-Munkadir (d. 130/747f.),[152] while a druggist chatting to a female customer is interrupted on the instructions of the Kūfan Wakīʿ ibn al-Jarrāḥ (d. 196/812).[153] There are also more serious incidents. A soldier with his hand between the thighs of a woman is confronted by the Kūfan Abū Nuʿaym al-Faḍl ibn Dukayn (d. 219/834),[154] and a man with a knife who had seized a woman is dealt with by the ascetic Bishr al-Ḥāfī (d. 227/841f.).[155]

Music appears in a variety of contexts.[156] The jug of wine at the party that provoked the ire of Ibn Masʿūd was accompanied by a singer with a mandolin.[157] Music at a wedding causes offence to the Wāsiṭī Aṣbagh ibn Zayd (d. 159/775f.).[158] The sound of a lute coming from a private house leads to a showdown between the lady of the house and the ascetic Muḥammad ibn Muṣʿab (d. 228/843).[159]

Other wrongs defy neat categorisation. One theme is the maltreatment of slaves and animals. Thus a man engaged in beating his slave is confronted by the ascetic Dahtham ibn Qurrān (*fl.* mid-second/eighth century),[160] and overloaded beasts of burden find a champion in ʿUmar ibn al-Khaṭṭāb.[161]

148 See below, note 245, and ch. 14, note 10.

149 We have this from one of those present, the Kūfan Zādhān (d. 82/701f.), who subsequently repents and is welcomed by Ibn Masʿūd (Baḥshal, *Taʾrīkh Wāsiṭ*, 198.1 (I owe this reference to Nurit Tsafrir); Ibn ʿAsākir, *Taʾrīkh*, 18:283.15; Dhahabī, *Siyar*, 4:281.8; Dhahabī, *Taʾrīkh al-Islām*, years 81–100, 65.6).

150 See below, 80f.

151 Ibn Ḥanbal, *ʿIlal*, 2:200 no. 2,003; Ibn Abī Ḥātim, *Taqdima*, 124.10; Abū Nuʿaym, *Ḥilya*, 7:14.24.

152 Ibn Abī ʾl-Dunyā, *Amr*, 89 nos. 42f.

153 Khallāl, *Amr*, 129 no. 101.

154 See below, 70.

155 Ghazzālī, *Iḥyāʾ*, 2:307.4.

156 The attitude to music encountered here (and generally in this book) is hostile. An early statement of the contrary view, that music is permitted, is found in Mufaḍḍal ibn Salama (*fl.* later third/ninth century), *Malāhī*, ed. G. ʿA. Khashaba, Cairo 1984, 8–13. For recent discussions of Islamic attitudes to music, see A. Shiloah, *Music in the world of Islam*, Aldershot 1995, ch. 4 (and see 62–4 on musical instruments); F. Shehadi, *Philosophies of music in medieval Islam*, Leiden 1995, part 2.

157 Cf. above, note 149, and see below, note 249.

158 Baḥshal, *Taʾrīkh Wāsiṭ*, 213.1 (I owe this reference to Nurit Tsafrir). The sound he hears is that of a drum (*ṭabl*) or a tambourine (*duff*).

159 See below, ch. 5, note 117.

160 See below, notes 189f.

161 Khallāl, *Amr*, 95 no. 31 (cf. below, ch. 5, note 168); Ibn Abī Zayd al-Qayrawānī (d. 386/996), *al-Jāmiʿ fī ʾl-sunan waʾl-ādāb waʾl-maghāzī waʾl-taʾrīkh*, ed. M. Abū ʾl-Ajfān and ʿU. Baṭṭīkh, Beirut and Tunis 1982, 157.9.

Meanwhile the more privileged may be rebuked for their inappropriate gait. A vain Qurashī is reproved for this by the Companion Abū Hurayra (d. 58/677f.).[162] The distinguished general Muhallab ibn Abī Ṣufra (d. 82/702) is dressed down by the Baṣran ascetic Mālik ibn Dīnār (d. 127/744f.) for his arrogant walk.[163] An unidentified ʿAlid is similarly told off by ʿAbdallāh ibn ʿAbd al-ʿAzīz al-ʿUmarī.[164] Sometimes only the context in which the wrongs occur is specified. Those that take place during the pilgrimage provoke an energetic response from Sufyān al-Thawrī, all the way to Mecca and back.[165] Sufyān also speaks of the market as a den of iniquity in which one will see nothing but wrongs.[166] An offence committed in the baths of Medina calls forth the reproof of Ibn al-Munkadir and his companions.[167]

Two of these incidents are worth a more detailed examination here for what they tell us about the character of our sources. The first is that just mentioned, the case of Ibn al-Munkadir in the baths. This man came of a distinguished family, and was known for his outstanding piety.[168] The standard version of the story comes from Mālik ibn Anas, a local source.[169] He tells us that when ʿUthmān ibn Ḥayyān al-Murrī was governor of Medina (in 94–6/713–15),[170] Ibn al-Munkadir and his companions reproved (*waʿaẓa*) some men over a matter relating to the baths (*ḥammāmāt*). As ill luck would have it, one of these men was a client of the governor, who

[162] Khallāl, *Amr*, 124f. no. 90.
[163] Abū Nuʿaym, *Ḥilya*, 2:385.14; Dhahabī, *Siyar*, 5:362.17; Dhahabī, *Taʾrīkh al-Islām*, years 121–40, 217.4; Gramlich, *Alte Vorbilder*, 1:100f. This is almost a case of confronting a *sulṭān* (for Muhallab's career, see *EI*², art. 'Muhallab ibn Abī Ṣufra' (P. Crone)); indeed in a version given by Ibn al-Jawzī, Muhallab is replaced by an unnamed governor of Baṣra (*Ṣifa*, 3:276.15). Mālik ibn Dīnār was a non-Arab who made a living of sorts as a copyist (van Ess, *Theologie*, 2:91–3; Gramlich, *Alte Vorbilder*, 1:59f., 63), so any authority he had must have been religious rather than social. When Muhallab asked him if he knew who he was talking to, Mālik gave him a suitably levelling ascetic reply. He also went to see Bashshār ibn Burd (d. 168/784f.) to reprove him for his love-poetry (van Ess, *Theologie*, 2:7, citing Abū ʾl-Faraj al-Iṣbahānī (d. 356/967), *Aghānī*, Cairo 1927–74, 3:170.10; van Ess's reference to *al-amr biʾl-maʿrūf* seems to be his own gloss on this source, though an appropriate one). [164] Ibn Abī ʾl-Dunyā, *Amr*, 93 no. 49.
[165] Dhahabī, *Siyar*, 7:259.7; cf. Abū Nuʿaym, *Ḥilya*, 7:13.21.
[166] *Ibid.*, 84.16. Cf. also below, 82, on the female Companion Samrāʾ bint Nahīk.
[167] See the following paragraph.
[168] Ibn Ḥibbān, for example, describes him as *min sādāt Quraysh wa-ʿubbād ahl al-Madīna wa-qurrāʾ al-tābiʿīn* (*Mashāhīr*, 65 no. 435).
[169] Fasawī, *Maʿrifa*, 1:659.14; Abū ʾl-ʿArab, *Miḥan*, 325.5. Van Ess adduces two shorter forms of this version, but overlooks the fact that they tell the same story (*Theologie*, 2:664 nn. 4, 6, citing Ibn Abī Zayd, *Jāmiʿ*, 155.13, and Dhahabī, *Taʾrīkh al-Islām*, years 81–100, 261.9).
[170] *Ibid.*, 261.7. For the date at which he was appointed, see also van Ess, *Theologie*, 2:664 n. 6, and for the date of his removal, Khalīfa ibn Khayyāṭ (d. 240/854f.), *Taʾrīkh*, ed. A. Ḍ. al-ʿUmarī, Najaf 1967, 323.14.

accordingly had Ibn al-Munkadir and his companions flogged for their temerity in forbidding wrong. The other version of the story is transmitted from a certain Rabīʿa[171] by ʿAbdallāh ibn Muṣʿab al-Zubayrī (*fl.* later second/eighth century);[172] again, this is local tradition. Here Rabīʿa relates that he and Ibn al-Munkadir went into the baths and there reproved a man (*waʿaẓnāhu*). This man then went to the governor and complained that there were Khārijites in the baths; the governor accordingly had them whipped, without bothering to inquire more closely into the report.[173] What is instructive about this story, in each of its versions, is that the narrators display no interest in the actual wrong (doubtless some form of sexual indecency) that Ibn al-Munkadir confronted in the baths of their city; the offence serves only to initiate a chain of events which issues in a collision with the governor. The presumption is thus that wrongdoing and reproof in the baths are not in themselves newsworthy, even locally, and that had the matter not escalated to a political level, we should not have heard of it.

The case of Abū Nuʿaym and the lascivious soldier teaches the same lesson. Abū Nuʿaym al-Faḍl ibn Dukayn was a Kūfan traditionist, a non-Arab who kept a shop selling clothing.[174] That he forbade wrong is something we learn only from this anecdote. The background is the anarchic years prior to the entry of al-Maʾmūn into Baghdad (in 204/819). The elders (*shuyūkh*) of the city had taken it upon themselves to maintain law and order, imprisoning and punishing offenders;[175] now that the caliph had arrived on the scene and authority had been restored, al-Maʾmūn proclaimed a ban on forbidding wrong. At this point Abū Nuʿaym came to Baghdad, and happened to see the soldier with his hand between the thighs of the woman. He confronted the soldier (*zajarahu*); the latter then took him to the chief of police, and the matter was reported to the caliph, who had Abū Nuʿaym brought before him. After he had been given an opportunity to display his scholarly credentials, al-Maʾmūn told him that the ban was not directed at people like him, but only against those who turned right into wrong. Abū Nuʿaym responded that this should have been made clear in the proclamation, and was released.[176] Again, the presumption is

[171] He is named as Rabīʿa ibn ʿUthmān al-Tamīmī. Tamīmī is an obvious error for Taymī. Rabīʿa ibn ʿUthmān al-Taymī (d. 154/770f.) is a known Medinese traditionist (see Ibn Ḥajar, *Tahdhīb*, 3:259f.), but it seems more likely that Rabīʿat al-Raʾy (d. 136/753f.) (a Taymī who likewise bore the *kunya* Abū ʿUthmān, *ibid.*, 258f.) is intended here; he was a client of the Āl al-Munkadir (Dhahabī, *Tadhkira*, 157.9).

[172] For him see Ibn Ḥazm, *Jamhara*, 123.3.

[173] Abū ʾl-ʿArab, *Miḥan*, 326.5.

[174] Mizzī, *Tahdhīb*, 23:197.3.

[175] Cf. below, ch. 5, note 172 and 107.

[176] Khaṭīb, *Taʾrīkh Baghdād*, 12:350.2 (cited in E. Tyan, *Histoire de l'organisation judiciaire en pays d'Islam*, Leiden 1960, 619 n. 1); Dhahabī, *Siyar*, 10:150.2; Dhahabī, *Taʾrīkh al-*

that had Abū Nuʿaym merely confronted the soldier without the subsequent escalation, we would not have come to know of the incident.

For good measure, we may add here the somewhat similar story of Ḥasan ibn al-Ṣabbāḥ al-Bazzār (d. 249/863), a Baghdādī traditionist of Wāsiṭī origin.[177] We are told that after al-Maʾmūn banned 'commanding right', Bazzār was brought before him for violating the ban. He was asked if he 'commanded right', and cheekily responded that he did not, but that he did 'forbid wrong'. The caliph, perhaps not finding this distinction entirely persuasive, had him flogged before releasing him.[178] Here the narrator gives us no indication whatever of the character of the wrong that Bazzār forbade. For biographers, clashes with high authority are intrinsically glamorous; exchanges with the man in the street are not.

So much for the wrongs themselves. How do our subjects react to them, or think one should react to them? Here, as with confronting the state, we find a spectrum both of thought and of practice. There are attitudes that strikingly play up the duty, and attitudes that just as strikingly play it down; in between there is a domain of moderation and qualification. Again, let us begin with the ends of the spectrum.

There is, of course, no shortage of commendations of forbidding wrong.[179] As Ḥudhayfa said, it is a fine thing;[180] someone who fails to do it is as a dead man among the living.[181] ʿUmar ibn al-Khaṭṭāb identifies commanding right and forbidding wrong as two of the components that make up Islam.[182] In a long and pious address, Sufyān al-Thawrī at one point exhorts the addressee to forbid wrong and be beloved of God.[183] But statements made in so general a vein do not commit one to very much.

Islām, years 211–20, 345.7. See also M. Muranyi in his edition of a fragment of the *Jāmiʿ* of ʿAbdallāh ibn Wahb (d. 197/813) under the subtitle *Die Koranwissenschaften*, Wiesbaden 1992, 134f. (but it should be remarked that the Miḥna, which was still in the future, plays no part in the story). Since Faḍl only arrives in Baghdad after al-Maʾmūn, this anecdote does not provide support for the idea that Faḍl had been 'active in the movement' of forbidding wrong in Baghdad (cf. I. M. Lapidus, 'The separation of state and religion in the development of early Islamic society', *International Journal of Middle East Studies*, 6 (1975), 380), nor does it suggest that he had provided the movement with its theological justification (van Ess, *Theologie*, 2:388, citing Lapidus).

177 Dhahabī, *Tadhkira*, 476.4.

178 Khaṭīb, *Taʾrīkh Baghdād*, 7:331.10; Ibn Abī Yaʿlā, *Ṭabaqāt*, 1:134.16; Dhahabī, *Tadhkira*, 476.13; Dhahabī, *Mīzān*, 1:500.2; Dhahabī, *Siyar*, 12:193.10; Dhahabī, *Taʾrīkh al-Islām*, years 241–50, 230.1. For al-Maʾmūn's ban on forbidding wrong, see further below, ch. 17, notes 21f.

179 See, in addition to the following references, below, ch. 14, note 6.

180 See above, note 40.

181 See above, ch. 3, note 28. Ḥudhayfa also has other sayings which play up the duty (see above, ch. 3, note 12, and below, ch. 5, note 173).

182 See above, ch. 3, note 25. Cf. also Ibn Saʿd, *Ṭabaqāt, al-qism al-mutammim*, 164.1.

183 Abū Nuʿaym, *Ḥilya*, 7:83.17.

The unpleasant consequences to which forbidding wrong may lead pose a sharper test, and the tendency to embrace such consequences can serve to define the activist end of our spectrum. This tendency finds several expressions in the anecdotal material.[184] Kurz ibn Wabara was a minor Kūfan ascetic who came to Jurjān in 98/716f. and settled there.[185] We learn that when he went out, he would command and forbid, getting himself beaten up to the point that he lost consciousness;[186] clearly he knew what to expect, and was not discouraged by it. After Ibn al-Munkadir was flogged on account of the episode in the baths,[187] the people of Medina responded by gathering around him; he seems to have calmed them by telling them that anyone worth his salt must expect to suffer in this line of activity.[188] When the ascetic Dahtham ibn Qurrān[189] admonished (*waʿaẓa*) a man who was whipping his slave, the man turned the whip on Dahtham. His companions rushed up in concern, but the pietist was in no hurry to escape from his ordeal. As he pointed out to them, Q31:17 contains an injunction to endure the consequences of commanding right and forbidding wrong, and he asked only to be left to do so.[190] Not everybody was such a glutton for punishment: a certain Ayyūb ibn Khalaf is asked why he does not perform the duty, and answers that he would indeed do so were he like Salm ibn Sālim; for Salm would have endured (*ṣabr kardī*) any unpleasant consequences, whereas he himself could not.[191]

Opinions encouraging such endurance are transmitted from several of our subjects.[192] ʿUmar ibn al-Khaṭṭāb would seem to approve of getting killed in the course of forbidding wrong.[193] 'Fortunate is the man who does not suffer (*lam yuṣibhu . . . adhā*) in this matter', states the pious ʿUmar

[184] In addition to the following references, see below, ch. 14, note 211.

[185] Sahmī (d. 427/1035f.), *Taʾrīkh Jurjān*, Hyderabad 1950, 295.11. Most of what we are told about Kurz relates to his piety and asceticism (see the entry on him in Dhahabī, *Siyar*, 6:84–6). I owe my knowledge of him to Amikam Elad.

[186] *Ibid.*, 85.6; Abū Bakr al-Dīnawarī (d. 333/944f.), *al-Mujālasa wa-jawāhir al-ʿilm*, Frankfurt am Main 1986, 190.24.

[187] See above, 69f.

[188] Abū ʾl-ʿArab, *Miḥan*, 326.13 (*lā khayr fī-man lā yuʾdhā fī hādhā ʾl-amr*).

[189] A native of Yamāma, he flourished (if that is the right word) towards the middle of the second/eighth century (he transmits from Yaḥyā ibn Abī Kathīr (d. 129/746f.), and to Abū Bakr ibn ʿAyyāsh (d. 193/809), see Mizzī, *Tahdhīb*, 8:496.4; for his provenance, see *ibid.*, 497.12). As a traditionist he was a disaster (see *ibid.*, 497.3, and the opinions that follow there), but he seems to have done better as a pietist; he rated inclusion in a list of articulate ascetics given by Jāḥiẓ (d. 255/868f.) (*al-Bayān waʾl-tabyīn*, ed. ʿA. M. Hārūn, Cairo 1948–50, 1:364.3).

[190] Zubayr ibn Bakkār, *Akhbār*, 523 no. 346; Ibn Abī ʾl-Dunyā, *Amr*, 94 no. 51. For the exegesis of Q31:17, see above, ch. 2, 28f.

[191] Wāʿiẓ-i Balkhī, *Faḍāʾil-i Balkh*, 157.4. For Salm, see above, 57. Compare the saying of Bishr al-Ḥāfī that only someone who can endure torment should forbid wrong (Abū Nuʿaym, *Ḥilya*, 8:337.12; I owe this reference to Michael Cooperson).

[192] Cf. also below, ch. 11, 256.

[193] See above, ch. 2, note 77.

ibn ʿAbd al-ʿAzīz (d. 101/720),[194] implying that such suffering is a normal accompaniment of the duty. According to Ḥasan al-Baṣrī, Q3:21 shows that those who perform the duty in the face of fear (*ʿinda ʾl-khawf*) have a standing close to that of the prophets.[195] Ibn Shubruma holds, on the analogy of holy war, that a single man can be expected to take on two men, commanding and forbidding them.[196] ʿAbdallāh ibn ʿAbd al-ʿAzīz al-ʿUmarī condemns any failure to perform the duty because one is in fear.[197] These last are particularly significant. It is usually unclear whether facing fearful odds is a duty or just an act of virtue; but for ʿUmarī, as for Ibn Shubruma within the limit of his ratio, it is plainly a duty.[198]

An obvious practical response to the dangers of forbidding wrong is for a group of men to perform it together. In fact it is not very common for private citizens to do this. In the course of the second civil war, Muḥammad ibn al-Ḥanafiyya (d. 81/700f.) found himself caught between the rival caliphs Ibn al-Zubayr (r. 64–73/684–92) and ʿAbd al-Malik (r. 65–86/685–705); he took the line that he would not give allegiance to either side until he saw what people at large would do.[199] At one point, he and his entourage made their way to Ayla, which was within the territories ruled by ʿAbd al-Malik, who soon told him to leave.[200] While in Ayla, according to one account, Ibn al-Ḥanafiyya and his party were treated with great respect; they forbade wrong, and no one was wronged in their vicinity.[201] But Ibn al-Ḥanafiyya was more than a private citizen, and there is perhaps a suggestion that his forbidding wrong implied a claim to political authority. In any case, the group was clearly not created for the purpose of forbidding wrong.

The same point applies in two cases encountered above. Ibn al-Munkadir in the baths had companions who participated in the reproof he administered, and shared the flogging to which he was then subjected.[202] Dahtham's companions came up as he was being whipped by the enraged slave-owner, and were ready to rescue him.[203] But again, these do not look like groups created for the purpose. In other instances, groups are indeed created for the

[194] Ibn Abī Zayd, *Jāmiʿ*, 156.2.
[195] Fakhr al-Dīn al-Rāzī, *Tafsīr*, 7:230.13 (cf. above, ch. 2, note 79).
[196] Abū ʿUbayd, *Nāsikh*, 101.13; Bukhārī, *Ṣaḥīḥ*, 3:247.18; Wakīʿ (d. 306/918), *Akhbār al-quḍāt*, ed. ʿA. M. al-Marāghī, Cairo 1947–50, 3:123.19 (drawn to my attention by Nurit Tsafrir); Jaṣṣāṣ, *Aḥkām*, 2:489.7. The argument goes back to the ratio established in Q8:66 with regard to *jihād*. [197] See above, note 86.
[198] Cf. Shuʿayb ibn Ḥarb's view that it was his *duty* to proceed against Hārūn al-Rashīd (see above, 59). [199] See EI^2, art. 'Muḥammad Ibn al-Ḥanafiyya' (F. Buhl).
[200] Abū Ḥanīfa al-Dīnawarī (d. 282/895), *al-Akhbār al-ṭiwāl*, ed. ʿA. ʿĀmir and J. al-Shayyāl, Cairo 1960, 309.6. [201] Ibn Saʿd, *Ṭabaqāt*, 5:79.3. [202] See above, 69f.
[203] See above, note 190.

purpose, but on a purely *ad hoc* basis. The ascetic Muḥammad ibn Muṣʿab, who was also a highly regarded Koran reciter, would use this skill to great effect to gather a crowd at the door of a house where a lute was being played.[204] Also instructive is the story of how ʿUmar ibn Maymūn al-Rammāḥ (d. 171/788) came to leave his native city of Balkh, where he held the office of judge for over twenty years.[205] One day he came upon a wrong which he was unable to handle on his own; he accordingly appealed to the neighbours (*hamsāyagān*) for help, but they did not respond to his call. Thereupon he swore an oath not to reside in a city in which he was denied help in forbidding wrong, and set off for Mecca.[206] His expectation that he could form such a group in the neighbourhood was presumably not unreasonable.[207] But the only case in the material considered in this chapter of a group dedicated to the continuing practice of forbidding wrong is Hishām ibn Ḥakīm's association of Syrians.[208]

We can move now to the other end of the spectrum. Here there is a background of attitudes which, while not disparaging the forbidding of wrong, regard its prospects with deep pessimism. Several early authorities predict the future demise or voiding of the duty.[209] Others lament that it is no longer performed in this day and age. The Companion ʿAbdallāh ibn ʿAmr ibn al-ʿĀṣ (d. 65/684f.), standing in the burnt-out Kaʿba after the Syrian siege of 64/683,[210] asks what has become of those who forbade wrong, and threatens divine retribution.[211] Mālik ibn Dīnār bemoans the fact that his generation has succumbed to the love of this world, neither commanding nor forbidding one another.[212] In two lines of verse, Bishr al-Ḥāfī lugubriously contrasts past generations with the present, and remarks that those who used to take action against every wrong (*al-munkirūna li-kulli amrin*

204 See below, ch. 5, note 117, and cf. above, note 159.
205 Madelung, 'The early Murji'a', 36; Khaṭīb, *Taʾrīkh Baghdād*, 11:182.11.
206 Wāʿiẓ-i Balkhī, *Faḍāʾil-i Balkh*, 124.7. 207 Cf. also below, ch. 5, 97f.
208 See above, note 97. For the case of ʿĪsā ibn al-Munkadir (d. after 215/830) in Egypt, see below, ch. 14, note 209.
209 For Ibn Masʿūd, see above, ch. 3, notes 38, 43. For Ḥudhayfa, see above, ch. 3, note 38, and Ghazzālī, *Iḥyāʾ*, 2:285.10. For Ibn ʿUmar, see above, ch. 3, notes 39, 44. For Kaʿb al-Aḥbār, see above, ch. 3, note 46. 210 For this event, see Khalīfa, *Taʾrīkh*, 250.11.
211 Azraqī (d. *c.* 250/864), *Akhbār Makka*, ed. R. Ṣ. Malḥas, Madrid n.d., 1:196.15.
212 Abū Nuʿaym, *Ḥilya*, 2:363.10; Bayhaqī, *Shuʿab*, 6:97 no. 7,596. Ḥasan al-Baṣrī complains rather that today, in contrast to the good old days, people command and forbid without practising what they preach (Abū Nuʿaym, *Ḥilya*, 2:155.6). This need not mean that such people should not command and forbid; on the question whether the sinner is obligated to perform the duty, Ḥasan's view is that he is so, since otherwise no one would perform it (Zamakhsharī, *Kashshāf*, 1:398.10 (to Q3:104); Ibn Abī 'l-Ḥadīd (d. 656/1258), *Sharḥ Nahj al-balāgha*, ed. M. A. Ibrāhīm, Cairo 1959–64, 7:170.2; cf. below, ch. 14, notes 20f., on the similar views of Saʿīd ibn Jubayr (d. 95/714) and Mālik).

munkarī) have departed this life.[213] Uways al-Qaranī (*fl.* first/seventh century), an ascetic of Yemeni background who settled in Kūfa,[214] treats a fellow-tribesman to a bucketful of gloom which includes the following: 'When a believer undertakes God's business, he retains no friends. By God, when we command them right and forbid them wrong, they take us as enemies and find accomplices in this among the reprobate, to the point that they have accused me of awful crimes.' None of this pessimism, however, actually disallows forbidding wrong. Indeed Uways goes on to declare: 'But by God, this will not stop me undertaking what is right on His behalf!'[215] Nonetheless, the tone is discouraging.

We can perhaps set against this background a set of responses to wrongdoing which can loosely be described as avoiding the duty (though not, it is to be hoped, evading it). When Aṣbagh ibn Zayd took offence at the music he heard at the wedding, he had already sat down at the table; on hearing the music, however, he immediately arose, and could not be prevailed on to stay.[216] Sufyān al-Thawrī counselled his addressee to be sparing in his visits to the market, since once there he would have a duty to command and forbid.[217] Some early authorities go so far as to prescribe emigration in the face of general wrongdoing.[218] Ibrāhīm ibn Adham (d. 161/777f.), a prominent ascetic from Balkh who migrated to Syria,[219] is asked his opinion of commanding right. His response to his inquirers is that these are times of divine wrath (*azminat al-ʿuqūbāt*); better that they should leave the world to the worldly and come to the Holy Land, to a place – the Temple Mount – where they will have no occasion to right any wrong (*lā tunkirūna munkaran*).[220] Another response which might sometimes be described as tantamount to avoidance of the duty is performance in the heart. Ibn Masʿūd insists that such performance is acceptable.[221] The Medinese Saʿīd ibn al-Musayyab (d. 94/712f.) holds that one should not gaze upon the henchmen of unjust rulers (*lā tamlaʾū aʿyunakum min aʿwān al-ẓalama*) without registering one's disapproval in one's heart (*illā*

213 Abū Nuʿaym, *Ḥilya*, 8:344.7; Khaṭīb, *Taʾrīkh Baghdād*, 7:77.10; Ibn ʿAsākir, *Taʾrīkh*, 10:215.8, and the versions there following.
214 See, for example, Ibn Ḥibbān, *Mashāhīr*, 100 no. 743.
215 Ibn Saʿd, *Ṭabaqāt*, 6:114.12.
216 See above, note 158. For walking out, see also below, ch. 5, note 111.
217 See above, note 166.
218 See below, ch. 12, note 11 (for Abū Ḥanīfa), ch. 14, note 24 (for Mālik), and ch. 17, note 171 (in general). A schema attributed to Ibn Masʿūd by Ghazzālī tends to suggest that such departure is the minimal response to wrongdoing (*Iḥyāʾ*, 2:284.1).
219 *EI*², art. 'Ibrāhīm b. Adham' (R. Jones).
220 Musharraf ibn al-Murajjā (fifth/eleventh century), *Faḍāʾil Bayt al-Maqdis*, ed. O. Livne-Kafri, Shfaram 1995, 190.6 (drawn to my attention by Amikam Elad).
221 See above, ch. 3, note 51.

bi-inkār min qulūbikum).[222] The captured ʿAlid rebel of Ṭālaqān, Muḥammad ibn al-Qāsim, found himself present at the revels with which the caliph al-Muʿtaṣim (r. 218–27/833–42) celebrated the Nawrūz of 219/834; he wept, and reminded God that he had never let up in his zeal to right this wrong (*taghyīr hādhā wa-inkārihi*).[223]

A much more radical attitude, though an uncommon one, is that in this day and age forbidding wrong is not a duty at all. Such a view is reported from no less an authority than Ḥasan al-Baṣrī. Asked if forbidding wrong is an obligation (*farīḍa*), he responds that it had indeed been so for the Israelites, but that a merciful God, taking into account the weakness of the Muslim community, had made it supererogatory (*nāfila*) for them.[224] Likewise Ibn Shubruma, in his reply to ʿAmr ibn ʿUbayd,[225] states that commanding right is supererogatory (*nāfila*); those who do not perform it out of weakness have a sufficient excuse, and should not be blamed for this.[226] In the same vein Fuḍayl ibn ʿIyāḍ, when asked about forbidding

222 Dhahabī, *Siyar*, 4:232.17. In practice, Saʿīd seems to have forbidden wrong in more overt ways. Thus he threw pebbles at the young Ḥajjāj to protest at the sloppiness of his prayer (Ibn Saʿd, *Ṭabaqāt*, 5:95.16; Dhahabī, *Siyar*, 4:226.5); and he told off a governor for marrying a fifth wife before the waiting period of the fourth was over (Ibn Saʿd, *Ṭabaqāt*, 5:91.2; Dhahabī, *Siyar*, 4:229.9). But the biographers do not characterise him as someone who forbade wrong, although Zuhrī as quoted by Ibn Saʿd ascribes to Saʿīd straight talk in the presence of rulers and others (*kalām bi-ḥaqq ʿinda ʾl-sulṭān wa-ghayrihim*, *Ṭabaqāt*, 2:2:131.20), and Dhahabī describes him as *qawwāl biʾl-ḥaqq* (*Tadhkira*, 54.9). Van Ess says that he was punished for *al-amr biʾl-maʿrūf* (*Theologie*, 2:664). However, the source he cites describes only the punishment to which Saʿīd was subjected, without mentioning the reason for which it was inflicted (Ibn Abī Zayd, *Jāmiʿ*, 156.1); and the motif of the hirsute shorts (*tubbān*) which appears here shows that the reference is to the second of the two occasions on which Saʿīd was flogged for withholding allegiance (Khalīfa, *Taʾrīkh*, 261.14 (year 68/687f.), 290.10 (year 84/703f.), and numerous other sources).

223 Abū ʾl-Faraj, *Maqātil al-Ṭālibiyyīn*, 585.11 (I owe this reference to Patricia Crone).

224 Khallāl, *Amr*, 86 no. 11 (the questioner is his pupil ʿAbd al-Wāḥid ibn Zayd (d. after 150/767)). This testimony has not been taken into account in the discussion of Ḥasan's attitude towards forbidding wrong in the secondary literature (Schaeder, 'Ḥasan al-Baṣrī', 50, 57f.; Madelung, *Qāsim*, 16f.; Madelung, 'Amr be maʿrūf', 993a). There is, however, a little work ascribed to Ḥasan in which forbidding wrong is explicitly categorised as a duty. This is his *Arbaʿ wa-khamsūn farīḍa*, for which see Ritter, 'Studien', 7f., and Sezgin, *Geschichte*, 1:593 no. 5. The work lists fifty-four duties which the believer must perform daily; ours is the nineteenth (ms. Princeton, Arabic, Third Series, no. 288, f. 201a.3; this volume is a collection of Ḥanafī creeds). Likewise Khallāl has a tradition in which Ḥasan tells his companions to command right, failing which they will become warning examples for others (*Amr*, 100f. no. 44).

225 Cf. above, note 44. Ibn Shubruma was a Kūfan of Arab stock; he held office as a *qāḍī*, and was on close terms with an ʿAbbāsid prince (*EI*², art. 'Ibn Shubruma' (J.-C. Vadet)).

226 Khallāl, *Amr*, 92 no. 24 (reading ʿUbayd for ʿUbayd Allāh), and the parallel versions in Ibn Abī ʾl-Dunyā, *Amr*, 130 no. 99, and Wakīʿ, *Quḍāt*, 3:92.2. The transmitters include the Kūfans Ḥasan ibn Ṣāliḥ ibn Ḥayy (d. 167/783f.) and Aḥwaṣ ibn Jawwāb (d. 211/826f.). But contrast the shorter version also given by Wakīʿ in which *nāfila* is replaced by *muftaraḍ* in the first (and here only) line (*ibid.*, 91.19; this version is transmitted by Ibn Shubruma's nephew, sc. ʿUmāra ibn al-Qaʿqāʿ, for whom see Ibn Ḥajar,

wrong, replies: 'This is not a time for speaking [out], but a time for weeping, supplication, humility, and prayer.'[227] On another occasion he is asked about 'commanding and forbidding', and does not enjoin it (*lam ya'mur bi-dhālika*).[228] The mood behind this trend is encapsulated in a dialogue between Bishr al-Ḥāfī and a certain Ṣāliḥ ibn Ṣāliḥ ibn ʿAbd al-Karīm:

BISHR: Ṣāliḥ, is your heart strong enough for you to speak out?
ṢĀLIḤ (AFTER A SILENCE): Bishr, do you command right and forbid wrong?
BISHR: No.
ṢĀLIḤ: And why not?
BISHR: If I'd known you would ask that, I wouldn't have answered you.[229]

This leaves us the middle range of the spectrum to examine. It can be characterised in terms of three basic, interrelated principles – or, if this is too strong a word, emphases. The first is that fear is a good reason not to proceed. ʿAlī ibn al-Ḥusayn (d. 94/712) condemns the omission of forbidding wrong unless one is in fear (*illā an yattaqī tuqātan*) – as when one fears a tyrant who may hasten to do one harm.[230] The point is well articulated by Wakīʿ ibn al-Jarrāḥ, who was a jurist as well as a traditionist: one should command and forbid only someone of whose sword or whip one is not in fear.[231] Likewise Fuḍayl ibn ʿIyāḍ, in what for him is a relatively activist vein, holds that a man who sees a wrong should not be silent unless he is in fear.[232]

The second principle is that one should only forbid wrong to someone who can be expected to accept the rebuke. As Awzāʿī, another jurist, put it when asked about forbidding wrong: 'Command one who will accept it from you (*mur man yaqbal minka*).'[233] Fuḍayl ibn ʿIyāḍ used to offer a similar counsel: 'You should only command one who will accept it from you (*innamā ta'mur man yaqbal minka*)'; he went on to contrast such prudent

Tahdhīb, 7:423f.). Van Ess cites Wakīʿ's versions, and notes Ibn Shubruma's view that the duty is supererogatory (*Theologie*, 2:286; and cf. M. Cook, 'Van Ess's second volume: testing a sample', *Bibliotheca Orientalis*, 51 (1994), cols. 25f.).

227 Ibn Abī 'l-Dunyā, *Amr*, 134 no. 102.

228 *Ibid.*, 92.2 (no. 47). Cf. also below, ch. 5, 106.

229 Khallāl, *Amr*, 91f. no. 22. Contrast the anecdote cited above, note 155, and the saying cited in note 191.

230 Ibn Saʿd, *Ṭabaqāt*, 5:158.13 (I owe this reference to Etan Kohlberg). The saying is a pastiche of Koranic verses, notably Q3:28, Q11:59, and Q20:45 (a reference to Pharaoh).

231 Khallāl, *Amr*, 89 no. 17; and cf. below, ch. 5, note 124; also ch. 11, note 14. Ibn al-Nadīm (d. 380/990) considers Wakīʿ to be one of the *fuqahā' aṣḥāb al-ḥadīth* (*Fihrist*, 314.16, 317.1).

232 Khallāl, *Amr*, 99 no. 39. The corollary is that he does not like it for a man to engage in commanding and forbidding by standing in a mosque or market rebuking people without actually seeing a wrong.

233 Ibn Abī 'l-Dunyā, *Amr*, 118 no. 83; Khallāl, *Amr*, 124 no. 89.

behaviour with the rashness of reproving someone in authority.[234] Ḥasan al-Baṣrī says that one should command and forbid only a believer who can be expected to listen, or someone whose ignorance can be remedied; but a man who draws a weapon and threatens to use it should be left alone.[235] The link between the first and second principles stands out in the formulations of Fuḍayl and Ḥasan: it is those who will not accept the rebuke whom one most often has reason to fear,[236] though there may of course be cases in which an offender can be expected to be recalcitrant but not dangerous.[237]

A corollary of this principle is that if in the event one's rebuke is not accepted, one should desist. Abū Hurayra reproves a young Qurashī for his vain conduct by quoting a Prophetic tradition; but when he later sees the youth persisting in his behaviour, he declines to repeat himself (*lā aʿūd*).[238] The same idea appears in a special context in Ḥasan al-Baṣrī's response to the question whether one should command and forbid one's parents: one should do so only if they accept it, and if not, one should be silent.[239] Other early authorities suggest that two or three unsuccessful rebukes are appropriate before one gives up the attempt.[240]

The third principle is that one should command and forbid nicely.[241] Sufyān al-Thawrī states that the duty should be performed with civility (*rifq*); if the offender does not accept it from you, he continues, concern yourself with your own soul – a course he considers apt in the circumstances of his day.[242] There is a clear link here with the second principle, as also in the saying of the Baṣran Sulaymān ibn Ṭarkhān (d. 143/761): 'No man whom you anger will accept [your rebuke] from you.'[243] Ibrāhīm ibn

234 See above, note 51.

235 Ibn Waḍḍāḥ, *Bidaʿ*, 230 = 360 no. 61 (from ʿAbdallāh ibn Shawdhab (d. 156/772f.), an itinerant Balkhī); Hūd ibn Muḥakkam, *Tafsīr*, 1:305.10 (to Q3:104); Qurṭubī, *Jāmiʿ*, 4:48.8 (to Q3:21). See also Abū Nuʿaym, *Dhikr akhbār Iṣbahān*, 1:192.11 (from the Baṣran ʿAwf (al-Aʿrābī) (d. 146/763f.)), where Ḥasan goes on to quote from Q5:105 (cf. above, ch. 2, 30f.; I owe this reference to Nurit Tsafrir).

236 Cf. the views of the extremist ʿAbdallāh ibn ʿAbd al-ʿAzīz al-ʿUmarī: he makes no concession to fear, and at the same time favours commanding even someone who will not accept it from one (see above, notes 85f.).

237 See below, ch. 14, 359f., for Mālik's view of such cases.

238 Khallāl, *Amr*, 124f. no. 90.

239 Ibn Abī 'l-Dunyā, *Amr*, 83 no. 37; ʿAbd al-Ghanī al-Maqdisī, *Amr*, 60f. no. 92. For Mālik's view of the question, see below, ch. 14, note 22.

240 See below, ch. 5, 99, for Ibn Ḥanbal, and below, ch. 11, 257f., for Jaʿfar al-Ṣādiq.

241 See also below, ch. 5, notes 92f., and ch. 14, note 10.

242 Ibn Abī Ḥātim, *Taqdima*, 124.15. Likewise he takes the view that to perform the duty one must be civil (*rafīq*), honest (*ʿadl*) and knowledgeable (*ʿālim*) (Khallāl, *Amr*, 96f. no. 32; cf. above, ch. 3, note 59, and below, ch. 5, note 74; also above, note 144). Contrast the harsher tone that appears in his saying that when you forbid wrong, you humiliate the hyprocrite (*ibid.*, 113 no. 67), and the incivility of his dealings with the caliphs (see esp. above, note 134).

243 *Ibid.*, 98 no. 38 (*mā aghḍabta rajulan fa-qabila minka*); and see *ibid.*, 100 no. 43.

Adham goes beyond civility: asked whether, on seeing or hearing that a man is acting wrongly, one should speak to him about it, he answers to the effect that this would be too aggressive (*hādhā tabkīt*); but one should drop a hint.[244] Examples of polite rebukes are to be found in the anecdotal material. Hearing of the Companion of the Prophet who had taken to drink in Syria, ʿUmar ibn al-Khaṭṭāb wrote to him simply quoting a Koranic passage which describes God as 'forgiver of sins, accepter of penitence', but also as 'terrible in retribution' (Q40:1–3); the man responded positively to the implied rebuke, and repented of his vice.[245] Ibn al-Munkadir is polite in reproving a man who is talking to a woman.[246] If Ḥasan ibn Ṣāliḥ ibn Ḥayy wanted to reprove one of his colleagues (*an yaʿiẓ akhan min ikhwānihi*), he would write the rebuke on his tablets, and hand it to him.[247]

It would probably be a mistake to assume that those who speak in favour of civility are to be understood as categorically opposing harsher measures. Certainly figures who belong firmly in the mainstream appear in the sources as recommending such measures or having recourse to them.[248] Ibn Masʿūd, on interrupting a group of revellers, pours out a jug of liquor and breaks a mandolin;[249] his companions would seize tambourines out of the hands of children and shred them.[250] We are not altogether surprised that Ibn ʿUmar, a harsh and inflexible pietist, should break mandolins over the heads of those who play them; but it is arresting to find this practice endorsed by the jurist Wakīʿ ibn al-Jarrāḥ.[251] Recourse to arms is not, of course, in evidence in these circles.[252]

One way of forbidding wrong nicely is to administer the rebuke in private, so that the offender is not subjected to public humiliation.[253] This idea finds a classic formulation in a saying of Umm al-Dardāʾ (d. after 81/700): 'Whoever admonishes his brother in private (*sirran*) graces him (*zānahu*);

244 *Ibid.*, 100 no. 42.
245 For references, see below, ch. 14, note 10; and cf. above, note 148.
246 See above, note 152.
247 Mizzī, *Tahdhīb*, 6:189.13; Ibn Abī 'l-Dunyā, *Amr*, 98 no. 57. But a parallel has *yughalliṭ* for *yaʿiẓ* (Ibn ʿAdī, *Kāmil*, 720.6); thus he would be correcting a colleague's faulty transmission of a tradition.
248 Cf. also below, ch. 5, 96, 97.
249 See above, notes 149, 157.
250 See below, ch. 5, note 21; and cf. Ṭabarī (d. 310/923), *Tahdhīb al-āthār*, ed. M. M. Shākir, Cairo 1982, *Musnad ʿAlī ibn Abī Ṭālib*, 240 nos. 377f. (in a section of the work cited in Gilliot, 'Islam et pouvoir', 130 n. 6), and Ibn Abī 'l-Dunyā (d. 281/894), *Dhamm al-malāhī*, in J. Robson (ed. and trans.), *Tracts on listening to music*, London 1938, 54.9.
251 Khallāl, *Amr*, 143 no. 126; cf. below, ch. 5, note 100, and *ibid.*, 146 no. 135. Ibn ʿUmar also destroys the hardware with which the games of backgammon and 'fourteen' (*arbaʿ ʿashra, shahārdah*) are played (Ibn Saʿd, *Ṭabaqāt*, 4:1:120.27; Ṭabarī, *Tahdhīb al-āthār*, *Musnad ʿAlī*, 241f. nos. 383–5; for the game of 'fourteen', see Shakir's note, *ibid.*, 241 n. 2).
252 Cf. also below, ch. 5, notes 109f.
253 Cf. also below, ch. 14, note 13.

whoever does so in public (*ʿalāniyatan*) disgraces him (*shānahu*).'[254] The examples we have encountered above relate to reproving rulers: Ibn ʿAbbās's counsel that, if you must rebuke a ruler, you should do so in private;[255] ʿIyāḍ ibn Ghanm's counter-reproof to Hishām ibn Ḥakīm;[256] and the governor's complaint to Ibn Abī Dhiʾb that Muḥammad ibn ʿAjlān had humiliated him by rebuking him in public.[257] In this last case, the governor makes the significant comment that, had the rebuke been private, he would have accepted it; in that event, we can assume that Ibn ʿAjlān would not have been thrown into jail.

4. DEFENDING PRIVACY

Less directly related to the spectrum of views set out above is concern with what we would call respect for privacy. There is no single category that corresponds to this in Islamic terms; rather, there are three basic, mutually supporting principles at work here. The first is the prohibition of spying and prying; this is enshrined in Q49:12.[258] The second is the duty not to divulge what would dishonour a Muslim; this is laid down in a Prophetic tradition.[259] The third is the sanctity of the home, which rests on Koranic stipulations regarding the way one should enter the homes of others (Q2:189, Q24:27).[260] All these values are strongly reflected in the materials we are concerned with in this chapter.

The prohibition of spying comes into play when Ibn Masʿūd is asked about a man whose beard drips with wine, and responds that God has forbidden spying (*tajassus*); we can take action, he says, only if the offence is out in the open (*in yaẓhar lanā shayʾ*),[261] which is perhaps to say that we must actually see the man drinking.[262]

The duty not to divulge finds expression in an anecdote about the Companion ʿUqba ibn ʿĀmir al-Juhanī (d. 58/677f.), who settled in Egypt and was Muʿāwiya's governor there in 44–7/665–7.[263] His secretary, Dukhayn al-Ḥajrī,[264] explained to him that he had neighbours who drank wine, and proposed to summon the police (*shuraṭ*) to arrest them.

[254] Khallāl, *Amr*, 101 no. 45. [255] See above, note 53. [256] See above, 61.
[257] See above, 62f. [258] See above, ch. 3, note 60. [259] See above, ch. 3, note 61.
[260] See also below, ch. 14, note 173.
[261] Abū Dāwūd, *Sunan*, 5:200 no. 4,890; Bayhaqī, *Shuʿab*, 6:99 no. 7,604; cf. above, ch. 3, note 60. Cf. also below, ch. 5, 99f., and ch. 14, note 202.
[262] Cf. also the tradition about God not punishing the common people for the hidden sins of the elite (see above, ch. 3, note 64).
[263] For his biography, see Ibn ʿAbd al-Barr, *Istīʿāb*, 1073f. no. 1824; for his governorship of Egypt, see Kindī (d. 350/961), *Wulāt*, in R. Guest (ed.), *The governors and judges of Egypt*, Leiden and London 1912, 36–8. [264] For whom see Mizzī, *Tahdhīb*, 8:476.

ʿUqba told him not to do this, but rather to counsel and threaten them (verbally). He did so, but to no effect; so he again proposed to call in the police. ʿUqba once more told him not to, and quoted a tradition he had heard from the Prophet: 'Whoever keeps hidden what would disgrace a believer (*man satara muʾminan*), it is as though he had restored a buried baby girl (*mawʾūda*) to life from her tomb.'[265]

The sanctity of the home is at the centre of an exchange which takes place in Baṣra between a certain Abū ʾl-Rabīʿ al-Ṣūfī and Sufyān al-Thawrī regarding the activities of what I take to be the officially appointed censors (*muḥtasiba*):

ABŪ ʾL-RABĪʿ: Abū ʿAbdallāh! When I'm with these censors, we go into the homes of these vile people (*khabīthīn*), clambering over the walls.
SUFYĀN: Don't they have doors?
ABŪ ʾL-RABĪʿ: Well yes, but we rush in so they don't escape.

Sufyān condemns this misconduct in no uncertain terms, and one of those present unkindly asks: 'Who let *him* in here?'[266]

In two of the three examples just given, the actual or potential enemy of privacy is not society but the state. This is typical for the material under examination here.[267] Saʿīd ibn al-Musayyab is asked whether, having come upon a drunkard, one is permitted not to report him to the authorities (*sulṭān*); he tells the questioner that he should rather conceal the man (*usturhu*) under his robe, if he is able to do so.[268] Most telling of all is a story told about ʿUmar ibn al-Khaṭṭāb, a caliph who in Sunnī sources has the image of a man with his heart in the right place, but a tendency to go too far. On this occasion he enters a man's home by climbing over the wall, and catches him engaged in wrongdoing. But the man retorts that, while he had indeed sinned in one respect, ʿUmar had sinned in three: he had spied, whereas God has prohibited this (Q49:12); he had entered through the roof, whereas God has commanded us to enter houses by their doors

[265] Khallāl, *Amr*, 108 no. 61 (and cf. *ibid.*, 106f. no. 57); Ibn Ḥanbal, *Musnad*, 4:153.24 (and cf. the parallel versions *ibid.*, 147.27, 158.12; also Abū Dāwūd, *Sunan*, 5:201f. no. 4,892). The tradition makes reference to the pre-Islamic Arabian practice of female infanticide (*waʾd*). Cf. also above, note 150.

[266] Khallāl, *Amr*, 96 no. 32. Sufyān was resident in Baṣra near the end of his life (van Ess, *Theologie*, 1:222), which would place the exchange around the year 160/776f. In giving the name of Sufyān's interlocutor as Abū ʾl-Rabīʿ, I follow the parallel in Ibn Ḥanbal (d. 241/855), *Waraʿ*, ed. Z. I. al-Qārūṭ, Beirut 1983, 154.11. The use of the plural *muḥtasiba* is puzzling; van Ess (citing the parallel in the *Waraʿ*) takes them to be self-appointed ('eine Bande religiöser Fanatiker', *Theologie*, 2:389), but this seems to me on balance to be the less likely alternative.

[267] The balance is rather different in the thinking of Ibn Ḥanbal (see below, ch. 5, 99f. and 102f.).

[268] Ibn Saʿd, *Ṭabaqāt*, 5:99.23, 101.26.

(Q2:189); and he had entered without pronouncing a greeting, whereas God has forbidden us to enter a house without first greeting those who live there (Q24:27). ʿUmar let the man be, merely stipulating that he should repent.[269]

It is striking that the attitudes manifested in this material are so uniformly in favour of privacy.[270] One reason for this is doubtless that the stand in favour of privacy is reinforced by a marked element of hostility and mistrust directed against the state. It is not out of concern for privacy that Sufyān al-Thawrī refuses to have anything to do with al-Mahdī's suggestion that they join forces, sallying forth into the market to forbid wrong together.[271] What we have here is rather a characteristic example of Sufyān's sullenness towards the authorities – his 'Staatsverdrossenheit', as van Ess has dubbed it.[272]

5. FINAL REMARKS

A final question may have arisen in the reader's mind on the basis of the material surveyed in this chapter: is it only men who command and forbid?

An early Ḥanbalite source describes a woman called Samrāʾ bint Nahīk, who had met the Prophet; she had a whip in her hand with which she chastised people, commanding right and forbidding wrong.[273] A biographer of the Companions devotes a few lines to this woman; what he has to say adds the details that she belonged to the tribe of Asad, lived to a great age, and did her commanding and forbidding in the markets.[274] Otherwise nothing is known of her, and it is unclear whether we are to think of her as self-appointed or as holding a public office. There may indeed be some confusion with a relatively well-known woman, Shifāʾ al-ʿAdawiyya, whom ʿUmar ibn al-Khaṭṭāb put in charge of some aspect of the market.[275] We do

[269] Ghazzālī, *Iḥyāʾ*, 2:297.23. For this story see further below, ch. 17, note 85.

[270] Contrast the view of Mālik that a neighbour who drinks wine and ignores a rebuke should be reported to the ruler (see below, ch. 14, note 18); cf. also below, ch. 5, notes 162f.

[271] Ibn Abī Ḥātim, *Taqdima*, 109.10; Abū Nuʿaym, *Ḥilya*, 7:43.21; Dhahabī, *Siyar*, 7:263.6; cf. also Ibn Abī Ḥātim, *Taqdima*, 107.17, 110.8; Abū ʾl-Shaykh, *Ṭabaqāt*, 2:114.16 (I owe this reference to Nurit Tsafrir); Abū Nuʿaym, *Ḥilya*, 7:43.10; Zaman, *Religion and politics*, 81 n. 41.

[272] Van Ess, *Theologie*, 1:224. Contrast Mālik's approval of commanding and forbidding at the behest of the ruler (see below, ch. 14, 361).

[273] Khallāl, *Amr*, 131 no. 106.

[274] Ibn ʿAbd al-Barr, *Istīʿāb*, 1863 no. 3,386, whence P. Chalmeta Gendron, *El 'señor del zoco' en España*, Madrid 1973, 57, 315f., 325. Chalmeta places her activity in the time of the Prophet, but Ibn ʿAbd al-Barr does not specify this.

[275] Ibn ʿAbd al-Barr, *Istīʿāb*, 1869.6 (no. 3,398); Ibn Ḥazm, *Jamhara*, 150.6, 156.15 (both sources are cited by Chalmeta, *El 'señor del zoco'*, 57, 315f., 328;); Mizzī, *Tahdhīb*, 35:207.14; Ibn Ḥajar, *Iṣāba*, 7:728.2 (no. 11,373).

not, then, find in this material a clear-cut instance of a woman forbidding wrong in a private capacity.

Alongside our lone and ambiguous woman we can nevertheless set a dog. Its owner was Sulaymān ibn Mihrān al-Aʿmash (d. 148/765), a noted Kūfan Shīʿite traditionist with a reputation for being boorish and disagreeable.[276] It was characteristic of his meanness towards students in search of traditions that when they visited him they would be harassed by a vicious dog. One day, however, they found that the dog had died, and eagerly rushed in. On seeing them, Aʿmash wept and remarked of the dog: 'He who used to command right and forbid wrong has perished!'[277]

As we have seen, the material surveyed in this chapter is relatively abundant, and its content is rich and sometimes colourful. Although it gives undue prominence to confrontations with rulers and governors, it is much more helpful than Koranic exegesis and tradition in conveying a sense of what the duty of forbidding wrong is about. This material does, however, lack coherence in two ways. First, in social terms it is somewhat eclectic: it does not permit a sustained focus on any one social milieu. Secondly, it is intellectually unsystematic, the residue of ideas which may or may not once have belonged to developed doctrinal systems which we can no longer hope to recover. The first defect will be remedied by turning to the early Ḥanbalites in the next chapter, and the second in due course by taking up the doctrines of the Muʿtazilites.

[276] *Encyclopaedia Iranica*, art. 'Aʿmaš' (E. Kohlberg).

[277] For this tradition, see Khaṭīb, *Sharaf aṣḥāb al-ḥadīth*, 134 no. 316; and cf. *ibid.*, 131 no. 309, 132 no. 311. I owe these references to Patricia Crone.

PART II

THE ḤANBALITES

CHAPTER 5

IBN ḤANBAL

1. INTRODUCTION

As we have seen, the study of forbidding wrong poses a problem of documentation. It is easy enough to find formal scholastic presentations of the duty; such accounts, as will appear from later chapters, are usually to be found in works on the fundamentals of the faith (*uṣūl al-dīn*) on the Sunnī side, and in handbooks of substantive law on the Shīʿite side. At the same time it is evident from the previous chapter that it is a relatively straightforward (though considerably more time-consuming) task to collect scattered information from biographical and historical sources bearing on the practice of the duty at a variety of times and places – items of information that caught the eye of an author, and particularly incidents which in some measure made political history. None of this material is to be despised. But what cannot be reconstructed from it is a convincing picture of the day-to-day agenda of the duty in a specific historical environment.

Fortunately there is one conspicuous exception to this: the milieu in which Ḥanbalism first took shape. The early Ḥanbalites were people with a taste for the concrete and specific, and a dislike for the theoretical and abstract.[1] Much early Ḥanbalite literature accordingly consists of responsa (where it does not consist simply of Prophetic traditions), and the questions that these address are often presented convincingly as ones that have arisen in everyday life and are currently on people's minds. This is particularly the case with a collection of responsa bearing on the duty of forbidding wrong.

[1] In a characterisation of the Ḥanbalite personality, the Ḥanbalite scholar Ibn ʿAqīl (d. 513/1119) wrote that Ḥanbalites accept only sciences that can be understood literally (*mā ẓahara min al-ʿulūm*), leaving aside whatever lies beyond them, and in particular the 'obscure sciences' (*al-ʿulūm al-ghāmiḍa*) (quoted in Ibn Rajab (d. 795/1393), *al-Dhayl ʿalā Ṭabaqāt al-Ḥanābila*, ed. H. Laoust and S. Dahan, Damascus 1951–, 1:184.14, and translated in G. Makdisi, *Ibn ʿAqīl et la résurgence de l'Islam traditionaliste au XIe siècle*, Damascus 1963, 479).

The collection in question was made by Abū Bakr al-Khallāl (d. 311/923).[2] Khallāl made it his life's work to collect the responsa of Ibn Ḥanbal (d. 241/855); he scarcely figures as an authority in his own right.[3] The text was published in 1395/1975 in a useful but unscholarly edition.[4] It contains some 250 traditions, though many, including the last ninety or so, are not directly concerned with forbidding wrong.[5] Of the 150 or so traditions that do concern us,[6] about two-thirds contain responsa (or relate opinions or actions) of Ibn Ḥanbal.[7] The variety of transmitters who appear between Ibn Ḥanbal and Khallāl is considerable.[8] Here, as else-

[2] For the work, see Sezgin, *Geschichte*, 1:511f. Sezgin notes a manuscript in the Ẓāhiriyya, Damascus (for this manuscript see M. N. al-Albānī, *al-Muntakhab min makhṭūṭāt al-ḥadīth* (part of the *Fihris makhṭūṭāt Dār al-Kutub al-Ẓāhiriyya*), Damascus 1970, 269 no. 956). He identifies the work as a part of Khallāl's *Kitāb al-jāmiʿ* (though it may rather belong to his *Kitāb al-sunna*).

[3] See Z. Aḥmad, 'Abū Bakr al-Khallāl – the compiler of the teachings of Imām Aḥmad b. Ḥanbal', *Islamic Studies*, 9 (1970), and C. Melchert, *The formation of the Sunni schools of law, 9th–10th centuries* CE, Leiden 1997, ch. 7 (with some material from our work, *ibid.*, 151).

[4] Abū Bakr al-Khallāl (d. 311/923), *al-Amr bi'l-maʿrūf wa'l-nahy ʿan al-munkar*, ed. ʿA. A. ʿAṭā, Cairo 1975; I owe my copy to the kindness of John Emerson. (There is also a Beirut reprint of 1986, in which the editor's introduction has been severely pruned; this was drawn to my attention by Amikam Elad, and a copy was obtained for me in Saudi Arabia by Abraham Udovitch.) The author and title of the work are named in the *incipit* (*ibid.*, 82.5). The division into chapters and the chapter headings are presumably Khallāl's; they were taken to be so by Ibn Mufliḥ (d. 763/1362) (see his *al-Ādāb al-sharʿiyya*, Cairo 1348–9, 1:180.15, 317.4, 322.3, quoting the chapter headings found at Khallāl, *Amr*, 114.2, 138.2, and 127.1 respectively). The editor's introduction is long and pious, but only a few pages (*ibid.*, 72–5) are devoted to the work itself. From what he says there, ʿAṭā based his edition on a Cairo University manuscript, which he does not further identify. He knew of the existence of the Damascus manuscript, but does not seem to have used it, and I have not seen it myself. There is also a manuscript in the library of the Hebrew University of Jerusalem to which my attention was drawn by Etan Kohlberg; he was subsequently kind enough to send me a copy. This text (MS AP AR° 158) runs to twenty-one folios, and bears the date 18 Rabīʿ al-Ākhir 859/1455 (f. 21a.12); it omits the last chapter of the printed text, ending with no. 236 (in ʿAṭā's numbering). This manuscript was collated with the printed text by Nurit Tsafrir in 1989, and I owe to her almost all references given below to the variants of the Jerusalem manuscript (hereafter J). At a late stage in my research, I encountered an earlier edition than ʿAṭā's, to which ʿAṭā makes no reference; this edition, by I. al-Anṣārī, was published in Cairo in 1389/1969 or soon after; it is based on the Ẓāhiriyya manuscript (Khallāl, *Amr*, ed. Anṣārī, 46.2), and likewise omits the last chapter found in the edition of ʿAṭā. I have collated this text for all cases where differences between ʿAṭā's edition and J are adduced below; where it offers a reading, this usually agrees with J (so, for example, the readings noted below, notes 11, 21, 79; an exception is the reading noted below, note 22).

[5] A good many of these traditions would fit better into a *kitāb al-bidaʿ*, being more concerned with the legal standing of the practices to which they relate than with what, if anything, should be done about them. For this genre, see M. Fierro, 'The treatises against innovations (*kutub al-bidaʿ*)', *Der Islam*, 69 (1992).

[6] Most of nos. 1–152, together with nos. 162f., 174, 240f.

[7] Of nos. 1–152, 104 fall into this category, and a further dozen are transmitted by Ibn Ḥanbal from earlier authorities.

[8] Usually there are either one or two links between them (forty-one and sixty-eight instances respectively), more rarely three or four (six and one instances respectively). Khallāl transmits

where, Khallāl was clearly collecting his material from a large number of sources; in at least three cases we can still locate the traditions in question in the collections from which he must have taken them.[9] Some relevant responsa not included by Khallāl survive here and there in other sources, and I have freely included these in my pool.[10] Khallāl's work was transmitted in Baghdad into at least the mid-sixth/twelfth century.[11]

As indicated, much of the interest of the work arises from its character. It is not a systematic account of the duty; indeed there are occasional contradictions between responsa.[12] But what it lacks in systematic coverage it

directly from some forty different authorities; only six of these are cited five times or more. The most frequently cited, Muḥammad ibn Abī Hārūn, appears in twenty *isnāds* (I have not been able to identify this transmitter; he is mentioned with the *laqab* 'al-Warrāq' in Ibn Abī Yaʿlā, *Ṭabaqāt*, 1:414.7).

9 These cases are as follows. (1) Khallāl cites authoritative sayings or doings of Ibn Ḥanbal nine times with the *isnād* Muḥammad ibn Abī Hārūn from Isḥāq (b. Ibrāhīm) (nos. 4, 15, 19, 86, 94, 113, 119f., 139; in no. 113 for 'Abā Isḥāq' read 'Isḥāq'). All these are to be found (with textual variants) in Isḥāq ibn Ibrāhīm ibn Hāniʾ al-Naysābūrī (d. 275/888f.), *Masāʾil al-imām Aḥmad ibn Ḥanbal*, ed. Z. al-Shāwīsh, Beirut and Damascus 1400 (2:173–8 nos. 1949, 1948, 1956, 1950, 1970, 1947, 1951f., 1955 respectively). All, except no. 1970, form a part of the *bāb al-amr waʾl-nahy* (173–5 nos. 1947–60). This chapter contains (alongside three irrelevant traditions) three responsa not taken up by Khallāl (nos. 1953, 1957, 1958); these will be cited in due course. (2) Khallāl cites responsa of Ibn Ḥanbal directly from Abū Dāwūd al-Sijistānī (d. 275/889) on six occasions (nos. 1, 25, 47, 63, 87, 133). All are to be found (with textual variants) in Abū Dāwūd's *Masāʾil al-imām Aḥmad*, Beirut n.d. (278.9 with 278.13, 278.15, 278.2, 278.17, 278.6, 279.3 with 279.6 respectively). These too form part of a *bāb fī ʾl-amr waʾl-nahy* (*ibid.*, 278–80). The traditions in this chapter from 279.15 on either do not relate to the topic, or are not ascribed to Ibn Ḥanbal, or both; this leaves two relevant responsa which are not taken up by Khallāl (*ibid.*, 279.8 and 279.11), and these too will be discussed in due course. (3) Much (but by no means all) of the material cited by Khallāl from Abū Bakr al-Marrūdhī (d. 275/888) appears in the chapter devoted to *al-amr biʾl-maʿrūf* in Ibn Ḥanbal, *Waraʿ*, 154–6. There are parallels here to Khallāl's nos. 26f., 21, 51, 32, 130, 114, 123 and 112, in that order; Khallāl has taken up all relevant material in the chapter. By way of contrast to these cases, the sole responsum quoted by Khallāl through Ibn Ḥanbal's son ʿAbdallāh (no. 115) does not seem to appear in ʿAbdallāh ibn Aḥmad ibn Ḥanbal (d. 290/903), *Masāʾil al-imām Aḥmad ibn Ḥanbal*, ed. Z. al-Shāwīsh, Beirut and Damascus 1981; likewise the only responsum that Khallāl quotes through Ibn Ḥanbal's son Ṣāliḥ (no. 28) does not seem to appear in Ṣāliḥ ibn Aḥmad ibn Ḥanbal (d. 266/880), *Masāʾil al-imām Aḥmad ibn Ḥanbal*, ed. F. Dīn Muḥammad, Delhi 1988 (drawn to my attention by Suliman Bashear). For a mongraphic study in this literature, see S. A. Spectorsky, *Chapters on marriage and divorce: responses of Ibn Ḥanbal and Ibn Rāhwayh*, Austin 1993.

10 Examples are given in the previous note. A good many of our responsa may also be found quoted in later Ḥanbalite sources, such as Ibn Mufliḥ's *Ādāb*; I have given references to such sources only when they have something to contribute to the text or understanding of the responsum.

11 See Khallāl, *Amr*, 81f. The date 501 (*ibid.*, 81.6) is better read 551, as in J (f. 1b.4).

12 For an example see below, note 147. A brief but more systematic account of the doctrine of Ibn Ḥanbal is offered by a Ḥanbalite scholar of a later epoch, Abū Muḥammad al-Tamīmī (d. 488/1095) (*Muqaddima*, *apud* Ibn Abī Yaʿlā, *Ṭabaqāt*, 2:279.20). However, the systematising tendency and technical terminology of this presentation render it suspect as evidence of Ibn Ḥanbal's own doctrine. I shall return to it in a later context (see below, ch. 6, notes 117, 135, 137f., 172).

gains in the richness and informality of its material, and in the directness with which this material seems to reflect the everyday concerns of the early Ḥanbalite community. A typical example may help to convey something of its flavour.[13] Ibn Ḥanbal is told by a disciple that one of his brethren is suffering greatly on account of the objectionable activities of his neighbours. They do three things: they drink liquor; they play lutes; and they commit offences which are coyly explained as having to do with women. The syndrome, once again, is wine, women and song. The victim, so the disciple reports, proposes to denounce them to the authorities (*sulṭān*). Ibn Ḥanbal disagrees; he should admonish them and forbid them, but the authorities are to be left out of it.

We can best survey this material in terms of three main questions. What are the offences most often encountered? In what contexts are they encountered? And what is to be done about them?

2. VARIETIES OF OFFENCE

The most commonly encountered forms of offence, to judge by the frequency of their occurrence in the responsa, were making music and drinking liquor – in that order. These are followed at some distance by sexual misconduct and a scatter of minor offences. On the whole, the menu is simple and repetitive.

We start, then, with the widespread and ramified offence of making music. There are three offensive instruments which are frequently encountered here: the mandolin (or so I shall translate the term *ṭunbūr*),[14] the drum (*ṭabl*)[15] and the lute (*ʿūd*).[16] The flute (*mizmār*) appears occasionally,[17] and a couple more instruments are mentioned once each.[18] An instrument of a different order which appears quite often is the homely tambourine (*daff*),[19] with or without jingles;[20] but attitudes to the tam-

[13] No. 57. (References in this form in this chapter are to Khallāl, *Amr*, unless otherwise specified.)

[14] Nos. 1, 16, 53, 58, *78, 102, 113–16, 119, 121, 123, 125, *126, 132f., *136, 139f. (An asterisk preceding the number of a tradition indicates that the authority quoted is not Ibn Ḥanbal.) In no. 123 there is also a reference to a small mandolin such as a boy might have. My translations or explanations of terms for musical instruments are based on Lane's *Arabic–English lexicon*; those as unlettered as I am in musical matters should note that a *ṭunbūr* is not a tambourine. Further information on musical instruments can be found in *EI*², articles 'Duff', 'Miʿzaf', 'Mizmār' (all by H. G. Farmer) and 'Malāhī' (A. Shiloah).

[15] Nos. 1, 53, 70–2, 75, 115, 119, 121, 129f., 139f. In no. 128 Ibn Ḥanbal equates the *ṭabl* with the *kūba* (cf. *Wörterbuch der klassichen arabischen Sprache*, Wiesbaden 1970–, 1:420 b 44).

[16] Nos. 57f., *76, *78, 102, 115f., 121, 124, 132f., 140.

[17] Nos. 70f., 102, and cf. no. *174 (*zammārat qaṣab*).

[18] Viz. the *barbaṭ* or Persian lute (no. *127), and the *miʿzafa*, perhaps a stringed instrument (no. *129).

[19] Nos. 137–48. Ibn Ḥanbal's views are to be found in nos. 137–43.

[20] From no. 140 it appears that a tambourine may include a bell (*jaras*).

bourine varied,[21] and Ibn Ḥanbal inclined to lenience.[22] We naturally come up against these instruments on occasions when they are in actual use.[23] But they also invite attention when on sale,[24] and many traditions are concerned with the appropriate response to the mere sighting of an offensive instrument.[25] It was not, of course, essential to possess an instrument in order to commit a musical offence: singing (*ghināʾ*) was one in itself.[26]

That we hear less of liquor than of music perhaps arises from the fact that it is at least possible to drink quietly – for all that drinking is likely enough to lead to rowdy behaviour,[27] or to be accompanied by music.[28] Various terms are used for liquor[29] and its containers,[30] and need not detain us here. The primary offence is of course drinking the liquor.[31] But it is also

[21] Extreme hostility marks the stance of the companions of Ibn Masʿūd (d. 32/652f.), who roamed the streets of Kūfa, seizing tambourines out of the hands of girls and children, and ripping them up (nos. 137, 138, 139, 143; cf. above, ch. 4, note 250). But Khālid ibn Maʿdān (d. 104/722f.) allows them at weddings (no. *144; more detail is given in a line omitted by haplography in the printed text, but preserved in J, f. 13b.17). Awzāʿī (d. 157/773) does not exclude their use at festivals (no. *145), the Kūfans permit them (no. *137), and the Prophet implicitly approves of their use by girls (no. *148).

[22] In one tradition Ibn Ḥanbal endorses the view of the companions of Ibn Masʿūd (no. 138), and in another he is uncertain (no. 137). But in the light of a Prophetic tradition, he regards the tambourine more favourably than the drum (in the continuation of no. 138), and we learn here that he does not follow the view of the companions of Ibn Masʿūd (no. 140). He sees no harm in the tambourine provided it is not accompanied by singing (nos. 141, 143, the latter referring to weddings – reading *al-zifāf* with the printed text, rather than *al-zuqāq* with J, f. 13b.13). He considers it desirable that a wedding be made public through the playing of tambourines (ʿAbdallāh ibn Aḥmad, *Masāʾil*, 320 no. 1183; I owe this reference to Susan Spectorsky). In general he is against the destruction of tambourines (nos. 139f.), though he approves of it in a funereal context (nos. 142f.).

[23] See, for example, nos. 53, 57f.

[24] No. 16 refers to a mandolin on sale in a Muslim market; no. 129 to the sale of drums, either by itinerant drum-sellers (*ṭabbāla*) or in the markets; no. 130 again refers to the sale of drums in the market.

[25] See, for example, nos. 115f., 119, 124. (For the question of concealed musical instruments, see below, note 147.)

[26] Nos. 54, 75. Curiously enough, Ibn al-Jawzī (d. 597/1201) tells us that Khallāl himself (together with his pupil ʿAbd al-ʿAzīz ibn Jaʿfar (d. 363/974), who transmits his *Amr*) considered singing to be permitted; he explains this away as referring to ascetic poetry (*Talbīs Iblīs*, Beirut n.d., 255.15). The same information is given about the views of Khallāl and ʿAbd al-ʿAzīz by Ibn Qudāma (d. 620/1223) (*Mughnī*, Cairo 1367, 9:174.21). Ibn Qudāma in turn had a heated disagreement with a younger contemporary who favoured the permissive view, Nāṣiḥ al-Dīn ibn al-Ḥanbalī (d. 634/1236) (Ibn Rajab (d. 795/1393), *al-Dhayl ʿalā Ṭabaqāt al-Ḥanābila*, ed. M. Ḥ. al-Fiqī, Cairo 1952–3, 2:195.8).

[27] No. 12 (if we read *yashrab* with the printed text as against *yaẓlim* with J, f. 2b.9); also Ibn Mufliḥ, *Ādāb*, 1:218.3. [28] No. 57.

[29] We find *nabīdh* (nos. 57, 73, 85, and cf. no. 7), *khamr* (nos. *61, 110f., 122), and *muskir* (nos. 111–13, 117, 120, 134, 139). In some cases the reference to liquor is implicit (e.g. nos. 118, 121).

[30] Liquor comes in jars (nos. 85, 112, 117, 120) or skins (nos. 110, 112, 118, 121). The term I translate 'jar' is *qinnīna*. I use 'skin' for *ziqq* (no. 110) and *qirba* (nos. 112, 118, 121). Note that one cannot know for certain that such a container contains liquor and not something permitted, such as vinegar, date-juice (*dibs*) or milk (nos. 120f.).

[31] Nos. 12, 57, *61, 73 (but for no. 12, cf. above, note 27).

a target of the duty when made,[32] sold,[33] stored,[34] and the like. There is no word of any concession to the relatively lenient delimitation of the category of forbidden drinks associated with the Ḥanafīs, though the existence of such views is mentioned.[35]

Turning to sexual misconduct, what we encounter in these responsa is fairly tame by modern Western standards, as no doubt by those of many of Ibn Ḥanbal's contemporaries.[36] The main problem is a domestic one: husbands divorce their wives, perhaps in a fit of temper, and then continue to cohabit with them.[37] Occasionally we find men and women associating a little too closely in the public domain. Thus you see a man of bad character with a woman,[38] a youth riding behind a woman,[39] or a druggist chatting to a female customer.[40] But the responsum with which we began is the only one in which there is a suggestion of something more flagrant.[41]

For the rest, the responsa deal with a miscellaneous collection of wrongs. Slovenliness and other shortcomings in the performance of the ritual prayer (*ṣalāt*) appear several times.[42] Groups of chess-players may sometimes be encountered[43] – one may happen to pass by such a

[32] In no. 7, a neighbour makes liquor (*yanbidh*) in a cooking-pot.

[33] In no. 122 a non-Muslim is openly selling liquor in a village, and it may happen that a Muslim buys some. [34] As in no. 85.

[35] The permissive Ḥanafī view of *nabīdh* is mentioned in our work in nos. *167 and *170. There is also a story recounted elsewhere in which Ibn Ḥanbal is brought face to face with *nabīdh* in the home of the traditionist Khalaf ibn Hishām al-Bazzār (d. 229/844), who in this respect at least followed Ḥanafī doctrine (*madhhab al-Kūfiyyīn*, cf. Khaṭīb, *Ta'rīkh Baghdād*, 8:327.3; Ibn Abī Ya'lā, *Ṭabaqāt*, 1:154.19). Ibn Ḥanbal turned his back on the liquor, and conducted his business with Khalaf; when pressed by Khalaf to take a stand on the matter, he responded: 'That's up to you, not me' (*ibid.*, 153.21). I have seen no discussion in the early Ḥanbalite material of the general question that arises here, namely whether one may treat as an offence conduct which is permitted by the school to which the putative offender belongs (cf. above, ch. 4, note 127).

[36] Contrast, for example, Jāḥiẓ (d. 255/868f.), *Risālat al-qiyān*, ed. and trans. A. F. L. Beeston, Warminster 1980, §37, §52, §58. [37] Nos. 80–3. [38] No. 95. [39] No. 96.

[40] No. *101.

[41] See above, note 13. The offence is referred to as *irtikāb al-maḥārim*, glossed as *amr al-nisā'* (no. 57).

[42] Nos. 36, 47, 86–8; also Abū Dāwūd, *Masā'il*, 279.11. In a long epistle on faulty prayer (Ibn Abī Ya'lā, *Ṭabaqāt*, 1:348–80), Ibn Ḥanbal stresses the obligation of the scholars (*ahl al-'ilm wa'l-fiqh*) to practise the duty in this connection (*ibid.*, 373.9, 375.10). In another responsum, Ibn Ḥanbal is asked about praying behind a man who recites the Koran in the *qirā'a* of Ḥamza; he replies that, if the man is likely to listen to you, you should forbid him (Isḥāq ibn Ibrāhīm, *Masā'il*, 2:174 no. 1953; for Ibn Ḥanbal's negative view of the *qirā'a* of the Kūfan Ḥamza ibn Ḥabīb al-Zayyāt (d. 156/772f.), later accepted as one of the Seven, see also Ibn Abī Ya'lā, *Ṭabaqāt*, 1:146.4, 146.23, 179.3, 229.1, 325.14, and cf. Nöldeke, *Geschichte des Qorāns*, 3:181).

[43] Nos. 133, 149–52; also Ājurrī (d. 360/970), *Taḥrīm al-nard wa'l-shaṭranj wa'l-malāhī*, ed. M. S. 'U. Idrīs, n.p. 1984, 161.3. (This responsum, in which Isḥāq ibn Manṣūr al-Kawsaj (d. 251/865) quotes Ibn Ḥanbal and Isḥāq ibn Rāhawayh (d. 238/853) in tandem, clearly derives from the as yet largely unpublished collection of Kawsaj noted in Sezgin, *Geschichte*, 1:509.)

group,[44] presumably in a public place. Chess-playing, though offensive, is less so than backgammon, which is scarcely met with here;[45] but with chess as with liquor, we hear nothing of any concession to those who adopt a more lenient view, in this case followers of Shāfiʿī (d. 204/820).[46] Other offences occasionally referred to are the display of images (*ṣuwar*),[47] scandalous talk and exchanges of insults,[48] fighting among boys,[49] living off (the profits of entertaining people with) a monkey,[50] depriving one's sisters of their rights of inheritance,[51] engaging in a certain kind of religious singing (*taghbīr*),[52] wailing for the dead (*niyāḥa*),[53] or using frogs and mice as bait (presumably to catch fish).[54] Ibn Ḥanbal responds to this last item in our catalogue of wrongs with the air of a man who has led too sheltered a life to have experienced the full wickedness of the world.

3. CONTEXTS OF OFFENCES

The contexts in which offences are encountered in the responsa can conveniently be ordered on a continuum from intimate to public.

A few offences take place within the home or family. One responsum deals with the natural reluctance of a man to reprove his kin,[55] another with the delicate predicament of a man whose mother does not wash or pray properly.[56] Yet others deal with the performance of the duty against one's father,[57] or against both parents.[58] One should speak up if they cultivate vines to make wine; if they pay no attention, one should move out.[59] Less clearly within the home, and in any case outside the bounds of the

44 Nos. 133, 152; Ājurrī, *Taḥrīm*, 161.3.

45 Various authorities are adduced against chess in nos. *153–8. Backgammon (*nard*) is encountered in no. 151, and referred to in nos. 152 and *155; also Ājurrī, *Taḥrīm*, 161.3.

46 See below, ch. 6, note 151.

47 See the responsum quoted in Ibn Qudāma, *Mughnī*, 7:8.4, and cf. Ibn Abī Yaʿlā, *Ṭabaqāt*, 1:234.7.

48 Nos. 15 (*kalām saw'*), 68 (two men call each other *ibn al-zānī*).

49 No. 27.

50 No. *104, quoting the view of Isḥāq ibn Rāhawayh, and cf. no. 105.

51 No. 84.

52 No. 103; on the standing of *taghbīr*, see the views of Ibn Ḥanbal and others in nos. 182–93, and for the term, see Lane, *Lexicon*, 2,223a.

53 No. 162. By contrast, the recitation of the Koran at funerals, initially treated by Ibn Ḥanbal as an offence, is permitted by him when he hears of an authoritative precedent (nos. 240f.; Ibn Abī Yaʿlā, *Ṭabaqāt*, 1:221.10).

54 Isḥāq ibn Ibrāhīm, *Masāʾil*, 2:175 no. 1958.

55 No. 64.

56 Abū Dāwūd, *Masāʾil*, 279.11. Even though she refuses to take instruction from her son on the grounds that she is older than he is, he should not cut off relations with her or beat her, but continue to instruct and admonish her politely.

57 Ibn Mufliḥ, *Ādāb*, 1:505.4. One should speak without any rudeness, or leave off; a father is not like a stranger (*ajnabī*).

58 *Ibid.*, 505.3.

59 *Ibid.*, 505.8, from Isḥāq ibn Ibrāhīm, *Masāʾil*, 2:136 no. 1768.

immediate family, is the lodger or tenant (*sākin*); Ibn Ḥanbal himself explodes at one who continues to cohabit with his divorced wife.[60]

A good many offences take place in the homes of others. Most of the responsa dealing with the offensive activities of one's neighbours presumably fall into this category.[61] Other responsa deal with situations which arise when one has been admitted to someone else's home and comes upon something offensive there.[62] In yet other cases the sound of music from a house assails one in the street.[63]

Finally, offences may be encountered directly in public places. In the street (*ṭarīq*), we find boys fighting[64] and brazen neighbours drinking liquor;[65] and where offences are encountered in passing (or being passed), the location is most likely to be the street.[66] In the market, people sell musical instruments,[67] and perhaps liquor.[68] In the mosque, people fail to pray properly.[69] An isolated responsum takes us out into the Sawād, the rural hinterland with its non-Muslim population.[70]

What is striking is that none of these contexts, with the exception of the last, necessarily takes us outside what might be called the home range of normal Ḥanbalite life. This is a point to which I shall return.

4. RESPONSES TO OFFENCES

The issues we need to attend to here are who should respond, and how, together with the conditions under which the duty lapses.

As to the question who is to perform the duty, the responsa have rather little to tell us. There are some slight indications regarding the standing of slaves and women. It is implicit in one responsum of Ibn Ḥanbal that a slave is not excluded from the obligation to command and forbid.[71]

60 No. 81. For the *sākin*, see below, note 221.

61 Nos. 7, 12, 21, 50f., 53, 57f., *61, 63, 73f., and cf. 72. In no. 7, J places the activity on the neighbour's doorstep (*ʿalā bāb dārihi*, f. 2a.14). In no. 74 the offence is explicitly located in a neighbour's home (*dār*); in no. 73, however, it is located in the street. That Ḥanbalites live in religiously mixed neighbourhoods is clear from a ruling of Ibn Ḥanbal's on the question whether one should greet (or respond to the greeting of) a Rāfiḍī neighbour (Ibn Abī Yaʿlā, *Ṭabaqāt*, 2:14.6).

62 See below, notes 139f.

63 Nos. 75, *76, *78.

64 No. 27.

65 No. 73.

66 Nos. 68, 111, 124, 133, 152.

67 Nos. 16, 129f.

68 One of Khallāl's chapter-headings refers to liquor containers which one passes in the markets (Khallāl, *Amr*, 134.2); but this location is not explicit in the responsa that follow (nos. 110–12).

69 No. 87. In other cases of defective prayer (see above, note 42), the location is not specified.

70 No. 122 (see below, note 155).

71 No. 150, where Ibn Ḥanbal tells a slave whose master sends him on errands to a group of chess-players that it is his duty to order them to desist. The slave's question was simply

Another case put to Ibn Ḥanbal concerns the wife of a man who fails to pray; she orders him to do so, but without effect. Ibn Ḥanbal's reply is that she should seek divorce.[72] There are no references to contemporary women performing the duty in public, but a tradition is quoted about one who did so in early Islamic times with a whip in her hand.[73] We may guess that every legally competent (*mukallaf*) Muslim is obligated, but this is nowhere stated.[74] We might expect that, in some matters at least, the religious scholars would be called upon to play a leading role, but again there is no indication of this in the responsa.[75]

A question that receives much greater attention is how the duty is to be performed. We can conveniently approach the issue through the three modes of performance established by the Prophetic tradition: performance may be with the hand, the tongue or the heart – the last being the minimum compatible with faith.[76] Let us take them in reverse order.

Performance 'with the heart' is, as might be expected, less than ideal; Ibn Ḥanbal refers to it as an 'easement' (*tashīl*).[77] But it has, of course, the sanction of authority – that of the Companion Ibn Masʿūd (d. 32/652f.),[78] as well as that of the Prophet. What Ibn Ḥanbal tends to say is that he hopes (*arjū*) that such performance will pass muster;[79] but it would seem that in the absence of contraindications,[80] some kind of action would be better.[81] There is nothing in the material to show that performance 'with the heart' (*bi'l-qalb*) involves anything more than an

whether he should greet them (for this issue, cf. below, note 82, and Ibn Ḥanbal (d. 241/855), *Zuhd*, Beirut n.d., 275.17).

72 Ibn Ḥanbal (d. 241/855), *Aḥkām al-nisāʾ*, ed. ʿA. A. ʿAṭā, Beirut 1986, 62 no. 205.

73 No. *106; the report is transmitted by Ibn Ḥanbal. On the woman in question, Samrāʾ bint Nahīk, see above, ch. 4, 82.

74 Sufyān al-Thawrī (d. 161/778) is quoted for his 'three qualities' saying (no. *32, see above, ch. 4, note 242), but this is presumably to be taken as moralising, not as a legal doctrine restricting the performance of the duty to the civil, honest and knowledgeable.

75 Elsewhere Ibn Ḥanbal lays emphasis on the responsibility of the scholars for performing the duty in relation to faulty prayer (see above, note 42).

76 The three modes are set out in these terms by Ibn Ḥanbal, though without explicit reference to the tradition, in no. 26. The tradition is nowhere quoted as such by Khallāl, but its wording appears also in no. 109, and partially in no. 19; in no. 18 it is referred to as 'the *ḥadīth* of Abū Saʿīd' (Abū Saʿīd al-Khudrī (d. 74/693) being the Companion who transmits the tradition). The frequent use of *ghayyara* as a term for the performance of the duty irrespective of mode (see, for example, nos. 1, 5, 13) is also likely to derive from this tradition. For a discussion of the tradition, see above, ch. 3, section 1.

77 No. 18.

78 No. 12. Cf. above, ch. 3, note 51.

79 Nos. 13–16, 25. (In no. 16, *bi-qalbihi* has dropped out in J, f. 3a.7.)

80 Viz. fear (nos. 12f., 16), impotence (nos. 15, 19, 21), or the ineffectiveness of previous reproofs (no. 21).

81 No. 25.

unobservable mental act,[82] so that 'with the heart' could just as well be rendered 'in the heart'.

Yet as the terms 'command' and 'forbid' suggest, the default mode is performance 'with the tongue'. A wide variety of locutions are used for this besides 'command' (*amara*)[83] and 'forbid' (*nahā*).[84] A man may speak to (*qāla li-*) the offender,[85] exhort him (*wa'aẓa*),[86] counsel him (*naṣaḥa*),[87] censure him (*wabbakha*),[88] shout at him (*ṣāḥa*),[89] and so forth.[90] Occasionally we are given actual words appropriate to the case, as when Ibn Ḥanbal tells a man who is praying sloppily: 'Hey you, straighten out your back when you bend and prostrate yourself, and pray properly!'[91] Most of this linguistic variation is without doctrinal significance, but there is one principle which bears on one's choice of words: other things being equal, one should perform the duty in a civil fashion.[92] Putting a man's back up by being rude to him is likely to be counterproductive.[93] But although in general one should speak politely, there are times when rudeness is in place – when the offender is a flagrant evildoer,[94] when a neighbour doesn't stop making liquor when told not to,[95] or when the neighbours are shameless enough to drink in the street.[96] According to one text of Khallāl's responsa, calling a man an evildoer (*fāsiq*) would be an example of speaking rudely.[97]

The final mode, performance 'with the hand', covers a considerable range of actions.[98]

[82] Cutting off relations with offenders is sometimes suggested by Ibn Ḥanbal's questioners (no. 84, and Abū Dāwūd, *Masā'il*, 279.13; cf. also no. 54); and in one responsum Ibn Ḥanbal states that players of chess and backgammon are not the sort of people to be greeted (Ājurrī, *Taḥrīm*, 161.3; Isḥāq ibn Rāhawayh takes the same view, except that if one intends to explain to them the error of their ways, one starts by greeting them, *ibid.*, 161.6). But such responses are not linked to performance 'with the heart', as is the case with some Imāmī authorities (see below, ch. 11, notes 81f.).

[83] See, for example, nos. 16, 74, 87. In no. 16, we find the specification *ya'mur bi-lisānihi*; the expression *ya'mur bi'l-ma'rūf bi-yadihi* is also possible, see no. 29, and cf. no. 55.

[84] See, for example, nos. 7, 50, 53.

[85] See, for example, nos. 64, 85, 87. In nos. 56 and 75, *takallama* is used. Occasionally the message is passed indirectly (nos. 36, 241).

[86] See, for example, nos. 57, 80, 88, and cf. *tudhakkiruhu 'llāh* in no. 80. [87] No. 84.

[88] No. 73. [89] Nos. 81, 95.

[90] In no. 19 we find *ghayyarta bi-lisānika*, echoing the diction of the Prophetic tradition.

[91] No. 86; see also no. 240.

[92] Tactful management (*mudārāt*) and civility (*rifq*), as opposed to rudeness (*ghilẓa*), are normally to be used (no. 33). The tradition that the companions of Ibn Mas'ūd would approach offenders with a civil 'easy there . . .' (*mahlan* . . .) is quoted three times (nos. *34f., *55). For civility, see also nos. 30, *32, 46, and Abū Dāwūd, *Masā'il*, 279.14. Ibrāhīm ibn Adham (d. 161/777f.) recommends a hint (*ta'rīḍ*) rather than an outright rebuke (*tabkīt*) (no. *42, see above, ch. 4, note 244); another tradition suggests private rather than public exhortation (no. *45, see above, ch. 4, note 254).

[93] Nos. *38, *43, 46 (or so I understand this tradition). [94] No. 33. [95] No. 7.

[96] No. 73. [97] No. 7. But J has *nabbādh* (f. 2a.15).

[98] Occasionally the nature of the action is unspecified (nos. 18, 25, 29, 109).

One of the more common is the destruction of offending objects. Thus the regular course of action against musical instruments is to break them.[99] (But breaking the instrument over the head of its owner, though sanctioned by weighty authority,[100] is not mentioned by Ibn Ḥanbal, and was not his style.) Containers of liquor get similar treatment[101] – though occasionally the liquor may be poured out, or otherwise spoilt, without damage to the container itself.[102] Chess-boards may be overturned, or picked up and thrown,[103] dramatically scattering the pieces.

Another class of actions is directed against the person of the offender. This may involve separating antagonists,[104] as when Ibn Ḥanbal goes out of his way to separate boys who are fighting,[105] or evicting an ex-wife whose former husband is cohabiting with her.[106] It may extend to intimidating offenders,[107] or even beating them.[108] But the level of violence envisaged is low. There is no question of using a sword or other weapon[109] – not even the widely available mud brick – and the only case in which we find Ibn Ḥanbal approving a beating concerns youths who get out of hand.[110] In any case, one way to resolve a confrontation with an offence is to remove oneself from the scene. Thus you might be called to a house to wash a dead body, hear a drum, and be unable to break it; so you walk out.[111]

All these forms of action presuppose that the believer is acting alone. He may indeed have no choice; in one case a man hears scandalous talk, but

[99] See, for example, nos. 113, 115f., 119, 121, 123–5, 129f. (No compensation is payable for the damage, see nos. 132f., 136, 139f.) In all these cases the verb used is *kasara*. There are occasional references to splitting (*shaqqa*), used for a flute (no. *174), and to ripping (*shaqqaqa*, *kharaqa*) in the case of tambourines (nos. *137–9, *143), although tambourines too may be 'broken' (*kasara*, nos. 139, 142f.). Such assaults on tambourines do not in general find favour with Ibn Ḥanbal (see above, note 22).

[100] No. *126; see above, ch. 4, note 251.

[101] They may be 'broken' (*kasara*, nos. 111–13, 121) or 'split' (*shaqqa*, no. 110). In no. 112, the verb *kasara* is used indifferently of a jar (*qinnīna*) or a skin (*qirba*); in no. 121 it is used of a skin.

[102] In no. 110, we learn that it is better to 'undo' (*ḥalla*) a skin (*ziqq*) of wine, but if one cannot, one should split it. But 'breaking' is preferred to pouring out in no. 112, whereas pouring out is approved in no. 122 (and cf. no. 134). One can spoil *nabīdh* by throwing into it salt or the like (no. 85). [103] Nos. 133, 152.

[104] No. 26. The parallel in Ibn Ḥanbal's *Waraʿ* (see above, note 9) is noted by van Ess (*Theologie*, 2:389 n. 18). [105] No. 27. [106] No. 82, and cf. no. 81.

[107] No. 74, and Ibn Mufliḥ, *Ādāb*, 1:218.3 (in the case of a blasphemous drunk).

[108] No. 107.

[109] No. 28. Use of a whip appears only in the tradition about Samrāʾ bint Nahīk (no. *106, see above, note 73).

[110] No. 107 (*al-fityān yatamarradūn* – the chapter-heading adds *biʾl-laʿib*); Ibn Ḥanbal sees no harm in beating them. By contrast, the questioner who in no. 30 asks if a beating (or blows, *ḍarb biʾl-yad*) is appropriate receives the laconic answer 'civility!' (*al-rifq*). The mother who will not listen to her son when he tells her to wash and pray properly should not be beaten by him (Abū Dāwūd, *Masāʾil*, 279.13, cf. above, note 56). For floggings that ought to be administered by the authorities, see below, note 168. [111] No. 130.

has no helpers (*aʿwān*) to assist him against the offender.[112] But it may be that he is able to enlist the help of a neighbour,[113] or to gather the neighbours and intimidate the offender.[114] He should seek the assistance of others against obdurate singers.[115] Simply making a fuss may help to gather a crowd, as Ibn Ḥanbal points out with regard to the case of some passers-by who saw singers disporting themselves in an upper room (*ʿulliyya*).[116] This technique was also used by the ascetic Muḥammad ibn Muṣʿab (d. 228/843). On hearing the sound of music coming from a house, he would knock at the door and demand the offending instrument in order to break it. If the inmates failed to cooperate, he would sit at the door and recite the Koran till a noisy crowd gathered round, and the inmates had second thoughts.[117] One might have expected such commotions to lead to excesses, but there is no indication of this.[118]

We can now turn to the circumstances in which one should not proceed with the duty. There are three main sources of contraindications: fear for one's own safety; the refusal of the offender to listen; and the demands of privacy.

Fear for one's own safety voids the obligation to perform the duty, other than in the heart. Thus one should not proceed if in peril of one's life,[119] if one fears a dangerous drunk,[120] or if one is up against a wrongdoer of whom one has reason to be afraid;[121] one should take action against the sale of mandolins in the market only if one is not in fear;[122] and so forth.[123] In particular, there is no obligation to proceed against an armed offender.[124] One should, of course, be prepared to put up with some degree of unpleasantness in the performance of the duty – such as being insulted.[125] But neither of the two allusions to martyrdom in Khallāl's responsa[126] relates to a con-

[112] No. 15. [113] No. 109. [114] No. 74. [115] No. 54.

[116] No. 75: *laʿalla ʾl-nās kānū yajtamiʿūn*.

[117] Nos. *76, *78; cf. above, ch. 4, notes 159, 204. For Muḥammad ibn Muṣʿab, who was highly regarded as a Koran-reciter, see Khaṭīb, *Taʾrīkh Baghdād*, 3:279–81; Ibn Abī Yaʿlā, *Ṭabaqāt*, 1:320f.

[118] Contrast the activities of the *muḥtasiba* (see below, note 137).

[119] No. 8 (*idhā khashiya ʿalā nafsihi*). In J, this is ascribed to Isḥāq ibn Rāhawayh (f. 2a.16).

[120] No. 12. [121] No. 13 (*inna minhum man yukhāf minhu*). [122] No. 16.

[123] The sense of no. 47 seems also to be that fear overrides the duty, in the light of the better text in Abū Dāwūd, *Masāʾil*, 278.3; and cf. also no. *39. Cases where a man is said to be unable to take on an offender, or not strong enough to do so (see, for example, nos. 15, 63), presumably come under the same rubric.

[124] No. 4 (mentioning sword and cudgel), and no. 5 (by implication, mentioning sword and whip); cf. no. *9 (Shuʿayb ibn Ḥarb (d. 196/811f.), mentioning sword and whip, see above, ch. 4, note 146), and no. *17 (Wakīʿ ibn al-Jarrāḥ (d. 196/812), mentioning sword and whip).

[125] No. 47 (*yushtam*). See also no. 29, where Ibn Ḥanbal declares the Prophetic tradition that the believer should not court humiliation (see above, ch. 3, note 53) to have no bearing on the performance of the duty.

[126] See nos. 2 and 3. The first refers to the case of a certain Ibn Marwān (see below, note

temporary context; this kind of heroism, though recollected, is not recommended. Elsewhere we find Ibn Ḥanbal being asked about a man who falls into the hands of Khārijite fanatics (*shurāt*), who demand that he dissociate from ʿAlī (r. 35–40/656–61) and ʿUthmān (r. 23–35/644–56) or die; his reply is that if they torture and beat him, he should tell them what they want to hear.[127]

What happens if one tells off an offender, but he ignores it? In some cases, this triggers escalation: if he doesn't listen, speak harshly to him,[128] pour out his liquor,[129] take the chess-set and throw it,[130] gather the neighbours and intimidate him.[131] But in other cases, the refusal of the offender to listen is a signal to leave off. If in the face of repeated expostulations your neighbour seems to be laughing at you, let him alone – you make one, two or three attempts, then give up. What else can you do?[132] If you pray in the mosque and the people there are not praying properly, talk to them about it, even if they are the majority of those present; but after telling them off two or three times to no effect, you give up.[133] In general, if you tell a man off and he won't listen, or doesn't stop, leave off.[134]

Finally, the demands of privacy may override the duty.[135] This severely limits any kind of gate-crashing of people's homes. It is Ibn Ḥanbal who transmits the dialogue in which Sufyān al-Thawrī (d. 161/778) expresses horror at the activities of what I understand to be the officially appointed censors (*muḥtasiba*)[136] who raid people's homes, climbing over the walls the better to surprise them.[137] It is a different matter if one finds oneself in the home of another for a legitimate reason, and there encounters something offensive.[138] Thus a man who had entered a home on some occasion was temporarily left on his own by the owner, who had gone into the

156). In the second, Ibn Ḥanbal remarks of one Ibn Abī Khālid (who is not further identified) and his courageous act (which is not specified) that 'he deemed his life of little account' (*qad hānat ʿalayhi nafsuhu*); the phrase is also used of Bilāl ibn Rabāḥ (d. *c.* 20/640) in the context of his persecution at the hands of the pagans of Mecca (see Ḥanbal ibn Isḥāq, *Miḥna*, 70.16, 72.8). [127] Isḥāq ibn Ibrāhīm, *Masāʾil*, 2:175 no. 1957.

[128] No. 7. [129] No. 122. [130] No. 133.

[131] No. 74. Cf. the practice of Muḥammad ibn Muṣʿab (nos. *76, *78; see above, note 117).

[132] No. 21. [133] No. 87. [134] Nos. 48, 55. Cf. also nos. 53, 56–8, *69, *89f.

[135] Of the three major relevant principles (see above, ch. 4, 80), it is only the duty not to divulge (*satr*) that is explicitly articulated here. The Prophetic tradition is quoted by ʿUqba ibn ʿĀmir (d. 58/677f.) in no. *61 (see above, ch. 4, note 265), and the root *s-t-r* appears also in nos. 114 and 152.

[136] For the official *muḥtasib*, see also below, ch. 17, notes 8f.

[137] No. *32; see above, ch. 4, 81. Van Ess suggests that later Ḥanbalites may have found authority for entering people's homes in responsa of Ibn Ḥanbal (*Theologie*, 2:389 n. 21); but those he cites would not support such conduct.

[138] But note the anecdote cited above, note 35, where Ibn Ḥanbal goes on to say that a man is in charge of his own home, and that it is not for a stranger to intervene (*laysa lil-khārij an yughayyir ʿalā ʾl-dākhil shayʾan*, Ibn Abī Yaʿlā, *Ṭabaqāt*, 1:154.6). We should perhaps see this in the context of conflicting legal views, as in the case in point.

house; he saw a jar beside him, opened it, and found it to contain liquor. Ibn Ḥanbal, far from reproving him for prying, told him that he should have thrown salt into it to spoil it.[139] A similar situation obtains if you are called to a house to wash a corpse, and encounter something offensive there.[140] But in general, there is a presumption against resorting to investigation (*taftīsh*) to discover or confirm offences. Thus if you hear the sound of music, but do not know where it is coming from, it is not your duty to proceed: 'Do not investigate what is not out in the open (*mā ghāba*).'[141] The same principle applies where a man is apparently cohabiting with his ex-wife, but claims to have legally remarried her.[142] Similarly, if you see a jar which you merely suspect to contain liquor, leave it alone and don't investigate.[143] An important distinction opposes an offensive object, whether musical or alcoholic, which is out in the open (*makshūf*) to one which is under cover (*mughaṭṭā*), such as a lute hidden by a garment.[144] An object out in the open should be destroyed.[145] But if it is concealed, most traditions say that it should be left alone,[146] though a few qualify or reverse this liberal view. Thus if you should catch sight of a concealed musical instrument, and it's clear to you what it is, you should break it.[147] Likewise you should break a concealed liquor container if you know it to contain liquor.[148] On the other hand, if chess-players cover the board, or move it behind them to hide it, you should take no action.[149] But where a man is cohabiting with his ex-wife (other than in the case already mentioned), privacy takes second place to the enormity of the offence. Thus a man in this situation may make a point of asking you not to tell his father-in-law what is going on; but you should tell on him all the same, so that the father-in-law can separate the couple.[150]

[139] No. 85.

[140] Nos. 130, 142, 163. In no. 98 the context is a visit to a sick man (reading *marīḍ* with J (f. 10a.18) for the nonsensical *rabaḍ* of the printed text).

[141] No. 71, and similarly no. 70.

[142] No. 80, quoting also the view of Ḥasan al-Baṣrī (d. 110/728).

[143] No. 117. Contrast his pronouncement in no. 85, where the questioner has already opened the jar (see above, note 139).

[144] For this example, see no. 116.

[145] Nos. 111–13, 115, 123f.; Ibn Abī Yaʿlā, *Ṭabaqāt*, 1:223.4. Abū Bakr al-Marrūdhī describes how he once met a woman who had a mandolin out in the open; he seized it, broke it, and stamped on it (Ibn al-Jawzī (d. 597/1201), *Manāqib al-imām Aḥmad ibn Ḥanbal*, ed. M. A. al-Khānjī, Cairo 1349, 285.5).

[146] Nos. 111, 113–16, 118.

[147] No. 119. No. 121 states without qualification that a concealed instrument is to be broken. Contrast no. 116, according to which an instrument concealed behind a garment is not to be broken, even if it is clear what it is. Abū Yaʿlā ibn al-Farrāʾ (d. 458/1066) remarks that the traditions from Ibn Ḥanbal differ on the question whether an offensive object which is concealed is to be broken if one knows what it is; he cites some of our responsa (Abū Yaʿlā, *al-Aḥkām al-sulṭāniyya*, ed. M. Ḥ. al-Fiqī, Cairo 1966, 296.18).

[148] No. 120, and similarly no. 121.

[149] No. 152.

[150] No. 83. One can also apparently take action oneself to expel her from the marital home (no. 82).

5. THE STATE

In this picture of the day-to-day performance of the duty among the early Ḥanbalites, two things are conspicuously absent – one implicitly, the other explicitly.

Implicitly absent is any tendency for Ḥanbalites to go looking for trouble in other parts of town. There is no indication that they were attempting to carry out the duty in quarters where the population might have been even less sympathetic to their values. They do not seek out Muʿtazilite preachers to revile and assault, or go raiding the brothels, or interfere in the pleasurable activities of the military and political elite. This is hardly surprising. Ḥanbalites as they appear in these responsa are ill-equipped to confront the immoral majority; they can hardly hope to dominate their own streets, let alone those of others.

Explicitly absent is the state: one seeks neither confrontation nor cooperation with it.

It is made very clear that one does not take the authorities as a target for the performance of the duty, for all that their misdeeds are doubtless frequent and flagrant. As Ibn Ḥanbal puts it, one should not expose oneself to the ruler (*sulṭān*) since 'his sword is unsheathed'.[151] He was once consulted by a fellow-Marwazī, Aḥmad ibn Shabbawayh (d. 229/843), who had arrived in Baghdad with the bold intention of going in to the caliph to 'command and forbid' him; he discouraged him on the ground of the risk he would be running.[152] Ibn Ḥanbal himself was urged by his uncle Isḥāq ibn Ḥanbal (d. 253/867) to take advantage of his involuntary presence at the court of al-Mutawakkil (r. 232–47/847–61) to go in to the caliph to command and forbid him; he refused.[153] Ibn Ḥanbal likewise

151 No. 19.

152 Ibn Abī Yaʿlā, *Ṭabaqāt*, 1:47.21 (*innī akhāf ʿalayka*), quoted in H. Laoust, *La profession de foi d'Ibn Baṭṭa*, Damascus 1958, 53 n. 2 (with the misreading 'Sibawaih' for 'Shabbawayh'). A continuation of the anecdote appears in Ibn Mufliḥ, *Ādāb*, 3:491.13. Here Ibn Ḥanbal refers the zealot to Bishr al-Ḥāfī (d. 227/841f.), who likewise discourages him: he fears that Ibn Shabbawayh would not have the requisite courage (*an takhūnaka nafsuka*), and that even if he did, his getting himself killed might prove to be the cause of the caliph's going to hell. Ibn Ḥanbal strongly endorses Bishr's view. This in turn is followed by a related pronouncement of Ibn Ḥanbal (*ibid.*, 492.2); here, however, he defers to the Prophetic tradition on speaking out in the presence of an unjust ruler (see above, ch. 1, note 18) once it is quoted to him.

153 Ibn Abī Yaʿlā, *Ṭabaqāt*, 1:112.3 (in the parallel in Ibn Mufliḥ, *Ādāb*, 3:492.6, 'Ḥanbal' has to be read in place of 'Ibrāhīm'). His uncle invokes the example of Isḥāq ibn Rāhawayh (d. 238/853), whom he describes as acting in this manner at the Ṭāhirid court; but Ibn Ḥanbal refuses to recognise his conduct as normative. Ibn Ḥanbal's view of Isḥāq ibn Rāhawayh is normally presented as highly favourable (see, for example, Khaṭīb, *Taʾrīkh Baghdād*, 6:350.8); Isḥāq's relations with ʿAbdallāh ibn Ṭāhir are likewise presented as good, not to say affable (see, for example, *ibid.*, 348.2, 353.13.)

quotes Sufyān al-Thawrī's rhetorical question: 'When the sea overflows, who can dam it up?'[154] The style is not Ibn Ḥanbal's, but the sentiment is his. In more prosaic tones, one of our responsa envisages a situation in which you encounter a Jewish or Christian vintner plying his trade openly, and with the knowledge of the authorities, in a village of the Sawād; if the authorities are indeed conniving at the offence, you have no reason to expose yourself to risk.[155] Only one tradition suggests that martyrdom might appropriately be incurred in carrying out the duty in the face of official hostility,[156] and armed insurrection is clearly out of the question.[157] It is not just that God has imposed a duty of obedience to the ruler. The state is much bigger than you are, and very dangerous; so you had best keep out of its way.

Equally one does not seek to enlist the ruler (*sulṭān*)[158] in the performance of the duty.[159] Ibn Ḥanbal repeatedly disapproves of such action,[160]

[154] No. *20 (see above, ch. 4, note 47). Early Ḥanbalite sources transmit advice to the same effect from Ibn ʿAbbās (d. 68/687f.) (see above, ch. 4, note 52) and Maymūn ibn Mihrān (d. 117/735f.) (see above, ch. 4, note 57).

[155] No. 122. (For *laysa* read *fa-aysh* with J, f. 12a.13.) Note, however, that the chapter-heading immediately preceding this tradition puts a different construction on the situation: one is not obliged to act when one knows that the ruler will do so (Khallāl, *Amr*, 141.2).

[156] Ibn Ḥanbal approves the conduct of a certain Ibn Marwān who was crucified (*ṣuliba*) in performing the duty (no. 2). In Anṣārī's edition of the *Amr*, his name appears as Muḥammad ibn Marwān (Khallāl, *Amr*, ed. Anṣārī, 3.16), and this is supported by the citation in Abū Yaʿlā, *Amr*, f. 102b.21. I am unable to identify him. In J we find a variant text of no. 1, in which Ibn Ḥanbal is asked whether a man may expect to be rewarded if he meets with something unpleasant at the hands of the authorities when he is acting against music-making; the answer is that he does indeed earn merit (f. 1b.14). This text has the support of the parallel in Abū Dāwūd, *Masāʾil*, 278.13.

[157] A poem of ʿAbdallāh ibn Shubruma (d. 144/761f.) is quoted in which he warns that the duty is not to be performed by unsheathing one's sword against the rulers (*aʾimma*) (no. *24; see above, ch. 4, notes 44, 226). A reply of Ḥudhayfa ibn al-Yamān (d. 36/656f.) on forbidding wrong, in which he condemns taking up arms against the ruler, is quoted in an early Ḥanbalite source (Ḥanbal, *Miḥna*, 99.3; see above, ch. 4, note 40).

[158] Terms other than *sulṭān* appear occasionally. In one case (no. 75) passers-by inform the *ṣāḥib al-khabar* (the local eyes and ears of the ruler, see R. Dozy, *Supplément aux dictionnaires arabes*, Leiden 1881, 1:347f.). In the case of the village vintner in the Sawād (no. 122), the governor (*ʿāmil*) is mentioned alongside the *sulṭān*. In an anecdote about the Egyptian Companion ʿUqba ibn ʿĀmir, the talk is of calling in the police (*shuraṭ*, no. *61; this anecdote, for which see above, ch. 4, 80f., is also referred to in no. 57).

[159] It is ironic that ʿAṭā includes in his introduction to Khallāl's work a eulogy of the institutionalisation of *al-amr biʾl-maʿrūf* in the contemporary Saʿūdī state (Khallāl, *Amr*, 67–9).

[160] Nos. 1, 51, 53–8; also below, note 163. In no. 1, in the printed text, he describes such a course as 'disapproved' (*makrūh*); however, the text of J (f. 1b.14), and the parallel text of Abū Dāwūd (*Masāʾil*, 278.13), carry a different sense (see above, note 156). In nos. 16 and 75 such a course is implicitly rejected. Another tradition in which the issue arises (Abū Dāwūd, *Masāʾil*, 279.8) is unclear to me. In no. 16, in J, one way of involving the ruler which is envisaged by the questioner is to get him to issue a proclamation about the matter at issue (f. 3a.4; a line has dropped out of the printed text here through haplography).

as in the responsum with which we began;[161] and cases where he is prepared to countenance it are rare indeed. In one such instance, he is told of the practice of certain fishermen (or hunters?) who use mice and frogs as bait. Confronted with this disturbing information, Ibn Ḥanbal responds that they should be told to stop it. He is then asked whether, if they persist, the authorities should be called in. The answer, unusually, is yes – then maybe they'll stop it.[162] The other such case concerns the question whether an incorrigible evil-doer may be denounced to the ruler; the answer again is yes – provided you know that the ruler will inflict the correct penalty (*ḥadd*).[163] The sequel then makes it clear that you are in fact unlikely to know this: Ibn Ḥanbal relates that they had had a noxious neighbour who was handed over to the authorities, received thirty lashes, and died.[164] In general, it seems, the ruler is likely to go too far against an offender;[165] and once you bring in the authorities, you are no longer in control of what happens.[166] Ibn Ḥanbal's reserve thus arises from the arbitrary and unpredictable character of political power.[167] You can have no confidence that the authorities will impose the legal punishment for the offence.[168] What they do will be too little or too much, and the chances are that they will act with lawless brutality.[169]

All this fits well with what we know of Ibn Ḥanbal's political attitudes, and of his life in general.[170] He was described, and described himself, as a

161 No. 57.

162 Isḥāq ibn Ibrāhīm, *Masāʾil*, 2:175 no. 1958. Cf. M. Cook, 'Early Islamic dietary law', *Jerusalem Studies in Arabic and Islam*, 7 (1986), 240, 277.

163 Compare a case in which Ibn Ḥanbal is asked whether the authorities should be called in to deal with a blasphemous drunk; the answer is no, because it is to be feared that they would not inflict the right penalty (Ibn Mufliḥ, *Ādāb*, 1:218.3). 164 No. 50.

165 No. 55 (*yataʿaddā ʿalayhi*). In one tradition, it seems that the likely response of the state is to fine the offender: they 'take something from him and ask him to repent' (no. 51).

166 No. 57.

167 Contrast the attitude of ʿUqba ibn ʿĀmir (see above, note 158), whose reluctance to see the police called in to deal with wine-drinking neighbours is motivated rather by concern for privacy.

168 Ibn Ḥanbal does occasionally discuss the legal punishments for offences in the responsa under study. Thus no. 102 concerns the punishment (*adab*) that the authorities should mete out to a music-maker – not more than ten lashes. I assume that the immediately following tradition on the beating of the perpetrator of *taghbīr* (no. 103, cf. above, note 52) also refers to punishment administered by the authorities, though this is not explicit. In no. *31, ʿUmar ibn al-Khaṭṭāb beats a camel-driver for cruelty to his camel.

169 Other traditions show a similar reluctance on the part of Ibn Ḥanbal to be responsible for a man's going to prison (no. 51, where the man dies there; no. 60; and cf. nos. *52, *62), or otherwise to involve the state in his affairs (no. 59).

170 See W. M. Patton, *Aḥmed ibn Ḥanbal and the Miḥna*, Leiden 1897, for what is still the best published account in a Western language. Though I shall not give further references to his work, Patton had access through late sources to a good deal of the material cited below, and one of his major sources remains of fundamental importance (see next note). A new study by Nimrod Hurvitz is in preparation.

man who kept clear of rulers.[171] Equally there is no indication that he had played any part in the popular movements that, back in the year 201/817, had sought to restore order on the streets of Baghdad in the chaotic conditions of the fourth civil war;[172] and indeed he explicitly condemned the action of the most prominent of the popular leaders, Sahl ibn Salāma,[173] though this must also have been connected with the latter's Muʿtazilism.[174] At no point during the long years of the Miḥna (218–34/833–48) did he feel it his duty to seek out a confrontation with the state; trouble always came knocking at his door, not the other way round.[175] And when

171 When Muḥammad ibn ʿAbdallāh ibn Ṭāhir (d. 253/867) was pressing to see him, he stated: *anā rajul lam ukhāliṭ al-sulṭān* (Abū Nuʿaym, *Ḥilya*, 9:220.2, quoting the account of Ibn Ḥanbal's life given by his son Ṣāliḥ (d. 266/880); for the career of Muḥammad ibn ʿAbdallāh ibn Ṭāhir in Baghdad, see *EI*², art. 'Muḥammad ibn ʿAbd Allāh' (K. V. Zettersteen and C. E. Bosworth)). ʿAbdallāh ibn Ṭāhir (d. 230/844) is said to have described Ibn Ḥanbal in the same terms to Isḥāq ibn Rāhawayh (Ṣāliḥ, *Sīra*, 41.9). In quoting Ṣāliḥ's biography of his father, I refer where possible (as in this case) to Aḥmad's edition, rather than to the citations in Abū Nuʿaym's *Ḥilya*. However, the material quoted by Abū Nuʿaym from *Ḥilya*, 9:206.16 onwards is not found in Aḥmad's edition, and for this I give references to Abū Nuʿaym. A further complication is that the first edition of Ṣāliḥ's work, that given by Dūmī in his monograph on Ibn Ḥanbal (A. ʿA. al-Dūmī, *Aḥmad ibn Ḥanbal bayn miḥnat al-dīn wa-miḥnat al-dunyā*, Cairo 1961, 266–303), reaches somewhat further than Aḥmad's: Dūmī's extra material (*ibid.*, 297.16–303.20) corresponds to Abū Nuʿaym, *Ḥilya*, 9:206.16–210.25. For this material I give references both to the *Ḥilya* and to Dūmī's edition. The versions of Dūmī and Aḥmad on the one hand, and of Abū Nuʿaym on the other, stem from different transmitters from Ṣāliḥ.

172 On these movements, see Lapidus, 'The separation of state and religion', 372–4; van Ess, *Theologie*, 3:173–5, 448. That they operated under the banner of *al-amr biʾl-maʿrūf* is a point to which I shall return (see below, note 190).

173 He disapproved of his enterprise, and reproved one of his followers, see Khallāl, *Musnad*, 25.15 (noted in van Ess, *Theologie*, 3:174). For brief descriptions of this rich work and its contents, see, in addition to the editor's introduction, C. Rieu, *Supplement to the catalogue of the Arabic manuscripts in the British Museum*, London 1894, 98–100 no. 168; H. Laoust, 'Les premières professions de foi hanbalites', in *Mélanges Louis Massignon*, Damascus 1956–7, 3:18–22. Incidentally, Laoust's statement that the fifth *juzʾ* of the work includes an enumeration of traditions concerned with *al-amr biʾl-maʿrūf* (*ibid.*, 21) is misleading, unless he had in mind the saying of Ḥudhayfa ibn al-Yamān which divides Islam into eight shares, of which the last two are *al-amr biʾl-maʿrūf* and *al-nahy ʿan al-munkar* respectively (quoted twice, Khallāl, *Musnad*, 396.20, 397.12; for this saying, which appears also as a Prophetic tradition, see Ibn Wahb, *Jāmiʿ*, fragment edited by M. Muranyi under the subtitle *Die Koranwissenschaften*, 134 line 19, and Muranyi's commentary thereto; Bayhaqī, *Shuʿab*, 6:94f. nos. 7,585f.).

174 See W. Madelung, 'Imam al-Qāsim ibn Ibrāhīm and Muʿtazilism', in *On both sides of al-Mandab: Ethiopian, South-Arabic and Islamic studies presented to Oscar Löfgren on his ninetieth birthday*, Swedish Research Institute in Istanbul, *Transactions*, 2 (1989), 43; W. Madelung, 'The vigilante movement of Sahl b. Salāma al-Khurāsānī and the origins of Ḥanbalism reconsidered', *Journal of Turkish Studies*, 14 (1990), 331; van Ess, *Theologie*, 3:174.

175 The problem of the appropriate response to the Miḥna is never discussed by Ibn Ḥanbal in terms of *al-amr biʾl-maʿrūf* (see, for example, Ḥanbal, *Miḥna*, 40.2, 44.6, 78.9; cf. Abū Yaʿlā, *Amr*, f. 102b.17). Nor does Ibn Ḥanbal seem to feel any obligation to speak out against official heresy at the Friday prayer (cf. below, note 244).

rebellion was mooted in traditionist circles in Baghdad against the heretical zeal of al-Wāthiq (r. 227–32/842–7), Ibn Ḥanbal is described as strongly opposing this dangerous project.[176] Again, there is no indication of his involvement in the abortive rising that ensued under the leadership of Aḥmad ibn Naṣr al-Khuzāʿī in 231/846[177] – though he seems to have gone along with the view that Aḥmad died a martyr's death.[178] When times changed, he sought to maintain the same distance from the orthodox caliph al-Mutawakkil as he had from his heretical predecessors. Such official orthodoxy, though a blessing to the Muslims at large,[179] did little for Ibn Ḥanbal personally except to complicate his life by rendering him the target of unwanted attention and largesse.[180] As he told his worldly uncle Isḥāq with regard to the food and presents that al-Mutawakkil pressed on him and his family: 'If you didn't accept them, they'd leave you alone.'[181]

6. CONCLUSION

The responsa of Ibn Ḥanbal give us a remarkable picture of the duty of forbidding wrong as it was understood and practised in the early Ḥanbalite milieu. Indeed this picture is perhaps the most lively we can hope to paint for any pre-modern Islamic society. But it is not one that we should attempt to generalise to other places and times in the traditional Islamic

176 Ḥanbal, *Miḥna*, 81.8; Ibn Abī Yaʿlā, *Ṭabaqāt*, 1:144.22; Khallāl, *Musnad*, 21.15. What particularly incensed the *fuqahāʾ* was the proposal to indoctrinate schoolchildren with the dogma of the created Koran (as noted in van Ess, *Theologie*, 3:470, where the proposal has, however, become an accomplished fact). Ibn Ḥanbal urged them rather to condemn the heresy in their hearts (*ʿalaykum biʾl-nukra bi-qulūbikum*). Another account of what is probably the same incident is also given by Khallāl (*Musnad*, 21.6).

177 The fate of Aḥmad ibn Naṣr is mentioned in passing in Ḥanbal, *Miḥna*, 84.3.

178 Ibn Ḥanbal is quoted as commending Aḥmad ibn Naṣr for his self-sacrifice (Khaṭīb, *Taʾrīkh Baghdād*, 5:177.15, and Ibn Abī Yaʿlā, *Ṭabaqāt*, 1:81.14, both from Abū Bakr al-Marrūdhī), and cf. *ibid.*, 2:289.17; but Ibn Abī Yaʿlā makes no direct reference to the rising anywhere in his *tarjama* of Aḥmad ibn Naṣr, *ibid.*, 1:80–2). Ibn Ḥanbal likewise sees no harm in praying over the severed head of Aḥmad ibn Naṣr (ʿAbdallāh ibn Aḥmad, *Masāʾil*, 141 no. 524; in no. 523, he has confirmed that one prays over the body of a martyr).

179 For Ibn Ḥanbal's endorsement of the view that the accession of al-Mutawakkil was a great blessing for the Muslims, see his letter in Abū Nuʿaym, *Ḥilya*, 9:216.10. The change of caliphal policy was, however, neither precipitate nor unqualified (see C. Melchert, 'Religious policies of the caliphs from al-Mutawakkil to al-Muqtadir', *Islamic Law and Society*, 3 (1996), 320–30).

180 For these tribulations, see the account given by his cousin (Ḥanbal, *Miḥna*, 84–109).

181 *Ibid.*, 105.9. What does not quite emerge in Ḥanbal's account, though amply documented in that of Ibn Ḥanbal's son Ṣāliḥ, is the extreme bitterness of the family quarrel that erupted as a result of the partiality of the family for the blandishments of al-Mutawakkil (see the extensive citations in Abū Nuʿaym, *Ḥilya*, 9:212–15).

world. For all that many of its themes recur elsewhere, the milieu of the early Ḥanbalites retains its own distinctive hues.

What stands out is the low-profile character of Ibn Ḥanbal's conception of the duty. As we have seen, one keeps out of the way of the state, neither confronting nor coopting the ruler. In this sense Ibn Ḥanbal's doctrine is a deeply apolitical one. At the same time it is a distinctly civilian one – as we saw, one neither uses weapons nor confronts them. There is also the tendency to leave off if the offender does not listen, and to take refuge in performing the duty in the heart. These features have parallels in the doctrines of other schools, but they are rarely used to such consistent effect.

More startling is the existence in Khallāl's collection of a trend of thought which casts doubt on the very idea that forbidding wrong is a duty, or even denies it this standing altogether. Such outright denial never appears in the mouth of Ibn Ḥanbal himself, but it is transmitted from two earlier authorities, Ḥasan al-Baṣrī (d. 110/728)[182] and ʿAbdallāh ibn Shubruma (d. 144/761f.).[183] Both regard forbidding wrong as a supererogatory activity (*nāfila*). Ibn Ḥanbal is less categorical. Asked whether forbidding wrong is obligatory, he replies that in these evil days it is too burdensome (*shadīd*) to impose, especially in the light of the easement in the Prophetic tradition[184] – a clear reference to the possibility of performing the duty in the heart. On another occasion he betrays a similar sense of the corruption of the times, remarking that 'this is no time for forbidding'.[185] Such minor hesitations are also apparent in other things he says on the subject.[186]

One way to interpret this early Ḥanbalite quietism is in terms of the adaptation of an activist heritage to a civilian society for which political quietism was an increasingly relevant option.[187] But even in the civil society

182 No. *11; see above, ch. 4, note 224.

183 No. *24; see above, ch. 4, note 226.

184 No. 18.

185 No. 19 (*laysa hādhā zamān nahy*).

186 In no. 1, in the printed text, Ibn Ḥanbal has pronounced it obligatory to proceed against a music-maker; he then adds that if a man does so, merit (*faḍl*) accrues to him. As it stands, this is puzzling. But in J, Ibn Ḥanbal, on being asked whether it is obligatory to proceed, replies: 'I don't know what's obligatory; if he acts, merit accrues to him' (f. 1b.13); and this text is supported by a parallel version of the responsum (Abū Dāwūd, *Masāʾil*, 278.11). In no. 14, he trusts that performance 'in the heart' will suffice (contrast no. 13, where a similar statement is immediately qualified). In no. 25, he hopes that performance 'in the heart' will be enough, but adds that it is 'more meritorious' (*afḍal*) to proceed 'with the hand'. In no. 29, he is asked about performance 'with the hand'; his answer is that, if a man has the strength for it, 'there is no harm in it' (*lā baʾs bihi*). Of these traditions, all except no. 1 are general statements about the duty at large. All go better with the view that performance of the duty (other than in the heart) is in fact optional. Cf. also the negative attitude towards *al-amr biʾl-maʿrūf* ascribed in Muʿtazilite sources to the Ḥashwiyya (see, for example, below, ch. 12, notes 208f.).

187 Cf. M. Cook, 'Activism and quietism in Islam: the case of the early Murjiʾa', in A. S. Cudsi and A. E. H. Dessouki (eds.), *Islam and power*, London 1981, 21f. I have not in general

of Baghdad in his own day, Ibn Ḥanbal's stance was far from universal. As mentioned above, the year 201/817 saw the emergence of popular movements aiming to restore public order in the absence of effective authority.[188] At least three leaders were active, Khālid al-Daryūsh, Sahl ibn Salāma, and the young Aḥmad ibn Naṣr.[189] All three acted under the banner of forbidding wrong.[190] What is more, Khālid and Sahl were separated by a significant doctrinal difference regarding the duty. Khālid (who was clearly the less successful leader) categorically opposed performing it against the ruler, and indeed is said to have handed over some of the criminals he apprehended to the authorities[191] (or what there was of them). Sahl, by contrast, proposed to fight anyone who opposed Koran and Sunna, irrespective of whether he was a ruler or not[192] – a view which may well reflect a Muʿtazilite affiliation. As we have already seen, the caliph al-Ma'mūn (r. 198–218/813–33) is said to have been moved by these worrisome events to declare a ban on forbidding wrong (sc. by private individuals).[193] Thirty years later, the duty was again prominent (according to some accounts) in the ideology of the rising planned by Aḥmad ibn Naṣr.[194] Ibn Ḥanbal was not, then, solidly representative of the urban

sought to distinguish *political* quietism (i.e. quietism in relation to the state) from *social* quietism (i.e. quietism in relation to the surrounding society). The two naturally tend to go together; but they need not always do so. The distinction was pointed out to me by David Marmer, with the apt example of Khālid al-Daryūsh (see below, note 191).

188 See above, note 172. I have also benefited from a sharp analysis of two of these movements in a graduate paper written for me by David Marmer in 1989.

189 For the role of the latter, see Ṭabarī, *Ta'rīkh*, series III, 1344.8 (under the year 231; Ṭabarī here gives a cross-reference to his account of the year 201 which is not honoured in the text of his work as we have it); a quotation from Ṣūlī (d. 335/947) *apud* Khaṭīb, *Ta'rīkh Baghdād*, 5:176.9 (both cited in van Ess, *Theologie*, 3:471); Azdī (d. *c.* 334/945), *Ta'rīkh al-Mawṣil*, ed. ʿA. Ḥabība, Cairo 1967, 341.15 (I owe this reference to Nurit Tsafrir). The quotation from Ṣūlī is a favourite of later sources (Ibn al-Jawzī, *Muntaẓam*, ed. ʿAṭā, 11:165.13; Mizzī, *Tahdhīb*, 1:508.6; Dhahabī, *Siyar*, 11:167.7; Dhahabī, *Ta'rīkh al-Islām*, years 231–40, 56.3; Ibn Ḥajar, *Tahdhīb*, 1:87.11).

190 For Aḥmad ibn Naṣr, who went into action on the east bank in the name of *al-amr bi'l-maʿrūf*, see the references given in the preceding note. For Khālid's appeal on the same basis to his neighbours, his family and the people of his quarter (*maḥalla*), see Ṭabarī, *Ta'rīkh*, series III, 1009.11; for Sahl's similar appeal, first to his neighbours and the people of his quarter, then to the population at large, see *ibid.*, 1009.18, and cf. Ibn al-Faqīh (*fl.* late third/ninth century), *Buldān*, in *Baghdād: Madīnat al-Salām*, ed. Ṣ. A. al-ʿAlī, Baghdad and Paris n.d., 80.16 (referring to his cause as *inkār al-munkar*).

191 Ṭabarī, *Ta'rīkh*, series III, 1009.15, 1010.9. 192 *Ibid.*, 1010.11.

193 See above, ch. 4, 70f.

194 See the continuation of the quotation from Ṣūlī cited above, note 189; Azdī, *Ta'rīkh al-Mawṣil*, 178.3 (I owe this reference to Nurit Tsafrir); ʿIzz al-Dīn ibn al-Athīr (d. 630/1233), *Kāmil*, ed. C. J. Tornberg, Leiden 1851–76, 7:14.5; and Ibn Kathīr (d. 774/1373), *al-Bidāya wa'l-nihāya*, Cairo 1351–8, 10:304.1. But Ṭabarī in his account (*Ta'rīkh*, series III, 1343–50) makes no reference to *al-amr bi'l-maʿrūf* in the context of the year 231. See also Lapidus, 'The separation of state and religion', 381, and van Ess, *Theologie*, 2:388.

society he belonged to. There was nevertheless something in his apolitical life and doctrines that spoke to the needs of this society in its more prudent moods. What he represented, an imperfectly realised aspiration to lead a life apart from the state, can best be grasped against the background of his own immediate circumstances.

Ibn Ḥanbal is perhaps the only ordinary citizen of third/ninth-century Baghdad whose life we can place in its concrete surroundings.[195] He lived near the north-western limits of the city.[196] His street (*zuqāq*) was a cul-de-sac:[197] at the open end there was a gate (*bāb al-zuqāq*) which could be closed to exclude outsiders,[198] and at the inner end there was a cluster of four homes (*manāzil*) belonging to Ibn Ḥanbal and his family.[199] One was the home of his uncle Isḥāq ibn Ḥanbal (d. 253/867), where his cousin Ḥanbal ibn Isḥāq (d. 273/886) also lived;[200] it was separated from Ibn Ḥanbal's home by a wall.[201] Another was the home of his eldest son Ṣāliḥ (d. 266/880);[202] it likewise adjoined Ibn Ḥanbal's, and there was a gate linking the two homes.[203] A third belonged to Ibn Ḥanbal's second son ʿAbdallāh (d. 290/903).[204] These five were the only adult males in the

195 The account of these surroundings given in this paragraph derives from sources which refer mainly to the later years of his life.

196 Each time a child was born to Ibn Ḥanbal, a family friend nicknamed 'Būrān' (or 'Fūrān' – the variants suggest an Iranian original 'Pūrān', cf. F. Justi, *Iranisches Namenbuch*, Marburg 1895, 255), who lived nearby (see below, note 227), would go out and buy a present either at the Bridge (al-Qanṭara) or at Bāb al-Tibn (Ibn al-Jawzī, *Manāqib*, 303.15). The Bridge was local, as we learn from another reminiscence (*ibid.*, 263.8), so presumably the Bāb al-Tibn was also close by. This gate is well known, and marked the north-western limit of the city (see G. Le Strange, *Baghdad during the Abbasid caliphate*, Oxford 1900, 115, and Map V no. 15); the Bridge is accordingly likely to be the Qanṭarat Raḥā Umm Jaʿfar (*ibid.*, 113, and Map V, no. 13). I do not know what to make of the statement that the 'one-eyed Tigris' (Dijla al-ʿAwrā') was behind Ibn Ḥanbal's home (Ibn al-Jawzī, *Manāqib*, 20.10); this term belongs in the neighbourhood of Baṣra, not Baghdad, unless it is a synonym for the 'Upper Harbour' of Le Strange's map.

197 For the cul-de-sac as a feature of Arab cities in a later period (but not, surprisingly, of those of Iraq), see A. Raymond, *The great Arab cities in the 16th–18th centuries: an introduction*, New York and London 1984, 15f.

198 See Ḥanbal, *Miḥna*, 67.20; Dhahabī (d. 748/1348), *Tarjamat al-imām Aḥmad* (extracted from his *Ta'rīkh al-Islām*), ed. A. M. Shākir, n.p. 1946, 76.6, 77.4; and Abū Nuʿaym, *Ḥilya*, 9:176.11 (*bāb al-darb*). Presumably such gates were widespread, but they do not seem to have ensured security at night: Ibn Ḥanbal is against going out in response to a shout after dark (no. 109).

199 That Ibn Ḥanbal's home was at the far end of the street appears from an account quoted in Abū Nuʿaym, *Ḥilya*, 9:176.13.

200 See for example Ḥanbal, *Miḥna*, 88.8.

201 *Ibid.*, 100.13. Ḥanbal could hear Ibn Ḥanbal reciting the Koran on his roof (*ibid.*, 110.2), and he could overlook Ibn Ḥanbal's home from his own roof (*ibid.*, 87.2).

202 See, for example, *ibid.*, 88.8, 113.5.

203 Ibn Ḥanbal had the gate closed up during the family quarrel (Abū Nuʿaym, *Ḥilya*, 9:213.23), but the children first opened a peephole (*kuwwa*) in it (*ibid.*, 214.8), and finally got it open again (*ibid.*, 215.3). See also Ibn al-Jawzī, *Manāqib*, 216.2.

204 See Ibn al-Jawzī, *Manāqib*, 264.7, 302.13, 403.6, and cf. Dhahabī, *Tarjama*, 76.2.

family;[205] with the exception of Ibn Ḥanbal's slave-girl Ḥusn,[206] women and children tend to be referred to only in general terms.[207] Ibn Ḥanbal's home, though described as cramped,[208] seems to have been quite a ramified affair: it contained at least three chambers (*buyūt*), upper rooms (*ghuraf*), and roofs (*suṭūḥ*),[209] not to mention an entrance-hall (*dihlīz*)[210] and a well.[211] Members of the family might sit at the gates of their homes,[212] and would sleep on the roofs of their houses in summer.[213] The local mosque, where his uncle led the prayer, and he himself would teach, was at his gate;[214] but during the quarrel with his family, Ibn Ḥanbal ceased to attend it, and instead went to a mosque located outside his street.[215] Beyond the family circle were the neighbours.[216] One of them, as we have seen, was a malefactor who perished while in the hands of the authorities.[217] But several of them were connected with Ibn Ḥanbal's scholarly activities.[218] Unlike his uncle, Ibn Ḥanbal seems to have been on good terms with his neighbours,[219] and they were people with whom he felt some solidarity: at one point he dismissed the idea of going into hiding on the grounds that it would put his family and neighbours at risk.[220] Among them were tenants of his (*sukkān*).[221] Weavers appear as both

205 Ḥanbal, *Miḥna*, 102.3, 108.12. The death of an uncle named ʿAbdallāh must have taken place at an earlier date (Ṣāliḥ, *Sīra*, 37.4).
206 See for example Ḥanbal, *Miḥna*, 100.12; Dhahabī, *Tarjama*, 38.16, 39.3.
207 See for example Abū Nuʿaym, *Ḥilya*, 9:207.9 (cf. Ṣāliḥ *apud* Dūmī, *Aḥmad ibn Ḥanbal*, 298.17); Ḥanbal, *Miḥna*, 88.8, 102.4.
208 Ibn al-Jawzī, *Manāqib*, 249.19.
209 Ḥanbal, *Miḥna*, 88.6 (reading *manzil* for *manzilay*, as in the parallel texts in Dhahabī, *Tarjama*, 59.10, and Dhahabī, *Siyar*, 11:267.8, but discarding the reading *sarāb* for *buyūt* found there).
210 See Ibn al-Jawzī, *Manāqib*, 209.14, 291.2; Ibn Abī Yaʿlā, *Ṭabaqāt*, 1:186.15.
211 Abū Nuʿaym, *Ḥilya*, 9:179.17 (*biʾr*). Ṣāliḥ's house too had its well (*ibid.*, 207.9 = Ṣāliḥ *apud* Dūmī, *Aḥmad ibn Ḥanbal*, 298.18).
212 Ḥanbal, *Miḥna*, 99.12.
213 *Ibid.*, 87.1, and cf. Abū Nuʿaym, *Ḥilya*, 9:207.22 (= Ṣāliḥ *apud* Dūmī, *Aḥmad ibn Ḥanbal*, 299.12).
214 Abū Nuʿaym, *Ḥilya*, 9:176.15; see also Ibn al-Jawzī, *Manāqib*, 384.19, and cf. *ibid.*, 209.9. For his teaching in the mosque, see *ibid.*, 189.15.
215 Abū Nuʿaym, *Ḥilya*, 9:214.17; Ibn al-Jawzī, *Manāqib*, 384.18. Cf. also Ṣāliḥ, *Sīra*, 34.6.
216 One's neighbourhood (*jiwār*) is defined by Ibn Ḥanbal as thirty homes around one's own (ʿAbdallāh ibn Aḥmad, *Masāʾil*, 384 no. 1393).
217 See above, note 164.
218 See Ibn Abī Yaʿlā, *Ṭabaqāt*, 1:137.12, 301.19, 334.1, 415.15. The last of these entries relates to Ibn Bukhtān, a friend of the family who had a shop (*dukkān*) at the Bridge (Ibn al-Jawzī, *Manāqib*, 263.8).
219 *Ibid.*, 218.3, 218.17.
220 Ḥanbal, *Miḥna*, 37.5.
221 One, whom Ibn Ḥanbal ejected from his home for cohabiting with his divorced wife, has already been mentioned (see above, note 60). Another retrieved a pair of scissors which Ibn Ḥanbal had dropped into the well; in return, Ibn Ḥanbal forgave him three months rent for the shop (*ḥānūt*) (Abū Nuʿaym, *Ḥilya*, 9:179.17). On his death-bed, Ibn Ḥanbal sent Ṣāliḥ to one of the tenants in connection with a purchase of dates (*ibid.*, 220.10). That these tenants, or some of them, were not living in Ibn Ḥanbal's own home is clear from a reference to the 'home of the tenants' (*dār al-sukkān*) (Ibn al-Jawzī, *Manāqib*, 274.11; Dhahabī, *Siyar*, 11:209.11).

neighbours[222] and tenants,[223] emphasising the humble character of the neighbourhood.[224] Another neighbour ran a butcher's shop.[225] Somewhere nearby there was a bath-house which Ibn Ḥanbal did not patronise,[226] and the home of the family's closest friend;[227] but it is not clear whether these were located in Ibn Ḥanbal's own street or outside it, and we do not know how far, if at all, his 'quarter' (*maḥalla*) extended beyond his street.[228] The family was not well-off, and Ṣāliḥ, who had too many mouths to feed, found it particularly hard to make ends meet.[229] But both Ibn Ḥanbal and his uncle had some income from property (*ghalla*).[230]

There was little in this lifestyle to force Ibn Ḥanbal into the proximity of the state, other than the gratuitous location of his home in a capital city. He was an Arab,[231] and as such a member of what had once been a political and military aristocracy; but it was not an identity he gloried in, or even made mention of.[232] He had a link to the incumbent dynasty through his

222 When a child of Ibn Ḥanbal's went missing, he turned up in one of the weavers' homes (Ibn al-Jawzī, *Manāqib*, 209.11). Ḥusn sells the yarn she has spun to one of them (*ibid.*, 302.5).

223 This is implicit *ibid.*, 266.11; and compare *ibid.*, 404.17 with *ibid.*, 223.17.

224 For the low status of weavers, see R. Brunschvig, 'Métiers vils en Islam', *Studia Islamica*, 16 (1962), esp. 50–5.

225 Ibn Abī Ya'lā, *Ṭabaqāt*, 1:430.6; Ibn al-Jawzī, *Manāqib*, 302.1; Dhahabī, *Tarjama*, 39.7.

226 One winter's day he scheduled a visit, but thought better of it and cancelled it (Ṣāliḥ, *Sīra*, 42.1); he had not entered a bath-house for fifty years (Ibn al-Jawzī, *Manāqib*, 247.16). Cf. also Dhahabī, *Tarjama*, 25.7.

227 Būrān (see above, note 196) makes frequent, sometimes intimate, appearances in the life of the family (see, for example, Ṣāliḥ, *Sīra*, 52.7; Abū Nu'aym, *Ḥilya*, 9:213.4, 215.7). That his home was close by we learn from an account of how Ibn Ḥanbal hid there at one stage during the Miḥna (Ḥanbal, *Miḥna*, 84.3). See also Ibn Abī Ya'lā, *Ṭabaqāt*, 1:195f. (giving his death date as 256/870).

228 In one account we read that his quarter was surrounded and searched by the authorities at a time when he was under suspicion (Abū Nu'aym, *Ḥilya*, 9:176.18).

229 See, for example, *ibid.*, 213.20. Ḥanbal ibn Isḥāq was also a poor man (Ibn Abī Ya'lā, *Ṭabaqāt*, 1:143.12).

230 According to Ibn Kathīr, Ibn Ḥanbal received 17 dirhems per month in income (*ghalla*) from property (*milk*) (*Bidāya*, 10:337.9). Ibn Kathīr does not give his source, but a reference to *ghallat al-dār* appears in Ibn Ḥanbal's will, see Abū Nu'aym, *Ḥilya*, 9:213.6, and cf. Ibn Abī Ya'lā, *Ṭabaqāt*, 1:195.12. For other references to this income, see for example *ibid.*, 10.13, 260.9; Ibn al-Jawzī, *Manāqib*, 224.5, 264.1; Dhahabī, *Siyar*, 11:320.1. For Isḥāq's income, see Abū Nu'aym, *Ḥilya*, 9:214.14.

231 For his standard genealogy, see Ṣāliḥ, *Sīra*, 27.1; also Dhahabī, *Tarjama*, 9.2, with variants and scholarly commentary. The 'master of the bridge' (*ṣāḥib al-jisr*) identifies him (in Persian) as an Arab (*Tāzīk*) as he returns home from his flogging (Ḥanbal, *Miḥna*, 67.19).

232 Ibn 'Asākir, *Ta'rīkh*, 5:257.15, 258.1; see also Ibn Abī Ya'lā, *Ṭabaqāt*, 1:249.6; Ibn al-Jawzī, *Manāqib*, 274.19; Dhahabī, *Tarjama*, 12.12. Madelung holds a very different view on this point; to establish Ibn Ḥanbal's Arab sentiments, he quotes a passage from a creed attributed to Ibn Ḥanbal which displays strong animosity to Shu'ūbism (Madelung,

Khurāsānian background:[233] his grandfather Ḥanbal had served the ʿAbbāsid cause at the time of the revolution,[234] and his father too had belonged to the ʿAbbāsid army.[235] This connection was vigorously exploited by his worldly uncle Isḥāq in his attempts to extricate his nephew from the Miḥna,[236] but again it meant nothing to Ibn Ḥanbal himself. At his interrogation he found occasion to put to the caliph the rhetorical question: 'Commander of the Faithful, a call (*daʿwa*) after the call of Muḥammad, peace be upon him?'[237] What remained for him of the fusion of religion and politics that had brought the Islamic world into being was little more than a duty and a ritual.[238] The duty was to obey the caliph[239] – in any matter, that is, that did not involve disobedience to God.[240] But in normal times, this was not an obligation that intruded much into the life of a man such as Ibn Ḥanbal. The ritual was the Friday prayer,[241] the residue of an earlier epoch in which the Muslim community could physically gather together in one place. To participate in this ritual meant to leave one's own immediate neighbourhood and attend at the official cathedral mosque[242] – for Ibn Ḥanbal the Great Mosque built originally by the

Religious trends, 23, citing Ibn Abī Yaʿlā, *Ṭabaqāt*, 1:34.18; and see also *ibid.*, 30.17, from the same creed). It is of course true that he was no friend to the Shuʿūbiyya (cf. Isḥāq ibn Ibrāhīm, *Masāʾil*, 1:200 no. 992). But the creed in question is one whose ascription to Ibn Ḥanbal was vigorously rejected by Dhahabī (*Siyar*, 11:286.18, 303.3), and perhaps rightly so.

233 He had been brought from Marw in his mother's womb (Ṣāliḥ, *Sīra*, 26.2). He could speak Persian, as emerges from a reminiscence of his grandson Zuhayr ibn Ṣāliḥ (d. 303/915f.) regarding a visit Ibn Ḥanbal received from the son of a maternal aunt in Khurāsān (Dhahabī, *Tarjama*, 34.20). Cf. also Ḥanbal, *Miḥna*, 53.19.

234 See Madelung, *Religious trends*, 22, citing al-Khaṭīb al-Baghdādī, *Taʾrīkh Baghdād*, 4:415.11; also Dhahabī, *Tarjama*, 12.4.

235 He is said to have been a commander (*qāʾid*) (see Madelung, *Religious trends*, 22, and Ibn al-Jawzī, *Manāqib*, 19.14), and to have belonged to the army of Marw (Dhahabī, *Siyar*, 11:179.7).

236 Ḥanbal, *Miḥna*, 43.11. Cf. also Abū Nuʿaym, *Ḥilya*, 9:205.13 (quoting a highly suspect account, see below, ch. 6, note 6). 237 Ḥanbal, *Miḥna*, 47.8.

238 In principle we should add to these *jihād*; but the part it played in Ibn Ḥanbal's life was slight. There is a report that he engaged in it while visiting Tarsus (Dhahabī, *Siyar*, 11:311.9), and he showed concern for the *thughūr* (*ibid.*, 311.11, with reference to Qazwīn; Ibn al-Jawzī, *Manāqib*, 196.6, 384.13).

239 See, for example, the statements that Ibn Ḥanbal makes to the authorities when they raid his house (Ḥanbal, *Miḥna*, 87.13, 88.4; cf. Khallāl, *Musnad*, 1.5).

240 Khallāl, *Musnad*, 1.7 (*al-samʿ waʾl-ṭāʿa mā lam yuʾmar bi-maʿṣiya*).

241 The ʿAbbāsids, in his view, were the right people to lead it, see Khallāl, *Musnad*, 1.12; Ibn Abī Yaʿlā, *Ṭabaqāt*, 1:144.20; and cf. *ibid.*, 26.17, 294.21, 330.10, 344.20, 421.11. These statements also mention less frequent rituals at which the ruler had the right to officiate, notably the two festivals and the pilgrimage.

242 For an anecdote which places Ibn Ḥanbal at the *masjid al-jāmiʿ* on a Friday with his eldest son, see Ṣāliḥ, *Sīra*, 34.8. The way there lay along a major road (*ṭarīq*) (see ʿAbdallāh ibn Aḥmad, *Masāʾil*, 129 no. 474).

caliph al-Manṣūr (r. 136–58/754–75).[243] But there too the contact could be minimal. Even in the period when the state was actively heretical, with an adherent of its false doctrine leading the prayer, Ibn Ḥanbal would still participate in this communal ritual; but on returning home he would make good the deficiency by repeating the prayer in private.[244]

It was through no choice of Ibn Ḥanbal's that the state burst into his world and shattered its peace. First came what he called the 'religious ordeal' (*fitnat al-dīn*), in which he was imprisoned, interrogated and flogged for refusing to pay lip-service to heresy; then, after his home and those of his family had been raided and searched in the middle of the night, came the 'worldly ordeal' (*fitnat al-dunyā*), a more insidious threat, because the favours lavished on him at the caliphal court corrupted his own family.[245] In both, he said, he wished he were dead.[246] As he lamented bitterly: 'I've been spared these people for sixty years, and now at the end of my life I'm afflicted with them.'[247] After the caliph had allowed him to go home, he was still pestered by the comings and goings of benevolent officialdom.[248] Even death did not fully release him: at his funeral, the Ṭāhirid

[243] This is shown by a report which has him attend the cathedral mosque on a Friday and pray in the 'Cupola of the Poets' (*qubbat al-shuʿarāʾ*) (Ibn al-Jawzī, *Manāqib*, 289.8). As Sabari has shown (S. Sabari, *Mouvements populaires à Bagdad à l'époque ʿabbasside*, Paris 1981, 15), this cupola, which owed its name to the weekly gathering of poets that took place under it (Khaṭīb, *Taʾrīkh Baghdād*, 8:249.6), was located in the Jāmiʿ al-Manṣūr (*ibid.*, 12:95.22).

[244] Ḥanbal, *Miḥna*, 79.15 (cf. Ibn al-Jawzī, *Manāqib*, 159.10). In the days of the orthodox al-Mutawakkil, by contrast, he attended and did not repeat the prayer (Ḥanbal, *Miḥna*, 80.6). At a late stage in the Miḥna, he did in fact cease to attend the Friday prayer, but this was because he was in hiding (*ibid.*, 80.5), or had received official orders to stay at home (Abū Nuʿaym, *Ḥilya*, 9:207.1 = Ṣāliḥ *apud* Dūmī, *Aḥmad ibn Ḥanbal*, 298.9).

[245] During his visit to the court he described them as 'my ruin' (*āfatī*) (Abū Nuʿaym, *Ḥilya*, 9:212.6). The agonising details given by Ṣāliḥ of such matters as Isḥāq's deception of his nephew (*ibid.*, 214.1), and of his own relapse after a period of probity (*ibid.*, 215.6), remind one of stories of the destruction of families by drug addiction at the present day. There are reports to the effect that Ibn Ḥanbal explained away his unwillingness to accept the state's money (*māl al-sulṭān*) as arising only from personal scrupulousness (Ibn Abī Yaʿlā, *Ṭabaqāt*, 1:204.6, and Ibn al-Jawzī, *Manāqib*, 259.6). These are hard to square with the biographical data, and one of them (the first) is transmitted, most tendentiously, by al-Mutawakkil's vizier ʿUbayd Allāh ibn Yaḥyā ibn Khāqān (d. 263/877) (for whom see D. Sourdel, *Le vizirat ʿabbāside*, Damascus 1959–60, 274–86).

[246] Abū Nuʿaym, *Ḥilya*, 9:211.21. For the parallelism between the two ordeals, see also Ibn Abī Yaʿlā, *Ṭabaqāt*, 1:265.8.

[247] Abū Nuʿaym, *Ḥilya*, 9:209.24, and cf. *ibid.*, 207.23 = Ṣāliḥ *apud* Dūmī, *Aḥmad ibn Ḥanbal*, 302.15, 299.15.

[248] Thus on one occasion the caliph's emissary, Yaḥyā ibn Khāqān, arrives outside the street with a large retinue in the pouring rain; with a fine sense of theatre, he dismounts there and proceeds up the street on foot, wading through the puddles till he reaches Ibn Ḥanbal's gate (Abū Nuʿaym, *Ḥilya*, 9:219.10). This Yaḥyā was frequently sent by al-Mutawakkil to ask Ibn Ḥanbal about this and that (Ibn Abī Yaʿlā, *Ṭabaqāt*, 1:401.6). He was the father of the vizier mentioned above, note 245 (see Sourdel, *Le vizirat ʿabbāside*, 273f.).

governor of Baghdad pushed in to perform the prayer in place of Ibn Ḥanbal's own son.[249]

Ibn Ḥanbal stood for unhesitating obedience to the ruler, except in disobedience to God. Yet it was obedience without a shadow of warmth or a hint of a smile.[250] He was neither an activist opponent of the caliphs[251] nor a loyalist pledged to their support.[252] He was ready to render unto Caesar the things which were Caesar's;[253] beyond that, what he asked most of all was to be left alone, and in that lies a key to his doctrine of forbidding wrong.

But just as his contemporaries refused to leave him alone, so also posterity was to impose on him a role he had never sought: that of founder and leader of a well-defined and often aggressive religious community. The circumstances of this community were to vary significantly over space and time in the millennium after his death. But in one way or another, their effect was to erode the foundations of Ibn Ḥanbal's apolitical politics.

249 Ḥanbal, *Miḥna*, 112.3.

250 Thus he caused great offence at court by greeting the caliph's son al-Muʿtazz as he would have any other Muslim (Ḥanbal, *Miḥna*, 107.7).

251 Here I find myself in disagreement with Lapidus's view that Ḥanbalism was marked by militant opposition to the caliphate ('The separation of state and religion', 383; see also *ibid.*, 370).

252 Madelung has a rather different view of the early Ḥanbalites, seeing them as committed to the 'unquestioning backing of the established caliphate', and to the revival of the spirit of the heroic age of Khurāsānian *jihād* against the infidel (Madelung, *Religious trends*, 25; Madelung, 'The vigilante movement of Sahl b. Salāma', 336f.).

253 Ibn Ḥanbal was once asked by a tradesman whether he should do business with the army (*jund*). He responded by asking, with one of his rare smiles, where the *dirham* was struck – wasn't it in their abode (*fī dārihim*)? (Ibn Abī Yaʿlā, *Ṭabaqāt*, 1:52.7; cf. Matt. 22:20.)

CHAPTER 6

THE ḤANBALITES OF BAGHDAD

1. INTRODUCTION

When we turn from Ibn Ḥanbal (d. 241/855) to the later development of Ḥanbalism, we no longer have a body of normative material so close to the life of the streets. Instead, we find ourselves looking through two rather different windows. On the one hand, we have formal, even systematic accounts of the duty from the pens of major Ḥanbalite scholars.[1] These accounts rather awkwardly seek to straddle the gap between the heritage of Ibn Ḥanbal's responsa on the one hand, and a fashionably systematising intellectual style on the other. What we lose here is the original sense of immediacy in the relationship of principle to practice. The other window is historical. After a period in which the Ḥanbalites play little part in the history of Baghdad, they rather suddenly acquire notoriety as troublemakers through the exploits of Barbahārī (d. 329/941) and his contemporaries. This activity then continues to be documented through the Būyid domination (334–447/945–1055) and far into the Seljūq period (447–590/1055–1194).[2] It gradually recedes, however, with the emergence of close ties between the Ḥanbalites and the ʿAbbāsid state; this happy relationship then lasts until the demise of the caliphate in 656/1258. What we have is thus largely a record of high principles on the one hand, and high drama on the other; but we no longer hear much of the daily round of forbidding wrong.[3]

[1] I have benefited from some references to Ḥanbalite discussions of *al-amr bi'l-maʿrūf* collected in Laoust, *La profession de foi d'Ibn Baṭṭa*, 53 n.2.

[2] For a useful consolidated account of this activity, see Sabari, *Mouvements populaires*, ch. 4.

[3] The Ḥanbalite biographers tell us from time to time that a scholar was noted for his performance of the duty. Thus (1) Jaʿfar ibn Muḥammad al-Nasāʾī, a transmitter from Ibn Ḥanbal, is said to have been *ammār bi'l-maʿrūf, nahhāʾ ʿan al-munkar* (Ibn Abī Yaʿlā, *Ṭabaqāt*, 1:124.10, adding that he is reported to have met his death in Mecca in the course of this activity). Similar statements are made about the following: (2) Ibn Baṭṭa al-ʿUkbarī (d. 387/997) (*ibid.*, 2:144.17; Khaṭīb, *Taʾrīkh Baghdād*, 10:372.14; Ibn al-Jawzī,

In what follows I shall first sketch this changing record of Ḥanbalite practice, and then turn to contemporary Ḥanbalite theory. At the end of the chapter I shall take up the question how far it is plausible to relate the two.

2. ḤANBALITE PRACTICE

The relative quietism that characterises the original Ḥanbalite attitude to forbidding wrong may well have continued for several decades after the death of Ibn Ḥanbal.[4] It is true that in Ḥanbalite sources we find references to an angry and aggressive Ḥanbalite populace at the time of his death,[5] and, indeed, already at the time of the Miḥna.[6] But this picture has no

Manāqib, 517.13); (3) Abū 'l-Ḥasan al-ʿUkbarī (d. 468/1076) (Ibn Rajab, *Dhayl*, ed. Laoust and Dahan, 1:14.20); (4) Abū 'l-Qāsim ibn Manda al-Iṣbahānī (d. 470/1078) (Ibn al-Jawzī (d. 597/1201), *Muntaẓam*, Hyderabad 1357–61, 8:315.8; Dhahabī, *Siyar*, 18:352.2 (I owe this reference to Nurit Tsafrir); Dhahabī, *Tadhkira*, 1166.12); Ibn Rajab, *Dhayl*, ed. Laoust and Dahan, 1:34.10; (5) Ibn al-Qawwās (d. 476/1084) (Ibn Abī Yaʿlā, *Ṭabaqāt*, 2:244.18, and Ibn al-Jawzī, *Manāqib*, 523.16; also Ibn Rajab, *Dhayl*, ed. Laoust and Dahan, 1:51.5, where the statement is followed by an anecdote about his public reproof of a man he had seen going naked in the bath-house); (6) Jaʿfar ibn Ḥasan al-Darzījānī (d. 506/1112) (Ibn Abī Yaʿlā, *Ṭabaqāt*, 2:257.9, and Ibn Rajab, *Dhayl*, ed. Laoust and Dahan, 1:136.17, the latter making reference to his *maqāmāt mashhūda* in this connection); (7) Aʿazz al-Baghdādī (d. after 560/1164) (Ibn Rajab, *Dhayl*, ed. Fiqī, 1:331.4); (8) Ibn al-Muqābala al-Bāmāwardī (d. 571/1175) (*ibid.*, 335.5); (9) Isḥāq al-ʿAlthī (d. 634/1236) (*ibid.*, 2:205.4). But with the exception of the latter (for whom see below, notes 101f., 201f.), these notices offer little beyond the bare statement. A more colourful case is that of (10) Aḥmad ibn ʿAlī al-ʿAlthī (d. 503/1110), who in his youth was a decorator, and would forbid his fellow-craftsmen to make images; he gave up the trade after an episode in which, in performance of the duty, he smashed images in the home of some exalted personage (*baʿḍ al-salāṭīn*) (Ibn Abī Yaʿlā, *Ṭabaqāt*, 2:255.6; the story is adduced from Ibn Rajab in I. Goldziher, *Le livre de Mohammed ibn Toumert*, Algiers 1903, 90, where the *nisba* is misread). We possess a fragment of a diary kept by the Baghdādī Ḥanbalite Ibn al-Bannāʾ (d. 471/1079) which covers a bit over a year; he notes the deaths in 460/1068 of two otherwise unknown Ḥanbalites who, he remarks, used to forbid wrong (G. Makdisi, 'Autograph diary of an eleventh-century historian of Baghdād', *Bulletin of the School of Oriental and African Studies*, 18–19 (1956–7), 241 §15 = 252, 244 §26 = 255).

4 For a survey of Ḥanbalism in this period, see H. Laoust, 'Le hanbalisme sous le califat de Bagdad', *Revue des Etudes Islamiques*, 27 (1959), 74–81.

5 See Ibn al-Jawzī, *Manāqib*, 418.5 (referring to Ibn Ḥanbal's funeral); *ibid.*, 503.15, and Ibn Abī Yaʿlā, *Ṭabaqāt*, 1:15.9 (for the period following his death).

6 The most dramatic of these accounts is transmitted from one Aḥmad ibn al-Faraj: people took up arms when Ibn Ḥanbal was taken to be examined, and were treated to a rousing speech of victory by their hero on his release (Abū Nuʿaym, *Ḥilya*, 9:204–6, esp. 204.11, 206.6). This account has rightly been called in question by Jadʿān (*Miḥna*, 151; and cf. Dhahabī's critical comments on another story of the Miḥna told by the same Aḥmad ibn al-Faraj, *Tarjama*, 52.17). For other accounts featuring at least the threat of popular violence, see Ibn al-Jawzī, *Manāqib*, 340.7, 340.15; Ibn Abī Yaʿlā, *Ṭabaqāt*, 1:240.6; Ibn al-Murtaḍā (d. 840/1437), *Ṭabaqāt al-Muʿtazila*, ed. S. Diwald-Wilzer, Wiesbaden 1961, 124.2. Töllner in his assessment of the Miḥna relies heavily on these accounts (H. Töllner, *Die türkischen Garden am Kalifenhof von Samarra*, Walldorf-Hessen 1971, 34–6, drawn to my attention by Matthew Gordon).

support from the earliest biographies of Ibn Ḥanbal,[7] and in any case the sources record no comparable incidents in the decades that follow.[8] The historical sources for this period make no mention of a Ḥanbalite role in the politics of Baghdad till near the end of the third/ninth century. Yet by the early fourth/tenth century, Ḥanbalite violence was rampant on the streets of Baghdad. This muscular Ḥanbalism was already noted by Goldziher, who spoke caustically but aptly of an evolution from an *ecclesia pressa* to an *ecclesia militans*, with a penchant for 'fanatical terrorism'.[9]

As it appears in our sources, the new style of Ḥanbalite politics is closely linked to the career of the preacher and demagogue Barbahārī (d. 329/941).[10] He is mentioned as the leader of the Ḥanbalites, and indeed of the Sunnī populace of Baghdad at large, as early as 296/908.[11] A few examples may serve to illustrate the range and character of this Ḥanbalite activism. When the celebrated scholar Abū Jaʿfar al-Ṭabarī died in 310/923, it is said that he had to be buried at night because the populace, apparently Ḥanbalite, prevented a public funeral, accusing him of Shīʿism (*rafḍ*).[12] In 317/929f., a serious riot took place between the Ḥanbalites and their opponents over a contentious point of Koranic interpretation[13] – and one that we know to have been dear to the heart of Barbahārī.[14] By

[7] In Ḥanbal's account, his cousin's Miḥna draws a large crowd – so much so that the markets are closed (Ḥanbal, *Miḥna*, 67.3); but the crowd is not portrayed as a violent one. In general, early Ḥanbalite sources do not in my experience support Madelung's view that proto-Ḥanbalism was 'a militant movement attempting to rule the streets' ('The vigilante movement of Sahl b. Salāma', 336).

[8] We are told that when Ibn Ḥanbal's disciple Abū Bakr al-Marrūdhī (d. 275/888) went on *jihād*, he involuntarily acquired a following which was estimated at 50,000 by the time he reached Sāmarrā' (Khaṭīb, *Ta'rīkh Baghdād*, 4:424.9; Ibn Abī Yaʿlā, *Ṭabaqāt*, 1:57.22); but there is no indication of any such support coming into play in the internal politics of Baghdad. Conversely, there is no lack of popular disturbances in this period (see Sabari, *Mouvements populaires*, 58–61, 62, 69), but no indication of a Ḥanbalite role in them.

[9] I. Goldziher, review of Patton, *Aḥmed ibn Ḥanbal and the Miḥna*, in *Zeitschrift der Deutschen Morgenländischen Gesellschaft*, 52 (1898), 158.

[10] For Barbahārī see Laoust, *Profession*, xxxiii–xli (summarized in his article 'Barbahārī' in *EI*[2]); Sabari, *Mouvements populaires*, 104–6; J. L. Kraemer, *Humanism in the Renaissance of Islam: the cultural revival during the Buyid age*, Leiden 1986, 61f. The select references to the primary sources in what follows are mostly to be found in these studies.

[11] Ibn al-Athīr, *Kāmil*, 8:12.6. Ibn al-Athīr gives him a divergent name (as opposed to *nisba*). The context is the attempted coup in which Ibn al-Muʿtazz lost his life; neither Ṭabarī nor Ibn al-Jawzī mention Barbahārī in their accounts of this event.

[12] Miskawayh (d. 421/1030), *Tajārib al-umam*, ed. H. F. Amedroz, Cairo 1914–16, 1:84.19 (speaking of the *ʿāmma*); Ibn al-Athīr, *Kāmil*, 8:98.3 (identifying the *ʿāmma* as the Ḥanbalites, and providing a further motivation for their hostility); but cf. the sceptical comments of F. Rosenthal, *General introduction*, in *The History of al-Ṭabarī*, vol. 1, Albany 1989, 77f.

[13] Ibn al-Athīr, *Kāmil*, 8:157.22; and see Rosenthal, *General introduction*, 74.

[14] Laoust, *Profession*, lxxix n. 187, citing Ibn Abī Yaʿlā, *Ṭabaqāt*, 2:43.20. The question in dispute is what God means by telling the Prophet: 'It may be that thy Lord will raise thee up to a laudable station (*maqāman maḥmūdan*)'(Q17:79). The Ḥanbalite view was that

323/935, Barbahārī was unquestionably a powerful man; the caliph himself was appalled at the number of his followers, brought to his notice by their lusty response to their leader's sneeze.[15] There could hardly be a more poignant contrast to Ibn Ḥanbal's dislike of being followed by anyone in the street.[16] Barbahārī and his followers zealously applied their power to taking action against innovators.[17] Or as unsympathetic accounts describe it, the Ḥanbalites went wild: they plundered shops,[18] raided the homes of military leaders and others to search for liquor, singing-girls or musical instruments, challenged men and women seen walking together in public,[19] and fomented ugly assaults on Shāfiʿites.[20] The chief of police responded by ordering that no two followers of Barbahārī might gather together in one place, and by making a good number of arrests.[21] The caliph himself then issued a decree threatening the Ḥanbalites with fire and sword if their misdeeds continued.[22] Yet the Ḥanbalites are again referred

on the day of the resurrection, God would place Muḥammad beside Him on His throne (Laoust, *Profession*, 113 n.1). Laoust draws attention to the extensive material on this Ḥanbalite shibboleth collected by Khallāl (*Musnad*, 60–99). This material reveals the earlier history of the controversy in Ḥanbalite circles. Whereas there is no indication that Ibn Ḥanbal himself was exercised by the issue, Ḥanbalite scholars of the following generation were outraged by the heretical views put about in Baghdad by a certain Tirmidhī (for the chronology, see Ahmed's comments in his edition of Khallāl's *Musnad*, 66 n. 1; the absence of any attempt to place the outrage of the disciples in the mouth of the master is, incidentally, a strong indication of the authenticity of Ibn Ḥanbal's responsa). The dispute flared up again in Tarsus in 292/904f. (*ibid.*, 68.14), at a time when it had died down in Baghdad (*ibid.*, 75.16). At an unspecified date, Ṭabarī is reported to have been involved in an unpleasant confrontation with the Ḥanbalites over this question; in the course of it, his house was pelted with enormous numbers of stones (*ḥijāra*) (see I. Goldziher, *Die Richtungen der islamischen Koranauslegung*, Leiden 1920, 94, 101f., with references; the account is a little suspect, if only because Baghdādī sources would speak of throwing mud bricks (*ājurr*), not stones). The whole issue has now been discussed at some length by Rosenthal (*General introduction*, 71–7, with a translation of part of Ṭabarī's commentary on the verse, *ibid.*, 149–51), and still more recently by Gilliot (C. Gilliot, *Exégèse, langue, et théologie en Islam: l'exégèse coranique de Tabari*, Paris 1990, 249–54) and van Ess (*Theologie*, 2:642f.). However, van Ess's view that the issue arose in the lifetime of Ibn Ḥanbal is not supported by the texts he cites; and his identification of the hated Tirmidhī with the respected Sunnī traditionist Abū Ismāʿīl al-Tirmidhī (d. 280/893) is hardly plausible; the latter was held in high esteem by Khallāl himself (Khaṭīb, *Taʾrīkh Baghdād*, 2:44.12), and was buried beside the grave of Ibn Ḥanbal (*ibid.*, 44.16).

15 For this sneeze and its repercussions, see Ibn Abī Yaʿlā, *Ṭabaqāt*, 2:44.16; also Hamadhānī (d. 521/1127), *Takmilat Taʾrīkh al-Ṭabarī*, ed. A. Y. Kanʿān, Beirut 1959, 113.15.

16 Ibn al-Jawzī, *Manāqib*, 282.14.

17 Ibn Abī Yaʿlā, *Ṭabaqāt*, 2:44.15.

18 Ṣūlī (d. 335/947), *Akhbār al-Rāḍī bi'llāh wa'l-Muttaqī lillāh*, ed. J. Heyworth Dunne, Cairo 1935, 65.4 (= trans. M. Canard, Algiers 1946–50, 1:114).

19 Ibn al-Athīr, *Kāmil*, 8:229.22. If they did not get a satisfactory answer, they beat the offender and handed him over to the chief of police.

20 *Ibid.*, 230.7.

21 Miskawayh, *Tajārib*, 1:322.1; and cf. Hamadhānī, *Takmilat Taʾrīkh al-Ṭabarī*, 113.12. The latter also mentions Ḥanbalite arson in the Shīʿite quarter of Karkh (*ibid.*, 115.4).

22 Miskawayh, *Tajārib*, 1:322.4. This decree shows Ḥanbalite opposition to the visiting of (ʿAlid) tombs (*qubūr al-aʾimma*) to have been one cause of the trouble (*ibid.*, 322.13).

to as a public nuisance in 327/939, when the chief of police was once more in action against them,[23] and again in 329/941.[24] In anecdotal references to the time of Barbahārī, Tanūkhī (d. 384/994) describes how the Ḥanbalites harassed pilgrims seeking to visit Karbalāʾ,[25] and tried to prevent the practice of mourning (*nawḥ*) for Ḥusayn and the family of the Prophet – it could be done only with official protection or in secret.[26] Barbahārī's Ḥanbalites were thus a serious problem for the police, and a tribulation for Baghdādīs who did not share their values.

Ḥanbalite activism no doubt continued through the Būyid period (334–447/945–1055), despite a lack of explicit attestation. Būyid Baghdad was the scene of repeated clashes between the Sunnī and Shīʿite populations of the city,[27] and it is more than likely that the Ḥanbalites played a central role in this conflict.[28] Confrontation between Sunnīs and Shīʿites did not, of course, end with the passing of the Būyids; it is enough to note that it remained a feature of the politics of Baghdad to the fall of the ʿAbbāsid caliphate.[29]

In the early Seljūq period there is also abundant evidence of Ḥanbalite activism on other fronts. Much energy was directed against time-honoured forms of moral turpitude.[30] In 461/1069, for example, a Ḥanbalite diarist of Baghdad records that Ibn Sukkara, a prominent Sharīf who seems to have belonged to the Ḥanbalite community, raided two groups in the neighbourhood of the caliphal palace (one unidentifiable, the other a Beduin delegation); he smashed musical instruments and poured out

23 Ṣūlī, *Akhbār*, 135.15 (= trans. Canard, 1:205f.).
24 Ṣūlī, *Akhbār*, 198.16 (= trans. Canard, 2:19).
25 Tanūkhī (d. 384/994), *Nishwār al-muḥāḍara*, ed. ʿA. al-Shāljī, Beirut 1971–3, 2:231.20.
26 *Ibid.*, 233.6. Barbahārī here orders his followers to seek out and kill a particularly fine performer of this art (*nāʾiḥa*).
27 H. Laoust, 'Les agitations religieuses à Baghdād aux IVe et Ve siècles de l'Hégire', in D. S. Richards (ed.), *Islamic civilisation 950–1150*, Oxford 1973, 170–5 (for the period from 381/991); Sabari, *Mouvements populaires*, 106–12.
28 Cf. Makdisi, *Ibn ʿAqīl*, 325 n. 1, and the discussion of Ḥanbalite numbers below, notes 48f.
29 See Sabari, *Mouvements populaires*, 119f. (to 488/1095); also Laoust, 'Agitations', 177, 181, 184 (to 485/1092). A few examples must suffice for the subsequent period. Ibn al-Athīr describes a flare-up of violence between quarters in 509/1115f. (*Kāmil*, 10:360.20; that the conflict was between Sunnīs and Shīʿites is strongly suggested by the more elaborate account he gives of the freakish peace of 502/1109, *ibid.*, 329.4). He describes a major conflict between the Shīʿite population of Karkh and the (Sunnī) population of the Bāb al-Baṣra quarter in 569/1173f. (*ibid.*, 11:271.12), and another in 581/1185f. (*ibid.*, 344.16), although Hartmann suggests a reduction in the level of conflict between the communities under the rule of the caliph al-Nāṣir (r. 575–622/1180–1225) (A. Hartmann, *an-Nāṣir li-Dīn Allāh*, Berlin and New York 1975, 196). Pseudo-Ibn al-Fuwaṭī (d. 723/1323) describes a pair of such conflicts in 653/1255 (*al-Ḥawādith al-jāmiʿa*, Baghdad 1351, 276.9; for this work, see *EI*², art. 'Ibn al-Fuwaṭī' (F. Rosenthal)).
30 Sabari, *Mouvements populaires*, 112–14; also Laoust, 'Agitations', 180.

liquor.[31] This, at least, was Ibn Sukkara's account of his exploits. Some of his victims, however, complained to the caliph that the Sharīf and his associates had attacked their houses and violated their privacy, when in fact, they claimed, they had no liquor in their possession. To this Ibn Sukkara retorted that he had actually seen the wrong (*munkar*) he had acted against[32] (sc. before he entered their homes). The matter caused a considerable stir, with responsa flying on the question whether Ibn Sukkara owed his victims compensation (*ḍamān*) for the instruments he had destroyed.[33] Then, in 464/1072, a younger Ḥanbalite scholar, Abū Saʿd al-Baqqāl (d. 506/1112), came upon a singing-girl who had just been performing for a Turk. Undeterred by the military connection, he grabbed her lute and cut its strings; she went back and complained to the Turk, who retaliated by raiding Abū Saʿd's home.[34] The incident had repercussions which will concern us shortly.

Alongside this activity against sin in the early Seljūq period, there was also a struggle with heresy in the guise of Ashʿarism, now prominent in Baghdad thanks to the patronage of the Seljūq vizier Niẓām al-Mulk (d. 485/1092).[35] Thus the same diarist records that in 461/1068 the same Ibn Sukkara took in hand the unseating of a provocative Ashʿarite preacher and the smashing of his chair (*kursī*).[36] But a more prominent role was played in this struggle by the Sharīf Abū Jaʿfar (d. 470/1077).[37] Makdisi aptly describes him as the 'exemple type' of the Ḥanbalite activist.[38] A great zealot against wrong (*munkar*) in general and heresy in particular, he had the backing of a group of companions who were not easily brushed aside.[39]

[31] Makdisi, 'Autograph diary', 281 §108 = 292. For the religious affiliation of Ibn Sukkara, cf. Makdisi, *Ibn ʿAqīl*, 335.

[32] Makdisi, 'Autograph diary', 282 §110 = 293. Note that Ibn Sukkara seems to have gone beyond the call of duty even on his own admission by ripping up tambourines (for *ḥaraqa* read *kharaqa*, see above, ch. 5, note 99) – unless, of course, he took an unusually negative view of them. At least one later Ḥanbalite scholar, ʿAbd al-Mughīth al-Ḥarbī (d. 583/1187), considered them to be prohibited even at weddings (Ibn Rajab, *Dhayl*, ed. Fiqī, 1:357.21), and ʿAbd al-Ghanī al-Maqdisī (d. 600/1203) is also said to have regarded them as forbidden (*ibid.*, 2:13.18). For an authoritative statement of the mainstream Ḥanbalite view that they are permitted, see Ibn Qudāma, *Mughnī*, 9:174.3.

[33] Makdisi, 'Autograph diary', 282f. §111, §115 = 293f. On compensation, cf. above, ch. 5, note 99.

[34] Ibn al-Jawzī, *Muntaẓam*, 8:272.10. This incident was already noted by Goldziher from a later source (I. Goldziher, 'Zur Geschichte der ḥanbalitischen Bewegungen', *Zeitschrift der Deutschen Morgenländischen Gesellschaft*, 62 (1908), 18 n.2).

[35] For a survey of this confrontation, see Makdisi, *Ibn ʿAqīl*, 340–75; also Laoust, 'Agitations', 178–84, and Sabari, *Mouvements populaires*, 114–18. My references to primary sources in what follows are mostly found in these studies.

[36] Makdisi, 'Autograph diary', 14f. §57 = 30f.

[37] For his career, see Makdisi, *Ibn ʿAqīl*, 240–8; also Laoust, *Profession*, civ–cviii.

[38] Makdisi, *Ibn ʿAqīl*, 240. [39] So Ibn Abī Yaʿlā, *Ṭabaqāt*, 2:238.6.

During the major Ḥanbalite–Ashʿarite disturbances of 469/1077, we find him and his companions defending their mosque against an Ashʿarite force, routing the attackers with a barrage of mud bricks.[40] When the caliph later sought to make peace between the contending parties, the Sharīf refused his overtures; conflicts of interest, he explained, can be patched up, but conflicts of doctrine, where the parties declare each other infidels, cannot be.[41] In 470/1078, after the death of the Sharīf, the conflict was renewed: an Ashʿarite preacher insulted the Ḥanbalites in a market-place, and was hit by a mud brick for his pains. (The mud brick was to the medieval inhabitants of Baghdad what the stone is to the geologically better endowed populations of the western Fertile Crescent.) The incident led to extensive fighting between quarters, and to the involvement of the military.[42] These hostilities between Ḥanbalism and Ashʿarism continued into the following century and beyond.[43] They upstaged, but did not end, the older Ḥanbalite conflict with Muʿtazilism.[44] Thus in 456/1064, a group of 'companions of ʿAbd al-Ṣamad' attacked a leading Muʿtazilite scholar of Baghdad on his home ground; after insulting and wounding him, they fled when his cries seemed likely to rouse the neighbourhood.[45]

This record suggests that the Ḥanbalites of the fourth/tenth and fifth/eleventh centuries were in no great awe of the state – though there seems to be only one case in which they actually repudiated their allegiance to it.[46] But if they were no longer appalled to find themselves in

[40] Ibn al-Jawzī, *Muntaẓam*, 8:305.19. [41] *Ibid.*, 306.21. [42] *Ibid.*, 312.16.

[43] In 521/1127f., for example, there were considerable commotions arising from the activities of an Ashʿarite preacher (Ibn al-Jawzī, *Muntaẓam*, 10:6.1); at one point he encountered a hail of bricks (or so I understand *rujima* in this context) and animal corpses in the market-place (*ibid.*, 6.13; a Ḥanbalite involvement in the disturbances of this year is explicit, *ibid.*, 6.16). These events were already recounted by Goldziher from a later source ('Zur Geschichte der ḥanbalitischen Bewegungen', 15f.). In 561/1165f. there were new troubles between Ḥanbalites and Ashʿarites, again brought on by a hostile preacher (Sibṭ ibn al-Jawzī (d. 654/1257), *Mirʾāt al-zamān*, vol. 8, Hyderabad 1951–2, 262.15). Six years later the Ashʿarite preacher Abū ʾl-Muẓaffar al-Barruwī (d. 567/1172) was reputed to have been poisoned by the Ḥanbalites because of his fanatical hostility towards them (*ibid.*, 292.8; this story too was known to Goldziher from a later source, see 'Zur Geschichte der ḥanbalitischen Bewegungen', 14). In the next century the Ḥanbalite ʿAbd al-Laṭīf ibn ʿAlī al-Baghdādī (d. 647/1249) was interrogated and put in prison for manifesting his adherence to traditionalist theology (Ibn Rajab, *Dhayl*, ed. Fiqī, 2:247.12).

[44] See Makdisi, *Ibn ʿAqīl*, 327–40; also Laoust, 'Agitations', 179f., and Sabari, *Mouvements populaires*, 114f.

[45] Ibn al-Jawzī, *Muntaẓam*, 8:235.23. For this traditionalist vigilante group and its exploits on this and other occasions, see Makdisi, *Ibn ʿAqīl*, 332–7. The group, though named after a well-known Shāfiʿite of the previous century, seems to have included Ḥanbalites among its members.

[46] Sabari adduces an account of the events of 464/1072 which culminates in a scene in which the Sharīf Abū Jaʿfar and his followers repudiate their allegiance to the caliph (*Mouvements populaires*, 112f., based on Sibṭ ibn al-Jawzī (d. 654/1257), *Mirʿāt al-zamān*, ms. Paris,

confrontation with the state, they were also, by the middle of the fifth/eleventh century, more willing to seek its cooperation in the duty of forbidding wrong. In 464/1072, as we saw, Abū Saʿd al-Baqqāl got himself into trouble by smashing a lute whose owner was dangerously well connected; the Ḥanbalites then gathered to consider what should be done. But instead of continuing with direct action, they addressed themselves to the caliph, demanding that he take measures against the brothels (*mawākhīr*), prostitutes (*mufsidāt*) and liquor-sellers. The caliph did what he could to comply – the problem being that the brothels were under the protection of the Seljūq governor of the city.[47] In this instance at least, the Ḥanbalites were prepared to take the state seriously as an agency for the performance of the duty.

This picture of Ḥanbalite activism in the fourth/tenth and fifth/eleventh centuries is in sharp contrast to the attitudes of Ibn Ḥanbal himself. How are we to explain the difference? It is not difficult to suggest the outline of an explanation. Two major changes had taken place in the circumstances of the Ḥanbalite community in Baghdad.

First, there were now many more Ḥanbalites. The geographer Muqaddasī in the second half of the fourth/tenth century tells us that Ḥanbalites and Shīʿites predominated in the population of the city,[48] and a century later the Shāfiʿite Niẓām al-Mulk allegedly conceded the Ḥanbalite predominance.[49] Modern scholars have followed suit.[50] The Ḥanbalites are thus likely to have derived increased confidence from their numbers. At the same time, some part of the Ḥanbalite expansion must have taken place through the

Bibliothèque Nationale, Arabe 1,506, f. 136a.11; for the events of this year, see also the following note). This remarkable incident does not seem to be cited by other scholars who have written on this period.

47 Ibn al-Jawzī, *Muntaẓam*, 8:272.13; and see Makdisi, *Ibn ʿAqīl*, 152f. Such action by the authorities was not entirely isolated; for example it recurred in 467/1075 (Ibn al-Jawzī, *Muntaẓam*, 8:293.24), 478/1085f. (*ibid.*, 9:17.9), and 479/1086 (*ibid.*, 26.6). In the first case the *muḥtasib* was involved. For two instances of Ḥanbalite exhortations to the authorities to forbid wrong in 461/1069, see Makdisi, 'Autograph diary', 284f. §126 = 296, 287 §130 = 298f.

48 Muqaddasī (*fl.* second half of the fourth/tenth century), *Aḥsan al-taqāsīm*, ed. M. J. de Goeje, Leiden 1906, 126.5. Compare also the statement of Ibn al-Athīr, in the context of the burial of Ṭabarī, that the number of Ḥanbalites in Baghdad was uncountably large (*Kāmil*, 8:98.12).

49 Ibn al-Jawzī, *Muntaẓam*, 8:312.9, translated in Makdisi, *Ibn ʿAqīl*, 365. The statement forms part of a letter which, if genuine, dates from the events of 469–70/1077–8 (*ibid.*, 366). In another letter, Niẓām al-Mulk speaks of the large numbers of the Ḥanbalites in Baghdad (*kathrat ʿadadihim fī tilka ʾl-buqʿa*, Sibṭ ibn al-Jawzī, *Mirʾāt*, ms. Paris, f. 169a.8, translated in Makdisi, *Ibn ʿAqīl*, 360).

50 *Ibid.*, 325 n. 1, 368; Laoust, 'Agitations', 179; W. Madelung, 'The spread of Māturīdism and the Turks', in *Actas do IV congresso de estudos árabes e Islâmicos, Biblos*, 46 (1970), 110 n. 3.

absorption of other traditionalist and popular circles of the third/ninth century, circles among which more activist dispositions had been in evidence – witness the events of 201/817 and 231/846.[51] Thus the make-up of the Ḥanbalite community had changed. We are told that a lower-class follower of Barbahārī once happened to pass by a heretic after drinking too much. The heretic was unwise enough to exclaim in disgust: 'These Ḥanbalites!' The drunk then turned back and explained to the heretic that there were three classes of Ḥanbalites: ascetics; scholars; and a third class, who slapped opponents like the heretic. He then proceeded to demonstrate his membership of the third class.[52] Though we might wish for a more sober analysis of the social character of Ḥanbalism, it is clear that the Ḥanbalites had become both more numerous and more violent.

Secondly, the state was now weaker. Early Ḥanbalism had taken shape in the metropolis of an empire. In the fourth/tenth and fifth/eleventh centuries, by contrast, the caliphate was a third-rate state whose powers were extensively, though unevenly, usurped by military regimes – those established by its own generals, by the Būyids, and finally by the Seljūqs. This meant two things. On the one hand, the caliphal state became less formidable, while the bifurcation of power provided endless opportunities for political manoeuvring by elements of Baghdādī society.[53] And on the other hand, a certain bond was established between the Ḥanbalites and the caliphate: they needed each other in the face of local Shīʿites and alien military rulers.[54] It is thus not hard to see how the Ḥanbalites could have lost a great deal of respect for political authority, and yet developed a new warmth towards the caliphate – their caliphate. Both these tendencies come together in an observation which Ibn al-Baqqāl (d. 440/1048) saw fit to make in the caliphal assembly (*dīwān*): the caliphate is like a tent with the Ḥanbalites as its ropes – if the ropes fail, the tent collapses.[55]

One instance of this rapprochement was the public alignment of the caliphate with traditionalist doctrine that marked the later part of the reign of al-Qādir (r. 381–422/991–1031) and that of his successor al-Qāʾim

[51] See above, ch. 5, notes 172–4, 177f., 188–94.

[52] Ibn Abī Yaʿlā, *Ṭabaqāt*, 2:43.16.

[53] This is a recurrent theme in the history of the period (see, for example, Sabari, *Mouvements populaires*, 108, and Makdisi, *Ibn ʿAqīl*, 363).

[54] The question arises whether improving relations between the Ḥanbalite elite and the authorities widened the gap between this elite and the Ḥanbalite masses. The opening up of such a gap is claimed by Glassen (see E. Glassen, *Der mittlere Weg: Studien zur Religionspolitik und Religiosität der späteren Abbasiden-Zeit*, Wiesbaden 1981, 61, 113, and cf. also 98f., 101); and she adduces sources which indeed attest the existence of a certain alienation of elite from masses in the late fifth/eleventh century (see especially Ibn Rajab, *Dhayl*, ed. Laoust and Dahan, 1:30.3, on an incident of 470/1077, and Ibn al-Jawzī, *Muntaẓam*, 9:48.9, on the disorders of 482/1089).

[55] Ibn Abī Yaʿlā, *Ṭabaqāt*, 2:190.1; see Makdisi, *Ibn ʿAqīl*, 297.

(r. 422–67/1031–75).[56] There is specific evidence for a Ḥanbalite role in a reaffirmation of the 'Qādirī creed' under al-Qā'im,[57] and for subsequent Ḥanbalite identification with it.[58]

Another indication of the change can be seen in Ḥanbalite attitudes towards state employment. Ibn Ḥanbal, of course, was against it. When a man burdened by debt asked him if he should pay off what he owed by entering the service of the authorities (*hā'ulā'*), the answer was negative; after all, he would not actually die of debt.[59] A commentator as late as Ibn ʿAqīl (d. 513/1119) still regarded the taking of public office as untypical of Ḥanbalite scholars, in contrast to their Ḥanafī and Shāfiʿite peers.[60] Yet here too there are indications of change. One case in point is the office of judge. Ibn Ḥanbal himself, of course, would not even consider such office,[61] and when a group of judges came to visit him on his death-bed, they were not admitted.[62] His elder son Ṣāliḥ (d. 266/880) had his father's principles but the morals of an ordinary mortal; he wept with shame when debt and too large a family forced him to don the black uniform of the ʿAbbāsid establishment[63] and take office as judge of Iṣbahān – what would his father think of him if he could see him now?[64] By contrast, there were no tears when Abū Yaʿlā ibn al-Farrā' (d. 458/1066) accepted the office in Baghdad. Naturally he refused until pressed, and stipulated various conditions, but in the manner of a man who knows a topos when he enacts one;[65] Ḥanbalite

[56] For the emergence and promulgation of the 'Qādirī creed' (*al-iʿtiqād al-Qādirī*), see Makdisi, *Ibn ʿAqīl*, 299–310.

[57] *Ibid.*, 346, citing Ibn Abī Yaʿlā, *Ṭabaqāt*, 2:197.17, on the role of Abū Yaʿlā ibn al-Farrā' (d. 458/1066).

[58] Makdisi, *Ibn ʿAqīl*, 363, translating Ibn al-Jawzī, *Muntaẓam*, 8:307.1.

[59] Ibn Abī Yaʿlā, *Ṭabaqāt*, 1:223.14. Compare his refusal to greet Aḥmad ibn Saʿīd al-Ribāṭī (d. after 243/857), who had been appointed to a *ribāṭ* by ʿAbdallāh ibn Ṭāhir (r. 213–30/828–45) (Ibn al-Jawzī, *Manāqib*, 272.6; Samʿānī, *Ansāb*, 6:69.11).

[60] The passage is translated in Makdisi, *Ibn ʿAqīl*, 478, from the quotation in Ibn Rajab, *Dhayl*, ed. Laoust and Dahan, 1:189.17; it appears already in Ibn al-Jawzī, *Manāqib*, 505.7.

[61] Shāfiʿī (d. 204/820) is reputed to have been tasteless enough to attempt to recruit the young Ibn Ḥanbal to be *qāḍī* of the Yemen for Hārūn al-Rashīd (*ibid.*, 270.7).

[62] Dhahabī, *Tarjama*, 77.10.

[63] Ibn Ḥanbal used to wear white (Khaṭīb, *Ta'rīkh Baghdād*, 4:416.10; Dhahabī, *Tarjama*, 12.7, 25.7), and he omitted to return the greeting of a man dressed in black (Ibn Abī Yaʿlā, *Ṭabaqāt*, 1:155.13). The prospect of having to wear black was one of his worst nightmares during his unwilling visit to al-Mutawakkil's court (Dhahabī, *Tarjama*, 66.4, 67.11). Ṣāliḥ compromised by taking off his uniform on returning home from his law-court (see the references in the next note).

[64] Ibn Abī Yaʿlā, *Ṭabaqāt*, 1:174.4; Khaṭīb, *Ta'rīkh Baghdād*, 9:318.6 (identifying the source of the anecdote as Khallāl's *Jāmiʿ*). He had previously been *qāḍī* of Tarsus (Ibn Abī Yaʿlā, *Ṭabaqāt*, 1:175.16).

[65] *Ibid.*, 2:199.1 (where Ibn Abī Yaʿlā is writing about his own father); and see Makdisi, *Ibn ʿAqīl*, 235f. For the topos, see A. J. Wensinck, 'The refused dignity', in T. W. Arnold and R. A. Nicholson (eds.), *A volume of Oriental studies presented to Edward G. Browne*, Cambridge 1922, esp. 497–9.

posterity felt no discomfort in referring to him by his official title as the Qāḍī Abū Yaʿlā. Whether this shift was accompanied by an actual increase in the number of Ḥanbalite judges is harder to tell. Ṣāliḥ was not the only Ḥanbalite to take such office in the generation after Ibn Ḥanbal,[66] and Ḥanbalite judges were by no means common even in the fifth/eleventh century.[67] But Ḥanbalite attitudes had changed.

This change can also be related to indications that Ḥanbalite scholars now had more extensive dealings with the court. In the fourth/tenth century we hear little of such ties. We are told that ʿAbd al-ʿAzīz ibn Jaʿfar (d. 363/974) enjoyed the favour of the ruler, presumably al-Muṭīʿ (r. 334–63/946–74),[68] and that Ibn Ḥāmid (d. 403/1012f.) could play a civilised role in a religious disputation at the caliph's court.[69] But beyond this we are scraping the barrel.[70] In the fifth/eleventh century, by contrast, such relations are more commonplace. Even Abū Saʿd al-Baqqāl, whom we met above in connection with his assault on a singing-girl's lute,[71] had another side to him: he used to preach in the presence of the caliph al-Mustaẓhir (r. 487–512/1094–1118) and other rulers,[72] and was not above making an approving reference to the Sasanian emperor Anūshirwān (ruled AD 531–79) in a sermon preached to Niẓām al-Mulk.[73] But the most striking instance was the scholar Abū Muḥammad al-Tamīmī (d. 488/1095), who enjoyed a career as a courtier and diplomat[74] which was almost without precedent in Ḥanbalite circles.[75] Already as a young man, he had gone along with the use of the un-Islamic title 'king of kings' in the Friday

[66] Ṣāliḥ's younger brother ʿAbdallāh (d. 290/903), the transmitter of the *Musnad*, was *qāḍī* of Ḥimṣ according to one source (Ibn Ḥazm, *Jamhara*, 319.8), and of the Khurāsān road according to another (Ibn Abī Yaʿlā, *Ṭabaqāt*, 1:188.8). His youngest brother Saʿīd was *qāḍī* of Kūfa (*ibid.*, 2:49.19), or deputised for one (Wakīʿ, *Quḍāt*, 3:199.2). Ibn Ḥanbal's pupil Aḥmad ibn Muḥammad al-Barthī (d. 280/893f.) was a *qāḍī* in Baghdad in the days of al-Muʿtamid (r. 256–79/870–92) (Ibn Abī Yaʿlā, *Ṭabaqāt*, 1:66.1).

[67] Makdisi's biographical notices show five Ḥanbalite *qāḍī*s (in addition to Abū Yaʿlā) with death dates ranging from 428/1037 to 513/1119 (*Ibn ʿAqīl*, 238, 251, 256, 256f., 269).

[68] Ibn Abī Yaʿlā, *Ṭabaqāt*, 2:122.3. This caliph is said to have played a part in deciding where ʿAbd al-ʿAzīz was to be buried (*ibid.*, 124.12), and to have had a scheme for erecting a dome over the grave of Ibn Ḥanbal (*ibid.*, 251.11).

[69] *Ibid.*, 177.6.

[70] There are two figures whom Ibn Abī Yaʿlā describes as enjoying close ties with the caliph al-Rāḍī (r. 322–9/934–40, at the height of Barbahārī's commotions). Whatever the historicity of the anecdotes he relates, both figures are too well known in other capacities for us to see them as present at court in the role of Ḥanbalite scholars. One is the philologist Ibn al-Anbārī (d. 328/940) (Ibn Abī Yaʿlā, *Ṭabaqāt*, 2:71.16, and cf. 71.2), and the other is the historian Ismāʿīl ibn ʿAlī al-Khuṭabī (d. 350/961) (*ibid.*, 119.2). In both cases the anecdotes are also related by the Khaṭīb (*Taʾrīkh Baghdād*, 3:184.20, and cf. 184.8; *ibid.*, 6:305.19), and they were doubtless taken from his work by Ibn Abī Yaʿlā.

[71] See above, note 34.

[72] Ibn Rajab, *Dhayl*, ed. Laoust and Dahan, 1:133.5.

[73] *Ibid.*, 134.17.

[74] See Makdisi, *Ibn ʿAqīl*, 269–74, esp. 271f.

[75] There are some indications that Abū ʿAlī al-Hāshimī (d. 428/1037) had played a similar role (see Makdisi, *Ibn ʿAqīl*, 269).

sermon (*khuṭba*);[76] Laoust aptly describes him as the representative of an 'ḥanbalisme gouvernmental plus opportuniste et plus souple'.[77]

This trend was to become even more pronounced in the next century and a half, despite or because of the revival of caliphal power against a background of continuing Ḥanbalite demographic weight in the city.[78] One Ḥanbalite scholar, Abū Manṣūr al-Jawālīqī (d. 540/1145), was in effect chaplain to the caliph al-Muqtafī (r. 530–55/1136–60).[79] Another, the famous Ibn Hubayra (d. 560/1165), was for sixteen years the caliph's vizier, and a very successful one;[80] and despite the more catholic – not to say idiosyncratic – ideological style of the caliph al-Nāṣir (r. 575–622/1180–1225), another Ḥanbalite scholar held the same office in 583–4/1187–8, though not with the same panache.[81] In the last decades of the caliphate, Ḥanbalites seem to have held positions in and around the state in larger numbers than ever before.[82] They served in various capacities, from that of mayor of the palace (*ustādh dār al-khilāfa*) downwards.[83] They likewise took office as judges[84] and censors (*muḥtasib*s).[85] Others were in one way or another close to the persons of the last caliphs; Hibatullāh ibn al-Ḥasan al-Ashqar (d. 634/1236), a teacher of Koranic recitation, boasted that his former pupils included the caliph, the vizier and the treasurer.[86] And

[76] Ibn al-Jawzī, *Muntaẓam*, 8:97.19, under the events of the year 429/1037f. (Ibn al-Jawzī refers to him only by his *nisba*, but no other member of the family can plausibly be understood here.) For this incident and its background, see W. Madelung, 'The assumption of the title Shāhānshāh by the Būyids and "the reign of the Daylam" (*dawlat al-Daylam*)', *Journal of Near Eastern Studies*, 28 (1969), esp. 181–3. Abū Yaʿlā devotes a section to the issue in his monograph on *al-amr biʾl-maʿrūf* (*Amr*, f. 116a.3).

[77] Laoust, 'Agitations', 179.

[78] Yāqūt (d. 626/1229) comments on the solidly Ḥanbalite populations of the Bāb al-Baṣra and Nahr al-Qallāʾīn quarters (*Muʿjam al-buldān*, ed. F. Wüstenfeld, Leipzig 1866–73, 4:255.11). Cf. also M. L. Swartz, 'The rules of the popular preaching in twelfth-century Baghdad, according to Ibn al-Jawzī', in G. Makdisi *et al.*, *Prédication et propagande au Moyen Age: Islam, Byzance, Occident*, Paris 1983, 226.

[79] Ibn Rajab, *Dhayl*, ed. Laoust and Dahan, 1:244.13, and cf. 245.7.

[80] See H. Mason, *Two statesmen of mediaeval Islam*, The Hague and Paris 1972, part I, and *EI*², art. 'Ibn Hubayra' (G. Makdisi).

[81] Hartmann, *an-Nāṣir*, 181–4, 285.

[82] For the role of Ḥanbalites at the court of al-Nāṣir, see *ibid.*, 180–95; and see, more generally, Laoust, 'Le hanbalisme sous le califat de Bagdad', 116–21.

[83] Ibn Rajab, *Dhayl*, ed. Fiqī, 2:48.5, 67.5, 121.14, 163.11, 176.9, 181.16, 202.4, 211.14, 218.14, 247.14, 248.10, 258.8, 262.10, 285.3. For Ḥanbalites as diplomats, see *ibid.*, 39.5, 262.11, and Hartmann, *an-Nāṣir*, 191f. (on Muḥyī ʾl-Dīn ibn al-Jawzī (d. 656/1258), the son of the celebrated preacher).

[84] Ibn Rajab, *Dhayl*, ed. Fiqī, 2:69.20, 121.14, 190.11, 265.22. Jamāl al-Dīn ibn al-Farrāʾ (d. 611/1214), a great-grandson of the famous Abū Yaʿlā ibn al-Farrāʾ, was a fourth-generation *qāḍī* (*ibid.*, 76.16). (Here and elsewhere, I have not always distinguished between full and deputy *qāḍī*s.)

[85] *Ibid.*, 121.14, 213.1, 258.17, 261.16, 262.9, 262.13. These include a son and three grandsons of Ibn al-Jawzī (see Hartmann, *an-Nāṣir*, 190–2, 290, and H. Laoust, 'Le hanbalisme sous les Mamlouks bahrides', *Revue des Etudes Islamiques*, 28 (1960), 1 n. 2).

[86] Ibn Rajab, *Dhayl*, ed. Fiqī, 2:211.20.

in the last quarter-century of the caliphate, the black economy of the ʿAbbāsid state was increasingly supplemented by the grey area of salaried employment in quasi-official institutions of learning, above all the Mustanṣiriyya (established in 631/1234). A good many Ḥanbalite scholars took advantage of these new opportunities.[87] There were still Ḥanbalites who maintained a traditional distance from the state; thus Shaykh Saʿd al-Miṣrī (d. 592/1196), who lived in Baghdad, would not visit the homes of potentates (*salāṭīn*).[88] But we hear little from such conservatives. All in all, we have here a period in which the role played by the Baghdādī Ḥanbalites in the state was greater than ever before – or since.[89]

At times, moreover, this symbiosis seems to have involved more than just the career-lines of individual Ḥanbalite notables. The policies of Ibn Hubayra and of the caliph al-Mustaḍīʾ (r. 566–75/1170–80) have been described as attempts to establish the power of the caliphate on a popular base through an appeal to the traditionalist loyalties of the populace.[90] The history of this relationship between caliph and populace remains to be written, if indeed it can be.[91] But one significant figure in it, the preacher

[87] *Ibid.*, 213.12, 219.20, 246.5, 248.9, 249.13, 259.18, 261.16, 262.9, 262.14 (all scholars who died in or before 656/1258). One Ḥanbalite, Abū Ṣāliḥ al-Jīlī (d. 633/1236), was given control over the entire *madrasa* system of Baghdad, and hired and fired even in the staunchly Shāfiʿite Niẓāmiyya (*ibid.*, 190.23; on this grandson of ʿAbd al-Qādir al-Jīlī, see Hartmann, *an-Nāṣir*, 194f.). The institution of the *madrasa* was not, of course, new to the Ḥanbalites of Baghdad in this period; for its role during the lifetime of Ibn al-Jawzī, see A. Hartmann, 'Les ambivalences d'un sermonnaire ḥanbalite', *Annales Islamologiques*, 22 (1986), 62f., 66.

[88] Ibn Rajab, *Dhayl*, ed. Fiqī, 1:385.23. Cf. also *ibid.*, 326.23, on ʿAṭṭār Shaykh Hamadhān (d. 569/1173), who never accepted appointment to a *madrasa* or *ribāṭ* (for the latter, cf. above, note 59).

[89] Few Ḥanbalites entered the bureaucracy under Mongol rule (for a couple of instances, see Ibn Rajab, *Dhayl*, ed. Fiqī, 2:291.20, 429.9), or even took the office of *ḥisba* (for an instance, see *ibid.*, 353.18). There were still Ḥanbalite *qāḍīs* (*ibid.*, 373.22, 411.6, 413.17, 436.5, 441.17), and Ḥanbalite scholars still took positions in the Mustanṣiriyya and other institutions of learning (see, for example, *ibid.*, 314.6, 317.23, 340.3, 344.7, 344.14, 374.1). But the symbiosis of late ʿAbbāsid times had fallen apart. Ibn al-Fuwaṭī (d. 723/1323) was felt to have gone too far in eulogising the Mongols and their henchmen (*ibid.*, 375.19), whereas no such reservations are expressed with regard to Muḥyī ʾl-Dīn ibn al-Jawzī's weekly eulogy of the caliph (*ibid.*, 259.8). Similarly, Ṣafī al-Dīn al-Baghdādī (d. 739/1338) gave up a career in the bureaucracy to return to the world of learning (*ibid.*, 429.9), whereas Muḥyī ʾl-Dīn had combined the two without apparent strain. I have no information on these matters in later centuries.

[90] M. L. Swartz (ed. and trans.), *Ibn al-Jawzī's Kitāb al-quṣṣāṣ waʾl-mudhakkirīn*, Beirut 1971, introduction, 28, 30; his documentation of this thesis is not, however, compelling. Cf. also Hartmann's remark: 'Die Ḥanbalīya hatte sich zum Wortführer der Legitimität des ʿabbāsidischen Chalifats in Bagdad entwickelt' (*an-Nāṣir*, 174).

[91] For the role of the populace in ridding the caliph of an overmighty general in 570/1175, see Swartz, *Quṣṣāṣ*, 32–4; but contrast the unpopularity of the Ḥanbalite vizier Ibn Yūnus a generation later (Hartmann, *an-Nāṣir*, 184). The basis of caliphal military power (such as it may have been) in this period also needs looking into (cf. *ibid.*, 178f., on al-Nāṣir's Turkish – and Ḥanafī – *mamlūks*).

Ibn al-Jawzī (d. 597/1201), is well known, and his relations with the caliphate have received some attention from scholars.[92] As a preacher he was immensely successful, the favourite of caliph and populace alike.[93] His position was more or less an official one.[94] He rejoiced at the presence of the great and powerful at his sermons,[95] and does not seem to have gone out of his way to tell them what they did not want to hear[96] – though at one point he wrote a tract against al-Nāṣir, doubtless when his relations with him turned sour after the fall of Ibn Yūnus.[97] Perhaps most striking of all, he takes pleasure in telling us how in 571/1176 he was given executive powers by the caliph to mount a crackdown on manifestations of extreme Shīʿism (*rafḍ*); the operation was to include the permanent imprisonment of offenders, and the demolition of their homes.[98] We have come a long way from the quietism of Ibn Ḥanbal on the one hand, and the rabble-rousing of Barbahārī on the other.

The more we hear about the entanglement of the Ḥanbalites in the web of direct and indirect state patronage, the less we tend to hear about forbidding wrong. Few Ḥanbalites are described as engaging in the activity in the last century or so of caliphal rule – though these few seem to have gone about it with some spirit.[99] Maḥmūd al-Naʿʿāl (d. 609/1212) was described in 572/1176f. as the leader of a group that took horrendous risks in the cause of duty. He once confronted a gathering of emirs and destroyed their supply of liquor; he was several times beaten up in the course of such incidents.[100] Another well-known performer was Isḥāq al-ʿAlthī[101] (d. 634/1236), who confronted everyone from the caliph downwards, and spent

92 See Swartz, *Quṣṣāṣ*, 27–34; Hartmann, *an-Nāṣir*, 186–9; and S. Leder, *Ibn al-Ǧauzī und seine Kompilation wider die Leidenschaft*, Beirut 1984, 31–8. Such references to primary sources as appear in what follows are mostly found in these discussions.

93 His preaching, as enthusiastically described by the traveller Ibn Jubayr (d. 614/1217), was pure theatre – exquisitely crafted, beautifully stage-managed, and emotionally well orchestrated (*Riḥla*, ed. W. Wright and M. J. de Goeje, Leiden and London 1907, 220–5; see also Swartz, 'The rules of the popular preaching', esp. 228–30, and Hartmann, 'Les ambivalences d'un sermonnaire ḥanbalite', 84–90).

94 See Swartz, *Quṣṣāṣ*, 31, and Leder, *Leidenschaft*, 35, for his position under al-Mustaḍīʾ. Earlier he had preached to the public at the home of Ibn Hubayra (Swartz, *Quṣṣāṣ*, 28, and Leder, *Leidenschaft*, 32).

95 *Ibid.*, 37. Cf. Ibn al-Jawzī's account of his after-dinner speech to the caliph and assembled dignitaries in 571/1176 (*Muntaẓam*, 10:259.22).

96 Note the flattering reference to the listening caliph as 'the perfect ruler' (*al-imām al-kāmil*) in Ibn Jubayr's account of his preaching (*Riḥla*, 224.2, and cf. 223.2).

97 Hartmann, *an-Nāṣir*, 188.

98 Ibn al-Jawzī, *Muntaẓam*, 10:259.4.

99 For earlier performers of the duty, see above, note 3; also below, note 112.

100 Ibn Rajab, *Dhayl*, ed. Fiqī, 2:64.7, noted in Laoust, 'Le hanbalisme sous le califat de Bagdad', 118 n. 326.

101 For Isḥāq al-ʿAlthī, see *ibid.*, 120, and Hartmann, *an-Nāṣir*, 192. (Both give the *nisba* as 'Ulthī; but the vocalisation with *fatḥa* is specified in Yāqūt, *Muʿjam*, 3:711.2, and Ibn Rajab, *Dhayl*, ed. Fiqī, 1:391.14.)

some time in prison in consequence; he wrote epistles in performance of the duty to the caliph and others.[102] Another ʿAlthī, ʿAbd al-Raḥīm ibn Muḥammad (d. 685/1286), carried out the duty (like Maḥmūd al-Naʿʿāl) with the help of a group of friends and followers.[103] Thereafter there is little mention of forbidding wrong among the Ḥanbalites of Baghdad.[104]

3. ḤANBALITE THEORY

In view of his historical role, it would be interesting to have a substantial account of Barbahārī's doctrine of forbidding wrong. But we have only a couple of incidental statements, both familiar in content. The first says that the duty is obligatory, except against someone whose sword or cudgel one fears.[105] The second states that it is to be performed by hand, tongue and heart, without use of the sword, and makes passing mention of privacy.[106] Both statements derive from a work of Barbahārī's characterised by expressions of a political quietism indistinguishable from Ibn Ḥanbal's;[107] neither gives any hint of the activities in which Barbahārī and his followers were engaged on the streets of Baghdad.

The views of many later Ḥanbalite figures are no better represented, though sometimes more interesting. It seems that Ibn Baṭṭa (d. 387/997) held that a man killed taking a stand against a wrong (***man ankara munkaran fa-qutila***) died a martyr (***shahīd***).[108] A quotation from a work of Ibn ʿAqīl which is largely lost stresses the centrality and exigence of the duty.[109] Ibn Hubayra offers what may well have been an original exegesis

[102] *Ibid.*, 2:205.5.

[103] *Ibid.*, 316.8; Salāmī (d. 774/1372), *Taʾrīkh ʿulamāʾ Baghdād*, ed. ʿA. al-ʿAzzāwī, Baghdad 1938, 92.15. (I assume him already to have been active before the fall of the caliphate; he was born in 612/1215.)

[104] For a couple of bare references, see Ibn Rajab, *Dhayl*, ed. Fiqī, 2:385.11, 446.20. Abū Ḥafṣ Sirāj al-Dīn (d. 749/1349), who lived in both Baghdad and Damascus, would perform the duty and confront the powerful (*al-kibār*) with things they would have preferred not to hear (Salāmī, *Taʾrīkh*, 162.7).

[105] Ibn Abī Yaʿlā, *Ṭabaqāt*, 2:35.11.

[106] *Ibid.*, 35.16. For the view that the duty may not be performed with the sword, see above, ch. 5, note 109, and cf. the anonymous view reported in Ashʿarī (d. 324/935f.), *Maqālāt al-islāmiyyīn*, ed. H. Ritter, Wiesbaden 1963, 452.4.

[107] Ibn Abī Yaʿlā, *Ṭabaqāt*, 2:21.19, 22.1, 34.1, 36.10 (but note the enthusiastic endorsement of Aḥmad ibn Naṣr, *ibid.*, 37.12). The work in question is Barbahārī's *Sharḥ Kitāb al-sunna* (*ibid.*, 18.18).

[108] Aḥmad ibn ʿUthmān al-Kabshī states that this was the view of his teacher, whom Abū Yaʿlā infers to be Ibn Baṭṭa (Abū Yaʿlā, *Amr*, f. 103a.3; for this pupil of Ibn Baṭṭa, see Ibn Abī Yaʿlā, *Ṭabaqāt*, 2:167.19).

[109] The passage is quoted indirectly from Ibn ʿAqīl's *Funūn* in Saffārīnī (d. 1188/1774f.), *Ghidhāʾ al-albāb*, ed. M. ʿA. al-Khālidī, Beirut 1996, 1:164.25; it appears also in a text by the Wahhābī Shaykh ʿAbd al-Raḥmān ibn Ḥasan (d. 1285/1869) (*Majmūʿat al-rasāʾil wa'l-masāʾil al-Najdiyya*, Cairo 1344–9, 4:414.1). See also G. Makdisi, *Ibn ʿAqil: religion and culture in classical Islam*, Edinburgh 1997, 168f.

of a difference of wording between Q28:20 and Q36:20; while the details are not worth going into, the effect is to underline the importance of the duty, and to emphasise the merit of facing death in the course of it, and of coming from afar to perform it.[110] He likewise muses that, but for the existence of malefactors, there would be no opportunity for the performer of the duty to show his mettle.[111] And on one occasion he considered it his duty to leave a distinguished scholarly gathering at his home to administer a reproof for a cry that had gone up in the private quarters on the death of his infant son.[112] In contrast to the statements of Barbahārī, this material is distinguished by a tone that is perceptibly different from that of Ibn Ḥanbal's responsa; but these attestations are too fragmentary to mean very much.[113]

Against this background, it is encouraging to find two Baghdādī Ḥanbalites who offer readily accessible formal accounts of forbidding wrong within the framework of larger works. One is the well-known Qāḍī Abū Yaʿlā ibn al-Farrāʾ (d. 458/1066).[114] The other is the Ṣūfī ʿAbd al-Qādir al-Jīlī (d. 561/1166),[115] the eponym of the Qādirī order. Of the two, Abū Yaʿlā is in Ḥanbalite terms the more authoritative, and I shall accordingly give his views priority. But much material is common to both accounts, and it is likely that ʿAbd al-Qādir borrowed directly or indirectly from his predecessor. Abū Yaʿlā also devoted a separate monograph to forbidding wrong, most of which is extant in manuscript.[116] Its treatment

[110] Ibn Rajab, *Dhayl*, ed. Fiqī, 1:269.3.

[111] *Ibid.*, 274.16. However, in another passage he counsels against the exposure of sinners (*ibid.*, 274.10).

[112] *Ibid.*, 263.10; the rendering in Mason, *Two statesmen*, 50f., captures the human interest of the anecdote, but garbles the reference to *al-amr bi'l-maʿrūf.*

[113] A more comprehensive treatment might have been provided by a monograph on *al-amr bi'l-maʿrūf* by the Baghdādī Abū Muḥammad al-Khallāl (d. 439/1047) (for whom see Sezgin, *Geschichte*, 1:232 no. 335), were it extant. That he wrote such a work is attested by citations in Ṣāliḥī, *Kanz*, 308.19, 375.4, and cf. *ibid.*, 332.24, 512.27, 612.6, 651.13 (with a chapter title), 669.9. However, the material quoted there goes back in one instance to Ibn Ḥanbal, and in others to the Prophet; no opinions of Abū Muḥammad himself are found. What is clearly the same work is cited in Ibn Mufliḥ, *Ādāb*, 1:215.18, 216.17, but without the details given in the *Kanz*. I take Abū Muḥammad to be a Ḥanbalite, though in the absence of an explicit statement of his school allegiance he could also be a Shāfiʿite.

[114] Abū Yaʿlā ibn al-Farrāʾ (d. 458/1066), *al-Muʿtamad fī uṣūl al-dīn*, ed. W. Z. Haddad, Beirut 1974, 194–8 §§350–9. The work is an abridgement made by the author himself from a longer version (see *ibid.*, 19.4, and Ibn Abī Yaʿlā, *Ṭabaqāt*, 2:205.8). For Abū Yaʿlā, see *EI*², art. 'Ibn al-Farrāʾ' (H. Laoust).

[115] ʿAbd al-Qādir al-Jīlī (d. 561/1166), *al-Ghunya li-ṭālibī ṭarīq al-ḥaqq*, Cairo 1322, 1:56–61. For ʿAbd al-Qādir, see *EI*², art. "Abd al-Ḳādir al-Djīlānī" (W. Braune).

[116] That Abū Yaʿlā wrote such a monograph is already mentioned by his son (Ibn Abī Yaʿlā, *Ṭabaqāt*, 2:205.18; see also Ibn Mufliḥ, *Ādāb*, 1:177.16). Most of this *Kitāb al-amr bi'l-maʿrūf wa'l-nahy ʿan al-munkar* is extant in a Ẓāhiriyya manuscript (Majmūʿ no. 3,779 =

tends to be richer though less clearly organised; I shall draw on it at a number of points, but will base my survey in the first instance on the treatment of the duty in Abū Yaʿlā's larger work. The title of this latter, with its reference to 'the fundamentals of the faith' (*uṣūl al-dīn*), is suggestive: the work provides a systematic theology in an intellectual style which is Muʿtazilite rather than Ḥanbalite in inspiration. This innovation is likely to have been a fairly recent one among the Ḥanbalites.[117] We thus have to do

Footnote 116 (*cont.*)
Majāmīʿ 42, item 7, ff. 96a–125a, for which see Y. M. al-Sawwās, *Fihris Majāmīʿ al-Madrasa al-ʿUmariyya fī Dār al-Kutub al-Ẓāhiriyya bi-Dimashq*, Kuwait 1987, 226); I am indebted to the Maktabat al-Asad for supplying me with a microfiche (in which, however, the first page in the text as bound, f. 96a, is unreadable). The opening of the text is missing; what we have begins at f. 97a. However, it would seem that the loss is not extensive, since Abū Yaʿlā at a later point (f. 113a.2) refers back to material found at f. 97a.15, and speaks of it as *fī awwal al-kitāb*. Two folios are misplaced: f. 96 belongs between ff. 106 and 108, and f. 107 after f. 115. The only identification of the work is the annotation by a later hand at the top of f. 97a: *min Kitāb al-amr biʾl-maʿrūf waʾl-nahy ʿan al-munkar lil-Qāḍī Abī Yaʿlā*. This is not in itself a very secure basis for identifying our text, but it seems to be right. Ibn Mufliḥ, who frequently quotes Abū Yaʿlā as 'the Qāḍī', does not usually specify which of his works he is citing; but on the one occasion on which he explicitly quotes the *Amr* (*Ādāb*, 1:178.10), the quotation (or at least the first part of it) agrees fairly well with a passage found in our text (*Amr*, f. 100b.14). There is a similar agreement between a passage in the *Amr* (f. 120a.2) and a quotation from the work in Ṣāliḥī's *Kanz* (471.18; cf. *Ādāb*, 1:288.13). That the work is indeed by Abū Yaʿlā finds a degree of confirmation from a number of points. First, there are frequent agreements (subject to paraphrasing and shortening) between the *Amr* and the citations from Abū Yaʿlā given by Ibn Mufliḥ without specification of the work cited (thus *Ādāb*, 1:185.10 = *Amr*, f. 97a.8; *Ādāb*, 292.9 = *Amr*, f. 100b.7; *Ādāb*, 175.3 = *Amr*, f. 102b.4). Second, there are numerous correspondences in the order of topics and in wording between the *Amr* and the *Muʿtamad*, and no significant differences of doctrine. For example, in both works the question of the respect due to the views of other law-schools is followed by the question of the obligation to perform the duty of a man who is himself an offender (*Amr*, 97b.3; *Muʿtamad*, §§352f.); likewise two passages on efficacy as a condition for obligation (*Amr*, f. 101a.13, 101a.20) have close parallels in the corresponding discussion in the *Muʿtamad* (§357). Third, the work stems from the right period, since the author speaks of the question of the use of royal titulature as one that had arisen in his time (*fī waqtinā*, *Amr*, f. 116a.3; cf. above, note 76). That the work is not a fragment from the unabridged *Muʿtamad* is indicated by numerous differences between the two over and above those attributable to the abridgement of the *Muʿtamad*. For example, the discussions of the absence of mortal danger as a condition for obligation agree in substance but diverge greatly in detail (*Amr*, f. 101b.6; *Muʿtamad*, §358); the topics covered in the *Muʿtamad* in §§355f. are allocated no systematic treatment in the *Amr*. This argument can be clinched thanks to the fact that Ibn Mufliḥ, shortly before the point at which he explicitly quotes from the *Amr*, also explicitly cites the corresponding passage from the *Muʿtamad* (*Ādāb*, 1:178.2 = opening of *Muʿtamad*, §357); it is clear from comparing the two citations that the work Ibn Mufliḥ knows as the *Amr* is indeed our text, and not some version of the *Muʿtamad*.

117 It may go back to Abū Yaʿlā's teacher Ibn Ḥāmid (d. 403/1012f.), who was the author of a *Sharḥ uṣūl al-dīn* (see Ibn Abī Yaʿlā, *Ṭabaqāt*, 2:171.7, and cf. Laoust, 'Le hanbalisme sous le califat de Bagdad', 93f.; for what may be a copy of an abridgement of Ibn Ḥāmid's work, see C. Brockelmann, *Geschichte der Arabischen Litteratur* (first edition, Weimar and Berlin 1898–1902; supplementary volumes, Leiden 1937–42; second edition, Leiden 1943–9), supplementary volumes, 2:966 no. 3). But this work may equally have been written in the traditionist style of Ibn Baṭṭa (d. 387/997) (cf. the

with a Ḥanbalite reception of a Muʿtazilite framework into which specific Ḥanbalite doctrines are inserted when their Muʿtazilite equivalents are deemed unacceptable; we shall encounter the original Muʿtazilite format, or something like it, in a later chapter.[118] In the summary that follows, the headings are mine, and I have rearranged some of the material.

1. *The obligation*

It is clear from the start, without any hint of hesitation, that we have to do with an obligation.[119] The scholastic issue raised and vigorously disposed of is simply the source of this obligation: is it revelation (*samʿ*) or reason (*ʿaql*)? The answer, of course, is revelation. This question, which would hardly have occurred to Ibn Ḥanbal, arises out of an awareness of Muʿtazilite doctrine, to which indeed Abū Yaʿlā makes specific reference.[120]

2. *Who is obligated?*

Every legally competent Muslim is obligated, subject to various conditions which will be taken up below; this holds true whether he is a ruler (*imām*), a scholar (*ʿālim*), a judge (*qāḍī*), or just an ordinary member of the community (*ʿāmmī*).[121] Curiously, the standard scholastic question whether the duty is individual or collective is not discussed by either author.[122] One

latter's work *al-Sharḥ wa'l-ibāna ʿalā uṣūl al-sunna wa'l-diyāna*, published in Laoust, *Profession*). Haddad, indeed, suggests that Abū Yaʿlā himself may have been the first Ḥanbalite to use the method of *kalām* (Abū Yaʿlā, *Muʿtamad*, introduction, 21). A similar systematising trend is jarringly evident at a later date in the account of Ibn Ḥanbal's views on *al-amr bi'l-maʿrūf* given by Abū Muḥammad al-Tamīmī (*Muqaddima*, *apud* Ibn Abī Yaʿlā, *Ṭabaqāt*, 2:279.20). [118] See below, ch. 9, section 3.

[119] Abū Yaʿlā, *Muʿtamad*, §350, and cf. the opening of §351; similarly ʿAbd al-Qādir, *Ghunya*, 1:56.15.

[120] Abū Yaʿlā, *Muʿtamad*, §351. The question is not discussed by ʿAbd al-Qādir. For Muʿtazilite views on this point, see below, ch. 9, notes 25, 64.

[121] *Ibid.*, §350. In the parallel passage in ʿAbd al-Qādir's *Ghunya*, the duty is limited to the free Muslim (see below, note 159). Instead of the term *ʿāmmī*, ʿAbd al-Qādir uses 'one of the *raʿiyya*' (*Ghunya*, 1:56.18).

[122] For this issue see, for example, above, ch. 2, note 19, and below, ch. 9, 216. The later Ḥanbalite scholar Ibn Ḥamdān (d. 695/1295) discusses the question in the course of a brief but dense scholastic account of the duty in his *Nihāyat al-mubtadiʾīn* (ms. London, British Library, Or. 11,851, ff. 21a–22b). He states that it is an individual duty (*farḍ ʿayn*) for someone witnessing an offence against which no one else takes action (*ibid.*, f. 21a.2); but the duty is voided for him if someone else in the town, village or quarter does act, as it is a collective obligation (*farḍ kifāya*) for one not individually obligated (*ibid.*, f. 21a.6). Thus forbidding wrong either is, or is tantamount to, a collective obligation. Ibn Mufliḥ echoes this account (*Ādāb*, 1:174.12, 181.9). For Ibn Ḥamdān and his work, see J. van Ess, 'Biobibliographische Notizen zur islamischen Theologie', *Die Welt des Orients*, 11 (1980), 127f. no. 7, with biographical data from Ibn Rajab, *Dhayl*, ed. Fiqī, 2:331f.

is obligated irrespective of whether one's own conduct is virtuous, for all that a virtuous man is more likely to obtain results; since nobody is perfect, the contrary view would have the effect of voiding the duty altogether.[123] However, Abū Yaʿlā's doctrine is not as egalitarian as it sounds. As we shall see, one condition for performing the duty is knowledge of the law, and this is unevenly distributed. There are things that are known to every one (*kull aḥad*) alike, irrespective of whether he belongs to the elite (*khāṣṣa*, i.e. the scholars) or the common people (*ʿāmma*, here in effect the laity). Thus every one knows that the five daily prayers are obligatory, that drinking wine is forbidden, and so forth, and in such cases forbidding wrong is as much a duty of laymen as it is of scholars. But there are other matters understood only by the elite, such as questions of theology. In cases of this latter kind, only a scholar can take the initiative in performing the duty; laymen are not obligated to act – and indeed are not permitted to do so – until they have been instructed by a scholar.[124]

3. *How is the duty to be performed?*

Abū Yaʿlā quotes the Prophetic tradition establishing the three modes (hand, tongue and heart) in his initial set of proof-texts,[125] but does not take up this taxonomy himself – perhaps because it was not present in the Muʿtazilite source that lies behind his account. All he offers is an insistence that forbidding wrong must be done nicely, supported by appropriate proof-texts.[126] He does not discuss the question of escalation in the event that good manners prove ineffective. He does, however, take up this theme in his monograph on the duty, devoting a section to the principle that one begins with the minimal response likely to prove effective and escalates to more drastic measures only as necessary.[127]

123 Abū Yaʿlā, *Muʿtamad*, §353; cf. ʿAbd al-Qādir, *Ghunya*, 1:59.9–11, 59.20–4 (where the intervening material seems to be out of place). The more detailed discussion given by Abū Yaʿlā in his *Amr* (f. 97b.3) adds nothing of interest, and omits the point about the voiding of the duty.

124 Abū Yaʿlā, *Muʿtamad*, §352 (to line 20); ʿAbd al-Qādir, *Ghunya*, 1:59.26. Cf. below, ch. 9, note 70.

125 Abū Yaʿlā, *Muʿtamad*, §350 (at the end); it likewise appears in ʿAbd al-Qādir's *Ghunya* at 1:57.14, but following a discussion of the modes (*ibid.*, 57.11). For the tradition, see above, ch. 3, section 1.

126 Abū Yaʿlā, *Muʿtamad*, §354 (quoting Q3:159 and the 'three qualities' tradition, for which see above, ch. 3, note 59). This becomes the third of ʿAbd al-Qādir's conditions at *Ghunya*, 1:58.4.

127 Abū Yaʿlā, *Amr*, f. 105b.20 (see esp. *ibid.*, f. 106b.4, and cf. f. 106a.20: *al-ashal faʾl-ashal*). He differentiates between *al-amr biʾl-maʿrūf* and *al-nahy ʿan al-munkar* in the application of this principle (*ibid.*, f. 106b.13). There is the same emphasis as in the *Muʿtamad* on performing the duty in a nice way, accompanied by the same proof-texts.

4. *What are the preconditions for going ahead with the duty?*

We can conveniently set these out, with a trifle more formality than Abū Yaʿlā,[128] in the following schema:

1 *Knowledge of law.* One must know the wrongfulness of the proposed target.[129] As we have seen, this establishes a distinction between scholars and laymen in certain matters.

2 *Knowledge of fact.* One must have definite knowledge of the reality of the evil in question (*al-ʿilm waʾl-qaṭʿ bi-ḥuṣūl al-munkar*). Mere supposition (*ẓann*) is not enough, contrary to the view of those who hold strong supposition to suffice.[130] (This latter view is Muʿtazilite.[131]) In his monograph, Abū Yaʿlā makes a more constricting point, namely that the (prospective) persistence (*istimrār*) of the offender in his offence is a condition for proceeding against him, since the object of the duty is to prevent wrong from happening, and what has already happened cannot be prevented.[132] Thus if the conduct of the offender indicates that he will not persist (*tark al-istimrār*), no action may be taken regarding what he has already done.[133] The appearance of the term 'persistence' (*istimrār*) in this context is interesting: it is also found in contemporary and later Imāmī sources written in the same style,[134] and doubtless derives from a common Muʿtazilite origin.

3 *It must not lead to a greater evil.* Abū Yaʿlā does not enlarge on this beyond his initial statement.[135]

Abū Yaʿlā also discusses the rather tepid attitude towards taking action 'with the hand' that marks Ibn Ḥanbal's responsa, but is not very clear as to his own position (*ibid.*, f. 106a.9, 106a.13). The following section (beginning at f. 106b.21, continued on f. 96a, and ending at f. 96b.2) deals with the breaking of musical instruments, opening with a statement that this may be done without compensation (*ḍamān*) (f. 106b.22).

128 In his *Amr*, Abū Yaʿlā includes a brief section (f. 115a.21) pulling together the conditions for obligation he has discussed elsewhere in the work. He lists five of them. The first corresponds to my condition (1), the second to my (5), the third to my (2), and the fifth to my (4); my (3) is not represented in this schema, while Abū Yaʿlā's fourth condition is that the supposed offence should not be a matter concerning which *ijtihād* is allowed. This fourth condition could be seen as a special case of the first. That apart, the schema has a markedly Muʿtazilite look about it (cf. below, ch. 9, 207–9). Elsewhere in the work (*ibid.*, f. 105a.8), Abū Yaʿlā devotes a section to the point that it is not a precondition for obligation that the offender be the only one perpetrating the wrong in question (cf. Ibn Mufliḥ, *Ādāb*, 1:297.15).

129 Abū Yaʿlā, *Muʿtamad*, §350 line 18; ʿAbd al-Qādir, *Ghunya*, 1:56.16, 56.18, restated as ʿAbd al-Qādir's first condition at 57.24.

130 Abū Yaʿlā, *Muʿtamad*, §356.

131 See below, ch. 9, note 71.

132 Abū Yaʿlā, *Amr*, f. 100b.7.

133 *Ibid.*, f. 115b.3.

134 See below, ch. 11, 276 no. (2) and note 186.

135 Abū Yaʿlā, *Muʿtamad*, §350 line 19 (understanding *aʿẓam minhu*); ʿAbd al-Qādir, *Ghunya*, 1:56.17. A similar formulation is ascribed to Ibn Ḥanbal by Abū Muḥammad al-Tamīmī (*Muqaddima*, *apud* Ibn Abī Yaʿlā, *Ṭabaqāt*, 2:280.4).

4 *It must be likely to succeed.* As Abū Yaʿlā states in his introductory formulation, one must be capable (*qādir*) of repelling the evil.[136] What if one is unlikely to succeed? Abū Yaʿlā takes up this question later in his presentation, and states that there are two antithetical pronouncements transmitted from Ibn Ḥanbal; however, these are not actually quoted in the abridged version of the work which is all we possess.[137] He goes on to say that the first view, which is that one should proceed, can be rationalised on the basis that the unlikely is not impossible: the offender may experience a change of heart.[138] Likewise the contrary view, which is also that of the 'dialecticians' (*mutakallimūn*), can be understood on the basis that the point is to get results.[139] The 'dialecticians' may be identified as the Muʿtazilites.[140]

5 *It must not involve personal risk.* Should performing the duty place one in mortal danger (*taghrīr bi'l-nafs*), there is no obligation. This is supported by reference to the two Koranic prohibitions of suicide (Q2:195, Q4:29) and to a couple of Prophetic traditions, of which the better known is that which states that a believer should not court humiliation.[141] But even when such fear voids the duty, it is still permissible to proceed – indeed to do so is the more virtuous course (*afḍal*).

136 Abū Yaʿlā, *Muʿtamad*, §350 line 19; similarly ʿAbd al-Qādir, *Ghunya*, 1:56.16. But ʿAbd al-Qādir seems to take *qudra* to refer not to the prospective efficacy of the action, but rather to the absence of personal risk (*ibid.*, 56.22, 56.25).

137 Abū Yaʿlā, *Muʿtamad*, §357. They do, however, appear in the citation from the full text in Ibn Mufliḥ, *Ādāb*, 1:178.2. The generalisation from the particular and specific injunctions of Ibn Ḥanbal that we see here (as equally at Abū Yaʿlā, *Amr*, f. 100b.15, and elsewhere in this text) is characteristic of the reformatting process that was required to turn Ḥanbalism into *kalām*, and is also illustrated by Abū Muḥammad al-Tamīmī's account of Ibn Ḥanbal's views (see the next note), and by the bare scholastic disjunctions to which divergent transmissions from Ibn Ḥanbal are reduced in Ibn Abī Yaʿlā (d. 526/1131), *al-Tamām li-mā ṣaḥḥa fī 'l-riwāyatayn wa'l-thalāth wa'l-arbaʿ ʿan al-imām*, ed. ʿA. M. A. al-Ṭayyār and ʿA. M. ʿA. al-Maddallāh, Riyāḍ 1414, 2:253–6 nos. 420f., 423.

138 Abū Muḥammad al-Tamīmī ascribes to Ibn Ḥanbal a different rationale: the point of the duty is to give warning and guidance (*al-tadhkira wa'l-irshād*) (see his *Muqaddima*, *apud* Ibn Abī Yaʿlā, *Ṭabaqāt*, 2:280.3).

139 Abū Yaʿlā, *Muʿtamad*, §357; ʿAbd al-Qādir, *Ghunya*, 1:57.19. The fuller discussion in Abū Yaʿlā's *Amr* (f. 100b.14, and see also f. 115b.7) seems to come down on the side of the view that having good reason to expect one's response to be successful is not a precondition for obligation (*ibid.*, f. 101b.2).

140 See below, ch. 9, note 73 (second view).

141 Abū Yaʿlā, *Muʿtamad*, §358; ʿAbd al-Qādir, *Ghunya*, 1:56.17, 56.26. Contrast Ibn Ḥanbal's comment on the tradition on avoiding humiliation (see above, ch. 5, note 125). For the tradition itself, see above, ch. 3, note 53. The discussion of mortal danger given by Abū Yaʿlā in his *Amr* (f. 101b.6) is to the same effect as that found in the *Muʿtamad*, but the specific content is very different. The next section (*Amr*, f. 102a.2) is concerned with the point – missing from the *Muʿtamad* – that non-mortal danger (as fear of blows, imprisonment, or loss of property) likewise voids the duty; the Muʿtazilites are said to hold the contrary view (*ibid.*, f. 102a.7; but contrast below, ch. 9, 209 no. (5)).

This latter point is worth examining in some detail. Abū Yaʿlā adopts the view he has stated across the board, regarding all such action as tending to 'the greater glory of the faith' (*iʿzāz al-dīn*). His use of the phrase in this context is an indication of Muʿtazilite influence;[142] more specifically, Abū Yaʿlā is adopting a view identified in Muʿtazilite sources as that of Abū 'l-Ḥusayn al-Baṣrī (d. 436/1044).[143] He contrasts the position he is taking with that of 'most' scholars,[144] who consider such an initiative to be permitted only in two cases. One of these is speaking out in the presence of an unjust ruler, and the other is asserting the true faith in the face of 'words of unbelief'.[145] Abū Yaʿlā's implicit endorsement of the virtue of speaking out in the presence of a tyrant, and thereby risking death, is interesting; as we have seen, this is an activity which, though supported by a well-known Prophetic tradition, was strongly discouraged by Ibn Ḥanbal.[146] What Abū Yaʿlā has to say in his monograph indicates that he is in fact somewhat fidgety on this delicate point. He includes a section on the question whether it is obligatory to speak out (*inkār*) against a ruler who is doing wrong.[147] In this section he says that the counselling and admonition of such a ruler (*waʿẓuhu wa-takhwīfuhu bi'llāh*) is indeed obligatory;[148] later, in connection with traditions that commend speaking out in the presence of an unjust ruler – and in one case getting killed for it – he observes that they show such counsel and admonition to be permissible.[149] Yet in another section he turns around and contests the application of the category of 'the greater glory of the faith' (*iʿzāz al-dīn*) to cases in which the performer is killed; such cases, he says, represent rather the humiliation of the faith (*idhlāl al-dīn*), while glory accrues only where the

[142] Cf. below, ch. 9, note 74, and ch. 10, note 112. The phrase does appear in Sunnī texts, but most occurrences there are either in contexts other than the danger condition (see below, ch. 12, notes 38, 117, and ch. 13, note 104, last citation), or else invite interpretation as reflecting Muʿtazilite influence or reference (see below, ch. 13, notes 41, 90). There is, however, one Shāfiʿite author who uses the term in the context of the danger condition without otherwise betraying such influence (see below, ch. 13, note 104).

[143] See below, ch. 9, note 74.

[144] So Abū Yaʿlā, *Muʿtamad*, §359 (*aktharuhum*). In the long discussion of the issue in his *Amr* (ff. 102b.14) he speaks specifically of the Muʿtazilites (*al-mutakallimūn*) (f. 103a.8), and includes considerable polemic against them. For Muʿtazilite views on the question, see below, ch. 9, 209 no. (5).

[145] Abū Yaʿlā, *Muʿtamad*, §359; ʿAbd al-Qādir, *Ghunya*, 1:57.3. Both cite Q31:17 and a Prophetic tradition that echoes its wording.

[146] Ibn Mufliḥ remarks that Ibn Ḥanbal's doctrine is against proceeding in this context (*Ādāb*, 1:179.12, referring to his fuller discussion *ibid.*, 3:491f.); see above, ch. 5, notes 152f. For the tradition, see above, ch. 1, note 18.

[147] Abū Yaʿlā, *Amr*, f. 98a.9. Most of this section is concerned to vindicate the Ḥanbalite rejection of recourse to arms against the views and objections of the Muʿtazilites (*al-mutakallimūn*, *ibid.*, f. 98b.2).

[148] *Ibid.*, f. 98a.11.

[149] *Ibid.*, f. 100a.1.

performer remains alive.[150] Pulled in conflicting directions by Ibn Ḥanbal and Abū ʾl-Ḥusayn, it would seem that Abū Yaʿlā is comfortable only with a prudent and moderate heroism.

This leaves a few miscellaneous points. One is that the duty is restricted by a recognition of the validity of the views of rival law-schools as norms governing the actions of their followers in matters in which independent judgement (*ijtihād*) is permitted by the scholars. Thus Ḥanbalites may not proceed against Ḥanafīs who are acting in accordance with a distinctive doctrine of their school, for example with regard to the existence of a category of permissible liquor (*nabīdh*). This tolerance is justified by a statement of Ibn Ḥanbal's to the effect that a scholar should not push people into following his own views.[151] A second point is that the performance of the duty is limited by the demands of privacy: no one should uncover an evil that is hidden from public view (*sutira*).[152] A related point is that if a man has no duty to proceed, he equally has no duty to involve the ruler (*imām*), though he may choose to do so.[153] This is another issue that seems to have given rise to some perplexity; there is perceptible strain between the negative views of Ibn Ḥanbal and a more positive tendency in evidence among later authorities.[154] It may be added that in a different part of his work, Abū Yaʿlā emphasises with much rhetoric that forbidding wrong includes the confutation of heresy.[155] Other points appear only in his monograph, and need not detain us.[156]

150 *Ibid.*, f. 103b.22; also f. 111a.10. Apart from a much later Shāfiʿite source (for which see below, ch. 13, note 90), I have not seen the phrase *idhlāl al-dīn* elsewhere in discussions of the danger condition; it may well be Abū Yaʿlā's own contribution.

151 Abū Yaʿlā, *Muʿtamad*, §352 line 20; ʿAbd al-Qādir, *Ghunya*, 1:60.5. The end of a more complex discussion of the issue is preserved in Abū Yaʿlā's *Amr* (f. 97a.1–97b.3; see also *ibid.*, f. 112b.22). A problem arises over chess-players: chess is permitted by the Shāfiʿites, yet Ibn Ḥanbal regards it as a fit target for the duty (ʿAbd al-Qādir, *Ghunya*, 1:60.9; and cf. Abū Yaʿlā, *Muʿtamad*, §352 line 4). For attitudes to chess in Khallāl's *Amr*, see above, ch. 5, notes 43–6; for the relative lenience of Shāfiʿite views, see the data collected in R. Wieber, *Das Schachspiel in der arabischen Literatur von den Anfängen bis zur zweiten Hälfte des 16. Jahrhunderts*, Walldorf-Hessen 1972, 184–91.

152 Abū Yaʿlā, *Muʿtamad*, §355; ʿAbd al-Qādir, *Ghunya*, 1:56.20. This would not, of course, preclude a private rebuke. Abū Yaʿlā's proof-texts for privacy are Q49:12 and a Prophetic tradition. He touches on the issue in his *Amr* (f. 107b.9).

153 Abū Yaʿlā, *Muʿtamad*, §358 line 20. The proof-text is the story of the Companion ʿUqba ibn ʿĀmir (see above, ch. 4, 80f.), within which is enclosed a version of the Prophetic tradition on *satr* (for which see above, ch. 3, note 61). ʿAbd al-Qādir makes reference to invoking the help of officialdom (the *aṣḥāb al-sulṭān*) in a slightly different context, as an apparently obligatory last resort (*Ghunya*, 1:59.1).

154 Ibn Ḥamdān speaks of a duty to help the authorities (*Nihāya*, f. 21b.7), and to report offences to them where appropriate (*ibid.*, ff. 21b.15, 22b.1); and see Ibn Mufliḥ, *Ādāb*, 1:219.2.

155 Abū Yaʿlā, *Muʿtamad*, 216 §389; see also Ibn Ḥamdān, *Nihāya*, f. 22a.19, and cf. f. 22a.11. Abū Yaʿlā gives a less rhetorical treatment of the matter in his *Amr* (ff. 112b.18).

156 For example, one should only attend parties where there is liquor and music if one is able

Most of the major points made by Abū Yaʿlā reappear in ʿAbd al-Qādir's presentation. The only significant exception is that ʿAbd al-Qādir does not discuss the source of the duty. He does, however, include in his account a good deal that is not in Abū Yaʿlā's. At a formal level, he offers definitions of the terms right (*maʿrūf*) and wrong (*munkar*),[157] and introduces a five-condition framework which at first sight looks Muʿtazilite, but is not.[158] At a substantive level he adds a number of points. He limits the duty to free Muslims – in contrast to the view that seems to have been taken by Ibn Ḥanbal himself.[159] He stresses, among his conditions, the need to proceed with the right intention,[160] to be persistent in the face of adversity,[161] and to practise what one preaches.[162] He urges that, at least in the first instance, one should remonstrate with the offender in private, going public and seeking the help of men of virtue (or even of officialdom) only if this fails.[163] He provides (out of context) proof-texts in support of martyrdom incurred in the performance of the duty.[164] Equally alien to the world of Ibn Ḥanbal is ʿAbd al-Qādir's willingness to envisage social conditions in which virtue prevails. On the one hand, of course, there are conditions under which performance of the duty involves serious personal risk; but on the other hand, he avers, we can have a situation in which the virtuous (*ahl al-ṣalāḥ*) enjoy the upper hand (*al-ghalaba*), and the ruler (*sulṭān*) is just.[165] We find in ʿAbd al-Qādir's presentation an idea not often found in Ḥanbalite circles: that the

to put a stop to the misconduct, since otherwise one risks appearing to condone such activities (*Amr*, f. 112b.5); a man notorious for his debauchery is to be prevented from being alone with a woman (*ibid.*, f. 113a.23); it is a duty to proceed against mutual imitation by the sexes (*ibid.*, f. 113b.5). In addition, Abū Yaʿlā gives extensive coverage to topics that are only indirectly connected to *al-amr bi'l-maʿrūf*: self-defence, duress and others. For what he has to say about rescue, cf. below, ch. 20, note 10.

157 ʿAbd al-Qādir, *Ghunya*, 1:59.25. Note that *ʿaql* appears here alongside Koran and *sunna*; Ibn Ḥamdān mentions only *sharʿ* in this connection (*Nihāya*, f. 21a.11).

158 ʿAbd al-Qādir, *Ghunya*, 1:57.23. These so-called conditions (*sharāʾiṭ*) are qualities a man needs in order to perform the duty, or to perform it well, rather than preconditions for his having an obligation to do so.

159 ʿAbd al-Qādir, *Ghunya*, 1:56.16; for Ibn Ḥanbal see above, ch. 5, note 71. ʿAbd al-Qādir's view is shared by Ibn Ḥamdān (*Nihāya*, f. 21b.10; and cf. Ibn Mufliḥ, *Ādāb*, 1:214.4). 160 Abd al-Qādir, *Ghunya*, 1:57.24.

161 *Ibid.*, 58.12. Abū Yaʿlā discusses this quality only in the context of the voluntary performance of the duty in the face of personal risk (*Muʿtamad*, 359).

162 ʿAbd al-Qādir, *Ghunya*, 1:58.16. As ʿAbd al-Qādir notes, this is in tension with the standard view which he reports from his teachers: that the righteous and the unrighteous alike are obligated by the duty (*ibid.*, 59.9). 163 *Ibid.*, 58.25.

164 These proof-texts are: Q2:207; ʿUmar's interpretation of this verse as referring to a man killed in performing the duty (see above, ch. 2, note 77); and two Prophetic traditions (for which see above, ch. 1, notes 18, 20) on speaking out in the presence of an unjust ruler (*ibid.*, 59.11).

165 *Ibid.*, 56.25. Cf. Ibn Ḥamdān's stipulation that one may not have recourse to the sword in performing the duty unless doing so together with the authorities (*Nihāya*, ff. 21a.10, 22b.2).

three modes correspond to a tripartite division of labour. In this hierarchic conception, performance 'with the hand' is for rulers (*imāms* and *sulṭāns*), performance 'with the tongue' for scholars (*ʿulamāʾ*) and performance 'in (or with) the heart' for the common people (*ʿāmma*).[166] This view does not go well with the general thrust of ʿAbd al-Qādir's presentation, but he makes no attempt at reconciliation. In point of fact all but two of these additional substantive points go back to a Ḥanafī source, the exceptions being the limitation of the duty to the free and the proof-texts for martyrdom.[167]

As the descent of this section into a miscellany makes clear, the systematisation of doctrine in the works of Abū Yaʿlā and ʿAbd al-Qādir is imperfect; and even before this descent began, I was tending to assist them by presenting their views somewhat more systematically than they do themselves.[168] Nevertheless, their accounts taken as a whole represent a style of intellectual activity quite unlike that of Ibn Ḥanbal. This invites us to ask whether the reworking of the substance of Ḥanbalite doctrine in these accounts is as far-reaching as the change in its form.

4. THEORY AND PRACTICE

As we saw in the previous chapter, the responsa of Ibn Ḥanbal do not present Ḥanbalism as a doctrine apt for the purposes either of rabble-rousers or of members of the political establishment. The heritage of the founder was thus in considerable tension with the historical roles of Ḥanbalism in Baghdad from the time of Barbahārī until the end of the ʿAbbāsid period. Do we then find that accounts of the duty given by authors contemporary with these later patterns of Ḥanbalite activity are better attuned to the circumstances of the day? In the case of the two brief statements which are all we have from Barbahārī, the answer is clearly negative.[169] Turning to Abū Yaʿlā and ʿAbd al-Qādir, it is just as clear that the answer is not strongly positive. Their accounts, as I have summarised them, cannot be read as expressions either of a heated populism or of symbiosis with the state. If, indeed, these formal accounts had been all that we had to go on, we could not have guessed at the activities of contemporary Ḥanbalites either in the streets or in the caliph's palace. The question remains, however, whether we might hope to identify weaker linkages. That is to say, if we read these accounts with the historical

[166] ʿAbd al-Qādir, *Ghunya*, 1:57.11. For parallels, see below, ch. 17, notes 29f.; also Maybudī, *Kashf*, 2:234.16. [167] See below, ch. 12, 312f.
[168] Cf. above, 131, 133. [169] See above, 128.

background in mind, can we point here and there to the pull of practice on theory?

The area in which such linkages can be found with the greatest plausibility is relations with the state. On the one hand, there is the more favourable view of commanding and forbidding a ruler, even in the face of personal risk;[170] this is associated with a generally warmer attitude towards heroism in forbidding wrong.[171] And on the other hand, there is the greater willingness to see the state in a positive light as a partner in carrying out the duty. Here, as we have seen, both authors are willing to countenance bringing in the authorities, and ʿAbd al-Qādir is ready to envisage conditions of just rule and of the predominance of the virtuous.[172] This is not a particularly rich yield; but we can eke it out by turning to the views of Ibn al-Jawzī, the leading Ḥanbalite figure in Baghdad in the latter part of our period.[173]

As a starting-point, let us consider some quotations that appear under Ibn al-Jawzī's name in a later compilation by Ibn Mufliḥ (d. 763/1362). At first sight these suggest a relatively aggressive approach to the execution of the duty, at least vis-à-vis fellow subjects. Thus Ibn al-Jawzī speaks freely in these passages of the use of violence by individuals where necessary, provided it is unarmed.[174] He takes the view that if one knows of a persistent evil in the market-place, and is capable of putting a stop to it, then it is one's duty not to sit at home, but rather to sally forth to confront the evil.[175] He also talks of entering other people's homes to carry out the duty, if the evidence against them warrants it.[176] Unfortunately, however, these points lose much of their interest when we realise that Ibn Mufliḥ is quoting from Ibn

170 See above, 135 no. (5) (Abū Yaʿlā). An extreme expression of a willingness to go up against the ruler is found in a dictum implausibly ascribed to Ibn Ḥanbal by ʿAbd al-Wāḥid ibn ʿAbd al-ʿAzīz al-Tamīmī (d. 410/1020): if you are able to depose a caliph who calls people to heresy (*bidʿa*), do so (Ibn Abī Yaʿlā, *Ṭabaqāt*, 2:305.11; for this uncle of Abū Muḥammad al-Tamīmī, see *ibid.*, 179.10).

171 See above, 134–6 no. (5) (Abū Yaʿlā), and note 164 (ʿAbd al-Qādir); cf. above, notes 108 (Ibn Baṭṭa), 110 (Ibn Hubayra).

172 See above, notes 153 (Abū Yaʿlā and ʿAbd al-Qādir), 165f. (ʿAbd al-Qādir), and cf. note 154 (Ibn Ḥamdān). Cf. also the positive attitude towards cooperation with the ruler against heretical doctrines (*al-madhāhib al-fāsida*) ascribed to Ibn Ḥanbal by Abū Muḥammad al-Tamīmī (*Muqaddima*, *apud* Ibn Abī Yaʿlā, *Ṭabaqāt*, 2:280.8). This orientation has already been linked by Laoust to Abū Muḥammad's state-friendly career (*Profession*, cxii, and cf. cixf.).

173 The numerous published works of Ibn al-Jawzī unfortunately do not include his *Minhāj al-wuṣūl ilā ʿilm al-uṣūl* (see his *Dafʿ shubah al-tashbīh*, ed. M. Z. al-Kawtharī, Cairo 1976, 26.2, describing the work as one on *uṣūl al-dīn*, and, for a manuscript, ʿA. al-ʿAlwachī, *Muʾallafāt Ibn al-Jawzī*, Baghdad 1965, 189 no. 464).

174 Ibn Mufliḥ, *Ādāb*, 1:195.6. He also admits here the possibility of armed bands operating with the permission of the ruler (*imām*).

175 *Ibid.*, 210.3.

176 *Ibid.*, 295.19, 320.5.

al-Jawzī's rifacimento of the famous *Revival of the religious sciences* (*Iḥyāʾ ʿulūm al-dīn*) of Ghazzālī (d. 505/1111).[177] Each of the passages in question simply adopts a formulation of Ghazzālī's,[178] thereby demonstrating no more than a certain acquiescence on the part of Ibn al-Jawzī.

However, the fact that Ibn al-Jawzī by and large takes his cue from Ghazzālī means that the points at which he decides to depart from his model can be very revealing. A comparison of what the two texts have to say about forbidding wrong throws up three illuminating instances of this. In each case Ibn al-Jawzī has seen fit to tone down Ghazzālī's politics in a sense favourable to the state.

1 In one passage Ghazzālī raises the question whether the permission of the ruler is required for the threat or use of blows in carrying out the duty; he leaves the question open.[179] Ibn al-Jawzī, by contrast, states that the (permission of the) ruler is required.[180]
2 There is a similar divergence on the question of the need for the ruler's permission for armed bands to operate. Ghazzālī prefers the view that such permission is not needed.[181] Ibn al-Jawzī, by contrast, states as the correct view that it is needed, and merely mentions the existence of the alternative view.[182]
3 Ghazzālī considers the question whether one may speak harshly (*takhshīn*) to rulers in cases where this involves danger only to oneself. His view is that such speech is not just permissible but commendable.[183] He then proceeds to fill a good many pages with illustrative sayings and doings of early Muslim worthies,[184] and concludes his discussion with a lament that the scholars of today no longer act in this courageous fashion.[185] Ibn al-Jawzī, by contrast, admits that such conduct is regarded as permissible by most scholars, but pronounces against it. He

[177] For Ghazzālī's account of *al-amr bi'l-maʿrūf* in his *Iḥyāʾ ʿulūm al-dīn*, see below, ch. 16. For Ibn al-Jawzī's *Minhāj al-qāṣidīn*, see ʿAlwachī, *Muʾallafāt Ibn al-Jawzī*, 188f. no. 463, and Hartmann, 'Les ambivalences d'un sermonnaire ḥanbalite', 103 n. 123. The *Minhāj al-qāṣidīn* has been published in an abridgement made by Aḥmad ibn ʿAbd al-Raḥmān ibn Qudāma al-Maqdisī (d. 689/1290) (*Mukhtaṣar Minhāj al-qāṣidīn*, Damascus 1389; on the identity of the abridger, I follow the remarks of M. A. Duhmān in his preface to a later Damascene printing of the work). For the relationship between the *Minhāj al-qāṣidīn* and Ghazzālī's *Iḥyāʾ*, see Aḥmad ibn Qudāma, *Mukhtaṣar*, 3.5.

[178] The correspondences are as follows: (1) Ibn Mufliḥ, *Ādāb*, 1:195.6; Aḥmad ibn Qudāma, *Mukhtaṣar*, 125.3; Ghazzālī, *Iḥyāʾ*, 2:304.23. (2) *Ādāb*, 1:210.3; *Mukhtaṣar*, 129.20; *Iḥyāʾ*, 2:313.23. (3) *Ādāb*, 1:295.19; *Mukhtaṣar*, 122.10; *Iḥyāʾ*, 2:297.21, 297.30. (4) *Ādāb*, 1:320.5; *Mukhtaṣar*, 122.19; *Iḥyāʾ*, 2:301.21.

[179] Ghazzālī, *Iḥyāʾ*, 2:289.9.

[180] Aḥmad ibn Qudāma, *Mukhtaṣar*, 120.12.

[181] Ghazzālī, *Iḥyāʾ*, 2:304.34.

[182] Aḥmad ibn Qudāma, *Mukhtaṣar*, 125.7.

[183] Ghazzālī, *Iḥyāʾ*, 2:314.5.

[184] *Ibid.*, 314–26.

[185] *Ibid.*, 326.19.

argues that its effect is to provoke the ruler to an offence worse than that which the rudeness is intended to curb, rulers being constitutionally unable to tolerate insult.[186] He too then devotes several pages to sayings and doings,[187] but ends with a contrast which effectively voids them. In the old days, he tells us, rulers – whatever their faults – appreciated the virtues of the scholars, and accordingly put up with their rudeness. In our time, however, it is better to flee from the presence of our rulers. If one cannot, then civility is the order of the day.[188] In short, for Ghazzālī it is the scholars who are not what they used to be; for Ibn al-Jawzī, by contrast, it is the rulers who have changed for the worse.[189]

This state-friendly tendency can also be detected elsewhere in Ibn al-Jawzī's works. He recommends that, in these evil days, one should seek to avoid putting oneself in the position of admonishing a ruler;[190] but he also emphasises that, if one does so, one should proceed only with the utmost tact,[191] and it is this latter counsel that seems generally to have informed his own practice.[192] We cannot, of course, infer that in this or other respects Ibn al-Jawzī spoke for all the Ḥanbalites of his day. Thus his younger contemporary Isḥāq al-ʿAlthī was, as we have seen, considerably more abrasive in his approach to admonishing the reigning caliph.[193] What the two nevertheless have in common is that neither displays the aversion to contact with the state that permeates Ibn Ḥanbal's responsa.

It is time to place these stray hints in a wider historical context. Between the third/ninth and sixth/twelfth centuries, Ḥanbalism had undergone a significant evolution, one which tended to bring it out of the sectarian ghetto and into the mainstream of Muslim life. In part, as we have seen, this was the result of the increased power that the Ḥanbalite community had come to enjoy in Baghdad, and of the fear and favour this power could elicit from non-Ḥanbalite rulers and neighbours. But it was also, in part, a matter of concessions on the part of the Ḥanbalites. It is this Ḥanbalite fence-mending of which Ibn al-Jawzī represents the culmination.

186 Aḥmad ibn Qudāma, *Mukhtaṣar*, 130.10. 187 *Ibid.*, 130–40. 188 *Ibid.*, 140.7.

189 In principle, these shifts could be the work of Aḥmad ibn Qudāma rather than of Ibn al-Jawzī; but the account the former gives of his editorial role (*Mukhtaṣar*, 2.8) goes against such a hypothesis.

190 Ibn al-Jawzī (d. 597/1201), *Ṣayd al-khāṭir*, ed. A. Abū Sunayna, Amman 1987, 410.8.

191 *Ibid.*, 409.8.

192 Cf. above, note 96. Ibn al-Jawzī wrote a work on admonishing rulers (*al-Shifāʾ fī mawāʿiẓ al-mulūk wa'l-khulafāʾ*, ed. F. ʿA. Aḥmad, Alexandria 1978; the editor aptly quotes the *Ṣayd al-khāṭir*, *ibid.*, 26f.). It is full of invocations of Sasanian monarchs and other religiously dubious characters. Much similar or identical material is also to be found in his work *al-Miṣbāḥ al-muḍīʾ* (ed. N. ʿA. Ibrāhīm, Baghdad 1976–7), which he wrote for his admirer the caliph al-Mustaḍīʾ. 193 See above, note 102.

One aspect of the adaption was formal rather than substantive, and it is nicely described by Ibn al-Jawzī himself, albeit from a somewhat egocentric perspective. At the beginning of a short tract against anthropomorphism, he explains that he had found the Ḥanbalite school disadvantaged in competition with its rivals by its literary deficiencies: whole genres of religious literature were missing as a result of the traditionist bias of the school. Ibn al-Jawzī therefore set about filling the gap, composing some 250 works, among them a treatise on dogmatics.[194] He is, of course, bound to admit that he was not the first Ḥanbalite scholar active in this latter field; he names three of his predecessors,[195] though he proceeds to dismiss them for reasons I shall come to.[196] Ibn al-Jawzī was thus taking the credit for a programme designed to bring Ḥanbalism into line with other schools.

The same pressures were also at work on the content of the Ḥanbalite tradition. The tract of Ibn al-Jawzī just cited is devoted to one of the sorest points of friction between Ḥanbalites and other Sunnīs: the allegation that Ḥanbalites are anthropomorphists (*mushabbiha*). Yet the purpose of the tract is not, as might have been expected, to refute this calumny,[197] but rather to excoriate major Ḥanbalite authorities of the past for having invited it. Previous Ḥanbalite works on dogmatics, Ibn al-Jawzī complains, were in this respect a disgrace to the school.[198] Another such issue arose out of the traditional Ḥanbalite partiality for the Umayyads in the face of the philo-ʿAlid sentiments widespread in mainstream Sunnism. Here the sore point was Ḥanbalite opposition to the cursing of the caliph Yazīd (r. 60–4/680–3), and here too Ibn al-Jawzī sought to bring his fellow-Ḥanbalites into line.[199]

194 For this work, see above, note 173.

195 Viz. Ibn Ḥāmid (see above, note 117), Abū Yaʿlā (cf. above, 129) and Ibn al-Zāghūnī (d. 527/1132) (see Makdisi, *Ibn ʿAqīl*, 265–7).

196 For all this, see Ibn al-Jawzī, *Dafʿ*, 24–6.

197 Contrast the outright rejection of the charge of Ḥanbalite anthropomorphism by Abū Yaʿlā (Ibn Abī Yaʿlā, *Ṭabaqāt*, 2:211.11) and Ibn ʿAqīl (Ibn al-Jawzī, *Muntaẓam*, 9:58.15, cited in Glassen, *Mittlere Weg*, 77 n. 141).

198 Ibn al-Jawzī, *Dafʿ*, 26.6. He cites such gems as Ibn Ḥāmid's statement that God has a face, though one may not affirm that He has a head; this is the kind of thing that makes Ibn al-Jawzī's flesh creep (*ibid.*, 31.10).

199 See *ibid.*, 29.3, and below, note 203. Ibn Ḥanbal's attitude to the question was non-committal (see Ibn Abī Yaʿlā, *Ṭabaqāt*, 1:246.6; and cf. *ibid.*, 347.8, 2:273.10). The Damascene Ḥanbalite ʿAbd al-Ghanī al-Maqdisī (d. 600/1203) took the view that Yazīd was a legitimate caliph whom one is free to love or not, but not to revile (Ibn Rajab, *Dhayl*, ed. Fiqī, 2:34.3). Ibn al-Jawzī's negative attitude to Yazīd contrasts with his lenience towards a man who made the mistake of supposing that ʿĀʾisha (d. 57/678) became a rebel (*ṣārat min jumlat al-bughāt*) when she fought against ʿAlī (r. 35–40/656–61) in the first civil war (Ibn al-Jawzī, *Muntaẓam*, 10:286.10).

This is not to say that Ibn al-Jawzī had everything his own way. He himself makes it clear that there were Ḥanbalites in his day who failed to appreciate his efforts to clean up their traditional theology.[200] Indeed we have excerpts from an eloquently offensive epistle addressed to Ibn al-Jawzī by an unreconstructed Ḥanbalite;[201] the writer is the same Isḥāq al-ʿAlthī, who as usual was performing the duty of forbidding wrong.[202] Another old-fashioned Ḥanbalite, ʿAbd al-Mughīth al-Ḥarbī (d. 583/1187), ceased to be on speaking terms with Ibn al-Jawzī over the question of the cursing of Yazīd; this did not prevent a vigorous literary polemic between them.[203] Nor were these the only issues on which Ibn al-Jawzī was at odds with conservative sentiment in his own school.[204] But for all this opposition, it is clear that Ibn al-Jawzī was a central figure in the development of Ḥanbalism.

Against this broader background, the links suggested above between the theory and practice of forbidding wrong from Barbahārī to Ibn al-Jawzī are plausible enough; and they mesh well with the general historical evolution of the Ḥanbalite community in the centuries after the death of its founder. Yet these links are a meagre harvest, and they do not make for satisfying intellectual history. It is tempting to conclude that the whole doctrine had long been in need of rethinking in the light of changed historical realities. But who, in a school as explicitly conservative as Ḥanbalism, could be expected to undertake such an enterprise?

If there was to be any answer to this question, it was unlikely to emerge from post-ʿAbbāsid Baghdad. Our knowledge of the history of the Ḥanbalite community of the city in this period is very sketchy,[205] but it must have suffered from the general decline of the city following the Mongol conquest. What is clear is that the centre of Ḥanbalite literary activity had

200 Ibn al-Jawzī, *Dafʿ*, 91.8 (on the *jamāʿa min al-juhhāl* who disliked his book); cf. also Ibn Rajab, *Dhayl*, ed. Fiqī, 1:414.13. 201 *Ibid.*, 2:205–11.

202 See particularly *ibid.*, 206.14 (citing Q5:79).

203 *Ibid.*, 1:356.3 (with information on the earlier history of the dispute); Mason, *Two statesmen*, 93f.; Hartmann, *an-Nāṣir*, 169f. Ibn al-Jawzī's contribution to the debate has now been published (Ibn al-Jawzī (d. 597/1201), *al-Radd ʿalā ʾl-mutaʿaṣṣib al-ʿanīd*, ed. M. K. al-Maḥmūdī, n.p. 1983); its keynote is the ascription of *ʿaṣabiyya ʿāmmiyya* to his opponent (*ibid.*, 7.2, 9.3, 12.14).

204 Cf. the quarrel over the question whether the *Musnad* of Ibn Ḥanbal contained traditions which were not 'sound' (*ṣaḥīḥ*) (Ibn al-Jawzī, *Ṣayd al-khāṭir*, 308.2; Ibn Rajab, *Dhayl*, ed. Fiqī, 1:357.18).

205 Laoust touched on the subject in some of his publications (see Laoust, 'Le hanbalisme sous le califat de Bagdad', 118 n. 325; H. Laoust, *Essai sur les doctrines sociales et politiques de Takī-d-Dīn Aḥmad b. Taimīya*, Cairo 1939, 493f.; Laoust, 'Le hanbalisme sous les Mamlouks bahrides', 1f., 39, 64f.). But he never made good his undertaking to write the history of the Ḥanbalites of Baghdad under the Īlkhāns (r. 654–736/1256–1335) (*ibid.*, 1 n. 2). For some information relating to this period, see above, notes 89, 104. Subsequent centuries have received even less attention.

shifted to the western Fertile Crescent, particularly Damascus. It was here that the Ḥanbalite biographical tradition now flourished. Incidental references in this tradition to Ḥanbalites who migrated westwards from Baghdad provide indirect testimony to the continuing existence of a Ḥanbalite community for two or three centuries after the fall of the city.[206] We again hear about Ḥanbalites in Baghdad towards the end of the twelfth/eighteenth century.[207] No doubt the community had maintained a continuous existence throughout the period, but its contribution to the intellectual history of Ḥanbalism was negligible.

[206] The half-dozen Baghdādīs to whom Mujīr al-Dīn al-ʿUlaymī (d. *c.* 927/1521) devotes biographies are all scholars who migrated westwards (***al-Manhaj al-aḥmad fī tarājim aṣḥāb al-imām Aḥmad***, ed. ʿA. al-Arnāʾūṭ *et al.*, Beirut 1997, 5:197f. no. 1486, 222–8 no. 1538, 232f. no. 1544, 244 no. 1559, 246 no. 1565, 314f. no. 1653, to which may be added Yūsuf ibn al-Ḥasan ibn ʿAbd al-Hādī (d. 909/1503), ***al-Jawhar al-munaḍḍad fī ṭabaqāt mutaʾakhkhirī aṣḥāb Aḥmad***, ed. ʿA. S. al-ʿUthaymīn, Cairo 1987, 171f. no. 201; I cite only cases where the scholar in question is explicitly indicated to have lived in Baghdad). The death dates of these scholars range from 807/1405 to 900/1495. Ḥanbalite scholars who stayed at home in Baghdad were either unknown to ʿUlaymī or ignored by him.

[207] Najm al-Dīn al-Ṭūrānī (d. *c.* 1184/1770f.) began a career in Baghdad before migrating to Istanbul (Kamāl al-Dīn al-Ghazzī (d. 1214/1799), ***al-Naʿt al-akmal li-aṣḥāb al-imām Aḥmad ibn Ḥanbal***, ed. M. M. al-Ḥāfiẓ and N. Abāẓa, Damascus 1982, 299.8; Murādī (d. 1206/1791), ***Silk al-durar***, Būlāq 1291–1301, 3:192.6). Likewise Jamīl al-Shaṭṭī (d. 1379/1959) dates the migration of his ancestors from Baghdad to Damascus around 1180/1766 (***Mukhtaṣar Ṭabaqāt al-Ḥanābila***, Damascus 1339, 155.2).

CHAPTER 7

THE ḤANBALITES OF DAMASCUS

1. INTRODUCTION

The shift of the Ḥanbalite metropolis from Baghdad to Damascus represents the first of two major geographical discontinuities in Ḥanbalite history. Up the end of the ʿAbbāsid caliphate, Baghdad had remained the undisputed centre of the Ḥanbalite school; and even after the Mongols sacked the city in 656/1258, the Ḥanbalite scholars of Baghdad retained a certain distinction. But it was the Ḥanbalites of Damascus, already prominent in late ʿAbbāsid times,[1] who now played the leading role in Ḥanbalite scholarship. It is to this milieu, for example, that we owe our first substantial Ḥanbalite law-book, the voluminous survey of Muwaffaq al-Dīn ibn Qudāma (d. 620/1223).[2] The result of this geographical shift was

[1] For the rise of Ḥanbalite scholarship in Damascus from the late fifth/eleventh century, and particularly under the Ayyūbids (570–658/1174–1260), see Laoust, 'Le hanbalisme sous le califat de Bagdad', 121–5, and L. Pouzet, *Damas au VIIe/XIIIe siècle*, Beirut 1988, 81–3.

[2] The *Mughnī* is a commentary on the early but frustratingly concise textbook of the Baghdādī Ḥanbalite Khiraqī (d. 334/945f.) (*Mukhtaṣar*, ed. M. Z. al-Shāwīsh, Damascus 1378). One part of Ibn Qudāma's work that bears on the duty of *al-amr bi'l-maʿrūf* is that dealing with the wedding feast (*walīma*) (Ibn Qudāma, *Mughnī*, 7:1–17; by contrast, the treatment of this topic in Khiraqī, *Mukhtaṣar*, 148f. contains nothing of interest to us). One may encounter various abominations at wedding feasts, notably music, liquor and images. This gives rise to two levels of discussion. The first is concerned with what exactly is prohibited under these headings. With regard to music, the main point established is the lawfulness of the tambourine, at least in this context (Ibn Qudāma, *Mughnī*, 7:10.11, and see also Ibn Qudāma, *Muqniʿ*, Cairo n.d., 223.20; on the status of the tambourine, see also above, ch. 5, notes 19–22, and ch. 6, note 32). With regard to images, the position is more complicated – it depends on what they are images of, and where they are placed (*ibid.*, 223.15, and Ibn Qudāma, *Mughnī*, 7:6.8). The second level of discussion concerns one's duty as a prospective guest. Ibn Qudāma's view is that, if one has prior knowledge of the abomination, one should attend only if able to take action to put a stop to it; if one encounters an abomination unexpectedly, and is unable to put a stop to it, one should leave (*ibid.*, 5.11, and cf. 6.5; similarly Ibn Qudāma, *Muqniʿ*, 223.13). If, however, the abomination is not out in the open, one may attend and eat (*ibid.*, 223.15, and Ibn Qudāma, *Mughnī*, 7:10.23). As to practicalities, an image is best neutralised by decapitating it (*ibid.*, 7.6). These issues are discussed in very similar terms in later Ḥanbalite law-books (see, for

that Ḥanbalite thought now evolved in a markedly different setting. Living as they did in a predominantly Shāfiʿite city, the Ḥanbalites of Damascus were a minority of the population[3] – albeit, as Madelung has put it, a vocal and respected one.[4] There could thus be no question of their dominating Damascene society, whether with or against the state; and Ḥanbalite demagoguery in the style of Barbahārī was never a serious option in Damascus.[5]

The attitude of the state was accordingly a key factor in determining how far the Ḥanbalite community was left out in the cold. Here there was a

Footnote 2 (*cont.*)
example, Majd al-Dīn ibn Taymiyya (d. 653/1255), *al-Muḥarrar fī ʾl-fiqh*, Cairo 1950, 2:40.9; Muḥammad ibn ʿAbd al-Wahhāb (d. 1206/1792), *Mukhtaṣar al-Inṣāf waʾl-Sharḥ al-kabīr*, Cairo n.d., 445.19). Another part of the law-book that is concerned with the identification of abominations, though not with the duty of forbidding them, is that dealing with probity (*ʿadāla*) as a precondition for the validity of testimony (Ibn Qudāma, *Mughnī*, 9:167–82). Several of the activities that can disqualify testimony are familiar to us: playing backgammon (*ibid.*, 170.14) or chess (*ibid.*, 171.2), making music in most forms (*ibid.*, 173.1, with the usual lenience towards the tambourine, *ibid.*, 174.3), going naked in the bath-house (Ibn Qudāma, *Muqniʿ*, 245.14). There are others which I have not noticed in discussions of *al-amr biʾl-maʿrūf*: eating in the market-place (Ibn Qudāma, *Mughnī*, 9:168.22), stretching out one's legs in company (*ibid.*, 169.1). The familiar question arises of someone who does something reprehensible which in his law-school is deemed permitted (*ibid.*, 181.19, and cf. 172.5 on chess). Again, much the same material recurs in later Ḥanbalite law-books (see, for example, Majd al-Dīn ibn Taymiyya, *Muḥarrar*, 2:266–9, and Ibn ʿAbd al-Wahhāb, *Mukhtaṣar*, 497.23).

3 As we read in an anecdote set in the late 520s/early 1130s: *hādhā ʾl-balad ʿāmmatuhu Shāfiʿiyya* (Ibn Rajab, *Dhayl*, ed. Laoust and Dahan, 238.17). At the end of the reign of Nūr al-Dīn (r. 541–69/1147–74), the Ḥanbalites held only two out of a score of *madrasas* in Damascus (N. Elisséeff, *Nūr ad-Dīn*, Damascus 1967, 758, 914); in 700/1300f. they held ten out of ninety-four (Pouzet, *Damas*, 426, but cf. 85). Moreover the Ḥanbalite population was concentrated in the Ṣāliḥiyya quarter outside the city proper (I. M. Lapidus, *Muslim cities in the later middle ages*, Cambridge, Mass. 1967, 85f.).

4 Madelung, 'The spread of Māturīdism', 110 n. 3; similarly R. S. Humphreys, *From Saladin to the Mongols: the Ayyubids of Damascus, 1193–1260*, Albany 1977, 190, 191.

5 Goldziher portrayed the Damascene Ḥanbalites as generally enjoying the support of 'das mit den Ḥanbaliten sympathisierende Volk' (Goldziher, 'Zur Geschichte der ḥanbalitischen Bewegungen', 24f.). In support of this he cited two passages from Subkī's biographies of Ashʿarite scholars of the city. The first is from the biography of Fakhr al-Dīn ibn ʿAsākir (d. 620/1223). Subkī alludes to clashes between this scholar and the Ḥanbalites, describing them as the kind of thing that commonly occurs between the Ashʿarites and the Ḥanbalite scum (*raʿāʿ al-Ḥanābila*), and adding that this Ibn ʿAsākir made a point of avoiding places where he was likely to encounter Ḥanbalites for fear of being assaulted (Subkī, *Ṭabaqāt*, 8:184.12). The second passage is from the biography of ʿIzz al-Dīn ibn ʿAbd al-Salām (d. 660/1262). Here Subkī describes how, thanks to the attitude of al-Malik al-Ashraf (r. 626–35/1229–37), the Ḥanbalites had the upper hand in the conflict between the two schools; when they found themselves alone with Ashʿarites in out-of-the-way places, they would revile them and beat them up (*ibid.*, 237.14; Goldziher's rendering is misleading in suggesting that Ḥanbalites could behave in this way wherever they encountered Ashʿarites). The passages are clearly evidence of violent tendencies among the Ḥanbalites, but they do not document the activity of a philo-Ḥanbalite mob. The only reference to such a mob that I have encountered is the common folk (*sūqa*) whom Nāṣiḥ al-Dīn ibn al-Ḥanbalī (d. 634/1236) threatened to mobilise when the Ḥanbalite position in the Umayyad Mosque was under attack (Abū Shāma (d. 665/1267), *Tarājim rijāl al-qarnayn al-sādis waʾl-sābiʿ*, ed. ʿI. al-ʿAṭṭār al-Ḥusaynī, Cairo 1947, 47.5, cited in Pouzet, *Damas*, 89).

gradual shift in its favour. The Zangid and early Ayyūbid state was not over-friendly. Nūr al-Dīn (r. 541–69/1147–74) was ambivalent,[6] Saladin (r. 570–89/1174–93) was strongly inclined to the Shāfiʿites,[7] and al-Malik al-ʿĀdil (r. 592–615/1196–1218) had a serious clash with the Ḥanbalites.[8] But the later Ayyūbids were better disposed towards them,[9] and in the first century of the rule of their Mamlūk successors (658–922/1260–1516), conditions improved still further. Thanks to the catholic policy adopted by the Mamlūks towards the four surviving Sunnī law-schools, there was now for the first time a Ḥanbalite judge in Damascus.[10] This did not lead to a high level of Ḥanbalite involvement in government: few Ḥanbalites took positions in the state bureaucracy,[11] or were even appointed to the office of censor.[12] On the other hand, salaried appointments in institutions of learning became a prominent feature in the careers of Ḥanbalite scholars from about the middle of the seventh/thirteenth century.[13] For a minority with no obvious claim to the favour of state or society, the Ḥanbalites had come to occupy a surprisingly comfortable position.

These conditions did not generate anything resembling the intimacy between the Ḥanbalites and the state that we saw in late ʿAbbāsid Baghdad. Some Ḥanbalites were indeed associated with major political figures: Ibn Najiyya (d. 599/1203) had close links with Saladin,[14] and Jamāl al-Dīn al-Maqdisī (d. 629/1232) was accused of being too well disposed towards rulers.[15] Other Ḥanbalites are described as enjoying the respect of kings.[16] But in general the Ḥanbalites were not intimately linked to the state. Yet they were not deeply alienated from it. One old-fashioned Ḥanbalite

6 See Madelung, 'The spread of Māturīdism', 155 n. 126.

7 See Madelung's characterisation of his religious affiliations, *ibid.*, 157–61.

8 *Ibid.*, 159f. n. 132.

9 Humphreys, *From Saladin to the Mongols*, 190f., 211. Humphreys, however, overstates the goodwill of al-Malik al-Muʿaẓẓam (r. 615–24/1218–27) towards the Ḥanbalites (see Madelung, 'The spread of Māturīdism', 160 n. 132; the final paragraph of this extended footnote helps to explain the vagaries of official treatment of the Ḥanbalites in this period).

10 For an illuminating account of Mamlūk policy against the background of the generally more partisan attitudes of earlier Sunnī regimes, see Madelung, 'The spread of Māturīdism', 164–6. This account does not seem to have been noted in the subsequent literature on the subject (see, for example, Pouzet, *Damas*, 107–12).

11 See Ibn Rajab, *Dhayl*, ed. Fiqī, 2:225.22, 378.14, for a couple of examples; also Pouzet, *Damas*, 94 n. 386.

12 For two instances, see Ibn Rajab, *Dhayl*, ed. Fiqī, 2:377.8, 441.2, and see Pouzet, *Damas*, 93f.

13 Ibn Rajab's references become numerous with the generation of scholars dying in the 680s/1280s (see for example Ibn Rajab, *Dhayl*, ed. Fiqī, 2:305.13, 311.10, 319.21, 321.7, 322.9).

14 *Ibid.*, 1:437.22 (and cf. *ibid.*, 437.1, on his relations with Nūr al-Dīn). His relations with Saladin are already noted from a later source in Goldziher, 'Zur Geschichte der ḥanbalitischen Bewegungen', 21.

15 Ibn Rajab, *Dhayl*, ed. Fiqī, 2:186.11.

16 *Ibid.*, 194.1, 304.20, 433.22.

scholar, Najm al-Dīn al-Shīrāzī (d. 586/1190), occupied no state office, and was glad to recall this on his death-bed.[17] Occasionally Ḥanbalites showed great reservation about accepting the office of judge: the first Ḥanbalite judge of Damascus, Ibn Abī ʿUmar al-Maqdisī (d. 682/1283), took the position against his will, and drew no salary for it.[18] Very rarely a Ḥanbalite scholar would even steer clear of income from scholastic endowments.[19] But if we set aside the case of ʿAbd al-Ghanī al-Maqdisī (d. 600/1203), there was little disposition on the part of the Ḥanbalite scholars of Damascus to get into confrontation with the state.

ʿAbd al-Ghanī was by any standards an unusual figure.[20] A man of electrifying presence,[21] he had a way of getting into trouble wherever he went.[22] He had no inhibitions about standing up to rulers. In Damascus he clashed more than once with al-Malik al-ʿĀdil. He was uncommonly rude to this ruler, but nonetheless got away with it.[23] Indeed al-ʿĀdil confessed to being terrified of ʿAbd al-Ghanī; when the latter came into his presence, he said, he felt as though a wild beast had come to devour him.[24] In the end, al-ʿĀdil expelled ʿAbd al-Ghanī from Damascus when he refused to back down in a recrudescence of the old theological quarrel between Ḥanbalites and Ashʿarites.[25] If Damascus could have supplied a suitable Ḥanbalite mob, and rulers as weak as those of Barbahārī's day, then ʿAbd al-Ghanī might have developed into a Damascene demagogue;[26] but as it was, he was something of a lone wolf.

The anecdotal record of forbidding wrong among the Ḥanbalites of Damascus is pretty much what might be expected against this background. ʿAbd al-Ghanī was, of course, a star performer.[27] He was a great breaker of

[17] *Ibid.*, 1:368.13. Ḥanbalites in this period were subject to criticism for their poverty and lack of office (*qillat al-manāṣib*) (*ibid.*, 377.9).

[18] *Ibid.*, 2:306.8. See also *ibid.*, 380.15, for Shams al-Dīn ibn Musallam (d. 726/1326).

[19] For Maḥāsin ibn ʿAbd al-Malik al-Ḥamawī (d. 643/1245), see *ibid.*, 234.7; for Fakhr al-Dīn al-Saʿdī (d. 690/1291), see *ibid.*, 327.1. The language used in the latter case is strong: *lam yatadannas min al-awqāf bi-shayʾ*.

[20] For his background, see J. Drory, 'Ḥanbalīs of the Nablus region in the eleventh and twelfth centuries', *Asian and African Studies*, 22 (1988); for ʿAbd al-Ghanī himself, see *ibid.*, 105f., 108 no. 15.

[21] For the effect of his presence in the streets of Iṣbahān and Cairo, see Ibn Rajab, *Dhayl*, ed. Fiqī, 2:14.10. [22] For incidents in Iṣbahān and Mosul, see *ibid.*, 19.18, 20.8.

[23] *Ibid.*, 13.8. [24] *Ibid.*, 14.4.

[25] Madelung, 'The spread of Māturīdism', 159f. n. 132; Goldziher, 'Zur Geschichte der ḥanbalitischen Bewegungen', 24. [26] Cf. Ibn Rajab, *Dhayl*, ed. Fiqī, 2:13.4.

[27] He was also the author of a short work on the duty (see Sibṭ ibn al-Jawzī, *Mirʾāt*, 8:520.15; Ibn Rajab, *Dhayl*, ed. Fiqī, 2:18.11); an autograph is extant in the Ẓāhiriyya (Majmūʿ no. 3,852 = Majāmīʿ 116, item 5, for which see Sawwās, *Fihris*, 623, no. 5), and it has now been edited (see above, ch. 3, note 27). As might be expected, this *Kitāb al-amr biʾl-maʿrūf waʾl-nahy ʿan al-munkar* is a collection of traditions on the subject, not a juristic analysis.

mandolins and flutes (*shabbābāt*).[28] On one occasion his target was mandolins which were being transported to a drinking-party given by members of the family of Saladin.[29] On another occasion he was pouring away wine when the irate owner drew his sword; ʿAbd al-Ghanī simply grabbed it.[30] In the time of al-Malik al-Afḍal (r. 582–92/1186–96), he once fell foul of the judge of the city as a result of his zeal in smashing musical instruments. He ignored the judge's summons, declaring the tambourine (*daff*) and flute (*shabbāba*) to be forbidden.[31] On receiving a second summons which made mention of the ruler's stake in the matter, he expressed the hope that God would strike the necks of both judge and ruler; on this occasion too, he got away with it.[32]

Although ʿAbd al-Ghanī was in a class by himself,[33] there are colourful references to the performance of the duty by one or two of his contemporaries. His brother ʿImād al-Dīn al-Maqdisī (d. 614/1218) was much given to it. He always corrected faulty prayer, and he was once beaten up when he took on a group of evil-doers and smashed the instruments of their depravity;[34] like his brother, he could be bad news for musicians.[35] Another contemporary, Sayf al-Dīn al-Maqdisī (d. 586/1190), lost a tooth while obeying the call of duty in Baghdad.[36] In the following century and a half, there are further references to Damascene scholars as performers of the duty;[37] but they are not very frequent, and they are marked by a certain perfunctoriness. This goes well with the increasingly integrated position of the Ḥanbalite community in the city.

At first sight the celebrated Ḥanbalite scholar Ibn Taymiyya (d. 728/1328) seems out of place in this setting. With his notorious disposition to rock the boat, he was in some ways a throwback to ʿAbd al-Ghanī. His

[28] Ibn Rajab, *Dhayl*, ed. Fiqī, 2:13.1. [29] *Ibid.*, 13.2. [30] *Ibid.*, 12.22.

[31] Cf. above, ch. 6, note 32.

[32] *Ibid.*, 13.15. All this material appears also in Dhahabī, *Siyar*, 21:454–6.

[33] A contemporary Ḥarrānian who perhaps bears comparison with him is Naṣrallāh ibn ʿAbdūs (d. before 600/1204). He poured out the wine of Saladin's brother-in-law Muẓaffar al-Dīn Gökböri (ruled Irbil 586–630/1190–1233, see *EI*², art. 'Begteginids' (C. Cahen)) at a time when the latter held Ḥarrān. When summoned to explain himself, Ibn ʿAbdūs denounced Muẓaffar al-Dīn to his face for his wrongdoing. Muẓaffar al-Dīn would have flogged him for this insulting behaviour, but was dissuaded because of the high standing Ibn ʿAbdūs enjoyed with the populace (Ibn Rajab, *Dhayl*, ed. Fiqī, 1:447.15, and cf. 447.9). [34] *Ibid.*, 2:95.21. [35] *Ibid.*, 100.23. [36] *Ibid.*, 1:372.7.

[37] I have noted the following: (1) Shihāb al-Dīn al-Maqdisī (d. 618/1221) (*ibid.*, 2:124.13); (2) Sayf al-Dīn ibn Qudāma (d. 643/1245) (*ibid.*, 241.13); (3) ʿIzz al-Dīn ibn Qudāma (d. 666/1267) (*ibid.*, 278.4); (4) Ibn al-Jayshī (d. 678/1279) (*ibid.*, 297.1); (5) Taqī al-Dīn al-Wāsiṭī (d. 692/1293) (*ibid.*, 330.18); (6) Ibn Taymiyya (d. 728/1328) (*ibid.*, 389.13); (7) Muḥammad ibn Aḥmad al-Tallī (d. 741/1340) (*ibid.*, 434.1). Similar statements are occasionally made about scholars outside Damascus and Baghdad (*ibid.*, 164.16, 425.9). For Ibn Taymiyya's performance of the duty, see further below, note 42.

abrasive personality and inability to compromise meant that he too was forever getting himself into trouble.[38] As Little puts it: 'It is Ibn Taymiyya's distinction that he opposed by word and deed almost every aspect of religion practiced in the Mamluk Empire.'[39] His frequent collisions with the authorities were marked by a whole succession of official investigations and imprisonments.[40] If we add to these dramatic events his popularity with the common people of Damascus,[41] and his occasional ventures into direct action,[42] it begins to look as if we have to reckon with a revival of Ḥanbalite populism.

In fact Ibn Taymiyya was playing a very different game. He made no attempt to cultivate street-power[43] – he was not a rabble-rouser, and mob scenes played little part in his life. At the same time, he maintained relations with the authorities in a style more reminiscent of Ibn al-Jawzī than of Barbahārī. He was closely associated with several military efforts directed against infidel (or allegedly infidel) enemies of the state.[44] He was available for consultation by rulers,[45] wrote letters of admonition to them,[46] and had close connections with several high-ranking members of the Mamlūk elite.[47] All in all, Ibn Taymiyya's confrontations with the authorities were a prominent, but in a sense episodic, feature of his career. Underlying them was a structural disposition to cooperate with the state, and it is cooperation rather than confrontation that is the keynote of his political thought.

[38] See D. P. Little, 'Did Ibn Taymiyya have a screw loose?', *Studia Islamica*, 41 (1975). The suggestion that he did have a screw loose comes from the contemporary traveller Ibn Baṭṭūṭa (d. 770/1368f.) (*ibid.*, 95).

[39] D. P. Little, 'Religion under the Mamluks', *The Muslim World*, 73 (1983), 180.

[40] For a summary of the record, see D. P. Little, 'The historical and historiographical significance of the detention of Ibn Taymiyya', *International Journal of Middle East Studies*, 4 (1973), 313.

[41] *Ibid.*, 324 (quoting Dhahabī).

[42] In 699/1300, he and a group of disciples toured the taverns of Damascus, smashing bottles and splitting skins (H. Laoust, 'La biographie d'Ibn Taimīya d'après Ibn Kaṯīr', *Bulletin d'Etudes Orientales*, 9 (1942–3), 124; Laoust suggests that this rampage had a background in the higher politics of the Mamlūk élite, *ibid.*, 124f.). In 704/1305, he led a small expedition to dispose of a sacred rock in a mosque (*ibid.*, 133). See also Little, 'Did Ibn Taymiyya have a screw loose?', 107.

[43] One biographer gives an account of a dialogue which took place in Cairo in 711/1311 in which Ibn Taymiyya steadfastly refused a timely offer of mob support against dangerous enemies (Shams al-Dīn ibn ʿAbd al-Hādī (d. 744/1343), *al-ʿUqūd al-durriyya*, ed. M. Ḥ. al-Fiqī, Cairo 1938, 286.8).

[44] See Laoust, 'Biographie', 120, 124, 125, 126, 130, 132, 134.

[45] See *ibid.*, 146–9, for his relations with al-Nāṣir Muḥammad ibn Qalāwūn in 709–12/1310–13.

[46] See Ibn ʿAbd al-Hādī, *ʿUqūd*, 51.2; Ibn Qayyim al-Jawziyya (d. 751/1350), *Asmāʾ muʾallafāt Ibn Taymiyya*, ed. Ṣ. al-Munajjid, Damascus 1953, 30 nos. 11f.

[47] See Laoust, 'Biographie', 120, 132f., 140, 148, 155 and the summary at 160.

2. IBN TAYMIYYA AND FORBIDDING WRONG

Ibn Taymiyya's writings include a short work devoted to the duty of forbidding wrong.[48] It has the air of being addressed to a lay audience, and not an exclusively Ḥanbalite one.[49] There is no discussion of the views of

[48] Ibn Taymiyya (d. 728/1328), *al-Amr bi'l-ma'rūf wa'l-nahy 'an al-munkar*, ed. Ṣ. al-Munajjid, Beirut 1984 (this edition was first published in Beirut in 1976). The work has been drawn on by T. Nagel in his *Staat und Glaubensgemeinschaft im Islam*, Zurich and Munich 1981, 2:122–4, 131f. The first edition of the work, by M. Ḥ. al-Fiqī, was published in Cairo in 1956; I have not seen it. In preparing his edition, Munajjid used a manuscript of his own, copied in 840/1436f. from an old exemplar (Ibn Taymiyya, *Amr*, 6f.). The work is something of a bibliographical puzzle. It appears in three contexts in the corpus of Ibn Taymiyya's writings: (a) as the independent work edited by Munajjid; (b) as the second of the two parts of his *Ḥisba* (*al-Ḥisba fī 'l-Islām*, Kuwait 1983, 69–124); and (c) as one of the several parts of his *Istiqāma* (ed. M. R. Sālim, Riyāḍ 1983, 2:198–311; Claude Gilliot kindly sent me a separate printing of the work from Sālim's edition of the *Istiqāma* which appeared in Cairo in 1997). Three points combine to suggest that the work was not originally an independent one. (1) It is not listed among Ibn Taymiyya's works by either Ibn 'Abd al-Hādī (d. 744/1343) or Ibn al-Qayyim (d. 751/1350) (Ibn 'Abd al-Hādī, *'Uqūd*, 26–67; Ibn al-Qayyim, *Asmā'*), nor by other biographers whose works I have consulted. This is not, however, conclusive: Ibn al-Qayyim is explicit that he can make no claim to know all his master's works (*ibid.*, 9.2), and Ibn 'Abd al-Hādī complains that these had already become a bibliographical nightmare in the lifetime of their author (*'Uqūd*, 65.9). (2) The work has no title in Munajjid's manuscript; the heading *min kalām . . . Ibn Taymiyya fī 'l-amr bi'l-ma'rūf wa'l-nahy 'an al-munkar* (Ibn Taymiyya, *Amr*, 7) is merely a copyist's description. Moreover, in a printing dependent on Fiqī's edition, the work is implicitly presented as an extract from some larger text, being described as *faṣl fī 'l-amr bi'l-ma'rūf wa'l-nahy 'an al-munkar* (Cairo n.d. (preface dated 1978), 5.2). (3) The work does not begin properly in Munajjid's edition: there are opening invocations, but no *ammā ba'd*. Yet if the work was not originally independent, neither does it seem to be an original part of the *Ḥisba*. The first part of that work (devoted, unlike the second, to the subject advertised by the title) is complete in itself: it ends with invocations appropriate to the end of a book, not to the end of a section within one (*Ḥisba*, 66.10). By elimination, then, our tract seems likely to be an original part of the *Istiqāma*, despite the looseness of the association of the various parts of that work. This is confirmed by the very early attestation of the *Istiqāma* in the form in which we now have it: the only known manuscript is dated 717/1317 (see *Istiqāma*, 2:348.16, and the editor's introduction, *ibid.*, 1:22f.); and it bears a *waqfiyya* dated 755/1354f. (*ibid.*, 21). But there is a final complication: all texts except that published by Munajjid are distinguished by a lacuna, lacking the material found in Munajjid's edition at *Amr*, 15.12–17.5. This material is missing at *Ḥisba*, 73.14, and at *Istiqāma*, 2:209.2 (but in this latter case the editor has filled the lacuna from an edition of the *Amr* based on Munajjid's, see *Istiqāma*, 210 n. 1, and, for the symbols, 198 n. 4); and it is also clear from Munajjid's introduction (*Amr*, 8) that the material is likewise missing in Fiqī's edition. (It is naturally also missing in the translation of the relevant passage from the *Ḥisba* in Laoust, *Essai*, 601–5; the lacuna is at 602.5.) That we do indeed have to do with a lacuna in these texts (and not with an interpolation in Munajjid's) is clear from the context: the *wa-li-hādhā qīla* . . . with which the text resumes makes little sense in the standard text, but is entirely logical in Munajjid's. The implication is that Munajjid's text preserves material already lost in a manuscript of 717/1317. Moreover, the lacuna falls in the middle of a folio in the manuscript of the *Istiqāma*; hence the source of the trouble cannot be the loss of a folio from this manuscript, and must antedate its copying.

[49] Ibn Taymiyya was firmly committed to the four-school doctrine (see, for example, Madelung, 'The spread of Māturīdism', 166 n. 150; Ibn Taymiyya, *Ḥisba*, 31.14, 36.12).

earlier scholars;[50] the style is somewhere between preaching and lecturing, and suffers from a marked tendency to digression.[51] The presentation thus has none of the systematic character of Abū Yaʿlā's. It equally lacks the rich and concrete detail that characterises Ibn Ḥanbal's responsa;[52] bar a passing reference to tomb-cults,[53] there is little in the work that makes direct reference to the realities of contemporary life.[54]

It is possible to retrieve from this text at least the outlines of a conventional doctrine of forbidding wrong, though this, as we shall see, is not where its main interest lies. As might be expected, Ibn Taymiyya makes much of the significance of the duty. It is what God's revelation is all about,[55] and it is closely linked to the duty of holy war.[56] Like holy war, it is a duty by which all are obligated until someone actually undertakes it;[57] it is thus a collective duty (*ʿalā ʾl-kifāya*), rather than one incumbent by its nature on each and every individual.[58] At the same time, no one on earth

Footnote 49 (*cont.*)
He even wrote a short work on the merits (*faḍāʾil*) of the four *imāms* – including, presumably, Abū Ḥanīfa (see Ibn ʿAbd al-Hādī, *ʿUqūd*, 46.13, and Ibn al-Qayyim, *Asmāʾ*, 27 no. 4; for similar works by other Ḥanbalite scholars, see Ibn Rajab, *Dhayl*, ed. Fiqī, 2:256.20, 435.11).

50 He once refers to the *Muʿtamad* of Abū Yaʿlā, but only for the Prophetic tradition of the three qualities (see above, ch. 3, note 59), which he then proceeds to quote in a rather different version (Ibn Taymiyya, *Amr*, 30.11, and cf. Abū Yaʿlā, *Muʿtamad*, 196.18 (§354); Ibn Taymiyya may, of course, have used the unabridged version of the book).

51 We are treated to a lengthy condemnation of miserliness (*bukhl*) (Ibn Taymiyya, *Amr*, 50.14–52.13), and to analyses of the meanings of the terms *islām* (*ibid.*, 72.6–74.2) and *sunna* (*ibid.*, 77.9).

52 A reference to the dispensation in favour of tambourines at weddings (*ibid.*, 59.4) is unusually specific, and places Ibn Taymiyya in the moderate mainstream of Ḥanbalite opinion on this point (cf. above, ch. 6, note 32). There are indeed responsa of Ibn Taymiyya which touch on *al-amr biʾl-maʿrūf*. In one, the questioners demand a plain answer to a question about vicious gossip (*ghība*), so that those who perform the duty will know what they are doing (*Majmūʿ fatāwā Shaykh al-Islām Aḥmad ibn Taymiyya*, collected and arranged by ʿA. Ibn Qāsim al-ʿĀṣimī, Riyāḍ 1381–6, 28:222.7). Another concerns a man who goes on pleasurable outings where he encounters abominations which he lacks the power to act against; what is more, he takes his wife with him (*ibid.*, 239.1). But such responsa are few and far between compared to those of Ibn Ḥanbal.

53 Ibn Taymiyya, *Amr*, 16.15. This was, of course, a favourite target of Ibn Taymiyya's honest indignation.

54 His listing of the main substantive matters in connection with which the duty arises is more an inventory of the law and faith of Islam than an identification of the concrete situations a believer is likely to encounter (Ibn Taymiyya, *Amr*, 15.15–17.3). He gives similar lists in other works (*al-Siyāsa al-sharʿiyya*, Beirut n.d., 66.16, and *ʿAqīdat ahl al-sunna waʾl-firqa al-nājiya*, Cairo 1358, 60.2; the latter is presumably the *ʿAdawiyya*, or epistle to the house of Shaykh ʿAdī ibn Musāfir (d. 557/1161f.), to which the bibliographers refer, see Ibn ʿAbd al-Hādī, *ʿUqūd*, 50.8, and Ibn al-Qayyim, *Asmāʾ*, 30 no. 6).

55 Ibn Taymiyya, *Amr*, 9.7; compare his *Ḥisba*, 12.10.

56 Ibn Taymiyya, *Amr*, 12.7, 15.5. In the first passage, he draws a contrast between the Muslim community and the Israelites: most of the *jihād* of the latter was devoted to expelling their enemies from their land, not to calling people to good or performing the duty of *al-amr biʾl-maʿrūf* (*ibid.*, 12.9). The completion (*itmām*) of the duty is by *jihād* (*ibid.*, 15.9).

57 *Ibid.*, 15.5.

58 *Ibid.*, 14.10, 15.3; similarly Ibn Taymiyya, *Ḥisba*, 12.15, 27.18, and Ibn Taymiyya,

is exempt from the scope of the duty.[59] It is to be performed in the three modes specified in the Prophetic tradition: with the hand, with the tongue and in (or with) the heart.[60] The emphasis is on civility (*rifq*)[61] – a respect in which Ibn Taymiyya was not noted for practising what he preached.[62] One must possess the knowledge requisite to distinguish right (*maʿrūf*) from wrong (*munkar*).[63] The benefit (*maṣlaḥa*) secured by performing the duty must outweigh any undesirable consequences (*mafsada*)[64] – a consideration which rules out attempts to implement it through rebellion.[65] One must nevertheless be prepared to display endurance (*ṣabr*) in the face of adverse reactions.[66] The obligation also turns on one's having the power (*qudra*) to act.[67] All this is familiar enough, but it leaves a good many questions unanswered. What, for example, is the place of women in the performance of the duty?[68] I have not found a sustained discussion of forbidding wrong elsewhere in Ibn Taymiyya's works.[69]

Majmūʿat al-rasāʾil waʾl-masāʾil, ed. M. Rashīd Riḍā, Cairo 1341–9, 1:154.11. This is an issue that Abū Yaʿlā and ʿAbd al-Qādir al-Jīlī omit to discuss (see above, ch. 6, note 122).

59 Ibn Taymiyya, *Amr*, 65.18.

60 *Ibid.*, 18.2. The Prophetic tradition is quoted earlier (*ibid.*, 15.7). For this tradition, see above, ch. 3, section 1.

61 *Ibid.*, 17.5, 29.2.

62 Cf. Little, 'Did Ibn Taymiyya have a screw loose?', 109, quoting Dhahabī.

63 Ibn Taymiyya, *Amr*, 28.12, 28.16.

64 *Ibid.*, 17.9, 21.2.

65 *Ibid.*, 20.3, 20.13. He contrasts this with the view of the Muʿtazila, who construe fighting against rulers as an integral part of the duty, and hence as one of their five principles (*ibid.*, 20.8; cf. below, ch. 9, 204, 224, 226). Ibn Ḥamdān likewise excludes performance of the duty against one's ruler other than verbally (*Nihāya*, f. 22b.3).

66 Ibn Taymiyya, *Amr*, 29.6. Cf. also Ibn Taymiyya, *Majmūʿ fatāwā*, 28:180.1, and Ibn Mufliḥ, *Ādāb*, 1:176.16.

67 Ibn Taymiyya, *Amr*, 23.5; also *ibid.*, 15.5. See too Ibn Taymiyya, *Ḥisba*, 12.14; Ibn Taymiyya, *Majmūʿ fatāwā*, 28:217.8, 219.11; Ibn Taymiyya, *ʿUbūdiyya*, Damascus 1962, 16.4; but contrast the quotation in *Majmūʿat al-rasāʾil waʾl-masāʾil al-Najdiyya*, 4:414.13.

68 Ibn Taymiyya's contemporary Umm Zaynab (d. 714/1315) had a reputation for zeal in the execution of the duty, in the course of which she did things men could not do (cf. below, ch. 17, note 135); we know at least that Ibn Taymiyya had a high opinion of her, and of her scholarship (Ibn Kathīr, *Bidāya*, 14:72.19, cited in Laoust, 'Le hanbalisme sous les Mamlouks bahrides', 61).

69 He does, of course, refer to it from time to time. For example, he gives the duty a brief sentence in one of his creeds (Ibn Taymiyya (d. 728/1328), *al-ʿAqīda al-Wāsiṭiyya*, in his *Majmūʿat al-rasāʾil al-kubrā*, Cairo 1966, 1:410.13, re-edited and translated in H. Laoust, *La profession de foi d'Ibn Taymiyya*, Paris 1986, 26.5 = 84). In one place, he defines *maʿrūf* (and *munkar*?) in terms of what natural moral sense (*fiṭra*) accepts or rejects (*Naqḍ al-manṭiq*, ed. M. Ḥ. al-Fiqī, Cairo n.d., 29.13; I owe this reference to Ilai Alon); in another, he defines them in terms of what is pleasing or displeasing to God (*Iqtiḍāʾ al-ṣirāṭ al-mustaqīm*, ed. M. Ḥ. al-Fiqī, Cairo 1950, 19.18). He stresses the inseparability of *al-amr biʾl-maʿrūf* and *al-nahy ʿan al-munkar* (*ibid.*, 297.12). His responsa attest his recognition of the claims of privacy (*Majmūʿ fatāwā*, 28:205.16, 217.11). He also discusses *hijra* as a mode of performance of the duty (*ibid.*, 211.5, 211.11). He has a couple of observations on doing it to *dhimmī*s (see Ibn Mufliḥ, *Ādāb*, 1:211.8, 297.5). And he refutes the simplistic view that there is no duty in matters over which the law-schools disagree (*masāʾil al-khilāf*) by distinguishing such questions from those actually admitting of independent legal judgment (*masāʾil al-ijtihād*) (see his *Bayān al-dalīl ʿalā buṭlān al-taḥlīl*, ed. F. S. ʿA. al-Muṭayrī, Damanhūr 1996, 210.4, 211.6; cf. above, ch. 6, note 151).

The interest of Ibn Taymiyya's rather haphazard treatment of the duty lies in two points. The first is that he displays a stronger, or at least a more vocal, tendency to utilitarianism than earlier Ḥanbalite authorities. Thus he speaks of 'the general rule' (*al-qāʿida al-ʿāmma*) according to which, when both costs (*mafāsid*) and benefits (*maṣāliḥ*) are associated with a given course of action, what matters is which is preponderant.[70] Shortly afterwards he discusses a situation in which good and evil form a single package, and the choice is between putting a stop to both, or allowing both to continue;[71] the same rule applies. This utilitarianism is a well-attested feature of Ibn Taymiyya's thought.[72] In his major work on politics, he tells us that in cases where costs and benefits have to be weighed, the proper course is to secure the greater benefit by sacrificing the lesser, and to avert the larger cost by accepting the smaller.[73] Likewise in his work on the office of censor (*ḥisba*), he stresses that one's duty is limited to taking the best course of action open to one; in real life, this will usually mean choosing the greater of two goods, or settling for the lesser of two evils.[74] None of this should be taken to imply the absolute sovereignty of utility. Indeed, Ibn Taymiyya's doctrine seems to have been less sweeping in this respect than was that of his contemporary and fellow-Ḥanbalite Najm al-Dīn al-Ṭūfī (d. 716/1316).[75] But the utilitarian idiom of costs and benefits, with its brushing aside of moral absolutes, is a strikingly pervasive feature of his political thought. Its bearing on the duty of forbidding wrong is nicely illustrated by a story told of his visit to the enemy camp during one of the

[70] Ibn Taymiyya, *Amr*, 20.13. [71] *Ibid.*, 21.10.

[72] For a general sketch of his doctrine of *maṣlaḥa*, see Laoust, *Essai*, 245–50. To the extent that I understand the issues, his attitude towards the concept is significantly less restrictive than that of Ibn Qudāma (compare Ibn Qudāma (d. 620/1223), *Rawḍat al-nāẓir*, Cairo 1378, 87.6, with Ibn Taymiyya, *Qāʿida fī ʾl-muʿjizāt waʾl-karāmāt*, in his *Majmūʿat al-rasāʾil waʾl-masāʾil*, 5:22.15, translated in Laoust, *Essai*, 246).

[73] Ibn Taymiyya, *Siyāsa*, 43.12. [74] Ibn Taymiyya, *Ḥisba*, 14.14.

[75] I adopt the vocalisation 'Ṭūfī' (in contrast to Kerr's 'Ṭaufī') on the authority of Ibn Ḥajar al-ʿAsqalānī (d. 852/1449), *al-Durar al-kāmina*, Hyderabad 1348–50, 2:154.6. Ṭūfī's doctrine of *maṣlaḥa* was analysed by Kerr (see M. H. Kerr, *Islamic reform: the political and legal theories of Muḥammad ʿAbduh and Rashīd Riḍā*, Berkeley and Los Angeles 1966, 97–102). Ṭūfī holds that utility takes precedence even over the revealed texts (*ibid.*, 97); Ibn Taymiyya does not (Ibn Taymiyya, *Amr*, 21.7). Since Kerr wrote, however, a work by Ṭūfī with a further discussion of *maṣlaḥa* has been published, and here his radical doctrine does not seem to find expression (Najm al-Dīn al-Ṭūfī (d. 716/1316), *Sharḥ Mukhtaṣar al-Rawḍa*, ed. ʿA. ʿA. al-Turkī, Beirut 1987–9, 3:204–17). In his commentary on the 'three modes' tradition in Nawawī's *Arbaʿīn* (cf. above, ch. 3, note 7), Ṭūfī applies a utilitarian perspective (the weighing of *maṣlaḥa* against *mafsada*) to the danger condition (*Sharḥ al-Arbaʿīn ḥadīthan al-Nawawiyya*, ms. Princeton, Yahuda 3,004 (= R. Mach, *Catalogue of Arabic manuscripts (Yahuda Section) in the Garrett Collection, Princeton University Library*, Princeton 1977, 64 no. 712), f. 100b.4, 100b.17), and to the question whether one should seek the permission of the ruler to perform the duty (*ibid.*, f. 101a.5).

Mongol invasions of Syria. The Mongols, as usual, were drunk; but when one of his companions wanted to reprove them for their drinking habits, Ibn Taymiyya restrained him on the grounds that the Muslims stood to suffer more if the Mongols renounced their liquor.[76]

The second point of interest in Ibn Taymiyya's discussion of forbidding wrong is that he seems to see the duty as one to be performed first and foremost (though not exclusively) by what the Koran calls 'those in authority' (*ulū 'l-amr*).[77] In one passage he states that the performance of the duty is obligatory for 'those in authority', whom he specifies as the scholars (*'ulamā'*), the political and military grandees (*umarā'*), and the elders (*mashāyikh*)[78] of every community (*ṭā'ifa*); it is their duty to carry out the duty vis-à-vis the common people subject to their authority (*'alā 'āmmat-ihim*).[79] In a subsequent passage he returns to the topic, enlarging on his original definition: 'those in authority' consist here of two groups (*ṣinf*), namely scholars (*'ulamā'*) and grandees (*umarā'*); they include kings (*mulūk*), elders (*mashāyikh*) and state functionaries (*ahl al-dīwān*) – but also anyone who has a following (*matbū'*).[80] Each of them should order and forbid what God has ordered and forbidden; each person subject to their authority should obey them in obedience to God, though not in disobedience to Him.[81] This emphasis on the role of constituted authority in forbidding wrong is attested elsewhere in Ibn Taymiyya's works; indeed he considers it to be the purpose of all state power to carry out the duty.[82] What is more, he provides a strikingly simple justification of this association of forbidding wrong with the authorities, and in particular with the state: successful performance of the duty is obviously and critically dependent on having the power (*qudra*) to execute it, and power is something of which those in authority naturally possess the lion's share.[83]

76 Ibn Qayyim al-Jawziyya (d. 751/1350), *I'lām al-muwaqqi'īn*, Beirut 1973, 3:5.9; *Majmū'at al-rasā'il wa'l-masā'il al-Najdiyya*, 3:127.20; and see Ibn Taymiyya, *Istiqāma*, 2:165.16.

77 Q4:59 (quoted at Ibn Taymiyya, *Amr*, 68.1).

78 Ibn Taymiyya also uses this term in a similar context in the same work (*ibid.*, 68.10), and in a parallel passage in his *'Aqīdat ahl al-sunna*, 59.18. He does not use it in his references to 'pouvoirs intermédiaires' in his *Siyāsa* (see 10.10, 82.4, 125.14). Nagel, translating the second passage of the *Amr*, renders the term 'die Lehrer . . . (der islamischen Gesetze und des Glaubens)' (*Staat und Glaubensgemeinschaft*, 2:123). But this reduces it to a synonym for *'ulamā'*, which it does not seem to be; the first passage of the *Amr* speaks of the *'ulamā' kull ṭā'ifa wa-umarā'uhā wa-mashāyikhuhā* (Ibn Taymiyya, *Amr*, 15.13).

79 *Ibid.*, 15.13.

80 *Ibid.*, 68.4. He also contrasts *ahl al-yad wa'l-qudra* with *ahl al-'ilm wa'l-kalām*.

81 *Ibid.*, 68.12.

82 Ibn Taymiyya, *Ḥisba*, 13.5; Ibn Taymiyya, *Siyāsa*, 65.9. He likewise considers that the authorities have more of a duty to display endurance and forbearance (*al-ṣabr wa'l-ḥilm*) in executing the duty than do their subjects (Ibn Taymiyya, *Majmū' fatāwā*, 28:180.10).

83 Ibn Taymiyya, *Ḥisba*, 12.14; and cf. his *Siyāsa*, 139.3.

3. IBN TAYMIYYA'S POLITICS

What then is the link between Ibn Taymiyya's utilitarianism on the one hand, and his emphasis on the role of the authorities in performing the duty on the other?

We can best begin by returning to the utilitarian aspect of his political thought.[84] Political morality, for Ibn Taymiyya, consists in doing one's best. Anyone in a position of authority who does this in good faith has done his duty, and is not to be held responsible for what he lacks the power to achieve.[85] Thus in making an appointment to a public office, the ruler's duty is to appoint the best man available (***al-aṣlaḥ al-mawjūd***); and provided that, in the absence of the right man for the job, he appoints the best man he can, he is a just ruler even if some undesirable consequences ensue.[86] In short, the ruler has a job to do, and he has nothing to be ashamed of provided he does it to the best of his abilities. More than that, all forms of political authority have the blessing of the holy law (***sharīʿa***), and all public offices are religious offices (***manāṣib dīniyya***).[87] Even writing an official letter, or keeping official accounts, are exercises of religious authority.[88] In practice, of course, the abuse of such authority is commonplace – rulers treat their subjects unjustly. But then subjects do the same to their rulers.[89]

What has disappeared in this brisk Islamic utilitarianism is the traditional Ḥanbalite queasiness over the exercise of political power. Back in the days of Ibn Ḥanbal, a certain Abū Muḥammad ʿAbda was once asked whether it was possible for a man to enter the service of the state (***ʿamal al-sulṭān***) and not to get blood on his hands; the answer, endorsed by Ibn Ḥanbal, was negative.[90] Ibn Taymiyya's political thought conveys no such sense

[84] For a recent introduction to Ibn Taymiyya's political thought, see Nagel, *Staat und Glaubensgemeinschaft*, 2:107–40.

[85] Ibn Taymiyya, *Siyāsa*, 143.12; similarly his *Ḥisba*, 16.4. In setting out views of this kind, Ibn Taymiyya sometimes invokes Q64:16: 'So fear God as far as you are able' (*Siyāsa*, 15.3, 43.9. 138.2).

[86] *Ibid*., 14.14. See also the subsequent discussion of the relative weight to be assigned to trustworthiness and competence when, as often happens, they are not to be had in the same man (*ibid*., 16.16). Here we learn that Abū Bakr (r. 11–13/632–4) retained Khālid ibn al-Walīd (d. 21/641f.) in his role of military leadership, despite his moral failings, because the benefits of doing so outweighed the costs (*li-rujḥān al-maṣlaḥa ʿalā ʾl-mafsada*) (*ibid*., 18.6).

[87] Ibn Taymiyya, *Ḥisba*, 16.3; cf. also his *Siyāsa*, 139.18. This view disregards the traditional Sunnī doctrine of the imamate, which for Ibn Taymiyya has no contemporary relevance (see Laoust, *Essai*, 282f., 293f.).

[88] Ibn Taymiyya, *Ḥisba*, 27.20.

[89] Ibn Taymiyya, *Siyāsa*, 38.5. Cf. also his *Majmūʿ fatāwā*, 28:180.13.

[90] Ibn Abī Yaʿlā, *Ṭabaqāt*, 1:132.23.

that power is inherently contaminated and contaminating. Nowhere, to my knowledge, does he directly confront an authoritative expression of this deeply felt revulsion.[91] There is, however, a key passage in one of his works in which he seeks to characterise and criticise this revulsion without naming names.[92] People, he tells us, fall into three groups with respect to their attitudes towards political power. The first group holds, in effect, that there can be no such thing as political morality; so it opts for politics without morality.[93] The second shares the premise, but opts for morality without politics.[94] The third group is, of course, the one that gets it right, avoiding the extreme positions of the other two by rejecting their shared premise.[95] The group that concerns us here is the second, moralistic group. Their moralism, he tells us, comes in two – very different – styles.[96] The first might be labelled quietist moralism. The quietist moralist, for all his uncompromising righteousness, is characterised by a certain timidity or meanness of spirit. This failing can lead him to neglect a duty the omission of which is worse than the commission of many prohibited acts; it can equally lead him to forbid the performance of a duty where this is tantamount to turning people aside from the way of God.[97] The second style can be labelled activist moralism. The activist moralist believes it to be his duty to take a stand against political injustice, and to do so by recourse to arms; thus he ends up fighting against Muslims in the manner of the Khārijites.[98] The distinction runs parallel to one that Ibn Taymiyya makes in his tract on forbidding wrong between those who fall short in the performance of the duty and those who go too far.[99] Now it cost Ibn Taymiyya nothing to take a firm stand against the Khārijites. But in condemning the quietist variety of moralism, he was dissociating himself from something perilously close to the attitude of the founder of his school.

[91] One way he might have taken around the responsa of Ibn Ḥanbal is suggested by a remark he makes about them in another context: many of them refer implicitly to the circumstances of particular individuals, and their rulings can thus be applied only in fully comparable cases (Ibn Taymiyya, *Majmūʿ fatāwā*, 28:213.1).

[92] Ibn Taymiyya, *Siyāsa*, 51f. The context is a discussion of gifts made by rulers for reasons of state.

[93] *Ibid.*, 51.3. (For *yaṭʿam* read *yuṭʿim*, as implied in Laoust's translation of the passage, see H. Laoust, *Le traité de droit public d'Ibn Taimīya*, Beirut 1948, 55.) Cf. Ibn Taymiyya, *Siyāsa*, 143.4. [94] *Ibid.*, 51.11; cf. *ibid.*, 143.3. [95] *Ibid.*, 52.7.

[96] The distinction is lost in Laoust's translation (*Traité*, 55f.), as also in Nagel's paraphrase (*Staat und Glaubensgemeinschaft*, 2:134), since both overlook the parallelism between the two *rubbamā*s (Ibn Taymiyya, *Siyāsa*, 51.13, 51.17). [97] *Ibid.*, 51.13.

[98] *Ibid.*, 51.17.

[99] For this distinction between the *muqaṣṣir* and the *muʿtadī*, see Ibn Taymiyya, *Amr*, 31.10, and cf. also *ibid.*, 18.12, 37.1, 64.13. Here again the Khārijites are mentioned (*ibid.*, 19.14, 64.15).

4. THE DAMASCENE ḤANBALITES AFTER IBN TAYMIYYA

The history of Damascene Ḥanbalism after the time of Ibn Taymiyya was long and in some ways distinguished, but it has relatively little to offer us. The intellectual drama is over: no subsequent Damascene Ḥanbalite was remotely comparable to Ibn Taymiyya in either authority or originality. At the same time the biographical record, though continuous, is thin and meagre in comparison to that of earlier centuries.[100]

Throughout this period, the Ḥanbalites must have remained a minority in Damascus.[101] Their relations with the state do not seem to have changed much in late Mamlūk times, though this period may have seen significant developments in the history of Syrian Ḥanbalism outside Damascus.[102] But there were two critical shifts associated with Ottoman rule (922–1337/1516–1918). The first was the Ottoman conquest itself. This, from the Ḥanbalite point of view, was an untoward event:[103] the centre of power was now more remote, and the new Hanafī rulers were less catholic in their attitudes to the Sunnī law-schools. But the effects

[100] The period is covered by four main sources, all devoted to Ḥanbalite biography. The first is the work of the Palestinian Mujīr al-Dīn al-ʿUlaymī (d. *c.* 928/1522); the relevant part (for the years 751–902/1350–1497) is *al-Manhaj al-aḥmad*, 5:91–322 nos. 1302–1654. The second is the work of the Damascene Ibn ʿAbd al-Hādī (d. 909/1503), *al-Jawhar al-munaḍḍad* (covering roughly the same period). The third is the work of the Damascene Shāfiʿite Kamāl al-Dīn al-Ghazzī (d. 1214/1799), *al-Naʿt al-akmal*; the relevant part is 52–340 (for the years 901–1207/1496–1792). For Ghazzī's sources, see *ibid.*, 25; most of those he mentions are published, and none of them is specifically concerned with the Ḥanbalites. The fourth is the work of Jamīl al-Shaṭṭī (d. 1379/1959), *Mukhtaṣar Ṭabaqāt al-Ḥanābila*; the relevant part is 145–86 (for the period from Ghazzī's time to his own). Also available is the work of Burhān al-Dīn ibn Mufliḥ (d. 884/1479) (*al-Maqṣad al-arshad fī dhikr aṣḥāb al-imām Aḥmad*, ed. ʿA. S. al-ʿUthaymīn, Riyāḍ 1990), but I have made less use of it. None of these works can compare in richness and variety with the classic biographical works of Ibn Abī Yaʿlā and Ibn Rajab, and the lack of an authentically Ḥanbalite biographical tradition covering the tenth to twelfth/sixteenth to eighteenth centuries is noteworthy.

[101] The only indication I have noted of the demographic position relates to the village of Dūmā in the Ghūṭa of Damascus. Here Ghazzī remarks that it was a distinctive feature of this village that all its inhabitants were Ḥanbalites (Ghazzī, *Naʿt*, 228.15).

[102] The period seems to have seen a rise of Ḥanbalite *qāḍīs*. ʿUlaymī, who mentions many of them in the towns of Syria, remarks in several cases that the *qāḍī* in question was the first (known) Ḥanbalite incumbent (for Baʿlabakk, see ʿUlaymī, *Manhaj*, 5:177.13 (no. 1447); for Ḥimṣ, see *ibid.*, 208.9 (no. 1508); for Jerusalem, see *ibid.*, 232.12 (no. 1544); for Ramla, see *ibid.*, 263.7 (no. 1593); for Hebron, see *ibid.*, 263.16 (no. 1593); for the last three, see also his *al-Uns al-jalīl bi-taʾrīkh al-Quds waʾl-Khalīl*, Najaf 1968, 2:261.18, 263.2, 263.10). Does this reflect an increase in the numbers of Ḥanbalites in the population, or in the acceptability of the school to the authorities? A curiosity of Ḥanbalite history in this period is the appearance of a couple of Ḥanbalites with hare-brained ideas of a caliphal restoration (ʿUlaymī, *Manhaj*, 5:178.1 (*apud* no. 1447), 256.13 (no. 1585)).

[103] This was also Goldziher's view ('Zur Geschichte der ḥanbalitischen Bewegungen', 28).

were hardly traumatic. A few Damascene Ḥanbalites continued to find their way into the patronage or employment of the central government,[104] though others still maintained their distance from the authorities.[105] And despite the fact that there was no longer a full Ḥanbalite judge in Damascus, the Ḥanbalite law-school continued to be recognised.[106] The second shift took place in the last decades of Ottoman rule, and marks the onset of modern times. As the reformed Ottoman state came to loom ever larger in Damascus, Ḥanbalites began to take advantage of the new educational and career opportunities that this opened up for them.[107] This process was to bring to an end the world of the Ḥanbalite scholars as we have known it in these chapters.

The duty of forbidding wrong played little part in this long history, though from time to time Ḥanbalite scholars still touched on it in passing, and a few even devoted separate works to it. In the generation after Ibn Taymiyya, his pupil Ibn Qayyim al-Jawziyya (d. 751/1350) referred to the duty from time to time, often repeating what his teacher had said already,[108] while Ibn ʿAbd al-Hādī (d. 744/1343) wrote a short work on

[104] See Ghazzī, *Naʿt*, 178.15, 327.8, and cf. 339.3 (the first is from Muḥibbī (d. 1111/1699), *Khulāṣat al-athar*, Cairo 1284, 4:158.20). Voll's findings on this point are thus to be modified slightly (see J. Voll, 'The non-Wahhābī Ḥanbalīs of eighteenth century Syria', *Der Islam*, 49 (1972), 278).

[105] See Ghazzī, *Naʿt*, 150.4, 297.3, 324.12. Shaykh ʿAbd al-Qādir al-Taghlibī (d. 1135/1723) went so far as to abstain from drinking the coffee served by the *qāḍī* of Damascus, and made his living from the work of his own hands as a book-binder (*ibid.*, 274.9, in a biography supplied by the editors; Murādī, *Silk al-durar*, 3:59.6).

[106] See M. A. Bakhit, *The Ottoman province of Damascus in the sixteenth century*, Beirut 1982, 119–22, and cf. 134; for the continuity of this system down to 1327/1909f., when the central government is described as decreeing the amalgamation of the *sharʿī* courts, see Ghazzī, *Naʿt*, 94.18, and Shaṭṭī, *Mukhtaṣar*, 81.2.

[107] Like his ancestors, Ḥasan al-Shaṭṭī (d. 1274/1858) made his living exclusively as a merchant, and was too scrupulous to involve himself in government (Shaṭṭī, *Mukhtaṣar*, 158.20). This is the last we hear of such attitudes. His son Muḥammad al-Shaṭṭī (d. 1307/1890) had a career in public office (*ibid.*, 168.8), and entertained 'reformist ideas' (*ārāʾ iṣlāḥiyya*, *ibid.*, 168.17, with particular reference to the idea of a railway from Damascus to Mecca). Muḥammad's son Murād al-Shaṭṭī (d. 1314/1897) in turn entered the civil service after a modern Ottoman schooling (*ibid.*, 172.9), and numbered 'patriotic enthusiasm' (*ḥamiyya waṭaniyya*) among his virtues (*ibid.*, 173.20). For further examples, see *ibid.*, 177.18, 178.1, 179.25. By this point our author has begun to speak of 'our Arab government' (*ḥukūmatunā al-ʿArabiyya*, *ibid.*, 178.6, 186.2; the work was published within a year of the expulsion of Fayṣal from Damascus by the French). For a sketch of the history of the family and its genealogy, see L. Schatkowski Schilcher, *Families in politics: Damascene factions and estates of the 18th and 19th centuries*, Stuttgart 1985, 177–9.

[108] The passage on the duty in his book on statecraft (Ibn Qayyim al-Jawziyya (d. 751/1350), *al-Ṭuruq al-ḥukmiyya fī 'l-siyāsa al-sharʿiyya*, ed. M. Ḥ. al-Fiqī, Cairo 1953, 237.18–238.3) is taken more or less verbatim from his teacher (Ibn Taymiyya, *Ḥisba*, 12.10–13.6). He likewise borrows from his teacher a critique of the view that *inkār* is not appropriate in matters on which the law-schools disagree (*masāʾil al-khilāf*) (*Iʿlām*, 3:288.2; cf. above, note 69). He argues at greater length than Ibn Taymiyya the position

forbidding wrong which seems to be lost.[109] Ibn al-Qayyim's pupil Ibn Rajab (d. 795/1393) also touched on the duty; thus he stressed the desirability of reproving offenders in private.[110] In the next century, Zayn al-Dīn al-Ṣāliḥī (d. 856/1452) compiled a massive treatise on forbidding wrong to which we will turn in a moment. Two centuries later, the well-known Egyptian Ḥanbalite Marʿī ibn Yūsuf (d. 1033/1623f.) wrote a further monograph on the subject, but this does not seem to survive.[111] A later scholar of the same century, the Damascene Ibn Faqīh Fiṣṣa (d. 1071/1661), left a brief account of the duty.[112] A century later the Palestinian Shams al-Dīn al-Saffārīnī (d. 1188/1774f.) gave a short summary of it in a versified creed, and expanded on this in his own commentary thereto; he also wrote on the topic at greater length in a commentary on a versified work by an earlier author.[113] What he had to say in all this is not, however, of any great interest. Finally the Damascene Muḥammad al-Shaṭṭī (d. 1307/1890) gave a couple of pages of a pamphlet to a discussion of the duty, but without contributing anything of consequence.[114] Doubtless many more such passages could be found in the

Footnote 108 (*cont.*)
that *maʿrūf* and *munkar* are to be defined in terms of natural moral sense (see above, note 69), explicitly refuting the view that they are by definition no more than what God has commanded or forbidden (Ibn Qayyim al-Jawziyya (d. 751/1350), *Miftāḥ dār al-saʿāda*, ed. M. Ḥ. Rabīʿ, Cairo 1939, 332.15). He also uses *inkār al-munkar* as a prime example of the way in which a legal obligation may be overridden by circumstances: where proceeding would bring about a worse evil (as with rebellion against unjust rule), it is not allowed (*Iʿlām*, 3:4.4). There are doubless further references to *al-amr bi'l-maʿrūf* elsewhere in his works.

[109] Ibn Rajab, *Dhayl*, ed. Fiqī, 2:439.4. The work is described as a single *juz'*.

[110] Ibn Rajab (d. 795/1393), *al-Farq bayn al-naṣīḥa wa'l-taʿyīr*, ed. N. A. Khalaf, Cairo n.d., 39.5. His discussion of the duty in his *Jāmiʿ al-ʿulūm wa'l-ḥikam* (see above, ch. 3, note 7) offers nothing of interest for views held in his own day.

[111] Ghazzī, *Naʿt*, 193.12, from Muḥibbī, *Khulāṣa*, 4:360.2.

[112] ʿAbd al-Bāqī al-Mawāhibī, known as Ibn Faqīh Fiṣṣa (d. 1071/1661), *al-ʿAyn wa'l-athar*, ed. ʿI. R. Qalʿajī, Damascus 1987, 48–50. He takes the unusual view that *al-amr bi'l-maʿrūf* is a collective duty for the collectivity, and an individual one for the individual (*ibid.*, 48.6).

[113] For the creed, see Saffārīnī (d. 1188/1774f.), *al-Durra al-muḍiyya*, in his *Lawāmiʿ al-anwār al-bahiyya*, Jedda 1380, 2:426.21, 430.5; for his commentary on it, see *ibid.*, 2:426–36. This work was epitomised by Ḥasan al-Shaṭṭī (d. 1274/1858) (see his *Mukhtaṣar Lawāmiʿ al-anwār al-bahiyya*, Damascus 1931, 193–6). Saffārīnī's *Ghidhā' al-albāb* is a commentary on the *Manẓūmat al-ādāb* of Muḥammad ibn ʿAbd al-Qawī al-Mardāwī (d. 699/1299) (see *ibid.*, 1:6.2, and Brockelmann, *Geschichte*, supplementary volumes, 1:459 no. 20). The long account of forbidding wrong and related topics which Saffārīnī gives here (*Ghidhā'*, 1:163–205) is largely a patchwork of quotations (for one of them, see above, ch. 6, note 109). It comes alive when he includes personal reminiscences: a story about a Christian convert to Islam who married his daughter to a Christian around 1142/1729 (*ibid.*, 184.17), and a reference to his reactions on perusing some Druze literature (*ibid.*, 194.20). For Saffārīnī's biography, cf. below, note 125.

[114] Muḥammad al-Shaṭṭī (d. 1307/1890), *Muqaddimat Tawfīq al-mawādd al-niẓāmiyya li-aḥkām al-sharīʿa al-Muḥammadiyya*, Cairo n.d., 10.9. This author is an incipiently modern figure (see above, note 107).

Ḥanbalite literature of these centuries; but of the three monographic treatments, it seems that only that of Ṣāliḥī is extant.

Zayn al-Dīn al-Ṣāliḥī was a cheerful and socially successful Damascene scholar; he was also a Qādirī Ṣūfī, and this aspect of his activities bulks large in his biography.[115] He wrote his work on forbidding wrong in two large volumes,[116] both of which have now been published in some fashion.[117]

[115] For the biography of Zayn al-Dīn ʿAbd al-Raḥmān ibn Abī Bakr ibn Dāwūd al-Ṣāliḥī, see Ibn Mufliḥ, *Maqṣad*, 2:84f. no. 571; Sakhāwī (d. 902/1497), *al-Ḍawʾ al-lāmiʿ*, Cairo 1353–5, 4:62f. no. 195; Ibn ʿAbd al-Hādī, *Jawhar*, 63 no. 68; Nuʿaymī (d. 927/1521), *al-Dāris fī taʾrīkh al-madāris*, ed. J. al-Ḥasanī, Damascus 1948–51, 2:202f. no. 616; ʿUlaymī, *Manhaj*, 5:240f. no. 1556. His father was a Ṣūfī saint and author of some note (Sakhāwī, *Ḍawʾ*, 11:31 no. 83; Brockelmann, *Geschichte*, supplementary volumes, 2:149 no. 10, and second edition, 2:146 no. 10). It is characteristic that when Ṣāliḥī cites ʿAbd al-Qādir al-Jīlī (d. 561/1166) in his work, he does so in a style that emphasises his Ṣūfī allegiance to him (*shaykh mashāyikhinā ʿAbd al-Qādir al-Kaylānī qaddasa ʾllāhu rūḥahu* and the like, *Kanz*, 112.14, 183.6, 199.19, 225.5).

[116] For the two volumes, see Sakhāwī, *Ḍawʾ*, 4:63.8 (and cf. Ibn ʿAbd al-Hādī, *Jawhar*, 63.8, and the editor's note thereto).

[117] The first volume was published by M. ʿU. Ṣumayda in Beirut in 1996 (this publication was drawn to my attention by Frank Stewart). The editor does not seem to have realised that he had only the first volume of the work, though this is apparent from a comparison of the four chapters (*abwāb*) that it contains with the ten announced by Ṣāliḥī (*Kanz*, 33.3 = 27.7 of Ṣumayda's edition). On the title-page, Ṣumayda gives the title as *al-Kanz al-akbar min* . . ., despite the fact that Ṣāliḥī himself states that he is naming his book *al-Kanz al-akbar fī ʾl-amr biʾl-maʿrūf waʾl-nahy ʿan al-munkar* (*ibid.*). Ṣumayda bases his edition on a Dublin manuscript which he identifies as Chester Beatty no. 3,732 (see *Kanz*, 7 no. 9 of his introduction); it is clear from the reproductions he gives of the first and last folios of his manuscript (*ibid.*, 9–12) that it is in fact no. 3,270 (for which see A. J. Arberry, *The Chester Beatty Library: a handlist of the Arabic manuscripts*, Dublin 1955–66, 2:8; this manuscript was drawn to my attention by Maribel Fierro prior to the appearance of Ṣumayda's edition, and I am grateful to the Chester Beatty Library for supplying me with a microfilm). A printing containing both volumes of the work appeared in Saudi Arabia in 1997, a year after Ṣumayda's edition. Whereas Ṣumayda's edition is a bad one, this is not really an edition at all. It is nevertheless the text that I cite when I give no indication to the contrary. According to the anonymous preface, it is based on these manuscripts (*Kanz*, 7): Chester Beatty no. 327 (read 3,270), and Cairo, Dār al-Kutub, Akhlāq 921, for the first volume; Berlin no. 167 (understand Landberg 167, see below), and Cairo, Dār al-Kutub, Akhlāq 287, for the second volume. The manuscripts on which I have relied in my own study of the work are the following. For the first volume, I used ms. Istanbul, Süleymaniye, Fatih 1,136 (185 folios), copied in Muḥarram 853/1449 (f. 185a.19) – that is to say, within the author's lifetime. Where I have occasion to cite this manuscript, I do so according to the newer and more correct of the two foliations. For the second volume, I used Berlin, Landberg 167 (171 folios); I am indebted to the Staatsbibliothek zu Berlin for sending me a microfilm. For this manuscript, which contains the last six of the ten chapters, see Ahlwardt, *Verzeichniss*, 5:10f. no. 5,397. Ahlwardt states that the date of copying is given by a later hand as 826/1422f.; but there is no mention of copying, and what the 'later' hand of the collator has in fact supplied is the omitted completion of the sentence beginning *intahā ʾl-taʾlīf* (f. 171b.10, reproduced in *Kanz*, 15; cf. the end of the Cairo manuscript of the second volume reproduced *ibid.*, 12, and *ibid.*, 881.10, where *min al-sinīn* is to be read for the printer's *min al-sabʿīn*). This, then, is the date of composition of the work. This manuscript was overlooked by Brockelmann, and I learnt of it only when Adam Sabra kindly brought me a printout of it from a microfilm in Cairo. He also informed me that there are copies of the work in the Dār al-Kutub, which can be identified with those mentioned in the Saʿūdī printing of the work (Taṣawwuf 921 and Akhlāq Taymūr 287; for the first, see Dār al-Kutub al-Miṣriyya,

Although Ṣāliḥī is not shy of speaking in his own voice, he is above all an assiduous compiler. He makes particularly extensive use of Ghazzālī, whom he doubtless regarded as a fellow-Ṣūfī – he explicitly quotes him some fifty-five times in his first volume and seventeen in the second;[118] and he depends on him for the bone-structure of his major doctrinal chapter.[119] He does, nevertheless, provide a substantial treatment of an idea that I have rarely seen elsewhere, and which strongly reflects his Ṣūfī concerns. When he introduces Ghazzālī's eight levels of response to wrong, he prefixes yet another: response through spiritual state (***inkār al-munkar bi'l-ḥāl***).[120] What he intends is most easily understood from the anecdotes that follow, in which Ṣūfī saints – including ʿAbd al-Qādir al-Jīlī – are able to right wrongs by invoking supernatural intervention; for example, they turn wine into honey, vinegar or water.[121] This is one of the rare examples of a distinctively Ṣūfī approach to forbidding wrong.

Footnote 117 (*cont.*)
Fihrist al-kutub al-ʿArabiyya al-mawjūda bi'l-Dār li-ghāyat sanat 1921, vol. 1, Cairo 1924, 349a); cf. the Cairo manuscript noted by Brockelmann (*Geschichte*, second edition, 2:124 no. 2, with errors in the author's name and death date); that mentioned without further details by Ṣumayda in his introduction (*Kanz*, 7 no. 1); and the likewise unidentified Cairo manuscript used by ʿAṭā in his edition of Khallāl's work (see Khallāl, *Amr*, 72f., 84 nn. 1f., 89 n. 1, 94 n. 1, 198 no. 36). I should add that Ṣāliḥī's work seems to have engendered two bibliographical muddles. The first regards the title of a short tract by the Shāfiʿite Abū Bakr ibn Qāḍī ʿAljūn (d. 928/1522) preserved under the same title (viz. *al-Kanz al-akbar fī 'l-amr bi'l-maʿrūf wa'l-nahy ʿan al-munkar*) in a Damascus manuscript (Ẓāhiriyya, Majmūʿ no. 3,745 *ʿāmm* = Majāmīʿ 8, item 7; see Brockelmann, *Geschichte*, supplementary volumes, 2:119 no. 2, and Sawwās, *Fihris*, 40 no. 7). However this title, which appears only on a title-page preceding the text (f. 98a), bears no relation to the content of the tract itself, which is about an alleged tomb of a member of the family of the Prophet in Damascus. I am grateful to the Maktabat al-Asad for supplying me with a copy. The second muddle – or such I suspect it to be – is the ascription by Ḥājjī Khalīfa (d. 1067/1657) of a work on forbidding wrong to another Ṣūfī of the time, namely ʿAbd al-Laṭīf ibn ʿAbd al-Raḥmān al-Maqdisī (also d. 856/1452), who, he says, completed it in Rabīʿ I, 853/1449 (*Kashf al-ẓunūn*, ed. Ş. Yaltkaya and R. Bilge, Istanbul 1941–3, 1398.20; for this scholar, see Brockelmann, *Geschichte*, second edition, 2:299f. no. 4, where the death date is from Ṭāshköprīzāde (d. 968/1561), *al-Shaqā'iq al-Nuʿmāniyya*, ed. A. S. Furat, Istanbul 1985, 69.1; also Sakhāwī, *Ḍaw'*, 4:327f. no. 901). This looks like a misattribution of a volume of Ṣāliḥī's *Kanz*, perhaps of the copy of the second volume which originally accompanied the Istanbul manuscript of the first.

118 His first quotation is, appropriately, the rhetorical passage with which Ghazzālī opens his discussion of *al-amr bi'l-maʿrūf* (Ṣāliḥī, *Kanz*, 31.3; cf. below, ch. 16, 428). My count leaves out cases where material deriving from Ghazzālī is appropriated without attribution, or attributed to intermediate sources.

119 This is Ṣāliḥī's second chapter (*ibid.*, 183–273); for the corresponding part of Ghazzālī's treatment, see below, ch. 16, 428–42. It is striking that Ṣāliḥī expresses no reservations about Ghazzālī's more radical notions; in particular, he transcribes Ghazzālī's eighth level (armed bands) without visible shock (*ibid.*, 270.2; cf. below, ch. 16, 441). In his second volume, he appropriates, embellishes and extends Ghazzālī's survey of common wrongs (*ibid.*, 720–58; cf. below, ch. 16, 442–6).

120 Ṣāliḥī, *Kanz*, 236.24; on this idea, see further below, ch. 16, 462–4. For Ghazzālī's eight levels, see below, ch. 16, 438–41.

121 *Ibid.*, 237.5–240.5.

Apart from this, what Ṣāliḥī has to offer us is bits and pieces.[122] One of the more interesting is his negative view of the saying that sets out the tripartite division of labour between rulers, scholars and the common people.[123]

Meanwhile the biographers make occasional reference to scholars who were assiduous in forbidding wrong, among them Ṣāliḥī himself.[124] But such statements tend to be perfunctory, and they become increasingly rare. For the study of forbidding wrong, there seems to be little more to be learnt from the Ḥanbalite communities of the Fertile Crescent.[125]

5. CONCLUSION

Until the rise of the Wahhābī movement in Najd, Ḥanbalite history was essentially a tale of two cities. But as we have seen, the circumstances of the Ḥanbalite communities of the two cities were strikingly different.

[122] Thus he includes a behavioural component – frowning – in the performance of the duty by or in the heart (*ibid.*, 76.18). He deals with reports that the Ḥashwiyya deny the obligatoriness of *al-amr bi'l-ma'rūf* (see below, ch. 9, notes 40, 63) by identifying the Ḥashwiyya as a subsect (*firqa*) of the Rāfiḍa (*ibid.*, 121.9; cf. below, ch. 9, note 63); interpreted in this way, such reports need occasion no embarrassment to Ḥanbalites.

[123] After quoting the saying anonymously, he remarks that it is a weak view (*qawl ḍa'īf*) (*ibid.*, 269.23). He himself sets out a mild version of the same idea (*ibid.*, 75.23, but note the caveat that follows, *ibid.*, 76.16). For the saying, see above, ch. 6, note 166.

[124] For (1) Ṣāliḥī, see Sakhāwī, *Ḍaw'*, 4:63.5. The other cases I have noted are: (2) Jamāl al-Dīn al-Maqdisī (d. 754/1353) (Ibn Ḥajar, *Durar*, 4:464.3 (no. 1268); Ibn Mufliḥ, *Maqṣad*, 3:141.7 (no. 1270); 'Ulaymī, *Manhaj*, 5:100.1 (no. 1308)); (3) Shihāb al-Dīn al-Zur'ī (d. 762/1360), a pupil of Ibn Taymiyya (Ibn Mufliḥ, *Maqṣad*, 1:198.12 (no. 176), and 'Ulaymī, *Manhaj*, 5:117.4 (no. 1338), with stress on his forwardness towards rulers); (4) Ya'qūb al-Kurdī of Ba'labakk (d. 813/1411) (Ibn 'Abd al-Hādī, *Jawhar*, 183.3 (no. 209)); (5) 'Umar al-Lu'lu'ī (d. 873/1468), a great admirer of Ibn Taymiyya (*ibid.*, 106.3 (no. 117)). To these might be added (6) Ibn al-Ḥabbāl (d. 833/1429), who agreed to accept appointment as Ḥanbalite *qāḍī* of Damascus only on various conditions, one of which was that he would take action against abominations (*yunkir al-munkar*) whoever the perpetrator might be (Nu'aymī, *Dāris*, 2:54.1); 'Ulaymī tells us that he was very severe with Turks and such (*Manhaj*, 5:212.5 (no. 1516)). Otherwise I have noted no Damascene performers of the duty in the works of 'Ulaymī, Ibn 'Abd al-Hādī, Ghazzī or Shaṭṭī.

[125] One of the most interesting of the lesser-known Ḥanbalite scenes of the Fertile Crescent is the rural Ḥanbalism of northern Palestine (the term *arḍ Filasṭīn* is used by 'Ulaymī, see *Manhaj*, 5:269.8 (no. 1593)). The existence of Ḥanbalite scholars living in the villages around Nāblus (and not simply stemming from them) is well attested in the sixth/twelfth century (see Drory, 'Ḥanbalīs of the Nablus region', 95–7, and D. Talmon Heller, 'The shaykh and the community: popular Ḥanbalite Islam in 12th–13th century Jabal Nablus and Jabal Qasyūn', *Studia Islamica*, 79 (1994)), and again in the twelfth and thirteenth/eighteenth and nineteenth centuries (see Ghazzī, *Na't*, 295.13, 302.4; Shaṭṭī, *Mukhtaṣar Ṭabaqāt al-Ḥanābila*, 171.9, 178.23). Ghazzī notes two Palestinian Ḥanbalites of the twelfth/eighteenth century as performers of *al-amr bi'l-ma'rūf*: 'Abd al-Ḥaqq al-Labadī (d. 1176/1762f.) (Ghazzī, *Na't*, 296.1) and Shams al-Dīn al-Saffārīnī (d. 1188/1774f.) (*ibid.*, 302.11; cf. *ibid.*, 303.17, and Murādī, *Silk al-durar*, 4:32.6). The latter is described with a vividness unusual in these sources.

In Baghdad, the Ḥanbalites made up a large part of the population, and were thus a potentially significant political constituency. As such, they could be mobilised either for or against the state. These alternatives of confrontation and cooperation are dramatised in the styles of the two charismatic Ḥanbalite preachers: on the one hand, there is the demagoguery and trouble-making of Barbahārī; and on the other, the theatricality and flattery of Ibn al-Jawzī. These poles, and the evolution from the one to the other, constitute a phase of Ḥanbalite history which was markedly out of tune with the original heritage of Ḥanbalism.

In Damascus, by contrast, the Ḥanbalites were only a minority; their relative scholastic distinction could never win them political weight as a community. But they lived in an increasingly benign political environment, and one in which a certain solidarity with the state was engendered by the exigencies of holy war against infidel invaders. Thus their minority status did not issue in a return to the quietly alienated politics of Ibn Ḥanbal. As in Baghdad, though not to the same extent, the community came to enjoy a positive relationship with the state. Thus in neither city did Ḥanbalite thought develop in a context similar to that in which it had originated.

In both cities, then, there was a tension between the heritage of the Ḥanbalite school and the actual circumstances of the community. Such a disparity called for some intellectual attention, if not resolution. Yet in Baghdad, Ḥanbalite discussions of forbidding wrong give only occasional and quite unsystematic expression to the tension. In Damascus, by contrast, Ibn Taymiyya succeeded in developing a style of political thought which was radically innovative, both in its implications for forbidding wrong and in general. It was not a style that had much future in the Ḥanbalite community of Damascus itself; for while Ibn Taymiyya was on the side of the state, the converse did not obtain. But his approach was to achieve a quite unexpected relevance to the political life of central Arabia some half a millennium later.

CHAPTER 8

THE ḤANBALITES OF NAJD

1. INTRODUCTION

We come now to the second, and more radical, of the two major geographical discontinuities of Ḥanbalite history. The scene shifts away from the great cities of the Fertile Crescent altogether; in their place we now encounter the scattered oases of the wilderness of Najd. The Ḥanbalite school seems to have been well established in this desolate region of Arabia as early as the ninth/fifteenth century.[1] Its situation here was naturally very different from what it was in the Fertile Crescent. Najdī Ḥanbalism had to come to terms with a tribal society that could barely be described as urban, and which lacked political organisation above the level of the local chief who held sway over a single oasis.[2] A further peculiarity of the position of the Ḥanbalite school in Najd was that it was not in serious competition with other sects or schools. For the first time in its history, Ḥanbalism had a society to itself. This is no doubt part of the reason why two-thirds of the pre-Wahhābī Najdī Ḥanbalite scholars known to us in the tenth to twelfth/sixteenth to eighteenth centuries were judges; who else could have filled these positions?[3] It would be interesting to know how this exotic

[1] For a useful survey of the Ḥanbalite biographical literature for Najd in the tenth to twelfth/sixteenth to eighteenth centuries, see U. M. Al-Juhany, 'The history of Najd prior to the Wahhābīs', University of Washington Ph.D. 1983, ch. 5. For some Syrian evidence of Najdī Ḥanbalism in the ninth/fifteenth century, see Ibn ʿAbd al-Hādī, *Jawhar*, 15 nos. 12f.; 40 no. 46; 112 nos. 128f. (and cf. 34f. of the introduction); M. Cook, 'The historians of pre-Wahhābī Najd', *Studia Islamica*, 76 (1992), 173 n. 40. Note also that the Syrian Ḥanbalite Dāwūd ibn Aḥmad (or Muḥammad) al-Balāʿī (d. *c.* 862/1457), though born in Ḥamāh, was of Najdī extraction (ʿUlaymī, *Maqṣad*, 5:250f. no. 1572; Ibn al-ʿImād (d.1089/1679), *Shadharāt al-dhahab*, ed. ʿA. and M. al-Arnāʾūṭ, Beirut 1986–93, 9:441.15).

[2] See Juhany, 'History of Najd', 175–82, 272–80. I am sceptical of Juhany's thesis of even a limited 'development of regional political powers' in late pre-Wahhābī Najd (*ibid.*, 275–9); cf. M. Cook, 'The expansion of the first Saudi state: the case of Washm', in C. E. Bosworth *et al.* (eds.), *Essays in honor of Bernard Lewis: the Islamic world from classical to modern times*, Princeton 1989, 667.

[3] Juhany, 'History of Najd', 252.

environment affected the practice of forbidding wrong. But we hear virtually nothing about it,[4] a circumstance which may reflect no more than the general paucity of information for the pre-Wahhābī period of Najdī history.

In 1158/1745f. an alliance was made which was to transform both the political structure of Najdī society and the relationship of Ḥanbalism to political authority within it. One of the parties to this alliance was a Ḥanbalite scholar, Muḥammad ibn ʿAbd al-Wahhāb (d. 1206/1792), who had come to the view that the religious practices of most so-called Muslims of his day were in reality polytheism (*shirk*), and as such an appropriate target for holy war. The other party was Muḥammad ibn Saʿūd (d. 1179/1765), the chief of Dirʿiyya, one of the larger Najdī oases. The outcome of this alliance was the rise of the militant Wahhābī movement, in symbiosis with what we can now begin to call the Saʿūdī state.[5] The transformation of the role of Ḥanbalism which this implied was far more drastic than any the tradition had undergone in Baghdad or Damascus. Ḥanbalism was now cast in the unfamiliar role of a doctrine of state-formation in a near-stateless tribal society, and in this role it functioned as the political ideology of three successive Saʿūdī states. What, then, was the place of forbidding wrong in this ideology?

2. THE FIRST SAʿŪDĪ STATE

The Wahhābī movement was a classic example of going to see what people were doing and telling them to stop it. We might therefore expect forbidding wrong to be central to Wahhābī thought and action from the start. And if we accept the testimony of Ibn Bishr (d. 1290/1873), one of our two major sources for the history of the first Saʿūdī state (1158–1233/1745f.–1818), this was indeed the case.

Before the appearance of Ibn ʿAbd al-Wahhāb, so Ibn Bishr tells us, manifestations of polytheism were rife in Najd, but there was no one to perform the duty against them.[6] On his father's death in 1153/1741, Ibn

[4] An epistle of ʿAbd al-Wahhāb ibn Sulaymān (d. 1153/1741), the father of the reformer, denounces the activities of certain Qādirīs in Ḥarma, and calls for action (*inkār*) to be taken against them with the hand and tongue (*Majmūʿat al-rasāʾil waʾl-masāʾil al-Najdiyya*, 1:525.7; for the rest of this chapter, the title of this work is abbreviated '*Majmūʿa*'). I saw no references to forbidding wrong in the Najdī biographies included in Ibn Ḥumayd (d. 1295/1878), *al-Suḥub al-wābila ʿalā ḍarāʾiḥ al-Ḥanābila*, n.p. 1989.

[5] This development is chronicled in H. S. Philby, *Saʿudi Arabia*, London 1955, ch. 2, and in other works cited in Cook, 'Expansion of the first Saudi state', 683 n. 32.

[6] Ibn Bishr (d. 1290/1873), *ʿUnwān al-majd fī taʾrīkh Najd*, Beirut n.d., 17.6 (*laysa lil-nās man yanhāhum ʿan dhālika fa-yaṣdaʿ biʾl-amr biʾl-maʿrūf waʾl-nahy ʿan al-munkar*). For an

ʿAbd al-Wahhāb set about doing just that in the oasis of Ḥuraymilāʾ;[7] in particular, he wished to carry out the duty against a servile group in the oasis who were notorious evil-doers.[8] When he moved to ʿUyayna, ʿUthmān ibn Muʿammar (d. 1163/1750), the local chief, assisted him, and the duty was publicly performed.[9] As the fortunes of Ibn ʿAbd al-Wahhāb began to rise, monotheism and forbidding wrong began to spread.[10] Subsequently, however, Ibn Muʿammar lost his nerve in the face of external pressure; Ibn ʿAbd al-Wahhāb then called upon him to persevere in his adherence to the cause of monotheism, the pillars of Islam and forbidding wrong.[11] When Ibn Muʿammar nevertheless defected, Ibn ʿAbd al-Wahhāb moved to Dirʿiyya, an oasis awash with polytheism, and made his historic alliance with Ibn Saʿūd. Once there, he performed the duty assiduously, and commanded the people of the oasis to study the meaning of the confession of faith 'There is no god but God'.[12] When the well-known Yemeni traditionalist Ibn al-Amīr al-Ṣanʿānī (d. 1182/1768) heard of Ibn ʿAbd al-Wahhāb's message of monotheism and forbidding wrong, he wrote a poem in his praise.[13] Likewise in his obituary notice on Ibn ʿAbd al-Wahhāb, Ibn Bishr remarks that he had treated the people of Najd justly, commanding right and forbidding wrong.[14] Here, then, we have an account of the career of Ibn ʿAbd al-Wahhāb in which the duty plays a central part.[15]

analysis of the general character of Ibn Bishr's account of the career of Ibn ʿAbd al-Wahhāb, see E. Peskes, *Muḥammad b. ʿAbdalwahhāb (1703–92) im Widerstreit*, Beirut 1993, 252–78.

7 Ibn Bishr, *ʿUnwān*, 19.1: *aʿlana biʾl-daʿwa waʾl-inkār waʾl-amr biʾl-maʿrūf waʾl-nahy ʿan al-munkar.* 8 *Ibid.*, 19.4. 9 *Ibid.*, 19.11.

10 *Ibid.*, 20.9: *wa fashā ʾl-tawḥīd waʾl-amr biʾl-maʿrūf waʾl-nahy ʿan al-munkar.*

11 *Ibid.*, 20.19. 12 *Ibid.*, 23.26.

13 *Ibid.*, 50.8. Ibn al-Amīr did indeed see Ibn ʿAbd al-Wahhāb's mission in terms of *al-amr biʾl-maʿrūf* (see the quotation from his *Dīwān* in Ḥ. al-Jāsir, 'al-Ṣilāt bayn Ṣanʿāʾ waʾl-Dirʿiyya', *al-ʿArab*, 22 (1987), 433). Compare the anti-Wahhābī polemist Ibn ʿAfāliq al-Aḥsāʾī, who in an epistle written not later than 1163/1750 speaks of the Wahhābīs carrying out their activities in the guise of (*fī ṣūrat*) *al-amr biʾl-maʿrūf* (epistle of Muḥammad ibn ʿAbd al-Raḥmān ibn ʿAfāliq al-Aḥsāʾī to ʿUthmān ibn Muʿammar, ms. Berlin, Pm. 25, f. 56b.5). For this text, see Ahlwardt, *Verzeichniss*, 2:477 no. 2,158, and Peskes, *Muḥammad b. ʿAbdalwahhāb*, 57; I am indebted to the Staatsbibliothek Preussischer Kulturbesitz for supplying me with a microfilm. The epistle can be dated not later than 1163/1750, since in that year Ibn Muʿammar was assassinated (Ibn Ghannām (d. 1225/1810f.), *Rawḍat al-afkār*, Bombay 1337, 2:16.7; Ibn Bishr, *ʿUnwān*, 30.5); Ibn ʿAfāliq himself died in the same or the following year, the best-supported date being early in 1163/1750 (ʿAbdallāh ibn ʿAbd al-Raḥmān ibn Ṣāliḥ al-Bassām, *ʿUlamāʾ Najd khilāl sittat qurūn*, Mecca 1398, 821.5). Ibn ʿAbd al-Wahhāb refers to an epistle of Ibn ʿAfāliq in one of his own (Ibn Ghannām, *Rawḍa*, 1:135.16). 14 Ibn Bishr, *ʿUnwān*, 84.20; and cf. *ibid.*, 83.24.

15 Ibn Bishr's comtemporary ʿAbd al-Laṭīf ibn ʿAbd al-Raḥmān (d. 1293/1876) likewise stresses Ibn ʿAbd al-Wahhāb's devotion to the duty (*Majmūʿa*, 3:372.12). For ʿAbd al-Laṭīf, see below, note 62.

Ibn Bishr then proceeds to chronicle the rest of the history of the first Saʿūdī state in the same vein. He describes successive Saʿūdī rulers as performers of the duty,[16] and says the same of Ibn ʿAbd al-Wahhāb's grandson Sulaymān ibn ʿAbdallāh (d. 1233/1818), whom he characterises as no respecter of persons in this connection.[17] He enters into some detail regarding the way in which forbidding wrong was carried out in the course of the pilgrimages to Mecca led by Saʿūd ibn ʿAbd al-ʿAzīz (r. 1218–29/1803–14) in the years 1223/1809, 1225/1811, 1226/1811 and 1227/1812.[18] Men were appointed to patrol the markets at the times of prayer and order people to pray; smoking vanished from the markets, or at least was no longer to be seen in public. When Ibn Bishr moves on to the chaotic years that followed the destruction of the first Saʿūdī state by the Egyptians, he devotes some purple passages to the disappearance of forbidding wrong and the moral and social disorders that flowed from this.[19] Thus he continues to present the duty as central to the Wahhābī enterprise to the end of the first Saʿūdī state and beyond.

There is nevertheless reason to doubt much of this testimony.[20] We are fortunately in a position to compare Ibn Bishr's account of early Saʿūdī

[16] Viz. ʿAbd al-ʿAzīz ibn Saʿūd (r. 1179–1218/1765–1803) (Ibn Bishr, *ʿUnwān*, 120.16), Saʿūd ibn ʿAbd al-ʿAzīz (r. 1218–29/1803–14) (*ibid.*, 171.27), and ʿAbdallāh ibn Saʿūd (r. 1229–33/1814–18) (*ibid.*, 207.8). He adds of Saʿūd that he frequently urged people to carry out the duty, both in his assemblies and in correspondence (see also his speech to two quarrelling tribal chiefs, *ibid.*, 170.14). [17] *Ibid.*, 208.25.

[18] *Ibid.*, 136.5 (1223/1809), 146.4 (1225/1811), 153.10 (1226/1811), 155.7 (1227/1812). Oddly, he makes no reference to such measures in his account of the original occupation of Mecca in 1217 (or rather 1218)/1803 (*ibid.*, 117.1); but the Meccan chronicler Aḥmad ibn Zaynī Daḥlān (d. 1304/1886) states that Saʿūd had a bonfire made of tobacco-pipes (*shiyash*) and stringed musical instruments, after recording the names of their owners (*Khulāṣat al-kalām*, Cairo 1305, 279.1, paraphrased in C. Snouck Hurgronje, *Mekka*, The Hague 1888–9, 1:150). He adds that the scholars of Mecca were made to study the *Kashf al-shubuhāt* of Ibn ʿAbd al-Wahhāb (Daḥlān, *Khulāṣat al-kalām*, 279.5). Daḥlān further reports that in 1221/1806 the Sharīf of Mecca issued orders to the people of Mecca and Jedda banning tobacco, requiring attendance at the mosque, and imposing readings of epistles of Ibn ʿAbd al-Wahhāb on the scholars; this, of course, was in deference to Saʿūdī views (*ibid.*, 292.29, and cf. Snouck Hurgronje, *Mekka*, 1:153). Burckhardt confirms that, as a result of the Saʿūdī conquest, the Meccans were 'obliged to pray more punctually than usual', and to desist from smoking in public; he mentions a bonfire of 'Persian pipes' in front of Saʿūd's headquarters (J. L. Burckhardt, *Notes on the Bedouins and Wahábys*, London 1831, 2:195). In addition, he attests roll-calls at prayers in Medina during the Saʿūdī occupation (*ibid.*, 199). See also below, note 49.

[19] Ibn Bishr, *ʿUnwān*, 209.13, 243.17, 297.2. For the antithesis between *al-amr biʾl-maʿrūf* and anarchy, compare also *ibid.*, 62.13. The examples of moral deterioration given by Ibn Bishr are music-making and neglect of prayer.

[20] I would accept the authenticity of his account of Saʿūd's pilgrimages; as we have seen (above, note 18), it is confirmed by non-Wahhābī sources. But it is also the only context in which Ibn Bishr's use of the terminology of *al-amr biʾl-maʿrūf* is matched by concrete historical detail – elsewhere his language merely embellishes his story. I thus tend to think that the conduct of the Saʿūdīs in the Ḥijāz represents an untypical response to a distinc-

history with that of a chronicler contemporary with the first Saʿūdī state, Ibn Ghannām (d. 1225/1810f.). In this earlier presentation, references to forbidding wrong are all but absent. In recounting Ibn ʿAbd al-Wahhāb's career, Ibn Ghannām makes a reference to his performance of the duty in ʿUyayna;[21] and he makes passing mention of it in a poem.[22] But that is all.

At the same time, forbidding wrong is not a prominent theme in the writings of Ibn ʿAbd al-Wahhāb. It is sometimes said that he devoted a separate work to the subject,[23] but this seems to be without firm foundation. As might be expected, he refers to the duty from time to time in his numerous extant works. Thus he includes it in two credal statements, in each case as the last item in a list.[24] He gives it a mention, but no more, in a commentary to Q3:100–8.[25] He briefly discusses the familiar issue of the appropriateness or otherwise of seeking to perform the duty in matters over which the law-schools differ.[26] He repeats familiar legal material

tive context: the prevalence of such laxity in such holy places. The alternative is to suppose that what was exceptional about the Ḥijāz was not what happened there but the quality of our evidence for it. This strikes me as possible but less likely.

21 Ibn Ghannām, *Rawḍa*, 2:2.4. There is no reference to the duty in the obituary notice that Ibn Ghannām devotes to Ibn ʿAbd al-Wahhāb (*ibid.*, 174–7). For an analysis of the general character of Ibn Ghannām's treatment of the career of Ibn ʿAbd al-Wahhāb, see Peskes, *Muḥammad b. ʿAbdalwahhāb*, 221–52.

22 Ibn Ghannām, *Rawḍa*, 2:217.7. Ibn Ghannām does not cover the Saʿūdī occupation of the Ḥijāz; his chronicle as we have it breaks off in 1212/1797f.

23 See, for example, K. al-Ziriklī, *Aʿlām*, Beirut 1979, 6:257b; ʿU. R. Kaḥḥāla, *Muʿjam al-muʾallifīn*, Damascus 1957–61, 10:269b. The oldest authority I know for this alleged work is Ṣiddīq Ḥasan Khān al-Qannawjī (d. 1307/1890) (*Abjad al-ʿulūm*, Bhopal 1295–6, 874.23, in a list of writings of Ibn ʿAbd al-Wahhāb which he states he had seen himself). It also appears in a list of the works of Ibn ʿAbd al-Wahhāb in a heavily edited version of the first volume of Ibn Bishr's chronicle (*al-Juzʾ al-awwal min kitāb ʿUnwān al-majd fī taʾrīkh Najd*, Baghdad 1328, 57.4); no such title is mentioned in the original (Ibn Bishr, *ʿUnwān*, 85.9), and the insertion is likely to be the work of the young Ibn Māniʿ (d. 1385/1965), who contributed to the editing of this version (cf. *al-Juzʾ al-awwal*, 57 n. 1).

24 ʿAbd al-Raḥmān ibn Qāsim al-ʿĀṣimī (d. 1372/1953), *al-Durar al-saniyya fī ʾl-ajwiba al-Najdiyya*, Beirut 1978, 1:30.13, 59.2. The first of these creeds appears in the Baghdad version of Ibn Bishr's chronicle (Ibn Bishr, *al-Juzʾ al-awwal*, 67–70), but not in the later and more authentic printings of the work; it is translated in R. Hartmann, 'Die Wahhābiten', *Zeitschrift der Deutschen Morgenländischen Gesellschaft*, 78 (1924), 179–84. Our passage is at Ibn Bishr, *al-Juzʾ al-awwal*, 70.17, and Hartmann, 'Die Wahhābiten', 184 §18. Hartmann points out the dependance of this creed, our article included, on Ibn Taymiyya's *Wāsiṭiyya* (*ibid.*, 186; cf. above, ch. 7, note 69). The second creed is quoted in extenso by Jabartī under the events of the year 1218/1803f. (Jabartī (d. 1240/1824f.), *ʿAjāʾib al-āthār*, ed. Ḥ. M. Jawhar *et al.*, Cairo 1958–67, 6:72–6; our passage is at *ibid.*, 76.10). It is not in fact clear in Jabartī's presentation who exactly is the author of the creed (*ibid.*, 72.12).

25 Ibn Ghannām, *Rawḍa*, 1:245.10. He says that a *ṭāʾifa mutajarrida* is here commanded to undertake the duty of calling to good and forbidding wrong, by which we may understand a group that exists solely for this purpose.

26 He offers the usual formula that there is no *inkār* in matters of *ijtihād* (*ibid.*, 2:163.5, in a letter to the scholars of Mecca written in 1204/1789f.). See also *Muʾallafāt al-Shaykh al-imām Muḥammad ibn ʿAbd al-Wahhāb*, ed. ʿA. Z. al-Rūmī *et al.*, Riyāḍ 1398, 3:2:33.8, and Ibn Qāsim, *Durar*, 1:136.11.

regarding the duties of the wedding-guest.[27] He ironically entertains the notion that his polemical opponents might consider themselves to be performing the duty against him.[28] But such references do not suggest any particular urgency or centrality of the duty in his conception of his mission.

Two passages in the works of Ibn ʿAbd al-Wahhāb merit closer attention in this connection. The first is a letter to the Wahhābīs of Sudayr.[29] What he emphasises here is the importance of tact in the performance of the duty. It should be performed in the first instance nicely and in private, and not in such a manner as to give rise to schism in the community. Indeed, if the offender is a ruler (*amīr*), it would seem that he should not be reproved in public at all.[30] The interest of these prescriptions lies in the fact that they are a response to current events. Although the circumstances that elicited this advice are not specified, it is clear from the letter that some men of religion in the oasis of Ḥawṭa had spoken out harshly against some evil, probably one committed by the local ruler, and that this had led to dissension. What is striking is that in this practical context of political damage limitation, Ibn ʿAbd al-Wahhāb felt no embarrassment about minimising the demands of the duty; clearly it had little bearing on the integrity of his mission. The second passage to be considered here is the only one I have encountered in which Ibn ʿAbd al-Wahhāb relates forbidding wrong to the struggle against polytheism. What is under discussion here is the part played by the scholars in this struggle; he states that they used to perform their role in the past,[31] and defines them as those who pit themselves against sin and heresy, to the extent that they are able to do so, by thought, word and deed.[32] In other words, he is here describing an earlier situation in which it was individual scholars, not rulers and armies, who carried on the struggle; the current phase of outright war on polytheism is something else again.

There are two other scholars of the first Saʿūdī period whose writings survive in sufficient bulk to make their views worth discussing: Ḥamad ibn Nāṣir ibn Muʿammar (d. 1225/1811) and Ibn ʿAbd al-Wahhāb's son ʿAbdallāh (d. 1242/1826f.).[33] Ḥamad, a pupil of Ibn ʿAbd al-Wahhāb,

[27] See above, ch. 7, note 2. [28] Ibn Ghannām, *Rawḍa*, 1:72.18, 226.8.

[29] *Ibid.*, 221–3. [30] *Ibid.*, 222.23.

[31] *Ibid.*, 1:92.10 (the passage is from his *Kashf al-shubuhāt*). Compare the complaint of two pupils of Ibn ʿAbd al-Wahhāb in an epistle to ʿAbdallāh ibn ʿĪsā al-Muways (d. 1175/1761f.) that, prior to the appearance of Ibn ʿAbd al-Wahhāb, their scholars (*ʿulamāʾunā*) had not performed the duty (*lā yaʾmurūn bi-maʿrūf wa-lā yanhawn ʿan munkar*) with regard to the many innovations of which they were guilty (Bassām, *ʿUlamāʾ Najd*, 606.11). Of Ibn ʿAbd al-Wahhāb himself they say that he 'commanded' and 'forbade' (*yaʾmuruhum wa-yanhāhum, fa-amara wa-nahā*, *ibid.*, 605.23, 606.3).

[32] Ibn Ghannām, *Rawḍa*, 1:92.20. He proceeds to quote the Prophetic tradition on the 'three modes' (*ibid.*, 92.25; for this tradition, see above, ch. 3, section 1).

[33] Some of ʿAbdallāh's writings are coauthored by one or more of his brothers; in what

touches on the duty in three of his responsa. In one, he is asked whether the obligation lapses once the offence has come to the notice of the ruler. He answers that it does not: if the ruler fails to perform the duty, you have the obligation to act yourself in so far as you are able. He stresses the primary importance of the ability (*istiṭāʿa*) to perform the duty, and the balancing of costs and benefits in deciding whether to do so.[34] In a second responsum, he is confronted with the view (attested in other schools) that if one is unable to perform the duty, one should emigrate. He pronounces against this suggestion. Emigration (*hijra*), he says, is obligatory where Muslims living in infidel lands are unable to practise their religion, and perhaps even if they are able to do so; but it is not appropriate in a land of mere misdeeds (*maʿāṣī*), as opposed to one of outright unbelief.[35] The third responsum is concerned with exceptions to the principle that one should not speak evil of a fellow-believer behind his back. One of these exceptions is seeking help in forbidding wrong. Here it is allowable to say: 'So-and-so is doing such-and-such, stop him!'[36] Again, the duty is hardly a major focus of attention, and no connection is made between it and holy war against polytheists.

ʿAbdallāh, the most prolific of Ibn ʿAbd al-Wahhāb's sons, makes some half-a-dozen references to the duty. Some are relatively uninteresting. He touches more than once on the issue of forbidding wrong with regard to matters in dispute between the law-schools.[37] He describes (not entirely accurately) an ancient clash of opinion within the Sunnī fold over the degree of activism appropriate in carrying out the duty;[38] the context is a scholastic dispute with a Zaydī polemicist regarding Sunnī attitudes to the rebellion of

follows I have treated these joint efforts as his. By way of completeness, it may be added that ʿAbdallāh's son Sulaymān mentions the duty alongside *jihād* in a call for solidarity among the believers against the infidel (printed in *Majmūʿat al-tawḥīd al-Najdiyya*, ed. Y. ʿA. al-Nāfiʿ, Cairo 1375, 369.19; also in *Majmūʿat al-tawḥīd*, Damascus 1962, 164.17, where the same text is wrongly ascribed to Ibn ʿAbd al-Wahhāb owing to the loss of initial material, see *ibid.*, 158.3, and contrast *ibid.*, 178.10).

34 *Majmūʿa*, 2:3:41.10. For this balancing of costs and benefits, cf. above, ch. 7, 154f.

35 *Ibid.*, 1:581.12.

36 *Ibid.*, 531.9; this text also appears *ibid.*, 4:817.6, without attribution. The point is not a new one, see for example Marʿī ibn Yūsuf (d. 1033/1623f.), *Ghāyat al-muntahā*, Riyāḍ 1981, 3:474.7.

37 *Majmūʿa*, 1:99.7, 225.6, 236.12 (and cf. 244.10). See also *ibid.*, 509.4 (apparently by his brother ʿAlī).

38 On the one hand there was the view that *al-amr bi'l-maʿrūf* is to be performed with the tongue and heart, but not with the hand or sword, nor by means of rebellion against even unjust rulers (*ibid.*, 4:70.5); on the other, there was the view that the sword must be unsheathed where there is no other way to put a stop to the evil (*ibid.*, 71.4). He includes Ibn Ḥanbal among the proponents of the first view (*ibid.*, 70.7), which is not quite right – as he should have known, Ibn Ḥanbal does not exclude performance with the hand (see above, ch. 5, 96f.). This account must derive from the heresiography of Ibn Ḥazm (d. 456/1064), where the same error appears (*Fiṣal*, Cairo 1317–21, 4:171.9).

Ḥusayn ibn ʿAlī (d. 61/680), not contemporary practice.[39] Elsewhere he takes up the duty in what are clearly contemporary contexts. In an open letter to the faithful,[40] he discusses it in general terms. He stresses a number of points: the sinfulness of being deterred from speaking out through fear or respect of persons,[41] the distinction between a hidden evil which harms only the evildoer and one out in the open which is detrimental to the public at large,[42] and the impropriety of taking exception when the duty is directed against one's own associates.[43] More specific than this is an epistle written in reaction to a rising tide of dishonesty in matters of booty (*maghnam*).[44] After stressing the overall importance of the duty, he says that anyone who knows of undeclared booty should counsel the offender and order him to turn it in – failing which he should report him to the commander (*amīr*); there is no excuse for inaction.[45] He goes on to make another general statement about the duty. It is, he says, an obligation incumbent on all subjects (*jamīʿ al-raʿiyya*); however, the ruler (*imām*) has an even stronger duty to engage in it, whether the offender in question is close by or far away.[46] A further epistle in which ʿAbdallāh responds to contemporary circumstances was written while he was in Mecca in 1218/1803f. during the Saʿūdī occupation.[47] He quotes a speech of Saʿūd to the Meccans in which the Saʿūdī ruler affirms that there are only two points at issue between the two sides: monotheism and forbidding wrong – of which latter only the name is to be found among the Meccans.[48] But when he comes to the practicalities of the duty, his tone is conciliatory. We forbid, he tells them, only innovations tending to polytheism; this apart, we tolerate such things as coffee, love-poems, eulogies of kings, the war-drum, and the tambourine at weddings – but not, of course, musical instruments at large.[49]

From these references it is clear that we have to do with a duty of some significance in the life of the community, but again it is not one central to

39 The tract in which the discussion occurs bears the title *Jawāb ahl al-sunna al-nabawiyya fī naqḍ kalām al-Shīʿa waʾl-Zaydiyya* (*Majmūʿa*, 4:47–221).
40 *Ibid.*, 1:27–32, coauthored by his brothers Ibrāhīm and ʿAlī.
41 *Ibid.*, 28.15.
42 *Ibid.*, 28.16.
43 *Ibid.*, 30.14. For *ṭārifa* read *ṭāʾifa*.
44 *Ibid.*, 17–21. This epistle is coauthored by his brother ʿAlī and by one Ḥamad (presumably Ḥamad ibn Nāṣir ibn Muʿammar).
45 *Ibid.*, 19.15.
46 *Ibid.*, 20.12. This passage is quoted without indication of source, and misattributed to Ibn ʿAbd al-Wahhāb, in M. K. Imām, *Uṣūl al-ḥisba fī ʾl-Islām: dirāsa taʾṣīliyya muqārina*, Cairo 1986, 128; the same misattribution already appears in ʿA. Ḥ. Abū ʿAliyya, *al-Dawla al-Suʿūdiyya al-thāniya*, Riyāḍ 1974, 249 (this work was drawn to my attention by Yitzhak Nakash). These two authors also share the anachronistic use of the term *hayʾa*, characteristic of the third Saʿūdī state (*ibid.*, 249f.; Imām, *Uṣūl al-ḥisba*, 131, 140; for the third Saʿūdī state, see below, section 4).
47 Sulaymān ibn Saḥmān (d. 1349/1930) (ed.), *al-Hadiyya al-sunniyya waʾl-tuḥfa al-Wahhābiyya al-Najdiyya*, Cairo 1344, 35–50.
48 *Ibid.*, 36.3.
49 *Ibid.*, 49.2.

the Wahhābī cause. This point can be underlined if we turn to a responsum which is the only one I have encountered in which ʿAbdallāh links forbidding wrong to the struggle against polytheism. Here the question relates to a situation in which the Wahhābī cause has made its appearance in some town, but, it seems clear, has not yet achieved political dominance there.[50] Suppose, he is asked, one of the people of the town accepts the truth of the doctrine, but is unwilling to engage in forbidding wrong, and instead expresses disapproval of fellow-monotheists who affirm their dissociation from the false religion of their ancestors. The answer is that under such circumstances a Muslim has the duty of emigration (*hijra*).[51] Again, forbidding wrong and the struggle against polytheism are linked only at a stage prior to military action.

To complete this survey, it may be added that there are a few references to forbidding wrong in epistles of the rulers ʿAbd al-ʿAzīz ibn Saʿūd (1179–1218/1765–1803) and Saʿūd ibn ʿAbd al-ʿAzīz. The duty is mentioned among the fundamentals of Islam, but without further elaboration.[52]

The significance of all this becomes apparent when we turn to a thoroughly tendentious letter written in 1231/1816 by the last ruler of the first Saʿūdī state, ʿAbdallāh ibn Saʿūd (r. 1229–33/1814–18). The addressee is Muḥammad ʿAlī (r. 1220–64/1805–48), the ruler of Egypt whose troops were shortly to bring the history of the state to a brutal conclusion.[53] This letter can be seen as a classic attempt at the insincere but politic placation of the infidel (*mudārāt al-kuffār*). In one passage, ʿAbdallāh offers an account of the wars the Wahhābīs had waged in propagating their cause. It was, he tells Muḥammad ʿAlī, their opponents who had started these wars – the Ḥijāzīs and others. The Saʿūdīs, on finding themselves in the position of victors over their irreligious enemies, had felt it their duty to impose the law of Islam on them. ʿAbdallāh then justifies this modest corrective measure by citing God and His Prophet – the first for one of the Koranic verses that mention forbidding wrong (Q22:41), the second for the well-known tradition of the 'three modes'. To these authorities he tactfully adds a third: the Saʿūdīs, he explains, had been confident that the misdeeds of their vanquished enemies had not enjoyed the approval of the (Ottoman) sultan.[54] With this elaborately insincere apologia we can appropriately contrast the real thing, a short epistle in which Ibn ʿAbd al-Wahhāb himself

[50] *Majmūʿat al-tawḥīd*, 432–4. This responsum is coauthored by his brother Ḥusayn (d. 1224/1809). [51] *Ibid.*, 432.2. The text at line 7 is unclear to me.

[52] Ibn Qāsim, *Durar*, 1:147.21, 149.13 (epistles of ʿAbd al-ʿAzīz); 156.18 (epistle of Saʿūd).

[53] The letter is published in ʿA. ʿA. ʿAbd al-Raḥīm, *al-Dawla al-Suʿūdiyya al-ūlā*, Cairo 1975, 435–7. For the dating of the letter, see ʿAbd al-Raḥīm's remarks, *ibid.*, 324f., aptly citing Ibn Bishr, *ʿUnwān*, 185.3. [54] ʿAbd al-Raḥīm, *Dawla*, 436.2.

sets out the doctrinal basis of Wahhābī militancy.[55] God, he points out in no uncertain terms, has ordered us to kill the polytheists wherever we find them, to capture them, surround them and ambush them (Q9:5). The Prophet, in turn, stated that he had been commanded to fight people till they converted to Islam.[56] Ibn ʿAbd al-Wahhāb's third authority is not the Ottoman sultan but the scholars: those of all schools have agreed on this same doctrine, with the exception of some ignorant so-called scholars who hold that anyone who pronounces the confession of faith is a Muslim. The choice, then, is simple: either to believe God and His Prophet, and dissociate from these ignoramuses, or to believe them and give the lie to God and His Prophet.[57]

The duty of forbidding wrong is a wide-ranging one. It includes the denunciation of polytheism by those not in a position to use military force against it; we have seen this in Ibn ʿAbd al-Wahhāb's remarks on the duty of the scholars to combat polytheism, and in his son ʿAbdallāh's responsum on the position of a Wahhābī believer in a society where the true doctrine is only beginning to spread. Equally, the duty includes action taken against routine misconduct within a Wahhābī-dominated society; this is illustrated by Ibn ʿAbd al-Wahhāb's emphasis on the importance of tact, by ʿAbdallāh's concern with undeclared booty, and by the campaign against vice waged by the Wahhābīs when in control of Mecca – a struggle strongly emphasised by Ibn Bishr, albeit underplayed by ʿAbdallāh. But neither of these aspects of the duty lay at the core of the Wahhābī enterprise, the essence of which was to pit against polytheism a political dominance created by military force. In principle, this too could be seen as an instance of forbidding wrong;[58] and in desperate straits, as we have seen, ʿAbdallāh ibn Saʿūd made a patently insincere attempt to portray the Wahhābī onslaught in such terms – it was no more than an adventitious combination of successful defensive warfare and subsequent performance of the duty. But it was simpler and more effective to identify the militant

[55] *Majmūʿa*, 4:41f.

[56] The wording of this well-known tradition quoted by Ibn ʿAbd al-Wahhāb is identical with that found in Bukhārī, *Ṣaḥīḥ*, 1:14.10.

[57] *Majmūʿa*, 4:41.11. Compare the third of the four basic principles enunciated by Ibn ʿAbd al-Wahhāb with regard to the distinction between believers and polytheists: the Prophet encountered people who practised a variety of forms of religion, ranging from the worship of the sun and moon to the cult of saints (*ṣāliḥūn*) and angels; he fought all of them without distinction (*Majmūʿat al-tawḥīd al-Najdiyya*, 255.14). The contemporary relevance of this point is accentuated by the fourth principle: the polytheists of our time are even worse than were those of the time of the Prophet (*ibid.*, 256.14).

[58] For Ibn Taymiyya's emphasis on the link between *al-amr bi'l-maʿrūf* and *jihād*, see above, ch. 7, note 56; and cf. the statement of ʿAbd al-Laṭīf ibn ʿAbd al-Raḥmān (d. 1293/1876) cited below, note 96.

monotheism of the Wahhābīs as holy war against the infidel. It was by bringing the frontier between Islam and polytheism back into the centre of the supposedly Muslim world that Wahhābism contrived to be a doctrine of state-formation and conquest. For a movement with so pointed and aggressive a programme, the idea of forbidding wrong was at once too general in conception, and too modest in its associations.

3. THE SECOND SAʿŪDĪ STATE

The second Saʿūdī state (1238–1305/1823–87) presents a rather different picture. References to forbidding wrong are more frequent in texts dating from this period, and its role in Wahhābī life is considerably more salient.

The importance of forbidding wrong is regularly stressed. Thus Turkī ibn ʿAbdallāh (r. 1238–49/1823–34), himself a noted performer of the duty,[59] emphasises the seriousness of neglecting it with regard to non-attendance at prayer.[60] Fayṣal ibn Turkī (r. 1249–54/1834–8 and 1259–82/1843–65) tells his people that it is one of the pillars (*arkān*) of Islam.[61] A prominent Wahhābī scholar of the age, ʿAbd al-Laṭīf ibn ʿAbd al-Raḥmān (d. 1293/1876),[62] echoes the same view, and describes the obligation as one of the most binding duties of Islam.[63] He warns against its neglect out of a desire to please,[64] and adduces a substantial array of proof-texts demonstrating its obligatoriness.[65] His father, ʿAbd al-Raḥmān ibn Ḥasan (d. 1285/1869),[66] the leading Wahhābī scholar at a somewhat

[59] Ibn Bishr, *ʿUnwān*, 300.21. [60] See his epistle, *ibid.*, 301.17.

[61] See his epistle *ibid.*, 348.29. He quotes a view of the *salaf* according to which Islam rests on ten pillars, of which *al-amr bi'l-maʿrūf* is one and *al-nahy ʿan al-munkar* another. For this epistle, see Philby, *Saʿudi Arabia*, 194, and R. B. Winder, *Saudi Arabia in the nineteenth century*, London 1965, 225.

[62] For this great-grandson of Ibn ʿAbd al-Wahhāb, see Winder, *Saudi Arabia*, 120 n. 1, 160; M. J. Crawford, 'Civil war, foreign intervention, and the question of political legitimacy: a nineteenth-century Saʿūdī qāḍī's dilemma', *International Journal of Middle East Studies*, 14 (1982), 232, 242. He is described as an assiduous performer of the duty (ʿAbd al-Raḥmān ibn ʿAbd al-Laṭīf Āl al-Shaykh, *Mashāhīr ʿulamāʾ Najd wa-ghayrihim*, Riyāḍ 1394, 95.14).

[63] See his epistle in *Majmūʿa*, 4:555.14. Echoing Ibn Taymiyya, he states that *al-amr bi'l-maʿrūf* is the purpose of God's revelation (*ibid.*, 555.18; cf. above, ch. 7, note 55).

[64] *Ibid.*, 557.13; also *ibid.*, 1:421.6.

[65] *Ibid.*, 4:555–7. A similar collection of proof-texts is given by Ḥasan ibn Ḥusayn (d. 1340/1922) in a short excursus on the duty (*Majmūʿa*, 1:441–3; he ends with the remark that he had compiled a separate work on *al-amr bi'l-maʿrūf*). For this descendant of Ibn ʿAbd al-Wahhāb, see Āl al-Shaykh, *Mashāhīr*, 142f.

[66] For this grandson of Ibn ʿAbd al-Wahhāb, see esp. Winder, *Saudi Arabia*, 65f., 204f., and Crawford, 'Civil war', 231f. He too is described as a zealous performer of the duty (Āl al-Shaykh, *Mashāhīr*, 81.5, 84.10, 86.7).

earlier date, is similarly concerned about neglect of the duty; he laments the feebleness with which it is currently performed,[67] and makes a general appeal for a more committed practice of it.[68] In an epistle distributed to the regions of Najd, he calls on everyone to practise it and to give their support to those who carry it out.[69] None of these authorities offers a comprehensive account of forbidding wrong, but the main points find mention.[70]

These texts also emphasise that the duty is incumbent on every member of the community. It is, of course, a collective duty. But both ʿAbd al-Raḥmān and his son stress that this does not make it any less onerous: in the event that no one undertakes to perform it, all who could have carried it out are guilty.[71] Thus it is not just the elite, but also ordinary individuals (***āḥād al-ʿāmma***) who are obligated.[72] Every one (***kull aḥad***) should ostracise those who visit the land of the polytheists for trade, and should manifest disapproval of their actions.[73] Likewise Fayṣal requires all who fear God to perform the duty,[74] and calls upon his subjects to do so to each other.[75]

67 See his epistle to Fayṣal in *Majmūʿa*, 4:380.18.

68 *Ibid.*, 381.3.

69 Ibn Bishr, *ʿUnwān*, 265.22, 266.14. On this epistle see Winder, *Saudi Arabia*, 87; the second passage is adduced in Crawford, 'Civil war', 233.

70 Turkī mentions that counsel (***nuṣḥ***) precedes punitive action (***taʾdīb***) (see his epistle in Ibn Bishr, *ʿUnwān*, 303.20). Fayṣal stipulates knowledge (*ibid.*, 309.23; cf. also *Majmūʿa*, 4:383.9). ʿAbd al-Raḥmān outlines the three modes (*ibid.*, 2:2:31.3), equating performance in the heart with ***karāha*** (*ibid.*, 32.8). He mentions that the capacity to perform the duty is a precondition for obligation (*ibid.*, 31.3, 32.8, and cf. *ibid.*, 4:381.1; see also the statement of ʿAbd al-Laṭīf, *ibid.*, 3:282.13). There is the inevitable discussion of the role of the tambourine at weddings: ʿAbd al-Raḥmān lays down that its use is acceptable in the daytime, but not at night, when those who are able to do so must put a stop to it (*ibid.*, 1:379.16, 4:408.7). For the collective character of the duty, see the following note.

71 *Ibid.*, 2:2:31.4; 4:380.21, 555.16. The last is adduced in Crawford, 'Civil war', 233.

72 ʿAbd al-Laṭīf in *Majmūʿa*, 4:555.13. ʿAbd al-Raḥmān addresses his exhortation to perform the duty to the ***maʿshar al-ikhwān min al-khāṣṣa waʾl-ʿāmma*** (*ibid.*, 381.3; see also *ibid.*, 423.8).

73 ʿAbd al-Laṭīf in *Majmūʿa*, 3:39.20. It should be explained that ʿAbd al-Laṭīf is here reinterpreting a responsum of his father's on the question (for this responsum, see *ibid.*, 1:380.17, 3:37.18, 4:409.7). ʿAbd al-Raḥmān had stated that offenders should be subjected to ostracism (***hajr***) and disapproval (***karāha***), but not abuse (***sabb***) or physical violence (***taʿnīf, ḍarb***). ʿAbd al-Laṭīf, perturbed by the lenience of this ruling, specifies that his father's prescription applies to individuals; the authorities, by contrast, should use punishment and imprisonment against offenders. The issue of such travel is discussed elsewhere in Wahhābī literature (see, for example, the significantly less negative responsum of Sulaymān ibn ʿAbdallāh (d. 1233/1818) on the question in *Majmūʿat al-tawḥīd al-Najdiyya*, 390f.). ʿAbd al-Laṭīf himself takes a more favourable view of a man who mixes with his polytheistic fellow-townsmen in the hope of winning them over to Islam (*Majmūʿa*, 3:127.15); he argues the point in terms of the greater utility (***al-maṣlaḥa al-rājiḥa***) of such action. For an earlier Ḥanbalite view, see Abū Yaʿla, *Amr*, f. 112a.1.

74 Ibn Bishr, *ʿUnwān*, 309.22. For this epistle, see Winder, *Saudi Arabia*, 99.

75 *Majmūʿa*, 4:383.9 (***taʾāmarū . . . wa-tanāhaw. . .***).

A more distinctive, and somewhat antithetical, feature of these texts is their stress on what might be called the officialisation of forbidding wrong.[76] One of the characteristic activities of the Saʿūdī rulers Turkī and Fayṣal was the writing of exhortatory epistles to their subjects in fulfilment of the duty,[77] and in order to urge them to perform it.[78] Thus Fayṣal states that it is through forbidding wrong that fundamental religious instruction is carried out, and hence that it is essential that there should be people to undertake the duty in every district.[79] He requires each emir to support those who carry out the obligation, just as they support him.[80] Likewise ʿAbd al-Laṭīf emphasises the duty of scholars and emirs to assist those who forbid wrong.[81] ʿAbd al-Raḥmān speaks of the ruler's duty to send out officials (*ʿummāl*) in charge of religious affairs, just as he sends out tax-collectors; they are to instruct the people, and to command and forbid them.[82]

There are other pointers to the official, not to say officious, character of the duty. Those charged with it engage in investigation (*tafaqqud*). Thus Turkī orders his emirs to seek out people who gather together to smoke tobacco.[83] ʿAbd al-Laṭīf says that the scholars and emirs should keep a check on the people of their towns with regard to prayer and religious instruction.[84] Performance of the pilgrimage is likewise to be monitored, since ordering subjects (*al-raʿiyya*) to discharge this obligation is part of the duty.[85] Holding religious meetings (*majālis*) is another aspect of the system; those known for their failure to attend are to be reported to the ruler.[86] Turkī further stipulates that people who obstruct the forbidding of wrong are to be punished with exile.[87] We also encounter the inevitable accompaniments of this official meddlesomeness: corrupt motives on the part of those performing the duty,[88] and sniggering on the part of those

76 It may be noted that these texts make no use of the terms *ḥisba* and *muḥtasib*.

77 Ibn Bishr, *ʿUnwān*, 304.1; Winder, *Saudi Arabia*, 87. Compare Fayṣal's exhortation to his subjects to perform the duty in his accession speech (Ibn Bishr, *ʿUnwān*, 309.1).

78 In addition to the references given elsewhere in this section, see Ibn Bishr, *ʿUnwān*, 365.1, where Fayṣal in 1265/1848f. urges the people of ʿUnayza to perform the duty at a time of incipient rebellion.

79 See his epistle *ibid.*, 309.16.

80 *Ibid.*, 309.24. They are in truth his *khāṣṣa*, those closest to him.

81 *Majmūʿa*, 3:343.17.

82 *Ibid.*, 4:381.5; and cf. *ibid.*, 2:2:7.18.

83 Ibn Bishr, *ʿUnwān*, 303.18.

84 *Majmūʿa*, 3:343.19. ʿAbd al-Raḥmān similarly equates keeping an eye on the prayer and instruction of fellow-townspeople with *al-amr biʾl-maʿrūf* (Ibn Bishr, *ʿUnwān*, 266.15).

85 ʿAbd al-Raḥmān in *Majmūʿa*, 2:2:10.4 (noted in Laoust, *Essai*, 528).

86 Turkī in Ibn Bishr, *ʿUnwān*, 303.19. Cf. his emphasis on people coming to the mosque to pray (*ibid.*, 301.10), and Fayṣal's instructions at the end of one of his epistles that the text be read in all mosques, and that the reading be repeated every two months (*ibid.*, 349.19; also Philby, *Saʿudi Arabia*, 194, and Winder, *Saudi Arabia*, 225).

87 Ibn Bishr, *ʿUnwān*, 303.21.

88 *Majmūʿa*, 2:2:35.10.

exposed to it.[89] And we have a most vivid description of the oppressiveness of this official system from the pen of the notoriously unreliable traveller Palgrave, who visited Riyāḍ in 1279/1862 – or at least, he claims to have done so.[90]

Why was forbidding wrong so prominent in the second Saʿūdī state, and why was it so heavily officialised? Clearly we are looking at an aspect of the intimate symbiosis of religious and political authority that was so marked a feature of the Saʿūdī state, in contrast to most regimes in the Islamic world at the time.[91] This symbiosis in turn may have owed something to the tribal environment, and something to the political thought of Ibn Taymiyya.[92] But this cannot account for the contrast between the first and second Saʿūdī states. Why should forbidding wrong, and its officialisation, have been so much more prominent in the latter than they had been in the former?[93]

89 Ḥamad ibn ʿAtīq (d. 1306/1888f.) gives as an example of irreligious mockery (*istihzāʾ*) a man who, on the arrival of those who perform the duty, says: 'The people of the cock (*ahl al-dīk*) have arrived', instead of 'the people of religion (*ahl al-dīn*') (*Majmūʿat al-tawḥīd*, 409.6, and cf. 409.10; for Ibn ʿAtīq, see Āl al-Shaykh, *Mashāhīr*, 244–54).

90 W. G. Palgrave, *Personal narrative of a year's journey through central and eastern Arabia*, London 1883, 243–50, 316–18. He states that the system had arisen, at least in the form in which he encountered it, only during the reign of Fayṣal, in reaction to a cholera epidemic. Fayṣal had convoked an assembly, and out of its deliberations emerged a system of twenty-two 'Zelators' whose task it was to wage war on vice in the capital and beyond. The Arabic term he translates as Zelator is, he tells us, 'Meddey'yee' (*muddaʿī?*) (*ibid.*, 243–5). At one point, however, he more credibly equates the terms 'Zelator' and 'Metow'waa'' (*ibid.*, 260), i.e. *muṭawwaʿ* (for this term, see Cook, 'Expansion of the first Saudi state', 672). The twenty-two were, he says, 'the real council of state' (*ibid.*, 249). He describes, very plausibly, the vices that the Zelators sought to stamp out (absence from prayer, smoking tobacco, making music and the like) (*ibid.*, 245), after which he goes on to their dress and mode of operation. This included 'unexpectedly entering the houses to see if there is anything incorrect going on there' (*ibid.*, 246) – a striking violation of privacy – and roll-calls of names in the mosques (*ibid.*, 248, 316f., with an account of an 'indignant Zelator' who collects 'a pious band armed with sticks and staves' to investigate absences from prayer). It is hard to know what to make of all this. As Winder has indicated, much of it is not substantiated by any other source (Winder, *Saudi Arabia*, 225 n. 1; and see *ibid.*, 222, for some general observations on the Palgrave problem). But Palgrave's account of roll-calls at prayers rings true: the device is attested under the first and third Saʿūdī states (see above, note 18, and below, notes 93, 106).

91 For the second Saʿūdī state in particular, see the remarks of Crawford, 'Civil war', 228.

92 Crawford advances the view that the relationship between religious and political power in the second Saʿūdī state was inspired by Ibn Taymiyya's ideas (*ibid.*). The claim is plausible, and although he does not document it, it gains some support from statements of Ibn Bishr. He tells us that Ibn Taymiyya's famous work *al-Siyāsa al-sharʿiyya* was one of the texts that used to be read in gatherings at the home of Turkī during his reign (Ibn Bishr, *ʿUnwān*, 300.13); and he recounts how the same text was read in the tent of Fayṣal, in the presence of ʿAbd al-Raḥmān ibn Ḥasan, during a campaign in 1262/1845f. (*ibid.*, 357.15, cited in Winder, *Saudi Arabia*, 226). To my knowledge, Ibn ʿAbd al-Wahhāb does not refer to the work, though he knows the corresponding work of Ibn al-Qayyim, *al-Ṭuruq al-ḥukmiyya fī ʾl-siyāsa al-sharʿiyya* (Ibn Ghannām, *Rawḍa*, 1:227.3, in an epistle to ʿAbd al-Wahhāb ibn ʿAbdallāh ibn ʿĪsā).

93 So far as I know, there is no evidence for the imposition of strict congregational discipline

The most plausible explanation of the contrast is changed historical circumstances. For the leaders of the second Saʿūdī state, as not for those of the first, the opportunities for territorial expansion were severely limited.[94] At a pinch they could still conquer al-Aḥsāʾ, but the Ḥijāz was now beyond their reach. Hence holy war against the infidel no longer possessed the same charm as a *raison d'être* for a Wahhābī polity. If the Saʿūdī state was not to lose its religious identity, it had to turn its righteousness inwards. Already under the first Saʿūdī state, the conquest of the Ḥijāz had exemplified a tendency for Saʿūdī rule over richer and more sophisticated territories to be accompanied by moral regimentation.[95] This pattern now reappeared, much enhanced, in the Najdī homeland itself. In effect, forbidding wrong within Wahhābī society had taken the place of holy war on its frontiers.[96] According to the distinguished Wahhābī scholar ʿAbdallāh ibn ʿAbd al-Raḥmān Abū Buṭayyin (d. 1282/1865),[97] the primary duty of the ruler is to ensure the adherence of his subjects to the laws of Islam – a duty which includes the practice of forbidding wrong; holy war against the infidel takes second place.[98] In such a setting, it is easy to understand the anachronistic pervasiveness of forbidding wrong in Ibn Bishr's account of the career of Ibn ʿAbd al-Wahhāb, and of the subsequent history of the first Saʿūdī state.

in Najd under the first Saʿūdī state. This observation is based on my general impressions, together with the detailed research on the region of Washm reported in Cook, 'Expansion of the first Saudi state', esp. 672–5. Roll-calls at prayers are attested for Medina during the first Saʿūdī occupation (see above, note 18).

94 Cf. Winder's characterisation of the history of the second Saʿūdī state (*Saudi Arabia*, 7), and his assessment of Fayṣal's overall strategy (*ibid.*, 228).

95 For the campaign against vice which attended the Saʿūdī occupation of the Ḥijāz under the first Saʿūdī state, see above, note 18. This pattern was repeated, with the emphasis on organisation characteristic of the second Saʿūdī state, at the conquest of al-Aḥsāʾ in 1245/1830 (for this event, see Winder, *Saudi Arabia*, 75–8). Turkī appointed an *imām* to each village, and provided for action to enforce attendance at prayer; he called for *al-amr bi'l-maʿrūf* to be performed, for religious meetings to be organised, and for religious instruction to be given to the ignorant (Ibn Bishr, *ʿUnwān*, 279.18; Winder, *Saudi Arabia*, 77, 86). Some decades later, the Saʿūdīs were again in occupation of al-Aḥsāʾ, and Pelly, who visited Riyāḍ in the spring of 1281/1865, heard in that or the following year a report that 'emissaries and moollas from the capital' had been sent to al-Aḥsāʾ 'to reprove the people for their laxness of life'; an example of such laxness was the open sale of tobacco in the markets (L. Pelly, *Report on a journey to the Wahabee capital of Riyadh in central Arabia*, Bombay 1866, 70f.).

96 The link between *al-amr bi'l-maʿrūf* and *jihād* (see above, ch. 7, note 56) is nevertheless restated by ʿAbd al-Laṭīf: the 'head and root' of the *maʿrūf* in *al-amr bi'l-maʿrūf* is monotheism (*tawḥīd*), just as that of the *munkar* in *al-nahy ʿan al-munkar* is polytheism (*shirk*); *jihād* is, so to speak, an enhanced form of commanding and forbidding (*qadr zāʾid ʿan mujarrad al-amr wa'l-nahy*) (*Majmūʿa*, 4:555.18). ʿAbd al-Laṭīf likewise states that those most deserving of being described as performing the duty in Q3:110 are those who call to monotheism (*ibid.*, 3:224.3). For the interpretation of *maʿrūf* and *munkar* in terms of monotheism and polytheism, an early theme of Koranic exegesis, see above, ch. 2, 22–4.

97 For Abū Buṭayyin see Winder, *Saudi Arabia*, 178f.; Ibn Ḥumayd, *al-Suḥub al-wābila*, 255–7 no. 383; Āl al-Shaykh, *Mashāhīr*, 235–8.

98 *Majmūʿa*, 2:3:170.18.

4. THE THIRD SAʿŪDĪ STATE

The third Saʿūdī state was brought into existence in 1319/1902 by the skill and energy of ʿAbd al-ʿAzīz ibn Saʿūd (r. 1319–73/1902–52). We can best divide its history into two parts: the initial phase of expansion culminating in the conquest of the Ḥijāz in 1343–4/1924–5, and the period from the conquest of the Ḥijāz to the present day. This conquest reflected the more favourable geopolitical environment of the Saʿūdī state after the demise of the reformed Ottoman Empire. In several ways it was to mark a turning-point in Saʿūdī history; in particular, it seems to have played a major role in the development of the official organisation of forbidding wrong. As we shall see, the balance of the evidence suggests that it was in the newly conquered Ḥijāz that the current Saʿūdī system of 'Committees for Commanding Right and Forbidding Wrong' took shape.

Unfortunately, our evidence for the quarter-century prior to the conquest of the Ḥijāz is thin. We possess a traditional Wahhābī creed from the pen of Muḥammad ibn ʿAbd al-Laṭīf (d. 1367/1948), a son of the well-known scholar whom we met in the context of the second Saʿūdī state.[99] This creed, written in 1339/1920f., takes the form of an open letter to the people of western Arabia.[100] It includes a brief reference to forbidding wrong: we are told that it is obligatory for whoever is capable of performing it, to the extent that they are able to do so, with the hand, tongue or heart.[101] From an earlier date – not later than 1335/1916f. – we have a brief discussion of forbidding wrong in a work written by Sulaymān ibn Saḥmān (d. 1349/1930) to cool the ardour of overenthusiastic laymen. He stresses the importance of considerations of utility, and of performing the duty with patience and kindness.[102] There is no hint in these doctrinal

[99] For Muḥammad ibn ʿAbd al-Laṭīf, see Āl al-Shaykh, *Mashāhīr*, 146f. For his father, see above, note 62.

[100] It is published in Ibn Saḥmān, *Hadiyya*, 101–10, and Ibn Qāsim, *Durar*, 1:283–90; for a translation, see Laoust, *Essai*, 615–24.

[101] Ibn Saḥmān, *Hadiyya*, 109.5; Ibn Qāsim, *Durar*, 1:289.12; Laoust, *Essai*, 623. He quotes the Prophetic tradition of the 'three modes' (for which see above, ch. 3, section 1). Ibn Qāsim's text is followed by a further letter from Muḥammad ibn ʿAbd al-Laṭīf to the people of western Arabia (*Durar*, 1:290f.), in which *al-amr bi'l-maʿrūf* finds a brief mention (*ibid.*, 291.4).

[102] Sulaymān ibn Saḥmān (d. 1349/1930), *Irshād al-ṭālib ilā ahamm al-maṭālib*, Cairo 1340, 36.14. He uses a variant of a well-known saying: the peformer of the duty must be knowledgeable (*ʿālim*), patient (*ḥalīm*) and civil (*rafīq*) (*ibid.*, 36.17; for the 'three qualities' tradition, cf. above, ch. 3, note 59). The text is printed from a copy made in 1335/1917 (*ibid.*, 63.16). For the question to which he is responding, see *ibid.*, 20.2. The general tenor of the work is indicated by his opening remarks: he stresses that it is undesirable for religiously minded laymen (*al-mutadayyinūn min al-ʿawāmm*) to meddle in matters beyond their competence (*ibid.*, 2.3), and he warns against those who rush to

texts of the officialisation of the duty that was so marked a feature of the second Saʿūdī state.

The scant material in the biographical sources for this period does, however, suggest a degree of institutionalisation. Thus when ʿAbdallāh ibn ʿAbd al-ʿAzīz al-ʿAnqarī (d. 1373/1953) was made imam of the mosque of Tharmadāʾ in 1321/1903f., he was given various additional functions, among which was the discharge of the duty (*muhimmat al-amr biʾl-maʿrūf*).[103] At the same time we hear little of purely individual performance.[104]

A clearer picture emerges from the foreign sources. Rihani, who visited Riyāḍ in 1341/1922–3, recounts that floggings were commonly inflicted in the city for smoking, non-attendance at prayer and other such offences.[105] In particular, he was told of regular roll-calls to check attendance at prayer in every mosque in the city. Offenders were visited by a group which Rihani refers to in English as a 'committee' and in Arabic as a 'delegation' (*wafd*); they were flogged if they did not mend their ways.[106] This fits well with the general characterisation of Saʿūdī religious organisation given by Philby on the basis of his travels towards the end of the First World War. Thus he speaks of the descendants of Ibn ʿAbd al-Wahhāb as constituting 'a recognised state hierarchy with its headquarters at Riyadh',[107] and he describes the role of this hierarchy in training and directing missionaries (*muṭawwaʿ*s) sent out to instruct the Beduin.[108]

declare others to be infidels (*ibid.*, 3.2). On Ibn Saḥmān, see Āl al-Shaykh, *Mashāhīr*, 290–322, from which it is clear that he was very close to Ibn Saʿūd.

103 Bassām, *ʿUlamāʾ Najd*, 583.19. I have noted two other relevant cases. The first concerns ʿAbdallāh ibn ʿAbd al-Laṭīf (d. 1339/1920), who was widely respected as a teacher. He is described in the traditional formula as *āmir biʾl-maʿrūf nāhī ʿan al-munkar*, with no indication of an official status in this respect (Āl al-Shaykh, *Mashāhīr*, 134.4; cf. also *ibid.*, 354.16). But he was also regarded as an authority by performers of the duty: *marjiʿ ahl al-ḥisba min al-āmirīn biʾl-maʿrūf waʾl-murshidīn* (*ibid.*, 134.14). The use of the term *ḥisba* is unusual in a Saʿūdī context, and the wording perhaps suggests a degree of organisation, at least on the part of those who consulted him. The second case is that of ʿUmar ibn Ḥasan (d. 1395/1975): he was appointed to an assistant role in the performance of the duty in 1336/1917f. (Āl al-Shaykh, *Mashāhīr*, 17.17, and cf. Bassām, *ʿUlamāʾ Najd*, 742.19).

104 Ḥamad ibn ʿAbd al-ʿAzīz al-ʿAwsajī (d. 1330/1911f.) is described as strong-hearted in *al-amr biʾl-maʿrūf* (*ibid.*, 227.13), without an indication of an official role; similarly ʿAbdallāh ibn Muḥammad ibn Sulaym (d. 1351/1932) (*ibid.*, 624.9).

105 A. Rihani, *Maker of modern Arabia*, Boston and New York 1928, 203; A. al-Rīḥānī, *Mulūk al-ʿArab*, Beirut 1924–5, 2:74.18.

106 He uses the term 'committee' in his *Maker of modern Arabia*, 204, but speaks of *wafd min al-ikhwān* in his *Mulūk al-ʿArab*, 2:75.25. The roll-calls and beatings had already been reported by an American doctor (and undercover missionary) who spent twenty days in Riyāḍ during the summer of 1335/1917 (P. W. Harrison, 'Al Riadh, the capital of Nejd', *The Moslem World*, 8 (1918), 418; for the year of Harrison's visit, see H. S. B. Philby, *The heart of Arabia: a record of travel & exploration*, London 1922, 1:97).

107 *Ibid.*, 297. 108 *Ibid.*, 297f.

In the light of subsequent developments, the key question here is how seriously we should take Rihani's use of the word 'committee'. His use of the term 'delegation' (*wafd*) when he writes in Arabic does not suggest a formal group with a permanent membership; we may accordingly suspect that his choice of the term 'committee' in English was influenced by later events. There are indeed accounts which claim that the committees antedated the conquest of the Ḥijāz, but they are late;[109] and as we shall see, the evidence for Mecca following the conquest indicates the emergence of a new institution, rather than the transplantation of an existing one.

The Saʿūdī conquest of the Ḥijāz, with its juxtaposition of Wahhābī puritanism and the laxer attitudes of the wider Muslim world, was a prescription for trouble. This was quickly evident from a serious confrontation which took place during the pilgrimage of 1344/1926 between the Wahhābīs and what they considered to be illegal music. As usual, the Egyptian soldiery were escorting their ceremonial palanquin (*maḥmal*) to the sound of bugles;[110] suddenly they found themselves being attacked by Ibn Saʿūd's most zealous troops, the Ikhwān. Such incidents, however, were nothing new,[111] and the considerable diplomatic reverberations of this one need not detain us.

It seems to have been continuing friction of a less dramatic kind that led to the emergence of a new institution in Mecca, the 'Committee for Commanding Right and Forbidding Wrong' (*Hay'at al-amr bi'l-maʿrūf wa'l-nahy ʿan al-munkar*).[112] According to a narrative published many

[109] A. Al-Yassini, *Religion and state in the Kingdom of Saudi Arabia*, Boulder and London 1985, 68; Imām, *Uṣūl al-ḥisba*, 133f. The two accounts, which manifestly go back to a common source, contain details that can be confirmed from elsewhere, notably the role of the young ʿUmar ibn Ḥasan (see above, note 103); but the biographical sources make no mention of the existence of the committees at that point. Yassini in turn attributes his information to interviews with the deputy director of the committees in Riyāḍ in 1400/1980 (*Religion and state*, 145 n. 22), suggesting a degree of dependence on oral tradition.

[110] See the contemporary account which appeared in the official Meccan newspaper *Umm al-qurā* (no. 78, 19 Dhū 'l-Ḥijja, 1344/1926, 1a); here the bugles are presented as a form of military communication innocent of musical intent. By contrast, a slightly later foreign report speaks of a band, 'this time equipped with modern musical instruments' (see the American report from Aden of 17 August 1926 reproduced in I. al-Rashid (ed.), *Documents on the history of Saudi Arabia*, Salisbury, N.C. 1976, 2:80). For the curious objects known as *maḥmals*, see *EI*², art. 'Maḥmal' (F. Buhl and J. Jomier).

[111] For the burning of the Egyptian *maḥmal* by the Wahhābīs in 1221/1807, shortly after the first Saʿūdī conquest of Mecca, see Daḥlān, *Khulāṣat al-kalām*, 294.31 (and cf. Snouck Hurgronje, *Mekka*, 1:152). Part at least of the friction was caused by the drums (*ṭabl*) and pipes (*zamr*) of the escort (Daḥlān, *Khulāṣat al-kalām*, 294.21, describing what had happened in the previous year; and see Jabartī, *ʿAjā'ib al-āthār*, 6:362.4, 7:47.5).

[112] I follow the conventional rendering of *hay'a* as 'committee'; the term is clearly a modern Ottoman rather than a traditional Najdī usage. It is curious that there seems to have been no official attempt to present the new institution as a revival of the role of the *muḥtasib*.

years later by Ibn Saʿūd's Egyptian retainer Ḥāfiẓ Wahba (d. 1387/1967), who played some part in the events, the object of the establishment of the committee was to check the aggressive behaviour of the Ikhwān towards the local Meccan population and, still more, the foreign pilgrims.[113] (It was, of course, crucial for the threadbare finances of the Saʿūdī state in this period that the pilgrim traffic not be disrupted.) Wahba explains that the Ikhwān, uncouth Beduin as they were, had no idea how to behave in a civilised environment; each of them considered himself individually entitled to take up his stick and execute God's law against the hapless Meccans.[114] This, in Wahba's view, rested on a doctrinal misapprehension, for the Prophetic injunction to take action against wrongs applied only in the time of the Prophet himself and such privileged ages; if it was open to anybody to take a stick to people today, the result would be anarchy.[115] Eventually Ibn Saʿūd came round to Wahba's way of thinking, curbed the excesses of the Ikhwān, and appointed a judge (*qāḍī*) whose mandate was to deal with the problems their activities were giving rise to. In this way, says Wahba, the institution was born; though just how the appointment of the judge led to the birth of the institution is left unclear.

Contemporary sources indicate the first such institution to have been set up in Mecca early in 1345/1926. An announcement by the governor in *Umm al-qurā*, the local newspaper, reports royal approval of the selection by the judicial authorities (*riʾāsat al-qaḍāʾ*) of a committee (*hayʾa*) to carry out the forbidding of wrong.[116] It names the chairman of the committee,

In addition to the references to the system given in what follows, the increasing external interest in Saʿūdī Arabia since the First World War has led to a proliferation of accounts of Saʿūdī affairs which touch on the committees in a vague and general fashion. For several such accounts, see the references given by Layish in his discussion of the committees (A. Layish, '*ʿUlamāʾ* and politics in Saudi Arabia', in M. Heper and R. Israeli (eds.), *Islam and politics in the modern Middle East*, New York 1984, 35f.; this discussion is useful for its citation of newspaper reports).

[113] Ḥ. Wahba (d. 1387/1967), *Jazīrat al-ʿArab fī ʾl-qarn al-ʿishrīn*, fourth edition, Cairo 1961, 309–12. This section was newly added to this edition (see the penultimate paragraph of Wahba's preface to it). The term he uses is *jamāʿat al-amr biʾl-maʿrūf* (not *hayʾa*; the same usage appears in the articles in *Umm al-qurā*, nos. 113–18, cited below, note 121, and in Bassām, *ʿUlamāʾ Najd*, 286.11). Wahba's memoirs are the sole source adduced by Goldrup for the establishment of the committees (L. P. Goldrup, 'Saudi Arabia: 1902–1932: the development of a Wahhabi society', University of California, Los Angeles, Ph.D. 1971, 402, 413 n. 19).

[114] Wahba, *Jazīrat al-ʿArab*, 310.12. He stresses that the Ikhwān could not behave in this fashion in al-Aḥsāʾ.

[115] *Ibid.*, 311.17. Did Wahba really take this view at the time, or is he retrojecting a later Egyptian discussion of performance of the duty 'with the hand' (see below, ch. 18, 523–5)?

[116] *Umm al-qurā*, no. 91, 3 Rabīʿ I, 1345 (= 10 September 1926), 2b. This is supported by the existence of a memorandum from Ibn Bulayhid (d. 1359/1940) to the king dated 20 Ṣafar, 1345/1926 in which he selects the first head of the committee in the Ḥijāz and some assistants for him (ʿAlī ibn Ḥasan al-Quranī, *al-Ḥisba fī ʾl-māḍī waʾl-ḥāḍir*, Riyāḍ 1994, 728.3). For Ibn Bulayhid, see below, note 120.

his deputy, the secretary, and the rest of the members.[117] As to the scope of the committee's duties, the announcement refers particularly to restraint of foul language and to prayer discipline, but offers nothing in the nature of a code. A British consular dispatch from Jedda, reporting the events of September 1926 (i.e. early 1345), likewise describes the formation of a committee 'to supervise morals, encourage collective prayers' and the like; surprisingly, it speaks of this as a 'fresh committee'.[118] That this was nonetheless the first establishment of such a committee finds some support in an argument from silence: we dispose of several earlier reports showing Saʿūdī concern with public morals in Mecca, but these reports make no reference to any committee.[119] A few months after the establishment of the committee, a series of articles appeared in *Umm al-qurā* on the subject of forbidding wrong. The first was by Ibn Bulayhid (d. 1359/1940), a Najdī judge who was in charge of the judicial apparatus in Mecca in 1344–5/1926–7.[120] The other six were written on his instructions by the young Damascene scholar Muḥammad Bahjat al-Bayṭār (d. 1396/1976), then director of the Saʿūdī Islamic Institute (*al-Maʿhad al-Islāmī al-Suʿūdī*), for distribution to the members of the committee and others.[121] There is a tendency in these articles to emphasise the role of the authorities; thus Ibn Bulayhid speaks

[117] For somewhat later listings of the membership of the committee, see *Umm al-qurā*, no. 149, 26 Rabīʿ II, 1346/1927, 3b; Quranī, *Ḥisba*, 728.10, quoting a royal order of 18 Muḥarram, 1347/1928; *Umm al-qurā*, no. 238, 12 Ṣafar, 1348/1929, 2b.

[118] Public Record Office, London, FO 371/11442, E 6016/367/91, report of N. Mayers dated 3 October 1926, f. 152, §34.

[119] Thus in 1344/1925, a long official document setting out the duties of the police (*shurṭa*) was published in *Umm al-qurā* (no. 34, 30 Muḥarram, 1344/1925, 4a–d); among these duties were enforcing prayer discipline, arresting and imprisoning those who smoked in public, arresting those using foul language in public, and the like. Some months later the newspaper published an official code of public morals; the official responsible for its enforcement was in this case to be the governor (*Umm al-qurā*, no. 68, 10 Shawwāl, 1344/1926, 5d). (For this code, see Goldrup, 'Saudi Arabia', 407f.; its promulgation is also reported in a British consular dispatch, E 3198/367/91, report of Jordan dated 1 May 1926, f. 129, and in 'Notizie varie', *Oriente Moderno*, 6 (1926), 289, drawn to my attention by Maribel Fierro.) Likewise British consular reports for the period February to June 1926 make occasional references to Wahhābī efforts to enforce public morals, and to problems arising from these efforts, but again they make no mention of a committee in this connection (E 1919/367/91, report of S. R. Jordan dated 1 March 1926, ff. 2f., §16; E 3790/367/91, report of Jordan dated 1 June 1926, f. 132, §7; E 4434/367/91, report of Jordan dated 5 July 1926, f. 136, §9). A recurring theme in these reports is Wahhābī hostility to smoking.

[120] *Umm al-qurā*, no. 111, 24 Rajab, 1345/1927. For his career, see Āl al-Shaykh, *Mashāhīr*, 344.

[121] See *Umm al-qurā*, no. 113, 8 Shaʿbān, 1345/1927, 1a; the articles are found in nos. 113–18. Bayṭār states that his articles are mere compilations from works such as Ibn Taymiyya's *Ḥisba*; and indeed his examples of *munkar* include throwing snow onto the streets (no. 117, 8 Ramaḍān, 1345/1927, 2a; the source is clearly Ghazzālī, *Iḥyāʾ*, 2:310.29, a work from which Bayṭār drew extensively). For Bayṭār's background and career, see ʿU. R. Kaḥḥāla, *al-Mustadrak ʿalā Muʿjam al-muʾallifīn*, Beirut 1985, 614f.; ʿA. al-Khaṭīb, *Muḥammad Bahjat al-Bayṭār: ḥayātuhu wa-āthāruhu*, Damascus 1976, esp. 15.

of the appointment of those who command and forbid,[122] and Bayṭār insists on the limits of what the individual Muslim may do.[123]

These contemporary sources also suggest two ways in which Wahba's account may be incomplete. First, they show that the Ikhwān were not the only troublemakers. In 1344/1926 a member of the Āl al-Shaykh, ʿAbdallāh ibn Ḥasan (d. 1378/1959), pulled a cigarette from the mouth of an Egyptian chauffeur and set about him with a stick; this led to a fight between them, after which the authorities had the chauffeur flogged, resulting in his death.[124] Secondly, Ibn Bulayhid may have played a significant part in the developments that led to the establishment of the system. One of his biographers quotes from an epistle which he addressed to the Ikhwān. In the course of it he reproves them for their well-intentioned but misguided efforts – including verbal abuse and physical violence – to forbid wrong; he stresses that the duty is not for the ill-informed, and that individuals are not to encroach on the role of the authorities.[125]

Whatever the exact circumstances of its origin, the institution was well established by 1347/1928f. In that year ʿAbd al-Wahhāb Maẓhar, who was on the staff of the Saʿūdī political agency in Cairo, published a short practical handbook for prospective pilgrims. In it he included a text promulgated by the committee which sets out, in twenty articles, the scope of the committee's activity.[126] The articles cover such matters as prayer-discipline,

122 *Umm al-qurā*, no. 111, 1a. 123 *Ibid.*, no. 117, 1d.

124 E 1919/367/91, report of Jordan dated 1 March 1926, ff. 2f., §16; and see E 6655/367/91, report of Mayers dated 3 November 1926, f. 158A, §24. Ibn Ḥanbal would not have been impressed (cf. above, ch. 5, note 164). For more sympathetic references to this cleric's zeal in *al-amr bi'l-maʿrūf*, see Āl al-Shaykh, *Mashāhīr*, 156.4, 162.7, and Bassām, *ʿUlamāʾ Najd*, 86.23. At the time he was *imām* and *khaṭīb* of the Holy Mosque; two years later he was appointed *qāḍī* of Mecca, to which was added the direction of *al-amr bi'l-maʿrūf* (*ibid.*, 83.25; Āl al-Shaykh, *Mashāhīr*, 154.9).

125 Bassām, *ʿUlamāʾ Najd*, 545.12. See also above, note 116.

126 ʿAbd al-Wahhāb Maẓhar, *Murshid al-ḥājj*, Cairo 1347, 47–50. It was Nallino who drew attention to this text, translating it in his monograph on Saudi Arabia (C. A. Nallino, *L'Arabia Saʿūdiana (1938)*, in his *Raccolta di scritti editi e inediti*, Rome 1939–48, 1:100–2). A British consular dispatch reports the promulgation of this 'list of twenty-one rules of conduct' in August 1928 (E 4770/484/91, report of F. H. W. Stonehewer-Bird dated 31 August, 1928, ff. 177f., §8), and contains a version of what is clearly the same document, despite additions, omissions and transpositions (*ibid.*, f. 178; I am grateful to Mike Doran for supplying me with copies of this and other reports of Stonehewer-Bird). These regulations do not seem to have been promulgated in *Umm al-qurā*, although a report dating from this period (no. 191, 12 Rabiʿ I, 1347/1928, 2a) mentions the prospect of the addition of new articles to the existing code (*niẓām*); see also Quranī, *Ḥisba*, 728.18. Another consular dispatch written the best part of a year earlier describes the 'new orders' issued by the 'Religious Committee' (E 5083/644/91, report of H. G. Jakins dated 6 November 1927, f. 192, §4); this description has a certain amount in common with Maẓhar's text, but seems to reflect a different document – again one that does not appear to have been published in *Umm al-qurā*.

liquor, smoking, the segregation of women, and the like. The final article is noteworthy in the context of the increasing officialisation of the duty: the headmen of quarters in the town are declared responsible for offences committed in their quarters, and would be deemed accomplices if they attempted to conceal them. He describes the committee as an official body made up of scholars and notables, both Ḥijāzī and Najdī.[127]

Further information on the early history of the institution is provided by some British reports from Jedda dating from a slightly later period. These reports describe a swing from a soft line to a hard one and back which took place in late 1348/early 1930, and a similar shift in early 1350/the summer of 1931. During the first, one dispatch describes the confiscation of mouth organs from small boys in Jedda;[128] the street-urchins subsequently took their revenge by waylaying the president of the local committee and pelting him with melon rind – the only instance of open resistance to the activities of the committees that I have encountered.[129] In the second period, Ibn Saʿūd had been trying to move away from Wahhābī puritanism, and to cultivate the image of a monarch 'who not only likes to see his people have a bit of fun, but is democratic enough to join in it' (the reference is to his participation in a Najdī war-dance).[130] In this relaxed atmosphere the committees had apparently disappeared.[131] Then, within a few months, the line shifted: the committees were reconstituted, and the war on vice took on a new lease of life. In addition to the traditional targets of the duty, we now encounter an instrument of music-making unknown to the Ḥanbalite lawbooks: the gramophone. Stocks of needles were seized, and it was said that as a result they could only be purchased from the police.[132] Shortly after this a plaintive report was penned by the Indian vice-consul Munshi Ihsanullah

127 Maẓhar, *Murshid al-ḥājj*, 47.9.

128 For this and other dispatches, see P. Sluglett and M. Farouk-Sluglett, 'The precarious monarchy: Britain, Abd al-Aziz ibn Saud and the establishment of the Kingdom of Hijaz, Najd and its Dependencies, 1925–32', in T. Niblock (ed.), *State, society and economy in Saudi Arabia*, London 1982, 41f.

129 E 2280/92/91, report of W. L. Bond dated 3 April 1930, f. 137, §10; I am indebted to Mike Doran for supplying me with a copy. I have not found evidence for the developments of this or the preceding year in *Umm al-qurā*.

130 FO 371/15298, E 1600/1600/25, report of Sir Andrew Ryan dated 6 March 1931, f. 146, §8. I am indebted to Yitzhak Nakash for supplying me with copies of this document and those cited in the following notes.

131 *Ibid.*, E 4167/1600/25, report of Sir Andrew Ryan dated 12 July 1931, f. 188, §6. According to Munshi Ihsanullah, the Indian vice-consul attached to the Legation in Jedda, the committee in Mecca had in fact been abolished (*ibid.*, E 4597, report dated 14 August 1931, f. 197, §1).

132 See Ryan's report cited in the previous note. The gramophone appears already in consular dispatches for 1347/1928; thus at one stage Christian owners of gramophones in Jedda were permitted to play them, but not to replace them when worn out (E 4286/484/91, report of Stonehewer-Bird dated 3 August 1928, f. 172, §12).

after his return from a visit to Mecca.[133] He was greatly disturbed by the shift of power from local to Najdī hands. Previously, he suggests, the committee had been something of a body of notables, where local figures would exercise a moderating influence, and in particular ensure that the well-to-do were properly treated; now, he reports, the committee had been given summary powers, and it was backed by groups of Najdī soldiers – twenty to a quarter, 260 in all – whose savage approach to prayer-discipline he found particularly appalling.[134]

I have not attempted to follow the later history of the committee system in detail. It seems that after its establishment in Mecca, it was rapidly extended to the rest of the Saʿūdī state.[135] We have already encountered

[133] This report is cited above, note 131. Some of its finest passages are quoted in J. S. Habib, *Ibn Saʾud's warriors of Islam: the Ikhwan of Najd and their role in the creation of the Saʾudi kingdom, 1910–30*, Leiden 1978, 119f. But note that the number of the document is E 4597 (not E 4957, as stated *ibid.*, 120 n. 39), and that what it describes is not the launching of the committee but its revival (cf. *ibid.*, 119).

[134] See Munshi Ihsanullah's report cited above, note 131, ff. 197f., §2, partially reproduced by Habib. I have not found much discussion of *al-amr biʾl-maʿrūf* in *Umm al-qurā* in this period. In a speech reported in 1350/1931, Ibn Saʿūd stresses to the Meccans the importance of the duty, and requests their cooperation in executing it – for it is the Meccans, as the proverb has it, who know best the streets of their town (*ahl Makka adrā bi-shiʿābihā*) (*Umm al-qurā*, no. 338, 18 Muḥarram, 1350/1931, 1c).

[135] Goldrup states that the committee system was extended to the towns of the Ḥijāz within a few months of its establishment, albeit without citing supporting evidence ('Saudi Arabia', 409). Elsewhere he quotes a document showing that a committee was indeed in place in Medina as early as Rabīʿ II, 1346/1927 (*ibid.*, 402, citing Ḥ. Wahba (d. 1387/1967), *Khamsūn ʿāman fī jazīrat al-ʿArab*, Cairo 1960, 271.4, and cf. *ibid.*, 269.3). He also cites a report which appeared about a year later in *Umm al-qurā* (Goldrup, 'Saudi Arabia', 409, citing *Umm al-qurā*, no. 191, 12 Rabīʿ I, 1347/1928). This report refers generally to the committees whose establishment had long before been ordered by the king in the Ḥijāz at large (*fī ʿumūm al-buldān al-Ḥijāziyya*), praising their activities but at the same time discussing plans for reforming them (*ibid.*, 1a–d); it goes on to mention one in Jedda (*ibid.*, 2a). A British consular dispatch adds the detail that the president of the latter committee was 'a young man of notoriously loose morals' (E 4770/484/91, report of Stonehewer-Bird dated 31 August 1928, f. 178, §8; an earlier instance of such a mismatch is noted in M. J. R. Sedgwick, 'Saudi Sufis: compromise in the Hijaz, 1925–40', *Die Welt des Islams*, 37 (1997), 359). There is a further reference to the committee in Jedda a few months later (*Umm al-qurā*, no. 214, 21 Shaʿbān, 1347/1929, 2b). In the same year Maẓhar speaks of the committee (in the singular) as having been established in the entire Ḥijāz (*Murshid al-ḥājj*, 47.7). Goldrup states that by the summer of 1348/1929 a directorate had been established in Riyāḍ responsible for all the committees in the country ('Saudi Arabia', 409f.). However, the report in *Umm al-qurā* that he cites as his source (no. 241, 26 Ṣafar, 1348/1929, 1b) does not bear him out; it does document the establishment of an official organisation for the execution of the duty in Riyāḍ itself (though without using the term *hayʾa*), and it refers in general terms to similar activity throughout the kingdom. Contrast the statement of the Saʿūdī biographers that ʿUmar ibn Ḥasan was put in charge of the committee(s) in Najd in 1345/1926f. (Āl al-Shaykh, *Mashāhīr*, 17.20; Bassām, *ʿUlamāʾ Najd*, 742.23, adding the Eastern Region). According to Nallino, who spent several weeks in Jedda in 1356–7/1938, there were committees in all cities of the kingdom (Nallino, *L'Arabia Saʿūdiana*, 100).

it in Jedda. The biographies of Saʿūdī scholars show them heading such committees in the Ḥijāz,[136] and they also attest their tenure of such office in Najd and al-Aḥsāʾ.[137] Thus by 1394/1974f., ʿUmar ibn Ḥasan (d. 1395/1975) bore the magnificent title of 'General Director of the Committees for Commanding Right in Najd, the Eastern Region and the Tapline'.[138] There has also been a move towards greater centralisation. Until 1396/1976, there were two mutually independent directorates, one in the Ḥijāz and the other in Najd;[139] in that year they were amalgamated into a unitary structure under a general director with the rank of cabinet minister.[140] Nor does the institution seem to have remained confined to urban settings: we hear of the existence of a committee in a village in the southern Ḥijāz with a population of 1,600 souls.[141]

This persistence and spread are striking. If the system was indeed the invention of the secular-minded Egyptian Ḥāfiẓ Wahba, then all one can say is that from his point of view it did not turn out to be a very felicitous one.[142] As we have seen, the institution did not work well as a buffer between Najdī fanaticism and the laxity of the Ḥijāzīs and the pilgrims. As first established, the original Meccan committee had about twice as many Meccan as Najdī members.[143] Yet this initially favourable balance was easily upset when the winds blew from the east. The very fact that the system outlived the Ikhwān shows that it had acquired effective support in other quarters.

How are we to interpret this survival? One line of thought, perhaps now abandoned in the face of recent developments, tended to see a process of emasculation at work as a result of bureaucratisation. Thus it was plausibly suggested that the system had tended to atrophy through the restriction

136 Āl al-Shaykh, *Mashāhīr*, 415.13, 514.14, and cf. 120.17; Bassām, *ʿUlamāʾ Najd*, 91 no. 7, 590 nos. 5 and 9, and cf. 286.11, 644.17, 891.11.

137 Āl al-Shaykh, *Mashāhīr*, 409.15, and cf. above, note 135. For the role of the committee in Qaṭīf and al-Aḥsāʾ in curtailing the public display of Shīʿism, see Ḥamza al-Ḥasan, *al-Shīʿa fī ʾl-Mamlaka al-ʿArabiyya al-Suʿūdiyya*, n.p. 1993, 2:398, and 415f. n. 30 (I owe this reference to Yitzhak Nakash).

138 Āl al-Shaykh, *Mashāhīr*, 15.8, and cf. 18.5. Most of the references to this work given in this and notes 136f. are found in Layish, '*ʿUlamāʾ* and politics in Saudi Arabia', 58 n. 19, 61 n. 93.

139 So Imām, *Uṣūl al-ḥisba*, 135, 140f.

140 Quranī, *Ḥisba*, 731.3 (quoting the text of the royal decree, and mentioning the appointment of a general director with the rank of minister which followed). According to Imām, the general director was given the status of minister in 1400/1980 (*Uṣūl al-ḥisba*, 142); Yassini, however, is in line with Quranī in dating this event to 1396/1976 (*Religion and state*, 70).

141 See ʿA. Shukrī, *Baʿḍ malāmiḥ al-taghayyur al-ijtimāʿī al-thaqāfī fī ʾl-waṭan al-ʿArabī*, Cairo 1979, 76, and, for the population, *ibid.*, 65 (drawn to my attention by Frank Stewart). See also Quranī, *Ḥisba*, 739.12, 760.5.

142 A British consular dispatch of 1347/1928 states that Wahba was strongly opposed to the committees (E 4956/484/91, report of Stonehewer-Bird dated 30 September 1928, f. 181, §4).

143 See *Umm al-qurā*, no. 91, 3 Rabīʿ I, 1345/1926, 2b.

of the scope of its activities and the curtailment of its powers[144] – processes which could be seen as an aspect of the general bureaucratisation of the role of the religious scholars in the modern Saʿūdī state.[145] At first sight it would go well with this that the institution received only the most cursory mention in the constitutional document issued by the Saʿūdī government in 1412/1992.[146] But another view, perhaps more prevalent today, is that the system, by entrenching forces of moral puritanism which might have dissipated long ago in a more secular climate, has provided the rising tide of Muslim fundamentalism with an institutional base.[147] In the absence of detailed information about the way the system works, all this remains fairly speculative.

Two relatively recent works do, however, shed some light on the activities of the committees. One is a book by a Wahhābī author on forbidding wrong.[148] Its significance in the present context is that it quotes from the

144 Quranī laments that the role of the committees from the 1380s/1960s on was not what it had been, and gives a long list of their previous functions (*Ḥisba*, 734.2); he mentions that they formerly had their own jails (*ibid.*, 735.9). See also Imām, *Uṣūl al-ḥisba*, 135f., 141; Yassini, *Religion and state*, 70; Layish, '*ʿUlamāʾ* and politics in Saudi Arabia', 53f. (but cf. 55).

145 Yassini, *Religion and state*, 67, 78f. However, not all Saʿūdī scholars were caught up in this process, see Layish, '*ʿUlamāʾ* and politics in Saudi Arabia', 32.

146 This document, entitled *al-Niẓām al-asāsī lil-ḥukm*, was published in the London paper *al-Sharq al-awsaṭ* on 2 March 1992; I am indebted to Sadik Al-Azm for showing me a copy. The reference to the state's performance of *al-amr biʾl-maʿrūf* comes in Article 23 (*ibid.*, 4b). See also F. G. Gause, *Oil monarchies*, New York 1994, 106 (and cf. *ibid.*, 96, 111).

147 So the article 'Everywhere in Saudi Arabia, Islam is watching' by Chris Hedges in *The New York Times*, 6 January 1993, A4. In this context we hear of oscillations in the level of activity of the committees reminiscent of those that characterised their early history. For an analysis of such a swing, see the anonymous article 'Fakhkh manṣūb wa-taṣfiya damawiyya qādima!' which appeared in *al-Jazīra al-ʿArabiyya*, no. 13, February 1992 (this monthly was published by the Saʿūdī Shīʿite opposition in London; I am indebted to Yitzhak Nakash for sending me a copy of the article).

148 Khālid ibn ʿUthmān al-Sabt, *al-Amr biʾl-maʿrūf waʾl-nahy ʿan al-munkar*, London 1995. This work was drawn to my attention by Bernard Haykel and Harry Bone; Nurit Tsafrir sent me a copy. No biographical information is given about the author, but it is clear that he is firmly located in a conservative Wahhābī tradition. Although he draws on a wide range of Sunnī literature, he makes frequent use of Ḥanbalite sources; for example, he gives references to Ibn Mufliḥ (d. 763/1362) (as *ibid.*, 274 n. 4) and Buhūtī (d. 1051/1641) (*ibid.*, 342 n. 2). He has a particular penchant for Wahhābī sources. Thus he invokes Ibn ʿAbd al-Wahhāb himself, quoting from two of his letters (*ibid.*, 191.14), and gives many references to Ibn Qāsim's collection *al-Durar al-saniyya* (see, for example, Sabt, *Amr*, 175 n. 1, 191 n. 1, 266 n. 1). Likewise no non-Wahhābī would quote the epistles of Ḥamad ibn ʿAtīq (*ibid.*, 57.9, 193.8, 266.18; for Ḥamad ibn ʿAtīq, see above, note 89). And as will be seen, one of his favourite sources is the responsa of Muḥammad ibn Ibrāhīm Āl al-Shaykh, a conservative Wahhābī authority (*ibid.*, 34–41, 222.5, 227.3, 273.8, 313.14, 314.3, 314.18, 340.8, 341.9, 345.8). On the other hand, our author does not seem to be close to the Saʿūdī dynasty; he never mentions the monarchy, and his book was published in London. Overall the work is rather bland, and his own references to the committees elsewhere in the volume (*ibid.*, 141.7, 367 no. 11) are supportive but uninteresting.

responsa of Muḥammad ibn Ibrāhīm Āl al-Shaykh (d. 1389/1969).[149] The most striking theme in these responsa, though a hardly surprising one, is the vein of hostility to which the activities of the committees give rise. A Meccan judge had allowed a man accused of drunkenness to attack the credibility of the testimony of the committee members; Ibn Ibrāhīm roundly condemns the judge.[150] Where members of committees have been over-zealous in the performance of their duties, he enjoins leniency; they have enemies among the reprobate who would be unduly encouraged if such lapses were dealt with severely.[151] Where members of committees go astray, they should be discharged only if they can be replaced with others known to be of better character.[152] In a case from Jedda involving serious sexual misconduct, the main informant had disappeared, leaving three witnesses among the committee members liable to the penalty for defamation (*qadhf*); Ibn Ibrāhīm rescues them by finding a loophole in the law, urging that to impose the prescribed penalty would diminish their authority in carrying out the duty.[153] This apart, these responsa do not have very much to tell us. We learn of a novel offence: the committee in Zilfī was concerning itself with young men who made it a practice to ride out into the countryside at night on their motorcycles.[154] A responsum dealing with the organisation of the committees states that they should be divided into three sections: one to patrol the markets and streets and arrest (but not beat) offenders; one responsible for the judicial process; and one charged with carrying out punishments.[155] There is, of course, no saying how far such a division of labour was ever realised in practice.

The other recent work that provides some concrete detail on the activities of the committees is a voluminous treatise on the institution of the censorship (*ḥisba*) in Islam by ʿAlī ibn Ḥasan al-Quranī. He includes a sympathetic study of the Saʿūdī committee system,[156] in the course of which he devotes some pages to its present functioning.[157] In particular,

[149] *Ibid.*, 34–41, 319f., 345–7. I do not have access to the work from which Sabt is quoting; it seems to be a collection of the responsa of Ibn Ibrāhīm in at least twelve volumes (*ibid.*, 40 n. 1, 41 n. 1). Muḥammad ibn Ibrāhīm, a grandson of ʿAbd al-Laṭīf ibn ʿAbd al-Raḥmān ibn Ḥasan, was Muftī of Saudi Arabia (*muftī ʾl-diyār al-Suʿūdiyya*) and in charge of the judicial apparatus (Āl al-Shaykh, *Mashāhīr*, 169.4).

[150] Sabt, *Amr*, 34.15. He accords no such immunity to the police (*ibid.*, 36.5).

[151] *Ibid.*, 37.10. [152] *Ibid.*, 40.4. [153] *Ibid.*, 40.15. [154] *Ibid.*, 319.13.

[155] *Ibid.*, 345.16. [156] Quranī, *Ḥisba*, 721–71.

[157] *Ibid.*, 735–51. Quranī had some access to documents and files (*ibid.*, 741.6), interviewed a high official in the organisation in 1410/1990 (*ibid.*, 753.19), was enabled to observe the activities of the Riyāḍ committee in the same year (*ibid.*, 758.3), and submitted legal questions on the institution to ʿAbd al-ʿAzīz ibn Bāz (d. 1420/1999) (*ibid.*, 865–77). As might be expected, he has all the right attitudes; for example, he would like to see the committees have their own jails again (*ibid.*, 771.13). His treatise

he gives an account of some of the offences encountered by the committee in Riyāḍ in 1404/1984. One was sodomy; the offenders were Filipinos in one case, Sri Lankan and British in another, but not, it seems, Saʿūdī. Two Saʿūdīs, however, were furtively engaged in pushing Eau de Cologne among young people. Another was peddling liquor (*ʿaraq*) together with two Yemenis; they were also found to have 2,555 forbidden pills in their possession. Four Yemenis had 3,773 Seconal pills. A young Saʿūdī picked up in an unusual state was found to have been sipping paint. A mixed group of Saʿūdīs and Yemenis had been producing liquor; the plant was raided and destroyed.[158] The pattern of wrongdoing in Riyāḍ in 1404/1984 was obviously not lacking in either variety or ethnic diversity.

As might be expected, there is little direct evidence of the practice of forbidding wrong outside this official framework.[159] The striking exception is ʿAbdallāh al-Qarʿāwī (d. 1389/1969) of ʿUnayza, a pupil of Ibn Ibrāhīm. One of his biographers, who owed his elementary education to Qarʿāwī, describes his teacher's activities in the town. In the course of forbidding wrong, he would roam the streets and markets, belabouring with his tongue and stick any man who held back from communal prayer, and any woman whose dress flaunted her sexuality; there is no indication that he did this in an official capacity.[160] Another biographer describes how, in the years after 1358/1940, Qarʿāwī mounted a large-scale (and officially approved) campaign to spread education in the extreme south-west of the country; he recounted in 1367/1948 how on Thursday evenings he would take his senior students out to visit the tribes to preach, instruct and forbid wrong, supervising his students' efforts and showing them how to perform the duty nicely.[161] But Qarʿāwī seems to have been an unusual figure.

5. CONCLUSION

In Arabia, as in the Fertile Crescent, the expanding bureaucracy of the modern state meant the end of Ḥanbalite history as we have known it in this study. But where the reformed Ottoman state and its successors effectively destroyed the traditional role of the Ḥanbalite scholars, either

seems to have originated in a doctoral dissertation submitted to the University of Medina (*ibid.*, 15.3). [158] *Ibid.*, 744.2. Seconal sodium is a sedative drug.

[159] A scholar of Ḥāʾil who died in 1391/1971 is still described in the traditional way as *āmir biʾl-maʿrūf nāhī ʿan al-munkar* (Āl al-Shaykh, *Mashāhīr*, 427.10).

[160] Bassām, *ʿUlamāʾ Najd*, 631.20.

[161] Āl al-Shaykh, *Mashāhīr*, 423.13; see also Bassām, *ʿUlamāʾ Najd*, 632.4. For the close connection between religious instruction and *al-amr biʾl-maʿrūf*, compare Habib, *Ibn Saʿud's warriors*, 133f.

absorbing them as individuals or pushing them aside, the rise of the modern state in Saʿūdī Arabia preserved that role by a kind of ossification, turning the scholars into an appanage, though not always a docile one, of the state bureaucracy.

These different outcomes were not arbitrary. What happened in the Fertile Crescent is in part a reflection of the position of the Ḥanbalites in the region since the fall of the ʿAbbāsid caliphate. They were a minority community, and one which, if not strongly alienated from political power, was far from identified with it. The Arabian development, by contrast, rests on the paradoxical emergence of a Ḥanbalite state within a solidly Ḥanbalite society, and one whose Ḥanbalite doctrine, refracted through the thought of Ibn Taymiyya, provided it with its *raison d'être*.[162]

Yet in Arabia, as in the Fertile Crescent, the tradition that we owe to Ibn Ḥanbal has effectively come to an end. Few things illustrate this more poignantly than the transformation of his strongly apolitical and individual doctrine of forbidding wrong into a bureaucratic function, discharged by a set of Committees for Commanding Right and Forbidding Wrong under the supervision of a general director with ministerial rank. The irony of this development is unlikely to be diminished should the system be reinvigorated by fundamentalist revolution.[163]

[162] It is noteworthy that traditional Saʿūdī scholars did not cite the views of Ibn Ḥanbal himself on the matters considered in this chapter. (I owe this observation to a question put to me by Nimrod Hurvitz.)

[163] What would a fundamentalist reform of the committees look like? Unfortunately the tract on *al-amr bi'l-maʿrūf* by Juhaymān al-ʿUtaybī (d. 1400/1980), the leader of the group that seized the Meccan sanctuary in 1400/1979, is largely what it claims to be, namely an abridgement of Ibn Taymiyya's tract on the subject (*Rasāʾil Juhaymān al-ʿUtaybī qāʾid al-muqtaḥimīn lil-Masjid al-Ḥarām bi-Makka*, ed. R. S. Aḥmad, Cairo 1988, 349–85). Even the introductory material (*ibid.*, 349–61) contains nothing of interest for the contemporary scene.

PART III

THE MU'TAZILITES AND SHĪ'ITES

CHAPTER 9

THE MUʿTAZILITES

1. INTRODUCTION

If the bias of Ḥanbalite thinking was towards the concrete, that of Muʿtazilite thought was towards the abstract. This, in the end, was to carry a certain cost. Whatever may have been the case in the early history of the school, it was becoming clear by the fourth/tenth century that Muʿtazilism could not make a Muslim. Instead it came to function as one element in a package, playing the part of a tradition of abstract scholastic thought that could be combined with a variety of other allegiances. One could be a Ḥanafī Muʿtazilite, a Zaydī Muʿtazilite, an Imāmī Muʿtazilite – even a Jewish Muʿtazilite. In these various symbioses, Muʿtazilism tended to represent something between a systematic body of substantive scholastic doctrine and an intellectual technique which, as we have seen, even the Ḥanbalites were eventually to find irresistible.

Muʿtazilism thus tended to become a tradition of socially and politically disembodied intellection. One implication of this is that we are unlikely to be very successful in linking the content of classical Muʿtazilite doctrines to the concrete historical environments in which they flourished. I shall accordingly make no attempt to do for Muʿtazilism what I did for Ḥanbalism; instead, what lies ahead is the history of ideas in a distinctly narrow sense. There will still be points at which we can link intellectual history to less cerebral realities, but they will be few and far between. We might hope that the situation would be different in the case of early Muʿtazilism; but unfortunately we know too little about its views on forbidding wrong to have much sense of what we are missing.

The symbiosis of originally distinct religious traditions in the classical packages also poses an organisational problem for this study. The course I shall take in this part of the book is as follows. In the present chapter, I shall be broadly concerned with Muʿtazilism as such. After surveying the little we know of early Muʿtazilite doctrines of forbidding wrong, I shall discuss in some detail the classical doctrines of the fourth/tenth century and later, regarding a few of which we are relatively well informed. In principle I shall not be concerned here with Zaydī or Imāmī Muʿtazilism as phenomena in their own right, though in practice I shall cross the border from time to time. The two following chapters will be devoted to the Zaydīs and Imāmīs respectively. In each case I shall begin with the pre-Muʿtazilite phase of sectarian thought, and go on to the history of the Muʿtazilite tradition in the sect.

2. EARLY MUʿTAZILITE DOCTRINE

If we take the Muʿtazilite school to have been founded by the Baṣrans Wāṣil ibn ʿAṭāʾ (d. 131/748f.) and ʿAmr ibn ʿUbayd (d. 144/761), then its origins go back to the early second/eighth century. The earliest Muʿtazilite author to have left us a systematic and substantial account of forbidding wrong, the Zaydī ʿAlid Mānkdīm (d. 425/1034), lived in northern Iran some three centuries later. This means that, for the first three hundred years of the movement, our material is fragmentary or summary at best. But it does raise some points of interest.

Forbidding wrong is, of course, one of the celebrated 'five principles' (*al-uṣūl al-khamsa*) of Muʿtazilism. However, there is no agreement among modern scholars as to the antiquity of this pentad.[1] Such uncertainty need not call in question the assumption that forbidding wrong was a Muʿtazilite precept from the beginning; given its prominence in the Koran, and in early Islamic thought in general, it would be surprising if it had not been. What is missing is specific evidence of the conception of the duty entertained in the time of Wāṣil and ʿAmr. It has been linked to early Muʿtazilite missionary activity,[2] and this derives a hint of support from its appearance in a poem of Ṣafwān al-Anṣārī (*fl.* later second/eighth century) describing the emissaries (*duʿāt*) sent out by Wāṣil ibn ʿAṭāʾ.[3] It has been connected with movements of local autonomy.[4] And not least, it has been

[1] Contrast the positive judgement of Madelung (*Qāsim*, 7) with the sceptical view of van Ess (J. van Ess, *Une lecture à rebours de l'histoire du Muʿtazilisme*, Paris 1984, 56; *Theologie*, 2:273). [2] Madelung, *Qāsim*, 16; van Ess, *Lecture*, 125; van Ess, *Theologie*, 2:387.

[3] Jāḥiẓ, *Bayān*, 26.8 (noted in van Ess, *Theologie*, 2:387). The duty is paired in the same line with 'fortifying God's religion against every infidel'. The poem, first brought into play by H. S. Nyberg (*The Encyclopaedia of Islam*, first edition, Leiden and London 1913–38, art. 'Muʿtazila', cols. 789a, 790a), is translated in W. M. Watt, 'Was Wāṣil a Khārijite?', in R. Gramlich (ed.), *Islamwissenschaftliche Abhandlungen: Fritz Meier zum sechzigsten Geburtstag*, Wiesbaden 1974, 310f., and most recently in van Ess, *Theologie*, 5:183f.; and see *ibid.*, 2:382–7. [4] Van Ess, *Lecture*, 103, 123, 127.

linked to rebellion against unjust rule.[5] This old allegation[6] is plausible, and it resonates with some of what the sources tell us about ʿAmr ibn ʿUbayd. Thus ʿAmr is reported to have said that the traditionists (*hāʾulāʾi ʾl-ḥashw*) were the ruin of the religion; they were the ones who held people back from standing up for justice (*al-qiyām biʾl-qisṭ*) and commanding right.[7] There is also the story transmitted by Kūfan traditionists that ʿAmr wrote to the Kūfan Ibn Shubruma (d. 144/761f.) urging him to forbid wrong, or reproaching him for not doing so; it may be significant that Ibn Shubruma's reply makes a point of saying that commanding right is not to be undertaken by taking up the sword against the authorities.[8] However, no explicit mention of rebellion is ascribed here to ʿAmr, and Ibn Shubruma's reference to it is only indirect evidence of what ʿAmr believed.

Once we reach the late second/eighth and early third/ninth century, we have credible reports that a few Muʿtazilite authors wrote on our topic: Abū Bakr al-Aṣamm (d. 200/815f.),[9] Jaʿfar ibn Mubashshir (d. 234/848f.),[10] and presumably Hishām al-Fuwaṭī (d. *c.* 230/844) in his work on the 'five principles';[11] other such reports are late and unreliable.[12] But we know almost nothing of actual Muʿtazilite views in this period. The heresiographer Ashʿarī (d. 324/935f.) tells us that Aṣamm stood outside the consensus of

[5] Madelung, *Qāsim*, 16, and cf. 18; W. M. Watt, *The formative period of Islamic thought*, Edinburgh 1973, 212, 231; van Ess, *Theologie*, 2:390, and cf. 4:675, 704.

[6] It appears in Ibn Taymiyya, *Amr*, 20.8; cf. also Mubarrad, *Kāmil*, 561.3.

[7] ʿAbd al-Jabbār ibn Aḥmad (d. 415/1025), *Faḍl al-iʿtizāl wa-ṭabaqāt al-Muʿtazila*, ed. F. Sayyid, Tunis 1974, 242.16 (cited in van Ess, *Lecture*, 123 n. 5, and van Ess, *Theologie*, 2:287). ʿAmr likewise held nothing to be more meritorious than standing up for justice (*al-qiyām biʾl-qisṭ*) and being killed for it (Ṭūsī, *Tibyān*, 2:422.18 (to Q3:21), cited in van Ess, *Theologie*, 2:287, 5:166; though there is no explicit reference to *al-amr biʾl-maʿrūf* here, this is the context in which Ṭūsī adduces it, cf. below, note 36). This saying is also quoted by al-Ḥākim al-Jishumī (d. 494/1101) in his Koran commentary to Q3:21 (see Zarzūr, *al-Ḥākim al-Jushamī*, 195.4). For the phrase *al-qiyām biʾl-qisṭ*, cf. Q4:135.

[8] See above, ch. 4, notes 44, 226. ʿAmr's exhortation is noted by van Ess (*Theologie*, 2:286, 390).

[9] J. W. Fück, 'Some hitherto unpublished texts on the Muʿtazilite movement from Ibn al-Nadīm's *Kitāb-al-Fihrist*', in S. M. Abdullah (ed.), *Professor Muḥammad Shafiʿ presentation volume*, Lahore 1955, 68.8, cited in *EI*[2], *Supplement*, art. 'Aṣamm', 89a (J. van Ess), and cf. van Ess, *Theologie*, 5:193 no. 12, and *ibid.*, 2:409 n. 5.

[10] Khayyāṭ (d. *c.* 300/912), *Intiṣār*, ed. and trans. A. N. Nader, Beirut 1957, 63.14 = 74; Fück, 'Some hitherto unpublished texts', 64.10; van Ess, *Theologie*, 6:274 no. 8.

[11] Fück, 'Some hitherto unpublished texts', 69.3 (*Kitāb uṣūl al-khams*); van Ess, *Theologie*, 6:222 no. 1.

[12] The report that Abū ʾl-Hudhayl (d. 227/841f?) wrote on the 'five principles' (cf. D. Gimaret, 'Les *Uṣūl al-ḫamsa* du Qāḍī ʿAbd al-Ǧabbār et leurs commentaires', *Annales Islamologiques*, 15 (1979), 68 n. 1), and so presumably on *al-amr biʾl-maʿrūf*, is probably to be discounted (see van Ess, *Lecture*, 56, and van Ess, *Theologie*, 3:223). That Jaʿfar ibn Ḥarb (d. 236/850f.) did so (cf. Gimaret, 'Les *Uṣūl al-ḫamsa*', 68, n. 1) is also unlikely (see W. Madelung, 'Frühe muʿtazilitische Häresiographie: das *Kitāb al-Uṣūl* des Ǧaʿfar b. Ḥarb?', *Der Islam*, 57 (1980), 227; van Ess, *Theologie*, 6:288 no. 4).

the Muʿtazilites, who consider forbidding wrong to be obligatory – provided they are able to perform it (*maʿa ʾl-imkān waʾl-qudra*) – with the tongue, hand and sword, in whatever way they are able to effect it.[13] However, he neglects to specify the nature of Aṣamm's dissent;[14] it is doubtless to be linked to a report that he wrote a work directed against 'those who favour the sword'.[15] With this quietism we may contrast the attitude of Sahl ibn Salāma, who in 201/817 was prepared to fight anyone in performance of the duty, irrespective of whether he was a ruler or not.[16]

Our information is slightly better for the later third/ninth and early fourth/tenth centuries. The earliest surviving work of Muʿtazilite doctrine, a polemical tract by Khayyāṭ (d. *c.* 300/912),[17] offers a definition of Muʿtazilism in terms of adherence to the 'five principles', with forbidding wrong listed in its classical fifth place.[18] From roughly the same period comes our oldest heresiographical account of the Muʿtazilite doctrine of forbidding wrong, the formulation of the ex-Muʿtazilite Ashʿarī already adduced in connection with Aṣamm; he too lists the 'five principles'.[19] Masʿūdī (d. 345/956), who may or may not have been a Muʿtazilite himself,[20] gives a brief account of Muʿtazilite doctrine: forbidding wrong is obligatory if one has the ability (*istiṭāʿa*) to perform it, by the sword and by less drastic means.[21] He likewise lists the 'five principles', defining

[13] Ashʿarī, *Maqālāt*, 278.7, translated in van Ess, *Theologie*, 5:198 no. 13.

[14] According to Ibn Ḥazm, he believed that *al-amr biʾl-maʿrūf* is not to be performed by deed (including recourse to arms) (*Fiṣal*, 4:171.10, translated in van Ess, *Theologie*, 5:198 no. 14, and cf. *ibid.*, 2:409; the passage is also adduced by van Ess in *EI*², *Supplement*, art. 'Aṣamm', 89a, where the suggestion that Aṣamm based his view on a deviant exegesis of Q3:104 seems unfounded). However, Ibn Ḥazm's presentation brackets Aṣamm with too wide a spectrum of quietist thought (from Ibn Ḥanbal to the Rāfiḍa, both of whom are misrepresented) for us to be able to put much weight on it.

[15] For this *Kitāb al-radd ʿalā man qāla biʾl-sayf*, see Fück, 'Some hitherto unpublished texts', 68.13, and cf. van Ess, *Theologie*, 2:409 and 5:193 no. 15. As noted by van Ess, Aṣamm held with the sword in the context of hostilities against the *ahl al-baghy* under the leadership of a just imam about whom there is consensus (*ibid.*, 2:409 and 5:207 no. 31, citing and translating Ashʿarī, *Maqālāt*, 451.12). Cf. also below, note 63.

[16] See above, ch. 5, notes 173f., 192.

[17] See *EI*², art. 'al-Khayyāṭ' (J. van Ess); van Ess, *Lecture*, 6f.

[18] Khayyāṭ, *Intiṣār*, 93.2 = 115 (cited in van Ess, *Lecture*, 56 n. 4).

[19] Ashʿarī, *Maqālāt*, 278.10, concluding Ashʿarī's survey of Muʿtazilism. In the thematic survey that constitutes the latter part of Ashʿarī's doxography, the account of *al-amr biʾl-maʿrūf* deals only with quietist views disallowing the use of the sword, and makes no mention of the Muʿtazilites (*ibid.*, 452.3); but he includes the Muʿtazilites among those approving the use of the sword in general (*ibid.*, 451.4), and sets out the conditions under which they hold with rebellion against (unjust) rule (*ibid.*, 466.5).

[20] See A. M. H. Shboul, *Al-Masʿūdī & his world*, London 1979, 38f.

[21] Masʿūdī (d. 345/956), *Murūj al-dhahab*, ed. C. Pellat, Beirut 1965–74, 4:59 §2,256. He adds that the duty is like *jihād* in that there is no distinction between fighting the infidel and fighting the reprobate (*mujāhadat al-kāfir waʾl-fāsiq*).

Muʿtazilism in terms of acceptance of them.[22] We also possess occasional opinions on specific questions attributed to Abū ʾl-Qāsim al-Balkhī, alias Kaʿbī (d. 319/931). Thus he holds that recourse to arms is permitted to subjects solely in the absence of a ruler (*imām*) or of someone appointed by him; if there is a ruler, recourse to arms is allowable only under conditions of overriding necessity (*ḍarūra*).[23] One reason this is interesting is that Abū ʾl-Qāsim belonged to the Baghdādī – as opposed to the Baṣran – school of Muʿtazilism,[24] in other words to the branch of the movement that is relatively underrepresented in the surviving literature.

The two scholars of this period whom we know best are the Jubbāʾīs, Abū ʿAlī (d. 303/916) and his son Abū Hāshim (d. 321/933), both members of the Baṣran school; yet even here, we have at our disposal only scattered references in later works. Mānkdīm and others give accounts of the views of the Jubbāʾīs on two main points. The first is the source of the obligation. Abū ʿAlī held it to be both reason and revelation, whereas Abū Hāshim held it to be revelation alone, except in so far as the mental anguish (*maḍaḍ wa-ḥarad*) of the spectator provides a reason for him to act in his own interest.[25] Altruism, we understand, is not a duty established

[22] *Ibid.*, 4:58 §2,254, and 60, §2,256.

[23] Ṭūsī, *Tibyān*, 2:549.22; and cf. Abū ʾl-Futūḥ-i Rāzī, *Rawḍ*, 3:141.16 (both to Q3:104). For another issue in connection with which his name is mentioned, see below, note 27.

[24] See *Encyclopaedia Iranica*, art. 'Abūʾl-Qāsem Kaʿbī', 361a (J. van Ess).

[25] So Mānkdīm (d. 425/1034), *Taʿlīq Sharḥ al-Uṣūl al-khamsa*, ed. ʿA. ʿUthmān, Cairo 1965 (published as ʿAbd al-Jabbār ibn Aḥmad (d. 415/1025), *Sharḥ al-Uṣūl al-khamsa*, see below, note 57), 142.3, and cf. *ibid.*, 742.1 (where Mānkdīm endorses Abū Hāshim's view as school doctrine), 743.11 (reporting an argument of Abū ʿAlī), 744.8 (again endorsing Abū Hāshim's view). It is assumed that the wrongs in question affect others (see *ibid.*, 145.1, and cf. below, 212f.). The disagreement is noted by Madelung ('Amr be maʿrūf', 993b), and the following citations will indicate how widely reported it is in the literature: al-Ḥākim al-Jishumī (d. 494/1101), *al-ʿUyūn fī ʾl-radd ʿalā ahl al-bidaʿ*, ms. Milan, Ambrosiana, B 66, f. 66a.6 (for this manuscript, see O. Löfgren and R. Traini, *Catalogue of the Arabic manuscripts in the Biblioteca Ambrosiana*, Vicenza 1975–, 2:89 no. 190); al-Ḥākim al-Jishumī (d. 494/1101), *Sharḥ ʿUyūn al-masāʾil*, ms. Leiden, Or. 2,584–B, f. 265a.14; al-Ḥākim al-Jishumī (d. 494/1101), *al-Tahdhīb fī tafsīr al-Qurʾān*, ms. Milan, Ambrosiana, F 184, f. 70a.6 (to Q3:104) (for this work and its manuscripts, see D. Gimaret, *Une lecture muʿtazilite du Coran: Le Tafsīr d'Abū ʿAlī al-Djubbāʾī (m. 303/915) partiellement reconstitué à partir de ses citateurs*, Louvain and Paris 1994, 17, 25f.; Gimaret kindly sent me a copy of the commentary to Q3:104–10); Farrazādhī (*fl.* late fifth/eleventh century), *Taʿlīq Sharḥ al-uṣūl al-khamsa*, ms. Ṣanʿāʾ, Great Mosque, *kalām* 73, f. 155a.1 (the character of this work has been analysed by Gimaret ('Les *Uṣūl al-ḫamsa*', 60–3), who kindly made available a microfilm of the manuscript (for this microfilm, see D. Gimaret, *Théories de l'acte humain en théologie musulmane*, Paris 1980, xvi no. 23); I am indebted to Adrien Leites for consulting the microfilm and making a copy of the relevant passage for me); Ibn al-Malāḥimī (d. 536/1141), *al-Fāʾiq fī uṣūl al-dīn*, ms. Ṣanʿāʾ, Great Mosque, *kalām* 53, f. 256b.6 (I am indebted to Wilferd Madelung for making available to me his microfilm of this manuscript); Zamakhsharī (d. 538/1144), *al-Minhāj fī uṣūl al-dīn*, ed. and trans. S. Schmidtke as *A Muʿtazilite creed of az-Zamaḫšarī*,

by reason. The second point is a subtle one: to command a supererogatory act is itself supererogatory, while to command an obligatory act is obligatory.[26] This view, Mānkdīm tells us, was introduced by Abū ʿAlī, earlier Muʿtazilites (*al-mashāyikh min al-salaf*) having failed to make the distinction.[27] Other views of the Jubbāʾīs appear here and there in the literature. Zaydī sources report from Abū ʿAlī such legal opinions as that one must have actual knowledge that a wrong is being committed before violating the privacy of a home.[28] Further opinions of Abū ʿAlī are found in later works of Koranic exegesis, and are likely to derive from his lost Koran commentary.[29] Here again the disagreement between him and Abū Hāshim over the source of obligation is mentioned.[30] He is also quoted for the view that the group which in Q7:164 saw no point in reproving the Sabbath-breakers[31] did so because they despaired of them; this would place them among the saved.[32] More interestingly, he is reported to have

Footnote 25 (*cont.*)
Stuttgart 1997, 77.4 (drawn to my attention by Etan Kohlberg; the chapter on *al-amr biʾl-maʿrūf* is translated *ibid.*, 40f.); Zamakhsharī, *Kashshāf*, 1:397.11; Ḥimmaṣī (d. early seventh/thirteenth century), *al-Munqidh min al-taqlīd*, Qumm 1412–14, 2:211.3; Sayf al-Dīn al-Āmidī (d. 631/1233), in a passage cited below, ch. 13, note 75; Muḥallī (d. 652/1254f.), *ʿUmdat al-mustarshidīn fi uṣūl al-dīn*, ms. Princeton, Arabic, Third Series, no. 347, 292.4 (the manuscript is paginated, not foliated; for this work, see ʿA. M. al-Ḥibshī, *Maṣādir al-fikr al-Islāmī fi ʾl-Yaman*, Sidon and Beirut 1988, 117); Ibn Abī ʾl-Ḥadīd, *Sharḥ Nahj al-balāgha*, 19:307.17; Abū Ḥayyān, *Baḥr*, 3:21.3; al-Muʾayyad Yaḥyā ibn Ḥamza (d. 749/1348f.), *al-Shāmil li-ḥaqāʾiq al-adilla*, ms. Leiden, Or. 2,587, ff. 181b.27, 182a.25, 187b.6 (for this work, see below, note 115); Ibn al-Murtaḍā (d. 840/1437), *al-Qalāʾid fi taṣḥīḥ al-ʿaqāʾid*, ed. A. N. Nādir, Beirut 1985, 149.8. For references to the position of Abū ʿAlī, see also Muwaffaq al-Shajarī (first half of the fifth/eleventh century), *Iḥāṭa*, ms. Leiden, Or. 8,409, f. 135b.8 (for this author and his work, see below, ch. 10, 241); also below, note 45 for Abū Ṭālib al-Nāṭiq (d. 424/1032f.), and note 30 for Ṭabrisī (d. 548/1153).

26 For this question, see below, 213.

27 Mānkdīm, *Taʿlīq*, 146.10, and cf. 745.3; and see Yaḥyā ibn Ḥamza, *Shāmil*, f. 183a.22, citing the *Mughnī* of ʿAbd al-Jabbār. Ibn al-Murtaḍā (d. 840/1437) credits the innovation to Abū Hāshim (*al-Durar al-farāʾid*, in the abridgement of Ṣārim al-Dīn al-Ḥayyī, ms. Berlin, Glaser 202, f. 243a.15 (for this manuscript, see Ahlwardt, *Verzeichniss*, 4:310 no. 4,910), and cf. Ibn al-Murtaḍā, *Qalāʾid*, 149.12, reading *yazīd* for *yurīd*). Jishumī states that Abū ʾl-Qāsim al-Balkhī did not distinguish in this way (*Sharḥ*, f. 266a.5; *ʿUyūn*, f. 66a.11), while Ibn al-Murtaḍā says that he believed it to be obligatory to command the supererogatory (*Durar*, f. 243a.13; *Qalāʾid*, 149.13).

28 Ibn Miftāḥ (d. 877/1472), *Muntazaʿ*, Cairo 1332–58, 4:587.2. For other such opinions of Abū ʿAlī in Zaydī sources, see Muwaffaq al-Shajarī, *Iḥāṭa*, f. 141a.9; ʿAlī ibn al-Ḥusayn ibn al-Hādī (*fl.* early seventh/thirteenth century), *Lumaʿ*, ms. London, British Library, Or. 3,949, f. 221a.11 (for this manuscript, see Rieu, *Supplement*, 219f. no. 342); Muḥallī, *ʿUmda*, 302.4.

29 For this work, see Gimaret, *Lecture*.

30 Zamakhsharī, *Kashshāf*, 1:397.11, and cf. Ṭabrisī, *Majmaʿ*, 1:484.5 (both to Q3:104, though not included thereto by Gimaret).

31 See above, ch. 2, 28.

32 Ṭūsī, *Tibyān*, 5:16.18; Ṭabrisī, *Majmaʿ*, 2:492.6; Gimaret, *Lecture*, 370. However, as Gimaret points out, Ṭabrisī has Abū ʿAlī suspend judgement on the fate of the group (*Majmaʿ*, 2:493.14).

held the opinion that forbidding wrong is an individual (as opposed to a collective) duty.[33] But the monograph that Abū ʿAlī devoted to forbidding wrong, and which might have given us a rounded picture of his views, does not survive.[34]

For the middle and later fourth/tenth century, we have direct access to some views of the Koranic exegete Rummānī (d. 384/994) and the celebrated Būyid vizier the Ṣāḥib ibn ʿAbbād (d. 385/995). Rummānī, like Abū ʾl-Qāsim al-Balkhī, belonged to the Baghdādī school.[35] He saw Q3:21, together with the tradition about standing up to an unjust ruler and getting killed for it, as proof that it was permissible to risk death in taking action against wrong (*inkār al-munkar*).[36] From his commentary to Q3:104 we learn his views on a number of points. He inclined to the view that the duty can be known by reason;[37] he held it to be a collective obligation;[38] and he approved of recourse to arms where necessary.[39] The Ṣāḥib ibn ʿAbbād, who was closely connected to the Baṣran school, has left us two very short accounts of the duty. Perhaps their most notable feature is their stress on an escalation (*irtiqāʾ*) which may lead in the end to the gravest measures, including the use of arms. The only condition he mentions is being able to perform the duty (*imkān* or *istiṭāʿa*).[40]

33 Ṭūsī, *Tibyān*, 2:548.14 (to Q3:104, not included by Gimaret); cf. above, ch. 2, note 17. What Ṭūsī says here is explicit enough. However Zajjāj, whom he yokes with Abū ʿAlī in connection with the interpretation of the *min* of Q3:104, does not himself raise the issue whether the duty is to be classified as individual or collective (see above, ch. 2, note 16); this in turn suggests that we cannot entirely trust Ṭūsī's report of Abū ʿAlī's position. For other comments of Abū ʿAlī on verses bearing on *al-amr biʾl-maʿrūf*, see Gimaret, *Lecture*, 674, 801.

34 For this work see D. Gimaret, 'Matériaux pour une bibliographie des Ǧubbāʾī', *Journal Asiatique*, 264 (1976), 283 no. 8; D. Gimaret, 'Matériaux pour une bibliographie des Jubbaʾi: note complémentaire', in M. E. Marmura (ed.), *Islamic theology and philosophy*, Albany 1984, 32 no. 8.

35 For Rummānī's school allegiance, see Ibn al-Murtaḍā, *Ṭabaqāt*, 110.11, and *EI*², art. 'Rummānī', 614b (J. Flanagan).

36 Ṭūsī, *Tibyān*, 2:422.16; Ṭabrisī, *Majmaʿ*, 1:423.31; cf. above, ch. 2, note 79, and ch. 1, note 18, respectively.

37 Rummānī (d. 384/994), *Tafsīr al-Qurʾān*, ms. Paris, Bibliothèque Nationale, Arabe 6,523, f. 62b.9 (partially reproduced in Ṭūsī, *Tibyān*, 2:549.11). For this manuscript, see Gimaret, *Lecture*, 18, 23; I am grateful to Adrien Leites for obtaining for me a copy of the commentary to Q3:104–10.

38 Rummānī, *Tafsīr*, f. 62a.14, 62b.14.

39 *Ibid.*, f. 62a.9 (copied in Ṭūsī, *Tibyān*, 2:549.16). Contrast the more restrictive view of his fellow-Baghdādī Abū ʾl-Qāsim al-Balkhī on this point (see above, note 23).

40 See al-Ṣāḥib ibn ʿAbbād (d. 385/995), *al-Ibāna ʿan madhhab ahl al-ʿadl*, in M. Ḥ. Āl Yāsīn (ed.), *Nafāʾis al-makhṭūṭāt*, Najaf and Baghdad 1952–6, 1:24.15; al-Ṣāḥib ibn ʿAbbād (d. 385/995), *al-Tadhkira fī ʾl-uṣūl al-khamsa*, also in Āl Yāsīn, *Nafāʾis al-makhṭūṭāt*, 2:94.17. Both are cited in E. Kohlberg, 'The development of the Imāmī Shīʿī doctrine of *jihād*', *Zeitschrift der Deutschen Morgenländischen Gesellschaft*, 126 (1976), 68 n. 30. In the first, the Ṣāḥib also mentions a group of the Ḥashwiyya who deny the obligatoriness of *al-amr biʾl-maʿrūf*.

We can conclude this survey of the first three centuries of Muʿtazilite doctrine with the well-known Shāfiʿite Muʿtazilite ʿAbd al-Jabbār ibn Aḥmad al-Hamadhānī (d. 415/1025), a representative of the Baṣran school. Though a considerable number of his works survive, among those that are definitely his we find only one that treats forbidding wrong.[41] It does so in two passages of a few lines each. The first begins with the point that commanding right may be either obligatory or supererogatory, depending on whether the right to be commanded is itself obligatory or supererogatory; by contrast, forbidding wrong is invariably obligatory, since all wrong (*munkar*) is evil (*qabīḥ*). ʿAbd al-Jabbār then goes on to escalation, stressing that one should not go beyond the minimum measure that is effective (he cites in support Q49:9). He ends the passage by stating that the duty of forbidding wrong lapses (and it is best not to proceed) when there is good reason to believe that it would lead to worse offences and greater harm. The second passage answers the question: 'Do you hold that one who does not forbid wrong disobeys God?' The reply is that this is indeed so if he is able to perform the duty (*in amkanahu dhālika*),[42] does not fear for his life or property, and believes (*ẓanna*) that he would be successful (*annahu yuqbal minhu*); if despite fear for his life he proceeds anyway, he acts virtuously. Another work which is very probably ʿAbd al-Jabbār's devotes a few lines to the grounds of obligation.[43] These are given as scripture, tradition (*sunna*) and consensus – but only the first is illustrated (here by Q5:78–9), further proofs being described as innumerable.

[41] ʿAbd al-Jabbār ibn Aḥmad (d. 415/1025), *al-Uṣūl al-khamsa*, *apud* Gimaret, 'Les *Uṣūl al-ḫamsa*', 82.7, 94.16 (the latter passage was drawn to my attention by Haggai Ben Shammai). (This work, for which see *ibid.*, 73, is translated in R. C. Martin *et al.*, *Defenders of reason in Islam*, Oxford 1997, 90–110.) ʿAbd al-Jabbār does not treat forbidding wrong in either his *Mughnī* or his *Muḥīṭ* to the extent that they are extant and published; but there are cross-references to such a discussion in the published volumes of the *Mughnī* (see J. R. T. M. Peters, *God's created speech*, Leiden 1976, 34; also *Mughnī*, ed. Ṭ. Ḥusayn *et al.*, Cairo 1960–9, 20:2:239.5).

[42] This, as we have seen, is commonly presented as a condition in other Muʿtazilite (not to mention non-Muʿtazilite) accounts, though the wording varies (cf. above, notes 13, 21, 40).

[43] ʿAbd al-Jabbār ibn Aḥmad (d. 415/1025), *Mukhtaṣar fī uṣūl al-dīn*, in M. ʿUmāra (ed.), *Rasāʾil al-ʿadl waʾl-tawḥīd*, Cairo 1971, 1:248.1. The title of the work is taken by ʿUmāra from the author's own description of it (*ibid.*, 168.5). He ascribes it to ʿAbd al-Jabbār on various grounds, none of them compelling (*ibid.*, 163–7). Some support for his view can, however, be found in the appearance near the beginning of the work of the statement that the principles of religion with which one must be acquainted are four, namely *tawḥīd*, *ʿadl*, *nubuwwāt*, and *sharāʾiʿ* (*ibid.*, 168.17); this is identical with a schema adduced by Mānkdīm from ʿAbd al-Jabbār's *Mukhtaṣar al-Ḥasanī* (*Taʿlīq*, 122.15, and cf. *ibid.*, 23, in the editor's introduction). However, the rest of what Mānkdīm says about this work in the same passage does not fit ʿUmāra's text (contrast Mānkdīm, *Taʿlīq*, 123.1 with ʿUmāra, *Rasāʾil*, 169.13). The ascription to ʿAbd al-Jabbār is accepted by Madelung (*Encyclopaedia Iranica*, art. ''Abd al-Jabbār', 117b item 3).

The author adds that reason declares it an act of benevolence (*iḥsān*) to restrain others from evil (*qabīḥ*). However, our knowledge of ʿAbd al-Jabbār's views is much more extensive than direct attestations would suggest. As will be seen in the next section, almost all classical Muʿtazilite treatments of the duty derive from his school, and on occasion they expressly quote him or make explicit reference to his opinions on one point or another. An exception is a short account that is in all probability the work of the Zaydī imam Abū Ṭālib al-Nāṭiq (d. 424/1032f.).[44] Like ʿAbd al-Jabbār, Abū Ṭālib was a pupil of the well-known Ḥanafī Muʿtazilite Abū ʿAbdallāh al-Baṣrī (d. 369/980),[45] and what he says can thus help us to work back to the generation preceding ʿAbd al-Jabbār.

Before we proceed to the classical accounts of forbidding wrong, we need to pull together the threads of these rather disjointed findings regarding early Muʿtazilite views. There are two issues worth raising here.

The first concerns the evolution of Muʿtazilite thought over time. That it evolved is something we can assume. Indeed in one instance our sources explicitly tell us that it did so: Abū ʿAlī introduced a distinction that had not been made by his predecessors.[46] But I have encountered no instance of a reported view of an early authority which we can identify as an archaism in relation to classical Muʿtazilite doctrines of forbidding wrong. The one possible candidate is the equation of forbidding wrong with rebellion against unjust rule, an attitude which has been seen as a casualty of the declining activism of the movement;[47] I shall return in a moment to the question whether the early Muʿtazilites actually made such an equation. This apart, my category of 'early Muʿtazilism' does not identify a stage in the development of the school when its doctrine of forbidding wrong was visibly different from what it later became. In the present (and probably future) state of our knowledge, early Muʿtazilism is simply Muʿtazilism which we do not know very much about.

The second issue is whether modern scholars are right to suppose that the early Muʿtazilite conception of the duty was a particularly activist one.

[44] This account is found in ms. Milan, Ambrosiana, Codex Griffini 27, ff. 63b.6–64a.22. Madelung, who kindly sent me a copy of the passage, has shown that the work in question is likely to be Abū Ṭālib al-Nāṭiq's *Mabādiʾ al-adilla fī uṣūl al-dīn* (as which I cite it below), and that it is in any case by a pupil of Abū ʿAbdallāh al-Baṣrī (d. 369/980) other than ʿAbd al-Jabbār (see W. Madelung, 'Zu einigen Werken des Imams Abū Ṭālib an-Nāṭiq bi l-Ḥaqq', *Der Islam*, 63 (1986)). For Abū Ṭālib al-Nāṭiq, see Madelung, *Qāsim*, 178–82.

[45] See *EI²*, *Supplement*, art. 'Abū ʿAbd Allāh al-Baṣrī' (J. van Ess). Abū ʿAbdallāh is not, however, mentioned in our passage; the only named Muʿtazilite authority here is Abū ʿAlī, adduced for his view that the duty is obligatory by reason (*ʿaqlan*) (Abū Ṭālib al-Nāṭiq, *Mabādiʾ*, f. 63b.7; for this issue, see above, note 25).

[46] See above, note 27.

[47] See van Ess, *Theologie*, 2:390, 4:675, 704; cf. also McDermott, *Mufīd*, 56, and the polemic of the Imāmī Shaykh al-Mufīd (d. 413/1022) cited *ibid.*, 124.

If we mean by this that they linked forbidding wrong to rebellion against unjust rule, the evidence we have considered above is inconclusive. With regard to ʿAmr ibn ʿUbayd, it is suggestive, but not much more.[48] It is noteworthy that the linkage is absent from Ṣafwān al-Anṣārī's poem,[49] as also from Abū ʾl-Qāsim al-Balkhī's chapter on Muʿtazilite rebels (*khurūj ahl al-ʿadl*).[50] The only instance in which the connection is explicit is the view attributed to Sahl ibn Salāma.[51] But if we leave aside the question of rebellion, there is much to be said for the view that early Muʿtazilism took a broadly activist stance with regard to forbidding wrong. With the possible exception of Abū Bakr al-Aṣamm,[52] the Muʿtazilites seem generally willing to contemplate recourse to arms in discharging the duty – in marked contrast to the Ḥanbalites. As we have seen, this theme appears in the accounts of Ashʿarī, Masʿūdī, Rummānī, and the Ṣāḥib ibn ʿAbbād;[53] and although Abū ʾl-Qāsim al-Balkhī himself significantly limits the use of arms,[54] he says of the Muʿtazilites in general that they agree on the obligation to carry out the duty with the sword, as well as through less drastic measures.[55] Reinforcing this embrace of the sword is a loud, if not quite deafening silence: there is no mention in all this of the third mode of standard Sunnī doctrine, performance in the heart.[56]

3. CLASSICAL MUʿTAZILISM: THE DOCTRINE OF MĀNKDĪM

There are three classical Muʿtazilite authorities whose views on forbidding wrong are known to us in some detail. Those of Mānkdīm (d. 425/1034) and al-Ḥākim al-Jishumī (d. 494/1101) are directly accessible in their own works. Those of Abū ʾl-Ḥusayn al-Baṣrī (d. 436/1044) are known from the works of a number of later scholars. All three are members of the school

[48] See above, 197. I am not concerned here with the wider question of the early Muʿtazilite attitude to rebellion, though it is worth noting that there never was a rebellion that was both historically significant and specifically Muʿtazilite. Indeed it has been argued with some force that early Muʿtazilism cannot be seen as a movement with a clear political identity (S. Stroumsa, 'The beginnings of the Muʿtazila reconsidered', *Jerusalem Studies in Arabic and Islam*, 13 (1990), 280–7, 293). [49] See above, note 3.

[50] Abū ʾl-Qāsim al-Balkhī, *Maqālāt*, *apud* ʿAbd al-Jabbār, *Faḍl al-iʿtizāl*, 115–19.

[51] See above, note 16. [52] See above, 197f. [53] See above, notes 13, 21, 39f.

[54] See above, note 23.

[55] Abū ʾl-Qāsim al-Balkhī, *Maqālāt*, *apud* ʿAbd al-Jabbār, *Faḍl al-iʿtizāl*, 64.12. The passage reappears in Abū Tammām, *Shajara*, 13.7 = 30.

[56] It does appear in the doctrine attributed by Ibn Ḥazm to Aṣamm and others, but this is not serious evidence (see above, note 14). It also figures in the account of Muʿtazilite doctrine given by Malaṭī (d. 377/987f.) (*Tanbīh*, ed. S. Dedering, Istanbul 1936, 30.12), but this is an even less reliable source. See also below, ch. 13, note 8, for a statement of Qaffāl al-Shāshī (d. 365/976) listing the three modes.

of ʿAbd al-Jabbār, who was himself in a line that went back through his teacher Abū ʿAbdallāh al-Baṣrī to the Jubbāʾīs. I shall proceed by giving pride of place to the account of Mānkdīm; it is relatively clear and systematic, and can stand as a model of what a classical Muʿtazilite doctrine of forbidding wrong is like. The book in question, itself based on a lost work of ʿAbd al-Jabbār which it frequently quotes, is a compendium of Muʿtazilite doctrine.[57] Mānkdīm discusses the duty in two extended passages,[58] which I summarise and merge in what follows.[59] In the notes I have added frequent references to other Muʿtazilite accounts of the duty,[60] but the more significant features of rival doctrines will be taken up in the next section. As will be seen, Mānkdīm's account has something in common with that of the Ḥanbalite Abū Yaʿlā ibn al-Farrāʾ (d. 458/1066),[61] but it is much more elaborate and sophisticated.

1. *Definitions*

Mānkdīm begins, logically enough, by defining the four terms making up the phrase 'commanding right and forbidding wrong'. Thus 'commanding' (***amr***) is telling someone below one in rank (***rutba***) to do something, while forbidding (***nahy***) is telling them not to; 'right' (***maʿrūf***) is any action of which the agent knows or infers the goodness (***ḥusn***), and 'wrong' (***munkar***) any action of which he knows or infers the badness (***qubḥ***).[62]

[57] The work is Mānkdīm's *Taʿlīq Sharḥ al-Uṣūl al-khamsa*, and I cite it as such; but as already noted, it was published as the *Sharḥ al-Uṣūl al-khamsa* of ʿAbd al-Jabbār. For the correct ascription and title, see Gimaret, 'Les *Uṣūl al-ḫamsa*', 49f., and the detailed discussion that follows there. For the relationship of the work to ʿAbd al-Jabbār's, see *ibid.*, 55, 66, and for Mānkdīm himself, see *ibid.*, 57–60.

[58] Mānkdīm, *Taʿlīq*, 141–8, 741–9. He has already discussed the question whether *al-amr biʾl-maʿrūf* is one of five irreducible principles of the faith (*uṣūl al-dīn*), referring to various views of ʿAbd al-Jabbār (*ibid.*, 122.14). The position he endorses is that there are in fact only two irreducible principles, namely the unity of God and His justice, and that the other three principles of Muʿtazilism – including *al-amr biʾl-maʿrūf* – fall under His justice (*ibid.*, 123.5).

[59] The numbering and headings of the sections are mine. Sections 1–12 are taken from the first passage, with parenthetical insertions of additional material from the second passage marked {. . .}. I do not cite material from the second passage when it merely repeats what is said in the first.

[60] As witnesses to the doctrine of Abū ʾl-Ḥusayn I cite Ibn al-Malāḥimī, Zamakhsharī, Ḥimmaṣī, Ibn Abī ʾl-Ḥadīd (d. 656/1258) and Yaḥyā ibn Ḥamza. I have also made reference to the account of Abū Ṭālib al-Nāṭiq.

[61] Cf. above, ch. 6, 129–36.

[62] Mānkdīm, *Taʿlīq*, 141.9 (the application of the terms *maʿrūf* and *munkar* to acts of God is restricted). Similar definitions of *maʿrūf* and *munkar* are given by Ibn al-Malāḥimī (*Fāʾiq*, f. 256a.18) and Ḥimmaṣī (*Munqidh*, 2:209.6), while Yaḥyā ibn Ḥamza defines all four terms (*Shāmil*, f. 181b.5). Cf. also Jishumī, *Tahdhīb*, f. 69a.16, 69b.9.

2. *Obligation*

Mānkdīm explains that there is no disagreement that commanding right and forbidding wrong are obligatory. {In the second passage he qualifies this by noting the dissent of an insignificant splinter-group of the Imāmīs.}[63] The only point at issue is whether the obligation is known to be such by reason (*ʿaql*), or by revelation (*samʿ*) alone. On this he reports disagreement within the Muʿtazilite fold: one view is that the obligation is known from both reason and revelation, the other that it is known only from revelation.[64] An exception is made on the latter view where the wrong being done to another is causing one emotional distress; here reason requires that one should proceed, simply to alleviate one's own discomfort. {In the second passage, Mānkdīm identifies the view that the obligation is known only from revelation as the correct school doctrine.}[65] The forms of revelation that establish the duty are Koran, tradition (*sunna*) and consensus (*ijmāʿ*). From the Koran, he adduces Q3:110: 'You were the best community brought forth to men, commanding right and forbidding wrong'; God would not have praised us so had commanding right and forbidding wrong not been obligatory. {The second passage adds Q31:17.}[66] Turning to tradition, he quotes a saying of the Prophet: 'No eye which sees God disobeyed should blink before righting the wrong or departing the scene.'[67]

[63] Mānkdīm, *Taʿlīq*, 741.5; Farrazādhī specifies that this group makes obligation conditional on the presence of a ruling imam (*imām muftarad al-ṭāʿa*, *Taʿlīq*, f. 154b.14). Compare Mānkdīm, *Taʿlīq*, 124.10, where he notes that Imāmī disagreement with the 'five principles' of the Muʿtazilites concerns *al-amr biʾl-maʿrūf.* Jishumī mentions as dissenters the Rāfiḍa, the Ḥashwiyya and Abū Bakr al-Aṣamm (*Sharḥ*, f. 264b.7, and cf. his *ʿUyūn*, f. 66a.1). His statement of the view of Aṣamm looks like a conflation of two statements made by Ashʿarī, rather than an independent testimony (cf. above, notes 13, 15). Yaḥyā ibn Ḥamza speaks of the dissent of an Imāmī sect (*baʿḍ firaq al-Imāmiyya*, *Shāmil*, f. 181b.25).

[64] For the earlier Muʿtazilite disagreement on this issue, see above, note 25.

[65] Mānkdīm, *Taʿlīq*, 742.6, adducing complex arguments which we can leave aside. Similar accounts are given by Abū Ṭālib al-Nāṭiq (*Mabādiʾ*, f. 63b.7), Jishumī (*Sharḥ*, f. 265a.14, and cf. his *ʿUyūn*, f. 66a.6), Ibn al-Malāḥimī (*Fāʾiq*, f. 256b.6), Ḥimmaṣī (*Munqidh*, 2:211.3), and Yaḥyā ibn Ḥamza (*Shāmil*, f. 181b.21). The last three set out the argument of Abū ʾl-Ḥusayn in favour of the rationalist view, namely that altruism leads to reciprocation, and is thus in the altruist's interest (*Fāʾiq*, f. 256b.14; *Munqidh*, 2:214.13; *Shāmil*, f. 182a.10). Ibn Abī ʾl-Ḥadīd and Zamakhsharī do little more than set out the disagreement between the Jubbāʾīs (see above, note 25). Cf. also the quotation from an unpublished volume of ʿAbd al-Jabbār's *Muḥīṭ* in A. ʿA. ʿĀrif, *al-Ṣila bayn al-Zaydiyya waʾl-Muʿtazila*, Beirut and Ṣanʿāʾ 1987, 351.3.

[66] Mānkdīm, *Taʿlīq*, 741.8.

[67] *Ibid.*, 142.11, 741.10 (*laysa li-ʿayn tarā ʾllāh yuʿṣā fa-taṭrif ḥattā tughayyir aw tantaqil*; similarly Farrazādhī, *Taʿlīq*, f. 154b.18). It is striking, though not perhaps surprising, that Mānkdīm does not cite a better-known tradition. This one is sparsely attested in Sunnī sources. One variant is quoted by al-Ḥakīm al-Tirmidhī (*fl.* late third/ninth century)

As to consensus, this is unproblematic in the absence of disagreement.[68]

3. *Conditions*

Having established the basis of the obligation, Mānkdīm now turns to the circumstances that trigger it. He gives a schema of five conditions (*sharāʾiṭ*) which must be satisfied for commanding right and forbidding wrong to be obligatory.[69] These conditions are as follows:

1 *Knowledge of law.* One must know that what one commands is indeed right and what one forbids wrong. Without this, one is in danger of commanding what is wrong and forbidding what is right, which is not permissible. More specifically, one must have actual knowledge of the

(*Nawādir al-uṣūl*, Beirut n.d., 22.1, whence Muttaqī, *Kanz*, 3:87 no. 5,614); another, ascribed to anonymous sources (*kāna yuqāl*) rather than to the Prophet, is given by Ibn Abī ʾl-Dunyā (*Amr*, 78 no. 34, whence ʿAbd al-Ghanī al-Maqdisī, *Amr*, 51 no. 67). On the Imāmī side, a wording almost identical with that of Ibn Abī ʾl-Dunyā is found in Ṭūsī (d. 460/1067), *Amālī*, Najaf 1964, 1:54.17, and subsequently in Ḥurr al-ʿĀmilī, *Wasāʾil*, 6:1:399 no. 25, and Majlisī, *Biḥār*, 100:77 no. 28. On the Zaydī side, the tradition is quoted in forms close to or identical with Mānkdīm's, and ascribed to the Prophet, by such authorities as Ṣuʿaytirī (d. 815/1412) (*Taʿlīq*, ms. Berlin, Glaser 145, f. 390a.13 (for this manuscript, see Ahlwardt, *Verzeichniss*, 4:295 no. 4,883)) and Ibn al-Murtaḍā (d. 840/1437) (*al-Baḥr al-zakhkhār*, ed. ʿA. M. Ṣadīq and ʿA. S. ʿAṭiyya, Cairo 1947–9, 5:470.2, and cf. the commentary thereto; also his *Qalāʾid*, 152.19 and his *Durar*, ff. 241b.4, 247a.22). Another version of the tradition is found in a Zaydī source contemporary with al-Hādī ilā ʾl-Ḥaqq (d. 298/911) (ʿAbdallāh ibn al-Ḥusayn, *Nāsikh*, f. 45b.6). The only version supplied with an *isnād* is that of Ibn Abī ʾl-Dunyā and the Imāmī sources. Here the tradition has an ʿAlid higher *isnād* which does not seem to be Imāmī, and may be Zaydī. The latest ʿAlid to appear, the polymath Abū Ṭāhir Aḥmad ibn ʿĪsā (*fl. c.* 200/815), is familiar to the ʿAlid genealogists (see, for example, ʿAlī ibn Abī ʾl-Ghanāʾim al-ʿUmarī (fifth/eleventh century), *al-Majdī fī ansāb al-Ṭālibiyyīn*, ed. A. al-Mahdawī al-Dāmghānī, Qumm 1409, 294.3, and cf. 292.10 for the chronology), but he is not included by the Imāmī biographers. In short, we cannot be certain whether we have to do with a Sunnī tradition adduced by ʿAbd al-Jabbār or a Zaydī tradition supplied by Mānkdīm. Ibn al-Malāḥimī, Zamakhsharī, and Ḥimmaṣī cite a much better known tradition at this point (Ibn al-Malāḥimī, *Fāʾiq*, f. 256a.25; Zamakhsharī, *Minhāj*, 77.5; Ḥimmaṣī, *Munqidh*, 2:210.1; for the tradition, see above, ch. 3, note 19). But Ḥimmaṣī also knows Mānkdīm's tradition (*ibid.*, 220.13), and Yaḥyā ibn Ḥamza cites both (*Shāmil*, f. 183a.5).

68 Mānkdīm, *Taʿlīq*, 142.1. Similarly Ibn al-Malāḥimī (*Fāʾiq*, f. 256a.22), Ḥimmaṣī (*Munqidh*, 2:209.14), and Yaḥyā ibn Ḥamza (*Shāmil*, f. 183a.10). See further below, 215.

69 Abū Ṭālib al-Nāṭiq gives a list of four conditions (which he refers to as *maʿānī*), starting with equivalents of Mānkdīm's in the order (5), (4), (3); his fourth condition, that one's *inkār al-munkar* should not itself be a *munkar* deserving of *inkār*, can be taken to correspond to Mānkdīm's (1) and (2) (*Mabādiʾ*, f. 64a.12). Jishumī gives pretty much the same conditions as Mānkdīm, but in the order (1), (4), (2), (5), (3) (*Sharḥ*, f. 266b.1). For the different overall approach to the conditions taken by writers in the school of Abū ʾl-Ḥusayn (including Ibn al-Malāḥimī, Zamakhsharī, Ḥimmaṣī, Ibn Abī ʾl-Ḥadīd and Yaḥyā ibn Ḥamza), see below, 222f.

point in question; just having good reason to believe (*ghalabat al-ẓann*) that something is right or wrong is not enough.[70]

2 *Knowledge of fact.* One must know the wrong to be in the making (*ḥāḍir*); for example, one might see the wherewithal for drinking or making music already assembled. Mānkdīm's treatment of this condition is very brief, but the parallels in other Muʿtazilite accounts make it clear that he is restricting the duty in a way that is significant (and to an extent counter-intuitive). The point of forbidding wrong, in this Muʿtazilite doctrine, is solely to have an impact on the future; blaming or punishing people for what they have already done are thus no part of the duty, except to the extent that they function as deterrents against recidivism. With regard to this condition, it suffices to have good reason to believe.[71]

3 *Absence of worse side-effects.* One must know that taking action will not lead to a greater evil (*maḍarra*). Thus if one knows – or has good reason

[70] Mānkdīm, *Taʿlīq*, 142.16. Jishumī gives a formidable account of the religious knowledge the performer must possess, but then quotes ʿAbd al-Jabbār to the effect that where the status of the wrong is obvious and generally agreed upon by the scholars, the layman is in the same position as a scholar – whereas if *ijtihād* is involved, only scholars can perform the duty (*Sharḥ*, f. 266b.4). For the equivalent of this condition in the school of Abū 'l-Ḥusayn, see Ibn al-Malāḥimī, *Fāʾiq*, f. 256b.23; Zamakhsharī, *Minhāj*, 78.1; Zamakhsharī, *Kashshāf*, 1:397.13, and cf. 396.9; Ḥimmaṣī, *Munqidh*, 2:216.7; Ibn Abī 'l-Ḥadīd, *Sharḥ*, 19:308.20; Yaḥyā ibn Ḥamza, *Shāmil*, f. 185b.28.

[71] Mānkdīm, *Taʿlīq*, 143.1. Jishumī expresses the condition in terms of the existence of signs that the offender is going to commit the offence (*amārāt al-iqdām*) (*Sharḥ*, f. 266b.2), and in expanding on this explains that what has already happened (*al-wāqiʿ*) cannot be prevented, and so cannot be taken as the target of the duty – unless to discourage the offender from doing such things in future (*ibid.*, f. 266b.12). In the school of Abū 'l-Ḥusayn, this condition is in effect divided into two: that the wrong has not already happened (which is a condition for it to be good to proceed), and that it looks as if it's going to happen (a condition for it to be obligatory to proceed) (Ibn al-Malāḥimī, *Fāʾiq*, f. 257a.4, 257a.15; Zamakhsharī, *Minhāj*, 78.2, 77.12; Zamakhsharī, *Kashshāf*, 1:397.13, 397.16; Ibn Abī 'l-Ḥadīd, *Sharḥ*, 19:309.4 (garbled), 309.16; Yaḥyā ibn Ḥamza, *Shāmil*, f. 186a.6, 186b.17). Ḥimmaṣī complicates the picture by omitting the first (cf. *Munqidh*, 2:216.11), and giving the second in a form that owes its key term (*amārāt al-istimrār*) to the account of the Sharīf al-Murtaḍā (d. 436/1044) (*ibid.*, 218.7; cf. below, ch. 11, 276, condition (2)); in other words, he speaks of an offence that is now in progress, and at the same time likely to recur in the future. On the handling of the conditions in the school of Abū 'l-Ḥusayn in general, see further below, 222f.; what concerns us here is the condition that the wrong has not already happened. The key word in this is *wāqiʿ* (see the wordings quoted below, note 123), used in the sense of 'having already happened'. The garbled wording of Ibn Abī 'l-Ḥadīd's *Sharḥ* at this point is no doubt the result of a failure (very likely his own) to understand this usage: *wāqiʿ* has thus been taken in the sense of 'real' or 'actual'. (For the temporal force of the participle here, compare Muwaffaq al-Shajarī, *Iḥāṭa*, f. 138a.20: *idh ikhrājuhu ʿan kawnihi fāʿilan li-mā qad faʿalahu lā yumkin*, where *fāʿilan* clearly has the sense of 'having done'.) One result of this Muʿtazilite doctrine is that the past tense of *faʿalūhu* in Q5:79 becomes a problem; Zamakhsharī seeks to explain it away (*Kashshāf*, 1:667.9; for this verse, see above, ch. 2, 15f.).

to believe – that telling off wine-drinkers will lead to the killing of Muslims or the burning of a quarter of a town, there is no obligation to proceed, nor is it good to do so.[72]

4 *Efficacy*. One must know – or have good reason to believe – that speaking out will have an effect (*taʾthīr*). However, there is disagreement as to whether or not it is still good to proceed even when it is not obligatory. Some say that it is good because it is tantamount to calling others to the faith (*istidʿāʾ al-ghayr ilā ʾl-dīn*); others say that it is bad because futile (*ʿabath*).[73] Mānkdīm does not state his own view on this point.

5 *Absence of danger to oneself*. One must know – or have good reason to believe – that one's action will not bring harm to one's person or property. This, however, depends on the kind of person one is. A man who will not be greatly affected by insults and blows is hardly exempted from the duty by such a prospect; on the other hand, one who would suffer and lose standing has no obligation. Again the question arises whether it is still good to proceed, even for someone who is not obligated to do so. In this case the answer is that it depends: if the man's suffering would be for the greater glory of the faith (*iʿzāz al-dīn*), then it is good that a man should act, but if not, not. This is how we should understand the case of Ḥusayn ibn ʿAlī (d. 61/680), who persisted in commanding right and forbidding wrong till he was killed.[74]

72 Mānkdīm, *Taʿlīq*, 143.3 (when this condition is picked up a little later, the quarter is specified to be a Muslim one, *ibid*., 146.2). For various versions of this condition, see above, 202 (ʿAbd al-Jabbār); Abū Ṭālib al-Nāṭiq, *Mabādiʾ*, f. 64a.13; Jishumī, *Sharḥ*, f. 266b.4, 266b.15; Ibn al-Malāḥimī, *Fāʾiq*, f. 257a.5; Zamakhsharī, *Minhāj*, 78.3; Zamakhsharī, *Kashshāf*, 1:397.15; Ḥimmaṣī, *Munqidh*, 2:216.11; Ibn Abī ʾl-Ḥadīd, *Sharḥ*, 19:309.6; Yaḥyā ibn Ḥamza, *Shāmil*, f. 186a.10.

73 Mānkdīm, *Taʿlīq*, 143.6; similarly Abū Ṭālib al-Nāṭiq, *Mabādiʾ*, f. 64a.13, and Jishumī, *Sharḥ*, f. 266b.2, 266b.10 (but without discussion of the point of disagreement). For the school of Abū ʾl-Ḥusayn (in which prospective efficacy is in the first instance a condition for it to be good to proceed, cf. below, note 151), see Ibn al-Malāḥimī, *Fāʾiq*, f. 257a.6; Zamakhsharī, *Minhāj*, 78.3, and his *Kashshāf*, 1:397.15, and cf. 396.12; Ḥimmaṣī, *Munqidh*, 2:216.13; Ibn Abī ʾl-Ḥadīd, *Sharḥ*, 19:309.10; Yaḥyā ibn Ḥamza, *Shāmil*, f. 186a.15. Yaḥyā quotes from ʿAbd al-Jabbār two antithetical views on the question whether it is still good to proceed, one espoused in his *Taʿlīq al-Muḥīṭ* (*ibid*., f. 186a.25), and the other in his *Mughnī* (*ibid*., f. 186b.4); he supports the more positive view cited from the *Mughnī*, which is also that of ʿAbd al-Jabbār in his *al-Uṣūl al-khamsa* (see above, 202).

74 Mānkdīm, *Taʿlīq*, 143.10 (I read *yuhmal* for *yajmul*). Jishumī's formulation of the danger condition is similar (*Sharḥ*, f. 266b.3, 266b.13), and his position on the question whether it is good to proceed is the same (*ibid*., f. 264b.17). In his Koran commentary he takes the view that Q3:21 shows it to be good to proceed with *al-amr biʾl-maʿrūf* even at risk to one's life; he comments that this confirms the view of the Muʿtazilites ('our teachers') that in the face of such danger it is best to go ahead for the greater glory of the faith (*iʿzāz al-dīn*) (see Zarzūr, *al-Ḥākim al-Jushamī*, 194.16, where the passage is quoted). Muḥallī does not use the phrase *iʿzāz al-dīn*, but makes the same point by distinguishing between people who serve as religious role models, for whom heroism is virtuous, and people who

4. *Escalation*

By what means is the duty to be performed? Here Mānkdīm sets out a basic principle: since the object of the exercise is simply to bring about good and put a stop to evil, one may not have recourse to drastic measures (*al-amr al-ṣaʿb*) where the purpose is achieved (*idhā ʾrtafaʿa ʾl-gharaḍ*)[75] by gentler ones (*al-amr al-sahl*). This is established by both reason and revelation. As to reason, when one of us has an objective, it is impermissible (*lā yajūz*) for him to take a difficult course where an easy one would suffice. As to revelation, God first commands us to try to put things right between groups of believers who are fighting each other, and only then does He go on to tell us to fight the group that is in the wrong (Q49:9), thus prescribing a process of escalation.[76] {The second passage approaches escalation from a different angle, establishing a difference between commanding right and forbidding

Footnote 74 (*cont.*)
do not fulfil such a role, for whom it is not (*ʿUmda*, 299.23). For the equivalent of the condition in the school of Abū ʾl-Ḥusayn (where it is a condition for obligation, cf. below, note 152), see Ibn al-Malāḥimī, *Fāʾiq*, f. 257a.17; Zamakhsharī, *Minhāj*, 77.13 (for *li-annahu* read *illā annahu*, *ibid.*, 77.17, and revise the translation accordingly); Zamakhsharī, *Kashshāf*, 1:398.1; Ḥimmaṣī, *Munqidh*, 2:218.18; Ibn Abī ʾl-Ḥadīd, *Sharḥ*, 19:309.19; and Yaḥyā ibn Ḥamza, *Shāmil*, f. 186b.28. Ibn al-Malāḥimī states that the distinction turning on *iʿzāz al-dīn* was made by ʿAbd al-Jabbār, and that it was rejected by Abū ʾl-Ḥusayn, who took the view that it is good to proceed in all such cases, because all alike involve *iʿzāz al-dīn* (*Fāʾiq*, f. 257a.24; similarly Ḥimmaṣī, *Munqidh*, 2:219.10, and Yaḥyā ibn Ḥamza, *Shāmil*, f. 187a.17 (endorsing the view of Abū ʾl-Ḥusayn)). We have already encountered this view in the doctrine of the Ḥanbalite Abū Yaʿlā (see above, ch. 6, note 142; and cf. below, ch. 10, note 112, for Ibn al-Murtaḍā). However, this forms part of an account in which Ibn al-Malāḥimī has already stated that, in cases where there is good reason to believe that one's action would be effective, it is the doctrine of 'our teachers' that it is wrong to proceed where the offence in question is less weighty than the danger courted (*Fāʾiq*, f. 257a.19; likewise Zamakhsharī, *Minhāj*, 77.13; Ḥimmaṣī, *Munqidh*, 2:219.2; Ibn Abī ʾl-Ḥadīd, *Sharḥ*, 19:310.2; Yaḥyā ibn Ḥamza, *Shāmil*, f. 187a.5). Ibn al-Malāḥimī goes on to a discussion of danger to property more elaborate than Mānkdīm's (*Fāʾiq*, f. 257b.1; similarly Ḥimmaṣī, *Munqidh*, 2:220.2, and Yaḥyā ibn Ḥamza, *Shāmil*, f. 187a.22). Abū Ṭālib al-Nāṭiq, having stated that the obligation turns on the absence of mortal danger (*Mabādiʾ*, f. 64a.13), quotes 'our teachers' as holding that where one has good reason to believe that proceeding will be for the greater glory of the faith (*iʿzāz al-dīn*), one may do so (*ibid.*, f. 64a.15); this suggests that the distinction was inherited by ʿAbd al-Jabbār, and not originated by him. The distinction does not in fact appear in the account of *al-amr biʾl-maʿrūf* given by ʿAbd al-Jabbār in his *al-Uṣūl al-khamsa*, but the treatment given there is after all very brief (see above, 202). Muwaffaq al-Shajarī reports a deviant Muʿtazilite view to the effect that heroism for the greater glory of the faith was commendable when Islam first began, but is no longer so now that the religion has spread and become dominant (*Iḥāṭa*, f. 138a.8).

75 This phrase recurs (*ibid.*, 148.17, 741.16; in the first passage, read *al-gharaḍ* for *al-farḍ*).

76 *Ibid.*, 144.1. Similarly above, 202 (ʿAbd al-Jabbār); Abū Ṭālib al-Nāṭiq, *Mabādiʾ*, f. 64a.9; Ibn al-Malāḥimī, *Fāʾiq*, f. 257b.4; Zamakhsharī, *Minhāj*, 77.8; Zamakhsharī, *Kashshāf*, 1:398.1; Ḥimmaṣī, *Munqidh*, 2:220.15; Ibn Abī ʾl-Ḥadīd, *Sharḥ*, 19:310.12; Yaḥyā ibn Ḥamza, *Shāmil*, f. 191a.20. Abū Ṭālib al-Nāṭiq's account is unusual in that he makes use of the 'three modes' of Sunnī doctrine (*qalb*, *lisān*, *yad*); but it seems clear from the context that by *karāhat al-qalb* he intends a manifestation of disapproval which could have a real impact on the offender.

wrong. In the first, the verbal act of commanding is all we are obligated to perform; we have no duty to force a man to pray. In the second, forbidding alone is not enough; rather, provided the conditions are satisfied, we have a duty actively to prevent the wrong being committed. Thus if we have a wine-drinker in our power, we should first forbid him gently (*biʾl-qawl al-layyin*);[77] if he continues, we should speak harshly to him (*khashshannā lahu ʾl-qawl*); if he persists, we should beat him (*ḍarabnāhu*); if even this does not deter him, we should fight him (*qātalnāhu*, sc. with weapons) till he desists.}[78]

5. *Manifesting disapproval*

At this point Mānkdīm quotes ʿAbd al-Jabbār asking himself a question.[79] Suppose that, by reason of the non-fulfilment of the specified conditions, someone is not obligated. Does he then have any other obligation in this context (*taklīf ākhar fī hādhā ʾl-bāb*)? The answer is that it depends on his character. If he is the sort of virtuous and respectable person who would never be supposed to approve of what was going on, he has no obligation. If, on the other hand, he is the kind of man who might be expected to go along with wrongdoing, he should make a point of manifesting his disapproval (*karāha*) in order to avoid any suspicion to the contrary – and also because doing so is benevolent and beneficial (*li-anna fīhi luṭfan wa-maṣlaḥa*).[80]

6. *Categories of wrong*

Wrongs (*manākir*) are the kind of thing that invites taxonomy, and Mānkdīm, again quoting ʿAbd al-Jabbār, now proceeds to provide it. He

77 Cf. Q20:44.

78 Mānkdīm, *Taʿlīq*, 744.13. Note that when Mānkdīm refers to fighting, he does not use the ugly word 'sword'. It is equally unmentioned in the accounts stemming from Abū ʾl-Ḥusayn (see the references given above, note 76). Abū Ṭālib al-Nāṭiq, however, speaks bluntly of arms (*silāḥ*) (*Mabādiʾ*, f. 64a.11, and see f. 64a.18), and Farrazādhī talks of the sword (*Taʿlīq*, f. 154b.23).

79 The formula used is: 'Then he (may God have mercy on him) asked himself'. Mānkdīm is here directly quoting ʿAbd al-Jabbār (see Gimaret, 'Les *Uṣūl al-ḫamsa*', 56). He continues to quote him through sections 6–8 below, and again in section 10, and also refers to him in the second passage in section 13. In the other sections it is not clear what is ʿAbd al-Jabbār's contribution and what is Mānkdīm's (cf. *ibid.*, 56f.), unless the introductory phrase 'know that . . . (*wa-ʾʿlam . . .*)' is a marker of the latter. It opens sections 4, 9, 11 and 12, and forms part of the opening of section 2; it also occurs twice in the second passage (*ibid.*, 744.13, 745.3, the latter a parallel to section 8).

80 Mānkdīm, *Taʿlīq*, 144.9. Note that this is the section in which Mānkdīm should have discussed the residual duty of performing *al-amr biʾl-maʿrūf* in one's heart – had he believed in it. He does not even speak of *karāhat al-qalb* in the sense in which it is used by Abū Ṭālib al-Nāṭiq (cf. above, note 76).

divides them up in two ways. His first partition of the field divides wrongs into those affecting oneself (*mā yakhtaṣṣ bihi*) and those that affect others (*mā yataʿaddāhu*).[81] Those affecting only oneself may in turn be subdivided into the significant (*mā yaqaʿ bihi ʾl-iʿtidād*) and the trifling (*mā lā yaqaʿ bihi ʾl-iʿtidād*). An example of a trifling wrong would be the theft of a dirhem from someone as rich as Korah; here reason establishes no obligation on the victim to rebuke the perpetrator {since he himself suffers no harm},[82] though revelation does so. An example of a significant wrong would be the theft of a poor man's only dirhem; here the poor man's obligation to respond is established by both reason and revelation. {The second passage fills in the details: the obligation is established by reason, because the poor man thereby averts harm (*ḍarar*) from himself, and this is an obligation; and by revelation, inasmuch as Q3:110 makes no distinction between cases where the harm affects only oneself and those where it affects others.}[83] As to wrongs that affect others, there is disagreement among the Muʿtazilites as to whether the duty to forbid such wrongs is established by both reason and revelation, or by revelation alone.[84] {The second passage makes no mention of this disagreement, and instead sets out the same distinction according to whether the wrong is significant or trifling; it specifies that there is a rational basis for the duty to forbid a significant wrong affecting others if it disturbs one.}[85] Thus far the first partition. The second partition of the field of wrongs set out by Mānkdīm (or ʿAbd al-Jabbār) is closely related to the first, but has a different starting-point. In one category he places wrongs that are excusable (*yataghayyar ḥāluhu*) if they result from duress (*ikrāh*), namely those in which the harm done affects only oneself: in the other he places wrongs that are not so excusable, namely those in which the harm affects (*yataʿaddā ilā*) others. Thus eating carrion, drinking wine or affirming unbelief are permitted if someone compels one to do them. However, in the last case one may not believe the words one is saying, but should inwardly affirm something like: 'It is you who are forcing me to say: "God is the third of three"' (cf. Q5:73). As for wrongs not excusable when perpetrated under duress, such as killing a Muslim or making false accusations of adultery (*qadhf*), these are not permitted. An exception is made where the wrongs involve only the property of others: it may be permissible to destroy the property of others

[81] It is not immediately clear from the text to whom or to what the pronominal suffixes refer. The second passage, however, specifies *mā yakhtaṣṣ al-mukallaf* (*sic*, *ibid.*, 745.10).

[82] *Ibid.*, 746.3. [83] *Ibid.*, 745.13. [84] *Ibid.*, 144.15; cf. section 2 (above, 206).

[85] *Ibid.*, 746.4 (cf. above, 206). Here again we see that, for Mānkdīm, altruism is not a duty founded in reason. The first division of wrongs is also given by Yaḥyā ibn Ḥamza (*Shāmil*, f. 184b.21).

under duress, subject to subsequent compensation (*ḍamān*).[86] Thus the fundamental distinction in both partitions is between harm to oneself and harm to others.

7. *Proceeding in the absence of obligation*

An action can be virtuous without being obligatory. Suppose that someone who is legally competent is nevertheless not obligated to perform the duty (sc. because the conditions are not satisfied); is it still good (*hal yabqā ʾl-ḥusn*) for him to proceed? The answer is that it depends. If the unfulfilled condition is one of the first three (viz. knowledge of law, knowledge of fact or absence of worse side-effects), then it is not good. If it is the fourth or fifth (viz. the efficacy or danger condition), then the situation is as already described in setting out those conditions.[87] This still leaves up in the air the question whether it is good to proceed without any prospect of success, but endorses heroism where it redounds to the greater glory of the faith.

8. *Obligation and supererogation*

The fact that an action can be virtuous without being obligatory now leads to a further question. If right (*maʿrūf*) can be either obligatory or non-obligatory, what is the status of the act of commanding such right? The answer is that it is obligatory to command the obligatory, but supererogatory (*nāfila*)[88] to command the supererogatory; the principle behind this is that the command cannot be more obligatory than what is commanded. We are given details of the history of this distinction among the Muʿtazilites.[89] Wrong (*munkar*), however, cannot be divided in this manner. It is thus obligatory to forbid any wrong without distinction, provided always that the conditions are satisfied. One cannot argue for a category of wrongs that are minor (*ṣaghīra*), and so do not have to be forbidden, since permitting a minor wrong is itself a major wrong (*kabīra*); moreover, the obligation arises from the badness (*qubḥ*) of the

86 Mānkdīm, *Taʿlīq*, 145.3. This second division of wrongs is likewise given by Yaḥyā ibn Ḥamza (*Shāmil*, f. 184a.25). The topic of duress is not normally treated within the doctrine of *al-amr biʾl-maʿrūf*, though some writers go on to discuss it immediately afterwards (see, for example, Ḥimmaṣī, *Munqidh*, 2:222.1), and Yaḥyā ibn Ḥamza himself includes a long treatment of it within his discussion of *al-amr biʾl-maʿrūf* (*Shāmil*, ff. 187b.20–190b.8). Cf. also Muwaffaq al-Shajarī, *Iḥāṭa*, 139a.1; Muḥallī, *ʿUmda*, 302.18.

87 Mānkdīm, *Taʿlīq*, 145.12. For the way this question is handled in the school of Abū ʾl-Ḥusayn, see below, 222f.

88 The second passage uses *mandūb ilayhi* (*ibid.*, 745.5).

89 See above, note 27.

wrong, and this is as much inherent in a minor wrong as it is in a major one.[90] The objection could be made that we cannot lump all wrongs together, since there are some about which expert opinion (*ijtihād*) may differ. The answer to this is essentially that expert opinion is concerned solely with determining whether something is wrong or not; once it has been established that it is wrong, there is no place for argument over the obligation to forbid it.[91]

9. *Relevance of law-schools*

Once again, Mānkdīm reverts to taxonomy, but in a different way. Wrongs are of two types, those known to be wrong by reason, and those known to be so by revelation. Examples of the first are injustice (*ẓulm*), lying and the like. It is obligatory to forbid all such wrongs; this does not depend on who is being forbidden, provided he is legally competent. The second type, those known to be wrong by revelation, subdivides into two groups: those on which expert opinion may not differ, and those on which it may do so. The first group includes such things as theft, adultery and drinking wine; it is obligatory to forbid all of this, and again it does not depend on who is being forbidden. The second group includes drinking a type of liquor (*muthallath*)[92] that is considered forbidden by some scholars but not by others.[93] In such a case, it does make a difference who is being forbidden. Thus if a Shāfiʿite sees a Ḥanafī drinking such liquor, he has no business forbidding him, whereas if a Ḥanafī sees a Shāfiʿite doing so, he should indeed forbid him. This does not, however, mean that a wrong thereby ceases to be one.[94]

[90] Read *tajwīzuhā* for *bi-jawzihā* (*ibid.*, 146.17), and *li-qubḥihi* for *li-ṣiḥḥatihi* (in the following line, cf. the parallel in the second passage, *ibid.*, 745.9).

[91] *Ibid.*, 146.9. The main lines of Mānkdīm's account in this section are standard Muʿtazilite doctrine (see above, 202 (ʿAbd al-Jabbār); Abū Ṭālib al-Nāṭiq, *Mabādi'*, f. 64a.5; Jishumī, *Sharḥ*, ff. 265a.4, 266a.5; Jishumī, *ʿUyūn*, f. 66a.11; Jishumī, *Tahdhīb*, f. 70a.8; Zamakhsharī, *Minhāj*, 77.2; Zamakhsharī, *Kashshāf*, 1:397.9; Ibn al-Malāḥimī, *Fā'iq*, f. 265a.21; Ḥimmaṣī, *Munqidh*, 2:209.9; Yaḥyā ibn Ḥamza, *Shāmil*, f. 183a.21; and, with regard only to wrongs, Ibn Abī 'l-Ḥadīd, *Sharḥ*, 19:307.15).

[92] Lane gives the sense as 'wine cooked until the quantity of two thirds of it has gone', or 'the expressed juice of grapes so cooked' (*Lexicon*, 349b).

[93] For the conflicting attitudes of Shāfiʿites and Ḥanafīs to this type of liquor, see Marghīnānī (d. 593/1197), *Hidāya*, Beirut 1990, 3–4:450.13. Cf. also above, ch. 5, note 35, and ch. 6, note 151.

[94] Mānkdīm, *Taʿlīq*, 147.5; cf. also Zamakhsharī, *Kashshāf*, 1:396.10, and the taxonomy of wrongs given by Ibn al-Malāḥimī (*Fā'iq*, f. 256b.25), Zamakhsharī (*Minhāj*, 78.4), Ibn Abī 'l-Ḥadīd (*Sharḥ*, 19:308.6), and Yaḥyā ibn Ḥamza (*Shāmil*, f. 184a.8). This latter taxonomy is taken up below, note 144.

10. *Back to consensus*

We come now to a point that might well have been considered earlier.[95] How, it could be asked, can one maintain that commanding right and forbidding wrong are obligatory (on the ground of consensus), when there are people who hold them to be so only if there is a legitimate ruler (*imām muftaraḍ al-ṭāʿa*)?[96] Essentially the answer is that one who takes this view must maintain one of two positions: either that they are not obligatory by either word (*qawl*) or deed (*fiʿl*) in the absence of a legitimate ruler; or that in such a situation they are not obligatory by deed, but are so by word.[97] But both views are without foundation, since the evidence of Koran, tradition and (antecedent?) consensus does not differentiate between a situation in which there is a legitimate ruler and one in which there is not.[98] Consequently no attention is paid to such views.

11. *Role of the ruler*

At this point, by an association of ideas, Mānkdīm takes up the role of the ruler in earnest. There are two varieties of the duty: what only rulers (*aʾimma*) can carry out, and what people at large (*kāffat al-nās, afnāʾ al-nās*) can undertake. Examples of the former are such tasks as inflicting the set punishments (*ḥudūd*), defending the Muslim heartland and frontiers, dispatching armies, and appointing judges and governors. Examples of the latter are taking action against wine-drinking, theft, adultery and the like; if, however, there is a legitimate ruler, then even in such cases it is better to have recourse to him.[99] {In fact most of what falls under the duty can

[95] It belongs above, 206f.

[96] This is a distorted version of an Imāmī view (see below, ch. 11, 266–8).

[97] The second view is closer to the actual Imāmī position. In the *Iḥāṭa* of Muwaffaq al-Shajarī, the question is raised how one can claim consensus on the obligatoriness of *al-amr biʾl-maʿrūf* when the Imāmīs do not consider it obligatory; the answer given is that this is not how things are, since what the Imāmīs actually hold is that it is obligatory by word but not by deed (f. 136b.21). Muḥallī states the Imāmī position in the same way (*ʿUmda*, 296.2).

[98] Mānkdīm, *Taʿlīq*, 148.1. Earlier Mānkdīm has stated that one who disagrees with the principle of *al-amr biʾl-maʿrūf* by denying its obligatoriness outright is an infidel; if, however, he accepts its obligatoriness but makes it conditional on the presence of an imam, then he is merely in error (*mukhṭiʾ*) (*ibid*., 126.7). Jishumī strongly endorses the view that there does not have to be an imam (*Sharḥ*, f. 265a.5; *ʿUyūn*, f. 66a.4).

[99] Mānkdīm, *Taʿlīq*, 148.9. Jishumī makes the same distinction (*Sharḥ*, f. 265a.5), but does not ascribe any preferential status to rulers in matters in which all can perform the duty. For the school of Abū ʾl-Ḥusayn, see Ibn al-Malāḥimī, *Fāʾiq*, f. 256b.1 (supporting the view that the duty is not restricted to rulers even in cases involving beating and fighting); Ḥimmaṣī, *Munqidh*, 2:210.5; Yaḥyā ibn Ḥamza, *Shāmil*, ff. 183a.10, 183b.28, and cf. ff. 181a.25, 184b.29 (tending to the same view); and the references given below, note 148.

only be performed by rulers.[100] This emphasis on forbidding wrong as the business of the state is in part contextual: the passage forms part of Mānkdīm's opening statement in his discussion of the imamate, and justifies considering this institution under the rubric of forbidding wrong.}

12. *Collective obligation*

Again Mānkdīm brings up a point that would have been better placed towards the beginning of his account. The purpose of the duty is to prevent right from being thwarted and wrong from occurring; so if this is achieved by one person, it ceases to obligate others. We accordingly classify the duty among the collective obligations (*furūḍ al-kifāyāt*),[101] as opposed to the individual ones.

13. *Proceeding against beliefs*

We now turn to the question of forbidding wrongs that take the form of beliefs (*iʿtiqādāt*). The basic point is that, with regard to the obligation to forbid wrongs, there is no difference between those that are mental acts (*afʿāl al-qulūb*) and those that are bodily acts (*afʿāl al-jawāriḥ*). What makes it obligatory to forbid them is that they are bad, and this is a quality shared by both categories of act. It may be objected that mental acts are unobservable, and thus hidden (*mughayyab*) from us, which would mean that there is no duty to forbid them. Our reply to this is that some mental acts are in fact ascertainable; thus we know from the way ʿAlids behave (*min ḥāl al-ʿAlawiyya*) how they hate the Umayyads and what they believe about them, just as we can be certain from the behaviour of a man who spends his life teaching and promoting a doctrine that he believes in it himself.[102] Presumably no duty arises in regard to mental acts that are not manifested in such ways.

100 Mānkdīm, *Taʿlīq*, 749.9. Ibn al-Malāḥimī likewise makes a transition here to his treatment of the imamate (*Fāʾiq*, f. 257b.15), while Yaḥyā ibn Ḥamza invokes the salience of the role of the imam to justify his presentation of *al-amr biʾl-maʿrūf* as an aspect of the imamate (*min jumlat tawābiʿ al-imāma*, *Shāmil*, f. 181a.25).

101 Mānkdīm, *Taʿlīq*, 148.16. Similarly Abū Ṭālib al-Nāṭiq, *Mabādiʾ*, f. 64a.7; Jishumī, *Tahdhīb*, ff. 69b.3, 70a.10; Ibn al-Malāḥimī, *Fāʾiq*, f. 256b.20; Zamakhsharī, *Minhāj*, 77.8; Zamakhsharī, *Kashshāf*, 1:396.8; Ibn Abī ʾl-Ḥadīd, *Sharḥ*, 19:308.3; Yaḥyā ibn Ḥamza, *Shāmil*, f. 190b.19. Ḥimmaṣī here follows the contrary view of Ṭūsī (*Munqidh*, 2:220.7; see below, ch. 11, note 156). Muwaffaq al-Shajarī takes the view that it can be either, and supports this with sophisticated arguments (*Iḥāṭa*, f. 138a.23).

102 Mānkdīm, *Taʿlīq*, 746.8. There follows a discussion of repentance of wrong beliefs (*ibid.*, 747.7) which, Mānkdīm remarks, ʿAbd al-Jabbār had placed at this point, although it really belongs elsewhere (*ibid.*, 746.9); we can disregard it. The parallel passage in

This concludes our survey of the doctrine of Mānkdīm. Before we leave him, however, there is one question that needs to be taken up. As already mentioned, Mānkdīm was both a Zaydī and a Muʿtazilite. In which doctrinal persona is he speaking in these passages? All the indications point to the Muʿtazilite persona. The work is devoted to the classic 'five principles' (*al-uṣūl al-khamsa*) of the Muʿtazilites; it is a commentary on a work by a non-Zaydī Muʿtazilite from which it quotes extensively;[103] the earlier scholastic authorities whose views it adduces are likewise non-Zaydī Muʿtazilites;[104] and in general, when Mānkdīm speaks of 'our teachers', the reference is to Muʿtazilites, not Zaydīs.[105] Even the adduction of Ḥusayn as an exemplar could well be of Muʿtazilite provenance.[106] Thus despite the uncertainty as to the extent of Mānkdīm's departure from the underlying work of ʿAbd al-Jabbār when not actually quoting it,[107] we can take it that his doctrine is in all essentials Muʿtazilite. In this sense, we can validly treat his account as representative of classical Muʿtazilism. It does not follow that all of it is equally representative. Certain sections of the summary given above belong to the core of Muʿtazilite doctrine on forbidding wrong; others are more peripheral.[108] At the same time, opinions differed on particular points. The next section should convey a sense of the extent – and the limits – of this variation.

4. CLASSICAL MUʿTAZILISM: RIVAL DOCTRINES

We can now turn from Mānkdīm to the other members of our trio, Abū 'l-Ḥusayn and Jishumī. In the case of Abū 'l-Ḥusayn, the discussion will centre on lines of transmission and differences of scholastic presentation. In the case of Jishumī, the focus will be on his strident political activism.

Farrazādhī's *Taʿlīq* includes an account of escalation in response to heresy (f. 155b.20): we start with kind words ('don't hold that belief, it's false, and leads to perdition and hellfire'), and end with recourse to the sword, executing the heretic after he has refused to repent for three days. Yaḥyā ibn Ḥamza likewise discusses action against heresies (*al-madhāhib al-fāsida*, *Shāmil*, f. 191b.22), but his treatment has little in common with Mānkdīm's. [103] See above, note 79. [104] See above, 199f.

[105] See Madelung, *Qāsim*, 182f. In our passages, the term *mashāyikhunā* occurs once (Mānkdīm, *Taʿlīq*, 745.3); it clearly refers to the Muʿtazilites, since it echoes the *mashāyikh min al-salaf* (*ibid.*, 146.11) of an earlier passage quoted from ʿAbd al-Jabbār.

[106] See above, 209, section 3, condition (5). For ʿAbd al-Jabbār's recognition of the imamate of Ḥusayn, see ʿAbd al-Jabbār, *Mughnī*, 20:2:149.7, cited in McDermott, *Mufīd*, 124; and cf. Madelung, *Qāsim*, 185f.

[107] For contrasting views on this point, compare McDermott, *Mufīd*, 7, with Gimaret, 'Les *Uṣūl al-ḥamsa*', 56f.; and see above, note 79.

[108] I would assign sections 1–4, 7–9 and 12 to the core.

Abū ʾl-Ḥusayn al-Baṣrī (d. 436/1044) was a Ḥanafī Muʿtazilite, a pupil of ʿAbd al-Jabbār who had a mind of his own;[109] he exercised a considerable influence on later Muʿtazilism, both Sunnī and Shīʿite.[110] No relevant work of his is extant, but we can reconstruct the outlines of his doctrine of forbidding wrong with fair confidence from the writings of five later scholars who were linked to his school: the Khwārazmians Ibn al-Malāḥimī (d. 536/1141)[111] and Zamakhsharī (d. 538/1144),[112] the Imāmī Ḥimmaṣī (d. early seventh/thirteenth century),[113] the Iraqi Ibn Abī ʾl-Ḥadīd (d. 656/1258),[114] and the Yemeni Zaydī al-Muʾayyad Yaḥyā ibn Ḥamza (d. 749/1348f.).[115] It is Ibn al-Malāḥimī's account[116] that stands in the clearest relationship to the heritage of Abū ʾl-Ḥusayn. The work in question (the *Fāʾiq*) is Ibn al-Malāḥimī's own abridgement of his larger theological treatise (the *Muʿtamad*), which in turn was based directly on a work of Abū ʾl-Ḥusayn (the *Taṣaffuḥ al-adilla*);[117] and at several points in his treatment of forbidding wrong he refers to Abū

[109] See *EI*², *Supplement*, art. 'Abū ʾl-Ḥusayn al-Baṣrī' (W. Madelung), and *Encyclopaedia Iranica*, art. 'Abūʾl-Ḥosayn al-Baṣrī' (D. Gimaret).

[110] See Ibn al-Malāḥimī (d. 536/1141), *al-Muʿtamad fī uṣūl al-dīn*, ed. M. McDermott and W. Madelung, London 1991, iii–x of the editors' introduction.

[111] For Ibn al-Malāḥimī's membership of the school of Abū ʾl-Ḥusayn, see *ibid.*, iii, vi, xif.

[112] For Zamakhsharī's links to the school of Abū ʾl-Ḥusayn, see W. Madelung, 'The theology of al-Zamakhsharī', in Union Européenne d'Arabisants et d'Islamisants, *Actas del XII Congreso*, Madrid 1986, 488–93.

[113] See Ibn al-Malāḥimī, *Muʿtamad*, viii; Kohlberg, *Ibn Ṭāwūs*, 19, 75, 354f. no. 590.

[114] For a general account of the religious affiliations of this somewhat protean figure, see *EI*², art. 'Ibn Abī ʾl-Ḥadīd', 685f. (L. Veccia Vaglieri).

[115] For Yaḥyā ibn Ḥamza and his relationship to the school of Abū ʾl-Ḥusayn, see Madelung, *Qāsim*, 221f. The Leiden manuscript Or. 2,587 contains the latter part of a Zaydī Muʿtazilite *kalām* treatise composed in 711–12/1311–12; the author is not named, but the title is given at the end of the manuscript as *al-Shāmil li-ḥaqāʾiq al-adilla al-ʿaqliyya wa-uṣūl al-masāʾil al-dīniyya* (see P. Voorhoeve, *Handlist of Arabic manuscripts in the Library of the University of Leiden*, Leiden 1957, 328; Or. 2,587, f. 194a.6). Now Yaḥyā ibn Ḥamza is known as the author of a work the title of which is given by Ḥibshī as *al-Shāmil li-ḥaqāʾiq al-adilla wa-uṣūl al-masāʾil al-dunyawiyya* (*sic*) (*Maṣādir al-fikr al-Islāmī fī ʾl-Yaman*, 620 no. 31, noting two eleventh/seventeenth-century manuscripts). That the Leiden manuscript does indeed contain the latter part of the *Shāmil* of Yaḥyā ibn Ḥamza is clinched by the quotations from a Cairo microfilm of the work given by ʿĀrif (*Ṣila*, 350–3); thus the quotation from the *Shāmil* footnoted in n. 9 corresponds to f. 182a.4 in the Leiden manuscript; that footnoted in n. 11 to f. 182a.28; and that footnoted in n. 15 to f. 181b.22. ʿĀrif's foliation is different from that of the Leiden manuscript, and his microfilm presumably derives from a copy found in Yemen. I am grateful to Gautier Juynboll for examining the Leiden manuscript for me, and to the Leiden University Library for supplying me with a microfilm. All references to the *Shāmil* of Yaḥyā ibn Ḥamza are to this manuscript.

[116] Ibn al-Malāḥimī, *Fāʾiq*, ff. 256a.17–257b.16. What is extant of Ibn al-Malāḥimī's much fuller *Muʿtamad* unfortunately contains no treatment of *al-amr biʾl-maʿrūf*.

[117] He explains in the preface to his *Muʿtamad* that this work is based on Abū ʾl-Ḥusayn's *Taṣaffuḥ al-adilla* (see the editors' introduction to the *Muʿtamad*, xi); in the preface to the *Fāʾiq* he describes it as a condensed version of the *Muʿtamad* (see *ibid.*, xiv, and *Fāʾiq*, f. 1b.6).

ʾl-Ḥusayn by name.[118] Zamakhsharī, by contrast, gives no indication of the provenance of the related material he incorporates, in a highly condensed form, in his well-known Koran commentary, as also in a short work on the principles of the faith which has recently been published.[119] Ibn Abī ʾl-Ḥadīd is a little more helpful in introducing his account:[120] he at least makes it clear that he took his material on forbidding wrong (he leaves aside commanding right) from Muʿtazilite authorities;[121] and at one point he refers to Abū ʾl-Ḥusayn.[122] When the three accounts are compared, it becomes evident that those of Zamakhsharī and Ibn Abī ʾl-Ḥadīd belong to a single tradition as against that of Ibn al-Malāḥimī.[123] An obvious hypothesis would be that both go back to a work of Abū ʾl-Ḥusayn other than that which is behind Ibn al-Malāḥimī's account.[124]

Turning to Ḥimmaṣī's account,[125] this can be seen as a conflation of material from two distinct lines of the Baṣran Muʿtazilite tradition. The first

[118] Ibn al-Malāḥimī, *Fāʾiq*, ff. 256b.15, 257a.9, 257a.22, 257a.25.

[119] Zamakhsharī, *Kashshāf*, esp. 1:397.9–398.8 (to Q3:104); Zamakhsharī, *Minhāj*, 77f.

[120] Ibn Abī ʾl-Ḥadīd offers a systematic account of the duty, or more precisely of *al-nahy ʿan al-munkar*, towards the end of his *Sharḥ Nahj al-balāgha* (*Sharḥ*, 19:307–11). He gives cross-references to discussion of the duty earlier in the work (*ibid.*, 305.13, 306.12); however, none of the earlier passages I have found offers a comparably systematic account. In one passage he mentions that he had treated the subject in his works on *kalām* (*kutubī al-kalāmiyya*) (*ibid.*, 16:65.5).

[121] It is presented as 'a summary of what our companions say' about the subject (*ibid.*, 19:307.10, and cf. 311.3); these companions are manifestly Muʿtazilites, since Ibn Abī ʾl-Ḥadīd remarks that they consider *al-amr biʾl-maʿrūf* as one of the 'five principles' (*ibid.*, 306.12; cf. *ibid.*, 16:65.2, presenting this directly as his own view (*ʿindanā*)).

[122] *Ibid.*, 19:308.1, stating that 'our *shaykh*' Abū ʾl-Ḥusayn inclined to Abū ʿAlī al-Jubbāʾī's view that reason shows *al-amr biʾl-maʿrūf* to be obligatory. Note also that, at two points, views that Ibn al-Malāḥimī explicitly characterises as those of Abū ʾl-Ḥusayn (*Fāʾiq*, f. 257a.22, 257a.25) are presented by Ibn Abī ʾl-Ḥadīd as standard doctrine without attribution (*Sharḥ*, 19:310.5, 310.11).

[123] This can be seen by comparing both the sequence of topics and the wording. With regard to sequence, the one respect in which Ibn Abī ʾl-Ḥadīd's *Sharḥ* departs significantly from the order of topics found in Ibn al-Malāḥimī's *Fāʾiq* is that it discusses the question who is to perform the duty before the question whom it is to be performed against; Zamakhsharī's treatments side with the *Sharḥ* (*Fāʾiq*, f. 257b.7; *Sharḥ*, 19:310.16; *Minhāj*, 78.7; *Kashshāf*, 1:398.3). With regard to wording, the formulation of the third condition for it to be good to proceed is typical: *Fāʾiq*: *wa-minhā an lā yakūn al-munkar wāqiʿan li-annahu yudhamm ʿalayhi baʿda ʾl-wuqūʿ lā an yumnaʿ ʿanhu* (f. 257a.4); *Sharḥ*: *wa-minhā an yakūn mā yanhā ʿanhu wāqiʿan li-anna ghayr al-wāqiʿ lā yaḥsun al-nahy ʿanhu wa-innamā yaḥsun al-dhamm ʿalayhi waʾl-nahy ʿan amthālihi* (19:309.4; the sense is garbled, one way to restore it being to move *ghayr* so that it precedes *wāqiʿan*); *Minhāj*: *wa-an yakūn al-amr ghayr wāqiʿ li-anna mā waqaʿa lā yunhā ʿanhu wa-lākin ʿan mithlihi* (78.2); *Kashshāf*: *wa-an lā yakūn mā yanhā ʿanhu wāqiʿan li-anna al-wāqiʿ lā yaḥsun al-nahy ʿanhu wa-innamā yaḥsun al-dhamm ʿalayhi waʾl-nahy ʿan amthālihi* (1:397.13).

[124] Elsewhere in his work Ibn Abī ʾl-Ḥadīd makes several references to Abū ʾl-Ḥusayn's *Ghurar* (*Sharḥ*, 4:10.3, 10:212.4, 17:158.13, 18:115.7, 227.11), and mentions his own commentary on it (*ibid.*, 5:157.2). However, he also knows the *Taṣaffuḥ* (*ibid.*, 3:236.15, 238.3).

[125] Ḥimmaṣī, *Munqidh*, 2:209–21.

line, and the source of the greater part of his account, is the school of Abū ʾl-Ḥusayn, who is mentioned several times.[126] Some of this material is taken from Ibn al-Malāḥimī.[127] Some of it cannot derive from this source,[128] and must therefore go back to some other work of Abū ʾl-Ḥusayn or his disciples.[129] But in general, we have no way to tell whether we have to do with material copied from this source, or with extensively paraphrased material from Ibn al-Malāḥimī.[130] The other line of the Baṣran Muʿtazilite tradition drawn on by Ḥimmaṣī is that represented by his fellow-Imāmīs the Sharīf al-Murtaḍā (d. 436/1044) and Abū Jaʿfar al-Ṭūsī (d. 460/1067).[131] Here again, while Ḥimmaṣī does not conceal his debt,[132] the extent of his borrowing is greater than his explicit acknowledgements would indicate.[133] It is clear, however, that he owes all this material to a single work of Ṭūsī.[134]

[126] *Ibid.*, 214.13, 217.7, 217.16, 219.6, 219.11.

[127] He is quoted twice as *ṣāḥib al-Fāʾiq* (*ibid.*, 214.20, 217.19). The first passage (*ibid.*, 214.17–215.3) is taken from Ibn al-Malāḥimī, *Fāʾiq*, f. 256b.16–20, the second (*Munqidh*, 2:217.19–218.4) from *Fāʾiq*, f. 257a.10–14. Two further passages are so close to the corresponding discussions in the *Fāʾiq* that they are likely to be unacknowledged borrowings (*Munqidh*, 2:218.18–219.12 and *Fāʾiq*, f. 257a.17–257b.1; *Munqidh*, 2:220.2–6 and *Fāʾiq*, f. 257b.1–4); the first has a parallel in Ibn Abī ʾl-Ḥadīd (*Sharḥ*, 19:309.19–310.11), but this is significantly more distant.

[128] The substantial quotation from Abū ʾl-Ḥusayn at *Munqidh*, 2:217.7–15 cannot derive from *Fāʾiq*, f. 257a.9, and that at *Munqidh*, 2:217.16–18 has no parallel in the *Fāʾiq*.

[129] The obvious candidate would be Abū ʾl-Ḥusayn's *Ghurar*, or a work deriving from it; this is what the editor of the *Munqidh* assumes (2:217 nn. 1f.), and cf. Ibn al-Malāḥimī, *Muʿtamad*, viii of the editors' introduction. The fact that the second quotation from Abū ʾl-Ḥusayn finds an unascribed parallel in Ibn Abī ʾl-Ḥadīd (*Sharḥ*, 19:309.10) would tend to bear this out.

[130] For example, *Munqidh*, 2:209.14–210.8 stands in such a relationship to *Fāʾiq*, f. 256a.22–256b.2; likewise *Munqidh*, 2:210.14–211.2 and *Fāʾiq*, f. 256b.3–6. In some instances Ibn Abī ʾl-Ḥadīd offers a closer parallel to the *Munqidh* than does the *Fāʾiq* (a case in point is *Munqidh*, 2:221.16–20; *Fāʾiq*, f. 257b.7–11; *Sharḥ*, 19:311.1–3; and cf. Zamakhsharī, *Minhāj*, 78.7–9, and Zamakhsharī, *Kashshāf*, 1:398.6–8). But in other instances Ibn Abī ʾl-Ḥadīd's version is yet more distant (a case in point is *Munqidh*, 2:209.6–13; *Fāʾiq*, f. 256a.18–22; *Sharḥ*, 19:307.15f.).

[131] Murtaḍā (d. 436/1044), *Dhakhīra*, ed. A. al-Ḥusaynī, Qumm 1411, 553–60; Abū Jaʿfar al-Ṭūsī (d. 460/1067), *Tamhīd al-uṣūl*, ed. A. Mishkāt al-Dīnī, Tehran 1362 sh., 301–6. These accounts will be considered among those of the Imāmī scholars (see below, ch. 11, section 3).

[132] For references to Murtaḍā, see *Munqidh*, 2:210.9, 213.10, 213.18, 220.9, 221.8; for references to Abū Jaʿfar al-Ṭūsī, see *ibid.*, 213.10, 213.17, 220.10, 221.7. He mentions both the *Dhakhīra* (*ibid.*, 213.10) and the *Tamhīd* (*ibid.*, 213.11, 220.11).

[133] Thus *Munqidh*, 2:213.1–8 is taken from *Tamhīd*, 302.7–13 (which is closer than *Dhakhīra*, 555.6–12); *Munqidh*, 2:218.9–11 is taken from *Tamhīd*, 303.5–7 (slightly closer than *Dhakhīra*, 556.10–12).

[134] A good example is *Munqidh*, 2:210.9–14, where Ḥimmaṣī explicitly quotes Murtaḍā; the quotation, though deriving ultimately from *Dhakhīra*, 560.6–9, reveals through its wording that it has been filtered through *Tamhīd*, 305.22–4. The parallel in Abū Jaʿfar al-Ṭūsī (d. 460/1067), *Iqtiṣād*, Qumm 1400, 150.10–13 is significantly less close. In general, there is no evidence in Ḥimmaṣī's discussion of *al-amr biʾl-maʿrūf* that he had direct access to the *Dhakhīra*, or made any use of the *Iqtiṣād*.

Ḥimmaṣī's own contribution is limited.[135] If we set aside the material derived from Murtaḍā and Ṭūsī, we can thus treat Ḥimmaṣī as a fourth representative of the school of Abū ʾl-Ḥusayn.

This leaves Yaḥyā ibn Ḥamza's account.[136] This treatment is clearly in the tradition of Abū ʾl-Ḥusayn, inasmuch as it adopts his binary schema of conditions.[137] Abū ʾl-Ḥusayn himself is mentioned from time to time,[138] as is Ibn al-Malāḥimī.[139] But Yaḥyā ibn Ḥamza seems also to be in direct contact with the works of ʿAbd al-Jabbār.[140] To all his material he brings a very clear and explicit expository format which, so far I can judge from the sources available to me, is his own. The similarities between all five of these representatives of the school of Abū ʾl-Ḥusayn[141] are extensive enough to suggest that they could ultimately stem from a single underlying text.

What of the relationship between all these accounts taken together and that of Mānkdīm? Here the similarities are not such as to suggest an origin in a common text. There is, however, a substantial identity of basic doctrines,[142] as might be expected given that both traditions stem from ʿAbd al-Jabbār. There are, of course, matters covered exclusively by Mānkdīm.[143] Equally there are others that appear only in the treatments of the duty under consideration here. Thus we find in several of these accounts a taxonomy of potential wrongs that contains significant elements to which Mānkdīm offers no parallel.[144] According to this classifiation, one category consists of things that are invariably wrong, such as injustice (*ẓulm*); we could call these intrinsic wrongs. The other category consists of things that may or may not be wrong; we could call these contingent wrongs. Within

135 The only substantial passage that looks like his own work (*Munqidh*, 2:213.17–214.12) is one in which he asks how one might support a certain view of Ṭūsī's against Abū Hāshim and Murtaḍā, and proceeds to supply an answer.

136 Yaḥyā ibn Ḥamza, *Shāmil*, ff. 181a–192b. For a digest, see A. M. Ṣubḥī, *Zaydiyya*, Cairo 1984, 306–11.

137 Yaḥyā ibn Ḥamza, *Shāmil*, ff. 185b.18–187b.4.

138 As *ibid.*, ff. 182a.10, 187a.14, 192a.26. No work of his is mentioned.

139 *Ibid.*, ff. 182a.23, 182b.14, 182b.28, 185a.22 (referring to him as 'al-Khwārazmī'). The last reference, on the question of the performance of the duty by infidels, could well be to Ibn al-Malāḥimī, *Fāʾiq*, f. 257b.12.

140 He makes several references to the *Mughnī* (Yaḥyā ibn Ḥamza, *Shāmil*, ff. 183a.22, 186b.4, 189b.9) and one to a *Taʿlīq al-Muḥīṭ* (*ibid.*, f. 186a.25).

141 For example, the account of varieties of wrong in the *Sharḥ* (19:308.6) makes it possible to decipher the parallel in the *Fāʾiq* (f. 256b.25).

142 Cf. the references given in the notes to my rendering of Mānkdīm's account, above, 205–16.

143 The main items here are the theme of Mānkdīm's section 5, and the substance of his section 13 (above, 211, 216). As already indicated (see above, note 108), neither belongs to the core of topics regularly associated with the duty.

144 Ibn al-Malāḥimī, *Fāʾiq*, f. 256b.25; Zamakhsharī, *Minhāj*, 78.4; Ibn Abī ʾl-Ḥadīd, *Sharḥ*, 19:308.6; Yaḥyā ibn Ḥamza, *Shāmil*, f. 184a.8. Ḥimmaṣī has no parallel. Cf. sections 6 and 9 of Mānkdīm's account (above, 211–13, 214; the overlap is greatest with section 9).

the latter category, we again distinguish. There are cases that turn on the thing itself, as with archery, which is good or bad depending on whether the purpose of the activity is military preparedness or social frivolity. And there are cases that turn on the person, as with playing chess, which may be forbidden for an adherent of one law-school but not for a member of another.

More centrally, these accounts fill a major gap in Mānkdīm's treatment of the duty by addressing two obvious questions: who is obligated to forbid wrong, and to whom?[145] The answer to the first question is every Muslim who is able to perform the duty and satisfies the conditions,[146] and perhaps in principle infidels too.[147] However, the imam and his deputies are better placed to undertake the duty where it involves fighting (*qitāl*).[148] The answer to the second question is every legally competent person (*mukallaf*) who satisfies the conditions.[149] At the same time the legally incompetent, such as boys and lunatics, should be restrained from doing harm to others, and boys should be broken in to religious duties such as prayer, even though these do not yet obligate them.

The most striking differences, however, relate to the conditions. One aspect of this is the way in which they are set out.[150] Where Mānkdīm has one set of five conditions for obligation, the accounts deriving from Abū ʾl-Ḥusayn have one set of five for it to be good to proceed,[151] and a further

145 Ibn al-Malāḥimī, *Fāʾiq*, f. 257b.7; Ibn Abī ʾl-Ḥadīd, *Sharḥ*, 19:310.16; Zamakhsharī, *Minhāj*, 78.7; Zamakhsharī, *Kashshāf*, 1:398.3. Ḥimmaṣī treats only the second issue (*Munqidh*, 2:221.16), while Yaḥyā ibn Ḥamza discusses these topics within a framework borrowed from Ghazzālī (see below, ch. 10, note 139).

146 Presumably this would include women; but for Yaḥyā ibn Ḥamza's negative view, in tacit response to Ghazzālī, see below, ch. 10, 247.

147 This question is raised by Ibn al-Malāḥimī, who inclined to give infidels some role (*Fāʾiq*, f. 257b.12); Yaḥyā ibn Ḥamza adopts Ghazzālī's negative view, but also quotes Ibn al-Malāḥimī's (*Shāmil*, f. 185a.19; for Ghazzālī's position, see below, ch. 16, 429f.).

148 Ibn al-Malāḥimī, *Fāʾiq*, f. 257b.13; Zamakhsharī, *Minhāj*, 78.8; Zamakhsharī, *Kashshāf*, 1:398.5; Ibn Abī ʾl-Ḥadīd, *Sharḥ*, 19:310.19.

149 Ibn al-Malāḥimī (*Fāʾiq*, f. 257b.7) and Yaḥyā ibn Ḥamza (*Shāmil*, f. 185b.7) include brief discussions of the immunity of the *ahl al-dhimma* in this connection.

150 Ibn al-Malāḥimī, *Fāʾiq*, f. 256b.22; Zamakhsharī, *Minhāj*, 77.12; Zamakhsharī, *Kashshāf*, 1:397.12; Ḥimmaṣī, *Munqidh*, 2:216.1; Ibn Abī ʾl-Ḥadīd, *Sharḥ*, 19:308.5; Yaḥyā ibn Ḥamza, *Shāmil*, f. 185b.18. Cf. section 3 of Mānkdīm's account (above, 207–9).

151 The relationship of this set of conditions to Mānkdīm's is as follows. The second, fourth and fifth conditions are essentially Mānkdīm's first, third and fourth. The first condition is a stipulation that unaided common sense would tend to include in the second (knowledge of law): that the supposed wrong which is the target of the duty must actually be bad (this condition is omitted in the account in Zamakhsharī's *Kashshāf*). The third condition is roughly speaking a weakened form of Mānkdīm's second (knowledge of fact): the wrong must not be one that has already happened (*wāqiʿ*, see above, notes 71, 123). Something is missing in Yaḥyā ibn Ḥamza's account of the first condition (*Shāmil*, f. 185b.21), but cf. his account of the difference between this and the second condition (*ibid.*, f. 186a.3).

set of three (or two) for it to be obligatory.[152] (Ḥimmaṣī's account, while retaining the binary structure, is in some respects divergent.[153]) Mānkdīm does not, of course, ignore the distinction between what is good and what is obligatory, but he handles it in a way that is structurally less prominent, and indeed less elegant.[154] So far as I can see, there is no question of substantive doctrine at issue here except in one respect. This concerns the danger condition, or more precisely, situations in which this condition is not met. In such cases it is agreed that the obligation is voided; but as we have seen, the question arises whether it might still be virtuous to proceed in the face of danger. Here the standard doctrine of the school of ʿAbd al-Jabbār makes its distinction between cases where heroism would be for the greater glory of the faith, and cases where it would not; the school of Abū 'l-Ḥusayn, by contrast, refuses to make this distinction, holding the greater glory of the faith to be at stake in all such cases.[155] This could reflect a greater zest for heroism on the part of Abū 'l-Ḥusayn; but it could also arise from a concern not to compromise the elegance of his two-set schema by including forms of the danger condition in both sets.

With al-Ḥākim al-Jishumī (d. 494/1101) we are moving towards Zaydī Muʿtazilism. A Ḥanafī Muʿtazilite of the school of ʿAbd al-Jabbār, Jishumī was himself an ʿAlid, recognised the Zaydī imams, and was in some sense a Zaydī.[156] Much of what he has to say about forbidding wrong is close to, or identical with, the doctrine of Mānkdīm.[157] The most conspicuous

[152] The first of these is roughly speaking the rest of Mānkdīm's second condition: one must believe that the wrong is going to happen (unless prevented), as when one sees a man failing to prepare for prayer although its set time is fast approaching. The second and third conditions are Mānkdīm's fifth: absence of danger to oneself or one's property respectively. (No specific mention of the third is made by Ibn Abī 'l-Ḥadīd and Zamakhsharī.) The distinction between the two sets of conditions has a faint echo among the Mālikīs (see below, ch. 14, 363f., 374f.).

[153] He omits the third condition of the first set (cf. *Fāʾiq*, f. 257a.4, and *Sharḥ*, 19:309.4; it would have found its place at *Munqidh*, 2:216.11); perhaps he regarded it as redundant in the light of the first condition of the second set. His discussion of this latter condition (*ibid.*, 218.7–17) mixes material from both the lines he draws on (cf. *Fāʾiq*, f. 257a.16 and *Sharḥ*, 19:309.16 on the one hand, and *Tamhīd*, 303.5–12 on the other); in particular, he takes the key term he uses to formulate the condition (*amārat al-istimrār*) from the *Tamhīd* (303.8). When he comes to the second and third conditions of the second set (absence of danger to person and property respectively), he is careful to distance himself from the implied approval of heroism (*Munqidh*, 2:218.18, 219.19; cf. below, ch. 11, note 211).

[154] He discusses it within his presentation of his fourth and fifth conditions, and returns to it in section 7 of his account (see above, 213).

[155] See above, note 74.

[156] See Madelung, *Qāsim*, 186–91; al-Ḥākim al-Jishumī (d. 494/1101), *Risālat Iblīs ilā ikhwānihi al-manāḥīs*, ed. Ḥ. al-Mudarrisī al-Ṭabāṭabāʾī, n.p. 1986, 8–11 of the editor's introduction (for the vocalisation of the *nisba*, see *ibid.*, 8 n. 4); Gimaret, *Lecture*, 25f.

[157] This is apparent from the references to Jishumī's views given in the notes to my rendering of Mānkdīm's account, above, 205–16.

respect in which it differs from it is a strongly activist tone which it shares with Zaydī Shīʿism.

This activism finds a particularly lively expression in a short polemical tract by Jishumī entitled 'The epistle of the devil to his baleful brethren'. Here Jishumī has the devil explain that he has disseminated quietist notions of rendering obedience to every usurper, with the purpose of subverting the imamate, the forbidding of wrong, and rebellion against unjust rule. His brethren, the devil continues, had accepted this infernal propaganda, and were busy relating traditions in support of it. The Muʿtazilites, by contrast, had vigorously opposed it: they stood for the imamate of the just and the forbidding of wrong, and transmitted traditions accordingly.[158]

It is thus more than dry scholasticism when Jishumī opens one of his systematic discussions of the duty with the statement that it is obligatory by word and sword.[159] How strongly he identifies forbidding wrong with resistance to unjust rule is apparent from his formulation of the contrary view espoused by the traditionists (Ḥashwiyya): 'Obedience (***inqiyād***) is due to whoever wins (***ghalaba***), even if he is an oppressor (***ẓālim***).'[160] And as might be expected, Jishumī repeats the view that it is good to forbid wrong even in the face of mortal danger, provided always that this would be to the greater glory of the faith.[161]

5. CONCLUSION

Three general features of Muʿtazilite views of forbidding wrong have become apparent in the course of this survey. The first is the consistently analytical style in which these views are presented.[162] Against the background of the Ḥanbalite attitudes discussed in the preceding chapters, the structured approach of the Muʿtazilites stands out in stark relief. Abū Yaʿlā's account does, of course, provide a significant parallel, but what he represents is precisely a Ḥanbalite appropriation of a Muʿtazilite format. It is no accident that in this chapter I have told no entertaining stories, and reported no casual conversations. Apart from Jishumī's impersonation of the devil, all is dialectic.

158 Jishumī, *Risālat Iblīs*, 97.8.

159 Jishumī, *ʿUyūn*, f. 65b.20; and cf. his *Sharḥ*, f. 264b.12. It should be noted that the relationship between these two works is not that of text and commentary; rather the *Sharḥ* is a much-expanded version of the *ʿUyūn*.

160 Jishumī, *Sharḥ*, f. 264b.8. The parallel passage in the *ʿUyūn* formulates their position on forbidding wrong simply as 'It is not obligatory' (f. 66a.1).

161 See above, note 74.

162 The account I have given in this chapter considerably underplays the dialectical intricacy that Muʿtazilite accounts of forbidding wrong can attain. The reader who does not find my presentation of Mānkdīm sufficiently advanced should try the account of the duty given by Muḥallī, a later representative of the same line (*ʿUmda*, 290–304).

This systematisation of Muʿtazilite thinking is by no means perfect: even Mānkdīm's account, after a well-organised start, tails off into a miscellany in which opportunities are missed and items are out of place.[163] The analytical impulse in Muʿtazilite thought is nonetheless a strong one. What pleased Abū ʾl-Ḥusayn about his presentation of the conditions of obligation is doubtless what pleases us: the result is more of a structure and less of a list.

The second feature of Muʿtazilite views is the underlying homogeneity of doctrine over space and time. The school of Abū ʾl-Ḥusayn differs from other members of the school of ʿAbd al-Jabbār on two related questions: how to organise the conditions of obligation, and how widely to apply the principle that it is virtuous to proceed for the greater glory of the faith.[164] Abū Ṭālib al-Nāṭiq, representing a tradition that goes back to the teacher of ʿAbd al-Jabbār, gives an account of the duty which diverges only in detail from those of the pupils of ʿAbd al-Jabbār.[165] At a still earlier date, the Jubbāʾīs disagree on the question of the source of the duty in a manner that sets the terms of all later presentations of the issue.[166] All this, of course, goes back to a single line of the Baṣran school; we know too little of the doctrines of other lines, or of the Baghdādī Muʿtazilites. But the little we do know, as in the case of the Baghdādī Rummānī, does not suggest that the blank areas on our map were filled with anything very exotic;[167] the same is true of the earlier Baghdādī Abū ʾl-Qāsim al-Balkhī.[168] I have already noted the lack of any positive evidence of doctrinal archaism among the early Muʿtazilites.[169] In sum, these and other divergences do not

163 Cf. above, ch. 6, 137f.

164 See above, 222f. Cf. also the anonymous disagreement reported by Mānkdīm regarding the question whether it is good to proceed if it will not work (see above, note 73).

165 See the references to his account in the notes to my summary of Mānkdīm's doctrine (above, 205–16). Only Abū Ṭālib al-Nāṭiq's use of the 'three modes' of Sunnī tradition stands out as an anomaly in the context of formal statements of Muʿtazilite doctrine (see above, note 76). Elsewhere this idea makes sporadic appearances, but in works that belong to other genres. Thus Jishumī refers to the 'three modes' tradition in his Koran commentary, where he endorses its categories, including performance in the heart (*Tahdhīb*, f. 70a.7). Likewise Ibn Abī ʾl-Ḥadīd seems quite receptive to the idea when he is not quoting Muʿtazilite school doctrine (see *Sharḥ*, 19:312.7, where he speaks of performance in the heart (*al-inkār biʾl-qalb*) as the last of the modes).

166 See above, note 25. As we have seen, Abū Hāshim's revelationist view is standard, but Abū ʿAlī had occasional sympathisers (see above, note 37, for Rummānī, and note 122, for Abū ʾl-Ḥusayn). 167 See above, 201.

168 For his rather restrictive view of recourse to arms, see above, note 23; for his failure to make a certain distinction with regard to obligatory and supererogatory acts, see above, note 27.

169 See above, 203. From the material covered in this chapter, it might appear that reference to 'being able to' perform the duty constitutes an archaic way of expressing some or all of the conditions that appear in the classical texts (cf. above, notes 13, 21, 40). But the fact that ʿAbd al-Jabbār still speaks this way (see above, note 42) counts against such a hypothesis; and Imāmī authors in the Muʿtazilite tradition continue the usage (see below, ch. 11, 278–80).

amount to deep cleavages; it would not be a wild guess that all the basic elements of the doctrine of forbidding wrong had been pretty much the same for all Muʿtazilites since the first half of the third/ninth century.

The third and final feature of the Muʿtazilite accounts of the duty is the activism that runs through them in varying degrees. To start with a negative point, most of these accounts are silent regarding performance in the heart, an idea with an obvious quietist potential.[170] At the same time, Muʿtazilite opinion is overwhelmingly in favour of heroism that redounds to the greater glory of the faith.[171] Most tellingly, all are willing to countenance lethal combat (*qitāl*) where the duty requires it. There may, however, be a significant nuance here. Mānkdīm and the writers in the tradition of Abū ʾl-Ḥusayn make no explicit reference to the use of weapons,[172] and either recommend recourse to the ruler, or emphasise that he is better placed to engage in such combat than ordinary believers.[173] Jishumī, by contrast, has no qualms about referring to the sword, and makes no such qualification.[174] It goes well with this that Jishumī, alone among the classical writers, identifies forbidding wrong with rebellion against unjust rule, and does so in a tone of marked enthusiasm.[175]

[170] For the exceptions, see above, notes 76, 165.

[171] See above, notes 7, 36, 74, 155. The only dissent comes from the anonymous view reported by Muwaffaq al-Shajarī (above, note 74).

[172] See section 4 of Mānkdīm's account (above, 210f.), and esp. note 78.

[173] See section 11 of Mānkdīm's account (above, 215f.), and above, note 148. Compare Abū ʾl-Qāsim al-Balkhī's restrictive view of recourse to arms (above, note 23).

[174] See above, notes 159 and 99 respectively. Yet Jishumī is one of the few Muʿtazilite authors to mention performance in the heart (see above, note 165).

[175] See above, 224. When ʿAbd al-Jabbār discusses the death of Ḥusayn ibn ʿAlī, he does not raise the issue of rebellion (see above, note 74). For two other instances of a strikingly activist tone in authors with Muʿtazilite links, see below, ch. 12, 336–8 (and cf. ch. 13, 347), and ch. 13, 340f.

CHAPTER 10

THE ZAYDĪS

1. INTRODUCTION

This and the following chapter are concerned with Shīʿite conceptions of forbidding wrong. Shīʿite Islam is a ramified phenomenon. But of the numerous Shīʿite sects that have existed at one time or another, only two will receive sustained attention in this study: the Zaydīs in this chapter, and the Imāmīs in the next. The reasons for this limitation are not far to seek. These sects have preserved large bodies of religious literature down to the present day, so that their doctrines are accessible to serious study. At the same time, they have always been sufficiently close to the mainstream of Islamic thought to support a body of ideas comparable to those of Sunnī Islam. The other major Shīʿite sect of Islamic history, the Ismāʿīlīs, has less to offer on both counts, but I shall devote a short excursus to it at the end of the chapter on the Imāmīs.

The Zaydīs and Imāmīs have much in common. Both are Shīʿite sects, both developed elaborate traditions of legal scholarship, and both adopted Muʿtazilite theology. But they also diverged in significant respects. The most important of these differences for the purposes of this study concern religious politics. Here both sects were firmly committed to doctrines of ʿAlid power, but they disagreed on two basic questions. The first was precisely who among the ʿAlids should rule: where the Zaydīs saw the family of the Prophet as a large and continuing pool of potential rulers, the Imāmīs were committed to a single line of imams which eventually ended in occultation. The second question was what, if anything, was to be done if the right ʿAlid was not in fact ruling: where the Zaydīs were activists, the Imāmīs were quietists. As will be seen, these contrasts strongly colour their respective conceptions of forbidding wrong.

2. EARLY ZAYDĪ DOCTRINE

The study of Zaydī Shīʿism is adversely affected by the fact that large numbers of Zaydī manuscripts remain unpublished.[1] At the same time, most Zaydī literature represents a form of the sectarian tradition already marked by an extensive adoption of Muʿtazilism. As a result our knowledge of pre-Muʿtazilite Zaydism is limited, both in general and in the specific case of the doctrine of forbidding wrong.[2]

One of the more accessible early Zaydī sources is a collection of traditions ascribed to Zayd ibn ʿAlī (d. 122/740). In substance its traditions are often more or less familiar from Sunnī sources, in which they are likely to be found with Kūfan chains of transmission; in form they are transmitted by Zayd from his ʿAlid forbears. The work contains some seven traditions that bear on forbidding wrong.[3] The doctrinal payload of these traditions is slight – they make much of the duty, but do not analyse it. They fall into two groups. The first relates forbidding wrong to holy war. Forbidding wrong is equivalent in virtue to holy war.[4] The dominance of the wicked no more vitiates forbidding wrong than unjust rule invalidates holy war or the pilgrimage.[5] One who performs the duty (and is killed) is a martyr (*shahīd*).[6] He has the same status as one who wages holy war in the way of God, irrespective of whether he is obeyed.[7] The second group is concerned with the prospects or consequences of the abandonment of forbidding wrong. Its decay will affect first the hand, then the tongue, then the heart.[8] If the community ceases to perform the duty, God will give the wicked power over them.[9] No community that fails to perform it

[1] As will be seen, I have made considerable use of Zaydī manuscripts in this chapter (as also in the preceding one); but those I have consulted are only a small proportion of those available, and more extensive research in them would refine and extend much of my analysis. I regret that I realised too late the possible interest of the one surviving Muṭarrifī dogmatic treatise for the Baghdādī Muʿtazilite tradition (cf. below, ch. 11, note 142).

[2] For pre-Muʿtazilite Zaydī doctrine in general, see Madelung, *Qāsim*, 44–86.

[3] Zayd ibn ʿAlī, *Majmūʿ al-fiqh*, 235–8 nos. 851, 853, 856; 273 no. 942; 294 nos. 994–6 (cited in Madelung, *Qāsim*, 56 n. 79). The first three of these traditions are in the *kitāb al-siyar*. On the *Majmūʿ al-fiqh*, see *ibid.*, 54–7.

[4] Zayd, *Majmūʿ*, 235f. no. 851 (from the Prophet).

[5] *Ibid.*, 236 no. 853 (from ʿAlī).

[6] *Ibid.*, 238 no. 856 (from the Prophet). The tradition has obvious Sunnī parallels in that it lists five categories of people who are accounted martyrs (see, for example, Muslim, *Ṣaḥīḥ*, 1,521 nos. 1,914f.); but the Sunnī versions make no reference to *al-amr biʾl-maʿrūf*.

[7] Zayd, *Majmūʿ*, 273 no. 942, also found in Abū Ṭālib al-Nāṭiq, *Amālī*, 295.15 (both from Zayd himself).

[8] Zayd, *Majmūʿ*, 294 no. 994 (from ʿAlī). For a Sunnī parallel, see Ibn Waḍḍāḥ, *Bidaʿ*, 231 = 361 no. 64 (the *isnād* is Kūfan; for ʿAbū Ḥanīfaʾ read ʿAbū Juḥayfaʾ); and cf. Abū Ṭālib al-Nāṭiq, *Amālī*, 295.21, with a similar *isnād*.

[9] Zayd, *Majmūʿ*, 294 no. 995 (from ʿAlī); Abū Ṭālib al-Nāṭiq, *Amālī*, 293.15 (from the Prophet). For Sunnī parallels, see above, ch. 3, note 19.

is deemed holy.[10] Two things are noteworthy about this small corpus of traditions. One is the activist strain evident in the first group,[11] with their linkage of forbidding wrong to holy war. The other is the fact that it is the traditions of the second group, not the first, that have close Sunnī parallels;[12] particularly striking here is the appearance in the second group of the notion of performance in the heart.[13]

The earliest Zaydī authority of whose opinions we know something in this field is the rather eirenic Qāsim ibn Ibrāhīm al-Rassī (d. 246/860f.).[14] In general, Qāsim has rather little to say about forbidding wrong.[15] I have noted three responsa in which he is asked about it. In the first he gives an anodyne definition of right (*maʿrūf*) and wrong (*munkar*) in terms of obedience and disobedience to God.[16] In the second he insists that one has a duty to reprove one's neighbours for such offences as drinking, even should this elicit their hostility, unless one is afraid that they will do one a mischief.[17] In a third responsum, he is asked at what point one incurs the duty to obey the imam, and whether he will make himself known; in the course of answering the latter question, Qāsim states that the imam will

10 Zayd, *Majmūʿ*, 294 no. 996 (from the Prophet). For Sunnī parallels, see above, ch. 3, note 36.

11 Cf. the long activist tradition quoted from ʿAlī with a partly ʿAlid *isnād* through Muḥammad al-Bāqir (d. *c.* 118/736) in Abū Ṭālib al-Nāṭiq, *Amālī*, 294.9. This tradition also appears in Imāmī sources ascribed to al-Bāqir himself; the key figure in the *isnād* is, however, a Ḥanafī (see below, ch. 11, 256).

12 In each case these are found with Kūfan *isnāds*.

13 Cf. also the tradition quoted in Abū Ṭālib al-Nāṭiq, *Amālī*, 299.8, with a Sunnī *isnād*.

14 On Qāsim ibn Ibrāhīm see Madelung, *Qāsim*, 86–152. Madelung in this study categorised Qāsim as in no real sense a Muʿtazilite, and declared spurious certain works of a marked Muʿtazilite character which the Zaydī tradition ascribes to him. Both these points were contested by B. Abrahamov (see the introduction to his *Al-Ḳāsim b. Ibrāhīm on the proof of God's existence*, Leiden 1990). Madelung, however, has maintained his position on both counts, and has adduced convincing new evidence in support of it (see his 'Imam al-Qāsim ibn Ibrāhīm and Muʿtazilism').

15 Abrahamov, who as is to be expected is concerned to maximise any Muʿtazilite resonances in Qāsim's thought, states that the idea, but not the term, appears in some passages of Qāsim's *Hijra* (*Ḳāsim*, 52). I have not seen this work, for which see Madelung, *Qāsim*, 138–40. Qāsim's view that one may not reside in a land in which wrong prevails and cannot be righted (or the like) is widely reported, as for example by Jishumī (*Sharḥ*, f. 270b.5, and his *ʿUyūn*, f. 68b.2) and Ibn al-Murtada (*Qalāʾid*, 152.15, and *Durar*, f. 247a.4); and it is shared among others by al-Mahdī Aḥmad ibn al-Ḥusayn (d. 656/1258) (*Mufīd*, ms. London, British Library, Or. 3,811, f. 134b.6; for this manuscript, see Rieu, *Supplement*, 221f. no. 346, item I); and see R. al-Sayyid, 'al-Dār wa'l-hijra wa-aḥkāmuhā ʿind Ibn al-Murtaḍā', *Ijtihād*, 3 (1991), 220. Abrahamov also cites the explicit discussion of the duty in a short work entitled *al-ʿAdl wa'l-tawḥīd* (ʿUmāra, *Rasāil*, 1:130.15, with emphasis on the sword). However, Madelung has shown the ascription of this work to Qāsim to be spurious (*Qāsim*, 97f., and 'Imam al-Qāsim ibn Ibrāhīm and Muʿtazilism', 47).

16 Qāsim ibn Ibrāhīm (d. 246/860f.), *Masāʾil manthūra*, ms. London, British Library, Or. 3,977, f. 24a.17 (for this collection, see Rieu, *Supplement*, 124–6 no. 203, item II).

17 Qāsim ibn Ibrāhīm, *Masāʾil*, f. 55a.17. He uses the term *taqiyya*, and cites Q3:28 (cf. below, ch. 12, note 204).

make himself known through forbidding wrong[18] – a rather pale adumbration of a classic Zaydī theme. Finally, there is a short text of Qāsim's from which forbidding wrong is strikingly absent. Here he sets out five Islamic principles which every Muslim must know.[19] The first three are indeed those of the classic Muʿtazilite schema. The last two, however, are conspicuously different, with forbidding wrong being replaced by a statement on the illegitimacy of making a living under unjust rule.[20] The practical import of this stance is not indicated; but given what we know of Qāsim's politics, it is unlikely to have been activist.[21]

The only other pre-Muʿtazilite Zaydī authority for whom I have attestations – all deriving from later sources – is al-Nāṣir al-Uṭrūsh (d. 304/917), a more typically Zaydī figure.[22] He is the only pre-Muʿtazilite Zaydī scholar cited in the account of forbidding wrong given by Ibn al-Murtaḍā (d. 840/1437) in his work on comparative law: he held that it was permissible for one to raid (*an yahjum*) a house if one had reason to believe (thanks to noise or the like) that a wrong was being perpetrated there.[23] He likewise took the view that no compensation is payable for breaking a wine-jar when one cannot otherwise pour out the wine.[24] These views look like isolated fragments of a larger picture that is mostly lost to us. One source, however, quotes from Uṭrūsh a brief scholastic account of forbidding wrong (*inkār al-munkar*): one should do it so far as one is able, by words if it seems likely to one (*idhā ghalaba fī ẓannihi*) that they will suffice, by the whip if words are of no avail, and finally, if one can, by the sword if the offender has not desisted; he adds that the performer of the duty is like a doctor.[25]

18 *Ibid.*, f. 57b.12; see Madelung, *Qāsim*, 143.

19 The text was published in E. Griffini, 'Lista dei manoscritti Arabi Nuovo Fondo della Biblioteca Ambrosiana di Milano', *Rivista degli Studi Orientali*, 7 (1916–18), 605f., item xv; it appears also in ʿUmāra, *Rasāʾil*, 1:142. On this text see Madelung, *Qāsim*, 103f., and Gimaret, 'Les *Uṣūl al-ḫamsa*', 66–8.

20 Griffini, 'Lista', 606.7; ʿUmāra, *Rasāʾil*, 1:142.15. The legality of earning a living is linked to *al-amr biʾl-maʿrūf* in the long activist tradition referred to above, note 11 (see, for example, Abū Ṭālib al-Nāṭiq, *Amālī*, 294.15).

21 See Madelung's commentary, *Qāsim*, 138 (and cf. *ibid.*, 68). ʿUmāra, who is interested in Zaydī texts for their political radicalism, reads the principle in an activist sense (*Rasāʾil*, 1:142 n. 2, quoted in turn in Y. ʿA. al-Faḍīl, *Man hum al-Zaydiyya?*, Beirut 1975, 93.9; this latter work was brought to my attention by Bernard Haykel).

22 For his anti-Muʿtazilite stance, see Madelung, *Qāsim*, 161–3. Uṭrūsh quotes a bland Prophetic exhortation to *al-amr biʾl-maʿrūf* near the beginning of his *ḥisba* manual (R. B. Serjeant, 'A Zaidī manual of ḥisbah of the 3rd century (H)', *Rivista degli Studi Orientali*, 28 (1953), 11.15, with an ʿAlid *isnād*), but this work, as might be expected, is not otherwise concerned with the individual duty.

23 Ibn al-Murtaḍā, *Baḥr*, 5:466.5; also ʿAlī ibn al-Ḥusayn, *Lumaʿ*, f. 221a.10, and cf. the scholion thereto.

24 Ibn Miftāḥ, *Muntazaʿ*, 4:587.7, and the scholion to ʿAlī ibn al-Ḥusayn, *Lumaʿ*, f. 221a.17.

25 See al-Manṣūr ʿAbdallāh ibn Ḥamza (d. 614/1217), *al-Durra al-yatīma*, ms. London,

This is a poor yield. It is not until Uṭrūsh that we encounter anything suggestive of an organised Zaydī doctrine of forbidding wrong. Before that, our only significant finding is the existence of an activist tendency articulated in early traditions, alongside a quietist mood that appears in the thought of Qāsim ibn Ibrāhīm. As we will see in the next section when we turn to Zaydī politics, it was the activist strain that was to prove typical of the Zaydī mainstream down the centuries.

3. ZAYDĪ ACTIVISM

The context in which forbidding wrong figures most prominently in the record of early Zaydism relates directly to the political activism that is characteristic of the sect. Zaydism laid claim to, and continued, an old ʿAlid pattern: rebellion against unjust rule with the aim of establishing a legitimate imamate. References to forbidding wrong are a recurring (though not an inevitable) feature of accounts of such ʿAlid risings.

As might be expected, these references are not confined to narrowly Zaydī sources and figures. Thus Abū Mikhnaf (d. 157/773f.), a Shīʿite historian well known to mainstream historiography, reports a speech made by Ḥusayn (d. 61/680) prior to the battle of Karbalāʾ in which he quotes the Prophet as condemning anyone who fails to take action against an unjust ruler (*lam yughayyir ʿalayhi*) by deed or word.[26] Abū ʾl-Faraj al-Iṣbahānī (d. 356/967), a Zaydī[27] but likewise well known to mainstream literature, has Jaʿfar al-Ṣādiq (d. 148/765) speak of rebellion for the sake of forbidding

British Library, Or. 3,976, f. 179b.19 (for this manuscript see Rieu, *Supplement*, 132 no. 210, item III), cited in E. Landau-Tasseron, 'Zaydī imams as restorers of religion: *iḥyāʾ* and *tajdīd* in Zaydī literature', *Journal of Near Eastern Studies*, 49 (1990), 255 n. 34.

26 Ṭabarī, *Taʾrīkh*, series II, 300.6 (I owe this reference to Nurit Tsafrir, who acutely read *yughayyir* for the *yuʿayyir* of the printed text); Abū Mikhnaf (d. 157/773f.), *Maqtal al-Ḥusayn*, Qumm 1362 sh., 85.9. Ḥusayn goes on to refer to himself as *aḥaqq man ghayyar*. Compare the speech that Abū Mikhnaf ascribes to ʿAbd al-Raḥmān ibn Abī Laylā (d. 82/701) at the battle of Jamājim, in which the latter in turn quotes ʿAlī at the battle of Ṣiffīn: whoever sees people being called to wrong, and disapproves of it in his heart (*ankarahu bi-qalbihi*), has acquitted himself of his duty; whoever speaks out against it has done better; and whoever responds with the sword has found the path of right guidance (*ibid.*, series II, 1,086.9, whence the *Nahj al-balāgha* of the Sharīf al-Raḍī (d. 406/1015) *apud* Ibn Abī ʾl-Ḥadīd, *Sharḥ*, 19:305.6; Ḥurr al-ʿĀmilī, *Wasāʾil*, 6:1:405 no. 8; Majlisī, *Biḥār*, 100:89 no. 69; Goldziher, *Le livre de Mohammed ibn Toumert*, 94f.). Cf. also the avowal of Zayd ibn ʿAlī that he would be ashamed to meet the Prophet at the resurrection if he had not performed the duty, apparently also transmitted by Abū Mikhnaf (Ibn ʿInaba (d. 828/1424), *ʿUmdat al-ṭālib*, ed. N. Riḍā, Beirut 1390, 207.20, a reference which I owe to Amikam Elad; the same avowal occurs with other *isnāds* in Abū Ṭālib al-Nāṭiq, *Amālī*, 100.24, 103.15).

27 That he was a Zaydī is stated by Abū Jaʿfar al-Ṭūsī (d. 460/1067) (*Fihrist*, ed. M. Ṣ. Āl Baḥr al-ʿUlūm, Najaf 1960, 223f. no. 896, cited in van Arendonk, *Débuts*, xv); and it finds support in his work (see his *Maqātil al-Ṭālibiyyīn*, 689.5, showing his participation in a sectarian Zaydī academic milieu; see also Madelung, *Qāsim*, 59 n. 102).

wrong.[28] He also recounts how Mūsā al-Kāẓim (d. 183/799), confronted with the head of the Ḥusayn ibn ʿAlī who was killed at Fakhkh in 169/786, pronounced him to have been one who commanded right and forbade wrong;[29] and he describes Ibn Ṭabāṭabā (d. 199/815) in his appeal to the people of Kūfa as calling them to forbid wrong.[30]

This theme is continued in accounts of properly Zaydī pretenders.[31] An example is Ḥasan ibn Zayd (d. 270/884), who established the first Caspian Zaydī state, though he does not seem to have claimed the imamate;[32] when he initiated his venture in 250/864, forbidding wrong was part of the terms of allegiance.[33] Similarly al-Nāṣir al-Uṭrūsh is described as setting up his rule in Daylam and Gīlān in 287/900 by converting pagans to Islam; thereafter he continued to rule there, commanding right and forbidding wrong, abolishing oppressive taxes and the like.[34] Clearly this link between forbidding wrong and state formation does not imply any denial of the individual Zaydī's duty to command and forbid. Indeed we have already encountered some pronouncements of Uṭrūsh on this aspect of the duty.[35] But the politically excited

[28] Jaʿfar is distinguishing between such rebellion and the role of the future Mahdī; the context is the rising of Muḥammad al-Nafs al-Zakiyya (d. 145/762) (*Maqātil*, 207.8). Cf. the anecdote quoted in Abū Ṭālib al-Nāṭiq, *Amālī*, 131.22, and van Arendonk, *Débuts*, 56 n. 1; cf. also *ibid.*, 54 n. 1.

[29] Abū ʾl-Faraj, *Maqātil*, 453.11. Cf. also Aḥmad ibn Sahl al-Rāzī (*fl.* later third/ninth century), *Akhbār Fakhkh*, ed. M. Jarrar, Beirut 1995, 149.9 (drawn to my attention by Etan Kohlberg).

[30] *Ibid.*, 523.13, on the authority of the Shīʿite Naṣr ibn Muzāḥim (d. 212/827f.); van Arendonk, *Débuts*, 96f. Of Ḥasan ibn al-Ḥasan ibn al-Ḥasan, who died in prison in 145/763, Abū ʾl-Faraj remarks that he followed the Zaydī path in *al-amr biʾl-maʿrūf* (*Maqātil*, 185.4). The Imāmī al-Shaykh al-Mufīd (d. 413/1022) has Zayd ibn ʿAlī going forth with the sword, commanding right and forbidding wrong (*Irshād*, Tehran n.d., 2:168.2).

[31] As noted by Madelung, 'Amr be maʿrūf', 993b. During his rebellion in Daylam in the reign of Hārūn al-Rashīd (r. 170–93/786–809), Yaḥyā ibn ʿAbdallāh had seventy learned missionaries whose message included *iẓhār al-amr biʾl-maʿrūf* (Rāzī, *Akhbār Fakhkh*, 197.8; on Yaḥyā, see van Arendonk, *Débuts*, 65–70). Cf. also the characterisation of the Batriyya in Nawbakhtī (alive in 300/912), *Firaq al-Shīʿa*, ed. H. Ritter, Istanbul 1931, 51.2, translated in van Ess, *Theologie*, 5:52.

[32] For his title *al-dāʿī ilā ʾl-ḥaqq*, see Madelung, *Qāsim*, 154f. A distinction is made by Abū Ṭālib al-Nāṭiq (d. 424/1032f.) between actual imams and ʿAlids who merely took the path of *al-amr biʾl-maʿrūf* and rebellion against the oppressors without claiming the imamate (see the passage from the introduction to his *Ifāda* published in R. Strothmann, 'Die Literatur der Zaiditen', *Der Islam*, 2 (1911), 74.3 of the Arabic text).

[33] Ibn Isfandiyār (writing 613/1216f.), *Tārīkh-i Ṭabaristān*, ed. ʿA. Iqbāl, Tehran n.d., 1:229.7, cited in Madelung, *Qāsim*, 154.

[34] W. Madelung (ed.), *Arabic texts concerning the history of the Zaydī Imāms of Ṭabaristān, Daylamān and Gīlān*, Beirut 1987, 88.9, 225.7. This report was drawn to my attention by Ella Landau-Tasseron from manuscript. Another source (which states that Uṭrūsh was successful only on his fifth attempt) likewise associates his venture with *al-amr biʾl-maʿrūf* (*ibid.*, 75.9).

[35] See above, 230. In his public statements Uṭrūsh remarks that the formerly pagan Gīlites and Daylamites now perform *al-amr biʾl-maʿrūf* (Abū Ṭālib al-Nāṭiq, *Amālī*, 204.14; Madelung, *Arabic texts*, 214.17); he speaks of how he calls to *al-amr biʾl-maʿrūf* (*ibid.*, 215.14); and he calls upon people to perform it (*ibid.*, 217.8; Abū Ṭālib al-Nāṭiq, *Amālī*, 201.19).

form of forbidding wrong associated with the Zaydī pretenders does tend to displace the duty of the ordinary individual from the centre of the stage.

This conjunction of forbidding wrong with political activism remains a prominent feature of the Zaydī tradition during and after the adoption of Muʿtazilite doctrine. The first major figure in the history of the Zaydī–Muʿtazilite symbiosis is al-Hādī ilā ʾl-Ḥaqq (d. 298/911), the founder of the Zaydī imamate in the Yemen.[36] We are fortunate in possessing a fair number of his works, together with an account of his career stemming from his immediate followers. This material has relatively little to say about forbidding wrong as a duty of the individual Muslim,[37] but a great deal that links it to the Zaydī conception of the imamate.[38]

Thus in a law-book written by a follower of al-Hādī, we find a polemic against the (typically Imāmī) view that the imam does not have to rebel; he need only be learned, pious and trustworthy. The Zaydī retort is that such a man is merely an authority on legal matters (*imām ḥalāl wa-ḥarām*), not one to whom obedience is due (*muftaraḍ al-ṭāʿa*), 'since he is sitting at home (*jālis fī baytihi*), neither commanding nor forbidding; for God does not enjoin obedience to one who sits [quietly at home] as He does to one who arises (*al-qāʾim*), commanding right and forbidding wrong.'[39]

[36] For his career, see van Arendonk, *Débuts*, 127–305. For his Muʿtazilism, which derived from the Baghdādī school, see Madelung, *Qāsim*, 163–8. A key passage at the beginning of his work *al-Manzila bayn al-manzilatayn* gives a list of five principles (*uṣūl*), including *al-amr biʾl-maʿrūf*, which are in fact the five principles of the Muʿtazilites (ms. London, British Library, Or. 3,798, f. 53b.22, and see Madelung, *Qāsim*, 164; for the *Manzila*, see Rieu, *Supplement*, 127–9 no. 206, item XVI, and van Arendonk, *Débuts*, 287–91). By contrast, the list given in al-Hādī's *Uṣūl al-dīn* (ms. London, British Library, Or. 3,798, f. 69a.26), while retaining *al-amr biʾl-maʿrūf*, drops the *manzila bayn al-manzilatayn* and adds the ʿAlid imamate (for this work, see Rieu, *Supplement*, 127–9 no. 206, item XIX, and van Arendonk, *Débuts*, 298f.).

[37] Even al-Hādī's treatment of *al-amr biʾl-maʿrūf* in his law-book has nothing to say on the subject (*al-Aḥkām fī ʾl-ḥalāl waʾl-ḥarām*, n.p. 1990, 1:503–5; the volume numbers in this printing are transposed).

[38] See the brief remarks of Landau-Tasseron, 'Zaydī imams', 255.

[39] Muḥammad ibn Sulaymān al-Kūfī (alive in 309/921), *Muntakhab*, Ṣanʿāʾ 1993, 14.12, cited in Madelung, *Qāsim*, 145 n. 264. This is a standard theme of Zaydī polemic against Imāmism. It is prominent in the *Ishhād* of the Zaydī polemist Abū Zayd al-ʿAlawī (*fl.* later third/ninth century), preserved in the refutation of the Imāmī Muʿtazilite Ibn Qiba al-Rāzī (d. not later than 319/931) (see H. Modarressi, *Crisis and consolidation in the formative period of Shīʿite Islam*, Princeton 1993, 193.4, 194.11, and cf. Ibn Qiba's retorts, *ibid.*, 196.16, 198.21, 200.16, 201.10); the date of this exchange cannot be earlier than 271/884 (*ibid.*, 169, and cf. 83 n. 161) nor later than 319/931 (*ibid.*, 117, 119). Three centuries later, the imam al-Manṣūr ʿAbdallāh ibn Ḥamza (d. 614/1217) replies to the assertion that God has not given the imam permission to rebel by saying that this is contrary to Islam, for God has ordered His servants in general, and the imams in particular, to perform *al-amr biʾl-maʿrūf* and *jihād*; so if a supposed imam claims that he has not been commanded to engage in such activities as *jihād*, the implementation of the *ḥudūd*, resistance to the oppressors (*ẓālimūn*), and *al-amr biʾl-maʿrūf*, we ask him: 'So what *were* you commanded to do, and to what purpose?' (*al-ʿIqd al-thamīn*, ms. London, British Library, Or. 3,976, f. 139b.19, cited in Landau-Tasseron, 'Zaydī imams', 255 n. 34; for this manuscript, see Rieu, *Supplement*, 132 no. 210, item I).

Elsewhere al-Hādī argues that commanding and forbidding are vested in the best members of the family of the Prophet (*khiyār āl Muḥammad*) to the exclusion of Pharaohs and tyrants (*jabābira*);[40] he adduces a set of Koranic proof-texts of which the first is Q22:41.[41] His polemical target here is the anthropomorphist predestinationists (in other words, the Sunnīs) who believe that God has Himself decreed the oppression they suffer; were they to come to know God as He really is, and then to set about commanding right and forbidding wrong, their prayers would be answered and they would be delivered from their oppressors.[42] The same linkage appears in a tradition quoted by al-Hādī to establish the Zaydī doctrine of the imamate. Here the Prophet states: 'Whoever of my descendants (*min dhurriyyatī*) commands right and forbids wrong is God's caliph on His earth . . .'[43]

The narrative of the career of al-Hādī in founding the Zaydī imamate in the Yemen is accordingly one in which forbidding wrong figures prominently.[44] The duty is central to the enterprise in which he is engaged: it is one of the things he does when he first calls people to his cause,[45] just as it is part of what the true ʿAlid does when he unsheathes his sword and

40 See al-Hādī ilā 'l-Ḥaqq (d. 298/911), *Kitāb fīhi maʿrifat Allāh*, in ʿUmāra, *Rasā'il*, 2:83–6.

41 *Ibid.*, 83.15. Cf. the Zaydī use of Q3:104 as a proof-text for the imamate noted by Landau-Tasseron ('Zaydī imams', 255 n. 36), and the similar appeal to Q3:110 at the end of the refutation of the Rawāfiḍ ascribed to Qāsim ibn Ibrāhīm (see the quotation in R. Strothmann, *Das Staatsrecht der Zaiditen*, Strasburg 1912, 42 n. 1; for the ascription of the work, see Madelung, *Qāsim*, 98f.).

42 See al-Hādī, *Kitāb fīhi maʿrifat Allāh*, 86.8. This is a fine yoking of Muʿtazilite dogmatic positions to Zaydī activism.

43 *Ibid.*, 83.2 (here al-Hādī immediately draws attention to the phrase *min dhurriyyatī*, which is not found in the Sunnī version of the tradition, see above, ch. 3, note 27); al-Hādī, *Aḥkām*, 1:505.22. The tradition was duly included by Qāḍī Ṣaʿda (d. 646/1248f.) in his collection of Prophetic traditions transmitted by al-Hādī (*Durar al-aḥādīth*, ed. Y. ʿA. al-Faḍīl, Beirut 1979, 48.4, whence Crone and Hinds, *God's caliph*, 98 n. 12, and Landau-Tasseron, 'Zaydī imams', 255 n. 35). Strothmann, who cited the tradition from manuscript, noted the marginal annotation of a reader: 'This is an explicit stipulation (*naṣṣ*) of the imamate of the descendants of the Prophet (*ahl al-bayt*)' (*Staatsrecht*, 43 and n. 2, with the comment that this reader was 'ein echter Zaidit').

44 A painfully spurious tradition has the Prophet predict the appearance in the Yemen of a descendant of his named Yaḥyā al-Hādī who would command right and forbid wrong, and through whom God would bring life to truth and death to falsehood (al-Manṣūr Sharaf al-Dīn ibn Badr al-Dīn (d. 670/1271f.), *Anwār al-yaqīn*, ms. London, British Library, Or. 3,868, f. 150a.4, cited in Landau-Tasseron, 'Zaydī imams', 255 n. 34; for this manuscript, see Rieu, *Supplement*, 331f. no. 538).

45 ʿAlī ibn Muḥammad al-ʿAlawī (*fl.* late third/ninth century), *Sīrat al-Hādī ilā 'l-Ḥaqq Yaḥyā ibn al-Ḥusayn*, ed. S. Zakkār, n.p. 1972, 17.8; cf. also *ibid.*, 92.4, and van Arendonk, *Débuts*, 135. In an extant written *daʿwa*, al-Hādī stresses the obligations of *jihād* and *al-amr bi'l-maʿrūf* (*Daʿwa*, ms. London, British Library, Or. 3,798, f. 85a.2, with a string of Koranic verses), and calls upon the addressee to join him in *al-amr bi'l-maʿrūf* (*ibid.*, f. 88b.7, and cf. f. 89b.24; for this text, see Rieu, *Supplement*, 127–9 no. 206, item XXIV, and cf. van Arendonk, *Débuts*, 302f.). In all the passages cited from this *daʿwa*, we find the expanded form *al-amr bi'l-maʿrūf al-akbar wa'l-nahy ʿan al-taẓālum wa'l-munkar*, as also at ʿAlawī, *Sīra*, 25.2.

proclaims his imamate.[46] It makes a simple meal of three buns and a little condiment shared by al-Hādī and one of his followers tantamount to a banquet.[47] It figures as a formal component of the allegiance done to al-Hādī by those who follow or submit to him.[48] It is one of the most salient roles of his governors[49] and emissaries.[50] It appears as a duty of the people at large, indeed of all believers.[51] It lies at the core of the enterprise in which his band of followers is engaged.[52] He tells the people of the localities that join his state to perform it.[53] Few of these references have much to say about concrete and particular wrongs;[54] several have rich associations with the tradition of ʿAlid insurrection against injustice.[55] Likewise after his death the absence of forbidding wrong, and the need for someone to undertake it, figure prominently in the story of the anarchy that ensued.[56]

The same idiom remains prominent in the later history of Zaydī state formation. Thus forbidding wrong appears repeatedly as an activity characteristic of (though far from confined to) imams and similar figures exercising religiously validated political power. This is readily illustrated from the annals of Caspian Zaydism. The imam al-Muʾayyad Aḥmad ibn al-Ḥusayn (d. 411/1020)[57] issued a call to his cause which deplored the conditions of anarchy and oppression that had arisen; among them he

46 *Ibid.*, 29.4. By contrast, the stay-at-home ʿAlid pretenders fail to do it (*ibid.*, 28.1, 28.10, the latter from Zayd ibn ʿAlī). He likewise stresses the role of armed conflict in the performance of the duty in a passage in his *Manzila* (f. 55a.3); most of the passage is quoted in ʿA. M. Zayd, *Muʿtazilat al-Yaman*, Ṣanʿāʾ and Beirut 1981, 180f.

47 ʿAlawī, *Sīra*, 57.3.

48 See the text of the form of allegiance, *ibid.*, 117.9, and the accounts of the submission of local rulers, *ibid.*, 115.6, 207.3.

49 See the text of his letter of appointment, *ibid.*, 45.1 (= van Arendonk, *Débuts*, 320.12, and cf. *ibid.*, 136f.); cf. also ʿAlawī, *Sīra*, 211.3. For particular instances, see *ibid.*, 80.5, 94.9, 115.16, 211.16, 212.17, 214.9, 214.19, 341.7. In another such document, *al-amr biʾl-maʿrūf* is a duty in which governors are to instruct their subjects (*ʿAhd*, London, British Library, ms. Or. 3,798, f. 179b.14, likewise using the expanded form; for this document, which in now printed in Kūfī, *Muntakhab*, 505–7, see Rieu, *Supplement*, 127–9 no. 206, item XXXV, and van Arendonk, *Débuts*, 302 and n. 2).

50 ʿAlawī, *Sīra*, 115.10. Cf. also *ibid.*, 298.10.

51 *Ibid.*, 25.2 (and cf. *ibid.*, 24.12, citing Q3:104 and Q3:110). See also *ibid.*, 22.6, 123.4.

52 *Ibid.*, 50.15, 51.1.

53 *Ibid.*, 211.12, 214.12, and cf. 52.6.

54 Cf. *ibid.*, 94.9 (mentioning unspecified *fawāḥish*), 115.6 (mentioning wine), 115.13 (mentioning a case of drunkenness); and see van Arendonk, *Débuts*, 164.

55 See ʿAlawī, *Sīra*, 22.6 (where *al-amr biʾl-maʿrūf* is associated with separating from the oppressors and fighting the wicked on the side of just imams descended from Ḥasan and Ḥusayn), 25.2 (associated with assistance to the imams – the caliphs descended from the prophets – and with a hard line against wicked and oppressive tyrants and those who follow them), 29.4 (associated with the ʿAlid imam who unsheathes his sword and plants his standard).

56 W. Madelung (ed.), *The Sīra of Imām Aḥmad b. Yaḥyā al-Nāṣir li-Dīn Allāh from Musallam al-Laḥjī's Kitāb Akhbār al-Zaydiyya bi l-Yaman*, Exeter 1990, 7.1, 7.16, 8.11, 8.19; cf. also *ibid.*, 46.20, 48.11, 62.17. This material derives from a contemporary source (see Madelung's introduction, vf.). The most interesting of these passages were drawn to my attention from manuscript by Ella Landau-Tasseron.

57 See Madelung, *Qāsim*, 177f.

mentioned that the practitioners of the duty had become few and impotent.[58] He went on to call people to assist him in his enterprise, and to help him in the task of forbidding wrong which he had undertaken.[59] After his death he was succeeded by his brother Abū Ṭālib al-Nāṭiq (d. 424/1032f.),[60] who continued to command right and forbid wrong in the tradition of the family of the Prophet till he died.[61] Later, between 472/1079f. and 490/1097, there were in effect two imams, al-Hādī al-Ḥuqaynī (d. 490/1097) and Abū ʾl-Riḍā al-Kīsumī (who died soon after).[62] When the timely sabotage of a bridge prevented what might have been an ugly encounter between their forces, they agreed to divide and rule: one reigned in Daylamān, while the other (Kīsumī) commanded right and forbade wrong in Gīlān.[63] Nearly a century later – in the 560s/1160s – ʿAlī ibn Muḥammad al-Ghaznawī, an ʿAlid from Ghazna, set up in Gīlān, though without claiming to be a full imam;[64] he established right and took action against wrongs.[65] As late as the second half of the eighth/fourteenth century a descendant of his, ʿAlī ibn Amīr Kiyā Malāṭī (d. 781/1379f.), was established as a fully fledged Zaydī imam;[66] our account of his career refers to forbidding wrong as a part of his role in such contexts as the duty of the imam to reduce a fractious local ruler to obedience,[67] and the forced conversion of a conquered Ismāʿīlī community to Zaydism.[68]

What is true of Caspian Zaydism is true also for its Yemeni offshoot. The imam al-Manṣūr al-Qāsim ibn ʿAlī al-ʿIyānī (d. 393/1003) sent out letters reminding his subjects that the terms of their mutual allegiance were the Book of God and the normative practice (*sunna*) of His Prophet, which include forbidding wrong and mutual help in performing it.[69] Two centuries later the terms of allegiance to the imam al-Manṣūr ʿAbdallāh ibn Ḥamza (d. 614/1217) included the Book of God, the normative practice

58 Madelung, *Arabic texts*, 311.11.

59 *Ibid.*, 314.2, quoting Q5:78 and Q3:110; cf. also 354.1

60 See Madelung, *Qāsim*, 178–82.

61 Madelung, *Arabic texts*, 320.16. Cf. his own statement of the duties of the imam in his *Taḥrīr*, *apud* Strothmann, *Staatsrecht*, 105.4.

62 See Madelung, *Qāsim*, 208f.

63 Madelung, *Arabic texts*, 145.5. Cf. also *ibid.*, 151.15, 332.5 (on the fate of Kīsumī's wine-bibbing son).

64 Madelung, *Qāsim*, 217f.

65 Madelung, *Arabic texts*, 159.2 (*aqāma ʾl-maʿrūf wa-azāla ʾl-manākir*). The text goes on to remark that he was a Zaydī in *uṣūl* and *furuʿ*.

66 *Ibid.*, 12f. of the introduction, citing Ẓahīr al-Dīn Marʿashī (ninth/fifteenth century), *Tārīkh-i Gīlān wa Daylamistān*, ed. M. Sutūda, Tehran 1347 sh., 41.8.

67 *Ibid.*, 55.18. It is also mentioned as the duty of such a ruler and his followers on submission to the imam (*ibid.*, 34.17).

68 Marʿashī, *Taʾrīkh*, 67.18. The conquest itself is presented as a consequence of the duty of the 'people of Islam' to see that *al-amr biʾl-maʿrūf* is carried out (*ibid.*, 66.12).

69 Ḥusayn ibn Aḥmad ibn Yaʿqūb (*fl.* later fourth/tenth century), *Sīrat al-imām al-Manṣūr biʾllāh*, ms. London, British Library, Or. 3,816, f. 40a.8 (for the distribution of the letter, see *ibid.*, f. 38a.3); and cf. also *ibid.*, ff. 42b.3, 57b.12, and cf. 111a.13, 112a.20. For this manuscript, see Rieu, *Supplement*, 328 no. 532.

of His Prophet, and forbidding wrong.[70] Another four centuries take us to the time of the imam al-Manṣūr al-Qāsim ibn Muḥammad (d. 1029/1620), who wrote a letter calling people to his cause in which the rhetoric of forbidding wrong is as conspicuous as ever.[71] At the same time the language retains its old formulaic quality. Even after so many centuries, we have little sense that this Zaydī tradition of forbidding wrong implied a concrete and practical programme of moral reform. In marked contrast to what we saw in the case of the later Saʿūdī state, we have here little more than a banner under which an ʿAlid can rebel, establish a state, and maintain his power.

4. THE ZAYDĪ LEGAL TRADITION

There was, of course, more to Zaydism than this inflammatory brand of religious politics. As we have seen, forbidding wrong was also a duty of the individual Zaydī believer, and it is regularly treated as such in legal works.[72] A good deal of what the scholars have to say here is Muʿtazilite, or heavily influenced by Muʿtazilism, as will be seen in the next section. But as might be expected, there is much in the legal tradition that seems to be independent of Muʿtazilite sources. We can best approach this material through a work on the legal doctrine of the imam al-Muʾayyad Aḥmad ibn al-Ḥusayn (d. 411/1020) put together by his disciple Abū ʾl-Qāsim al-Hawsamī. Although al-Muʾayyad was a Muʿtazilite,[73] it hardly shows in the part of the work that concerns us. In what follows I shall reproduce the substance of his treatment,[74] respecting the order of topics found in it.

[70] The wording of the *bayʿa* is quoted in Muḥallī (d. 652/1254f.), *al-Ḥadāʾiq al-wardiyya*, ms. London, British Library, Or. 3,786, f. 167a.7 (for this manuscript, see Rieu, *Supplement*, 329f. no. 534).

[71] This incomplete *daʿwa* is found in Jurmūzī (d. 1077/1667), *al-Nubdha al-mushīra*, ms. London, British Library, Or. 3,329, ff. 52b–54a (= 88–90 in the published facsimile, n.p. n.d.); note the borrowing at f. 53a.20 (= 89.23) of some of the rousing language of the long activist tradition mentioned above, note 11. For this manuscript, see Rieu, *Supplement*, 336f. no. 543.

[72] The Zaydīs are like the Imāmīs, and unlike the Sunnīs, in including discussion of *al-amr biʾl-maʿrūf* in their law-books. But the two Shīʿite sects differ with regard to the location of the topic in the law-book: whereas the Imāmīs place it in the *kitāb al-jihād*, which normally follows the discussion of the rites of pilgrimage, the Zaydīs treat it in their *kitāb al-siyar*, which includes both *jihād* and the imamate, and is placed at the end of the law-book. For more details on the Imāmī practice, see below, ch. 11, note 2.

[73] See Madelung, *Qāsim*, 177.

[74] Viz. al-Muʾayyad Aḥmad ibn al-Ḥusayn (d. 411/1020), *Ifāda*, ms. London, British Library, Or. 4,031, ff. 80b.19–81b.9 (for this manuscript see Rieu, *Supplement*, 216f. no. 338). I have also consulted a Berlin manuscript of the work and made use of its readings where I had difficulty with the London manuscript (ms. Berlin, Glaser 188, ff. 12a.16–13a.1; for this manuscript, see Ahlwardt, *Verzeichniss*, 4:292f. no. 4,878, item 1); but unless otherwise indicated, my references are to the London manuscript. I have also made some use of the parallel passages and further materials found in ʿAlī ibn al-Ḥusayn, *Lumaʿ*, ff. 220b–223a.

The account opens with a general statement about the manner of taking action against wrongs (*kayfiyyat izālat al-munkar*). Whoever has good reason to think that he is able to do so has a duty to proceed against wrong. If words suffice, he should not resort to blows; but if neither words nor blows are enough, he can escalate further as the situation requires, since the sole object is to eliminate the wrong.[75] This formulation is quite likely to derive from a Muʿtazilite source, but it does not have to: Uṭrūsh had said much the same.[76]

With these generalities out of the way, the account turns to detail. There is no overall structure; the following topics are addressed in succession:

1 *Smashing offending objects:* With regard to objects used in wrongful activities – mandolins and the like – a distinction is made between those normally used for illicit purposes (even if a licit use is possible) and those used for both licit and illicit purposes (such as cups and bottles). Objects in the first category are to be smashed,[77] and the bits returned to the owner; those in the second are not to be smashed.[78]

2 *Dealing with wine:* The basic techniques for dealing with wine or the like are to pour it out or to put into it something such as dung (*sarqīn aw ʿadhira*) which will render it unfit for consumption.[79] However, dung (*zibl*) – or sand (*raml*)? – is not to be put into amphorae (*dinān*) because of the inconvenience (*taʿab*) this gives rise to.[80] If you see a man carrying a jar with wine in it, you pour it out; if the jar gets broken in the process, you are – rather surprisingly – liable for its cost.[81] If the

[75] Muʾayyad, *Ifāda*, f. 80b.20; cf. ʿAlī ibn al-Ḥusayn, *Lumaʿ*, f. 220b.10, with explicit reference to killing.

[76] See above, 230. That we are not in a Sunnī milieu is underlined by the absence of any mention of performance in the heart, and perhaps by the implicit authorisation of recourse to arms.

[77] For the uncompromising Zaydī attitude to musical instruments, compare the view of Uṭrūsh in Serjeant, ʿA Zaidī manual of ḥisbahʾ, 17.7, and cf. below, note 124.

[78] Muʾayyad, *Ifāda*, f. 80b.22. Authority for such smashing is found in the Koranic account of Abraham's treatment of the idols of his people (Q21:58), and in an anecdote about the harsh reaction of ʿAlī to some chess-players he encountered. The anecdote about ʿAlī is quoted from al-Hādī, *Aḥkām*, 1:553.1; for the severe Zaydī attitude to chess, see also Serjeant, ʿA Zaidī manual of ḥisbahʾ, 17.1 (where a version of the same anecdote follows). A later Zaydī source states that objects in the second category may be broken only by the authorities (*ahl al-wilāyāt*) (Ibn Miftāḥ, *Muntazaʿ*, 4:589.3). For the smashing of offending objects in Ibn Ḥanbal's responsa, compare above, ch. 5, note 99; and cf. ch. 7, notes 28f.

[79] A later source also names urine as a possible additive (*ibid.*, 4:587.23, in the scholia).

[80] The readings *zibl* and *raml* are those of the London and Berlin manuscripts respectively; the reading in the parallel passage in ʿAlī ibn al-Ḥusayn's *Lumaʿ* is ambiguous (f. 221a.19), while in Ṣuʿaytirī's *Taʿlīq* it is clearly *raml* (f. 391a.24). We may perhaps have to do with Caspian realia which were already obscure to Yemeni copyists.

[81] In the *Ifāda* mention is made of the contrary opinion of the Ḥanafī Abū Yūsuf (d.

only way to pour out the wine is to break the jar, you may do so subject to compensation. If you do not know for sure that there is wine in the jar, but have good reason to think there is, you must proceed; if afterwards it turns out that you were wrong, you are liable for compensation.[82]

3 *Entering a home:* When you hear the sound of music – such as singing or the noise of musical instruments – coming from inside a home (*dār*), and recognise (the signs of) wine-drinking, it is your duty to enter the home. Likewise if you know (or just have good reason to think) that there is wine there, you must go in and pour it out.[83]

4 *Turning in a drunk:* On the other hand, if you come across a drunk, you have no duty to turn him over (*rafʿ*) to the authorities (*ḥākim*). You should keep the matter quiet, and counsel him.[84]

5 *Unjust rulers:* When a reprobate ruler (*sulṭān fāsiq*) calls people to establish right and eliminate wrong, the Muslims may not assist him. However, it is permissible to seek his help in forbidding wrong. If one thinks that by addressing oneself orally or in writing to an unjust ruler (*mutaghallib*) one may be able to persuade him to release someone he has wrongfully imprisoned, or the like, one should do so. What if there are two unjust rulers (*ẓālimān*), one worse than the other, and the less bad seeks the help of the Muslims against his rival, and the Muslims in question have reason to believe that their help will be effective in getting rid of the worse ruler, and that the less bad one will expend the taxes he collects from the Muslims in ways advantageous to the faith? The answer is that it is still impermissible to assist the less bad ruler in any wrongdoing, and the taxes he collects are illegal. On the other

182/798) (al-Muʾayyad had studied Ḥanafī law, see Madelung, *Qāsim*, 177, and cf. 179); cf. also the position mentioned in a scholion to the parallel passage in ʿAlī ibn al-Ḥusayn's *Lumaʿ* (f. 221a.15) that there is no duty to pour out wine when this would lead to (the obligation to pay) compensation, and the view of Uṭrūsh cited above, note 24.

82 Muʾayyad, *Ifāda*, f. 81a.1. For the treatment of vessels containing wine in Ibn Ḥanbal's responsa, see above, ch. 5, notes 101f.; for the question of compensation, see ch. 5, note 99, and cf. ch. 6, note 33; for the problem of uncertainty, cf. ch. 5, notes 143, 148.

83 *Ibid.*, f. 81a.8. For the view of Uṭrūsh, see above, 230; and cf. Ṣuʿaytirī, *Taʿlīq*, f. 391a.20; ʿAlī ibn al-Ḥusayn, *Lumaʿ*, f. 221a.8. Confronted with the problem of the sound of music, Ibn Ḥanbal says one should reprove the offenders, but he does not say that one should push one's way in (see his responsum cited above, ch. 5, note 63; cf. also ch. 6, note 32).

84 *Ibid.*, f. 81a.10. Cf. the view of al-Muʾayyad that if one has a neighbour who gives one trouble, and one knows that if one hands him over to the ruler he will harm him (in some unlawful way), one may not involve the ruler (ʿAlī ibn al-Ḥusayn, *Lumaʿ*, f. 222a.13, in the scholion; also Ṣuʿaytirī, *Taʿlīq*, f. 391b.26, and Ibn Miftāḥ, *Muntazaʿ*, 4:592.15, in the scholia). For the problem of involving the authorities as dealt with in Ibn Ḥanbal's responsa, see above, ch. 5, 90, 102f.; and cf. ch. 4, note 268.

hand, (cooperating with him with a view to) eliminating the worse ruler is permissible, indeed obligatory.[85]

6 *Conduct of boys:* Boys must be prevented from wearing silk, golden rings, anklets or earrings, and from drinking wine and the like.[86]

7 *Errors in Korans:* If you find a mistake in someone else's Koran, you must erase it. If, however, you would damage the Koran, whereas someone more skilful than you could erase the mistake without such damage, you are not obliged to act.[87]

8 *Conduct of women:* When women speak up (*idhā aẓharna kalāmahunna*), they are not to be forbidden or rebuked. This point is supported from cases of women at the beginning of Islam who spoke to men, transmitted what they had seen and heard from the Prophet, or even gave legal opinions.[88] You do have a duty against a woman who makes a habit of so raising her voice when declaiming poetry or singing that she can be heard outside her home (*min warāʾ al-dār*). How could this be permitted, when it is disapproved of for a woman to recite even the call to prayer because she would have to raise her voice to do so?[89]

9 *Minstrels:* Finally, two points are made about minstrels. First, the question is raised of an otherwise virtuous and pious Muslim who listens to minstrels (*qawwālūn*) and enjoys their melodies. The answer is that this is to be considered a sin, and the man a sinner. Second, suppose that a male and a female minstrel inside a home are singing amorous verses in a manner that is liable to excite someone outside it; do the Muslims have a duty to stop them? The answer is that they do.[90]

As already indicated, there is not much in this account that evokes either Muʿtazilite scholasticism or Zaydī activism – though the opening statement

[85] Muʾayyad, *Ifāda*, f. 81a.11. Note also the view that when confronting the wicked (*fussāq*) without an imam, the Muslims may appoint someone to discipline the malefactors, and turn the matter over to him (ʿAlī ibn al-Ḥusayn, *Lumaʿ*, f. 221a.6).

[86] Muʾayyad, *Ifāda*, f. 81a.20. However, beating, wounding, and killing are not admissible in such a context, though they may be required to deal with boys whose actions harm others, as in cases of arson (ʿAlī ibn al-Ḥusayn, *Lumaʿ*, f. 221a.2). The prohibition of beating does not, of course, apply to the boy's legal guardian (*walī*) (Ṣuʿaytirī, *Taʿlīq*, f. 391a.15).

[87] Muʾayyad, *Ifāda*, f. 81a.22. For the point about the more skilful eraser, compare Ibn Miftāḥ, *Muntazaʿ*, 4:588.7. In ʿAlī ibn al-Ḥusayn's *Lumaʿ* we also find provisions regarding books of *zindīqs* and anthropomorphists: these may be burnt and compensation paid to the owner, or, better, (the offending passages) may be dealt with by blacking out (*taswīd*) and the expurgated books returned to the owner (f. 221b.5). In the scholia to the *Muntazaʿ*, the term *taswīd* is glossed *ṭams*, i.e. obliteration (4:588.24).

[88] Muʾayyad, *Ifāda*, f. 81a.24. We can take it that what is problematic about women speaking up is the temptation (*fitna*) it may give rise to for men (cf. Ṣuʿaytirī, *Taʿlīq*, f. 391a.25). Note that no mention is made of women performing *al-amr biʾl-maʿrūf*.

[89] Muʾayyad, *Ifāda*, f. 81b.1.

[90] *Ibid.*, f. 81b.4.

could be an example of the first, and item (5) of the second. What it offers is rather the kind of detailed guidance on the everyday practicalities of the duty that we found in the responsa of Ibn Ḥanbal.[91] There is the same simple menu, predominantly wine and music. Several of the main themes are shared: breaking instruments and vessels, pouring out or spoiling wine, and the problems raised by uncertainty and liability for compensation. There is, of course, no identity of views on the finer points. The Zaydīs seem less inclined to smash vessels than the Ḥanbalites, but harsher in their choice of pollutant – dung rather than salt – for spoiling wine.[92] There are also topics considered in our Zaydī text which are not covered by Ibn Ḥanbal, such as mistakes in Korans. But it is striking that two legal traditions with such different political attitudes should agree in their negative view of turning in a drunk to the authorities,[93] and the overall similarity in the character of the material is unmistakable.

That this material represents for the most part a Zaydī legal tradition distinct from Muʿtazilism is confirmed by the treatment of forbidding wrong given by a follower of al-Muʾayyad more distinguished than Abū ʾl-Qāsim al-Hawsamī, namely the ʿAlid Muwaffaq al-Shajarī (first half of the fifth/eleventh century).[94] His account falls into two main parts. The first is a thoroughly Muʿtazilite analysis comparable in coverage, style and doctrine to Mānkdīm's.[95] The second is more practical in scope, and deals with questions relating to musical instruments, amphorae, blasphemous books (***kutub al-ilḥād***), Biblical texts, toys, images, chess, backgammon, liquor of contested status, vessels of gold and silver and the like.[96] The treatment is somewhat more theoretical than that of al-Muʾayyad, but broadly similar. Now in this part of his account Muwaffaq, unlike al-Muʾayyad, cites numerous authorities. He once cites a Muʿtazilite,[97] and quite often makes reference to Sunnī views.[98] But overall, his pattern of citation places him firmly in the Zaydī legal tradition.[99] What is true for Muwaffaq is likely to be true also for al-Muʾayyad. The roots

[91] Cf. above, notes 78, 82–4.

[92] For the views of Ibn Ḥanbal on these points, see above, ch. 5, notes 101f.

[93] See above, note 84. [94] For this scholar, see Madelung, *Qāsim*, 182, 183f.

[95] Muwaffaq, *Iḥāṭa*, ff. 135b.3–138b.25. The only authorities named are Abū ʿAlī and Abū Hāshim (*ibid.*, ff. 135b.8, 136a.6, 137a.6).

[96] *Ibid.*, ff. 141a.4–144b.13. The intervening passage deals with duress (*ikrāh*).

[97] *Ibid.*, f. 141a.9, citing Abū ʿAlī (see above, ch. 9, note 28).

[98] See, for example, *ibid.*, f. 141a.8 (Shāfiʿite doctrine), f. 141a.10 (a view of Abū Ḥanīfa), and cf. f. 143b.19 (an action of ʿUmar).

[99] See, for example, *ibid.*, f. 141a.19 (citing an action of the Amīr al-Muʾminīn – i.e. ʿAlī – with the comment that his actions and words are definitive proof for us), 141b.16 (citing the consensus of the Prophet's family (*ijmāʿ ahl al-bayt*) as indefeasible), 141a.13 (citing Qāsim ibn Ibrāhīm in the *Masāʾil* of Nayrūsī), 141a.7 (citing Yaḥyā ibn al-Ḥusayn, i.e. al-Hādī). For Nayrūsī (third/ninth century), see Madelung, *Qāsim*, 133, 160.

of this legal tradition doubtless go back to the early evolution of Zaydism in Kūfa.

We have thus identified the two major components of the properly Zaydī heritage with respect to forbidding wrong: a political activism which is unmistakably Zaydī, and a legalistic tradition which is presumably so. Apart from their common Zaydī origin, they have little intrinsic connection to each other. Alongside these components, as we have already seen in the case of Muwaffaq al-Shajarī, we find a scholastic doctrine of the duty which is manifestly Muʿtazilite.

5. THE ZAYDĪ–MUʿTAZILITE SYMBIOSIS

Probably the best-known Zaydī Muʿtazilite is the Yemeni Ibn al-Murtaḍā (d. 840/1437), whose writings became standard works and attracted much attention from later commentators.[100] As he explains in one of them, forbidding wrong is a topic that receives double coverage.[101] It is treated once under the rubric of theology (*ʿilm al-kalām*) – the basic principles of the faith (*uṣūl al-dīn*), knowledge of which is incumbent on every legally competent Muslim; he observes that any comprehensive Zaydī or Muʿtazilite work in the field includes it. And it is discussed again in the exposition of substantive law (*ʿilm al-furūʿ*).[102] When Ibn al-Murtaḍā treats the subject himself in the theological context, his account is solidly Muʿtazilite.[103] By contrast, when he treats it in the legal context, he mixes Muʿtazilite scholasticism with a legal tradition close to that of al-Muʾayyad. No systematic account of his theological treatment of the duty is called for; what he has to say falls squarely within the tradition of ʿAbd al-Jabbār with which we are already familiar.[104] The following survey will therefore concentrate on the mixture found in his legal works, which is typical for what I have called the Zaydī–Muʿtazilite symbiosis.

Ibn al-Murtaḍā includes a brief, highly concentrated treatment of forbidding wrong at the end of an epitome of Zaydī law which he composed during his years in prison following an unsuccessful imamate.[105] This terse

[100] For the biography of Ibn al-Murtaḍā, see Shawkānī (d. 1250/1834), *al-Badr al-ṭāliʿ*, Cairo 1348, 1:122–6. In what follows I leave aside his *Ṭabaqāt al-Muʿtazila*. He there refers only once to *al-amr biʾl-maʿrūf*, stating that its obligatoriness is one of the things the Muʿtazilites agree on (*Ṭabaqāt*, 8.10).

[101] Ibn al-Murtaḍā, *Durar*, f. 240b.9.

[102] Cf. above, note 72.

[103] *Ibid.*, ff. 240b.8–244b.15; cf. also the very brief coverage in Ibn al-Murtaḍā, *Qalāʾid*, 149f.

[104] See above, ch. 9, section 3. There is no sign of influence from the school of Abū ʾl-Ḥusayn, except on one point (cf. below, notes 110, 112). I shall include a few points of interest from the *Durar* in the notes to what follows.

[105] Ibn al-Murtaḍā (d. 840/1437), *Azhār*, ed. Ṣ. Mūsā, Beirut 1975, 529–31 (the editor gives the title as *ʿUyūn al-Azhār* to include his own footnoted commentary). The work was a standard textbook of Zaydī law for students (Shawkānī (d. 1250/1834), *al-Sayl al-jarrār*,

statement of his views can be filled out from the account he gives in a much larger work on comparative law.[106] To convey a sense of the character of the material, I shall follow the text of the epitome, with parenthetical expansions from the larger work.

Ibn al-Murtaḍā's opening lines[107] are considerably more elaborate than the introductory statement of al-Mu'ayyad's account,[108] but he leaves aside such theoretical questions as the basis of the obligation in revelation, whether the duty is also grounded in reason, and whether it is individual or collective. {In the larger work he touches on the first point, but not on the others.}[109] He does, however, attend to the practical matter of the conditions of obligation: rather than mentioning only the ability to carry off the task, as al-Mu'ayyad does, he works in four of the five standard conditions. {In the larger work he sets out the full schema of five conditions, which are essentially those of Mānkdīm; but the order is not the same, and one condition is slightly different.}[110] He also specifies that every legally competent

ed. M. I. Zāyid, Beirut 1985, 1:3.7). The writing is so dense that, taken on its own, much of it would be unintelligible. I have also used the standard commentary on the *Azhār* by Ibn Miftāḥ (*Muntaza'*, 4:582–97, with numerous scholia reproduced at the foot of the page; it is stated on the title-page that the copy from which the text was printed derives from one that had belonged to Shawkānī). Shawkānī describes this commentary as that on which students relied down to his own day (*Badr*, 1:394.16); as he remarks, the work is an abridgement of a larger commentary written by Ibn al-Murtaḍā himself (*ibid.*, 394.19). The scholia are rich in detail culled from a variety of Zaydī sources. Among other things, they raise a very practical question which I have not seen discussed elsewhere: how exactly is one's obligation to right a wrong affected by the physical distance intervening between oneself and it? (Ibn Miftāḥ, *Muntaza'*, 4:582.21, and cf. 583.20, 585.20; an idea advanced in the first passage is that the obligation is extinguished beyond a one-mile radius).

106 Ibn al-Murtaḍā, *Baḥr*, 5:464–8 (cited in Madelung, 'Amr be ma'rūf', 993b). This account incorporates a good many passages from the *Azhār*, but changes their order, adds much new material, and gives divergent opinions with attribution.

107 Ibn al-Murtaḍā, *Azhār*, 529.15. 108 Cf. above, 238.

109 Ibn al-Murtaḍā, *Baḥr*, 5:464.10. In the *Durar* he deals adequately with the first two questions (f. 241a.25, 241b.13), but on the third he merely quotes a statement that all who consider *al-amr bi'l-ma'rūf* obligatory hold it to be a collective obligation (*ibid.*, 241b.11). With Najarī (d. 877/1473), by contrast, we have clear statements that it is a collective duty (see his *Shāfī al-'alīl*, ed. A. 'A. A. al-Shāmī, Ṣan'ā' and Beirut 1987–, 1:422.2, and the citation from his commentary to the introductory books of the *Baḥr* in Strothmann, *Staatsrecht*, 92 n. 5, stating that the Zaydīs and Mu'tazilites agree on this point). The *Muntaza'* is similarly explicit (Ibn Miftāḥ, *Muntaza'*, 4:582.8). See also above, ch. 9, note 101.

110 Ibn al-Murtaḍā, *Baḥr*, 5:465.4. The fifth condition is that one must know, or at least think, that if one takes no action, the wrong will happen (*ibid.*, 466.2). In the *Durar*, where the order is different again, the corresponding condition requires that the right or wrong in question should not already be past (*lam yafūtā*) (f. 242a.13). With regard to the condition that proceeding should not lead to (worse) side-effects, Ibn al-Murtaḍā here notes an unusual contrary view: if the offender reacts by doing something worse, the entire responsibility is his (*ibid.*, f. 242b.9). It should be added that there is no trace in any of Ibn al-Murtaḍā's accounts of Abū 'l-Ḥusayn's distinctive approach to the conditions (cf. above, ch. 9, 222f.). In his *Luma'*, 'Alī ibn al-Ḥusayn introduces his brief statement of the conditions by making a distinction between those that must be satisfied for it to be good to proceed, and those that must hold for it to be obligatory; but he then goes on to list the usual five conditions (f. 220a.5; similarly Muḥallī, *'Umda*, 298.13).

Muslim is subject to the obligation,[111] slips in a statement that when the conditions (which ones?) are not satisfied it is usually bad to proceed,[112] makes the usual point about tolerating the divergences of rival law-schools,[113] and restricts taking action against a minor who is not in one's charge[114] – all this in just over five lines. He further states that escalation may extend to killing.[115] {In the larger work he charts a more elaborate escalation: admonition, insult, smashing up musical instruments, clubbing people with sticks, confronting them with arms – but in the public interest he reserves the gathering of an army (*jaysh*) to the imam.}[116] So far, then, almost all of what Ibn al-Murtaḍā has to say is in the Muʿtazilite tradition.

Then follows a passage similar in content to al-Mu'ayyad's guidance on

[111] In the scholia to the *Muntazaʿ* we find the view that the infidel too is obligated (Ibn Miftāḥ, *Muntazaʿ*, 4:582.14; cf. above, ch. 9, note 147).

[112] Ibn al-Murtaḍā contradicts himself in his fuller discussions of the question whether, if the obligation is voided by danger, it is still good to proceed. In the *Baḥr* he takes the usual view that it depends on whether such action would be for the greater glory of the faith, though he also quotes the contrary view of Yaḥyā ibn Ḥamza (d. 749/1348f.), with citation of Q9:111 (*Baḥr*, 5:465.14). In the *Durar*, however, Ibn al-Murtaḍā rejects the view that one may distinguish those cases in which the greater glory of the faith comes into play from those in which it does not (f. 242a.25). The latter, unlike the former, aligns him with Yaḥyā ibn Ḥamza on the side of Abū 'l-Ḥusayn against ʿAbd al-Jabbār (cf. above, ch. 9, note 74; note, however, that Yaḥyā ibn Ḥamza does not cite Q9:111 in his discussion of danger to oneself in his *Shāmil*). In the *Muntazaʿ* the view is raised (and rejected) that it might be good to proceed even when one lacks actual knowledge of the law (Ibn Miftāḥ, *Muntazaʿ*, 4:583.7; also Ṣuʿaytirī, *Taʿlīq*, f. 390a.27).

[113] Cf. above, ch. 9, 214. In the *Baḥr* he mentions a view of Yaḥyā ibn Ḥamza that the imam is exempt from this restriction, but indicates doubt about this (*Baḥr*, 5:466.12; cf. also ʿAlī ibn al-Ḥusayn, *Lumaʿ*, f. 220b.14 and the scholion thereto, and Ṣuʿaytirī, *Taʿlīq*, f. 391a.9); however, this view does not appear in the discussion of the relevance of disagreement among law-schools in Yaḥyā ibn Ḥamza's *Shāmil* (f. 184a.21). In the *Muntazaʿ* consideration is given to such contentious matters as exposure of the knee (Ibn Miftāḥ, *Muntazaʿ*, 4:585.5) and the procedure to be adopted if one does not know the law-school of the putative offender (*ibid.*, 586.2); a scholion excludes tolerance in matters on which there is consensus among the *ahl al-bayt*, such as drinking *muthallath* and singing (*ibid.*, 585.28; for *muthallath*, see above, ch. 9, notes 92f.). Ṣuʿaytirī (or his source) states that those who hold that every *mujtahid* is right (*kull mujtahid muṣīb*) are in favour of tolerance, whereas those who hold that truth is one (*al-ḥaqq wāḥid*) are against it (*Taʿlīq*, f. 391a.13).

[114] The text runs: *wa-lā ghayr walī ʿalā ṣaghīr bi'l-iḍrār illā ʿan iḍrār*, which sums up all the main points made in earlier discussions (see above, note 86). Elsewhere Ibn al-Murtaḍā includes lunatics in the analysis (*Baḥr*, 5:466.13); Ibn Miftāḥ extends it to animals (*Muntazaʿ*, 4:586.9). See also ʿAlī ibn al-Ḥusayn, *Lumaʿ*, f. 221a.6, in the scholion; above, ch. 9, note 149.

[115] Elsewhere Ibn al-Murtaḍā contrasts the positive attitude of the Muʿtazilites towards the use of the sword in *al-amr bi'l-maʿrūf* with the negative view of the Ḥashwiyya and the Imāmī view that the presence of the imam is required (*Qalā'id*, 149.3; *Durar*, f. 241a.20). In the *Muntazaʿ* a distinction is made: individuals may kill in *inkār al-munkar*, but only the authorities may do so in *al-amr bi'l-maʿrūf* (*ibid.*, 583.2; and cf. ʿAlī ibn al-Ḥusayn, *Lumaʿ*, f. 220b.13).

[116] Ibn al-Murtaḍā, *Baḥr*, 5:466.8. He notes the contrary view of Ghazzālī (for which see below, ch. 16, 441). In fact Ghazzālī's account – at one remove – lies behind the whole set of escalatory stages (see below, ch. 16, 438–41). The intermediary source can be identified as a work of Yaḥyā ibn Ḥamza (*Tasfiyat al-qulūb*, Cairo 1985, 490–4). See below, 246.

practicalities, though it adds to it here and there.[117] Thus Ibn al-Murtaḍā allows uninvited entry when there is good reason to believe that a wrong is being committed.[118] {In the larger work he rules out spying on people, quoting Q49:12; the duty applies to what is out in the open.}[119] He goes on to pouring out what is suspected to be wine,[120] subject to compensation in the event of error.[121] There is a new provision that one should correct errors that affect the sense in works of religious guidance,[122] but the treatment prescribed for books containing unbelief is familiar.[123] Likewise musical instruments not normally used for any other purpose are to be smashed or ripped, subject to the return of the pieces to the extent that they retain any value, unless they are withheld by way of punishment.[124] He then treats decorative art (where the problem begins with free-standing images of whole animals) and slander.[125] {In the larger work a long list of wrongs against which action should be taken is inserted, divided according to context.}[126] The next topic is the question of unjust rulers. It is obligatory to assist an oppressor (*ẓālim*) in establishing a right or eliminating a wrong, and to aid the less bad against the worse oppressor, provided this does not strengthen him in his oppression.[127] Finally Ibn

[117] Ibn al-Murtaḍā, *Azhār*, 530.7; cf. above, 238–40.

[118] Cf. above, 239 item (3). In the *Baḥr* this is given as the view of Uṭrūsh (see above, note 23). Shawkānī in his commentary on the *Azhār* puts forward the view that actual knowledge is required here, but then in effect takes it back (*Sayl*, 4:591.6). In both works Ibn al-Murtaḍā adds that one should enter even an unlawfully possessed property (*Azhār*, 530.7; *Baḥr*, 5:466.7); in other words, the duty overrides respect for the rights of the true owner. [119] *Ibid.*, 466.5.

[120] Shawkānī again requires actual knowledge (*Sayl*, 4:591.13). For an exposition of the complexities of the law of vinegar, see Ibn Miftāḥ, *Muntazaʿ*, 4:587.10.

[121] Cf. above, 238f. item (2).

[122] In the scholia to the *Muntazaʿ*, some doubt is expressed on this point other than in cases where the legal status (lawful, forbidden, etc.) of an action is at stake, or where the text in question is a Koran (*ibid.*, 588.18).

[123] Cf. above, note 87.

[124] Cf. above, 238 item (1). The reference to punishment (*ʿuqūba*) is out of place in the context of *al-amr biʾl-maʿrūf*. Shawkānī adds as a condition for return to the owner that it must not be possible to reuse the pieces in making a new instrument (*Sayl*, 4:593.4). For brief statements of the Zaydī law of music, see Ibn al-Murtaḍā, *Baḥr*, 5:27.5 (singing), 30.6 (instruments) (cited in Serjeant, 'A Zaidī manual of ḥisbah', 17 n. 7).

[125] On these topics see also ʿAlī ibn al-Ḥusayn, *Lumaʿ*, 221b.3, 222a.3.

[126] Ibn al-Murtaḍā, *Baḥr*, 5:466.15. The framework and a good many of the examples derive from Ghazzālī's survey of common wrongs (for which see below, ch. 16, 442–6), again through Yaḥyā ibn Ḥamza's recension (*Taṣfiya*, 494–505). That Ibn al-Murtaḍā was using the *Taṣfiya* rather than the *Iḥyāʾ* itself is indicated by such agreements as the following: (1) Ibn al-Murtaḍā and Yaḥyā both use the word *dībāj* in a context in which Ghazzālī does not (*Baḥr*, 5:466.18; *Taṣfiya*, 496.1; *Iḥyāʾ*, 2:308.14); (2) Ibn al-Murtaḍā and Yaḥyā use the term *ḍāriya* where Ghazzālī does not (*Baḥr*, 5:466.20; *Taṣfiya*, 499.21; *Iḥyāʾ*, 2:310.32).

[127] Cf. above, 239f. item (5). This is not a topic discussed in the mainstream Muʿtazilite tradition on *al-amr biʾl-maʿrūf*. Yaḥyā ibn Ḥamza briefly considers the question whether those who hold illegitimate power (*al-fussāq min umarāʾ al-ẓulm wa-ahl al-jawr*) have a duty to right wrongs (*Shāmil*, f. 185a.24), but even this is isolated.

al-Murtaḍā turns to relations with the wicked in general. One can be on friendly terms with a wicked man (*fāsiq*) in the interests of the faith; more than this is forbidden.[128]

In all this there was little that was new, and little that would change for some centuries to come. The only significant exception is some traces of an encounter with the thought of Ghazzālī, from whom the escalatory schema cited above ultimately derives.[129] The encounter had in fact taken place a century earlier; the Zaydī protagonist was the imam al-Muʾayyad Yaḥyā ibn Ḥamza (d. 749/1348f.), more familiar in this study as a Muʿtazilite in the school of Abū ʾl-Ḥusayn.[130] Yaḥyā must have owed his knowledge of Ghazzālī's *Revival of the religious sciences* to the Yemeni Shāfiʿites.[131] One of his books can fairly be described as a Zaydī recension of this work of Ghazzālī,[132] and it includes an account of forbidding wrong abridged from parts of Ghazzālī's treatment with some degree of modification.[133] In the case of the escalatory schema, Yaḥyā reproduces Ghazzālī's succession of stages,[134] including the gathering of armed supporters. But Yaḥyā takes issue with Ghazzālī on this last stage, adopting the position that such activity is not for individuals, and endorsing this as the view of the Zaydī and Muʿtazilite authorities.[135] We are thus treated to a somewhat unusual spectacle: the view of a Sunnī scholar is rejected by a Zaydī imam as too activist.[136] This, in fact, is Yaḥyā's only serious challenge to Ghazzālī's doctrine of forbidding wrong in this work.

But Yaḥyā's encounter with Ghazzālī's thought was not limited to this context.[137] His account of forbidding wrong in his major theological

[128] Ibn al-Murtaḍā, *Azhār*, 531.5. The discussion of unjust rulers clearly goes back to al-Muʾayyad, and that of relations with the wicked has a precedent in his school (see the treatment of interaction with a wicked neighbour quoted from a *Taʿlīq al-Ifāda* in ʿAlī ibn al-Ḥusayn, *Lumaʿ*, f. 222b.1). There is no treatment of these topics in the discussion of *al-amr biʾl-maʿrūf* in the *Baḥr*. Shawkānī in his commentary to the *Azhār* makes a series of points which considerably soften Ibn al-Murtaḍā's view (*Sayl*, 4:601.3).

[129] See above, note 116.

[130] For Yaḥyā ibn Ḥamza, see above, ch. 9, note 115.

[131] See below, ch. 16, notes 160f., 184.

[132] As noted in Ḥibshī, *Maṣādir*, 618 no. 13.

[133] Yaḥyā ibn Ḥamza, *Taṣfiya*, 484–515, abridged from Ghazzālī, *Iḥyāʾ*, 2:280–5, 301–5, 307–26. Yaḥyā inserts occasional references to Zaydī doctrine on this point or that (*Taṣfiya*, 494.1, 495.5, 500.17–501.7); he customises Ghazzālī's references to heretics so that they now refer to predestinationists and anthropomorphists (*ibid.*, 496.7, 503.9; cf. *Iḥyāʾ*, 2:308.19, 312.15); he omits the discussion of snow as a public nuisance (*ibid.*, 310.29, cf. *Taṣfiya*, 499.16); he makes an egregious prosopographical error whereby he presents Sufyān al-Thawrī (d. 161/778) as a contemporary of the caliph al-Muʿtaḍid (r. 279–89/892–902) (*ibid.*, 512.19; cf. *Iḥyāʾ*, 2:325.29); and so forth.

[134] Yaḥyā ibn Ḥamza, *Taṣfiya*, 490–4.

[135] *Ibid.*, 494.1.

[136] For Yaḥyā's understandable stress on the role of the imam in *al-amr biʾl-maʿrūf*, cf. also *Taṣfiya*, 506.1, where he inserts a passage not found at *Iḥyāʾ*, 2:314.5. For Ghazzālī's radical tendencies – unexpected in the Sunnism of his day – see below, ch. 16, 456f.

[137] Ḥibshī notes a pamphlet of Yaḥyā's refuting Ghazzālī's lenient view of *samāʿ* (*Maṣādir*, 620 no. 36).

treatise[138] is likewise influenced by Ghazzālī. Here he introduces a schema, central to Ghazzālī's presentation, in which forbidding wrong is analysed in terms of four basic elements (*arkān*).[139] However, the substantive doctrine which Yaḥyā presents within this framework differs from Ghazzālī's in some respects, most strikingly in excluding women and slaves from performing the duty.[140] Women are excluded for two reasons: first, because of their frivolity and impotence; and second, because the law does not give them authority (*walāya*) over themselves, let alone over such weighty matters.[141] Slaves are likewise excluded for two reasons: the first is their low status in people's eyes, which renders them unsuitable to undertake the duty; the second, omitted in our text, should presumably have been the same lack of authority that afflicts women.[142]

If Yaḥyā allowed Ghazzālī to shape some of his discussion of forbidding wrong in a major theological treatise, it is not unlikely that he did the same in his major legal work;[143] but I do not have access to the relevant part of it, if indeed it is extant.[144] Be this as it may, the intrusion of Ghazzālī's thought into the Zaydī heritage is significant. We see in it an early example of a Sunnī penetration of the sect that was to become increasingly pervasive with the passing of the centuries.

6. THE SUNNISATION OF ZAYDISM

Almost all the Zaydī material considered so far in this chapter, whether Muʿtazilite or not, is consistent on two points. One is the absence of the

138 For the *Shāmil* of Yaḥyā ibn Ḥamza, see above, ch. 9, note 115. There are explicit references to Ghazzālī in the work (as at ff. 3b.19, 4b.20), but not in the discussion of *al-amr bi'l-maʿrūf*.

139 *Ibid.*, f. 185a.4–185b.17; compare Ghazzālī, *Iḥyā'*, 2:285–305, for which see below, ch. 16, 428f. and the exposition that follows there. Yaḥyā does not adopt Ghazzālī's distinctive *ḥisba* terminology, but the equivalences are clear. His discussion is much less extensive than Ghazzālī's.

140 Yaḥyā ibn Ḥamza, *Shāmil*, f. 185a.7, specifying that the performer of the duty must be, among other things, male and free. Note also Yaḥyā's categorical exclusion of boys (*ibid.*, f. 185a.9; contrast below, ch. 16, 429). Likewise the discussion of Islam as a prerequisite for the performance of the duty (*ibid.*, f. 185a.19) owes nothing to Ghazzālī's discussion of the issue (see below, ch. 16, 429f.), and uses material from Ibn al-Malāḥimī (see above, ch. 9, note 139). Similarly the discussion of restraint of boys from wrongdoing is in the Muʿtazilite tradition (*ibid.*, f. 185b.4; cf. above, ch. 9, 222, and below, ch. 16, 438).

141 *Ibid.*, f. 185a.12. The view that a woman possesses no authority over herself is no doubt linked to the doctrine that only her guardian (*walī*) can give her in marriage; but I do not have access to a statement of Yaḥyā ibn Ḥamza's view on this point.

142 *Ibid.*, f. 185a.16.

143 For the *Intiṣār* of Yaḥyā ibn Ḥamza, see Ḥibshī, *Maṣādir*, 617 no. 8. The full title of the work as given there suggests that it may have served as a major source for Ibn al-Murtaḍā's *Baḥr*.

144 That it covered *al-amr bi'l-maʿrūf* is confirmed by a later author's citation (see below, note 146). Ibn al-Murtaḍā twice cites views of Yaḥyā which cannot be taken from the *Shāmil* (see above, notes 112f.); their most likely source is the *Intiṣār*.

notion of performing the duty in the heart.[145] The other is the endorsement of recourse to arms where necessary[146] – a recourse which fits effortlessly into the long Zaydī tradition of rebellion against unjust rule. On both points, Zaydism and Muʿtazilism were in accord.[147] However, the later history of Yemeni Zaydism is marked by two parallel phenomena: the decay of the Muʿtazilite tradition,[148] and the penetration of the sect by Sunnī traditionism.[149] The result was that Zaydī conceptions of forbidding wrong

[145] In Zaydī texts earlier than those about to be discussed, I know of very few instances of this idea. One is the tradition in the *Majmūʿ al-fiqh* (see above, note 8, for this tradition and a Sunnī parallel; and cf. above, note 13, for what seems to be a Sunnī tradition in a Zaydī work). Another instance is found in a tract ascribed to Qāsim ibn Ibrāhīm (for the ascription, see above, note 15). Here the discussion of *al-amr bi'l-maʿrūf* in some ways fits well into the Zaydī Muʿtazilite tradition: the author speaks positively of recourse to the sword, and refers to the use of the tongue as the minimal (*adnā*) form of the duty (*al-ʿAdl wa'l-tawḥīd*, in ʿUmāra, *Rasā'il*, 1:130.18; something seems to be missing before *bi-kull*). Then follows a reference to *inkār . . . bi'l-qalb*, combined with determination to act once it becomes possible to do so (*ibid.*, 130.20). The only other unusual feature of this discussion is that reference is made to the duty to avoid offenders socially (*ibid.*, 130.15, 131.2; it is not presented as performance with the heart). For whatever reason, this theme is not usually included in Zaydī or Muʿtazilite accounts of *al-amr bi'l-maʿrūf* (for what might be a Muʿtazilite exception see below, ch. 12, note 206)). For a third instance, see above, ch. 9, note 76. Note, however, that ʿAbdallāh ibn al-Ḥusayn (al-Hādī's brother) speaks of the duty as one to be carried out against offending Muslims by hand and tongue, according to one's ability (*Nāsikh*, f. 45b.1) – with no mention of the heart. The idea is likewise absent from the scholia to Ibn Miftāḥ's *Muntazaʿ*.

[146] Contrary opinions are rare. Ṣuʿaytirī quotes from the *Intiṣār* (sc. of Yaḥyā ibn Ḥamza) the view that, when action against a wrong requires killing and fighting, this is for the imams to undertake, and not for individual Muslims (*Taʿlīq*, f. 390b.31; cf. above, note 135, also above, ch. 9, note 23). Less sweeping qualifications are also found. Thus one view is that, if what is at issue is a matter of *sharʿ* (e.g. prayer) as opposed to *ʿaql* (e.g. repayment of a debt), then under the rubric of *al-amr bi'l-maʿrūf* (as opposed to *al-nahy ʿan al-munkar*) the use of the sword is restricted to the imam (see ʿĀrif, *Ṣila*, 349f., and particularly the quotation from Najarī, *ibid.*, 350.8). ʿĀrif states that this is a Zaydī position upheld against the Muʿtazilite view. See also above, note 115.

[147] With regard to recourse to arms, this agreement is pointed out by Najarī (see the passage quoted in Strothmann, *Staatsrecht*, 92 n. 5).

[148] Madelung, *Qāsim*, 221. Imam al-Manṣūr al-Qāsim ibn Muḥammad (d. 1029/1620) still discusses *al-amr bi'l-maʿrūf* in the old scholastic tradition in his *al-Asās li-ʿaqā'id al-akyās*, ed. A. N. Nādir, Beirut 1980, 176–8. He takes the unusual view that the prospective inefficacy of one's action does not dispense one from the obligation to proceed (*ibid.*, 176.13); this is a view characteristic of Nawawī (d. 676/1277), and could reflect Shāfiʿite influence (see below, ch. 13, 352f.). He also transmits a subtle point I have not seen elsewhere: if, by the time one has reflected on the correct point in the escalatory sequence at which to pitch one's intervention, the wrong will already have been committed, then one should act without reflection (*ibid.*, 177.19). For Qāsim's Muʿtazilism (and formal anti-Muʿtazilism), see Madelung, *Qāsim*, 220.

[149] An early representative of this trend is Ibn al-Murtaḍā's contemporary Ibn al-Wazīr (d. 840/1436). For example, he attacks such Zaydī *ḥadīth* collections as there were as worthless (*al-Rawḍ al-bāsim fī 'l-dhabb ʿan sunnat Abī 'l-Qāsim*, Cairo n.d., 1:89.20), and asks rhetorically how one can rely on them in preference to the works of the (Sunnī) traditionists (*ibid.*, 91.6). Shawkānī remarks approvingly of him that he writes like Ibn Ḥazm and Ibn Taymiyya, and not like his (Zaydī) contemporaries and successors (*Badr*, 2:91.16); he takes his biographical entry on Ibn al-Wazīr as an opportunity for a long statement of his own Sunnising traditionist views (*ibid.*, 83–90). Contrast the dismissive

were increasingly assimilated to those of Sunnī Islam. Most obviously, the notion of performance in the heart became ever more commonplace, followed eventually by the repudiation of rebellion against unjust rule.

Already in the tenth/sixteenth century Bahrān al-Ṣaʿdī (d. 957/1550) composed a work tracing the traditions quoted in Ibn al-Murtaḍā's work on comparative law to the classical Sunnī collections.[150] He includes the standard Sunnī 'three modes' tradition, with its reference to performance in the heart as the minimal form of faith[151] – unnecessarily, since characteristically Ibn al-Murtaḍā had not adduced it. In the eleventh/seventeenth century, the Sunnising Maqbalī (d. 1108/1696f.)[152] remarks that, in treating the subject of forbidding wrong in one of his works, he had adorned his discussion with some seventy Prophetic traditions – most of which can only have been Sunnī.[153] In the twelfth/eighteenth century Ibn al-Amīr al-Ṣanʿānī (d. 1182/1768), a well-known traditionist who at one point had some sympathy for the Wahhābīs,[154] was able to take the idea of performance in the heart for granted. He used it in a philo-Wahhābī pamphlet to refute the idea that a consensus established by silence legitimises the toleration of polytheistic practices among (supposed) Muslims: since the duty could be performed in the heart, it followed that the silence of earlier authorities could not be read as consent.[155] He applied the same argument in refuting the view that such a consensus validated the failure of the Muslims to expel the Jews from the Yemen in accordance with the Prophet's instructions.[156]

attitude to Sunnī *ḥadīth* of al-Mahdī al-Ḥusayn ibn al-Qāsim (d. 404/1013f.): 'most of the *ḥadīth* of this community (*umma*) is noxious, hypocritical and frivolous' (cited in Strothmann, 'Die Literatur der Zaiditen', 73).

150 Bahrān al-Ṣaʿdī (d. 957/1550), *Jawāhir al-akhbār*, printed at the foot of the page in Ibn al-Murtaḍā, *Baḥr*.

151 Ṣaʿdī, *Jawāhir*, 5:464.19, mentioning its appearance in Muslim and elsewhere. For this tradition, see above, ch. 3, section 1.

152 Shawkānī regards Maqbalī as a man after his own heart: on the one hand an opponent of *taqlīd*, and on the other an enemy of the extreme Shīʿism of the Yemeni 'Jārūdiyya' (*Badr*, 1:288.10, 289.5, 291.10).

153 Maqbalī (d. 1108/1696f.), *al-Manār fī 'l-mukhtār*, Beirut and Ṣanʿāʾ 1988, 2:505.7. For his use of Sunnī materials, compare his bruising discussion of the traditional inclusion of the Shīʿite *ḥayya ʿalā khayri 'l-ʿamal* in the Zaydī *adhān* (*ibid.*, 1:145–7). Qāsim al-Manṣūr, by contrast, still happily cites the consensus of the family of the Prophet (*ijmāʿ al-ʿitra*) (*Asās*, 177.16, 178.15).

154 See M. Cook, 'On the origins of Wahhābism', *Journal of the Royal Asiatic Society*, series 3, 2 (1992), 200f.

155 Ibn al-Amīr al-Ṣanʿānī (d. 1182/1768), *Taṭhīr al-iʿtiqād ʿan adrān al-ilḥād*, ed. M.ʿA. Khafājī, Cairo 1954, 46–8, esp. 46.17, 47.2 (echoing the three modes tradition). For negative attitudes to the idea of consensus established by silence in *uṣūl al-fiqh*, see H. Modarressi Tabātabāʾi, *Kharāj in Islamic law*, London 1983, 86.

156 Ibn al-Amīr al-Ṣanʿānī (d. 1182/1768), *Subul al-salām*, Beirut 1960–71, 4:62.20 (with reference to the three modes, *ibid.*, 62.25). He observes that his argument is an original one (*ibid.*, 62.29).

The culminating figure in the Sunnisation of Zaydism was Shawkānī (d. 1250/1834).[157] One of his works was a commentary on Ibn al-Murtaḍā's epitome of Zaydī law.[158] When he reached the section on forbidding wrong, he formally laid out the doctrine of the three modes, and stressed the Prophetic authority behind them.[159] Performance in the heart, he noted, is an unobservable mental act.[160] A less formal appeal to the notion occurred in his lifetime during a visit by a Saʿūdī embassy to Ṣanʿāʾ in 1222–3/1807–8. The Saʿūdī ambassador accused the Yemenis of unbelief because of their failure to confront the imam and his followers with regard to their current misdeeds. The Yemeni historian Jaḥḥāf (d. 1243/1827f.), a pupil of Shawkānī,[161] responded that forbidding wrong is divided into parts; since the Yemenis were unable to perform it with the hand or tongue, they were left only with the third part, viz. performance in their hearts.[162] The assimilation of this notion can be set alongside the adoption by Shawkānī of the characteristic Sunnī traditionalist rejection of rebellion against unjust rulers.[163]

This development did not mean that Shawkānī and those who thought like him took the duty less seriously than their forbears. Shawkānī himself regarded forbidding wrong as a matter of overriding importance for the welfare of the Muslim community at large, and of the people of Yemen in particular.[164] Nor was this just a matter of generalities. He describes a

[157] For a recent discussion of this key figure, see B. Haykel, 'Al-Shawkānī and the jurisprudential unity of Yemen', *Revue du Monde Musulman et de la Méditerranée*, 67 (1994). The publication of the author's dissertation will much advance our understanding of Shawkānī and of the wider trend in the history of Yemeni Zaydism which he represents (B. A. Haykel, 'Order and righteousness: Muḥammad ʿAlī al-Shawkānī and the nature of the Islamic state in Yemen', Oxford D.Phil. 1997).

[158] On this work, see H. ʿA. al-ʿAmri, *The Yemen in the 18th & 19th centuries*, London 1985, 152–64 (this study was drawn to my attention by Frank Stewart).

[159] Shawkānī, *Sayl*, 4:586.11; cf. also *ibid.*, 587.4, 587.20, 600.9. Again, compare his negative stance towards the inclusion of *ḥayya ʿalā khayri ʾl-ʿamal* in the *adhān* (*ibid.*, 1:205.4).

[160] *Ibid.*, 4:587.7 (*amr kāʾin fī ʾl-qalb lā yaẓhar fī ʾl-khārij*). The other noteworthy feature of Shawkānī's commentary is his diatribe against the law-schools (*ibid.*, 588.15), inevitably triggered by Ibn al-Murtaḍā's concession to their differences.

[161] On Jaḥḥāf, see A. F. Sayyid, *Maṣādir taʾrīkh al-Yaman fī ʾl-ʿaṣr al-Islāmī*, Cairo 1974, 289–91 no. 15. Shawkānī states that Jaḥḥāf was his pupil (*Badr*, 2:60.21).

[162] Jāsir, 'al-Ṣilāt bayn Ṣanʿāʾ wa'l-Dirʿiyya', 447.

[163] See Shawkānī (d. 1250/1834), *al-Durar al-bahiyya*, in his *al-Darārī al-muḍiyya*, Cairo 1986, 505.2, together with the torrent of quietist traditions in his own commentary thereto (*ibid.*, 505.8; there is a brief confrontation with the old Zaydī activism, *ibid.*, 506.16). His son's commentary to the *Durar* conveys the same message (Aḥmad al-Shawkānī (d. 1281/1864), *al-Sumūṭ al-dhahabiyya*, ed. I. B. ʿAbd al-Majīd, Beirut 1990, 326.17).

[164] For a general statement of its importance, see Shawkānī (d. 1250/1834), *Rafʿ al-rība*, printed with his *Sharḥ al-ṣudūr bi-taḥrīm rafʿ al-qubūr*, ed. M. Ḥ. al-Fiqī, n.p. 1366, 32–7. For similar rhetoric in a pamphlet on the problems of the Yemen, see Shawkānī's

scholar of whom he approved, ʿAbdallāh ibn Luṭf al-Bārī al-Kibsī (d. 1173/1759f.), as a noted performer of the duty,[165] and is pleased to recount an anecdote set in the streets of Sanʿāʾ in which our scholar separated a lascivious soldier from a woman, ignoring the abuse that was heaped upon him in consequence, but refusing to have recourse to the state.[166] In short, Shawkānī had not joined the Ḥashwiyya. The notion of performance in the heart, for all that it lends itself to quietism, does not preclude an active engagement in forbidding wrong.[167] More significantly, Shawkānī holds that performance with the hand extends where necessary to fighting (*muqātala*), and that someone who thereby gets himself killed is a martyr (*shahīd*).[168] Yet this conception of forbidding wrong is no longer a distinctively Zaydī one.[169]

al-Dawāʾ al-ʿājil, printed in the same volume, 51f., and cf. 56.2 (on this tract, see ʿAmri, *The Yemen*, 121–3).

165 Shawkānī, *Badr*, 1:393.4, 394.6. Kibsī shared Shawkānī's hostility to *taqlīd* (*ibid.*, 393.7).

166 *Ibid.*, 393.8. Compare the incident noted above, ch. 4, 70.

167 In three instances we have seen performance in – or with – the heart mentioned by Muʿtazilite or Zaydī writers who also speak of recourse to arms: in a work ascribed to Qāsim ibn Ibrāhīm (see above, note 145), in one likely to have been written by Abū Ṭālib al-Nāṭiq (see above, ch. 9, notes 76, 78), and in the Koran commentary of al-Ḥākim al-Jishumī (see above, ch. 9, notes 159, 165). Pseudo-Qāsim, like Shawkānī, is speaking of a performance confined within the heart; al-Nāṭiq, by contrast, has in mind a performance with the heart which is externally manifested, while Jishumī's intention is not clear.

168 Shawkānī, *Sayl*, 4:586.14, 587.3. I have not, however, seen Shawkānī speak of the sword in connection with the duty, except in one purely rhetorical context (Shawkānī, *Rafʿ al-rība*, 36.1). This is in marked contrast with traditional Zaydī formulations (see above, notes 15, 25, 115, 145, 147, but cf. the restrictive views cited above, note 146).

169 It is a pity that Shawkānī's traditional Zaydī antagonist, Ibn Ḥarīwa (d. 1241/1825), was executed well before his vigorous rebuttal of the *Sayl* reached the topic of forbidding wrong (I owe this information to Bernard Haykel; see his 'Order and righteousness', esp. 231–4). A relatively recent commentator on the *Azhār*, Qāḍī Aḥmad ibn Qāsim al-ʿAnsī (d. 1390/1970) (*al-Tāj al-mudhhab li-aḥkām al-madhhab*, Ṣanʿāʾ n.d. (preface to this edition dated 1380/1960), 4:468–79 sections 473f.), retains much detail from the old Zaydī commentarial tradition (for the one-mile radius, see *ibid.*, 470.6), and still mentions predestinationism and anthropomorphism as leading heresies (*ibid.*, 475.20 and n. 1); but he cites Sunnī *ḥadīth* as authoritative (*ibid.*, 469.10, 477 n. 1), regards only the Koran readings of the Seven as permissible (*ibid.*, 475.17), and speaks of unobservable performance in the heart (*ibid.*, 471.1 and n. 1); modernity makes its appearance with his insistence that the kind of printed pictures we have today do not count as images (*ibid.*, 477 n.1). I am indebted to Bernard Haykel for drawing this work to my attention and supplying me with a copy of the relevant pages (and see his 'Order and righteousness', 276f.).

CHAPTER 11

THE IMĀMĪS

1. INTRODUCTION

The Imāmīs provide the richest and most continuous documentation of the doctrine of forbidding wrong of any sect or school. Though early Imāmī literature is less abundant than that of Sunnī tradition or the Ḥanbalite law-school in the same period, it is far more plentiful than the fragmentary Muʿtazilite and Zaydī record. Thereafter we have at our disposal a succession of Imāmī discussions of the duty which is more or less unbroken from the fifth/eleventh century till the present day. We owe this wealth of material to three circumstances. First, the Imāmīs, like the Zaydīs,[1] made it a practice to give a place to forbidding wrong in their law-books.[2] Secondly, and unlike the Zaydīs, the Imāmīs waxed numerous over the centuries, and generated a literary heritage that was commensurately large. Thirdly, recent developments in Iran have helped to make this heritage increasingly available in print. We can accordingly set out to write a

[1] See above, ch. 10, note 72.

[2] Their standard practice is to place it towards the end of the *kitāb al-jihād*. This arrangement is first found with Ṭūsī (d. 460/1067) in his *Nihāya*, and is standard in Imāmī law-books thereafter (except that Ibn al-Barrāj (d. 481/1088) in his *Muhadhdhab* and the Muḥaqqiq (d. 676/1277) in his *Sharāʾiʿ* make *al-amr biʾl-maʿrūf* a separate *kitāb* following close after that on *jihād*). Earlier law-books do not conform to this classical pattern. Ibn Bābawayh (d. 381/991f.) clearly does not regard *al-amr biʾl-maʿrūf* as a legal topic at all, since he covers it in the doctrinal section of his *Hidāya* and omits it altogether from his *Muqniʿ*, as also from his *Faqīh*. Mufīd (d. 413/1022) in his *Muqniʿa* and Sallār (d. 448/1056) in his *Marāsim* do cover the topic, but at or near the end of the law-book in association with their *kitāb al-ḥudūd waʾl-ādāb*. In his collections of traditions, Ṭūsī adopts the classical pattern in his *Tahdhīb* (thus overriding the arrangement of the *Muqniʿa* on which it is a commentary), and does not cover the topic in the *Istibṣār*. The puzzle is that the *Kāfī* of Kulaynī (d. 329/941) exhibits the classical pattern – which suggests that, at this point at least, the arrangement of the *Kāfī* as we have it may be the work of a later redactor (compare Modarressi, *Crisis and consolidation*, 102 and n. 259). Full references for the law-books mentioned in this note will be given below, notes 5, 65–74. In his Koran commentary, Abū ʾl-Futūḥ-i Rāzī (first half of the sixth/twelfth century) states that the topic of *al-amr biʾl-maʿrūf* belongs in the detailed discussion of the imamate (*furūʿ-i abwāb-i imāmat*), which in turn belongs to the *uṣūl al-dīn* (*Rawḍ*, 3:141.17 (to Q3:104)); this statement very probably derives from the same Sunnī source as the traditions which follow it.

more sustained narrative of the history of the doctrine in Imāmism than is possible for any other sect or school. But against the continuity of the record must be set its narrowness of focus. What the Imāmī scholars have to offer is repeated coverage of doctrinal issues of a kind familiar from the Muʿtazilite tradition. It is in the nature of this material that it displays only a limited number of points of contact with the outside world. There seems to be no substantive Imāmī equivalent to the treatment of forbidding wrong in the Zaydī legal tradition, let alone the responsa of Ibn Ḥanbal, and to this extent the Imāmī story is a much more restricted one.

For the purposes of this study, the history of Imāmī thought can conveniently be divided into three periods. The first I shall refer to as the early Imāmī period. This is the epoch in which the imams were still present in the community, and Muʿtazilism did not yet dominate Imāmī theology. It was in this context that Imāmī tradition and the earliest Imāmī Koranic exegesis took shape. The second period is that of the classical Imāmī scholars, beginning in the fourth/tenth century and ending – somewhat arbitrarily – in the eighth/fourteenth. The third is that of the later scholars from the eighth to fourteenth/fourteenth to twentieth centuries, including the establishment of an Imāmī state in Iran, but excluding the origins and aftermath of the Iranian revolution. We begin, then, with the early Imāmī period, as reflected in the body of tradition to which it gave rise.

2. IMĀMĪ TRADITION

We can conveniently define the classical core of Imāmī tradition on forbidding wrong as those traditions on the subject that are shared by the authors of two of the classical 'four books' of Imāmī tradition, namely Kulaynī (d. 329/941)[3] and Abū Jaʿfar al-Ṭūsī (d. 460/1067).[4] There are some twenty of these traditions in all.[5] The other two of the 'four books' do not treat the topic.[6]

[3] Kulaynī, *Kāfī*, 5:55–64, at the end of the *kitāb al-jihād*. Kulaynī divides his material into five chapters; the first two (*ibid.*, 55–61) contain the most significant traditions.

[4] Ṭūsī, *Tahdhīb*, 6:176–82. These traditions form a single chapter, again at the end of the *kitāb al-jihād*.

[5] Kulaynī has thirty-three traditions in all, twenty-one of them in his first two chapters. Ṭūsī has twenty-four. All of Ṭūsī's traditions bar the last three are also in Kulaynī's chapters, and this common stock of twenty-one traditions contains all the traditions of any importance; seventeen of them will be cited in what follows. Of the seventeen, approximately four are from the Prophet, three from Muḥammad al-Bāqir (d. *c.* 118/736), nine from Jaʿfar al-Ṣādiq (d. 148/765), and one from ʿAlī al-Riḍā (d. 203/818). The predominance of traditions from al-Ṣādiq is characteristic of Imāmī tradition in general. The three traditions at the end of Ṭūsī's chapter are taken from al-Shaykh al-Mufīd (d. 413/1022), *Muqniʿa*, Qumm 1410, 808.10; this is clear from the order of the traditions, and from the way in which the second is abbreviated.

[6] Viz. the *Faqīh* of Ibn Bābawayh, and Ṭūsī's *Istibṣār*.

Much of this material need not detain us long, and this for two reasons. In the first place, about half of the traditions consist of exhortation without doctrinal content. They emphasise the great importance of forbidding wrong,[7] its future decay,[8] the dire consequences to the community of failure to perform it,[9] and the like.[10] In the second place, about half the material is already familiar from Sunnī tradition[11] – though much of it appears in the mouths of Jaʿfar al-Ṣādiq (d. 148/765) and others of the twelve imams,[12] and is transmitted with recognisably Imāmī chains of transmission.[13]

If we concentrate on the traditions that have something substantive to say, we can readily detect a quietist strain which befits the general character of early Imāmism. Nevertheless, most of the ideas pressed into service here are ones familiar from Sunnī tradition. The following, all from Jaʿfar al-Ṣādiq, are cases in point. In one tradition he avers that forbidding wrong is a matter of counselling the faithful and instructing the ignorant, but not of confronting someone armed with a whip or a sword.[14] Asked about the

[7] Kulaynī, *Kāfī*, 5:58 no. 9 = Ṭūsī, *Tahdhīb*, 6:176 no. 4; Kulaynī, *Kāfī*, 5:59 no. 11 = Ṭūsī, *Tahdhīb*, 6:177 no. 6; Kulaynī, *Kāfī*, 5:59 no. 15; cf. also Kulaynī, *Kāfī*, 5:55f. no. 1 = Ṭūsī, *Tahdhīb*, 6:180f. no. 21; *ibid.*, 181 no. 23.

[8] Kulaynī, *Kāfī*, 5:59 no. 14 = Ṭūsī, *Tahdhīb*, 6:177 no. 8; and cf. also Kulaynī, *Kāfī*, 5:55f. no. 1 = Ṭūsī, *Tahdhīb*, 6:180f. no. 21.

[9] Kulaynī, *Kāfī*, 5:56 no. 3 = Ṭūsī, *Tahdhīb*, 6:176 no. 1; Kulaynī, *Kāfī*, 5:56f. no. 4 = Ṭūsī, *Tahdhīb*, 6:176 no. 2; Kulaynī, *Kāfī*, 5:57 no. 5 = Ṭūsī, *Tahdhīb*, 6:176 no. 3; Kulaynī, *Kāfī*, 5:59 no. 13 = Ṭūsī, *Tahdhīb*, 6:177 no. 7; Kulaynī, *Kāfī*, 5:56 no. 2 = Ṭūsī, *Tahdhīb*, 6:180 no. 20; *ibid.*, 181 no. 22; Kulaynī, *Kāfī*, 5:57f. no. 6 (for this last, see also Nagel, *Staat und Glaubensgemeinschaft*, 1:221, citing other sources).

[10] Kulaynī, *Kāfī*, 5:58 no. 7; and cf. Ṭūsī, *Tahdhīb*, 181f. no. 24. All this and further exhortatory material is consolidated into a chapter on the theme (*al-ḥathth ʿalā ʾl-amr biʾl-maʿrūf*) in Muḥsin al-Fayḍ (d. 1091/1680), *Wāfī*, Tehran 1375, 9:28–30; by contrast, the other two chapters of his that concern us amount to only a page (*ibid.*, 30f.).

[11] I have noted Sunnī parallels in the following cases: (1) Kulaynī, *Kāfī*, 5:56 no. 3 = Ṭūsī, *Tahdhīb*, 6:176 no. 1: see above, ch. 3, note 19 (and cf. note 23). (2) Kulaynī, *Kāfī*, 5:57 no. 5 = Ṭūsī, *Tahdhīb*, 6:176 no. 3: cf. Ibn Waḍḍāḥ, *Bidaʿ*, 234 = 365 no. 82, and Muttaqī, *Kanz*, 3:81 nos. 5,583f. (3) Kulaynī, *Kāfī*, 5:58 no. 9 = Ṭūsī, *Tahdhīb*, 6:176 no. 4: see Abū Yaʿlā al-Mawṣilī (d. 307/919), *Musnad*, ed. Ḥ. S. Asad, Damascus and Beirut 1984–8, 12:229f. no. 6,839; Abū ʾl-Layth al-Samarqandī (d. 373/983), *Tanbīh al-ghāfilīn*, ed. ʿA. M. al-Wakīl, Jedda 1980, 97.12. (4) Kulaynī, *Kāfī*, 5:58f. no. 10 = Ṭūsī, *Tahdhīb*, 6:176f. no. 5: cf. Ibn Abī ʾl-Dunyā, *Amr*, 138 no. 109; Haythamī, *Zawāʾid*, 7:276.2; Muttaqī, *Kanz*, 3:67 no. 5,518; *ibid.*, 81 no. 5,585. (5) Kulaynī, *Kāfī*, 5:59 no. 14 = Ṭūsī, *Tahdhīb*, 6:177 no. 8 = Ḥimyarī (*fl.* later third/ninth century), *Qurb al-isnād*, Najaf 1950, 37.12: see above, ch. 3, note 38. (6) Kulaynī, *Kāfī*, 5:60 no. 1 = Ṭūsī, *Tahdhīb*, 6:178 no. 10: see above, ch. 3, note 62. (7) Kulaynī, *Kāfī*, 5:60 no. 2 = Ṭūsī, *Tahdhīb*, 6:178 no. 11: see Qurṭubī, *Jāmiʿ*, 4:48.8. (8) Kulaynī, *Kāfī*, 5:63f. nos. 4f. = Ṭūsī, *Tahdhīb*, 6:180 nos. 17f.: see above, ch. 3, note 53. (9) Kulaynī, *Kāfī*, 5:56 no. 2 = Ṭūsī, *Tahdhīb*, 6:180 no. 20: see above, ch. 3, note 36. (10) Kulaynī, *Kāfī*, 5:57f. no. 6: ʿAbd al-Ghanī, *Amr*, 42f. no. 54, and cf. 50 no. 66. (11) Ṭūsī, *Tahdhīb*, 6:181 no. 23: see above, ch. 3, note 28. As might be expected, much of the parallel Sunnī material is found with Kūfan *isnāds*.

[12] Taking the eleven instances given in the previous note, three are from the Prophet (quoted in each instance through Jaʿfar al-Ṣādiq), two from ʿAlī, one from Muḥammad al-Bāqir, four from Jaʿfar al-Ṣādiq, and one from ʿAlī al-Riḍā.

[13] But cf. below, note 21.

[14] Kulaynī, *Kāfī*, 5:60 no. 2 = Ṭūsī, *Tahdhīb*, 6:178 no. 11; cf. above, note 11, item (7).

(Sunnī) Prophetic tradition on standing up to an unjust ruler,[15] he explains it away as applying only where the ruler will accept the admonition.[16] The believer, he affirms in a similar vein, should not court humiliation by exposing himself to an ordeal he cannot withstand.[17] In the same way the occasional references to performance of the duty in the heart appear in material with Sunnī associations. Thus Jaʿfar al-Ṣādiq holds that it is enough that God should know a believer's disapproval from his heart,[18] and Muḥammad al-Bāqir (d. *c.* 118/736) urges the faithful to perform the duty in their hearts, as well as verbally and physically.[19] The only tradition that formally sets out the three modes (here heart, hand and tongue) is one placed in the mouth of ʿAlī without a chain of transmission.[20] A tradition of some doctrinal interest in this connection has ʿAlī identify the minimal form of disapprobation (*adnā ʾl-inkār*) as meeting offenders with 'frowning faces' (*wujūh mukfahirra*).[21] This formulation would preclude any performance of the duty that was confined to the heart; yet even here, the 'frowning faces' are a theme familiar from Sunnī tradition.[22]

Yaʿqūbī (d. 284/897f.) knows this as a saying of ʿAlī al-Riḍā (*Taʾrīkh*, ed. M. T. Houtsma, Leiden 1883, 2:551.12; I owe this reference to Michael Cooperson).

15 See above, ch. 1, note 18.

16 Kulaynī, *Kāfī*, 5:60.7 no. 16 = Ṭūsī, *Tahdhīb*, 6:178.6 no. 9; see also Ibn Bābawayh (d. 381/991f.), *Khiṣāl*, Najaf 1971, 6 no. 16; Majlisī, *Biḥār*, 100:75 no. 19; and cf. below, note 36. (Such further references could be given for almost all the traditions discussed in this section, but will be supplied only for the more significant ones.) Cf. above, ch. 3, note 55.

17 Kulaynī, *Kāfī*, 5:63f. nos. 4f. = Ṭūsī, *Tahdhīb*, 6:180 nos. 17f.; cf. above, note 11, item (8).

18 Kulaynī, *Kāfī*, 5:60 no. 1 (the version in Ṭūsī, *Tahdhīb*, 6:178 no. 10 has *niyyatihi* for *qalbihi*); cf. above, note 11, item (6).

19 Kulaynī, *Kāfī*, 5:56.4 no. 1 = Ṭūsī, *Tahdhīb*, 6:181.5 no. 21. The activist tone and Sunnī linkage of this tradition will be discussed below, 256.

20 Ṭūsī, *Tahdhīb*, 6:181 no. 23; cf. above, note 11, item (11). Cf. also Raḍī, *Nahj al-balāgha*, *apud* Ibn Abī ʾl-Ḥadīd, *Sharḥ*, 19:306.6. Several exhortatory traditions under consideration in this section have parallels in the *Nahj al-balāgha* which I have not otherwise indicated.

21 Ṭūsī, *Tahdhīb*, 6:176f. no. 5 (the version in Kulaynī, *Kāfī*, 5:58f. no. 10 is from the Prophet, and does not contain the phrase *adnā ʾl-inkār*). The *isnād* contains an apparently Sunnī transmitter from al-Ṣādiq, viz. Ismāʿīl ibn Abī Ziyād al-Sakūnī (see al-ʿAllāma al-Ḥillī (d. 726/1325), *Rijāl*, ed. M. Ṣ. Baḥr al-ʿUlūm, Najaf 1961, 199 no. 3, describing him as a Sunnī (*ʿāmmi*), and Barqī (d. 274/887f.) (attrib.), *Rijāl*, Tehran 1342 sh., 28.7, stating that he transmits from Sunnīs (*ʿawāmm*); cf. also Ibn Ḥajar, *Tahdhīb*, 1:300.9, and 333f. no. 601). For a version in a Zaydī source with a Ḥasanid *isnād*, see al-Murshad Yaḥyā ibn al-Ḥusayn (d. 477/1084f.), *Amālī*, Cairo 1376, 2:230.29.

22 See above, note 11, item (4) (and cf. Ibn al-Murtaḍā, *Durar*, f. 246a.5, for a parallel in a Zaydī source). The social avoidance of offenders is also a theme in traditions from al-Ṣādiq. In one he accuses his followers of not cutting off social interaction with the offender (Ṭūsī, *Tahdhīb*, 6:181f. no. 24: *lā tahjurūnahu*). In another he is asked what to do if offenders within the community do not accept a rebuke; he replies that social relations with them should be cut off (*uhjurūhum wa-ʾjtanibū majālisahum*) (Kulaynī, *Kāfī*, 8:162 no. 169 (in the *Rawḍa*); Ḥurr al-ʿĀmilī, *Wasāʾil*, 6:1:415 no. 3; Majlisī, *Biḥār*, 100:85f. no. 58; similarly Ḥurr al-ʿĀmilī, *Wasāʾil*, 6:1:415 no. 5, and Majlisī, *Biḥār*, 100:88 no. 66, translated in Nagel, *Staat und Glaubensgemeinschaft*, 1:222).

In general there is not much activism to be found in this material, but there is one conspicuous exception: a long activist tradition from Muḥammad al-Bāqir.[23] In harsh rhetorical language, he foretells that in the last days (*fī ākhir al-zamān*)[24] there will be people who, despite their pious observances, do not consider forbidding wrong to be obligatory unless they are safe from harm (*idhā aminū ʾl-ḍarar*). They thereby brush aside the noblest of duties, for forbidding wrong is the way of the prophets and saints, and is fundamental to the moral and physical well-being of society. The faithful should therefore perform it in (or with) their hearts, speak out with their tongues, and strike the foreheads of the evil-doers. If the evil-doers comply, well and good; if not, the faithful should fight them (*jāhidūhum bi-abdānikum*) while hating them in their hearts.[25] Apart from its discordant activism, two things cast suspicion on the Imāmī credentials of this tradition. First, it is also known to the Zaydīs.[26] Secondly, the chain of transmission is unusual in that its key figure is Abū ʿIṣma, judge of Marw.[27] This transmitter is no Imāmī: he can be identified as the Ḥanafī Murjiʾite Nūḥ ibn Abī Maryam al-Marwazī (d. 173/789f.).[28] The rest of the chain of transmission, in both the Imāmī and Zaydī versions, is unhelpful.[29] But taken together, these points suggest that this violently activist tradition was not of Imāmī provenance.

Three traditions belonging to our core remain to be discussed. The first is the most interesting.[30] Here Jaʿfar al-Ṣādiq is asked an explicitly doctrinal question: is forbidding wrong incumbent on the entire community (*al-*

23 Kulaynī, *Kāfī*, 5:55f. no. 1 = Ṭūsī, *Tahdhīb*, 6:180f. no. 21; see also Fayḍ, *Wāfī*, 9:28.12; Ḥurr al-ʿĀmilī, *Wasāʾil*, 6:1:394f. no. 6, 401f. no. 6, and 403f. no. 1.

24 Such predictions are a familiar theme, see above, ch. 3, 39f.

25 My summary omits much detail, including a final anecdote about the prophet Shuʿayb which is paralleled in Sunnī sources (see for example Abū ʾl-Layth al-Samarqandī, *Tanbīh*, 96.8, and Ghazzālī, *Iḥyāʾ*, 2:285.10; in both the prophet is Joshua). Note the absence of any reference to the imam in the context of violence against offenders.

26 See above, ch. 10, note 11. The text in this transmission is shorter and visibly corrupt; it contains neither of the references to the heart found in the Imāmī version.

27 So Kulaynī and Ṭūsī. The Zaydī version has simply ʿAbū ʿIṣmaʾ.

28 See van Ess, *Theologie*, 2:549–51, and Cook, ʿVan Ess's second volumeʾ, 27–33. A pupil of Abū Ḥanīfa, he had a bad reputation as a traditionist among the Sunnī experts. His identity is pointed out in a scholion to the tradition in Fayḍ, *Wāfī*, 9:28, right-hand margin; the scholiast concludes that the tradition is to be relied on for the soundness of its content rather than its *isnād*.

29 As to the higher part of the *isnād*, in both versions Abū ʿIṣma transmits from Jābir (sc. the Kūfan Jābir ibn Yazīd al-Juʿfī (d. 128/745f.)) from Muḥammad al-Bāqir; the Zaydī *isnād* then continues through al-Bāqir's forebears to ʿAlī. As to the lower *isnād*, the Imāmīs and Zaydīs have different transmitters from Abū ʿIṣma; neither seems to be identifiable.

30 Kulaynī, *Kāfī*, 5:59f. no. 16 = Ṭūsī, *Tahdhīb*, 6:177f. no. 9; see also Fayḍ, *Wāfī*, 9:30.27; Ḥurr al-ʿĀmilī, *Wasāʾil*, 6:1:400 no. 1; Majlisī, *Biḥār*, 100:93 nos. 92f.; al-Nūrī al-Ṭabarsī (d. 1320/1902), *Mustadrak al-Wasāʾil*, Qumm 1407–8, 12:187f. no. 6. This tradition was selected by Bahāʾ al-Dīn al-ʿĀmilī (d. 1030/1621) as the twelfth in his collection of forty traditions (*Kitāb al-arbaʿīn*, Tabrīz 1378, 103.8).

umma jamīʿan)? He answers in the negative: it is incumbent on the strong who can expect obedience and know right from wrong (*al-qawī al-muṭāʿ al-ʿālim biʾl-maʿrūf min al-munkar*), not on the weak and ignorant; he then supports this answer with Koranic exegesis.[31] He goes on to draw a significant practical conclusion: 'For one who knows this, there can be no objection if in this time of truce (*hudna*) [he does not forbid wrong] when he lacks strength, the power of numbers, and the prospect of being obeyed (*idhā kāna lā quwwa lahu wa-lā ʿadad*[32] *wa-lā ṭāʿa*).'[33] Here, in this application of the idea of a truce between the Imāmīs and their (Sunnī) enemies, we have a very Imāmī notion.[34] Nevertheless the transmitter from Jaʿfar al-Ṣādiq is reported to have been a non-Imāmī.[35]

The second tradition returns to the theme of confrontation with the unjust ruler. Here Jaʿfar al-Ṣādiq avers in quietist vein that there is no reward for one who comes to grief in such a venture.[36]

The third tradition tells us what Jaʿfar al-Ṣādiq would do when he came upon a group of people engaged in a dispute (*yakhtaṣimūn*): before moving on, he would three times admonish them in a loud voice to fear God.[37] This

31 He cites Q3:104, interpreting this as restrictive (*khāṣṣ*) rather than general (*ʿāmm*) in scope (cf. above, ch. 2, 17–20; note that Ṭūsī himself holds the contrary view, see above, ch. 2, note 17). This exegesis is then buttressed with a parallel (Q7:159), after which the term *umma* is defined. Thus the tone of the discussion is scholastic, despite the absence of the formal concept of a collective obligation (*farḍ ʿalā ʾl-kifāya*).

32 In Kulaynī's text this is corrupted to *ʿudhr*.

33 The transmitter then appends al-Ṣādiq's quietist interpretation of the (Sunnī) tradition on standing up to an unjust ruler (see above, note 16).

34 See Kohlberg, 'Development', 78, citing Majlisī's commentary to a tradition extolling *taqiyya* in which al-Ṣādiq states that 'people are in [a state of] truce (*hudna*)' (*Biḥār*, 75:426 no. 84; the tradition itself is from Kulaynī, *Kāfī*, 2:217 no. 4). Note the surprising lack of invocations of *taqiyya* as an antidote to *al-amr biʾl-maʿrūf* in our tradition and others of quietist tendency.

35 Masʿada ibn Ṣadaqa is described as a Batrī Zaydī in one source (Kashshī, *Rijāl*, 390.5), and as a Sunnī (*ʿāmmī*) in another (Ṭūsī, *Rijāl*, 137 no. 40). He is known to the Sunnī *rijāl* literature (see Ibn Ḥajar al-ʿAsqalānī (d. 852/1449), *Lisān al-Mīzān*, Hyderabad 1329–31, 6:22f. no. 83; Ibn Ḥajar notes a case where he transmits a spurious tradition from al-Ṣādiq in the *Kanjarūdiyyāt*, an impeccably Sunnī source for which see Kattānī (d. 1345/1927), *al-Risāla al-mustaṭrafa*, Damascus 1964, 93.9).

36 Kulaynī, *Kāfī*, 5:60f. no. 3 = Ṭūsī, *Tahdhīb*, 6:178 no. 12; see also Ibn Bābawayh (d. 381/991f.), *ʿIqāb al-aʿmāl*, ed. ʿA. A. al-Ghaffārī with the *Thawāb al-aʿmāl*, Tehran 1391, 296.13; Fayḍ, *Wāfī*, 9:31.3; Ḥurr al-ʿĀmilī, *Wasāʾil*, 6:1:401 no. 3; Majlisī, *Biḥār*, 100:92 no. 88; Nūrī, *Mustadrak*, 12:187 no. 5. Yaʿqūbī knows this saying as ʿAlī al-Riḍā's (*Taʾrīkh*, 2:551.14; I owe this reference to Michael Cooperson). I have not seen Sunnī parallels to this formulation.

37 Kulaynī, *Kāfī*, 5:59 no. 12 = *ibid*., 61 no. 4 = Ṭūsī, *Tahdhīb*, 6:180 no. 19; see also Fayḍ, *Wāfī*, 9:31.10; Ḥurr al-ʿĀmilī, *Wasāʾil*, 6:1:394 no. 3; Majlisī, *Biḥār*, 100:92 no. 86; Nūrī, *Mustadrak*, 12:181 no. 16. Elsewhere al-Ṣādiq uses this rebuke against a man who is blocking the way, but gives up when it becomes clear that the man is inured to rebuke (Kulaynī, *Kāfī*, 5:61 no. 5; Fayḍ, *Wāfī*, 9:31.12; for the point of the tradition, see the latter part of the scholion in the left-hand margin, and the summary in Ḥurr al-ʿĀmilī, *Wasāʾil*, 6:1:401 no. 4).

is, in effect, an answer to the question how long one should persist in reproving people who do not listen.[38] Again, the transmitter from Jaʿfar al-Ṣādiq seems not to be an Imāmī.[39]

If we widen our coverage of Imāmī tradition to include other early sources and, still more, the compilations of the Ṣafawid period, we encounter a good deal of further material; but it does not greatly affect the overall picture.

One feature of this material worth noting is that it provides further evidence of the penetration of Sunnī material into Imāmī tradition. Even the standard Sunnī 'three modes' tradition makes its appearance,[40] as does that of the 'three qualities'.[41] Likewise the term 'put right' (*ghayyara*), well established in Sunnī tradition and absent from the Imāmī traditions considered above,[42] is quite common in this additional material, and that from an early date.[43] Most of these occurrences are ascribed to the

[38] Cf. above, ch. 5, 99.

[39] Ghiyāth ibn Ibrāhīm is described as a Batrī Zaydī (Ṭūsī, *Rijāl*, 132.6).

[40] See Ḥurr al-ʿĀmilī, *Wasāʾil*, 6:1:407.4 no. 12; Majlisī, *Biḥār*, 100:85.16 no. 57; Nūrī, *Mustadrak*, 12:192 no. 7. All are from the Prophet; the last is closest to the Sunnī wording, and is taken from Ibn Abī Jumhūr al-Aḥsāʾī (*fl.* late ninth/fifteenth century), *ʿAwālī al-laʾālī*, ed. M. al-ʿArāqī, Qumm 1983–5, 1:431 nos. 128f. A much earlier source in which the tradition is found is Isḥāq ibn Wahb (writing after 334/946), *al-Burhān fī wujūh al-bayān*, 276.7; but despite the author's clear Imāmī affiliation (cf. *ibid.*, 277.18), he quotes other well-known Sunnī traditions (*ibid.*, 276.17, 277.11). This work was drawn to my attention by Etan Kohlberg. For the Sunnī tradition, see above, ch. 3, section 1. The saying of ʿAlī regarding the decay of *al-amr biʾl-maʿrūf* (see above, ch. 10, note 8) also finds a parallel (Ḥurr al-ʿĀmilī, *Wasāʾil*, 6:1:406 no. 10; Majlisī, *Biḥār*, 100:89 no. 71; Nūrī, *Mustadrak*, 12:194 no. 4; and see also Raḍī, *Nahj al-balāgha*, *apud* Ibn Abī ʾl-Ḥadīd, *Sharḥ*, 19:312.3). The notion of performance in the heart further appears in a Sunnī tradition quoted with a Sunnī *isnād* (Ṭūsī, *Amālī*, 2:88.9; Majlisī, *Biḥār*, 100:77 no. 29; Nūrī, *Mustadrak*, 12:189f. no. 1; for Sunnī sources, see above, ch. 3, note 47).

[41] See Ibn Bābawayh, *Khiṣāl*, 105 no. 79; Ḥurr al-ʿĀmilī, *Wasāʾil*, 6:1:403 no. 10, and 419 no. 3; Majlisī, *Biḥār*, 100:91 no. 79; Nūrī, *Mustadrak*, 12:187 no. 4 (all from al-Ṣādiq); *ibid.*, 189 no. 9 (from ʿAlī); Abū ʾl-Riḍā al-Rāwandī (sixth/twelfth century), *Nawādir*, Beirut 1988, 97.16; Ibn al-Ashʿath (*fl.* first half of fourth/tenth century), *al-Jaʿfariyyāt aw al-Ashʿathiyyāt*, published with Ḥimyarī's *Qurb al-isnād*, Tehran n.d., 88.11 (whence Nūrī, *Mustadrak*, 12:186 no. 1); Majlisī, *Biḥār*, 100:87 no. 64 (all from the Prophet). For the Sunnīs, see above, ch. 3, note 59. For other traditions on the qualities needed to perform the duty, see Jaʿfar al-Ṣādiq (d. 148/765) (attrib.), *Miṣbāḥ al-sharīʿa*, Beirut 1961, 81.7, 82.3.

[42] There is one possible exception. The tradition from al-Ṣādiq stating that it is sufficient for the dignity (*ʿizz*) of the believer who sees a wrong that God should know his disapprobation from his heart or his intention (see above, note 18) is found in a variant text with *ghiyaran* for *ʿizzan*. This is the text given in Majlisī's commentary on Kulaynī's *Kāfī* (Majlisī (d. 1110/1699), *Mirʾāt al-ʿuqūl*, ed. H. al-Rasūlī *et al.*, Tehran 1404–11, 18:407f. no. 1), and as he remarks (*ibid.*, 408.12), *ghiyar* here could be taken in the sense of *taghyīr al-munkar* (see also Majlisī (d. 1110/1699), *Malādh al-akhbār*, ed. M. al-Rajāʾī, Qumm 1406–7, 9:472.8). For this variant, see also Ḥurr al-ʿĀmilī, *Wasāʾil*, 6:1:408f. no. 1 (from Kulaynī); ʿAlī ibn al-Ḥasan al-Ṭabrisī (*fl.* later sixth/twelfth century), *Mishkāt al-anwār*, Najaf 1965, 49.20, whence Majlisī, *Biḥār*, 100:92 no. 85. The Sunnī versions offer no parallel at this point in the tradition.

[43] It appears in two variants of a tradition found in the collection of Ḥimyarī, who flourished in the later third/ninth century: (1) *Qurb al-isnād*, 37.17, from the Prophet with an Imāmī *isnād* through Masʿada ibn Ṣadaqa (for *yataghayyar* read *yughayyar*); see also Ḥurr

Prophet,[44] but we also find the usage in the mouths of ʿAlī[45] and Jaʿfar al-Ṣādiq.[46]

The rest of this material modifies the picture already given in places, but without substantially changing it. A touch of scholastic language appears in a letter from ʿAlī al-Riḍā (d. 203/818) to al-Maʾmūn (r. 198–218/813–33) in which he states that the duty is incumbent when possible (*idhā amkana*) in the absence of fear for oneself.[47] Yet elsewhere ʿAlī al-Riḍā refuses to rebuke offenders who belong to his own household, citing a saying of his father's that 'counsel is harsh' (*al-naṣīḥa khashina*).[48] Other traditions suggest a positive attitude towards confrontation with unjust rulers – in marked contrast to the negative views we encountered above.[49]

al-ʿĀmilī, *Wasāʾil*, 6:1:407 no. 1 (second part); Majlisī, *Biḥār*, 100:74f. no. 15 (from Ḥimyarī); *ibid.*, 78 no. 35; (2) Ḥimyarī, *Qurb al-isnād*, 38.1 (a variant with a similar *isnād*, but from ʿAlī); see also Ḥurr al-ʿĀmilī, *Wasāʾil*, 6:1:407 no. 1 (first part); Majlisī, *Biḥār*, 100:75 no. 16; *ibid.*, 78f. no. 36. This tradition is familiar from Sunnī sources (see above ch. 3, note 64). At the same time, the oldest Imāmī Koran commentaries contain the usage in a tradition cited by Muḥammad al-Bāqir from the *kitāb ʿAlī* telling the story of Q7:163–6 (Qummī, *Tafsīr*, 1:245.14; ʿAyyāshī, *Tafsīr*, 2:34.9; see also Fayḍ, *Ṣāfī*, 2:248.12; Baḥrānī (d. 1107/1695f.), *al-Burhān fī tafsīr al-Qurʾān*, Tehran 1375, 2:42.21, 43.34). For the term *kitāb ʿAlī*, see E. Kohlberg, 'Authoritative scriptures in early Imāmī Shīʿism', in E. Patlagean and A. Le Boulluec (eds.), *Les retours aux écritures*, Louvain and Paris 1993, 300f.

44 See the first variant adduced in the previous note; the 'three modes' tradition and the tradition with the Sunnī *isnād* cited above, note 40; a tradition using the term *ghiyar* (Ḥurr al-ʿĀmilī, *Wasāʾil*, 6:1:410f. no. 8); and an unusual tradition regarding a white bird that reproves believers who have been remiss in performing the duty at home by crying *ghayyir! ghayyir!* (Ibn al-Ashʿath, *Jaʿfariyyāt*, 89.5, whence Nūrī, *Mustadrak*, 12:200f. no. 3).

45 See above, note 43.

46 See above, note 42; also Ibn Bābawayh, *ʿIqāb al-aʿmāl*, 310.18, whence Ḥurr al-ʿĀmilī, *Wasāʾil*, 6:1:408 no. 3, and Majlisī, *Biḥār*, 100:78 no. 34.

47 See Ḥurr al-ʿĀmilī, *Wasāʾil*, 6:1:402 no. 8, and Majlisī, *Biḥār*, 100:77 no. 27, both from Ibn Bābawayh (d. 381/991f.), *ʿUyūn akhbār al-Riḍā*, Najaf 1970, 2:124.6 (the full text shows that the letter as we have it cannot in fact be earlier than 260/874, see *ibid.*, 121.2). The statement is also ascribed to al-Ṣādiq (Ḥurr al-ʿĀmilī, *Wasāʾil*, 6:1:398f. no. 22).

48 See *ibid.*, 402 no. 7, and Majlisī, *Biḥār*, 100:76 no. 25, both from Ibn Bābawayh, *ʿUyūn akhbār al-Riḍā*, 1:226 no. 38.

49 Thus Ḥusayn ibn ʿAlī (d. 61/680) – or ʿAlī himself – describes *al-amr biʾl-maʿrūf* as (among other things) 'opposing tyrants' (*mukhālafat al-ẓālim*) (see Fayḍ, *Wāfī*, 9:30.6, Ḥurr al-ʿĀmilī, *Wasāʾil*, 6:1:403.6 no. 9, and Majlisī, *Biḥār*, 100:79.15 no. 37, all from Ibn Shuʿba (mid-fourth/tenth century), *Tuḥaf al-ʿuqūl*, ed. ʿA. A. al-Ghaffārī, Tehran 1376, 237.12, translated in Nagel, *Staat und Glaubensgemeinschaft*, 2:271; this speech appears already in Ibn al-Iskāfī (third/ninth century), *al-Miʿyār waʾl-muwāzana*, ed. M. B. al-Maḥmūdī, Beirut 1981, 275.6; for the authorship of this work, assuming it to be correctly identified, see the editor's note following the title-page). ʿAlī in one of his speeches describes speaking out in the presence of an unjust ruler (*kalimat ʿadl ʿinda imām jāʾir*) as the best form of *al-amr biʾl-maʿrūf* (Raḍī, *Nahj al-balāgha*, *apud* Ibn Abī ʾl-Ḥadīd, *Sharḥ*, 19:306.10, whence Majlisī, *Biḥār*, 100:89 no. 70, translated in Nagel, *Staat und Glaubensgemeinschaft*, 1:221). Muḥammad al-Bāqir speaks of the reward that awaits someone who goes to an unjust ruler and commands him to fear God (al-Shaykh al-Mufīd (d. 413/1022) (attrib.), *Ikhtiṣāṣ*, ed. ʿA. A. al-Ghaffārī, Tehran 1379, 261.16, whence Nūrī, *Mustadrak*, 12:178 no. 5; Ḥurr al-ʿĀmilī, *Wasāʾil*, 6:1:406 no. 11). Nagel takes the view that such texts are older than the quietist material in Imāmī sources (*Staat und Glaubensgemeinschaft*, 1:222).

As might be expected, Ḥusayn ibn ʿAlī (d. 61/680) is a figure in whom forbidding wrong and righteous rebellion are associated; pilgrims to the tomb of the martyr are to testify that he commanded right and forbade wrong.[50]

Finally, there are two traditions that bear on the relationship between forbidding wrong and the imamate. In one, al-Bāqir foretells that the world will not end until God sends a member of the family of the Prophet who will take action against all wrongs he encounters (*lā yarā munkaran illā ankarahu*).[51] The implication is, perhaps, that wrongs will not be much righted in the meantime. The other tradition is placed in the mouth of the Prophet on the day of Ghadīr Khumm. He exhorts the faithful to perform the duty, and ends with the arresting statement that there can be no commanding right or forbidding wrong without the presence of an infallible imam (*illā maʿa imām maʿṣūm*).[52] In general, however, Imāmī tradition does little to relate forbidding wrong to the imamate.

Early Imāmī Koranic exegesis is a different matter. Here, as in Zaydism,[53] there is a strain of sectarian exegesis which construes certain Koranic verses on forbidding wrong as references to the imams.[54] This strain is already present in the oldest extant Imāmī Koran commentaries, themselves drawing on earlier traditions. Thus ʿAlī ibn Ibrāhīm al-Qummī (alive in 307/919) interprets Q9:111–12 to refer to the imams; his argument is along the lines

[50] Majlisī, *Biḥār*, 101:163.21, 171.17, 172.18, 209.18, 230.2, 231.4, 267.3, 345.15, 360.8; Ibn Qūlawayh (d. 368/978), *Kāmil al-ziyārāt*, ed. ʿA. al-Amīnī al-Tabrīzī, Najaf 1356, 203.9, 207.7, 208.14, 209.6, 210.4, 210.16, 213.3, 220.10, 229.12 (similar formulae are prescribed for pilgrims visiting the tombs of ʿAlī (*ibid.*, 43.8) and ʿAlī al-Riḍā (*ibid.*, 312.13)); several of these variants include reference to *jihād*. I am indebted to Etan Kohlberg for supplying me with one of these references and putting me on the track of the rest.

[51] This tradition appears in two of our earliest sources: Ḥimyarī's *Qurb al-isnād* (where it is quoted by ʿAlī al-Riḍā in a letter to a follower, *ibid.*, 204.16); and the *aṣl* of Jaʿfar ibn Muḥammad ibn Shurayḥ al-Ḥaḍramī (*apud* Ḥ. al-Muṣṭafawī (ed.), *al-Uṣūl al-sitta ʿashar*, Qumm 1405, 63.4; on this *aṣl*, see E. Kohlberg, '*Al-uṣūl al-arbaʿumiʾa*', *Jerusalem Studies in Arabic and Islam*, 10 (1987), 145 no. 68, and 154 no. 5). I have not seen this tradition in the Imāmī books on the *ghayba*. Cf. also below, note 63.

[52] Aḥmad ibn ʿAlī al-Ṭabrisī (*fl.* early sixth/twelfth century), *Iḥtijāj*, Najaf 1966, 1:82.1, whence Nūrī, *Mustadrak*, 12:182.16 no. 20. The tradition is transmitted by al-Bāqir, with an apparently Imāmī *isnād*.

[53] Some of the Imāmī material discussed below is in fact of Zaydī origin (see below, notes 60, 63).

[54] I leave aside the story that Jaʿfar al-Ṣādiq in an exchange with Abū Ḥanīfa identified the Koranic term *maʿrūf* with ʿAlī, and *munkar* with his enemies, since though manifestly Shīʿite it is not attested in old Imāmī sources (van Ess, *Theologie*, 2:389, citing Abū Ḥayyān al-Tawḥīdī, *al-Baṣāʾir waʾl-dhakhāʾir*, 8:162 no. 561 (with a Ḥanafī parallel), and Majlisī, *Biḥār*, 10:208f., no. 10 (ultimately from Kalbī (d. 146/763f.)); this story was first drawn to my attention by Nurit Tsafrir). But for a similar equation of *munkar* with the enemies of the imams, see *ibid.*, 24:303.8, likewise from al-Ṣādiq.

that those who command right (*maʿrūf*) are those who know all that is right, and only the imams answer to this description.[55] The same identification is reported by his contemporary ʿAyyāshī.[56] At Q3:110 these exegetes, or their sources, go beyond exegesis to emend the text itself: as originally revealed, they tell us, the verse read not 'the best community' (*khayra ummatin*) but 'the best imams' (*khayra aʾimmatin*); again the argument is clinched in Qummī's version by reference to forbidding wrong.[57] Already in ʿAyyāshī's commentary, however, other views are also reported.[58] This sectarian strain survives down the centuries in Imāmī exegesis alongside more conventional approaches;[59] it can be found in commentaries to Q3:104,[60] Q3:110,[61]

[55] Qummī, *Tafsīr*, 1:306.1. Qummī adds an anecdote in which ʿAlī Zayn al-ʿĀbidīn (d. 94/712) refers the verses to the imams (*ibid.*, 306.8).

[56] ʿAyyāshī, *Tafsīr*, 2:113 no. 142.

[57] Qummī, *Tafsīr*, 1:10.3, 110.1, both from Jaʿfar al-Ṣādiq; ʿAyyāshī, *Tafsīr*, 1:195 nos. 128f., again from al-Ṣādiq, who in the first tradition is reporting the reading of ʿAlī. A version close to Qummī's appears in a short work of Saʿd ibn ʿAbdallāh al-Qummī (d. 301/913f.) (see Majlisī, *Biḥār*, 92:60.12). On all this see E. Kohlberg, 'Some notes on the Imāmite attitude to the Qurʾān', in S. M. Stern *et al.* (eds.), *Islamic philosophy and the classical tradition: essays presented by his friends and pupils to Richard Walzer*, Oxford 1972, 211f., and M. M. Bar-Asher, 'Variant readings and additions of the Imāmī-Šīʿa to the Quran', *Israel Oriental Studies*, 13 (1993), 42, 53 item 9.

[58] ʿAyyāshī gives a further tradition on Q3:110 (again from al-Ṣādiq) in which the canonical text is assumed (*Tafsīr*, 1:195 no. 130, noted in Bar-Asher, 'Variant readings', 53 n. 51).

[59] Cf. the material cited from Imāmī commentaries above, ch. 2.

[60] Qummī, *Tafsīr*, 1:108.21 (with an exegesis of Muḥammad al-Bāqir's referring the verse to the family of Muḥammad and those who follow them); Ṭabrisī, *Majmaʿ*, 1:484.1 (reporting al-Ṣādiq's reading *aʾimma* for *umma* both here and in Q3:110); Fayḍ, *Ṣāfī*, 1:339.11 (quoting Qummī). Both reports reappear in the commentary of Baḥrānī (*Burhān*, 1:308.12, 307.29, respectively), and see also Sharaf al-Dīn al-Astarābādī (tenth/sixteenth century), *Taʾwīl al-āyāt al-ẓāhira*, Qumm 1407, 1:118f. no. 33 (with Astarābādī's endorsement, *ibid.*, 119.2), and Majlisī, *Biḥār*, 24:153f. nos. 4f. Qummī's report derives from the commentary of Abū ʾl-Jārūd (first half of the second/eighth century), the eponym of the Jārūdiyya (cf. above, ch. 10, note 152) – in other words, from a Zaydī source (on this work see W. Madelung, 'The Shiite and Khārijite contribution to pre-Ashʿarite *kalām*', in P. Morewedge (ed.), *Islamic philosophical theology*, Albany 1979, 136 n. 51).

[61] Abū ʾl-Futūḥ-i Rāzī, *Rawḍ*, 3:148.19 (reporting that in their exegeses the *ahl al-bayt* refer this verse to themselves and the infallible imams); *ibid.*, 150.9 (similarly referring the verse to the imams); Miqdād, *Kanz*, 1:406.14 (on referring the verse to the infallible imams); Abū ʾl-Maḥāsin al-Jurjānī, *Jilāʾ al-adhhān*, 2:102.13 (derivative from Rāzī's first passage); Astarābādī, *Taʾwīl*, 1:121.9 (referring the verse to the infallible imam, and going on to quote from Qummī); Kāshānī, *Manhaj*, 2:300.13 (echoing both of Rāzī's passages); Fayḍ, *Ṣāfī*, 1:342.17 (quoting Qummī and ʿAyyāshī), and cf. *ibid.*, 343.4; Baḥrānī, *Burhān*, 1:308.30 (quoting Qummī); Baḥrānī *Burhān*, Tehran 1295–1302, 1:190.26 (quoting ʿAyyāshī; the modern edition as available to me is defective at this point); Majlisī, *Biḥār*, 24:153–5 nos. 1f., 5f., 12 (with the reading *aʾimmatin*); *ibid.*, nos. 1f., 8, 10–12 (referring the verse to the family of the Prophet and the like); Aḥmad al-Jazāʾirī (d. 1151/1738f.), *Qalāʾid al-durar*, Najaf 1382–3, 2:205.9, 206.13 (referring the verse to Muḥammad, ʿAlī and the imams, and citing Qummī and others). Cf. also above, ch. 2, note 25.

Q9:112[62] and Q22:41.[63] Its status, however, seems to be somewhat marginal, and its near-absence from the commentary of Abū Jaʿfar al-Ṭūsī (d. 460/1067) is perhaps a testimony to its lack or loss of mainstream respectability.[64]

To sum up, there is no scarcity of material on forbidding wrong in early Imāmī literature, and what it offers is by no means identical with what we find in Sunnī sources for the same period. Yet it soon becomes evident that forbidding wrong was not the locus of a strong and distinctive development in Imāmī thought – in contrast, for example, to precautionary dissimulation (*taqiyya*). Much of the material is merely exhortatory, and much of it echoes – and most probably derives from – the Sunnī heritage. It is true that early Imāmī Koranic exegesis links forbidding wrong to the imamate in a manner not paralleled in Sunnī exegesis; but this linkage is one we have already encountered in Zaydism. Here and there we can see Imāmī quietism at work in the traditions, but the message is by no means consistent.

3. THE CLASSICAL IMĀMĪ SCHOLARS

In this section I shall consider the views of the Imāmī scholars of the period from the fourth/tenth to the early eighth/fourteenth century – from Ibn Bābawayh (d. 381/991f.) to the ʿAllāma (d. 726/1325). I shall bring together works of law, theology and Koranic commentary. It will be simplest to analyse the material in terms of a small number of recurrent topics.

62 Ṭabrisī, *Majmaʿ*, 3:76.8 (probably from Qummī); Astarābādī, *Taʾwīl*, 1:211.6 (citing Ṭabrisī); Fayḍ, *Ṣāfī*, 2:381.23 (citing Qummī); Baḥrānī, *Burhān*, 2:167.3 (citing ʿAyyāshī).

63 Qummī, *Tafsīr*, 2:85.2 (simply referring the verse to the imams); Ṭabrisī, *Majmaʿ*, 4:88.19 (quoting Muḥammad al-Bāqir saying: 'We're them, by God!'); Fayḍ, *Ṣāfī*, 3:382.2 (quoting from Qummī a report (not found in his work as we have it) offering an eschatological exegesis of Muḥammad al-Bāqir which refers the verse to the family of Muḥammad, the Mahdī and his companions; and cf. *ibid.*, 382.7). Baḥrānī gives the second of these as taken from the commentary of Abū ʾl-Jārūd (*Burhān*, 3:96.16). Following Astarābādī, he also gives four traditions from the imams to the same effect from a work of Muḥammad ibn al-ʿAbbās (Astarābādī, *Taʾwīl*, 1:342–4 nos. 22–5; Baḥrānī, *Burhān*, 3:95.20; here the fourth tradition is a variant of the same tradition from Abū ʾl-Jārūd). The work in question is the *Taʾwīl mā nazala . . . fī ʾl-nabī wa-ālihi* of Muḥammad ibn ʿAbbās known as Ibn al-Juḥām (alive in 328/939f.) (see Kohlberg, *Ibn Ṭāwūs*, 369–71 no. 623). See also Majlisī, *Biḥār*, 24:164–7 nos. 6–8, 10f. (including three of Ibn al-Juḥām's traditions); Furāt ibn Ibrāhīm al-Kūfī (*fl.* later third/ninth century), *Tafsīr*, Najaf n.d., 98.3, 99.4 (both quoting al-Bāqir, the second eschatological), 100.10 (from Zayd ibn ʿAlī (d. 122/740), on the Qāʾim of the family of Muḥammad).

64 Ṭūsī strongly hints that Q3:110 refers to the imam(s) (*Tibyān*, 2:558.14, followed by Rāwandī (d. 573/1177f.), *Fiqh al-Qurʾān*, ed. A. al-Ḥusaynī, Qumm 1397–9, 1:360.19), but quotes none of the traditions found in the other commentaries.

Of the six that I will discuss in detail, the first two show the Imāmīs departing significantly from the Baṣran Muʿtazilite tradition with which the last two chapters have familiarised us. Then follow three cases in which they adhere to this tradition in more or less the same manner as the Zaydīs. With regard to the final topic, the conditions of obligation, the Imāmī record combines overall adherence with a telling divergence on one particular point.

1. *The three modes*

The first noteworthy feature of the accounts of forbidding wrong given by the Imāmī scholars of this period is the prominence of the doctrine of the 'three modes'. As we have seen, this schema was known to Imāmī tradition, but it had not been particularly salient there.

Ibn Bābawayh (d. 381/991f.), in the oldest account we possess,[65] states that a man must take a stand against wrong (*ʿalā ʾl-ʿabd an yunkir al-munkar*) with his heart, his tongue and his hand (*bi-qalbihi wa-lisānihi wa-yadihi*); (if he cannot do this, then with his heart and his tongue;)[66] if he cannot do this, then with his heart (*fa-in lam yaqdir fa-bi-qalbihi*). Further accounts of this kind, in which the modes are presented in the same de-escalating sequence, are to be found in works of al-Shaykh al-Mufīd (d. 413/1022),[67] Sallār (d. 448/1056),[68] Ṭūsī (d. 460/1067),[69] Ibn al-Barrāj

[65] Ibn Bābawayh (d. 381/991f.), *Hidāya*, printed with his *Muqniʿ*, Qumm and Tehran 1377, 11.7; the passage is translated (with an omission) in McDermott, *Mufīd*, 316 n. 4. Unfortunately, this seems to be the only surviving account of the duty by Ibn Bābawayh. In a concise description of the Imāmī faith he lists *al-amr biʾl-maʿrūf*, but without expanding further (*Amālī*, Tehran 1404, 652.13).

[66] The passage enclosed in parentheses is not in the text of the *Hidāya* as we have it; but it appears in a citation from the *Hidāya* given by Majlisī (*Biḥār*, 100:71 no. 2, where we also find *yughayyir* for *yunkir*).

[67] Mufīd, *Muqniʿa*, 809.8. In another work, Mufīd speaks of performance with the tongue and hand, but makes no mention of the heart (*Awāʾil al-maqālāt*, Tabrīz 1371, 98.4, translated in McDermott, *Mufīd*, 279).

[68] Sallār (d. 448/1056), *Marāsim*, ed. M. al-Bustānī, Beirut 1980, 260.7, speaking of *thalāthat aḍrub*. He adds a somewhat obscure statement about escalation (*ibid.*, 260.9). Sallār was a pupil of Mufīd and Murtaḍā (ʿAbdallāh Afandī al-Iṣbahānī (d. 1130/1717f.), *Riyāḍ al-ʿulamāʾ*, ed. A. al-Ḥusaynī, Qumm 1401, 2:438.2).

[69] The account given by Ṭūsī in his *Nihāya* is dominated by the 'three modes', referred to as *al-anwāʿ al-thalātha* (Ṭūsī (d. 460/1067), *Nihāya*, Beirut 1970, 299.10). The presentation of the de-escalatory sequence is complicated by Ṭūsī's choice to deal separately with *al-amr biʾl-maʿrūf* (*ibid.*, 299.16) and *al-nahy ʿan al-munkar* (*ibid.*, 300.9). In his *Jumal* he likewise refers to the 'three modes' (here *thalāthat aqsām*, *al-Jumal waʾl-ʿuqūd*, ed. M. W. Khurāsānī, Mashhad 1347 sh., 161.3). He does not cover *al-amr biʾl-maʿrūf* in his *Mabsūṭ*. An impression of his discussion of it in his *Nihāya* can be obtained from the translation in A. K. S. Lambton, *State and government in medieval Islam*, Oxford 1981, 243f.

(d. 481/1088),[70] and Ibn Abī ʾl-Majd (sixth/twelfth century?).[71] Ibn Ḥamza (alive in 566/1171), followed by Yaḥyā ibn Saʿīd (d. 689/1290), presents the matter differently: one starts with the tongue; if this does not work, one escalates to violence; if one is unable to do any of this, one confines one's performance to the heart.[72] With the Muḥaqqiq (d. 676/1277) the original sequence has been reversed: one first tries with the heart;[73] if one knows that this will not work, one moves to the tongue; failing that, one has recourse to the hand.[74] The ʿAllāma follows the Muḥaqqiq in adopting this escalatory sequence.[75]

This difference of presentation is analysed by the ʿAllāma in one of his works.[76] He remarks that he does not see much to argue about, and that the dispute should be seen as verbal rather than substantive.[77] There is no doubt something to be said for this. The de-escalatory sequence makes sense as a statement that one does as much as one can. The escalatory sequence, by contrast, makes sense as a statement that one does no more than is necessary.[78] Any sensible view will implicitly or explicitly combine these points: one does as much as is necessary and possible.

[70] Ibn al-Barrāj (d. 481/1088), *Muhadhdhab*, Qumm 1406, 1:341.3 (in an account that clearly follows Ṭūsī's *Nihāya*). The sequence is de-escalatory, though not fully spelled out. Ibn al-Barrāj was a pupil of Ṭūsī and his deputy (*khalīfa*) in Syria (ʿAbdallāh Afandī, *Riyāḍ*, 3:141.6, 142.5).

[71] Ibn Abī ʾl-Majd (sixth/twelfth century?), *Ishārat al-sabq*, ed. I. Bahādurī, Qumm 1414, 146.9. For *biʾl-lisān* at 146.12 we must surely read *biʾl-qalb*; as it stands, the text identifies performance with the tongue as the irreducible minimum.

[72] Ibn Ḥamza al-Ṭūsī (alive in 566/1171), *Wasīla*, ed. M. al-Ḥassūn, Qumm 1408, 207.9; Yaḥyā ibn Saʿīd (d. 689/1290), *al-Jāmiʿ lil-sharāʾiʿ*, *apud Silsilat al-yanābīʿ al-fiqhiyya*, Beirut 1990, vol. 9: *al-Jihād*, 239.15.

[73] For what this means, see below, note 81.

[74] See al-Muḥaqqiq al-Ḥillī (d. 676/1277), *Sharāʾiʿ al-Islām*, ed. ʿA. M. ʿAlī, Najaf 1969, 1:343.2, and similarly his *al-Mukhtaṣar al-nāfiʿ*, Tehran 1387, 139.9. He speaks of three *marātib*.

[75] See al-ʿAllāma al-Ḥillī (d. 726/1325), *Tabṣirat al-mutaʿallimīn*, *apud* Ṣādiq al-Shīrāzī, *Sharḥ Tabṣirat al-mutaʿallimīn*, Qumm 1406, 1:299.3; and his *Taḥrīr al-aḥkām*, n.p. 1314, 1:157.31; *Irshād al-adhhān*, ed. F. al-Ḥassūn, Qumm 1410, 1:352.15; *Qawāʿid al-aḥkām*, Qumm 1413–, 1:525.2; *Tadhkirat al-fuqahāʾ*, n.p. n.d., 1:458.38; *Muntahā ʾl-maṭlab*, n.p. 1333, 993.24. He uses the term *marātib* in the accounts of the *Taḥrīr*, *Tadhkira*, and *Muntahā*.

[76] See al-ʿAllāma al-Ḥillī (d. 726/1325), *Mukhtalaf al-Shīʿa*, Qumm 1412–, 4:474.10 (using the term *martaba* for 'mode'). He reports the views of Ibn Ḥamza and Sallār correctly, but surprisingly he ascribes Ibn Ḥamza's position also to Ṭūsī; the Muḥaqqiq's view (and his own in his other works) is adduced anonymously.

[77] *Ibid.*, 474.16 (*al-taḥqīq anna ʾl-nizāʿ lafẓī*). The analysis that he then gives is not, however, entirely cogent, since he has to interpret Sallār's view in terms of the notion that performing *al-amr biʾl-maʿrūf* with the hand means setting a good example; this, as we shall see, is a view put forward by Ṭūsī and his pupil Ibn al-Barrāj (see below, note 83), but not by Sallār.

[78] Escalation was, of course, a familiar concept, and one that did not need to be expressed in terms of the 'three modes' (see Murtaḍā, *Dhakhīra*, 559.18; Abū ʾl-Ṣalāḥ al-Ḥalabī (d. 447/1055), *al-Kāfī fī ʾl-fiqh*, ed. R. Ustādī, Iṣfahān 1403, 267.7; Ṭūsī, *Iqtiṣād*, 150.3; Ṭūsī, *Tamhīd al-uṣūl*, 305.15; Ṭūsī, *Tibyān*, 2:549.17 (to Q3:104); *ibid.*, 566.2 (to Q3:114), whence Rāwandī, *Fiqh al-Qurʾān*, 1:362.16 (also to Q3:114); *ibid.*, 359.1 (to Q3:110), borrowed from Zamakhsharī, *Kashshāf*, 1:398.1 (to Q3:104)).

Within this framework, there are two variations that are really matters of classification. First, it is not obvious where such responses as avoiding or turning away from the offender belong in the three-mode schema. Ṭūsī, the oldest source to confront the problem, describes avoidance as 'a kind of action' (*ḍarb min al-fiʿl*), and is followed by Ibn al-Barrāj.[79] Ibn Ḥamza, again followed by Yaḥyā ibn Saʿīd, sees such responses as actions taking the place of verbal rebukes.[80] The Muḥaqqiq, by contrast, regards them as performance with the heart,[81] and he is followed in this by the ʿAllāma.[82] The second variation is Ṭūsī's view (loyally followed by his pupil Ibn al-Barrāj) that in the case of commanding right (as opposed to forbidding wrong), performance with the hand means setting a good example for others.[83]

Yet there are other accounts that ignore the entire schema of the 'three modes'. This is the case with Murtaḍā (d. 436/1044)[84] and Abū 'l-Ṣalāḥ (d. 447/1055f.),[85] and with certain works of Ṭūsī.[86] Ibn Idrīs (d. 598/

[79] Ṭūsī, *Nihāya*, 300.14; Ibn al-Barrāj, *Muhadhdhab*, 1:341.20.

[80] Ibn Ḥamza, *Wasīla*, 207.10 (*rubbamā yaqūmu 'l-fiʿl fī dhālika maqām al-qawl*); Yaḥyā ibn Saʿīd, *Jāmiʿ*, 239.17.

[81] Muḥaqqiq, *Sharāʾiʿ*, 1:343.5, and cf. his *Mukhtaṣar*, 139.11. He indicates that there are degrees in such responses: *iẓhār al-karāha* is less drastic than *iʿrāḍ* and *hajr*. For Mufīd and Ṭūsī, by contrast, performance in the heart is clearly no more than an unobservable mental act (see Mufīd, *Muqniʿa*, 809.12, 810.3, implying that this mode is not affected by external constraints; Ṭūsī, *Nihāya*, 300.2, speaking of 'belief in the obligation of *al-amr bi'l-maʿrūf* in the heart'; and see also Abū 'l-Ṣalāḥ, *Kāfī*, 265.3, and Ibn al-Barrāj, *Muhadhdhab*, 1:341.8).

[82] ʿAllāma, *Taḥrīr*, 1:157.31; and his *Irshād*, 1:352.15; *Qawāʿid*, 1:525.2; *Tadhkira*, 1:458.39; *Muntahā*, 993.24 (where the root *hjr* is misspelled *ḥjr*); and cf. his *Mukhtalaf*, 4:475.5. The ʿAllāma recognises that performance in the heart may also be an unobservable mental act (*Qawāʿid*, 1:525.2; and cf. his *Mukhtalaf*, 4:475.3).

[83] Ṭūsī, *Nihāya*, 299.16 (the usual view also appears, *ibid.*, 300.4); Ibn al-Barrāj, *Muhadhdhab*, 1:341.9. The idea finds an echo in Yaḥyā ibn Saʿīd (*Jāmiʿ*, 239.18), and the ʿAllāma has ingenious though inappropriate recourse to it in his *Mukhtalaf* (4:475.7), but essentially it died with Ṭūsī and his immediate school.

[84] This is true not just for the brief accounts in his *Jumal* and *Muqaddima*, but also for the elaborate discussion in his *Dhakhīra* (Murtaḍā (d. 436/1044), *Jumal al-ʿilm wa'l-ʿamal*, ed. A. al-Ḥusaynī, Najaf 1387, 39.12; *Muqaddima fī 'l-uṣūl al-iʿtiqādiyya*, in M. Ḥ. Āl Yāsīn (ed.), *Nafāʾis al-makhṭūṭāt*, Najaf and Baghdad 1952–6, 2:82.5; *Dhakhīra*, 553–60).

[85] This despite the fact that Abū 'l-Ṣalāḥ's *Kāfī* gives a reasonably detailed account of the duty. He was a pupil of Murtaḍā and Ṭūsī (ʿAbdallāh Afandī, *Riyāḍ*, 5:464.17).

[86] There is no trace of the 'three modes' in his *Iqtiṣād* or *Tamhīd* (in both of which he seems to be following the presentation of Murtaḍā's *Dhakhīra*); nor is the schema in evidence in the accounts of school doctrine found in his *Tibyān*. However, his cross-reference to his *Sharḥ Jumal al-ʿilm* (sc. his *Tamhīd*) at *Tibyān*, 2:549.15 (to Q3:104) is replaced in the commentary of Abū 'l-Futūḥ-i Rāzī with an account of the 'three modes' (*sih martaba*, with the usual de-escalatory sequence) (*Rawḍ*, 3:141.12). Note also Ṭūsī's statement that *inkār* 'with the hand' is to be done only against one who commits a 'bodily' offence (*min maʿāṣī 'l-jawāriḥ*) or rebels against a legitimate imam (*Tibyān*, 2:566.7 (to Q3:114), whence Rāwandī, *Fiqh al-Qurʾān*, 1:363.2). There is likewise no mention of the 'three modes' in Ḥimmaṣī's account (*Munqidh*, 2:209–21).

1202) makes no systematic use of it.[87] Even Mufīd in one of his works makes no reference to performance in the heart.[88]

What is the origin of the 'three modes' doctrine as adopted by the Imāmī scholars? A Muʿtazilite origin can be excluded: the doctrine is not at home there, and in any case it is already attested for Ibn Bābawayh, an Imāmī traditionalist. This helps to explain the absence of the schema from the doctrine of Murtaḍā and derivative sources. But equally, the doctrine is hardly to be seen as a direct inheritance from Imāmī tradition, since as we have seen, it is only weakly attested there.[89] The likelihood is thus that the source of the doctrine is Sunnī traditionalism, where the notion is prominent thanks to its embodiment in the standard Sunnī Prophetic tradition on forbidding wrong.[90] The Imāmī reception of the doctrine presumably took place in the interval between the formation of Imāmī tradition and the lifetime of Ibn Bābawayh. This adoption no doubt owed something to the simple elegance of the schema and the lack of any principle of comparable systematising power in Imāmī tradition. But it also illustrates the fact that the Imāmī assimilation of Muʿtazilism was less thorough-going than that of the Zaydīs.

2. *The imam's permission*

A second noteworthy element in the accounts of the Imāmī scholars is the doctrine that when forbidding wrong involves violence, or some level of violence, the permission of the imam or of someone appointed by him is required.[91] This point is often presented within the framework of the 'three modes', and we can therefore consider it here.

Most authorities espouse this doctrine in some form, even when recognising the existence of a contrary view. It may take the form that permission

87 He does, however, interpolate references to performance 'with the hand' into the passage he quotes from Ṭūsī's *Iqtiṣād* (Ibn Idrīs (d. 598/1202), *Sarāʾir*, Qumm 1410–11, 2:23.8; cf. Ṭūsī, *Iqtiṣād*, 150.3); and references to tongue and heart are found in a passage he quotes at *Sarāʾir*, 2:24.2 from Ṭūsī's *Nihāya*, 300.14.

88 See above, note 67.

89 See above, notes 20, 40. The tradition that Ibn Bābawayh adduces in the *Hidāya* makes no reference to the 'three modes' (*Hidāya*, 11.10; for this tradition, see above, note 14). One of the two traditions quoted by Mufīd sets out the 'three modes' (*Muqniʿa*, 808.14); it is the saying of ʿAlī noted above, note 20. This latter tradition is also quoted by the ʿAllāma (*Muntahā*, 993.32), who is more given to quoting traditions than any previous Imāmī jurist since Mufīd.

90 On the Sunnī side, too, the apparently temporal ordering of the modes in this tradition (hand, then tongue, then heart) eventually came to be seen as problematic (see ʿAlī al-Qārī, *Mubīn*, 191.3, and Ismāʿīl Ḥaqqī Brūsevī, *Sharḥ*, 338.1; ʿAlī al-Qārī remarks that to his knowledge he is the first to deal with the problem).

91 See Ḥ. Mudarrisī Ṭabāṭabāʾī, *Zamīn dar fiqh-i Islāmī*, Tehran 1362 sh., 1:112, with references to numerous sources.

is needed where killing or wounding is involved; so Mufīd in one of his works,[92] Sallār,[93] the Muḥaqqiq,[94] and the ʿAllāma in one of his works.[95] Elsewhere, however, we may find suggestions of a lower or higher threshold: thus Mufīd in another of his works,[96] Ṭūsī in one of his works,[97] and Ibn al-Barrāj[98] seem to extend the requirement to all forms of violence, whereas Ibn Ḥamza appears to restrict it to killing.[99] These authors also use

92 Mufīd, *Muqniʿa*, 809.15 (*wa-laysa lahu ʾl-qatl waʾl-jirāḥ illā bi-idhn sulṭān al-zamān al-manṣūb li-tadbīr al-anām*); a few lines below he speaks of 'shedding blood' (*safk al-dimāʾ*, *ibid.*, 810.1).

93 Sallār, *Marāsim*, 260.16 (restricting such action to the *sulṭān* or someone acting under his orders). Of his teachers, he here follows Mufīd rather than Murtaḍā.

94 Muḥaqqiq, *Sharāʾiʿ*, 1:343.11 (stating that the view requiring *idhn al-imām* is the more widely accepted (*al-aẓhar*)); Muḥaqqiq, *Mukhtaṣar*, 139.14 (requiring the permission of the imam or of his appointee).

95 ʿAllāma, *Tabṣira*, 1:300.1 (requiring *idhn al-imām* for wounding); cf. his *Irshād*, 1:353.1 (where he gives this as an opinion, though without mentioning an alternative).

96 Mufīd, *Awāʾil al-maqālāt*, 98.6 (making *basṭ al-yad* subject to appointment or permission on the part of the *sulṭān*; for *wa-lan yajūz taghayyur hādhā ʾl-sharṭ al-madhkūr*, read *wa-lā yajūz bi-ghayr hādhā ʾl-sharṭ al-madhkūr*). This passage is translated in McDermott, *Mufīd*, 279; he identifies the *sulṭān* as 'the *de facto* holder of power', but see below, note 108.

97 In his *Nihāya*, Ṭūsī makes it clear that, at least in the case of *inkār al-munkar*, even blows require permission (*ibid.*, 300.9; for *al-amr biʾl-maʿrūf*, see *ibid.*, 300.4). The imam is referred to as *sulṭān al-waqt al-manṣūb lil-riyāsa*, or simply as *al-sulṭān* (cf. below, note 108). Ṭūsī does not however limit performance in the absence of permission to the heart, as indicated in A. A. Sachedina, *The just ruler (al-sultān al-ʿādil) in Shīʿite Islam*, New York and Oxford 1988, 145. In parallel passages in his *Iqtiṣād* (150.9) and *Tamhīd* (305.20), Ṭūsī states that the dominant Imāmī view (*al-ẓāhir min madhhab/madhāhib shuyūkhinā al-Imāmiyya*) is that this kind of performance of the duty (the context leaves it unclear exactly what is intended) is for the imams or for someone who has their permission (the *Tamhīd* adds the invocation *ʿalayhim al-salām*, which may or may not be from Ṭūsī himself). In his *Tibyān*, Ṭūsī states that 'most of our companions' believe that this kind of performance of the duty (in the context, armed conflict) needs the permission of the *sulṭān al-waqt*, whereas 'those who disagree with us' hold otherwise (*Tibyān*, 2:549.20 (to Q3:104), and see *ibid.*, 566.4 (to Q3:114)). Puzzlingly, Ibn Idrīs states that in his *Tibyān* (though not in his *Iqtiṣād* and *Nihāya*) Ṭūsī firmly espoused Murtaḍā's view (*Sarāʾir*, 2:23.18, whence ʿAllāma, *Mukhtalaf*, 4:475.17; ʿAllāma, *Taḥrīr*, 1:158.1; Madelung, 'Amr be maʿrūf', 995b; Sachedina, *Just ruler*, 145). Yet the text of the *Tibyān* as we have it is clearly old: parallel passages with a wording identical to Ṭūsī's are already found in a work of the sixth/twelfth century (Rāwandī, *Fiqh al-Qurʾān*, 1:358.4, 362.17), and the sense is likewise reproduced in the Persian of Abū ʾl-Futūḥ-i Rāzī (*Rawḍ*, 3:141.14 (to Q3:104), speaking of the need for *dastūrī-i imām*). The stipulation of the need for the imam's permission does have a distinctly intrusive look in both the passages of the *Tibyān* in which we find it; but this can readily be understood as a result of its insertion by Ṭūsī himself into material taken from Muʿtazilite sources that made no mention of it. Thus Ṭūsī's first pronouncement on the issue follows a statement enjoining recourse to arms where necessary; this latter is taken from Rummānī (d. 384/994), who makes no reference to the imam's permission (compare Ṭūsī, *Tibyān*, 2:549.16 with Rummānī, *Tafsīr*, f. 62a.9, both to Q3:104).

98 Ibn al-Barrāj, *Muhadhdhab*, 1:341.12 (speaking of *al-imām al-ʿādil*, or one appointed by him). Again, he is following Ṭūsī's *Nihāya*.

99 Ibn Ḥamza, *Wasīla*, 207.12. He requires permission from the appropriate authority (*man lahu dhālika*) for action involving *talaf* (or for any kind of *taʾdīb*?).

a variety of terms to refer to the imam;[100] some allow for permission being granted by an appointee of his, while others do not mention this. But despite the variations, there is no indication of explicit disagreement within this camp.[101]

A few authorities, however, reject the whole requirement.[102] Murtaḍā does so quite explicitly,[103] and he is followed by Ibn Idrīs,[104] and by the ʿAllāma in most of his works.[105] Yaḥyā ibn Saʿīd is in the same camp.[106]

Finally, there are authors who do not mention the issue at all. This is the case with Ibn Bābawayh, Abū ʾl-Ṣalāḥ and Ibn Abī ʾl-Majd. This is not

[100] These terms are given in the preceding notes.

[101] It is thus unclear to me how far Madelung is right to single out certain scholars (he names the Muḥaqqiq and the ʿAllāma) as holding 'an intermediate position' ('Amr be maʿrūf', 995b).

[102] Sachedina takes the view that there is a consensus among the Imāmī scholars on the issue (see his *Just ruler*, 142, 144f.). However, if this had been so, the ʿAllāma would not have needed to discuss the question in his *Mukhtalaf* (see below, note 105). Sachedina's view may be based on the interpretations noted below, notes 103, 105.

[103] Murtaḍā, *Dhakhīra*, 560.4. He says that some have held that performance involving injury (*al-iḍrār wa'l-īlām*) can only be carried out as punishment (*ʿuqūbatan*), and that this can only be inflicted by the imams (*al-aʾimma*) or at their command. He then argues that this is wrong, because such punishment is deliberate – in contrast to injury inflicted in the course of *al-amr bi'l-maʿrūf*, which is an unintended consequence. This argument is quoted by Ṭūsī (see especially *Iqtiṣād*, 150.11, whence later sources); he proceeds to refute it. A different understanding of the argument as quoted by Ṭūsī seems to lie behind Sachedina's view that Murtaḍā requires the imam's permission (*Just ruler*, 145).

[104] Ibn Idrīs, *Sarāʾir*, 2:23.18 (*huwa ʾl-aqwā wa-bihi uftī*). Ibn Idrīs has just quoted views of Ṭūsī and Murtaḍā. Ḥimmaṣī, whose account of the issue mixes material from Ṭūsī's *Tamhīd* and the school of Abū ʾl-Ḥusayn (see above, ch. 9, notes 130, 134), espouses the rejection of the requirement in accordance with the views of both Murtaḍā and the school of Abū ʾl-Ḥusayn (*Munqidh*, 2:210.5–211.2).

[105] ʿAllāma, *Taḥrīr*, 1:157.34 (setting out the rival views), 158.1 (endorsing the view that permission is not needed as the stronger (*al-aqwā*)); similarly his *Muntahā*, 993.34, 994.1. In his *Mukhtalaf* he gives an account of the disagreement among the Imāmī scholars on the issue based on the analysis of Ibn Idrīs, to which he adds the views of Sallār and Ibn al-Barrāj, and the silence of Abū ʾl-Ṣalāḥ (*ibid.*, 4:475.10). He himself again endorses the view of Murtaḍā (*ibid.*, 476.3). In support of this view, the ʿAllāma adduces the following arguments: the unrestricted scope (*ʿumūm*) of the duty; two Imāmī traditions (including the long activist one) which do not speak of permission, and are presumably read by him as indications that it is not required; the point that the duty is obligatory for the good order of the world (*li-maṣlaḥat al-ʿālam*), and so like other goods is not dependent on any condition (read *fa-lā yaqifān ʿalā sharṭ ka-ghayrihimā min al-maṣāliḥ*); and finally the fact that it is obligatory for the imam and the Prophet, and is therefore obligatory for us in the same way, since they are our mandatory role models (*li-wujūb al-taʾassī*). Those who take the other view, he adds, have argued from the sanctity of life (*wujūb ʿiṣmat al-nufūs*) and the prohibition of shedding blood (*taḥrīm al-iqdām ʿalā irāqat al-dimāʾ*). The occurrence of the word *ʿiṣma* in this passage may be behind Sachedina's view that some Imāmī scholars hold infallibility to be necessary for the use of force in *al-amr bi'l-maʿrūf* (*Just ruler*, 101, 144f.). In two other works, the ʿAllāma merely notes the existence of divergent views on the issue (*Tadhkira*, 1:458.43; *Qawāʿid*, 1:525.6).

[106] Yaḥyā ibn Saʿīd, *Jāmiʿ*, 239.16, stating the view that such permission is unnecessary to be the more sound (*aṣaḥḥ*).

necessarily significant: some authors mention the issue in one work but not in another.[107]

It is not difficult to see why such a doctrine would find favour with the Imāmī scholars. Since the imam was by their time in occultation, and had no designated representative among the community, such a requirement would mean that violence (or the specified level of violence) could not be employed in forbidding wrong until such time as the imam returned.[108] The doctrine can thus be seen as of a piece with the quietist tendency that characterises Imāmism in this period.[109]

What this leaves is the question where the doctrine comes from. It has no significant basis in Imāmī tradition,[110] and it is in line with this that it makes no appearance in Ibn Bābawayh's account of the duty. Instead, it is first encountered in a work of Mufīd – promptly to be rejected by Murtaḍā. Mufīd was a Baghdādī Muʿtazilite, whereas Murtaḍā was aligned with the ultimately more successful Baṣran school.[111] Could we then have to do with a piece of Baghdādī Muʿtazilite doctrine? A quotation from the Baghdādī Abū 'l-Qāsim al-Balkhī (d. 319/931) given by Ṭūsī in his Koran commentary runs as follows:[112] 'Other people [i.e. people other than the ruler] may only do this [i.e. have recourse to arms in the course of forbidding wrong] when there is no imam, nor anyone appointed by him; when there is one, no one should do this except under conditions of necessity.' The first part of this view was formally irrelevant to the Imāmī situation: it was a matter of faith that there was an imam, whether he was present or

107 Thus Murtaḍā does not mention it in his *Jumal* or *Muqaddima*, and Ṭūsī omits it in his *Jumal*.

108 That the various terms employed by the scholars (see above, notes 92–9) refer to the imam seems clear from such equivalences as that in Ṭūsī's discussion of the execution of the *ḥadd* punishments between *sulṭān al-zamān al-manṣūb min qibal Allāh* and *al-imām* (*Nihāya*, 300.19). There has been some dispute as to whether the Imāmī jurists did or did not use some of these terms to refer to a just ruler who was not the imam (see N. Calder, 'Legitimacy and accommodation in Safavid Iran: the juristic theory of Muḥammad Bāqir al-Sabzavārī (d. 1090/1679)', *Iran*, 25 (1987), 91f., 104 nn. 21f., with discussion of other views, including that of Madelung; above, note 96; also Sachedina, *Just ruler*, 103, and, in the context of *al-amr bi'l-maʿrūf*, S. A. Arjomand, *The shadow of God and the hidden Imam*, Chicago and London 1984, 62). Calder takes the rather isolated view that in the usage of the jurists these terms refer only to the imam; on the basis of the limited body of texts considered here, I would tend to agree with him.

109 McDermott aptly characterises Mufīd's doctrine of *al-amr bi'l-maʿrūf* as expressed in his *Awā'il al-maqālāt* as 'mild' (*Mufīd*, 279).

110 See above, note 52, for the rather marginal tradition that is the only exception known to me.

111 McDermott, *Mufīd*, 4f., 396.

112 Ṭūsī, *Tibyān*, 2:549.22 (to Q3:104) (cf. above, ch. 9, note 23), whence Abū 'l-Futūḥ-i Rāzī, *Rawḍ*, 3:141.16. Rāzī's rendering includes the phrase *bī dastūrī-i imām*; this may be his own addition, or it may represent a reference to the permission of the imam which has dropped out of our text of the *Tibyān*. Note that Balkhī's view seems not to have been the only one among the Baghdādī Muʿtazilites (see above, ch. 9, note 39, on Rummānī).

not. It is the second part that may represent the source of the Imāmī doctrine.[113] Baṣran Muʿtazilite doctrine, by contrast, goes no further than the view that in such a context it is better to have recourse to the imam, if there is one.[114] Supposing that Baghdādī Muʿtazilism was indeed the source of the doctrine, the next question would be whether it was imported into Imāmism by Mufīd himself, or had already been received at an earlier stage.[115] Hostile sources frequently say that the Imāmīs (or Rāfiḍīs) denied that forbidding wrong could be performed in the absence of their imam;[116] we can take such claims to be polemical misstatements of the doctrine of the imam's permission. For what it is worth, none of these testimonies seems to be old enough to indicate that the doctrine antedated Mufīd.

3. *Reason and revelation*

A third element, which is likely to belong to the Baṣran Muʿtazilite heritage, is the discussion of the basis of the obligation: is it founded in both reason and revelation, or in revelation alone?[117] For the Baghdādī view of

[113] This may help to explain the difficulty we encounter when we ask whether the jurists are referring to an absent imam or to a present usurper. The language they are using would derive from a tradition that was concerned with an imam who, if he existed at all, was present.

[114] See above, ch. 9, notes 99, 148. The passage in Zamakhsharī's Koran commentary (*Kashshāf*, 1:398.5) is taken up by Rāwandī (*Fiqh al-Qurʾān*, 1:359.7).

[115] It is unfortunate that we have no information as to the views of the fourth/tenth-century jurists (and theologians) Ibn Abī ʿAqīl and Ibn al-Junayd on *al-amr biʾl-maʿrūf* (for these scholars, see H. Modarressi Tabātabāʾi, *An introduction to Shīʿī law*, London 1984, 35–9). Their contemporary Isḥāq ibn Wahb in one passage discusses performance of the duty with the tongue, whip and sword, the latter to be used against various armed malefactors (*muqātilūn*, *bughāt*, *māriqūn*), with no mention of the imam's permission (*Burhān*, 276.2). However, this author is too literary in his interests, and too prone to use Sunnī materials (see above, note 40), for his silence to be significant. In another passage he discusses the ways in which the common people (*raʿiyya*) may get above themselves and need to be curbed by the ruler and his vizier; one such case is when they undertake *al-amr biʾl-maʿrūf* without having received the permission of their ruler (*sulṭān*) to do so (*ibid.*, 422.8). The whole discussion in this passage is, however, political rather than juridical in character.

[116] This has been noted by Madelung ('Amr be maʿrūf', 995a). For relatively early authors making such allegations, see Mānkdīm, *Taʿlīq*, 148.1, 741.6; Māwardī (d. 450/1058), *Adab al-dunyā waʾl-dīn*, ed. M. al-Saqqā, Cairo 1973, 102.21 (in the context of wrongdoing by a group, without naming the sect); Muwaffaq al-Shajarī, *Iḥāṭa*, f. 137a.17 (speaking of *al-amr biʾl-maʿrūf* by deed, with mention of the *sharṭ al-imām*; and cf. *ibid.*, f. 136b.21); Ibn Ḥazm, *Fiṣal*, 4:171.12; Abū Yaʿlā, *Muʿtamad*, 194 §350; Juwaynī, *Irshād*, 368.5; Jishumī, *ʿUyūn*, f. 66a.4, and *Sharḥ*, f. 265a.10; Farrazādhī, *Taʿlīq*, f. 154b.14; Ghazzālī, *Iḥyāʾ*, 2:288.27. Jishumī also offers a more graphic formulation: 'The Rāfiḍa hold that it is not obligatory until the *qāʾim* comes forth' (*Sharḥ*, f. 264b.7). Cf. above, ch. 9, notes 63, 96–8.

[117] See Madelung, 'Amr be maʿrūf', 995a; also Sachedina, *Just ruler*, 143f. No one, of course, is suggesting that the duty is founded in reason alone.

the matter we have only the position of Rummānī (d. 384/994), who inclined to the rationalist side.[118] The standard Baṣran position seems to have been that the duty is known only by revelation, except in cases reducible to self-interest.[119] There was, however, excellent precedent for the view that the duty is known by reason as well as revelation, for such had been the doctrine of Abū ʿAlī (d. 303/916), in contrast to his son Abū Hāshim (d. 321/933); and at a later date Abū ʾl-Ḥusayn al-Baṣrī (d. 436/1044) is said to have inclined to this view.[120] Confronted with this divergence, the Imāmī scholars tended to opt for the standard view.[121] It appears first in works of Murtaḍā;[122] he is followed by Abū ʾl-Ṣalāḥ,[123] Ṭūsī both in his doctrinal works[124] and in his Koran commentary,[125] Ibn Abī ʾl-Majd,[126] Ibn Idrīs,[127] Naṣīr al-Dīn al-Ṭūsī (672/1274),[128] and the ʿAllāma

118 See above, ch. 9, note 37. 119 See above, ch. 9, 206.

120 See above, ch. 9, note 25 for Abū ʿAlī, and note 65 for Abū ʾl-Ḥusayn.

121 Several of them, however, do not explicitly raise the issue: Mufīd, Sallār, Ibn al-Barrāj, Ibn Ḥamza and the Muḥaqqiq. (I am not sure on what basis Madelung states that the Muḥaqqiq held the revelationist view, see his 'Amr be maʿrūf', 995a.) Zihdāzī (or Zihdārī) (early eighth/fourteenth century) in his commentary on the *Sharāʾiʿ* merely notes the fact of the dispute, and refers the reader to the science of *kalām* (*Īḍāḥ taraddudāt al-Sharāʾiʿ*, ed. M. al-Rajāʾī, Qumm 1408, 1:263.6; for this work, see Modarressi, *Introduction*, 67).

122 Murtaḍā, *Jumal*, 39.15; Murtaḍā, *Dhakhīra*, 553.8. In the latter Murtaḍā devotes a couple of pages to the issue, stating and refuting arguments for a rational basis. As usual I make no attempt to analyse such arguments, but two of them should be noted for reference below: the argument (in favour of a rational basis) that the duty is *luṭf* (*ibid.*, 553.15, refuted *ibid.*, 555.6); and the argument (against such a basis) that, if rational, the duty would be incumbent on God, with intolerable consequences (*ibid.*, 554.1, 554.5). For the first, cf. Mānkdīm, *Taʿlīq*, 742.16; for the second, *ibid.*, 742.12.

123 Abū ʾl-Ṣalāḥ, *Kāfī*, 264.9. The two arguments just noted for Murtaḍā reappear in this presentation.

124 Ṭūsī, *Iqtiṣād*, 146.15 (stating that this is the view of the majority of *mutakallimūn* and *fuqahāʾ*, and endorsing it as correct); Ṭūsī, *Tamhīd*, 301.5 (again clearly stating his preference for the view). Madelung's statement of Ṭūsī's position ('Amr be maʿrūf', 995a) is thus to be modified. In the *Tamhīd*, Ṭūsī goes on to reproduce Murtaḍā's account of the arguments for and against the rationalist view, though not accepting all of it (*ibid.*, 301.11; he mentions his source as the *Dhakhīra*, *ibid.*, 302.13). In the *Iqtiṣād*, he makes a general statement that he has found no good arguments for the rationalist position, but refers to his *Sharḥ al-Jumal* (i.e. the *Tamhīd*) for the details (*Iqtiṣād*, 147.2).

125 Ṭūsī, *Tibyān*, 2:549.11 (to Q3:104), 565.16 (to Q3:114), 5:299.19 (to Q9:71). What Ṭūsī says is repeated by Abū ʾl-Futūḥ-i Rāzī (*Rawḍ*, 3:141.9 (to Q3:104)), Ṭabrisī (*Majmaʿ*, 1:484.4 (to Q3:104)), and Rāwandī (*Fiqh al-Qurʾān*, 1:357.14 (to Q22:41, but taken from Ṭūsī's commentary to Q3:104), 362.10 (to Q3:114)). The formulations that appear here differ from those found in the *kalām* works of Ṭūsī and others, and may represent a different tradition. 126 Ibn Abī ʾl-Majd, *Ishāra*, 146.3.

127 Ibn Idrīs, *Sarāʾir*, 2:21.15. Here again, Ibn Idrīs takes over Ṭūsī's account from the *Iqtiṣād*; he rearranges it a bit, inserts statements of his own view and of Murtaḍā's, and draws attention to Ṭūsī's second thoughts.

128 Naṣīr al-Dīn al-Ṭūsī (d. 672/1274), *Tajrīd al-iʿtiqād*, *apud* al-ʿAllāma al-Ḥillī (d. 726/1325), *Kashf al-murād*, Beirut 1979, 455.2.

in some of his works.[129] Yet two of these scholars also pronounce in favour of the view that the duty has a basis in reason: Ṭūsī[130] and the ʿAllāma.[131] The range of opinion thus perpetuates that already established in Baṣran Muʿtazilism.

4. *The doctrine of divisibility*

A fourth element, which possesses a certain diagnostic interest, can be labelled the doctrine of divisibility. According to this doctrine in its standard form, right can be divided into the obligatory and the supererogatory, with the corollary that it is obligatory to command obligatory right, and supererogatory to command supererogatory right; wrong, by contrast, cannot be divided in such a way, so that it is obligatory to forbid all wrong without distinction. This doctrine first appears in Imāmī sources with Murtaḍā, who never fails to make these points.[132] He is followed in this by Ṭūsī,[133] Ibn al-Barrāj,[134] Ibn Abī ʾl-Majd,[135] Abū ʾl-Futūḥ-i Rāzī (first half of the sixth/twelfth century),[136] Rāwandī (d. 573/1177f.),[137] Ibn Idrīs,[138] Naṣīr al-Dīn al-Ṭūsī,[139] the Muḥaqqiq,[140]

[129] In two of them he clearly pronounces the revelationist view the stronger (*aqwā*) (ʿAllāma, *Taḥrīr*, 1:527.24; *Muntahā*, 992.37), and he is still more uncompromising in his *Nahj al-mustarshidīn* (*apud* Miqdād al-Suyūrī (d. 826/1423), *Irshād al-ṭālibīn*, ed. M. al-Rajāʾī, Qumm 1405, 380.13). In another the text is most easily read to imply the same view (ʿAllāma, *Tadhkira*, 1:458.25). Madelung's statement of the ʿAllāma's position ('Amr be maʿrūf', 995a) is thus to be modified.

[130] Ṭūsī, *Iqtiṣād*, 147.9; Ṭūsī, *Tamhīd*, 302.14. Ṭūsī here develops the *luṭf* argument, drawing from the contrary an unacceptable consequence; he presents this as his strong opinion (*yaqwā fī nafsī*). Ḥimmaṣī, without offering a clear statement of his own view, seems to side with Ṭūsī here (*Munqidh*, 2:213.17).

[131] ʿAllāma, *Qawāʿid*, 1:524.3 (declaring the rationalist view the stronger); ʿAllāma, *Tabṣira*, 1:298.2 (stating only the rationalist view); ʿAllāma, *Mukhtalaf*, 4:471.3 (pronouncing Ṭūsī's second thoughts more plausible (*al-aqrab*)). In the *Mukhtalaf*, as in other works such as the *Tadhkira* and the *Muntahā*, the ʿAllāma explicates Murtaḍā's argument (stated in a form that has little in common with that found in the *Dhakhīra*) that, if based on reason, the duty would bind God; in the *Mukhtalaf* he then goes on to indicate that he does not find this argument persuasive (*fīhi naẓar*), and to adduce the argument from *luṭf* in favour of 'our' position (*ibid.*, 4:472.3; cf. also his *Ajwibat al-masāʾil al-Muhannāʾiyya*, Qumm 1401, 166.7). Another version of this explication appears in the commentary on the *Qawāʿid* written by the ʿAllāma's son (Fakhr al-Muḥaqqiqīn (d. 771/1370), *Īḍāḥ al-fawāʾid*, n.p. 1387–9, 1:397.22); he also confirms that his father held the rationalist view, with which he himself disagrees (*ibid.*, 398.15).

[132] Murtaḍā, *Dhakhīra*, 553.4; Murtaḍā, *Jumal*, 39.12; Murtaḍā, *Muqaddima*, 82.6 (this last in a three-line account of the duty).

[133] Ṭūsī, *Iqtiṣād*, 148.4; Ṭūsī, *Jumal*, 160.8; Ṭūsī, *Tamhīd*, 301.7; Ṭūsī, *Tibyān*, 2:549.3; likewise Ḥimmaṣī, *Munqidh*, 2:209.9.

[134] Ibn al-Barrāj, *Muhadhdhab*, 1:340.12.

[135] Ibn Abī ʾl-Majd, *Ishāra*, 146.13.

[136] Abū ʾl-Futūḥ-i Rāzī, *Rawḍ*, 3:141.3.

[137] Rāwandī, *Fiqh al-Qurʾān*, 1:356.16.

[138] Ibn Idrīs, *Sarāʾir*, 2:22.19. This passage, like most of his account, is lifted from Ṭūsī's *Iqtiṣād*.

[139] Naṣīr al-Dīn al-Ṭūsī, *Tajrīd*, *apud* ʿAllāma, *Kashf*, 455.2.

[140] Muḥaqqiq, *Sharāʾiʿ*, 1:341.12; also his *Mukhtaṣar*, 1:139.3.

and the ʿAllāma.[141] A few scholars subscribe to the division of right, but not to the indivisibility of wrong. Thus Ibn Ḥamza divides wrong in the same way as right,[142] while Abū ʾl-Ṣalāḥ advances an equivalent distinction without recourse to the term 'wrong'.[143] Sallār divides right, but does not discuss the question whether wrong is divisible.[144] We can be confident that the standard view is a piece of Baṣran Muʿtazilite doctrine. The mainstream Imāmī view does not appear before Murtaḍā, and is identical with that set out by Mānkdīm (d. 425/1034) and others;[145] Mānkdīm also tells us explicitly that the distinction between the two kinds of right was an innovation of the Baṣran scholarch Abū ʿAlī al-Jubbāʾī (d. 303/916).[146]

5. *Individual or collective?*

A fifth element is the discussion of the question whether the duty is an individual or a collective obligation.[147] This is another area in which it is likely that much of what the Imāmī scholars have to say derives from the Baṣran Muʿtazilite tradition, though this cannot be proved. The issue is, of course, widely discussed among the Islamic sects and schools, the usual conclusion being that the duty is collective: once somebody undertakes it, others cease to be obligated. This is likewise the mainstream Muʿtazilite view.[148] But in

[141] ʿAllāma, *Irshād*, 1:352.12; ʿAllāma, *Nahj al-mustarshidīn*, *apud* Miqdād, *Irshād*, 380.12; ʿAllāma, *Qawāʿid*, 1:524.7; ʿAllāma, *Tabṣira*, 1:299.1; ʿAllāma, *Tadhkira*, 1:458.15; ʿAllāma, *Taḥrīr*, 1:157.15; ʿAllāma, *Muntahā*, 992.2. In his *Mukhtalaf* (4:474.1), the ʿAllāma adduces the views of Ṭūsī (for the indivisibility of wrong) and Ibn Ḥamza (for its divisibility), and pronounces in favour of Ṭūsī's view on the ground that wrong is evil by definition. He is clearly aware of the desire for symmetry that motivates the contrary view; in this connection he finds Abū ʾl-Ṣalāḥ's formulation particularly neat (see below, note 143).

[142] He says that to forbid a wrong (*munkar*) which is forbidden (*maḥẓūr*) is obligatory, while to forbid one that is only disapproved (*makrūh*) is merely recommended (*mandūb*) (Ibn Ḥamza, *Wasīla*, 207.7). For what may be a contemporary Zaydī parallel, see ʿA. M. Zayd, *Tayyārāt Muʿtazilat al-Yaman fī ʾl-qarn al-sādis al-hijrī*, Ṣanʿāʾ 1997, 294.12, reporting the view of Sulaymān al-Muḥallī from manuscript (this work was drawn to my attention by Bernard Haykel). This author was a Muṭarrifī (see EI^2, art. 'Muṭarrifiyya' (W. Madelung), with further references).

[143] He says that it is obligatory to forbid what is evil (*qabuḥa*), but merely commendable (*mandūb*) to forbid what is only disapproved (*karuha*) (Abū ʾl-Ṣalāḥ, *Kāfī*, 264.2). Similarly Yaḥyā ibn Saʿīd states that forbidding what it would be better (*awlā*) to abstain from is supererogatory (Yaḥyā ibn Saʿīd, *Jāmiʿ*, 239.13). Compare the account of the issue given by the Zaydī Muʿtazilite Muḥallī (d. 652/1254f.), in the course of which he observes that one may 'forbid' (though not in the literal sense) something that is not actually wrong (*munkar*), such as eating with the left hand (*ʿUmda*, 291.20).

[144] Sallār, *Marāsim*, 260.5.

[145] See above, ch. 9, 213f.; also Muwaffaq, *Iḥāṭa*, f. 136a.21, and Muḥallī, *ʿUmda*, 291.17.

[146] See above, ch. 9, notes 26f.

[147] For a brief account of the Imāmī positions on the question against the wider background, see Madelung, 'Amr be maʿrūf', 995a.

[148] For Baghdādī Muʿtazilism, see above, ch. 9, note 38, on Rummānī. For Baṣran Muʿtazilism, see above, ch. 9, 216; also ch. 10, note 109 (for later Zaydī authorities). For the link between this doctrinal question and the interpretation of Q3:104, see above, ch. 2, note 19.

Muʿtazilism, as elsewhere, the individual view found occasional adherents. One of them, it seems, was none less than Abū ʿAlī.[149]

Among the Imāmī scholars, as might be expected, the mainstream view that the duty is collective was well represented. It is adopted by both Mufīd,[150] representing the Baghdādī Muʿtazilite tradition, and Murtaḍā,[151] representing the Baṣran, and accordingly it does not lack followers: Abū ʾl-Ṣalāḥ,[152] Ibn Idrīs,[153] Yaḥyā ibn Saʿīd,[154] and, with relative single-mindedness, the ʿAllāma.[155] Ṭūsī, however, went against the mainstream by consistently favouring the individual view.[156] His prestige ensured this view a considerable popularity among subsequent scholars. It was adopted by Ibn Abī ʾl-Majd,[157] Ibn Ḥamza,[158] the Muḥaqqiq,[159] Zihdāzī,[160] and those who followed in the wake of Ṭūsī's Koran commentary;[161] Ibn al-Barrāj devised a compromise position according to which the duty was sometimes collective and sometimes individual.[162] Ibn Idrīs, an ever-ready critic of Ṭūsī, would seem to have been the first to break with his view.

What evidence is there to link either position as found in the Imāmī sources with Baṣran Muʿtazilism? In the case of the individual view, there is none: we have Ṭūsī's argument for his position,[163] but no non-Imāmī

[149] See above, ch. 2, note 17, and ch. 9, note 33. [150] Mufīd, *Awāʾil al-maqālāt*, 98.4.
[151] Murtaḍā, *Dhakhīra*, 560.10. [152] Abū ʾl-Ṣalāḥ, *Kāfī*, 267.3.
[153] Ibn Idrīs, *Sarāʾir*, 2:22.17 (stating the collective position to be the more prevalent (*al-aẓhar*) among 'our companions').
[154] Yaḥyā ibn Saʿīd, *Jāmiʿ*, 239.10 (with mention of the contrary view, *ibid.*, 239.19).
[155] In six of his works he comes down squarely on the collective side of the fence (ʿAllāma, *Mukhtalaf*, 4:473.9; ʿAllāma, *Muntahā*, 993.10; ʿAllāma, *Nahj al-mustarshidīn*, *apud* Miqdād, *Irshād*, 381.10; ʿAllāma, *Qawāʿid*, 1:524.3; ʿAllāma, *Tabṣira*, 1:298.2; ʿAllāma, *Taḥrīr*, 1:157.25). In three works he does not seem to offer a clear-cut opinion (*Irshād*, 1:352.12; *Ajwiba*, 171f. no. 22; *Tadhkira*, 1:458.31).
[156] Ṭūsī, *Iqtiṣād*, 147.15, and cf. 151.1; Ṭūsī, *Jumal*, 160.7; Ṭūsī, *Nihāya*, 299.9; Ṭūsī, *Tamhīd*, 301.4, and cf. 301.23, 306.3; Ṭūsī, *Tibyān*, 2:549.10 (to Q3:104), 5:300.1 (to Q9:71). Ḥimmaṣī explicitly endorses Ṭūsī's view (*Munqidh*, 2:220.13).
[157] Ibn Abī ʾl-Majd, *Ishāra*, 146.3. [158] Ibn Ḥamza, *Wasīla*, 207.2.
[159] Muḥaqqiq, *Mukhtaṣar*, 139.2; Muḥaqqiq, *Sharāʾiʿ*, 1:341.9 (both endorsing the individual view as more in accord with basic principles (*ashbah*)).
[160] Zihdāzī, *Īḍāḥ*, 1:263.5 (endorsing it as stronger (*aqwā*)).
[161] Abū ʾl-Futūḥ-i Rāzī, *Rawḍ*, 3:140.20, 141.8 (to Q3:104); Rāwandī, *Fiqh al-Qurʾān*, 1:357.4 (to Q3:104), and cf. 358.14 (in the commentary to Q3:110). Ṭabrisī does not commit himself to Ṭūsī's view in his commentary to Q3:104 as we have it (*Majmaʿ*, 1:483.23, 484.3), but he follows Ṭūsī to Q9:71 (*ibid.*, 3:50.7).
[162] Ibn al-Barrāj, *Muhadhdhab*, 1:340.3. His view is cited by the ʿAllāma (*Mukhtalaf*, 4:473.12), and anonymously by Rāwandī (*Fiqh al-Qurʾān*, 1:357.5). Roughly, he says that the duty is collective in a case in which someone performs the duty successfully, with the result that others cease to be obligated; but it is tied to individuals in a case in which someone tries but fails, and no other individual acting alone discharges it, with the result that it becomes an individual duty obligating everyone equally – until such time as the object is achieved. Cf. the view of the Ḥanbalite Ibn Ḥamdān (d. 695/1295) (see above, ch. 6, note 122).
[163] Viz. the generality (*ʿumūm*) of the relevant Koranic verses and traditions (Ṭūsī, *Iqtiṣād*,

Muʿtazilite material to compare it with. In the case of the collective view we are better served. There is a much-repeated utilitarian argument for this position which recurs in various wordings. According to this argument, the object of the duty is to get results – to bring it about that the right thing happens and the wrong thing does not. If someone undertakes the duty successfully, the object is thereby attained; consequently, it makes no sense for others to continue to be obligated. This argument is advanced in a number of Imāmī sources[164] and reported in others.[165] It is also attested for non-Imāmī Baṣran Muʿtazilism, in the accounts of Mānkdīm and others;[166] thus despite the lack of an adequate Baghdādī Muʿtazilite control, it is a reasonable hypothesis that we have here a piece of Baṣran argumentation adopted by the Imāmīs.[167]

The significance of the disagreement is not immediately obvious from these texts.[168] On the one hand, those who consider the duty a collective one concede that in some circumstances it becomes individual.[169] In this way, the ʿAllāma argues, the collective view is no different from the compromise put forward by Ibn al-Barrāj.[170] And on the other hand, the individualists are not denying that the obligation ceases when someone else has successfully performed it. The defining characteristic of an individual duty is that one's obligation does not lapse merely because someone else undertakes it,[171] and Ṭūsī explicitly subscribes to this.[172] But once the duty has been performed successfully, there is no longer a wrong to right, and hence

147.16; Ṭūsī, *Tamhīd*, 301.5). In the *Iqtiṣād*, Ṭūsī goes on to give his Koranic proof-texts (Q3:104, Q3:110, Q31:17), but remarks that the innumerable traditions would take too long to quote. In his accounts of Ṭūsī's argument, the ʿAllāma generously supplies the traditions (see particularly *Mukhtalaf*, 4:472.14); but it seems quite likely that he chose them himself.

164 Murtaḍā, *Dhakhīra*, 560.12; Abū 'l-Ṣalāḥ, *Kāfī*, 267.3; ʿAllāma, *Muntahā*, 993.10; cf. also the reworking of the idea in Ibn al-Barrāj, *Muhadhdhab*, 1:340.3. In the version of Murtaḍā and in the parallel in Ibn al-Barrāj (*ibid.*, 340.10), the passage continues with a qualification about the ability to perform the duty (*tamakkun*).

165 Ṭūsī, *Iqtiṣād*, 150.18; Ṭūsī, *Tamhīd*, 305.24; ʿAllāma, *Mukhtalaf*, 4:473.7; ʿAllāma, *Tadhkira*, 1:458.32. The qualification regarding *tamakkun* appears in both of Ṭūsī's versions.

166 For Mānkdīm and the school of Abū 'l-Ḥusayn, see above, ch. 9, 216.

167 To this a rather peripheral borrowing can be added. In his commentary to Q3:104, Zamakhsharī supports the view that the *min* of Q3:104 is partitive on the ground that only someone who knows how to go about the duty can perform it properly (*Kashshāf*, 1:396.8). This argument is borrowed by Ṭabrisī (*Jawāmiʿ*, 1:230.20, see above, ch. 2, note 21), and then refuted by Rāwandī (*Fiqh al-Qur'ān*, 1:358.14).

168 Madelung describes the individual view as 'heightening the responsibility of every Muslim' for the duty ('Amr be maʿrūf', 995a).

169 See Murtaḍā, *Dhakhīra*, 560.10; Abū 'l-Ṣalāḥ, *Kāfī*, 267.3; and the reporting in Ṭūsī, *Iqtiṣād*, 150.18, and his *Tamhīd*, 305.24.

170 ʿAllāma, *Mukhtalaf*, 4:473.16.

171 Cf. the remark of Jaṣṣāṣ (d. 370/981) that 'if it were not a collective obligation, it would not cease to obligate the rest when someone undertakes it' (*Aḥkām*, 2:29.25).

172 Ṭūsī, *Tibyān*, 2:548.13 (to Q3:104); similarly Rāwandī, *Fiqh al-Qur'ān*, 1:356.14 (also to Q3:104).

no continuing obligation. What, then, is the point at issue? An answer is to be found only in later texts.[173]

6. *The conditions of obligation*

Only one major ingredient of these accounts remains to be discussed: the set of conditions (*shurūṭ, sharāʾiṭ*) under which forbidding wrong is held to be obligatory. A convenient point of reference, and the root of most subsequent accounts, is the following list given by Murtaḍā:[174]

1 The person who proposes to carry out the duty must know that the supposed offence is indeed wrong (*ʿilm al-munkir bi-kawnihi munkaran*; we may designate this condition 'knowledge of law').

2 He has to have evidence that the offence is going to continue in the future (*an yaḥṣul hunāka amārat al-istimrār ʿalā ʾl-munkar*; 'evidence of persistence').

3 He must consider it possible that his attempt will work (*tajwīz al-munkir taʾthīr inkārihi fī ʾl-iqlāʿ ʿan al-munkar*; 'possibility of efficacy').[175]

4 He must not thereby place himself in mortal danger (*an yartafiʿ khawfuhu ʿalā nafsihi idhā ankar al-munkar*; 'no mortal danger').

5 Nor must he risk his property (*an lā yakhāf ʿalā mālihi matā ankar al-munkar*; 'no danger to property').

6 His action against the wrong must not itself be an occasion of something evil happening (*an lā yakūn fī inkārihi ʾl-munkar mafsada*; 'no untoward side-effects').

Most subsequent Imāmī lists of conditions can readily be seen to be variants of this six-condition schema. Sometimes the schema is repeated without significant change: the same six conditions are given in the same order by Ṭūsī in his longer theological works,[176] and by Ibn Idrīs.[177] More

[173] See below, 290–2. Zihdāzī, who pronounces for Ṭūsī's view, disputes the inference that the (continued) obligation of others is pointless (*wa-namnaʿ khuluww taklīf al-bāqīn ʿan al-fāʾida*, *Īḍāḥ*, 1:263.5); but he does not enlarge on the question.

[174] Murtaḍā, *Dhakhīra*, 555.15. A detailed exposition follows there.

[175] Murtaḍā notes that some replace this condition with one requiring that he should think that it actually will work (*ẓann al-munkir anna inkārahu yuʾaththir*).

[176] Ṭūsī, *Iqtiṣād*, 148.7; Ṭūsī, *Tamhīd*, 302.18. In the first, condition (3) is given with *yaẓunn* and *yujawwiz* as alternatives; in the second, Ṭūsī follows Murtaḍā. In both works he also reproduces the detailed exposition given by Murtaḍā in a pretty similar form.

[177] Ibn Idrīs, *Sarāʾir*, 2:23.2, taken as usual from Ṭūsī's *Iqtiṣād*.

often, the number of conditions is reduced by amalgamating some or all of conditions (4), (5) and (6); Murtaḍā himself is said to have held that an amalgamation of all three was possible.[178] Thus Ibn Abī ʾl-Majd amalgamates (4) and (5),[179] as does Ibn Ḥamza;[180] the Muḥaqqiq amalgamates all three to produce a four-condition schema,[181] and the ʿAllāma in general follows him.[182] Occasionally the process is taken even further: in addition to such amalgamation, condition (2) is dropped. This is seen in one work of Murtaḍā,[183] in one of Ṭūsī,[184] and elsewhere.[185] The elements of diction

[178] Ṭūsī states that Murtaḍā often said this in his teaching (*tadrīs*), and himself endorses it as the stronger view (*al-aqwā*) (*Tamhīd*, 302.22; in his *Iqtiṣād*, 148.10, he makes the same point, but without reference to Murtaḍā, and this is copied by Ibn Idrīs in his *Sarāʾir*, 2:23.5).

[179] Ibn Abī ʾl-Majd, *Ishāra*, 146.8. Since he does not number his conditions, the change is minimal.

[180] Ibn Ḥamza, *Wasīla*, 207.2. With regard to (6), he stipulates that carrying out *al-amr biʾl-maʿrūf* should not lead to a greater evil (*lā yuʾaddī ilā akthar minhu*); for this compare Mānkdīm, *Taʿlīq*, 143.3 (*maḍarra aʿẓam minhu*), and below, ch. 14, notes 33, 37.

[181] Muḥaqqiq, *Sharāʾiʿ*, 1:342.2 (where the inclusion of mortal danger and danger to property under untoward side-effects is spelled out); Muḥaqqiq, *Mukhtaṣar*, 139.5 (where it is assumed). He also reverses the order of conditions (2) and (3). The account of the 'possibility of efficacy' condition in the *Sharāʾiʿ* goes on to say that if one has good reason to believe (*law ghalaba ʿalā ẓannihi*) or knows that it will not work, one has no obligation; this would suggest that *jawwaza* implies something more than a remote possibility of success.

[182] ʿAllāma, *Irshād*, 1:352.13; ʿAllāma, *Muntahā*, 993.12; ʿAllāma, *Qawāʿid*, 1:524.10; ʿAllāma, *Tabṣira*, 1:298.2; ʿAllāma, *Tadhkira*, 1:458.33; ʿAllāma, *Taḥrīr*, 1:157.27. The topic is not treated in the *Mukhtalaf*, which would indicate that the ʿAllāma found no differences of opinion worth discussing. The ʿAllāma usually adopts the Muḥaqqiq's reversal of conditions (2) and (3), and in some of his works (the *Muntahā*, *Tadhkira* and *Taḥrīr*) expands on the 'possibility of efficacy' condition in the same way as the Muḥaqqiq (see the previous note). The conditions mentioned by Madelung in his account of Imāmī views are the second and fourth of this four-condition schema ('Amr be maʿrūf', 995b). In his *al-Bāb al-ḥādī ʿashar*, however, the ʿAllāma presents a four-condition schema which does not reverse conditions (2) and (3), and gives a deviant formulation of (2): the right or wrong has to be something that will actually happen (*mimmā sa-yaqaʿān*) (*apud* Miqdād al-Suyūrī (d. 826/1423), *al-Nāfiʿ yawm al-ḥashr*, Beirut 1988, 127.21; cf. above, ch. 9, note 71); while in two works he espouses a three-condition schema (see below, note 185).

[183] Murtaḍā, *Jumal*, 39.18 (with implied amalgamation of (4) and (5)). Murtaḍā's shortest account of the duty gives no list of conditions, mentioning only that there should be no untoward side-effects (*mafsada*) (*Muqaddima*, 82.5).

[184] Ṭūsī, *Jumal*, 160.11 (with the amalgamation of all three spelled out), whence doubtless Rāwandī, *Fiqh al-Qurʾān*, 1:358.19.

[185] This schema is followed by Naṣīr al-Dīn al-Ṭūsī (*Tajrīd*, *apud* ʿAllāma, *Kashf*, 455.18), and hence by the ʿAllāma in his commentary thereto (*ibid.*, 455.19). More surprisingly, the ʿAllāma adopts the same schema in his *Nahj al-mustarshidīn* (*apud* Miqdād, *Irshād*, 381.6). It also appears in a work likely to be by ʿImād al-Dīn Ṭabarī (*fl.* second half of the seventh/thirteenth century) (*Muʿtaqad al-Imāmiyya* (in Persian), ed. M. T. Dānishpazhūh, Tehran 1961, 340.12). It is conceivable that Ashʿarite influence could have played some part in the appearance of the three-condition schema (cf. below, ch. 13, 351).

shared by all these accounts confirm their close genetic links.[186] Their general origin is not far to seek: Murtaḍā was a Baṣran Muʿtazilite, and these accounts show a broad family resemblance to those of Mānkdīm on the one hand,[187] and (more distantly) of the school of Abū ʾl-Ḥusayn on the other.[188]

There are nevertheless Imāmī accounts that stand outside this tradition. What they have in common is that being able to perform the duty is stipulated as a condition for obligation. Though not found in the sources considered so far,[189] this feature is in fact so widespread that in itself it has little genetic significance.[190] Most of the accounts exhibiting it do not present a formal list of conditions at all.[191] The two clear exceptions are Abū ʾl-Ṣalāḥ and Yaḥyā ibn Saʿīd. Abū ʾl-Ṣalāḥ presents a list of five conditions which in

186 Note particularly the use of the term *istimrār* in most formulations of condition (2); it is not common in non-Imāmī sources, which tend to use very different wordings to make the same or a similar point (for exceptions, see above, ch. 6, notes 132f., and Muwaffaq, *Iḥāṭa*, ff. 137b.8, 138a.19 (*yastamirr*)). For the versions lacking condition (2), the use of *jawwaza* in condition (3) constitutes a comparable linkage.

187 See above, ch. 9, 207–9. In terms of Murtaḍā's conditions, Mānkdīm's list runs (1), (2), (6), (3), (4+5). Here Mānkdīm formulates condition (2) in terms of the offence being *ḥāḍir*; condition (6) in terms of greater evil; condition (3) in terms of knowing or having good reason to believe; and he qualifies condition (4+5) (it depends on the person).

188 See above, ch. 9, 222f. Among the Imāmīs, only Ḥimmaṣī reproduces this schema, albeit with some modification (*Munqidh*, 2:216.1–220.6; see above, ch. 9, note 153 for details). In other Imāmī accounts, the structure is of course very different from that which characterises the school of Abū ʾl-Ḥusayn, and there are divergences in the conditions that go beyond wording. There is, however, an element in common as between one of the accounts reflecting the doctrine of Abū ʾl-Ḥusayn and those of Murtaḍā and Ṭūsī: the impropriety of taking action against what one does not know to be wrong is compared to that of asserting what one does not know to be true (Ibn Abī ʾl-Ḥadīd, *Sharḥ*, 19:309.1; Murtaḍā, *Dhakhīra*, 555.21 (for *yaʿmaluhu* read *yaʿlamuhu* twice); Ṭūsī, *Iqtiṣād*, 148.13; Ṭūsī, *Tamhīd*, 302.25).

189 Ibn Abī ʾl-Majd is an exception: after setting out his list of conditions, he goes on to say that when they are satisfied, and given *istiṭāʿa* and *mukna*, there is obligation with the hand, tongue and heart (*Ishāra*, 146.9). The other accounts deriving from Murtaḍā's present the list as complete in itself.

190 For its appearance in non-Imāmī Muʿtazilite sources, see above, ch. 9, note 42. For its appearance in Sunnī sources, see for example Abū Yaʿlā, *Muʿtamad*, 194 §350; Ghazzālī, *Iḥyāʾ*, 2:292.10.

191 So Ibn Bābawayh, *Hidāya*, 11.8; Mufīd, *Muqniʿa*, 809.6; Sallār, *Marāsim*, 260.4; Ṭūsī, *Nihāya*, 299.10, 300.1; Ṭūsī, *Tibyān*, 2:549.16 (to Q3:104) (whence Rāwandī, *Fiqh al-Qurʾān*, 1:357.20); Ibn al-Barrāj, *Muhadhdhab*, 1:341.4. Cf. also above, note 47, for a formulation ascribed to al-Riḍā. Ibn Qiba (d. not later than 319/931) likewise stresses that obligation depends on being able to perform the duty (*ṭāqa*, *imkān*) (*Naqḍ Kitāb al-ishhād*, *apud* Modarressi, *Crisis and consolidation*, 194.1, 200.18). Rāwandī (*Fiqh al-Qurʾān*, 1:359.5 (to Q3:110)) borrows such a formulation from Zamakhsharī (*Kashshāf*, 1:398.4 (to Q3:104)). Ibn Ṭāwūs (d. 664/1266) tells his son that the devil may seek to persuade him that he is unable to perform the duty (*annaka mā taqdir ʿalā ʾl-inkār*) (*Kashf al-maḥajja*, Najaf 1950, 102.7); the burden of the passage is that one should avoid situations in which the duty to protest is incurred, since these of necessity bring upon one either human or divine displeasure (see Kohlberg, *Ibn Ṭāwūs*, 18f.).

some ways clearly belongs to the same family as Murtaḍā's, and yet in others is notably deviant.[192] The second of his conditions is being able to perform the duty (*al-tamakkun min al-amr wa'l-nahy*). If for the sake of argument we assume that Abū 'l-Ṣalāḥ's set of conditions and Murtaḍā's are equivalent, this would imply that Abū 'l-Ṣalāḥ's second condition is tantamount to Murtaḍā's (4) and (5) – in other words, that to be able to act is to be free of danger.[193] But the assumption could well be wrong: in Yaḥyā ibn Sa'īd's otherwise less interesting set of conditions, a person's being able to perform the duty (*tamakkunuhu min dhālika*) replaces Murtaḍā's possibility of efficacy.[194]

There are also accounts in this group that, without presenting a formal list of conditions, have more to say about the relevant issues. Three in particular share features that set them apart from others in the group, as also from the lists given by Abū 'l-Ṣalāḥ, Murtaḍā and others. All three are found in legal works: those of Mufīd,[195] Ṭūsī[196] and Ibn al-Barrāj.[197] In each case, after stipulating that one must be able to perform the duty,[198] the account goes on to treat danger, and specifies that this can be danger 'now or in the future'.[199] Although there is nothing conceptually

[192] Abū 'l-Ṣalāḥ, *Kāfī*, 265.3. Leaving aside his second condition (which will be discussed in a moment), the order is the same for the four common conditions. Two of them (Murtaḍā's (3) and (6)) use the same terminology (note especially the use of *tajwīz* in condition (3)). The other two, however, use quite different wording. Under (1), he speaks in terms of *ḥusn* and *qubḥ*, rather than *ma'rūf* amd *munkar* (compare the similar usage of Ibn al-Malāḥimī, *Fā'iq*, f. 256b.23; Ibn Abī 'l-Ḥadīd, *Sharḥ*, 19:308.20; Zamakhsharī, *Minhāj*, 78.1; Zamakhsharī, *Kashshāf*, 1:397.13 (to Q3:104)). Under (2), he speaks of having good reason to believe in the occurrence (*wuqū'*) of the evil in the future (compare the use of the same term in the wording of a related condition in the accounts of Ibn Abī 'l-Ḥadīd, *Sharḥ*, 19:309.16, and Zamakhsharī, *Kashshāf*, 1:397.16 (to Q3:104); and cf. Zamakhsharī, *Minhāj*, 77.12, and Ibn al-Malāḥimī, *Fā'iq*, f. 257a.15). Like Murtaḍā, Abū 'l-Ṣalāḥ follows his list with a detailed discussion of the conditions; but for the most part the material is different. At one point (*Kāfī*, 266.1) he reports an argument also adduced by Zamakhsharī (*Kashshāf*, 1:396.12 (to Q3:104), 2:171.25 (to Q7:164); and cf. Zamakhsharī, *Minhāj*, 78.3): it is bad to attempt to perform the duty against collectors of tolls (*aṣḥāb al-ma'āṣir*) because it is futile (Abū 'l-Ṣalāḥ goes on to reject this argument, *Kāfī*, 266.12). All this suggests that he was influenced by the school of Abū 'l-Ḥusayn.

[193] Unfortunately Abū 'l-Ṣalāḥ's treatment of this condition in his subsequent discussion does not help to elucidate it further (*Kāfī*, 260.16).

[194] Yaḥyā ibn Sa'īd, *Jāmi'*, 239.10. Likewise Mufīd's account in his *Muqni'a* distinguishes between being able to perform the duty and absence of danger (*ibid.*, 809.8). Ṭūsī's account in his *Nihāya* at one point distinguishes them (*ibid.*, 299.11), but at another identifies them (*ibid.*, 300.1). Ghazzālī, by way of comparison, interprets being able (*qādir*) to perform the duty to include both absence of danger and expectation of success (*Iḥyā'*, 2:292.13).

[195] Mufīd, *Muqni'a*, 809.6.

[196] Ṭūsī, *Nihāya*, 299.10.

[197] Ibn al-Barrāj, *Muhadhdhab*, 1:341.4.

[198] The terms used are *imkān* (and *tamakkana*), *tamakkana*, and *mutamakkin* respectively.

[199] The wordings are *fī 'l-ḥāl wa-mustaqbalihā*, *lā fī 'l-ḥāl wa-lā fī mustaqbal al-awqāt*, and *lā fī ḥāl al-amr wa'l-nahy wa-lā fī-mā ba'd hādhihi 'l-ḥāl min mustaqbal al-awqāt* respectively.

remarkable about this phrasing of the condition, it is unusual. The fact that it occurs in a work of Mufīd means that it does not derive from the Baṣran Muʿtazilite tradition. Since in each case it appears in accounts couched in the language of the 'three modes', it could in principle stem from a traditionalist source. But given the nexus of jargon with which it is associated, a Baghdādī Muʿtazilite origin seems more likely.[200] The phrase is scarcely found after Ibn al-Barrāj;[201] its virtual disappearance could thus be seen as an instance of the displacement of the Baghdādī by the Baṣran heritage.

A final point, and one of more substantive interest, arises over the question what happens when the conditions for obligation are not satisfied: is it still good to proceed? In principle, this question can arise with reference to several of the conditions.[202] In practice, it arises most pressingly with regard to danger. The standard view in the Baṣran Muʿtazilite tradition would seem to have been that it is good to be a hero, at least if this is for the greater glory of the faith (*iʿzāz lil-dīn*). Such is the view of ʿAbd al-Jabbār,[203] Mānkdīm[204] and Abū 'l-Ḥusayn.[205] This attitude can also be found among the Sunnīs.[206] The Imāmīs, by contrast, will have none of this, or very little.[207] Sallār, the most adventurous in this regard, goes no further than to allow that there are cases not involving mortal danger where suffering is rewarded, as when one is subjected to abuse (*sabb*) or to

[200] Another unusual element in Mufīd's account in his *Muqniʿa* is the stipulation of a *sharṭ al-ṣalāḥ* (*ibid.*, 809.7). In his *Awāʾil al-maqālāt*, he states that *al-amr biʾl-maʿrūf* with the tongue is obligatory on condition (a) that it is needed (*bi-sharṭ al-ḥāja ilayhi*) to instruct someone and (reading *wa-* for *aw*) (b) that it is known – or there is good reason to believe – that it will be advantageous (*wa-ḥuṣūl al-ʿilm biʾl-maṣlaḥa bihi aw ghalabat al-ẓann bi-dhālika*) (*ibid.*, 98.4). The terms *ṣalāḥ* and *maṣlaḥa* in these two works presumably refer to the same condition; at a guess, it might be equivalent to conditions (3) and (6) of Murtaḍā's schema. In the *Awāʾil al-maqālāt*, Mufīd also refers to the imam's permission as a condition (*sharṭ*), a usage not found elsewhere in the Imāmī sources. Here too we may have residues of distinctively Baghdādī doctrine.

[201] Yaḥyā ibn Saʿīd uses the phrase *fī 'l-ḥāl aw al-maʾāl* (*Jāmiʿ*, 239.12), and much later it reappears in this form in Najafī (d. 1266/1850), *Jawāhir al-kalām*, Najaf and Tehran 1378–1404, 21:371.13, whence Khwānsārī (d. 1405/1985), *Jāmiʿ al-madārik*, Tehran 1383–92, 5:404.17.

[202] See above, ch. 9, 213, 222f. I have seen no comparably systematic statement in the Imāmī sources.

[203] See also above, ch. 9, 202 and note 74. For the view of the Baghdādī Muʿtazilite Rummānī, see above, ch. 9, note 36.

[204] See above, ch. 9, 209, condition (5). Similarly Ibn al-Murtaḍā and Yaḥyā ibn Ḥamza (see above, ch. 10, note 112). [205] See above, ch. 9, notes 74, 155.

[206] Thus for Abū Yaʿlā (d. 458/1066), see above, ch. 6, note 142; for Ghazzālī (d. 505/1111), see below, ch. 16, note 42; for Ibn al-ʿArabī (d. 543/1148), see below, ch. 14, 366.

[207] Isḥāq ibn Wahb condemns heroism in the performance of the duty as stupidity (*jahl*) tantamount to provoking a wild beast (*Burhān*, 277.3). If this can be taken to represent an Imāmī view (cf. above, notes 40, 115), it is an early attestation.

the loss of a bit of one's property (*dhahāb baʿḍ mālihi*).[208] Murtaḍā rejects outright the view that courting danger to one's property in forbidding wrong can be good,[209] and goes on to deny that enduring death can be justified even in terms of the glory of the faith.[210] He is followed by Ṭūsī in his longer doctrinal works.[211] Thereafter the issue is scarcely discussed. We might see this departure from well-established Baṣran doctrine as mandated by the tradition from Jaʿfar al-Ṣādiq according to which a man who exposes himself to an unjust ruler gets no reward for his suffering.[212] But no reference is made to this tradition.[213] It therefore seems more likely that this was one of the few cases in this period where the development of Imāmī doctrine was driven by practical considerations.

These six topics apart, there is little in the classical Imāmī accounts that calls for attention. Some scholars commence with definitions of key terms,[214] again continuing a Baṣran Muʿtazilite tradition.[215] A couple of themes familiar elsewhere are notably absent. The Imāmīs scarcely discuss the question whether a man who is himself an offender is obligated to

208 Sallār, *Marāsim*, 260.11. His contemporary Abū ʾl-Ṣalāḥ takes a position that implicitly rejects heroism, though the point is not spelled out (*Kāfī*, 266.17).

209 Murtaḍā, *Dhakhīra*, 557.19. He holds that it makes no difference whether a lot of property is at stake or a little (*ibid.*, 558.7).

210 *Ibid.*, 558.9; cf. his presentation of the issue, *ibid.*, 557.13. By contrast, he has a favourable view of heroism for the greater glory of the faith in the case of a man who is under pressure to make professions of unbelief (*ibid.*, 562.9); he goes on to argue that in such a case getting killed cannot be considered an evil (*mafsada*) (*ibid.*, 562.15).

211 Ṭūsī, *Iqtiṣād*, 149.9; Ṭūsī, *Tamhīd*, 304.1. Cf. also his *Tibyān*, 2:422.19, followed by Ṭabrisī, *Majmaʿ*, 1:423.32 (both to Q3:21). Likewise Ṭūsī firmly rejects the idea that speaking out in the presence of an unjust ruler and getting killed for it can be good (*Tamhīd*, 307.2, invoking the duty of *taqiyya*; cf. Murtaḍā, *Dhakhīra*, 562.13). On the other hand, Ṭūsī allows for a bit of unpleasantness (*baʿḍ al-mashaqqa*) in performing the duty (*Tibyān*, 8:279.19 (to Q31:17); Rāwandī mentions abuse and blows which are not life-threatening, *Fiqh al-Qurʾān*, 1:361.7 (also to Q31:17)). For Ṭūsī's invocation of *taqiyya* in this context, compare Isḥāq ibn Wahb, *Burhān*, 277.8, and cf. above, note 34. Ḥimmaṣī does not adopt the categorical position of Murtaḍā and Ṭūsī; but he distances himself from the contrary analysis which he reproduces from the school of Abū ʾl-Ḥusayn, and carefully sits on the fence (*Munqidh*, 2:218.18, 219.19).

212 For this tradition, see above, note 36.

213 The ʿAllāma quotes the tradition, but only to make the point that the obligation is voided in such cases (*Muntahā*, 993.23).

214 Abū ʾl-Ṣalāḥ, *Kāfī*, 264.6 (defining *amr* and *nahy*); Ḥimmaṣī, *Munqidh*, 2:209.6 (defining *maʿrūf* and *munkar*); Muḥaqqiq, *Sharāʾiʿ*, 1:341.3 (defining *maʿrūf* and *munkar*); ʿAllāma, *Muntahā*, 991.35; ʿAllāma, *Tadhkira*, 1:458.3; ʿAllāma, *Taḥrīr*, 1:157.12 (each defining – with one omission – *amr* and *nahy*, *maʿrūf* and *munkar*, *ḥasan* and *qabīḥ*). The ʿAllāma in these works notes that *ḥasan* and *qabīḥ* are asymmetric: technically, the former includes the permitted, the recommended, the obligatory and the disapproved, while the latter comprises only the forbidden. See also his *Nahj al-mustarshidīn*, *apud* Miqdād, *Irshād*, 380.2.

215 Compare the definitions of *amr* and *nahy*, *maʿrūf* and *munkar* with which Mānkdīm opens his discussion (see above, ch. 9, 205).

forbid wrong;[216] and they have almost nothing to say about the impropriety (or otherwise) of seeking to carry out the duty in matters on which other law-schools hold differing views.

Overall, the classical Imāmī doctrine of forbidding wrong is one that reflects the realities of the lecture-room rather than the street. There are only two clear exceptions to this. One is the retention of the doctrine of the imam's permission, despite what I take to be its no longer fashionable Baghdādī Muʿtazilite source, and its rejection by Murtaḍā. The other is the condemnation of heroism – in striking departure from the predominant Baṣran strain of Muʿtazilism. Both points reflect an underlying quietism which is in sharp contrast to Zaydism. Turning to the lecture-room, it is remarkable that despite the abundance of Imāmī tradition on the subject of forbidding wrong, the doctrine of the classical jurists owes little to that earlier stage of Imāmī thought. Instead, it mixes elements that we can assign with greater or lesser plausibility to Sunnī traditionalism, Baghdādī Muʿtazilism and Baṣran Muʿtazilism. While the traditionalist element maintains its position, the Baghdādī strain of Muʿtazilism seems to be displaced by its Baṣran rival, to the point that only the doctrine of the imam's permission can be seen as a plausible Baghdādī survival. Be this as it may, the fusion of Muʿtazilite and traditionalist thought again sets Imāmī doctrine apart from that of the Zaydīs.

4. THE LATER IMĀMĪ SCHOLARS

The history of Imāmī scholasticism from the eighth to the fourteenth/fourteenth to twentieth centuries is in some respects strikingly conservative; but in others it displays a creativity unparalleled at the time in other sects or schools. This paradox is clearly in evidence in the case of forbidding wrong. On the one hand, the agenda of discussion down the centuries continues to be that set by the classical jurists. Indeed many of the relevant works of the later scholars are commentaries on the standard texts of the classical period.[217] Yet on the other hand, the attitude of these scholars to the works

216 An author who does consider the issue is Isḥāq ibn Wahb (*Burhān*, 276.9), in a discussion in which he quotes and correctly ascribes Jesus's mote and beam saying (cf. I. Goldziher, 'Matth. VII. 5 in der muhammedanischen Literatur', *Zeitschrift der Deutschen Morgenländischen Gesellschaft*, 31 (1877), 765–7). This saying appears already in Abū ʿUbayd al-Qāsim ibn Sallām (d. 224/838f.), *Amthāl*, ed. ʿA. Qaṭāmish, Damascus and Beirut 1980, 74 no. 152 (with further references), see *EI*², art. 'Mathal', 819b (R. Sellheim); also in Jāḥiẓ, *Kitmān al-sirr*, 162.13. Rāwandī's treatment of the question (*Fiqh al-Qur'ān*, 1:359.13 (to Q3:110)) is borrowed from Zamakhsharī (*Kashshāf*, 1:398.8 (to Q3:104)).

217 In addition to the works cited below, there are also some monographic treatments of *al-*

upon which they are commenting is not unduly respectful. What is more, their thinking is often more supple and sophisticated than that of their predecessors, and they show little inhibition about displaying this. The upshot is a widespread tendency in these later works to subvert the classical Imāmī doctrine of forbidding wrong without replacing it with anything better. This tendency is readily apparent if we run through the topics considered in the previous section.

1. *The three modes*

With regard to the modes of performance of the duty, the setting of the discussion among the later scholars remains recognisably classical. Virtually all of them talk the language of the three modes (heart, tongue and hand),[218] even if they go on to question some part of the classical heritage. As before, there is emphasis on the principle of escalation,[219] and the order in which the modes are listed is usually escalatory; but the de-escalatory

amr bi'l-ma'rūf from this period which I have not seen (see Modarressi Tabātabā'i, *Introduction*, 170; also S. H. al-Ṭuʿma, 'al-Makhṭūṭāt al-ʿArabiyya fī khizānat Āl al-Marʿashī fī Karbalā'', *al-Mawrid*, 3, no. 4 (1974), 285 no. 3 (I owe this reference to Maribel Fierro)).

218 Thus Najafī remarks that he has found no disagreement among the scholars with regard to the number of the modes (*marātib*) (*Jawāhir*, 21:374.15).

219 See al-Shahīd al-Awwal (d. 786/1384), *al-Durūs al-sharʿiyya*, Qumm 1412–14, 2:47.9, and his *al-Lumʿa al-Dimashqiyya*, Tehran 1406, 46.8; Miqdād al-Suyūrī (d. 826/1423), *al-Tanqīḥ al-rā'iʿ*, ed. ʿA. al-Kūhkamarī, Qumm 1404, 1:594.20; Miqdād al-Suyūrī, *Nāfiʿ*, 129.12; Miqdād al-Suyūrī, *Kanz*, 1:405.4, 407.12 (whence Kāshānī, *Manhaj*, 2:295.4 (to Q3:104)); Ibn Ṭayy (d. 855/1451), *al-Durr al-manḍūd*, ed. M. Barakat, Shīrāz 1418, 103.9; al-Shahīd al-Thānī (d. 965/1557f.), *Masālik al-afhām*, Qumm 1413–, 3:104.21; al-Shahīd al-Thānī (d. 965/1557f.), *al-Rawḍa al-bahiyya*, ed. M. Kalāntar, Najaf 1386–90, 2:416.5; Abū 'l-Fatḥ al-Jurjānī, *Tafsīr*, 2:101.3; Kāshānī, *Manhaj*, 2:294.4 (to Q3:104); Muqaddas al-Ardabīlī (d. 993/1585), *Majmaʿ al-fā'ida*, ed. M. al-ʿArāqī *et al.*, Qumm 1402–, 7:541.11; Bahā' al-Dīn al-ʿĀmilī (d. 1030/1621), *Jāmiʿ-i ʿAbbāsī*, n.p. 1328, 146.21; Jawād al-Kāẓimī (writing 1043/1633), *Masālik al-afhām*, ed. M. T. al-Kashfī and M. B. al-Bihbūdī, Tehran *c.* 1347 sh., 2:374.16; Sabzawārī (d. 1090/1679f.), *Kifāyat al-aḥkām*, n.p. 1269, 82.16; Muḥsin al-Fayḍ (d. 1091/1680), *Mafātīḥ al-sharā'iʿ*, ed. M. Rajā'ī, Qumm 1401, 2:56.20; Muḥsin al-Fayḍ (d. 1091/1680), *al-Maḥajja al-bayḍā' fī tahdhīb al-Iḥyā'*, ed. ʿA. A. al-Ghaffārī, Tehran 1339–42 sh., 4:108.9 (this account of *al-amr bi'l-maʿrūf*, in an Imāmī recension of Ghazzālī's *Iḥyā'*, was first drawn to my attention by Basim Musallam); Muḥsin al-Fayḍ (d. 1091/1680), *Nukhba*, n.p. 1303, 110.4; Aḥmad al-Jazā'irī, *Qalā'id*, 2:204.7; Kāshif al-Ghiṭā' (d. 1227/1812), *Kashf al-ghiṭā'*, Iṣfahān n.d., 420.19; Mīrzā Abū 'l-Qāsim Qummī (d. 1231/1815f.), *Jāmiʿ al-shatāt* (in Persian), ed. M. Raḍawī, Tehran 1371– sh., 1:421.23; Najafī, *Jawāhir*, 21:378.6 (remarking that he finds no disagreement on the point), 378.22, 380.10; Khū'ī (d. 1413/1992), *Minhāj al-ṣāliḥīn*, *apud* Taqī al-Ṭabāṭabā'ī al-Qummī, *Mabānī Minhāj al-ṣāliḥīn*, Qumm 1405–11, 7:157.1, 158.1; Khumaynī (d. 1409/1989), *Taḥrīr al-Wasīla*, Beirut 1981, 1:476 no. 1; 477f. nos. 1–4; 479f. no. 1; 481 no. 13, and throughout the discussion. Escalation is often referred to as *tadarruj* in these texts.

sequence can still be found.[220] At some points the classical schema is refined or embellished. Thus a more sophisticated handling of the relationship between the escalatory and de-escalatory orderings of the modes makes its appearance.[221] The discussions of escalation also become richer in detail; thus twisting ears is assigned its place in the spectrum.[222]

More subversive developments are found regarding the old and ambiguous notion of performance through the heart. The distinction between performing the duty *within* the heart (an unobservable mental act) and doing it *by means* of the heart (manifesting disapproval through outward and visible signs) is now generally assumed, and sometimes very clearly stated.[223] More significantly, it is regularly argued that performance in (or even with) the heart does not properly speaking fall under forbidding wrong at all, since it does not involve commanding or forbidding.[224] Performance with the heart is, however, generally accepted as part of forbidding wrong. But here the sequencing of the first and second modes is cleverly and convincingly attacked: a performance with the heart, such as cutting someone dead, may in fact be a harsher measure than a performance with the tongue, such as gently rebuking them.[225] The implication is the collapse of the second mode and what is left of the first into one.[226]

220 For the escalatory sequence, see Miqdād, *Tanqīḥ*, 1:594.15 (cf. *ibid*., 593.7); Miqdād, *Nāfiʿ*, 129.12; Kāshānī, *Manhaj*, 2:294.5 (to Q3:104); Aḥmad al-Jazāʾirī, *Qalāʾid*, 2:202.6; Khwānsārī, *Jāmiʿ*, 5:407.14; Khūʾī, *Minhāj*, 7:157.2; Khumaynī, *Taḥrīr*, 1:476.10, 477.22, 479.22. For the de-escalatory sequence, see Abū ʾl-Maḥāsin al-Jurjānī, *Jilāʾ al-adhhān*, 2:99.16 (to Q3:104).

221 In one of his works al-Shahīd al-Awwal (d. 786/1384) discusses what he calls the mutual inversion (*taʿākus*) of the sequences; he describes the de-escalatory sequence as ordered with respect to strength (*qudra*), and the escalatory sequence as ordered with respect to efficacy (*taʾthīr*) (*al-Qawāʿid wa'l-fawāʾid*, ed. ʿA. al-Ḥakīm, Najaf 1980, 2:202.11). This passage is not found in the Shahīd's Vorlage, the *Furūq* of the Mālikī Qarāfī (d. 684/1285), but it reappears in Miqdād al-Suyūrī (d. 826/1423), *Naḍd al-Qawāʿid al-fiqhiyya*, ed. ʿA. al-Kūhkamarī, Qumm 1403, 265.4; the latter also has a less illuminating discussion of the question in his *Tanqīḥ* (1:593.18), with a conclusion (*ibid*., 594.15) questioning the ʿAllāma's view (above, note 77) that the dispute is merely verbal. See also Najafī, *Jawāhir*, 21:379.15.

222 Miqdād, *Tanqīḥ*, 1:595.7; Ibn Ṭayy, *Durr*, 104.3; al-Shahīd al-Thānī, *Masālik*, 3:105.6; Najafī, *Jawāhir*, 21:378.12.

223 For particularly explicit formulations of the distinction, see al-Shahīd al-Thānī, *Masālik*, 3:103.14; Bahāʾ al-Dīn, *Arbaʿīn*, 106.17; Mīrzā-yi Qummī, *Jāmiʿ*, 1:421.14.

224 Miqdād, *Tanqīḥ*, 1:593.19 (but cf. *ibid*., 594.20); Karakī (d. 940/1534), *Jāmiʿ al-maqāṣid*, Qumm 1408–11, 3:486.15; Karakī, *Fawāʾid al-Sharāʾiʿ*, f. 138b.7; al-Shahīd al-Thānī, *Masālik*, 3:103.19; al-Shahīd al-Thānī, *Rawḍa*, 2:417.5; Muqaddas, *Majmaʿ*, 7:540.11; Bahāʾ al-Dīn, *Arbaʿīn*, 107.10; Najafī, *Jawāhir*, 21:368.1, 376.9, 377.1, 377.18; Muḥsin al-Amīn (d. 1371/1952), *Sharḥ Tabṣirat al-mutaʿallimīn*, Damascus 1947, 95.19; Khwānsārī, *Jāmiʿ*, 5:408.5, 409.7; Khumaynī, *Taḥrīr*, 1:477 no. 7; Taqī al-Qummī, *Mabānī*, 7:156.12.

225 The first to make this point seems to have been Muqaddas al-Ardabīlī (*Majmaʿ*, 7:542.9). It reappears in Kāshif al-Ghiṭāʾ, *Kashf*, 420.20; Mīrzā-yi Qummī, *Jāmiʿ*, 1:421.24; Najafī, *Jawāhir*, 21:379.5, 380.16; Khwānsārī, *Jāmiʿ*, 5:410.7; Khumaynī, *Taḥrīr*, 1:478 no. 6.

226 As indicated by Khūʾī (*Minhāj*, 7:157.2).

Very occasionally the undermining of classical doctrine reached further. Miqdād al-Suyūrī (d. 826/1423) considered the possibility of defining 'commanding' (*amr*) in a manner that does not limit it to a verbal act, but he addressed the issue only in the context of resolving a problem of definition.[227] In a hypothetical vein, Muqaddas al-Ardabīlī (d. 993/1585) observed that, were it not for the consensus on the point, the permissibility of any kind of violence in the performance of the duty would be problematic.[228] Bahā' al-Dīn al-ʿĀmilī (d. 1030/1621) suggested in passing that it did not really make sense to speak of 'commanding' or 'forbidding' except with reference to some kinds of verbal performance, but he accepted that it was a convention of legal usage to do so.[229] Najafī (d. 1266/1850) found it worthwhile to refute such doubts.[230] None of this is of great significance. But a contemporary scholar, Taqī al-Qummī, has set out this line of argument in earnest – most likely following the lead of his teacher Khū'ī (d. 1413/1992). In this account, neither the first nor the third mode qualifies for inclusion in the concept of forbidding wrong, nor does so classic an instance of the second mode as counselling someone.[231]

2. *The imam's permission*

The question whether the imam's permission is needed where performance of the duty involves a high level of violence is regularly discussed. The general tendency is to perpetuate the view of the majority of the classical scholars that this permission is necessary, or to restrict such measures to the imam or his deputy outright.[232] By contrast, the minority view to

[227] Miqdād, *Irshād*, 382.2.

[228] Muqaddas, *Majmaʿ*, 7:543.5; and see Sabzawārī, *Kifāya*, 82.32, and Mīrzā-yi Qummī, *Jāmiʿ*, 1:422.14.

[229] Bahā' al-Dīn, *Arbaʿīn*, 107.10. He refers to the usage as employment of a metaphor (*tajawwuz*), but says that it has in effect become the literal usage of the lawyers (*ḥaqīqa sharʿiyya*). The verb *tajawwaza* had already been used by al-Shahīd al-Thānī with regard to the practice of the scholars in treating performance in the heart as though it belonged to *al-amr bi'l-maʿrūf* (*Rawḍa*, 2:417.8).

[230] Najafī, *Jawāhir*, 21:381.13, 382.6. He says that despite the plain sense of the words 'command' and 'forbid' (*ẓāhir lafẓ al-amr wa'l-nahy*), what is meant by *al-amr bi'l-maʿrūf* is not just verbal activity (*mujarrad al-qawl*).

[231] See Taqī al-Qummī, *Mabānī*, 7:156.14 (on performance with the heart), 156.17 (on *waʿẓ* and *naṣīḥa*), 157.8 (on *ḍarb*, *shatm* and *sabb*), 157.12 (a general statement rejecting Najafī's view as unproven assertion). There is no indication of a political agenda behind this radical attack on the traditional scholastic doctrine.

[232] Thus al-Shahīd al-Awwal remarks that the most plausible view (*al-aqrab*) is that wounding and killing should be made over to the imam (*tafwīḍuhumā ilā 'l-imām*) (*Durūs*, 2:47.10, cited in Sachedina, *Just ruler*, 145); Miqdād considers them a duty of the imam (*waẓīfa imāmiyya*) (*Kanz*, 1:405.5, whence Kāshānī, *Manhaj*, 2:294.4); Karakī endorses the need for the imam's permission, citing the danger of disorder (*thawarān al-fitna*) (*Jāmiʿ*, 3:488.20, and *Fawā'id*, f. 139a.5; see also Mudarrisī Ṭabāṭabā'ī, *Zamīn*, 1:112

the contrary held by the ʿAllāma and others hardly survives in this period.[233] This does not, however, mean that the question had been resolved and that the later scholars did no more than repeat what their predecessors had said. There are new developments in several directions.

One interesting innovation is the occasional expression of the idea that, in the absence of the imam, a suitably qualified jurist (*al-faqīh al-jāmiʿ lil-sharāʾiṭ, al-faqīh al-jāmiʿ li-sharāʾiṭ al-fatwā*) can undertake such performance of the duty. This idea appears in the early Ṣafawid period,[234] though without becoming particularly prominent; as we will see, it reappears in a modified form with Khumaynī (d. 1409/1989).[235]

At the same time classical thought is undermined from various directions. A subtle attack is mounted by al-Shahīd al-Thānī (d. 965/1557f.). He distinguishes wounding and killing. Wounding by itself, he suggests, may not require the imam's permission. Killing may indeed be a matter for the imam; but this is scarcely a concession to the classical view, since he also argues that killing can have no place in forbidding wrong. The reason this is so is that killing someone in such a context is self-defeating: dead men cannot obey orders.[236] More radical still is the criticism of Muqaddas al-Ardabīlī. Wounding and killing, he points out, are not instances of commanding and forbidding; consequently the obligatoriness of wounding

Footnote 232 (*cont.*)
n. 42); Najafī endorses the classical doctrine in a long and heated argument laying particular emphasis on the same theme (*Jawāhir*, 21:383.12; he ends with the remark that such a duty is rare or non-existent these days, *ibid.*, 385.21).

233 Sabzawārī inclines to it (*Kifāya*, 83.3), and al-Shahīd al-Awwal adopts it in his *Ghāyat al-murād* (Qumm 1414–, 1:509.6; contrast his view in the *Durūs* as cited in the previous note).

234 Karakī suggests that such a jurist may undertake such action during the *ghayba* on the analogy of his role in the execution of the *ḥudūd* (*Jāmiʿ*, 3:488.20; *Fawāʾid*, f. 139a.5; likewise al-Shahīd al-Thānī, *Masālik*, 3:105.16). Cf. also Najafī, *Jawāhir*, 21:385.18 (speaking in similar terms of the *nāʾib al-ghayba*). For the 'qualified jurist' in other contexts, see N. Calder, 'Judicial authority in Imāmī Shīʿī jurisprudence', *British Society for Middle Eastern Studies Bulletin*, 6 (1979), 105; N. Calder, 'Zakāt in Imāmī Shīʿī jurisprudence, from the tenth to the sixteenth century AD', *Bulletin of the School of Oriental and African Studies*, 44 (1981), 479f.; W. Madelung, 'Shiite discussions on the legality of the *kharāj*', in R. Peters (ed.), *Proceedings of the ninth Congress of the Union Européenne des Arabisants et Islamisants*, Leiden 1981, 194 n. 5; Modarressi Tabātabāʾi, *Kharāj in Islamic law*, 157f.; A. J. Newman, 'The nature of the Akhbārī/Uṣūlī dispute in late Ṣafawid Iran, Part 2: the conflict reassessed', *Bulletin of the School of Oriental and African Studies*, 55 (1992), 257–9.

235 See below, ch. 18, note 243.

236 See al-Shahīd al-Thānī, *Rawḍa*, 2:416.11, and al-Shahīd al-Thānī, *Masālik*, 3:105.12 (Sachedina's report of al-Shahīd al-Thānī's position is misleading, *Just ruler*, 145); similarly Sabzawārī, *Kifāya*, 83.3. Najafī criticises the distinction between wounding and killing on the ground that the first leads to the second (*Jawāhir*, 21:385.13). The point that dead men cannot obey orders is also made in a Zaydī source (ʿAlī ibn al-Ḥusayn, *Lumaʿ*, f. 220b.14, in the scholion), but there with respect only to killing in *al-amr biʾl-maʿrūf* as opposed to *al-nahy ʿan al-munkar* (cf. above, ch. 10, note 115).

and killing cannot simply be extrapolated from that of commanding and forbidding (a line of argument later revived in the account of Taqī al-Qummī).[237] In the next century the moderate Akhbārī Muḥsin al-Fayḍ (d. 1091/1680) remarks impatiently that the issue is a waste of time. Anyone who satisfies the demanding preconditions for performing the duty will know best what to do in any given situation.[238] With Kāshif al-Ghiṭā' (d. 1227/1812), a pupil of Bihbahānī (d. 1206/1791f.), we have perhaps a tendency to shift the issue into the domain of the set punishments (*ḥudūd*).[239]

3. *Reason and revelation*

With regard to the question whether the duty can be grounded in reason as well as revelation, the later scholastic tradition is fairly conservative. The negative view of the great majority of the classical scholars, though at first under some pressure, regains its predominance;[240] meanwhile the rationalist position has distinguished adherents down to the early Ṣafawid

[237] Muqaddas, *Majmaʿ*, 7:542.20, and cf. Taqī al-Qummī, *Mabānī*, 7:158.18.

[238] Fayḍ, *Mafātīḥ*, 2:57.5 (*al-baḥth ʿanhu qalīl al-jadwā, li-anna 'l-jāmiʿ lil-sharā'iṭ adrā bi-mā yaqtaḍīhi 'l-ḥāl*); Fayḍ, *Maḥajja*, 4:108.13 (mentioning also that it is better (*awlā*) not to proceed to such measures). In his *Nukhba*, by contrast, he requires that the judicial authority (*al-ḥākim*) be informed and give permission (110.9). The argument that one who satisfies the preconditions will know best harks back to the Imāmī tradition in which al-Ṣādiq confines *al-amr bi'l-maʿrūf* to strong and authoritative persons who know right from wrong (see above, note 30). Fayḍ later uses the same argument from the same tradition to explain his decision to omit Ghazzālī's account of common wrongs (*Maḥajja*, 4:112.1). One wonders why he should bother to give any account at all of *al-amr bi'l-maʿrūf*. Indeed, in a letter written in Persian in 1072/1661f. to a zealot in Māzandarān who wished to mobilise the state against Ṣūfīs and Christians and to obtain from it a delegation of the office of censor (*amr al-ḥisba*), Fayḍ invokes only the reference to truce in the tradition (*zamān zamān-i hudna ast*, see M. T. Dānishpazhūh, 'Dāwarī-i Fayḍ-i Kāshānī miyān-i pārsā wa dānishmand', *Nashriyya-i Dānishkada-i Adabiyyāt-i Tabrīz*, 9 (1336 sh.), 127.19). He goes on to tell the zealot that it will take him several wrongs to put a stop to one, that not everyone knows what is right and wrong (the zealot himself being a conspicuous example), and that it would be better for him to reform himself and his close companions, and forget anything more (*ibid.*, 128.7).

[239] Kāshif al-Ghiṭā', *Kashf*, 420.21 (stating that escalation stops short of wounding and killing except in the context of the *ḥudūd* (*illā fī maqām al-ḥadd*)), and cf. *ibid.*, 420.38. Despite the fact that the execution of the *ḥudūd* is regularly taken up immediately after the end of the discussion of *al-amr bi'l-maʿrūf*, it is rare for earlier authors to bring the *ḥudūd* into their analysis of *al-amr bi'l-maʿrūf* (for an analogy drawn by Karakī, see above, note 234; for a contrast drawn between them, see Muqaddas, *Majmaʿ*, 7:543.13).

[240] Revelationist positions are adopted more or less strongly by the following: Fakhr al-Muḥaqqiqīn (*Īḍāḥ*, 1:398.15); Abū 'l-Maḥāsin al-Jurjānī (*Jilā' al-adhhān*, 2:99.16 (to Q3:104)); Karakī (*Jāmiʿ*, 3:485.17, with some caution); Kāshānī (*Manhaj*, 2:294.1 (to Q3:104), with a classical exception); Muqaddas al-Ardabīlī (*Majmaʿ*, 7:530.11, and cf. his *Zubdat al-bayān*, ed. M. B. al-Bihbūdī, Tehran n.d., 321.18); Bahā' al-Dīn al-ʿĀmilī (*Jāmiʿ*, 146.12); Jawād al-Kāẓimī (*Masālik*, 2:374.7, with the same classical exception); Najafī (*Jawāhir*, 21:358.6).

period,[241] but thereafter pretty much drops out.[242] The Akhbārī scholars scarcely discuss the question.[243] With regard to argumentation, the later scholars are for the most part content to repeat the arguments of the classical sources,[244] though here and there new twists emerge.[245] Only the approach of Muqaddas al-Ardabīlī smacks of radicalism. He declares the discussion to be of no consequence, and leaves aside the arguments of his predecessors, on the ground that the whole issue is academic. Since we now know our duty from revelation, it is pointless to inquire whether or not we could have known it in its absence.[246]

4. *The doctrine of divisibility*

The classical scholars had never quite articulated the dilemma they faced with regard to the question of the divisibility of right and wrong. The need for a tidy and comprehensive doctrine called for a certain symmetry: since there was a category of supererogatory right (***mandūb***) which it was supererogatory to command, it seemed appropriate to match it with a category of low-grade wrong (***makrūh***) which it was supererogatory to abstain from, and by the same token supererogatory to forbid. Yet this logic came to grief on the accepted meanings of the words: 'right' (***maʿrūf***) was wide enough to include both the obligatory and the supererogatory, whereas 'wrong' (***munkar***) was a narrower term, covering only the forbidden.

241 It is maintained by al-Shahīd al-Awwal (*Durūs*, 2:47.6; *Lumʿa*, 46.6; *Qawāʿid*, 2:201.2, not derived from Qarāfī, and repeated in Miqdād, *Naḍd*, 364.3); Miqdād al-Suyūrī (*Kanz*, 1:404.14); Ibn Ṭayy (*Durr*, 103.3); al-Shahīd al-Thānī (*Rawḍa*, 2:409.7); and Abū 'l-Fatḥ al-Jurjānī (*Tafsīr*, 2:100.1). The positions of the two Shahīds are noted in Sachedina, *Just ruler*, 144.

242 For an exception, see Kāshif al-Ghiṭā', *Kashf*, 419.31. For the adoption of the essence of the rationalist position by a contemporary scholar, see Ḥusayn al-Nūrī al-Hamadānī, *al-Amr bi'l-maʿrūf wa'l-nahy ʿan al-munkar*, Tehran 1990, 61.10.

243 In his adaptation of Ghazzālī's *Iḥyā'*, Fayḍ transcribes without comment a statement that includes, among the proofs that *al-amr bi'l-maʿrūf* is obligatory, *ishārāt al-ʿuqūl al-salīma* (*Maḥajja*, 4:96.8, from Ghazzālī, *Iḥyā'*, 2:281.9). The absence of Akhbārī discussion of the point was drawn to my attention by Shohreh Gholsorkhi.

244 For the two most-repeated arguments, see above, note 122.

245 On behalf of Ṭūsī, Miqdād produces an unusual riposte to the old argument from divine liability (*Irshād*, 384.3, and cf. his *Tanqīḥ*, 1:592.16). Karakī makes the point that there does not have to be a general answer – the rationalist view could be true of some instances (*afrād*) of right or wrong but not of all (*Jāmiʿ*, 3:485.15, and cf. Muqaddas, *Majmaʿ*, 7:530.20, implausibly reading such a position into al-Shahīd al-Awwal, *Durūs*, 2:47.6). Muqaddas al-Ardabīlī also mounts some subtle and, I think, new arguments to show that reason cannot be relied on to discern the entire duty (*Majmaʿ*, 7:530.11). Kāshif al-Ghiṭā' comes up with some typically idiosyncratic reasons why the duty should be rationally binding (*Kashf*, 419.32).

246 Muqaddas, *Majmaʿ*, 7:530.3. He then goes on to give the arguments of his own mentioned in the previous note.

In the post-classical period this dilemma becomes explicit.[247] Doubtless connected to this is a major shift in alignment: whereas in the classical period only Abū 'l-Ṣalāḥ and Ibn Ḥamza had given play to the pull of symmetry, this is now the rule,[248] and those who continue to ignore symmetry in the classical manner are in a minority.[249] There is, however, less consensus as to how this shift is to be validated. Some take the bull by the horns, or at least toy with the idea of doing so, and consider redefining 'wrong' (*munkar*) to include both the forbidden and the merely disapproved.[250] One scholar finds a place for forbidding the disapproved under the wing of commanding the supererogatory.[251] A Sunnī idea that is introduced but makes little headway places it under the very different rubric of 'helping one another to piety and godfearing' (*al-taʿāwun ʿalā 'l-birr wa'l-taqwā*, cf. Q5:2).[252] Many are content not to confront the problem at all.

The only other point of note is the late appearance of the suggestion that, but for the consensus to the contrary, commanding the supererogatory and

[247] Miqdād, *Tanqīḥ*, 1:592.21; Muqaddas, *Majmaʿ*, 7:529.6.

[248] See al-Shahīd al-Awwal, *Durūs*, 2:47.8; al-Shahīd al-Awwal, *Lumʿa*, 46.6; al-Shahīd al-Awwal, *Qawāʿid*, 2:205.8 (based on Qarāfī (d. 684/1285), *Furūq*, Cairo 1344–6, 4:257.15, and repeated in Miqdād, *Naḍd*, 267.5); Miqdād, *Tanqīḥ*, 1:593.5; Miqdād, *Kanz*, 1:407.15 (whence Kāshānī, *Manhaj*, 2:295.6 (to Q3:104)); Ibn Ṭayy, *Durr*, 103.4; al-Shahīd al-Thānī, *Masālik*, 3:100.8 (but cf. his *Rawḍa*, 2:414.8); Abū 'l-Fatḥ al-Jurjānī, *Tafsīr*, 2:97.11; Muqaddas, *Majmaʿ*, 7:529.6; Bahāʾ al-Dīn, *Jāmiʿ*, 146.8; Jawād al-Kāẓimī, *Masālik*, 2:374.9; Fayḍ, *Nukhba*, 109.18 (contrast his works cited in the following note); al-Ḥurr al-ʿĀmilī (d. 1104/1693), *Bidāyat al-hidāya*, ed. M. ʿA. al-Anṣārī, n.p. n.d., 2:59.12; Kāshif al-Ghiṭāʾ, *Kashf*, 419.31; Najafī, *Jawāhir*, 21:357.16, 365.19 (quoting and approving the view of Abū 'l-Ṣalāḥ); Muḥsin al-Amīn, *Sharḥ Tabṣirat al-mutaʿallimīn*, 95.18; Khwānsārī, *Jāmiʿ*, 5:398.15, 399.8; Khumaynī, *Taḥrīr*, 1:463 no. 1.

[249] Miqdād, *Irshād*, 380.12 (in contrast to his works cited in the previous note); Karakī, *Jāmiʿ*, 3:485.20 (dismissing those who would divide *munkar* on the grounds that its plain sense (*al-mutabādir min al-munkar*) goes against this); Fayḍ, *Mafātīḥ*, 2:54.15; Fayḍ, *Maḥajja*, 4:106.12; Aḥmad al-Jazāʾirī, *Qalāʾid*, 2:201.23 (but cf. the alternative suggestion mentioned *ibid.*, 202.2).

[250] Thus Muqaddas al-Ardabīlī remarks that it would be best (*al-aḥsan*) to apply the term *munkar* in a wider sense to include the disapproved (compare Abū 'l-Fatḥ al-Jurjānī, *Tafsīr*, 2:97.11), but that most scholars do not do this on semantic grounds which he considers trivial (*hayyin*) (*Majmaʿ*, 7:529.6). Jawād al-Kāẓimī mentions the widening of the sense of *munkar* as an option (*Masālik*, 2:374.11), and Aḥmad al-Jazāʾirī reports the idea (*Qalāʾid*, 2:202.2). Najafī refers to it in one passage (*Jawāhir*, 21:357.11, noting the semantic objection), and in another states that but for conventional usage (*iṣṭilāḥ*), one could divide wrong in the manner of Ibn Ḥamza (*ibid.*, 365.14, again mentioning the semantic problem). Khwānsārī introduces the idea as an option (*Jāmiʿ*, 5:398.16), and soon after says that there can be no doubt about it (*ibid.*, 399.8). The alternative course for restoring symmetry – to redefine *maʿrūf* to include only the obligatory – finds no takers (cf. Jawād al-Kāẓimī, *Masālik*, 2:374.10, and al-Shahīd al-Thānī, *Rawḍa*, 2:414.3).

[251] See al-Shahīd al-Thānī, *Masālik*, 3:100.12 (with the remark that this is the best view (*al-awlā*)); cf. Najafī, *Jawāhir*, 21:357.14, 363.3).

[252] See al-Shahīd al-Awwal, *Qawāʿid*, 2:205.10, taken from Qarāfī, *Furūq*, 4:257.16, and repeated in Miqdād, *Naḍd*, 267.7.

forbidding the disapproved might themselves be obligatory, despite the status of the conduct being commanded or forbidden.[253]

5. *Individual or collective?*

We left the classical scholars inclined to the view that the duty of forbidding wrong is a collective one, with some opposition arising from Ṭūsī's unusual but influential espousal of the contrary position. Overall this balance is continued among the later scholars, though the appeal of Ṭūsī's view seems gradually to have diminished. The great majority thus opt for the collective view, whether firmly or with reservations.[254] By contrast, few scholars take up a clear position in favour of the individual view,[255] and the only jurist of note among them is Karakī (d. 940/1534).[256] Yet this

[253] Najafī, *Jawāhir*, 21:363.16 (referring only to *al-amr biʾl-maʿrūf*); Khwānsārī, *Jāmiʿ*, 5:399.11, 408.12. This is a challenge to the heritage of Abū ʿAlī al-Jubbāʾī (d. 303/916) (see above, ch. 9, note 27).

[254] See al-Shahīd al-Awwal, *Lumʿa*, 46.6; al-Shahīd al-Awwal, *Qawāʿid*, 2:201.2 (not derived from Qarāfī, and repeated in Miqdād, *Naḍd*, 264.3); al-Shahīd al-Thānī, *Masālik*, 3:100.18; al-Shahīd al-Thānī, *Rawḍa*, 2:413.7; Abū ʾl-Fatḥ al-Jurjānī, *Tafsīr*, 2:101.1 (and compare *ibid.*, 104.7, on Q3:104, but contrast *ibid.*, 103.8, on Q3:110); Kāshānī, *Manhaj*, 2:293.7 (to Q3:104); Muqaddas, *Majmaʿ*, 7:534.4; Muqaddas, *Zubda*, 321.17; Bahāʾ al-Dīn, *Arbaʿīn*, 105.20 (cf. below, note 258); Jawād al-Kāẓimī, *Masālik*, 2:372.13 (on Q3:104; but later he remarks that the dispute is tantamount to a verbal one, *ibid.*, 373.13); Sabzawārī, *Kifāya*, 81.39; Fayḍ, *Mafātīḥ*, 2:55.17; Fayḍ, *Maḥajja*, 4:106.21 (and see *ibid.*, 96.13, repeating Ghazzālī's espousal of the collective view at *Iḥyāʾ*, 2:281.12); Kāshif al-Ghiṭāʾ, *Kashf*, 420.11; Mīrzā-yi Qummī, *Jāmiʿ*, 1:418.11; Najafī, *Jawāhir*, 21:362.6 (taking a firm line only on performance by hand); Khumaynī, *Taḥrīr*, 1:463f. no. 2 (the ramifications and qualifications in nos. 3–7 do not affect the principle); Khūʾī, *Minhāj*, 7:138.7, question 1; Taqī al-Qummī, *Mabānī*, 7:140.15, 141.13.

[255] Fakhr al-Muḥaqqiqīn knows his own mind, for he tells us that of the two views, it is 'the latter' (*al-akhīr*) that in his opinion is the stronger (*Īḍāḥ*, 1:398.20). Unfortunately this is ambiguous: 'the latter' is the individual view if he is still thinking of the statement of the ʿAllāma on which he is commenting (cf. *ibid.*, 397.16), but it is the collective view if he is referring to his own immediately preceding statement (*ibid.*, 398.17). The first seems more likely, making him an individualist, as is Ibn Ṭayy (*Durr*, 103.3). Abū ʾl-Maḥāsin al-Jurjānī firmly identifies with the view that the duty is an individual one (*Jilāʾ al-adhhān*, 2:99.15 (to Q3:104)), and it is likewise endorsed by Aḥmad al-Jazāʾirī (*Qalāʾid*, 2:201.15, 201.21). The fact that both these works are Koran-centred renders them somewhat separate from the mainstream of legal thought. Miqdād, incidentally, is notably evasive: he either fails to express a view of his own (as in the *Irshād*, *Tanqīḥ* and *Nāfiʿ*), or suggests both (*Kanz*, 1:406.8 (to Q3:110), 406.19 (to Q3:104)); the one exception is the *Naḍd*, where he is transcribing al-Shahīd al-Awwal's *Qawāʿid* (see above, note 254).

[256] Karakī, *Jāmiʿ*, 3:485.10. The same view is implicit in his commentary to Muḥaqqiq, *Sharāʾiʿ*, 1:341.9. The Muḥaqqiq had begun by saying that the duty is collective, being voided when a suitable person undertakes it (*yasquṭ bi-qiyām man fīhi kifāya*); Karakī comments that the more correct view is that (in addition) the offender must desist (*al-aṣaḥḥ: waʾl-iqlāʿ*), and he makes it clear in what follows that this renders the obligation an individual one (*Fawāʾid*, f. 138a.12). A contemporary scholar holds the duty to be individual in some contexts and collective in others (Nūrī, *Amr*, 62.10).

appearance of conservatism is misleading. What it conceals is a remarkable evolution in the clarity and sophistication with which the issue is presented. For the first time in this discussion, we learn what is actually at stake.

We can conveniently begin with a helpfully concrete illustration in a work of Bahāʾ al-Dīn al-ʿĀmilī. Let us suppose that we have in town a man who fails to pray and drinks wine. Assume further that in the town there are ten men each of whom thinks he might successfully undertake the duty. Now imagine that we are at the stage at which one of them has just undertaken the righting of the wrong; he can be expected to succeed, but his success still lies in the future. In this situation has the duty lapsed for the other nine? Or is it their duty to join him in the effort until such time as success is actually achieved?[257] Bahāʾ al-Dīn finds it plausible to say that, unless the nine think that their participation would be efficacious in expediting matters, they no longer have an obligation; accordingly he would describe the duty as a collective one. If, however, one takes the view that they still have an obligation to join in, then the duty is individual.[258] In other words, we can think in terms of three phases. In the first phase, there is a wrong which no one has yet undertaken to put right; here everyone who satisfies the conditions is obligated, and if no one steps forward, then all are at fault. In this phase it is of no practical significance whether one calls the duty individual or collective. Now we come to the second phase, in which there is a wrong and someone who has undertaken to put it right; he can be expected to succeed, and (let us further assume) the participation of others would not help to achieve this any faster. In this phase, the individualist holds that the rest are still obligated, whereas the collectivist holds that they are not. In the third phase the wrong has been put right (or, perhaps, it has emerged that it cannot be put right by means that satisfy the conditions); in this phase, obviously, no one is obligated, and once again it makes no difference how one categorises the duty. Only in the interval between the first man's initiative and the actual achievement of success is there any practical difference between the two views.

Bahāʾ al-Dīn was not himself an inventor, merely an effective populariser. The elements of the analysis are older than his day,[259] and indeed go back to Ibn al-Barrāj and the classical scholars.[260] It is, however, in the works of al-Shahīd al-Thānī that the analysis is first clearly set out.[261] Thereafter it

[257] Bahāʾ al-Dīn, *Arbaʿīn*, 104.19.
[258] *Ibid.*, 105.17; and cf. Bahāʾ al-Dīn, *Jāmiʿ*, 146.13, where he favours this latter view.
[259] See al-Shahīd al-Awwal, *Ghāyat al-murād*, 1:507.6, whence Miqdād, *Kanz*, 1:406.9 (and cf. Miqdād, *Irshād*, 385.9); Karakī, *Jāmiʿ*, 3:485.10; Karakī, *Fawāʾid*, f. 138a.12.
[260] See above, note 162, for the rather clumsy compromise put forward by Ibn al-Barrāj.
[261] See al-Shahīd al-Thānī, *Masālik*, 3:101.6; al-Shahīd al-Thānī, *Rawḍa*, 2:413.9.

belongs to the mainstream.[262] Further sophistication is brought to it by Muqaddas al-Ardabīlī, who argues that the puzzle lies less in the substantive law of forbidding wrong than in the general concept of a collective obligation.[263]

6. *The conditions of obligation*

By and large, the later scholars follow the schemas of conditions devised by the classical scholars. Those who are commenting on earlier works accept the lists they find there without protest.[264] Those who write independently usually give lists that agree with the standard four-condition schema used by the Muḥaqqiq and the ʿAllāma,[265] with occasional variation in the order of the conditions;[266] the three-condition schema is also found, but it is rarer.[267] A few scholars make limited additions to the four-condition schema: al-Shahīd al-Awwal (d. 786/1384) adds two conditions,[268] while

262 Kāshānī, *Manhaj*, 2:293.17 (to Q3:104); Muqaddas, *Majmaʿ*, 7:531.17, 532.8; Fayḍ, *Mafātīḥ*, 2:56.4; Fayḍ, *Maḥajja*, 4:107.5 (and cf. his *Nukhba*, 110.2); Mīrzā-yi Qummī, *Jāmiʿ*, 1:418.14; Najafī, *Jawāhir*, 21:362.1, 362.14. Jawād al-Kāẓimī's remark that the dispute is pretty much verbal (*kaʾl-lafẓī*, *Masālik*, 2:373.13) misses the point that it does in fact have practical consequences (*lahu thamara*, as Muqaddas al-Ardabīlī puts it, *Majmaʿ*, 7:531.8).

263 *Ibid.*, 532.4, 532.17, and cf. 534.10; similarly Najafī, *Jawāhir*, 21:362.22. The only other development of note in the argumentation is the appearance of the idea that what Najafī calls 'continuing practice' (*al-sīra al-mustamirra*) indicates the duty to be collective (Muqaddas, *Majmaʿ*, 7:533.10; Najafī, *Jawāhir*, 21:362.9, and cf. *ibid.*, 362.17; Taqī al-Qummī, *Mabānī*, 7:144.17).

264 In the only case where an author makes a substantial change to a text he is following, this text is a Mālikī one. Qarāfī (*Furūq*, 4:255.18) had set out a three-condition schema of a well-known Mālikī kind (see below, ch. 14, note 121). Here al-Shahīd al-Awwal gives Qarāfī's three conditions with a gratuitous change of order, placing absence of harmful consequences (*mafsada*) first (*Qawāʿid*, 2:201.7); he then adds as a further condition absence of danger to the performer of the duty (*ibid.*, 202.7, cf. Qarāfī's further discussion of *mafsada*, *Furūq*, 257.17), while remarking that this could be covered by his first condition. As usual, Miqdād follows the Shahīd (*Naḍd*, 264.7).

265 Bahāʾ al-Dīn, *Jāmiʿ*, 146.14 (leaving aside his first condition, for which see below, note 268); Sabzawārī, *Kifāya*, 82.1; Fayḍ, *Mafātīḥ*, 2:54.17; Fayḍ, *Maḥajja*, 4:106.14; Fayḍ, *Nukhba*, 110.1; Aḥmad al-Jazāʾirī, *Qalāʾid*, 2:202.3; Mīrzā-yi Qummī, *Jāmiʿ*, 1:419.4; Khumaynī, *Taḥrīr*, 1:465.19, 467.9, 470.4, 472.1.

266 See al-Shahīd al-Awwal, *Lumʿa*, 46.7; Ibn Ṭayy, *Durr*, 103.6; Miqdād, *Kanz*, 1:405.1; Bahāʾ al-Dīn, *Arbaʿīn*, 106.8.

267 Kāshānī, *Manhaj*, 294.2 (to Q3:104); Ḥurr al-ʿĀmilī, *Bidāya*, 2:59.3.

268 He begins by stipulating that *taklīf* is a condition, which it obviously is (cf. Najafī, *Jawāhir*, 21:374.8; he is followed in this by Bahāʾ al-Dīn (*Jāmiʿ*, 146.15)); and he ends by making it a condition (according to the stronger view) that no one else is thought to be undertaking the duty in one's place (*ʿadam ẓann qiyām al-ghayr maqāmahu*) (*Durūs*, 2:47.2). The formulation of the persistence condition is similar to that given by the ʿAllāma in *al-Bāb al-ḥādī ʿashar* (see above, note 182). The six conditions are introduced as conditions of obligation, but at the end the Shahīd remarks that some of them are conditions of permissibility (*jawāz*). None of this is found in the account the Shahīd gives in his *Lumʿa* (see above, note 266).

Khū'ī adds one.[269] Only Kāshif al-Ghiṭā' departs entirely from the classical tradition, producing an untidy collection of no fewer than fourteen conditions.[270] At the same time there is little change in the mainstream with regard to the wording of the individual conditions. One innovation is that from the early Ṣafawid period honour (*ʿirḍ*) is included alongside person and property in the danger condition.[271]

In scholastic terms, the main development lies rather in the more systematic handling of two subsidiary questions that arise with all or most of the conditions. The first is what degree of certainty is required to satisfy the various conditions; the second is whether, when a given condition is not satisfied, it is still permissible to proceed.

For the first question a brief indication of the overall weight of scholarly opinion will suffice. With regard to the knowledge condition, the issue is scarcely raised.[272] With regard to the efficacy condition, the tendency is to make the condition easily satisfied: as the standard classical wording (*tajwīz al-ta'thīr*) might suggest, a possibility of success is generally – though not always – taken as a sufficient basis for obligation.[273] With regard to the other two conditions, by contrast, the tendency is to render them easily voided. For the persistence condition the tendency of the classical wording is again sustained: a mere sign that the offence will not be continued or repeated is often considered enough for the duty to

[269] Khū'ī's fourth condition is that the law should be actually binding (*munajjaz*) on the supposed offender in respect of his offence, in other words that he should not have a good excuse (*maʿdhūr*) for his action or omission (Khū'ī, *Minhāj*, 7:149.7; cf. Khumaynī, *Taḥrīr*, 1:475 nos. 22f.). This condition voids the obligation in cases of disagreement among the jurists.

[270] Kāshif al-Ghiṭā', *Kashf*, 420.11. Here conditions (2), (3), (5) (perhaps with (4), (9), (10) and (13)) and (7) are close to the standard four, while (1) and (6) are the added conditions of the *Durūs* (see above, note 268). Of the rest, (8) seems redundant since he holds the duty to be collective; (11) is that the offender must understand the meaning of the command; (12) relates to duties which, like prayer, are tied to a specific time-frame; (14) is that the offender must be someone whom one is permitted to look at and touch, though arguably this would be covered by the classical *mafsada* condition. Incidentally, Kāshif al-Ghiṭā' is one of the few scholars to bring *al-amr bi'l-maʿrūf* into relation with *taqiyya* (*ibid.*, 420.11, and 420.13, condition (4); cf. above, notes 34, 211, and the apt observations of Madelung, 'Amr be maʿrūf', 995af.).

[271] See al-Shahīd al-Thānī, *Rawḍa*, 2:415.5; Bahā' al-Dīn, *Arbaʿīn*, 106.14; Najafī, *Jawāhir*, 21:371.12; Khwānsārī, *Jāmiʿ*, 5:404.16; Khumaynī, *Taḥrīr*, 1:472 no. 1; Khū'ī, *Minhāj*, 7:150.6.

[272] But see al-Shahīd al-Thānī, *Rawḍa*, 2:415.1.

[273] See particularly al-Shahīd al-Awwal, *Durūs*, 2:47.3 (formulating the condition as *imkān al-ta'thīr*), and al-Shahīd al-Thānī, *Masālik*, 3:102.10 (endorsing this view); also al-Shahīd al-Thānī, *Rawḍa*, 2:415.6, 416.1; Muqaddas, *Majmaʿ*, 7:536.18 (cf. also *ibid.*, 539.14, and Muqaddas, *Zubda*, 353.21); Sabzawārī, *Kifāya*, 82.2 (inclining towards a more restrictive view); Mīrzā-yi Qummī, *Jāmiʿ*, 1:417.11 no. 490 (taking a similar view); Najafī, *Jawāhir*, 21:368.7 (worrying over the more restrictive wording of the Muḥaqqiq, for which see above, note 181); Khumaynī, *Taḥrīr*, 1:467.9, and no. 1.

lapse.[274] Likewise for the danger condition the usual view is that the mere supposition (*ẓann*) of untoward consequences suffices to void the duty.[275]

Turning to the second question, the conditions fall into two groups. On the one hand there is the efficacy condition: just as this condition is easily satisfied, so also its voiding leaves one free to proceed.[276] On the other hand we have the conditions where the usual view is that voiding renders it forbidden to proceed. This is the case with the knowledge condition (in so far as it is discussed in this context),[277] the persistence condition,[278] and, with occasional qualification, the danger condition.[279] The qualification usually takes the form that it is permissible to proceed in the case of bearable loss, particularly to property.[280]

Sometimes, however, the qualifications begin to erode the condition itself. Before modern times, this is scarcely encountered. In a way this is surprising, since the long activist tradition had condemned those who perform the duty only when safe (*idhā aminū ʾl-ḍarar*).[281] But this had been largely ignored by the scholars, despite its direct contradiction of

[274] For discussions of the question see, for example, al-Shahīd al-Thānī, *Masālik*, 3:102.22 (expressing some doubt); Muqaddas, *Majmaʿ*, 7:537.17; Najafī, *Jawāhir*, 21:370.14; Khumaynī, *Taḥrīr*, 1:470 no. 2; Khūʾī, *Minhāj*, 7:148.2. Mīrzā-yi Qummī is asked whether one may construe the conduct of Muslims as licit even when this is barely plausible (*Jāmiʿ*, 1:417.7 no. 490), and replies that in such cases one should proceed with the duty, but not forbid the conduct in question categorically (*ibid.*, 417.13).

[275] See al-Shahīd al-Awwal, *Durūs*, 2:47.12; al-Shahīd al-Thānī, *Masālik*, 3:102.16; al-Shahīd al-Thānī, *Rawḍa*, 2:416.2; Mīrzā-yi Qummī, *Jāmiʿ*, 1:417.11 no. 490; Najafī, *Jawāhir*, 21:373.4; Khūʾī, *Minhāj*, 7:151.1 (for the qualification that follows there, see below, ch. 18, notes 209f.).

[276] See al-Shahīd al-Awwal, *Durūs*, 2:47.13; al-Shahīd al-Awwal, *Qawāʿid*, 2:202.5 (mentioning that it is also recommended; this derives from Qarāfī, *Furūq*, 4:256.1, and is repeated in Miqdād, *Naḍd*, 264.15); al-Shahīd al-Thānī, *Masālik*, 3:102.18; al-Shahīd al-Thānī, *Rawḍa*, 2:416.3; Kāshif al-Ghiṭāʾ, *Kashf*, 420.13 (describing it as *sunna* to proceed; cf. also *ibid.*, 420.10).

[277] See al-Shahīd al-Awwal, *Qawāʿid*, 2:202.2 (taken from Qarāfī, *Furūq*, 4:255.22, and repeated in Miqdād, *Naḍd*, 264.12; Muqaddas, *Majmaʿ*, 7:539.8). Kāshif al-Ghiṭāʾ takes the view that uncertainty (*iḥtimāl*) makes it a matter of *sunna* (rather than obligation) to proceed (*Kashf*, 420.13).

[278] See al-Shahīd al-Awwal, *Durūs*, 2:47.14; al-Shahīd al-Thānī, *Masālik*, 3:103.11; Muqaddas, *Majmaʿ*, 7:539.8; Najafī, *Jawāhir*, 21:370.3.

[279] See al-Shahīd al-Awwal, *Durūs*, 2:47.13; al-Shahīd al-Awwal, *Qawāʿid*, 2:202.8 (not from Qarāfī, repeated in Miqdād, *Naḍd*, 265.1); al-Shahīd al-Thānī, *Masālik*, 3:102.19; al-Shahīd al-Thānī, *Rawḍa*, 2:415.6, 416.3; Muqaddas, *Majmaʿ*, 7:539.8; Khumaynī, *Taḥrīr*, 1:472 no. 4. The qualifications mentioned by some of these scholars will be taken up in the following notes. Mīrzā-yi Qummī is unusual in giving an account in which obligation turns on the principle that one must choose the lesser evil (*aqall-i qabīḥayn*), see *Jāmiʿ*, 1:420.22.

[280] So al-Shahīd al-Awwal, *Qawāʿid*, 2:202.8 (not taken from Qarāfī, and repeated in Miqdād, *Naḍd*, 265.1); Muqaddas, *Majmaʿ*, 7:539.10; Khumaynī, *Taḥrīr*, 1:472 nos. 4f. Cf. the view of Sallār among the classical jurists (see above, note 208, and cf. also note 211)).

[281] See above, 256.

the danger condition.[282] Instead, we find a continuing rejection of flirtation with danger.[283] Occasionally this is enlivened with explicit polemics against the Sunnī weakness for the temptations of heroism. Thus al-Shahīd al-Awwal, in adapting a work of the Mālikī Qarāfī (d. 684/1285), refutes his arguments on this question one by one.[284] Likewise Muḥsin al-Fayḍ, in making his recension of Ghazzālī's *Revival of the religious sciences*, interrupts him to disallow rudeness (*al-takhshīn fī 'l-qawl*) to rulers,[285] and again to discard his stories about Sunnīs (*ahl al-ḍalāl*) who courted death by confronting tyrants out of a hidden desire for status and popularity.[286] Recent scholars, however, have moved sharply in the other direction.[287]

This new radicalism was, however, political rather than intellectual, and as such will not concern us in this chapter. There was no accompanying effort to redo the whole edifice of conditions. There were ancient doubts about the knowledge condition,[288] and these continued.[289] But beyond this the scholars showed little disposition to return to the drawing-board. The only radical account in intellectual terms is that of Taqī al-Qummī,

[282] Attempts to explain it away were made by Sabzawārī (*Kifāya*, 82.7), Ḥurr al-ʿĀmilī (*Wasāʾil*, 6:1:402.5), and Najafī (*Jawāhir*, 21:372.12). However, the four interpretations listed by Ḥurr al-ʿĀmilī include the duty to endure slight harm (*al-ḍarar al-yasīr*) and the virtue (*istiḥbāb*) of enduring great harm (*al-ḍarar al-ʿaẓīm*); Najafī responds sceptically to this, and rules out the second altogether.

[283] See the references given above, note 279.

[284] Qarāfī had stated that some held it permissible to court danger to oneself, and gave their arguments, including of course the tradition about speaking out in the presence of an unjust ruler (*Furūq*, 4:257.17; for the tradition, see above, ch. 1, note 18); by the end of the presentation, it seems that Qarāfī is speaking in his own voice (*ibid.*, 258.8). For the Shahīd's responses to these arguments of the Sunnīs (*al-ʿāmma*), see *Qawāʿid*, 205.15, repeated in Miqdād, *Naḍd*, 267.11. For the relationship between the two works, cf. above, esp. notes 221, 248, 252, 264, 276f.

[285] Fayḍ, *Maḥajja*, 4:112.19; cf. Ghazzālī, *Iḥyāʾ*, 2:314.8.

[286] Fayḍ, *Maḥajja*, 4:113.2; cf. Ghazzālī, *Iḥyāʾ*, 2:314.17. He does quote one story about a man who reproved the caliph al-Manṣūr (r. 136–58/754–75) after getting a guarantee of safety from him (*Maḥajja*, 4:113.7, from Ghazzālī, *Iḥyāʾ*, 2:321.10); the man turned out to be Khaḍir (*Maḥajja*, 4:117.9, cf. Ghazzālī, *Iḥyāʾ*, 323.8). Compare also Fayḍ's remark that a man who courts death by reproving those who hold political power is likely to be condemned to hell for his violation of the prohibition of suicide (Q2:195) (*Maḥajja*, 4:111.16, and cf. 113.4).

[287] See below, ch. 18, 533–40.

[288] Suppose I know (say from reliable witnesses) that someone is acting wrongly, but do not know just what it is that is wrong about his conduct; could it not be said that I am still obligated, but now have the added duty of first finding out what it is that is wrong? This argument first appears with Karakī (*Jāmiʿ*, 3:486.6; *Fawāʾid*, f. 138a.17, whence Najafī, *Jawāhir*, 21:366.12); it is taken up by al-Shahīd al-Thānī (*Masālik*, 3:101.18), and by Muqaddas al-Ardabīlī (*Majmaʿ*, 7:535.16), who goes on to suggest a counter-argument. Najafī refutes the argument (*Jawāhir*, 21:367.6). Cf. also below, ch. 18, 543.

[289] Khwānsārī, *Jāmiʿ*, 5:403.1; Khūʾī, *Minhāj*, 7:146.4 (where the words *wa-law ijmālan* take account of Karakī's argument); Taqī al-Qummī, *Mabānī*, 7:147.4 (rejecting the condition outright; and cf. *ibid.*, 146.20, on the duty to find out); and cf. Khumaynī, *Taḥrīr*, 1:471 no. 12. I detect no political overtones in these discussions.

who rejects the knowledge and danger conditions,[290] and has doubts about the efficacy condition.[291]

There is not much else about the formulation of Imāmī doctrine in this period that needs attention. The classical practice of defining the key terms of the duty continues.[292] Here Miqdād al-Suyūrī correctly identifies one particular twist of definition as characteristic of Abū 'l-Ḥusayn al-Baṣrī (d. 436/1044), as against the majority of the Muʿtazila.[293] At the same time the two topics mentioned above for their conspicuous absence or near-absence from classical discussions[294] now appear: the question whether the sinner is obligated,[295] and the problem of disagreements between scholars as to what is and is not wrong.[296] These developments clearly reflect Sunnī influence,[297] as does the occasional use of a terminology stemming from Ghazzālī in which terms normally associated with the role of the official censor (*ḥisba* and *iḥtisāb*) appear as synonyms for forbidding wrong.[298]

[290] See the preceding note, and below, ch. 18, note 210.

[291] See Taqī al-Qummī, *Mabānī*, 7:148.13.

[292] Miqdād, *Irshād*, 381.12–383.4; Miqdād, *Kanz*, 1:404.12; Miqdād, *Nāfiʿ*, 128.1; Ibn Fahd al-Ḥillī (d. 841/1437f.), *al-Muhadhdhab al-bāriʿ*, ed. M. al-ʿArāqī, Qumm 1407–13, 2:321.12; al-Shahīd al-Thānī, *Masālik*, 3:99.7; Abū 'l-Fatḥ al-Jurjānī, *Tafsīr*, 2:97.4; Kāshānī, *Manhaj*, 2:293.2 (to Q3:104); Bahāʾ al-Dīn, *Arbaʿīn*, 104.3; Najafī, *Jawāhir*, 21:356.10; Khwānsārī, *Jāmiʿ*, 5:398.10.

[293] The feature in question is the insistence on *istiʿlāʾ* as opposed to plain *ʿuluww* in the definition of *amr* (Miqdād, *Irshād*, 381.18, and cf. his *Kanz*, 1:404.12, and his *Nāfiʿ*, 128.1). This is found in all the works of the ʿAllāma in which he offers a definition of the term (for references, see above, note 214). The term *istiʿlāʾ* does indeed appear in Abū 'l-Ḥusayn al-Baṣrī's definition of *amr* (*al-Muʿtamad fī uṣūl al-fiqh*, ed. M. Hamidullah, Damascus 1964–5, 49.19). Cf. also Yaḥyā ibn Ḥamza, *Shamil*, f. 181b.9.

[294] See above, 281f.

[295] Miqdād, *Kanz*, 1:408.5, whence Kāshānī, *Manhaj*, 2:295.15 (to Q3:104); Bahāʾ al-Dīn, *Arbaʿīn*, 107.15 (with his own view at 108.5); Jawād al-Kāẓimī, *Masālik*, 2:375.3; Fayḍ, *Mafātīḥ*, 2:55.5; Aḥmad al-Jazāʾirī, *Qalāʾid*, 2:203.7; Najafī, *Jawāhir*, 21:373.5, 374.4; Khwānsārī, *Jāmiʿ*, 5:406.9 (from the *Jawāhir*), 407.5 (offering an opinion of his own); Khumaynī, *Taḥrīr*, 1:475 no. 20; Taqī al-Qummī, *Mabānī*, 7:152.13, 154.6. Aḥmad al-Jazāʾirī is alone in dismissing the view that the sinner is obligated (*lā yakhfā mā fīhi*).

[296] The standard Sunnī restriction of the duty in connection with matters on which the law-schools differ makes an appearance in al-Shahīd al-Awwal's recension of the *Furūq* of the Mālikī Qarāfī (al-Shahīd al-Awwal, *Qawāʿid*, 2:201.11, reflecting Qarāfī, *Furūq*, 4:257.7, and repeated in Miqdād, *Naḍd*, 264.10). Mīrzā-yi Qummī enlarges on the principle, giving examples of a familiar kind: one is grape-juice which has been boiled, but not until the loss of two-thirds of its volume, and the other is the use of tambourines by women at weddings (*Jāmiʿ*, 1:419.6). Though later endorsed by Khumaynī (*Taḥrīr*, 1:466 no. 2, and cf. *ibid.*, 476 no. 24), this principle never becomes a regular part of the discussion of *al-amr bi'l-maʿrūf*. Cf. also above, note 269.

[297] Likewise the only appearance of the question of the sinner that I have noted in a classical Imāmī text stems from Zamakhsharī (see above, note 216). The issue is domesticated in the Imāmī environment by bringing the infallible imam into the argument (so Bahāʾ al-Dīn, *Arbaʿīn*, 108.12, followed by Fayḍ, *Mafātīḥ*, 2:55.11).

[298] See al-Shahīd al-Awwal, *Durūs*, 2:47.1 (assuming the heading *kitāb al-ḥisba* to be his);

More interesting developments take place in the treatment accorded to Imāmī tradition. The classical scholars had, of course, quoted traditions in their accounts of forbidding wrong, sometimes in considerable numbers.[299] But they had not made it their business to argue closely from them; and perhaps for this reason, they had shown no interest in the reliability of their transmission. This remains true down to the early Ṣafawid period. The first indication that something has changed is the frequency with which Muqaddas al-Ardabīlī uses traditions to argue for specific points of doctrine.[300] He makes particularly effective use of the tradition from Jaʿfar al-Ṣādiq on the strong who can expect obedience, finding in it authority for three of the four conditions.[301] In this he is followed more or less closely by Bahāʾ al-Dīn al-ʿĀmilī[302] and Muḥsin al-Fayḍ.[303] Subsequently Majlisī in his commentaries on the traditions collected by Kulaynī and Ṭūsī indicates the transmission-status of the individual traditions;[304] Aḥmad al-Jazāʾirī (d. 1151/1738f.) then uses such information to set aside the tradition about the strong.[305] These trends leave their mark on subsequent scholarship. Thus Najafī gives space to interpreting awkward traditions,[306] while

Kāshānī, *Manhaj*, 2:305.23 (to Q3:114; there is a parallel in Fayḍ, *Ṣāfī*, 1:344.4); Bahāʾ al-Dīn, *Arbaʿīn*, 104.15, 106.16, 108.14 (whence doubtless Fayḍ, *Mafātīḥ*, 2:55.12); Fayḍ, *Maḥajja*, 4:110.13, 112.2; and cf. Fayḍ, *Nukhba*, 108.7, and Fayḍ, *Wāfī*, 9:6.2, where *kitāb al-ḥisba* appears as the heading of a book that includes the topics normally covered in the *kitāb al-jihād*; Muḥammad Mahdī al-Narāqī (d. 1209/1794f.), *Jāmiʿ al-saʿādāt*, ed. M. Kalāntar, Najaf 1963, 2:240.18 (and some fourteen instances in the following ten pages; these disappear in the Persian rendering of the work by his son, see Aḥmad Narāqī (d. 1245/1829), *Miʿrāj al-saʿāda*, Qumm 1371 sh., 515–21). As is clear from these references, the Ghazzālian terminology entered the Imāmī tradition well before Muḥsin al-Fayḍ made his recension of the *Iḥyāʾ*. The innovatory character of this usage was noted by Murtaḍā Muṭahharī (d. 1399/1979) ('Amr ba-maʿrūf wa nahy az munkar', *Guftār-i māh*, 1 (1339–40 sh.), Tehran n.d., 79.11). Muṭahharī also cited an Imāmī lexicographer who defines *ḥisba* as *al-amr biʾl-maʿrūf* (Ṭurayḥī (d. 1085/1674f.), *Majmaʿ al-baḥrayn*, ed. A. al-Ḥusaynī, Najaf and Tehran 1381–95, 2:41a.17). For Ghazzālī's terminology, see below, ch. 16, 428f. [299] Cf. above, note 89.

[300] Muqaddas, *Majmaʿ*, 7:539.7, 539.12, 541.13, 543.16, 544.17. Cf. Modarressi Tabātabāʾi, *Introduction*, 53.

[301] Muqaddas, *Majmaʿ*, 7:537.5. For this tradition, see above, 256f.

[302] Bahāʾ al-Dīn, *Arbaʿīn*, 106.15.

[303] Fayḍ, *Mafātīḥ*, 2:56.14; Fayḍ, *Maḥajja*, 4:107.18; and cf. the resonances of the same tradition, *ibid.*, 106.13, 112.2. The three-tradition schema of Ḥurr al-ʿĀmilī (*Bidāya*, 2:59.3) may belong in this lineage, though it could also reflect a classical model (cf. above, notes 183–5, 267).

[304] Majlisī, *Mirʾāt*, 18:399–413; Majlisī, *Malādh*, 9:466–76. On this showing, the tradition about the strong is weak (*ḍaʿīf*, see Majlisī, *Mirʾāt*, 18:406.20, and his *Malādh*, 9:470.11), and the long activist tradition is flawed by an interrupted *isnād* (*mursal*, see Majlisī, *Mirʾāt*, 18:399.14, and his *Malādh*, 9:476.13). In general, the treatment is harsh: out of the twenty-one traditions of Ṭūsī which Majlisī categorises, only five have acceptable ratings.

[305] Aḥmad al-Jazāʾirī, *Qalāʾid*, 2:201.14 (*ḍaʿf sanadihā*).

[306] Najafī, *Jawāhir*, 21:361.8 (connecting the tradition about the strong with the just imam), 372.12 (on *idhā aminū ʾl-ḍarar* in the long activist tradition). Compare Khwānsārī, *Jāmiʿ*, 5:405.11, 411.2.

Khwānsārī (d. 1405/1985) is aware of problems over the reliability of traditions, though he has no wish to exploit them.[307] By contrast, the account of Taqī al-Qummī, with its characteristic iconoclasm, uses considerations of transmission to trash the bulk of the relevant traditions.[308] I leave the politically tendentious treatment of traditions by some modern scholars to a later chapter.[309]

The background to most of these developments is obviously the Akhbārī controversy and its aftermath.[310] What is just as striking is the absence of any distinctive views on substantive questions among the scholars with Akhbārī sympathies.

Overall, what we see in this period of Imāmī scholasticism is increasing sophistication within a familiar, if somewhat eroded, classical framework[311] – and this without benefit of any continuing contact with Muʿtazilism. We have encountered numerous examples of this: the way the later scholars handle the tension between the escalatory and de-escalatory ordering of the modes; their exclusion of performance within the heart from the scope of forbidding wrong; their attack on the classical treatment of the first and second modes as an ordered set; their concern for symmetry in the analysis of the problem of the divisibility of right and wrong; the clarity with which they identify what is at issue between the individual and collective accounts of the duty; their more systematic treatment of the conditions with respect to the problems raised by uncertainty and the issue of the permissibility of proceeding when a condition is not satisfied. Indeed on occasion one has the sense that the later scholars are running rings around their less agile classical predecessors. Alongside this runs a new disposition (by no means confined to Akhbārī scholars) to take Imāmī tradition seriously, whether by arguing from its specific content or by testing its credentials of transmission.

So much for the lecture-room. What of the street? Over the bulk of the period considered here, there are few developments that can plausibly be

[307] *Ibid.*, 402.7, and cf. 411.6.

[308] See Taqī al-Qummī, *Mabānī*, 7:144.15 (setting aside the string of traditions he begins to quote *ibid.*, 141.15), and the repeated dismissals that appear subsequently (*ibid.*, 146–8, 151, 153–6). He makes no exception for the tradition about the strong (*ibid.*, 146.16, 147.10), nor for the long activist tradition (*ibid.*, 154.17), though this does not prevent him using these traditions to his advantage when it suits him (*ibid.*, 141.13, 151.10, and cf. 160.7). No tradition is at any stage in the argument pronounced sound.

[309] See below, ch. 18, notes 227, 241.

[310] For the place in this controversy of Muḥsin al-Fayḍ, the Akhbārī who has been cited most in this section, see E. Kohlberg, 'Aspects of Akhbari thought in the seventeenth and eighteenth centuries', in N. Levtzion and J. O. Voll (eds.), *Eighteenth-century renewal and reform in Islam*, Syracuse 1987, 136–46.

[311] This reflects the general evolution of Imāmī law (see Modarressi Tabātabāʾī, *Introduction*, 50, 51, 56, 57).

seen as responses to changing real-world conditions. The virtual disappearance of the view that the imam's permission is not needed for serious violence – a view supported by no less an authority than the ʿAllāma – could perhaps be correlated with the political establishment of Imāmism under the Ṣafawids (907–1135/1501–1722) and their successors. The emergence early in the Ṣafawid period of the idea that a suitably qualified jurist can nevertheless undertake such action is no doubt part of a changing view of clerical authority in Imāmī Shīʿism; but this innovation of Karakī's was largely ignored by his successors until Khumaynī. If we leave it aside, there is nothing in the development of the formal Imāmī doctrine of forbidding wrong that would suggest an enhancement of the authority of the clergy.[312] All in all, this is a surprisingly meagre yield when we consider the extent of the changes that Imāmism was undergoing in this period, and the expression these found in doctrinal disputes in other fields.[313] As we found with Imāmī tradition, so also with the juristic thought of the Imāmīs: forbidding wrong is just not a particularly sensitive point in the interaction of Imāmī scholasticism with political and social realities.

Against this background, the last few decades appear as a period of dramatic change. On the intellectual side, the most interesting phenomenon is the attack on several hallowed features of the scholastic tradition represented by Taqī al-Qummī. As we have seen, his account rejects the inclusion of the non-verbal first and third modes within forbidding wrong, does considerable damage to the four conditions (rejecting two of them, while throwing doubt on a third), and savages most of the relevant Imāmī traditions. These intellectual pyrotechnics are not, however, associated with any discernible political agenda. The political shift of recent decades is to be found in the thought of scholars who in purely intellectual terms were far

312 Thus al-Ḥurr al-ʿĀmilī states that the duty must be performed by the elite vis-à-vis the masses, and vice versa (*Bidāya*, 2:59.6), while Khūʾī emphasises that it is not one confined to any one category (*ṣinf*) of people, but obligates scholars and laity alike (*Minhāj*, 7:152.4). That such formal doctrine may not tell the whole story is suggested by a responsum of Mīrzā-yi Qummī (*Jāmiʿ*, 1:422f. no. 493). The question concerns a person who has the capacity (*qābilīyat*) for *al-amr biʾl-maʿrūf* and is learned, but fears that if he seeks clerical authority (*marjaʿīyat-i mardum*), this will have deleterious effects on his character; yet there is nobody else to undertake the role. The answer is that such a man should indeed choose pastoral care (*qaḍā-yi ḥawāyij-i ʿibād*) because of the importance of this work. The question takes it for granted that *al-amr biʾl-maʿrūf* is a characteristic of clerical authority (he may have in mind the implementation of the *ḥadd* punishments, though there is no explicit mention of them). We also find included here in the *kitāb al-amr biʾl-maʿrūf* two questions concerning clerical education which make no specific reference to the duty (*ibid.*, 424 no. 498 (*sic*), and 424f. no. 496).

313 Cf. Madelung, 'Shiite discussions on the legality of the *kharāj*'; Modarressi Tabātabāʾi, *Kharāj in Islamic law*, 47–59; and more generally, Calder, 'Legitimacy and accommodation in Safavid Iran'.

less radical; again, this political development will be taken up in a later chapter.[314]

Overall, what is lacking in the Imāmī scholastic literature, classical and post-classical, is concrete and colourful detail. In Imāmī society, as elsewhere, there was more to forbidding wrong than dry scholastic doctrine. Thus the responsa of Mīrzā-yi Qummī (d. 1231/1815f.) deal with a variety of questions which the systematic accounts of the duty given by the Imāmī scholars do not consider. Is it a husband's duty to command and forbid his wife?[315] Is it one's duty to command right to one's father in all modes, or should one distinguish between speaking gently, which is a duty, and speaking harshly, which is not?[316] What exactly counts as blameworthy singing for legal purposes, and what if elegies and scripture are recited with vocal tremor (*larzish*)?[317] Must compensation be paid for broken wine-jars?[318] Likewise Ṣafawid rulers, in their official attempts to execute the duty by curbing the pleasures of their delinquent subjects, had very specific notions of the wrongs they were seeking to right: wine-taverns, ale-houses, establishments that were the haunts of drug-addicts, story-tellers, prostitutes, and gamblers; pigeon-fancying; the shaving of beards; the playing of mandolins and other musical instruments; the pursuit of beardless youths, and the employment of such youths in bath-houses.[319] There is also biographical material. Thus Āghā Buzurg al-Ṭihrānī (d. 1389/1970) in his biographies of scholars who died in the fourteenth/twentieth century makes occasional references to their zeal, steadfastness or courage in forbidding wrong.[320] He describes them in much the same terms as we find

314 See below, ch. 18, section 3.

315 Mīrzā-yi Qummī, *Jāmiʿ*, 1:417 no. 489. The answer is that it most certainly is; here the duty includes religious instruction.

316 *Ibid.*, 424 no. 495. The distinction is correct.

317 *Ibid.*, 418 no. 491. Tremor is not in itself singing.

318 *Ibid.*, 423f. no. 494. The question is not directly answered.

319 See the firman of Shāh Ṭahmāsp (r. 930–84/1524–76) published in R. Jaʿfarīyān, *Dīn wa siyāsat dar dawra-i Ṣafawī*, Qumm 1370 sh., 434.17. For a similar list in another firman of the same ruler, see *ibid.*, 439.20 (mentioning also backgammon and *taʿziya*-performances). Matters had not changed much by the end of the Ṣafawid period, as is attested by the lists of evils found in two firmans of Shāh Sulṭān Ḥusayn (r. 1105–35/1694–1722) (*ibid.*, 442.11, 444.16), albeit a richer range of animal sports appears here (*ibid.*, 443.7, 445.8). These firmans were drawn to my attention by Kambiz Eslami. See also R. Jaʿfarīyān, 'Amr bah maʿrūf wa nahy az munkar dar dawra-i Ṣafawī', *Kayhān-i Andīsha*, 82 (1377 sh.).

320 Āghā Buzurg al-Ṭihrānī (d. 1389/1970), *Nuqabāʾ al-bashar fi ʾl-qarn al-rābiʿ ʿashar* (in his *Ṭabaqāt aʿlām al-Shīʿa*), Najaf 1954–68, 19.14, 94.13, 201.10, 333.3, 337.8, 438.16, 502.14, 568.22, 882.5, 1212.5, 1325.19, 1377.11, 1434.1, 1435.9. Most of these scholars died in the first half of the century. He also notes two scholars who wrote epistles about *al-amr biʾl-maʿrūf*, or in performance of the duty (*ibid.*, 212.3, 948.19). For a slightly earlier period, see, for example, Muḥammad Ḥasan Khān Iʿtimād al-Salṭana (d. 1313/1896), *Chihil sāl-i tārīkh-i Īrān*, ed. I. Afshār, Tehran 1363–8 sh., 193.15, 207.6, 219.25, 774.3.

in Sunnī biographical writing; thus their willingness to court danger and suffer harm appears as a virtue.[321] But only for one scholar does he enlarge on general characterisation with anecdotal material.[322] Much more such evidence could doubtless be found. But these themes were not caught in the net of the traditional scholastic discussion of the duty. This discussion was in any case losing steam thanks to a tendency in the last phase of pre-modern Imāmī literature to omit from the law-book the entire treatment of holy war; since forbidding wrong was traditionally part of this treatment, it became an inadvertent casualty of this omission.[323]

5. EXCURSUS: THE ISMĀʿĪLĪS

At the core of Ismāʿīlism was a fusion of gnostic cosmological speculation with Islamic religious politics. The gnostic component, esoteric and antinomian, was hardly fertile soil for so exoteric and law-oriented a conception as forbidding wrong. The political component, however, inevitably committed the Ismāʿīlīs to having a concept of legitimate political authority, something pre-Islamic gnostics had no need for. At the same time, the esoteric core of Ismāʿīlī religion was at most times and places embedded in an exterior more in conformity with the prevailing Islamic environment; and this exoteric form of the religion could easily become the reality that many Ismāʿīlīs actually lived by. All this meant that forbidding wrong, though not central to Ismāʿīlī thought, was bound to feature in it.

[321] Āghā Buzurg, *Nuqabāʾ al-bashar*, 568.23 (*wa-law kāna fī dhālika khaṭar ʿalayhi*), 1377.12 (*lā yubālī bi-mā qad yatarattab ʿalā dhālika min maḍarr*); and cf. *ibid.*, 94.14, 333.4.

[322] *Ibid.*, 1377.19. This scholar, Shaykh Muḥammad ʿAlī al-Khurāsānī al-Najafī, died in 1383/1964, and his encounter with modernity is reflected in an anecdote about his rebuke of a barber who had to shave beards in order to make a living (*ibid.*, 1378.3; cf. below, ch. 18, note 28).

[323] Cf. below, ch. 18, notes 200, 207; for the placing of *al-amr biʾl-maʿrūf* in the *kitāb al-jihād*, see above, note 2. Muḥammad Karīm Khān Kirmānī (d. 1288/1871), the founder of the Kirmānī branch of Shaykhism, notes the tendency of the jurists to omit the *kitāb al-jihād*, and gives as the reason the pointlessness of investigating the topics it covers (*Risāla dar jawāb-i suʾālāt-i Niẓām al-ʿUlamāʾ*, translated from the Arabic by Ḥusayn Āl-i Hāshimī, Kirmān n.d., 79.6). Particularly in the case of the Shaykhīs, there was a doctrinal basis for this omission in the deferment of (offensive) *jihād* until the return of the imam (see, for example, *ibid.*, 79.2, speaking of *ḥurmat-i jihād dar zamān-i ghaybat*; for the wider Imāmī background, see Kohlberg, 'Development', 79–86). Muḥammad Karīm Khān went so far as to extend this deferment to most cases of *al-amr biʾl-maʿrūf* (*Sī faṣl*, Kirmān 1368, 38.5: *dar bisyārī az jāhā sāqiṭ ast tā ẓuhūr-i imām*). He nevertheless devoted a work to the legal aspects of *al-amr biʾl-maʿrūf* (see Abū ʾl-Qāsim Khān Kirmānī (d. 1389/1969), *Fihrist*, Kirmān n.d., 2:221.14, on his unpublished *Niẓām al-bashar*, and cf. the responsum mentioned *ibid.*, 246 item 4). Though he omitted the topic from his law-book (*ibid.*, 214.10), he covered it in his collection of traditions (*Faṣl al-khiṭāb*, Kirman 1392, 651–4, drawn to my attention by Etan Kohlberg).

In terms of Ismāʿīlī notions of political authority, forbidding wrong is in the first instance something done by imams. In 302/915, during the first Fāṭimid invasion of Egypt, the future caliph al-Qāʾim (r. 322–34/934–46) spoke in the mosque of Alexandria of the vicious morals of the rulers of the day, and averred that there had been no one to command right or forbid wrong until the appearance of 'the meek and lowly ʿAbdallāh', sc. ʿUbaydallāh al-Mahdī (r. 297–322/909–34), the first Fāṭimid caliph.[324] The caliph al-Muʿizz (r. 341–65/953–75) speaks of the evil alcoholic, sexual and musical proclivities of his subjects, and of the mission God has conferred on 'us' (sc. the imams) to command right and forbid wrong among them.[325] The Fāṭimid missionary (*dāʿī*) Aḥmad ibn Ibrāhīm al-Naysābūrī (*fl.* later fourth/tenth century) refers both Q3:104 and Q3:110 to the imams.[326] Perhaps the most famous, not to say notorious, attempt by a ruler to impose a puritan morality on his subjects was that of the Fāṭimid caliph al-Ḥākim (r. 386–411/996–1021);[327] and as might be expected, there are indications that this was done under the aegis of forbidding wrong.[328]

The duty is likewise associated with the main representatives of the imam, the missionaries (*dāʿīs*). Abū ʿAbdallāh al-Shīʿī (d. 298/911), who established the Fāṭimid state in North Africa, took action against liquor and all publicly visible wrongs after he had conquered Ifrīqiya;[329] and in a reassuring letter sent out to neighbouring parts of the Islamic world, he described his career in North Africa as one of – among other things – commanding

324 S. M. Stern, *Studies in early Ismāʿīlism*, Jerusalem and Leiden 1983, 118.6.

325 Qāḍī Nuʿmān (d. 363/974), *al-Majālis wa'l-musāyarāt*, ed. Ḥ. al-Faqī *et al.*, Tunis 1978, 92.9 (I owe this reference to Sumaiya Hamdani). For other references to *al-amr bi'l-maʿrūf* as a duty of imams, see *ibid.*, 137.20, 251.24. Failure to perform the duty was among the causes of Umayyad domination (*ibid.*, 93.2).

326 For Q3:104, see Aḥmad ibn Ibrāhīm al-Naysābūrī (*fl.* later fourth/tenth century), *al-Risāla al-mūjaza al-kāfiya fī adab al-duʿāt*, *apud* V. Klemm, *Die Mission des fāṭimidischen Agenten al-Muʾayyad fī d-dīn in Šīrāz*, Frankfurt am Main 1989, 266.6 (for Naysābūrī's work, see *ibid.*, 65); for Q3:110, see his *Ithbāt al-imāma*, ed. M. Ghālib, Beirut 1984, 68.4 (for this work, see I. K. Poonawala, *Biobibliography of Ismāʿīlī literature*, Malibu 1977, 91f.). Cf. also *Rasāʾil Ikhwān al-Ṣafā*, ed. K. al-Ziriklī, Cairo 1928, 4:30.20, and, for Imāmī parallels, above, 260–2.

327 H. Halm, 'Der Treuhänder Gottes: Die Edikte des Kalifen al-Ḥākim', *Der Islam*, 63 (1986), esp. 21–6, 56–9.

328 Maqrīzī (d. 845/1442), *Ittiʿāẓ al-ḥunafāʾ*, ed. J. al-Shayyāl and M. Ḥ. M. Aḥmad, Cairo 1967–73, 2:77.3, and cf., for example, *ibid.*, 44.3 (*rafʿ al-munkarāt*), 89.2 (*tatabbuʿ al-munkarāt wa'l-manʿ minhā*); Ibn Saʿīd al-Maghribī (d. *c.* 685/1286), *al-Nujūm al-zāhira*, ed. Ḥ. Naṣṣār, Cairo 1970, 74.1, and cf. 61.16. For the sources behind these sources, see Halm, 'Der Treuhänder Gottes', 15–17. We lack a first-hand Fāṭimid justification of the measures, but the remarks of al-Muʿizz on his subjects would fit such a context (see above, note 325).

329 Qāḍī Nuʿmān (d. 363/974), *Risālat iftitāḥ al-daʿwa*, ed. W. al-Qāḍī, Beirut 1970, 215.3.

right and forbidding wrong.[330] Naysābūrī, having stated that Q3:104 refers to the imams, then proceeds to extend it to missionaries, insisting however on their duty to practise what they preach.[331] In another passage, he includes forbidding wrong among the dignified and sober activities that should characterise the missionary's circle.[332] Ḥasan-i Ṣabbāḥ (d. 518/1124), according to a Nizārī Ismāʿīlī account of his life preserved in non-Ismāʿīlī sources, commanded right and forbade wrong during his long reign (483–518/1090–1124) at Alamūt; there is specific mention of liquor and music.[333] An account of the Yemeni missionary Ibrāhīm ibn al-Ḥusayn al-Ḥāmidī, who held office from 546/1151 to his death in 557/1162, describes him as forbidding wrong and commanding right (in that order); the context suggests that the terms are a natural description of what a missionary did.[334]

This role of forbidding wrong in Ismāʿīlī religious politics invites comparison with Zaydism. What is striking is how much more muted the idiom seems to be in the Ismāʿīlī context. Consider, for example, the career of Abū ʿAbdallāh al-Shīʿī, an instance of sectarian state-formation very similar in some respects to Zaydī initiatives in the same period. We possess a lively and detailed account of the process in a work of Qāḍī Nuʿmān (d. 363/974); yet it makes no reference to forbidding wrong other than as already indicated.[335] It is hard to imagine a comparable Zaydī text being so sparing.

[330] *Ibid.*, 220.1.

[331] Naysābūrī, *Risāla*, 266.7. For the theme of setting oneself to rights, cf. Naysābūrī, *Ithbāt*, 68.3, and Qāḍī Nuʿmān (d. 363/974), *al-Himma fī ādāb atbāʿ al-aʾimma*, ed. M. K. Ḥusayn, n.p. n.d., 132.10. [332] Naysābūrī, *Risāla*, 220.2.

[333] See F. Daftary, *The Ismāʿīlīs: their history and doctrines*, Cambridge 1990, 367, citing Juwaynī (d. 681/1283), *Tārīkh-i jahān-gushā*, ed. Muḥammad Qazwīnī, Leiden and London 1912–37, 3:210.2; Rashīd al-Dīn (d. 718/1318), *Jāmiʿ al-tawārīkh: qismat-i Ismāʿīliyān wa Fāṭimīyān wa Nizāriyān wa dāʿiyān wa rafīqān*, ed. M. T. Dānishpazhūh and M. Mudarrisī Zanjānī, Tehran 1338 sh., 124.11; Abū ʾl-Qāsim Kāshānī (*fl.* early eighth/fourteenth century), *Zubdat al-tawārīkh*, section on the Ismāʿīlīs, ed. M. T. Dānishpazhūh, Tabrīz 1343 sh., 145.7. For the relationship between these accounts, see Daftary, *The Ismāʿīlīs*, 327–9.

[334] A. Hamdani, 'The dāʿī Ḥātim ibn Ibrāhīm al-Ḥāmidī (d. 596 H/1199 AD) and his book *Tuḥfat al-qulūb*', *Oriens*, 23–4 (1974), 286, beginning of the Arabic text (from the *Nuzhat al-afkār* of the *dāʿī* Idrīs ʿImād al-Dīn (d. 872/1468)).

[335] See above, notes 329f. Nagel, in a reference to the role of *al-amr biʾl-maʿrūf* in the movement of Abū ʿAbdallāh al-Shīʿī (*Staat und Glaubensgemeinschaft*, 1:229), cites Qāḍī Nuʿmān (d. 363/974), *Daʿāʾim al-Islām*, ed. A. ʿA. A. Fayḍī, Beirut 1991, 1:34.17. This passage gives an exegesis of Q3:104 as showing Muslims at large ('the people of the *qibla*') to be infidels; but it has no bearing on the implementation of *al-amr biʾl-maʿrūf*. It is doubtless taken from an Imāmī source (compare ʿAyyāshī, *Tafsīr*, 1:195 no 127, and Baḥrānī, *Burhān*, 1:308.6).

I have encountered only one formal account of forbidding wrong in the Ismāʿīlī sources I have consulted.[336] It is found in a work of the Yemeni missionary ʿAlī ibn Muḥammad ibn al-Walīd, who held office from 605/1209 to his death in 612/1215.[337] His account consists mostly of Koranic quotations. In the residue he offers a number of rather ordinary ideas. He sets out the usual three modes,[338] and mentions repeatedly that the duty is contingent on one's being able to perform it. Worth noting is his mention of precautionary dissimulation (*taqiyya*) as a reason for not proceeding with the duty.[339] Only one thing, however, sets his account apart from the mainstream of Islamic doctrine: he states explicitly that the duty (here conjoined to 'calling to the faith') is to be performed only by scholars, to the exclusion of others (*al-ʿulamāʾ dūna ghayrihim*).[340] It has been suggested, quite plausibly, that this might represent a later addition to the text.[341] Whether this is so or not, we have here an unabashed assertion of clerical authority scarcely paralleled elsewhere.

Some of the material analysed in this excursus could be seen as reflecting interaction with a Sunnī environment. The earliest attestations, the letter of Abū ʿAbdallāh al-Shīʿī and the speech of al-Qāʾim in Alexandria, invite such a gloss. But this cannot be true of the material as a whole; the activities of Ḥasan-i Ṣabbāḥ at Alamūt were not a public relations campaign directed at a Sunnī audience. So the value was unquestionably an authentic element of the Ismāʿīlī tradition. What we seem to lack is any indication as to how it related to the central ideas of Ismāʿīlism. Was it spirited away by symbolic interpretation? Was it given some startlingly concrete connotation? Ibn Abī ʾl-Ḥadīd makes the statement that the (Nizārī) Ismāʿīlīs justify their practice of assassination in terms of forbidding wrong;[342] but to my knowledge this is not attested in the literature of the Nizārīs themselves.

[336] The absence of the duty from the extant legal works of Qāḍī Nuʿmān is likely to reflect a conception of the proper contents of a law-book formed under Sunnī or, more likely, early Imāmī influence (for the Imāmīs, see above, note 2).

[337] ʿAlī ibn Muḥammad ibn al-Walīd (d. 612/1215), *Tāj al-ʿaqāʾid*, ed. ʿA. Tāmir, Beirut 1967, 111f. no. 59, translated or summarised in W. Ivanow, *A creed of the Fatimids*, Bombay 1936, 48f. no. 59 (for the work, see Poonawala, *Biobibliography*, 157).

[338] He gives them in the order tongue, hand and heart (Ibn al-Walīd, *Tāj*, 112.15).

[339] *Ibid.*, 112.17; cf. above, notes 34, 211, 270. [340] *Ibid.*, 111.3.

[341] Ivanow, *Creed*, 49, in his commentary to the account; he speaks of it as 'intended to uphold the interests of the priestly class'. Contrast the statement later in the account that the believer (and so presumably not just the scholar) is obligated (Ibn al-Walīd, *Tāj*, 112.15). [342] Ibn Abī ʾl-Ḥadīd, *Sharḥ*, 19:311.18.

PART IV

OTHER SECTS AND SCHOOLS

CHAPTER 12

THE ḤANAFĪS

1. INTRODUCTION

The Ḥanafīs were the oldest of the Sunnī law-schools.[1] But unlike the Ḥanbalites, they were slow in developing a distinct theological identity.[2] Abū Ḥanīfa (d. 150/767f.) had held views on theological questions, or at least such views were later ascribed to him; a tradition going back to these views was established among the Ḥanafīs of Samarqand, and eventually became known as Māturīdism. By the fifth/eleventh century this tradition was predominant in Transoxania, whence it spread to the Turks. Yet prior to this development, and for a while thereafter, Ḥanafīs subscribed to a variety of theological persuasions. There were Ḥanafī Muʿtazilites and Ḥanafī traditionalists, together with a second peculiarly Ḥanafī school, the Najjāriyya; we even encounter a Ḥanafī Ashʿarite.[3] But the brute force of history, in the shape of the Turkish invasion of the fifth/eleventh century and the subsequent domination of the Turks, was to sweep away this diversity, and establish Māturīdism as the theological face of Ḥanafism.

Our knowledge of Ḥanafī views of forbidding wrong is accordingly dominated by the Māturīdite heritage, and it is on the material preserved there that most of this chapter is inevitably based. We are not wholly ignorant of the Ḥanafī Muʿtazilites, since some of their literature survived both within and outside the Ḥanafī mainstream; one work stemming from this milieu will be considered at the end of this chapter.[4] But the only strictly

[1] The history of the formation and spread of the Ḥanafī law-school as a whole has yet to be written, but for a substantial contribution see N. Tsafrir, 'The spread of the Ḥanafī school in the western regions of the ʿAbbāsid caliphate up to the end of the third century AH', Princeton Ph.D. 1993.

[2] For what follows, see Madelung, 'The spread of Māturīdism', and his *Religious trends*, ch. 3.

[3] For these non-Māturīdite Ḥanafī persuasions, see Madelung, 'The spread of Māturīdism', 112–16.

[4] We have already encountered two Koran-centred works that were preserved among non-Muʿtazilite Sunnīs: the *Aḥkām al-Qurʾān* of Jaṣṣāṣ (d. 370/981), and the *Kashshāf* of

doctrinal residue of this heritage with which we will be concerned here is a single passage from the Koran commentary of Zamakhsharī (d. 538/1144). We have no solid information regarding attitudes to forbidding wrong among the Ḥanafī traditionalists, and none at all for the Najjāriyya.

2. THE ḤANAFĪS BEFORE THE OTTOMANS

The Ḥanafīs were a product of the Kūfan Murji'ite milieu of the second/eighth century. Pre-Ḥanafī Kūfan Murji'ites doubtless had views on the subject of forbidding wrong, but we know nothing of them.[5] With Abū Ḥanīfa, the eponymous founder of the law-school, we are better served. Much of what we are told of his opinions has already been discussed, but it will be useful to resume this rather disparate material here. Most generally, the duty is the second of five doctrinal points – a creed of sorts – ascribed to him in an early Ḥanafī text.[6] In two sources he is pressed on the question of rebellion against unjust rule under the aegis of forbidding wrong. In each case he agrees that forbidding wrong is a divinely imposed duty, and he does not categorically deny that it could sanction such activity. But he does in practice discourage it: it is not something that

Footnote 4 (*cont.*)
Zamakhsharī (d. 538/1144). As might be expected, the distribution of the manuscripts of the *Aḥkām al-Qur'ān* suggests that it was preserved primarily among Ḥanafīs (see Sezgin, *Geschichte*, 1:445). We have also met with two systematic theological works that were preserved by the Zaydīs, the *Minhāj* of Zamakhsharī and the *Fā'iq* of Ibn al-Malāḥimī (d. 536/1141), who was likewise doubtless a Ḥanafī. For Zamakhsharī and Ibn al-Malāḥimī, see above, ch. 9, section 4. Jaṣṣāṣ will be discussed below, section 7.

[5] The only primary source I know of which imputes a doctrinal position regarding *al-amr bi'l-ma'rūf* to non-Ḥanafī Murji'ites is Abū Tammām's *Shajara*, itself likely to be dependent on the heresiography of Abū 'l-Qāsim al-Balkhī (d. 319/931) (see above, ch. 1, note 28). He tells us that the Ghaylāniyya and all of the Murji'a hold that Muslims have a duty to forbid wrong in any way they can, by the sword, the tongue, the hand or the heart (*ibid.*, 80.11 = 79). In his historically rather worthless heresiography, by contrast, the Ḥanafī Makḥūl al-Nasafī (d. 318/930) quotes Q9:71 (noting that it does not reserve *al-amr bi'l-ma'rūf* to the *umarā'*) and the tradition about speaking out in the presence of an unjust ruler (see above, ch. 1, note 18) in order to refute the Bida'iyya, a sect which he classes as Murji'ite, and to which he imputes a belief in unconditional obedience to rulers (M. Bernand, 'Le *Kitāb al-radd 'alā l-bida'* d'Abū Muṭī' Makḥūl al-Nasafī', *Annales Islamologiques*, 16 (1980), 123.18; cf. Rudolf, *Al-Māturīdī*, 105); but there is no indication that the sect itself held a view on *al-amr bi'l-ma'rūf*. Ibn Mufliḥ (d. 763/1362) quotes a statement from Ibn Taymiyya (d. 728/1328) to the effect that some Murji'ites are inclined to abandon *al-amr bi'l-ma'rūf* in the belief that this constitutes avoidance of sedition (*Ādāb*, 1:177.11); but the example given is the Ḥanafī Māturīdī (d. *c.* 333/944) (see below, note 29). Cf. also Lambton, *State and government in medieval Islam*, 310, and Athamina, 'The early Murji'a', 124.

[6] See above, ch. 1, note 25. The replies Abū Ḥanīfa gives in the versions of the story in which he is asked about the duty by Ja'far al-Ṣādiq (d. 148/765) are blandly uninteresting (for this anecdote, see above, ch. 11, note 54).

one man can undertake on his own;[7] even if undertaken by a leader and his followers, it will cause more harm than good.[8] One Ḥanafī source nevertheless tells us that Abū Ḥanīfa held forbidding wrong to be obligatory by word and sword.[9] Abū Ḥanīfa also transmits a couple of Prophetic traditions endorsing martyrdom incurred in rebuking unjust rulers.[10] He takes the view that, if the community as a whole is acting wrongfully, one should emigrate.[11] In late sources, Abū Ḥanīfa appears as the author of the saying setting out the tripartite division of labour.[12] Finally, a good many sources relate in one form or another a relevant legal opinion of Abū Ḥanīfa: if someone breaks a mandolin – presumably in the course of forbidding wrong – then he owes compensation for it.[13] Such material cannot add up to a systematic account of the duty, and its authenticity is by no means assured; but for so early a figure it is not to be sneezed at. It suggests that the topic gave rise to considerable tension in early Ḥanafī thought.

Yet if we expect to find here the beginnings of a rich Ḥanafī literary tradition on forbidding wrong, we shall be disappointed. Like the Sunnīs in general, the Ḥanafīs do not treat the topic in their law-books.[14] What is more surprising is that, with few exceptions, they do not treat it in works

[7] See above, ch. 1, 7. [8] See above, ch. 1, note 26.

[9] See below, note 198, and cf. above, ch. 1, note 28. [10] See above, ch. 1, notes 19f.

[11] Abū Ḥanīfa, *al-Fiqh al-absaṭ*, 48.4 (*wa-'khruj ilā ghayrihim*). He invokes Q4:97, Q29:56, a Prophetic tradition with the standard Ḥanafī *isnād*, and an anonymous Companion tradition.

[12] See below, note 132, and ʿAlī al-Qārī, *Mubīn*, 188.20 (an incomplete version stating that *al-amr biʾl-maʿrūf* by hand is reserved for the authorities (*umarāʾ* and *wulāt*) because of their power, others being confined to doing it with the tongue).

[13] So ʿAbdallāh ibn Aḥmad ibn Ḥanbal, *Sunna*, 207 no. 323. Kāsānī (d. 587/1191) indicates that the view relates to musical instruments in general (*Badāʾiʿ al-ṣanāʾiʿ*, Cairo 1327–8, 5:144.28), and contrasts the position of Abū Yūsuf (d. 182/798) and Shaybānī (d. 189/805) (I am indebted to Baber Johansen for directing me to this passage); Kāsānī also mentions an analogous disagreement regarding the ripping of wine-skins (*ibid.*, 129.30). (For the concept of *māl* which is in play here, see B. Johansen, 'Commercial exchange and social order in Ḥanafite law', in C. Toll and J. Skovgaard-Petersen (eds.), *Law and the Islamic world past and present*, Copenhagen 1995, 89f.) See also Sunāmī (*fl.* early eighth/fourteenth century), *Niṣāb al-iḥtisāb*, ed. M. Y. ʿIzz al-Dīn, Riyāḍ 1982, 190.18 (for Sunāmī, whose *nisba* is Indian, see 10–13 of the editor's introduction, and M. Izzi Dien, *The theory and the practice of market law in medieval Islam*, Warminster 1997, 1–7); ʿAlī al-Qārī, *Mubīn*, 188.16 (indicating that Abū Ḥanīfa held that such things should not be destroyed). For Abū Yūsuf's view, see also *ibid.*, 188.15, and above, ch. 10, note 81.

[14] Quite why the Sunnīs should not have given *al-amr biʾl-maʿrūf* a place in their law-books is hard to say; the Ḥanbalite Abū Yaʿlā describes the duty as one of the *ʿibādāt sharʿiyya* (*Amr*, ff. 102a.1, 102a.17, 105a.15). The Ḥanafīs do, of course, touch on it on occasion, just as the Ḥanbalites do (see above, ch. 7, note 2). Thus Kāsānī takes a hard-line view regarding a home from which the sound of music is heard: one should enter without leave, since *taghyīr al-munkar* is a duty (*farḍ*) which otherwise could not be performed (Kāsānī, *Badāʾiʿ*, 5:125.3; also Ibn Qayyim al-Jawziyya (d. 751/1350), *Ighāthat al-lahfān*, ed. M. S. Kaylānī, Cairo 1961, 1:245.20, where the view is attributed to Abū Yūsuf); and cf. the references to Kāsānī in the preceding note and below, note 48.

of theology either.[15] The result is a scarcity of sustained, systematic accounts of the duty from Ḥanafī scholars. Instead, we often have to make do with scattered material which is soft in doctrinal content.

The Ḥanafī law-school originated in Iraq, and Iraq may have remained its most important centre for some centuries.[16] But thanks to the Turkish invasion of the fifth/eleventh century, it was the Ḥanafism of the north-eastern corner of the Islamic world that was swept to prominence.[17] Under the rule of the Sāmānids (263–395/875–1005), the Ḥanafīs of this region seem to have become relatively well disposed towards the state, something they had not been under ʿAbbāsid rule.[18] It is against this background that the duty receives some attention in works of – or ascribed to – two major Ḥanafī scholars of Samarqand: Abū Manṣūr al-Māturīdī (d. *c.* 333/944), after whom the theological school to which he belonged was eventually named,[19] and Abū ʾl-Layth al-Samarqandī (d. 373/983).[20]

There are two works ascribed to Māturīdī which have something of interest to say about the duty.[21] The first, the ascription of which to Māturīdī seems to be quite arbitrary,[22] offers a commentary on two of Abū

[15] An insignificant exception is a short work on theology ascribed to Ṭaḥāwī (d. 321/933), where *al-amr biʾl-maʿrūf* is included in a list of religious duties which he affirms (*Fuṣūl fī uṣūl al-dīn*, ms. Princeton, Arabic, Third Series, 288, f. 125a.9, *faṣl* 187; this work is not Ṭaḥāwī's well-known *ʿaqīda*). [16] Cf. below, 334, on Jaṣṣāṣ.

[17] On this process see the works of Madelung already cited (above, note 2).

[18] See Madelung, 'The early Murjiʾa', 36–9. This earlier hostility is perhaps reflected in the long activist tradition transmitted by the Shīʿites from the Marwazī Ḥanafī Nūḥ ibn Abī Maryam (d. 173/789f.) (see above, ch. 11, note 28).

[19] See *EI*², articles 'Māturīdī' and 'Māturīdiyya' (W. Madelung).

[20] See *Encyclopaedia Iranica*, art. 'Abūʾl-Layṯ Samarqandī' (J. van Ess).

[21] It is also treated in his Koran commentary (see above, ch. 2, notes 17, 44, 47, 54). It may be noted that in defining *maʿrūf* and *munkar* in his commentary to Q3:110, he offers alternative rationalist and revelationist glosses (*Taʾwīlāt*, f. 46a.22); contrast A. Bardakoğlu, 'Hüsn ve kubh konusunda aklın rolü ve İmam Mâturîdî', in *Ebû Mansur Semerkandî Mâturîdî*, Kayseri 1986, 43, and cf. below, note 35.

[22] For the authorship of the *Sharḥ al-Fiqh al-akbar*, see H. Daiber, *The Islamic concept of belief in the 4th/10th century*, Tokyo 1995 (with a new edition of the text). Daiber argues convincingly that the ascription to Māturīdī (which I use below as a bibliographical convenience) is false (*ibid.*, 5–7), and makes a serious case for the authorship of Abū ʾl-Layth al-Samarqandī (*ibid.*, 7–10). However, if the work was indeed by so well known a figure, it remains puzzling that it should be ascribed in some copies to scholars whom we are unable even to identify. One of these is a certain Khāṭirī (*ibid.*, 3 n. 15; 17, manuscripts S and F; to which may be added ms. Istanbul, Süleymaniye, M. Arif M. Murad 177 (see f. 74b.2)). The other is a certain Jūzajānī (Daiber, *Islamic concept of belief*, 3, where Daiber mistakenly takes Jūzajānī to be the author of a distinct work); a case in point is ms. Istanbul, Süleymaniye, Fatih 3,139, where the usual *incipit* of the work is put in the mouth of this Jūzajānī (see f. 117b.2). Since the scribe of this manuscript states that he was copying from a manuscript of 565/1169f. (f. 151a.15), this gives us a *terminus ante quem* for Jūzajānī earlier than the usual 687/1288. All the manuscripts of this work that I cite here and below are in the Süleymaniye; one of them (Esat Efendi 1,581) was used by Daiber.

Ḥanīfa's positions noted above. First, in response to Abū Ḥanīfa's inclusion of forbidding wrong in his creed, the commentator states that the duty is at issue between 'us' and the 'Mujbira'. The 'Mujbira' deny the duty on the basis of Q5:105;[23] the commentator declares this verse irrelevant, and locates the source of the duty in Q3:104.[24] The 'Mujbira' are presumably the traditionists, who are regularly accused of denying the duty.[25] That 'we' should affirm its obligatoriness is unsurprising. Secondly, in response to Abū Ḥanīfa's condemnation of rebellion by a leader and his followers, the commentator – as might be expected – takes a firmly quietist line.[26] More surprisingly, he states that Abū Ḥanīfa's ruling against rebellion on the grounds of its adverse consequences shows that commanding right and forbidding wrong are no longer in effect in our time;[27] he explains that these activities are now entirely of this kind (he means that they are directed only to bloodshed and plunder), and not motivated by disinterested virtue (*lā ʿalā wajh al-ḥisba lillāh*).[28] Does the commentator really mean to say that forbidding wrong in general – and not just rebellion under its aegis – has lapsed in his time, despite the fact that, in refuting the 'Mujbira', he states it to be obligatory? Or is he simply using 'forbidding wrong' as a synonym for righteous rebellion in this passage? If we turn to the second work ascribed to Māturīdī which touches on the duty, we encounter a similar statement: commanding and forbidding are not in effect in our time, not being motivated by disinterested virtue (*li-annahu lā ʿalā wajh al-ḥisba*); the author goes on to say that for this reason armed rebellion against an

23 Cf. above, ch. 2, 30f.

24 Māturīdī, *Sharḥ al-Fiqh al-akbar*, 4.1 (commenting on Abū Ḥanīfa, *al-Fiqh al-absaṭ*, 40.10), whence Wensinck, *Creed*, 107; Daiber, *Islamic concept of belief*, 39–41, lines 48–56. (For the relationship between the two texts, see van Ess, 'Kritisches', 331f., and Daiber, *Islamic concept of belief*, 214.) The passage appears without significant variation in the manuscripts cited above, note 22.

25 See below, 336f.

26 Māturīdī, *Sharḥ al-fiqh al-akbar*, 13.15 (commenting on Abū Ḥanīfa, *al-Fiqh al-absaṭ*, 44.10); Daiber, *Islamic concept of belief*, 97–100, lines 334–46, with commentary *ibid.*, 228–30.

27 The wording is: *irtafaʿā fī hādhā ʾl-zamān, fī hādhā ʾl-zamān murtafiʿān*. The most interesting variant concerns the second reference to the duty no longer being in effect. This is attributed to Abū Muṭīʿ al-Balkhī (d. 199/814) in many manuscripts (cf. Daiber, *Islamic concept of belief*, 99 n. 9; also Fatih 3,137, f. 22a.5; likewise Fatih 5,392, f. 68b, where the commentary of Jūzajānī appears in the margin). However, in two manuscripts I have noted the alternative reading *qāla ʾl-faqīh* (Esat Efendi 1,581, f. 205a.20 (a reading not noted by Daiber); Fatih 3,139, f. 129b.10 (a manuscript not used by Daiber)); for this phrase, see Daiber, *Islamic concept of belief*, 6, arguing plausibly that the author of the work uses it to refer to himself. It may be noted that there is no trace of this doctrine in Māturīdī's *Taʾwīlāt* to Q3:104 (ff. 44b–45a) or Q3:110 (f. 46a–b).

28 Māturīdī, *Sharḥ al-fiqh al-akbar*, 14.3 (corrupt); Daiber, *Islamic concept of belief*, 100, lines 345f.

unjust ruler is impermissible.[29] The concern with rebellion is again close, but the formulation appears to be general.[30] This is the first we hear among the Ḥanafīs of the doctrine that the duty has lapsed, though it is not quite the last: as we shall see, something of the kind was reinvented in Ottoman Syria.[31] It suggests an unusually – though not uniquely – quietist view of the duty.

Abū ʾl-Layth's longest treatment of forbidding wrong is found in a well-known pietistic work of his.[32] But it is in the nature of such works that it sets out no systematic doctrine, and indeed the passage consists overwhelmingly of a succession of quotations from Koran and tradition.[33] Interspersed among them we find such points as the following. Abū ʾl-Layth mentions that a certain Prophetic tradition shows that being able to carry out the duty (*qudra*) is a condition for it (to be obligatory); he glosses this as meaning that the virtuous (*ahl al-ṣalāḥ*) must enjoy predominance (*al-ghalaba*).[34] He defines right (*maʿrūf*) as what is in accordance with revelation and reason, and wrong (*munkar*) as the contrary.[35] He says that the duty should be performed in private (*fī ʾl-sirr*) where possible; if this does not work, one should do it in public (*fī ʾl-ʿalāniya*), calling upon the help of the virtuous.[36] He quotes the tripartite saying that performance with the hand is for rulers (*umarāʾ*), with the tongue for scholars

[29] Māturīdī (d. *c.* 333/944), *ʿAqīda*, in Y. Z. Yörükân, *İslâm akaidine dair eski metinler*, Istanbul 1953, 17 no. 27 (= 26 no. 27). One or other of these passages, or a parallel, was known to Ibn Taymiyya as Māturīdī's (Ibn Mufliḥ, *Ādāb*, 1:177.13). Daiber categorically rejects the ascription of the work to Māturīdī (*Islamic concept of belief*, 5, 10); though he may well be right, it should be noted that this ascription was already established in the eighth/fourteenth century (see further the following note).

[30] It was taken to be so by Tāj al-Dīn al-Subkī (d. 771/1370) in his work *al-Sayf al-mashhūr fī sharḥ ʿAqīdat Abī Manṣūr*: he objects that the duty remains in effect in the view of the Muslims at large (ms. Istanbul, Süleymaniye, Hacı Mahmud 1,329, f. 25b.7). For this work, which is concerned to play down credal differences between Māturīdism and Ashʿarism (see, for example, f. 2a.4), see Sezgin, *Geschichte*, 1:605 no. 3.

[31] See below, 327f. For attestations of such views elsewhere, see above, ch. 3, 40–2, and ch. 5, 106.

[32] Abū ʾl-Layth, *Tanbīh*, 96–105. That the work is semi-popular is suggested by the way in which Abū ʾl-Layth will sometimes restate the meaning of a Koranic verse or tradition in simpler language (as *ibid.*, 103.6, 103.14).

[33] Note that when he quotes the 'three-modes' tradition, his Māturīdite commitment leads him to gloss *aḍʿaf al-īmān* as *aḍʿaf fī ʾl ahl al-īmān* (*ibid.*, 100.14; the same gloss appears in his *Bustān al-ʿārifīn*, printed in the margin of his *Tanbīh al-ghāfilīn*, Cairo n.d., 128.20). For the doctrinal issue here (whether faith can increase and decrease), see Wensinck, *Creed*, 45, 125, 138, 194.

[34] Abū ʾl-Layth, *Tanbīh*, 98.7; compare the view of ʿAbd al-Qādir al-Jīlī (see above, ch. 6, note 165), who cites the same Prophetic tradition.

[35] *Ibid.*, 98.15; cf. ʿAbd al-Qādir al-Jīlī (see above, ch. 6, note 157). This may be governed by the 'it is said' of *ibid.*, 98.11; compare Abū ʾl-Layth, *Tafsīr*, 1:289.17. For such definitions in general, cf. above, ch. 2, 25.

[36] Abū ʾl-Layth, *Tanbīh*, 99.7; cf. ʿAbd al-Qādir al-Jīlī (see above, ch. 6, note 163).

(*ʿulamāʾ*), and in (or with) the heart for the rest of society (*ʿāmma*); others say that whoever is able to right a wrong should do so.[37] Commanding right is to be embarked on only for the sake of God and to secure the greater glory of the faith (*iʿzāz al-dīn*), not as an ego-trip (*li-ḥamiyyat nafsihi*).[38] One who commands right needs five things: knowledge; pure intentions; sympathy, so that he performs the duty gently; perseverance; and to practise what he preaches.[39] To emigrate from a land of misdeeds (*maʿāṣī*) is to follow the example of Abraham and the Prophet;[40] but it is acceptable to stay on, provided one can fulfil one's religious duties and disapproves of the wrongdoing around one.[41]

The other works of Abū ʾl-Layth are on the whole disappointing. In his Koran commentary he ventures no relevant opinions in his own name. In a short work on prayer he mentions forbidding wrong in passing as an example of a collective duty.[42] However, in another popular work he sets out quite a complicated account of the way in which the standing of forbidding wrong varies with the prospects of efficacy and harm to the performer.[43] If it seems likely to work (whether or not the performer will come to harm?), it is obligatory. If it will not work, and the performer will meet with verbal abuse, it is better for him to abstain. If what confronts him is the prospect of a beating, it depends whether he can endure it:[44] if he cannot, it is better to abstain, but if he can, there is no harm in proceeding – indeed it puts him in the position of one who wages holy war. If it will not work, but at the same time will not put him in harm's way, the choice is his – though it is better to proceed. Altogether, this may not be

37 *Ibid.*, 101.1; cf. ʿAbd al-Qādir al-Jīlī (see above, ch. 6, note 166). Abū ʾl-Layth reports the same anonymous saying in his *Tafsīr*, 1:289.20 (to Q3:104), and in his *Bustān*, 128.31. Cf. the position of Makḥūl (above, note 5).

38 Abū ʾl-Layth, *Tanbīh*, 101.3, with a long story about a zealot who set out to cut down a sacred tree; compare ʿAbd al-Qādir al-Jīlī (see above, ch. 6, note 160). Here and elsewhere, I adopt the expression 'ego-trip' to render an idea that recurs in the sources in various wordings. The phrase *iʿzāz al-dīn* occurs sporadically in Ḥanafī texts (see Muḥammad ibn ʿUthmān al-Balkhī (d. 830/1426f.) (attrib.), *ʿAyn al-ʿilm*, *apud* ʿAlī al-Qārī, *Sharḥ ʿAyn al-ʿilm*, 1:429.3; and below, note 117); but the Ḥanafīs do not, to my knowledge, use it in the context of the danger condition (cf. above, ch. 6, note 142).

39 Abū ʾl-Layth, *Tanbīh*, 101.22; the whole list reappears, with much additional material, in ʿAbd al-Qādir al-Jīlī's five conditions (see above, ch. 6, notes 158, 160–2).

40 *Ibid.*, 103.10 (the verb used is *kharaja*). Cf. above, note 11.

41 *Ibid.*, 104.1 (the verb used is *hājara*).

42 A. Zajączkowski, *Le Traité arabe Mukaddima d'Abou-l-Lait as-Samarkandī en version mamelouk-kiptchak*, Warsaw 1962, 99.1 (with an interlinear Qipchaq translation). In his Koran commentary Abū ʾl-Layth reports an anonymous view that Q3:104 does not impose the duty on all, since not everybody can do it well; only those who know are obligated (*Tafsīr*, 1:289.19).

43 Abū ʾl-Layth, *Bustān*, 127.36. All the material cited here, and in notes 33 and 37 above, forms part of the eighty-fourth chapter of the work.

44 For this distinction, compare Wāʿiẓ-i Balkhī, *Faḍāʾil-i Balkh*, 157.4.

a particularly activist approach to the issues, but it shows no sign of the quietism associated with Māturīdī.

Between the Sāmānid and the high Ottoman periods, the Ḥanafī record is surprisingly threadbare. The Bukhāran scholar Imāmzāda (d. 573/1177f.) gives a short, exhortatory account of the duty.[45] It shows no links with the earlier Ḥanafī literature we have looked at, and for the most part proceeds by quoting, paraphrasing or expanding on traditions. At the same time its tone is enthusiastic. There is a marked absence of counsels of prudence in the face of danger: Muslims should be zealous and unyielding, with no fear even of getting killed, and should speak out in the presence of unjust rulers.[46] The question might thus be raised whether this work reflects a literary tradition somewhat apart from the Māturīdite mainstream, but I am not in a position to answer it.[47] The jurist Marghīnānī (d. 593/1197) in a series of responsa makes obligation turn on prospective efficacy: it is this that determines whether one may attend a wedding feast at which there is (musical) wrongdoing, whether one should correct someone's error in Koran recitation, whether one should write to the father of an offender informing him of his son's misdeeds, or whether one should draw someone's attention to an impurity larger than a dirhem in their dress.[48] Abū 'l-Barakāt al-Nasafī (d. 701/1301) touches briefly on forbidding wrong in his Koran commentary, explaining that it is a collective obligation, and one that can be accomplished only by someone who

[45] See Imāmzāda (d. 573/1177f.), *Shirʿat al-Islām*, ms. Princeton, Garrett 836H, ff. 101a.11–102a.10 (for this manuscript, see P. K. Hitti *et al.*, *Descriptive catalog of the Garrett Collection of Arabic manuscripts in the Princeton University Library*, Princeton and London 1938, 506 no. 1693). The text is also available in print in the commentary of Yaʿqūb ibn Seyyid ʿAlī (d. 931/1524f.) (*Sharḥ Shirʿat al-Islām*, Istanbul 1326, 495–506). Since comparison shows the text as given in this commentary to be virtually complete, all further references will be to this text, and not to the manuscript.

[46] Imāmzāda, *Shirʿa*, 497.6, 499.18. The commentator is not insensitive to this rather reckless tone (Yaʿqūb, *Sharḥ*, 499.9).

[47] A somewhat similar work, but lacking the enthusiastic tone, is the *Khāliṣat al-ḥaqāʾiq* of Fāryābī (d. 607/1210) (ms. Princeton, Garrett 1026H (for this manuscript, see Hitti, *Catalog*, 631 no. 2,076, item 3); *al-amr biʾl-maʿrūf* is treated in the twenty-third chapter, here ff. 93b.4–94b.2).

[48] Marghīnānī (d. 593/1197), *al-Tajnīs waʾl-mazīd*, ms. Istanbul, Süleymaniye, Yeni Cami 533, quire 20, f. 3a.22; quire 21, f. 2a.23, 2a.28, 2b.9; and cf. the general rule, *ibid.*, f. 2b.12. He also states that the sinner is obligated (*ibid.*, f. 2a.21). The quires in this manuscript are numbered, and consist of ten folios each. With regard to the immoral wedding-feast, Marghīnānī's view is that if one's declining the invitation will prevent the wrongdoing, it is one's duty not to go; otherwise there is no harm in going and enjoying the food, while not listening to the music. A similarly accommodating tendency is apparent in Kāsānī's treatment of the question (*Badāʾiʿ*, 5:128.23); he quotes a statement of Abū Ḥanīfa to the effect that he had endured the sound of music on one such occasion (*ibid.*, 128.31). Ḥanafī law is thus significantly less likely to cause social embarrassment in this context than that of the Ḥanbalite Ibn Qudāma (see above, ch. 7, note 2).

knows right from wrong, and understands the principle of escalation.[49] A younger contemporary in a treatise on the office of the censor (*ḥisba*) sets out differences between the officially appointed censor (*al-muḥtasib al-manṣūb*) and the ordinary believer who engages in forbidding wrong (*al-mutaṭawwiʿ*);[50] he also repeats a good deal of earlier material.[51] Taftazānī (d. 793/1390) treats the duty at some length in one of his works[52] and more briefly in another;[53] but apart from a couple of quotations from a Ḥanafī source,[54] these seem to represent a Shāfiʿite and Ashʿarite tradition, and will accordingly be discussed in the next chapter. Ibn al-Malak (*fl.* early eighth/fourteenth century) gives a commentary on the 'three modes' tradition[55] which is pillaged by authors of the Ottoman period.[56]

Alongside this fragmented material there are occasional references to forbidding wrong in the biographical literature. Among the Ḥanafī or semi-Ḥanafī figures of the second/eighth century, Dāwūd ibn Nuṣayr al-Ṭāʾī (d. 165/781f.) poured cold water on the idea of going in to rulers to command and forbid them,[57] whereas ʿAbdallāh ibn Farrūkh (d. 175/791)

[49] Abū 'l-Barakāt al-Nasafī, *Madārik*, 1:240 n. 2 (to Q3:104); he depends – directly or indirectly – on Zamakhsharī (*Kashshāf*, 1:396.8). Likewise heavily dependent on Zamakhsharī is Sīwāsī (d. 803/1400f.) in his *ʿUyūn al-tafsīr* (ms. Princeton, Yahuda 5,766, ff. 69b–70a, particularly f. 70a.10, which is from Zamakhsharī, *Kashshāf*, 1:397.16). Sīwāsī also works in a reference to the tripartite division of labour (*ʿUyūn*, f. 70a.7). For this manuscript, see Mach, *Catalogue*, 36f. no. 394.

[50] Sunāmī, *Niṣāb al-iḥtisāb*, 24f., 189–91. The idea goes back to Māwardī (d. 450/1058) (*al-Aḥkām al-sulṭāniyya*, ed. A. M. al-Baghdādī, Kuwait 1989, 315.5; cf. below, ch. 13, note 45).

[51] Compare, for example, Sunāmī, *Niṣāb al-iḥtisāb*, 190.3, 196.7, with Abū 'l-Layth, *Bustān*, 127.36 (cf. above, note 43), and Abū 'l-Layth, *Tanbīh*, 101.3 (cf. above, note 38) respectively.

[52] Taftazānī (d. 793/1390), *Sharḥ al-Maqāṣid*, ed. ʿA. ʿUmayra, Beirut 1989, 5:171–5 (the work is a commentary on his own *Maqāṣid*). For the Ashʿarite character of this work in general, see Gimaret, *Théories de l'acte humain*, 162–4; the account of *al-amr bi'l-maʿrūf* leans heavily on that given by Juwaynī (*Irshād*, 368–70).

[53] Taftazānī, *Sharḥ ḥadīth al-Arbaʿīn*, 105. The work is a commentary on the collection made by Nawawī (d. 676/1277) (see above, ch. 3, note 7), and in its discussion of *al-amr bi'l-maʿrūf* it cites Nawawī's commentary on Muslim (*ibid.*, 105.9) and the *Iḥyāʾ*, sc. of Ghazzālī (*ibid.*, 105.24). Its literary connections are thus markedly Shāfiʿite, though I do not know the identity of the *Rawḍa* to which it refers (*ibid.*, 105.18). For a slightly later commentary on the same work of Nawawī by the Ḥanafī Burhān al-Dīn al-Khujandī (d. 851/1447f.), see Ḥājjī Khalīfa, *Kashf al-ẓunūn*, 59.35; Brockelmann, *Geschichte*, supplementary volumes, 1:683 no. 8a (and probably no. 28); second edition, 1:499 no. 8a. I have not seen it.

[54] Taftazānī, *Sharḥ al-Maqāṣid*, 5:174.17, 175.12. The first relates to the question of the views of rival law-schools, the second to the proper escalation in response to varying degrees of nakedness (exposure of the knee, the thigh, and finally the genitals).

[55] Ibn al-Malak (*fl.* early eighth/fourteenth century), *Mabāriq al-azhār*, ed. A. ʿA. ʿAbd al-Raḥīm, Beirut 1995, 1:105f. no. 83. The work is a commentary on the *Mashāriq al-anwār* of Ṣaghānī (d. 650/1252). One substantial passage goes back to Zamakhsharī (see below, note 92).

[56] See below, notes 83, 92–4.

[57] See above, ch. 4, note 56. I owe the term 'semi-Ḥanafī' to Nurit Tsafrir; for some of the figures considered in this paragraph, even that may be too much to claim.

associated forbidding wrong with rebellion against unjust rule.[58] Figures mentioned for their performance of the duty are Salm ibn Sālim al-Balkhī (d. 194/810),[59] ʿUmar ibn Maymūn al-Rammāḥ (d. 171/788), and Abū Muṭīʿ al-Balkhī (d. 199/814).[60] A trickle of later Ḥanafī scholars are also mentioned as engaging in forbidding wrong: Naṣr ibn Ziyād (d. 233/847f.), who was chief judge in Nīshāpūr;[61] Yūsuf ibn Yaʿqūb al-Tanūkhī (d. 329/941);[62] Ismāʿīl ibn Abī Naṣr al-Ṣaffār (d. 461/1068f.), who was killed for it in Bukhārā by the Qarakhānid ruler Shams al-Mulk Naṣr (r. 460–72/1068–80);[63] ʿImād al-Dīn al-Lāmishī (d. 522/1128), who would go in to kings and speak the truth in their faces;[64] and Muḥammad ibn Yaḥyā al-Zabīdī (d. 555/1160), whose commanding and forbidding got him expelled from Damascus around 506/1112.[65] The most interesting of these figures is Ibn Farrūkh, since he illustrates that early equation of forbidding wrong with rebellion which had so embarrassed Abū Ḥanīfa.

3. THE COMMENTATORS OF THE OTTOMAN PERIOD

Visiting the city of Laodicea (the modern Denizli) in western Anatolia, the traveller Ibn Baṭṭūṭa (d. 770/1368f.) was moved to comment: 'The people of this city do not take action against offences (*lā yughayyirūn al-munkar*), nor do the people of this entire region (*iqlīm*).'[66] He went on to give a vivid picture of the prostitution of Greek slave-girls. He was told that their owners included the judge of the town, and that these prostitutes freely entered the bath-houses in the company of their clients.

By the high Ottoman period, things were somewhat less relaxed; but the change affected social mores rather than politics. Ottoman Ḥanafism had its roots in the accommodationist tradition of the Sāmānid north-east, and was comfortable with it. As we would expect from this, forbidding wrong was not in general much discussed in the Ottoman context, and it did not take on the overtly political character that it possessed for Abū Ḥanīfa's interlocutors. In any case, much of the discussion in Ottoman religious

[58] See below, ch. 14, 385. [59] See above, ch. 4, note 71.
[60] For ʿUmar ibn Maymūn, see above, ch. 4, note 206; for Abū Muṭīʿ, see above, ch. 4, note 68.
[61] Ibn Abī ʾl-Wafāʾ, *Jawāhir*, 2:194.1. I owe this and the following references to Nurit Tsafrir.
[62] Khaṭīb, *Taʾrīkh Baghdād*, 14:322.4.
[63] Samʿānī, *Ansāb*, 8:318.13. I take him to be a Ḥanafī since his father seems to have been one (Ibn Abī ʾl-Wafāʾ, *Jawāhir*, 1:137.2). [64] *Ibid.*, 210.9; Samʿānī, *Ansāb*, 13:464.6.
[65] Ibn Abī ʾl-Wafāʾ, *Jawāhir*, 2:142.13.
[66] Ibn Baṭṭūṭa (d. 770/1368f.), *Riḥla*, ed. C. Defrémery and B. R. Sanguinetti, Paris 1853–8, 2:272.2.

literature represents little more than the momentum of literary traditions; often it is a by-product of the writing of commentaries on earlier works which happened to touch on the duty.[67]

One such work is, of course, the Koran. Thus Abū ʾl-Suʿūd (d. 982/1574) discusses forbidding wrong in commenting on Q3:104. There is nothing significantly new about the points he makes,[68] though I am not able to pin down the precise sources he is using.[69] The treatment of the verse by Ismāʿīl Ḥaqqī Brūsevī (d. 1137/1725)[70] is more transparent in this respect. Leaving aside some traditions, and some passages taken from Abū ʾl-Suʿūd,[71] we find here a remarkable literary fossil: material lifted from Zamakhsharī which in some measure perpetuates the doctrine of the Ḥanafī Muʿtazilite Abū ʾl-Ḥusayn al-Baṣrī.[72]

For a somewhat more interesting genre, we can turn to the commentaries on the little collection of forty traditions put together by Nawawī (d. 676/1277), since he included among them the 'three modes' tradition.[73] Two Ḥanafī commentaries of this period are those of ʿAlī al-Qārī al-Harawī (d. 1014/1606)[74] and, again, Ismāʿīl Ḥaqqī.[75]

Though the commentary of ʿAlī al-Qārī provides one of the richer treatments of the duty in Ḥanafī literature, its sources are largely Shāfiʿite. This is not altogether surprising. It was Nawawī, a Shāfiʿite, who put the collection together; it was Nawawī who wrote the classic exposition of the 'three modes' tradition;[76] and it was the Shāfiʿites who produced most of the subsequent commentaries on the forty traditions.[77] Though it is hard to be

67 I have not attempted to be comprehensive in my coverage of this literature. For example, while I cite Yaʿqūb ibn Seyyid ʿAlī's *Sharḥ Shirʿat al-Islām*, I give no systematic treatment of it.

68 Abū ʾl-Suʿūd, *Irshād*, 1:528–530. He stresses that the duty, while incumbent on all, is a collective one, and that it requires knowledge of law and of the principle of escalation to perform it correctly (*ibid.*, 528.9).

69 He has material in common with Zamakhsharī (cf. *Irshād*, 1:528.15 with *Kashshāf*, 1:396.11) and Bayḍāwī (cf. *Irshād*, 1:528.20 with *Anwār*, 2:35.13); some of what he shares with Zamakhsharī is not found in Bayḍāwī.

70 Ismāʿīl Ḥaqqī Brūsevī (d. 1137/1725), *Rūḥ al-bayān*, Istanbul 1389, 2:73–5.

71 *Ibid.*, 73.25, 73.32, 74.27; cf. Abū ʾl-Suʿūd, *Irshād*, 1:528.9, 528.18, 530.1.

72 Ismāʿīl Ḥaqqī, *Rūḥ al-bayān*, 2:73.29, 74.1, 74.16; cf. Zamakhsharī, *Kashshāf*, 1:396.10, 397.3, 397.9. For Abū ʾl-Ḥusayn, see above, ch. 9, 218. For the fortunes of this passage in mainstream Ḥanafī literature, see also below, note 92.

73 For this genre, see above, ch. 3, note 7.

74 ʿAlī al-Qārī, *Mubīn*, 188–94.

75 Ismāʿīl Ḥaqqī, *Sharḥ al-Arbaʿīn ḥadīthan*, 336–41. The somewhat later commentary of Muḥammad Ḥayāt al-Sindī (d. 1163/1750) is notable for its weepiness with regard to the corruption of the times (*Sharḥ al-Arbaʿīn al-Nawawiyya*, ed. Ḥ. A. al-Ḥarīrī, Dammām 1995, 105.9).

76 Nawawī, *Sharḥ Ṣaḥīḥ Muslim*, 1:380–6. In his own commentary to his *Arbaʿīn*, he gives only a brief treatment of the tradition which will hardly concern us (*Sharḥ matn al-Arbaʿīn*, 91f.).

77 Two relevant commentaries are those of Taftazānī (see above, note 53) and Ibn Ḥajar al-Haytamī (d. 974/1567) (*Fatḥ*, 244–8).

sure in exactly what form ʿAlī al-Qārī had access to this Shāfiʿite tradition, it is clear that he drew on it extensively.[78] At the same time, the only non-Shāfiʿite source I can identify in his account is Ḥanbalite.[79] He seems insensitive to the non-Māturīdite background of the material he is adopting.[80]

In what ways, then, does ʿAlī al-Qārī represent a Ḥanafī tradition[81] – or, indeed, himself? There are a number of doctrinal points he puts forward that do not derive from the non-Ḥanafī sources with which I have compared his account; but their Ḥanafī provenance is not thereby secured. Thus he affirms that death incurred in performance of the duty is rewarded;[82] he discusses the problem of the descending order in which the modes are presented in the tradition;[83] he mentions the unusual idea that the immersion of the mystic in the depths of absolute existence might be an excuse – though an unconvincing one – for not performing the duty;[84] he speculates that performance in the heart may actually mean performance by means of the heart through the mustering of a sort of mental energy (*himma*) which, through divine intervention, may actually bring about the desired result.[85]

There is, however, one theme which we can with some confidence identify as a Ḥanafī contribution. ʿAlī al-Qārī tends to see the duty within a notably hierarchical conception of society. He quotes the tripartite saying assigning the modes by social categories.[86] Unlike most authors who

[78] There are numerous parallels with Nawawī's *Sharḥ Ṣaḥīḥ Muslim* (e.g. ʿAlī al-Qārī, *Mubīn*, 188.13; Nawawī, *Sharḥ*, 1:382.4); three with Taftazānī's *Sharḥ ḥadīth al-Arbaʿīn* (ʿAlī al-Qārī, *Mubīn*, 189.14, 189.19, 189.21; Taftazānī, *Sharḥ*, 105.7, 105.9, 105.12); and a good many further parallels with Ibn Ḥajar al-Haytamī's *Fatḥ* (e.g. ʿAlī al-Qārī, *Mubīn*, 188.7, 190.12; Ibn Ḥajar al-Haytamī, *Fatḥ*, 244.20, 246.4). Nawawī and Taftazānī may be among ʿAlī al-Qārī's immediate sources; my impression is that Ibn Ḥajar al-Haytamī is drawing on a common source.

[79] ʿAlī al-Qārī quotes and acknowledges the *Ghunya* of ʿAbd al-Qādir al-Jīlī at *Mubīn*, 194.12 (cf. *Ghunya*, 1:59.25); he quotes it without acknowledgement at *Mubīn*, 193.27 (cf. *Ghunya*, 1:57.24). The first passage, on the distinction between wrongs that members of the laity may seek to put right and those with regard to which only scholars are qualified to act, goes back to the Ḥanbalite Abū Yaʿlā (see above, ch. 6, note 124), who in turn is likely to have it from a Muʿtazilite source (cf. above, ch. 9, note 70 on the doctrine of ʿAbd al-Jabbār). The second, about the importance of undertaking the duty with good intentions, goes back to none other than Abū 'l-Layth al-Samarqandī (see above, note 38). That ʿAlī al-Qārī should be indebted to a Ḥanbalite for Muʿtazilite and Ḥanafī material shows how far the processes of inter-school borrowing had reached by his time.

[80] The phrase *aḍʿaf al-īmān* in the tradition is problematic from a Māturīdite point of view (cf. above, note 33, and the words *al-īmān yazīd wa-yanquṣ* in Nawawī's chapter heading, *Sharḥ Ṣaḥīḥ Muslim*, 1:380.18); but ʿAlī al-Qārī, unlike Ismāʿīl Ḥaqqī, does not respond strongly (*Mubīn*, 189.11; cf. below, note 94).

[81] For what he has to say about Abū Ḥanīfa see above, notes 12f.

[82] *Ibid.*, 190.14.

[83] *Ibid.*, 191.3. Cf. also Ibn al-Malak, *Mabāriq*, 1:105.13, whence Yaʿqūb, *Sharḥ*, 500.9, and above, ch. 11, 263f.

[84] ʿAlī al-Qārī, *Mubīn*, 193.19.

[85] *Ibid.*, 194.17; cf. above, ch. 7, 162, and below, ch. 16, 462–4. Faith, as he says, can move mountains (*himmat al-rijāl tahudd al-jibāl*).

[86] *Ibid.*, 188.21; he is quoting a Ḥanafī source, the *Khizānat al-muftīn* of Ḥusayn ibn

mention this saying, he is prepared to take it seriously as doctrine. He extends the category of scholars (*ʿulamāʾ*) to include saints (*awliyāʾ*), and that of officers of state (*umarāʾ*) to include (other) powerful people (*aqwiyāʾ*). He takes pride in the fact that he has not seen this analysis in the works of earlier commentators.[87] It is of a piece with this, though less distinctive, that he uses material that lays stress on the role of the scholars, and on the failings of those of the day.[88] Likewise it is typical that a passage he cites with explicit approval from a Ḥanbalite source concerns the differing roles of scholars and laity in performing the duty.[89] In short, he can be taken to represent the accommodationist tendencies of Ḥanafism.

Ismāʿīl Ḥaqqī, as might be expected, makes extensive use of ʿAlī al-Qārī's commentary.[90] He also has a couple of acknowledged borrowings from Ghazzālī (d. 505/1111),[91] and as in his Koran commentary he appropriates a substantial block of material deriving from Zamakhsharī,[92] thereby rendering the thought of Abū ʾl-Ḥusayn into Turkish. Towards the end of his account he has a good deal of material whose sources I have mostly

Muḥammad al-Samʿānī (writing in 740/1339, see Ḥājjī Khalīfa, *Kashf al-ẓunūn*, 703.22). He also works a version of the saying into his commentary on the *ʿAyn al-ʿilm* (*Sharḥ ʿAyn al-ʿilm*, 1:438.21). [87] ʿAlī al-Qārī, *Mubīn*, 191.11.

[88] *Ibid.*, 191.25, 192.16. He speaks of them as being among those individually obligated (*mimman yataʿayyan ʿalayhi*) to perform the duty (*ibid.*, 191.26). The first passage at least is not his own, since there is a close parallel in the commentary of the Mālikī Tāj al-Dīn al-Fākihānī (d. 734/1234) on the tradition (*al-Manhaj al-mubīn*, ms. Princeton, Garrett 749H, f. 99a.12; for this manuscript, see Hitti, *Catalog*, 434 no. 1432).

[89] See above, note 79.

[90] The first two pages of his treatment consist largely of passages from the first two pages of ʿAlī al-Qārī's – rearranged, paraphrased and translated into Turkish. There are also a few further borrowings later in the account (cf., for example, Ismāʿīl Ḥaqqī, *Sharḥ*, 339.21, with ʿAlī al-Qārī, *Mubīn*, 190.12).

[91] Ismāʿīl Ḥaqqī, *Sharḥ*, 338.4, 340.4. The first is Ghazzālī's five stages of escalation (*Iḥyāʾ*, 2:289.3, cf. below, ch. 16, 431); the second is a statement of the importance of performing the duty against heresy (*ibid.*, 299.26, cf. below, ch. 16, 437).

[92] Ismāʿīl Ḥaqqī gives an account of the conditions for forbidding wrong (*Sharḥ*, 339.14–340.4) which is at once a truncated and expanded version of Zamakhsharī, *Kashshāf*, 1:397.12–398.1. His expansions include the pleasing argument that you cannot rebuke a man simply because he has a pot of wine beside him, since after all he also has with him the means of adultery (*anın yanında ālet-i zinā dakhı vardır*) (*Sharḥ*, 339.18). Expansions apart, the passage overlaps that in his Koran commentary (see above, note 72), but is closer to a block of material found in Ibn al-Malak, *Mabāriq*, 1:106.3 (whence Yaʿqūb, *Sharḥ*, 496.2), and in Rajab ibn Aḥmad al-Āmidī (writing 1087/1676), *al-Wasīla al-Aḥmadiyya*, Istanbul 1261, 2:761.6. Thus *wuqūʿ al-maʿṣiya* at *Rūḥ*, 2:74.20 preserves the wording of *Kashshāf*, 1:397.16; by contrast, the other sources mentioned have the paraphrase *annahu yafʿaluhu*, to which the *işleyeceğine* of Ismāʿīl Ḥaqqī, *Sharḥ*, 339.17 corresponds (Ibn al-Malak, *Mabāriq*, 1:106.6; Yaʿqūb, *Sharḥ*, 496.3; Rajab, *Wasīla*, 2:761.8). On the other hand, all these versions reflect a common source downstream of the *Kashshāf*, since they share an ordering of the conditions that departs from Zamakhsharī's and, more seriously, the total loss of Abū ʾl-Ḥusayn's basic distinction between the conditions under which it is good to proceed and the conditions of obligation to do so.

been unable to identify; some of this, and much of the material inserted in among the earlier borrowings, is doubtless his own.[93]

Unlike ʿAlī al-Qārī, Ismāʿīl Ḥaqqī displays a marked Māturīdite allegiance.[94] He also allows his account to take on a little more historical colour; he is, after all, writing in his vernacular, which ʿAlī al-Qārī was not. Thus where ʿAlī al-Qārī spoke of the powerful, Ismāʿīl Ḥaqqī gives as an instance 'the notables of every town'.[95] In one respect, however, his thinking is significantly in tune with ʿAlī al-Qārī's. He too seems to take the tripartite division of labour seriously. What the hand wields is the sword and the spear; these are to be used to destroy churches, taverns and the like. The work of the tongue is proofs and demonstrations; these are to be used to eliminate the doubts and superstitions of the people. The role of the heart is to avow and submit (*iʿtirāf ve idhʿān*).[96] He also sees fit to insert an explicit condemnation of rebellion against the state (*sulṭān*),[97] and modifies the doctrine of Ghazzālī to exclude harshness when a subject (*raʿiyet*) rebukes a ruler (*sulṭān*).[98] He does retain a positive attitude towards martyrdom incurred in forbidding wrong,[99] but in general he too shows accommodationist tendencies.

The case of Ismāʿīl Ḥaqqī brings us to another characteristic form of Ḥanafī literary dependence on non-Ḥanafī sources: the appropriation, whether acknowledged or not, of material from Ghazzālī. The oldest example we possess is perhaps a Ḥanafī abridgement of Ghazzālī's *Revival*

[93] He slips in a reference to opium addicts (*ibid.*, 339.24), and discusses Ṣūfīs, who are not to be declared innovators (*ehl-i bidʿat*) since of their twelve groups, one is orthodox (*ehl-i sünnet*) (*ibid.*, 340.8; for his borrowing of a passage from the Koran commentary of Muḥyī 'l-Dīn ibn al-ʿArabī (d. 638/1240), see below, ch. 16, note 279). On the other hand, the point that the notion of changing in the heart makes no literal sense (*ibid.*, 337.25) is not his, since it appears already in Rajab, *Wasīla*, 2:760.24, and before that in Ibn al-Malak, *Mabāriq*, 1:105.12, and Nawawī, *Sharḥ matn al-Arbaʿīn*, 92.7.

[94] He repeats material which rises to the challenge posed by *aḍʿaf al-īmān*, setting out the doctrine of 'the Ḥanafīs' on faith as against that of Shāfiʿī (Ismāʿīl Ḥaqqī, *Sharḥ*, 338.21; cf. Yaʿqūb, *Sharḥ*, 500.23, and before him Ibn al-Malak, *Mabāriq*, 1:106.9; contrast Khādimī (d. 1176/1762f.), *Barīqa Maḥmūdiyya*, Cairo 1348, 3:245.5).

[95] Ismāʿīl Ḥaqqī, *Sharḥ*, 337.14 (*her şehrde vüjūh ül-qavm gibi*); cf. above, note 87. Cf. his reference to the workings of patronage in protecting wrongdoers in his time (*ibid.*, 337.15).

[96] *Ibid.*, 340.21. He writes as if performance other than in the heart is for officers of state and scholars (*ibid.*, 337.21).

[97] *Ibid.*, 337.19. This is appended to a passage taken from ʿAlī al-Qārī (*Mubīn*, 189.14), who there commends not stirring up sleeping *fitna*.

[98] Ismāʿīl Ḥaqqī, *Sharḥ*, 338.8 (cf. above, note 91). Ismāʿīl Ḥaqqī is drawing on Ghazzālī, *Iḥyāʾ*, 2:291.11, 292.2 (cf. below, ch. 16, 432); but he simplifies the discussion in a quietist direction, and ignores Ghazzālī's explicit approval of harshness to rulers in cases where this will not cause harm to others (*ibid.*, 314.5, cf. below, ch. 16, 446).

[99] Ismāʿīl Ḥaqqī, *Sharḥ*, 339.27; cf. above, note 82.

of the religious sciences.[100] The treatment of forbidding wrong found in this abridgement[101] is unremarkable except, perhaps, for the omission of all mention of the use of weapons and of the participation of armed helpers.[102] Other authors quote passages from Ghazzālī in the course of their works: such is the case with Yaʿqūb ibn Seyyid ʿAlī (d. 931/1524f.),[103] Kemālpāshāzāde (d. 940/1534),[104] Maḥmūd ibn Muḥammad al-Qarabāghī (tenth/sixteenth century?)[105] and later authors.[106]

The first Ottoman scholar – though not, as we shall see, the last – to engage in wholesale plagiarisation of Ghazzālī's analysis of forbidding wrong was Ṭāshköprīzāde (d. 968/1561).[107] Beyond the fact of literary dependence, the most interesting feature of his account is his toning down of Ghazzālī's views on the use of violence by ordinary believers in the performance of the duty. Thus one significant question on which Ṭāshköprīzāde departs from Ghazzālī's doctrine is the circumstances under which the permission of the authorities is required. Ghazzālī had set out a schema of five levels (*marātib*) of response to wrong: (1) informing one

[100] Balkhī, *ʿAyn al-ʿilm*, *apud* ʿAlī al-Qārī, *Sharḥ ʿAyn al-ʿilm*. Internal evidence establishes the Ḥanafī allegiance of the author (*ibid.*, 1:48.1), but does not help with his identity or date. The work is often, and perhaps correctly, ascribed to Muḥammad ibn ʿUthmān al-Balkhī (see Ismāʿīl Pāshā al-Baghdādī (d. 1339/1920), *Hadiyyat al-ʿārifīn*, Istanbul 1951–5, 2:187.3, with the death date 830/1426f.; Brockelmann, *Geschichte*, supplementary volumes, 1:749 no. 17). I follow this ascription; ʿAlī al-Qārī, however, knows only that the author of the *ʿAyn al-ʿilm* was an Indian or Balkhī scholar (*Sharḥ ʿAyn al-ʿilm*, 1:3.3). [101] *Ibid.*, 433–49.

[102] *Ibid.*, 442.3. ʿAlī al-Qārī in his commentary mentions helpers, but not weapons (*ibid.*, 442.19).

[103] He makes extensive use of the *Iḥyāʾ* in his commentary on Imāmzāda's *Shirʿat al-Islām*, mostly with acknowledgement. Thus substantial quotations of analytical material are found in his *Sharḥ Shirʿat al-Islām*, 501.20, 503.12, 504.30 (from Ghazzālī, *Iḥyāʾ*, 2:292.13, 302.14, and 291.11 respectively). Ghazzālī is referred to as *al-imām al-Ghazzālī* (*Sharḥ*, 502.16, 504.30), or simply as *al-imām* (*ibid.*, 501.20, 503.12).

[104] Kemālpāshāzāde (d. 940/1534), *al-Risāla al-munīra*, n.p. 1296, 35.10, quoting the opening of Ghazzālī's discussion of *al-amr biʾl-maʿrūf* in his *Kīmiyā-yi saʿādat* (cf. below, ch. 16, note 4); for this epistle, see Atsız, 'Kemalpaşa-oğlu'nun eserleri', *Şarkiyat Mecmuası*, 7 (1972), 117f. no. 170.

[105] Maḥmūd ibn Muḥammad al-Qarabāghī (tenth/sixteenth century?), *Muḥāḍarāt*, ms. Qumm, Marʿashī Library, no. 473, f. 35a.1 (quoting *Iḥyāʾ*, 2:313.27); f. 35b.2 (quoting *Iḥyāʾ*, 2:286.2). The discussion of *al-amr biʾl-maʿrūf* in this source occupies ff. 34a–35b. I take the author to be a Ḥanafī (he refers to Abū Ḥanīfa at f. 34a.4, and cf. f. 35b.7). The main indications of dating are a mention of Dawānī (d. 908/1502) on the one hand (f. 34b.5), and the date of copying – 1039/1630 – on the other (for this, and a description of the manuscript, see M. Marʿashī and A. Ḥusaynī, *Fihrist-i nuskhahā-yi khaṭṭī-i Kitābkhāna-i ʿumūmī-i ḥaḍrat-i Āyatullāh al-ʿuẓmā Najafī Marʿashi*, Qumm 1354– sh., 2:78f. no. 473).

[106] For Ismāʿīl Ḥaqqī, see above, notes 91, 98. See also below, notes 145, 154, and, for modern times, below, section 5.

[107] Ṭāshköprīzāde (d. 968/1561), *Miftāḥ al-saʿāda*, ed. K. K. Bakrī and ʿA. Abū ʾl-Nūr, Cairo 1968, 3:301–10.

who acts wrongly out of ignorance; (2) polite admonition; (3) harsh language; (4) forcible prevention through attacking offending objects; and (5) the threat or actual use of violence against the person of the offender.[108] Of the fifth, he says that it is arguable (*inna fīhā naẓaran*) whether or not it needs the permission of the authorities;[109] Ṭāshköprīzāde, by contrast, holds that for Ghazzālī's fifth stage the permission of the ruler (*idhn al-imām*) is required.[110] He displays a similar attitude when he comes to a passage in which Ghazzālī says that someone performing the duty (*al-muḥtasib*, in his distinctive terminology) will use weapons where he has to, provided this will not lead to disorder (*fitna*), for wrong must be prevented by any means possible.[111] Ṭāshköprīzāde, however, prefers to take this to refer to the officially appointed censor (*al-muḥtasib*, in normal usage), for he immediately adds that the individual subject (*ʿāmmī*) is never under any circumstances to take up arms.[112] Ghazzālī then turns to the question of enlisting the support of armed helpers (*aʿwān*), and notes that there is disagreement as to whether this requires the permission of the ruler (*idhn al-imām*).[113] Some say that this is not for individual subjects (*āḥād al-raʿiyya*), since it leads to disorder; others say that no such permission is needed, which is the more logical (*aqyas*) position, and accordingly endorsed by Ghazzālī – though he adds that such eventualities will be rare. Ṭāshköprīzāde likewise mentions both views, but comes down on the other side of the fence: such action is not allowed without permission, since it may lead to disorder, though but for this logic would allow it.[114]

The other Ḥanafī author of this period who depends heavily on Ghazzālī is ʿIṣmat Allāh ibn Aʿẓam ibn ʿAbd al-Rasūl (d. 1133/1720f.), a resident of Sahāranpūr in northern India who in 1091/1680f. wrote a work on forbidding wrong.[115] This work is a free rendering of Ghazzālī's

[108] See below, ch. 16, 431. This schema seems to be a primitive version of the eight levels (*darajāt*) set out later in the account (see below, ch. 16, 438–41).
[109] Ghazzālī, *Iḥyāʾ*, 2:289.9.
[110] Ṭāshköprīzāde, *Miftāḥ*, 3:303.9. Contrast the doubt expressed by Khādimī regarding Ṭāshköprīzāde's view on this point (*Barīqa*, 3:244.16).
[111] Ghazzālī, *Iḥyāʾ*, 2:304.26; cf. below, ch. 16, 441.
[112] Ṭāshköprīzāde, *Miftāḥ*, 3:307.18.
[113] Ghazzālī, *Iḥyāʾ*, 2:304.34; cf. below, ch. 16, 441.
[114] Ṭāshköprīzāde, *Miftāḥ*, 3:307.23.
[115] ʿIṣmat Allāh ibn Aʿẓam ibn ʿAbd al-Rasūl (d. 1133/1720f.), *Raqīb bāb al-maʿrūf waʾl-munkar*, ms. London, India Office, Delhi (Persian) 219, ff. 1a–32b; note that folios 7 and 8 should be transposed. For this manuscript, see C. A. Storey, A. J. Arberry and R. Levy, *Catalogue of the Arabic manuscripts in the Library of the India Office*, vol. 2, London 1930–40, 276f. no. 1697. The author gives his name (mentioning also his residence in Sahāranpūr), the date of composition and the title (which is a chronogram) at the beginning of the work (*Raqīb*, f. 1a.6, 1a.17). Levy states the title as *Kitāb bayān al-amr biʾl-maʿrūf waʾl-nahy ʿan al-munkar*; this, however, is a misundertanding of the author's

treatment of the duty, the overall structure of which it retains despite the addition of some chapters.[116] When following Ghazzālī, he freely recasts, omits, or adds material,[117] but the changes are rarely of much significance. In particular, he shows little discomfort with Ghazzālī's views on the role of violence. On the question of the need for permission from the authorities, he reproduces Ghazzālī's view;[118] he does the same when he comes to the right of the individual to have recourse to arms where necessary,[119] and even with regard to the gathering of armed bands[120] – though in this last instance he adds that anyone performing the duty should consider the question very carefully.[121] This may reflect a difference between the high Ottoman and late Moghul contexts, or it may simply mean that ʿIṣmat Allāh is under-supplied with views of his own. Certainly there is little in his work that speaks to the conditions of his own place and time.[122]

4. BIRGILI AND HIS HEIRS

One Ottoman scholar who wrote on the duty directly, and not simply as a commentator on an earlier text, was Birgili Meḥmed Efendi (d. 981/1573).[123] He mentions the duty of forbidding wrong without elaboration

description of his work: *wa-inna hādhā kitāb fī bayān al-amr biʾl-maʿrūf waʾl-nahy ʿan al-munkar* (f. 1a.16). Levy adds a useful table of contents. There has been some confusion about the date of the death of ʿIṣmat Allāh; I follow ʿAbd al-Ḥayy al-Ḥasanī (d. 1341/1923), *Nuzhat al-khawāṭir*, Hyderabad 1947–70, 6:181.10 (with a description of the *Raqīb*). I am indebted to Yohanan Friedmann for assistance with this author.

116 In the table of contents given by Levy, the following have no equivalent in the *Iḥyāʾ*: the introduction (on the meaning of *maʿrūf* and *munkar*); the fifth chapter (on heretics who believe in not bothering people); the seventh chapter (on government); and the concluding section (on the Rāshidūn). In the seventh chapter, the list of the twenty rights of Muslim subjects against their ruler includes the duty of the latter to command right and forbid wrong (*Raqīb*, f. 31a.5). ʿIṣmat Allāh gives no indication of the extent of his dependence on Ghazzālī.

117 For example, he transposes Ghazzālī's second and fourth *rukn*s (*ibid.*, ff. 9b.20, 11b.21; cf. below, ch. 16, 428f. and note 11), and inserts into Ghazzālī's survey of common wrongs a long treatment of cemeteries (*ibid.*, ff. 14b.13–16b.13). He introduces the phrase *iʿzāz dīn Allāh* (*ibid.*, f. 8a.24, and cf. f. 8b.6), though not in the context of the danger condition (cf. above, note 38).

118 *Ibid.*, f. 8a.12.

119 *Ibid.*, f. 10b.25.

120 *Ibid.*, f. 10b, line 14 of the passage in the right margin.

121 *Ibid.*, f. 11a.8.

122 This is an Indian writer for whom common people express themselves in Persian (*ibid.*, f. 12a.9, 17a.8). He does, however, update Ghazzālī's survey of common wrongs (see below, ch. 16, 442–6) with a reference to the reek of tobacco (*ibid.*, f. 13a.13), and he addresses an Indian heresy in his diatribe against those who hold with leaving people alone and being friendly to every infidel sect (*ibid.*, ff. 17a.7–19a.17; see below, ch. 16, 467f.).

123 I use the form 'Birgili' (rather than 'Birgivī' or the like) in the light of the comments of Atsız, *İstanbul kütüphanelerine göre Birgili Mehmet Efendi (929–981 = 1523–1573) bibliografyası*, Istanbul 1966, 1.

in a little popular handbook of religious obligations written in Turkish.[124] This in turn caused the commentators on this work to attend to the subject;[125] the only point of interest amid the old and familiar ideas they present is that harsh talk seems to be something for state officials to undertake.[126] Birgili gives a more substantial treatment of the duty in a pietistic work written in Arabic and heavily loaded with traditions.[127] Most of what he has to say there is again familiar: the duty is collective given the power to perform it and the absence of (anticipated) harm;[128] the sinner too is obligated;[129] one must not merely forbid offenders, but also avoid socialising with them;[130] harsh talk is in place where polite talk does not suffice.[131] But two things are suggestive enough to give us pause. First, the saying about the tripartite division of labour is quoted, and even attributed to Abū Ḥanīfa, but only as a minority view;[132] most scholars, Birgili says, hold that all three modes are incumbent on everyone, and this is what one goes by in giving legal opinions.[133] Abū ʾl-Layth, by contrast, had merely mentioned the two views one after the other.[134] Secondly, Birgili holds that one may proceed even where this will lead to certain death; one thereby enters the ranks of the most excellent of martyrs[135] – he quotes the appropriate traditions.[136] This endorsement of martyrdom is not, of course, new among the Ḥanafīs,[137] but the language he uses is uncharacteristically

[124] Birgili (d. 981/1573), *Risāla* (in Turkish), n.p. 1300, 44.2. For the work, see Atsız, *Birgili Mehmet Efendi*, 5. It was popular in both senses: there are 110 manuscripts of it in Istanbul alone (*ibid.*, 6–11).

[125] Qāḍīzāde Aḥmed ibn Meḥmed Emīn (d. 1197/1783), *Jawhara-i bahiyya-i Aḥmadiyya* (in Turkish), Būlāq 1240, 256f.; Ismāʿīl Niyāzī (thirteenth/nineteenth century), *Sharḥ-i Niyāzī ʿalā ʾl-Qūnawī* (in Turkish), Istanbul 1264, 277f. The latter is a commentary on that of ʿAlī Ṣadrī al-Qūnawī, for whom I have no biographical information. For Qūnawī's commentary, I have also consulted ms. Princeton, Third Series 190, f. 75a.3.

[126] Niyāzī, *Sharḥ*, 278.8. Qāḍīzāde adduces the tripartite saying (Qāḍīzāde, *Jawhara*, 256.23).

[127] Birgili (d. 981/1573), *al-Ṭarīqa al-Muḥammadiyya*, Cairo 1937, 147f. For the work, see Atsız, *Birgili Mehmet Efendi*, 15; there are no fewer than 221 manuscripts in Istanbul (*ibid.*, 16–32). The weight of traditions in the work is reminiscent of Imāmzāda's *Shirʿat al-Islām* and Fāryābī's *Khāliṣat al-ḥaqāʾiq*; whether we should see in this an indication of the persistence of a traditionalist trend in Ḥanafism, antithetical to the predominant Māturīdite theology, is more than I can say.

[128] Birgili, *Ṭarīqa*, 147.3.

[129] *Ibid.*, 147.11.

[130] *Ibid.*, 148.15.

[131] *Ibid.*, 148.19.

[132] *Ibid.*, 147.9; he adds that it was on this ground that Abū Ḥanīfa held compensation to be payable for broken musical instruments (cf. above, note 13). In the commentary of Khwājazāde al-Aqshehrī (eleventh/seventeenth century), Abū Ḥanīfa's division of labour is dubbed *al-tawzīʿ waʾl-taqsīm* (*Ḥāshiya ʿalā ʾl-Ṭarīqa al-Muḥammadiyya*, ms. Istanbul, Süleymaniye, Fatih 2,607, f. 92a.10).

[133] Birgili, *Ṭarīqa*, 147.7.

[134] See above, note 37.

[135] *Ibid.*, 147.21.

[136] *Ibid.*, 148.4.

[137] Cf. above, notes 10, 82, 99. See also ʿAlī ibn Muḥammad al-Pazdawī (d. 482/1089), *Uṣūl*, *apud* ʿAbd al-ʿAzīz ibn Aḥmad al-Bukhārī (d. 730/1329f.), *Kashf al-asrār*, Istanbul 1308, 2:317.1 (in the margin), with Bukhārī's commentary, *ibid.*, 317.6; Pazdawī's statement is quoted in Kemālpāshāzāde, *al-Risāla al-munīra*, 34.28.

enthusiastic: the duty, according to the scholars, is even more binding than holy war (*al-ḥisba ākad min al-jihād*), since in the latter it is not permitted to take a course involving certain death without military benefit. A zealous, almost radical tone can be detected here, antithetical to the prevailing Ḥanafī climate of accommodation.

Since Birgili quotes both Q3:104 and the 'three modes' tradition, the commentators on his work have the opportunity to discuss them once again. I will spare the reader what I have also spared myself, namely any attempt to identify systematically their unacknowledged sources. Let us concentrate rather on Birgili's radical tone: do the commentators share it, dislike it, or merely bypass it in the humdrum process of exposition? Two of the three commentaries available to me are rather colourless. That of Rajab ibn Aḥmad al-Āmidī (writing in 1087/1676) offers only one feature of interest: the space given to the point that one must not undertake the duty as an ego-trip.[138] Khādimī (d. 1176/1762f.) gives some attention to resolving the tension Birgili had set up between the 'three modes' tradition and the saying about the tripartite division of labour.[139] This saying, he opines, should be taken as an account of how things usually are (*maḥmūl ʿalā ʾl-aʿamm al-aghlab*): in normal circumstances it is indeed the case that those in a position to execute the duty by hand are attached to the state apparatus, and so forth; but exceptional cases will arise where the doctrine set out in the tradition does not work out in accordance with the saying. This looks like a rehabilitation of the accommodationist perspective with which Ḥanafīs had traditionally felt comfortable. But these are straws in the wind. Much more significant than either of these is the commentary we owe to the Damascene Ḥanafī ʿAbd al-Ghanī al-Nābulusī (d. 1143/1731).[140]

ʿAbd al-Ghanī does not have much of interest to say about the tripartite formula. He does his job as a commentator by explicating it when he gets to it.[141] Later he refers back to the 'three modes' tradition in a way that shows that he has taken Birgili's point;[142] yet towards the end of his

[138] The point is of course an old one, and what Rajab has to say is derivative. He quotes a passage on the theme that goes back to Abū ʾl-Layth (*Wasīla*, 2:763.2; cf. above, note 38). He returns to it with a story he owes to Sunāmī about a Ṣūfī who pours out jars of wine, but leaves one intact when he finds that his ego is becoming involved (for this story, see below, ch. 16, note 257). He quotes a saying, also taken from Sunāmī, that the Ṣūfīs make it a condition (of obligation) that one's ego should not be involved (see below, ch. 16, note 252).

[139] Khādimī, *Barīqa*, 3:245.13. Of the attribution of the saying to Abū Ḥanīfa he remarks that this appears not to be a well-known transmission (*ibid.*, 245.16).

[140] ʿAbd al-Ghanī al-Nābulusī (d. 1143/1731), *al-Ḥadīqa al-nadiyya*, Istanbul 1290, 2:290–9. [141] *Ibid.*, 292.1. [142] *Ibid.*, 293.14.

discussion he would seem to have forgotten that there was ever anything problematic about the saying.[143]

By contrast, there is nothing muted about his reaction to Birgili's enthusiastic comparison of forbidding wrong with holy war.[144] In effect, ʿAbd al-Ghanī sets out a new and chastening doctrine of the duty. It rests on two pillars.

The first is a firm distinction between forbidding wrong and censorship (*ḥisba*) – two terms that the influence of Ghazzālī had tended to render synonymous among Ḥanafīs[145] and others alike. So on the one hand we have forbidding wrong, which is a quite general duty to command right and forbid wrong – that and no more.[146] It is purely a matter of the tongue, and carries with it no power or duty of enforcement. Either people listen or they don't: 'No compulsion is there in religion' (Q2:256).[147] And on the other hand we have censorship (*ḥisba*), the duty to enforce right conduct (*ḥaml al-nās ʿalā ʾl-ṭāʿa*).[148] This activity is reserved to the authorities (*ḥukkām*),[149] with one qualification: when an offence is actually being committed (and not after the event), the ordinary believer may intervene

[143] *Ibid.*, 298.1. By contrast, a Ḥanafī author who sees a clear doctrinal distinction here is ʿAbdallāh ibn Ibrāhīm al-Mīrghanī (d. 1207/1792f.), who wrote a credal poem and a commentary thereon in the style of the Mālikī Laqānī (d. 1041/1631) (cf. below, ch. 14, 374). Mīrghanī remarks that the plain sense of the 'three modes' tradition is that the modes apply to everyone, and that this is the view of the Mālikīs, Shāfiʿites and many Ḥanafīs; however, some (of the latter) hold to the tripartite division of labour (*Baḥr al-ʿaqāʾid*, ms. Princeton, Yahuda 5,246, f. 216a.11; for this manuscript, see Mach, *Catalogue*, 201 no. 2,351). He also quotes from Marghīnānī (d. 593/1197) the view that no layman may proceed against a judge, a *muftī*, or a scholar well known for his learning, since this is bad manners, and where the conduct arises from necessity (*ḍarūra*) the layman may fail to understand this (*ibid.*, f. 216a.14). In general, as might be expected from an author writing in the tradition of Laqānī, Mīrghanī is very much aware of Mālikī and Shāfiʿite views; thus his three conditions of obligation (*ibid.*, f. 216b.11) clearly derive from such a source (cf. below, ch. 13, note 92, and ch. 14, notes 32–4).

[144] The key passage begins at ʿAbd al-Ghanī, *Ḥadīqa*, 2:294.9, and continues to 296.22.

[145] Leaving aside authors in direct literary dependence on Ghazzālī, the term *ḥisba* is clearly being used interchangeably with *al-amr bi'l-maʿrūf* in the saying of the scholars quoted by Birgili at *Ṭarīqa*, 147.21; cf. also the use of the phrase *marātib al-iḥtisāb* in ʿAbd al-Aḥad al-Nūrī (d. 1061/1651), *Mawʿiẓa ḥasana*, Istanbul 1263, 49.9 (I am grateful to Şükrü Hanioğlu for obtaining for me a copy of Nūrī's discussion of *al-amr bi'l-maʿrūf*).

[146] ʿAbd al-Ghanī, *Ḥadīqa*, 2:293.30, 294.9. The first passage suggests that the paradigmatic form of *al-amr bi'l-maʿrūf* is preaching.

[147] He also quotes Q10:99 and Q18:29 to the same effect. I have not seen Q2:256 used in this way elsewhere, but such a move is already blocked by Taftazānī on the ground that the verse is abrogated (*Sharḥ al-Maqāṣid*, 5:172.2, 173.2; for the view that the verse is abrogated, see Ṭabarī, *Tafsīr*, 5:414.3).

[148] ʿAbd al-Ghanī, *Ḥadīqa*, 2:294.5, 294.13.

[149] *Ibid.*, 292.19, 293.31, 296.30. As to the term *ḥukkām*, in one passage he glosses *umarāʾ* as *ḥukkām al-siyāsa* and *ḥukkām* as *qāḍī*s and *muḥtasib*s (*ibid.*, 292.1); in another he glosses *amīr* as *ḥākim* (*ibid.*, 297.11). The separation between forbidding wrong and the exercise of state authority (*wilāya*, *ḥukm*) is strikingly absent from ʿAbd al-Ghanī's entry on *al-amr bi'l-maʿrūf* in his work on the interpretation of dreams (*Taʿṭīr al-anām fī taʿbīr al-manām*, Cairo n.d., 1:24.11; I owe this reference to Mona Zaki).

(but has no duty to do so).[150] The proof of this position is taken from the role of the ordinary believer in criminal law: if you see a man committing adultery with a woman, then at the time of the crime (but not thereafter) you may (but do not have to) kill him if other means of prevention do not work.[151] Failure to make this distinction between forbidding wrong and censorship is common among supposed scholars in our time, and leads to disastrous results.[152] ʿAbd al-Ghanī's tone in this part of his argument is discouraging, but his substantive doctrine would not in itself preclude much of the activity that is usually part of forbidding wrong.

This is not the case with the second pillar of ʿAbd al-Ghanī's doctrine, which might be described as neo-Māturīdite.[153] He lays great stress on having the right motives, and laments the prevalence of the wrong ones in his time: people set out to command and forbid because they crave an ego-trip, or see it as a way to establish a role of power and dominance in society, or to gain the attention of important people, or to win fame, or to attain proximity to the portals of rulers.[154] What is significant here, apart from the unusual elaboration of the theme, is the doctrinal conclusion he draws from this moralising: those whose motives are corrupt are obligated not to undertake the activity.[155] And who in this age of ours could even think, let alone be sure, that his motives were pure?[156] Certainly not those whose obsession with prying into the faults of others makes them blind to their own; so the chances of any scholar in this day and age attaining the martyrdom of which Birgili spoke are negligible.[157] What we need, in short, is less self-righteousness and more self-knowledge.[158] This is something that

[150] ʿAbd al-Ghanī, *Ḥadīqa*, 2:294.14, 295.21.

[151] *Ibid.*, 294.28. Ibn al-Humām (d. 861/1457), by contrast, regards such action as ***min bāb izālat al-munkar biʾl-yad*** (*Fatḥ al-qadīr*, Cairo 1970, 5:346.5; I owe this reference to Everett Rowson). [152] ʿAbd al-Ghanī, *Ḥadīqa*, 2:295.22. [153] Cf. above, 311f.

[154] *Ibid.*, 294.19, 296.9; I give only the highlights of this diatribe. The theme has already made its appearance earlier in the commentary with a passage taken from Ghazzālī (*ibid.*, 291.26; cf. Ghazzālī, *Iḥyāʾ*, 2:302.14).

[155] He construes the likelihood of impure motives as an instance of prospective harm (***ḍarar***) to the performer, and hence as voiding the duty under classical doctrine (ʿAbd al-Ghanī, *Ḥadīqa*, 2:294.18). These psychological hazards (he speaks of them as ***mafāsid***), unlike the danger of getting killed or the prospect of inefficacy, actually render the activity forbidden, because they are internal to the performer himself (*ibid.*, 296.5).

[156] *Ibid.*, 296.1. He has just explained that Birgili, in speaking of someone who proceeds when death is assured, must be referring to a person who is certain that he is free of the wrong motives (cf. also *ibid.*, 296.12). This is as close as ʿAbd al-Ghanī comes in this discussion to criticising Birgili overtly. [157] *Ibid.*, 296.14.

[158] This theme also appears in a letter of 1111/1699, in which ʿAbd al-Ghanī discourages his correspondent from busying himself with judging others and engaging in ***al-amr biʾl-maʿrūf***; instead, he should be oblivious to the vices of others, and spend his time examining his own soul (ʿAbd al-Ghanī al-Nābulusī (d. 1143/1731), *Murāsalāt*, ed. B. ʿAlāʾ al-Dīn, Damascus 1996(?), 328.16; this passage was drawn to my attention in proofs by Barbara von Schlegell). ʿAbd al-Ghanī's leading proof-text is Q5:105 (*ibid.*, 329.3; cf. above, ch. 2, 30f.). For an earlier adumbration of the theme, cf. above, note 138.

can only be attained through a deep knowledge of Ṣūfism, which alone confers knowledge, not just of the holy law, but also of how to practise it.[159] The combination of the redrawn distinction between forbidding wrong and censorship on the one hand, and of the Ṣūfī critique of egotistical and self-righteous pietism on the other, effectively closes the door to the activity Birgili had considered so binding. What is all this about?

We have here one of those rare but rewarding moments when a tradition of academic commentary suddenly gets real. Birgili had been more than an author of much-copied books. He was the inspiration of the Qāḍīzādeli movement, a puritanical reformism which gripped eleventh/seventeenth-century Istanbul under the successive leadership of Qāḍīzāde Meḥmed Efendi (d. 1045/1635f.), Usṭuvānī Meḥmed Efendi (d. 1072/1661), and Vānī Meḥmed Efendi (d. 1096/1684f.).[160] These men, and others like them, held official positions as preachers in the major mosques of Istanbul, combining popular followings with support from within the Ottoman state apparatus. Their prime target was none other than Ṣūfī innovation – the religious tradition to which ʿAbd al-Ghanī was so strongly committed.

Prior to this period, forbidding wrong does not seem to have been a prominent feature of the Ottoman religious scene.[161] For the Qāḍīzādeli preachers, however, it was a way of life, and one they engaged in with a wealth of contemporary reference and a conspicuous disrespect for persons.[162] Their followers likewise made it their business to command and

159 ʿAbd al-Ghanī, *Ḥadīqa*, 2:296.16; he quotes Shādhilī (d. 656/1258). The ignoramuses who set themselves up as devotees of the duty – manifestly lacking such wisdom – delude themselves by reading and misconstruing traditions (*ibid.*, 295.26).

160 For a survey of the Qāḍīzādeli movement, see M. C. Zilfi, *The politics of piety: the Ottoman ulema in the postclassical age (1600–1800)*, Minneapolis 1988, esp. ch. 4; for a fuller study, see S. Çavuşoğlu, 'The Ḳāḍīzādeli movement', Princeton Ph.D. 1990. A reverberation of the movement in Cairo in 1123/1711 is discussed in R. Peters, 'The battered dervishes of Bab Zuwayla: a religious riot in eighteenth-century Cairo', in N. Levtzion and J. O. Voll (eds.), *Eighteenth-century renewal and reform in Islam*, Syracuse 1987; note the appeal to *al-amr biʾl-maʿrūf* (*ibid.*, 95, 103).

161 I have only noted one explicit reference to it in the biographies of Ottoman scholars compiled by Ṭāshköprīzāde: he describes Mollā ʿArab (d. 938/1531) – by no means a typical Ottoman scholar – as performing the duty while residing in Constantinople (*al-Shaqāʾiq al-Nuʿmāniyya*, 414.14). Nevʿīzāde ʿAṭāʾī (d. 1045/1635) in his continuation of Ṭāshköprīzāde's work describes Birgili as performing the duty in his preaching (*Ḥadāʾiq al-ḥaqāʾiq fī takmilat al-Shaqāʾiq* (in Turkish), n.p. 1268, 180.17, and cf. Kātib Chelebi (d. 1067/1657), *Mīzān al-ḥaqq* (in Turkish), Istanbul 1306, 122.5).

162 Zilfi, *The politics of piety*, 137f., 163. As a contemporary epistle puts it, instructing people in their basic religious duties becomes incumbent on preachers (*wuʿʿāẓ*) as an individual duty by virtue of the very fact that they sit on their chairs (*bi-julūsihim ʿalā ʾl-karāsī*), since the sole point of sitting on these chairs is *al-amr biʾl-maʿrūf*, and such instruction is a form of this (*Risāla-i durar-i ghawwāṣ* (in Arabic), ms. Istanbul, Süleymaniye, Kasidecizade 663, f. 69b.3; this epistle follows immediately, and in the same hand, on one

forbid: one of them got into trouble in eastern Anatolia when he felt it his duty to mutilate the illustrations in a fine copy of the Persian national epic (the *Shāhnāma*), an action which he regarded as an instance of forbidding wrong; the local authorities instead considered it vandalism, and had him flogged for it.[163] Not that the response of the authorities was always so negative. The Shaykh al-Islām Zekerīyāzāde Yaḥyā Efendi (d. 1053/1644), who was not in principle well disposed towards the Qāḍīzādelis, remarked that he had found 'the hypocrites' (*mürā'īler*) to be courageous in forbidding wrong, and respected by the ignorant masses; so that although their hypocrisy was harmful to themselves, it could be expedient in respect of others.[164] But it could also be dangerous: on one occasion the Qāḍīzādelis made an appeal to all members of Muḥammad's community to gather the next day with weapons of war to assist in the cause of forbidding wrong.[165] All in all, forbidding wrong was undoubtedly the occasion of much friction between the Qāḍīzādelis and their opponents.

Yet at the time no clear doctrinal issue seems to have emerged with regard to the duty.[166] It was indeed an item on the long list of points of

copied in 1085/1674f. (f. 63a.11); I suspect it to be the work of Vānī Meḥmed Efendi, the author of the first epistle in the volume (f. 1b.1)).

163 R. Dankoff, *Evliya Çelebi in Bitlis*, Leiden 1990, 294–9. The Pasha tells the zealot that he has no commission to forbid wrong (*sen nehy-i münker etmeğe me'mur degilsin*, *ibid.*, 296.29). The incident is cited in Çavuşoğlu, 'The Ḳāḍīzādeli movement', 258.

164 Na'īmā (d. 1128/1716), *Tārīkh*, Istanbul 1283, 6:238.21, cited in Çavuşoğlu, 'The Ḳāḍīzādeli movement', 152. For the theme of Qāḍīzādeli hypocrisy, compare Na'īmā's remark that people such as the Qāḍīzādelis adopt the outward form of *al-amr bi'l-ma'rūf* in order to become famous (*taḥṣīl-i şöhret ve san içün*) (*Tārīkh*, 6:228.7, cited in Çavuşoğlu, 'The Ḳāḍīzādeli movement', 10f.).

165 Na'īmā, *Tārīkh*, 6:235.18, cited in Çavuşoğlu, 'The Ḳāḍīzādeli movement', 147.

166 Çavuşoğlu summarises a discussion of the performance of the duty by the preacher from a work of 'Abd ül-Mejīd Sīvāsī (d. 1049/1639), Qāḍīzāde's leading opponent: he should avoid causing mischief, respect privacy, have pure motives, refrain from naming names, hold back if his preaching would be ineffective or counter-productive, and speak nicely ('The Ḳāḍīzādeli movement', 253–8). This is clearly a call for restraint, and the references to purity of motive and anonymity may have contemporary relevance, but the ideas are standard. Çavuşoğlu notes Sīvāsī's references to the *Mawāqif* of Ījī (d. 756/1355) and to the *Kashshāf* of Zamakhsharī (*ibid.*, 256); and indeed a key doctrinal passage in Sīvāsī's account (*Durar-i 'aqā'id* (in Turkish), ms. Istanbul, Süleymaniye, Mihrimah Sultan 300, f. 72b.12) is more or less a translation from Ījī (*Mawāqif*, with the *Sharḥ* of al-Sayyid al-Sharīf al-Jurjānī (d. 816/1413), ed. T. Soerensen, Leipzig 1848, 331.22). She adds that Qāḍīzāde does not discuss these questions in his writings, and indeed his *Tāj al-rasā'il* (in Turkish) (ms. Istanbul, Süleymaniye, Hacı Mahmud 1,926) and his *Risāla qāmi'a lil-bid'a* (ms. Istanbul, Süleymaniye, Serez 3,876, ff. 47a–76a) make only occasional and uninteresting references to the duty. Vānī Meḥmed Efendi, if indeed he is the author of the *Risāla-i durar-i ghawwāṣ* – itself an exercise in *al-amr bi'l-ma'rūf* (see ff. 63b.10, 64b.7) – refers the reader to his epistle on *al-amr bi'l-ma'rūf* (f. 73b.1), but to my knowledge it does not survive. Another opponent of the Qāḍīzādelis who discusses *al-amr bi'l-ma'rūf* is 'Abd al-Aḥad al-Nūrī (*Maw'iẓa ḥasana*, 49–57); but he says nothing of significance in the present context.

contention between the two parties.[167] Hence Kātib Chelebi (d. 1067/1657), in a little work that he contributed to the controversy, devoted a section to forbidding wrong,[168] and in the course of it set out a rather rambling account of the conditions of obligation borrowed from Ashʿarite sources.[169] His purpose in piling up caveats was to cool the ardour of latter-day 'pretenders' (*müddeʿīler*),[170] in other words the Qāḍīzādelis. But while he stated that the common people were ignorant of the restrictions he dwelt on, he gave no indication that the Qāḍīzādelis themselves subscribed to a doctrine that formally sanctioned their more reckless activities.[171] The clash articulated in Kātib Chelebi's tract was not between rival doctrines of forbidding wrong, but rather between the zeal of the Qāḍīzādelis and his own realism and common sense. As he remarks elsewhere in the work, once an innovation (*bidʿat*) has become firmly rooted, it is fatuous to try to eradicate it in the name of forbidding wrong; the plain fact is that, for better or worse, people will not give up what they are accustomed to.[172] It is only with ʿAbd al-Ghanī al-Nābulusī that the friction over the practice of forbidding wrong is elevated to the level of a doctrinal dispute.

5. THE ḤANAFĪS IN THE LATE OTTOMAN PERIOD

Around the time when the Ottoman sultanate was abolished, Osman Nuri [Ergin] (d. 1381/1961) published the first volume of his monumental

167 See, for example, Naʿīmā, *Tārīkh*, 6:230.9, where it is the fifteenth of sixteen points.

168 Kātib Chelebi, *Mīzān al-ḥaqq*, 91–6 (= *The balance of truth*, trans. G. L. Lewis, London 1957, 106–9). 'Kātib Chelebi' is an alias of Ḥājjī Khalīfa.

169 He states that he has the analysis from two sources: one is the *Abkār al-afkār* of Āmidī (d. 631/1233); the other is the *Mawāqif* of Ījī, with the commentary thereon of al-Sayyid al-Sharīf al-Jurjānī (Kātib Chelebi, *Mīzān al-ḥaqq*, 92.3). His exposition of *al-amr bi'l-maʿrūf* is indeed manifestly related to the latter (*Mawāqif*, 331f.), but owes more to the former (*Abkār al-afkār*, ms. Istanbul, Süleymaniye, Aya Sofya 2,166, ff. 310a-311a; I am much indebted to Şükrü Hanioğlu for locating this discussion in the manuscript and obtaining a copy for me). For the conditions themselves, see below, ch. 13, 349f.

170 Kātib Chelebi, *Mīzān al-ḥaqq*, 95.3.

171 For the ignorance of the common people, see *ibid.*, 95.15. At the beginning of his account he states that the Muslim scholars disagree, some of them holding that *al-amr bi'l-maʿrūf* is obligatory absolutely (*muṭlaq vājibdir*), others that it is not (*ibid.*, 91.15). In fact, of course, no Muslim scholars held it to be obligatory without any conditions. The wording seems to derive from Jurjānī's quotation of a passage in which Āmidī draws a contrast: some Rāfiḍīs make the obligatoriness of *al-amr bi'l-maʿrūf* dependent on the imam, but everyone else holds it to be obligatory 'absolutely' (*muṭlaqan*), i.e. without reference to the imam (Jurjānī, *Sharḥ al-Mawāqif*, *apud* Ījī, *Mawāqif*, 331.7; the word *muṭlaqan* is not used by Āmidī himself at *Abkār*, f. 310a.14, but does appear at f. 310a.25). Thus there is no reference in these ancient dialectical cobwebs to the Qāḍīzādelis.

172 Kātib Chelebi, *Mīzān al-ḥaqq*, 75.1 (*bir bidʿat bir qavmın arasında yerleşüb qarārdāde olduqdansonra ʿemr bil-maʿrūf ve nehy ʿan il-münkerdir' diyü khalqı menʿ edüb andan döndürmek ārzūsında olmaq ʿaẓīm ḥamāqat ve jehldir*).

treatise on municipal affairs. Here, as background to his treatment of the role of the censor (*muḥtasib*) in urban life, he gave an account of the doctrine of forbidding wrong.[173] Osman Nuri was a product of the Westernising reforms of the late Ottoman period, but he did not choose to show it here. Instead, he presented an analysis of the duty which is immediately recognisable to the discerning reader as Ghazzālī's. He himself may not, however, have been aware of this. Indeed he stated quite explicitly where he had found his material: he was relying exclusively on a series of articles written by the sometime Shaykh al-Islām Ḥaydarīzāde Ibrāhīm Efendi (d. 1349/1931), and published in a well-known Islamist weekly a few years before.[174] He did in fact reproduce this material with great fidelity,[175] and we can accordingly leave his account aside and go back to his immediate source.

Unlike Osman Nuri, Ḥaydarīzāde saw no reason to name his sources. He opens his first article by remarking on a flurry of recent pronouncements on forbidding wrong that had appeared in the press,[176] and proposes to contribute some clarifications. The following three paragraphs present some of the main Koranic verses bearing on the duty, together with comments; the succession of the verses and the comments make it clear that his source is Ghazzālī.[177] Then, after a brief transition, he switches to a more surprising source: the rest of the article, bar a short concluding paragraph,

173 Osman Nuri [Ergin] (d. 1381/1961), *Mejelle-i umūr-i belediye*, Istanbul 1330–8 *mālī*, 1:314–26, drawn to my attention by Şükrü Hanioğlu. The first volume, which was in fact the last to appear, was published in 1338 *mālī*/1922.

174 *Ibid.*, 315.1. Ḥaydarīzāde Ibrāhīm Efendi's articles were published in Turkish in 1336–7/1918 under the title 'Amr bi'l-maʿrūf, nahy ʿan al-munkar' in the weekly *Sebīl ür-Reşād* (15 (1334–5 *mālī*), 65b–66b, 108a–110a, 139b–140b, 161a–162b). For the biography of Ḥaydarīzāde, who came from Irbil and spent his last years in Iraq, see A. Altunsu, *Osmanlı şeyhülislâmları*, Ankara 1972, 252f. (with an incorrect Christian death date; this work was drawn to my attention by Şükrü Hanioğlu); B. A. al-Ward, *Aʿlām al-ʿIrāq al-ḥadīth*, Baghdad 1978–, 1:37f. no. 25; ʿA. al-Ḥasanī, *Taʾrīkh al-wizārāt al-ʿIrāqiyya*, Sidon 1965–9, 1:196f., with a photograph (both works drawn to my attention by Yitzhak Nakash); also S. H. Longrigg, *ʿIraq, 1900 to 1950*, London 1953, 152.

175 With few and insignificant variations, he copied word for word the second, third and fourth of Ḥaydarīzāde's articles. He made no use of the first article, of which at least the opening paragraphs would have been in place; perhaps he did not have a copy to hand.

176 A considerable part is played by *al-amr bi'l-maʿrūf* in the rhetoric of two translated articles by the Egyptian ʿAbd al-ʿAzīz Chāwīsh (d. 1347/1929) which had appeared in *Sebīl ür-Reşād* under the title 'Tefsīr-i Qurʾān-i kerīm' (14 (1331–4 *mālī*), 137a–138a, 234b–235b); but it is not clear that Ḥaydarīzāde is responding to these articles in any specific way. For Chāwīsh, see Ziriklī, *Aʿlām*, 4:17b–c.

177 Ḥaydarīzāde, 'Amr bi'l-maʿrūf', 65b.15; Ghazzālī, *Iḥyāʾ*, 2:281.10. In principle he could have been using Ghazzālī indirectly, but I have noted nothing that would indicate this here or in his later articles; the *Iḥyāʾ* had in any case been available in print for several decades. Ḥaydarīzāde's dependence on Ghazzālī is pointed out in H. Karaman, 'İslâmda içtimaî terbiye ve kontrol', in H. Karaman, *İslâmın ışığında günün meseleleri*, Istanbul 1988, 691.

is doxographic material taken from the treatment of the duty by Ibn Ḥazm (d. 456/1064) in his heresiography.[178] In all this, Ḥaydarīzāde is a far less faithful copyist than Osman Nuri, and he occasionally introduces minor points of his own; but the ultimate provenance of the bulk of the material is beyond doubt.

In the second article he goes back to Ghazzālī, whom he follows despite a good deal of omission.[179] He also diverges from him on a significant point. While there is no indication that Ḥaydarīzāde knew Ṭāshköprīzāde's account, he shares his negative attitude towards the use of violence by ordinary believers in forbidding wrong.[180] So just like Ṭāshköprīzāde, he insists with regard to Ghazzālī's five levels that the permission of the authorities is indispensable for the fifth.[181] Moreover, he returns to this issue at the end of his article in a paragraph that is clearly his own.[182] Here he states that, given the requirements of our time and the present organisation of the state (*zamānın bugünkü īcābātiyle devletin teşkīlāt-i ḥāḍırasına naẓaran*), the third, fourth and fifth levels would all run foul of the criminal law (*cezāyı müstelzim aḥvālden ʿadd edilmiş*); accordingly, the view of those scholars who hold the permission of the authorities to be a condition for the performance of the duty is to this extent to be accepted. This shift away from Ghazzālī's position is likely to reflect two things: one is the pressure of modern conditions, as acknowledged by Ḥaydarīzāde; the other is the traditional Ḥanafī inclination not to rock the boat.[183] The only other point of interest in this article is the retention of Ghazzālī's explicit inclusion of women among those obligated to perform the duty.[184] The third article continues to follow Ghazzālī, with only minor departures.[185] The fourth does the same, breaking off somewhat arbitrarily with

[178] Ḥaydarīzāde, 'Amr bi'l-maʿrūf', 65b.36; Ibn Ḥazm, *Fiṣal*, 4:171.8. He follows Ibn Ḥazm as far as *ibid.*, 174.23, though towards the end he tends to skip more and more material. The *Fiṣal* too had been available in print for some time.

[179] The section covered is Ghazzālī, *Iḥyāʾ*, 2:285.29–290.20. Ḥaydarīzāde at one point mentions Ghazzālī, but not in such a way as to indicate the extent of his dependence on him ('Amr bi'l-maʿrūf', 109a.26).

[180] See above, 321f.

[181] *Ibid.*, 109b.4, and cf. 109b.12.

[182] *Ibid.*, 110a.34.

[183] Ḥaydarīzāde does not quote the tripartite saying, for all that it had been a favourite of the Ḥanafīs. It does, however, appear in the commentary of Meḥmed Vehbī (d. 1368–9/1949) to Q3:104 (*Khulāṣat al-bayān* (in Turkish), Istanbul 1341–3, 3:156.9).

[184] Ḥaydarīzāde, 'Amr bi'l-maʿrūf', 108b.1 (contrast the silence of Ṭāshköprīzāde, *Miftāḥ*, 3:302.11). Other Ḥanafī authors who include women are Rajab (*Wasīla*, 2:761.18), ʿIṣmat Allāh (*Raqīb*, f. 6b.3), ʿAbd al-Ghanī (*Ḥadīqa*, 2:297.4), and Mīrghanī (*Baḥr*, f. 216b.4). The context in which ʿAbd al-Ghanī makes the point is remarkable: he is commenting on the word *rajul* in a tradition about standing up to an unjust ruler and getting killed for it.

[185] Ḥaydarīzāde consolidates Ghazzālī's discussion of the individual soldier who courts certain death in war with the infidel (compare Ḥaydarīzāde, 'Amr bi'l-maʿrūf', 140a.28 with Ghazzālī, *Iḥyāʾ*, 2:292.30); this may reflect the fact that he was writing in the last

a discussion of damage caused to property by animals.[186] The abrupt ending of the series may reflect the pressures of office: it was a month after the publication of the last article that Ḥaydarīzāde first became Shaykh al-Islām.[187]

6. CONCLUSION

The sources used in this chapter could doubtless be considerably extended. But the material surveyed above is enough to establish two things about the Ḥanafī treatment of forbidding wrong.

The first is a certain weakness in the Ḥanafī literary tradition on the subject. Nowhere in Ḥanafī literature have I found an account of the duty that could be described as coherent, systematic and at the same time authentically Ḥanafī. In particular, we have seen a tendency for the Ḥanafī tradition to be penetrated by Shāfiʿite materials, a process nowhere more evident than in the wholesale adoption of Ghazzālī's analysis by a number of Ḥanafī writers.

The second noteworthy feature of the Ḥanafī tradition is what I have called its accommodationist tendencies. As we have seen, the leitmotivs of this disposition were the recurrent theme of the tripartite division of labour, and a nagging discomfort with the more abrasive aspects of Ghazzālī's doctrine.[188] That the Ḥanafīs would incline in this direction was not a foregone conclusion, as we will see in the excursus that follows. But

months of the First World War (for the way in which this touched him, cf. his poem *ʿIrāq ordusuna khiṭāb* of 1335/1917, Istanbul 1335 *mālī*). He also moves Ghazzālī's discussion of the performer's need for knowledge, scrupulousness and good temper to what is perhaps a more logical position (*Iḥyāʾ*, 2:305.9; Ḥaydarīzāde, 'Amr bi'l-maʿrūf', 140b.5).

186 The article corresponds to Ghazzālī, *Iḥyāʾ*, 2:297.7–301.15, with extensive omissions towards the end. By breaking off at this point, Ḥaydarīzāde fails to go on to cover Ghazzālī's eight levels (*ibid.*, 301–5), his account of commonplace evils (*ibid.*, 307–13), and his long anecdotal section on the performance of the duty against rulers (314–26). With regard to this last, it should be noted that Ḥaydarīzāde does not suppress incidental references to rebuking unjust rulers earlier in Ghazzālī's account (see Ḥaydarīzāde, 'Amr bi'l-maʿrūf', 109b.8, 140a.13).

187 For his various brief tenures of this office, see İ. H. Danişmend, *İzahlı Osmanlı tarihi kronolojisi*, Istanbul 1947–61, 4:561f.

188 For the tripartite division of labour, see above, notes 12, 37, 49, 86, 96, 126, 132, 139, 141–3, 183; and see also ʿAlī ibn Shihāb al-Dīn al-Hamadānī (d. 786/1385), *Dhakhīrat al-mulūk* (in Persian), Lahore 1905, 131.5 (translating and glossing the 'three modes' tradition; this author seems to have shifted from the Ḥanafī to the Shāfiʿite law-school, see J. K. Teufel, *Eine Lebensbeschreibung des Scheichs ʿAlī-i Hamadānī*, Leiden 1962, 12). The Turkish Islamist Mehmet Şevket Eygi sets out the tripartite division in a piece published in *Millî Gazete* for 2 August 1999 under the title 'Kara para' (I am indebted to Şükrü Hanioğlu for supplying me with a copy from the paper's web site). For the toning down of Ghazzālī, see above, notes 98, 102, and 321f., 332; but contrast 323.

there is a consistent line running from the embarrassment of Abū Ḥanīfa at the hands of the goldsmith, through the Sāmānids, and on to the state Ḥanafism of the Ottoman period; it is this bent that is for the most part typical of the Ḥanafism we know from the literary heritage of the school. It was to be the historical role of Ḥanafism to live in symbiosis, not to say collaboration, with Turkish military and political power.[189] In the hard light of history, this development may appear as an adventitious consequence of the geography of the fourth/tenth-century Islamic world. But among Abū Ḥanīfa's followers the belief arose that he had received a supernatural assurance that his school would continue 'as long as the sword remains in the hands of the Turks'.[190] It is characteristic of this symbiosis that even the Qāḍīzādeli radicals owed their positions to the patronage of the Ottoman state.[191]

7. EXCURSUS: JAṢṢĀṢ

Against the background of the Ḥanafī literary tradition as described in this chapter, one Ḥanafī scholar whose views stand out as anomalous is Abū Bakr al-Rāzī, better known as Jaṣṣāṣ (d. 370/981). This scholar spent most of his life in Baghdad, where he steadfastly resisted the attempts of the caliph al-Muṭīʿ (r. 334–63/946–74) to appoint him chief judge.[192] His work on Koranic law contains two significant chapters on forbidding wrong.[193] The immediate problem is to disentangle the allegiances represented in this material: Ḥanafī, traditionalist, and Muʿtazilite.

The Ḥanafī allegiance is obvious from the work as a whole, in which the views of the founding fathers of the Ḥanafī law-school are repeatedly cited on questions of law. In the chapters that concern us, however, no such place is allotted to their opinions on forbidding wrong; instead, their

[189] There were Ḥanafīs outside the range of this phenomenon, but for the purposes of this study I know almost nothing about them. One who touched on the duty was the Aḥsāʾī Abū Bakr al-Mullā al-Ḥanafī (d. 1270/1853) in his *Naẓm al-Jawāhir* (printed at the end of his *Qurrat al-ʿuyūn al-mubṣira*, Damascus n.d., 2:340); thus he speaks of the need to command and forbid one's leaders (*ruʾūs*) (*ibid.*, 340.9). For this scholar, see Muḥammad ibn ʿAbdallāh Āl ʿAbd al-Qādir, *Tuḥfat al-mustafīd bi-taʾrīkh al-Aḥsāʾ fī ʾl-qadīm waʾl-jadīd*, Riyāḍ and Damascus 1960–3, 2:106–9.

[190] Rāwandī (writing 599/1202f.), *Rāḥat al-ṣudūr* (in Persian), ed. M. Iqbál, London 1921, 17.21.

[191] Zilfi notes their significant failure to take on the blood-curdling misdeeds of the Janissaries (*The politics of piety*, 167).

[192] Khaṭīb, *Taʾrīkh Baghdād*, 4:314.8, and cf. 314.3.

[193] Jaṣṣāṣ, *Aḥkām*, 2:29–36, 486–9. The *aḥkām al-Qurʾān* genre, a form of Koran commentary devoted to legal topics, was well established in his time (see Ibn al-Nadīm, *Fihrist*, 57.7; Ḥājjī Khalīfa, *Kashf al-ẓunūn*, 20.3; also below, ch. 14, note 50). Ḥājjī Khalīfa notes two earlier Ḥanafī works of this kind, and Ibn al-Nadīm characterises Jaṣṣāṣ's work as Ḥanafī (*ʿalā madhhab ahl al-ʿIrāq*).

teachings are cited only in incidental references to more narrowly legal questions.[194] Nor does Jaṣṣāṣ make any use of the early Ḥanafī sources familiar to us.[195] Thus it is only indirectly, through the anecdote about Abū Ḥanīfa and the goldsmith,[196] together with the tradition transmitted to him by Abū Ḥanīfa,[197] that we learn anything from these chapters about earlier Ḥanafī views of forbidding wrong. This is curious; elswhere in the work we read that Abū Ḥanīfa believed in the obligatoriness of forbidding wrong by word and sword.[198]

The second allegiance is immediately obvious from the profusion of traditions that Jaṣṣāṣ quotes in the course of his presentation. He has two from Abū Dāwūd al-Ṭayālisī (d. 204/819),[199] nine from Abū Dāwūd al-Sijistānī (d. 275/889),[200] a battery of mostly exegetical traditions from Abū ʿUbayd (d. 224/838f.),[201] another exegetical tradition from ʿAbd al-Razzāq ibn Hammām al-Ṣanʿānī (d. 211/827),[202] and some six sayings quoted without full chains of transmission.[203] All told, this material comprises a little over a third of the entire coverage of the duty. It would thus be surprising if Sunnī traditionalism had no visible impact on the substance of the views advanced in these chapters. If we look for the tell-tale notion of performance in the heart, we shall not be disappointed: Jaṣṣāṣ duly sets

194 On such points he cites Abū Ḥanīfa (Jaṣṣāṣ, *Aḥkām*, 2:31.28, 31.29), Shaybānī (d. 189/805) (*ibid.*, 31.27, 36.14), and his own teacher Abū ʾl-Ḥasan al-Karkhī (d. 340/952) (*ibid.*, 36.11; cf. Khaṭīb, *Taʾrīkh Baghdād*, 4:314.2).

195 Jaṣṣāṣ does not draw on Abū Ḥanīfa's views as found in the *Fiqh absaṭ* (see above, ch. 1, notes 24–6). He also passes by the two traditions on *al-amr biʾl-maʿrūf* found in Abū Yūsuf's *Kharāj* (10.19, 11.2), citing the first from Abū Dāwūd (Jaṣṣāṣ, *Aḥkām*, 2:31.7 = Abū Dāwūd, *Sunan*, 4:509f. no. 4,338), and ignoring the second.

196 Jaṣṣāṣ, *Aḥkām*, 2:33.5 (see above, ch. 1, note 4).

197 *Ibid.*, 34.17 (see above, ch. 1, note 20). The key figure in the *isnād* of this tradition is Abū Bishr al-Muṣʿabī (d. 323/935), a Marwazī who had a reputation as a staunch Sunnī but a great liar in matters of *ḥadīth* (see Dhahabī, *Tadhkira*, 803f. no. 793, and Samʿānī, *Ansāb*, 12:292.8); he was presumably a Ḥanafī.

198 Jaṣṣāṣ, *Aḥkām*, 1:70.21 (drawn to my attention by Patricia Crone).

199 *Ibid.*, 2:30.6, 30.18.

200 *Ibid.*, 30.11, 30.21, 30.28, 31.5, 31.10, 34.13, 486.10, 486.14, 487.6. Jaṣṣāṣ uses the recension of Ibn Dāsa (d. 346/957f.), for which see J. Robson, 'The transmission of Abū Dāwūd's *Sunan*', *Bulletin of the School of Oriental and African Studies*, 14 (1952), 581f.; for the death date of Ibn Dāsa, see Dhahabī, *Tadhkira*, 863.15.

201 Jaṣṣāṣ, *Aḥkām*, 2:486.24, 486.30, 487.1, 487.21, 488.11, 488.26, 488.30, 489.1, 489.4, 489.6. These traditions are taken from the chapter on *al-amr biʾl-maʿrūf* in Abū ʿUbayd, *Nāsikh*, 98–101. He also makes occasional use of Abū ʿUbayd's own comments (compare Jaṣṣāṣ, *Aḥkām*, 2:487.2, 489.8 with Abū ʿUbayd, *Nāsikh*, 100.3, 101.20). A citation of an exegetical view of Saʿīd ibn Jubayr (d. 95/714) missing from the text of Abū ʿUbayd's work (cf. *Nāsikh*, 100.1, 100.3, 100.7, and Burton's comment, *ibid.*, 167 of the English section) can be restored from Jaṣṣāṣ, *Aḥkām*, 2:486.30.

202 *Ibid.*, 34.27. This tradition derives from his Koran commentary (ʿAbd al-Razzāq, *Tafsīr*, 1:130.9); it appears also in Ṭabarī, *Tafsīr*, 7:104 no. 7,622 (both to Q3:110).

203 Jaṣṣāṣ, *Aḥkām*, 2:32.17, 32.23, 33.27, 34.25, 487.32, 488.4. Several of these are exegetical.

out the doctrine of the three modes (*manāzil*), namely hand, tongue and heart.[204]

Yet our author seems also to have been a Muʿtazilite, like other leading Ḥanafī scholars of his day.[205] This is not, however, obvious from his doctrine of forbidding wrong as set out in these chapters. Jaṣṣāṣ makes no mention of any Muʿtazilite authorities. It is true that many of his positions are broadly similar to those found in Muʿtazilite accounts;[206] but with one exception, none of his doctrines look distinctively Muʿtazilite. The exception is his attitude to the use of the sword in performance of the duty. This attitude appears in two passages that have a strong claim to be considered Muʿtazilite.[207]

The first is an impassioned polemic against the spineless attitudes of ignorant anthropomorphist traditionists.[208] They alone – in effect – deny the duty. They reject resort to arms in the execution of the duty, calling all such action sedition (*fitna*).[209] They hold that injustice and murder may be

204 *Ibid.*, 30.3 (where the term *manāzil* appears), and cf. 30.16, 487.14. The three modes tradition is cited more than once (*ibid.*, 30.10, 30.14, 486.12). In several places performance in the heart is linked to *taqiyya* (*ibid.*, 32.16, 487.17, 487.29, 488.22, and cf. 486.4).

205 See Madelung, 'The spread of Māturīdism', 112. He was the author of works of *kalām* as well as of *fiqh* (Ibn al-Murtaḍā, *Ṭabaqāt*, 130.12), and is quoted for the remark that it was Abū ʿAlī al-Jubbāʾī (d. 303/916) who made the science of *kalām* easy (*ibid.*, 80.2). His Muʿtazilism is, however, called in question in A. K. Reinhart, *Before revelation: the boundaries of Muslim moral thought*, Albany 1995, 46f.

206 Thus the duty is imposed by Koran, tradition and consensus (Jaṣṣāṣ, *Aḥkām*, 2:486.2, and cf. 33.21). It is collective (*farḍ ʿalā ʾl-kifāya*), not individual (*farḍ ʿalā kull aḥad fī nafsihi*) (*ibid.*, 29.19, 33.22). Drastic action is not permitted where lesser measures will suffice (*ibid.*, 31.23). Though no formal set of conditions is advanced, some points are familiar: personal danger releases one from the obligation to act (*ibid.*, 30.4, 32.8, 487.30); likewise there is no duty to attempt the impossible (*ibid.*, 30.4, 487.14, 487.31, and cf. 30.16, 31.17), and the obligation to speak out lapses where nothing would be achieved by it (*ibid.*, 32.12, 488.23). If we see a wicked man (*fāsiq*) performing *al-amr biʾl-maʿrūf*, it is our duty to assist him (*ibid.*, 3:119.27). We also find discussions of the obligation of the sinner to perform *al-amr biʾl-maʿrūf* (*ibid.*, 2:33.23), of one's duty to avoid offenders (*an yujānibahum wa-yuẓhir hijrānahum*) whom one is unable to confront (*ibid.*, 30.31, 32.13), and of the question whether heresy (i.e. false belief short of unbelief, see *ibid.*, 36.7) is to be tolerated (*ibid.*, 35.27) – the answer being that it depends in the first instance on whether the heretic is a progagandist (*dāʿī*) (*ibid.*, 35.28).

207 Note also the definition of *maʿrūf* in terms of reason (*ʿaql*) (*ibid.*, 3:38.10) without reference to revelation (cf. above, ch. 2, note 54).

208 He refers to them as *qawm min al-ḥashw wa-juhhāl aṣḥāb al-ḥadīth* (*ibid.*, 2:34.2) – in other words, the Sunnī traditionists. Fighting the *fiʾa bāghiya* is included alongside *al-amr biʾl-maʿrūf*, with citation of Q49:9. In another passage Jaṣṣāṣ states that some traditionists (*qawm min al-ḥashw*) hold that one may only fight the *ahl al-baghy* with sticks and sandals, but not with the sword (*ibid.*, 3:400.3); he has already remarked that fighting the *ahl al-baghy* is a form of *al-amr biʾl-maʿrūf* (*ibid.*, 399.30). Elsewhere in the work he lashes out at the ignorant traditionists (*aghmār aṣḥāb al-ḥadīth*) who are responsible for the demise of *al-amr biʾl-maʿrūf*, with the result that unjust rulers have taken over the affairs of Islam (*ibid.*, 1:70.31).

209 *Ibid.*, 2:34.3.

committed by a ruler with impunity (*lā yunkar ʿalayhi*), while other offenders may be proceeded against by word or deed – but not with arms.[210] The point is not, in the writer's view, an academic one. It is these attitudes that have led to the present sorry state of Islam – to the domination of the reprobate, of Magians, of enemies of Islam; to the collapse of the frontiers of Islam against the infidel; to the spread of injustice, the ruin of countries, and the rise of all manner of false religions.[211] All this, we learn, is a consequence of the abandonment of the duty to command right and forbid wrong, and of standing up to unjust rulers (*al-inkār ʿalā ʾl-sulṭān al-jāʾir*). We cannot tell whether this attack is original to our author, or culled by him from some earlier source; that it may be the latter is suggested by the oddity of his simultaneously attacking the traditionists and adducing their traditions as authoritative. The historical references, such as they are, would fit the third/ninth century as well as the fourth/tenth.[212] In any case, the betrayal of forbidding wrong by the traditionists (Ḥashwiyya) is, as we have seen, a favourite theme of the Muʿtazilites.[213]

The second passage is a variant on the same basic theme: the use of the sword against unjust rule.[214] Jaṣṣāṣ is considering situations in which it is within one's power to put a stop to some evil, and accordingly one's duty to do so. Where words or blows will not suffice, one will have an obligation to resort to arms and, if necessary, to kill the offender; if need be, one will do so without prior warning, since such warning may defeat the purpose of the action. Examples of relevant criminal behaviour are then adduced, of which the most prominent is the collection of non-canonical taxes (*al-ḍarāʾib waʾl-mukūs*).[215] It is the duty of Muslims to kill such tax-collectors; every man should do this whenever he can, and without giving them prior warning.[216] This does not, of course, imply that the believer is committed to anti-fiscal suicide missions. If he fears for his life, he is entitled to leave

210 *Ibid.*, 34.6. The passage is borrowed in Abū Ḥayyān al-Gharnāṭī, *Baḥr*, 3:20.19.

211 He names *zandaqa*, *ghuluww*, dualist doctrines, the Khurramiyya and Mazdakism (Jaṣṣāṣ, *Aḥkām*, 2:34.11).

212 The complaint about the domination of Magians could well refer to the power held by the 'Magians' Faḍl ibn Sahl (d. 202/818) and his brother Ḥasan (d. 236/851) under the Caliph al-Maʾmūn (r. 198–218/813–33) (cf. W. Madelung, 'New documents concerning al-Maʾmūn, al-Faḍl b. Sahl and ʿAlī al-Riḍā', in W. al-Qāḍī (ed.), *Studia Arabica et Islamica: Festschrift for Iḥsān ʿAbbās*, Beirut 1981, 344).

213 See above, ch. 9, notes 7, 40, 63, 160.

214 Jaṣṣāṣ, *Aḥkām*, 2:31.19.

215 *Ibid.*, 32.3. The passage is cited in Abū Ḥayyān, *Baḥr*, 3:20.23.

216 Cf. the Prophetic tradition 'When you meet a tax-collector (*ʿashshār*), kill him!' (Ibn ʿAbd al-Ḥakam, *Futūḥ Miṣr*, 231.15). This positive thinking may be contrasted with the more sober view of Zamakhsharī, for whom the attempt to rebuke and restrain tax-collectors (*aṣḥāb al-maʿāṣir, makkāsūn*) is a prime example of the kind of futile activity (*ʿabath*) that would make one a figure of fun (for references, see above, ch. 11, note 192).

tax-collectors alone. But he should still conduct himself towards them with as much incivility as he can muster,[217] and he should avoid socialising with them.[218]

In short, if we leave aside the few specifically Ḥanafī elements in Jaṣṣāṣ's account, we can see it as a curious blend of traditionalist and Muʿtazilite elements: the traditionalist notion of performance in the heart appears side by side with the Muʿtazilite relish for the sword.[219] But as we have seen, it was a Māturīdite rather than a Muʿtazilite (or traditionalist) Ḥanafism that represented the wave of the future. The Ottoman Empire of the Shaykh al-Islām Abū 'l-Suʿūd Efendi had no elective affinity for a brand of Ḥanafism that gloried in the killing of tax-collectors.

217 The term for this unpleasantness is *ghilẓa* (Jaṣṣāṣ, *Aḥkām*, 2:32.9, and cf. Q9:123). The goldsmith's speech to Abū Muslim was *ghalīẓ* (*ibid.*, 33.18).

218 As far as Jaṣṣāṣ himself is concerned, the Khaṭīb records no clash with the authorities more strenuous than his assiduous refusal to accept the office of *qāḍī 'l-quḍāt* (see above, note 192).

219 Compare also the vigour of Jaṣṣāṣ's reaction to the threat posed to *al-amr bi'l-maʿrūf* by Q5:105 (cf. above, ch. 2, 30f.): he devotes the greater part of his second chapter on the duty (from *ibid.*, 486.17) to damage control on this score, at the same time leaning heavily on the notion of performance in the heart to make his case (*ibid.*, 487.15).

CHAPTER 13

THE SHĀFIʿITES

1. INTRODUCTION

In this chapter we shall be concerned with doctrines of forbidding wrong among members of the Shāfiʿite law-school.[1] It is convenient to bring the Shāfiʿites together in this fashion, but not much more. The law-schools of Sunnī Islam were, in general, real social communities in a way in which its theological schools were not, and it was primarily within these communities that literary heritages were either transmitted or allowed to die out. Yet the Shāfiʿite tradition proper was a legal one, and here, as elsewhere in Sunnism, forbidding wrong was not included within the compass of the law-book – for all that the well-known Shāfiʿite Ashʿarite Juwaynī (d. 478/1085) thought it should have been.[2] The topic was thus left to the theologians. There was, however, no such thing as Shāfiʿite theology. The theological doctrines of Shāfiʿī (d. 204/820) himself, even to the extent that they were transmitted, were of no great importance to Shāfiʿites;[3] and his views on forbidding wrong, fine and upstanding though they doubtless were, are not transmitted at all. It was not until the fifth/eleventh century that the Shāfiʿites acquired a theological identity in the shape of Ashʿarism. Even then it was one that they shared with the Mālikīs, and it met with

[1] I leave aside the Qāḍī ʿAbd al-Jabbār (d. 415/1025), for whom see above, ch. 9, 202. His Muʿtazilism was by no means unique among the Shāfiʿites (see Halm, *Ausbreitung*, 33, and cf. below, note 6); but it was nevertheless an untypical theological allegiance for a Shāfiʿite, and his works were not transmitted within the Shāfiʿite school.

[2] Juwaynī, *Irshād*, 368.3, cited in Madelung, 'Amr be maʿrūf', 993b; Juwaynī (d. 478/1085), *Ghiyāth al-umam*, ed. F. ʿA. Aḥmad and M. Ḥilmī, Alexandria 1979, 177.12. Juwaynī states that the lawyers have handed over the topic to the *mutakallimūn*, whose custom it is to treat the duty under *uṣūl*. Fakhr al-Dīn al-Rāzī likewise remarks in one place that the conditions of obligation are discussed in works of *kalām* (*Tafsīr*, 8:178.23 (to Q3:104)), and in another that the rules of forbidding wrong are a major topic in *ʿilm al-uṣūl* (*ibid.*, 16:204.24 (to Q9:112)).

[3] See Madelung, *Religious trends*, 27f., contrasting the Shāfiʿites with the Ḥanbalites and Ḥanafīs.

continued resistance from traditionalist Shāfiʿites.[4] The role of Ashʿarism as an imported theology was thus comparable to that of Muʿtazilism among the Zaydīs, Imāmīs and Ḥanafīs. This analogy might suggest the appropriateness of a chapter on Ashʿarite doctrines of forbidding wrong parallel to that on the Muʿtazilites. In fact, however, the analogy breaks down. Though we have much detailed information about Ashʿarite theological doctrines prior to their reception among the Shāfiʿites, this does not extend to forbidding wrong.[5] The impression we are left with is that the duty was far less central to Ashʿarite concerns than it was to those of the Muʿtazilites. And if we juxtapose such later accounts as we find among the Shāfiʿites and Mālikīs, we are hard put to it to find anything that looks like a common core of Ashʿarite doctrine. The subject-matter of this chapter is accordingly the views that Shāfiʿites have held on forbidding wrong, with no implication that there was such a thing as a generally accepted Shāfiʿite – or indeed Ashʿarite – view.

In practice, the major distinction to be made among the Shāfiʿites who will concern us is not between Ashʿarites and others but, quite simply, between Ghazzālī (d. 505/1111) and the rest. His account is at once so monumental, so distinctive and so widely influential that I shall accord it a chapter on its own. The present chapter will thus be somewhat in the nature of *Hamlet* without the Prince of Denmark; we shall look first at the Shāfiʿites before Ghazzālī, and secondly at the Shāfiʿites after Ghazzālī.

2. THE SHĀFIʿITES BEFORE GHAZZĀLĪ

Our earliest information about the views of Shāfiʿite scholars on forbidding wrong seems to date from a surprisingly late period: the fourth/tenth century. The first scholar for whom I have any material is Abū Bakr al-Qaffāl al-Shāshī (d. 365/976), who may have been a Muʿtazilite.[6] All we have from him are some brief comments on Q3:110.[7] The tone is strongly activist. The

[4] See *ibid.*, 28f.; Madelung, 'The spread of Māturīdism', 109f.; Halm, *Ausbreitung*, 32–40.

[5] Abū Yaʿlā makes a reference to the view preferred by the Mālikī Ashʿarite Bāqillānī (d. 403/1013) on the question whether the prospect of being beaten or imprisoned – but not actually killed – is enough to void the duty (*Amr*, f. 102a.9). The syntax leaves it tantalisingly unclear on which side of the fence Bāqillānī came down.

[6] For Qaffāl and his theological allegiance, see Halm, *Ausbreitung*, 33, 35f., 112f.; but see also Reinhart, *Before revelation*, 19–21.

[7] Fakhr al-Dīn al-Rāzī, *Tafsīr*, 8:191.4, 191.23, 192.6 (noted in Roest Crollius, 'Mission and morality', 272); cf. also below, note 16. I identify Rāzī's Qaffāl as ours (i.e. as al-Qaffāl al-Kabīr) on the strength of the remarks of Nawawī (d. 676/1277) as quoted in Suyūṭī (d. 911/1505), *Ṭabaqāt al-mufassirīn*, ed. ʿA. M. ʿUmayr, Cairo 1976, 109.14, and the explicit statement of Suyūṭī himself, *ibid.*, 110.6. Rāzī's most likely source, direct or indirect, is Qaffāl's own Koran commentary, a work singled out for its pernicious Muʿtazilism (see Halm, *Ausbreitung*, 35, translating Subkī, *Ṭabaqāt*, 3:201.14).

verse, it will be remembered, declares the Muslim community the best to have been brought forth. Remarking that the mode of commanding right may be by heart, tongue or hand, Qaffāl attributes the superiority of the Muslims to the fact that their practice of forbidding wrong extends to fighting (*qitāl*); this, he says, is the most stringent mode of performance of the duty, since it involves the risk of being killed.[8] From what we know of Qaffāl's biography, this was not just a rhetorical flourish. He was among 'the disorderly Khurāsān rabble' who appeared in Rayy in 355/966 on their way to defend the frontiers of Islam against the Byzantines and Armenians; significantly, they justified their depredations as forbidding wrong.[9]

Our earliest Shāfiʿite set piece on the duty is found in a work by a pupil of Qaffāl, the Transoxanian scholar, judge and diplomat Abū ʿAbdallāh al-Ḥalīmī al-Jurjānī (d. 403/1012).[10] In this treatise on the 'branches of the faith', forbidding wrong rates a chapter as the fifty-second of seventy-seven branches.[11] Ḥalīmī quotes scripture and traditions extensively, and what he has to say in his own voice is not particularly systematic. A good deal of it is too familiar to detain us long. He establishes the obligatoriness of forbidding wrong with reference to Koran and normative tradition (*sunna*).[12] He deploys the three modes, supported by the usual tradition from the Prophet.[13] He insists on the minimal duty of avoiding intercourse with offenders,[14] but enjoins emigration – where possible – in order to get away from evil-doers who cannot be restrained.[15] More striking is a passage reminiscent of Qaffāl, but in this case triggered by Q9:67, on the connection between forbidding wrong and holy war. Here he stresses the lack of any fundamental distinction; we are given to understand that both duties are reducible to calling people to Islam, and backing the call with violence (*qitāl*) where necessary.[16]

This apart, the tone of Ḥalīmī's account is strongly accommodationist. Though he does not mention the tripartite saying so often quoted among

[8] Fakhr al-Dīn al-Rāzī, *Tafsīr*, 8:191.23. The rest of the passage is explicitly concerned with *jihād* against unbelief.

[9] Miskawayh, *Tajārib*, 6:223.8, 223.12, adduced in H. F. Amedroz, 'The Hisba jurisdiction in the Ahkam Sultaniyya of Mawardi', *Journal of the Royal Asiatic Society*, 1916, 292f.

[10] For Ḥalīmī see Halm, *Ausbreitung*, 103. For his activity as a diplomat, see also Sahmī, *Taʾrīkh Jurjān*, 156.16.

[11] Ḥalīmī (d. 403/1012), *al-Minhāj fī shuʿab al-īmān*, Damascus 1979, 3:215–23; the text is frequently corrupt. I am indebted to Wilferd Madelung for referring me to this work. Bayhaqī's *Shuʿab al-īmān* is a recension of Ḥalīmī's work in which traditions appear with full *isnāds* (see Bayhaqī's initial statement, *ibid.*, 1:28.14), and in much greater numbers; much of Ḥalīmī's discussion is repeated there, though in a text which is no less corrupt (*ibid.*, 6:81.7, 84.22, 87.5, 88.9). [12] Ḥalīmī, *Minhāj*, 3:216.8.

[13] *Ibid.*, 217.12, and cf. 219.8, 219.21, and cf. 222.2. [14] *Ibid.*, 223.5.

[15] *Ibid.*, 222.15 (read *faʾl-khurūj min baynihim*).

[16] *Ibid.*, 216.9; the passage reappears in part in Qurṭubī, *Jāmiʿ*, 4:47.11.

the Ḥanafīs, he presents what is in some degree the same division of labour in a more elaborate form, and in his own voice. For Ḥalīmī the set of believers who are qualified to undertake the duty is an explicitly restricted one.[17] Leaving aside for the moment a relaxation which he introduces at the end of his argument, Ḥalīmī limits the duty to two kinds of people: the ruler (*sulṭān al-Muslimīn*,[18] or simply *sulṭān*), and the righteous scholar (*al-ʿālim al-muṣliḥ*).[19] It is in the first instance on the ruler that the duty falls,[20] since he alone has executive power.[21] Since he is not omnipresent, the ruler should appoint a watch-dog in each town (*balad*) and village (*qarya*); this appointee should be a learned and trustworthy man of strong and sound character.[22] Whenever he[23] hears of a wrong that needs to be put right, he should act. It makes no difference to the ruler's duty whether he is himself an offender.[24] When the ruler does not perform the duty (*ʿinda imsāk al-sulṭān*), it falls upon others – namely the righteous scholars of the community.[25] They are all of them obligated to perform the duty, so far as they are able, in the three familiar modes, even to the extent of seeking assistance where this is appropriate;[26] but they are not to presume to encroach on the executive powers of the ruler by inflicting penalties.[27] There is no mention of resort to arms or killing on their part.

What if a prospective performer of the duty (other than the ruler) lacks one or other of the two requisite qualities? He might be a scholar, but not a righteous one. In such a case Ḥalīmī does not budge from his view.[28] Such a man would be better occupied reforming his own character, and lacks the moral authority needed to carry out the duty vis-à-vis others.[29] But what of a righteous Muslim (*min ṣulaḥāʾ al-Muslimīn*) who is not an outstanding scholar (*min al-ʿulamāʾ al-mubarrizīn*)? Ḥalīmī considers this question pretty much as an afterthought, and states (but God knows best)

17 Ḥalīmī, *Minhāj*, 3:216.17. The beginning of this passage reappears in Qurṭubī, *Jāmiʿ*, 4:47.13.
18 So Ḥalīmī, *Minhāj*, 3:216.18.
19 So *ibid.*, 217.14.
20 *Ibid.*, 216.18; 'in the first instance' is my addition.
21 Specifically the powers of carrying out *ḥadd* punishments, making decisions relating to discretionary floggings (*taʿzīr*), making arrests and releasing prisoners, and imposing banishment (*nafy*) and torture (*taʿdhīb*) if the ruler considers them politic (*ibid.*, 216.18).
22 *Ibid.*, 216.20. Ḥalīmī does not use the term *muḥtasib*.
23 Sc. the ruler's appointee.
24 *Ibid.*, 219.5. As will be seen, the ruler is in this respect an exception, the reason given being that 'rulership is just that' (*al-salṭana hiya hādhā*) – i.e. were the ruler to cease to command and forbid, he would thereby cease to be a ruler.
25 *Ibid.*, 219.7.
26 *Ibid.*, 217.7. Read *yazjur* for *yuʾakhkhir*, *ṭāqatihi* for *ṭāʿatihi*, and *yuṭīq* for *yuṭbiq*, *ibid.*, 217.8; read *lā yuṭīq* for *yuṭīq*, *ibid.*, 217.9. For these readings, compare Bayhaqī, *Shuʿab*, 6:85.14, and Ṣāliḥī, *Kanz*, 190.27.
27 Ḥalīmī, *Minhāj*, 3:217.10.
28 *Ibid.*, 218.13. He claims the support of two traditions, *ibid.*, 218.23.
29 *Ibid.*, 218.13, 219.8. In indicating that such a man is not even permitted to undertake the duty (*ibid.*, 218.21), Ḥalīmī espouses a view which, though widely discussed, is almost always rejected.

that if such a man forbids an evil the status of which is apparent even to the unlearned (*al-ʿāmma*), then his standing in the matter is the same as that of the righteous scholar.[30]

It goes well with this that a vein of sensitivity to the social context of the duty runs through Ḥalīmī's account of it.[31] Thus he concerns himself with situations in which the duty is best deferred. On encountering a man in his cups, you might pour away what is left of his liquor, but it would be unwise to speak to him, and pointless, until he has sobered up.[32] Equally he emphasises that one who undertakes the duty must be discriminating.[33] He must know when to be kind and when to be harsh, how to talk to people of every class (*ṭabaqa*) in a manner appropriate to each, and how to ensure that his initiative is not counter-productive.[34] He is not bound to take action leading to the public disgrace of the offender;[35] he could speak in general terms about the evil in question in public, but without identifying the offender, or he could privately send him a message about it.

All in all, Ḥalīmī's approach – in contrast to that of his teacher – is marked by respect for constituted authority and social hierarchy, perhaps even by a certain urbanity. In effect, he expresses the accommodationist tendency we encountered in Ḥanafism better than the Ḥanafīs themselves.

We meet similarly antithetical styles among Shāfiʿites of the fifth/eleventh century. Views reminiscent of Ḥalīmī's are briefly expressed by Abū Isḥāq al-Shīrāzī (d. 476/1083) in an Ashʿarite creed.[36] There are those whose duty it is to punish wrongdoing; these are caliphs and their subordinates. There are those who are obligated to take verbal action (*an yughayyir bi'l-lisān*). And there are those who are not obligated at all.[37] But as we will see, most accounts dating from this period do not share this tendency.

[30] *Ibid.*, 222.12.

[31] Cf. his unusual view that tambourines may be permitted to women, but not to men (Subkī, *Ṭabaqāt*, 4:339.8).

[32] Ḥalīmī, *Minhāj*, 3:217.20, with what is obviously the continuation at line 22.

[33] *Ibid.*, 218.3.

[34] This does not apply in the case of a ruler, who does not need to be tactful – unless he is a powerless ruler, in which case he finds himself in the same boat as the righteous scholar (*ibid.*, 218.6).

[35] *Ibid.*, 219.9 (or so I understand the tenor of the passage).

[36] Abū Isḥāq al-Shīrāzī (d. 476/1083), *ʿAqīdat al-salaf*, *apud* his *al-Maʿūna fī 'l-jadal*, ed. ʿA. Turkī, Beirut 1988, 101f. no. 36, and M. Bernand, *La Profession de foi d'Abū Isḥāq al-Šīrāzī*, Cairo 1987, 71.17. For Abū Isḥāq, see *Encyclopaedia Iranica*, art. 'Abū Esḥāq al-Šīrāzī' (W. Madelung). There is, however, some doubt as to the attribution of this text to Abū Isḥāq (see W. Madelung's review of Bernand's edition, *Journal of the Royal Asiatic Society*, 1989, 135f., where two corrections are also given to the reading of our passage; in Turkī's edition, read *al-umma mujmiʿa* for *wa-li-ummat Muḥammad*). Abū Isḥāq's contemporary Abū 'l-Qāsim al-Qushayrī (d. 465/1072) also mentions the duty in a creed (quoted in Subkī, *al-Sayf al-mashhūr*, f. 42b.1), but he says nothing of interest, beyond declaring rebellion against unjust rule to be impermissible.

[37] Note that he does not say that they are obligated to perform the duty in the heart.

A case in point is a discussion of the duty by the celebrated Māwardī (d. 450/1058).[38] He organises his account around an unusual distinction: there are cases in which the offence is committed by isolated individuals, and there are those in which it is the work of a group. In cases of the first kind, it is universally agreed that it is the duty of anyone who witnesses the wrong to command and forbid the wrongdoers, provided he is able to do so;[39] the only disagreement concerns the question whether this obligation is grounded in reason or revelation.[40] This is, of course, a favourite Muʿtazilite issue, and what follows is in fact a Muʿtazilite analysis within which is included a typically Muʿtazilite account of the danger condition.[41] In cases of the second kind, which are likely to include what we would call political conflicts, opinions differ.[42] Some traditionists (*aṣḥāb al-ḥadīth*) deny the obligatoriness of taking action against such a wrong, and recommend that one should stay quietly at home; another school – clearly the Imāmīs – defers the obligation until the appearance of their expected (imam); yet others, including Aṣamm (d. 200/815f.), make it conditional on agreement on a just imam.[43] But the great majority of theologians (*jumhūr al-mutakallimīn*) hold it to be obligatory to proceed if the conditions are satisfied; here it is necessary that one have capable helpers, since without them one risks being killed without attaining the goal, a course which reason condemns. Presumably Māwardī shares this view. This account may not share Qaffāl's forcefulness, but it shows no accommodationist tendencies.

This is in some tension with what Māwardī says about the duty of the individual to forbid wrong in his well-known treatise on government. His primary concern there is with the role of the officially appointed censor (*muḥtasib*).[44] He deals with the duty of the individual only at the begin-

[38] Māwardī, *Adab*, 101–3. On Māwardī, see *EI*², *s.n.* (C. Brockelmann). It may be noted that he makes no mention of the doctrine of the three modes.

[39] Māwardī, *Adab*, 101.14. [40] *Ibid.*, 101.17.

[41] Cf. above, ch. 9, 206 and 209 no. (5). The account of the danger condition does not reflect the views of Abū ʾl-Ḥusayn, since a distinction is made between cases that do and do not involve the greater glory of the faith (*iʿzāz dīn Allāh*, *ibid.*, 102.10); but I see nothing to preclude its derivation from the school of ʿAbd al-Jabbār. Māwardī was later accused of Muʿtazilite tendencies on the basis of his Koran commentary (see Subkī, *Ṭabaqāt*, 5:270.1, cited in *EI*², art. 'Māwardī'); it is not clear to me whether he was in any sense an Ashʿarite.

[42] Māwardī, *Adab*, 102.18.

[43] For the traditionists, cf. above, ch. 12, 336f.; for the Imāmīs, cf. above, ch. 11, note 116, for Aṣamm, cf. above, ch. 9, note 15.

[44] Māwardī's account of the *muḥtasib* is read by Laoust as an attempt to cut back on the unofficial forbidding of wrong in favour of the power of the state, and not entirely without reason (H. Laoust, 'La pensée et l'action politiques d'al-Māwardī', *Revue des Etudes Islamiques*, 36 (1968), 36–8; cf. also Lambton, *State and government*, 311; Glassen, *Mittlere Weg*, 23).

ning of his chapter on the censor, setting out nine differences between the individual and official duties.[45] For the most part the distinctions he makes are straightforward, and need not detain us; for example, the duty is an individual one for the censor, but a collective one for others, and he alone may be paid a salary for it from the public treasury. Two of Māwardī's distinctions, however, are arresting. The second of the nine distinctions is that the official censor may not be distracted from his duties – by pressure of other business, so to speak – because these duties *are* his business; by contrast, such distraction is permissible for the individual, since his activity is supererogatory (*min nawāfil ʿamalihi*). This contrasts with Māwardī's statement in the same text that individuals are subject to a collective obligation. The sixth distinction is that the official censor has the right to engage helpers, whereas the individual does not. This seems to contradict the account Māwardī gives in his other work of cases in which the offence is committed by a group. In both instances, the effect is to lower the profile of the duty of the individual Muslim; it is hardly accidental that Māwardī expresses such views in a handbook written to instruct the political authorities.[46]

The next major figure of concern to us is the Ashʿarite Juwaynī (d. 478/1085). As usual, much of what he says is familiar and requires little attention. He discusses the grounding of the obligation in consensus, setting aside the alleged dissent of the Rāfiḍa.[47] He distinguishes matters in which laymen can tell right from wrong from those in which it takes scholarly judgement (*ijtihād*) to do so; in the former, in contrast to the latter, it is for laymen and scholars alike to command and forbid.[48] He takes the usual view of disagreements between law-schools,[49] and of the obligation of the wrongdoer to forbid wrong himself.[50] He states that the obligation is a collective one, going on to say that if in every district (*ṣuqʿ*)

[45] Māwardī, *al-Aḥkām al-sulṭāniyya*, 315.4. This became a favourite schema; it is reproduced by such authors as the Ḥanbalite Abū Yaʿlā (*al-Aḥkām al-sulṭāniyya*, 284.9), the Shāfiʿite Ibn al-Ukhuwwa (d. 729/1329) (*Maʿālim al-qurba fī aḥkām al-ḥisba*, ed. R. Levy, London 1938, 11.10, with omission of Māwardī's fifth difference), and the Mālikī ʿUqbānī (d. 871/1467) (*Tuḥfat al-nāẓir*, ed. A. Chenoufi, *Bulletin d'Etudes Orientales*, 19 (1965–6), 177.22; ʿUqbānī rewrites the first difference to remove Māwardī's categorisation of *al-amr bi'l-maʿrūf* as a collective duty where the ordinary believer is concerned). It is also taken up in Chalmeta, *El 'señor del zoco'*, 613f.

[46] Laoust, however, goes too far in this direction. He reads too much into the first, third and fourth differences; he also gives a misleading rendering of the ninth, inasmuch as he does not make it clear that the customary matters it relates to are those about which the law is silent ('La pensée', 36f.). [47] Juwaynī, *Irshād*, 368.4. [48] *Ibid.*, 368.15.

[49] *Ibid.*, 369.5. He states it as school doctrine that every *mujtahid* is right; but he adds that it comes to the same thing if one believes only one to be right, but does not know his identity. [50] *Ibid.*, 369.9.

someone appropriate undertakes it, others are relieved of it.[51] And he rules out any kind of spying.[52]

More interesting are the passages that make it clear that he is no accommodationist. He emphasises that the duty is not reserved to rulers (*wulāt*), but extends to individual Muslims (*āḥād al-Muslimīn*); the proof of this is again consensus, for in early Islamic times such individuals would command and forbid the rulers themselves, and did so with the approval of the Muslims at large.[53] Later he stresses that taking action (*fiʿl*) where words (*qawl*) do not suffice is permissible for subjects in the case of a grave sin, so long as it does not lead to armed conflict; this latter is for the ruler (*sulṭān*).[54] This sounds prudently non-Muʿtazilite. But he then goes on to say something which was on occasion to take away the breath of posterity.[55] If the ruler of the time (*wālī al-waqt*) acts in a manifestly unjust fashion, and does not respond to verbal admonition, then it is for 'the people of binding and loosing' (*ahl al-ḥall waʾl-ʿaqd*) to prevent him, even if this means doing battle with him.[56]

Rather like Māwardī, Juwaynī speaks about the duty in a different tone in a work concerned mainly with the imamate.[57] Here again he says that the duty extends to all Muslims (*kāffat al-Muslimīn*), provided they possess the requisite firmness and understanding.[58] He then limits subjects to restrained verbal initiatives, to the exclusion of armed conflict; in such cases they should turn the matter over to the rulers.[59] No mention is made here of the problem of the unjust ruler. Juwaynī does, however, go on to say that, subject to some restriction, individual Muslims are not excluded

[51] *Ibid.*, 369.11.

[52] *Ibid.*, 370.6. For *taqnīr* read *tanqīr*, as in the quotation in Nawawī, *Sharḥ Ṣaḥīḥ Muslim*, 1:385.25.

[53] Juwaynī, *Irshād*, 368.10.

[54] *Ibid.*, 369.14. Note that action and words are mentioned as modes, but not performance in the heart; by contrast, Abū Bakr ibn Maymūn in his commentary on the *Irshād* mentions performance in the heart among the three modes (*Sharḥ al-Irshād*, ed. A. Ḥ. A. al-Saqqā, Cairo 1987, 607.23; I do not know the date of this commentary, except that the manuscript used by the editor was copied in 782/1380 (*ibid.*, 7 of the editor's introduction)). Later Ashʿarite authors who mention performance in the heart include Fakhr al-Dīn al-Rāzī (*Tafsīr*, 8:177.17, 179.22 (to Q3:104)) and Ibn al-Ukhuwwa (*Maʿālim*, 22.8, in a scholastic passage on the duty quoted from an unnamed scholar; Ibn al-Ukhuwwa describes himself as an Ashʿarite, *ibid.*, 3.4). An earlier writer close to Ashʿarism who mentions performance in the heart is Rāghib al-Iṣbahānī (*fl.* later fourth/tenth century), stating the view of 'most *mutakallimūn*' (*Muḥāḍarāt al-udabāʾ*, Beirut 1961, 1:134.13; for his theological stance, see *EI*², art. 'Rāghib al-Iṣfahānī', 390b (E. K. Rowson)).

[55] Juwaynī, *Irshād*, 370.3; cf. the negative reaction of Nawawī (*Sharḥ Ṣaḥīḥ Muslim*, 1:385.23). On the other hand, Abū Bakr ibn Maymūn endorses Juwaynī's position (*Sharḥ al-Irshād*, 608.6).

[56] Should we see here Juwaynī's settled opinion, or an ill-tempered response to the Seljūq persecution of the Ashʿarites in 445/1053f. which drove him into exile (cf. Madelung, *Religious trends*, 33)?

[57] Juwaynī, *Ghiyāth al-umam*, 176f.

[58] *Ibid.*, 176.10.

[59] *Ibid.*, 176.11. In contrast to the doctrine of the *Irshād*, this would seem to exclude physical action short of armed conflict on the part of subjects.

from performing the duty in the market-place – acting for God's sake (*muḥtasibūn*), as he puts it.[60]

A contemporary of Juwaynī from whom we have a brief account of the duty is the little-known Ashʿarite Mutawallī (d. 478/1086).[61] He grounds the obligation in Koran, tradition and – so it seems from a damaged passage – the continuing practice of the Muslims; he implies that it is a collective obligation. He makes the same distinction as Juwaynī between matters that do and do not require scholarly judgement (*ijtihād*),[62] and in language very similar to Juwaynī's he states that performing the duty by word and action is not reserved to the rulers (*a'imma*), but extends to individual subjects (*āḥād al-raʿiyya*) as long as it does not lead to fighting.[63]

We may end this survey with an account of the duty by Kiyā al-Harrāsī (d. 504/1110), an Ashʿarite contemporary of Ghazzālī who, like him, was a pupil of Juwaynī.[64] Here, however, he is following in the footsteps of the Ḥanafī Muʿtazilite Jaṣṣāṣ (d. 370/981).[65] Thus he states that where words are not enough, one may if necessary proceed as far as killing the offender;[66] he goes on from this to a discussion of the view of the scholars on self-defence and rescue, in which he reports them as holding that one may kill collectors of illegal taxes without warning.[67] What is noteworthy is his willingness to adopt or quote these views without protest.

In sum, we find among early Shāfiʿite authorities no homogeneous doctrine of forbidding wrong. In particular, they differ with respect to the level of activity they allow to individuals. But the accommodationist tone of Ḥalīmī's account turns out on balance to be uncharacteristic. As to what might constitute a properly Ashʿarite doctrine of the duty, we are left pretty much in the dark.[68]

60 *Ibid.*, 177.4.

61 Mutawallī (d. 478/1086), *Mughnī*, ed. M. Bernand, Cairo 1986, 66.1. The text is problematic, the scribe having left several blanks in the manuscript. See also Madelung's review of Bernand's edition in *Journal of the Royal Asiatic Society*, 1988, 173.

62 Mutawallī, *Mughnī*, 66.8. He says that where *ijtihād* is needed, action is reserved to the rulers (*a'imma*).

63 *Ibid.*, 66.7; compare Juwaynī, *Irshād*, 370.1. Both use the phrase *naṣb qitāl.*

64 See Halm, *Ausbreitung*, 58f.

65 Kiyā al-Harrāsī (d. 504/1110), *Aḥkām al-Qur'ān*, ed. M. M. ʿAlī and ʿI. ʿA. ʿI. ʿAṭiyya, Cairo 1974–5, 2:62–7 (to Q3:104). The treatment follows that of Jaṣṣāṣ's work of the same title; thus Harrāsī begins with the point that the duty is a collective one, and ends with its application to heresy. His discussion, however, is much less full, and only at one point does he insert substantial material of his own (*ibid.*, 67.4–11). It may be noted that he quotes the 'three modes' tradition (*ibid.*, 63.5), but otherwise makes no reference to performance in the heart. For Jaṣṣāṣ's account, see above, ch. 12, 334–8.

66 *Ibid.*, 64.4; he bases this on Q49:9. Cf. Jaṣṣāṣ, *Aḥkām*, 2:31.17.

67 Harrāsī, *Aḥkām*, 2:65.7. Cf. Jaṣṣāṣ, *Aḥkām*, 2:32.3.

68 The silence of the known Ashʿarites discussed above (in contrast to Ḥalīmī) regarding performance in the heart is suggestive, but by no means conclusive.

The biographies of early Shāfiʿites make only occasional reference to the performance of the duty. The Naysābūrī Abū ʾl-ʿAbbās al-Sarrāj (d. 313/925) used to command right and forbid wrong riding on his donkey, telling his teaching assistant (*mustamlī*) ʿAbbās to do away with this and break that (*Yā ʿAbbās! ghayyir kadhā! iksir kadhā!*).[69] In another anecdote he is brought in to remonstrate with the ruler, but embarrasses everybody by bringing up a point about the ritual of prayer in the mosque, instead of furthering the material interests of the city.[70] Abū ʿAlī al-Manīʿī (d. 463/1071) was likewise a performer of the duty, and received the attention and respect of rulers in this connection; the Seljūq sultan Alp Arslan (r. 455–65/1063–73) was said to have remarked of him that 'there is in my kingdom someone who does not fear me but only God'.[71]

3. THE SHĀFIʿITES AFTER GHAZZĀLĪ

After Ghazzālī, the Shāfiʿite literary record is an anti-climax, though still richer than that of the Ḥanafīs. Accounts of forbidding wrong are found in a variety of literary contexts, of which the best represented are works of theology on the one hand and commentaries on the 'three modes' tradition on the other. (Creeds are disappointing.[72]) Neither stream is particularly impressive. The theological literature, to which for our purposes there is no Ḥanafī parallel, starts fairly strongly with Sayf al-Dīn al-Āmidī (d. 631/1233), but peters out over the following centuries.[73] The

69 Subkī, *Ṭabaqāt*, 3:108.15, 109.1; Dhahabī, *Siyar*, 14:394.13 (I owe this reference to Nurit Tsafrir); Ibn Kathīr (d. 774/1373), *Ṭabaqāt al-fuqahāʾ al-Shāfiʿiyyīn*, ed. A. ʿU. Hāshim and M. Z. M. ʿAzab, Cairo 1993, 1:218.19; and cf. Isnawī (d. 772/1370), *Ṭabaqāt al-Shāfiʿiyya*, ed. ʿA. al-Jubūrī, Baghdad 1970–1, 2:34.7.

70 Subkī, *Ṭabaqāt*, 3:109.3.

71 *Ibid.*, 4:301.8. I have noted a couple of further instances from this period. One is Abū ʾl-Naḍr al-Ṭūsī (d. 344/955) (Isnawī, *Ṭabaqāt*, 2:162.5; Ibn Kathīr, *Ṭabaqāt*, 1:269.15); the other is Abū ʿAbdallāh al-Khabbāzī (d. 497/1103f.), a pupil of Abū Isḥāq al-Shīrāzī (*ibid.*, 2:503.1, and cf. Subkī, *Ṭabaqāt*, 4:348 n. 3).

72 Madelung's observation that later Sunnī creeds rarely refer to *al-amr biʾl-maʿrūf* ('Amr be maʿrūf', 993b) holds good for the Shāfiʿites. A rare exception is the *ʿAqīda* of Ibn Daqīq al-ʿĪd (d. 702/1302), who was both a Mālikī and a Shāfiʿite, in the commentary of Ibrāhīm ibn Abī Sharīf al-Maqdisī (d. 923/1517), *al-ʿIqd al-naḍīd*, ms. Princeton, Yahuda 879, ff. 30a–31a (in red). For this manuscript, see Mach, *Catalogue*, 195 no. 2,285; but note that I hesitantly follow the title-page of the manuscript in ascribing the commentary to Burhān al-Dīn Ibrāhīm rather than to his brother Kamāl al-Dīn Muḥammad (d. 906/1500); cf. Sakhāwī, *Ḍawʾ*, 1:135.3. For two fifth/eleventh-century creeds that mention the duty, see above, note 36.

73 It is frustrating that we do not seem to possess a formal account of the duty by Fakhr al-Dīn al-Rāzī (d. 606/1210), the leading Ashʿarite authority of the whole period. He does, of course, discuss some issues in his Koran commentary (see, for example, *Tafsīr*, 3:47.5 (to Q2:44), 8:178.26 (to Q3:104), for the obligation of the sinner); but for the core topic

commentaries on the 'three modes' tradition, though more numerous than those of the Ḥanafīs, exhibit the same rather unstructured character. With the exception of one monographic treatment of forbidding wrong, such other accounts as I have found here and there are rather similar in style to these commentaries. In the Shāfiʿite case, moreover, the dust of the scholastic tradition was not disturbed by any equivalent of the Qāḍīzādelis and the lively reaction they provoked. I shall accordingly deal with the later Shāfiʿites rather summarily.

Āmidī treats the duty in his monumental theological treatise.[74] He devotes two sections to it. The first includes a discussion of the basis of forbidding wrong. He states that it is Ashʿarite and Sunnī doctrine that it is founded in revelation, not reason,[75] and gives a brief exposition which makes reference to consensus, Koran and tradition.[76] However, the dominant theme of this section is an argument against the view that the duty can only be performed on the authority of the imam. He ascribes this view to some of the Rāfiḍa; everyone else agrees that forbidding wrong is obligatory whether the imam enjoins it or not.[77] His main argument is that we know that individual Companions after the death of the Prophet commonly performed the duty without seeking any such authority, and later generations have followed suit.[78] Quite why he should invest such energy in refuting this alleged Rāfiḍite position is unclear to me. The second section is unusual in setting out no fewer than seven conditions for obligation, and in referring to them as 'restrictions' (*quyūd*).[79] The schema was ignored by Shāfiʿite posterity; Kātib Chelebi had a use for it because he wished to discourage Qāḍīzādeli activism by emphasising the sheer number of restrictions.[80] The individual items on the list contain no real surprises,

of the conditions of obligation, he refers us to the theological literature (*kutub al-kalām*, *ibid.*, 178.23). Much the same is true on a smaller scale for Bayḍāwī (thus for his treatment of the obligation of the sinner, see *Anwār*, 2:35.17 (to Q3:104)).

74 Āmidī, *Abkār al-afkār*, ff. 310a–311a. For this work, see Gimaret, *Théories*, 153f. The account of *al-amr bi'l-maʿrūf* shows no dependence on Ghazzālī.

75 Āmidī, *Abkār*, f. 310a.14, and cf. f. 310b.18. He mentions the views of the Jubbāʾīs in a passage echoed by the Shāfiʿite Maḥmūd ibn Abī 'l-Qāsim al-Iṣfahānī (d. 749/1349) in his commentary on the *Tajrīd* of Naṣīr al-Dīn al-Ṭūsī (*Tasdīd*, ms. Princeton, Yahuda 2,220, f. 223b.12; for this manuscript, see Mach, *Catalogue*, 261 no. 3,062).

76 Āmidī, *Abkār*, f. 310a.24, 310b.3.

77 *Ibid.*, f. 310a.13. The text is corrupt; a better text is found in the citation of the passage by Jurjānī (d. 816/1413) in his commentary to Ījī (*Mawāqif*, 331.7). Jurjānī gives a shortened and somewhat rearranged paraphrase of the whole section (*ibid.*, 331.7–22).

78 Āmidī, *Abkār*, f. 310a.18. Compare Juwaynī and Mutawallī (above, 347, and note 53); also Ghazzālī (below, ch. 16, note 29).

79 *Ibid.*, ff. 310b.19–311a.21. Here too Jurjānī draws on Āmidī, but not for the structure of the presentation.

80 Katīb Chelebi, *Mīzān al-ḥaqq*, 92–5 (= trans. Lewis, 106–8); cf. above, ch. 12, note 169.

all being already familiar in one way or another.[81] All in all, Āmidī's account is a substantial one, if only by Ash'arite standards. But it is too isolated to be representative of a continuing Ash'arite tradition.[82]

The treatment of the duty in two works of 'Aḍud al-Dīn al-Ījī (d. 756/1355) is altogether slighter.[83] In contrast to Āmidī, he confines himself to two conditions of obligation.[84] Of the commentators, the Ḥanafī Ash'arite Jurjānī (d. 816/1413) has nothing of significance to add in his own name.[85] Dawānī (d. 908/1502) is more forthcoming,[86] but the only

[81] In summary the restrictions are as follows. (1) The performer must be legally competent. (Katīb Chelebi extends this to include the offender; this aligns him with what Ghazzālī says in his *Kīmiyā-yi sa'ādat* as opposed to his *Iḥyā'* (see below, ch. 16, note 71), and also with the scholastic account quoted in Ibn al-Ukhuwwa, *Ma'ālim*, 22.11.) (2) The performer must know right from wrong in the case, which does not mean that he must be a scholar (and the sinner is obligated; Āmidī's treatment of this point is quoted in Ibrāhīm al-Laqānī (d. 1041/1631), *Hidāyat al-murīd*, ms. Princeton, Yahuda 504, f. 283a.16; for this manuscript, see Mach, *Catalogue*, 200 no. 2,337). (3) The alleged offence must actually be one. (The combination of these last two points is reminiscent of the school of Abū 'l-Ḥusayn, see above, ch. 9, note 151.) (4) It must not be a matter of dispute between law-schools. (5) It must be the case that no one else undertakes the duty, since it is not an individual but rather a collective obligation; it suffices if a single person undertakes it in each district (*nāḥiya*). (The idea of a single person in each district is an echo of Juwaynī, see above, note 51.) (6) There must be expectation of success (Katīb Chelebi elaborates that the chances must be against it resulting in harm; for *khalq iṣrār* read *khalqa iḍrār* at *Mīzān al-ḥaqq*, 94.1); but if there is no prospect of success, it is still commendable as a public affirmation of Islamic norms (*iẓhār sha'ā'ir al-Islām*). (Cf. the quotation ascribed to Āmidī in Laqānī, *Hidāya*, f. 282b.3, whence Bājūrī (d. 1276/1860), *Tuḥfat al-murīd*, *apud* Laqānī, *Jawharat al-tawḥīd*, Cairo n.d., 203.10.) (7) There must be no spying or prying. Outside this framework of restictions, Āmidī adds in the course of a final argument that the performer must have reason to believe that the offence in question will take place (*Abkār*, f. 311a.24; his use of the terms *amārāt* and *istimrār* in this connection is reminiscent of Imāmī usage (cf. above, ch. 11, 276 no. (2)). Note that Āmidī is silent on the danger condition, perhaps inadvertently; hence Katīb Chelebi's elaboration of the sixth restriction.

[82] It may be noted in passing that Āmidī makes no mention of performance in the heart (cf. above, notes 54, 68).

[83] Ījī (d. 756/1355), *al-'Aqīda al-'Aḍudiyya*, *apud* Dawānī (d. 908/1502), *Sharḥ 'alā 'l-'Aqā'id al-'Aḍudiyya*, printed in the margin of the *Ḥāshiya*s thereto of Siyālkūtī (d. 1067/1657) and Muḥammad 'Abduh (d. 1323/1905), Cairo 1322, 211.3; and his *Mawāqif*, 331f. All the points mentioned in the *'Aḍudiyya* are covered in the *Mawāqif*. In the latter he discusses familiar topics: obligatoriness and supererogation, the collective character of the duty, and the conditions of obligation. He also remarks, in a manner reminiscent of Juwaynī, that whereas 'we' regard the subject as belonging to positive law (*furū'*), the Mu'tazilites consider it under theology (*uṣūl*) (*Mawāqif*, 331.6; cf. above, note 2).

[84] One is that one must think it will not lead to disorder (*fitna*), or fail to achieve its purpose – though (in this latter case) it is still virtuous to proceed for the glory of Islam (*iẓhāran li-shi'ār al-Islām*) (*ibid.*, 331.24; cf. above, note 81, no. (6)). The other is that there must be no spying (backed by Koran, tradition and an appeal to the practice (*sīra*) of the Prophet) (*ibid.*, 332.3).

[85] Jurjānī, *Sharḥ*, *apud* Ījī, *Mawāqif*, 331f. Elsewhere this Ḥanafī Ash'arite provides revelationist definitions of *ma'rūf* and *munkar* (al-Sayyid al-Sharīf al-Jurjānī (d. 816/1413), *Ta'rīfāt*, ed. 'A. 'Umayra, Beirut 1987, 275.14, 290.5; cf. also Shayzarī (*fl.* later sixth/twelfth century), *Nihāyat al-rutba*, ed. S. B. al-'Arīnī, Cairo 1946, 6.4, whence Ibn Bassām (seventh or eighth/thirteenth or fourteenth century?), *Nihāyat al-rutba*, ed. Ḥ. al-Sāmarrā'ī, Baghdad 1968, 10.6, and Ibn al-Ukhuwwa, *Ma'ālim*, 8.15, and cf. 22.5).

[86] Dawānī, *Sharḥ*, 211.3. However, a good many of the points he supplies in this commen-

notable point is his formal division of the category of wrong (*munkar*) into the forbidden (*ḥarām*) and the disapproved (*makrūh*).[87]

The last free-standing theological account of forbidding wrong is by Saʿd al-Dīn al-Taftazānī (d. 793/1390), accompanied by his own commentary.[88] Taken together, the two works give a fairly substantial coverage of the duty. The backbone of the account is taken from Juwaynī, suitably paraphrased,[89] but there is a liberal admixture of other elements.[90] The string of topics is as usual a familiar one.[91] Taftazānī's doctrine of the conditions of obligation, unlike those of his predecessors, is a triad: (1) knowledge of the law (*al-ʿilm bi-wajh al-maʿrūf*); (2) the prospect of efficacy (*tajwīz al-taʾthīr*); and (3) the absence of undesirable consequences (*intifāʾ al-mafsada*).[92] This triad is reminiscent of that of the Mālikī Ibn Rushd (d. 520/1126);[93] but any hypothesis that the two triads might go back to a common Ashʿarite source is complicated by the fact that there are also occasional parallels in unusually stripped-down versions of the conditions given in Imāmī sources.[94]

The other main genre that concerns us, commentary on the 'three modes' tradition, goes back to Nawawī (d. 676/1277), the Damascene Shāfiʿite traditionist and jurist. Nawawī included the tradition in his selection of forty traditions,[95] and accordingly discussed it briefly in his own commentary on that collection.[96] At the same time he treated the tradition at much greater

tary to the *ʿAḍudiyya* are already present in, if not taken from, the *Mawāqif*. The glosses of Siyālkūtī to Dawānī are uninteresting.

87 *Ibid.*, 211.4. Ījī introduces the category of *makrūh*, but does not specify whether it is a species of *munkar* (*Mawāqif*, 331.4; cf. also Taftazānī, *Sharḥ al-Maqāṣid*, 5:171.21, and the scholastic account quoted in Ibn al-Ukhuwwa, *Maʿālim*, 22.6). Bayḍāwī (*Anwār*, 2:35.17 (to Q3:104)) follows Zamakhsharī (*Kashshāf*, 1:397.10) in explicitly denying the divisibility of wrong. For Imāmī parallels to Dawānī's view, see above, ch. 11, notes 142, 250; the same view appears in Bājūrī, *Tuḥfa*, 202.7.

88 Taftazānī, *Sharḥ al-Maqāṣid*, 5:171–5; cf. above, ch. 12, note 52.

89 This dependence is not acknowledged, but at one point Taftazānī expressly cites him (*ibid.*, 174.11); compare the echoes of Juwaynī noted for Āmidī and Ījī (see above, notes 78, 81, 83). Taftazānī too has the idea of one person performing the duty in each district (*buqʿa*, *ibid.*, 174.23).

90 Thus the idea of a duty to proceed *iʿzāzan lil-dīn* is considered and dismissed with a reference to *idhlāl* (*ibid.*, 173.21). This is a clear echo of Muʿtazilite doctrine, though hardly an accurate representation of it (see above, ch. 9, 209 no. (5), and cf. also ch. 6, note 142); but for the use of the term *idhlāl* in a Ḥanbalite source, cf. above, ch. 6, note 150. For his citation of a Ḥanafī source, see above, ch. 12, note 54.

91 Thus he deals with the grounds of obligation, obligation and supererogation, the correct understanding of Q5:105, the conditions of obligation, the role of individual subjects and laymen, matters in dispute between the law-schools, the obligation of the sinner, the collective character of the obligation and, somewhat unsually, the duties of the official *muḥtasib*.

92 *Ibid.*, 172.4 (in the *Maqāṣid*); similarly 173.15 (in the commentary).

93 See below, ch. 14, 363f.

94 See above, ch. 11, notes 183–5. The wording of the *Maqāṣid*, such as it is, is surprisingly close to that found in Naṣīr al-Dīn al-Ṭūsī's *Tajrīd*; a possible link between the two might be Iṣfahānī's commentary on the *Tajrīd* (*Tasdīd*, f. 224a.10).

95 See above, ch. 3, note 7.

96 Nawawī, *Sharḥ matn al-Arbaʿīn*, 91f.

length in his commentary on Muslim,[97] a genre he inherited from his Mālikī predecessors.[98]

Whatever one might have expected, Nawawī's approach is not very different in style or content from the theological presentations we have already considered.[99] The range of topics covered is much the same – the grounds of obligation (with the familiar references to the views of Shīʿites and Muʿtazilites),[100] the collective character of the duty, and so forth; however, no formal schema of conditions is in evidence. There is no indication of allergy to Ashʿarism: Juwaynī is quoted several times, and with respect.[101] The main difference is the presence in Nawawī's account of a note of moral urgency missing in the theological literature: he lays great stress on the importance of the duty and its present sorry state.[102]

There is, however, one curious doctrinal deviation. The usual view, expressed also in the theological literature considered above, is that there is no duty where the initiative will not be successful.[103] ʿIzz al-Dīn ibn ʿAbd al-Salām (d. 660/1262) explains this straightforwardly enough: forbidding wrong is a means to an end, and if the end does not stand, neither does the means.[104] Nawawī, by contrast, states it as the view of the scholars that the duty is not voided because one thinks it will not work (*li-kawnihi lā yufīd fī ẓannihi*).[105] One's duty is to command and forbid, not that the offender should comply (*innamā ʿalayhi ʾl-amr waʾl-nahy lā ʾl-qabūl*).[106] Likewise in his commentary to his forty traditions, Nawawī

[97] Nawawī, *Sharḥ Ṣaḥīḥ Muslim*, 1:380–6.

[98] He quotes the commentary of Qāḍī ʿIyāḍ (d. 544/1149) at two points (*ibid.*, 380.20, 385.6). The first passage corresponds to ʿIyāḍ, *Ikmāl al-Muʿlim*, ms. Dublin, Chester Beatty, no. 3,836, f. 44b.21, the second to f. 45a.18. For this manuscript, see Arberry, *Handlist*, 4:25.

[99] A real traditionalist commentary on the tradition is that of the Ḥanbalite Ibn Rajab (d. 795/1393) (*Jāmiʿ*, 346–52).

[100] Nawawī, *Sharḥ Ṣaḥīḥ Muslim*, 1:382.6. Both references are taken (without acknowledgement) from ʿIyāḍ (*Ikmāl*, f. 45a.16).

[101] Nawawī, *Sharḥ Ṣaḥīḥ Muslim*, 1:382.7, 383.3, 385.19, 385.23 (all are passages from the *Irshād*). In the first passage Juwaynī is referred to as *al-imām Abū ʾl-Maʿālī Imām al-Ḥaramayn*. Subkī describes Nawawī as an Ashʿarite (*Ṭabaqāt*, 1:132.3, and his *Qāʿida fī ʾl-jarḥ waʾl-taʿdīl*, ed. A. Abū Ghudda, Aleppo 1968, 25.7).

[102] Nawawī, *Sharḥ Ṣaḥīḥ Muslim*, 1:383.21, 386.14. Nawawī practised what he preached (see below, note 135).

[103] For an isolated Sunnī exception not dependent on Nawawī, see below, ch. 16, note 41. For similar Ibāḍī views, see below, ch. 15, notes 48, 180f.

[104] ʿIzz al-Dīn ibn ʿAbd al-Salām (d. 660/1262), *Qawāʿid al-aḥkām*, Cairo n.d., 1:109.5 (*al-wasāʾil tasquṭ bi-suqūṭ al-maqāṣid*). It does, however, remain commendable (*wa-yabqā ʾl-istiḥbāb*). Elsewhere he remarks with reference to *al-amr biʾl-maʿrūf* that risking life is lawful for the greater glory of the faith (*iʿzāz al-dīn*) (see the quotations in Subkī, *Ṭabaqāt*, 8:228.8, and cf. Ṣāliḥī, *Kanz*, 130.10). (For his use of the phrase *iʿzāz al-dīn* in another context, see his *Qawāʿid*, 1:106.1; for the phrase, cf. above, note 90.)

[105] Nawawī, *Sharḥ Ṣaḥīḥ Muslim*, 1:382.17. He does not owe this view to ʿIyāḍ.

[106] *Ibid.*, 382.12, 382.19. He quotes Q51:55 and Q5:99. The first verse states that 'the reminder profits (*tanfaʿu*) the believers'; thus Nawawī could have made his point in a less

affirms – here in his own voice – that someone who is able to perform the duty verbally must do so even if he will not be listened to, just as one must greet a person even if one knows that he will not return the greeting.[107]

The subsequent Shāfiʿite commentaries base themselves on Nawawī's to a greater or lesser extent.[108] No two are the same, but they are not sufficiently different to merit separate treatment. A good indication of the way in which they belong to a common tradition is their marked tendency to repeat or otherwise take note of Nawawī's rejection of the view that obligation turns on the prospect of success;[109] this rejection is much less in evidence among non-Shāfiʿite commentators.[110] (As might be expected, Nawawī's view also crops up in other Shāfiʿite works.)[111] The latest of these

drastic fashion by arguing that the performance of the duty achieves something even when the offender is obdurate. [107] Nawawī, *Sharḥ matn al-Arbaʿīn*, 92.1.

[108] That of Ibn Daqīq al-ʿĪd (*Sharḥ al-Arbaʿīn*, 55–7) is so dependent on Nawawī as to need no further discussion. The others I have consulted are those of Ibn Faraḥ al-Ishbīlī (d. 699/1300) (*Sharḥ al-Arbaʿīn*, ms. Princeton, Yahuda 4,161, ff. 61b–65a; for this manuscript, see Mach, *Catalogue*, 64 no. 711; the author, despite his provenance, was a Shāfiʿite); Taftazānī (*Sharḥ ḥadīth al-Arbaʿīn*, 105); Ibn Ḥajar al-Haytamī (*Fatḥ*, 244–8); Fashnī (writing 978/1570) (*al-Majālis al-saniyya*, Cairo 1278, 133–6); Shabshīrī (d. *c.* 990/1582) (*al-Jawāhir al-bahiyya*, ms. Princeton, Garrett 753H, ff. 101b–102b; for this manuscript, see Hitti, *Catalog*, 435 no. 1436); Munāwī (d. 1031/1622) (*Taʿlīq*, ms. Princeton, Garrett 752H, ff. 126a–128a; for this manuscript, see Hitti, *Catalog*, 435 no. 1435); and Nabarāwī (writing 1243/1828) (*Sharḥ ʿalā ʾl-Arbaʿīn*, Cairo 1960, 171–4). An oddity in this company is the commentary of ʿIzz al-Dīn Muḥammad ibn Jamāʿa (d. 819/1416) (*al-Tabyīn fī sharḥ al-Arbaʿīn*, ms. Princeton, Yahuda 4,010, ff. 75b–76b; for this manuscript, see Mach, *Catalogue*, 64f. no. 714); this discussion draws heavily on the commentary of the Ḥanbalite Ṭūfī (note particularly the utilitarian formulations, *ibid.*, 76a.3, 76a.7; cf. above, ch. 7, note 75). It is worth noting that Taftazānī explicitly extends the obligation to women and slaves (*Sharḥ ḥadīth al-Arbaʿīn*, 105.16).

[109] Ibn Faraḥ, *Sharḥ*, f. 62b.7; Ibn Ḥajar al-Haytamī, *Fatḥ*, 245.11 (stating Nawawī's position, but noting widespread adherence to the contrary view); Fashnī, *Majālis*, 134.30; Shabshīrī, *Jawāhir*, f. 102a.14; Munāwī, *Taʿlīq*, f. 128a.3; Nabarāwī, *Sharḥ*, 172.20; also Muʿīn al-Dīn ibn Ṣafī al-Dīn al-Ījī (alive in 911/1506), *Sharḥ al-Arbaʿīn*, ms. Princeton, Garrett 117W, f. 141b.5; for this manuscript, see Hitti, *Catalog*, 435f. no. 1437, and for the author, Najm al-Dīn al-Ghazzī (d. 1061/1651), *al-Kawākib al-sāʾira*, ed. J. S. Jabbūr, Beirut 1945–58, 1:307f.); Muṣliḥ al-Dīn al-Lārī (d. 979/1572), *Sharḥ al-Arbaʿīn*, ms. Princeton, Yahuda 5,067, f. 142a.5 (for this manuscript, see Mach, *Catalogue*, 65 no. 715; for the author, a Shāfiʿite who later became a Ḥanafī, see *EI*², art 'Lārī' (H. Sohrweide)). The exceptions are Taftazānī, who instead gives a statement of the usual view, adding that it is nevertheless commendable to proceed *iẓhāran li-shiʿār al-Islām* (*Sharḥ ḥadīth al-Arbaʿīn*, 105.15 – for his view in his *Sharḥ al-Maqāṣid*, cf. above, notes 90, 92), and Ibn Jamāʿa (cf. the previous note).

[110] Most of the non-Shāfiʿite commentaries I have seen do not mention Nawawī's deviant view (see, for example, Ibn Rajab, *Jāmiʿ*, 350.12, 351.3; ʿAlī al-Qārī, *Mubīn*, 189.27; Ismāʿīl Ḥaqqī, *Sharḥ*, 340.3). But for the adoption of Nawawī's view in a Ḥanbalite source, see Ṣāliḥī, *Kanz*, 128.2.

[111] Ibn Abī Sharīf al-Maqdisī follows it in his commentary to the *ʿAqīda* of Ibn Daqīq al-ʿĪd (*ʿIqd*, f. 30a.16), as does the jurist Shirbīnī (d. 977/1570) (*Mughnī ʾl-muḥtāj*, Cairo 1933, 4:211.16). Bājūrī remarks that 'most of the scholars, like the Shāfiʿites' deny that efficacy is a condition (*Tuḥfa*, 203.11); this observation, unlike most of Bājūrī's discussion of this condition, is not found in his Vorlage (Laqānī, *Hidāya*, f. 282a.19).

commentaries I have consulted, that of Nabarāwī (active in 1257/1842), ends on an appropriate note. After quoting Nawawī's lament about the sad state of forbidding wrong in his day,[112] Nabarāwī remarks that if that is how matters stood in the sixth/twelfth century (*sic*), what can we say of our own time?[113]

What this leaves is a monograph on the duty by Ibn al-Naḥḥās (d. 814/1411),[114] a Damascene who settled in Damietta.[115] The work, which he wrote in less than two months in 810–11/1408,[116] is rather similar in character to that written a few decades later by Zayn al-Dīn al-Ṣāliḥī (d. 856/1452),[117] though considerably less substantial.[118] Like Ṣāliḥī, he relies primarily on Ghazzālī for the doctrinal bedrock of his account, adopting his structures, echoing his formulations, and including a score of attributed quotations from him;[119] but he includes material from many other sources, mainly though by no means exclusively Shāfiʿite.[120] He occasionally claims ideas as his own, but they are not in themselves particularly noteworthy ones.[121] He pronounces clearly in favour of the performance of the duty by women in so far as they are able,[122] but he expresses no view of his own on Ghazzālī's most violent level of performance of the duty,[123] and he does not take sides over Nawawī's rejection of the efficacy condition.[124] He includes much tradition (*ḥadīth*) and much exhortation; his intended audience seems not to be restricted to the learned.[125]

For the period after Ghazzālī, the biographical literature offers numerous examples of Shāfiʿites known for their performance of the duty.

[112] Nabarāwī, *Sharḥ*, 173.21. [113] *Ibid.*, 174.3.

[114] Ibn al-Naḥḥās (d. 814/1411), *Tanbīh al-ghāfilīn*, ed. ʿI. ʿA. Saʿīd, Beirut 1987. This work was brought to my attention by Larry Conrad and Maribel Fierro, and a copy was kindly obtained for me by Margaret Larkin. [115] Sakhāwī, *Ḍawʾ*, 1:203.14.

[116] Ibn al-Naḥḥās, *Tanbīh*, 536.18.

[117] See above, ch. 7, 161–3. It is quite possible that Ṣāliḥī knew his predecessor's work and was influenced by it, but I have noticed no specific evidence of this.

[118] It is in fact only the first quarter of the book (15–130) that really concerns us. The rest consists in large part of a massive catalogue of sins (major and minor) and of things the Prophet forbade (*ibid.*, 131–426), and this is followed by a lengthy survey of wrongs and innovations (*ibid.*, 427–531). The survey owes its general conception to Ghazzālī (cf. below, ch. 16, 442–5), and quotes him from time to time (*ibid.*, 435.1, 460.12, etc.); but most of the material in it derives from other sources, or is the work of Ibn al-Naḥḥās himself. After the first quarter of the book, direct references to *al-amr biʾl-maʿrūf* occur only sporadically (as *ibid.*, 167.1, 316.4).

[119] He does not, however, adopt Ghazzālī's *ḥisba* terminology (cf. below, ch. 16, 428f.).

[120] The author most frequently cited is Nawawī. [121] See *ibid.*, 30.22, 112.17.

[122] *Ibid.*, 20.12 (with reference to Q9:71), 33.8 (also including slaves).

[123] *Ibid.*, 59.2; cf. below, ch. 16, 441. [124] *Ibid.*, 118.4.

[125] He glosses the terms *shuraṭ* (explaining that the singular is *shurṭī*) and *mawʾūda* (*ibid.*, 38.10).

Instances from the sixth/twelfth century are Abū Ḥafṣ al-Hamadhānī (d. 554/1159),[126] Ibn ʿAsākir (d. 571/1176),[127] Silafī (d. 576/1180),[128] Muḥammad ibn ʿAbd al-Karīm al-Rāfiʿī (d. 580/1184),[129] Bawāzījī (d. 582/1186f.),[130] Khubūshānī (d. 587/1191)[131] and Shihāb al-Dīn al-Ṭūsī (d. 596/1200).[132] By far the most colourful of these figures is Khubūshānī. A series of anecdotes stresses his fearlessness in confrontation with political power, whether Fāṭimid or Ayyūbid; once when Saladin (r. 564–89/1169–93) refused to comply with a petition of his regarding illegal taxes, Khubūshānī went so far as to poke at the ruler with a stick, knocking off his headgear.[133] Such examples occur sporadically thereafter. They include authorities as well known as ʿIzz al-Dīn ibn ʿAbd al-Salām,[134] Nawawī[135] and Ibn Ḥajar al-Haytamī (d. 974/1567),[136] and also lesser figures such as ʿAbd al-Fattāḥ ibn Nūḥ of Qūṣ (d. 708/1309),[137] the Damascene Aḥmad ibn ʿAbd al-Wahhāb (d. 800/1398)[138] and Jaʿfar ibn

[126] Subkī, *Ṭabaqāt*, 7:248.12; Isnawī, *Ṭabaqāt*, 2:7.14; Ibn Kathīr, *Ṭabaqāt*, 2:647.17.

[127] Isnawī, *Ṭabaqāt*, 2:217.5; Ibn Kathīr, *Ṭabaqāt*, 2:695.10. Both note his scant deference (*iltifāt*) to rulers.

[128] Subkī, *Ṭabaqāt*, 6:38.8; Ibn Kathīr, *Ṭabaqāt*, 2:686.16. He dealt with many offences in his neighbourhood, and once prevented a group who sang the Koran (*yaqraʾūn biʾl-alḥān*) from doing so.

[129] Rāfiʿī (d. 623/1226), ***al-Tadwīn fī akhbār Qazwīn***, ed. ʿA. al-ʿUṭāridī, Beirut 1987, 1:382.4. Rāfiʿī here devotes a short section to his father's zeal in *al-amr biʾl-maʿrūf*, and describes the psychosomatic symptoms he was sometimes subject to when unable to right a wrong. Cf. also *ibid.*, 2:2.3, 3:214.6. I owe these references to Nurit Tsafrir.

[130] Subkī, *Ṭabaqāt*, 7:89.6; Isnawī, *Ṭabaqāt*, 1:269.1.

[131] Subkī, *Ṭabaqāt*, 7:14.16; Ibn Kathīr, *Ṭabaqāt*, 2:730.1.

[132] Subkī, *Ṭabaqāt*, 6:397.8. Subkī also tells us that Ibn al-Bazrī (d. 560/1165) was of the opinion that a man has a duty to order his wife to pray, and to beat her if she does not (*ibid.*, 7:253.19).

[133] *Ibid.*, 16.10; and cf. Ibn Kathīr, *Ṭabaqāt*, 2:730.20.

[134] Subkī, *Ṭabaqāt*, 8:209.5; Isnawī, *Ṭabaqāt*, 2:198.4 (noting his contempt for kings); and cf. Ibn Kathīr, *Ṭabaqāt*, 2:874.13. His zeal for the duty seems to have been directed primarily against heresy and innovation, specifically Ḥanbalism (Subkī, *Ṭabaqāt*, 8:223.4, 228.8, 253.2, and cf. 218.7, 238.11).

[135] *Ibid.*, 397 n. 1, mentioning his enounters with Baybars (r. 658–76/1260–77); also Isnawī, *Ṭabaqāt*, 2:477.15 (speaking of confrontations with kings and lesser figures); Ibn Kathīr, *Ṭabaqāt*, 2:912.12 (with a similar comment); Sakhāwī (d. 902/1497), *Tarjamat Shaykh al-Islām . . . Abī Zakariyyāʾ Muḥyī ʾl-Dīn al-Nawawī*, ed. M. Ḥ. Rabīʿ, Cairo 1935, 3.1, 34.13, 47.5, 56.11, 56.25, 57.18, 57.23, 63.16.

[136] Shawkānī, *Badr*, 1:109.16.

[137] Subkī, *Ṭabaqāt*, 10:87.10.

[138] Ibn Qāḍī Shuhba (d. 851/1448), *Ṭabaqāt al-Shāfiʿiyya*, ed. ʿA. Khān, Hyderabad 1978–9, 3:198.9 (in the context of religious instruction during the pilgrimage). Other such figures are: ʿAbdallāh ibn Marwān al-Fāriqī (d. 703/1303) (ʿAfīf al-Dīn al-Maṭarī al-ʿUbādī (d. 765/1363f.), *Dhayl Ṭabaqāt al-fuqahāʾ al-Shāfiʿiyyīn*, *apud* Ibn Kathīr, *Ṭabaqāt*, 3:185.9; for the author, see C. Gilliot, 'Textes arabes anciens édités en Egypte au cours des années 1994 à 1996', *MIDEO*, 23 (1997), 287f.); Ibn Shihāb al-Isnāʾī (d. 707/1307f.) (Isnawī, *Ṭabaqāt*, 1:159.6); Ṣadr al-Dīn al-Yāsūfī (d. 789/1387) (Ibn Qāḍī Shuhba, *Ṭabaqāt*, 3:208.2); Burhān al-Dīn ibn Abī Sharīf al-Maqdisī (d. 923/1517) (Ghazzī, *Kawākib*, 1:104.5, and cf. above, note 72). The latter was a Damascene of Ẓāhirite tendencies who apparently practised *al-amr biʾl-maʿrūf* in a phase of his life when he had dropped out of academia and taken up asceticism.

Ḥasan al-Barzanjī (d. 1177/1764).[139] A dramatic incident involved the Cairene Nūr al-Dīn al-Bakrī (d. 724/1324), who with much popular support confronted Muḥammad ibn Qalāwūn (r. 693–741/1293–1341 with intermissions) over the Coptic question in 714/1314. He quoted the tradition on standing up to an unjust ruler, and when the infuriated sultan asked if the reference was to himself, Bakrī accused him of giving the Copts power over the Muslims.[140]

All in all, three features of the Shāfiʿite record after Ghazzālī stand out. One is the continuing dependence on Juwaynī, which is the more striking in that Juwaynī's account, though forceful, was neither extended nor comprehensive. The second feature, which goes well with this, is the relative immunity of the Shāfiʿites to the accommodationist tendences of the mainstream of the Ḥanafīs. The accounts of Ḥalīmī and Abū Isḥāq al-Shīrāzī do not reappear in the later tradition. The only Shāfiʿite author to quote the saying about the tripartite division of labour is Munāwī (d. 1031/1622);[141] the only jurist with views reminiscent of Ḥalīmī's is ʿAbd al-Barr al-Ujhūrī (later eleventh/seventeenth century), who apparently held that the common people had no business commanding or forbidding, and considered it inappropriate for a scholar to perform the duty unless he was dressed like one.[142] The final feature of the Shāfiʿite record is the lack of any firm structure of school doctrine comparable to that of the Muʿtazilites. A telling example of this is the fact that no two of the major Shāfiʿite authorities have the same number of conditions of obligation.

139 For this Shāfiʿite *muftī* of Medina, see Jabartī (d. 1240/1824f.), *ʿAjāʾib al-āthār*, Beirut n.d., 1:403.16; for the date of his death, I follow Murādī, *Silk al-durar*, 2:9.26.

140 See Subkī, *Ṭabaqāt*, 10:370.10; Ibn Qāḍī Shuhba, *Ṭabaqāt*, 2:361.7, and 362 nn. 15, 21; D. Richards, 'The Coptic bureaucracy under the Mamlūks', in *Colloque international sur l'histoire du Caire*, Cairo n.d., 378. Nuwayrī (d. 733/1333), in a passage quoted by Richards from manuscript, remarks with apparent disapproval that Bakrī had no official mandate or permission to engage in *al-amr bi'l-maʿrūf*.

141 Munāwī, *Taʿlīq*, f. 127b.14; for *lil-ʿamal* read *lil-ʿulamāʾ*.

142 See ʿAbd al-Barr al-Ujhūrī (later eleventh/seventeenth century), *Fatḥ al-qarīb*, ms. Princeton, Yahuda 5,504, f. 95a.18, 95b.5 (where *laysa* has dropped out before *lābisan*; for this manuscript, see Mach, *Catalogue*, 200 no. 2,339). The work is a commentary on the *Jawharat al-tawḥīd* of the Mālikī Ibrāhīm al-Laqānī, from whose own commentary (*Hidāya*, f. 283b.11) Ujhūrī has doubtless taken the stipulation about dress; Laqānī himself, however, gives it only as the view of a certain authority (*baʿḍ al-aʾimma*).

CHAPTER 14

THE MĀLIKĪS

1. INTRODUCTION

In contrast to the Shāfiʿites, the Mālikīs preserved a considerable amount of material regarding the views of their Medinese founder, Mālik ibn Anas (d. 179/795), on non-legal matters. They did not, however, adhere strongly to this heritage in the manner of the Ḥanbalites, nor did they elaborate it into a specifically Mālikī theology comparable to Māturīdism. Instead they adopted Ashʿarism. In this they resembled the Shāfiʿites; but for whatever reasons, the Mālikī reception of Ashʿarism does not seem to have provoked the sustained opposition within the school that characterises the Shāfiʿite case.[1] Indeed the Shāfiʿite Subkī (d. 771/1370) describes the Mālikīs as the Ashʿarites *par excellence* (*akhaṣṣ al-nās biʾl-Ashʿarī*), explaining that he had never heard of a non-Ashʿarite Mālikī;[2] and in

[1] This reception has been studied with particular reference to Ifrīqiya and Spain. For Ifrīqiya, see H. R. Idris, 'Essai sur la diffusion de l'aš'arisme en Ifrîqiya', *Les Cahiers de Tunisie*, 1 (1953); H. R. Idris, *La Berbérie orientale sous les Zīrīdes*, Paris 1962, 700–5. For Spain, see M. Fierro, 'La religión', in M. J. Viguera Molíns (ed.), *Los reinos de taifas: al-Andalus en el siglo XI* (= *Historia de España Menéndez Pidal*, tomo VIII–I), Madrid 1994, 414f., and the bibliography there cited; Fierro stresses the central role of Bājī (d. 474/1081). Clear evidence that there was at one time strong opposition to Ashʿarism in the west is to be found in some responsa of Ibn Rushd discussed in V. Lagardère, 'Une théologie dogmatique de la frontière en al-Andalus aux XIe et XIIe siècles: l'aš'arisme', in *Anaquel de Estudios Árabes*, 5 (1994), 93–7; see particularly Ibn Rushd (d. 520/1126), *Fatāwā*, ed. M. Ṭ. al-Talīlī, Beirut 1987, 804.2, 943.9. Ibn Ṭumlūs (d. 620/1223f.) speaks of a lingering but no longer virulent hostility (*al-Madkhal li-ṣināʿat al-manṭiq*, ed. M. Asín, Madrid 1916, 11.13). Ibn Khuwāzmindād, an eastern Mālikī of the fourth/tenth century, regarded every *mutakallim*, Ashʿarite or other, as a heretic (Ibn ʿAbd al-Barr, *Jāmiʿ*, 943.6, and cf. ʿIyāḍ (d. 544/1149), *Tartīb al-madārik*, ed. A. B. Maḥmūd, Beirut n.d., 4:606.14; for *al-Miṣrī* at Ibn ʿAbd al-Barr, *Jāmiʿ*, 942.19, read *al-Baṣrī* with Ibn Ḥajar, *Lisān al-Mīzān*, 5:291.12 (I owe this reference to Joseph Braude)). Ibn ʿAbd al-Barr (d. 463/1071) himself takes a strong line against *ahl al-kalām* of all kinds, but without making specific mention of Ashʿarites (*Jāmiʿ*, 944.8, and cf. *ibid.*, 938.7 (invoking the view of Mālik), 942.15).

[2] Subkī, *Ṭabaqāt*, 3:367.14; he notes that other schools are known to have had Muʿtazilite or anthropomorphist wings. He later says that all Mālikīs are Ashʿarites (*al-Mālikiyya kulluhum Ashāʿira*, *ibid.*, 377.18); but he follows this with statements about the prominence

another context he refers to the western Ashʿarites as particularly rigid in their adherence to the exact doctrines of Ashʿarī himself.[3] An incidental but significant effect of this shared Ashʿarism was to make the membrane between Mālikism and Shāfiʿism particularly permeable.

The history of Mālikī doctrines of forbidding wrong has to be seen against this background. I shall first consider the opinions transmitted from Mālik himself. These do not add up to a comprehensive doctrine, but they deal with several significant issues. I shall then turn to views contemporary with the Ashʿarite phase of Mālikī thought. I have, however, already noted the absence of any specifically Ashʿarite doctrine of forbidding wrong.[4] As we shall see, the later Mālikī doctrine of the duty possesses little coherence as a tradition, and the continuing influx of Shāfiʿite ideas only tends to accentuate this instability. At the same time, and in marked contrast to the Shāfiʿite case, there is no equivalent within the school to the dominating figure of Ghazzālī (d. 505/1111).

After discussing Mālikī doctrine, I shall give separate treatment to Mālikī practice. Far more than the Shāfiʿite sources, Mālikī works contain significant amounts of material bearing directly on the practice of the duty. Broadly speaking, this material falls into two categories. The first reflects the characteristic milieu of the early centuries of Mālikī history: urban populations under relatively strong state authority in such cities as Medina, Fusṭāṭ, Qayrawān and Cordoba. Here we find a practice of forbidding wrong comparable to that of the early Ḥanbalites, though not so emphatically quietist. The second category of material arises from the subsequent spread of Mālikism among North African tribal populations with political proclivities of a kind that had previously been articulated in Khārijite or Shīʿite idioms. Here, in contrast to the earlier – and continuing – urban environment, forbidding wrong can take on politically activist overtones more characteristic of sectarian Islam.

2. EARLY MĀLIKĪ DOCTRINE

We are told that the Egyptian Ibn Wahb (d. 197/813) heard Mālik state, regarding the question of someone who sees something that invites commanding or forbidding, that worthy scholars (*ahl al-khayr wa'l-fiqh*) hold

Footnote 2 (*cont.*)
of Ashʿarism among the Ḥanafīs and Ḥanbalites which shed some doubt on his credibility (for the strength of Subkī's Ashʿarite bias, cf. G. Makdisi, 'Ashʿarī and the Ashʿarites in Islamic religious history', *Studia Islamica*, 17 (1962), 57–60).

[3] Subkī, *Ṭabaqāt*, 6:244.7. He makes special reference to Māzarī (d. 536/1141) as an Ashʿarite fundamentalist (*ibid.*, 244.1, 245.2).

[4] See above, ch. 13, 340.

differing opinions;[5] what these opinions might be we are not told. When he speaks in his own voice, however, Mālik is clearly of the view that forbidding wrong is a good thing.[6] Thus he is asked about offences committed 'among us' against public morality: a Muslim openly carries wine around, or he walks in the street with a young woman to whom he chats, and when challenged claims that she is his freedwoman (*hiya mawlātī*). Should one not step out and do something to stop this kind of thing? Mālik replies that he thoroughly approves of such action, and would like to see it happen.[7] We could hardly expect him to say less.

More interestingly, the views attributed to Mālik offer a fragmentary account of the conditions for the duty which is to some extent reminiscent of the efficacy–harm matrix later propounded by the Ḥanafī Abū 'l-Layth al-Samarqandī (d. 373/983).[8] In one passage, Mālik is asked about a man who commands another to act rightly, when he knows that the offender will not obey him, and at the same time the offender is someone like a neighbour or brother of whom he is not in fear. He replies that he sees no harm in it,[9] if he treats him nicely, since God may bestow success on his effort (despite his negative expectation). In support, Mālik quotes a Koranic passage in which God tells Moses and Aaron to speak gently to Pharaoh 'that haply he may be mindful, or perchance fear' (Q20:44), and goes on to relate an anecdote about how 'Umar ibn al-Khaṭṭāb (r. 13–23/634–44)

[5] Ibn Abī Zayd, *Jāmi'*, 158.1. This and other opinions quoted below are found in a chapter on *fitan*, *fasād al-zamān*, *al-amr bi'l-ma'rūf*, and other topics (*ibid.*, 153–9; for this association of topics, cf. above, ch. 3, note 37). Ibn Abī Zayd states that most of what is in the book is taken *min majālis Mālik wa-min Muwaṭṭa'ihi* (*Jāmi'*, 301.8). The phrase *majālis Mālik* doubtless refers to such works as the *Majālis* of Ibn al-Qāsim (d. 191/806) or the *Majālis* of Aṣbagh ibn al-Faraj (d. 225/840) (see Abū Bakr ibn Khayr (d. 575/1179), *Fahrasa*, ed. F. Codera and J. Ribera Tarrago, Beirut n.d., 254.1, 254.16). The *Muwaṭṭa'* is not in question where materials on *al-amr bi'l-ma'rūf* are concerned. It does contain a saying related by 'Umar ibn 'Abd al-'Azīz (d. 101/720) to the effect that God will not hold the common people responsible for the sins of the elite (*khāṣṣa*) unless evils (*munkar*) are committed in public (*jihāran*) (Mālik, *Muwaṭṭa'*, 991 no. 23; for parallels, see above, ch. 3, note 64); the commentators could have taken this as an invitation to treat *al-amr bi'l-ma'rūf* at length, but those I have checked do not do so (see, for example, Bājī (d. 474/1081), *Muntaqā*, Cairo 1332, 7:316.16).

[6] In addition to what follows, there is a brief exhortation to *al-amr bi'l-ma'rūf* in an epistle attributed to Mālik (*Risāla fī 'l-sunan wa'l-mawā'iẓ wa'l-ādāb*, Cairo 1937, 6.12; for this work, see Sezgin, *Geschichte*, 1:464, item II).

[7] 'Utbī (d. 255/869), *Mustakhraja*, *apud* Ibn Rushd (d. 520/1126), *al-Bayān wa'l-taḥṣīl*, ed. M. Ḥajjī *et al.*, Beirut 1984–91, 9:360.2 (for this work, which was drawn to my attention by Maribel Fierro, see M. Muranyi, *Materialien zur mālikitischen Rechtsliteratur*, Wiesbaden 1984, section III. 1, esp. 53–5); Ibn Abī Zayd, *Jāmi'*, 157.11.

[8] See above, ch. 12, note 43; the same schema is used by Ghazzālī, see below, ch. 16, 432f.

[9] Ibn Rushd in his commentary makes the point that this is a clear indication that Mālik held that *al-amr bi'l-ma'rūf* is not actually obligatory in such circumstances (Ibn Rushd, *Bayān*, 17:84.19).

once performed the duty gently, and this worked.[10] In another passage, Mālik provides an alternative justification for proceeding in such circumstances: even if one is disobeyed, one is still bearing witness against the offender.[11] What then if one does fear harm, while again not expecting success? This problem is posed to Mālik by (Muṣʿab) al-Zubayrī (d. 236/851): there are people who, if he commands them, comply; but there are others who instead make him suffer – the poets lampoon him, and the reprobates beat him up and imprison him. What should he do? Mālik's answer is that if he is in fear of them and thinks that they will not comply, he should leave off, and disapprove only in his heart,[12] this being permissible.[13] In sum, we know what Mālik thought in the absence of a prospect of success, with and without a prospect of harm. But we have no statement of his views in cases where success is to be anticipated. Presumably he held it obligatory to proceed in the absence of danger, but we are left to guess at his attitude in its presence.

Another area in which we have a cluster of views from Mālik is the relationship between commanding right and the state. We may first consider the question of rebuking the political authorities for their misdeeds. Mālik states that it is the duty of every Muslim – or scholar – to go in to the ruler or the like (*dhū sulṭān*), and to command good and forbid evil to him; it is for this purpose alone that the scholar enters into the presence of the ruler.[14] In another passage, however, his attitude seems less resolute. When asked whether a man should command and forbid a governor (*wālī*) or the like, his answer is that he should do so if he expects that the offender will comply. To the further question whether one may omit doing so if there is no such expectation, he replies that he does not know.[15] Elsewhere a saying of Mālik is quoted to the effect that he had met seventeen Successors, and had not heard that they had admonished unjust rulers.[16] It is curious that

[10] ʿUtbī, *Mustakhraja*, *apud* Ibn Rushd, *Bayān*, 17:84.5; similarly, but less fully, Ibn Abī Zayd, *Jāmiʿ*, 156.12 (where for *yuṭīquhu* read *yuṭīʿuhu*), and Bājī (d. 474/1081), *Sunan al-ṣāliḥīn*, ms. Leiden, Or. 506, f. 115b.2; also ʿIyāḍ, *Madārik*, 1:187.2, stressing the importance of doing it nicely. For Bājī's *Sunan al-ṣāliḥīn*, see Abū Bakr ibn Khayr, *Fahrasa*, 277.10, and Brockelmann, *Geschichte*, second edition, 1:534; for the manuscript, see Voorhoeve, *Handlist*, 347. I am indebted to Maribel Fierro for bringing the work to my attention and sending me a copy of the relevant pages.

[11] Ibn Abī Zayd, *Jāmiʿ*, 156.10.

[12] This can be read as an implicit reference to the doctrine of the three modes; the other two terms, however, do not appear in these sayings of Mālik.

[13] ʿIyāḍ, *Madārik*, 1:186.21. In another anecdote Mālik upbraids a man who had been badly beaten up as a result of his folly in rebuking a powerful figure at the gate of his own house and in the presence of his retinue (*ibid.*, 141.11).

[14] *Ibid.*, 207.18, without indication of source. Cf. also *ibid.*, 207.16.

[15] Ibn Abī Zayd, *Jāmiʿ*, 157.1.

[16] Mālikī, *Riyāḍ*, 395.5; cf. Ṣāliḥī, *Kanz*, 671.13.

none of these sayings explicitly raises the question of danger, since a ruler or governor, unlike a neighbour or brother, is someone one is likely to be in fear of. Mālik's response to Muṣʿab al-Zubayrī perhaps bears on the question, if we take it that the imprisonment of which Muṣʿab complains was inflicted by the authorities.[17]

The other issue that arises in relation to the state is cooperation. Here Mālik's attitudes are distinctly positive. He holds that where a neighbour openly drinks wine and the like, and ignores a rebuke, he should be reported to the imam.[18] More significantly, he is asked to comment on a situation in which a man who wishes to take action is unable to do so without recourse to the authorities (*lā yaqwā ʿalayhi illā bi-sulṭān*); he approaches a ruler (*atā sulṭānan*), who invites him to undertake the task (of enforcing public morality). The man accepts on condition that he is not to sit in any appointed place, nor to have anything to do with set punishments, but is (solely) to command and forbid. Does Mālik approve of such a man undertaking the duty at the command of the ruler (*bi-amr al-sulṭān*)? Mālik replies that if he is able to perform it, and does it right, he should indeed undertake it.[19]

Apart from this, only disparate observations are transmitted from Mālik. With regard to the question who may perform the duty, one issue on which he pronounces is the question whether the sinner is obligated. Here Mālik quotes Saʿīd ibn Jubayr (d. 95/714), who used to say that, were only those who are themselves blameless to forbid wrong, then nobody would ever do so.[20] In a parallel passage, Mālik himself endorses this view, and asks rhetorically who can be considered blameless.[21] With regard to the targets of the duty, he mentions parents and Qadarīs. Asked if one should command and forbid one's parents, his answer is yes, but with becoming humility (cf. Q17:24).[22] In response to a query about relations with Qadarīs, Mālik, while holding that one should avoid normal social relations with them, nevertheless states that one should command and forbid them.[23] Finally he

[17] See above, note 13.

[18] Ibn Farḥūn (d. 799/1397), *Tabṣirat al-ḥukkām*, ed. Ṭ. ʿA. Saʿd, Cairo 1986, 2:187.14 (from Ibn Wahb); ʿUqbānī, *Tuḥfa*, 21.12. The two versions differ considerably in wording; ʿUqbānī attributes his to the *Nawādir* of Ibn Abī Zayd.

[19] ʿUtbī, *Mustakhraja*, *apud* Ibn Rushd, *Bayān*, 9:360.6; similarly Ibn Abī Zayd, *Jāmiʿ*, 157.14 (read *fa-mā* for *mimmā*).

[20] ʿUtbī, *Mustakhraja*, *apud* Ibn Rushd, *Bayān*, 18:37.7.

[21] *Ibid.*, 330.6 (with mention of Rabīʿa, sc. the Medinese Rabīʿat al-Raʾy (d. 136/753f.), as the transmitter from Saʿīd to Mālik); similarly Ibn Abī Zayd, *Jāmiʿ*, 158.12. ʿIyāḍ quotes the passage in a slightly different form as a saying of Mālik (*Madārik*, 1:185.21, without indication of source).

[22] Ibn Abī Zayd, *Jāmiʿ*, 157.5.

[23] ʿIyāḍ, *Madārik*, 1:176.2 (mentioning Ibn Wahb as one source).

takes the view that one may not continue to reside in a land of wrongdoing in which the righteous ancestors are reviled; God's earth is wide (cf. Q4:97).[24]

It is curious that we have no views on forbidding wrong from the transmitters of the doctrine of Mālik in the late second/eighth and third/ninth centuries. This is in striking contrast to the abundance of their surviving views on legal points.[25]

3. LATER MĀLIKĪ DOCTRINE

In the absence of any single mainstream doctrine of forbidding wrong among the later Mālikīs, this section will take the form of a survey of a rather disparate body of sources. First, I shall discuss two authors of the fifth/eleventh and early sixth/twelfth centuries who present what might be an Ashʿarite doctrine of the duty. Second, I shall consider Koranic exegesis written by Mālikīs who lived from the sixth/twelfth to the ninth/fifteenth century. Third, I shall abstract some relevant material from the works of authors primarily concerned with the role of the censor (*muḥtasib*), i.e. the official supervision of morals and markets; these range in date from the third/ninth to the ninth/fifteenth century. Fourth, I shall examine an assemblage of commentaries of one sort or another, many of them late. I shall conclude with a discussion of monographs on forbidding wrong.

Despite a reference to a stray view of the eastern Mālikī Ashʿarite Bāqillānī (d. 403/1013) on a point of detail,[26] it is only with Bājī (d. 474/1081), a major figure in the introduction of Ashʿarism into Muslim Spain, that we can even begin to place our subject on the map. Unfortunately the works in which he might have set out a systematic doctrine of forbidding wrong do not survive;[27] we are thus reduced to using the rather skimpy doctrinal statements that he includes in his account of the duty in an ascetic work.[28] Some of what he has to say is not very different in

[24] Ibn Abī Zayd, *Jāmiʿ*, 156.6.

[25] Thus the treatment in a major law-book of the period of the testimony of poets, singers, professional mourners and those who play chess or backgammon reveals nuances in the Mālikī assessment of what is offensive about their practices; for example, Mālik holds that poets may give evidence provided they do not use their art for purposes of extortion (Saḥnūn (d. 240/854), *Mudawwana*, Beirut n.d., 5:153.7; and cf. Ibn ʿAbd al-Barr (d. 463/1071), *Kāfī*, Riyāḍ 1980, 895.12, 896.11, 898.9). But this does not touch on the question of what the individual Muslim is to do about these dubious characters.

[26] See above, ch. 13, note 5.

[27] Cf. Abū Bakr ibn Khayr, *Fahrasa*, 255f.

[28] Bājī, *Sunan*, ff. 114a–116a (for this work, see above, note 10). It is only in a few places that Bājī speaks with his own voice; the bulk of the material consists of Koranic quotations, traditions and sayings of early figures. In a testament to his two sons, Bājī exhorts them to perform the duty, but without further elaboration (J. ʿA. Hilāl, 'Muqaddimat waṣiyyat al-

texture from the sayings of Mālik: if one cannot take action against a wrong, one must avoid being present;[29] the sinner is not excluded from forbidding wrong, but the initiative of a virtuous person is more likely to be accepted;[30] one should do it nicely unless one knows in advance that the wrongdoer will be obstinate.[31] But the outstanding feature of his account is an unmistakably scholastic analysis of the conditions. These he presents as a triad.[32] Two are conditions for it to be permissible to proceed. The first is that the performer must be someone who knows right from wrong. The second is that it must be assured that his action will not bring about a wrong equal to or greater than the one he is acting against; suppose, for example, that were he to reprove a wine-bibber, this would lead to a situation in which he or someone else would be killed. If one of these two conditions is not satisfied, he may not proceed by tongue, but should do so in his heart.[33] If both conditions are satisfied, it is permissible to proceed, but not yet obligatory. What renders it obligatory is fulfilment of the third condition: that the performer should know or have good reason to believe that the wrongdoer will comply.[34] Given the historical role of Bājī in the spread of Ashʿarism and the scholastic character of this doctrine, it seems likely that he obtained it from an eastern Ashʿarite source. But we have no confirmation of this.[35]

A later Andalusian author in the same tradition is the elder Ibn Rushd (d. 520/1126). Here again, he is not writing in a genre conducive to a full-dress doctrinal presentation.[36] It is, however, immediately clear that he is using the same three-condition schema as Bājī, though the wording is

Qāḍī Abī ʾl-Walīd al-Bājī li-waladayhi', *Majallat al-Maʿhad al-Miṣrī*, 1 no. 3 (1955), 36.11, brought to my attention by Maribel Fierro). [29] Bājī, *Sunan*, f. 115a.9.

[30] *Ibid.*, f. 115b.8. [31] *Ibid.*, f. 115b.12. [32] *Ibid.*, ff. 114b.15, 115a.12.

[33] This may perhaps represent the intrusion of an idiom used by Mālik (see above, note 12), since the term is not common in Shāfiʿite Ashʿarite sources (see above, ch. 13, notes 54, 68, 82).

[34] Bājī adds, however, that if he is not in danger (but has no expectation of success), he should manifest his condemnation to avoid any appearance of approval (*ibid.*, f. 115a.3).

[35] Cf. above, ch. 13, 351, for eastern parallels to Bājī's triad. The dichotomy between conditions of permissibility and obligation is paralleled in the doctrine of the Muʿtazilite Abū ʾl-Ḥusayn (see above, ch. 9, 222f.).

[36] The material is found in two contexts. One is the *Bayān*, in which he is commenting on the sayings of Mālik quoted in the *Mustakhraja*. The other is a work introductory to the *Mudawwana* (Ibn Rushd (d. 520/1126), *al-Muqaddamāt al-mumahhadāt*, ed. M. Ḥajjī and S. A. Aʿrāb, Beirut 1988, 3:425–8). However, this latter treatment is largely identical with that of the *Bayān*: apart from two passages, the whole section runs parallel to *Bayān*, 9:360–3. Much of the first passage which does not appear there is found *ibid.*, 17:84.9–16 (with transposition), leaving only a passage on rebuking one's parents (*Muqaddamāt*, 3:426.17–20, cf. Ibn Abī Zayd, *Jāmiʿ*, 157.5) unaccounted for in the *Bayān*. The second passage is a brief reference to the three modes (*Muqaddamāt*, 3:427.18). In what follows, I shall cite only the *Bayān*.

never close enough to suggest direct dependence.[37] Like Bājī, though again in different words, he endorses the view that it is not a condition for forbidding wrong that one be sinless (*maʿṣūm*).[38]

The rest of what Ibn Rushd has to offer is not found in Bājī's discussion. Prompted by Mālik,[39] he takes a favourable view of the performance of the duty at the ruler's command.[40] He states that only the authorities are able to deal with offences of the kind in question across the board (*jumlatan*). They have the duty to do so by appointing someone to see to it; it is commendable for such a person to respond to the imam's request if he knows that he is able to carry out the duty.[41] One who is not called upon to assume an official role should take action against such offences as obtrude upon him, subject to the three conditions; but to go out of one's way in this regard is obligatory only for the imam, and commendable for others only when they have the power to do so (with effect).[42] Unlike the three-condition schema, this has the look of an *ad hoc* response to the view of Mālik on which he is commenting.

Two views advanced by Ibn Rushd are more arresting. The first is his position that forbidding wrong is an individual duty (*farḍ ʿalā ʾl-aʿyān*) provided the conditions are satisfied;[43] this is an unusual view, or at least an unusual way of putting things, particularly among Sunnīs.[44] The second is something he says in connection with Q5:105, with its suggestion that the believers should look to their own souls and ignore the misdeeds of others. Unremarkably, he refers this injunction to a time in which forbidding wrong will be ineffective.[45] He then observes how much his own day resembles such a time[46] – whereas under conditions in which a helper can be found to assist in the cause of justice, no one may remain silent in the face of offences, or neglect to take action against them.[47] What is striking here is the suggestion that the future in which the duty will lapse may

37 Ibn Rushd, *Bayān*, 9:360.13, paraphrased *ibid.*, 17:84.21, and 18:37.15, 330.18. Cf. also above, note 9. Note that Ibn Rushd does not include Bājī's qualification (see above, note 34).

38 *Ibid.*, 37.10, 330.10. He uses the term *maʿṣūm* because he has just made the point that not even prophets are perfect.

39 Cf. above, note 19.

40 *Ibid.*, 9:361.12.

41 He quotes the injunction of Q5:2 to 'help one another to piety and godfearing'.

42 Similarly *ibid.*, 18:331.6, quoting Q22:41.

43 *Ibid.*, 38.1, quoting two Koranic verses and a Prophetic tradition; also *ibid.*, 330.16. Cf. his remark that *al-amr biʾl-maʿrūf* is obligatory for every Muslim (*ibid.*, 9:360.13).

44 For Imāmīs holding this view, see above, ch. 11, 274, 290; for a possible Muʿtazilite case, see above, ch. 9, note 33.

45 *Ibid.*, 9:362.6, with citation of appropriate Prophetic traditions (for which see above, ch. 3, notes 40, 47). Compare Mālikī, *Riyāḍ*, 74.13, and Dabbāgh, *Maʿālim*, 1:212.10, both commenting on an unusual Prophetic tradition.

46 *Wa-mā ashbaha zamānanā bi-hādhā ʾl-zamān.*

47 Ibn Rushd, *Bayān*, 9:363.7.

already have arrived; this is a view found in tradition, but rare among later scholars.[48]

Let us turn now to works of Koranic exegesis written by Mālikīs. Much of what they say is, of course, part of an exegetical tradition which is not specifically Mālikī. However, there are passages in which the exegetes stand back from the detailed exposition of the Koranic verses and give general accounts of the duty; these are more likely to represent school doctrine, and are thus worth examination here. Two of the works I shall draw on are straightforward Koran commentaries, namely those of the Andalusian Ibn ʿAṭiyya (d. 541/1146) and the North African Thaʿālibī (d. 873/1468f.).[49] Three proclaim in their titles that they belong to the genre of specifically legal Koran commentary, namely the works of the Andalusians Abū Bakr ibn al-ʿArabī (d. 543/1148), Qurṭubī (d. 671/1273) and Ibn al-Faras al-Gharnāṭī (d. 597/1201); we could reasonably expect these to contain a stronger dose of school doctrine than the general commentaries,[50] though this is by no means assured, and Qurṭubī's commentary does not really belong to the genre.[51]

Much of what the exegetes have to say is banal. In contrast to the unusual formulation of Ibn Rushd, the duty is held to be a collective one[52] – although according to Ibn al-ʿArabī it may become an individual one under some conditions.[53] A brief account that appears in several commentaries[54]

[48] It makes no appearance in the systematic discussion of the verse in Ibn al-ʿArabī (d. 543/1148), *al-Nāsikh wa'l-mansūkh*, ed. ʿA. al-ʿAlawī al-M'daghrī, Morocco 1988, 2:204.14. For tradition, cf. above, ch. 3, 40–2.

[49] I leave aside that of Abū Ḥayyān al-Gharnāṭī (d. 745/1344), since despite his Andalusian origin he ended up as a non-Mālikī living in Egypt (for his *madhhab*, see Ibn Ḥajar, *Durar*, 4:304.11).

[50] For the genre of legal commentaries, typically entitled *Aḥkām al-Qurʾān*, see above, ch. 12, note 193. Ibn al-ʿArabī was not the first Mālikī author of such a work: for example, he was preceded by Ismāʿīl ibn Isḥāq al-Jahḍamī (d. 282/896) (see Sezgin, *Geschichte*, 1:475f. no. 20), whose work was known to Ibn al-ʿArabī's pupil Abū Bakr ibn Khayr al-Ishbīlī (d. 575/1179) (*Fahrasa*, 51.11) and survives in fragments (Muranyi, 'Neue Materialien zur *tafsīr*-Forschung', 252).

[51] Thus one of these authors includes in his commentary to Q3:104 a brief discussion of the treatment of heretics (Ibn al-Faras al-Gharnāṭī (d. 597/1201), *Aḥkām al-Qurʾān*, fragment edited by M. I. Yaḥyā under the title *Tafsīr sūratay Āl ʿImrān wa'l-Nisāʾ min kitāb Aḥkām al-Qurʾān*, Miṣrātā 1989, 75.6); this is in fact a paraphrase of a passage in the *Aḥkām al-Qurʾān* of the Ḥanafī Jaṣṣāṣ (d. 370/981) (see above, ch. 12, note 206).

[52] Ibn ʿAṭiyya, *Muḥarrar*, 3:187.16; Ibn al-ʿArabī, *Aḥkām*, 292.15; Qurṭubī, *Jāmiʿ*, 4:165.14; Thaʿālibī, *Jawāhir*, 1:355.7; Ibn al-Faras, *Aḥkām*, 74.5 (all to Q3:104).

[53] Ibn al-ʿArabī, *Aḥkām*, 292.17 (to Q3:104)); and cf. *ibid.*, 406.6 (to Q4:25), where he describes individuals as God's deputies in *al-amr bi'l-maʿrūf*, and his *ʿĀriḍa*, 9:13.16, where he states that the duty is incumbent on everyone.

[54] Ibn ʿAṭiyya, *Muḥarrar*, 5:166.10; Qurṭubī, *Jāmiʿ*, 6:253.17 (a summary, with attribution to Ibn ʿAṭiyya); Thaʿālibī, *Jawāhir*, 1:573.6 (unattributed, with one minor expansion of Ibn ʿAṭiyya's text) (all to Q5:79).

sums up the consensus of opinion on the duty as follows: forbidding wrong is obligatory for anyone who can sustain it, provided that he does it nicely, and that it will not cause harm to him or his fellow-believers; if for any of these reasons it is not feasible, he should perform the duty in his heart,[55] and avoid socialising with the offender; finally, according to expert opinion, it is not required that one who performs the duty should himself be free of sin[56] – rather it is for sinners to forbid each other. There is nothing in this to detain us.

There are, however, some more interesting points in these commentaries.[57] One is a disagreement regarding the extent to which fear of unpleasant consequences voids the duty. As Ibn al-ʿArabī says, there is no disagreement that when a man fears for his life, he ceases to be obligated; but there is disagreement on the question whether it is nevertheless commendable (*yustaḥabb*) to expose oneself to injury or death.[58] Elsewhere he observes that most scholars consider it permissible to do so in such a case if there is an expectation of success, whereas it would be pointless in the absence of such an expectation; his own view, however, is that if a man's intention is pure, he should go ahead whatever the circumstances.[59] This is a notably strong view.[60] Qurṭubī in turn quotes the passage, and despite an initial reservation, he finds support in Q3:21, which refers to the killing of those who command justice (*alladhīna yaʾmurūna biʾl-qisṭi*).[61] Likewise Ibn ʿAṭiyya states that, while fear of unpleasant consequences voids the

55 For this see also Ibn al-ʿArabī, *Aḥkām*, 293.3 (to Q3:104), and Ibn ʿAbd al-Barr (d. 463/1071) as quoted in Qurṭubī, *Jāmiʿ*, 4:48.3 (to Q3:21). For the views of Ibn ʿAbd al-Barr on *al-amr biʾl-maʿrūf*, see also above, ch. 2, note 85.

56 Similarly Ibn al-ʿArabī, *Aḥkām*, 266.11 (to Q3:21), 292.19 (to Q3:104) (contrasting this view with that of unspecified 'innovators' (*mubtadiʿa*)); Qurṭubī, *Jāmiʿ*, 4:47.18 (to Q3:21) (likewise referring to the 'innovators'). The only scholar known to me who holds a contrary view is the Shāfiʿite Ḥalīmī (d. 403/1012) (see above, ch. 13, notes 28f.).

57 I leave aside a rare scholastic point raised by Ibn al-ʿArabī: is it all the same whether the offence is against divine or human rights? He says that he has seen no statement on the question by 'our scholars', and gives it as his own view that human rights take precedence (*Aḥkām*, 267.4, to Q3:21).

58 Ibn al-ʿArabī, *Aḥkām*, 145.11 (to Q2:207); he suggests that Q2:207 supports the view that it is commendable. In another formulation of his, security of property as well as of person is a condition for obligation (*ʿĀriḍa*, 9:13.16).

59 Ibn al-ʿArabī, *Aḥkām*, 266.21 (to Q3:21) (read *ʿindī* for *ʿindahu*, *ibid.*, 267.1, as in the citation of the passage at Qurṭubī, *Jāmiʿ*, 4:48.18, likewise to Q3:21). For a refutation of the view that this is tantamount to suicide (cf. Q2:195), Ibn al-ʿArabī refers the reader to his *Sharḥ al-mushkilayn* (cf. also *Aḥkām*, 266.7), which does not appear to be extant.

60 Ibn al-ʿArabī himself takes the opposite view in a passage in another work in which he gives it as his opinion that in forbidding wrong it is *not* permissible to take action that would lead to one's death (Ibn al-ʿArabī (d. 543/1148), *al-Qabas fī sharḥ Muwaṭṭaʾ Mālik ibn Anas*, ed. M. A. Walad Karīm, Beirut 1992, 583.3, this time referring us to a book of his on *uṣūl*; this passage was drawn to my attention by Etan Kohlberg).

61 Qurṭubī, *Jāmiʿ*, 4:48.16. He also adduces Q31:17.

obligation, accepting such consequences secures one a greater reward.[62] But their sober formulations hardly compare with Ibn al-ʿArabī's enthusiastic commendation of martyrdom.

Ibn al-ʿArabī is not, however, an activist, as is clear from his attitude towards the question of recourse to arms. He states that if there is no other way to perform the duty, one should leave off; recourse to arms is reserved to the ruler (*sulṭān*), since it could otherwise lead to sedition (*fitna*), and so to an evil greater than that which one is seeking to prevent.[63] Qurṭubī and Ibn al-Faras, by contrast, allow killing where necessary.[64]

A final point of interest is the idea found among the exegetes that the content of forbidding wrong depends on one's position in the social and political hierarchy. Some of this is unremarkable. Thus Ibn ʿAṭiyya states that the duty is one imposed on the community in general (*bi'l-jumla*), but that beyond that point people differ in their obligations. Those in authority (*wulāt al-amr wa'l-ru'asā'*) are obligated in all circumstances; others are only obligated under certain conditions, of the kind already familiar.[65] In another passage, however, he says that people are on different levels (*marātib*) with regard to forbidding wrong. The duty of the scholars (*ʿulamā'*) is to instruct the rulers (*tanbīh al-ḥukkām wa'l-wulāt*) and ease them into the highroad of learning (*ḥamluhum ʿalā jāddat al-ʿilm*); that of the rulers is to take action against (*taghyīr*) evils through their strength and power; that of the rest – the lay subjects, we might say – is to bring matters to the attention of the authorities, after verbal protest. This, he adds, refers to an ongoing evil; if the ordinary believer sees an incidental misdeed (such as robbery or fornication), he should himself take such action as he can.[66] This position, however, involves a significant limitation of action on the part of ordinary believers. In yet another passage he goes a step further. Speaking of the scholars, he says that it is they who should perform the duty while the rest of the community follows them, since performance requires extensive learning.[67] These views are echoed by other commentators.[68] Thus Qurṭubī

62 Ibn ʿAṭiyya, *Muḥarrar*, 3:187.19 (to Q3:104).
63 Ibn al-ʿArabī, *Aḥkām*, 293.8 (to Q3:104). He makes an exception for episodic crime: if one sees one man killing another, the only course of action may be armed intervention.
64 See Qurṭubī, *Jāmiʿ*, 4:49.5 (to Q3:21), citing Q49:9; Ibn al-Faras, *Aḥkām*, 74.13 (to Q3:104). 65 Ibn ʿAṭiyya, *Muḥarrar*, 8:286.13 (to Q9:112).
66 *Ibid.*, 3:188.4 (to Q3:104).
67 *Ibid.*, 186.18 (to Q3:104). It is not entirely clear that Ibn ʿAṭiyya himself endorses this view.
68 Cf. Qurṭubī, *Jāmiʿ*, 4:165.12 (to Q3:104), where he states that those who command right must be scholars (*ʿulamā'*), and *ibid.*, 12:73.6 (to Q22:41), where he quotes a saying of the Ṣūfī Sahl ibn ʿAbdallāh al-Tustarī (d. 283/896) to the effect that it is not for ordinary people to command right to rulers or scholars. Thaʿālibī reproduces two of Ibn ʿAṭiyya's passages (*Jawāhir*, 1:354.13, 355.9 (to Q3:104)).

quotes the saying about the tripartite division of labour.[69] And in another passage he states that forbidding wrong is not appropriate for everyone, and that only the ruler (*sulṭān*) should undertake it, since executive power is in his hands; he should appoint a righteous, strong, learned and trustworthy man in every town to see to it.[70] This latter passage is unlikely to be of Mālikī origin, since a fuller version is found in the work of the Shāfiʿite Ḥalīmī (d. 403/1012).[71] Indeed the whole hierarchic theme seems to lack roots in the wider Mālikī tradition.

We can now move on to the writers on the official oversight of morals and markets.[72] As might be expected, they do not in general have much to say about the individual duty. The earliest of them, the western Mālikī Yaḥyā ibn ʿUmar (d. 289/902), offers no general discussion of forbidding wrong, but shows frequent concern for public morals. Thus he discusses such problems as nudity and the presence of women in public baths,[73] the mourning practices of women,[74] and their coquettish habit of wearing squeaky sandals.[75] There is, however, only one passage in which he seems to be concerned with the duty of the individual Muslim.[76] Here the bath-keeper has admitted women who have no reason to be there; do Muslim onlookers (*al-nāẓirūn al-Muslimūn*)[77] have the duty of raiding the establishment and expelling the women? Yaḥyā's answer is that in such a situation he (*sic*) should not burst in, but rather order the women to get dressed and veiled, and then to leave; (if they fail to heed the warning and offend again) he should punish them as he sees fit. This is a surprising prescription for a private citizen, and perhaps suggests that we should understand 'guardians' rather than 'onlookers'. Like Yaḥyā, most of the later writers on market regulation proceed to the official duty without any prior discussion of forbidding wrong.[78] There are, however,

69 Qurṭubī, *Jāmiʿ*, 4:49.3 (to Q3:21); for this saying, see above, ch. 6, note 166.
70 *Ibid.*, 47.13 (to Q3:21, quoting Q22:41).
71 Ḥalīmī, *Minhāj*, 3:216.17–21; see above, ch. 13, 342.
72 On market supervision in Muslim Spain in general, see Chalmeta, *El 'señor del zoco'*.
73 Yaḥyā ibn ʿUmar (d. 289/902), *Aḥkām al-sūq*, in M. ʿA. Makkī, 'Kitāb aḥkām al-sūq li-Yaḥyā ibn ʿUmar al-Andalusī', *Revista del Instituto Egipcio de Estudios Islámicos en Madrid*, 4 (1956), 123f. §33. He does not use the term *muḥtasib*.
74 *Ibid.*, 124f. §§34f.
75 *Ibid.*, 126 §36.
76 *Ibid.*, 142f. §56. Even in the context of the wedding-feast (*walīma*), which Yaḥyā treats at some length and with special reference to varieties of music-making, the duty of the individual to command and forbid is not discussed; the question is only whether he should be present (*ibid.*, 119–22 §31).
77 E. García Gómez likewise translates this phrase as 'los musulmanes que lo ven' ('Unas "Ordenenzas del zoco" del siglo IX', *Al-Andalus*, 22 (1957), 307).
78 Saqaṭī at the beginning of his treatise quotes a couple of the relevant Koranic verses (Q3:104, Q3:110), but proceeds to the official activity of the *muḥtasib* without discussing the individual duty (*Ādāb al-ḥisba*, ed. G.-S. Colin and E. Lévi-Provençal, Paris 1931, 2.2,

two interesting exceptions: the North Africans Ibn al-Munāṣif (d. 620/1223) and ʿUqbānī (d. 871/1467).

It will be simplest to begin with ʿUqbānī. He is, of course, primarily concerned with the duties of an appointed official, rather than with those of the individual Muslim – though it is not in fact always clear which he is discussing.[79] The opening chapters of his work nevertheless provide an unusually extensive account of the individual duty in which two things strike the eye.

The first is ʿUqbānī's debt to Ibn Rushd. He reproduces the latter's three-condition schema,[80] and also his analysis of Q5:105 as referring to a time in which forbidding wrong can no longer be practised[81] – with the obvious comment that, if the age of Ibn Rushd was such a time, how much more so must our own be.[82] But Ibn Rushd's coverage of the duty is too incomplete to fill out a work of the scope of ʿUqbānī's, and at the same time the latter makes no attempt to draw on the materials offered by the Mālikī Koran commentators.

Hence the second noteworthy feature of ʿUqbānī's treatment: the importation of Shāfiʿite material from the east. The early chapters of the book make intensive use of a brief account of forbidding wrong in a minor work by Ghazzālī (d. 505/1111).[83] In particular, ʿUqbānī depends on Ghazzālī for his account of the conditions under which fear of the consequences to oneself dispenses one from obligation – an aspect of the duty at best implicitly covered in the three-condition schema. He does, however, take issue with Ghazzālī's view that in the face of such danger it is still meritorious to

3.12; the editors incline to date the treatise to the end of the fifth/eleventh century or the first half of the next century, *ibid.*, ix). Ibn ʿAbdūn does no more than mention *taghyīr al-munkar* in his introduction (E. Lévi-Provençal (ed.), *Trois traités hispaniques de ḥisba*, Cairo 1955, 3.4; he demonstrably belongs to the early Almoravid period, see E. Lévi-Provençal, 'Un document sur la vie urbaine et les corps de métiers à Séville au début du XIIe siècle: le traité d'Ibn ʿAbdūn', *Journal Asiatique*, 224 (1934), 180f.). Ibn ʿAbd al-Raʾūf makes general reference to the duty only in his doxology (Lévi-Provençal, *Trois traités*, 69.3, 69.7). Jarsīfī, like Saqaṭī, proceeds directly to *ḥisba* (*ibid.*, 119.4; on the uncertain dates of the last two authors, see *ibid.*, v of the French preface).

79 Starting from the discussion of the illegality of fines (ʿUqbānī, *Tuḥfa*, 13.16), it is clear that his primary concern is with the official duty, though at times he still touches on the individual duty (see, for example, *ibid.*, 21.8). Most of what goes before can be taken to refer to the individual duty (or to the duty in general), though this only becomes explicit in a cross-reference near the end of the work (*ibid.*, 177.14).

80 *Ibid.*, 4.17 (cf. above, note 37). He refers here to Ibn Rushd's *Bayān*, and also to his *Muqaddamāt*; cf. ʿUqbānī, *Tuḥfa*, 141f. of the French section.

81 ʿUqbānī, *Tuḥfa*, 5.16 (cf. above, 364f.). 82 *Ibid.*, 6.3.

83 See *ibid.*, 5.3, 6.9, 6.20, 8.7, corresponding to Ghazzālī (d. 505/1111), *Kitāb al-arbaʿīn fī uṣūl al-dīn*, Cairo 1344, 85.10, 86.9, 86.14, 88.15, respectively. ʿUqbānī regarded Ghazzālī as one of the luminaries of his age (*Tuḥfa*, 6.4), but does not seem to have had access to the *Iḥyāʾ*.

proceed, preferring the contrary view, which he extrapolates from Ibn Rushd's position;[84] he correctly notes that Ghazzālī's view was shared by ʿIzz al-Dīn ibn ʿAbd al-Salām (d. 660/1262), also a Shāfiʿite,[85] but makes no reference to Ibn al-ʿArabī.[86] Towards the end of the work, ʿUqbānī borrows from another celebrated Shāfiʿite scholar, Māwardī (d. 450/1058), whom he quotes on the qualifications required of the censor,[87] and on the nine differences between the official and individual duties of forbidding wrong.[88]

The bulk of ʿUqbānī's material, however, derives from his fellow-Mālikī Ibn al-Munāṣif.[89] In the latter part of his work, Ibn al-Munāṣif had covered much of the same ground, and for the most part ʿUqbānī simply appropriates his material through a process of paraphrase, accompanied by occasional rearrangement and a certain amount of omission and interpolation.[90] In the part of the work that concerns us, there is in fact only one passage where ʿUqbānī makes it his business to think for himself, namely that in which he disagrees with Ghazzālī.[91] We can therefore set ʿUqbānī aside at this point and go back to Ibn al-Munāṣif.

What then is the origin of Ibn al-Munāṣif's material?[92] As might be expected, it contains echoes of earlier Mālikī thought, though they are not particularly numerous. He cites only one opinion of Mālik himself in the passages that properly concern us, and he does so in a form he does not seem to owe to a Mālikī source.[93] He does not quote Ibn

[84] ʿUqbānī, *Tuḥfa*, 6.12. [85] Cf. above, ch. 13, note 104. [86] Cf. above, 366.

[87] *Ibid.*, 177.13 = Māwardī, *al-Aḥkām al-sulṭāniyya*, 316.4.

[88] ʿUqbānī, *Tuḥfa*, 178.1; see above, ch. 13, note 45. The rewriting of the first difference noted there is likely to reflect ʿUqbānī's loyalty to Ibn Rushd's doctrine of the individual, as opposed to collective, nature of *al-amr biʾl-maʿrūf* (cf. above, note 43).

[89] On Ibn al-Munāṣif see M. J. Viguera Molins, 'La censura de costumbres en el *Tanbīh al-ḥukkām* de Ibn al-Munāṣif (1168–1223)', in Instituto Hispano-Árabe de Cultura, *Actas de las II Jornadas de Cultura Árabe e Islamica (1980)*, Madrid 1985, 591–3. ʿUqbānī's use of the *Tanbīh* was noted by Chenoufi (*apud* ʿUqbānī, *Tuḥfa*, 142 of the French section), followed by Viguera Molins ('La censura de costumbres', 594).

[90] Broadly speaking, ʿUqbānī, *Tuḥfa*, 3–13 corresponds to Ibn al-Munāṣif (d. 620/1223), *Tanbīh al-ḥukkām*, ed. ʿA. Manṣūr, Tunis 1988, 309–23. More precisely, the correspondences are as follows: 3.3–12 and 4.3–17 = 309.3 to 311.4; 7.3 to 8.13 = 314.13 to 317.4; 8.13 to 9.17 = 311.8 to 313.14; 9.21 to 13.14 = 317.6 to 323.8. Most of the material in the *Tanbīh* thus reappears in the *Tuḥfa*; the longest passage omitted is 314.3–10. The greater part of what ʿUqbānī adds is quotation: passages from Ibn Rushd and Ghazzālī, most of which have already been discussed; and additional *ḥadīth*s and related material (as at *Tuḥfa*, 3.12–23, 8.7–10, 10.19 to 11.4). Only once in these pages does ʿUqbānī make explicit reference to his predecessor's work, when he quotes an anecdote Ibn al-Munāṣif relates about one of his teachers (*Tuḥfa*, 11.19, citing *Tanbīh*, 320.19). I am indebted to Maribel Fierro for drawing my attention to the *Tanbīh* and sending me a copy of the relevant part.

[91] See above, note 84. The passage begins with a *qultu*.

[92] Neither Ibn al-Munāṣif himself nor his modern editor has anything of value to say about his sources in their respective introductions (*ibid.*, 15, 20.3, 20.19).

[93] This is Mālik's citation and approval of a saying of Saʿīd ibn Jubayr (*ibid.*, 317.2; cf. above,

Rushd, though he is surely indebted to him, directly or indirectly, on two points of doctrine: the division of the conditions for performance of the duty into those that render it permissible and those that render it obligatory,[94] and a tilt towards the view that the duty is an individual one.[95] He does not seem to draw on Mālikī Koranic exegesis. Often I have not been able to establish whether Ibn al-Munāṣif was writing his own script, or whether he was following some earlier source, Mālikī or other. There is, however, one unmistakable linkage: though he does not quote Ghazzālī, he is heavily indebted to his *Revival of the religious sciences*.

This debt is immediately obvious from Ibn al-Munāṣif's use of the characteristic battery of technical terms devised by Ghazzālī for the analysis of the duty.[96] Closer examination of Ibn al-Munāṣif's account shows that with this terminology has come much of the structure of Ghazzālī's presentation. Three of its major structural components are easily recognised: the account of the conditions that the performer of the duty does and does not have to satisfy;[97] the escalatory schema of levels of response to offences;[98] and the survey of commonplace wrongs.[99] Yet the Ghazzālian heritage in Ibn al-Munāṣif, though extensive, is heavily eroded. Basic structures of Ghazzālī's account are missing.[100] Within those that survive there is much

notes 20f.). The wording of Ibn al-Munāṣif's version (*wa-aʿjaba Mālikan dhālika*) resembles that found in Ghazzālī, *Iḥyāʾ*, 2:286.24.

[94] Ibn al-Munāṣif, *Tanbīh*, 314.16, 315.10; cf. above, notes 32, 37.

[95] His formulation is guarded: *al-qiyām bi-taghyīr al-munkar wājib mutaʿayyin wa-farḍ mutaʾakkid fī baʿḍ al-aḥwāl* (*ibid.*, 310.3, whence ʿUqbānī, *Tuḥfa*, 4.3, without the qualification; cf. also Ibn al-Munāṣif, *Tanbīh*, 310.7, 310.11, 315.12, 316.13, 332.2). For Ibn Rushd's view, see above, note 43. In neither of these cases is there any sign of literary borrowing.

[96] Ibn al-Munāṣif sets out the three basic categories (*uṣūl*) as *al-muḥtasib*, *nafs al-iḥtisāb*, and *al-manākir al-muḥtasab fīhā* (*ibid.*, 314.5). This leaves out one of Ghazzālī's four pillars (*arkān*), namely *al-muḥtasab ʿalayhi*; but Ibn al-Munāṣif later uses the phrase (*ibid.*, 315.5). For Ghazzālī's terms, see below, ch. 16, 428f. ʿUqbānī prefers to drop this distinctive terminology when appropriating Ibn al-Munāṣif's material.

[97] *Ibid.*, 314.12; cf. below, ch. 16, 429–33.

[98] *Ibid.*, 320.10; cf. below, ch. 16, 431 and 438–41. Ibn al-Munāṣif's account owes the term *marātib* and the set of five levels to Ghazzālī's first sketch of his schema, but to some extent he appears to draw on Ghazzālī's fuller eight-level analysis when he expands on each level in turn; thus Ibn al-Munāṣif's account of his third level (*ibid.*, 322.1) contains an echo of the corresponding passage in Ghazzālī's fuller presentation (*Iḥyāʾ*, 2:302.30, cf. below, ch. 16, 439f.). Cf. also Ibn al-Munāṣif, *Tanbīh*, 317.14, where Ghazzālī's initial five levels are condensed to three.

[99] *Ibid.*, 329–46; cf. below, ch. 16, 442–6. Ibn al-Munāṣif speaks of *al-manākir al-maʾlūfa* (*ibid.*, 330.2) and *al-manākir al-muʿtāda* (*ibid.*, 330.10), Ghazzālī of *al-munkarāt al-maʾlūfa fī ʾl-ʿādāt* (*Iḥyāʾ*, 2:307.12).

[100] Thus Ibn al-Munāṣif's account lacks Ghazzālī's analysis (as opposed to survey) of wrongs (cf. below, ch. 16, 435–7), and omits consideration of one of Ghazzālī's favourite themes, namely rebuking rulers (cf. below, ch. 16, 446).

reshuffling, adding and dropping.[101] And despite verbal echoes of Ghazzālī's text here and there,[102] there is no sustained passage of Ibn al-Munāṣif which runs parallel to one of Ghazzālī's, even as a paraphrase. The extent of these changes goes far beyond anything that was required by the shift in focus from the individual to the official aspect of the duty.[103]

From a historical point of view, this is perhaps unfortunate. Where an author depending on Ghazzālī is generally faithful to his source, any deliberate and substantive departure from it is likely to be significant. In the present case, such a relationship no longer obtains. There is, however, one point of some interest. In two places Ibn al-Munāṣif, following Ghazzālī, finds himself considering armed conflict and the gathering of bands as a limiting case of individual response to wrongdoing – the issue being whether such activity requires the permission of the ruler. In the first passage, Ghazzālī merely remarks that the issue needs looking into, and will be discussed later;[104] Ibn al-Munāṣif by contrast states unambiguously that the ruler's permission is required, except in emergencies.[105] In the second passage, Ghazzālī comes out in favour of the view that such undertakings are allowed even without the permission of the ruler;[106] Ibn al-Munāṣif follows suit, but then backs away with the observation that such matters are best referred to the authorities, again with the exception of emergencies.[107]

Was Ibn al-Munāṣif's access to Ghazzālī's account of forbidding wrong direct or indirect? There is no way to be sure, but the degree of literary erosion that intervenes between the two texts rather suggests that it was indirect. One possibility is that the reshaping was the work of those who

[101] Thus the order in which Ibn al-Munāṣif considers the conditions to be satisfied by the performer is different. In the survey of wrongs he transposes the sections on the market and the street, omits the sections on bath-houses and hospitality, and adds a section concerned with divorce (Ibn al-Munāṣif, *Tanbīh*, 334–7). The single most interesting change is perhaps the appearance in Ibn al-Munāṣif's survey of wrongs of a concern, quite absent from Ghazzālī, with the large numbers of people who simply fail to perform the ritual prayer at all (*ibid.*, 330.11, 331.20, 332.24, and cf. *ibid.*, 332.16, 332.19).

[102] Compare, for example, *ibid.*, 314.16 with Ghazzālī, *Iḥyā'*, 2:286.12 (on the ineligibility of the unbeliever to perform the duty); Ibn al-Munāṣif, *Tanbīh*, 315.21 (*li-iẓhār sha'ā'ir al-dīn*) with Ghazzālī, *Iḥyā'*, 2:292.22 (*li-iẓhār sha'ā'ir al-Islām*; for the context, see below, ch. 16, 433 case (3)); Ibn al-Munāṣif, *Tanbīh*, 344.22 with Ghazzālī, *Iḥyā'*, 2:310.10 (on the fraudulent reconditioning of old clothes; cf. below, ch. 16, 443). These examples could easily be multiplied; but at the same time, it would not be implausible to attribute any one of them to coincidence.

[103] For Ibn al-Munāṣif's repeated references to the duties of the authorities, which serve to make them the prime agents of the performance of the duty in his account, see, for example, *Tanbīh*, 310.15, 325.5 (and the rest of the section), 329.4, 329.15, 330.15, 331.7, 332.4, 332.13, 333.2, 336.10, 337.12, 338.3; for his distinctly less frequent references to individuals, see, for example, *ibid.*, 310.15, 330.15, 332.2.

[104] Ghazzālī, *Iḥyā'*, 2:289.13; cf. below, ch. 16, note 28.

[105] Ibn al-Munāṣif, *Tanbīh*, 317.18.

[106] See below, ch. 16, 441.

[107] *Ibid.*, 323.3.

had previously adapted and abridged Ghazzālī's work. We know of at least three such efforts among the scholars of the Muslim west in this period.[108] A generation or two before Ibn al-Munāṣif, a certain Abū ʿAlī al-Masīlī (*fl.* second half of the sixth/twelfth century) wrote a work on the model of Ghazzālī's, and was known for this as 'Abū Ḥāmid al-Ṣaghīr'; the work was later described as widely available and popular.[109] A slightly earlier contemporary of his, Ibn al-Rammāma (d. 567/1172), made an epitome of Ghazzālī's work.[110] Before this the well-known Andalusian scholar Ṭurṭūshī (d. 520/1126), who resided in Alexandria, had composed a work in which he is described as emulating (*yuʿāriḍ bihi*) Ghazzālī's.[111] Another possibility is that Ibn al-Munāṣif was drawing on a tradition of earlier books of the same kind as his own. The truth might, of course, involve a combination of the two, and we have no way to reconstruct it.

The bulk of the Mālikī literature we have still to consider consists of commentaries of one sort or another. First, as in other schools, there is discussion of the 'three modes' tradition.[112] This may occur in the context of commentaries on one of the classical collections of traditions, that of Muslim (d. 261/875). The Mālikīs played a major role in the development of commentaries on this work;[113] examples are those of ʿIyāḍ (d. 544/1149), Aḥmad ibn ʿUmar al-Qurṭubī (d. 656/1258), and Ubbī (d. 827/1423f.), all western Mālikīs. Alternatively, treatment of the 'three modes' tradition

[108] I leave aside the epitome of the *Iḥyāʾ* contained in ms. Madrid, Junta, no. 21 (in the library of the Consejo Superior de Investigaciones Científicas), since its coverage of the *kitāb al-amr bi'l-maʿrūf* retains none of Ghazzālī's analysis (ff. 68a–70a; for this manuscript, see J. Ribera and M. Asín, *Manuscritos árabes y aljamiados de la Biblioteca de la Junta*, Madrid 1912, 95–7 no. 21). I am indebted to Maribel Fierro for sending me a copy of the relevant part of the text, and for the information that it is probably a work of ʿAlī ibn ʿAbdallāh al-Khazrajī (d. 539/1145). I owe my knowledge of the existence of this manuscript to P. S. van Koningsveld.

[109] M. al-Manūnī, '*Iḥyāʾ ʿulūm al-dīn* fī manẓūr al-gharb al-Islāmī ayyām al-Murābiṭīn wa'l-Muwaḥḥidīn', in *Abū Ḥāmid al-Ghazzālī: dirāsāt fī fikrihi wa-ʿaṣrihi wa-taʾthīrihi*, Rabat 1988, 133, citing Ghubrīnī (d. 704/1304f.), *ʿUnwān al-dirāya*, ed. ʿA. Nuwayhiḍ, Beirut 1969, 33.14, 34.3. Manūnī's article is by far the richest study of the fortunes of Ghazzālī's *Iḥyāʾ* in the west.

[110] Manūnī, '*Iḥyāʾ*', 132f. Ibn al-Rammāma was *qāḍī* of Fez.

[111] The composition of this work was already noted by Goldziher from a biographical entry on Ṭurṭūshī (*Le livre de Mohammed ibn Toumert*, 37); see now the remarks of M. Fierro in her translation of Ṭurṭūshī's *al-Ḥawādith wa'l-bidaʿ*, Madrid 1993, 73–5 no. 26, and the addenda, 177, citing Manūnī's article. Manūnī publishes extracts from the introduction to a work partially preserved in manuscript which answers to the description of Ṭurṭūshī's work ('*Iḥyāʾ*', 135–7, and see *ibid.*, 130; for *al-Nawawī* at 135.8, read *al-Thawrī*). It was Maribel Fierro who pointed out to me the possibility that Ṭurṭūshī's work might be a link between Ghazzālī's and Ibn al-Munāṣif's.

[112] For this tradition, see above, ch. 3, section 1.

[113] See the listing of the earliest extant commentaries on the *Ṣaḥīḥ* of Muslim in Sezgin, *Geschichte*, 1:136f. The classic commentary is, however, that of Nawawī (d. 676/1277) (cf. above, ch. 13, 351–3).

may find its place in the familiar genre of commentaries on the collection of forty traditions put together by the Shāfiʿite Nawawī (d. 676/1277);[114] I have used those of Tāj al-Dīn al-Fākihānī (d. 734/1334) and Shabrakhītī (d. 1106/1694f.), both Egyptian Mālikīs. Secondly, there are the commentaries on the law-book of Khalīl (d. 767/1365), who at one point mentions the duty as an instance of a collective obligation.[115] Here I have made use of some half-a-dozen published commentaries, most of them Egyptian.[116] Thirdly, the versified creed of the Egyptian Mālikī Ibrāhīm al-Laqānī (d. 1041/1631) precipitated a tradition of commentary to which he and his son ʿAbd al-Salām (d. 1078/1668) were the first contributors. A widespread feature of all this literature, familiar from other schools, is its somewhat disintegrated character: often it seems that the commentator is simply putting together a patchwork of excerpts from earlier sources. This in turn makes it a rather unrewarding literature to discuss at length, and I shall accordingly confine myself to picking out a few significant themes.

The first is the relative weakness of the indigenous Mālikī tradition. There are few echoes in these commentaries of the oldest stratum of Mālikī literature on forbidding wrong;[117] a rare exception is the commentary on Khalīl of the Andalusian Mawwāq (d. 897/1492), who adduces several views from Mālik.[118] We hear more of the three-condition schema of Bājī and Ibn Rushd; though it has no roots in the original Mālikī heritage, it could be described as Mālikī by association.[119] As a doctrinal complex, it proved a good survivor, and as such an exception to the rule. Outside the commentaries, we have already noted its adoption by ʿUqbānī;[120] to him we can add the well-known Egyptian scholars Qarāfī (d. 684/1285)[121] and Ibn al-Ḥājj (d. 737/1336f.),[122] together with Ibn Zakrī of Tlemsen

[114] Cf. above, ch. 3, note 7.

[115] Khalīl ibn Isḥāq, *Mukhtaṣar*, 111.5. He has nothing of substance to say about it.

[116] On these commentaries, see the introduction to I. Guidi and D. Santillana (trans.), *Il 'Muḫtaṣar' o Sommario del diritto malechita di Ḫalīl ibn Isḥāq*, Milan 1919, 1:x.

[117] Cf. above, note 93.

[118] Mawwāq (d. 897/1492), *al-Tāj wa'l-iklīl*, in the margin of Ḥaṭṭāb (d. 954/1547), *Mawāhib al-jalīl*, Cairo 1328–9, 3:348.16 (these views are already familiar to us, see above, notes 11, 15, 22, 13 respectively). Mawwāq gives his main source as Ibn Yūnus (al-Ṣaqalī) (d. 451/1059), for whom see Sezgin, *Geschichte*, 1:467, 471 no. 4. The third view, on rebuking one's parents, also appears in Laqānī, *Hidāya*, f. 283a.4. Note also the saying of Mālik bearing on emigration quoted in Ubbī (d. 827/1423f.), *Ikmāl Ikmāl al-Muʿlim*, ed. M. S. Hāshim, Beirut 1994, 1:252.15 (cf. above, note 24).

[119] For this schema, see above, notes 32, 37.

[120] See above, note 80, with explicit reference to the works of Ibn Rushd. For an echo in Ibn al-Munāṣif, see above, 94.

[121] Qarāfī, *Furūq*, 4:255.18.

[122] Ibn al-Ḥājj (d. 737/1336f.), *Madkhal*, Cairo 1929, 1:70.22, with explicit reference to Ibn Rushd's *Bayān*. He adds a fourth condition (*ibid.*, 71.12). For the genre to which the *Madkhal* belongs, see Fierro, 'The treatises against innovations (*kutub al-bidaʿ*)', esp. 207–9. It is not the practice of the authors of these works to include general accounts of *al-amr bi'l-maʿrūf*; for the doctrine that might be extrapolated from the oldest of them,

(d. 900/1494f.).[123] Among the commentators on the 'three modes' tradition, the schema is included by Fākihānī,[124] and has an echo in Shabrakhītī.[125] It is the central and most stable element in the late Egyptian commentaries and supercommentaries on Khalīl,[126] though two of them remark that one of the conditions is logically redundant.[127] In their commentaries to Laqānī's creed, both father and son adduce the schema.[128] From them it was inherited by the Shāfiʿite Bājūrī (d. 1276/1860) in his commentary on Laqānī's creed[129] – an unusual but not isolated instance of Mālikī material penetrating Shāfiʿite scholarship.[130] The indications are that it is Ibn Rushd rather than Bājī who lies behind all this.[131] From the relative success of this schema, we might be led to expect that the other distinctive feature of the doctrine of Ibn Rushd, his view that the duty is an individual and not a collective one, would have achieved a similar acceptance from Mālikī posterity. This, however, was not the case. Although Ibn Rushd's prestige seems to have exerted some pull on later scholars,[132] the

that of the Andalusian Ibn Waḍḍāḥ (d. 287/900), see his *Bidaʿ*, 104f. of the editor's introduction.

123 He deploys the schema in a responsum directed against the destruction of the Jewish synagogues of Tuwāt undertaken by Maghīlī (d. 909/1503f.) (Wansharīsī (d. 914/1508), *al-Miʿyār al-muʿrib*, ed. M. Ḥajjī *et al.*, Rabat 1981, 2:223.25). For the background to this controversy, see J. O. Hunwick, 'Al-Ma[g]hîlî and the Jews of Tuwât: the demise of a community', *Studia Islamica*, 61 (1985); for Ibn Zakrī, see *ibid.*, 172.

124 Fākihānī, *Manhaj*, f. 96a.19. The source is likely to be Ibn Rushd, since Fākihānī quotes him on performing the duty to one's parents (*ibid.*, f. 96b.13; cf. above, note 36).

125 Shabrakhītī (d. 1106/1694f.), *al-Futūḥāt al-wahbiyya bi-sharḥ al-Arbaʿīn al-Nawawiyya*, Cairo 1280, 477.12.

126 ʿAbd al-Bāqī al-Zurqānī, *Sharḥ*, 3:108.17; Kharashī (d. 1101/1690), *Sharḥ*, Būlāq 1317–18, 3:109.21; Dardīr (d. 1201/1786), *al-Sharḥ al-kabīr*, Cairo 1292, 1:261.19; Ṣāwī (d. 1241/1825f.), *Bulghat al-sālik*, Cairo 1952, 1:355.21; Ṣāliḥ ʿAbd al-Samīʿ al-Ābī (fourteenth/twentieth century), *Jawāhir al-iklīl*, Cairo n.d., 1:251.25. For a western commentary which includes the schema, but adds two further conditions, see Muḥammad al-Amīn ibn Aḥmad Zaydān al-Jakanī (d. *c.* 1325/1907), *Sharḥ*, ed. Ḥ. ʿA. M. Aḥmad Zaydān, Beirut 1993, 2:289.1 (this author is said by his grandson to have been much given to *al-amr biʾl-maʿrūf*, *ibid.*, 1:14.15). The three-condition schema is the only element retained from the commentaries in Guidi and Santillana, *Il 'Muḫtaṣar'*, 1:386f. no. 6.

127 Zurqānī, *Sharḥ*, 3:108.19; Dasūqī (d. 1230/1815), *Ḥāshiya*, Cairo n.d., 2:174.19 (*lā yakhfā anna ẓann al-ifāda yastalzim ʿadam al-taʾdiya ilā munkar akbar minhu*).

128 Ibrāhīm al-Laqānī, *Hidāya*, ff. 281a.1, 281b.3, 282a.19, 282b.9 (with much interpolated material), citing Qarāfī; ʿAbd al-Salām ibn Ibrāhīm al-Laqānī (d. 1078/1668), *Itḥāf al-murīd*, Cairo 1955, 262.8. In general, Mālikī creeds (like Sunnī creeds at large) tend not to refer to *al-amr biʾl-maʿrūf*; for an exception which could be reckoned either Mālikī or Shāfiʿite, see above, ch. 13, note 72.

129 Bājūrī, *Tuḥfa*, 203.1.

130 For another example, see above, ch. 13, note 98.

131 See above, notes 120, 122, 124; likewise Bannānī (d. 1163/1750) in his comments on Zurqānī's *Sharḥ* identifies the schema as Ibn Rushd's (*Ḥāshiya*, in the margin of Zurqānī, *Sharḥ*, 3:108.12, with a reference to Ibn Rushd, *Bayān*, 9:360.13).

132 As we have seen, Ibn al-Munāṣif tends to describe the duty as an individual one (see above, note 95), as does ʿUqbānī (see above, notes 88 and 95). Cf. also Qarāfī, *Furūq*, 4:256.1, where no general statement is made on the question. Contrast the much stronger influence of Abū Jaʿfar al-Ṭūsī (d. 460/1067) among his fellow-Imāmīs on this issue (see above, ch. 11, 274).

usual view among Mālikīs, as among others, is that forbidding wrong is a collective duty (though one that becomes individualised under certain conditions).[133]

As might be expected, the weakness of the Mālikī tradition is also evident in the adoption of Shāfiʿite material – a dependence we have already noted in Ibn al-Munāṣif and ʿUqbānī.[134] Thus our commentators quote Māwardī (d. 450/1058),[135] Juwaynī (d. 478/1085),[136] Āmidī (d. 631/1233),[137] Subkī (d. 771/1370)[138] and Taftazānī (d. 793/1390).[139] But the Shāfiʿite on whom they draw most often is not, as one might have expected, Ghazzālī,[140] but rather Nawawī. Leaving aside the commentary of Ibn Daqīq al-ʿĪd (d. 702/1302), who was both a Mālikī and a Shāfiʿite,[141] the first Mālikī I have noted who is heavily dependent on Nawawī is Fākihānī; at one point he quotes and approves a purple passage by Nawawī on the decay of the duty.[142] Ubbī in his exposition of the 'three modes' tradition draws considerably more material from Nawawī than he does from his fellow-Mālikī ʿIyāḍ – for all that he presents his work as a revision of the latter's.[143]

[133] For the Koranic exegetes, see above, notes 52f.; for Khalīl, see above, note 115; see also Aḥmad ibn ʿUmar al-Qurṭubī (d. 656/1258), *Mufhim*, Damascus and Beirut 1996, 1:233.17, 234.3; Fākihānī, *Manhaj*, f. 96a.1; Ubbī, *Ikmāl*, 1:251.16, paraphrasing Nawawī, *Sharḥ Ṣaḥīḥ Muslim*, 1:382.13; Ibrāhīm al-Laqānī, *Hidāya*, f. 279a.11; ʿAbd al-Salām al-Laqānī, *Itḥāf*, 261.18.

[134] See above, 369f., 371f., and cf. note 71. Dependence on the east had, of course, been a feature of the western receptions of both Mālikism and Ashʿarism.

[135] Fākihānī, *Manhaj*, ff. 97a.11, 98a.23 (both through Nawawī); Shabrakhītī, *Futūḥāt*, 477.23 (from Nawawī?).

[136] Ubbī, *Ikmāl*, 1:253.7 (through Nawawī); Mawwāq, *Tāj*, 3:348.10 (a sequence of quotations from the *Irshād*, very likely direct); Ibrāhīm al-Laqānī, *Hidāya*, ff. 280b.6, 281a.3 (perhaps largely but not entirely through Nawawī). For the early transmission of Juwaynī's *Irshād* in the Muslim west, see J. M. Fórneas, 'De la transmisión de algunas obras de tendencia aš ʿarī en al-Andalus', *Awrāq*, 1 (1978), 7f. no. 5a (I am indebted to Maribel Fierro for bringing this article to my attention and sending me a copy). There was a copy of the *Irshād* in the mosque library of Qayrawān in 693/1294 (see I. Shabbūḥ, 'Sijill qadīm li-maktabat jāmiʿ al-Qayrawān', *Majallat Maʿhad al-Makhṭūṭāt al-ʿArabiyya*, 2 (1956), 364 no. 93). For Juwaynī's account of *al-amr biʾl-maʿrūf*, see above, ch. 13, 345f.

[137] For Ibrāhīm al-Laqānī's quotations from Āmidī, see above, ch. 13, note 81; he acknowledges that he has the first quotation noted there through the *Shāmil* of the western Mālikī Ibn ʿArafa (d. 803/1401) (for this work, cf. Brockelmann, *Geschichte*, supplementary volumes, 2:347).

[138] Shabrakhītī, *Futūḥāt*, 479.16.

[139] Ibrāhīm al-Laqānī, *Hidāya*, 279a.12, the first of many citations.

[140] Cf. above, 369f., 371f. Our commentators ignore him.

[141] See above, ch. 13, notes 72, 108.

[142] Fākihānī, *Manhaj*, f. 98b.9, quoting Nawawī, *Sharḥ*, 1:383.21. He includes a substantial quotation from ʿIyāḍ which, ironically, he is likely to owe to Nawawī (Fākihānī, *Manhaj*, f. 98a.8, to be compared with Nawawī, *Sharḥ*, 1:385.6; the quotation begins and ends at exactly the same point in both sources).

[143] Ubbī, *Ikmāl*, 1:250.9–254.10 (where Ubbī marks the provenance of his material with appropriate sigla). The title *Ikmāl Ikmāl al-Muʿlim* places the work in the tradition of ʿIyāḍ's *Ikmāl al-Muʿlim*.

The elder Laqānī likewise quotes Nawawī.[144] An anonymous but relatively recent Mauritanian epistle draws on Nawawī's purple passage.[145] That such material should flow between the two schools is not surprising; in addition to their shared Ashʿarism, they were in continuing contact in Egypt. That the flow is overwhelmingly from the Shāfiʿites to the Mālikīs[146] is also not hard to explain: it reflects on the one hand the relative provinciality of the Mālikī west, and on the other the dominance of Shāfiʿism in the crucial Egyptian context.

Was anything of substance at stake in this process of easternisation? I have noted only two cases of clearcut doctrinal differences. The first is the question whether the duty is individual or collective. Here imported Shāfiʿite material may have helped to deny a future to Ibn Rushd's unusual view that the duty is primarily an individual one.[147] In this case, then, the imported views represented the mainstream of Islamic thought against a western anomaly. In the second case, the question was whether to maintain the efficacy condition; here the roles were reversed. According to Ibn Rushd's three-condition schema, prospective efficacy is a necessary condition for obligation;[148] as we have seen, this schema was rather successful in the west,[149] and at the same time its inclusion of the efficacy condition is standard doctrine. Nawawī, on the other hand, insisted that there was no such condition.[150] Nawawī's view appears in four of the Mālikī sources I have used: in all three of the commentaries on the 'three modes' tradition that postdate Nawawī's,[151] and in the elder Laqānī's exposition of his own creed.[152] But these authors do not show much awareness of the problem this

144 Ibrāhīm al-Laqānī, *Hidāya*, ff. 279a.16, 279a.19, 280a.16, 283b.13, and cf. 282b.4.

145 Anon., *Risāla fī 'l-amr bi'l-maʿrūf wa'l-nahy ʿan al-munkar*, Institut Mauritanien de Recherche Scientifique, Nouakchott, ms. 2,764, 9.10 (there is also a quotation from Ghazzālī at 9.19). For this manuscript, see C. Stewart *et al.*, *General catalogue of Arabic manuscripts at the Institut Mauritanien de Recherche Scientifique*, Urbana and Nouakchott 1992, 3:287 no. 2,565. The title is merely a cataloguer's description, though apt; the addressees are the Banū Daymān (as at 1.20; for this Berber-speaking scholarly lineage, see H. T. Norris, 'Muslim Sanhāja scholars of Mauritania', in J. R. Willis (ed.), *Studies in West African Islamic history*, vol. 1, London 1979, 147, 155f., 158f.). I am indebted to Maribel Fierro for sending me a copy from a microfiche in the library of the Instituto de Cooperación con el Mundo Árabe, Madrid. I have not been able to make out much of the text.

146 For counter-examples, see above, note 130. Another instance is a quotation from a commentary on Muslim by an Andalusian which appears in two Shāfiʿite works (Ibn Faraḥ al-Ishbīlī, *Sharḥ al-Arbaʿīn*, f. 64a.18, and Ibn Ḥajar al-Haytamī, *Fatḥ al-mubīn*, 248.21, both citing Aḥmad al-Qurṭubī, *Mufhim*, 1:232.17). 147 Cf. above, notes 132f.

148 See above, 363f. (but note Bājī's qualification, above, note 34).

149 See above, note 80 and 374f.

150 See above, ch. 13, 352f. Compare the view of Mālik's cited above, note 11.

151 Fākihānī, *Manhaj*, f. 97b.8; Ubbī, *Ikmāl*, 1:252.12 (from Nawawī); Shabrakhītī, *Futūḥāt*, 480.20. 152 Ibrāhīm al-Laqānī, *Hidāya*, f. 282b.5 (quoting Nawawī).

poses. Fākihānī and Shabrakhītī simply include the two views at different points in their commentaries without noting the disagreement.[153] For Ubbī the issue does not arise, since he does not quote the three-condition schema; he does, however, indicate a commitment to Nawawī's position by adducing and refuting Zamakhsharī's contrary view.[154] Laqānī presents Nawawī's view within the framework of the three-condition schema, and seems not to distinguish it from weakened forms of the efficacy condition.[155]

A final question worth raising about these commentators is the degree of activism they espouse. On the virtue of heroism they are divided. ʿIyāḍ has no patience for heroism, and waxes polemical against those who think otherwise;[156] he perhaps has in mind his contemporary Ibn al-ʿArabī.[157] Qarāfī, on the other hand, strongly favours it.[158] With regard to recourse to arms, all the authors who discuss the issue insist that the matter be referred to the authorities;[159] here ʿIyāḍ is in agreement with Ibn al-ʿArabī.[160] More than among the Shāfiʿites,[161] the tripartite division of labour is occasionally mentioned with at least implicit approval.[162] But Ibn al-Ḥājj points out that, while the saying may hold in general, there are many instances in which someone who is neither in authority nor a scholar may be obligated to take physical action.[163]

The last genre we need to consider under the heading of Mālikī doctrine is the monographic treatment of the duty. The earliest such work I know of was by a certain Abū Ṭālib ʿUmar ibn al-Rabīʿ al-Khashshāb (d. 345/

153 Fākihānī, *Manhaj*, ff. 96a.23, 97b.8; Shabrakhītī, *Futūḥāt*, 477.17, 480.20.

154 Ubbī, *Ikmāl*, 1:252.13. The quotation from Zamakhsharī does not resemble the latter's statement of the efficacy condition in his commentary to Q3:104 (*Kashshāf*, 1:397.15).

155 Contrast the Shāfiʿite Bājūrī, who in his commentary to Laqānī's creed underlines the disagreement (see above, ch. 13, note 111).

156 ʿIyāḍ, *Ikmāl*, f. 45a.27, 45b.6 (taking a stand against *man raʾā ʾl-inkār biʾl-taṣrīḥ bi-kull ḥāl wa-in qutila wa-nīla minhu kull adhā*), whence Nawawī, *Sharḥ Ṣaḥīḥ Muslim*, 1:385.12, 385.17, and Ubbī, *Ikmāl*, 1:252.24.

157 See above, 366.

158 Qarāfī, *Furūq*, 4:257.17; Ibrāhīm al-Laqānī quotes from this passage (*Hidāya*, f. 281b.6). Ibn al-Ḥājj likewise permits heroism (*Madkhal*, 1:71.12).

159 ʿIyāḍ, *Ikmāl*, f. 45b.3, whence Aḥmad al-Qurṭubī, *Mufhim*, 1:234.5, Nawawī, *Sharḥ*, 1:385.15, and Ubbī, *Ikmāl*, 1:252.23; Shabrakhītī, *Futūḥāt*, 478.22.

160 See above, 367.

161 See above, ch. 13, note 141, for my only Shāfiʿite example.

162 *Ibid.*, 482.5; ʿAdawī (d. 1189/1775), *Ḥāshiya*, in the margins of Kharashī, *Sharḥ*, 3:110.5. A letter from the ruler of Bornu which was received in Cairo in 794/1391f. sets out the division of labour (Qalqashandī (d. 821/1418), *Ṣubḥ al-aʿshā*, Cairo 1913–19, 8:118.12, translated in J. F. P. Hopkins and N. Levtzion, *Corpus of early Arabic sources for West African history*, Cambridge 1981, 348; I take the passages printed in parentheses to be the ruler's glosses on the text he is quoting). ʿAbd al-Qādir al-Jazāʾirī (d. 1300/1883) sets out the tripartite division of labour as if it were standard doctrine (*al-Mawāqif fī ʾl-taṣawwuf waʾl-waʿẓ waʾl-irshād*, Damascus 1966–7, 294.6, 1284.26; I owe these references to Itzchak Weismann). ʿAbd al-Qādir clearly thinks of the third mode as performance within the heart (*ibid.*, 294.12), whereas Shabrakhītī states that action by the heart involves the manifestation of disapproval (*Futūḥāt*, 481.4).

163 Ibn al-Ḥājj, *Madkhal*, 1:70.18.

956f.); some seventeen passages from it are quoted by the Damascene Ḥanbalite Zayn al-Dīn al-Ṣāliḥī (d. 856/1452).[164] The author was an Egyptian and seems to have been a Mālikī, though I lack conclusive indications on the latter point.[165] The next known author of a monograph is the Toledan ascetic Abū Muḥammad ibn Dhunayn (d. 424/1032f.); himself a devotee of the duty, he composed a work (*dīwān*) on it of which we have only the title.[166] Thereafter there is a gap until ʿUthmān dan Fodio (d. 1232/1817), the founder of the Sokoto caliphate in what is now northern Nigeria; a pamphlet of his on the subject is extant, and though I have not seen it, its content is clearly doctrinal.[167] Of these works, the only one on which I have more to say is that of ʿUmar ibn al-Rabīʿ.[168]

164 Ṣāliḥī, *Kanz*, 131.16, 187.5, 188.5, 188.21, 206.13, 207.2, 222.22, 240.15, 250.9, 258.2 – probably resumed at 259.15 – 262.16, 560.16, 650.11, 674.19, 683.15, 837.25, and cf. 236.15, 733.17. The full form of the author's name appears *ibid.*, 188.5, 650.11. In five of the passages (*ibid.*, 187.5, 222.22, 240.15, 258.2 (read *kitābihi*, as in ms. Fatih 1,136, f. 90a.8), 674.19) Ṣāliḥī uses the phrase *fī kitābihi al-Amr biʾl-maʿrūf* (*waʾl-nahy ʿan al-munkar*) to refer to the work; this establishes its monographic character and title. Was Ṣāliḥī's access to it direct? His mention of a *bāb al-inkār ʿalā aṣḥāb al-malāhī* (*Kanz*, 262.17) is a weak indication that it was. It is usually but not always clear where the quotations end.

165 My only significant source of biographical information on him is Ibn Ḥajar, *Lisān*, 4:304–6 no. 854. From this I take him to be Egyptian because he died in Egypt (*ibid.*, 306.1) and transmitted to the Egyptian Ḥasan ibn Ismāʿīl al-Ḍarrāb (d. 392/1002) (*ibid.*, 304.19; for Ibn al-Ḍarrāb, see Sezgin, *Geschichte*, 1:213 no. 262); and I take him to be Mālikī because of his appearance in two works on *gharāʾib Mālik* (Ibn Ḥajar, *Lisān*, 4:304.19, 305.3). Stray references given by Maqrīzī (d. 845/1442) confirm that he was Egyptian: he is described as *imām jāmiʿ Miṣr* (*Muqaffā*, ed. M. Yaʿlāwī, Beirut 1991, 1:515.13), and a younger traditionist heard from him in Egypt (*ibid.*, 6:274.11; I was put on the track of these references by Maribel Fierro).

166 Ibn Bashkuwāl (d. 578/1183), *Ṣila*, ed. ʿI. al-ʿAṭṭār, Cairo 1955, 258.1 (giving the title as *Kitāb al-amr waʾl-nahy*), cited in Chalmeta, *El 'señor del zoco'*, 405 no. 50. On Ibn Dhunayn, see M. Marín, 'Familias de ulemas en Toledo', *Estudios onomástico-biográficos de al-Andalus*, vol. 5, Madrid 1992, 252.

167 See B. Y. Muhammad and J. Hunwick, *Handlists of Islamic manuscripts: Nigeria*, section 1, *The Nigerian National Archives: Kaduna State*, vol. 1, London 1995, 75 no. 191 (drawn to my attention by Maribel Fierro); also J. O. Hunwick, *The writings of central Sudanic Africa* (= *Arabic literature of Africa*, vol. 2), Leiden 1995, 59 no. 2. The text as described by the cataloguers opens with the words: 'As for the proofs of the obligatoriness of *al-amr biʾl-maʿrūf*. . .'

168 I have not attempted to cover works that are exercises in performing the duty rather than expositions of it. Examples of such works are a pair of recent Mauritanian texts by Aḥmad al-Karīm ibn al-Mukhtār ibn Ziyād (writing *c.* 1398/1978) catalogued in U. Rebstock, *Sammlung arabischer Handschriften aus Mauretanien*, Wiesbaden 1989, 53 nos. 630f. (both in the possession of al-Mukhtār ibn Bābā al-Ḥājjī, Dār al-Barka). The first, described as a *Risāla ṭawīla fī ʾl-ḥathth ʿalā ʾl-maʿrūf waʾl-nahy ʿan al-munkar*, is much concerned about the twin wrongs committed by men who shave their beards and women who dress improperly. The second, described as a *Naẓm fī ʾl-amr biʾl-maʿrūf waʾl-nahy ʿan al-munkar*, is a verse treatment of such themes; it includes a section devoted specifically to *al-amr biʾl-maʿrūf* which, however, says nothing of interest (*Naẓm*, ff. 11a–12a; the work is followed in the manuscript by endorsements from other scholars, including one dated 1399/1979 and another dated 1400/1980, *ibid.*, ff. 15b.9, 18a.12). I am indebted to Frank Stewart for drawing my attention to these items, and to Ulrich Rebstock for sending me copies and supplying me with further information.

Ibn al-Rabīʿ's monograph may well have been a comprehensive treatment of the duty. Ṣāliḥī quotes him on a variety of topics. Thus in one passage he condemns any attempt to evade the obligation by misinterpreting scripture (*ta'wīl*); in another he avers that forbidding wrong carries a greater reward than holy war, since saving Muslims from sinning and going to hell is more meritorious than fighting the infidel.[169] But for whatever reason, the bulk of the material that Ṣāliḥī quotes from Ibn al-Rabīʿ is concentrated in a single area: the duty of ordinary Muslims with regard to commonplace wrongs as limited by the role of the authorities on the one hand and the claims of privacy on the other.[170] To begin with the authorities, punishment is for them alone to inflict.[171] They also have a fairly extensive duty of raiding wrongdoers in their homes. This applies if the offenders are gathering to drink liquor, or selling it, or making music that is audible to the Muslims in their homes and streets – activities that amount to holding the faithful in contempt.[172] But where the nuisance is confined to the wrongdoer's own abode, and no criminal offence against others is involved, the demands of privacy come first: the believer's home (*bayt al-mu'min*) is then his castle (*ḥirz lahu*).[173]

Where does this leave the ordinary believers? In the first place, they have a duty of admonition (*waʿẓ*) which applies whether or not the wrongdoing is private. They should respond in this way whether the music is audible or inaudible,[174] whether the offence is open profanity in the streets[175] or something between the sinners and God.[176] In the second place, where admonition is insufficient, they have a duty to bring the wrongdoing to the notice of the authorities, provided the latter can be expected to act within

[169] Ṣāliḥī, *Kanz*, 131.16, 206.13. The second passage continues with an exposition of the idea that in *al-amr bi'l-maʿrūf* one man should be willing to take on two (cf. above, ch. 4, note 196). For the first theme, see also *ibid.*, 837.25 (for *al-sā'il* read *al-ta'wīl*, with ms. Berlin, Landberg 167, f. 150a.9). Other themes treated are the efficacy and danger conditions (*ibid.*, 650.11, with reference also to absence of helpers), and the duty of the weak to emigrate from lands in which they are unable to right manifest wrongs (*ibid.*, 683.15); God will not recognise weakness (*ḍaʿf*) as an excuse for those who fail to do their duty (*ibid.*, 207.2).

[170] I leave aside a discussion of musical instruments in the hands of the *dhimmīs* (*ibid.*, 222.22), and another concerned with the object-specific grounds for breaking or not breaking musical instruments, wine-bottles and the like (*ibid.*, 258.2, 259.15). Here Ibn al-Rabīʿ makes the tart observation that the only known alternative use for musical instruments is as firewood (*ibid.*, 259.20); but he makes room for the tambourine in the usual fashion (*ibid.*, 258.3). [171] *Ibid.*, 188.14, 241.6, 262.24.

[172] *Ibid.*, 188.10, 241.4, 262.21. The phrase *istikhfāf bi'l-Muslimīn* appears *ibid.*, 241.8, 262.20.

[173] *Ibid.*, 188.18 (read *yahjumū* for *yajmaʿū*, with ms. Istanbul, Süleymaniye, Fatih 1,136, f. 62a.6), 240.22. [174] *Ibid.*, 262.18, 262.22.

[175] *Ibid.*, 188.21. There is no obligation to admonish if the man is not the kind who will listen. [176] *Ibid.*, 188.18.

the bounds of the law.[177] This duty, however, is limited by the demands of privacy: it applies to drinking-parties, profanity in the streets, the sale of wine in homes and audible music,[178] but not where the offence is between the offenders and God.[179] Finally, there is the duty of ordinary believers to take direct action. This applies where they are unable to secure the attention of the authorities, and may thus have the duty of taking action to break up a liquor party, or raiding the homes of people making audible music.[180] They likewise have a duty to act in emergencies, raiding homes where rape or murder is about to be committed,[181] answering calls for help against violence, and even killing the aggressor where necessary.[182] But they also have a regular right or duty to take action in the markets and streets, be it against the sale of liquor,[183] or the carrying or sale of musical instruments.[184]

There is nothing very unusual about the concerns of Ibn al-Rabīʿ as displayed in this limited corpus of material. But it does suggest that his book, which has no echoes in Mālikī literature, may have represented a more comprehensive and impressive account of the duty than any other we have considered in this chapter.

4. MĀLIKĪ PRACTICE

The Mālikī practice of forbidding wrong begins with Mālik himself in Medina. Most of what we are told about him concerns his relations with the authorities. Contrary to what one might have expected, the tone of the sources is not straightforwardly hagiographical. Within the school, of course, we hear only good news; yet even here, there is an undertone of embarrassment, as if the impression had to be avoided that Mālik mixed too often and too easily with those in power. There is a concern to show that Mālik made no concessions to the corrupting and intimidating ambience of the caliphal presence, and that in any case his visits were justified by the results. Mālik caught Hārūn al-Rashīd (r. 170–93/786–809) in the act of playing chess, and rebuked him to good effect.[185] His predecessor al-Manṣūr (r. 136–58/754–75) had asked Mālik to let him know of any

177 *Ibid.*, 187.5, 188.6. 178 *Ibid.*, 188.5, 188.21, 241.3, 262.18. 179 *Ibid.*, 188.18.
180 *Ibid.*, 188.8, 262.22. *A fortiori* they have the right or duty to act thus if the authorities order them to do so (*ibid.*, 188.12, 241.5, and cf. 560.16). 181 *Ibid.*, 188.15.
182 *Ibid.*, 250.10, 250.17. He speaks here of the duty of the Muslim community (*jamāʿat al-Muslimīn*, a term that also appears *ibid.*, 258.17).
183 *Ibid.*, 241.7; cf. also *ibid.*, 258.18 (defective and corrupt, see ms. Fatih 1,136, f. 90a.22), 259.15.
184 *Ibid.*, 259.15; cf. also *ibid.*, 250.13, where no limitation to public places is mentioned or implied. 185 ʿIyāḍ, *Madārik*, 1:208.7.

undesirable actions on the part of his governors;[186] he was to forbid them wrong, and they were to comply.[187] Less grandiosely, Mālik protested that if he did not visit the authorities, not a single normative custom (*sunna*) of the Prophet would be put into practice in Medina.[188] And not to worry: he swore that whenever he went in to see someone in authority, it was God's habit to remove from his heart the awe that such figures inspire, and enable him to come out with the truth.[189]

Thus far the Mālikī version. Outside the school, we encounter an image that is different, but not wholly unexpected. It takes the form of an unfavourable comparison between Mālik and the Medinese traditionist Ibn Abī Dhiʾb (d. 159/775f.). In the presence of the authorities (*umarāʾ*), we are told, Ibn Abī Dhiʾb would speak out, commanding and forbidding; meanwhile Mālik would say nothing.[190] With this we can compare Mālik's response to the question why he absented himself from the Friday prayer for twenty-five years: he feared that he might see some offence (*munkar*) and have to take action against it (*an ughayyirahu*).[191] In sum, Mālik's record in commanding and forbidding was at best ambivalent.

Against this background, the practice of forbidding wrong in the next stage of Mālikī history is surprisingly robust. This is roughly the period from the late second/eighth to the early fourth/tenth century. The bulk of the evidence concerns scholars living in the cities of Ifrīqiya, above all Qayrawān; but I shall also include some material from other regions, particularly Spain and Egypt. The context is overwhelmingly urban: when the inhabitants of Toledo found the devotion of Ibn ʿUbayd (*fl.* first third of the fourth/tenth century) to the duty too much to bear, he retired to a village.[192] It is unfortunate that this is a period for which we have little doctrinal treatment of the duty.

We can begin with the range of offences encountered in this literature. They are hardly exotic. The commonest have to do with music, whether the offenders actually make it[193] or merely carry around the means for

[186] *Ibid.*, 209.12. [187] *Ibid.*, 209.19. [188] *Ibid.*, 208.14 (reading *ākhiran* for *ākhar*).
[189] *Ibid.*, 208.12
[190] Ibn Ḥanbal, *ʿIlal*, 1:511 no. 1195, and Fasawī, *Maʿrifa*, 1:686.12, 686.17 (both sources cited in van Ess, *Theologie*, 2:684f.); also Khaṭīb, *Taʾrīkh Baghdād*, 2:302.12, 302.16 (with haplography); Ibn Abī Yaʿlā, *Ṭabaqāt*, 1:251.15, 251.18; Mizzī, *Tahdhīb*, 25:638.4, 638.9; Dhahabī, *Siyar*, 7:148.9. The direct or indirect authority for this material is Ibn Ḥanbal (d. 241/855). For Ibn Abī Dhiʾb, see above, ch. 4, 56.
[191] Dhahabī, *Siyar*, 8:66.16, from Abū Muṣʿab (d. 242/857).
[192] ʿIyāḍ, *Madārik*, 4:458.2.
[193] Mālikī, *Riyāḍ*, 381.16 (concerning Qayrawān in the period 261–75/875–88f.); *ibid.*, 393.7 (Sūsa in approximately the same period); ʿIyāḍ, *Madārik*, 3:231.23 (Qayrawān in the mid-third/ninth century).

doing so.[194] Wine-drinking, surprisingly, is not prominent,[195] and other offences appear only sporadically: robbing a woodcutter of his wood,[196] doing something wrong at a funeral,[197] following a noisy and innovatory religious practice,[198] engaging in sexual misconduct,[199] abducting a girl.[200] One scholar went so far as to upbraid another for failing to rebuke (*lā tunkir wa-lā tughayyir*) his brother, who had just come in from the countryside, and was talking endlessly in a religious circle about matters of rain and grain.[201] The contexts in which these offences are met with are usually implicitly or explicitly public;[202] this would apply even in a case where a passing scholar heard the noise of singing coming from a private house while on his way to the mosque.[203] In two cases, both involving music, the scene is no less than the residence of the ruler.[204]

As to the manner of performing the duty, it is often verbal, as in the case of the polite insistence with which the passing scholar dealt with the singing he encountered on the way to the mosque. Indeed one anecdote equates forbidding wrong with preaching (*wa'ẓ*).[205] But methods varied. While one scholar is said to have performed the duty nicely,[206] another seized and smashed a lute or mandolin.[207] Performance is normally by

194 Abū 'l-'Arab al-Tamīmī (d. 333/945), *Ṭabaqāt 'ulamā' Ifrīqiya wa-Tūnis*, ed. 'A. al-Shābbī and N. Ḥ. al-Yāfī, Tunis 1968, 201.4 (= Mālikī, *Riyāḍ*, 303.7) (first half of the third/ninth century); Khushanī (d. 361/971), *Quḍāt Qurṭuba*, ed. 'I. al-'Aṭṭār al-Ḥusaynī, n.p. 1372, 142.7 (later third/ninth century).

195 It is mentioned alongside music-making as an offence that was unknown in Sūsa in the good old days, apparently up to the second half of the third/ninth century (Mālikī, *Riyāḍ*, 394.6); and it appears in association with singing in a story of mid-third/ninth-century Qayrawān ('Iyāḍ, *Madārik*, 3:232.3).

196 Abū 'l-'Arab, *Ṭabaqāt*, 123.1 (mid-second/eighth century).

197 Mālikī, *Riyāḍ*, 276.2, and 'Iyāḍ, *Madārik*, 2:599.10 (first half of the third/ninth century). The offence is not specified, but probably related to improper mourning.

198 For Yaḥyā ibn 'Umar's unsuccessful reproof to certain silk-workers of Qayrawān in such a connection, see Mālikī, *Riyāḍ*, 401.19. As pointed out to me by Maribel Fierro, Ṭurṭūshī quotes the passage from Mālikī with the addition of the remark that Yaḥyā was zealous (*shadīd*) in *al-amr bi'l-ma'rūf* (Ṭurṭūshī (d. 520/1126), *al-Ḥawādith wa'l-bida'*, ed. 'A. Turkī, Beirut 1990, 260 no. 231 = trans. Fierro, 315 no. 231).

199 'Iyāḍ, *Madārik*, 3:360.19 (early fourth/tenth century).

200 Khushanī, *Quḍāt*, 108.3 (towards the middle of the third/ninth century).

201 Abū 'l-'Arab, *Ṭabaqāt*, 127.9 = Mālikī, *Riyāḍ*, 213.1 (mid-second/eighth century). The pietist in turn was rebuked, and accepted the rebuke.

202 Cf. the explicit concern of the second/eighth-century scholar Rabāḥ ibn Yazīd with *public* offences (Abū 'l-'Arab, *Ṭabaqāt*, 123.5).

203 'Iyāḍ, *Madārik*, 3:231.23 (mid-third/ninth century).

204 The references are given above, in notes 194f. 205 *Ibid.*, 4:504.22.

206 Dabbāgh, *Ma'ālim*, 2:160.9, on Ibn Ṭālib (d. 275/888f.) (the phrase *layyin al-qawl* is not found in the parallel passages at Mālikī, *Riyāḍ*, 376.12, and 'Iyāḍ, *Madārik*, 3:195.14). Saḥnūn describes the second/eighth-century scholar Ibn Ashras as severe (*shadīd*) in performing the duty (Abū 'l-'Arab, *Ṭabaqāt*, 223.11; Mālikī, *Riyāḍ*, 170.20; 'Iyāḍ, *Madārik*, 1:329.18) – which suggests that he was not particularly nice about it.

207 Abū 'l-'Arab, *Ṭabaqāt*, 201.4; and his *Miḥan*, 467.5; Mālikī, *Riyāḍ*, 303.7 (on Marwān ibn Abī Shaḥma, a contemporary of Saḥnūn).

solitary individuals, though this could prove problematic.[208] However, one Egyptian scholar, ʿĪsā ibn al-Munkadir (d. after 215/830), had a group (*ṭāʾifa*) of companions who forbade wrong with him;[209] likewise the Qayrawānī Ibn bint al-Mahdī (*fl.* early fifth/eleventh century) is said to have had such followers (*atbāʿ*).[210] Some scholars seem to have approached the duty fairly recklessly. One Ifrīqiyan would act the moment he saw an offence, without fear of anybody at all;[211] an eastern Mālikī was killed by the Daylamites while performing the duty.[212] Finally, the last resort of emigration is envisaged by the pietists of Sūsa as they seek to put an end to the music-making of their ruler.[213]

What is striking about this material, at least in Ifrīqiya where it is richest, is how much of it concerns interaction between scholars and rulers. Here, in contrast to the doctrinal literature, the context in which we hear of forbidding wrong is most commonly that of confrontation with the authorities. Buhlūl ibn Rāshid (d. 183/799f.) took exception to an offence committed by some of the governor's men; they ripped his fur garment, but were afterwards officially punished for it.[214] His contemporary Rabāḥ ibn Yazīd stepped in when followers of the same governor were robbing a woodcutter; they set hands on Rabāḥ, and were in turn attacked by bystanders.[215] Marwān ibn Abī Shaḥma, a contemporary of Saḥnūn (d. 240/854), smashed a eunuch's lute or mandolin at court, and when upbraided by the ruler offered no apology.[216] Some seventy pietists of Sūsa, determined to

[208] The Qayrawānī pietist Abū Maysara (d. 337/948f.) chanced on a woman who was letting a man have his way with her. He cried out and went for them, whereupon the man fled; the woman, however, embarrassed him by clinging to him and then claiming that he had tried to seduce her; she left him with the advice not to undertake such action (*lā tughayyir al-munkar*) unless he had someone with him (ʿIyāḍ, *Madārik*, 3:360.19).

[209] Kindī (d. 350/961), *Quḍāt*, in R. Guest (ed.), *The governors and judges of Egypt*, Leiden and London 1912, 440.2; ʿIyāḍ, *Madārik*, 2:583.1. This association had begun before he became *qāḍī* in 212/827, but continued thereafter, with the result that he would interrupt his official duties to go off and take action against abominations reported by these associates. In another connection, his associates are described as ascetics (*ṣūfiyya*, Kindī, *Quḍāt*, 440.15), a circumstance which seems to have disturbed ʿAbdallāh ibn ʿAbd al-Ḥakam (d. 214/829), who sent one of his sons to command and forbid Ibn al-Munkadir over conduct that was causing wide concern; but these efforts were brushed aside by the latter (ʿIyāḍ, *Madārik*, 2:583.13). Another Egyptian of this period, Ashhab ibn ʿAbd al-ʿAzīz (d. 204/820), is described by Saḥnūn as most assiduous in performing the duty (*āmaruhum bi'l-maʿrūf*), but without further details (*ibid.*, 449.8).

[210] *Ibid.*, 4:769.17.

[211] Mālikī, *Riyāḍ*, 239.17, on Ismāʿīl ibn Rabāḥ al-Jazarī (d. 212/827f.).

[212] Abū Isḥāq al-Shīrāzī, *Ṭabaqāt al-fuqahāʾ*, 140.1, on Isḥāq ibn Aḥmad al-Rāzī (d. 335/946) (but cf. the parallel text in ʿIyāḍ, *Madārik*, 4:473.13). I owe this reference to Nurit Tsafrir.

[213] Mālikī, *Riyāḍ*, 393.10, 394.3; cf. above, note 24, and Abū 'l-ʿArab, *Ṭabaqāt*, 123.7.

[214] *Ibid.*, 118.6. [215] *Ibid.*, 123.1.

[216] *Ibid.*, 201.2; and his *Miḥan*, 467.5; Mālikī, *Riyāḍ*, 303.6.

put an end to their ruler's music-making, proceeded to his residence, filled the courtyard, and demanded entry; the ruler capitulated to their wishes.[217] In the same vein it is often observed that this scholar or that was not in fear of the ruler.[218] Not surprisingly, such conduct was regarded as dangerous. Ḥamdīs al-Qaṭṭān, a companion of Saḥnūn, was asked whether he would command and forbid a ruler who sinned; his answer was negative.[219] On the other hand, it is clear that rulers knew the part they were supposed to play in these little dramas. Members of the Aghlabid family, which ruled Ifrīqiya from 184/800 to 296/909, used to visit the blind Abū Muḥammad al-Anṣārī to derive blessing from him. But on one occasion the saint refused to admit Ziyādat Allāh I (r. 201–23/817–38) and his retinue. The enraged ruler responded: 'Listen you, we've come to you so you can command us right, and we then hasten to do it, and forbid us wrong, and we then restrain ourselves from it. But [instead] you've humiliated me and kept me out here, me, your ruler!' His protest was of course in vain, and after further slights he departed, full of appreciation for the saint.[220]

There are even a couple of cases in Ifrīqiya of scholars who associated forbidding wrong with rebellion against unjust rule. One was Ibn Farrūkh (d. 175/791). He at one stage took the view that rebellion against unjust rulers (*a'immat al-jawr*) was appropriate when as many men were gathered together forbidding wrong as were present at the Battle of Badr (2/624); but he later changed his mind. His own attempt at revolt fizzled out when only two men showed up to join him at the appointed place.[221] But Ibn Farrūkh, though adopted into the Mālikī biographical tradition, was a Persian Ḥanafī.[222] A later figure reported to have held such views is

217 *Ibid.*, 393.7.

218 Thus a Mālikī source recollects that the Successor Sa'd ibn Mas'ūd al-Tujībī, sent to Ifrīqiya by 'Umar ibn 'Abd al-'Azīz, was *qalīl al-hayba lil-mulūk fī ḥaqq yaqūluhu* (Mālikī, *Riyāḍ*, 66.16). Similar things are said of others: Ibn Farrūkh (d. 175/791) (*ibid.*, 113.15; Dabbāgh, *Ma'ālim*, 1:238.11); 'Abd al-Khāliq al-Qattāt, a companion of Buhlūl (Mālikī, *Riyāḍ*, 232.4); Ibn Abī Ḥassān al-Yaḥṣubī (d. 227/841f.) ('Iyāḍ, *Madārik*, 2:482.11); Saḥnūn (Abū 'l-'Arab, *Ṭabaqāt*, 184.10; Mālikī, *Riyāḍ*, 249.9, 279.1; 'Iyāḍ, *Madārik*, 2:602.15); and Ibn Ṭālib (Mālikī, *Riyāḍ*, 376.9).

219 *Ibid.*, 395.3. He quotes the Prophetic tradition that a believer should not court humiliation (see above, ch. 3, note 53), and a saying of Mālik cited above, note 16. On the other hand, he believes in *jihād* against a ruler who seeks to impose heresy (*bid'a*) (*ibid.*, 395.7).

220 *Ibid.*, 318.5.

221 'Iyāḍ, *Madārik*, 1:346.7 (I owe this reference to Nurit Tsafrir). Other sources, however, omit the reference to *al-amr bi'l-ma'rūf* (Abū 'l-'Arab, *Ṭabaqāt*, 108.11, 109.1; Mālikī, *Riyāḍ*, 118.3; Dabbāgh, *Ma'ālim*, 1:247.10; Dhahabī, *Ta'rīkh al-Islām*, years 171–80, 215.7, 215.17). Reference to the number of men present at the Battle of Badr in the context of righteous rebellion is more familiar as a Shī'ite idea (see Madelung, *Qāsim*, 91f.; al-Shaykh al-Mufīd (d. 413/1022), *al-Risāla al-thālitha fī 'l-ghayba*, in his *'Iddat rasā'il*, Qumm n.d., 390.2).

222 'Iyāḍ, *Madārik*, 1:346.16; Ibn Abī 'l-Wafā', *Jawāhir*, 1:279f. no. 245.

ʿAbdallāh ibn Muḥammad ibn al-Ashajj (d. 286/899f.); he too seems to have been a Ḥanafī. Summoned before the Aghlabid Ibrāhīm II (r. 261–89/875–902), he explained that he believed in rebellion against unjust rulers given the support of the number of men present at Badr and agreement on an imam; but he did not, he said, hold with righting wrongs by committing worse ones (*taghyīr al-munkar bi-ashadd minhu*).[223]

At the other end of the spectrum, I have not noted any instance of formal cooperation with the authorities in the manner approved by Mālik.[224] The only arguable exception would be the role of Ibn Ṭālib (d. 275/888f.) in Qayrawān. The responsibilities placed upon this scholar by Ibrāhīm II included banishing public immorality from the city, and his impact on the musical life of its inhabitants is said to have been considerable.[225] He was, however, judge of Qayrawān. A negative attitude towards involving the state is enshrined in an anecdote about Muḥammad ibn Waḍḍāḥ (d. 287/900), another figure adopted by the Mālikī biographers. He suffered from a neighbour who used to drink and sing, and considered putting the matter into the hands of the authorities; but he changed his mind on recollecting that in a similar case Saḥnūn had taken no such action.[226]

When we move on to later centuries, we enter a period marked by some significant changes in the geography of the Mālikī law-school. In the north, Spain and its rich urban environments were gradually lost to the Mālikīs, as they were to Islam at large. When Yçe de Chebir of Segovia, writing his 'Brebiario çunní' in Castillian in AD 1462, instructs Muslims to 'stand in the way of those who are disobeying the law or normative custom (*sunna*), because those who commit the sin and those who stand by and do nothing are equal in sin',[227] it is no longer entirely clear that what he has in mind is precisely forbidding wrong. In the south, the large-scale expansion of Mālikī Islam across the Sahara brought it into contact and confrontation with a very different milieu. Just how exotic this could be is indicated by a

223 Dabbāgh, *Maʿālim*, 2:232.6 (I owe this reference to Nurit Tsafrir). For his Ḥanafī affiliation, see M. Ben Cheneb, *Classes des savants de l'Ifrīqīya*, Beirut n.d., 193.14.

224 See above, 361.

225 Mālikī, *Riyāḍ*, 381.15; ʿIyāḍ, *Madārik*, 3:205.12. We are told that Saḥnūn was the first *qāḍī* to give attention to *ḥisba* (in Ifrīqiya), and to order people to take action against offences (Mālikī, *Riyāḍ*, 276.19, and cf. *ibid.*, 279.8; ʿIyāḍ, *Madārik*, 2:600.6).

226 *Ibid.*, 617.8 (cited from manuscript in M. Talbi, 'Kairouan et le malikisme espagnol', in *Etudes d'orientalisme dédiées à la mémoire de Lévi-Provençal*, Paris 1962, 328, which in turn was brought to my attention by Maribel Fierro).

227 'Estorba á los desobedeçedores da la Ley ó Çunna, que hazedores y consentidores yguales son en el peccado' (Yçe de Chebir (writing AD 1462), 'Brebiario çunní', in *Memorial histórico español*, published by the Real Academia de la Historia, vol. 5, Madrid 1853, 252.15, translated in L. P. Harvey, *Islamic Spain 1250–1500*, Chicago and London 1990, 90.

problem regarding the customs of the town of Jenne brought to the notice of the North African jurist Maghīlī (d. 909/1503f.) by the ruler of Songhay: 'All the most beautiful girls walk naked among people with no covering at all.'[228] But the most important development is perhaps one that took place within North Africa itself: the extension of the Mālikī horizon to include the tribal hinterlands. Their religiosity, with its heady combination of Ṣūfism and tribal politics, stands in marked contrast to the urban scholarly milieu with which we have been concerned so far.[229]

In the traditional urban milieu, the practice of the duty doubtless continued in the old way, though the documentation I have seen is less rich than for early Ifrīqiya. We have already encountered the devotion of the Toledan Ibn ʿUbayd to forbidding wrong.[230] Likewise one reason for the troubles Abū ʿUmar al-Ṭalamankī (d. 429/1038) brought upon himself towards the end of his life is said to have been his harsh and ill-natured way of going about the duty (*inkār al-munkar*).[231] A late source says that the well-known scholar Abū ʿImrān al-Fāsī (d. 430/1039) was expelled from Fez by those in power there for forbidding wrong.[232] Ibn al-Zubayr (d. 708/1308) of Jaén is described as undertaking the duty; mention is made of his zeal against heretics and his confrontations (*waqāʾiʿ*) with rulers.[233] Ibn Qunfudh (d. 810/1407f.) describes the efforts of a pious man he met in Fez in righting wrongs (*taghyīr al-munkar*), and the support he enjoyed in this at all levels of society.[234] In 871/1466 the preacher (*khaṭīb*) of a mosque in Oran was replaced because of something the ruler heard that he

228 J. O. Hunwick (ed. and trans.), *Sharīʿa in Songhay: the replies of al-Maghīlī to the questions of Askia al-Ḥājj Muḥammad*, Oxford 1985, 40.10 = 90. Maghīlī characterises this custom as *munkar min akbar al-manākir* (*ibid.*, 46.6 = 95). While he clearly regards this and other offences as primarily a matter for the authorities, he also states that every believer who is able to do so has a duty to act (*an yughayyir tilka 'l-manākir*, *ibid.*, 41.5 = 90).

229 As will be seen, the following paragraphs draw extensively on the body of material assembled and analysed in M. García-Arenal, 'La práctica del precepto de *al-amr bi-l-maʿrūf wa-l-nahy ʿan al-munkar* en la hagiografía magrebí', *Al-Qanṭara*, 13 (1992).

230 See above, note 192; also García-Arenal, 'Práctica', 147. For an earlier Toledan devotee, Dāwūd ibn Hudhayl (d. 315/927f.), see Khushanī (d. 361/971), *Akhbār al-fuqahāʾ wa'l-muḥaddithīn*, ed. M. L. Ávila and L. Molina, Madrid 1992, 89.4 (brought to my attention by Maribel Fierro).

231 See M. I. Fierro, 'El proceso contra Abū ʿUmar al-Ṭalamankī a través de su vida y de su obra', *Sharq al-Andalus*, 9 (1992), 118 (and cf. 124), citing phrases from Dhahabī, *Siyar*, 17:568.13, and his *Tadhkira*, 1099.17.

232 Ibn al-Aḥmar (d. 807/1404f.), *Buyūtāt Fās al-kubrā*, Rabat 1972, 44.19, cited in García-Arenal, 'Práctica', 148.

233 Ibn Ḥajar, *Durar*, 1:86.3, cited indirectly in Chalmeta, *El 'señor del zoco'*, 487. I leave aside two further cases mentioned by Chalmeta, since both are *qāḍī*s (*ibid.*, 486 nos. 74f.).

234 Ibn Qunfudh al-Qusanṭīnī (d. 810/1407f.), *Uns al-faqīr*, ed. M. al-Fāsī and A. Faure, Rabat 1965, 79.3 (on Abū ʿAlī al-Rajrājī). Ibn Qunfudh left Morocco in 777/1375f. or 778/1376f., and wrote in 787/1385f. (see the editors' French introduction, vi, viii).

had said by way of forbidding wrong.[235] The familiar theme of confrontation with political power is present in three of these instances; but in no case is confronting power an attempt to appropriate it.

The same is broadly true for the motley collection of tenth/sixteenth-century scholars and saints treated by Ibn ʿAskar (d. 986/1578), a biographer whose interests are centred in the Moroccan Rīf.[236] He remarks on the performance of the duty by eight of his subjects, usually describing them as unyielding (*shadīd al-shakīma*) in it, but offering little in the way of further detail.[237] Some of these are first and foremost Ṣūfīs,[238] and some have tribal backgrounds.[239] None of them are manifestly contenders for political power. Indeed one responded to the prevalence of wrong by migrating with his family to Medina.[240] Another would speak harshly to rulers when rebuking them, but seems to have been more interested in his vast supernatural following.[241] A third was a mentor of the founders of the Saʿdian dynasty (r. 916–1069/1510–1659), but not apparently a political actor in his own right.[242] What is perhaps significant, however, is a sense that even if they were not aspiring politicians, they could have been. We are told of one Ṣūfī, who would speak out against unjust rule, that the rulers feared possible subversion on the part of his followers and family – though this was not until after his death.[243] The scholars of Fez were able to undermine the position of Maghīlī with their ruler by telling him that Maghīlī's real aim was political power, not forbidding wrong.[244] None of this suggests any confusion in principle between forbidding wrong and subversion; but the last example does hint at some blurring in practice.

There are in fact many instances in the history of the Muslim west of forbidding wrong as part of the repertoire of those who made it their business to subvert or create states. We have already encountered the views and abortive practice of Ibn Farrūkh.[245] The Andalusian rebel Ibn al-Qiṭṭ used the slogan of forbidding wrong when he launched his rebellion in

[235] R. Brunschvig, *Deux récits de voyage inédits en Afrique du Nord au XVe siècle*, Paris 1936, 65.14 = 133, cited in Chalmeta, *El 'señor del zoco'*, 630.

[236] Ibn ʿAskar (d. 986/1578), *Dawḥat al-nāshir*, ed. M. Ḥajjī, Rabat 1976. Most of the relevant material from this work is cited in García-Arenal, 'Práctica', 158–60. The work is in striking contrast to the earlier collection of biographies of Ṣūfīs composed by Ibn al-Zayyāt (d. *c.* 628/1230) (*al-Tashawwuf ilā rijāl al-taṣawwuf*, ed. A. al-Tawfīq, Rabat 1984); here I have not noted a single Ṣūfī credited with performing the duty (though on the day of his death one of them upbraided his contemporaries for failing to do so, *ibid.*, 428.9).

[237] Ibn ʿAskar, *Dawḥa*, 8.4, 14.24, 63.5, 88.5, 97.31, 102.3, 103.2, 130.17 (nos. 3, 4, 49, 80, 94, 99, 100, 132). [238] Nos. 3, 94, 99. [239] Nos. 3, 49, 94.

[240] No. 49.

[241] No. 99. He had over seventy thousand followers among the *jinn* (*ibid.*, 102.11).

[242] No. 80. [243] No. 100. [244] *Ibid.*, 131.15 (no. 132). [245] See above, 385.

288/901.[246] A more typical case is that of Abū Rakwa (d. 397/1007), the Andalusian pretender who raised the Banū Qurra of Cyrenaica against the Fāṭimids. While insinuating himself into the affections of this tribe, he practised asceticism, taught their children the Koran, and engaged in the reform of morals (*taghyīr al-munkar*).[247] Here the performance of the duty is not in itself an act of subversion or state formation, but it leads to it. We find the same pattern, attended with much greater eventual success, in the case of Ibn Yāsīn (d. 450/1058f.) and the establishment of the Almoravid dynasty (r. 454–541/1062–1147),[248] in the case of Ibn Tūmart (d. 524/1130) and the establishment of the Almohad dynasty (r. 524–668/1130–1269),[249] and in the case of Muḥammad al-Mahdī (d. 923/1517) and the establishment of the Saʿdian dynasty.[250] The Saʿdians in turn were challenged by the rebel Abū Maḥallī (d. 1022/1613).[251] A hostile anecdote about his youth recounts that he and his coeval Maḥammad ibn Abī Bakr al-Dilāʾī (d. 1046/1636) once spent the day in contrasting pursuits: Abū Maḥallī in fractious and fruitless attempts to forbid wrong, and Ibn Abī Bakr in washing his clothes, saying his prayers and the like.[252] It was, of course, Abū Maḥallī who developed the pretensions to temporal power that led to his early death, whereas Ibn Abī Bakr lived to a ripe old age as the head of a major centre of religious culture in Dilāʾ.[253] Muḥammad al-Tāhartī, who had messianic pretensions and a significant tribal following in south-western Morocco in the later 1030s/1620s,[254] was rebuked in a

[246] Ibn Ḥayyān (d. 469/1076), *Muqtabis*, ed. M. M. Antuña, Paris 1937, 133.13, cited in García-Arenal, 'Práctica', 147; and see M. I. Fierro Bello, *La heterodoxia en al-Andalus durante el periodo omeya*, Madrid 1987, 108–11.

[247] Maqqarī (d. 1041/1631f.), *Nafḥ al-ṭīb*, ed. I. ʿAbbās, Beirut 1968, 2:658.14; and see J. Aguadé, 'Abū Rakwa', *Actas del IV Coloquio Hispano-Tunecino*, Madrid 1983, 13, and García-Arenal, 'Práctica', 147f.

[248] ʿIyāḍ, *Madārik*, 4:781.8 (speaking of *taghyīr al-manākir*); Ibn Abī Zarʿ (*fl. c.* 700/1300), *Rawḍ al-qirṭās*, ed. C. J. Tornberg, Uppsala 1843–6, 1:78.19 (speaking of *al-amr biʾl-maʿrūf*). Here the problem was that among the Ṣanhāja men were marrying six, seven, or ten wives each (*ibid.*, 78.17). Cf. also *ibid.*, 79.14, 79.17, 81.21, and García-Arenal, 'Práctica', 149f.

[249] See below, ch. 16, 458f.; also García-Arenal, 'Práctica', 156f.

[250] García-Arenal, 'Práctica', 160f., citing E. Fagnan (trans.), *Extraits inédits relatifs au Maghreb*, Algiers 1924, 340.

[251] Cf. García-Arenal, 'Práctica', 161, and *EI*², *Supplement*, art. 'Abū Maḥallī' (G. Deverdun).

[252] Yūsī (d. 1102/1691), *Muḥāḍarāt*, ed. M. Ḥajjī, Rabat 1976, 106.4 (I was directed to this source by Houari Touati). In the fuller version quoted by Ifrānī (d. *c.* 1155/1742), Ibn Abī Bakr objects to Abū Maḥallī's plan for the day on the ground that the conditions for *taghyīr al-munkar* do not obtain (*Nuzhat al-ḥādī*, ed. O. Houdas, Paris 1888, 204.23; cf. also *ibid.*, 204.14, 205.10).

[253] Cf. *EI*², *Supplement*, art. 'Dilāʾ' (C. Pellat).

[254] See M. Ḥajjī, *al-Ḥaraka al-fikriyya biʾl-Maghrib fī ʿahd al-Saʿdiyyīn*, n.p. 1976–8, 231 (this work was drawn to my attention by Maribel Fierro).

similar tone by a literary antagonist: 'We call you . . . to repent from what you are doing, and to adhere to the normative custom (*sunna*) in commanding right with what it entails (*bi-mā fīhi*); for rebelling against the authorities (*al-umarāʾ*) leads only to the corruption of the good order of mankind.'[255] These examples could doubtless be multiplied.[256]

Where then is the theory that goes with this aggressive style of practice? It is not to be found in the Mālikī doctrines we have surveyed.[257] Nor does it appear in the sources from which our historical examples are taken. Perhaps we should not look for it anywhere; people do not have to have theories in order to do things. But it is certainly worth inquiring, as Mercedes García-Arenal has done, whether there was in fact some unusually virulent strain of doctrine behind any or all of these instances, and more particularly those that clearly belong within the Mālikī community. An obvious local source would be the views of Ibn Ḥazm (d. 456/1064). In one discussion of forbidding wrong he strongly supports recourse to arms where necessary, and holds that the ruler should be deposed for the slightest act of injustice (*jawr*) should he fail to reform and submit to the appropriate penalty.[258] In another discussion he maintains that, if an unjust Qurashī ruler is challenged by a rebel more just than he, it is our duty to fight for the rebel since doing so is righting a wrong (*taghyīr munkar*).[259] But Ibn Ḥazm's message, though appropriate, was scarcely heard by posterity.[260]

255 Quoted *ibid.*, 234, from manuscript.

256 See García-Arenal, 'Práctica', 157f., and the references given there, for the cases of Saʿāda (d. 705/1305f.) in the tribal society of the Zāb, and of Yaʿqūb al-Khāqānī (d. *c.* 825/1422) in the anarchic conditions of Fez in 817/1414f. (the latter invites comparison with the popular leaders who emerged in Baghdad in 201/817, for whom see above, ch. 5, 107). In the first case the source speaks of *taghyīr al-munkar* (Ibn Khaldūn (d. 808/1406), *ʿIbar*, Beirut 1956–9, 6:81.8), in the second of *al-amr bi'l-maʿrūf* (Ibn Ḥajar al-ʿAsqalānī (d. 852/1449), *Inbāʾ al-ghumr*, ed. Ḥ. Ḥabashī, Cairo 1969–72, 3:295.14, cited indirectly by García-Arenal). Elsewhere Ibn Khaldūn comments in general terms that many pious laymen and jurists foolishly rebel against unjust rule when they have no chance of success, appealing to these same slogans (*Muqaddima*, ed. E. M. Quatremère, Paris 1858, 1:287.2, cited in Abou El Fadl, 'The Islamic law of rebellion', 274 n. 835).

257 Cf. above, 360f., 367, 372, 378.

258 Ibn Ḥazm, *Fiṣal*, 4:171–6, esp. 175.24 (and cf. García-Arenal, 'Práctica', 148). This passage is a devastating polemic against the quietism of the traditionists and others. In the course of it Ibn Ḥazm refers the reader to his *Īṣāl* (read so for *Ittiṣāl*) *ilā fahm maʿrifat al-khiṣāl* for detailed discussion of the traditions adduced by the quietists (*Fiṣal*, 4:172.20); this work may be extant in an abridged form (see Brockelmann, *Geschichte*, supplementary volumes, 1:695 no. 11).

259 Ibn Ḥazm (d. 456/1064), *Muḥallā*, ed. A. M. Shākir, Beirut n.d., 9:362.15. In this work Ibn Ḥazm devotes two sections to *al-amr bi'l-maʿrūf* – something unusual in a Sunnī law-book. The first is anodyne (1:26f. no. 48). The second (*ibid.*, 9:361f. nos. 1,772f.) contains the doctrine just mentioned (and cf. also *ibid.*, 362.10). Note also his endorsement of righteous rebellion under the banner of *al-amr bi'l-maʿrūf* (*ibid.*, 11:98.18, cited in Madelung, 'Amr be maʿrūf', 994a).

260 As pointed out in García-Arenal, 'Práctica', 163f.

The alternative hypothesis, cautiously advanced by García-Arenal, is that a key role in making such activity doctrinally respectable in Mālikī circles was played by Ghazzālī.[261] As we have seen, Ghazzālī was prepared to countenance armed conflict and the gathering of bands in the course of forbidding wrong.[262] While we have no evidence that the particular passage in which he expressed this view was influential in the Maghrib, the impact of his work as a whole in the Muslim west is beyond dispute.[263] Thus the hypothesis that Ghazzālī's views on violence worked on the minds of western Mālikīs, and especially the Ṣūfīs among them, is not implausible.

5. CONCLUSION

As we have seen in this chapter, there is a fair amount of source-material bearing on the theory and practice of forbidding wrong among the Mālikīs. But it does not add up to a well-developed, continuing and distinctive Mālikī heritage. This is evident in both literary and substantive terms.

From a literary point of view, the material we have considered is fragmented. There is a real if limited body of doctrine handed down from Mālik himself, but it plays only a rather restricted part in the subsequent history of Mālikī thought.[264] Ibn al-Rabīʿ, to judge by the little that survives, must have written an account of forbidding wrong more elaborate than anything we possess today in Mālikī literature; but his work seems to have had little impact.[265] There is something of a new departure in the doctrines of Bājī and Ibn Rushd, but they have little residue apart from the persistence of the three-condition schema.[266] Thereafter the dominant literary theme is the borrowing of material from the Shāfiʿites, as by Ibn al-Munāṣif, ʿUqbānī and the commentators.[267]

In terms of substantive doctrine the same unevenness is apparent, particularly with regard to the politics of the duty. Thus Mālik's cooperative attitude towards the state has virtually no resonance in the record of practice in Ifrīqiya.[268] The hierarchical conception of the duty is a pronounced feature of Koranic exegesis, but makes little appearance elsewhere.[269] Mālikī attitudes towards heroism may be positive, as in the case of Ibn al-ʿArabī or Qarāfī, or negative, as in the case of ʿIyāḍ or ʿUqbānī.[270] Recourse

261 *Ibid.*, 154–6, 163–4. 262 See above, 372; and see below, ch. 16, 441.
263 Cf. above, 369–73, and below, ch. 16, 453–8.
264 See above, section 2; for Ibn Rushd as a commentator on Mālik, cf. above, notes 39f.
265 See above, 378–81.
266 See above, 362–5, and, for the persistence of the schema, above, note 80 and 374f.
267 See above, 369f., 371f., 376f. 268 Cf. above, 361 and 386.
269 See above, 367f., and notes 162f. 270 See above, 366f., and notes 84, 156–8.

to arms on the part of subjects gets no support at the level of doctrine – witness the views of Ibn al-ʿArabī, Ibn al-Munāṣif and the commentators;[271] but in later centuries it becomes a conspicuous feature of practice among Mālikīs.[272]

In addition to these points, there are perhaps two main historical reasons why the picture of the relations between theory and practice presented in this chapter is a rather unsatisfying one. The first is the very success of the Mālikīs in propagating their school over a wide area with a diversity of political and social conditions; this means that the accumulated body of their thought is not readily susceptible of analysis as a response to a specific historical setting. The second reason is more like bad luck: the evidence for theory and the evidence for practice tend to come from different periods and milieus of Mālikī history.

[271] See above, 367, 372, and notes 159f.

[272] See above, 388–90.

CHAPTER 15

THE IBĀḌĪS

1. INTRODUCTION

In the early Islamic period, the Khārijite sects were comparable in number and significance to those of the Shīʿites. In the long run, however, they were far less successful. Within a few centuries, the only surviving Khārijite sectarians were the Ibāḍīs, and they are consequently the only Khārijite group whose doctrines can be investigated systematically on the basis of their own writings. The pattern of distribution of the Ibāḍīs was similar to that of the medieval Zaydīs: having died out in the centre of the Islamic world, they gradually came to be confined to two widely separated peripheral regions. In the Ibāḍī case, these were Oman in the east and parts of North Africa (Jerba, the Jabal Nafūsa, and the Mozab) in the west. Unlike the Zaydīs, the Ibāḍīs survived the centuries in both their peripheral habitats, and today each of them preserves an Ibāḍī literary heritage. Of the two heritages, that of the eastern Ibāḍīs is by now the more extensively published, in large part thanks to the existence in Oman – as not in North Africa – of an Ibāḍī state.[1]

One implication of this is that we know rather little about the views of non-Ibāḍī Khārijites on forbidding wrong. What we are told in non-Khārijite sources is, however, very consistent: the duty is regularly associated with Khārijite political activism.[2] Thus Ibn Abī ʾl-Ḥadīd, in making the point that forbidding wrong is a major religious principle, states that it was the value espoused by the Khārijites who rebelled against the state

[1] For a survey of the history and doctrines of the sect as a whole, see *EI*², art. 'Ibāḍiyya' (T. Lewicki).

[2] This association is well known to the secondary literature (see, for example, J. Wellhausen, *Die religiös-politischen Oppositionsparteien im alten Islam*, Berlin 1901, 13); Madelung has dubbed it the 'Kharijite interpretation' of *al-amr biʾl-maʿrūf* ('Amr be maʿrūf', cols. 993a–b). For an example, see Ājurrī (d. 360/970), *Sharīʿa*, ed. M. Ḥ. al-Fiqī, Riyāḍ 1992, 33.4.

(*sulṭān*), since they did so only in response to what they knew or believed to be the injustice of those in authority.[3] Early sources provide some support for this observation. Thus an account is preserved from Abū Mikhnaf (d. 157/773f.) in which forbidding wrong appears in a Khārijite proclamation on the occasion of the secession to Ḥarūrāʾ in the year 37/657.[4] A heresiography which is likely to be the work of Jaʿfar ibn Ḥarb (d. 236/850f.) states that the Khārijite heresiarch Nāfiʿ ibn al-Azraq (d. 65/685) outlawed precautionary dissimulation (*taqiyya*), and held any quietist Khārijite who did not go forth (*lam yakhruj*) commanding right and forbidding wrong to be an infidel.[5] According to Haytham ibn ʿAdī (d. *c.* 206/821) as quoted by Balādhurī (d. 279/892f.), the Khārijite rebel Saʿīd ibn Bahdal (d. 127/744f.) had been a follower of a Khārijite leader called Saʿīd ibn Marwān al-Ḍaʿīf, who owed his sobriquet to his reply when asked if he did not command right and forbid wrong: he was physically weak (*ḍaʿīf al-badan*) and lacked followers (*aʿwān*). This attitude is implicitly contrasted with the activism of Saʿīd ibn Bahdal himself.[6]

There is no reason to doubt the historicity of this association of forbidding wrong with rebellion among the Khārijites. However, two qualifications may be in place. First, the linkage is not peculiar to the Khārijites; as we have seen, it is found elsewhere, and is particularly prominent among the Zaydīs. Even a staunch Ḥanbalite such as Ibn Qayyim al-Jawziyya (d. 751/1350) finds the idea of rebellion with the aim of righting wrong (*inkār al-munkar*) perfectly intelligible; it is just that it is overridden by consideration of the adverse consequences it would lead to, which render it the root of all evil.[7] Secondly, the linkage need not imply that rebellion

[3] Ibn Abī ʾl-Ḥadīd, *Sharḥ*, 19:311.15. See also Ibn Taymiyya as quoted in Ibn Mufliḥ, *Ādāb*, 1:177.8 (and cf. above, ch. 7, note 99).

[4] Ṭabarī, *Taʾrīkh*, series I, 3,349.13, cited in van Ess, *Theologie*, 2:388 n. 9; Balādhurī (d. 279/892f.), *Ansāb al-ashrāf*, ed. M. B. al-Maḥmūdī, Beirut 1974, 342.8, cited from manuscript in E. R. Fığlalı, *İbâdiye'nin doğuşu ve görüşleri*, Ankara 1983, 57 n. 28. In another report from Abū Mikhnaf, the Khārijite leader ʿAbdallāh ibn Wahb al-Rāsibī (d. 38/658) calls the leading Khārijites to *al-amr biʾl-maʿrūf* (Balādhurī, *Ansāb*, ed. Maḥmūdī, 362.15).

[5] J. van Ess, *Frühe muʿtazilitische Häresiographie: Zwei Werke des Nāšiʾ al-Akbar (gest. 293 H.) herausgegeben und eingeleitet*, Beirut 1971, 69.2 of the Arabic text; and see K. Lewinstein, 'The Azāriqa in Islamic heresiography', *Bulletin of the School of Oriental and African Studies*, 54 (1991), 260f. For the probable authorship of this text, see Madelung, 'Frühe muʿtazilitische Häresiographie: das *Kitāb al-Uṣūl* des Ǧaʿfar b. Ḥarb?'. The heresiographer goes on to speak of a quietist sect which emerged from the Azāriqa after their military defeat, the Khāzimiyya (for whom see Madelung, *Religious trends*, 63–5). This group forbade the *ḥajj* in the context of *taqiyya*, but held that once they undertook the duty of commanding and forbidding (*al-amr waʾl-nahy*) and *taqiyya* ceased, pilgrimage would become a duty (van Ess, *Frühe muʿtazilitische Häresiographie*, 69.7 of the Arabic text; and see Madelung, *Religious trends*, 63f.).

[6] Balādhurī (d. 279/892f.), *Ansāb al-ashrāf*, ms. Istanbul, Reisülküttap 598, f. 116a.31; cf. Ashʿarī, *Maqālāt*, 121.3. I am indebted to Chase Robinson for drawing my attention to both passages and supplying me with a copy of the first.

[7] Ibn Qayyim al-Jawziyya, *Iʿlām*, 3:4.4. Cf. Ḥasan al-Baṣrī's response to the news of a

was all there was to the duty among the Khārijites; it may simply have been the aspect that attracted most attention from outsiders. It is only quite incidentally that we hear that, in Medina in the late first/seventh century, people who rebuked others in the baths were liable to be stereotyped as Khārijites.[8]

It goes without saying that this material does not permit us to characterise the doctrine of the early Khārijites, apart from the obvious point that they cannot have assigned great weight to the adverse consequences of rebellion against unjust rule. Wellhausen went so far as to remark that it was characteristic of the Khārijites to implement the duty without any regard for circumstances.[9] But this, though a fine literary touch, should not be mistaken for a formal statement of the Khārijite doctrine of forbidding wrong across the board.[10]

Once we turn from the Khārijites at large to the Ibāḍīs, we can begin to draw on the literature of the sectarians themselves. Most of this literature was written in Oman and North Africa. There is, however, a significant body of Ibāḍī texts that date back to the period when Ibāḍī scholarly activity was still centred in the heartlands of the Islamic world, above all in Baṣra. Unfortunately this literature – in so far as it is accessible to me – has very little to say about forbidding wrong. A minor exception is an epistle ascribed to Abū Sufyān Maḥbūb ibn al-Raḥīl (*fl.* later second/eighth century).[11] The writer includes forbidding wrong in a list of things for which the sect stands.[12] More interestingly, he has a passage in which he laments how, in these evil times, someone (*wāḥidunā*) could say that, if only he were to be commanded right and forbidden wrong, he would not be a helper of the oppressors (*ẓālimūn*) or a friend to those who profess obedience to them.[13] A similar spirit is prominent in an early Omani text, an epistle of Shabīb ibn ʿAṭiyya (*fl.* mid-second/eighth century) directed

rebellion initiated by a Khārijite: while seeking to right a wrong, he had fallen into a worse one (see above, ch. 4, note 43). [8] See above, ch. 4, note 173.

[9] Wellhausen, *Die religiös-politischen Oppositionsparteien*, 13: 'die rücksichtslose Betätigung desselben zur Zeit und zur Unzeit kennzeichnet die Chavârig'.

[10] Cf. Lambton, *State and government*, 310. That the Khārijites considered *al-amr bi'l-maʿrūf* to be an unconditional duty is a favourite theme of the Imāmī Murtaḍā Muṭahharī (d. 1399/1979) (see his *Jādhiba wa dāfiʿa-i ʿAlī ʿalayhi 'l-salām*, Tehran 1391, 124f., last paragraph of the footnote; his *Āshnāʾī bā ʿulūm-i Islāmī*, Qumm n.d., 2:34.15; his 'ʿAdālat az naẓar-i Islām', in his *Bīst guftār*, n.p. 1357 sh., 46.1; and his *Sayrī dar sīra-i aʾimma-i aṭhār*, Tehran and Qumm 1367 sh., 38.17).

[11] Darjīnī (seventh/thirteenth century), *Ṭabaqāt al-mashāyikh bi'l-maghrib*, ed. I. Ṭallāy, n.p. n.d., 279–89 (but note the second *ammā baʿd* at 284.3). Darjīnī says the epistle was written to ʿAbdallāh ibn Yaḥyā (d. 130/747f.), which makes no sense chronologically (see van Ess, *Theologie*, 2:202 and n. 100). For Abū Sufyān, see *EI*², art. 'Maḥbūb b. al-Raḥīl al-ʿAbdī' (T. Lewicki).

[12] Darjīnī, *Ṭabaqāt*, 289.8. He glosses *maʿrūf* as *ṭāʿa*[*t Allāh*], and *munkar* as *maʿṣiyat Allāh*.

[13] *Ibid.*, 288.12.

against the quietist traditionists of mainstream Islam.[14] Thus he reviles the mainstream (*al-sawād al-aʿẓam*) as those who have disregarded God's rights and gone home, abandoning the struggle for justice (*al-qiyām bi'l-qisṭ*) and the forbidding of wrong.[15] Here we find the same association of forbidding wrong with rebellion against unjust rule that marks accounts of the Khārijites at large.[16] It is also found in non-Khārijite accounts of the Ibāḍīs. Thus Abū 'l-Faraj al-Iṣbahānī (d. 356/967) quotes from Madā'inī (d. *c.* 228/842) a speech of the Ibāḍī rebel ʿAbdallāh ibn Yaḥyā al-Kindī (d. 130/747f.) in Yemen; here forbidding wrong figures among a list of beliefs and duties to which the rebels call people.[17] Likewise an elegy for the rebels also quoted by Abū 'l-Faraj describes them as 'forbidding wrong to whoever they met' (*nāhīna man lāqaw ʿani 'l-nukri*).[18] To return to Ibāḍī sources, a passage in the same vein is found in an epistle ascribed to Sālim ibn Dhakwān (*fl.* 70s/690s), in any event an early source.[19] The author states that, in the view of the sect, one should affiliate to women and slaves (*al-mar'a wa'l-mamlūk*) who 'go forth' (sc. to join fellow-members of the sect who are in rebellion) with the right intentions. His proof-text is Q9:71: 'And the believers, the men and the women (*wa'l-mu'minūna wa'l-mu'minātu*), are friends one of the other; they command right, and forbid wrong . . .'[20] There is a clear link here to wider Khārijite attitudes to rebellion. Incidentally, this is not the last time that we will be concerned with Ibāḍī views on the role of women in forbidding wrong.[21]

14 For this epistle, see Cook, *Early Muslim dogma*, 57.

15 Shabīb ibn ʿAṭiyya (*fl.* mid-second/eighth century), *Sīra*, in S. I. Kāshif (ed.), *al-Siyar wa'l-jawābāt li-ʿulamā' wa-a'immat ʿUmān*, Oman 1986–8, 2:378.16; and see also *ibid.*, 354.2, 358.17, 370.11. I owe my copies of all texts cited from the second volume of Kāshif, *Siyar*, to Patricia Crone.

16 Darjīnī also quotes from the mother of a certain Nāfiʿ ibn Khalīfa, whom I am unable to date, an account of the *qurrā'* in the days before the Khārijites split (in 64/683f.), according to which they believed in fighting the tyrants (*qitāl al-jabābira*) and in *al-amr bi'l-maʿrūf* (*Ṭabaqāt*, 235.4). Compare the quotation from the third/ninth-century Omani Ibāḍī Abū 'l-Mu'thir al-Ṣalt ibn Khamīs in Sālimī (d. 1332/1914), *Tuḥfat al-aʿyān*, Cairo 1961, 1:86.4; I am indebted to Lesley Wilkins for sending me this volume and several other Omani publications cited in this chapter.

17 Abū 'l-Faraj al-Iṣbahānī, *Aghānī*, 23:227.1 (translated in van Ess, *Theologie*, 2:196).

18 Abū 'l-Faraj, *Aghānī*, 23:251.4, whence I. ʿAbbās, *Shiʿr al-Khawārij*, Beirut 1974, 224 no. 123, line 11, and cf. ʿAbbās's introduction, 10. The poet, ʿAmr ibn al-Ḥusayn al-ʿAnbarī, is described as a Kūfan Ibāḍī (Abū 'l-Faraj, *Aghānī*, 23:234 n. 1).

19 For the dating and ascription of this epistle see Cook, *Early Muslim dogma*, esp. ch. 10, and van Ess, *Theologie*, 1:171–4. A full edition, translation and study of the epistle is being published by P. Crone and F. Zimmermann.

20 Sālim ibn Dhakwān (*fl.* 70s/690s), *Sīra*, in Hinds Xerox, 192.6. The proof-text clearly provides more explicit support with regard to women than slaves.

21 See below, 402, 415f., 422, 423f. For the military role of women among the early Khārijites, see Kohlberg, 'Medieval Muslim views on martyrdom', 6 n. 5, and the examples collected in the forthcoming study of Crone and Zimmermann. Since women were unusually prominent in early Khārijite sects, it would not be surprising if they were also given to commanding right and forbidding wrong; but I have not come across an example.

2. THE WESTERN IBĀḌĪS

The link between forbidding wrong and political power remains prominent in Western Ibāḍī sources. As among the Zaydīs, the duty is associated with sectarian state-formation – with rebellion against unjust rule and the exercise of the legitimate authority of the imam. The connection with rebellion, though much less common than among the Zaydīs, was noted by Goldziher in the case of the Nukkārī Ibāḍī rebel Abū Yazīd Makhlad ibn Kaydād (d. 336/947).[22] The linkage with the imamate is more frequently attested. Thus in the context of a dispute over the authority of the second imam of the Rustumid dynasty of Tāhart (161–296/778–909), ʿAbd al-Wahhāb ibn ʿAbd al-Raḥmān (r. 171–208/788–824), the view was put forward that the imam was bound to act only in the presence of a regular congregation (*jamāʿa maʿlūma*).[23] When the leading eastern Ibāḍī authorities were consulted on this, they rejected the idea, ridiculing the notion that, among other things, the imam could not forbid wrong except in the presence of the congregation.[24] In an anecdote likewise set in Tāhart, the imam – perhaps Aflaḥ (r. 208–58/824–72) – refers to his duty to forbid wrong.[25] Janāwunī (first half of the sixth/twelfth century) in one version of his creed mentions 'commanding and forbidding' as a subject of disagreement in the community:[26] the orthodox (*muwaḥḥidūn*) agree that forbidding wrong is an obligation, whereas certain heretics (the Nukkāth) deny this, holding the imamate not to be obligatory.[27] The later

[22] Goldziher, *Livre*, 96; for this rebellion of 332–6/944–7 against the Fāṭimids, see *EI*², art. 'Abū Yazīd al-Nukkārī' (S. M. Stern). Goldziher's authority was Ibn Khaldūn, according to whom Abū Yazīd engaged in *al-ḥisba ʿalā 'l-nās wa-taghyīr al-munkar* (*ʿIbar*, 4:84.16); see also I. ʿAbbās, 'Maṣādir thawrat Abī Yazīd Makhlad ibn Kaydād', *al-Aṣāla*, 6 (1977), 30.

[23] Darjīnī, *Ṭabaqāt*, 48.16. This incident forms part of the confused story of the Nukkārī schism (see *EI*², art. 'Nukkār' (T. Lewicki)).

[24] Darjīnī, *Ṭabaqāt*, 50.3 (*wa-lā yanhā ʿan munkar*). Otherwise, they held, everyone and no one would be an imam. In the chronicle of Abū Zakariyyāʾ al-Warjlānī (*fl.* late fifth/eleventh century), however, the corresponding wording is *wa-lā yanhā ʿan fasād* (*Siyar al-aʾimma wa-akhbāruhum*, ed. I. al-ʿArabī, Algiers 1982, 91.8).

[25] Darjīnī, *Ṭabaqāt*, 293.14. A responsum of imam Aflaḥ regarding *al-amr bi'l-maʿrūf* is noted in W. Schwartz, *Die Anfänge der Ibaditen in Nordafrika*, Wiesbaden 1983, 74 n. 7; for the manuscript cited, see *ibid.*, 301 no. 18.

[26] R. Rubinacci, 'La professione di fede di al-Ǧannāwunī', in Istituto Universitario Orientale di Napoli, *Annali*, new series, 14 (1964), 586. The other version, which presents the matter in a somewhat different light, will be taken up below, notes 34, 41.

[27] *Ibid.*, 587f., and cf. 563 (for Janāwunī, see *EI*², art. 'Abū Zakariyyāʾ al-Djanāwunī' (A. de Motylinski and T. Lewicki)). The Nukkāth are doubtless the Nafāthiyya, for whom see T. Lewicki, 'Les subdivisions de l'Ibāḍiyya', *Studia Islamica*, 9 (1958), 79. There is a similar association of *al-amr bi'l-maʿrūf* with the imamate in the rhetoric of Abū ʿAmmār ʿAbd al-Kāfī (*fl.* mid-sixth/twelfth century), *Mūjaz*, *apud* ʿA. Ṭālibī, *Ārāʾ al-Khawārij al-kalāmiyya*, Algiers 1978, 2:224.2, 226.1, 233.3 (for Abū ʿAmmār, see *EI*², *Supplement*, art. 'Abū ʿAmmār' (J. van Ess)).

third/ninth-century chronicler Ibn Ṣaghīr remarks on the arrangements made by the imam Abū 'l-Yaqẓān (r. 260–81/874–94) for a group to command right and forbid wrong in the markets.[28] A residual association of the duty with political authority is apparent in an anecdote told about Yakhlaf ibn Yakhlaf (second half of the sixth/twelfth century), long after the demise of the Ibāḍī imamate in North Africa.[29] One winter morning after he and his pupils had performed the dawn prayer, he jokingly inquired who would give them breakfast in return for being appointed emir over them. He had in mind one Mūsā ibn Ilyās al-Mazātī, who took up the offer. When they left, Yakhlaf remarked to Mūsā that he could not himself assume the role of emir, but that he would have a son whom he should call Aflaḥ after the Rustumid imam of that name. Mūsā did indeed have such a son, who grew up to command right and forbid wrong, and was obeyed and followed in every good enterprise he undertook.[30]

What of the duty of the ordinary individual? A short letter of imam ʿAbd al-Wahhāb to the people of Tripoli opens with the statement that Islam consists of the confession of faith, the affirmation of revelation, forbidding wrong, performance of prayer, payment of the alms-tax and the like;[31] from the company it keeps here, the duty would seem to be one of individuals. The third/ninth-century author who preserves this letter adopts a similar formulation himself.[32] The mention of the duty in Ibāḍī creeds[33] presumably refers at least in part to the individual duty. Janāwunī in one version of his creed states it as orthodox doctrine that God has imposed the duty on His servants at every moment (*ḥīn*) and time (*awān*) according to their capacity (*ʿalā qadr al-ṭāqa*).[34] Similarly ʿĀmir ibn ʿAlī al-Shammākhī (d. 792/1389f.) states that forbidding wrong is obligatory at every time (*fī kull zamān*) according to a person's capacity (*ʿalā qadr al-ṭāqa*).[35] A third such Ibāḍī creed, that of Ibn Jumayʿ (eighth/fourteenth century), does no

[28] Ibn Ṣaghīr (later third/ninth century), *Akhbār al-aʾimma al-Rustumiyyīn*, ed. Ḥ. ʿA. Ḥasan, Cairo 1984, 287.6; and cf. 269.8 (mentioning *al-iḥtisāb ʿalā 'l-fussāq*). These passages appear in Barrādī (later eighth/fourteenth century), *Jawāhir*, Cairo 1302, 177.4, 177.10. [29] Darjīnī, *Ṭabaqāt*, 518.23.

[30] *Ibid.*, 519.11. Darjīnī remarks that he had himself witnessed the conduct of the son.

[31] Ibn Sallām (third/ninth century), *Kitāb fīhi badʾ al-Islām wa-sharāʾiʿ al-dīn*, ed. W. Schwartz and Sālim ibn Yaʿqūb, Wiesbaden 1986, 93.5, and cf. 93.12.

[32] *Ibid.*, 86.3. [33] Noted by Madelung ('Amr be maʿrūf', 993a).

[34] See above, note 27. The other version is the same in substance, but uses the phrase *fī kull zamān* (see the text published in P. Cuperly, 'Une profession de foi ibāḍite', *Bulletin d'Etudes Orientales*, 32–3 (1980–1), 53.4, and cf. the listing of *al-amr bi'l-maʿrūf* at 48.35; for the sources of the two versions, see *ibid.*, 21).

[35] ʿĀmir ibn ʿAlī al-Shammākhī (d. 792/1389f.), *Diyānāt*, published in P. Cuperly, *Introduction à l'étude de l'Ibāḍisme et de sa théologie*, Algiers 1984, 336.16. For translations, see *ibid.*, 333; ʿA. K. Ennāmi, *Studies in Ibāḍism*, Beirut 1972, 152 item 5; also Madelung, 'Amr be maʿrūf', 993a (rendering only the relevant article).

more than mention forbidding wrong.[36] These short statements do not tell us much, but they have one interesting feature. While the reference to capacity is widespread Islamic doctrine, the insistence that the duty obtains at all times is unusual. What were the Ibāḍī scholars seeking to exclude?

The clue can perhaps be found in a view reported by Darjīnī (seventh/thirteenth century) to have been held by a scholar of the second half of the fourth/tenth century, Abū Mūsā ʿĪsā ibn al-Samḥ al-Zawāghī.[37] Zawāghī held some controversial views. That which concerns us was to the effect that while the believers are in a state of concealment (*kitmān*), they have no obligation to command or forbid.[38] Now the state of concealment, as opposed particularly to manifestation (*ẓuhūr*), is a basic concept of Ibāḍī religious politics.[39] It precludes the existence of an imamate, so that Ibāḍīs in this state are obliged to accommodate themselves to the rule of tyrants; but it does not preclude forbidding wrong.[40] Moreover, Janāwunī in one version of his creed seems to associate the view that the duty lapses in the absence of manifestation and the imamate with a heretical group among the Ibāḍīs, the Nukkāth.[41] Posterity therefore hastened to explain away Zawāghī's deviant view by saying that he was referring only to commanding and forbidding non-Ibāḍīs (*ahl al-khilāf*).[42] This, as Darjīnī goes on to say, is an acceptable view, and close

[36] Ibn Jumayʿ (eighth/fourteenth century), *ʿAqīda*, in Aḥmad ibn Saʿīd al-Shammākhī (d. 928/1522) and Dāwūd ibn Ibrāhīm al-Talātī (d. 967/1560), *Muqaddimat al-tawḥīd wa-shurūḥuhā*, ed. Ibrāhīm Aṭfayyish, Cairo 1353, 43.1, 56.1, noted in Madelung, 'Amr be maʿrūf', 993a. For this creed, which Ibn Jumayʿ translated from an older Berber version, see Rubinacci, 'Professione', 553f., 567–76; also Ennāmi, *Studies*, 174 (whence I adopt the vocalisation 'Jumayʿ'). The only point of note in the commentaries is that Talātī, after listing the 'three modes', adds the tripartite division of labour as an anonymous saying (Shammākhī and Talātī, *Muqaddima*, 43.11); this saying is typically – though not exclusively – Ḥanafī (see below, ch. 17, notes 29f.). The editor – a nephew of the well-known Muḥammad ibn Yūsuf Aṭfayyish (d. 1332/1914) – firmly rejects the idea of such a division of labour in a footnote (*ibid.*, 43 n. 1).

[37] On Zawāghī see Darjīnī, *Ṭabaqāt*, 365–7.

[38] *Ibid.*, 366.5 (*inna ʾl-amr waʾl-nahy marfūʿān ʿan ahl al-kitmān, lā yalzamuhum min dhālika shayʾ*). [39] Ennāmi, *Studies*, 234–8.

[40] *Ibid.*, 235, citing the *Masāʾil al-tawḥīd* of Abū ʾl-ʿAbbās Aḥmad ibn Muḥammad ibn Bakr (d. 504/1110f.) (for which see *ibid.*, 170, and A. K. Ennami, 'A description of new Ibadi manuscripts from North Africa', *Journal of Semitic Studies*, 15 (1970), 73); P. Cuperly, 'L'Ibâḍisme au XIIème siècle: la ʿAqîda de Abû Sahl Yaḥyâ', *IBLA* (= *Revue de l'Institut des belles lettres arabes*), 42 (1979), 295, translating a similar passage from the *ʿaqīda* of a scholar of about the sixth/twelfth century (for whom see *ibid.*, 70–3). It is even permissible for Ibāḍīs to take office under tyrants if they are capable of commanding them right and forbidding them wrong (Ennāmi, *Studies*, 237, citing Warjlānī, *Dalīl*, 3:64.7).

[41] Cuperly, 'Une profession de foi ibāḍite', 53.5. In substance this version is like that quoted above, note 27, except that it adds the explanation: *wa-qad ʿalimnā annahu lā yaṣiḥḥ al-amr biʾl-maʿrūf waʾl-nahy ʿan al-munkar illā biʾl-imāma waʾl-ẓuhūr*; I take it that it is the Nukkāth who are speaking, but the passage seems confused. For the Nukkāth, see above, note 27. [42] Darjīnī, *Ṭabaqāt*, 366.10.

to one expressed by Abū Muḥammad Jamāl, a scholar of the first half of the fourth/tenth century:[43] you are not obliged to rebuke non-Ibāḍīs for anything which is allowable in their law but not in yours,[44] and to abstain from such censure is not to throw to the winds the duty of forbidding wrong. However, Darjīnī concludes, this is not the view of most of our scholars; they consider it a duty to forbid all wrongs without distinction, provided one is not unable to do so or in fear. This last points to an underlying doctrine of forbidding wrong in line with mainstream Islamic views. The insistence on the obligatoriness of the duty at all times can thus be understood as a rejection of Zawāghī's deviation.

The earliest sustained account of the duty known to me from the western Ibāḍīs is that of Sulaymān ibn Yakhlaf al-Mazātī (d. 471/1078f.),[45] but it does not in fact have much to offer. The familiar point is made that the obligatoriness of forbidding wrong turns on how far people are able to perform it (*ʿalā qadr ṭāqatihim*).[46] More interesting is the appearance of the three modes (here *maʿānī*), albeit in a variant form.[47] Here the first case is that in which one is able to put a stop to the wrong; one's duty is to do just that, whether by saying something or by recourse to one's whip or sword (*immā bi-kalāmihi aw bi-sawṭihi aw bi-sayfihi*); there is no mention of the hand as such. The second case is that in which one is unable to put a stop to the wrong; here one still has the obligation to forbid it verbally (*fa-ʿalayhi nahyuhu bi-lisānihi*). The third case is that in which one is unable to forbid the wrong, and is in fear of being killed or beaten up; here one's duty is to right the wrong in one's heart (*fa-l-yughayyir bi-qalbihi*). Again the basic ideas are standard, but the duty to forbid even when this

[43] For Abū Muḥammad, see *ibid.*, 345–9. He had reason to have a view on the topic, since he used to pray in a congregation composed mostly of *ahl al-khilāf* (*ibid.*, 347.10); we can identify them as Mālikīs, since Darjīnī describes them as following a ritual practice – *qunūt* (prayers directed against enemies) at the dawn prayer – which was characteristic of the Mālikīs and Shāfiʿites (see *EI*[2], art. 'Ḳunūt' (A. J. Wensinck), and Ibn Ḥazm, *Muḥallā*, 4:145.13; for Ibāḍī rejection of this practice, see Ennāmi, *Studies*, 106, and below, note 120). Abū Muḥammad also rebuked a dishonest vendor in Madyan while he was on pilgrimage, slapping him and aptly quoting Q26:181 (Darjīnī, *Ṭabaqāt*, 349.4).

[44] Compare also the view reported by Aṭfayyish (d. 1332/1914) that there is no commanding and forbidding between us and non-Ibāḍī Muslims (*lā amr wa-lā nahy baynanā wa-bayna qawminā*) (*Taysīr al-tafsīr*, Cairo 1981–, 2:137.17, to Q3:104; the employment of *qawm* in this sense is standard Ibāḍī usage).

[45] For Mazātī see Darjīnī, *Ṭabaqāt*, 425–9; *EI*[2], art. 'Mazātī' (T. Lewicki).

[46] Sulaymān ibn Yakhlaf al-Mazātī (d. 471/1078f.), *Tuḥaf*, ms. Bārūnī, Kābāw, Jabal Nafūsa, f. 21a.12. For the work, see Ennāmi, *Studies*, 168f., and, for this manuscript, Ennami, 'Description of new Ibadi manuscripts', 72f. My copy of the relevant passage is taken from a xerox of the manuscript kindly loaned to me by Elizabeth Savage; the xerox quality is poor towards the bottom of each page.

[47] Sulaymān ibn Yakhlaf, *Tuḥaf*, f. 21b.6. He makes no reference to the tradition behind the schema.

will be ineffective is noteworthy,[48] as is the approval of the use of the sword. There is also a set piece on the duty in a work by a pupil of Sulaymān ibn Yakhlaf, Tabghūrīn al-Malshūṭī (second half of the fifth/eleventh century),[49] but it has nothing significant for us, being concerned largely with holy war and the imamate.

By far the longest treatment of forbidding wrong in any western Ibāḍī source known to me is that of Jayṭālī (d. 750/1349f.).[50] Its length is easily explained: the work in which it is found is essentially an Ibāḍī recension of Ghazzālī's *Revival of the religious sciences*.[51] His discussion of forbidding wrong by and large follows and paraphrases that of Ghazzālī, to whom he refers quite frequently by name.[52] This does not, of course, prevent him from incorporating other material. Some of this is non-Ibāḍī: the discussion of the question whether the duty is grounded in reason, or in revelation alone, is taken from the Shāfiʿite Māwardī (d. 450/1058),[53] while anecdotes about the virtuous in the presence of the powerful are borrowed from a work of the Mālikī Ṭurṭūshī (d. 520/1126).[54] Other material which Jayṭālī cites or refers to is Ibāḍī: he invokes such sources as the transmission of the scholars of the Jabal Nafūsa (*riwāyat mashāyikh al-Jabal*),[55] 'what we have heard' (*mā balaghanā*) of the Ibāḍī heroes of the past,[56] and stories of early Ibāḍīs (*ḥikāyāt al-salaf*).[57] But it is his handling of Ghazzālī's text that is the primary focus of interest.

48 Compare the view of Nawawī (above, ch. 13, p. 352f.), and below, notes 179–81, 209. It is this duty that drives the reshaping of the schema.

49 Tabghūrīn al-Malshūṭī (second half of the fifth/eleventh century), *Uṣūl al-dīn*, in ʿA.K. Ennāmī, 'Studies in Ibāḍism', Cambridge Ph.D. 1971, vol. 2, second item, 35–8. For this work, see Ennāmi, *Studies*, 169f.; van Ess, 'Untersuchungen zu einigen ibāḍitischen Handschriften', 54f. no. 10. Van Ess notes the treatment of *al-amr wa'l-nahy* in the eighth chapter of the work, and the structural similarity of the work to Muʿtazilite dogmatic treatises.

50 Jayṭālī (d. 750/1349f.), *Qanāṭir al-khayrāt*, Oman 1983, 2:129–217 (excluding the chapter on *jihād*, *ibid.*, 130–45). On Jayṭālī, see *EI*², art. 'Djayṭālī' (T. Lewicki). He himself was well known for his performance of the duty (see Aḥmad ibn Saʿīd al-Shammākhī (d. 928/1522), *Siyar*, ed. A. S. al-Siyābī, Muscat 1987, 2:195.23, 197.13, 197.15).

51 See Ennāmī, 'Studies in Ibāḍism', vol. 2, English introduction, 8f.; for the relationship between the treatments of ritual purity in the two works, see R. Rubinacci, 'La purità rituale secondo gli Ibāḍiti', in Istituto Universitario Orientale di Napoli, *Annali*, new series, 6 (1954–6), 6. Ghazzālī's account of *al-amr bi'l-maʿrūf* is discussed below, ch. 16.

52 Jayṭālī, *Qanāṭir*, 2:159.8, 185.4, 185.12, 187.14, 188.12, 189.9, 195.12, 210.21.

53 *Ibid.*, 155.11, paraphrasing Māwardī, *Adab*, 101.17. The borrowing is not acknowledged, and may not be direct (cf. below, notes 203f.). Māwardī's account in turn is likely to stem from a Muʿtazilite source (see above, chapter 13, notes 40f.).

54 There are acknowledged borrowings from the *Sirāj al-mulūk* at Jayṭālī, *Qanāṭir*, 2:194.10, 199.6; for the first, see Ṭurṭūshī (d. 520/1126), *Sirāj al-mulūk*, Cairo 1935, 64.19, and for the second, *ibid.*, 51.7.

55 Jayṭālī, *Qanāṭir*, 2:153.5.

56 *Ibid.*, 165.2.

57 *Ibid.*, 178.9.

In what ways does Jayṭālī intervene to alter the content or emphasis of Ghazzālī's doctrine? Some of his initiatives concern relatively isolated points. He makes reference to the 'three modes'.[58] He inserts rationalist explanations of the terms 'right' (*ma'rūf*) and 'wrong' (*munkar*) which are alien to Ghazzālī.[59] Rather surprisingly, he not only adopts Ghazzālī's statement that the duty obligates slaves and women,[60] but works in similar formulations in other parts of Ghazzālī's text;[61] he also quotes from the scholars of the Jabal Nafūsa an anecdote in which one old woman exhorts another not to give up her share of commanding and forbidding.[62]

But by far the most prominent intervention of Jayṭālī's is his enhancement of the activist flavour of Ghazzālī's account. Ghazzālī at one point states that a subject proceeding against a ruler may have recourse only to informing and counselling;[63] Jayṭālī reproduces this, but distances himself from it by describing it as the view of the non-Ibāḍīs (*qawmunā*).[64] He goes on to remark that there has been disagreement over the question of rebellion against unjust rulers (*al-khurūj 'alā 'l-salāṭīn al-jawara*), though he declines to go into this here. Later Ghazzālī considers the question whether it is lawful for individual subjects to form an armed band in performance of the duty; he notes that there have been divergent views on this, and presents the arguments on both sides before coming down in favour – but with the reassurance that such eventualities will be rare.[65] Jayṭālī, by contrast, makes no mention of contrary views, and endorses the formation of armed bands in God's cause as no great matter (*dhālika ghayr kabīr*).[66] With regard to speaking harshly to rulers, Ghazzālī takes the view that this is permissible and commendable, but only if an adverse response will bring harm solely upon oneself.[67] Jayṭālī explicitly quotes this from Ghazzālī,[68] and then goes on to give his own view (*alladhī 'indī*). He holds that, provided one's sole purpose is to right the wrong (*inkār al-munkar*) and proclaim the truth, it makes no difference who is harmed; Ibāḍīs in the past had suffered greatly at the hands of tyrants as a consequence of the

58 *Ibid.*, 154.22, inserted at a point corresponding to Ghazzālī, *Iḥyā'*, 2:285.26. What Jayṭālī offers is close to the wording of the relevant Sunnī tradition.

59 Jayṭālī, *Qanāṭir*, 2:146.21, 168.2 (contrast Ghazzālī, *Iḥyā'*, 2:297.9). This has a precedent in the Koran commentary of the third/ninth-century North African Ibāḍī Hūd ibn Muḥakkam (*Tafsīr*, 2:50.17 (to Q7:157), 149.5 (to Q9:67), 150.21 (to Q9:71), 171.1 (to Q9:112)).

60 Jayṭālī, *Qanāṭir*, 2:156.6, corresponding to Ghazzālī, *Iḥyā'*, 2:286.3.

61 Jayṭālī, *Qanāṭir*, 2:154.20, 167.12; contrast Ghazzālī, *Iḥyā'*, 2:285.26, 296.32.

62 Jayṭālī, *Qanāṭir*, 2:153.5.

63 Ghazzālī, *Iḥyā'*, 2:292.2.

64 Jayṭālī, *Qanāṭir*, 2:163.15.

65 Ghazzālī, *Iḥyā'*, 2:304.33.

66 Jayṭālī, *Qanāṭir*, 2:175.2 (the context precludes reading *kathīr* for *kabīr*). However, he adds 'God knows best' to Ghazzālī's statement that someone killed in performing the duty is a martyr.

67 Ghazzālī, *Iḥyā'*, 2:314.5.

68 Jayṭālī, *Qanāṭir*, 2:187.4.

rebellions of their coreligionists, but this had never been taken as a reason not to rebel.[69] To give examples, he says, would make the book too long; but elsewhere he inserts brief references to Ibāḍī martyrs.[70]

A much more recent account, at least in the form in which we have it, is found in a catechism of 1332/1914.[71] Ghazzālī's influence is again obvious from the formulation of the escalatory sequence of responses.[72] This apart, two points are noteworthy. One is an unusual rider to the standard view that spying is illegal: someone who learns of an offence by spying has the dual duty of forbidding the offence and repenting of his intrusion.[73] The other is a clear distinction between non-verbal manifestations of disapproval (showing one's anger and contempt, frowning, social avoidance) and performance of the duty within one's heart (*bi-qalbihi*).[74]

As might be expected, the Ibāḍī biographical literature preserves occasional accounts of scholars known for their performance of the duty. When in the first half of the fourth/tenth century a heresy arose over a point of dietary law, Abū Ṣāliḥ Jannūn, a scholar who was given to waxing wroth on behalf of God and to undertaking the righting of wrongs (*taghyīr al-munkar*), took action with a group of his pupils to prevent the heresy from spreading.[75] A scholar of the second half of the fourth/tenth century, Abū Nūḥ Saʿīd ibn Zanghīl, seems to have engaged in righting wrongs (*taghyīr al-manākir*) as part of the normal pattern of his activity with his pupils.[76] In the second half of the sixth/twelfth century, both Abū Nūḥ Yūsuf and his son Abū Zakariyyāʾ Yaḥyā were strong in anger on God's behalf when they engaged in righting wrongs (*inkār al-munkar*).[77]

Before leaving the western Ibāḍīs, one negative point is worth making. After the Ibāḍī imamate in North Africa came to an end in 296/909, a

[69] *Ibid.*, 187.8.

[70] *Ibid.*, 164.23, 188.3, 188.11. He also refers to stories about Ibāḍī authorities who had peformed the duty nicely (*ibid.*, 178.9); but again, actually telling these stories would make the book too long.

[71] ʿAlī ibn Muḥammad al-Mundhirī (writing 1332/1914), *Mukhtaṣar al-Adyān li-taʿlīm al-ṣibyān*, in I. Aṭfayyish (ed.), *al-Majmūʿa al-qayyima*, Bahlā and Beirut 1989, 280.5, and cf. 253.5. I do not know the identity of the *Adyān* of which this is an epitome (see *ibid.*, 282.9); I take Mundhirī to be a western Ibāḍī.

[72] *Ibid.*, 280.8 (for Ghazzālī's levels, see below, ch. 16, 438–41). The material could have come through Jayṭālī (cf. *Qanāṭir*, 172–5), but there is nothing to prove it.

[73] Mundhirī, *Mukhtaṣar*, 280.7. [74] *Ibid.*, 280.13.

[75] Darjīnī, *Ṭabaqāt*, 107.7; for the biography of Abū Ṣāliḥ, see *ibid.*, 341–5. For the heresy of the Farthiyya see Lewicki, 'Les subdivisions de l'Ibāḍiyya', 81.

[76] Darjīnī, *Ṭabaqāt*, 145.17. For Abū Nūḥ, see *ibid.*, 353. Compare the activity of a gathering of teachers (*mashāyikh*) and pupils (*talāmidha*) in the time of Sulaymān ibn Yakhlaf al-Mazātī (Abū Zakariyyāʾ, *Siyar al-aʾimma*, 285.8).

[77] Darjīnī, *Ṭabaqāt*, 510.2. For other examples, see Shammākhī, *Siyar*, 1:128.24, 151.10, 163.10, 211.1; 2:24.9, 188.1, 195.23, 201.9, and cf. 92.6; also above, notes 30, 43, 50.

marked institutionalisation of clerical life developed among the North African Ibāḍīs, sometimes associated with considerable clerical power over the laity; the system is documented from as early as the beginning of the fifth/eleventh century, and in modern times is best known from the form it took in the Mozabite pentapolis.[78] One might have expected forbidding wrong to have figured prominently in such a context, but in fact this does not seem to have been the case.[79] A reference to the duty in the oldest extant clerical code is noteworthy in that it makes the righting of wrongs among the disciples of a teacher subject to his authority.[80]

3. THE EASTERN IBĀḌĪS

Of the the various eastern Ibāḍī communities that once existed, only that of Oman succeeded in surviving the centuries. Though more isolated in its region than the western communities, it was also politically more fortunate. Where the western Ibāḍīs lacked an imamate after the fall of the Rustumid dynasty in 296/909, a comparable trauma in Oman in 280/893 was less final; the Ibāḍī imamate experienced several subsequent revivals, and finally disappeared a little under half a century ago.

One implication of this for our topic is that the eastern tradition generated, or perhaps simply preserved, a great deal more literature reflecting the inevitable political quarrels that developed around the imamate. In the rather sanctimonious rhetoric of these disputes, forbidding wrong makes quite frequent appearances. An example is an open letter of the third/

[78] See *EI*², art. 'Ḥalḳa' (T. Lewicki), and, for a more detailed account of the system in the Mozab, S. Faath, *Die Banû Mîzâb: Eine religiöse Minderheit in Algerien zwischen Isolation und Integration*, Scheessel 1985, 60–79.

[79] Aṭfayyish makes the point that commanding and forbidding are not restricted to scholars (*'ulamā'*) (*Hīmyān*, 4:203.18 (to Q3:104)).

[80] In the code of conduct for students drawn up by Abū 'Abdallāh Muḥammad ibn Bakr (d. 440/1048f.) (for whom see T. Lewicki, 'Les historiens, biographes et traditionnistes ibāḍites–wahbites de l'Afrique du Nord du VIIIe au XVIe siècle', *Folia Orientalia*, 3 (1961), 29–31), and preserved by Darjīnī and Barrādī, there is a section devoted to the proper times for doing things. We read here in Darjīnī's version: 'The time to right wrongs is when they come to light; it is not restricted to a [particular] time (*waqt taghyīr al-munkar matā ẓahara, lā yanḥaṣir ilā waqt*). The teacher must take the initiative or give his permission, or someone more suited must take the initiative' (*wa-yushtaraṭ taqaddum al-shaykh aw bi-idhnihi aw taqaddum al-amthal*) (*Ṭabaqāt*, 182.8). Barrādī's version reads: *wa-yushtaraṭ fī inkār al-munkar taqdīm* [*sic*] *al-shaykh aw idhnuhu, wa-waqt inkārihi matā ẓahara, wa-lā yanḥaṣir fī waqt ghayr ẓuhūrihi* (*Jawāhir*, 217.7). Darjīnī's version is translated, and Barrādī's adduced in a footnote, by Rubinacci in his study of the code (R. Rubinacci, 'Un antico documento di vita cenobitica musulmana', in Istituto Universitario Orientale di Napoli, *Annali*, new series, 10 (1960), 76 and n. 319; Rubinacci gives a photographic reproduction of the Cracow manuscript of the *Ṭabaqāt*, which has a text differing slightly from the printed text, see plate I lines 3f.).

ninth-century scholar Abū 'l-Mu'thir al-Ṣalt ibn Khamīs regarding the civil war of the 270s/880s.[81] He describes Mūsā ibn Mūsā (d. 278/891), the scholar behind the deposition of the imam Ṣalt ibn Mālik in 272/886, as claiming to be engaged in forbidding wrong.[82] This, he says, stirred up the ignorant rabble, including those who loved commanding right but did not know right from wrong.[83] As if this was not bad enough, Mūsā's candidate for the imamate, Rāshid ibn al-Naẓr (r. 272–7/886–90), failed to forbid wrong in the matter of the burning of a house belonging to a member of the family of the deposed imam.[84] Then there was an incident of plundering by Rāshid's forces. If they claimed it was the work of interlopers, they admitted that they had been penetrated by people to whom they could not forbid wrong. They should have shown their disapproval (*inkār*) of the offence and corrected it (*yughayyirūhu*), whoever did it. Indeed Mūsā was asked to do so, but refused on grounds of fear; since he could in fact have done so, his refusal to perform the duty was tantamount to acquiescence.[85] Other writers of such political pamphlets make similar, if less intensive, use of the language of forbidding wrong.[86]

That the focus on the role of the imam is less marked here than in Zaydism is doubtless a reflection of the difference between Shīʿite and Khārijite conceptions of the relative significance of imam and congregation. Nevertheless eastern Ibāḍī sources frequently link forbidding wrong and the imamate in the same kind of way as the Zaydīs. Thus Muḥammad ibn Maḥbūb ibn al-Raḥīl (d. 260/873), in a letter to his Ibāḍī brethren in the west, says that the Muslims should dissociate from an imam who fails to forbid wrong.[87] Bisyawī, an authority of the fourth/tenth or fifth/eleventh century, identifies the imams as the 'best community' of Q3:110

[81] For Abū 'l-Mu'thir, see *EI*², art. 'Abū 'l-Mu'thir al-Bahlawī' (T. Lewicki). This civil war plays a role in the discussion of religious politics among the Omani scholars comparable to that of the civil war of 35–40/656–61 in Islam generally. It is surprising that it did not lead to a formal and lasting sectarian split in Omani Ibāḍism.

[82] Abū 'l-Mu'thir al-Ṣalt ibn Khamīs (third/ninth century), *al-Aḥdāth wa'l-ṣifāt*, in Kāshif, *Siyar*, 1:27.7. [83] *Ibid.*, 28.14. [84] *Ibid.*, 48.1.

[85] *Ibid.*, 52.11, 53.10. Cf. also *ibid.*, 51.3, 52.9, 56.10, 65.8, 81.7, and a further epistle of Abū 'l-Mu'thir, also in Kāshif, *Siyar*, 1:256.14, 261.15.

[86] See the epistle of Munīr ibn al-Nayyir al-Jaʿlānī upbraiding the imam Ghassān ibn ʿAbdallāh (r. 192–207/808–23), *ibid.*, 1:245.17, 246.4, 252.1; that of Abū 'l-Ḥawārī (*fl. c.* 300/912) to some Ibāḍīs of Ḥaḍramawt, *ibid.*, 338.12, 365.11 (for this scholar, see below, note 105); that of Abū Qaḥṭān Khālid ibn Qaḥṭān (third/ninth century) quoting a letter of Ṣalt ibn Mālik (r. 237–72/851–86), *ibid.*, 128.8, 128.16; that of Qāḍī Muḥammad ibn ʿĪsā al-Sirrī to the imam Rāshid ibn ʿAlī (d. 513/1119f.), *ibid.*, 411.1, 417.2.

[87] Muḥammad ibn Maḥbūb ibn al-Raḥīl (d. 260/873), *Sīra*, in Kāshif, *Siyar*, 2:242.15, and cf. *ibid.*, 261.4, 267.9. In this letter he also lays emphasis on the duty of the scholars and others to forbid wrong to the imams (*ibid.*, 239.10, 240.2, 248.13). For the Zaydī linking of forbidding wrong and the imamate, see above, ch. 10, section 3.

when they command right and forbid wrong.[88] The duty is readily mentioned in the context of the 'seller' (*shārī*) imam, who with his followers (*shurāt*) 'sells' himself to God in pursuit of martyrdom.[89] Thus Abū 'l-Mu'thir in one of his epistles speaks of the imam who has sold himself to God for the forbidding of wrong.[90] Likewise a twelfth/eighteenth-century compiler has a chapter on imams who sold themselves (to God) for the righting of wrong (*fī inkār al-munkar*).[91] An abortive rising in the mid-thirteenth/nineteenth century involved no imam, but demonstrates the linkage between forbidding wrong and righteous rebellion. Forty men, against the wishes of their relatives, resolved on 'selling' themselves to God, donned shrouds, and went forth to command right and forbid wrong. However, the group went to pieces after they agreed to accept presents sent by the sultan, and they all went home.[92]

Forbidding wrong was also a standard part of the formula by which allegiance to a new imam was offered and accepted. It features in general juristic prescriptions,[93] and in numerous reports relating to particular imams.[94] The duty also appears in other ways in accounts of the inceptions of imamates. According to Abū 'l-Mu'thir, when the Muslims prevail, their leaders

[88] Bisyawī, *Jāmiʿ*, 4:192.18. Elsewhere, in a polemic directed against the Rāfiḍa, he argues that their supposed imam cannot in fact be one, since he does not command right and forbid wrong (*Sīra*, in Kāshif, *Siyar*, 2:134.15; cf. above, ch. 10, note 39 on Zaydī polemic against the Imāmīs). For Bisyawī, see below, note 110.

[89] For this politically activist Ibāḍī (and broadly Khārijite) conception and its Koranic foundation, see Ennāmi, *Studies*, 231–4.

[90] Kāshif, *Siyar*, 1:263.7. Compare Muḥammad ibn Maḥbūb, *Sīra*, *ibid.*, 2:243.1, 255.3.

[91] Izkawī (twelfth/eighteenth century), *Kashf al-ghumma*, ms. London, British Library, Or. 8,076, f. 265b.13 (and cf. *ibid.*, f. 279a.20).

[92] Sālimī, *Tuḥfa*, 2:225.19; J. C. Wilkinson, *The Imamate tradition of Oman*, Cambridge 1987, 233. Sālimī's understanding is that they appointed no imam, and instead reached decisions by consultation (*shūrā*) among themselves (*ibid.*, 226.12); he does not fault this.

[93] See, for example, Abū ʿAbdallāh al-Kindī (d. towards 508/1114), *Bayān al-sharʿ*, Oman 1982–93, 28:111.4, 111.22, 112.7 (I owe my references to this volume of this work to Patricia Crone); J. C. Wilkinson, 'The Ibāḍī *imāma*', *Bulletin of the School of Oriental and African Studies*, 39 (1976), 539; Wilkinson, *Imamate tradition*, 170 (and cf. also *ibid.*, 159, 177f.).

[94] I have noted the cases of Wārith ibn Kaʿb (r. 179–92/796–808) (Sālimī, *Tuḥfa*, 1:115.1, on the authority of Bisyawī); Muhannā ibn Jayfar (r. 226–37/841–51) (Kindī, *Bayān*, 28:112.22; Sālimī, *Tuḥfa*, 1:150.3); Rāshid ibn al-Walīd (second quarter of the fourth/tenth century?) (*ibid.*, 280.21; Izkawī (twelfth/eighteenth century), *Kashf al-ghumma*, ed. A. ʿUbaydalī, Nicosia 1985, 306.15 (this publication is an edition of select chapters of the *Kashf al-ghumma*, the attribution of which to Izkawī the editor rejects); for this imam, see Wilkinson, *Imamate tradition*, 349 n. 19); Rāshid ibn Saʿīd (fourth or fifth/tenth or eleventh century) (Kindī, *Bayān*, 28:111.8; Sālimī, *Tuḥfa*, 1:304.5; for this imam, see Wilkinson, *Imamate tradition*, 210); Nāṣir ibn Murshid (r. 1034–59/1625–49) (Sālimī, *Tuḥfa*, 2:21.20); ʿAzzān ibn Qays (r. 1285–7/1868–70) (*ibid.*, 247.9); Sālim ibn Rāshid al-Kharūṣī (r. 1331–8/1913–20) (Muḥammad ibn ʿAbdallāh al-Sālimī (writing 1380/1961), *Nahḍat al-aʿyān*, Cairo n.d., 152.6, 184.2).

gather and choose as imam the most outstanding of them in – among other things – strength to forbid wrong.[95] The election of Nāṣir ibn Murshid (r. 1034–59/1625–49), the first Yaʿrubī imam, was the outcome of consultations about the appointment of an imam to command right and forbid wrong.[96] In 1262/1846 a gathering at Rustāq was to set up an imam who would command right and forbid wrong, but nothing came of it.[97]

Once in office, a new imam acted accordingly. Nāṣir ibn Murshid travelled around the country, receiving the submission of local communities and performing the duty.[98] When Aḥmad ibn Saʿīd (ruled *c.* 1167–88/1754–75), the first ruler of the reigning Āl Bū Saʿīd dynasty, had taken office, and all fair-minded people had submitted to him, he proceeded to command right and forbid wrong.[99] After this initial phase of a reign we tend to hear rather less about forbidding wrong. However, Sulṭān ibn Sayf (r. from 1059/1649 to *c.* 1091/1680), the second Yaʿrubī imam, is described as not ceasing to command right and forbid wrong till he died.[100] At the same time imams instructed their provincial governors to perform the duty.[101] Sending out military expeditions likewise serves the purpose of forbidding wrong.[102] And so on, and so forth.[103]

95 Abū 'l-Mu'thir, *Aḥdāth*, in Kāshif, *Siyar*, 1:77.10.

96 Ibn Qayṣar (writing 1050/1640), *Sīrat al-imām Nāṣir ibn Murshid*, ed. ʿA. Ḥ. al-Qaysī, Oman 1983, 14.18; Izkawī, *Kashf al-ghumma*, ed. ʿUbaydalī, 348.20, and cf. 349.2; Ibn Ruzayq (writing 1274/1857), *al-Fatḥ al-mubīn*, ed. ʿA. ʿĀmir and M. M. ʿAbdallāh, Oman 1977, 262.3, and cf. 262.7 (for which see also his *al-Shuʿāʿ al-shāʾiʿ*, ed. ʿA. ʿĀmir, Cairo 1978, 204.7); Sālimī, *Tuḥfa*, 2:3.11.

97 Ibn Ruzayq, *Fatḥ*, 548.14 (and see Sālimī, *Tuḥfa*, 2:218.6). For this incident, see also R. G. Landen, *Oman since 1856*, Princeton 1967, 70 n. 37; Wilkinson, 'The Ibāḍī *imāma*', 543; Wilkinson, *Imamate tradition*, 172. Ibn Ruzayq's turn of phrase here is noteworthy; he does not speak of *al-amr bi'l-maʿrūf* in his account of those Āl Bū Saʿīd rulers who were not imams.

98 Ibn Ruzayq, *Fatḥ*, 265.9 (Nizwā), 265.23 (Manḥ), 266.4 (Samad al-Sha'n).

99 *Ibid.*, 364.10.

100 *Ibid.*, 292.2; Ibn Ruzayq, *Shuʿāʿ*, 258.1. The same is said of Wārith ibn Kaʿb (*ibid.*, 33.9), while ʿAbd al-Malik ibn Ḥumayd (r. 207–26/823–41) continued until he became too old and decrepit (*ibid.*, 38.8). Ibn Ruzayq also associates *al-amr bi'l-maʿrūf* with other imams (*Shuʿāʿ*, 39.4, 82.16, 267.18), and includes it in a general statement about the just imam (*ibid.*, 10.10).

101 Sālimī, *Tuḥfa*, 1:184.5 (imam Ṣalt ibn Mālik); *ibid.*, 309.18 (imam Rāshid ibn Saʿīd); Ibn Qayṣar, *Sīra*, 49.2, 64.2, and Sālimī, *Tuḥfa*, 2:27.7, 27.17, 30.2, 30.14, 32.14, 33.2, 33.20, 34.18 (imam Nāṣir ibn Murshid); Ibn Ruzayq, *Fatḥ*, 291.5, and Sālimī, *Tuḥfa*, 2:49.3 (imam Sulṭān ibn Sayf); Muḥammad al-Sālimī, *Nahḍa*, 267.6, 267.18 (imam Kharūṣī); and cf. *ibid.*, 432.17, 434.6 (imam Khalīlī (r. 1338–73/1920–54) in appointments of *qāḍīs*).

102 See Sālimī, *Tuḥfa*, 1:249.10, in a quotation from Abū 'l-Ḥawārī. Cf. also *ibid.*, 317.19.

103 For further material, see *ibid.*, 2:23.21, 176.12, 223.3, 230.18, 250.2; Muḥammad al-Sālimī, *Nahḍa*, 169.9, 179.14. In an aberration induced by the diplomatic history of the last imamate, imam Khalīlī in a letter written shortly before his death to the king of Saudi Arabia expresses his hope that God will include the king among those who command right and forbid wrong under the terms of Q22:41 (*ibid.*, 443.4; the letter is not free of modern political diction).

The great bulk of the Omani material on forbidding wrong is, however, juristic in nature. The older material consists of collections of the opinions of jurists on specific questions; where these authorities are named and known, they are often scholars of the third/ninth century. Some of these opinions relate to the duties of those in authority, particularly imams, some to the duties of ordinary Muslims, and much is of unclear reference. Such material is preserved in a number of compilations, of which I have used four. The first is ascribed to Faḍl ibn al-Ḥawārī (d. 278/892),[104] the second to Abū ʾl-Ḥawārī Muḥammad ibn al-Ḥawārī (*fl. c.* 300/912),[105] the third to Abū ʿAbdallāh al-Kindī (d. towards 508/1114)[106] and the fourth to Abū Bakr al-Kindī (d. *c.* 557/1161).[107] Accounts of forbidding wrong in works by individual authors first appear with scholars of the fourth or fifth/tenth or eleventh century: Ibn Baraka,[108]

104 Faḍl ibn al-Ḥawārī (d. 278/892), *Jāmiʿ*, Oman 1985, 3:190–228 (all my references are to the third and last volume; I am indebted to Lesley Wilkins for procuring me a copy of this work). As with many recent publications of eastern Ibāḍī texts, including most of those used in this study, the work is printed, not edited; there is no introduction, and the state of the text leaves a lot to be desired. The work as now constituted cannot have been compiled by Faḍl ibn al-Ḥawārī, since on occasion it refers back to the time of the imam Rāshid ibn Saʿīd (*ibid.*, 191.16, 193.3, cf. above, note 94; it also cites a responsum of Abū ʾl-Ḥawārī, *ibid.*, 225.12, 227.15). For Faḍl ibn al-Ḥawārī, see Wilkinson, *Imamate tradition*, 209. His death date seems to be secure; but in general, the reader should be aware that there is often great uncertainty as to the dating of Omani scholars.

105 Abū ʾl-Ḥawārī Muḥammad ibn al-Ḥawārī (*fl. c.* 300/912), *Jāmiʿ*, Oman 1985, 1:127–31 (all my references are to the first of the five volumes; again, I am indebted to Lesley Wilkins for procuring me a copy of this work). For Abū ʾl-Ḥawārī, see Wilkinson, *Imamate tradition*, 189, 196. But here again, the compiler cannot be Abū ʾl-Ḥawārī. The first discussion in the work opens with the words *min al-kitāb al-mansūb ilā Abī ʾl-Ḥawārī* (*Jāmiʿ*, 11.5), and later the compiler adduces the views of Abū ʾl-Ḥasan (*ibid.*, 16.16) and Abū Saʿīd (*ibid.*, 23.12); the former is to be identified with Abū ʾl-Ḥasan al-Bisyawī, and the latter with Abū Saʿīd al-Kudamī – both scholars who seem to have lived in the fourth/tenth or fifth/eleventh century (see below, notes 109f.). In any case, the chapter on *al-amr biʾl-maʿrūf* is described as an addendum (*min al-iḍāfa ilā ʾl-kitāb*, *ibid.*, 127.2).

106 Kindī, *Bayān*, 29:7–98 (apart from the references given above, notes 93f., all references to 'Kindī, *Bayān*' are to the twenty-ninth volume of this work; I am grateful to Khaled Abou El Fadl for lending me his copy). For this work, see G. R. Smith, 'The Omani manuscript collection at Muscat', *Arabian Studies*, 4 (1978), 166–9. Here too, the identity of the work is somewhat problematic; the compiler refers several times to the *Bayān al-sharʿ* as the source from which he draws (Kindī, *Bayān*, 16.7, 16.9, 16.16, 70.1), and at one point (*ibid.*, 69.12) he quotes from the supposedly later *Muṣannaf* (for this work see the next note).

107 Abū Bakr al-Kindī (d. *c.* 557/1161), *Muṣannaf*, Cairo and Maṭraḥ 1979–84, 12:5–80 (all my references to 'Abū Bakr al-Kindī, *Muṣannaf*' are to the twelfth volume of this work). For this work, see Smith, 'The Omani manuscript collection at Muscat', 163–6. While the ascription may be sounder than in the previous cases, it is not unproblematic: at one point a certain Muḥammad (ibn) ʿAbd al-Salām is quoted for an event that took place in Nizwā in 886/1481f. (Abū Bakr al-Kindī, *Muṣannaf*, 39.3), and the same authority is also quoted elsewhere (*ibid.*, 32.18, 56.14, 59.15).

108 Ibn Baraka (fourth/tenth century), *Jāmiʿ*, ed. ʿI. Y. al-Bārūnī, Oman 1971–3, 1:180–4

Kudamī[109] and Bisyawī.[110] The later authorities whose discussions of the duty are available to me are Shaqṣī (*fl. c.* 1034/1625),[111] Khalīlī (d. 1287/1871)[112] and Sālimī (d. 1332/1914).[113]

The picture given by the early sources of the wrongs that concerned Ibāḍī jurists is a rich one, but in large part it is already familiar from the repertoires of other sects and schools. There is the usual matter of liquor; thus action should be taken against those who gather to drink, including women who do so.[114] The same goes for those who gather to make music, men and women;[115] as will be seen, various instruments are considered, not to mention singing.[116] There is a measure of local colour in the attention

(all my references are to this first volume). On Ibn Baraka see *EI*², art. 'Ibn Baraka' (T. Lewicki), and J. C. Wilkinson, 'Bio-bibliographical background to the crisis period in the Ibāḍī Imāmate of Oman', *Arabian Studies*, 3 (1976), 151f. Both date him to the fourth/tenth century, as do Crone and Zimmermann in their forthcoming study.

109 Kudamī (fourth/tenth century), *Muʿtabar*, Ruwī 1984, 2:211–13 (I owe my xerox of this text to Wafa Al-Zaid, and have not seen the work itself). For Kudamī, see Wilkinson, 'Bio-bibliographical background', 147f. (but note that Darjīnī in the passage referred to indirectly by Wilkinson (*Ṭabaqāt*, 2:445.3) does not in fact mention Abū Saʿīd al-ʿUmānī); J. C. Wilkinson, 'The Omani manuscript collection at Muscat', *Arabian Studies*, 4 (1978), 196, assigning him to the fourth/tenth and early fifth/eleventh century. In dating him to the fourth/tenth century I follow Crone and Zimmermann in their forthcoming study.

110 Bisyawī, *Jāmiʿ*, 4:184–93 (all my references are to this volume); Bisyawī, *Mukhtaṣar*, Oman n.d., 275–7; also his *Sīra*, in Kāshif, *Siyar*, 2:146–74. For Bisyawī or Bisyānī, see Wilkinson, 'Bio-bibliographical background', 152, dating him to the fifth/eleventh century; Crone and Zimmermann in their forthcoming study redate him to the fourth/tenth century.

111 Shaqṣī (*fl. c.* 1034/1625), *Manhaj al-ṭālibīn*, Cairo and Muscat *c.* 1979–, 8:6–39 (all my references are to this eighth volume). For Shaqṣī see Wilkinson, 'Bio-bibliographical background', 144.

112 Khalīlī (d. 1287/1871), *Tamhīd qawāʿid al-īmān*, Oman 1986–7, 7:5–77 (all my references are to this seventh volume of the work, which I cite only for points of particular interest). I owe my knowledge of this work to Joachim Düster. The chapter on *al-amr bi'l-maʿrūf* begins and ends with responsa of Khalīlī (*ibid.*, 5–28, 72–7). In between we find a long extract from a *Kitāb ighāthat al-malhūf bi'l-sayf al-mudhakkar* (read so) *fī 'l-amr bi'l-maʿrūf wa'l-nahy ʿan al-munkar* (*ibid.*, 29–72); this is doubtless the epistle of Khalīlī mentioned by the younger Sālimī with the title *al-Sayf al-mudhakkar fī 'l-amr bi'l-maʿrūf wa'l-nahy ʿan al-munkar* (Muḥammad al-Sālimī, *Nahḍa*, 331.19). Saʿīd ibn Khalfān al-Khalīlī was the major figure in the religious movement in the interior of Oman that issued in the imamate of ʿAzzān ibn Qays.

113 Sālimī (d. 1332/1914), *Jawhar al-Niẓām*, Cairo 1381, 487–93 (the relevant material is actually at 487–9). The work is a revised version of a twelfth/eighteenth-century work (see *ibid.*, 2.11, 3.5). I owe my copy of this text to Patricia Crone.

114 Faḍl, *Jāmiʿ*, 192.9; Kindī, *Bayān*, 34.20, 97.7; Abū Bakr al-Kindī, *Muṣannaf*, 69.3. For women, see Kindī, *Bayān*, 81.12; Abū Bakr al-Kindī, *Muṣannaf*, 33.3, 72.1, 148.8. But there would seem to be nothing wrong with women innocently gathering and sitting together in the street (Kindī, *Bayān*, 38.8).

115 Faḍl, *Jāmiʿ*, 218.4; Abū 'l-Ḥawārī, *Jāmiʿ*, 129.11; Kindī, *Bayān*, 50.15; Abū Bakr al-Kindī, *Muṣannaf*, 64.12; Shaqṣī, *Manhaj*, 20.3.

116 Kindī, *Bayān*, 57.9 (classifying singing as a grave sin), 58.14, 79.18; Abū Bakr al-Kindī, *Muṣannaf*, 58.3, 60.5.

given to African and Indian music (*la'b al-Zanj wa'l-Hind*).[117] As often, puritanism is as much opposed to uninhibited grief as to uninhibited pleasure, and the behaviour of women in mourning appears repeatedly as a target of the duty.[118] Another kind of shrieking (*zu'āq*) that meets with disapproval seems to be practised by men, particularly in warfare.[119] Various practices of non-Ibāḍīs constitute wrongs to be righted,[120] and so forth; as Shaqṣī observes, it would take too long to go into it all.[121]

It is noteworthy that the attitudes of the jurists are not uniformly hard-line in all these matters. The single most prominent motive behind the softer views is military. One jurist who considers playing chess a grave sin allows it when the object is instruction in military strategy.[122] Another describes male shrieking as a wrong and a residue of the Jāhiliyya, but relents when asked to consider it as a war-cry intended to rally the troops and strike fear into the enemy; he expresses the hope that it may then be permitted, though his preference would be for the use of the Islamic war-cry 'God is greatest!'[123] Likewise Muḥammad ibn Maḥbūb permitted the Ḥaḍramīs to use a certain kind of drum (the *duhra*)[124] for military pur-

[117] Faḍl, *Jāmi'*, 218.13 (for *al-ribḥ* read *al-Zanj*); Abū 'l-Ḥawārī, *Jāmi'*, 129.18; Kindī, *Bayān*, 50.21, and cf. 42.21; Abū Bakr al-Kindī, *Muṣannaf*, 66.14.

[118] Faḍl, *Jāmi'*, 194.5, 196.1; Abū 'l-Ḥawārī, *Jāmi'*, 128.14, 130.18, 132.17 (the latter two passages mention both men and women); Kindī, *Bayān*, 33.8, 77.4; Abū Bakr al-Kindī, *Muṣannaf*, 30.9, 33.3, 58.6; Shaqṣī, *Manhaj*, 11.15, 22.5. One of the early Ibāḍī imams of Ḥaḍramawt used to send even free women to prison for such conduct (Faḍl, *Jāmi'*, 194.10; Kindī, *Bayān*, 77.15; Abū Bakr al-Kindī, *Muṣannaf*, 59.2). A later Ḥaḍramī imam includes *nawḥ al-nā'iḥāt* among the various wrongs he is committed to banning (Abū Isḥāq Ibrāhīm ibn Qays (fifth/eleventh century), *Dīwān al-sayf al-naqqād*, ed. Sulaymān al-Bārūnī, n.p. n.d., 12.16 (cf. 2.14 of Bārūnī's introduction); for this imam, see Wilkinson, 'Bio-bibliographical background', 152f.). The terms most frequently used in these contexts are *nawḥ* and *ṣurākh*; but for a narrow definition of *nawḥ*, see Kindī, *Bayān*, 77.11, 81.16.

[119] Faḍl, *Jāmi'*, 190.12; Kindī, *Bayān*, 37.20; Abū Bakr al-Kindī, *Muṣannaf*, 61.2, 61.14; Shaqṣī, *Manhaj*, 22.5.

[120] An example is the practice of *qunūt* in prayer by non-Ibāḍī Muslims (Faḍl, *Jāmi'*, 228.4; Kindī, *Bayān*, 67.3; Abū Bakr al-Kindī, *Muṣannaf*, 43.8; Shaqṣī, *Manhaj*, 17.10; cf. above, note 43). More generally, Ibn Baraka is of the view that one may not sit in the gatherings of proponents of a heresy (*bid'a 'an aḥad ahl al-madhāhib*) except with the purpose of engaging in disputation with them, and with the expectation of some success in converting them (*Jāmi'*, 182.9, whence Kindī, *Bayān*, 26.6, and Abū Bakr al-Kindī, *Muṣannaf*, 66.4).

[121] Shaqṣī, *Manhaj*, 12.8.

[122] Kindī, *Bayān*, 48.11, and cf. 57.17, 58.9; Abū Bakr al-Kindī, *Muṣannaf*, 63.16. Reference is made to the Shāfi'ite view (Kindī, *Bayān*, 58.3; Abū Bakr al-Kindī, *Muṣannaf*, 64.4; cf. above, ch. 6, note 151, and, for the military motive in particular, Wieber, *Schachspiel*, 189f.). The jurist in question, Abū 'l-Qāsim Sa'īd ibn Quraysh, must have been a figure of the later fourth/tenth century or so, if he is the father of the *qāḍī* Ḥasan ibn Sa'īd ibn Quraysh who was present at the writing of a letter in 443/1052 (Sālimī, *Tuḥfa*, 1:313.8).

[123] Faḍl, *Jāmi'*, 190.12; Kindī, *Bayān*, 37.20; Abū Bakr al-Kindī, *Muṣannaf*, 61.2 (with ascription to Kudamī); Shaqṣī, *Manhaj*, 22.5.

[124] It is defined by Shaqṣī as a small, long drum (*ṭabl ṣaghīr ṭawīl*, *Manhaj*, 20.9). As pointed out to me by Shohreh Gholsorkhi, this is most likely to be an Iranian loan-word (cf.

poses.[125] Such use of the instrument was, however, a controversial matter, as reports relating to the reign of imam Muhannā ibn Jayfar (r. 226–37/841–51) make clear. One jurist recollects that in the coastal city of Ṣuḥār, Maṭṭār and his men had not been prevented from use of this drum, and he wonders what the doctrine of the scholars concerned can have been;[126] we know from elsewhere that this Maṭṭār and his men were Indians, a military force which the imam maintained in Ṣuḥār.[127] Another jurist states that a certain Abū 'l-Ḥawārī al-Maʿnī used to object to the Indian who beat the drum in the camp (sc. at Nizwā in the Omani interior), and distanced himself from the imam in consequence.[128] More striking than any of this is the discussion of the question whether the imam may overlook the misdeeds of his own followers in wartime; one view accepts this concession, the other rejects it.[129] The emphasis on military efficacy is doubtless linked to the resilience of the imamate in Oman.

Accommodating views can also be inspired by less martial considerations. To take the case of musical instruments, the jurists will consider – though not necessarily adopt – a kinder view of an instrument if it meets one or more of the following criteria: it is not actually being played;[130] it is being played without the accompaniment of singing, revelry or partying;[131] it could in principle be used for some legitimate purpose;[132] it is being used by children at play rather than by adults.[133] They also look more favourably (or less disfavourably) on some instruments than on others.[134] The results are complex, and the jurists frequently disagree, but a couple

Persian *duhul*), though given the association of the instrument with Indians in our texts, it is worth noting that it is also widely represented in Indo-Aryan languages (see R. L. Turner, *A comparative dictionary of the Indo-Aryan languages*, London 1966, 318 no. 5,608).

125 See Faḍl, *Jāmiʿ*, 221.14; Kindī, *Bayān*, 51.19, 58.17; Abū Bakr al-Kindī, *Muṣannaf*, 56.18; cf. also Faḍl, *Jāmiʿ*, 222.2, 226.9; Kindī, *Bayān*, 43.1, 46.15, 50.1, 52.1; Abū Bakr al-Kindī, *Muṣannaf*, 61.6, 63.2; Shaqṣī, *Manhaj*, 20.18, 22.7.

126 Faḍl, *Jāmiʿ*, 218.13; Abū 'l-Ḥawārī, *Jāmiʿ*, 129.19; Kindī, *Bayān*, 50.21; Abū Bakr al-Kindī, *Muṣannaf*, 66.14. Two of the three scholars mentioned here, Sulaymān ibn al-Ḥakam and Waḍḍāḥ ibn ʿUqba, are included by Abū 'l-Muʾthir in a list of scholars contemporary with Muḥammad ibn Maḥbūb (Kāshif, *Siyar*, 1:24.13); for the third, Mūsā ibn ʿAlī (d. 230/844), see Wilkinson, *Imamate tradition*, 154f.

127 See Izkawī, *Kashf al-ghumma*, ed. ʿUbaydalī, 262.5, and the editor's n. 2 thereto.

128 Faḍl, *Jāmiʿ*, 219.3; Abū 'l-Ḥawārī, *Jāmiʿ*, 130.4; Kindī, *Bayān*, 51.4.

129 *Ibid.*, 41.2.

130 See, for example, *ibid.*, 47.9, 49.11, 51.13.

131 See, for example, *ibid.*, 47.16, 50.16, 56.3 (singing); 47.13, 50.15, 55.6 (revelry and partying).

132 See, for example, *ibid.*, 51.7, 56.16, 58.11.

133 Faḍl, *Jāmiʿ*, 209.10; Kindī, *Bayān*, 51.15 (but cf. 51.11, 98.2); Abū Bakr al-Kindī, *Muṣannaf*, 63.10, 80.10.

134 One of the instruments they dislike most is the *zammāra*, a wind-instrument which is to be destroyed in all circumstances, even if the owner is all alone (see, for example, Kindī, *Bayān*, 50.19).

of examples will serve to illustrate their attitudes. They have a soft spot for a large and mournful pipe of some kind (the *qaṣaba kabīra*), considering it permissible to listen to its music – provided this is not accompanied by singing and partying – in order to focus one's thoughts on death and the next world; one third/ninth-century scholar saw his father listen and weep.[135] On a somewhat more cheerful note, some jurists are prepared to allow the tambourine provided it is not associated with revelry,[136] though others are unrelenting.[137] One view here is that it is acceptable to strike it once or twice – but not more – in order to publicise a wedding.[138] Similar complexities arise with regard to vessels that contain – or are denied to contain, or formerly contained, or may in future contain – liquor.[139] Altogether, the Ibāḍī scholars should probably not be thought of as in principle more puritanical than any others; their attitude to joking was perhaps a little more liberal than Ghazzālī's.[140]

Who is supposed to deal with all these offences? Here the role of the authorities bulks large. The duty divides into two parts: that which obligates people in general (*al-kāffa*) in so far as they are able to undertake it, and that which obligates the imams of justice and their officers (*umarāʾ*) to the exclusion of the people at large (*al-ʿāmma*).[141] In the context of the 'three modes' tradition, one jurist remarks that the 'hand' of the imam extends further than that of anyone else.[142] Likewise the imams and their officers are described as singled out (*makhṣūṣūn*) to undertake the duty.[143] There are also indications that the imams may have had followers whose business it was to execute it. The 'sellers' (*shurāt*), who were in principle political activists who had sold themselves to God in pursuit of martyrdom, may in practice have tended to degenerate into a rather disorderly tribal militia;[144] but they also appear to have had some role in policing Ibāḍī

135 Faḍl, *Jāmiʿ*, 218.10; Abū ʾl-Ḥawārī, *Jāmiʿ*, 129.18; Kindī, *Bayān*, 55.15; Abū Bakr al-Kindī, *Muṣannaf*, 64.14. The son, Ziyād ibn al-Waḍḍāḥ, was a contemporary of Muḥammad ibn Maḥbūb (he is mentioned in the list cited above, note 126).

136 Faḍl, *Jāmiʿ*, 220.16, 221.6, 225.5; Kindī, *Bayān*, 48.16, 49.1; and cf. Shaqṣī, *Manhaj*, 20.13.

137 Faḍl, *Jāmiʿ*, 219.11, 221.10, 226.2; Abū ʾl-Ḥawārī, *Jāmiʿ*, 128.20, 129.5; Kindī, *Bayān*, 48.1, 49.4; Abū Bakr al-Kindī, *Muṣannaf*, 55.17; Shaqṣī, *Manhaj*, 20.15.

138 Abū Bakr al-Kindī, *Muṣannaf*, 56.4, and cf. 55.11.

139 See, for example, Kindī, *Bayān*, 93–8.

140 Abū Bakr al-Kindī, *Muṣannaf*, 68.5; cf. below, ch. 16, 445.

141 See Faḍl, *Jāmiʿ*, 197.4 (corrupt), and Abū Bakr al-Kindī, *Muṣannaf*, 23.4, from Abū ʾl-Mundhir Bashīr ibn Muḥammad ibn Maḥbūb (*fl.* late third/ninth century, see Wilkinson, *Imamate tradition*, 190, 191); also Shaqṣī, *Manhaj*, 6.7.

142 Faḍl, *Jāmiʿ*, 209.5 (*yad al-imām absaṭ min yad ghayrihi*). This is from Abū Muḥammad, i.e. Ibn Baraka.

143 Kindī, *Bayān*, 32.17; Abū Bakr al-Kindī, *Muṣannaf*, 24.11.

144 Wilkinson, *Imamate tradition*, 184f.

society.[145] A passage concerned with the offence of unsheathing arms in the market-place or street mentions that it is a particularly grave matter if a man does so against 'sellers' who are commanding him right and forbidding him wrong.[146] Very often, however, it is simply unclear whether the jurists, in speaking of the performance of the duty, have in mind those in authority or others.[147]

Much of what the jurists have to say about the duty of ordinary people is familiar and unsurprising; for example, the 'three modes' doctrine is well established.[148] It will be more rewarding here to leave aside the gentler end of the spectrum – white lies calculated to make the offender desist,[149] scowling[150] and the like – and concentrate on performance involving action. Here individuals cannot, of course, inflict punishment, though Kudamī allows that in exceptional cases they may achieve a recognition that entitles them to do this.[151] He goes on to say that individuals have a duty to right wrongs in any way they can, and that since there cannot in principle be a limit to this, it may extend to beating and fighting.[152] This activism is not isolated. We learn that a significant duty of ordinary people (*al-kāffa*) is to come to the aid of those seeking it, whether they are commanded to give this assistance by the imams or not; if the authorities are to hand, well and good, but if not, and if the wrongdoers will not desist unless they are fought (*illā bi-jihādihim*), then people have the right to

145 From an account of an event of 886/1481f. (see above, note 107) we learn that the *shurāt* had such a role in Nizwā at that time (Abū Bakr al-Kindī, *Muṣannaf*, 39.5).

146 Kindī, *Bayān*, 196.7; Abū Bakr al-Kindī, *Muṣannaf*, 85.10; cf. also Faḍl, *Jāmiʿ*, 191.9 (for *al-shirk* read *al-shirā'*), 223.12, 227.3; Kindī, *Bayān*, 56.3, 93.3. 93.8; Abū Bakr al-Kindī, *Muṣannaf*, 22.4, 30.1, 63.5, 74.10; Shaqṣī, *Manhaj*, 6.7, 14.9, 27.1. There are other references to persons undertaking the duty which are suggestive of official functionaries (Kindī, *Bayān*, 87.20; Abū Bakr al-Kindī, *Muṣannaf*, 30.5, 40.6, 149.1; and cf. Bisyawī, *Mukhtaṣar*, 275.21, 276.19). However, the term *muṭawwaʿ* does not appear in the texts I have used, though it seems to have been in common use around the time of the imamate of ʿAzzān ibn Qays (r. 1285–7/1868–70) (see Sālimī, *Tuḥfa*, 2:225.16 (where the term is explained as meaning a pietist); Wilkinson, *Imamate tradition*, 232f., 237, 242; Landen, *Oman*, 297f., 308f.; J. G. Lorimer, *Gazetteer of the Persian Gulf*, Calcutta 1908–15, 1:2374f.).

147 See, for example, Abū Bakr al-Kindī, *Muṣannaf*, 79.2 (not a trivial ambiguity, since it relates to raiding homes).

148 Abū 'l-Ḥawārī, *Jāmiʿ*, 127.7 (from a responsum of Abū 'l-Ḥawārī); Kindī, *Bayān*, 12.3, 22.11; Abū Bakr al-Kindī, *Muṣannaf*, 28.3 (and cf. 22.10); Bisyawī, *Jāmiʿ*, 190.1 (but with a twist for which see below, notes 180, 209); Bisyawī, *Mukhtaṣar*, 276.12; Kudamī, *Muʿtabar*, 211.18; and cf. Abū 'l-Mu'thir al-Ṣalt ibn Khamīs (third/ninth century), *Sīra*, in Kāshif, *Siyar*, 2:317.14. The 'three modes' tradition is likewise known to the Ibāḍīs (Faḍl, *Jāmiʿ*, 209.3; Kindī, *Bayān*, 17.14; Abū Bakr al-Kindī, *Muṣannaf*, 22.7).

149 Kindī, *Bayān*, 17.5; Abū Bakr al-Kindī, *Muṣannaf*, 30.12; Shaqṣī, *Manhaj*, 14.12.

150 Abū Bakr al-Kindī, *Muṣannaf*, 20.3.

151 Kindī, *Bayān*, 23.14.

152 *Ibid.*, 23.19.

fight them.[153] Curiously, and in contrast to the western Ibāḍīs, there is no explicit mention of the sword.[154]

Much of the action prescribed or described is less drastic than this. A contemporary of Muḥammad ibn Maḥbūb drives away a female mourner (*bākiya*) at a funeral.[155] We likewise find individuals engaged in such standard activities as pouring out liquor and breaking musical instruments. Two scholars of the third/ninth century hold that subjects (*raʿiyya*) may take such action in the absence of an imam when the nuisances in question directly affect them.[156] In one anecdote we are told that a man was walking in the market of Ṣuḥār, and saw someone with a drum (*duhr*); he broke it, whereupon the owner reported him to Muḥammad ibn Maḥbūb, who merely ordered him to return the fragments.[157] We also encounter more intrusive responses. Thus a jurist states that there is disagreement on the question whether a man who hears of a drinking party in a home may enter it without asking leave; but he himself seems to favour the hard-line view of the question, for he goes on to say that one may climb over the wall if denied leave to enter, though one should not damage the wall.[158]

There is also a more accommodationist strain in evidence among the jurists – to a surprising extent the same ones. In this view, that part of the duty which is incumbent on the authorities may be performed by ordinary people (*al-ʿāmma*) only by way of counselling (*mawʿiẓa*) and talk of hell-fire.[159] Whereas the imams and their officers are singled out for the duty, subjects are obliged only to counsel people.[160] In the absence of imams, the duty of the Muslims regarding such wrongs is to give good counsel (*al-mawʿiẓa al-ḥasana*, cf. Q16:125);[161] but when the imams are there, the

[153] Faḍl, *Jāmiʿ*, 197.8 (for *juhhāl* read *jihād* in lines 13 and 18); Kindī, *Bayān*, 31.19; Abū Bakr al-Kindī, *Muṣannaf*, 23.9 (from Bashīr); Shaqṣī, *Manhaj*, 9.4, and cf. 16.2; also Bisyawī, *Mukhtaṣar*, 275.16, 276.2. [154] Cf. above, 400.

[155] Kindī, *Bayān*, 78.20.

[156] Faḍl, *Jāmiʿ*, 222.16 (from Muḥammad ibn Maḥbūb and – I think – his son Bashīr); *ibid.*, 202.3 (from Bashīr?); Kindī, *Bayān*, 52.5 (from Bashīr); and cf. *ibid.*, 35.7; Abū Bakr al-Kindī, *Muṣannaf*, 26.13.

[157] Faḍl, *Jāmiʿ*, 226.14; Kindī, *Bayān*, 50.6; Abū Bakr al-Kindī, *Muṣannaf*, 57.8. Muḥammad ibn Maḥbūb was *qāḍī* of Ṣuḥār (Sālimī, *Tuḥfa*, 163.18).

[158] Abū Bakr al-Kindī, *Muṣannaf*, 78.11 (from a certain Ḥasan ibn Aḥmad), and cf. the parallel in Kindī, *Bayān*, 85.1. On the question of raiding people's homes, see below, 417f.

[159] Faḍl, *Jāmiʿ*, 197.7 (from Bashīr; read *illā bi'l-mawʿiẓa*); Kindī, *Bayān*, 31.17; Abū Bakr al-Kindī, *Muṣannaf*, 23.7 (from Bashīr); Shaqṣī, *Manhaj*, 11.3. Compare Bisyawī's statement that performance which requires the use of the hand and the infliction of punishment is for the authorities (*al-ḥākim wa'l-quwwām bi'l-ḥaqq*) whereas counselling and talk of hell-fire is for the Muslims in general (*Mukhtaṣar*, 275.21).

[160] Faḍl, *Jāmiʿ*, 198.12 (from Bashīr?); Kindī, *Bayān*, 32.17; Abū Bakr al-Kindī, *Muṣannaf*, 24.11 (from Bashīr?).

[161] Faḍl, *Jāmiʿ*, 201.3; Kindī, *Bayān*, 34.13; Abū Bakr al-Kindī, *Muṣannaf*, 26.1.

matter should be made over to them.[162] We likewise encounter the view that it is not for subjects to beat people: if an offender will only stop when beaten, then this is a matter for the authorities.[163] There is even the view of Muḥammad ibn Maḥbūb that you have no right to break musical instruments; instead you should refer the matter to the authorities (*ulū 'l-amr*) so that they can punish the offender.[164]

Just who are the ordinary people we have been talking about? Here the Ibāḍī jurists raise two rather unusual questions. The first concerns the 'people of prayer' (*ahl al-ṣalāt*) – in other words, those we would call Muslims, whether Ibāḍī or non-Ibāḍī, as opposed to the 'Muslims' proper, whom we would call Ibāḍīs.[165] According to one third/ninth-century jurist, the form of the duty that obligates all is likewise incumbent on all the 'people of prayer' (one consequence of this is that one may under certain conditions seek aid from an unjust non-Ibāḍī ruler against other non-Ibāḍīs, since all of them are obligated).[166] I have not seen comparable Sunnī or Shīʿite discussions.

The second question concerns the performance of the duty by women – an obvious but often neglected issue in discussions of forbidding wrong. Here the position of Muḥammad ibn Maḥbūb is unbendingly negative. It is his view that forbidding wrong is not a universal obligation (*laysa bi-farḍ ʿalā kull*), and his proof is that if it were one, it would obligate women.[167] The exclusion of women from obligation is thus a premise, not a conclusion. He likewise states that a woman is obligated to perform the duty in her heart, but not with her tongue.[168] At the other extreme we have the position of Ibn Baraka, who takes the view that the righting of wrongs is a duty incumbent on whoever can discharge it, man or woman; women should sally forth to perform it just as men do (*an yakhrujna ilayhi ka-mā yakhruj al-rijāl*).[169] Kudamī, though less sweeping than Muḥammad ibn

[162] Faḍl, *Jāmiʿ*, 201.18; Kindī, *Bayān*, 32.1. Likewise there is no harm in reporting to the authorities a man seen in suspicious circumstance (*ibid.*, 24.3).

[163] Abū 'l-Ḥawārī, *Jāmiʿ*, 127.19 (from a responsum of Abū 'l-Ḥawārī); Kindī, *Bayān*, 23.2, 35.15 (from Ibn Baraka). Contrast the view of Bashīr that subjects are not to take it upon themselves to beat people unless this is the only way to stop them (Abū Bakr al-Kindī, *Muṣannaf*, 29.2; and cf. Faḍl, *Jāmiʿ*, 202.5; Kindī, *Bayān*, 35.12).

[164] *Ibid.*, 48.18; Abū Bakr al-Kindī, *Muṣannaf*, 54.13.

[165] The term *ahl al-ṣalāt* thus includes *ahl al-khilāf* and *qawmunā* (cf. above, notes 42, 44).

[166] Faḍl, *Jāmiʿ*, 198.4; Kindī, *Bayān*, 32.9; Abū Bakr al-Kindī, *Muṣannaf*, 24.3 (from Bashīr); also Shaqṣī, *Manhaj*, 9.12.

[167] Abū Bakr al-Kindī, *Muṣannaf*, 22.3; in the parallel passage in Faḍl, *Jāmiʿ*, 191.8, the words *ʿalā kull* have dropped out, while in Kindī, *Bayān*, 21.3, the text reads *ʿalā kull ḥāl*.

[168] Faḍl, *Jāmiʿ*, 190.10; Kindī, *Bayān*, 21.1.

[169] Abū Bakr al-Kindī, *Muṣannaf*, 12.6 (from Abū Muḥammad, i.e. Ibn Baraka).

Maḥbūb, clearly inclines in his direction. He refers to the view that women have no obligation to speak out, although if they do so in a manner that does not involve sexual self-display (*tabarruj*), this is unobjectionable (*ḥasan*).[170] The reference to female self-display invokes God's words to the wives of the Prophet: 'Remain in your houses; and display not your finery, as did the pagans of old' (Q33:33). Kudamī then continues by saying that he does not care for women taking upon themselves the hazards of sallying forth, since they are excused from speaking up; let them rather remain at home, as God has ordered them.[171] Shaqṣī is more liberal: they are not obligated to perform the duty by deed, but are to do so verbally if they can, failing which they do it in the heart;[172] in other words, women differ from men only in having no obligation to act as opposed to speak.

The jurists offer no formal listing of the conditions of obligation, but the categories with which they operate are familiar. They have one very general notion, that of being able to perform the duty,[173] and two more specific conceptions. One of these is not being in fear. Thus if you fear that some evil which you cannot avert will befall you if you act or speak, you perform the duty in your heart.[174] The early jurists show no disposition to explore this condition further.[175] There is, however, one unusual feature of their discussion, namely the frequency with which they seem to speak of precautionary dissimulation (*taqiyya* or *tuqāt*).[176] Muḥammad ibn Maḥbūb states that the obligation holds firm unless one finds oneself in a situation that makes such dissimulation permissible (*ḥāl yujawwiz lahu 'l-taqiyya*).[177]

170 *Ibid.*, 26.17 (from Abū Saʿīd, i.e. Kudamī).

171 *Ibid.*, 27.1.

172 Shaqṣī, *Manhaj*, 13.12.

173 See, for example, Abū 'l-Ḥawārī, *Jāmiʿ*, 127.3; Abū Bakr al-Kindī, *Muṣannaf*, 12.6, 22.9, 28.3.

174 Abū 'l-Ḥawārī, *Jāmiʿ*, 127.9 (from a responsum of Abū 'l-Ḥawārī); see also Ibn Baraka, *Jāmiʿ*, 180.7, whence Abū Bakr al-Kindī, *Muṣannaf*, 23.1; *ibid.*, 65.11 (from Kudamī).

175 Contrast Ibn Baraka, who holds that it is not permitted for a single individual to proceed against a group unless he will be safe and successful, and justifies this with the observation that God has not obligated a man to fight more than two men (cf. Q8:66) (*Jāmiʿ*, 182.14; Kindī, *Bayān*, 26.11; compare the view of Ibn Shubruma (d. 144/761f.), above, ch. 4, note 196). He further explains that the Prophetic tradition on speaking out in the presence of an unjust ruler and getting killed for it (*Jāmiʿ*, 183.5, and Kindī, *Bayān*, 26.17) assumes a prior expectation of safety in this world and the next, or that the ruler will accept the rebuke (*Jāmiʿ*, 183.11; Kindī, *Bayān*, 27.1).

176 For the use of the word *taqiyya* (or *tuqāt*), see, for example, Abū 'l-Muʾthir, *Sīra*, in Kāshif, *Siyar*, 2:317.14; Bisyawī, *Jāmiʿ*, 190.2; Bisyawī, *Mukhtaṣar*, 276.1; Kindī, *Bayān*, 18.1, 20.1, 21.6, 41.4, 43.8; and the references in the next two notes.

177 Faḍl, *Jāmiʿ*, 191.10; Kindī, *Bayān*, 21.6; Abū Bakr al-Kindī, *Muṣannaf*, 22.5; cf. also *ibid.*, 30.2 (a parallel passage, but apparently from Muḥammad ibn ʿAbd al-Salām, for whom see above, note 107), and Shaqṣī, *Manhaj*, 14.10 (suggesting that there is disagreement as to whether *taqiyya* dispenses). In his *Sīra* to the western Ibāḍīs, Muḥammad ibn Maḥbūb again makes reference to *taqiyya* as dispensing (or not dispensing) one from the duty to forbid wrong (Kāshif, *Siyar*, 2:241.1, 243.1, 249.5).

One elaborate account of the fear condition is in fact couched in such terms: if one goes to reprove a group, but is unable to do so, or they do not accept one's reproof, one may not sit with them unless one has fears (*illā an yattaqī minhum tuqātan*) concerning their reaction to one's departure; these may relate to one's property, life or religion.[178] The other conception is having an expectation that what one says will find acceptance (*qabūl*) on the part of the wrongdoer. It is, however, a matter of disagreement whether this is a condition of obligation.[179] An early authority takes the view that the duty still holds even when the offender will not accept it, provided you are not in fear of him.[180] A later compromise view is that in such a case one has a duty to reprove the offender once only, anything more being supererogation.[181]

How does one adjudicate between the claims of forbidding wrong and those of privacy? Here the discussion is concerned with a single, though major, issue: the conditions under which one can enter a home without leave in order to right a wrong.[182] Such cases fall into two categories. In one, what is at stake is the prevention of immoral conduct – such as drunken revels,[183] or fornication.[184] In the other, it is the rescue of a victim.[185] In general, the first move is to ask leave to enter.[186] If this is refused, there is an opinion that one should not enter at all;[187] but in the

178 Kindī, *Bayān*, 19.19, and Abū Bakr al-Kindī, *Muṣannaf*, 65.11 (from Kudamī); for the wording, cf. Q3:28. In both passages I read *aw lam* for *wa-lam*. Cf. also Kudamī, *Muʿtabar*, 211.18.

179 So Abū Bakr al-Kindī, *Muṣannaf*, 22.11 (from an anonymous authority).

180 Abū ʾl-Ḥawārī, *Jāmiʿ*, 127.12, adducing Q7:164–5 in support (from a responsum of Abū ʾl-Ḥawārī). This position is also implicit in Bisyawī's reshaping of the 'three modes' doctrine: 'by word and deed if he can; if he cannot, by speaking with his tongue . . .' (*Jāmiʿ*, 190.1; but cf. his *Mukhtaṣar*, 276.1, which seems to state the contrary). Compare Nawawī's view (above, ch. 13, 352f.).

181 Ibn Baraka, *Jāmiʿ*, 180.4, whence Kindī, *Bayān*, 24.5, and Abū Bakr al-Kindī, *Muṣannaf*, 22.16. The same view is put forward by the fifth/eleventh-century Ḥaḍramī imam Abū Isḥāq Ibrāhīm ibn Qays (*Mukhtaṣar al-khiṣāl*, Oman 1983, 193.12). Cf. also Abū ʾl-Ḥawārī, *Jāmiʿ*, 128.5, and Sālimī, *Tuḥfa*, 1:300.15.

182 There are, of course, homes that can regularly be entered without leave (e.g. one in which a merchant keeps shop, or that of a judge who holds court there), and there are situations in which any home may be so entered which may have nothing to do with the perpetration of a wrong (e.g. a house on fire, or a house of mourning) (Kindī, *Bayān*, 84.11, 87.7, 88.20, 89.3).

183 *Ibid.*, 84.4, 85.1, 88.17, 89.8, 90.21; Abū Bakr al-Kindī, *Muṣannaf*, 78.11.

184 Kindī, *Bayān*, 84.1, 89.5, 90.18.

185 Bisyawī, *Mukhtaṣar*, 275.17; Kindī, *Bayān*, 84.13, 85.12, 85.19, 86.4, 87.17, 88.20. Such a situation is said at one point to 'count as' a wrong (*yakūn bi-manzilat al-munkar*, *ibid.*, 86.8).

186 The exception would be when the wrongdoer is likely to take advantage of the warning to make good his escape (*ibid.*, 86.20, and cf. Abū Bakr al-Kindī, *Muṣannaf*, 77.9; Shaqṣī, *Manhaj*, 24.3).

187 This is given as one of the views that have been held (Kindī, *Bayān*, 84.20, 87.3, 87.12). Cf. also *ibid.*, 85.6, and Abū Bakr al-Kindī, *Muṣannaf*, 78.14.

usual view, what happens next depends primarily on the extent to which those outside the home know what is going on inside it. In the case of immoral conduct, relevant considerations include prior suspicion,[188] information received,[189] clear indications,[190] and sounds coming from the home.[191] If one is not in fact sure that the drink being consumed there is forbidden, one should not enter without leave.[192] In the case of rescue, the appropriate action turns mainly on the victim's cries for help, which should conform to certain formulae.[193] If there is a risk of encountering a female victim – who might be unveiled or even partly naked – one should announce one's entry appropriately: 'Cover up! We're coming in!'[194] The discussion is quite thorough as far as it goes; but it has nothing to say about the prohibition of spying, nor does it deal with the casuistry of bulging cloaks concealing musical instruments.

The issues considered above represent an agenda already established by the third/ninth-century jurists, though one to which, as we have seen, later authorities continued to contribute. What does not emerge from this treatment is the changed intellectual atmosphere that can be sensed elsewhere in the works of the scholars of the fourth or fifth/tenth or eleventh century – Ibn Baraka, Kudamī and Bisyawī. In general, these authors are characterised by a more developed intellectual style than the earlier jurists. Thus Ibn Baraka presents much of his material in a dialectic format: 'If someone were to say . . . the answer would be . . .', and the like;[195] Bisyawī likewise makes some use of this device.[196] These authors also tend to deploy more sustained and sophisticated arguments than the early jurists.[197] What we see

188 As where the people concerned are *ahl al-rayb* (Kindī, *Bayān*, 88.14, and cf. Abū Bakr al-Kindī, *Muṣannaf*, 79.2).

189 Kindī, *Bayān*, 85.1, 88.14; Abū Bakr al-Kindī, *Muṣannaf*, 78.11. What if a group put pressure on a man to come with them to take action against a wrong they hear (sc. music), but he says he hears nothing? The answer is that unless he knows of the wrong in the same way as they do, or is given proof of it, he has no obligation (Kindī, *Bayān*, 38.16).

190 *Ibid.*, 85.3, 85.16, 86.8, 87.1; Abū Bakr al-Kindī, *Muṣannaf*, 78.11, 79.2.

191 Kindī, *Bayān*, 89.10. Compare the fact that a woman who raises her voice in her own home in a quarrel with a member of her family, or in laughter, can be told to lower it (*ibid.*, 80.1).

192 *Ibid.*, 84.7, 89.8, 90.22. The question is raised whether, when the violence is between husband and wife, one should refrain from entering until it is established that he is beating her wrongfully; the answer is that the duty of rescue is unchanged (*ibid.*, 86.11). It likewise makes no difference whether the victim is a boy or an adult, a free person or a slave (*ibid.*, 86.18).

193 Thus a woman who is being beaten up by her husband should call out *wā ghawthāh bi'llāh* or *wā ghawthāh bi'l-Muslimīn*; failing that, one does not enter without leave (*ibid.*, 84.13, 89.1; and cf. 85.15, 86.7, 88.3).

194 *Ibid.*, 84.13, 88.22, and cf. 85.19.

195 See, for example, Ibn Baraka, *Jāmi'*, 180.12. Compare his use of the term *ghalabat al-ẓann*, unknown to the early jurists (*ibid.*, 180.7, and cf. 180.8); the same terminology is used by Abū Isḥāq (*Mukhtaṣar al-khiṣāl*, 193.12).

196 Bisyawī, *Jāmi'*, 188.9.

197 In the case of Kudamī I am rather taking this on trust: either the state of the text or the

here is doubtless a development associated with a certain openness to the intellectual currents of the wider Islamic world.

As might be expected, this is accompanied by the first appearance of some of the more conceptual questions relating to forbidding wrong.[198] Unlike the earlier jurists, Bisyawī concerns himself with the definition of terms.[199] He is likewise familiar with the concept of a collective obligation.[200] As to the teasing question of the obligation of the sinner, Kudamī reports the view that only the trusted and truthful (*ahl al-ṣidq al-ma'mūnūn*), whether laymen (*ḍuʿafā'*) or scholars (*ʿulamā'*), are to undertake the duty, and insists that he knows of no disagreement on this point;[201] but though what he says is relevant to the question, he does not really seem to be addressing it.[202] As will be seen in a moment, one highly intellectual issue, the dispute as to whether the duty is grounded in revelation alone or also in reason, makes its appearance with the younger Kindī. All in all, we have here a measure of penetration of the eastern Ibāḍī tradition by wider scholastic concerns, but it does not go very deep.

This picture is reinforced by the near-absence of literary borrowing from non-Ibāḍī sources. The only work of the period in which there is a clear (though unacknowledged) case of such dependence is the younger Kindī's, the passage in question being concerned with the dispute over reason and revelation.[203] We have already met this passage in a work by Māwardī, who in turn is likely to have had it from a Muʿtazilite source; and we have also seen it appear in the work of an eighth/fourteenth-century western

limits of my comprehension render much of what he says opaque to me, particularly with regard to the question what one may and may not be ignorant of in relation to the duty (*Muʿtabar*, 212.2; and compare the passage from his *Istiqāma* quoted in Jumayyil ibn Khamīs al-Saʿdī (*fl.* early thirteenth/nineteenth century), *Qāmūs al-sharīʿa*, Zanzibar 1297–9, 8:22.19).

198 There is, however, one piece of scholastic thought that appears surprisingly early, namely what I have dubbed in the Imāmī context, where it is standard, the doctrine of divisibility (cf. above, ch. 11, 272f.). According to this view, as espoused by Bashīr, all wrong must be righted, whereas right is of two kinds: the obligatory, which it is obligatory to command, and the supererogatory, which it is supererogatory to command (Kindī, *Bayān*, 27.13). Bashīr was a contemporary of Abū ʿAlī al-Jubbā'ī (d. 303/916), who is identified by one Muʿtazilite source as the originator of the doctrine (see above, ch. 9, note 27).

199 More precisely, he provides both an anthropocentric explanation of why *maʿrūf* and *munkar* are so called, and a revelationist definition of what the terms comprise (*Jāmiʿ*, 188.12). The first reappears anonymously in Kindī, *Bayān*, 8.7, and Abū Bakr al-Kindī, *Muṣannaf*, 5.4, the second with attribution, *ibid.*, 8.17.

200 Bisyawī, *Sīra*, in Kāshif, *Siyar*, 2:171.9; cf. also Shaqṣī, *Manhaj*, 6.9.

201 Kudamī, *Muʿtabar*, 213.2.

202 Cf. also Abū Bakr al-Kindī, *Muṣannaf*, 29.15; Shaqṣī, *Manhaj*, 14.5.

203 Abū Bakr al-Kindī, *Muṣannaf*, 10.17–11.18 (without attribution).

Ibāḍī.[204] In three other instances I suspect mining of non-Ibāḍī sources, but have not succeeded in identifying them.[205]

Religious and geographical distance thus seem to have conspired to insulate the eastern Ibāḍī tradition from any far-reaching Sunnī (let alone Shīʿite) influence in this period.[206] Geographical distance alone seems to have been equally effective in excluding any serious western Ibāḍī influence.[207] At least where forbidding wrong is concerned, links between the two branches of the sect are few and far between. The most striking common feature – and it can hardly be a coincidence – is the passage from Māwardī just discussed. The only other shared material I have noted is a particular paraphrasing of the 'three modes' tradition.[208] A significant doctrinal link is the view, attested in both east and west, that the duty to speak out does not lapse even when it will have no effect, and the associated reshaping of the 'three modes' doctrine.[209] In each case, however, the eastern attestation is earlier than the western, which makes it unlikely that

[204] See above, note 53. Kindī's version is closer than Jayṭālī's to Māwardī's original, and fuller. On the other hand, Jayṭālī preserves features of Māwardī's text lost in Kindī's version (examples are the initial *innamā*, and the point that were the duty binding in reason, it would obligate God). This could mean that Jayṭālī was using a version other than Kindī's, but equally it could reflect the defective transmission of Kindī's text.

[205] The first is Bisyawī's philological explanation as to why *maʿrūf* and *munkar* are so called (see above, note 199). The second is a general characterisation of the duty quoted from Muḥammad ibn ʿAbd al-Salām (Abū Bakr al-Kindī, *Muṣannaf*, 29.11, and cf. Shaqṣī, *Manhaj*, 14.1; for this scholar, see above, note 107). Each of these passages also has a parallel in Khalīlī (d. 1287/1871) (attrib.), *al-Akhbār wa'l-āthār*, Oman 1984, 1:82.14, 80.16 respectively, though in the latter case the parallel is rather deviant (I owe my copy of these passages to Patricia Crone). This work, which does not in fact seem to be Khalīlī's (see the note following the title-page of the first volume), also reproduces – without ascription – Abū 'l-Layth al-Samarqandī's account of the five things one needs in order to perform *al-amr bi'l-maʿrūf* (*ibid.*, 80.20; see above, ch. 12, note 39). The third passage is concerned with *al-amr bi'l-maʿrūf* as controlling one's own ego (*nafs*) (Shaqṣī, *Manhaj*, 12.10–13.10); it is manifestly Ṣūfī in style and content.

[206] The story might have been a very different one if the Ibāḍīs had not lost the cosmopolitan sea-port of Ṣuḥār, and if Iraq had retained its metropolitan status in the Muslim world. There were Qadarīs and Murji'ites in third/ninth-century Ṣuḥār under Ibāḍī rule (see the epistle of Hāshim ibn Ghaylān to imam ʿAbd al-Malik ibn Ḥumayd in Kāshif, *Siyar*, 2:38.5, whence Abū Bakr al-Kindī, *Muṣannaf*, 42.18, and, indirectly, Wilkinson, *Imamate tradition*, 164), together with Shīʿites, one of whom was a Muʿtazilite (see Faḍl, *Jāmiʿ*, 228.8, and Kindī, *Bayān*, 67.7; I follow Kindī's text).

[207] That there were contacts between the two wings of the sect is, of course, well known. Barrādī provides a list of works by eastern Ibāḍīs which includes a good number by Omani authors (*Jawāhir*, 218.14), and he gives a report according to which Darjīnī had composed his *Ṭabaqāt* as part of an exchange of books with Oman (*ibid.*, 11.4, and see EI^2, art. 'Dardjīnī' (T. Lewicki)).

[208] Here *aḍʿaf al-īmān* becomes *aḍʿaf al-inkār* (Bisyawī, *Mukhtaṣar*, 276.12; Kudamī, *Muʿtabar*, 211.23; Kindī, *Bayān*, 12.3, 17.14; Jayṭālī, *Qanāṭir*, 2:154.22).

[209] For Sulaymān ibn Yakhlaf, see above, 400f.; for the eastern parallels, see above, notes 180f. The two reshapings of the 'three modes' doctrine are parallel in thought, but do not show much closeness in language.

the eastern Ibāḍīs were the borrowers. The doctrinal link might, of course, go back to an original common heritage.

This relative isolation is no doubt one reason why such external intellectual stimulus as there was did not lead to any drastic reshaping of the eastern Ibāḍī tradition. There is nothing to compare with the subordination of archaic traditional materials to the demands of an intellectually sophisticated academic culture which marks the work of the Ḥanbalite Abū Yaʿlā, or still more of the Imāmī Shīʿite scholars of the classical period. Ibāḍī scholars such as Bisyawī did introduce one rather daring innovation: they established a strong, though not very clear, connection between forbidding wrong and the old Ibāḍī doctrine of affiliation and dissociation (*walāya* and *barāʾa*).[210] Thus Bisyawī holds that commanding right and forbidding wrong are linked to affiliation and dissociation (*min amr al-walāya waʾl-barāʾa*), since affiliation is owed to those who are obedient to God and do what is right, and dissociation to those who act wrongly and disobey Him;[211] and it is clear that the targets of the two duties are bound to overlap in practice – the dishonest tradesman, for example, is a typical object of forbidding wrong, and is also liable to dissociation.[212] Later authors maintain the linkage.[213] But this apart, there is not much change down the centuries.

A later Ibāḍī scholar whose work may serve to illustrate this stability is Shaqṣī (*fl. c.* 1034/1625), who in his compendium of Ibāḍī law gives a substantial account of forbidding wrong. In the main this represents a version of the juristic tradition which has been superficially tidied up and equipped with suitable prolegomena. Shaqṣī's deference to the tradition does not prevent him from expressing occasional views of his own. Thus in his discussion of musical instruments, he states it as his personal view that in this time of ours tambourines should not be tolerated at all, even to publicise weddings; on the other hand, explicitly reversing the bias of old tradition (*al-athar al-qadīm*), he holds that in our time the drum (*ṭabl*) should not be considered an evil, especially in such contexts as war.[214] Every time has its own ruling, he observes, as does every town.[215] This is

[210] For this doctrine as developed in Ibāḍism, see Ennāmi, *Studies*, ch. 6.

[211] Bisyawī, *Sīra*, in Kāshif, *Siyar*, 2:147.15. Despite the heading *dhikr al-amr biʾl-maʿrūf*, most of this section (*ibid.*, 146–74) is in fact about *walāya* and *barāʾa*. Likewise a significant part of the discussion found under the heading *al-amr biʾl-maʿrūf* in Bisyawī's *Jāmiʿ* is concerned with *walāya* and *barāʾa* (185–8).

[212] Bisyawī, *Sīra*, in Kāshif, *Siyar*, 2:157.17. Cf. also Ennāmi, *Studies*, 203f., 211.

[213] See Abū Bakr al-Kindī, *Muṣannaf*, 10.3, 56.4; cf. also 63.16 (this last from Saʿīd ibn Quraysh, for whom see above, note 122).

[214] Shaqṣī, *Manhaj*, 20.15.

[215] *Ibid.*, 21.1 (*kull zamān lahu ḥukm wa-kull balad lahu ḥukm*). A little later, commenting on the same issue of the military use of the drum, he remarks that it all depends on intention (*al-aʿmāl biʾl-niyyāt*, *ibid.*, 22.8).

a practical point of view, and indeed an engaging one, but it is not intellectually ambitious; it mostly leaves the tradition where it falls.

An even later illustration of the continuity of the tradition is the versified treatment of the duty by Sālimī.[216] Thus he still cites the opinion of Muḥammad ibn Maḥbūb on drums.[217] Some new offences have nevertheless appeared in the meantime: Banians cremate their dead among the faithful,[218] tobacco and drugs have made their appearance.[219] Sālimī likewise repeats the restrictive view that performance by hand is for the authorities, while others should make do with the tongue.[220] But the remarkable feature of his discussion is the attention he gives to the question of women performing the duty.[221] He begins by stating a negative view which stems directly from the tradition: a woman is to perform the duty in her heart, not with her tongue.[222] But he then states that Khalīlī[223] (d. 1287/1871) had taken the radical – but not altogether new – position that women are to perform the duty by word and deed; he based himself on Q9:71, which speaks even-handedly of men and women as commanding right and forbidding wrong, thus implying equality (*tasāwī*) in this respect.[224] Sālimī professes to be impressed by the logic of this position, but seeks to neutralise it by invoking the duty of women to keep their voices down; this excuses them, and provides a basis for what he describes as the majority view, since one wrong cannot be put right by another.[225]

216 In addition to the account in his *Jawhar*, Sālimī also has a brief and uninteresting mention of *al-amr bi'l-ma'rūf* in his *Madārij al-kamāl* (Oman 1983, 147.3). For Sālimī, see Wilkinson, 'Bio-bibliographical background', 141f.; Wilkinson, *Imamate tradition*, 253f.

217 Sālimī, *Jawhar*, 489.8 (cf. the references given above, note 125, esp. Faḍl, *Jāmi'*, 222.2, Kindī, *Bayān*, 46.15, 52.1, and Abū Bakr al-Kindī, *Muṣannaf*, 63.2). Another early jurist whom he cites is *Bashīr najl Muḥammad* (Sālimī, *Jawhar*, 487.9), whom I take to be Bashīr ibn Muḥammad ibn Maḥbūb; however, the view he ascribes to him – that the duty is grounded in reason – seems unlikely to be his, and has no basis in the tradition as known to me (indeed Abū Bakr al-Kindī, *Muṣannaf*, 6.6 would support the contrary).

218 Sālimī, *Jawhar*, 489.1. Cf. the friction that arose between imam 'Azzān ibn Qays and the Banians of Muscat over the use of drums and the like at Hindu religious ceremonies (Landen, *Oman*, 309).

219 Sālimī, *Jawhar*, 489.16 (the terms used are *tutun* and *banj*). For the war on tobacco in Muscat under the imamate of 'Azzān ibn Qays, see Landen, *Oman*, 309. Some decades later, we are told that imam Kharūṣī would flog smokers, whereas imam Khalīlī would imprison them (Muḥammad al-Sālimī, *Nahḍa*, 199.23).

220 Sālimī, *Jawhar*, 487.21.

221 *Ibid.*, 487.23. The discussion continues for thirteen lines.

222 Cf. above, note 168.

223 He refers to him as *al-muḥaqqiq al-Khalīlī*, sc. Sa'īd ibn Khalfān al-Khalīlī (see above, note 112).

224 Sālimī, *Jawhar*, 488.2. Sālim ibn Sayf ibn Ḥamad al-Aghbarī, a recent or contemporary Omani scholar (his father was politically active in 1373/1954, see Wilkinson, *Imamate tradition*, 308f.), in his versification of the *Ghāyat al-maṭlūb* of 'Āmir ibn Khamīs al-Mālikī (d. 1346/1928), takes a similarly positive line: a woman is obligated to put things right (*an tughayyir*) as far as she is able, and to counsel imams and others (Aghbarī, *al-Naẓm al-maḥbūb*, Oman 1984, 208.22).

225 Sālimī, *Jawhar*, 488.7.

We can best end this survey of Omani authors by going back a few decades to Khalīlī, who at least in literary terms stands somewhat apart from the mainstream of the eastern tradition.[226] What is unprecedented about his discussion of forbidding wrong is his extensive dependence on a western Ibāḍī work, that of Jayṭālī,[227] and through it on Ghazzālī.[228] Thus he makes frequent use of Ghazzālī's characteristic terminology,[229] and retains in a heavily eroded form some of the outlines of his presentation.[230] But without question, the single most interesting feature of Khalīlī's account is his treatment of the duty of women to forbid wrong.[231] Through Jayṭālī, he is confronted with Ghazzālī's inclusion of slaves and women.[232] He promptly moves to exclude slaves, making personal freedom a precondition for obligation;[233] he explains that the slave has no power to act (*lā yaqdir ʿalā shayʾ*), and no right to involve himself in such matters, as opposed to the service of his master – unless, perhaps, his master has given him permission.[234] With regard to women, his view is positive, but more complex than appears from Sālimī's account of it. He begins by quoting the statement of Muḥammad ibn Maḥbūb that a woman is to

226 Our concern here is with the long extract from his *Ighāthat al-malhūf* which occupies the greater part of the treatment of *al-amr biʾl-maʿrūf* in his *Tamhīd* (see above, note 112).

227 For Jayṭālī's *Qanāṭir al-khayrāt*, see above, 401–3. Khalīlī refers to the work as *al-Qanāṭir al-maghribiyya* (*Tamhīd*, 7:41.1, and cf. 35.7, 54.11), and to its author as al-Shaykh Ismāʿīl or al-Shaykh Ismāʿīl al-Maghribī (*ibid.*, 52.11, 53.3). Although in his discussion of heroism he is able to cite a positive view of Kudamī's against the negative position of Ibn Baraka (for which cf. above, note 175), the attention he gives to the question undoubtedly reflects the influence of Jayṭālī (*ibid.*, 51.1; cf. above, notes 67–70). In one of his responsa he makes general reference to a view of the Maghāriba (*ibid.*, 21.4).

228 He refers twice to Ghazzālī (*ibid.*, 35.6, 52.11), and speaks also of a work he calls the *Ghazzāliyyāt* (*ibid.*, 40.19, 54.11). Cf. also his attribution of material to 'our scholars and others from among our people (*qawmunā*)' (*ibid.*, 33.15). But I noted no evidence of direct access to Ghazzālī's work.

229 He uses the terms *ḥisba* (*ibid.*, 52.6, 55.17), *muḥtasib* (*ibid.*, 49.8, 56.9), *muḥtasab fīhi* (*ibid.*, 54.15), and above all *iḥtisāb* (*ibid.*, 49.5, etc.).

230 For example, the obligation is established by citing a mass of proof-texts, with separate sections dealing with Koran, Prophetic traditions, and non-Prophetic traditions, in that order (*ibid.*, 31–42, cf. below, ch. 16, 428). There is a recognisable parallelism with regard to much of the analysis that then follows (*ibid.*, 45–57, cf. below, ch. 16, 428–41); but thereafter we are in unfamiliar territory. Even where the parallelism is evident, it may be faint. Thus Ghazzālī's eight levels (*darajāt*) of reaction to a wrong (see below, ch. 16, 438–41), which survive as such in Jayṭālī's work (*Qanāṭir*, 2:171–5), have been reduced by Khalīlī to three *marātib* (*Tamhīd*, 7:56.16; there is mention of the sword, *ibid.*, 57.4, but not of armed bands). Major components of Ghazzālī's treatment of the duty which do not appear at all are his survey of common wrongs (see below, ch. 16, 442–6), and his collection of anecdotes on forbidding wrong to rulers (see below, ch. 16, 446); both had been retained by Jayṭālī (*Qanāṭir*, 2:178–87, 187–217).

231 Khalīlī, *Tamhīd*, 7:53.1–15. Cf. also a responsum in which he rules that suitably covered women who need to buy and sell in the market should not be prevented from doing so (*ibid.*, 24.19). 232 See above, notes 60f.; and cf. *ibid.*, 49.6. 233 *Ibid.*, 49.10.

234 *Ibid.*, 49.14.

perform the duty in her heart, and has no duty to speak out.[235] To this he opposes the view of Jayṭālī, which he then justifies, just as Sālimī indicates, by invoking Q9:71: God has made all the believers partners (*sharrakahum*) in forbidding wrong.[236] His problem is how to interpret the view of Muḥammad ibn Maḥbūb, and he does so by setting out the way in which the duty of women is limited by their segregation. A woman is the most appropriate person to forbid the wrongdoing of other women, and she is likewise obligated with regard to males with whom she is properly on intimate terms (*dhawū 'l-maḥārim*). What cannot be her duty is forbidding wrong in a gathering of men of doubtful character, since her very presence there would in itself constitute a wrong. But this is not, we should note, a point about the impropriety of women exercising authority over men: if a woman is in a position to exercise power (*sulṭān wa-yad*) over wrongdoers, and no other Muslim is taking action against them, then it is her duty to send someone to forbid them.[237]

Perhaps reflecting the relative autarky of the eastern Ibāḍī tradition for most of its history, two genres of literature that provide some illumination in the western Ibāḍī context are almost absent in the east. One is creeds; very few eastern examples are known to me. There is a creed loosely ascribed to Ibn Ibāḍ (later first/seventh century),[238] though the fact that it refers to Muʿtazilites and Ismāʿīlīs obviously points to a much later date.[239] This text contains a bare reference to forbidding wrong.[240] Another such text is a chapter on the beliefs of the Omanis (*ʿaqīdat ahl ʿUmān*) put together by Sālimī;[241] here too the duty appears only as an item in a list.[242]

235 *Ibid.*, 53.1; see above, note 168, and cf. note 222.

236 *Ibid.*, 53.3. He formulates Jayṭālī's view in the language of the three modes.

237 For all this, see *ibid.*, 53.7.

238 Izkawī, *Kashf al-ghumma*, ff. 244b.3–248b.9; translation in E. Sachau, 'Über die religiösen Anschauungen der Ibaditischen Muhammedaner in Oman und Ostafrika', *Mittheilungen des Seminars für Orientalische Sprachen*, 2 (1899), 62–9. The sections and headings of the translation are the work of Sachau. Izkawī (or his source) attributes the creed to Ibn Ibāḍ at the outset, but it is not clear how much of the text this attribution is supposed to include; nor is the creed presented as a document written by Ibn Ibāḍ. My only (though probably sufficient) reason for regarding the creed as an eastern text is the fact that we find it in an Omani source.

239 That the ascription is hard to sustain was pointed out by Rubinacci ('Professione', 567; however, I do not find his suggestion of an influence from the doctrine of Ghazzālī convincing).

240 Izkawī, *Kashf al-ghumma*, f. 246a.3. The paragraphing and headings introduced by Sachau in his translation ('Anschauungen', 65) are misleading at this point; the text does not in fact intend to link *al-amr bi'l-maʿrūf* to the pilgrimage.

241 Sālimī, *Tuḥfa*, 1:79–85 (drawn to my attention by Patricia Crone).

242 *Ibid.*, 84.21. The list derives from a work of the second/eighth-century Wā'il ibn Ayyūb (*Nasab al-Islām*, in Kāshif, *Siyar*, 2:46.14; I owe this reference to Patricia Crone).

The other missing genre, more surprisingly, is biography. Students of Sunnī Islam are, of course, thoroughly spoilt by the richness and precision of the biographical traditions of the Sunnī law-schools. No significant Islamic community, however, is as poorly served as the eastern Ibāḍīs.[243] Hence we lack biographical documentation of the activity of individuals in forbidding wrong. Occasionally, of course, comparable information appears in other sources. Thus Abū 'l-Mu'thir, in his open letter,[244] praises a certain Bashīr ibn al-Mundhir (a contemporary of Muḥammad ibn Maḥbūb) who, though not perhaps an outstanding scholar, was a great Ibāḍī leader, strong in forbidding wrong.[245] Here, as elsewhere in the letter, the primary emphasis is political. Around the beginning of the tenth/sixteenth century, one Muḥammad ibn Ismāʿīl saw a man chasing a naked woman whom he had come upon while she was washing; our hero grappled with the pursuer and brought him down, while the woman escaped. The story is preserved only because it made political history: people were sufficiently impressed with Muḥammad ibn Ismāʿīl's strength in forbidding wrong that he was chosen to be imam, ruling from 906/1500f. to his death in 942/1536.[246] A couple of more recent scholars are described as performers of the duty.[247]

4. CONCLUSION

By way of conclusion, two comparisons are worth making with regard to the substance of Ibāḍī doctrine.

The first is between western and eastern Ibāḍism. As we have seen, these represent two distinct historical communities with largely separate literary heritages. Before Khalīlī there are only occasional links between them: one shared literary borrowing,[248] the unusual doctrine that the verbal obligation does not lapse when the offender will not listen,[249] the equally unusual interest in women as performers of the duty.[250] But there are also differences

[243] Hence the chronological shakiness of the biographical data on eastern Ibāḍī scholars referred to in the footnotes of this section. In the case of the western Ibāḍīs we rarely have precise death dates, but it is not usually a problem to situate a scholar in the right half of the right century. [244] See above, 404f.

[245] Abū 'l-Mu'thir, *Aḥdāth*, in Kāshif, *Siyar*, 1:24.15. For this Bashīr ibn al-Mundhir, see Wilkinson, *Imamate tradition*, 174.

[246] Izkawī, *Kashf al-ghumma*, ed. ʿUbaydalī, 321.3; for this imam, see Wilkinson, *Imamate tradition*, 215f.

[247] For one who died in 1336/1918, see Muḥammad al-Sālimī, *Nahḍa*, 252.13; for one who died in 1364/1945, see *ibid.*, 420.20. [248] See above, note 204.

[249] See above, note 209. The main Sunnī parallel to this is the doctrine of Nawawī (d. 676/1277) (see above, ch. 13, 352f.).

[250] See above, 402, 415f., 422, 423f., and cf. 396.

which are likely to reflect the very different political histories of the two wings of the sect. In Oman, the resilience of the imamate down the centuries finds obvious and direct expression in the frequency with which the Omani sources link forbidding wrong to this institution;[251] the same history may be behind the relative indulgence with which the scholars view military matters.[252] In the west, the vacuum left by the disappearance of the imamate was filled in part by clerical organisation and authority; this, however, seems to have left little mark on conceptions of forbidding wrong.[253] The demise of the imamate does, nevertheless, seem to have had one interesting effect: it made the western scholars less cautious about the role of the individual performer. There is little in the west to compare with the accommodationist strain in the eastern tradition. We find no equivalents to the view that subjects are only to give counsel, are not to inflict beatings or even to break musical instruments,[254] and should leave performance 'by hand' to the authorities.[255] By contrast, one western scholar speaks of 'the sword' like a Muʿtazilite,[256] while another consistently enhances the individual activism of Ghazzālī's doctrine.[257] This is not surprising: as in Zaydism, more room for imams means less for others.

The second comparison is with the doctrines of the other Islamic sects and schools. The significant point here is that if we leave aside the close association of forbidding wrong with righteous rebellion and state-formation which the Ibāḍīs share with the Zaydīs, Ibāḍī views do not diverge in any systematic way from those of the Islamic mainstream. The most unusual features of the Ibāḍī material are the doctrine of the persistence of the verbal duty and the recurrent attention to women. This hardly suggests a distinctively Khārijite heritage, though the second of these features has possible echoes in the wider Khārijite milieu of early Islam.[258] This leaves us with two ways to imagine the relationship between the Khārijite and the specifically Ibāḍī doctrines of the individual duty. We can see Ibāḍism as a late and much softened version of the Khārijite heritage. Or we can suppose that the tenor of the Ibāḍī doctrine of forbidding wrong was not so different from the views that were in fact to be found among the early Khārijite sects. Neither of these guesses can be substantiated; the second is perhaps more economical.

[251] See above, 405–7. [252] See above, 410f.
[253] See above, 403f. As we have seen, the same is true even of Imāmī Shīʿism (see above, ch. 11, note 312). [254] See above, 414f.
[255] See above, notes 159, 220. Such a view makes an isolated appearance in the west when reported by Talātī (see above, note 36). [256] See above, 400.
[257] See above, 402f. [258] See above, note 21.

CHAPTER 16

GHAZZĀLĪ

1. INTRODUCTION

Ghazzālī (d. 505/1111) in the title of his major work promised a revival of the religious sciences (*Iḥyāʾ ʿulūm al-dīn*).[1] It was not a humble title, and must have given grave offence to many of his contemporaries,[2] but he meant it and lived up to it. Though not as intellectually systematic as some Muʿtazilites, nor as clever as the later Imāmī scholars, his characteristic disregard for the settled habits of his colleagues enabled him to rethink the entire doctrine of forbidding wrong in a way that was to prove immensely influential far beyond the boundaries of his law-school.

Ghazzālī's account of the duty takes up the ninth book of the second 'quarter' (*rubʿ*) of the work, and is larger than most of those we have considered by an order of magnitude.[3] It is also, as might be expected from

[1] At the beginning of the work Ghazzālī speaks of his decision to write a book *fī iḥyāʾ ʿulūm al-dīn* (*Iḥyāʾ*, 1:7.4, and cf. 8.13), but does not explicitly give it a title. In later works, however, he treats the phrase as a title, speaking of his *Kitāb iḥyāʾ ʿulūm al-dīn* (see, for example, *al-Maqṣad al-asnā*, ed. F. A. Shehadi, Beirut 1971, 115.11, 127.8).

[2] Ṭurṭūshī (d. 520/1126) commented acidly that the book was more like 'The killing of the religious sciences' (*Imātat ʿulūm al-dīn*) (see Fierro's introduction to her translation of his *Kitāb al-ḥawādith waʾl-bidaʿ*, 63, from Dhahabī, *Siyar*, 19:495.1; and cf. Wansharīsī, *Miʿyār*, 12:184.4). A later scholar, Sulaymān al-Andalusī (d. 634/1237), objected that the religious sciences had never died, and so were in no need of revival (Ghubrīnī, *ʿUnwān al-dirāya*, 280.7, quoted in Manūnī, '*Iḥyāʾ*', 134).

[3] Ghazzālī, *Iḥyāʾ*, 2:280–326 (these are large, dense pages; all references below are to the second volume). I sometimes have occasion to correct the text of the edition of the *Iḥyāʾ* I have used, which is not a particularly good one; where I cite no authority for my correction, it is simply the reading of the Cairo 1967–8 edition (2:391–455), but where the two agree in error, I adduce parallels from elsewhere. For a complete translation, see L. Bercher ('L'obligation d'ordonner le bien et d'interdire le mal selon Al-Ghazali', *IBLA* (= *Revue de l'Institut des belles lettres arabes*), 18 (1955), 20 (1957), 21 (1958), 23 (1960)); for a partial translation, see L. Veccia Vaglieri and R. Rubinacci, *Scritti scelti di al-Ghazālī*, Turin 1970, 233–89. For an epitome, see G.-H. Bousquet, *Ghazâlî, Ih'ya 'oulоûm ed-dîn ou Vivification des sciences de la foi: analyse et index*, Paris 1955, 187–96. For brief summaries, see H. Laoust, *La politique de Ġazālī*, Paris 1970, 128–30, and Madelung, 'Amr be maʿrūf', 994a–995a. Extensive use is made of Ghazzālī's account in B. Musallam, 'The ordering of Muslim societies', in F. Robinson (ed.), *The Cambridge illustrated history of the Islamic world*, Cambridge 1996, 174–86.

Ghazzālī, highly organised, and in a manner that in some ways departs radically from earlier treatments. Ghazzālī himself wrote a shorter Persian recension of the work; even here, the discussion of forbidding wrong is still substantial.[4] I shall begin by presenting his doctrine in an extended summary.

2. THE DOCTRINE OF GHAZZĀLĪ: A SUMMARY

Introduction

After a brief rhetorical introduction on the vital importance of the duty, its virtual disappearance in this day and age, and the near-absence of anyone seeking to revive it, Ghazzālī turns to business and announces the four chapters he will devote to the topic.[5]

1. Obligation

The first chapter is concerned primarily with the obligatoriness of forbidding wrong.[6] Ghazzālī begins by stating that, apart from consensus (*ijmāʿ al-umma*) and common sense (*ishārāt al-ʿuqūl al-salīma*), this obligatoriness is established by Koran, Prophetic traditions (*akhbār*)[7] and non-Prophetic traditions (*āthār*). Consensus and common sense get no further hearing. Instead, several pages are devoted to scripture and traditions, interspersed with comments; thus he remarks that Q3:104 establishes the duty to be collective.[8]

2. Basic components of the duty

Terminology. The second chapter treats the basic components (*arkān*) and conditions (*shurūṭ*) of the duty,[9] and represents the analytical core of

[4] Ghazzālī (d. 505/1111), *Kīmiyā-yi saʿādat*, ed. Ḥ. Khadīvjam, Tehran 1368 sh., 1:499–524; all references below are to the first volume. I have noted the more significant differences between the Arabic and the Persian recensions in the notes. Occasionally they carry a faint suggestion that the Persian may in places represent a more primitive version of the text, as opposed to a revision or simplification of it (see below, notes 36, 50, 116); but I have encountered nothing conclusive in this respect. Ghazzālī also gives a short account of *al-amr biʾl-maʿrūf* in his *al-Arbaʿīn fī uṣūl al-dīn*, 84–9. In this account he makes some use of the terminology of the *Iḥyāʾ* (as at *Arbaʿīn*, 85.19, 88.11), and at one point gives a reference to the work (*ibid.*, 86.14); but while virtually every point he makes is found in the *Iḥyāʾ*, he does not reproduce the structure of the account he gives there.

[5] Ghazzālī, *Iḥyāʾ*, 280.26. In the *Kīmiyā* there are only three chapters, the fourth being omitted.

[6] *Iḥyāʾ*, 281–5.

[7] A few of the traditions he adduces as *akhbār* are in fact non-Prophetic.

[8] *Ibid.*, 281.12.

[9] *Ibid.*, 285–307.

Ghazzālī's doctrine. He first introduces parenthetically an unfamiliar terminology: the term *ḥisba*, he states, is a general term (*ʿibāra shāmila*) for commanding right and forbidding wrong.[10] Ringing changes on the root from which this term is formed, he then sets out the four basic components of the duty: the person who does it (*al-muḥtasib*), the person against whom it is done (*al-muḥtasab ʿalayhi*), the matter regarding which it is done (*al-muḥtasab fīhi*), and the actual process of doing it (*nafs al-iḥtisāb*).[11] Each of these has its conditions.

I. THE FIRST COMPONENT: THE PERFORMER.

Of the four components, it is the first that receives the lengthiest discussion.[12] The initial summary states that the conditions for performing the duty are that one be (1) legally competent (*mukallaf*), (2) a Muslim, and (5)[13] able to do it (*qādir*).[14] This excludes lunatics, boys, unbelievers and the infirm (*ʿājiz*); it includes individual subjects (even if they do not have official permission), sinners, slaves and women.[15] The discussion that follows is slightly untidy in relation to this summary, though identical in upshot. Ghazzālī treats in succession five candidate conditions, namely the three already mentioned together with (3) probity (*ʿadāla*) and (4) official permission (*kawnuhu maʾdhūnan min jihat al-imām waʾl-wālī*); the former are sustained, while the latter are discarded, which accounts for their omission in the initial summary.

Condition (1): legal competence With regard to legal competence, he stresses that it is a condition only for being obligated; a boy who is approaching puberty and knows what he is doing may proceed against wrongs, for all that he has no duty to do so.[16]

Condition (2): belief Turning to belief, Ghazzālī makes his point with a rhetorical question: since the duty consists in coming to the aid of the faith, how could one of its enemies perform it?[17] He returns to the issue at the

[10] *Ibid.*, 285.29; he has already used the term incidentally, *ibid.*, 284.17. In the Persian he makes use of *ḥisbat* to translate *al-amr biʾl-maʿrūf* and related terms in traditions (see, for example, *Kīmiyā*, 500.22, 501.17, 501.19). For the question which sense of the word *ḥisba* lies behind Ghazzālī's choice of it, see below, 447–9.

[11] In the discussion that follows he will reverse the order of the second and third components. The last is rendered in Persian as *chigūnagī-i iḥtisāb* (*ibid.*, 502.6).

[12] *Iḥyāʾ*, 286–97.

[13] The reason for this numbering will appear very shortly.

[14] The Persian spells out what the Arabic takes for granted: the duty is incumbent on all Muslims (*Kīmiyā*, 502.3); whoever belongs to the religion is included (*har kih az ahl-i dīn ast ahl-i ḥisbat ast, ibid.*, 502.9).

[15] *Iḥyāʾ*, 286.2. By contrast, Ghazzālī held the view that neither slaves nor women could be judges (*Wajīz*, Cairo 1317, 2:237.15).

[16] *Iḥyāʾ*, 286.5.

[17] *Ibid.*, 286.12. Ghazzālī implicitly equates *muslim* and *muʾmin*.

end of his discussion of probity.[18] An infidel (*dhimmī*), he says there, may not physically prevent a Muslim from doing wrong, since this would be exercising power over him (*tasalluṭ*). For him to tell a Muslim not to commit adultery is likewise forbidden, because it displays a pretension to authority over him (*iẓhār dāllat al-iḥtikām ʿalā ʾl-Muslim*), and is thus a humiliation (*idhlāl*) of the Muslim – not that such an offender is not deserving of humiliation, simply that he should not suffer it from an infidel, who deserves it more than he does.[19]

Supposed condition (3): probity Then follows a long discussion of probity, that is to say the question whether the sinner is obligated. In the course of this we reach the familiar conclusion that he is, with an appeal to the argument that, were sinners excluded, there would be no one left to perform the duty.[20] Much of the argumentation consists of the kind of dialectic of which Ghazzālī is supposed to disapprove; its highlight is the case of the fastidious rapist who reproves his victim when she unveils her face while he ravishes her.[21] The major concession made by Ghazzālī is that the sinner whose sin is well known is not obligated to counsel virtue in others, since his counsel (*waʿẓ*) would be ineffective.[22]

Supposed condition (4): official permission The discussion of the question of official permission is even longer.[23] The condition is rejected, and the alleged contrary view of the Rāfiḍa is brushed aside. When they come to the law-courts claiming their rights, they are to be mocked with the argument that the time for this has not yet come, since the true imam has yet to go forth.[24] There is no analogy between the position of the individual Muslim subject and that of the unbeliever; the authority (*ʿizz al-salṭana waʾl-iḥtikām*) exercised in the performance of the duty by the individual Muslim no more requires the permission of the ruler than does informing the ignorant.[25] Ghazzālī then proceeds to treat the

[18] *Ibid.*, 288.17.
[19] The summary of Bousquet (*Ghazâlî*, 189) is misleading in indicating that the unbeliever may proceed verbally against a Muslim. However, such a view is attested elsewhere (ʿAlī al-Qārī, *Sharḥ ʿAyn al-ʿilm*, 1:442.9, and cf. Nabarāwī, *Sharḥ ʿalā ʾl-Arbaʿīn*, 171.19).
[20] *Iḥyāʾ*, 286.14. Laoust reverses Ghazzālī's position (*La politique de Ġazālī*, 128).
[21] *Iḥyāʾ*, 287.15. This teasing example also appears in Fakhr al-Dīn al-Rāzī, *Tafsīr*, 3:47.8 (to Q2:44), 8:179.6 (to Q3:104).
[22] *Iḥyāʾ*, 287.34. As ʿAlī al-Qārī (d. 1014/1606) points out, this is tantamount to saying that where counsel is concerned, probity is indeed a condition – which, he says, contradicts what has previously been said (*Sharḥ ʿAyn al-ʿilm*, 1:439.9).
[23] *Iḥyāʾ*, 288.24. In the *Kīmiyā* (504.2) Ghazzālī equates such permission with the writing of a letter of appointment to the (office of) *ḥisba* (*manshūr-i ḥisbat nibishtan*).
[24] *Iḥyāʾ*, 288.27. [25] *Ibid.*, 288.32.

matter less sweepingly. There are five levels (*marātib*) of performance of the duty:[26]

informing;
polite counselling;
harsh language;
physical action against objects;
the threat or use of violence against the person.

With regard to the first four, there can be no question of any need for the ruler's permission.[27] Thus we know that harsh language may be used against the ruler himself, so how could it require his permission? The fifth level is problematic: it may require gathering helpers, and this can lead to fighting (*qitāl*) and armed conflict (*shahr al-asliḥa*), and so to general disorder (*fitna ʿāmma*).[28] But in general, the persistence of the early Muslims in performing the duty against rulers demonstrates their consensus that no such permission is needed from them.[29]

Excursus: inferiors against superiors Ghazzālī then raises the general question of performance of the duty against the grain of authority – by the son against the father, by the slave against the master, by the wife against the husband, by the pupil against the teacher, and by the subject against the ruler.[30] Is it the same unqualified duty as when it goes in the other direction, or is it different? The answer that Ghazzālī puts forward is that there is no basic difference in principle, but that there are variations in detail. He takes son and father as an example. Here the son may proceed at the first two levels, but not at the last two (he means the third and fifth). As for the third (he means the fourth), it depends. Analogy would indicate that the son could and should take action against offending objects

26 *Ibid.*, 289.3 (reduced to four in the *Kīmiyā*, 504.6, through the omission of the first). He refers here to his later discussion of these levels, which we shall come to under the fourth component (see below, 438–41). There he refers to them, however, not as *marātib* but as *darajāt*, and their number has swollen to eight.

27 The Persian is more vivid: here Ghazzālī remarks of the equivalent of the fourth level that whoever is a believer has been invested with this authority (*salṭanat*) without the permission of the ruler (*sulṭān*) (*Kīmiyā*, 504.15).

28 He again refers to his later discussion (below, 441). The Persian is more conservative: it is best for such gathering of helpers not to be effected without the ruler's permission (*ibid.*, 504.19).

29 Anecdotal support follows (*Iḥyāʾ*, 289.18): the frame-story of the 'three modes' tradition, a man who confronted the caliph al-Mahdī (r. 158–69/775–85), another who told off Hārūn al-Rashīd (r. 170–93/786–809), Sufyān al-Thawrī (d. 161/778) rebuking al-Mahdī, a man who went about commanding and forbidding and was unsuccessfully challenged by al-Maʾmūn (r. 198–218/813–33) for doing so without his permission. These anecdotes are omitted in the Persian.

30 *Ibid.*, 291.11.

in his father's possession; but it is plausible to say that he should weigh the extent of the wrong against the degree of aggravation and anger that will be caused by such action.[31] What goes for the son applies also to the slave and the wife.[32] The subject, however, is more restricted.[33] He can have recourse to the first two levels, but as to the third (again, he seems to mean the fourth), it depends: proceeding at this level may damage the ruler's majesty (*hayba*), which is forbidden,[34] but so also is silence in the face of wrong; the conflict can only be resolved by weighing the two considerations against each other. The pupil, on the other hand, is less restricted, since the scholar who does not practise his learning is owed no respect.[35]

Condition (5): power Finally, there is the condition that one must have the power to perform the duty.[36] One who lacks the strength to perform it (*al-ʿājiz*) need do so only in his heart.[37] What is intended here is not subjective weakness (*al-ʿajz al-ḥissī*). Rather, weakness consists in the knowledge either that one will come to harm[38] or that one's action will be ineffective. Working through the various possibilities generates four cases:[39]

1 It will be ineffective and cause one harm: in such a case there is no obligation, and it may even be forbidden to proceed.[40] One will, however, have a duty to stay away from the wrongdoing, staying at home as much as possible; but there is no need to resort to emigration (*hijra*) as long as one is not compelled to participate in wrongdoing, as by rendering assistance to unjust rulers.

[31] I read *qalīlan* for *qarīban* twice at *ibid.*, 291.23 (cf. Yaʿqūb, *Sharḥ Shirʿat al-Islām*, 505.16). [32] *Iḥyāʾ*, 291.32. [33] *Ibid.*, 292.2.

[34] Cf. the traditions quoted *ibid.*, 292 n. 2. [35] *Ibid.*, 292.6.

[36] *Ibid.*, 292.10. The Persian leaves out this condition, but takes up the question of harm at the end of the discussion of the third component (*Kīmiyā*, 509.11; more precisely, the paragraph begins as a translation of *Iḥyāʾ*, 300.34, then follows Ghazzālī's cross-reference to *ibid.*, 292.10, and continues from there).

[37] This is the first mention of performance in the heart. The tradition that follows suggests that scowling might come under this heading (contrast below, note 82).

[38] For *bal yaltaḥiq bihi mā yakhāf ʿalayhi makrūhan* (*ibid.*, 292.13), we find *bal yataḥaqqaq idhā khāfa ʿalayhi makrūhan* in the citation of the passage in Yaʿqūb, *Sharḥ Shirʿat al-Islām*, 501.21; however, Jayṭālī has the same reading as in our text of the *Iḥyāʾ* (*Qanāṭir*, 2:164.4), as does ʿAlī al-Qārī (*Sharḥ ʿAyn al-ʿilm*, 1:443.4). I speak of 'knowledge' that one will come to harm, not just of 'fear', since Ghazzālī goes on to speak in this way himself (as at *Iḥyāʾ*, 292.16, 292.24), and later makes it clear that this is deliberate (*ibid.*, 293.26).

[39] *Iḥyāʾ*, 292.15.

[40] The Persian agrees that there is no obligation, but says that proceeding is permitted, indeed rewarded; the tradition about standing up to an unjust ruler and getting killed for it is adduced in support (*Kīmiyā*, 509.15). There is no mention of staying at home or emigrating.

2 It will be effective and safe: in such a case it is obligatory.

3 It will be ineffective but safe: in such a case the ineffectiveness voids the obligation, but it is still virtuous to proceed as an assertion of the claims of Islam (*li-iẓhār sha'ā'ir al-Islām*).[41]

4 It will be effective but will cause one harm: in such a case there is again no obligation to proceed, but it is virtuous to do so, as is shown by the tradition about speaking out in the presence of an unjust ruler.[42] How does this tally with the Koranic injunction 'cast not yourselves by your own hands into destruction' (Q2:195)? Here Ghazzālī draws an analogy with holy war. A lone Muslim may hurl himself at the ranks of the enemy and be killed where this will be to the advantage of the Muslims, as by damaging the morale of the enemy. In the same way, it is permissible and indeed virtuous for someone forbidding wrong to expose himself to being beaten up or killed where such action will be effective in righting the wrong, discrediting the wrongdoer or encouraging[43] the faithful.

Where there is no such prospect of success in the face of danger, to proceed is pointless and doubtless forbidden.[44] This is also the case when the backlash would cause harm to others, and not just to the performer, thus bringing about a new wrong.[45] Likewise when putting a wrong to rights would lead others to commit a wrong, the better view is that one may not proceed.[46] But on this point one can also take the opposite view, and some have done so.[47] These are questions of law (*masā'il fiqhiyya*) on which no certainty is to be attained, and in such cases it would make sense to consider the relative weight of the two wrongs. Such fine points (*daqā'iq*) are a matter of judgement (*ijtihād*); the layman (*'āmmī*) would be well advised to stick to open-and-shut cases such as wine-drinking, adultery and failure to pray, since if he tackles more complex cases he is likely to do more harm than good. In this respect those who would restrict forbidding wrong to official appointees have a point.[48]

[41] The Persian, by contrast, says it is obligatory to proceed verbally (*ibid.*, 509.21), while in the *Arba'īn*, 86.3, it is recommended. The Persian thus provides a parallel to the doctrine of Nawawī (d. 676/1277) (see above, ch. 13, 352f.) and to Ibāḍī views (see above, ch. 15, note 209).

[42] The Persian agrees, but does not adduce the tradition at this point (*Kīmiyā*, 510.3).

[43] Read *taqwiya* for *tawqiya* at *Iḥyā'*, 293.6. [44] *Ibid.*, 293.6.

[45] *Ibid.*, 293.10. Harm to others is treated somewhat more systematically in the Persian (*Kīmiyā*, 512.14). [46] For *al-afkār* read *al-inkār 'alā* at *Iḥyā'*, 293.13.

[47] Cf. above, ch. 10, note 110, for another reference to such a view. I do not know of anyone who actually held it.

[48] It will be obvious that Ghazzālī's presentation is untidy at this point: he is trying to take account of something like the 'no untoward side-effects' condition (cf. above, ch. 11, 276 condition (6)), but without giving it a formal place in his framework.

Loose ends Ghazzālī has not quite finished with his 'power' condition. We now get a string of minor points related to it.

(1) Degree of certainty Does one have to have actual knowledge regarding the safety or efficacy of proceeding against a wrong?[49] The answer is negative: in general it is enough in this respect to have good reason to believe (*al-ẓann al-ghālib*). What then if the action probably will not work, but it just might, and there is no prospect of coming to harm? This is disputed, the better answer being that to proceed is obligatory in such a case. What if one probably will not come to harm, but one might? The answer here is that it is obligatory to proceed, since there is always some possibility of coming to harm. What if one confronts even odds? This is disputable, but the more plausible answer is that it is obligatory to proceed.

(2) Subjectivity of expectations Does not expectation of coming to harm in practice vary with the cowardice or courage of the person concerned?[50] For the apprehensive, distant eventualities loom terrifyingly close; the foolhardy, by contrast, recognise disaster only when it has already struck. The answer is that we take as our standard a balanced and sensible personality.

(3) Degrees of harm Just how much anticipated harm voids the duty?[51] After all, some degree of unpleasantness is always to be expected in such situations. Here Ghazzālī offers an elaborate analysis of harm, the details of which we can dispense with. His central distinction is between loss of an actual good and deprivation of the prospect of acquiring one.[52] The latter does not as a general rule dispense one from performing the duty, since it can be called 'harm' (*ḍarar*) only in a metaphorical sense; it is nevertheless possible to envisage cases where it would be plausible to allow exceptions, though such cases must always be a matter of judgement. By contrast, loss of an actual good does dispense. Here, in cases of harm to the person or property, there will be a lower limit below which harm is not considered, an upper limit above which it must be considered, and a grey area in between where one has to use one's judgement.[53] Similarly with social

49 *Ibid.*, 293.26.

50 *Ibid.*, 294.5. This too is a little untidy: it looks like an unrecognised recurrence of the point about subjective weakness. The Persian alludes to this point (*Kīmiyā*, 510.22), but does not develop it as is done here; instead, it presents the analysis of degrees of certainty as the solution to this problem.

51 *Iḥyā'*, 294.20; *Kīmiyā*, 511.6.

52 *Iḥyā'*, 294.31, 295.22.

53 Here, as in several other passages, Ghazzālī uses *ijtihād* for the kind of exercise of judgement that any normal person has to engage in.

standing (*jāh*): the prospect of being paraded around the town bare-headed and bare-footed[54] is one thing, that of merely having to walk on foot rather than ride a horse is another.[55]

(4) Self-destructiveness How about a case in which someone is about to cut off one of his own limbs, and we can only stop him by fighting him, which may lead to his death?[56] Would this not be absurd, since the limb would perish with the man? Ghazzālī's answer is a startling reminder that he is not a utilitarian like Ibn Taymiyya:[57] we should indeed fight such a man, because our purpose is not to preserve either his life or his limb, but to prevent sin and wrongdoing; our killing him in the process is not a sin, unlike his cutting off his own limb. But would this not imply that we should kill him pre-emptively in a case in which we know that, if allowed to go off on his own, he will proceed to injure himself?[58] The answer is no, because we cannot in fact know with certainty what he will do.

(5) Sins past, present, and future Pondering this case leads Ghazzālī to some general reflections. Generally, one must make a temporal distinction: a sin may already have been committed, be in the process of being committed, or be anticipated.[59] In the first case what remains is to punish the sinner, and this of course is for rulers, not for individuals. In the second case, the obligation is in full force for individuals and subjects (*al-āḥād wa'l-ra'iyya*). The third case is less clear, since something may intervene to prevent the actual commission of the sin. In such cases individuals may only counsel and exhort. An apparent exception would be a situation in which it is just a matter of time before the sin is committed, as when youths hang around the doors of women's bath-houses to stare at the women as they enter and leave. But a more careful consideration of such cases will show that they in fact involve an actual sin, not just an anticipated one, so that the use of force by individuals is appropriate.

II. THE SECOND COMPONENT: THE WRONG

The second component is the matter with regard to which the duty is to be performed (*mā fīhi 'l-ḥisba*).[60] The initial summary defines this as all

[54] *Ibid.*, 294.33: *al-ṭawāf bihi fī 'l-balad ḥāsiran ḥāfiyan*. The Persian has: *sar-barahna ba-bāzār bīrūn barand* (*Kīmiyā*, 512.4).
[55] *Iḥyā'*, 295.30. Being exhibited in such a way would destroy a man's *murū'a*; walking on foot would not. [56] *Ibid.*, 296.20. This discussion is not found in the Persian.
[57] Compare above, ch. 7, 154f. This contrast is noted by Madelung ('Amr be ma'rūf', 995a).
[58] *Iḥyā'*, 296.26.
[59] *Ibid.*, 296.29, likewise not found in the Persian. My paragraphing at this point is convenient but somewhat misleading; this general analysis is properly an elaboration of the last point made about self-destructiveness. [60] *Ibid.*, 297.6.

wrongs that are currently in existence, are apparent to the performer without recourse to prying, and can be known to be wrong without expert legal judgment (*ijtihād*). This gives us four conditions.

Condition (1): being a wrong By this is meant that we have to do with something that is against the law.[61] The concept of a wrong (***munkar***) is appropriate here, rather than the more restricted notion of a sin (***maʿṣiya***): there can be no sin without a sinner, but there can indeed be a wrong without a sinner, as when a boy or a madman drinks wine; and such a wrong is a proper target of the duty. Nor does the distinction between major and minor sins have a bearing on the duty.[62]

Condition (2): being current This excludes action against past or future wrongs.[63]

Condition (3): being apparent without prying Ghazzālī deals here with the familiar prohibition of spying on people, invoking appropriate authorities.[64] One may not raid a home unless the wrong is apparent to those outside it, as in the case of loud music or drunken cries, or the aroma of drink where the indications are that it is illicit. Similarly one may not challenge a sinner who has something concealed in his robe, unless there is some special reason to suspect him; it could be a bottle of wine, but then again it might be vinegar – a sinner needs his vinegar like anyone else, and people have all sorts of reasons for concealing things. If there is an aroma, the case is disputable, though the answer is plausibly that one should proceed; similarly if the garment is thin enough to reveal the outlines of a musical instrument. In general, one may learn of a wrong of this kind by encountering indications of it; but one has no right to go looking for such signs.

Condition (4): being known without recourse to scholarly judgement Whatever is within the domain of scholarly judgement (***ijtihād***) cannot be the object of the duty.[65] Thus a Ḥanafī has no business rebuking a Shāfiʿite for eating lizard or hyena, and so forth.[66] But may one reprove a member of one's own law-school for a violation that is permitted in some other law-

[61] *Ibid.*, 297.9. The Persian treats this condition in the same way (*Kīmiyā*, 506.2).
[62] This looks like a disavowal of a view suggested by a formulation of Ghazzālī's teacher Juwaynī (*Irshād*, 369.14).
[63] *Iḥyāʾ*, 297.16. Somewhat inelegantly, we have already dealt with this point (see above, 435). [64] *Ibid.*, 297.21. [65] *Ibid.*, 298.12.
[66] Shāfiʿite school doctrine permits eating these animals, whereas that of the Ḥanafīs forbids or disapproves (see the tabulation in Cook, 'Early Islamic dietary law', 259).

school? The answer would seem to be that one may, since people should stick to the views of their own school. But this would lead to the somewhat bizarre conclusion that a Shāfiʿite could rebuke a Ḥanafī who joined him in eating a lizard, telling him in effect that while there was nothing wrong with eating lizard in itself, it was wrong for a Ḥanafī to do it. This leads us into yet more paradoxical cases. Altogether Ghazzālī's conclusion is that the duty is in some measure applicable in such cases: the Ḥanafī cannot rebuke the Shāfiʿite for something he himself considers lawful, but the Shāfiʿite may rebuke a fellow Shāfiʿite since they share the same legal position.[67] However, Ghazzālī does not condemn the opposing view that the duty applies only where the matter is known quite definitely to be a wrong, as with wine and pork.[68]

Excursus: the slippery slope of relativism But how far is such relativism to extend?[69] If we are bound to respect the views of other law-schools, does this not have the alarming implication that we must show the same tolerance for the views of Muʿtazilites, anthropomorphists and philosophers? Ghazzālī resolves this by distinguishing between legal questions, in which it makes sense to say that every jurist exercising scholarly judgement (*mujtahid*) is right, and theological questions, where it does not and the falsity of wrong views is plain. But he faces the objection that in practice this does not help: the heretic still thinks he is right and calls you a heretic, just as you know yourself to be right and call him one. Ghazzālī replies that this can be taken account of in the following manner. In the case of a town to which heresy is a stranger, the townspeople may carry out the duty without the permission of the ruler. But if the town is split and proceeding would be an invitation to disorder, then it is not for individuals to act independently of the ruler. For all the importance of performing the duty against heresy, this limitation has to be observed.

III. THE THIRD COMPONENT: THE OFFENDER

The offender must be such that the behaviour in question is wrong in relation to him.[70] The minimal criterion for this is that he be human; he does not have to be legally competent, as we have seen.[71] By contrast, restraining

67 Read *al-Shāfiʿī* for *al-Ḥanafī*, *Iḥyāʾ*, 298.35.

68 The Persian, by contrast, dismisses this view (*Kīmiyā*, 507.22).

69 *Iḥyāʾ*, 299.6. For the historical background to what follows, see Madelung, *Religious trends*, 32–7.

70 *Iḥyāʾ*, 299.32.

71 See above, 436. The Persian is different (*Kīmiyā*, 508.16; contrast above, note 61). Here Ghazzālī says that legal competence is indeed a condition, otherwise the action would not be a sin; thus restraining boys and madmen is not part of the duty. He also says that the offender must possess no immunity (*ḥurmat*), such as the father has to certain modes of performance of the duty (see above, 431f.).

an animal does not come within the purview of the duty. The reason for this is that forbidding wrong (*ḥisba*) is preventing a wrong out of respect for a right of God (*al-manʿ ʿan munkar li-ḥaqq Allāh*).[72] When we stop a boy drinking wine, it is in deference to a right of God that we do so. By contrast, when we stop an animal doing damage to property, we are motivated by respect for the right of the owner; our object is not really to restrain the animal, but rather to preserve a Muslim's property.[73] Again, we see that for Ghazzālī the duty is not a utilitarian one.

IV. THE FOURTH COMPONENT: THE PROCESS

Two topics fall under this rubric. One is the levels (*darajāt*) of performance; the other is its norms (*ādāb*).[74]

The eight levels We start with the escalating sequence of eight levels of performance of the duty. These levels are as follows.[75]

Level (1): seeking information The first level is seeking information (*taʿarruf*) about wrongs that are being committed.[76] This, as we already know, is forbidden. One is not to go around eavesdropping for the sound of music, sniffing to detect the aroma of wine, feeling a garment in search of the shape of a flute, or collecting gossip from a man's neighbours. It would be different if one heard the unsolicited testimony of two good witnesses to the effect that a man was a drinker, or whatever; one could then enter his house without leave.

72 *Iḥyāʾ*, 300.4. In the Persian the purpose is specified as *iẓhār-i shaʿāʾir-i Islām* (*Kīmiyā*, 509.5).

73 Ghazzālī here gives a brief discussion of this latter duty (*Iḥyāʾ*, 300.18), despite the fact that it is no part of *ḥisba*. From this he goes on to the question of the duty of someone who comes across lost property (*luqaṭa*) to preserve it (*ibid.*, 300.36). In both cases a relevant consideration is the inconvenience (*taʿab*) one suffers through involving oneself in such action – whereas inconvenience (as opposed to harm) has no bearing on the duty of *al-amr biʾl-maʿrūf* (*ibid.*, 300.32). With regard to cases to which the consideration is relevant, Ghazzālī handles the question very characteristically: there is a lower limit below which we disregard inconvenience, and an upper limit above which there is no duty to put up with it; in between there is a grey area of the kind humans just have to live with (*ibid.*, 301.11). The Persian renders *taʿab* as *ranj*, and adds the point that one's time is something one has a right to, and is not obligated to expend for the sake of someone else's property (*Kīmiyā*, 509.9).

74 *Iḥyāʾ*, 301.16; *Kīmiyā*, 512.19.

75 There are now eight *darajāt*, as opposed to the five *marātib* we encountered earlier (see above, note 26). Note that performance in the heart does not appear among these levels (cf. above, note 37, and below, note 82). The Imāmīs Qāḍī Saʿīd al-Qummī (writing 1107/1696) and Mahdī al-Narāqī (d. 1209/1794f.), by contrast, feel constrained to replace Ghazzālī's first level with performance in the heart (Qāḍī Saʿīd al-Qummī, *Sharḥ Tawḥīd al-Ṣadūq*, ed. N. Ḥabībī, Tehran 1415–16, 1:742.16; Mahdī al-Narāqī, *Jāmiʿ al-saʿādāt*, 2:246.14). They are probably influenced by Fayḍ, *Maḥajja*, 4:108.9; Narāqī is followed by his son in his Persian rendering of his father's work (*Miʿrāj al-saʿāda*, 519.8).

76 *Iḥyāʾ*, 301.20.

Level (2): informing The second level is informing the ignorant (*taʿrīf*).[77] Thus if you see a rustic (*sawādī*)[78] praying incorrectly, you know that this is the result of ignorance, since if he did not want to pray correctly he would not be attempting to pray at all. He should be told about his shortcomings nicely. Instructing people carries with it the suggestion that they are ignorant or stupid, and this is something they do not appreciate; indeed they are more touchy about revealing their ignorance than they are about exposing their private parts. You tell such a man that people aren't born knowing, that we too were ignorant in matters of prayer till those who knew better instructed us, that perhaps his village lacks a scholar, or has one who is remiss in giving instruction in prayer, and so forth, to make it painless for him. Hurting a Muslim is just as wrong as silence in the face of his wrongdoing.

Level (3): exhortation The third level is forbidding by exhortation (*waʿẓ, nuṣḥ, takhwīf biʾllāh*).[79] This is for someone who is doing wrong even though he knows it to be wrong, or persists in it after he has learnt it to be so. This may involve repeating to him relevant traditions and anecdotes about early Muslims, all this to be done nicely and sympathetically. There is a mortal peril to be avoided here, namely that the scholar becomes puffed up with his sense of his own superior knowledge, and of the inferiority of the person he is instructing – an attitude which is a greater wrong than the one he is seeking to right.[80] Only someone who knows his own faults is safe from this, for there is a tremendous egotistical pleasure to be had from knowing better and assuming authority over others. One can detect this vice in oneself by a simple introspective test. Ask yourself what would please you more, for the offender to be corrected by your intervention, or for the agent of correction to be someone else, perhaps the offender himself? Anyone who finds the duty unwelcome and wishes someone else would do it for him should in fact go ahead, because his motives are genuinely religious. But if it is the other way round, then he is simply looking for an ego-trip, and should start by reforming himself.

Level (4): harsh language The fourth level is harsh language (*al-sabb waʾl-taʿnīf biʾl-qawl al-ghalīẓ al-khashin*).[81] One turns to this when good manners do not work and the offender begins to manifest obduracy and contempt. This does not mean having recourse to bad language or falsehood,

[77] *Ibid.*, 301.29.
[78] The Persian has *rūstāʾī* (*Kīmiyā*, 513.11). The term *sawādī* is derogatory: though it might be accurate to say 'You *sawādī*!' to someone, it would not be polite (see *Iḥyāʾ*, 302.33).
[79] *Ibid.*, 302.10. [80] For *dhālika* read *dhull*, *ibid.*, 302.15. [81] *Ibid.*, 302.30.

but rather saying things that are fair comment, such as: 'You libertine! You fool! You ignoramus! Don't you fear God?' But if someone knows that this will not be effective, or that speaking out in this way will get him beaten up, he should manifest his anger silently by frowning and scowling.[82]

Level (5): physical action The fifth level is physical action (*al-taghyīr bi'l-yad*).[83] This refers to the destruction of offending objects (breaking musical instruments and the like) and to the use of force to eject someone from somewhere (for example, to drag someone in a state of major ritual impurity out of a mosque). Not all wrongs admit of such action. Moreover, one should not proceed in this fashion if one can get the offender to perform the action himself. Nor should one go further than is necessary: if one can get him out by grabbing his arm, one should not drag him by his foot or his beard, just as a musical instrument that can be rendered non-functional by being broken should not be ripped to pieces,[84] and wine should be poured out where possible without breaking the vessels containing it. One example of a case in which breaking vessels is justified would be bottles with narrow necks; here pouring out the wine might expose one to danger, or simply take up too much of one's time. But where there are no such difficulties, breaking vessels renders one liable to compensation.

Excursus: the question of preventive measures It might be argued that it is justifiable to go beyond the demands of the immediate occasion in order to diminish the likelihood of future offences (*zajr*).[85] However, preventing future offences, like punishing past ones, is not for individual subjects, who are permitted to act only to eliminate wrongs in the present. A ruler, by contrast, may judge it appropriate to break vessels containing wine as a preventive measure.[86]

Level (6): the threat of violence The sixth level is the threat of violence (*al-tahdīd wa'l-takhwīf*), as when you tell a man 'Stop that, or I'll break your head!'[87] Where possible, one should threaten such violence before actually

[82] Ghazzālī says that this is his duty provided he knows that he will not be beaten up for it, and that in such a case it is not enough for him to perform the duty in the heart (*al-inkār bi'l-qalb*) (*ibid.*, 303.4). Here there is no concept of performance by (as opposed to within) the heart (cf. above, note 37). [83] *Ibid.*, 303.6.

[84] The text has *wa-lā yaḥriq* (*ibid.*, 303.18); I read *wa-lā yakhriq*, since the Persian has *rīza rīza na-kunad* (*Kīmiyā*, 515.15). [85] *Iḥyā'*, 303.27.

[86] There is a curious difference between the Arabic and the Persian here. While both are concerned to explain away the fact that vessels were broken when the prohibition of wine was first introduced in Islam, the Persian states that this practice was abrogated (*mansūkh*) (*Kīmiyā*, 516.2), whereas the Arabic denies this (*Iḥyā'*, 303.32). [87] *Ibid.*, 304.12.

inflicting it. One should not threaten to do something impermissible, like kidnapping a man's wife, though it is allowable to exaggerate one's real intentions.

Level (7): actual violence The seventh level is actual violence (*mubāsharat al-ḍarb*) involving the infliction of blows with the hand and foot, but not the use of weapons.[88] This is permitted to individuals if and to the extent that it is necessary, observing the principle of minimal escalation (*tadrīj*). If the use of weapons is needed, this too is admissible as long as it does not lead to disorder (*fitna*). Thus if someone the other side of a river has seized a woman or is playing a flute, one may take up one's bow and shout 'Let her go or I'll shoot you!' If he does not desist, one may proceed with one's threat, though one should not shoot to kill.

Level (8): armed helpers The eighth level is collecting armed helpers (*aʿwān*) where one cannot accomplish the duty on one's own.[89] In such a case the offender may gather helpers too, resulting in a pitched battle. There is disagreement as to whether this needs the ruler's permission. Some say that individual subjects may not do this because it leads to anarchy (*taḥrīk al-fitan wa-hayajān al-fasād wa-kharāb al-bilād*).[90] Others take the more logical (*aqyas*) view that such permission is unnecessary, since once individuals are allowed to take action at the lower levels, there is no way to draw a line that excludes the formation of armed bands (*tajnīd al-junūd*). Their situation is no different from that of individual fighters engaging in holy war; in each case those who are killed are martyrs. In general it is uncommon for matters to reach such a pass in forbidding wrong, but the obligation is there in principle.[91]

The norms Having dispatched the levels, we come to the other topic included under the fourth component, namely the norms (*ādāb*). Detailed norms have already been set out in discussing each level; here, Ghazzālī says, we need only treat the subject in a general way.[92] What it all comes down to is three qualities which the performer of the duty must possess.

88 *Ibid.*, 304.23. The Persian includes the use of a stick (*chūb*) as an option at this point (*Kīmiyā*, 516.15). 89 *Iḥyāʾ*, 304.33.

90 Murtaḍā al-Zabīdī (d. 1205/1791) comments that this has been a frequent occurrence in conflict between Sunnīs and Shīʿites in Khurāsān, with ruinous consequences (*Itḥāf al-sāda*, Cairo 1311, 7:48.3; in general this extensive commentary on the *Iḥyāʾ* is rather unrewarding for our purposes).

91 Laoust reverses Ghazzālī's position (*La politique de Ġazālī*, 130). In the Persian, Ghazzālī does not take sides in the dispute (*Kīmiyā*, 517.6).

92 *Iḥyāʾ*, 305.8. The word *bāb* is to be omitted in the heading.

Quality (1): knowledgeableness The first quality the peformer must have is knowledgeableness (*ʿilm*): he must know the occasions, limits, modes and contraindications of forbidding wrong.[93]

Quality (2): scrupulousness The second quality is scrupulousness (*waraʿ*), which he needs in order to ensure that he acts in conformity with what he knows.[94] A man might know perfectly well that he was going too far, but do so for some motive of his own. At the same time he must be scrupulous if people are to accept what he tells them; a corrupt person (*fāsiq*) who attempts the duty will only meet with scorn.

Quality (3): even temperament The third quality is an even temperament (*ḥusn al-khulq*).[95] The performer of the duty needs this both to restrain his own anger and to endure the backlash that his action will provoke.

Further thoughts on the norms There follows a rather unstructured passage with many traditions and anecdotes.[96] Ghazzālī first talks about the importance of these three norms. He then takes up some further themes. He stresses the need to do right as well as command it; to endure the unpleasant consequences of forbidding wrong; to minimise one's wants and avoid being beholden to others so that one is free to perform the duty;[97] and, once again, to do it nicely.

3. *Wrongs that are commonly met with*

Introductory Ghazzālī begins his third chapter by emphasising that it is impossible to give an exhaustive account of all the wrongs that may be encountered.[98] Instead he offers a representative selection.[99] He notes at this point that wrongs are divided into the disapproved (*makrūh*) and the forbidden; where he speaks of a wrong without qualification, we are to understand a forbidden wrong. It is commendable (*mustaḥabb*) to prevent a disapproved wrong, and disapproved to remain silent about it. However,

[93] *Ibid.*, 305.11. [94] *Ibid.*, 305.12. [95] *Ibid.*, 305.15. [96] *Ibid.*, 305.20.

[97] *Ibid.*, 306.4. This point, like the previous one, is presented as one of the norms (*ādāb*), but in what relationship they stand to the three norms already set out is not made clear.

[98] *Ibid.*, 307.12.

[99] The Persian has a less abrupt introduction: it opens with the observation that the world is full of wrongs in this day and age, and goes on to the need to do what one can about them (*Kīmiyā*, 520.7).

in a case where the offender is unaware that what he is doing is disapproved, it is one's duty to inform him.[100]

(1) Wrongs in the mosque These wrongs include sloppy prayer, faulty recitation of the Koran, the practice whereby pairs of muezzins make a duet of the call to prayer, needless repetitions of the call to prayer after daybreak, the preacher (*khaṭīb*) who wears black robes made mostly of silk, storytellers and preachers (*wuʿʿāẓ*) who mix heresy into what they say, the sale of medicines and the like,[101] not to mention the presence of madmen, boys and drunks in the mosque.[102] These are just Ghazzālī's leading examples; I have left aside his numerous subordinate instances, as also most of his qualifications. Thus with regard to preachers, he warns against the young, elegantly dressed preacher whose delivery is full of poetry and gesture and whose circle is frequented by women.[103]

(2) Wrongs in the market-place The evils Ghazzālī mentions here fall into three categories.[104] The first is commercial dishonesty: concealment of defects in goods; discrepancies in weights and measures; passing off reconditioned second-hand clothes as new. The second is engaging in transactions that violate legal prescriptions: failure to make a proper contract; the inclusion of defective conditions; usurious transactions; and other defective dispositions. The third is the sale of forbidden goods: musical instruments; toy animals (*ashkāl al-ḥayawānāt al-muṣawwara*) sold for small boys during festivals; gold and silver vessels; silk clothes such as can only be worn by men, or are locally known to be worn only by them. It is evident that Ghazzālī is concerned here with the duty of the individual Muslim, not that of the officially appointed censor. He makes this clear in the case of dishonesty regarding profit margins: if a man says 'I bought these goods for – say – ten and I'm taking a profit of such-and-such', and he is lying, then anyone who is aware of this has a duty to inform the prospective buyer of the deceit.

100 *Iḥyāʾ*, 307.15. This passage is actually at the beginning of the section on wrongs in mosques. The introduction of such a basic doctrinal distinction at this point in Ghazzālī's account is distinctly untidy.

101 Such commercial activity in mosques need not be forbidden in itself; though best avoided, it may be tolerated occasionally unless it is disrupting prayer (*ibid.*, 309.6).

102 It is not in itself forbidden for boys to play in the mosque. The case is similar to that of commercial activity: a mosque is not a playground (*ibid.*, 309.13).

103 *Ibid.*, 308.26. The Persian specifies young women (*Kīmiyā*, 521.12), and has further material on the abuse of mosques, e.g. as places to settle financial accounts with peasants (*ibid.*, 521.19).

104 *Iḥyāʾ*, 309.32. The corresponding Persian text (*Kīmiyā*, 522.1) includes polemic against the observance of the Zoroastrian festivals of Nawrūz and Sada among Muslims.

(3) Wrongs in the street These include not just permanent encroachments but also temporary obstructions, unless they cause no inconvenience or are the kind of thing that everyone has to have recourse to (as temporarily placing on the street a load of firewood one is taking home, or tethering an animal there).[105] Streets are for public use (*mushtarakat al-manfaʿa*). The list continues with such evils as unnecessarily transporting loads of thorns in narrow alleys, overloading animals, slaughtering on the street, scattering watermelon rind, discharging water from spouts into narrow lanes, leaving puddles, mud and snow on the streets (though the rights and duties of individuals are limited in this matter), and keeping dogs that bother passers-by.

(4) Wrongs in the bath-house Here the problem starts with the image (*ṣūra*) that one finds at the entrance to the bath-house, or inside it.[106] One's duty is to deface this image; if it is too high to reach, one should try one's luck at another bath-house. Images of trees and such are not a problem. Then follow the issues of nudity, touching and impurity that inevitably arise in such places. In addition, there is the matter of slippery surfaces and the liabilities to which they give rise.[107]

(5) Wrongs of hospitality Finally, there are the wrongs committed in receiving and entertaining people (*ḍiyāfa*).[108] These include laying out silk coverings for men, using censers and the like made of silver or gold, hanging curtains with images on them, and listening to musical instruments or singing-girls. To these we can add the scandal of women[109] gathering on roofs to watch men when there are youths among them who could give rise to temptation. All this requires action, and if one cannot rise to the occasion, one has to leave. So also if forbidden food is served, or the house is one occupied illegally, or someone present is drinking wine or wearing silk or has a golden signet ring,[110] or a heretic is holding forth

[105] *Iḥyāʾ*, 310.13. The heading speaks of major thoroughfares (*shawāriʿ*, Persian *shāhrāh*), not the alleys typical of residential quarters, but some remarks apply more to the latter.

[106] *Ibid.*, 311.1. [107] The Persian adds wasting water (*Kīmiyā*, 523.22).

[108] *Iḥyāʾ*, 311.23. The Persian likewise terms these wrongs *munkarāt-i mihmānī* (*Kīmiyā*, 524.3), but refers to them in the introduction to the chapter as wrongs that occur in homes (*khānahā*) (*ibid.*, 520.11). But wrongs occurring in homes are not as such a category accessible to *ḥisba*; it is being an invited guest that exposes one to them and triggers the duty. [109] Again the Persian specifies young women (*ibid.*, 524.6).

[110] From the references to silk and gold it is clear that Ghazzālī assumes the gathering to be male. There follows another discussion of the restraining of boys from committing wrongs, at the end of which Ghazzālī takes a dim view of the practice of piercing a girl's ears so she can wear golden earrings (*Iḥyāʾ*, 312.4).

about his heresy,[111] or some joker is regaling the party with ribald and untruthful humour.[112] (Humour that is neither untruthful nor indecorous is acceptable in moderation, provided it does not become a habit.) Further relevant wrongs are extravagance and wastefulness.[113]

(6) Other wrongs There are many other wrongs, and no way to enumerate them all.[114] You can think for yourself of the corresponding wrongs associated with informal gatherings (*majāmiʿ*),[115] the courts of judges, offices of state (*dawāwīn al-salāṭīn*), colleges and the like.[116] Every locale has its wrongs.

(7) Of wrongs in general. Anyone who in this day and age sits at home, wherever that may be, is in some measure guilty of failing to instruct people and bring them to right conduct.[117] Ignorance of the law regarding the conditions for prayer prevails among most urban populations, let alone those of the villages and the wildernesses, such as the Beduin, the Kurds or the Turcomans. It is mandatory that there should be found in every[118] mosque and quarter (*maḥalla*) of the town a scholar (*faqīh*) to teach people their religion, and similarly in every village. Likewise it is the duty of every scholar who has discharged his individual duties and is free to undertake a collective one to go out into the rural hinterland of his town, and to the Beduin, the Kurds and the like, and to give them religious instruction. He should, incidentally, take his own food with him, since theirs is usually unlawful.[119] Once one scholar undertakes this duty, others are dispensed from it. In the same way, every layman who understands the conditions of prayer has a duty to instruct others; but the responsibility weighs more heavily on scholars. If you know that people are praying wrongly in the mosque, you cannot just sit at home, and much the same goes for the market-place. Every Muslim has the duty of first setting himself to rights, and then, successively, his household, his neighbours, his quarter, his town, the surrounding countryside, the wilderness with its Beduin, Kurds or whatever, and so on to the uttermost ends of the earth. If somebody closer takes action, then those further away are dispensed

[111] *Ibid.*, 312.15. One does not have to leave if the heretic keeps quiet about his heresy, though one should make no secret of one's distaste for him. [112] *Ibid.*, 312.17.

[113] *Ibid.*, 312.23. [114] *Ibid.*, 313.5.

[115] Murtaḍā al-Zabīdī explains these as *mawāḍiʿ tajtamiʿ fihā ʾl-nās* (*Itḥāf*, 7:63.1).

[116] At this point the Persian text ends abruptly (*Kīmiyā*, 524.17). [117] *Iḥyāʾ*, 313.9.

[118] Insert *kull* (*ibid.*, 313.12).

[119] The reason Ghazzālī gives is that most of their food is acquired illegally; he does not mention that such populations might also be expected to be ignorant or lax in matters of dietary law.

from doing so; otherwise all are guilty. This is a matter of considerably more importance than hair-splitting academic investigations.

4. *Commanding and forbidding rulers*

Ghazzālī begins his fourth and final chapter by referring back to his earlier discussion of the levels (*darajāt*) of performance.[120] Where the wrongdoer is a ruler, there is no problem with the first two levels, namely informing and exhorting; but individual subjects may not have recourse to the use of force or violence, since this leads to disorder (*fitna*) and to consequences worse than the original wrong. What of harsh language – expressions such as 'You tyrant (*ẓālim*)! You who have no fear of God!'? If its use brings harm to others, it is not permitted; but if one fears only for oneself, it is permitted, and indeed commendable.[121] Thus the early Muslims would expose themselves to such risks, knowing that to be killed in such a case was martyrdom.[122] Ghazzālī now quotes a series of seventeen anecdotes to illustrate their courage and plain speaking.[123] This is how things used to be; today, alas, the scholars are silent, or if they do speak out, they are ineffectual, all because of their love of the things of this world.[124]

3. THE ACHIEVEMENT OF GHAZZĀLĪ

Ghazzālī's account of forbidding wrong is a remarkable one, and to the best of my knowledge it is almost entirely his own.[125] He does, of course, incorporate much previous thinking into his analysis; for example, the efficacy–harm matrix is an idea we have already encountered in a work of Abū 'l-Layth al-Samarqandī (d. 373/983).[126] But here, as elsewhere, the affinities are not accompanied by the sustained verbal similarities that would point to literary dependence.[127] Only for traditions and anecdotes about early Muslims is Ghazzālī straightforwardly dependent on earlier literature.

[120] *Ibid.*, 314.1. He seems in fact to be thinking of his original five-level schema (see above, note 26), not his later eight-level version (see above, 438–41), except that he merges the fourth and fifth levels.

[121] Compare the rather different account given above, 431f.

[122] Appropriate traditions are quoted. [123] *Ibid.*, 314–26. [124] *Ibid.*, 326.17.

[125] I find nothing in Ghazzālī's account that invites categorisation as Ashʿarite (on the question of his relationship to Ashʿarism, cf. G. Makdisi, 'The non-Ashʿarite Shafiʿism of Abū Ḥāmid al-Ghazzālī', *Revue des Etudes Islamiques*, 54 (1986), and R. M. Frank, *Al-Ghazālī and the Ashʿarite school*, Durham and London 1994).

[126] See above, 432f., for Ghazzālī's version, and above, ch. 12, 313, for Abū 'l-Layth's.

[127] For a straw in the wind, see below, note 147.

One aspect of Ghazzālī's originality is the impressive architecture of his account. Even the best of earlier analyses – notably those of the Muʿtazilites – tended to proceed by stringing together a succession of topics only one of which, the conditions of obligation, was given much internal structure. Ghazzālī, by contrast, operates with two distinct structural levels: the four basic components (*arkān*) and, within each, a set of subordinate elements – conditions, levels or qualities, as the case may be. This is very typical of Ghazzālī. Thus schemas in which a topic is broken down into a small number of components – usually between three and five – are common in his handbook of Shāfiʿite law.[128] There too we sometimes find subordinate sets of conditions, levels, qualities and the like.[129] A further similarity is that in a good many cases we find that the naming of the components in his handbook involves some degree of ringing changes on roots, though cases in which a single root provides designations for all the components of a set – as it does in our case[130] – are relatively uncommon.[131] As might be expected, the naming of the four components of forbidding wrong seems to be very much a terminological innovation of Ghazzālī.[132]

What Ghazzālī fails to explain is just why he chose the word *ḥisba* as a general term for forbidding wrong, and I am not entirely clear why he did so. There is, of course, the obvious point that, in order to ring his changes, he needed a single term that would cover both commanding right and forbidding wrong. But why this one? The modern reader tends to assume that Ghazzālī is implying an analogy between the duty of the individual to forbid wrong and the obligation of the officially appointed censor

[128] See, for example, Ghazzālī, *Wajīz*, 1:106.5 (*iʿtikāf*), 159.10 (*rahn*), 183.6 (*ḍamān*), 188.3 (*wakāla*). I noted over thirty instances of such sets of *arkān* in the book, and there are doubtless more of them.

[129] Thus in the treatment of *rahn*, the component *al-marhūn* contains three conditions (*sharāʾiṭ*) (*ibid.*, 159.12; for similar sets of conditions, see, for example, *ibid.*, 188.4, 195.17, 246.5). The component *al-ṣīgha* in the treatment of *waqf* contains three levels (*marātib*) (*ibid.*, 245.17; similarly *ibid.*, 2:232.18). There are also components containing sets of *aṭrāf* (*ibid.*, 121.5), *khiṣāl* (*ibid.*, 125.13), *darajāt* (*ibid.*, 207.17), and the like.

[130] For his terms for these components, see above, 428f.

[131] An example in which there is no ringing of changes is *hiba*, where the three components are *al-ṣīgha*, *al-mawhūb* and *al-qabḍ* (*ibid.*, 1:249.4). An example where the phenomenon appears, but is not carried through, is *dhabḥ*, where the four components are *al-dhābiḥ*, *al-dhabḥ*, *al-āla* and *nafs al-dhabḥ* (*ibid.*, 2:205.18). I noted five cases where all components are designated by forms of the same root. An example is *ʿāriya*, where the four components are *al-muʿīr*, *al-mustaʿīr*, *al-mustaʿār*, and *ṣīghat al-iʿāra* (*ibid.*, 1:203.14). The others instances I noted are *rahn* (*ibid.*, 159.11, but cf. 162.8), an aspect of *shufʿa* (*ibid.*, 214.20), *luqaṭa* (*ibid.*, 250.18), and an aspect of *qiṣāṣ* (*ibid.*, 2:121.3). The device is also used by the younger Ibn Rushd (d. 595/1126) in his *Bidāyat al-mujtahid* (Cairo 1970–4), with some development; thus the three components of *hiba* appear there as *al-wāhib*, *al-mawhūb lahu*, and *al-hiba* (*ibid.*, 2:359.9).

[132] In addition to the pattern of ringing changes on the root, compare the terms *nafs al-iḥtisāb* and *nafs al-dhabḥ* (for the latter, see the previous note).

(*muḥtasib*) to police morals and markets – for all that Ghazzālī has nothing to say about the duties of the censor. Such analogies do indeed appear in our sources, though not very frequently, and they are based on the obvious fact that both individual and censor have a duty to forbid wrong. Thus a Ṣūfī who has gone on a rampage against the caliph's wine supply is brought before him; asked who he is, he replies: 'A censor (*muḥtasib*).' When the caliph asks him who appointed him to the censorship (*ḥisba*), he cleverly replies: 'He who appointed you to the imamate.'[133] More significantly for our purposes, Ghazzālī's fellow-Shāfiʿite Māwardī (d. 450/1058) at the beginning of his chapter on the censorship defines the term *ḥisba* as commanding right and forbidding wrong, though he then goes on to distinguish systematically between the individual performer of the duty (*al-mutaṭawwiʿ*) and the official censor (whom alone he terms *al-muḥtasib*).[134] But while this provides a limited precedent, it does not tell us what Ghazzālī had in mind in basing his terminology on the term *ḥisba*. My own feeling is that the key element in the background is the idea of doing something for God's sake, without personal or worldly motives of any kind.[135] This makes sense inasmuch as someone who forbids wrong, if not corruptly motivated, is doing something precisely for God's sake – and not with a view to furthering his own interests, legitimate or otherwise.[136] The problem is, of course, that forbidding wrong is far from being the only thing that can or should be done for God's sake.[137] And with the single

[133] *Iḥyāʾ*, 326.5; Dhahabī, *Siyar*, 14:76.6; Dhahabī, *Taʾrīkh al-Islām*, years 291–300, 71.14. For the story, see below, note 257. For similar anecdotes, see below, note 226, and ch. 19, note 139. [134] Māwardī, *Aḥkām*, 315.3.

[135] One does, of course, stand to attain a reward in the next life.

[136] It is, I think, for this reason that we sometimes find the verb *iḥtasaba* used in older sources in contexts connected with *al-amr biʾl-maʿrūf*. See, for example, above, ch. 4, note 97; Ibn Saʿd, *Ṭabaqāt*, 5:313.1, where the word should be vocalised *yaḥtasibu* (for this passage, cf. above, ch. 4, note 78); Juwaynī, *Ghiyāth*, 177.6; Khwāja ʿAbdallāh Anṣārī (d. 481/1089), *Ṭabaqāt al-ṣūfiyya* (in Persian), ed. M. S. Mawlāʾī, n.p. 1362 sh., 397.5 (I owe this reference to Gerhard Böwering). See also above, ch. 12, notes 28f.

[137] For example, a witness who has come all the way from Seville to give evidence in Cordoba is asked by the suspicious *qāḍī*: 'Are you doing this for God's sake (*muḥtasib*) or for your own profit (*muktasib*)?' (Khushanī, *Quḍāt*, 158.2, cited in Chalmeta, *El 'señor del zoco'*, 405). It is, as it happens, from Muslim Spain that modern scholars have most energetically collected examples of the use of the term *muḥtasib* and related forms (for the period prior to Ghazzālī, see *ibid.*, 403–8, and M. Fierro, 'El proceso contra Ibn Ḥātim al-Ṭulayṭulī', *Estudios onomástico-biográficos de al-Andalus*, vol. 6, Madrid 1994, 191, 196). Some of this material displays usages that would not be out of place in the east. However, the term *muḥtasib* is often used in these texts to refer to someone who makes a practice of doing things for God's sake; such variously meddlesome and pious activities could include *al-amr biʾl-maʿrūf*, but were clearly not confined to it. What made this western usage possible was doubtless the fact that, in the west in contrast to the east, the term *muḥtasib* was not in common use in the sense of censor.

exception of Māwardī's initial definition of *ḥisba*, I have encountered no cases in texts written before the time of Ghazzālī in which forms related to this term are unmistakably being used synonymously with forbidding wrong. But perhaps there was enough in the air;[138] and once we accept Ghazzālī's choice of root, the rest of his terminology makes good sense against the background of his legal thought.

All this is not to say that Ghazzālī's architecture is by any means flawless. There is still a good deal about his account that is untidy or not thought through, as I have had occasion to point out from time to time. The chapter on the obligatoriness of forbidding wrong is deficient in analysis;[139] as a result, the question whether wrongs can be divided into the forbidden and the merely disapproved, and of the effect of these categories on the duty, is not dealt with till the beginning of the section on wrongs in mosques.[140] Likewise the eight levels of performance of the duty seem to represent a development from an earlier five-level schema which still survives in two passages.[141] Other passages balloon with too much unstructured material, as with the string of topics I have labelled 'loose ends',[142] and the passage I have called 'further thoughts on the norms'.[143] The last chapter, on rebuking rulers, covers the same ground as the latter part of the 'excursus' to the discussion of the question of official permission.[144] Altogether, there is no denying that Ghazzālī could have used the services of a good copy-editor.[145] But such lapses are likely to be the result of writing too much and too fast. They are not a reflection of any limitation in Ghazzālī's conception of what constitutes clear and effective analysis, nor do they detract from his extraordinary willingness to modify or abandon traditional ways of handling the subject.

The other aspect of his account that is often original is the handling of the practicalities of the duty. It is rare for a scholar to tell us whether it is incumbent on slaves and women to forbid wrong, and still more so for him to mention peasants, Beduin, Kurds and Turcomans.[146] The whole passage

[138] In addition to the usages already noted, there is a suggestive lexicographical explanation of the verb *iḥtasaba* as meaning to reprove someone for something: *wa-'ḥtasabta ʿalayhi kadhā idhā ankartahu ʿalayhi* (Jawharī (d. *c.* 398/1007), *Ṣiḥāḥ*, ed. A. ʿA. ʿAṭṭār, Cairo 1377, 110a.20; see also Lane, *Lexicon*, 565f.). This usage may, of course, be confined to lexicography.

[139] For the lack of a discussion of the question whether or not the duty can be grounded in reason, cf. above, note 8.

[140] Cf. above, notes 8, 100.

[141] See above, notes 26, 120.

[142] See above, 434f.

[143] See above, 442.

[144] See above, 431f.

[145] See also above, notes 11, 48, 50, 63.

[146] For slaves and women, see above, note 15, and cf. above, 431f.; for the inhabitants of the countryside, see above, note 78, and 445f.

on the duties of scholars not just within their urban environments but also outside them represents a very unusual perspective.[147] The survey of commonly encountered wrongs is (so far as I know) unprecedented, both as an idea and in most of its detail.[148] Equally striking is the freedom with which Ghazzālī brings psychological insights to bear in doctrinal questions, as with his remarks on the subjectivity of expectations,[149] the psychology of ignorance,[150] and the lure of the ego-trip.[151] Such insights are not themselves necessarily new, but they are new to the genre. Ghazzālī also displays a very real sense of what can and cannot be determined by laying down rules in advance. He has a vivid awareness that life is full of problematic cases and grey areas, and that individuals have to make judgements about them as best they can.[152] All in all, there is a great deal of fresh air in Ghazzālī's account.

4. THE LEGACY OF GHAZZĀLĪ

This is not the place to consider whether the religious sciences were moribund in Ghazzālī's time, and whether he succeeded in his aim of reviving them. It is enough that the book he devoted to this project, the *Revival of the religious sciences*, was extraordinarily successful down the centuries. The reasons for this success go beyond the particular qualities I have picked out from his account of forbidding wrong. But at least one of these, effective organisation, was already highlighted in the traditional Muslim world. The Spanish doctor and philosopher Ibn Ṭumlūs (d. 620/1223f.) describes how people were attracted by the unprecedentedly well-ordered and well-arranged character of Ghazzālī's works,[153] while the Imāmī Muḥsin al-Fayḍ (d. 1091/1680) comments on the clarity and good arrangement of the *Revival*.[154]

The wide diffusion of the work, and consequently of its account of forbidding wrong, is documented by a mass of evidence that remains largely

[147] See above, 445f. There is, incidentally, a parallel between Ghazzālī's point about the indefinitely widening horizons of *al-amr bi'l-ma'rūf* (*Iḥyā'*, 313.27–30) and a very similar idea of Galen's (see the text in P. Kraus, '*Kitāb al-akhlāq* li-Jālīnūs', *Majallat Kulliyyat al-ādāb bi'l-Jāmi'a al-Miṣriyya*, 5 (1937), 39.12–14; English translation in J. N. Mattock, 'A translation of the Arabic epitome of Galen's book *Peri ēthōn*', in S. M. Stern *et al.* (eds.), *Islamic philosophy and the classical tradition*, Oxford 1972, 248 (I owe this reference to Baki Tezcan)). But the parallel is isolated, and the wordings are quite different.

[148] See above, 442–6. [149] See above, note 50. [150] See above, 439.

[151] See above, 439. [152] See above, notes 48, 53, 73.

[153] Ibn Ṭumlūs, *Madkhal*, 12.17, quoted in Manūnī, '*Iḥyā'*', 132. He speaks of *jūdat al-niẓām wa'l-tartīb*.

[154] Fayḍ, *Maḥajja*, 1:1.8, speaking of *ḥusn al-bayān wa'l-taḥrīr wa-jūdat al-tartīb wa'l-taqrīr*. The words we should take seriously (because they do not rhyme) are *bayān* and *tartīb*.

unstudied.[155] In attempting to sketch the fortunes of the work, I have arranged the material I have collected in terms of sects and schools, since these are the prime categories of this study; but it should be remembered that to a large extent the literary vector is likely to have been Ṣūfī.

The interest rapidly generated by the work among Ghazzālī's fellow-Shāfiʿites is nicely illustrated by the case of his pupil Abū ʾl-Fatḥ ibn Barhān (d. 518/1124). This Ibn Barhān was a grossly overworked teacher who at one time held a position at the Niẓāmiyya. When asked by his students to teach the *Revival*, he at first refused for lack of time, but eventually agreed to put on the course in the middle of the night.[156] Thereafter two phenomena are worthy of note among the Shāfiʿites. One is the existence of people who had the work by heart, or nearly so.[157] The other is the proliferation of epitomes.[158] There was one by Ghazzālī's brother Aḥmad (d. *c.* 520/1126),[159] one by the Yemeni Yaḥyā ibn Abī ʾl-Khayr al-ʿImrānī (d. 558/1163),[160] one by the Yemeni Muḥammad ibn Saʿīd

[155] For the manuscripts of the work, see Brockelmann, *Geschichte*, supplementary volumes, 1:748 no. 25, and second edition, 1:539 no. 25; ʿA. Badawī, *Muʾallafāt al-Ghazālī*, Cairo 1961, 98–112. For a rich study of the reverberations of a controversial theological idea of Ghazzālī's, see E. L. Ormsby, *Theodicy in Islamic thought: the dispute over al-Ghazālī's 'best of all possible worlds'*, Princeton 1984, esp. ch. 2.

[156] Subkī, *Ṭabaqāt*, 6:30.14, whence H. Laoust, 'La survie de Ġazālī d'après Subkī', *Bulletin d'Etudes Orientales*, 25 (1972), 158 no. 2.

[157] For Abū Ṭālib al-Rāzī (d. *c.* 522/1128), see Subkī, *Ṭabaqāt*, 7:180.9, whence Laoust, 'Survie', 158 no. 4; for Sharaf al-Dīn al-Mawṣilī (d. 622/1225), who used to teach the book from memory, see below, note 162; for Bilālī (d. 820/1417), see below, note 211. With these we may compare a Tunisian who memorised the work (Ibn al-Zayyāt, *Tashawwuf*, 179.15, noted in Manūnī, '*Iḥyāʾ*', 132 no. 3).

[158] A general idea of the number of epitomes made of the book can be obtained from Brockelmann, *Geschichte*, supplementary volumes, 1:748f. no. 25, 750 no. 29; second edition, 1:539f. no. 25, 540f. no. 29; and Badawī, *Muʾallafāt*, 114–18 (listing twenty-six epitomes). For two modern epitomes, see below, ch. 18, notes 8, 155. I have looked at all published and unpublished epitomes that were easily accessible to me.

[159] Aḥmad al-Ghazzālī made a one-volume abridgement of the *Iḥyāʾ* which he called the *Lubāb al-Iḥyāʾ* (Subkī, *Ṭabaqāt*, 6:60.7, whence Laoust, 'Survie', 158 no. 3). The work is extant (see M. Bouyges, *Essai de chronologie des oeuvres de al-Ghazali*, Beirut 1959, 135f. no. 219; also Brockelmann, *Geschichte*, second edition, 1:539f. no. 1, and Badawī, *Muʾallafāt*, 114 no. 1). I have consulted ms. Princeton, Garrett 1079H (for this manuscript, see Hitti, *Catalog*, 448 no. 1482). The treatment of the *kitāb al-amr biʾl-maʿrūf* (ff. 28b–30a) is uninteresting.

[160] Subkī, *Ṭabaqāt*, 7:338.6, whence Laoust, 'Survie', 161 no. 20; Jaʿdī (*fl.* later sixth/twelfth century), *Ṭabaqāt fuqahāʾ al-Yaman*, ed. F. Sayyid, Cairo 1957, 181.4; Janadī (d. 732/1331f.), *al-Sulūk fī ṭabaqāt al-ʿulamāʾ waʾl-mulūk*, ed. M. ʿA. Ḥ. al-Akwaʿ al-Ḥiwālī, Yemen 1983–, 1:344.5; Yāfiʿī (d. 768/1367), *Mirʾāt al-janān*, Hyderabad 1337–9, 3:323.14. The work has been identified with an epitome of the *Iḥyāʾ* preserved in a Bankipore manuscript (Arabic 841, see Brockelmann, *Geschichte*, supplementary volumes, 1:748 no. 1a; Badawī, *Muʾallafāt*, 115 no. 5; *Catalogue of the Arabic and Persian manuscripts in the Oriental Public Library at Bankipore*, Calcutta and Patna 1908–46, 13:24f. no. 841). The title-page of the manuscript offers the title *Mukhtaṣar al-Iḥyāʾ*, which is certainly an accurate description, but gives the author's name as Muḥyī

al-Qurayẓī (d. 575/1179), judge of Laḥj,[161] two by Sharaf al-Dīn al-Mawṣilī (d. 622/1225),[162] one by a certain Jamāl al-Dīn Muḥammad ibn ʿAbdallāh al-Khwārazmī al-Shāfiʿī (d. 679/1280f?),[163] one by the Cairene Ṣūfī Bilālī (d. 820/1417),[164] and doubtless others. At the same time, many Shāfiʿites writing on forbidding wrong after the time of Ghazzālī quote or make use of his treatment of the subject. Such is the case with Ibn al-

Footnote 160 (*cont.*)
ʾl-Dīn Abū Zakariyyāʾ Yaḥyā ibn Muḥammad ibn Mūsā, with a ***nisba*** which might be read as al-Najabī (unvowelled, with the second and third consonants unpointed). By contrast, the biographical sources usually give the Yemeni scholar's ***kunya*** as Abū ʾl-Ḥusayn, say nothing of the ***laqab*** or ***nisba*** found in the manuscript, and mention Muḥammad ibn Mūsā only as a distant ancestor. However, Ḥājjī Khalīfa (d. 1067/1657), referring to what is likely to be the same work, gives the author's name as Abū Zakariyyāʾ Yaḥyā ibn Abī ʾl-Khayr al-Yamanī (***Kashf al-ẓunūn***, 24.31), and the same form appears already in Yāfiʿī, ***Mirʾāt***, 3:318.9. So the identification is plausible, though in the absence of internal evidence it is hard to feel confident of it. The abridgement of Ghazzālī's account of forbidding wrong (***Mukhtaṣar al-Iḥyāʾ***, ff. 63b.12–67a.13) is in any case disappointing. Ghazzālī's analysis disappears, though the term ***ḥisba*** is used in one passage (***ibid.***, f. 64b.7); what remains is mostly anecdotes about rebuking rulers. I am much indebted to the Khuda Bakhsh Oriental Public Library for sending me a microfilm of the relevant parts of the manuscript.

161 Jaʿdī, ***Ṭabaqāt***, 225.11; Janadī, ***Sulūk***, 1:433.13.

162 He twice made epitomes of the ***Iḥyāʾ***, one large and one small, and used to teach from the book from memory (Ibn Khallikān (d. 681/1282), ***Wafayāt al-aʿyān***, ed. I. ʿAbbās, Beirut 1971–2, 1:108.8 (remembering him from personal experience as an incomparable lecturer in Irbil, ***ibid.***, 108.17); similarly Subkī, ***Ṭabaqāt***, 8:39.5, whence Laoust, 'Survie', 164 no. 36). One of the two epitomes survives (Sharaf al-Dīn al-Mawṣilī (d. 622/1225), ***Rūḥ al-Iḥyāʾ wa-rawḥ al-aḥyāʾ***, ms. Oxford, Bodleian, Pocock 240, item 2; see Brockelmann, ***Geschichte***, second edition, 1:540 no. 3; Badawī, ***Muʾallafāt***, 115 no. 3; and J. Uri, ***Bibliothecae Bodleianae codicum manuscriptorum orientalium catalogus***, first part, Oxford 1787, 62 no. 71). The whole work occupies less than thirty not very dense folios, and Ghazzālī's ***kitāb al-amr biʾl-maʿrūf*** is reduced to less than a page (f. 53a.19–53b.16); so this must surely be the smaller of the two epitomes. I am indebted to Chase Robinson for examining the manuscript for me and sending me copies of the relevant parts.

163 Jamāl al-Dīn Muḥammad ibn ʿAbdallāh al-Khwārazmī al-Shāfiʿī (d. 679/1280f?), ***Dhukhr al-muntahī fī ʾl-ʿilm al-jalī waʾl-khafī***, ms. London, British Library, Add. 7,275. For this work, see Brockelmann, ***Geschichte***, second edition, 1:540 no. 6, and Badawī, ***Muʾallafāt***, 115 no. 6; for the manuscript, see ***Catalogus codicum manuscriptorum orientalium qui in Museo Britannico asservantur, Pars secunda, codices Arabicos amplectens***, London 1846–52, 337 no. 740. The name of the author and the title of the work are given on a title-page in the same hand as the rest of the text, but do not appear in the body of the work. There is also a fragmentary manuscript in Cairo, for which see ***Fibrist al-kutub al-ʿArabiyya al-maḥfūẓa biʾl-Kutubkhāna al-Khidīwiyya al-Miṣriyya***, Cairo 1305–10, 7:297.23. The cataloguers give the same title, but state the name of the author somewhat differently, adding among other things that he was a Meccan; they also supply the death date of 679/1280f., which is adopted by Brockelmann and Badawī. I have not succeeded in identifying the author in the biographical literature. He certainly post-dates Ibn al-Jawzī (d. 597/1201), since he mentions his ***Minhāj al-qāṣidīn*** (Khwārazmī, ***Dhukhr***, f. 2b.5; cf. above, ch. 6, note 177). To judge from his introductory remarks, he was a Ṣūfī; note, for example, the oppositions ***ẓāhir/bāṭin*** (***ibid.***, ff. 1b.25, 2a.25), ***sharīʿa/ḥaqīqa*** (***ibid.***, ff. 2b.1), and ***muʿāmala/mukāshafa*** (***ibid.***, f. 2a.2, 2a.13). His epitome of Ghazzālī's treatment of forbidding wrong (***ibid.***, ff. 116b–121a) offers nothing of interest.

164 The work is extant, see below, note 211.

Ukhuwwa (d. 729/1329),[165] ʿAlī ibn Shihāb al-Hamadānī (d. 786/1385),[166] Taftazānī (d. 793/1390),[167] Ibn al-Naḥḥās (d. 814/1411),[168] Dawānī (d. 908/1502),[169] Khunjī (d. 927/1521),[170] Fashnī (writing in 978/1570),[171] Bājūrī (d. 1276/1860),[172] and doubtless others[173] – but not, significantly, Āmidī (d. 631/1233)[174] or Nawawī (d. 676/1277).[175]

More striking is the appearance of epitomes and customised versions of the work among other sects and schools. On the Sunnī side, we have already encountered this phenomenon among the Mālikīs.[176] Here Ṭurṭūshī (d. 520/1126) remarks in the introduction to his recension that, of the

165 For example, compare Ibn al-Ukhuwwa, *Maʿālim*, 7.11–8.11, with *Iḥyāʾ*, 286.2–13. Most of the material of *Maʿālim*, 14–22 is likewise from Ghazzālī's account (the parallels are largely unremarked by the editor).

166 Hamadānī devotes the seventh chapter of his work on rulership to *al-amr biʾl-maʿrūf* (*Dhakhīra*, 157–93; for the work in general, see Teufel, *Lebensbeschreibung*, 43–6). The structure is taken from Ghazzālī, together with most of the material. Though Hamadānī is writing in Persian, his source is the *Iḥyāʾ*, not the *Kīmiyā* (compare, for example, the wording on noxious dogs in *Dhakhīra*, 191.2, with that found in *Iḥyāʾ*, 310.32, and *Kīmiyā*, 523.11). For Hamadānī's school allegiance, see above, ch. 12, note 188.

167 Taftazānī summarises Ghazzālī's doctrine in a few lines in his commentary on the 'three modes' tradition (*Sharḥ ḥadīth al-Arbaʿīn*, 105.24). On the other hand, he owes little or nothing to Ghazzālī in the account of *al-amr biʾl-maʿrūf* in his *Sharḥ al-Maqāṣid* (5:171–5, for the sources of which see above, ch. 13, 351).

168 Ibn al-Naḥḥās relies on Ghazzālī for the doctrinal bedrock of his account, but does not use his *ḥisba* terminology (see above, ch. 13, note 119).

169 Dawānī seems to be borrowing Ghazzālī's wording on the duty to stay at home (*Sharḥ*, 211.8; compare *Iḥyāʾ*, 292.17, and cf. above, 432 case (1)).

170 Ghazzālī is the main source behind the chapter on the *muḥtasib* in Khunjī (d. 927/1521), *Sulūk al-mulūk*, ed. M. ʿA. Muwaḥḥid, Tehran 1362 sh., 175–99. Khunjī's borrowing may be acknowledged (as 176.17–177.22, cf. *Iḥyāʾ*, 301.20–305.7), unacknowledged (as 184.21–187.10, cf. *Iḥyāʾ*, 289.21–291.9), or credited to an intermediate source (as 188.10–189.9, cf. *Iḥyāʾ*, 297.7–299.5). Khunjī's account was brought to my attention by Mark Tulloss.

171 Fashnī in his commentary to the 'three modes' tradition cites Ghazzālī for the case of the fastidious rapist (*Majālis*, 135.4; cf. above, note 21).

172 Bājūrī likewise cites Ghazzālī for the fastidious rapist in his commentary on the versified creed of Laqānī (*Tuḥfa*, *apud* Laqānī, *Jawharat al-tawḥīd*, 202.11).

173 A version of Ghazzālī's survey of common wrongs turns up (without mention of his name) in an edition of the popular Egyptian catechism of Jurdānī (d. 1331/1912f.) (see the translation in A. Jeffery, *A reader on Islam*, The Hague 1962, 512–15; the last section does not stem from Ghazzālī). See also Shirbīnī, *Mughnī*, 4:211.12.

174 Cf. above, ch. 13, 349f.

175 Cf. above, ch. 13, 351f. Although he made no use of Ghazzālī's account in his commentary on the 'three modes' tradition, he nevertheless ends the rather uninteresting section on *al-amr biʾl-maʿrūf* in his later *Adhkār* by referring the reader not only to his own commentary, but also to the *Iḥyāʾ*, which he says is the best place to go for the doctrinal aspects (*shurūṭ wa-ṣifāt*) of forbidding wrong (Nawawī (d. 676/1277), *al-Adhkār al-muntakhaba min kalām Sayyid al-Abrār*, Cairo 1988, 418.13; I owe this reference to Mona Zaki).

176 See above, ch. 14, 373 for Ṭurṭūshī (d. 520/1126), Ibn al-Rammāma (d. 567/1172), Abū ʿAlī al-Masīlī (*fl.* second half of the sixth/twelfth century), and also Khazrajī (d. 539/1145). Ismāʿīl Pāshā al-Baghdādī ascribes an epitome of the *Iḥyāʾ* to Wādī Āshī (d. 657/1259) (*Hadiyyat al-ʿārifīn*, 2:126.29; I owe this reference to Maribel Fierro).

countless works on piety (*taqwā*), the *Revival* is the best, but that it suffers from a number of faults which he proceeds to list.[177] Among the Ḥanbalites, it was Ibn al-Jawzī (d. 597/1201) who went to work in this way.[178] Someone going into spiritual retreat wanted a book to take with him, and chose the *Revival*, claiming it to be unique of its kind (*infirāduhu fī jinsihi*); Ibn al-Jawzī responded by pointing out the hidden faults of the book, and undertaking to remedy them in his recension.[179] Among the Ḥanafīs, we possess an epitome of the work which may date from the early ninth/fifteenth century, on which ʿAlī al-Qārī (d. 1014/1606) wrote a commentary which in effect restores much material omitted by the epitomiser.[180] On the Ibāḍī side, there is the recension of Jayṭālī (d. 750/1349f.);[181] the background to this is perhaps the popularity of the work in North Africa under the Almohads (r. 524–668/1130–1269).[182] On the Shīʿite side, both the Zaydīs and Imāmīs have their versions of the work – though not, so far as I know, the Ismāʿīlīs. The Zaydīs owe their recension to the imam al-Muʾayyad Yaḥyā ibn Ḥamza (d. 749/1348f.);[183] this version is likely to reflect the currency of the work among the Yemeni Shāfiʿites.[184] The Imāmī recension was produced by Muḥsin al-Fayḍ (d. 1091/1680);[185] he explains that the *Revival*, for all its considerable virtues, was unfortunately written by Ghazzālī before his conversion to Shīʿism, and that consequently much of it is based on false Sunnī principles (*uṣūl ʿāmmiyya fāsida*).[186] The relative

177 See the passage published in Manūnī, '*Iḥyā*'', 135.10. Compare also the remark of Qāḍī ʿIyāḍ (d. 544/1149) reported by his son that it would be good to make an epitome of the *Iḥyāʾ* containing only its sound elements (*mā fīhi min khāliṣ al-ʿilm*) (Muḥammad ibn ʿIyāḍ (d. 575/1179f.), *al-Taʿrīf bi'l-Qāḍī ʿIyāḍ*, ed. M. Sharīfa, n.p. n.d., 106.12, cited in S. Ghurāb, 'Ḥawl iḥrāq al-Murābiṭīn li-*Iḥyāʾ* al-Ghazzālī', in *Actas del IV Coloquio Hispano-Tunecino*, Madrid 1983, 153). 178 See above, ch. 6, note 177.

179 Aḥmad ibn Qudāma, *Mukhtaṣar*, 3.1; also Ibn al-Jawzī, *Muntaẓam*, ed. Hyderabad, 9:170.6. 180 See above, ch. 12, 320f.

181 See above, ch. 15, 401–3, and cf. 423f.

182 For this see Manūnī, '*Iḥyā*'', 132–4.

183 For the *Taṣfiya* of Yaḥyā ibn Ḥamza, see above, ch. 10, 246; for the influence of Ghazzālī in Yaḥyā ibn Ḥamza's *Shāmil*, see above, ch. 10, 246f.

184 See above, notes 160f., for two epitomisers in this milieu. A third Yemeni Shāfiʿite, Muḥammad ibn ʿUmar al-ʿImrānī (d. 572/1176f.), is known to have set about copying the *Iḥyāʾ* (Jaʿdī, *Ṭabaqāt*, 193.7; Janadī, *Sulūk*, 1:392.12).

185 See above, ch. 11, note 219. He entitles his recension *al-Maḥajja al-bayḍāʾ fī tahdhīb al-Iḥyāʾ*, or, if you prefer, *fī iḥyāʾ al-Iḥyāʾ* (Fayḍ, *Maḥajja*, 1:3.17). In the *kitāb al-amr bi'l-maʿrūf*, Muḥsin al-Fayḍ is a fairly drastic editor: he introduces Imāmī traditions (see, for example, *Maḥajja*, 4:102.4, 107.6), freely discards Ghazzālī's analysis as based on the false principles of the Sunnīs (*uṣūluhum al-fāsida*, *ibid.*, 106.7), and turns the sectarian knife after recounting an anecdote of Ghazzālī's in which a libertine caught in the act rebukes ʿUmar for intrusion (*ibid.*, 109.11); see also above, ch. 11, notes 285f. (on rudeness to rulers). It is striking that Muḥsin al-Fayḍ, despite his initial complimentary remark on Ghazzālī's organisation of his material (see above, note 154), makes little use of the schemas set out by Ghazzālī in the *kitāb al-amr bi'l-maʿrūf*.

186 Fayḍ, *Maḥajja*, 1:1.6. For a sceptical review of the Imāmī reports of Ghazzālī's conver-

dates at which the various Muslim sects and schools get their recensions are suggestive of the relative distance between each of them and the Shāfiʿites: the Mālikīs by or even before the beginning of the sixth/eleventh century, the Ḥanbalites later in the sixth/eleventh century, the Zaydīs and Ibāḍīs in the eighth/fourteenth century, the Imāmīs in the eleventh/seventeenth.[187] But even the Christians had their version.[188]

At the same time the work was often mined by other non-Shāfiʿite authors writing on forbidding wrong. We have seen this among the Mālikīs with Ibn al-Munāṣif (d. 620/1223),[189] among the Ḥanbalites with Zayn al-Dīn al-Ṣāliḥī (d. 856/1452),[190] among the Ḥanafīs with a whole series of authors,[191] and likewise among the Imāmīs.[192] Ghazzālī's terminology further left its mark on Koranic exegesis.[193]

But the work did not please everyone. The controversy surrounding it was most visible in the west, where the book is likely to have been available as early as 495/1101f.[194] It was the target of hostile tracts among the

sion, see Khwānsārī (d. 1313/1895), *Rawḍat al-jannāt*, Tehran and Qumm 1390–2, 8:3–19 (I am indebted to Etan Kohlberg for this reference).

187 The Imāmīs had, of course, heard of Ghazzālī long before Muḥsin al-Fayḍ: Ibn Ṭāwūs (d. 664/1266) has citations from the *Iḥyāʾ* (Kohlberg, *Ibn Ṭāwūs*, 188 no. 188). If the Ḥanafīs had not made themselves a version of the *Iḥyāʾ* before the ninth/fifteenth century, this is surprisingly late.

188 See below, appendix 2.

189 See above, ch. 14, 371f. Note also that Ibn al-Zayyāt (*Tashawwuf*, 100.13) quotes a prayer recommended by Khaḍir from the *kitāb al al-amr biʾl-maʿrūf* of the *Iḥyāʾ* (322.35).

190 See above, ch. 7, 162 (and cf. ch. 8, note 121, on the use of the book by Bayṭār (d. 1396/1976) in his articles in *Umm al-qurā*).

191 See the information given above, ch. 12, regarding the following authors: Yaʿqūb ibn Seyyid ʿAlī (d. 931/1524f.) (note 103), Kemālpāshāzāde (d. 940/1534) (note 104), Ṭāshköprīzāde (d. 968/1561) (321f.), Qarabāghī (tenth/sixteenth century?) (note 105), ʿIṣmat Allāh of Sahāranpūr (d. 1133/1720f.) (322f.), Ismāʿīl Ḥaqqī (d. 1137/1725) (notes 98f.), ʿAbd al-Ghanī al-Nābulusī (d. 1143/1731) (note 154), and Ḥaydarīzāde (d. 1349/1931) (331–3), whence Osman Nuri (d. 1381/1961) (330f.). For two cases of Ḥanafīs using *ḥisba* and *iḥtisāb* in Ghazzālī's sense, see above, ch. 12, note 145.

192 For the appearance of the Ghazzālian terminology of *al-amr biʾl-maʿrūf* among the Imāmīs well before Muḥsin al-Fayḍ, see above, ch. 11, note 298. A later author who incorporates much Ghazzālian material left aside by Muḥsin al-Fayḍ is Mahdī al-Narāqī. Thus he includes Ghazzālī's levels of response (*Jāmiʿ al-saʿādāt*, 2:246.13) and his survey of common wrongs (*ibid.*, 249–51; both are carried over in his son's Persian rendering, *Miʿrāj al-saʿāda*, 519.5, 519.26); Muḥsin al-Fayḍ, by contrast, includes only one of Ghazzālī's levels (*Maḥajja*, 4:110.13), and dismisses Ghazzālī's survey as useless (*ibid.*, 111.22). For Narāqī's use of Ghazzālī's *ḥisba* terminology, abandoned by his son, see above, ch. 11, note 298. Qāḍī Saʿīd al-Qummī had likewise adopted Ghazzālī's schema of levels (*Sharḥ Tawḥīd al-Ṣadūq*, 1:742.16), editing them in a manner that may in turn have influenced Narāqī.

193 See above, ch. 2, note 36.

194 Abū Bakr ibn al-ʿArabī (d. 543/1148) heard it from Ghazzālī himself in 490/1097 (F. Jabre, 'La biographie et l'oeuvre de Ghazālī reconsidérées à la lumière des *Ṭabaqāt* de Sobkī', *MIDEO*, 1 (1954), 87f., citing Ibn al-ʿArabī, *al-ʿAwāṣim min al-qawāṣim*, ed. ʿA. Ṭālibī, in his *Ārāʾ Abī Bakr ibn al-ʿArabī al-kalāmiyya*, Algiers n.d., 2:30.10). Ibn al-ʿArabī returned from his travels in 495/1101f. (*ibid.*, 290.2, cited in Manūnī, '*Iḥyāʾ*', 126 n. 7).

scholars;[195] one of them, the same Ṭurṭūshī who made a recension of the work, pronounced that the *Revival* ought to be burnt.[196] It was also the object of official persecution on the part of rulers of the Almoravid dynasty (r. 454–541/1062–1147).[197] We have the text of an edict sent to Valencia in 538/1143 by the Almoravid ruler Tāshufīn ibn ʿAlī (r. 537–40/1142–6) ordering that special efforts be made to root out and burn copies of the works of Ghazzālī, with binding oaths to be administered to those suspected of concealing them.[198]

Just as the book as a whole could disturb people, so also Ghazzālī's treatment of forbidding wrong. As we have seen, his views on this subject are marked by a certain flirtation with radicalism.[199] In this Ghazzālī may have owed something to his teacher Juwaynī,[200] and he may also have been reacting to the Ḥanafī chauvinism of the Seljūq rulers of his day. The duty of course extends to every one,[201] not just rulers and scholars. More remarkably, he is prepared to allow individual subjects to have recourse to weapons where necessary,[202] and even to sanction the formation of armed bands to implement the duty without the permission of the ruler.[203] And while there is no question of countenancing rebellion, Ghazzālī is no accommodationist: he displays great enthusiasm for men who take their lives in their hands and rebuke unjust rulers in harsh and uncompromising language.[204] In espousing such views Ghazzālī may have been pushing

[195] For Ṭurṭūshī, see Fierro's discussion of his epistle to one Ibn al-Muẓaffar in her introduction to her translation of his *Ḥawādith*, 61–4 no. 19. For Ibn Ḥamdīn (d. 508/1114), *qāḍī* of Cordoba, see Manūnī, '*Iḥyāʾ*', 127 n. 11. For Māzarī (d. 536/1141, if this is the right Māzarī), see *ibid.*, 130f. (with remarks on the question which Māzarī is the author of the work in question). For Ilbīrī (d. 537/1142f.), see *ibid.*, 131.

[196] See the text from his epistle to Ibn al-Muẓaffar published in Ghurāb, 'Iḥrāq', 162.4; also in Wansharīsī, *Miʿyār*, 12:187.13.

[197] For the literary sources, see Manūnī, '*Iḥyāʾ*', 127–30. Ghurāb is inclined to view the historicity of the burning with scepticism, or as having happened only on a small scale (see his summing-up in his 'Iḥrāq', 155). His main arguments are that the literary sources, which are of the Almohad period, are biased against the Almoravids (*ibid.*, 150), and that the biographies of Ibn Ḥamdīn make no mention of the burning (*ibid.*, 145). Each of these points has merit, but given Ṭurṭūshī's approval of the burning of the book, and the edict of 538/1143, what the literary sources tell us is entirely plausible.

[198] Ḥ. Muʾnis, 'Nuṣūṣ siyāsiyya ʿan fatrat al-intiqāl min al-Murābiṭīn ilā ʾl-Muwaḥḥidīn', *Majallat al-Maʿhad al-Miṣrī lil-dirāsāt al-Islāmiyya fī Madrīd*, 3 (1955), 113.4, cited in Manūnī, '*Iḥyāʾ*', 128. Cf. the shocked marginal protest transcribed by Muʾnis in his footnote.

[199] As noted by Madelung ('Amr be maʿrūf', 994a; cf. Lambton, *State and government*, 312).

[200] Cf. above, ch. 13, 346.

[201] Note particularly the formulations of the Persian (above, notes 14, 27).

[202] See above, 441, and contrast Juwaynī's view (above, ch. 13, note 54). This difference is noted by Madelung ('Amr be maʿrūf', 994b).

[203] See above, note 91.

[204] Note how the need to respect the majesty (*hayba*) of rulers (see above, note 34) has been forgotten by the time we get to the chapter on rebuking them (see above, note 121).

against the limits of Sunnī political attitudes to established authority, and on occasion his nerve seems to falter.[205] It is not surprising that posterity had more or less extensive reservations with regard to these matters.

It was Ghazzālī's views on armed bands that provoked the most widespread dissent. Scholars borrowing his account often modified it to recommend or require the permission of the ruler for such activity: so the Ḥanbalite Ibn al-Jawzī,[206] the Mālikī Ibn al-Munāṣif,[207] an epitomiser writing in 689/1291,[208] the Zaydī Yaḥyā ibn Ḥamza (speaking also for the Muʿtazilites),[209] Hamadānī,[210] the Shāfiʿite Ṣūfī Bilālī,[211] and the Ḥanafī Ṭāshköprīzāde (d. 968/1561).[212] Some exclude the use of arms by individuals, as does Ṭāshköprīzāde,[213] or even deny them recourse to physical

[205] At the point at which the Arabic allows the formation of armed bands without official permission, the Persian sits on the fence (see above, note 91); and in an earlier passage the Persian favours such permission (see above, note 28).

[206] See above, ch. 6, note 182.

[207] See above, ch. 14, notes 105, 107.

[208] ʿAlī ibn Muḥammad ibn Aḥmad al-Rāzī (writing 689/1291), *al-Mustakhlaṣ min Iḥyāʾ ʿulūm al-dīn*, ms. Istanbul, Süleymaniye, Aya Sofya 2,097, f. 86b.20, stating that it is best not to seek helpers without the command of the ruler, since the common people (*ʿawāmm*) cannot be trusted to persist in the path of the law unless there is someone to restrain them (*illā bi-wāziʿ*). The work is mentioned by Brockelmann (*Geschichte*, second edition, 1:540 no. 4) and Badawī (*Muʾallafāt*, 115 no. 4); I have not been able to identify the author, and do not know to which law-school he belonged (doubtless he was a Shāfiʿite or a Ḥanafī). The manuscript contains Persian interlinear glosses (see, for example, ff. 85b, 86b).

[209] See above, ch. 10, note 135, and cf. note 116.

[210] Hamadānī, *Dhakhīra*, 168.20 (cf. above, note 28). But when he comes to Ghazzālī's main discussion of the issue (cf. above, 441), he gives us Ghazzālī's eighth level without flinching (*ibid.*, 179.2).

[211] Shams al-Dīn Muḥammad ibn ʿAlī al-Bilālī (d. 820/1417), *Jannat al-maʿārif* (alternative title: *Iḥyāʾ al-Iḥyāʾ fī ʾl-taṣawwuf*), ms. Istanbul, Süleymaniye, Fatih 2,604, f. 45a.17, stating that if helpers are needed, it depends on the ruler's permission. This epitome of the *Iḥyāʾ* was written in 807/1405 (*ibid.*, f. 95b.11); it is mentioned by Brockelmann (*Geschichte*, supplementary volumes, 1:749 nos. 10, 18, and the correction *ibid.*, second edition, 1:540 no. 18) and Badawī (*Muʾallafāt*, 116 no. 10, 117 nos. 18, 21, 118 no. 26). Bilālī, a Shāfiʿite living in Cairo, was above all a Ṣūfī (Sakhāwī, *Ḍawʾ*, 8:178f. no. 439); he was a devotee of the *Iḥyāʾ*, which he almost knew by heart, and his epitome was a considerable success, particularly with the Maghribīs (*ibid.*, 178.8, 178.24).

[212] See above, ch. 12, note 114 (and cf. also note 102).

[213] See above, ch. 12, note 112. In an anonymous Persian mirror for princes written a couple of generations after Ghazzālī by an author familiar with his *Iḥyāʾ* and *Kīmiyā*, we read that the use of arms by the common people (*ʿawāmm*) is a matter of dispute among the scholars; most theologians (*ahl-i uṣūl*) hold that such action is reserved to the ruler (*pādishāh*), but some jurists (*fuqahā*) permit it if it works (anon., *Baḥr al-fawāʾid* (in Persian), ed. M. T. Dānishpazhūh, Tehran 1345 sh., 187.11 = J. S. Meisami (trans.), *The sea of precious virtues*, Salt Lake City 1991, 130; and cf. *ibid.*, 189.19 = 132). The work was written in Syria for a ruler of Marāgha during the reign of the caliph al-Muqtafī (r. 530–55/1136–60) (see Meisami's introduction to her translation). The author was such a firm believer in Ḥanafī–Shāfiʿite détente that his school affiliation is not made explicit; though Meisami considers him a Shāfiʿite, he might be the Ḥanafī Abū Bakr ibn Aḥmad al-Balkhī (d. 553/1158), who taught in Marāgha before moving to Aleppo (see Madelung, 'The spread of Māturīdism', 149; also Ibn al-ʿAdīm (d. 660/1262), *Bughyat al-ṭalab*, ed. S. Zakkār, Damascus 1988–9, 4,341–3).

violence of any kind without the ruler's permission, as do Ibn al Jawzī,[214] Bilālī,[215] and Ṭāshköprīzāde.[216] Several are unhappy with Ghazzālī's celebration of heroic incivility to rulers: so Ibn al-Jawzī,[217] Hamadānī,[218] Bilālī[219] and the Imāmī Muḥsin al-Fayḍ.[220] There are, of course, authors who transcribe Ghazzālī's views without protest;[221] this may reflect approval, or simply the habit of copying from great books. But it is only the western Ibāḍī Jayṭālī who actually outdoes Ghazzālī in activism: he strongly endorses armed bands, favours speaking out against unjust rulers even where this will bring harm to others, and makes clear his positive attitude to righteous rebellion.[222]

One figure whom it is tempting to see as an heir of Ghazzālī's activist doctrine of forbidding wrong is the Moroccan Mahdī Ibn Tūmart (d. 524/1130), the founder of the Almohad movement. That there is some linkage between this movement and Ghazzālī is clear. Though the story of Ibn Tūmart's encounter with Ghazzālī is likely to be apocryphal,[223] he did study with Ṭurṭūshī,[224] who as we have seen was the author of a recension of the *Revival*. It was, moreover, in part thanks to the rise of the Almohads that the work achieved widespread popularity in the western Islamic world.[225] At the same time, forbidding wrong is a prominent theme in the biography of Ibn Tūmart, particularly in the context of his long journey home from the east.[226] He is reported to have been thrown into the sea for

[214] See above, ch. 6, note 180.
[215] Bilālī, *Jannat al-maʿārif*, f. 45a.8, reserving beating to the imam.
[216] See above, ch. 12, note 110. [217] See above, ch. 6, notes 186–8.
[218] Hamadānī's version of Ghazzālī's first treatment of this question (see above, note 33) rules out anything that goes beyond informing and counselling as impossible (*Dhakhīra*, 171.18); and he simply omits the whole chapter which Ghazzālī devotes to rebuking rulers (cf. *ibid*., 193.20).
[219] Bilālī, *Jannat al-maʿārif*, f. 45a.9, stating that the ruler may only be informed or counselled; again, this is with regard to Ghazzālī's first treatment of the issue.
[220] See above, ch. 11, notes 285f.
[221] See, for example, above, ch. 13, note 123, on the Shāfiʿite Ibn al-Naḥḥās; above, ch. 7, note 119, on the Ḥanbalite Zayn al-Dīn al-Ṣāliḥī; and above, ch. 12, notes 118–21, on the Ḥanafī ʿIṣmat Allāh of Sahāranpūr. Wansharīsī (d. 914/1508) lists Ghazzālī's treatment of *al-amr biʾl-maʿrūf* among the unexceptionable parts of the *Iḥyāʾ* (*Miʿyār*, 12:184.15), but without going into detail.
[222] See above, ch. 15, 402f. As might be expected, modern Muslim reactions to Ghazzālī's activism have been more mixed than those of pre-modern times (see above, ch. 12, 332, and below, ch. 18, notes 86f. and 526–8).
[223] See R. Le Tourneau, *The Almohad movement in North Africa in the twelfth and thirteenth centuries*, Princeton 1969, 6–9. For a recent attempt to rehabilitate the story, see M. Fletcher, 'Ibn Tūmart's teachers: the relationship with al-Ghazālī', *Al-Qanṭara*, 18 (1997).
[224] See Fierro's introduction to her translation of Ṭurṭūshī, *Ḥawādith*, 98f. no. 28.
[225] See Manūnī, '*Iḥyāʾ*', 132f.
[226] See, in addition to the references given in the following notes, ʿAbd al-Wāḥid al-Marrākushī (writing 621/1224), *Muʿjib*, ed. R. Dozy, Leiden 1881, 128.10, 129.4; Ibn

such activity on the ship he boarded at Alexandria.[227] In Bijāya he scattered a mixed crowd of men and women, who were celebrating the end of the Ramaḍān fast, by laying about him right and left with a cudgel.[228] In Tlemsen he disrupted a wedding procession, breaking tambourines and sweeping the bride from the saddle.[229] In Āgarsīf he took exception to a crucifixion, protesting that only the dead should be crucified, not the living.[230] But unfortunately the sources, and in particular Ibn Tūmart's extant writings, tell us nothing of his doctrine of forbidding wrong.[231] Any attempt to trace its affinities must accordingly be pure speculation.[232]

5. EXCURSUS: THE ṢŪFĪS

Ghazzālī was, among other things, a Ṣūfī. Ṣūfism, however, is a somewhat vague term, and should probably remain so.[233] We might be tempted to see Ṣūfism as a kind of alternative Islam, were it not that in many historical contexts it simply was Islam. What is clear is that the Ṣūfīs are not a group comparable to the sects and schools with which we have been concerned in previous chapters. Rather they represent a domain of piety to which neither religious law nor religious politics are central. In itself, of course, this does not say very much. The Ṣūfī persuasion can take any form from a scrupulously observant asceticism to a wild antinomian mysticism,

Abī Zarʿ, *Rawḍ al-qirṭās*, 1:111.6, 111.16, 111.22 (emphasising that Ibn Tūmart had no official permission to perform the duty), 111.26, 112.1 (implying that *qudra* is a condition of obligation); and above all Baydhaq (sixth/twelfth century), *Taʾrīkh al-Muwaḥḥidīn*, *apud* E. Lévi-Provençal (ed.), *Documents inédits d'histoire almohade*, Paris 1928, 53.1, 60–63, 66.16. For modern discussions of this record, see, for example, Goldziher, *Livre*, 96f.; Le Tourneau, *Almohad movement*, 15f.; Chalmeta, *El 'señor del zoco'*, 481–3; García-Arenal, 'Práctica,' 156. Cf. also the letters of Ibn Tūmart in Lévi-Provençal, *Documents inédits*, 6.1, 8.17. In one anecdote, Ibn Tūmart is asked at whose command he engages in *ḥisba*; his answer is 'God and His Prophet' (Baydhaq, *Taʾrīkh*, 53.2, cited by García-Arenal). [227] ʿAbd al-Wāḥid, *Muʿjib*, 129.6.

[228] Baydhaq, *Taʾrīkh*, 52.10. [229] *Ibid.*, 60.4.

[230] *Ibid.*, 62.1. Ibn Tūmart is attacking a practice which is in accord with Mālikī law (see *EI*², art. 'Ṣalb' (F. E. Vogel); Saḥnūn, *Mudawwana*, 6:299.9).

[231] For an attempt to get round this silence by extending to *al-amr biʾl-maʿrūf* what Ibn Tūmart says about *al-qiyām bi-amr Allāh*, see ʿA. al-Najjār, *al-Mahdī Ibn Tūmart*, n.p. 1983, 276–8, whence doubtless A. Ben Hamadi, 'Y a-t-il une influence khāriǧite dans la pensée d'Ibn Tūmart?', in *Mélanges offerts à Mohamed Talbi*, Tunis 1993, 20f. (drawn to my attention by Maribel Fierro). Najjār cites Ibn Tūmart (d. 524/1130), *Aʿazz mā yuṭlab*, *apud* Goldziher, *Livre*, 256.12 (= ed. ʿA. Ṭālibī, Algiers 1985, 238.10).

[232] The linkage with Ghazzālī was plausibly suggested by Goldziher (*Livre*, 96), followed by García-Arenal ('Práctica', 156). A less plausible line of speculation has led some scholars to the Khārijites (D. Urvoy, 'La pensée d'Ibn Tūmart', *Bulletin d'Etudes Orientales*, 27 (1974), 35; Ben Hamadi, 'Y a-t-il une influence khāriǧite?', 17–22).

[233] I should emphasise that Ṣūfī literature is not one I read in the course of a normal day. Hence my documentation in this section is likely to be relatively poor, and my understanding of it somewhat crude. But I think the main outlines of what follows are correct.

from an abject political quietism to a ferocious political activism. But either way, religious law and politics – the domains within which forbidding wrong is at home – are not constituents of Ṣūfism as such.

It is accordingly fruitless to go in search of anything that could be called the Ṣūfī theory of forbidding wrong. Indeed an inspection of the tables of contents of the classical handbooks of Ṣūfism rapidly reveals that forbidding wrong is just not a Ṣūfī topic.[234] There are, of course, some Ṣūfīs who give space to forbidding wrong, but in these instances there is usually little or nothing to indicate that they are writing as Ṣūfīs. An obvious example is Ghazzālī himself. As we have seen, his treatment is long and highly individual; yet there is little in it that could be characterised as specifically Ṣūfī. Suggestive points might be his recourse to psychological insight,[235] his warning against the temptation of the ego-trip,[236] and his recommendation that one minimise one's dependence on others (*taqlīl al-ʿalāʾiq*).[237] But these points are marginal to the account as a whole.[238] Another example is Ṣūfī Koranic exegesis; a Ṣūfī commentator is naturally bound to give some attention to those verses that speak of forbidding wrong. A case in point is the well-known Ṣūfī writer Qushayrī (d. 465/1072).[239] In his comments on Q3:104 and Q3:110, he departs from mainstream exegesis by ignoring the standard scholastic issues and adopting a straightforward moralistic and pietistic tone. But despite some Ṣūfī colouring, there is nothing in what he says that amounts to a Ṣūfī interpretation of the duty.[240]

This lack of any intrinsic link between Ṣūfism and forbidding wrong does not, of course, carry the implication that they were incompatible. Ṣūfīs were Muslims like anyone else. Ḥārith al-Muḥāsibī (d. 243/857f.), an early moralist and mystic,[241] says of the gnostics (*ahl al-maʿrifa biʾllāh*) that the basis of their way includes sincere cultivation of forbidding wrong.[242] Sahl

[234] Likewise in looking through Sulamī's biographies of Ṣūfīs, I found only two sayings that mention forbidding wrong, and in neither case were the sentiments distinctively Ṣūfī (Sulamī (d. 412/1021), *Ṭabaqāt al-Ṣūfiyya*, ed. N. Shurayba, Cairo 1969, 226.9, 508.10; for a biographical reference, see below, note 265). [235] See above, 439.

[236] See above, 439, and below, 461f. [237] See above, note 97.

[238] For another instance of a Ṣūfī whose account of forbidding wrong shows little Ṣūfī influence, see below, note 258.

[239] For Qushayrī see *EI*², art. 'Ḳushayrī' (H. Halm).

[240] Qushayrī (d. 465/1072), *Laṭāʾif al-ishārāt*, ed. I. Bisyūnī, Cairo n.d.–1971, 1:270.8, 282.6 (where a Ṣūfī colouring appears in the definitions of *maʿrūf* and *munkar*). His commentary on the other major verses bearing on forbidding wrong has nothing noteworthy to offer, but see also below, note 259. As might be expected, there is a much stronger Ṣūfī colouring in the commentary on the same verses of Muḥyī ʾl-Dīn ibn al-ʿArabī (d. 638/1240), *Tafsīr*, Beirut 1968, 1:206.17, 209.19; on this see also below, note 279.

[241] For a brief account of his life and thought, see *EI*², art. 'Muḥāsibī' (R. Arnaldez).

[242] Ḥārith al-Muḥāsibī (d. 243/857f.), *Risālat al-mustarshidīn*, ed. ʿA. Abū Ghudda, Aleppo 1974, 100.5.

al-Tustarī (d. 283/896), a major figure in early Ṣūfism,[243] developed a Ṣūfistic conception of a religious leader appointed by God; he describes this leader as, among other things, establishing the forbidding of wrong.[244] At the same time people referred to in the sources as Ṣūfīs freely engage in forbidding wrong. The Baghdādī Abū 'l-Ḥusayn al-Nūrī (d. 295/907f.), about to break a boatload of amphorae containing the caliph's wine, was addressed by the boatman as a 'meddlesome Ṣūfī' (ṣūfī fuḍūlī).[245] Under conditions of political chaos in Alexandria in the year 200/816, we are told that there appeared in the city 'a group called the Ṣūfīs' (ṭā'ifa yusammawn al-ṣūfiyya) who commanded right, or so they claimed, and challenged the local governor (sulṭān); they were led by a certain Abū 'Abd al-Raḥmān al-Ṣūfī, who was one of their number.[246] How we should understand their activity is not clear: was their intention to enforce moral puritanism on the population, to restore public order, or to seize power by outright rebellion? But whatever it was, commanding right was the name of their game.[247]

Beyond this general compatibility, there are two points at which the Ṣūfīs have something of their own to say about forbidding wrong, for all that these contributions do not amount to a Ṣūfī theory of the duty as a whole.

The first is a matter of ascetic psychology. Forbidding wrong can be an act of great altruism, but it can also become an ego-trip. The point is made by authorities of such widely different periods as Dāwūd al-Ṭā'ī (d. 165/781f.), a precursor of Ṣūfism;[248] Ghazzālī, who gives the theme characteristic development;[249] and 'Abd al-Ghanī al-Nābulusī (d. 1143/1731), who uses it to discourage forbidding wrong altogether.[250] The insight is not one attainable only by Ṣūfīs. It was also vouchsafed to Abū 'l-Layth al-Samarqandī (d. 373/983), who illustrated it with a story about a zealot who set out to cut down a sacred tree.[251] But sensitivity to the lure of egotism has at least an elective affinity with Ṣūfism. Sunāmī in the early eighth/fourteenth century clearly regarded it as a Ṣūfī idea, since he

---

[243] For a short account of his life and thought, see EI², art. 'Sahl al-Tustarī' (G. Böwering).
[244] Abū Nuʿaym, Ḥilya, 10:190.16 (aqāma 'l-amr bi'l-maʿrūf wa'l-nahy ʿan al-munkar), translated in G. Böwering, The mystical vision of existence in classical Islam, Berlin and New York 1980, 65. This passage was drawn to my attention by Maribel Fierro.
[245] Iḥyā', 325.34; and cf. Dhahabī, Siyar, 14.76.3, and his Ta'rīkh al-Islām, years 291–300, 71.10. For the story, see below, note 257; for Nūrī, see EI², art. 'Nūrī, Abū 'l-Ḥusayn' (A. Schimmel).   [246] Kindī, Wulāt, 162.2. I owe this reference to Patricia Crone.
[247] There are other examples. For Abū 'l-Rabīʿ al-Ṣūfī, a doubtless younger contemporary of Sufyān al-Thawrī (d. 161/778), see above, ch. 4, 81. For the companions of the Egyptian ʿĪsā ibn al-Munkadir (d. after 215/830), see above, ch. 14, note 209.
[248] See above, ch. 4, note 56.   [249] See above, 439.   [250] See above, ch. 12, 327f.
[251] See above, ch. 12, note 38, and cf. above, ch. 6, note 160.

remarks that the Ṣūfis add to the conditions for forbidding wrong that one's ego should not be involved – if it is, one should not proceed.[252] Likewise ʿAbd al-Ghanī gives the idea an explicit Ṣūfī reference by insisting that only a deep understanding of Ṣūfism can provide us with the requisite self-knowledge to assay our motives.[253]

Two anecdotes related by Ghazzālī and others may serve to illustrate the sensibility behind this thinking. One concerns Abū Sulaymān al-Dārānī (d. 205/820f.), an ascetic of Dārayyā near Damascus.[254] He relates that he once heard a caliph say something objectionable, and wanted to take a stand against it (*an unkir ʿalayhi*). But he knew that he would lose his life if he did so, and decided not to. What stopped him, he explained, was not the prospect of being killed; rather it was that there were many people present, and he feared that he might be motivated by vanity.[255] The second anecdote is about Abū ʾl-Ḥusayn al-Nūrī, whom we met as a 'meddlesome Ṣūfī'.[256] It starts with the observation that he was a man given to minding his own business, but would right a wrong if he saw one. One day at the riverside he noticed a boat with a suspicious cargo of thirty amphorae. He pressed the boatman to tell him what was in them, and learnt that the cargo was wine belonging to the caliph al-Muʿtaḍid (reigned 279–89/892–902). Nūrī thereupon broke all but one of the amphorae. For this he was taken before the caliph, who, among other things, was curious to know why he had left that single amphora intact. Nūrī explained that in the course of his rampage his inner state had changed: at first he had acted because God was demanding that he do so, but when he came to the last amphora, he became aware of self-conceit, and desisted.[257]

The second contribution of the Ṣūfis to forbidding wrong is more dramatic, and at the same time incontrovertibly their own. The idea is that Ṣūfis can use their spiritual powers to right wrongs in ways that bypass the clumsy recourse to hand and tongue that is the lot of ordinary mortals. This is what the Qādirī Ṣūfī Zayn al-Dīn al-Ṣāliḥī calls righting wrongs through spiritual

[252] Sunāmī, *Niṣāb*, 198.13, whence Rajab ibn Aḥmad al-Āmidī, *Wasīla*, 2:770.1. Cf. above, ch. 12, note 138. [253] See above, ch. 12, note 159.

[254] He was sufficiently well remembered for Samʿānī to go to Dārayyā to visit his tomb (*Ansāb*, 5:271.4).

[255] Ghazzālī, *Iḥyāʾ*, 292.27; and see Khaṭīb, *Taʾrīkh Baghdād*, 10:249.3, and Ibn al-Jawzī, *Ṣifa*, 4:223.17, where the caliph is al-Manṣūr (r. 136–58/754–75) and his offence is specified. Ghazzālī's version, though historically vaguer, is conceptually richer.

[256] See above, note 245, and also note 133.

[257] Ghazzālī, *Iḥyāʾ*, 325.29; and cf. Dhahabī, *Siyar*, 14:76.1, translated in Gramlich, *Alte Vorbilder*, 1:386f., and Dhahabī, *Taʾrīkh al-Islām*, years 291–300, 71.8. The same story is told, anachronistically, about the Ṣūfī Abū Bakr al-Shiblī (d. 334/945f.) (Sunāmī, *Niṣāb*, 198.14, whence Rajab, *Wasīla*, 769.22).

state (*inkār al-munkar bi'l-ḥāl*); he goes on to illustrate the technique with a collection of nine anecdotes.[258] But he was clearly not the inventor of the idea, since he quotes an earlier Ṣūfī, who practised the method, as saying: 'Inwardly righting a wrong through state is better than outwardly righting it through words.'[259] A contemporary of Ṣāliḥī, the Egyptian Ṣūfī Ibrāhīm al-Matbūlī (d. 877/1472),[260] integrated this technique into an old schema by giving the tripartite division of labour a Ṣūfī twist. Action with the hand, he said, is for the authorities, who beat but are not beaten, and action with the tongue is for scholars who practise what they preach. But action with the heart is for the gnostics (*ʿārifūn*), whose contempt for themselves precludes their forbidding others. Instead, such a man will turn to God in his heart to stop the wrongdoing, and in that way the offender will desist. This, he says, is taking action against wrong in a real sense (*fa-hādhā huwa 'l-taghyīr ḥaqīqatan*), whereas merely registering a protest in the heart is not.[261]

Again, some anecdotes may help to convey what is involved here. One concerns the well-known ascetic Bishr al-Ḥāfī (d. 227/841f.). He once disarmed a brawny man who had seized a woman and was wielding a knife.[262] To all appearances, he did no more than brush shoulders with the man in passing, at which the would-be rapist collapsed. When asked what had come over him, the miscreant revealed that the passing stranger had told him that God was watching him, whereupon his legs gave way under him. He took ill and died soon after. A second anecdote tells how the Ṣūfī whose adage was quoted above responded to a request that he demonstrate his method.[263] Sitting on a bench in the street, he waited till a mule went by carrying jars of wine. He then pointed at the load and said: 'That's it!' The mule tripped, and the jars broke. After this had happened three times, he said: 'That's how to right wrongs!' (*hākadhā yakūn al-inkār*).[264] A third

[258] See above, ch. 7, notes 120f. This is the only element in Ṣāliḥī's monumental account of the duty that is explicitly Ṣūfī. The idea is echoed by ʿAlī al-Qārī (see above, ch. 12, note 85).

[259] Ṣāliḥī, *Kanz*, 238.13: *inkār al-munkar bi'l-bāṭin min ḥayth al-ḥāl atamm min inkārihi bi'l-ẓāhir min ḥayth al-qāl*. This Ṣūfī is one Abū ʿAbdallāh Muḥammad al-Qurashī, for whom see perhaps Shaʿrānī (d. 973/1565), *al-Ṭabaqāt al-kubrā*, Cairo 1954, 1:159f. no. 281. Note also a Ṣūfī Koran exegesis to Q5:63 (Ṣāliḥī, *Kanz*, 237.2) which is taken from Qushayrī, *Laṭā'if*, 2:131.5.

[260] For Matbūlī see Sakhāwī, *Ḍaw'*, 1:85f.; Brockelmann, *Geschichte*, supplementary volumes, 2:151 no. 23.

[261] Quoted in Shabrakhītī, *Futūḥāt*, 481.8, through Shaʿrānī. For a shorter version, see Shaʿrānī (d. 973/1565), *Lawāqiḥ*, Cairo 1961, 801.10 (I owe this reference to Mona Zaki); here Matbūlī mentions that such Ṣūfī action against wrongs is rare.

[262] *Iḥyā'*, 307.4 (cf. above, ch. 4, note 155). The story also appears in Ṣāliḥī, *Kanz*, 239.10, doubtless from Ghazzālī, among Ṣāliḥī's examples of righting wrongs by *ḥāl*.

[263] See above, note 259.

[264] Ṣāliḥī, *Kanz*, 238.14 (where a line has been lost through haplography, see Ṣumayda's edition, 233.1).

case shows how the spiritual power of a saint may reinforce a rebuke administered in the normal way. Bunān al-Ḥammāl (d. 316/928), an Iraqi who settled in Egypt and was an outstanding ascetic, is described by some of his biographers as commanding right.[265] This reflects a story in which he commanded right to Ibn Ṭūlūn (ruled Egypt 254–70/868–84),[266] or gave offence to his son Khumārawayh (r. 270–82/884–96),[267] as a result of which he was thrown to a wild beast. He emerged from this experience, as Amedroz put it, 'with Daniel's impunity';[268] his only concern, he explains, had been over the ritual purity of the animal's saliva when it licked him. There is nothing distinctively Ṣūfī about Bunān's commanding right; but his relations with the wild beast reflect a spiritual power which mere scholars do not possess.

We also find among Ṣūfīs attitudes that are to some degree antithetical to forbidding wrong. Thus Sahl al-Tustarī lists a set of conditions under which one should shrink from forbidding wrong (*fa-iyyākum wa'l-amr bi'l-ma'rūf wa'l-nahy 'an al-munkar*): when the ruler oppresses his subjects, when the judges take bribes, when the scholars consort with the ruler and so forth.[269] Though presented as a future contingency, these conditions are such familiar symptoms of moral decay that the passage can easily be read as discouraging the forbidding of wrong in the present. But there is nothing specifically Ṣūfī about this way of thinking,[270] and the same is true of a saying of Sahl according to which it is not for ordinary people to command rulers or scholars.[271] Another example of such cold water is provided by some rather obscure passages in the letters of the Andalusian Ṣūfī Ibn al-'Arīf (d. 536/1141).[272] The tendency of these passages is unmistak-

[265] Sulamī, *Ṭabaqāt al-Ṣūfiyya*, 291.5; Abū Nu'aym, *Ḥilya*, 10:324.10; Anṣārī, *Ṭabaqāt*, 397.1. I am indebted to Gerhard Böwering for references to key sources for Bunān.

[266] Abū Nu'aym, *Ḥilya*, 10:324.11, 324.15; Khaṭīb, *Ta'rīkh Baghdād*, 7:101.19; Qushayrī (d. 465/1072), *Risāla*, Cairo 1966, 138.10 = R. Gramlich, *Das Sendschreiben al-Qušayrīs über das Sufitum*, Wiesbaden 1989, 83f. no. 45, with further references; Anṣārī, *Ṭabaqāt*, 397.5 (where the animal is explicitly identified as a lion); Ibn al-Jawzī, *Muntaẓam*, ed. Hyderabad, 6:217.7; Ibn al-Jawzī, *Ṣifa*, 2:449.6; Dhahabī, *Siyar*, 14:489.8; Dhahabī, *Ta'rīkh al-Islām*, years 301–20, 509.15. In these versions, we are not told what right Bunān commanded, and indeed Qushayrī does not even mention the cause of his being thrown to the beast.

[267] Dhahabī, *Siyar*, 14:489.2; Dhahabī, *Ta'rīkh al-Islām*, years 301–20, 509.8. In this version, which Dhahabī cites from Sulamī, Bunān makes Khumārawayh's Christian vizier dismount and tells him to behave as his religious status requires.

[268] Amedroz, 'Hisba jurisdiction', 295, citing Dhahabī's *Ta'rīkh al-Islām* from manuscript.

[269] Sahl al-Tustarī (d. 283/896), *al-Mu'āraḍa wa'l-radd*, ed. M. K. Ja'far, Cairo 1980, 110.3. For this work, see Böwering's remarks in *EI*², art. 'Sahl al-Tustarī', 840b.

[270] For other examples of it, see above, ch. 3, 40–2; ch. 4, 76f.; ch. 5, 106.

[271] Qurṭubī, *Jāmi'*, 12:73.6 (to Q22:41); cf. above, ch. 2, notes 22f.

[272] Ibn al-'Arīf (d. 536/1141), *Miftāḥ al-sa'āda*, ed. 'I. 'A. Dandash, Beirut 1993, 169.24, 174.6, 179.1 (these passages were drawn to my attention by Maribel Fierro). For this

ably to play down forbidding wrong. One who sees a public wrong (*munkaran ẓāhiran bayyinan*) should concern himself with his own soul (*fa-ʿalayhi bi-khāṣṣat nafsihi*); righting wrongs (*taghyīr al-munkar*) as an individual duty is incumbent only on rulers through the use of the police (*shurat*) and the like,[273] on scholars through counselling and explaining, and on friends through civility and counselling.[274] Rebuking rulers is circumscribed with such conditions as privacy, civility and purity of intention.[275] Only a ruler may use a whip or the like, and only a friend may administer a verbal admonition; not to divulge the offence of a Muslim is better than rebuking him in public, except in the case of rulers and scholars who have a duty to do so. Others, it seems, have no business aspiring to forbid wrong.[276] Ibn al-ʿArīf in these views goes beyond standard doctrine in limiting the duty, and his overall mood is deflating. But again, there is little that is identifiably Ṣūfī, and nothing to suggest an intrinsic tension between Ṣūfism and forbidding wrong.

We would nevertheless expect such a tension to manifest itself towards the antinomian end of the Ṣūfī spectrum.[277] From a mystical perspective, forbidding wrong should appear as a matter of externals, a desiccated pietism which is irrelevant to the inner values of Ṣūfism;[278] and for a thorough-going antinomian, there is in any case no wrong to forbid. Yet in the material I have come upon, the existence of this tension is evident mainly from its denial. The famous mystic Muḥyī ʾl-Dīn ibn al-ʿArabī (d. 638/1240) took the view that those who 'call to good' in Q3:104 must be upright gnostics (*ʿārifūn ulū ʾstiqāma*), like the 'elders of the way' (*shuyūkh al-ṭarīqa*). They must be gnostics since those who do not know God cannot know the good; someone in this category (*ghayr al-muwaḥḥid*) may call people to obey something other than God. But even a gnostic (*muwaḥḥid*) who is not upright may command something he deems right which is in fact wrong, and the other way around. This is often

Ṣūfī, see *EI*², art. 'Ibn al-ʿArīf' (A. Faure); M. Fierro, 'La religión', in M. J. Viguera Molíns (ed.), *El retroceso territorial de al-Andalus* (= *Historia de España Menéndez Pidal*, tomo VIII–II), Madrid 1997, 487–9. Fierro remarks aptly that his doctrine of *al-amr biʾl-maʿrūf* is innocuous (*ibid.*, 497 n. 61). [273] I understand *maʿnāhā* for *maʿnāhu*.

[274] Ibn al-ʿArīf, *Miftāḥ*, 169.24; similarly *ibid.*, 179.3. [275] *Ibid.*, 170.5.

[276] *Ibid.*, 174.6.

[277] Consider, for example, the milieu described in A. T. Karamustafa, *God's unruly friends: dervish groups in the Islamic later middle period, 1200–1550*, Salt Lake City 1994, 17–23.

[278] That forbidding wrong is a part of exoteric religion is perhaps suggested in a couple of references made to it by Jalāl al-Dīn Rūmī (d. 672/1273) in his *Mathnawī* (ed. and trans. R. A. Nicholson, London 1925–40, 5:299 = 6:284 (VI, 480), 5:390 = 6:373 (VI, 2,065)). However, there is no indication of esoteric hostility to forbidding wrong (*ibid.*, 5:392 = 6:374 (VI, 2,093)). The only other reference to the duty in the *Mathnawī* is uninteresting (*ibid.*, 5:222 = 6:209 (V, 3,497)).

the case with those who have attained a high mystical state and live in seclusion (*man balagha fī maqām al-jamʿ wa-ʾḥtajaba biʾl-ḥaqq ʿan al-khalq*).[279] Ibn al-ʿArabī likewise held that when a saint (*walī*) becomes aware of an offence through spiritual channels (*kashf*), this does not void his obligation in law (*sharʿ*) to forbid the offence. God, he declares, has imposed on us the duty of taking action against wrongs (*izālat al-munkar*), even if our spiritual perception tells us that the offence is predestined to happen (*muḥattam al-wuqūʿ*; the light of *kashf* does not extinguish the light of *sharʿ*).[280] Similar thinking appears in a letter of Ibn ʿAbbād al-Rundī (d. 792/1390), likewise a Ṣūfī from Andalusia.[281] He is responding to people who have been troubled by a saying of a deceased Ṣūfī; he endorses the saying, but unfortunately does not quote it. He then goes on to explain that there is in fact no contradiction between, on the one hand, excusing people's misdeeds by looking upon them with the eye of the mystic (*ʿayn al-tawḥīd*), and on the other, commanding right and forbidding wrong to them. He gives two reasons for this. The first is somewhat technical: forbidding wrong relates only to what may happen in the future, and not to the past. One who commands and forbids tells people to do this or not to do that; he does not ask them why they have already done something – except for the purpose of instruction, which looks to the future. By contrast, the eye of the mystic (*naẓar al-muwaḥḥid*) looks to what is already past.[282] The second reason is that the mystic is considering things from the viewpoint of esoteric truth (*ḥaqīqa*), whereas forbidding wrong is a matter of exoteric law (*sharīʿa*), and between the two there is no contradiction. Ibn ʿAbbād ends by expressing his surprise that his addressees should have failed to see something so obvious.[283]

A suggestion that forbidding wrong belongs to a relatively low level of Ṣūfī sainthood can perhaps be found in a passage quoted by ʿAbd al-Ḥaqq al-Bādisī, who completed a collection of biographies of saints of the Moroccan Rīf in 711/1311f.[284] In his introduction, he quotes from one

[279] Ibn al-ʿArabī, *Tafsīr*, 1:206.17, 207.6. The passage appears without attribution in Ismāʿīl Ḥaqqī's commentary to the verse (*Rūḥ al-bayān*, 2:75.8).

[280] Quoted in Shabrakhītī, *Futūḥāt*, 479.22. I do not know whether the passage is to be found in one of Ibn al-ʿArabī's numerous extant works.

[281] See EI^2, art. 'Ibn ʿAbbād' (P. Nwyia).

[282] Ghazzālī likewise excludes the past from the domain of forbidding wrong, but has a different view of the future (see above, 435).

[283] Ibn ʿAbbād al-Rundī (d. 792/1390), *al-Rasāʾil al-kubrā*, Fez 1320, 150.1. I owe my knowledge of this passage to Maribel Fierro, who drew my attention to the brief summary in P. Nwyia, *Ibn ʿAbbād de Ronda*, Beirut 1961, 159.

[284] ʿAbd al-Ḥaqq al-Bādisī (writing 711/1311f.), *al-Maqṣad al-sharīf*, ed. S. Aʿrāb, Rabat 1982. For the date of writing, see *ibid.*, 151.6.

of his biographees, ʿAlī ibn Muḥammad al-Marrākushī (*fl.* mid-seventh/thirteenth century), a typology of saints which moves in three stages from the most sociable to the least so.[285] The first group comprises those who live in the world, making a living as other people do, but leading scrupulously virtuous and observant lives; one aspect of this is their cultivation of forbidding wrong.[286] By contrast, there is no mention of it in the accounts of the other two types of saint.

Yet with the exception of ʿAbd al-Ghanī's frontal attack on the puritans of his day,[287] and some passing remarks of the emir ʿAbd al-Qādir al-Jazāʾirī (d. 1300/1883),[288] a full-blown Ṣūfī rejection of forbidding wrong is hardly to be found. The only parallel I can adduce to ʿAbd al-Ghanī's polemic is a position mercilessly rebutted in a work on forbidding wrong by the Indian Ḥanafī ʿIṣmat Allāh of Sahāranpūr (d. 1133/1720f.). Though he mostly follows Ghazzālī's account, he does insert some discussions of topics not covered by Ghazzālī, and the most interesting of these is a refutation of the views of certain heretics (*malāḥida*).[289]

These heretics take as their doctrine the principle of leaving people in peace (*tark taʿarruḍ al-khalq wa-īdhāʾihim*) and having pacific relations with everyone (*ṣulḥ al-kull*). Worse yet, they claim this to be the doctrine of the Ṣūfīs, and hold to the literal meaning of a saying widely current among the common people (*ʿawāmm*): 'Do not bother [anyone], and do whatever you wish; for in our law there is no sin other than this.'[290] They ingratiate themselves with every errant sect of infidels – Jews, Brahmins, Zindīqs and others – and hate the Muḥammadan community.[291] This is as much as he tells us about the heretics and their views. They were clearly Muslims, in their own view if not in that of our author: they claim that their

[285] For this typology, see García-Arenal, 'Práctica', 158, and A. Sebti, 'Hagiographie du voyage au Maroc médiéval', *Al-Qanṭara*, 13 (1992), 174f. (both ascribing the typology to Bādisī himself). For ʿAlī ibn Muḥammad al-Marrākushī, who settled in Bādis in the 640s/1240s, see Bādisī, *Maqṣad*, 72–5, 146.16. [286] *Ibid.*, 21.1.

[287] See above, ch. 12, 327f.

[288] ʿAbd al-Qādir al-Jazāʾirī (d. 1300/1883), *Mawāqif*, Damascus 1966–7, 294.10 (I owe this reference to Itzchak Weismann). Jazāʾirī argues that the mystic is not covered by the tripartite division of labour, and is thus not obligated by the duty. Cf. also a remark by ʿAlī al-Qārī noted above, ch. 12, note 84.

[289] This is the fifth chapter of the work (ʿIṣmat Allāh, *Raqīb*, ff. 17a.7–19a.17; cf. above, ch. 12, notes 116, 122).

[290] *Ibid.*, f. 17a.7. The saying is given in Persian (*mabāsh dar pay-i āzār-u har chih khwāhī kun; kih dar sharīʿat-i mā ghayr az īn gunāhī nīst*), and is repeated *ibid.*, f. 17b.24, with a suggestion as to how to explain it away; its source is a poem of Ḥāfiẓ-i Shīrāzī (d. 791/1389) (*Dīwān*, ed. B. Khurramshāhī, Tehran 1373 sh., 76.6). Compare this hemistich in the verses later quoted from Jāmī (d. 898/1492): *kas mayāzār wa har chih khwāhī kun* (ʿIṣmat Allāh, *Raqīb*, f. 18b.23; Jāmī, *Mathnawī-i haft awrang*, ed. M. Gīlānī, Tehran 1337 sh., 102.8). Jāmī attacks this view as that of the old antinomians (*mubāḥīyān-i kuhun*). [291] ʿIṣmat Allāh, *Raqīb*, f. 19a.5.

doctrine is Ṣūfī, and are refuted by appeals to Muslim authority. They were presumably a feature of the Indian environment: the principle of having pacific relations with everyone (*ṣulḥ-i kull*) was one well known in Moghul India, where it justified friendly interaction with the followers of native Indian religions.[292]

ʿIṣmat Allāh begins his refutation by impaling the heretics on the horns of a dilemma. Either they accept what the authoritative texts (*nuṣūṣ*) say about forbidding wrong, or they do not. If they do not accept them, they have abandoned Islam, and there is no possibility of dialogue with them (*lā khiṭāb maʿahum*); if they do accept them, their doctrine collapses.[293] Were leaving people alone pleasing to God, He would not have sent the prophets, nor established their laws (*sharāʾiʿ*), nor called to Islam, nor voided other religions, but would rather have left people to their own devices, untroubled by divine visitations; nor would He have imposed on them the duty of holy war, which involves suffering and death for both Muslims and infidels.[294] He further emphasises that Ṣūfīs – pantheists included – have made it abundantly clear that they neither practise nor preach an indiscriminate toleration.[295] What is more, distinguished Ṣūfīs have written on forbidding wrong.[296] Even apart from all this, the fact that the prophets were sent to command right and forbid wrong is enough to establish that it is both good and obligatory.[297] In short, if leaving people alone were praiseworthy, then forbidding wrong would not be a religious duty.[298]

It is hard to tell from this polemic whether the heretics had mounted an explicit attack on the doctrine of forbidding wrong. But even if they had not, the encounter throws into striking relief the less eirenical aspects of the Muslim duty. What it does not do is to help us to identify any overall view of forbidding wrong that we could describe as characteristically Ṣūfī.

[292] See, for example, A. Ahmad, *Studies in Islamic culture in the Indian environment*, Oxford 1964, 126. I have not been able to find a systematic discussion of the idea.

[293] ʿIṣmat Allāh, *Raqīb*, f. 17a.10. [294] *Ibid.*, f. 17a.17.

[295] *Ibid.*, f. 18a.7, 18a.22. However, he quotes no direct and explicit Ṣūfī statements endorsing forbidding wrong.

[296] *Ibid.*, f. 18a.24. He adduces the chapter on forbidding wrong in the *Ghunya* of ʿAbd al-Qādir al-Jīlī (d. 561/1166) (see above, ch. 6, note 115), the treatment of the subject in the *Iḥyāʾ* of Ghazzālī, and the chapter in the *Dhakhīrat al-mulūk* of Hamadānī (see above, note 166). [297] ʿIṣmat Allāh, *Raqīb*, f. 19a.3. [298] *Ibid.*, f. 19a.7.

CHAPTER 17

CLASSICAL ISLAM IN RETROSPECT

1. INTRODUCTION

Of the preceding sixteen chapters, some were devoted to particular bodies of religious literature dating from the early centuries of Islam: the Koran and Koranic exegesis, tradition and biographical literature. Other chapters – the majority – dealt successively with the literature of each of the surviving sects and schools: the Ḥanbalites at different times and places; the Muʿtazilites and their Shīʿite heirs; the Ḥanafīs, Shāfiʿites, Mālikīs and Ibāḍīs; and finally, Ghazzālī (d. 505/1111) and the Ṣūfīs. In the course of this extended survey, many themes have recurred again and again, so that the reader by now has a sense of the standard elements of the theory and practice of forbidding wrong. However, the extent of the survey, and the vast amount of detail it contains, mean that the reader may at times have been unable to see the wood for the trees. Hence one of the purposes of the present chapter is to pull together and amplify some of the themes that have been scattered here and there in the preceding chapters. In doing this I shall not attempt to produce a unified version of the scholastic doctrines of forbidding wrong that have been examined above. Instead, I shall pick out a number of themes which seem to me to be of particular historical significance. I shall also be making a preliminary effort to step back from the whole phenomenon of forbidding wrong in classical Islam, and to see it in some kind of perspective. By classical Islam I mean here Islam as it was in the period between the formation of the religion as we know it and the onset of drastic change in reaction to the impact of the West.

The phenomenon of forbidding wrong belongs in the first instance to the public space of Muslim society. We can think of this space as hemmed in by fortified enclosures on two sides. On one side lie the massive ramparts of the state, the citadels and palaces of rulers. On the other side lie the myriad diminutive forts that constitute the private domains of individual Muslims, each in his castle. Neither rulers nor ordinary Muslims are immune to the human proclivity for wrongdoing. But there the symmetry ends. In looking towards the ramparts of the state, the prospective forbidder of wrong is obliged to contemplate the vast and intimidating concentration of power located behind them. When he faces towards the castles of individual Muslims, by contrast, the balance of power is more equal. By and large, then, intrusion is likely to be a stronger temptation than subversion. But even sinners have their rights of privacy, and these rights are considerable.

The next two sections of this chapter will accordingly be devoted to politics and privacy respectively. In the final two sections I shall return to the public space between the two sets of fortifications, and consider what might be called the social locus of forbidding wrong.

2. THE POLITICS OF FORBIDDING WRONG

The state looms large in our picture in more than one way. In the first place, it makes its own claims to forbid wrong. In sects to which doctrines of the imamate are of central importance, there is likely to be emphasis on forbidding wrong as a role of the imam. As we have seen, this is particularly salient in Zaydism, and a noteworthy feature of Imāmism, Ismāʿīlism and Ibāḍism.[1] We likewise find Sunnī caliphs forbidding wrong. Thus we are told that this activity was part of the daily routine of the caliph al-Manṣūr (r. 136–58/754–75).[2] The caliph al-Muhtadī (r. 255–6/869–70) built a dome under which he would sit rendering justice to all; he commanded right and forbade wrong, forbidding liquor and singing-girls.[3] The Almohad caliph ʿAbd al-Muʾmin (r. 524–58/1130–63) was constantly engaged in forbidding wrong.[4] The activity extended to other Sunnī rulers who took themselves seriously in Islamic terms. An obvious example would be the rulers of the second Saʿūdī state.[5] A rather trite mirror for princes of the mid-sixth/twelfth century emphasises the duty incumbent on the ruler (*sulṭān*) to forbid wrong owing to his position of supremacy; in the

[1] See above, ch. 10, section 3; ch. 11, 260–2, 302; ch. 15, 397f., 405–7, and cf. 404f.

[2] Ibn Kathīr, *Bidāya*, 10:125.17 (I owe this reference to Nurit Tsafrir).

[3] Masʿūdī, *Murūj*, 5:92 no. 3,111, whence Zaman, *Religion and politics*, 114. In 321/933 the caliph al-Qāhir (r. 320–2/932–4) forbade liquor and singing, ordering that singing-girls be sold at prices that took no account of their musical talents; he then had them bought up for his own use at firesale prices (Ibn al-Athīr, *Kāmil*, 8:204.6). In this case the source does not, however, speak of 'forbidding wrong', and the same is true of a good many other references to such activity on the part of rulers.

[4] Ibn al-Qaṭṭān (*fl.* mid-seventh/thirteenth century), *Naẓm al-jumān*, ed. M. ʿA. Makkī, Tetouan n.d., 149.6, 149.11 (I owe this reference to Maribel Fierro).

[5] See above, ch. 8, notes 60, 77.

case of a ruler (*pādishāh*), the author avers, forbidding wrong is more important than praying by night or fasting by day.[6] It is accordingly the business of any legitimate ruler to forbid wrong; that, as the Shāfiʿite Ḥalīmī (d. 403/1012) put it, is what rulership is[7] – or at least, what it should be.

The forbidding of wrong by the state is not confined to the ruler. The official we hear most of in this connection is, of course, the officially appointed censor (*muḥtasib*),[8] whose role is readily presented in the sources in terms of forbidding wrong.[9] But he is far from alone. Among the Ismāʿīlīs, we have seen that forbidding wrong is one of the functions of the missionaries (*dāʿīs*), key figures in the organisation of the movement.[10] Among the western Ibāḍīs, a third/ninth-century imam appointed a group to forbid wrong in the markets,[11] while among their eastern brethren the 'sellers' (*shurāt*) may have played a similar role.[12] Among the Sunnīs, the governor of Egypt in 169–71/786–7, ʿAlī ibn Sulaymān al-ʿAbbāsī, made forbidding

[6] Anon., *Baḥr al-fawāʾid*, 312.11 = trans. Meisami, 217. [7] See above, ch. 13, note 24.

[8] See the broad survey in *EI*², art. 'Ḥisba' (C. Cahen *et al.*). Whatever the history of the institution, the term seems to have been well established by the early ʿAbbāsid period (see A. H. Morton, '*Ḥisba* and glass stamps in eighth- and early ninth-century Egypt', in Y. Rāġib (ed.), *Documents de l'Islam médiéval*, Cairo 1991, 24–7; Morton gives a survey of hitherto known material on the earliest attested *muḥtasibs*, and adds significant new evidence). It may be noted that the Baṣran Iyās ibn Muʿāwiya (d. 122/739f.) is said in one source to have been in charge of the *ḥisba* in Wāsiṭ (Balādhurī (d. 279/892f.), *Ansāb al-ashrāf*, vol. 6, part 2, ed. K. Athamina, Jerusalem 1993, 197 no. 341; I owe this reference to Michael Lecker). According to a further passage of Balādhurī, this appointment took place in the reign of Yazīd ibn ʿAbd al-Malik (r. 101–5/720–4) (cited from manuscript in I. Ṣ. al-ʿAmad, 'Nuṣūṣ turāthiyya ḥawla wujūd muḥtasib fī 'l-mujtamaʿ al-Qurashī qabla 'l-Islām', *Majallat Majmaʿ al-Lugha al-ʿArabiyya al-Urdunnī*, 41 (1991), 67 n. 46; see also Chalmeta, *El 'señor del zoco'*, 344, and van Ess, *Theologie*, 2:128). Another figure worth considering is the Baṣran ʿAwwām ibn Ḥawshab (d. 148/765f.), though he is not referred to in the sources as a *muḥtasib*. He belonged to a successful Arab family in Baṣra; both his father and brother held the office of chief of police (*shurṭa*) (Ibn Ḥazm, *Jamhara*, 325.2; Mizzī, *Tahdhīb*, 22:429.7). In a distinctive phrase repeated in several of the sources, he is said to have had the role of forbidding wrong (*kāna ṣāḥib amr biʾl-maʿrūf wa-nahy ʿan al-munkar*) (Ibn Saʿd, *Ṭabaqāt*, 7:2:60.14; Fasawī, *Maʿrifa*, 2:254.1; Baḥshal, *Taʾrīkh Wāsiṭ*, 114.17, 115.2 (I owe these references to Nurit Tsafrir); Mizzī, *Tahdhīb*, 22:429.11; Dhahabī, *Siyar*, 6:355.1; Dhahabī, *Taʾrīkh al-Islām*, years 141–60, 246.9; Ibn Ḥajar, *Tahdhīb*, 8:164.7). In all but one instance, the statement goes back to Yazīd ibn Hārūn (d. 206/821). The wording is unusual, and the suggestion of the editor of Baḥshal (*Taʾrīkh Wāsiṭ*, 114 n. 65) that ʿAwwām was a *muḥtasib* may be in place. It goes well with this that the only example of his forbidding wrong that I have seen in the sources is his visits to the money-changers (*ṣayārifa*), whom he used to admonish (*ibid.*, 114.18).

[9] Māwardī, *Aḥkām*, 315.3, whence Abū Yaʿlā, *Aḥkām*, 284.8; Shayzarī, *Nihāyat al-rutba*, 6.3, whence Ibn Bassām, *Nihāyat al-rutba*, 10.4; Sunāmī, *Niṣāb*, 13.1 (quoting Māwardī); Osman Nuri, *Mejelle-i umūr-i belediye*, 1:314.12. Compare also Samʿānī, *Ansāb*, 12:113.4, defining *ʿamal al-iḥtisāb* as commanding right and forbidding wrong. However, by no means all writers on *ḥisba* make such statements (cf. above, ch. 14, note 78).

[10] See above, ch. 11, 302f. [11] See above, ch. 15, note 28.

[12] See above, ch. 15, notes 144–6.

wrong a theme of his governorship, cracking down on music, liquor and newly built churches.[13] Clear-cut instances of the institutionalisation of forbidding wrong below the level of the ruler come from the second, and still more the third, Saʿūdī states.[14] There are also historical examples of a phenomenon we have encountered in the scholastic literature: the private citizen who forbids wrong with the permission of the ruler. Thus in Damascus in 758/1357, a pietist (*baʿḍ al-fuqarāʾ*) complained to the viceroy about the evils rampant in the city, and received his permission to take action against them; he then gathered a group (*jamāʿa*) which shared his views, attracted a large popular following, and created such a threat to public order that the authorities stepped in to suppress the movement.[15]

If the state made it its business to forbid wrong in this fashion, there was also a danger that it might seek to transform this business into a monopoly.[16] This is not, of course, what a virtuous Islamic ruler would do. The caliph ʿUthmān (r. 23–35/644–56) is said to have announced at the beginning of his reign: 'Whoever of you sees a wrong, let him put it right (*fal-yughayyirhu*); if he lacks the strength to do so, let him refer it to me (*fal-yarfaʿhu ilayya*).'[17] There are nevertheless accounts that portray the caliphs ʿAbd al-Malik (r. 65–86/685–705) and al-Maʾmūn (r. 198–218/813–33) as banning the forbidding of wrong. How seriously, or how literally, should we take them?

According to Abū Hilāl al-ʿAskarī (writing in 395/1005), ʿAbd al-Malik was 'the first to forbid commanding right'.[18] What he proceeds to quote is an account of a chastening sermon addressed by ʿAbd al-Malik to the Medinese in the year 75/695; according to one version, he promised in the course of it to strike off the head of anyone who commanded him to fear God.[19] In a similar vein, Jāḥiẓ (d. 255/868f.) says that until the time

[13] Kindī, *Wulāt*, 131.8, cited in Morton, '*Ḥisba* and glass stamps', 24. Likewise Shams al-Dīn Luʾluʾ, a major figure in Ayyūbid affairs till he was killed in a civil war in 648/1251, is described as a pious man who forbade wrong (Ibn Kathīr, *Bidāya*, 13:180.15; for his death, see Humphreys, *From Saladin to the Mongols*, 318f.) – though he might have done so in a private capacity. [14] See above, ch. 8, 177f., 182–91.

[15] Ibn Qāḍī Shuhba (d. 851/1448), *Taʾrīkh*, ed. ʿA. Darwīsh, Damascus 1977–97, 3:115.8 (this passage and its interest were drawn to my attention by Tamer El-Leithy). For the scholastic discussion of permission, see, for example, above, ch. 11, 266–70, 285–7; ch. 14, 361; ch. 16, 430f.; and cf. ch. 13, note 140.

[16] 'Eine starke Obrigkeit drängte natürlich darauf, dass nur ihr dieses Recht zustehe' (Van Ess, *Theologie*, 2:387f.).

[17] Balādhurī (d. 279/892f.), *Ansāb al-ashrāf*, vol. 5, ed. S. D. F. Goitein, Jerusalem 1936, 25.1, cited in A. Noth and L. I. Conrad, *The early Arabic historical tradition*, Princeton 1994, 92. Note the similarity of the initial wording to the 'three modes' tradition (see above, ch. 3, section 1).

[18] Abū Hilāl al-ʿAskarī (writing 395/1005), *Awāʾil*, ed. W. Qaṣṣāb and M. al-Miṣrī, Riyāḍ 1981, 1:347.3. An earlier parallel makes ʿAbd al-Malik the first to cut out people's tongues for forbidding wrong (Jaṣṣāṣ, *Aḥkām*, 1:71.14).

[19] Abū Hilāl, *Awāʾil*, 1:348.2 (cited in van Ess, *Theologie*, 2:388 n. 14); Jaṣṣāṣ, *Aḥkām*, 1:71.16.

of ʿAbd al-Malik and Ḥajjāj (d. 95/714), there was still 'a remainder forbidding corruption in the earth' (Q11:116); these two put a stop to this activity, punishing and killing those who engaged in it, with the result that people 'forbade not one another any wrong that they committed' (Q5:79).[20] If we take these accounts to be reliable, they depict ʿAbd al-Malik as an authoritarian with no tolerance for criticism; but they do not suggest a prohibition of forbidding wrong as such. With regard to al-Ma'mūn, there are indeed, as we have seen, anecdotes which state unambiguously that he prohibited the forbidding of wrong.[21] In two of these accounts, however, he makes a crucial distinction: he only prohibits the forbidding of wrong by people who do not know what they are doing. These reports are doubtless to be read against the background of the popular movements that forbade wrong in the streets of Baghdad in 201/817.[22]

A much more serious feature of the state than any tendency to claim a monopoly of forbidding wrong was the scale of its activity in committing it. The power of the state equipped it with the capacity to be the biggest wrongdoer of all, and this capacity was amply exploited by the unjust rulers whose misdeeds constituted the fabric of Islamic political history. How, then, were the scholars to respond to the painfully ambivalent presence of the state? Here was an institution that on the one hand engaged in forbidding wrong in what were often manifestly desirable, indeed necessary, ways, and yet on the other hand was accumulating an appalling record of wrongs which themselves stood in need of being forbidden. Were the scholars then to accommodate the state or confront it?

We have encountered many examples of a tendency on the part of the scholars to accommodate the ruler and his functionaries. There are occasional statements which, if taken seriously, would suggest that forbidding wrong should be left to the ruler altogether.[23] More commonly it is indicated in one way or another that the state should play the main role.[24]

[20] Jāḥiẓ (d. 255/868f.), *Banū Umayya* (= *Nābita*), in his *Rasā'il*, ed. Ḥ. al-Sandūbī, Cairo 1933, 296.21 (I owe this reference to Ilai Alon).

[21] See above, ch. 1, note 34; ch. 4, 70f. In another such anecdote, al-Ma'mūn is in dispute with a man who presumes to forbid wrong without having any official standing to do so; al-Ma'mūn tries to claim the privilege of forbidding wrong for the family of the Prophet on the basis of Q22:41, and is politely rebuffed (Ghazzālī, *Iḥyā'*, 2:290.29).

[22] See above, ch. 5, 107.

[23] See above, ch. 3, note 56; ch. 13, note 20; ch. 14, note 70. There is also a rather laconic passage in which Jāḥiẓ says that commanding right and forbidding wrong can be done only with the sword and whip (*Kitmān al-sirr*, 163.10). The point of the observation in context is that verbal performance is a waste of time; he is perhaps implying that the duty should be left to the state. This passage, which was first drawn to my attention by Larry Conrad, has since been cited by Athamina as representing a prevalent opinion arising from early confrontations with the Khārijites ('The early Murji'a', 124 n. 76); but to my knowledge, the view is isolated.

[24] See above, ch. 7, 155; ch. 8, note 46; ch. 9, note 99; ch. 14, note 103; ch. 15, notes 141–3, 162.

Frequently some level of violence, especially armed violence, is made over to the authorities,[25] or it is said that it can only be engaged in with the ruler's permission.[26] This latter idea is not restricted to narrowly scholastic contexts. The fourth/tenth-century Imāmī secretary Isḥāq ibn Wahb, in a passage on situations in which the common people may need to be reined in by the state, mentions a scenario in which they set about forbidding wrong without having received the permission of their ruler, neglecting their economic activities in the process.[27] Qazwīnī (d. 682/1283f.) in his account of Gīlān gives a remarkable account of an annual scholars' carnival. He says that it is a local custom that every year the scholars (*fuqahāʾ*) seek permission from the ruler (*amīr*) to command right. Once they have his permission, they round up everyone and flog them. If a man swears that he has neither drunk nor fornicated, the scholar will ask him his trade; if he says he is a grocer, the scholar infers that he cheats his customers, and flogs him anyway.[28] The view that violence is reserved for the authorities is also implied in the saying setting out the tripartite division of labour, according to which performance of the duty 'with the hand' is for the agents of the state (*umarāʾ*); this saying is particularly common (and first attested) among the Ḥanafīs,[29] but it can be found elsewhere.[30] We also encounter a willingness to refer cases of wrongdoing to the state,[31] and to cooperate with the state in dealing

[25] See above, ch. 9, notes 23, 148; ch. 10, notes 116, 135, 146, and cf. note 115; ch. 12, 326f.; ch. 13, notes 54, 59; ch. 14, notes 63, 107, 159; ch. 15, notes 163, 164, 220; ch. 16, note 276. Cf. also above, ch. 5, note 109; ch. 6, notes 106, 165; ch. 12, note 112; ch. 13, 342, 343; ch. 14, notes 66, 271; ch. 15, note 159; ch. 16, notes 273f.

[26] See above, ch. 6, notes 180, 182; ch. 11, 266–70, 282, 285–7, 299, ch. 12, notes 110, 114, 181; ch. 14, note 105; ch. 16, 457f. The idea is most at home among the Imāmīs, where despite some opposition it is school doctrine. Elsewhere it has a curious origin. Ghazzālī mocks the Imāmī doctrine and rejects it, even for armed conflict (see above, ch. 16, 430); he sticks to this position even in the context of armed helpers (see above, ch. 16, 441). Non-Imāmīs who cannot stomach the radicalism of these views then react to them by declaring the ruler's permission to be required in such cases, and are thus in the position of inadvertently importing an Imāmī doctrine.

[27] See above, ch. 11, note 115.

[28] Qazwīnī (d. 682/1283f.), *Āthār al-bilād*, ed. F. Wüstenfeld, Göttingen 1848, 237.9, cited in Goldziher, *Livre*, 91f.

[29] For Ḥanafī attestations, see above, ch. 12, notes 12, 37 (the earliest attestation of the saying), 49, 86, 126, 132, 139, 141–3, 183, 188, and cf. note 96.

[30] See above, ch. 6, note 166 (where the attestation in the *Ghunya* derives from a Ḥanafī source); ch. 7, note 123; ch. 13, note 141; ch. 14, notes 69, 162; ch. 15, note 36. See also ʿAbd al-Qādir al-Jazāʾirī, *Mawāqif*, 294.6, 1284.26 (I owe these references to Itzchak Weismann).

[31] See above, ch. 5, notes 162f.; ch. 6, notes 153f.; ch. 14, notes 18, 66, 177; and cf. ch. 6, note 19, and ch. 8, 171. Incidentally, informing the authorities of the unlawful activities of one's neighbours seems to have been quite common in twelfth/eighteenth-century Aleppo (A. Marcus, 'Privacy in eighteenth-century Aleppo: the limits of cultural ideals', *International Journal of Middle East Studies*, 18 (1986), 177; A. Marcus, *The Middle East*

with them.[32] At the same time the scholars endorse the idea that the ruler should appoint someone to see to the duty; such functionaries may be identified as censors (*muḥtasibs*),[33] though this is not always the case.[34] One should even be prepared to accept such appointment onself.[35] Ideas of this kind are sufficiently widespread that they cannot be dismissed as marginal.

Yet such accommodationist views may also be called in question. The claims of rulers to forbid wrong may be scorned. Thus a pupil of a Raqqan scholar who died in 161/777f. reports his teacher's unfavourable reaction to the public reading of a letter from some caliph; the content of the letter is described as commanding right and forbidding wrong.[36] The caliph ʿAbd al-Malik on one occasion forbade wrong from the pulpit; a member of the congregation called out to him that he and his likes did not practise what he preached.[37] One account even describes ʿAbd al-Malik as the first caliph to command wrong and forbid right.[38] At the same time we regularly encounter the view that individual subjects may resort to violence, including armed violence; it may even be held permissible for them to form armed bands.[39] The need for the ruler's permission for armed violence may

on the eve of modernity: Aleppo in the eighteenth century, New York 1989, 117; Marcus lists some forty references to court records from the years 1159–84/1746–70).

32 See above, ch. 6, notes 153f., 165, 172; and cf. above, ch. 10, notes 85 (a balanced Zaydī view of the question of cooperation with an unjust ruler in forbidding wrong), 127; also above, ch. 6, note 47.

33 Here matters can, of course, be confused by Ghazzālī's influential terminology, in which the term *muḥtasib* refers to the ordinary believer who forbids wrong (see above, ch. 16, 429; for an example, see above, ch. 14, note 79). But the distinction was always clear enough in principle. Thus Khunjī (d. 927/1521), after setting out what he calls the legal sense of the term, has no problem stating the difference: 'One must know that in this sense one can call anyone who commands right and forbids wrong a *muḥtasib*, but in common usage (*ʿurf-i ʿāmm*) this term *muḥtasib* has come to be used for someone appointed by the ruler (*manṣūb az qibal-i sulṭān*) to command right and forbid wrong' (*Sulūk al-mulūk*, 176.8). Cf. also the lists of the differences between the two drawn up by Māwardī (d. 450/1058) (see above, ch. 13, 344f., and ch. 16, note 134) and Sunāmī (see above, ch. 12, note 50). Rare examples of scholarly writers who have something to say about the official *muḥtasib* in discussing forbidding wrong are the exegete Niẓām al-Dīn al-Naysābūrī (*fl.* early eighth/fourteenth century) (see above, ch. 2, note 36) and Taftazānī (d. 793/1390) (see above, ch. 13, note 91).

34 See above, ch. 13, notes 22, 89; ch. 14, notes 41, 70f.

35 See above, ch. 14, notes 19, 41.

36 Qushayrī (d. 334/945f.), *Taʾrīkh al-Raqqa*, ed. Ṭ. al-Naʿsānī, Ḥamāh 1959, 76.8 (I owe this reference to Nurit Tsafrir). For the death date of Abū 'l-Muhājir al-Kilābī, see Mizzī, *Tahdhīb*, 10:159.8.

37 Sibṭ ibn al-Jawzī (d. 654/1257), *Mirʾāt al-zamān*, ms. London, British Library, Add. 23,277, f. 58a.22 (I owe this and the following reference to Amikam Elad).

38 *Ibid.*, f. 58a.11. The inversion is Koranic: in Q9:67, it is the hypocrites who command wrong and forbid right.

39 For violence in general, see below, note 188; for armed bands, see above, ch. 16, 441 and notes 221f.

likewise be denied.[40] The saying about the tripartite division of labour, often rather mindlessly repeated, is sometimes scrutinised and found wanting.[41] The idea of reporting the wrongdoing of one's fellows to the state may be rejected,[42] and cooperation with the state may regarded as out of the question.[43]

At the other end of the spectrum from the tendency to accommodate the state is the urge to confront it. This takes two characteristic forms which have significantly different constituencies: rebuke and rebellion.

As we have seen, the biographical and anecdotal record is full of sympathetically presented examples of pious Muslims harshly rebuking rulers, governors and their henchmen, often at great risk to themselves;[44] sometimes they are able to get away with it,[45] sometimes they are martyred for their pains.[46] This activity has the sanction of the Prophetic tradition according to which it is the highest form of holy war to speak out in the presence of an unjust ruler and – in some versions – be killed for it.[47] It is occasionally suggested that it is a duty to forbid wrong in this fashion,[48] and in any case the activity is widely regarded with favour.[49] This attitude gains support from the more general view that to forbid wrong in the face of danger, though not a duty, is commendable,[50] and that someone who loses his life in the process is accordingly a martyr.[51]

Yet these views, though widespread, are again not universal. There are those who take a more or less negative view of going up against rulers,[52] and more generally of courting danger.[53] A painless resolution is to render

40 See above, ch. 11, 268; ch. 16, 441, and cf. note 221.
41 See above, ch. 7, note 123; ch. 12, notes 132f., 143, and cf. note 139; ch. 14, note 163.
42 See above, ch. 4, note 268; ch. 5, notes 160f.; ch. 10, note 84; ch. 14, note 226.
43 Cf. above, ch. 5, 102f.
44 See above, ch. 1, 3; ch. 3, 33; ch. 4, 56–67, note 60, and cf. note 163; ch. 6, note 102; ch. 7, 148f., and note 33; ch. 12, note 64; ch. 13, notes 133, 140; ch. 14, 381f. (but cf. 382), 384f., and notes 241, 243; ch. 16, note 123.
45 As above, ch. 4, 59. 46 As above, ch. 1, 3.
47 For this tradition see above, ch. 1, 6f.
48 See above, ch. 4, 59; ch. 6, note 148; ch. 14, note 14.
49 See, in addition to the references in the previous note, above, ch. 6, notes 145, 149 (but cf. note 150), 170; ch. 11, note 49; ch. 12, notes 10, 46, 211, and cf. note 186; ch. 15, notes 67–9; ch. 16, notes 29, 42, 121–3, 204.
50 See above, ch. 6, 134–6 no. (5), and notes 110, 171; ch. 9, 202, and notes 36, 74, 171; ch. 10, note 112; ch. 12, notes 46, 82, 135f.; ch. 13, note 104; ch. 14, 366f., and notes 158, 270; ch. 15, notes 67–70, 227; ch. 16, 433 no. (4); and cf. ch. 5, note 156.
51 See above, ch. 1, note 20; ch. 6, notes 108, 164; ch. 10, notes 6, 168; ch. 12, notes 99, 135; ch. 16, notes 91, 122.
52 See above, ch. 1, 10f. (a ruler's perspective); ch. 4, 53–6, 61, and cf. 63–5, and note 146; ch. 5, 101f.; ch. 6, 140f. no. (3), and notes 146, 190f.; ch. 8, note 30; ch. 11, notes 16, 36, 285f.; ch. 12, note 98, and cf. note 126; ch. 14, note 219, and cf. note 15; and cf. ch. 15, note 175; ch. 16, note 255.
53 See above, ch. 3, notes 53f.; ch. 11, 280f., 282, and notes 17, 279f., 283f.; ch. 14, notes 84, 156, 270; and cf. ch. 12, note 157.

tribute to heroism, but to relegate it to the heroic age of the past. Thus Khaṭṭābī (d. 388/998), in a chapter on the depravity of rulers (*fasād al-a'imma*) and the need to have as little to do with them as possible (*al-iqlāl min ṣuḥbat al-salāṭīn*), quotes the Prophetic tradition on speaking out in the presence of an unjust ruler.[54] He then laments the corruption of the age: who is there today who goes in to rulers and does not tell them what they want to hear? Who today counsels them, and which of them would listen? The soundest course in these times, and that best calculated to preserve one's faith, is to have as little to do with them as possible.[55]

The other form taken by confrontation with the state is rebellion.[56] Favourable attitudes to forbidding wrong through rebellion are less common, but they do exist. The role of forbidding wrong as a rebel slogan is familiar to historians of the early centuries of Islamic history. We have already encountered several examples of this.[57] To these we could add those of Jahm ibn Ṣafwān (d. 128/746) in late Umayyad Transoxania,[58] Yūsuf al-Barm in Khurāsān in 160/776f.,[59] Mubarqaʿ in Palestine in 227/841f.,[60] and the ʿAbbāsid who rebelled in Armenia in 349/960, taking the title al-Mustajīr bi'llāh.[61] Attitudes favourable to this form of forbidding wrong are also reported from early Muslims who did not always get as far as actual rebellion.[62] Thus Ibn Farrūkh (d. 175/791) considered that it was time to rebel against unjust rulers when as many men commanding right were gathered together as had been present at the Battle of Badr.[63] Such attitudes also characterise the early Khārijites,[64] the

54 Khaṭṭābī (d. 388/998), *ʿUzla*, ed. Y. M. al-Sawwās, Damascus and Beirut 1987, 227.9.

55 *Ibid.*, 228.5. Cf. also above, ch. 6, notes 187f., and the deviant view reported by Muwaffaq al-Shajarī, above, ch. 9, note 74.

56 The linkage between *al-amr bi'l-maʿrūf* and rebellion is noted, for example, in Lambton, *State and government*, 313.

57 For the events of the years 201/817 and 231/846 in Baghdad, see above, ch. 4, notes 36–8, and ch. 5, 107. For ʿAlid and Zaydī examples, see above, ch. 10, section 3. For instances from the western Islamic world, see above, ch. 14, 388–90. For the early Khārijites, see above, ch. 15, 393f. For the Ibāḍīs, see above, ch. 15, 395f., and notes 22, 92. Where we depend on the chroniclers, they usually give no further indication as to what the slogan meant to these rebels; with the Zaydīs and Ibāḍīs we are more fortunate.

58 ʿAbd al-Qāhir al-Baghdādī (d. 429/1037f.), *al-Milal wa'l-niḥal*, ed. A. N. Nādir, Beirut 1970, 145.3: *wa-kāna yuẓhir al-amr bi'l-maʿrūf wa'l-nahy ʿan al-munkar wa-yakhruj bi'l-silāḥ ʿalā 'l-sulṭān*. In the parallel passage in Ashʿarī's *Maqālāt* (279.9) the linkage, as pointed out to me by Fritz Zimmermann, is not explicit.

59 Yaʿqūbī, *Ta'rīkh*, 2:478.15; and see E. L. Daniel, *The political and social history of Khurasan under Abbasid rule, 747–820*, Minneapolis and Chicago 1979, 166f.

60 Ṭabarī, *Ta'rīkh*, series III, 1320.3, noted in van Ess, *Theologie*, 2:388 n. 13.

61 Miskawayh, *Tajārib*, 2:177.7 (I owe this reference to Patricia Crone); Ibn al-Athīr, *Kāmil*, 8:394.5. Cf. also Ṭabarī, *Ta'rīkh*, series II, 137.11, 143.8, 150.6, with regard to Ḥujr ibn ʿAdī (d. 51/671f.) (I owe the first reference to Amikam Elad).

62 See above, ch. 1, 7f.; ch. 4, 51, and cf. note 72; ch. 5, note 192; ch. 14, 385f.

63 See above, ch. 14, 385. Each had to be a better man than Ibn Farrūkh himself (Abū 'l-ʿArab, *Ṭabaqāt*, 108.14).

64 See above, ch. 15, 393f.

Ibāḍīs,[65] the Zaydīs[66] and at least one Muʿtazilite;[67] in addition they are, so to speak, embalmed in the Imāmī heritage.[68] Very occasionally we find such views adopted by Sunnī scholars of later centuries. Thus Ibn Ḥazm (d. 456/1064) in developing his doctrine of forbidding wrong takes the view that it is obligatory to reprove the ruler for any act of injustice, however small. If the ruler desists and submits to the appropriate penalty, well and good; if not, he must be deposed and another appointed in his place.[69] Usually, of course, such ideas are condemned in Sunnī circles.[70] Thus we have seen how Abū Ḥanīfa (d. 150/767f.), though he does not deny that the duty might in principle make rebellion mandatory, seeks to override this alarming implication by invoking the likely costs of such action.[71]

The ambiguity of the concept of forbidding wrong in this connection can be illustrated by a curious paradox. While forbidding wrong can express the claims of rebels to political authority, it can also provide an alibi for those who do not wish to challenge an incumbent state too openly or directly. One instance of this is found in a letter of imam Yaḥyā Ḥamīd al-Dīn of the Yemen (r. 1322–67/1904–48) written in 1326/1909, during a period in which the Ottoman governor had adopted a conciliatory policy, and Yaḥyā's rebellion was more or less in abeyance.[72] Here Yaḥyā speaks of the grant of autonomy he is seeking from the Ottomans as 'the transfer into our hands of the execution of the important duty of commanding right and forbidding wrong in the region of Yemen'.[73] Another such case is Muḥammad ibn ʿAlī al-Idrīsī (r. 1326–41/1908f.–1923),[74] who in the last years of Ottoman rule established a state in ʿAsīr which was later annexed by the Saʿūdīs. In the early years of his venture, he liked to portray himself as a local religious reformer who was loyal to the Ottoman state.[75]

65 See above, ch. 15, 395f., and note 69.

66 See above, ch. 10, 233f.

67 See above, ch. 9, 224, and cf. notes 5–8, 175.

68 See above, ch. 11, note 50, and cf. also note 342 on the Nizaris.

69 Ibn Ḥazm, *Fiṣal*, 4:175.24; see above, ch. 14, notes 258f. Compare also above, ch. 13, notes 55f.

70 See above, ch. 4, 52f.; ch. 5, note 157; ch. 7, notes 65, 108 (and cf. ch. 15, note 7); ch. 10, note 163; ch. 12, notes 26, 29, 97; ch. 16, 446.

71 See above, ch. 1, notes 22f., 26; ch. 12, notes 7f. Likewise Ibn Khaldūn condemns those who rebel ineffectually in the name of forbidding wrong (see above, ch. 14, note 256) for their foolishness in acting when they lack the power (*qudra*) without which there is no obligation – not because what they are doing is intrinsically sinful.

72 For this period, see M. W. Wenner, *Modern Yemen 1918–1966*, Baltimore 1967, 46.

73 So the Turkish translation of his letter of 15 Dhū 'l-Ḥijja, 1326/1909 (Istanbul, Başbakanlık Arşivi, Hariciye Siyasî, 107/49, 9.1, made available to me by Şükrü Hanioğlu).

74 The date 1326/1908f. (which I take from M. A. ʿI. al-ʿAqīlī, (*Min ta'rīkh*) *al-Mikhlāf al-Sulaymānī*, Riyāḍ 1958 and Cairo n.d., 2:56.10) is not to be taken too seriously.

75 See J. Reissner, 'Die Idrīsīden in ʿAsīr', *Die Welt des Islams*, 21 (1981), 170f. (this study was drawn to my attention by Mark Sedgwick).

In this connection, he described himself as commanding right and forbidding wrong, both in correspondence with the Ottoman authorities,[76] and in propaganda directed to the local population.[77] Others spoke of him in the same vein.[78] Likewise the activity of Maghīlī (d. 909/1503f.) in forbidding wrong laid him open to the accusation that his aim was political power.[79] The concept also lends itself to indeterminate situations: the movements aiming to restore public order in Baghdad in 201/817,[80] or the activity of the Ṣūfis in Alexandria in the previous year.[81]

In conclusion, what the scholars have to say about the politics of forbidding wrong is marked by sharp issues and strong tensions. One basic issue, which presupposes a certain capacity for doing right on the part of the ruler, is whether the state is to be accorded a monopoly of legitimate violence in forbidding wrong. The other major issue is whether the state should be confronted for its own wrongdoing, and if so, how. What is striking is the very different way in which opinion is stacked on these two issues. With regard to the question of the monopoly of violence, the balance of opinion is fairly even; those who espouse the idea and those who reject it are alike part of the mainstream. By contrast, with regard to forbidding wrong in the face of the delinquency of the ruler, there is a clear mainstream position: rebuke is endorsed while rebellion is rejected.

3. PRIVACY AND FORBIDDING WRONG

The issues discussed by the scholars in connection with privacy are ramified. The underlying problem, however, is a straightforward clash of

[76] Istanbul, Başbakanlık Arşivi, Bâb-i Âlî Evrak Odası, 271645, enclosing a letter from the Idrīsī dated 22 Jumādā I, 1327/1909. In this letter he emphasises that he is not rebelling against Ottoman rule (*laysa fī hādhihi 'l-da'wa khurūj 'alā 'l-dawla*, line 24); nevertheless he says that it is quite true that, as his addressees have heard, he is commanding right and forbidding wrong to the stream of tribesmen who are coming to see him (line 4). This document, and the further enclosure cited in the next note, were made available to me by Şükrü Hanioğlu.

[77] See his pamphlet (*manshūr*) *apud* 'Aqīlī, *Mikhlāf*, 2:157.3, 161.8, 163.7 (and cf. the Koranic quotations *ibid.*, 156.6). The first of these passages is translated by Reissner ('Die Idrīsīden in 'Asīr', 171). Though I have adduced the Idrīsī in a pre-modern context, it should be noted that he was not untouched by modern influences: in the third of these passages he describes forbidding wrong as 'that Islamic natural right' (*dhālika 'l-ḥaqq al-ṭabī'ī al-Islāmī*). A further enclosure in the source mentioned in the previous footnote is a hortatory pamphlet (*risāla*) by the Idrīsī in which he quotes Q9:71, Q3:104, and Q22:41, with brief comments (f. 2a.4), and makes other references to the duty (ff. 3b.10, 4a.3, 5b.7).

[78] See the passage of 1331/1913 from *al-Manār* cited in Reissner, 'Die Idrīsīden in 'Asīr', 171, and 'Aqīlī, *Mikhlāf*, 2:56.8, 59.12, 59.17, 65.4. But Sharīf Ḥusayn of Mecca (r. 1326–43/1908–25) in 1327/1909 telegraphed his Ottoman overlords denouncing the Idrīsī as a Khārijite following the path of the Khārijites of old, who used forbidding wrong as a pretext for rebellion against Islamic states (telegram of 29 Rajab, 1327/1909, Istanbul, Başbakanlık Arşivi, Bâb-i Âlî Evrak Odası, 272199; this document was made available to me by Şükrü Hanioğlu).

[79] See above, ch. 14, note 244.

[80] See above, ch. 5, 107.

[81] See above, ch. 16, note 246.

two values: while it is a good thing to stop wrongdoing, it is a bad thing to violate privacy.[82] How then are the conflicting demands of these two values to be reconciled?[83]

A basic principle we encounter here is that, to trigger the duty, a wrong must in some way be public knowledge. Wrongs that are private in the sense that we do not know about them are beyond the scope of the duty;[84] we have no business going on fishing expeditions for the purpose of uncovering hidden wrongs. We may not spy and pry,[85] or raid a home on the off-chance of discovering wrongdoing in it.[86] Such wrongdoing is not in the public domain, and consequently, as is already pointed out in a Prophetic tradition, it harms only the wrongdoer.[87]

While this principle is simple enough to grasp, it may not always be easy to apply. There is a considerable grey area between knowledge and ignorance, a domain ruled by inference and suspicion. Should we, for example, raid a home from which we hear the sound of music? The usual answer is that we should,[88] though there are some hesitations, nuances and contrary views.[89] More generally, whereas some require only that one have good reason to believe that wrong is being done before one enters a

[82] As one Mālikī author stated, the believer's home is his castle (see above, ch. 14, note 173).

[83] I shall leave out of consideration emergencies involving rescue (see, for example, above, ch. 14, note 181; ch. 15, note 192).

[84] 'Do not investigate what is not out in the open' (see above, ch. 5, note 141). See also above, ch. 4, note 261; ch. 10, note 119; ch. 14, note 202. As Ibn Taymiyya (d. 728/1328) puts it: 'Manifest wrongs (*al-munkarāt al-ẓāhira*) must be acted against (*yajib inkāruhā*), in contrast to hidden ones (*al-bāṭina*), the [divine] punishment of which afflicts only the perpetrator' (*Majmūʿ fatāwā*, 28:205.16).

[85] See above, ch. 10, note 119; ch. 13, notes 52, 81 no. (7), 84; ch. 15, note 73; ch. 16, 436, 438. For the story of the sins of the caliph ʿUmar, one of which was spying, see above, ch. 4, note 269. The story is widely quoted, see, for example, Māwardī, *Aḥkām*, 331.5; Dawānī, *Sharḥ*, 211.30; Zurqānī, *Sharḥ*, 3:108.35. For another anecdote about ʿUmar, in which the Companion ʿAbd al-Raḥmān ibn ʿAwf (d. 32/652f.) brings up the prohibition of spying, see Fasawī, *Maʿrifa*, 1:368.6 (inserting *qultu* before *arā*).

[86] For allegations of such behaviour, see above, ch. 6, notes 19, 32; ch. 8, note 90.

[87] See above, ch. 3, note 60; Ḥimyarī, *Qurb al-isnād*, 37.17 (for further Imāmī references, see above, ch. 11, note 43); and cf. Ghazzālī, *Iḥyāʾ*, 2:285.13 (from the Syrian *tābiʿī* Bilāl ibn Saʿd), and above, ch. 8, note 42. Ibn al-Rabīʿ describes such wrongdoing as being between the offenders and God (see above, ch. 14, notes 176, 179). Cf. the saying noted above, ch. 3, note 64, and ch. 4, n. 262.

[88] See above, ch. 10, note 83, and cf. note 23; ch. 12, note 14; ch. 14, note 180; ch. 15, note 158 (also noting a contrary view); ch. 16, 436; and cf. ch. 10, notes 89f., and ch. 14, note 203.

[89] Khallāl, *Amr*, 117 no. 75 (cf. above, ch. 5, note 63). For Māwardī's view that the *muḥtasib* should not actually enter the home, see below, note 106, and contrast the view of Ibn al-Rabīʿ on the duty of the authorities in such cases (see above, ch. 14, note 172). Regarding some finer points, Ibn Ḥanbal says that you have no duty if you do not know where the sound is actually coming from (see above, ch. 5, note 141), while the Ibāḍīs say that you have no obligation if others can hear the sound of wrongdoing, but you yourself cannot hear it (see above, ch. 15, note 189).

home,[90] others require actual knowledge.[91] Likewise Ghazzālī is inclined to the view that the aroma of liquor is enough to proceed on,[92] whereas it would seem that, in the opinion of Ibn Masʿūd (d. 32/652f.), it is not enough even for a man's beard to be dripping with wine.[93] What if we discern under someone's robe a shape that looks uncommonly like a bottle of liquor or a lute? Here the views of Ibn Ḥanbal (d. 241/855) are mutually inconsistent.[94] What of a suspicious jar? Again, Ibn Ḥanbal's views seem not to hold together;[95] likewise one Zaydī authority says that one should proceed if one has good reason to believe that the jar contains wine,[96] whereas another requires actual knowledge in such a case.[97] What if a couple walking in the street look as if they might be unmarried? The caliph al-Ma'mūn would seem to be a champion of their right to a presumption of innocence against intrusive busybodies;[98] Mālik (d. 179/795), on the other hand, seems closer on this issue to the zealot whom al-Ma'mūn is ridiculing.[99]

If we do know, then the duty is activated. The severity of our response may, however, be mitigated by the Prophetic injunction not to disclose the shameful aspects of the lives of outwardly respectable Muslims.[100] Thus this principle of 'covering up' (*satr*) may stand in the way of our reporting such wrongoing to the state,[101] and it provides a convincing rationale for the preference for rebuking offenders in private.[102]

An important feature of these Muslim ideas of privacy, and one relevant to forbidding wrong, is what might be called their procedural rather than substantive character. That is to say, we do not seem to have here the notion that certain kinds of behaviour are inherently private, and as such immune to public scrutiny. What is protected is not 'private life' but rather

90 See above, ch. 10, notes 23, 83, 118; cf. also ch. 6, note 176; ch. 15, notes 187–91; ch. 16, 436, 438.
91 See above, ch. 9, note 28, and cf. ch. 10, note 118, and ch. 15, note 192.
92 See above, ch. 16, 436.
93 See above, ch. 4, note 261. Compare Ibn Ḥanbal's view that it is enough to void the duty for chess-players to cover the board or move it behind them (see above, ch. 5, note 149).
94 See above, ch. 5, notes 144–7. For the distinctions Ghazzālī makes on this question, see above, ch. 16, 436. 95 See above, ch. 5, notes 139, 143.
96 See above, ch. 10, note 82. 97 See above, ch. 10, note 120.
98 See above, ch. 1, 10f.
99 See above, ch. 14, note 7. Cf. also above, ch. 6, note 19, on the activity of Ḥanbalite zealots in the days of Barbahārī (d. 329/941). Ibn Ḥanbal says that one should accept the word of a man who claims to have remarried his ex-wife (see above, ch. 5, note 142).
100 See above, ch. 3, note 61; ch. 4, note 265; and cf. ch. 6, note 152; ch. 16, note 276.
101 See above, ch. 4, note 265, and cf. note 268.
102 See Ibn Taymiyya, *Majmūʿ fatāwā*, 28:217.11. For this preference, see above, ch. 4, 79f.; ch. 6, note 163; ch. 7, note 110; ch. 8, note 30; ch. 12, note 36; ch. 13, note 35; ch. 16, note 276.

'hidden sin': behaviour that happens not to be public knowledge – or more precisely, not known to others who might otherwise be obligated to forbid it. Wrongdoing that is confined within a home can still trigger the duty for others who live in that home: a wife may be obligated to rebuke her husband, and a son his parents.[103] Likewise someone from outside the home who for any reason happens to be there, and encounters wrongdoing, may be obligated to do something about it.[104] One view that makes this point very sharply concerns the duty of a person who has learnt of wrongdoing by spying: on the one hand he has to repent of his spying, and on the other he has to forbid the wrong.[105] The difference between Muslim thinking and that of the modern West is thus not simply that there is no single Muslim concept corresponding to the Western notion of privacy. It is also that the Muslim concepts are of a significantly different kind.[106]

It is perhaps in part for this reason that the Muslim discussion of privacy and forbidding wrong has a very different texture from the discussion of the political issues. While the views of the scholars are not entirely homogeneous on questions of privacy, this inhomogeneity does not seem to have generated any burning issues or dramatic polarisations of opinion.

There is another illustration of this phenomenon which is worth considering here in some detail: the sketchy treatment of the performance of the duty by women and slaves, two categories of persons juridically precluded from participating in the public life of Muslim society on the same terms as free adult males.

Let us start with women. In some ways it seems obviously inappropriate for women to exercise the authority presupposed by forbidding wrong, except perhaps in restricted contexts. Men are a step above them (Q2:228), and are the managers of their affairs (Q4:34). At the same time, the place of women is in the home (cf. Q33:33), and for them to be seen or heard

[103] See above, ch. 4, note 239; ch. 5, 93, and cf. note 72; ch. 11, notes 315f.; ch. 13, note 132; ch. 14, note 22; ch. 16, 431f.

[104] See above, ch. 5, notes 139–40, but cf. note 138.

[105] See above, ch. 15, note 73.

[106] I shall return to this point (see below, ch. 20, 593f.). A passage that does perhaps suggest a distinction of the Western type occurs in the discussion of the duty of the official *muḥtasib* given by Māwardī. The *muḥtasib* – like anyone else – has no right to spy into 'forbidden things which have not become manifest' (*Aḥkām*, 330.1, with parallel text in Abū Yaʿlā, *Aḥkām*, 295.16; Māwardī requires him to investigate manifest wrongs, while not imposing this on the individual, see Māwardī, *Aḥkām*, 315.10, and Abū Yaʿlā, *Aḥkām*, 284.15). What then if he (presumably the *muḥtasib*) hears the sound of music coming from a home? The answer is that he takes action against it (*ankarahā*) outside the home, without pushing his way in, since the wrong (that concerns him) is a public (*ẓāhir*) one, and it is not his business to uncover a further private (*bāṭin*) one (Māwardī, *Aḥkām*, 331.8; Abū Yaʿlā, *Aḥkām*, 297.5, with a better text, which I follow).

outside it poses a risk of sexual temptation. They also lack judgement.[107] Yet in other ways it seems obvious that they too should command and forbid. Unlike children, they are subject to the law just as men are; and in one verse God specifically includes the female believers (*al-muʾmināt*) among those who command right and forbid wrong (Q9:71). The question cries out for some incisive and yet nuanced thinking at once to establish their duty and to settle its boundaries. Surprisingly, we get very little of this; most authors pass by the issue in silence,[108] and those who do not are often laconic at best. It is, however, worth bringing together the views of those scholars – disproportionately Ibāḍī – who have something to say on the matter.[109]

Outright nay-sayers are in a minority, but they can be found. The eastern Ibāḍī Muḥammad ibn Maḥbūb (d. 260/873) takes it for granted that women are not obligated,[110] and Sālimī (d. 1332/1914) supports this view by invoking the duty of women to keep their voices down.[111] The Zaydī al-Muʾayyad Yaḥyā ibn Ḥamza (d. 749/1348f.) excludes them from forbidding wrong, and gives two reasons for this: first, their frivolity and weakness; and second, the fact that the law does not even give them authority over themselves, let alone in such a weighty matter as forbidding wrong.[112] There is an interesting difference of approach here: whereas for Yaḥyā ibn Ḥamza women are intrinsically incapable of forbidding wrong, for Sālimī their exclusion arises from an extrinsic legal restriction on their public behaviour. Turning to the Sunnīs, the negative view is less prominent here. An exegetical opinion adduces women as an example of those who are unable to perform the duty.[113] The eastern Ṣūfī Yaḥyā ibn Muʿādh

[107] Thus Thaʿlabī (d. 427/1035) mentions their intellectual deficiency (*nuqṣān ʿaqlihā*) in a list of the fifteen negative qualities with which Eve and her daughters have been afflicted (*Qiṣaṣ al-anbiyāʾ*, Beirut n.d., 29.5). He justifies this by citing a tradition in which some women ask the Prophet what this supposed deficiency consists in; in reply he points out that a woman's testimony is worth only half that of a man (cf. Q2:282).

[108] For example, we have no statements on the question from the classical Muʿtazilite authors (cf. above, ch. 9, note 146), the pre-modern Imāmī jurists, or Ibn Taymiyya (cf. above, ch. 7, note 68). Imāmī sources quote the advice of ʿAlī (r. 35–40/656–61) that when women tell one to do something perfectly proper one should nevertheless do the opposite (*in amarnakum biʾl-maʿrūf fa-khālifūhunna*) so that they do not seek to get their way in improper things (see, for example, Kulaynī, *Kāfī*, 5:517 no. 5; Mufīd, *Ikhtiṣāṣ*, 226.15; al-Ḥurr al-ʿĀmilī, *Wasāʾil*, 7:1:128.14). The wording might be taken to suggest that the saying is about *al-amr biʾl-maʿrūf*, but the scholars do not mention it in their discussions of this topic; and in another wording there is no mention of commanding right (Raḍī, *Nahj al-balāgha*, *apud* Ibn Abīʾl-Ḥadīd, *Sharḥ*, 6:214.7). I owe most of these references to Avraham Hakim.

[109] For the Ibāḍī role in general, see above, ch. 15, notes 250, 258. For the early roots of this, see above, ch. 15, notes 20f.

[110] See above, ch. 15, notes 167f.

[111] See above, ch. 15, note 225.

[112] See above, ch. 10, notes 140f.

[113] See above, ch. 2, note 20.

(d. 258/872) once spoke on forbidding wrong; a woman objected that her sex was exempt from this obligation (*hādhā wā jib qad wuḍiʿa ʿannā*), to which Yaḥyā responded that this might be so as far as hand and tongue were concerned, but not in the case of the heart.[114] The practical difference between his position and that of his female interlocutor is not a substantial one. Nabarāwī (writing in 1243/1828) finds in the 'three modes' tradition an assertion of the dominance of males over females, though he does not tell us whether this excludes women from performing the duty altogether.[115]

Positive views are well represented among the Ibāḍīs and Sunnīs. The western Ibāḍī Jayṭālī (d. 750/1349f.), in adopting Ghazzālī's account of forbidding wrong, not only retained his inclusion of women, but also took the trouble to insert the point in a couple of other passages.[116] Among the eastern Ibāḍīs, Ibn Baraka (fourth/tenth century) wanted women to sally forth to forbid wrong like men,[117] while Khalīlī (d. 1287/1871) as reported by Sālimī held that women should perform the duty by word and deed, since Q9:71 placed them on the same footing as men.[118] Among the Sunnīs, by far the most important authority to specify the inclusion of women was Ghazzālī, though he did not argue the point.[119] This was a direct invitation to those who followed his account to do likewise – as some did,[120] though others did not.[121] His view probably influenced further scholars indirectly. Thus the inclusion of women is a feature of some commentaries on the 'three modes' tradition,[122] and is found in works of Ibn al-Naḥḥās (d. 814/1411),[123] Ibn Ḥajar al-Haytamī (d. 974/1567),[124] ʿAbd al-Ghanī al-Nābulusī (d. 1143/1731),[125] and Mīrghanī (d. 1207/

[114] Ibn Qayyim al-Jawziyya, *Iʿlām*, 2:176.20. He speaks of *silāḥ al-qalb*; if this is not just rhetoric, it suggests that he was thinking of performance by (rather than in) the heart.

[115] Nabarāwī, *Sharḥ*, 171.21 (*wa-fīhi taghlīb al-dhukūr li-quwwatihim ʿalā 'l-ināth*).

[116] See above, ch. 15, notes 60f. [117] See above, ch. 15, note 169.

[118] See above, ch. 15, note 224, and compare also the later view cited there. Khalīlī's position was actually more complex (see below, note 132).

[119] See above, ch. 16, note 15.

[120] Khwārazmī, *Dhukhr*, f. 117a.19; ʿIṣmat Allāh, *Raqīb*, f. 6b.3; Ḥaydarīzāde, 'Amr bi'l-maʿrūf', 108b.1.

[121] Instances are Hamadānī, *Dhakhīra*, 166.1, and Ṭāshköprīzāde, *Miftāḥ*, 3:302.11.

[122] Taftazānī, *Sharḥ ḥadīth al-Arbaʿīn*, 105.16; Muḥammad ibn Aḥmad al-Ḥanafī (writing 812/1410), *Sharḥ al-Arbaʿīn*, ms. London, British Library, Or. 12,543, f. 92b.8 (for the date of writing, see *ibid.*, f. 111b.9; I take the author's name on trust from the British Library catalogue, see R. Vassie (ed.), *A classified handlist of Arabic manuscripts acquired since 1912*, London 1995–, 2:56 no. 370); Muṣliḥ al-Dīn al-Lārī, *Sharḥ al-Arbaʿīn*, f. 141b.5; also Rajab, *Wasīla*, 761.18.

[123] See above, ch. 13, note 122. He invokes Q9:71.

[124] Ibn Ḥajar al-Haytamī (d. 974/1567), *al-Zawājir ʿan iqtirāf al-kabāʾir*, Cairo 1980, 600.25. See also Shirbīnī, *Mughnī*, 4:211.13 (quoting Ghazzālī).

[125] See above, ch. 12, note 184.

1792f.).[126] To my knowledge, the only Sunnī who makes the point before Ghazzālī is Ibn Ḥazm.[127]

There are also a few intermediate positions. One way to articulate such a position was in terms of the three modes. We have already noted a view confining the obligation of women to performance in the heart, close though this is to excluding women altogether.[128] The eastern Ibāḍī jurist Shaqṣī (*fl. c.* 1034/1625) states that women are not obligated to perform the duty by deed, but should do it verbally if they can.[129] It would also be possible to formulate a compromise position by taking account of the fact that women are less able to perform the duty than men, though I have not seen this done.[130] Views that explicitly address the questions of privacy that arise in connection with women are found among the eastern Ibāḍīs. Kudamī (fourth/tenth century) holds that women are excused from forbidding wrong verbally, but notes the view that they may do so provided they do not flaunt their sexuality; his preference is for them to stay at home.[131] Khalīlī makes a sharp distinction: on the one hand a woman is obligated with regard to other women and to males within her family, but on the other hand it is improper for her even to be present in a male gathering that includes wrongdoers – though if she is in a position to do so, it could well be her duty to send someone to forbid them.[132] It is possible that these eastern Ibāḍī jurists – Kudamī, Shaqṣī and Khalīlī – were highly unusual in their attitudes; but it is just as likely that they were giving formal articulation to something widely accepted as common sense. Thus what they prescribe fits well with what I have been told of recent practice in traditional religious circles in Iran.

Occasionally there is anecdotal or biographical attestation of the forbidding of wrong by women. The case of a rather shadowy female Companion of the Prophet, Samrā' bint Nahīk, has already been considered;[133] as we

[126] See above, ch. 12, note 184.

[127] Ibn Ḥazm (d. 456/1064), *al-Iḥkām fī uṣūl al-aḥkām*, ed. A. M. Shākir, Cairo 1345–7, 3:81.22; and cf. his *Muḥallā*, 9:430.7. In general, writers on *uṣūl al-fiqh* do not seem to mention forbidding wrong when discussing how the masculine gender is to be construed in Koran and *ḥadīth*.

[128] See above, note 114. This view is also attributed to the eastern Ibāḍī Muḥammad ibn Maḥbūb (d. 260/873) (see above, ch. 15, note 168, and cf. note 222).

[129] See above, ch. 15, note 172.

[130] Shaqṣī's wording perhaps carries the suggestion that women are less able to administer verbal rebukes than men (see the previous note). Compare the view that women are unable to perform the duty (see above, note 113), the inclusion of weakness among the grounds on which Yaḥyā ibn Ḥamza excludes women (see above, note 112), and Nabarāwī's remark on the strength of males (above, note 115).

[131] See above, ch. 15, notes 170f.

[132] See above, ch. 15, note 237.

[133] See above, ch. 4, 82f., and ch. 5, note 73.

saw, we cannot be sure that she had not been officially appointed to discharge the duty. Jayṭālī tells of an old woman of the Jabal Nafūsa who urged another not to give up her share of commanding and forbidding.[134] Umm Zaynab (d. 714/1315) had a reputation for performing the duty, including doing things that men could not do; but this too may in part reflect the tenure of an office.[135]

The scholars seem to have been significantly less interested in slaves than they were in women. This difference is particularly striking in the case of Ibāḍism. Here only Jayṭālī and Khalīlī, both prompted by Ghazzālī, address the issue – Jayṭālī to include slaves, Khalīlī to exclude them on the grounds that they lack the power to act and their business is the service of their masters.[136] Nevertheless, those who consider the question of women often mention slaves alongside them. On the one hand, Ibn Ḥazm, Ghazzālī and several later authors do so to include them,[137] while a responsum of Ibn Ḥanbal presupposes that a slave is subject to the duty.[138] And on the other, Yaḥyā ibn Ḥamza mentions slaves along with women to exclude them, giving as reasons their low status and, presumably, lack of authority;[139] they are likewise excluded by the Ḥanbalite ʿAbd al-Qādir al-Jīlī (d. 561/1166).[140]

Overall, the sparsity of the discussion is striking. The Muʿtazilites and Imāmīs do not raise the question of women and slaves at all. The Sunnīs offer no reasoned discussion. Only one Zaydī and one Ibāḍī do this for both categories; and only the Ibāḍīs manifest a continuing interest in the question of women, or directly address the implications of their segregation.[141] We are left to wonder whether the scholars felt the answers to be so obvious that they went without saying, or the questions to be so tricky that they were best left alone.

[134] See above, ch. 15, note 62.

[135] See above, ch. 7, note 68. I owe to Adam Sabra the information that Umm Zaynab was in charge of a hospice in Cairo (the Ribāṭ al-Baghdādiyya) which housed divorced or separated women in conditions of strict discipline (Maqrīzī (d. 845/1442), *Khiṭaṭ*, Būlāq 1270, 2:428.3).

[136] For Jayṭālī, see above, ch. 15, notes 60f.; for Khalīlī, see above, ch. 15, note 233. Cf. also note 20.

[137] Ibn Ḥazm, *Muḥallā*, 9:430.5; for Ghazzālī, see above, ch. 16, note 15; for Jayṭālī, see the previous note; for Taftazānī, see above, ch. 13, note 108; for Ibn al-Naḥḥās, see above, ch. 13, note 122; Muḥammad ibn Aḥmad al-Ḥanafī, *Sharḥ*, f. 92b.8; Ibn Ḥajar al-Haytamī, *Zawājir*, 600.25; Shirbīnī, *Mughnī*, 4:211.13 (quoting Ghazzālī); ʿIṣmat Allāh, *Raqīb*, f. 6b.3; Mīrghanī, *Baḥr*, f. 216b.4; Ḥaydarīzāde, 'Amr bi'l-maʿrūf', 108b.1.

[138] See above, ch. 5, note 71.

[139] See above, ch. 10, notes 140, 142.

[140] See above, ch. 6, note 159.

[141] There is also a resonance of this in the case of Umm Zaynab (see above, note 135).

4. THE SOCIAL CONTEXT OF FORBIDDING WRONG

According to an account attributed to Ibn ʿAbbās (d. 68/687f.), the eight gardens of Paradise have eight golden gates, typically named for those who practise a particular duty or virtue, and whose privilege it will be to enter the abode of bliss by that gate.[142] The fourth is 'the gate of those who command right and forbid wrong'.[143] What sorts and conditions of men are destined to use this gate?

One thing that is clear is that this will be an overwhelmingly urban population. Our biographical material is, of course, almost solidly urban. Our doctrinal material is likewise urban centred. Ibn Ḥanbal's numerous responsa on forbidding wrong include only one with a rural setting.[144] Ghazzālī betrays the urban character of his world when he tells us that it is the duty of every scholar who can do so to go out from his town (*balad*) to the rural population (*ahl al-sawād*) around it.[145] In the same way he says that every Muslim must begin with himself, extending his efforts till they embrace his town, and after that the people of the countryside.[146] Ismāʿīl Ḥaqqī (d. 1137/1725) thinks of the powerful as 'the notables of every town'.[147] When the people of Toledo could not endure the zeal of Ibn ʿUbayd (*fl.* first third of the fourth/tenth century) in forbidding wrong among them, he retired to a village.[148] Against this background the rural Ḥanbalism of Palestine stands out as something of an exception in the Sunnī world, though doubtless it would not have looked out of place in some Zaydī and Ibāḍī environments.[149]

Within this predominantly urban society, what is the social locus of forbidding wrong? The obvious and inescapable answer is the scholarly elite.[150]

142 Kisāʾī, *Qiṣaṣ al-anbiyāʾ*, 17f.
143 *Ibid.*, 18.4 (*bāb al-āmirīn biʾl-maʿrūf waʾl-nāhīn ʿan al-munkar*).
144 See above, ch. 5, notes 70, 155.
145 Ghazzālī, *Iḥyāʾ*, 2:313.13 (see above, ch. 16, 445f.); in the same passage he opposes *balad* to *qarya* (*ibid.*, 313.12). Likewise when we tactfully tell a rustic who does not know how to pray properly that perhaps his village lacks a scholar (see above, ch. 16, 439), it seems that we are not in his village; presumably we are in town.
146 *Ibid.*, 313.27.
147 See above, ch. 12, note 95.
148 See above, ch. 14, note 192.
149 For Palestine, see above, ch. 7, note 125. The eastern Ibāḍī scholar Muḥammad ibn Maḥbūb, in a letter to his western brethren, considers the question whether it is more appropriate for a group (*qawm*) possessed of virtue and knowledge to sit at home responding to requests for *fatwās*, or instead to go out to the countryside and the villages (*al-sawād waʾl-qurā*) commanding right and forbidding wrong, with men and women gathering around them and making them presents of food and other goods when they depart (*Sīra*, in Kāshif, *Siyar*, 2:250.3).
150 In a happy phrase of A. Morabia, forbidding wrong 'fut, surtout, l'apanage des ulémas' (*Le ǧihâd dans l'Islam médiéval*, Paris 1993, 315; I owe this reference to Giorgio Vercellin).

This does not mean, of course, that the duty is restricted to scholars. As is regularly emphasised, it is incumbent on Muslims at large,[151] and not just on scholars.[152] That it is not intended to be confined to a religious elite is likewise suggested by the much-repeated doctrine that the sinner too is obligated;[153] though the point is sometimes made that a virtuous man has a better chance of success,[154] it is most uncommon for the duty of the sinner to be denied outright.[155] The obligation to forbid wrong is, of course, subject to knowledge of right and wrong in the case in point.[156] But this need not be unduly restrictive. While there are wrongs that it takes a scholar to evaluate, there are others that require no such expertise, and can thus be tackled by laymen.[157]

There is, nevertheless, a tendency to make scholars rather than laymen the primary agents of the duty. A widespread example of this is the relevant part of the saying about the tripartite division of labour: performance with the tongue is for scholars, while the common people should do it with (or within) their hearts.[158] Some scholars express similar views in different terms,[159] or in other ways lay great emphasis on the role of the scholars, or even use language that would restrict the duty to them.[160] The biographical record is naturally heavily biased towards the exploits of scholars, since it is they who get the biographies. Sometimes the assumption of the centrality of the scholars is revealed unthinkingly, as when Ghazzālī, lamenting the decay of the art of rebuking rulers, complains that today the *scholars* are silent;[161] it does not occur to him to mention the Muslims at large. Occasionally a scholar's sense of the dignity of his estate is expressed in the

[151] See above, ch. 6, note 121; ch. 8, notes 46, 72; ch. 9, note 149; ch. 10, notes 75, 111; ch. 11, note 312; ch. 13, notes 53, 58, 60, 63; ch. 14, note 228; ch. 15, note 141; ch. 16, 429, 445f., and note 201. [152] Cf. above, ch. 2, note 23.

[153] See above, ch. 4, note 212; ch. 6, note 123; ch. 11, notes 216, 295, 297; ch. 12, notes 48, 129, 206; ch. 13, notes 73, 81 no. (2), 91; ch. 14, notes 20f., 56; ch. 16, notes 15, 20f. For a discussion of the question by Ibn Ḥazm, see his *Risālat al-talkhīṣ*, edited with his *al-Radd ʿalā Ibn Naghrīla al-Yahūdī* by I. ʿAbbās, Cairo 1960, 178–82 (drawn to my attention by Etan Kohlberg).

[154] So above, ch. 6, note 123; ch. 14, note 30; and ch. 16, note 22.

[155] So above, ch 13, notes 28f.; and cf. ch. 6, note 162, and ch. 15, note 201.

[156] See above, ch. 6, note 129; ch. 7, note 63; ch. 8, note 70, and cf. 125; ch. 9, note 70; ch. 11, 276 no. (1); ch. 12, notes 39, 49; ch. 13, notes 58, 81 no. (2), 92; ch. 14, 363; ch. 16, note 93.

[157] See above, ch. 6, note 124; ch. 9, note 70; ch. 12, notes 79, 89; ch. 13, note 48, and cf. note 62; ch. 16, note 48, and cf. 445f.; and cf. ch. 15, note 201.

[158] See above, notes 29f. For scholars who find the saying problematic, see above, note 41.

[159] See above, ch. 13, 342 (but cf. note 30), note 142, and cf. note 37; ch. 14, note 67; and cf. ch. 16, notes 274, 276.

[160] See above, ch. 2, notes 22f.; ch. 11, notes 340f.; ch. 12, note 88; and cf. above, ch. 7, notes 79f., and ch. 11, note 31. [161] See above, ch. 16, note 124.

stipulation that laymen are not to rebuke scholars,[162] and there is even the view that the scholars themselves are not to forbid wrong unless they are dressed as scholars.[163] But this kind of thing is uncommon; even in societies in which we have reason to believe that clerical authority was considerable, the formal doctrine of forbidding wrong does not usually reflect this.[164]

Leaving aside the explicit statements the scholars make from time to time about their role in forbidding wrong, it could fairly be said that the broad character of the duty as they shaped it in their doctrines was one fitted to their own social role. The essence of the duty is the exercise of moral authority; any support this authority gains from the power of a state or the violence of a mob is extrinsic. A paradigmatic figure here might be Ibn Karrām (d. 255/869), the founder of the Karrāmiyya.[165] With a group of his disciples he once encountered some young men who had seated themselves and were engaged in drinking wine.[166] The indignant disciples wanted to right this wrong and put a stop to the drinking, but Ibn Karrām told them to hold off so that he could show them how to command right. He then went up to the tipplers and greeted them. One of them stood up and handed Ibn Karrām a cup; Ibn Karrām took the cup, and addressed them. He referred to their custom of talking about those they loved (*aḥibbāʾ*) as they drank, and suggested that instead they contemplate their own mortality. On this theme he waxed so eloquent that the young men arose, broke the instruments of their depravity, and repented.[167] The doctrinal analogue of this anecdote is the frequent emphasis on performing the duty nicely.[168] That the authority in play is moral is also evident when the refusal of the offender to comply is sooner or later accepted as a regrettable but not undignified outcome of an attempt to forbid wrong.[169] The same

[162] See above, ch. 12, note 143, and ch. 16, note 271. [163] See above, ch. 13, note 142.

[164] See above, ch. 11, note 312, and ch. 15, 403f.

[165] See *EI*², art. 'Karrāmiyya' (C. E. Bosworth).

[166] Abū Ḥafṣ al-Samarqandī (second half of the fifth/eleventh century), *Rawnaq al-majālis*, ms. Istanbul, Süleymaniye, Aya Sofya 1,832, f. 54b.15 (my access to this manuscript is through a typewritten copy); ʿUthmān ibn Yaḥyā ibn ʿAbd al-Wahhāb al-Mīrī, *Mukhtaṣar Rawnaq al-majālis*, Damascus and Beirut 1985, 76.9. For Samarqandī's work, see van Ess, *Ungenützte Texte zur Karrāmīya*, 30–41 (for the manuscript here cited, see *ibid.*, 35 n. 136, and for Mīrī's epitome, *ibid.*, 41). Ibn Karrām is referred to as *al-imām al-zāhid Abū ʿAbdallāh* (see *ibid.*, 31, with reference to our passage).

[167] Samarqandī, *Rawnaq*, f. 55b.1; Mīrī, *Mukhtaṣar*, 77.12.

[168] See above, ch. 3, note 59; ch. 4, 78f.; ch. 5, notes 92f.; ch. 6, note 126; ch. 7, note 61; ch. 8, notes 30, 102, 161; ch. 12, note 39; ch. 13, note 34; ch. 14, notes 10, 31, 55; ch. 16, 439, 442; and cf. ch. 15, note 70.

[169] On this question, see above, ch. 4, 78; ch. 5, notes 132–4; ch. 11, note 37; ch. 13, note 81 no. (6), and 352; ch. 14, notes 11, 151–5; ch. 15, notes 48, 180f., 209; ch. 16, note 41.

is true of such notions as performing the duty in or with the heart,[170] and avoiding it by emigration[171] or otherwise.[172] To these we can perhaps add the counsels of despair which discourage the forbidding of wrong altogether, at least in these evil times.[173] For despite all that is wrong with the world, God is still in His heaven, ultimately though not proximately vindicating the moral order for which the scholars speak.

Against this background, the association of the duty with violence looks anomalous, and to an extent it is. One thing that is striking here is the frequency with which the scholars yoke forbidding wrong to holy war.[174] The goldsmith of Marw describes his denunciation of Abū Muslim as waging holy war against him with his tongue,[175] and the tradition he enacts through his death identifies speaking out against an unjust ruler as the highest form of holy war.[176] It is argued on the analogy of holy war that one forbidder of wrong should be prepared to take on two men.[177] The Imāmīs treat forbidding wrong as a part of holy war, inasmuch as they assign it a place in the section of the law-book that deals with that topic.[178] Others invert the relationship, considering holy war to be a part of forbidding wrong.[179] Perhaps it is immaterial which is part of which. Ḥalīmī

[170] See above, ch. 3, notes 5, 51; ch. 4, notes 221f.; ch. 5, 95f., and note 184; ch. 7, notes 60, 122; ch. 8, notes 70, 101; ch. 9, notes 76, 165, but cf. notes 56, 170; ch. 10, notes 13, 145, 151, 155f., 160, 162, 167; ch. 11, 263f., 283f., and notes 18–20, 81f., 338; ch. 12, notes 85, 93, 204, 219; ch. 13, notes 13, 54; ch. 14, notes 12, 55, 162; ch. 15, notes 48, 74, 168, 174, 222; ch. 16, note 82, but cf. note 75; and above, notes 114, 128. For the role of the heart in the saying about the tripartite division of labour, see above, notes 29f. See also Ṭabarī, *Tahdhīb al-āthār*, *Musnad ʿAlī*, 243.6, and Muqātil, *Khams miʾa*, 279.15 (giving something close to the 'three modes' tradition on his own authority; the text is corrupt, read *bi-fiʿl* and *bi-qawl*).

[171] See above, ch. 4, notes 218, 220; ch. 7, note 69; ch. 12, notes 11, 40f.; ch. 13, note 15; ch. 14, notes 24, 213, 240; but cf. ch. 8, note 35, and ch. 16, 432 no. (1).

[172] See above, ch. 4, 75; ch. 5, note 111; ch. 7, note 2; ch. 14, notes 29, 191; ch. 16, 432 no. (1), and note 110.

[173] See above, ch. 2, note 85; ch. 3, 42; ch. 4, 76f.; ch. 5, 106; ch. 11, note 33; ch. 12, notes 27, 29f.; ch. 14, notes 46–8, 82; ch. 15, notes 38, 41; ch. 16, notes 269, 272. There is an analogy here between the Imāmī notion of *hudna* (see above, ch. 11, note 33) and the Ibāḍī notion of *kitmān* (see above, ch. 15, note 38).

[174] See, in addition to what follows, above, ch. 2, notes 25f., 29, 45, 78, and cf. note 6; ch. 3, notes 31–3; ch. 4, note 39; ch. 8, notes 33, 58, 96; ch. 10, notes 4–7, 39, 45; ch. 11, notes 50, 323; ch. 12, 313; ch. 13, note 8; ch. 16, notes 43, 91; Ibn Ḥazm, *Fiṣal*, 4:175.6; Ṣāliḥī, *Kanz*, 61.22. For a statement of three differences between *al-amr biʾl-maʿrūf* and *jihād*, see the gloss *apud* Ibn Miftāḥ, *Muntazaʿ*, 4:582.10. The second difference is that old men and women may be killed in the course of *al-nahy ʿan al-munkar*, but not in *jihād* (for this see also Ṣuʿaytirī, *Taʿlīq*, f. 390b.27).

[175] See above, ch. 1, note 2. [176] See above, ch. 1, note 18.

[177] See above, ch. 4, note 196; and cf. ch. 14, note 169, and ch. 15, note 175.

[178] See above, ch. 11, note 2; for the Zaydīs, cf. ch. 10, note 72. The Shāfiʿite Ḥalīmī (d. 403/1012) would regard such an arrangement as valid in principle (*Minhāj*, 3:216.13).

[179] For Jaṣṣāṣ (d. 370/981), *jihād* is a species (*ḍarb*) of *al-amr biʾl-maʿrūf* (*Aḥkām*,

(d. 403/1012) tells us that there is no fundamental difference between them: both involve calling people to Islam, and if need be fighting them in this cause.[180] Indeed some authors elevate forbidding wrong above holy war: one remarks that it is the more binding duty,[181] another that it earns the greater reward.[182] One scholar made the observation – perhaps a trifle parochial or premature – that since the infidel threat had so diminished in his day, what remained was spiritual struggle, speaking out, and forbidding wrong.[183] Such views can, of course, be understood as a way for the scholars to make their own activities seem as portentous, or more so, than those of generals: the cumulative effect is perhaps more militant than martial.[184]

Violence does, of course, play a much more concrete part in the duty, and sometimes quite vividly. There is an unmistakable thrill of violence in the rhetoric of Zaydī insurrection,[185] and we catch it again in the long activist tradition transmitted by the Imāmīs.[186] The image of the Ḥanafī Salm ibn Sālim al-Balkhī (d. 194/810) girt with his sword, or talking of raising 100,000 swords against the caliph, is of a piece with this.[187] But in general, those who leave ordinary people free to resort to violence, where the exigencies of forbidding wrong require it, do so in a prosaic and legalistic fashion.[188] Others are quite obviously civilian in their approach, as with those who make over armed violence to the political authorities, or allow it only in cooperation with them, or with their permission.[189] Ḥasan al-Baṣrī speaks as a civilian when he contrasts the swords of the rulers with

3:119.26). For Fakhr al-Dīn al-Rāzī (d. 606/1210), it belongs under the heading (*bāb*) of *al-amr bi'l-ma'rūf* (*Tafsīr*, 16:205.1 (to Q9:112)); a few lines further down, he remarks that the main part of the duty (*ra's al-amr bi'l-ma'rūf . . . wa-ra'īsuhu*) is *jihād* (*ibid.*, 205.7). For Ibn Taymiyya, the 'completion' of *al-amr bi'l-ma'rūf* is by *jihād* (see above, ch. 7, note 56). For Shāṭibī (d. 790/1388), the duty of *jihād* which was imposed in Medina was a branch (*far'*) of *al-amr bi'l-ma'rūf*, which was already established in Mecca (*Muwāfaqāt*, 3:50.6). For Najafī (d. 1266/1850), *jihād* is an element of *al-amr bi'l-ma'rūf* (*Jawāhir*, 21:361.16, speaking of *jamī' afrād al-amr bi'l-ma'rūf allatī minhā 'l-jihād*). [180] See above, ch. 13, note 16, and cf. above, ch. 9, note 21.

[181] See above, ch. 12, 325. [182] See above, ch. 14, note 169.

[183] Ṣāliḥī, *Kanz*, 62.1. The scholar is not named.

[184] Compare 'Onward Christian soldiers marching *as* to war'.

[185] See above, ch. 10, section 3. [186] See above, ch. 11, 256.

[187] See above, ch. 4, notes 70, 72.

[188] For views to the effect that individuals may have recourse to violence, see above, ch. 9, notes 13, 21, 39f., 53, 55, 78, 159, 172–4; ch. 10, notes 25, 75, 115f.; ch. 12, notes 9, 118–20, 198, 207 (and cf. 209), 214–16; ch. 13, notes 8, 16, 66f.; ch. 14, notes 258f.; ch. 15, 400, and notes 66, 152–4; ch. 16, notes 88, 91, 202f.

[189] For such ideas, see above, notes 25f. There is occasional mention of the performance of the duty with offensive weapons of a lowlier sort. One example is the use of sandals (see above, ch. 12, note 208; Malaṭī, *Tanbīh*, 30.1; Rummānī, *Tafsīr*, f. 62a.11); another would be sticks (see, for example, above, ch. 8, note 160; ch. 12, note 208).

'our' tongues,[190] as do the Ḥanbalites and Imāmīs when they free us from any duty to confront an armed man.[191]

To forbid wrong calls for a number of sterling qualities, such as a certain zeal,[192] and a degree of extrovert confidence – something with which ʿAbd al-Ghanī al-Maqdisī (d. 600/1203) was particulary well endowed.[193] Performing the duty can also take considerable courage. This courage is of two kinds: the active component is a moral courage which consists in 'not fearing the reproach of any reproacher' (Q5:54),[194] while the passive element is a capacity to 'bear patiently whatever may befall thee' (Q31:17).[195] It was courage of these kinds that the goldsmith of Marw displayed when he got himself killed by Abū Muslim (d. 137/755), attacking him verbally since he lacked the strength to do so physically.[196] But this is by no means the courage of a knight in shining armour. It is, after all, almost universally accepted that fear or the prospect of harm are good reasons not to proceed with the duty,[197] a point of view that is prudent but hardly chivalrous.[198] Useful though it may prove on occasion, proficiency

[190] See above, ch. 4, note 50.

[191] See above, ch. 5, note 124; ch. 6, note 105; ch. 11, note 14; and cf. ch. 4, notes 146, 231.

[192] For the psychosomatic symptoms reported by Sufyān al-Thawrī (d. 161/778) and the elder Rāfiʿī (d. 580/1184) in connection with the duty, see the references given above, ch. 4, note 130, and ch. 13, note 129.

[193] See above, ch. 7, 148f. Abū ʿAlī al-Rajrājī, who forbade wrong in Fez in the second half of the eighth/fourteenth century, is a striking exception: shy, solitary and painfully modest (Ibn Qunfudh, *Uns al-faqīr*, 77.20; cf. above, ch. 14, note 234).

[194] The phrase is often evoked, especially by biographers, in the context of forbidding wrong. See, for example, Dhahabī, *Siyar*, 8:332.4 (ʿAbdallāh ibn ʿAbd al-ʿAzīz al-ʿUmarī (d. 184/800f.), for whom see above, ch. 4, 58f.); *ibid.*, 21:454.6, and Ibn Rajab, *Dhayl*, 2:12.21 (ʿAbd al-Ghanī). For other such cases, see the references given above, ch. 6, note 3 nos. (4) (reference to Ibn al-Jawzī) and (9); ch. 8, notes 16 (first reference), 17, 124 (first reference to Āl al-Shaykh), 159f.; ch. 11, note 320 (ninth, eleventh and twelfth references); ch. 12, note 161 (first reference); ch. 13, notes 128 (second reference), 138 (last reference); ch. 14, notes 126 (on Jakanī), 166 (first reference); ch. 15, note 77 (third and fourth references to Shammākhī). See also Ghazzālī, *Iḥyāʾ*, 2:280.31. One does not, of course, evoke the verse when expressing disapproval; thus the Damascene Ḥanafī Ibn al-Ṭabbākh (d. 1006/1598) is described as bigoted (*shadīd al-taʿaṣṣub*) in his constant hostility to other scholars, which he manifested in the guise of forbidding wrong (Muḥibbī, *Khulāṣa*, 1:22.27; I owe this reference to Baki Tezcan).

[195] See above, ch. 2, notes 72f.; ch. 4, 72; ch. 6, note 161; ch. 7, note 66; ch. 12, notes 39, 44; ch. 16, note 97.

[196] See above, ch. 1, note 2.

[197] See above, ch. 4, notes 231f.; ch. 5, 98f.; ch. 6, notes 105, 141; ch. 9, 202, and note 74; ch. 10, note 17; ch. 11, 276 no. (4), and notes 47, 275, 339; ch. 12, notes 128, 206, 217; ch. 13, notes 41, 92; ch. 14, notes 13, 33, 55; ch. 15, 400, and note 174, and cf. note 85; ch. 16, notes 40, 42, 82, and cf. 434f. (an elaborate discussion of degrees of harm). For views that would seem to reject the danger condition, see above, ch. 4, note 86, and ch. 11, note 25, and cf. note 282.

[198] The French knight Geoffroi de Charny (d. AD 1356), speaking of good knights, writes as follows: 'No one can and should excuse himself from bearing arms in a just cause, whether for his lord or for his lineage or for himself or for the Holy Church or to defend and

in the martial arts is nowhere near the core of the scholars' conception of forbidding wrong. When ʿAbd al-Ghanī grabs the sword with which an irate wrongdoer attacks him in response to his intervention,[199] we pause to admire his prowess and to wonder if, in another life, he might not have been a great warrior. But as it is, his reaction is quite incidental to his identity as a scholar.[200] The annals of forbidding wrong are a record of moral, not martial, triumphs.

A final point is that the forbidder of wrong, unlike any sensible man of the sword, typically confronts wrongdoing alone. It is true that from time to time we hear of the performance of the duty by groups. Usually such groups would seem to be *ad hoc*: someone encounters a wrong and proceeds to gather the neighbours, or otherwise collects a few men to help him confront it.[201] Sometimes it appears that we have to do with groups that already exist for some other reason, and happen to encounter wrongdoing.[202] But there are also cases of what seem to be dedicated groups, in other words groups that exist for the express purpose of righting wrongs.[203] A group that forbade wrong in this way is described by Ibn ʿAqīl (d. 513/1119) from his own lifetime. He says that in the days of the caliph al-Qāʾim (r. 422–67/1031–75), one Abū Bakr al-Aqfālī, when he arose to right a wrong (*li-inkār munkar*), would take with him a following of pietists such as would eat only from the work of their own hands, men like a

uphold the faith or out of pity for men and women who cannot defend their own rights (*pour pitié d'ommes et de fammes qui ne peuent leur droit deffendre*). In such cases they should commit themselves eagerly, boldly, and gladly to such deeds of arms and adventures, fearing nothing' (R. W. Kaeuper and E. Kennedy, *The Book of Chivalry of Geoffroi de Charny*, Philadelphia 1996, 176 line 14 = 177). Our scholars are likewise innocent of the erotic undercurrent of chivalrous courage, whereas for Charny it is because love of a lady inspires a knight to great deeds that 'all good men-at-arms are rightly bound to protect and defend the honor of all ladies against all those who would threaten it by word or deed' (*ibid.*, 94 line 17 = 95).

199 See above, ch. 7, note 30.

200 Contrast the case of the eastern Ibāḍī Muḥammad ibn Ismāʿīl, whose prowess in grappling with a rapist led to his election to a role of military and political leadership in 906/1506f. (see above, ch. 15, note 246).

201 See above, ch. 4, note 204; ch. 5, 97f.; ch. 12, note 36; ch. 13, 344; ch. 15, note 189; ch. 16, 441; and cf. ch. 4, notes 206f., and ch. 14, note 47. Ibrāhīm ibn Isḥāq al-Ḥarbī (d. 285/899), a Baghdādī and a pupil of Ibn Ḥanbal, defined the 'stranger' (*gharīb*) in his time as a virtuous man living among virtuous folk who assist him when he forbids wrong (Khaṭīb, *Taʾrīkh Baghdād*, 6:36.12; I owe this reference to Nurit Tsafrir); the implication, of course, is that this would be quite unusual in the evil time in which he lives. Only Ṣāliḥī (d. 856/1452) states explicitly that it is a duty to assist in this way (*Kanz*, vol. 2, f. 144a.6, invoking the consensus of the scholars; in the printed text the whole of f. 144 has been omitted at 827.20); but only Māwardī denies to individuals the right to find helpers, and he contradicts himself on the point in his different works (see above, ch. 13, note 46, and contrast 344). Cf. also above, note 15.

202 See above, ch. 4, notes 201, 202, and cf. note 203; ch. 15, notes 75f.

203 See above, ch. 4, notes 97, 208; ch. 6, notes 39, 45, 100, 103; ch. 14, notes 209f.

certain Abū Bakr al-Khabbāz.[204] All told, I have encountered perhaps half-a-dozen definite instances of this phenomenon, which is not very many. The sources show no particular tendency to romanticise such activity; Ibn Karrām's disciples are relegated to the role of spectators during his star performance in rebuking the dissolute young men.[205]

5. THE SCHOLARS AND THE WIDER SOCIETY

If the scholars, in their thinking about how to forbid wrong, had a tendency to be thinking of themselves, does this mean that the value meant nothing to the rest of society? There are two issues worth looking at here. One is the place, if any, of forbidding wrong in the moral codes of social groups other than the scholars.[206] The other is the impact of the performance of the duty by scholars on the society around them.

We can best begin by reducing the first question to a more realistic one. There existed in the Islamic world culturally significant intellectual traditions which lay outside, or somewhat outside, the boundaries of religion, and in this sense can be described as profane.[207] Two of the most widespread, medicine and astrology, are obviously of no concern to us.[208] What does call for our attention is the broad range of profane ethical thought, from abstract philosophical reflection in the Greek tradition to practical counsels in the Persian tradition; within it we can to some extent include the ethical literature associated with what might be called the youth culture (*futuwwa*) of the medieval Islamic brotherhoods.[209] The question, then, is whether forbidding wrong appears among the moral values discussed in this body of ethical writing.

My admittedly cursory inspection of this literature suggests that forbidding wrong is no more a topic there than it is in the Ṣūfī handbooks.[210] On

[204] Ibn al-Jawzī, *Talbīs Iblīs*, 166.20. I have not been able to identify the two persons named, who may have been as plebeian as their *nisba*s suggest; doubtless they lived in Baghdad. The passage is translated in Makdisi, *Ibn ʿAqil*, 169.

[205] See above, note 166.

[206] My attempt to address this issue originated in a question put to me by Abbas Amanat at a conference in 1993.

[207] I do not, of course, mean by this that they were free of religious elements, nor that they were anti-religious.

[208] As a curiosity, it may be mentioned that references to forbidding wrong can be found in astrological predictions (see Mūsā ibn Nawbakht (*fl.* first half of the fourth/tenth century), *al-Kāmil fī asrār al-nujūm*, ed. and trans. A. Labarta, Madrid 1982, 93.8, 93.11, 94.4, 106.11 = 163f., 177).

[209] See *EI*², art. 'Futuwwa' (C. Cahen and F. Taeschner).

[210] Cf. above, ch. 16, note 234. This observation is based in the first instance on checking the tables of contents (and, where relevant, the indices) of the primary and secondary works cited in a bibliographically helpful review by D. Gutas of a recent publication on Muslim ethics (*Journal of the American Oriental Society*, 117 (1997), 171–5). I have also

one level this might seem surprising. The question what duty one has to prevent or discourage wrongdoing by others is one that, once raised, has an obvious relevance in almost any ethical system, religious or profane. We can hardly suppose that the philosophers took seriously the position maintained by the religious scholars that forbidding wrong is grounded in revelation to the exclusion of reason[211] (with occasional dissentient voices).[212] Doubtless we are up against the conservatism of intellectual genres, although in the domain of profane ethical writing, genres of diverse origins were by no means sealed off from one another. Whatever the explanation, the fact is that the idea of forbidding wrong scarcely crossed the boundary between religious and profane literature. This negative finding should fortify us against any temptation to imagine that the value had come to permeate everyday life for the non-religious élite, let alone the mass of society.

Before we leave this question, there are a few unusual passages from writings on ethics which are worth examining in some detail, precisely because in one way or another they seem to cross the boundaries between religious and profane traditions.

One of these passages is from the pen of Ibn Sīnā (d. 428/1037), who as a philosopher is a prime example of a writer in a profane tradition. While the passage in question is found in a work intended to present the basic principles of philosophy,[213] the chapter in which it occurs sets out the distinguishing characteristics of the gnostic élite (*ʿārifūn*).[214] What Ibn Sīnā is presenting here is in fact a kind of philosophical Ṣūfism,[215] and he did this with such success that the chapter was described by a commentator as the best-ordered account of the Ṣūfī sciences ever written.[216] At a certain point in this account, Ibn Sīnā devotes a few lines to the attitude of the 'gnostic' (*ʿārif*) to forbidding wrong.[217] The gnostic, he tells us, does not concern himself with spying and prying (*al-tajassus wa'l-taḥassus*). When he does witness a wrong (*munkar*), his insight into divine predestination

consulted C.-H. de Fouchécour, *Moralia: les notions morales dans la littérature persane du 3e/9e au 7e/13e siècle*, Paris 1986.

211 See above, ch. 6, note 120; ch. 9, notes 25, 65; ch. 11, 270–2, 287f.; ch. 13, note 75; and cf. ch. 13, note 40, and ch. 15, notes 53, 203.

212 See above, ch. 9, notes 25, 37, 64, 122; ch. 11, notes 130f., 241; and cf. ch. 15, note 217, and ch. 16, 428.

213 Ibn Sīnā (d. 428/1037), *al-Ishārāt wa'l-tanbīhāt*, ed. J. Forget, Leiden 1892, 2.5 (promising *uṣūlan wa-jumalan min al-ḥikma*).

214 *Ibid.*, 198.14.

215 Cf. the section on mysticism in *Encyclopaedia Iranica*, art. 'Avicenna', 3:79f. (D. Gutas).

216 Ibn Sīnā (d. 428/1037), *al-Ishārāt wa'l-tanbīhāt*, with the commentary of Nāṣir al-Dīn al-Ṭūsī (d. 672/1274), Tehran 1377–9, 3:363.15 (quoting the commentary of Fakhr al-Dīn al-Rāzī).

217 Ibn Sīnā, *Ishārāt*, ed. Forget, 205.17, cited in Goldziher, *Livre*, 89. Goldziher gives a partial translation (or rather paraphrase).

(*qadar*) is such that he is moved by compassion rather than anger. When he commands right (*idhā amara bi'l-ma'rūf*), he does so with the civility of someone giving friendly counsel (*bi-rifqi nāṣiḥin*), not with the harshness of a reproacher (*bi-'unfi mu'ayyirin*). But if the right at stake is the supreme mystical attainment (? *idhā jasuma 'l-ma'rūf*), he sometimes conceals it from those who are unworthy of it (*ghāra 'alayhi min ghayr ahlihi*).[218]

This is quite clearly a passage about forbidding wrong as it is understood by the Muslim scholars. Several of its key terms are immediately familiar, and most of the ideas are within the boundaries of mainstream Muslim thinking. What lies outside the mainstream is the élitism that marks the passage. The gnostic acts with civility not because he thinks it will work better, but rather because of his superior insight. Likewise the last allusive sentence is deliberately esoteric. Such ideas are alien to law-centred Islam. It is nevertheless remarkable that Ibn Sīnā should have felt it appropriate at this point to adopt not just the terminology, but also some of the substance, of the Muslim conception of forbidding wrong.[219]

Another passage to be examined here comes from a work on ethics by Ibn Ḥazm, a writer whom we usually encounter as a representative of the religious tradition. In this work, however, he does not narrowly confine himself within this tradition.[220] At no point does he expressly discuss forbidding wrong; but one topic that he does raise from time to time is advice (*naṣīḥa*) and counselling (*wa'ẓ*). Thus he urges that one do this nicely, invoking in support the authority of God and the Prophet.[221] The passage that particularly concerns us addresses the question how many times one should give (the same piece of) advice. The answer is twice. The first time it is a religious obligation (*farḍ wa-diyāna*), and the second time it is a warning and reminder (*tanbīh wa-tadhkīr*); whereas a third time it would be a rebuke and reproach, beyond which lies only violence – kicks, blows and worse. But this limitation does not apply in matters of religion (*ma'ānī 'l-diyāna*): here a man must keep repeating the advice, whether he suffers or not in consequence, and whether the recipient likes it or not.[222] The passage is tantalisingly brief. There is no explicit mention of forbidding

[218] Cf. the commentary of Naṣīr al-Dīn al-Ṭūsī (Ibn Sīnā, *Ishārāt*, with the commentary of Ṭūsī, 3:392.21; I owe this reference to Nizam Ahmad).

[219] Cf. also the passage by Judah ha-Levi (d. AD 1141) cited below, ch. 19, note 68.

[220] He lists as paragons of intelligence Ḥasan the Baṣrian, Plato the Athenian, and Buzurjmihr the Persian (Ibn Ḥazm (d. 456/1064), *al-Akhlāq wa'l-siyar*, ed. and trans. N. Tomiche, Beirut 1961, 22 §42), and he describes the contents of the work as arising from his own experience of life (*ibid.*, 12 §2).

[221] *Ibid.*, 45f. §152, 60f. §218.

[222] *Ibid.*, 42 §140.

wrong, and yet we are at least very close to it. We learn that advice as such is a religious duty, but that its subject-matter may or may not be a matter of religion, and that different norms apply in either case. Is forbidding wrong then something confined to matters of religion, a special case of a wider ethical value more typically concerned with profane matters? It would be asking too much of the passage to seek a clear-cut answer from it.

The third passage is less interesting. Ibn al-Miʿmār (d. 642/1244) was a Baghdādī Ḥanbalite writer on what I have called youth culture (*futuwwa*). At one point he gives a list of two hundred qualities which the young man (*fatā*) is to cultivate or avoid. Among the positive qualities, he includes forbidding wrong; but he has little to say about it.[223] The company it keeps in the list suggests superficial borrowing from the religious tradition.[224]

As indicated, all three authors can loosely be thought of as crossing the borders between religious and profane thought. But none of them helps us to address the question why the duty to prevent wrongdoing by others should be so well developed on one side of the fence, and yet virtually unknown on the other.

Just as we find little adoption of forbidding wrong in the literature of profane ethics, so also we find surprisingly little in the way of principled criticism of it outside the religious tradition. Even the strongest attacks on the practice of forbidding wrong will be found to appeal to Islamic values, or at least conform to them. Consider the encounter between the caliph al-Maʾmūn and the shrouded zealot.[225] This is an unusual story in that it invites us to identify squarely with the caliph;[226] in that sense we can see it as a fine articulation of the 'thèse caliphale'.[227] The story can also be relied

[223] For the list, see Ibn al-Miʿmār (d. 642/1244), *Futuwwa*, ed. M. Jawād *et al.*, Baghdad 1958, 256–61, translated in F. Taeschner, *Zünfte und Bruderschaften im Islam: Texte zur Geschichte der Futuwwa*, Zurich and Munich 1979, 165–8. For the mention of forbidding wrong, see Ibn al-Miʿmār, *Futuwwa*, 257.2.

[224] Compare the inclusion of *al-amr biʾl-maʿrūf* among some verbal formulae employed in a colourful *futuwwa* ritual described in a responsum of Taqī al-Dīn al-Subkī (d. 756/1355) (*Fatāwā*, Cairo 1355–6, 2:548.24; I owe this reference to Megan Reid). Subkī condemns the ritual as incontrovertible *bidʿa*, but has no objection to the reference to *al-amr biʾl-maʿrūf* (*ibid.*, 549.17, 550.6). [225] See above, ch. 1, 10f.

[226] There is another story in which the caliph is likewise confronted by a shrouded figure who is there to speak out and get himself killed (Ghazzālī, *Iḥyāʾ*, 2:325.11, cited in Amedroz, 'Hisba jurisdiction', 294; Ibn al-Naḥḥās, *Tanbīh*, 70.6). But here the point of view is quite different: al-Maʾmūn kills his antagonist, who promptly appears in Paradise.

[227] It is hardly coincidental that the author to whom we owe the story, Zubayr ibn Bakkār (d. 256/870), is remembered as the exceedingly well-paid tutor of the caliph's son (Khaṭīb, *Taʾrīkh Baghdād*, 8:469.7). As the title *Muwaffaqiyyāt* given to his work indicates, it was believed to have been written for al-Muwaffaq (d. 278/891) (see, for example, Ibn al-Nadīm, *Fihrist*, 161.10, where for *al-lugha* read *allafahu*). If this is correct, then the youthful prince was being instructed in the ways of his great-uncle.

on to warm the heart of any secularist.[228] The caliph is clear-headed, sober and responsible; the zealot is fanatical, pretentious and stupid. But the caliph's position is in no way that of a secularist. It is not just that he derives considerable moral advantage from the placement of the story in the context of holy war against the infidel. More than that, he mounts no argument that has its point of departure outside the religious tradition of Islam. The same is true of the sharp observation of Kātib Chelebi (d. 1067/1657) that it is sheer stupidity to attempt to uproot well-established innovations in the name of forbidding wrong.[229] Here too there is a tone with which a secularist could readily identify; but what Kātib Chelebi actually says can be understood as no more than an application of the efficacy condition.[230] A third example is ʿAbd al-Ghanī al-Nābulusī's attack on the meddlesome puritans of his day.[231] His argument is idiosyncratic, and perhaps unsustainable; but it invokes nothing outside the religious tradition of Islam.

What makes it possible to attempt these comparisons between the religious and profane ethical traditions of the cultural élites is the fact that each side has left a direct literary record. This is not the case with the common people. We do nevertheless have some indications of their reactions to unwanted forbidders of wrong. For most of this we are indebted as usual to the scholars, who never tired of pointing out that forbidding wrong was an activity likely to provoke negative responses. By far the most insistent of these responses can be rendered as: 'Mind your own business! This has nothing to do with you!' The scholars did not, of course, approve of this response, and did not portray it sympathetically. Ibn Masʿūd says that it is one of the worst of sins when someone is told to fear God, and responds: 'Look to yourself!' (*ʿalayka bi-nafsika*).[232] ʿUmar ibn ʿAbd al-ʿAzīz (d. 101/720) complains of people who propose to cultivate their own gardens (*innā lanā fī anfusinā shughlan wa-lasnā min al-nās fī shayʾ*).[233] The devil tells a zealot who purposes to take his axe and cut down a sacred tree: 'What's it got to do with you?' (*mā laka wa-lahā*).[234] Abū ʾl-Ḥusayn al-Nūrī (d. 295/907f.), pressing his inquiries regarding the thirty amphorae containing the caliph's wine, is described by the boatman in charge of them as a 'meddlesome Ṣūfī' (*ṣūfī fuḍūlī*).[235] Ibn Ḥanbal predicts that a time will come when the believer who sees occasion to forbid wrong will be declared

[228] As it obviously did in Jadʿān's case (cf. above, ch. 1, note 31).
[229] See above, ch. 12, note 172.
[230] Cf. his sustained appeal to the scholastic conditions of obligation in his effort to discourage forbidding wrong in general (see above, ch. 12, notes 168–70, and ch. 13, notes 80f.).
[231] See above, ch. 12, 326–8.
[232] ʿAlī al-Qārī, *Mubīn*, 193.16; cf. also Imāmzāda, *Shirʿat al-Islām*, *apud* Yaʿqūb ibn Seyyid ʿAlī, *Sharḥ*, 506.19.
[233] Ibn ʿAbd al-Ḥakam, *Sīrat ʿUmar ibn ʿAbd al-ʿAzīz*, 163.2.
[234] Abū ʾl-Layth al-Samarqandī, *Tanbīh*, 101.11.
[235] See above, ch. 16, note 245.

a busybody (*hādhā fuḍūlī*).[236] In this day and age, laments Ibn al-Naḥḥās (d. 814/1411), one who performs the duty is reviled for his meddlesomeness (*qīla mā akthara fuḍūlahu*), while one who fawns on people is praised for his ability to get along with them.[237] We also hear about this reaction in a less rhetorical and more juristic vein when the Ḥanafī scholars list irreligious statements the utterance of which may constitute unbelief. One man says to another: 'Go to the home of so-and-so and command him right!'; the other replies: 'What wrong has he done to me (*dar ḥaqq-i man chih jafā karda*) that I should command him right?'[238] Or he may reply 'What has he done to me?', or 'How has he bothered me (*marā az ū chih āzār ast*)?', or 'What have I to do with such meddlesomeness (*fuḍūlī*)?'[239] Or he may say to someone who is commanding right: 'What a commotion we have here! (*chih ghawghā āmad!*)'.[240] Nor are we exclusively dependent on the scholars to articulate this counter-cultural value for us. The poets express it directly. Ḥāfiẓ (d. 791/1389) says that it is nothing to do with you whether he is good or bad; in the end each of us will reap what he himself has sowed.[241] He tells the ascetic not to find fault with the profligate; the sins of others will not be debited to his account.[242] He asks the preacher (*wāʿiẓ*) what all the fuss is about, and tells him to go about his own business (*kār-i khwud*).[243] The poems of Ḥāfiẓ are not, of course, folk-poetry, but they had wide resonance in the traditional culture of Iran.

In itself, however, minding one's own business is perfectly Islamic. As the Prophet says, one of the things that makes a good Muslim is that he stays clear of what does not concern him (*tarkuhu mā lā yaʿnīhi*).[244] Nūrī,

236 Ṣāliḥī, *Kanz*, 308.23 (reading *fuḍūlī* with ms. Fatih 1,136, f. 106b.17). God's business will be seen as meddlesomeness (*fuḍūl*). 237 Ibn al-Naḥḥās, *Tanbīh*, 17.2.

238 Qāḍī Khān (d. 592/1196), *Fatāwā*, Cairo 1282, 3:603.21. The scholars hold the reply to be unbelief.

239 ʿĀlim ibn al-ʿAlāʾ al-Ḥanafī (compiling in 777/1375f.), *al-Fatāwā al-Tātārkhāniyya*, ed. S. Ḥusayn, Karachi 1990–, 5:503.4. All these and other replies are unbelief.

240 *Ibid.*, 503.3. If he means this in a derogatory sense, it is to be feared that he has fallen into unbelief. The material cited in the the last three notes can also be found with the offending utterances in Arabic (see, for example, Badr al-Rashīd (d. 768/1366f?), *Alfāẓ al-kufr*, published under the title *Tahdhīb risālat al-Badr al-Rashīd fī alfāẓ al-kufr*, Beirut 1991, 48.15). I do not know the source of the death date given for this author.

241 Ḥāfiẓ, *Dīwān*, 77.2. Note that Ḥāfiẓ takes a purely individualist view of the consequences of sin which the scholars would firmly reject. 242 *Ibid.*, 77.1.

243 *Ibid.*, 35.1. Ḥāfiẓ also makes frequent reference to the hypocrisy of the representatives of formal religion, as when he describes the prayer-leader of the city being carried home in a drunken stupor with his prayer-mat on his back (*ibid.*, 285.5), and asks why those who enjoin repentance do it so little themselves (*ibid.*, 199.2).

244 Mālik, *Muwaṭṭaʾ*, 903 no. 3 (and cf. *ibid.*, 990 no. 17); Sulamī (d. 412/1021), *ʿUyūb al-nafs wa-mudāwātuhā*, edited with his *Jawāmiʿ ādāb al-Ṣūfiyya* by E. Kohlberg, Jerusalem 1976, 85 §25, and the numerous references to further sources given by the editor. For a collection of sayings to the same effect, see Khaṭṭābī, *ʿUzla*, 134–6; one of these equates *mā lā yaʿnīka* with *faḍl* (*ibid.*, 134.11; cf. the term *fuḍūlī*). The many virtues of Ibn al-Mubārak (d. 181/797) included *tark al-kalām fī mā lā yaʿnīhi* (Mizzī, *Tahdhīb*, 16:18.7).

it will be remembered, was a man given to minding his own business (*qalīl al-fuḍūl, lā yas'al ʿammā lā yaʿnīhi*),[245] for all that the boatman regarded him as a meddlesome Ṣūfī (as events were to prove, with some reason). God tells the believers to 'look after your own souls', since those who are astray cannot harm them – provided, of course, they are 'rightly guided' (Q5:105).[246] The issue, in other words, is not whether one should mind one's own business, but rather just what the limits of one's business should be. Clearly those who invoked this value against unwanted commanding and forbidding had their own ideas as to these limits. What our sources scarcely tell us is what these ideas were.[247] Had they been more generous in this respect, we might perhaps have been better placed to discern values alien to those of the scholars to whom we owe our sources.

That forbidding wrong was primarily a matter for the scholars does not mean that it was socially irrelevant. For all that it bulks disproportionately large in the record it has left behind it, the religious élite of Islamic societies was a significant one. Sometimes, perhaps often, the more zealous forbidders of wrong were at loggerheads with their societies, as in the case of Ibn ʿUbayd and his withdrawal from Toledo.[248] But in other cases the sources mention the support they enjoyed – we might even speak of their constituencies. The Ḥanbalite Barbahārī (d. 329/941) is a case in point.[249] Another Ḥanbalite, Ibn ʿAbdūs of Ḥarrān (d. before 600/1204), got away with pouring out the ruler's wine because of his standing with the common people of the city.[250] Abū ʿAlī al-Rajrājī enjoyed wide support for his activity in Fez in the second half of the eighth/fourteenth century.[251] Ibn Baṭṭūṭa (d. 770/1368f.) describes an ascetic preacher in Harāt with whom the townspeople had entered into agreement to right wrongs (*taghyīr al-munkar*); they would put right any wrong, even if it took place at the court

[245] See above, ch. 16, note 257.
[246] For this verse and the problem to which it gave rise, see above, ch. 2, 30f., and ch. 3, 35.
[247] For one exception, see below, ch. 20, note 20. There were doubtless many in traditional Islamic societies who felt that a pietist telling others to pray was a busybody, whereas someone who protected women and the weak against harassment and oppression was a hero (cf. W. M. Floor, 'The political role of the Lutis in Iran', in M. E. Bonine and N. R. Keddie (eds.), *Modern Iran*, Albany 1981, 88, 94; I am indebted to Houchang Chehabi and Margaret Larkin for bibliographical leads in this connection). But the people can also be found on the side of the pietists. In the incident recounted by Ibn Qāḍī Shuhba (see above, note 15), the authorities paraded a group of pietists in chains, proclaiming 'This is how people are punished who interfere in what is none of their business' (*hādhā jazā' man yataʿarraḍ li-mā lā yaʿnīhi, Ta'rīkh*, 3:116.4); this provoked strong popular disapproval.
[248] See above, ch. 14, note 192. For other examples, see above, ch. 4, notes 186, 205f.
[249] See above, ch. 6, 116–18.
[250] See above, ch. 7, note 33.
[251] See above, ch. 14, note 234.

of the ruler.[252] He adds a story in which six thousand of them saw to it that the prescribed punishment for drinking was inflicted on the ruler in his palace.[253]

Some of this may have articulated no more than a populist resentment against the luxurious living of those who could better afford it. But there must also have been instances where forbidding wrong meshed with the society's interests and grievances. This is likely enough to have been the case when Khubūshānī (d. 587/1191) knocked off the headgear of Saladin (r. 564–89/1169–93) while protesting against illegal taxes.[254] A clear-cut example is the incident of 714/1314 when Nūr al-Dīn al-Bakrī (d. 724/1324) confronted the Mamlūk sultan over the Coptic question.[255] The expectation that scholars would forbid wrong in such a fashion lies behind the frustration engendered on one occasion by Abū 'l-ʿAbbās al-Sarrāj (d. 313/925): instead of furthering the material interests of his city, he rebuked the ruler on a point of ritual which was of no interest to anyone.[256] But representation of the interests of society against its rulers seems to have been only a small part of forbidding wrong.[257]

Why there was no neat fit between such representation and forbidding wrong can be illustrated from a passage in one of the epistles of Badīʿ al-Zamān al-Hamadhānī (d. 398/1008). He is urging prudence on a notable who is thinking of protesting at the fiscal exactions of Maḥmūd of Ghazna (r. 388–421/998–1030). 'Do you wish', he asks, 'to share with Ḥamza in his martyrdom and be his partner in lordship, though you feel the pain of blows, hate fetters and loathe chains, and fear disgrace, and you mix in society and are pleased when people's hopes are fixed on you?'[258] There is no way the notable can win: 'One who orders what is good, if he aims at wide influence or abundant wealth or far-flung fame and is killed short of his plan, has achieved nothing and his hopes are deceived. If he seeks the next world and mixes with it some of what I have listed and a touch of what I have mentioned, he will be written down among the

[252] Ibn Baṭṭūṭa, *Riḥla*, 3:69.5, cited in Goldziher, *Livre*, 94.
[253] Ibn Baṭṭūṭa, *Riḥla*, 3:70.1. [254] See above, ch. 13, note 133.
[255] See above, ch. 13, note 140. [256] See above, ch. 13, note 70.
[257] It is striking that there are no instances of it in the recorded activity of the early forbidders of wrong whom I classified as notables (see above, ch. 4, 56–8).
[258] Badīʿ al-Zamān al-Hamadhānī (d. 398/1008), *Rasāʾil*, *apud* Ibrāhīm Afandī al-Aḥdab al-Ṭarābulusī, *Kashf al-maʿānī waʾl-bayān ʿan Rasāʾil Badīʿ al-Zamān*, Beirut 1890, 488.2, translated in D. S. Richards, 'The *Rasāʾil* of Badīʿ al-Zamān al-Hamadhānī', in A. Jones (ed.), *Arabicus Felix*, Reading 1991, 154 (I owe this reference to Patricia Crone). Ḥamza is Ḥamza ibn ʿAbd al-Muṭṭalib (d. 3/625), the 'lord of the martyrs' (cf. above, ch. 1, note 20). On prospective loss of social standing as a reason for not forbidding wrong, compare Ghazzālī's discussion (see above, ch. 16, notes 54f.).

polytheists.'[259] Notables are precisely the people with the most to lose in abrasive interactions with rulers, and local interests can usually be furthered, if at all, by less confrontational means.

All in all, it is hard to resist a sense that, in their thinking about forbidding wrong, the scholars were wrestling with something that was in a way too big for them. Left to themselves, scholars will always invent reasons why other people should listen to them; but the Muslim conception of forbidding wrong goes far beyond this. The disparity between the content of the duty and the normal lifestyle of scholars is particularly noticeable in the early centuries with respect to violence. It generates a rich vein of early comedy: we have only to think of Ḥasan ibn Ṣāliḥ ibn Ḥayy (d. 167/783f.) seeking in vain for someone to crucify him,[260] or Ibn Farrūkh (d. 175/791) abandoning his attempted rebellion when only two men showed up to join him.[261] For most of Islamic history, it may be apt to describe forbidding wrong as an apanage of the scholars.[262] But there is enough of a mismatch to give us cause to wonder how it was that they came into such an apanage – and whether they could hope to retain it under modern conditions.

[259] Badīʿ al-Zamān, *Rasāʾil*, 489.5, as translated by Richards.
[260] See above, ch. 4, note 33. [261] See above, ch. 14, note 221.
[262] See above, note 150.

PART V

BEYOND CLASSICAL ISLAM

CHAPTER 18

MODERN ISLAMIC DEVELOPMENTS

1. INTRODUCTION

When treating the pre-modern period of Islamic thought in the preceding chapters, it made sense to organise the bulk of the material in terms of sects and schools. One of many respects in which the Western impact has profoundly changed the Islamic world is that these affiliations have tended to lose their former salience. The significant divisions within Islamic thought are no longer those between Ḥanafīs and Shāfiʿites, or Ashʿarites and traditionalists. Even the lines of division between Sunnīs, Zaydīs and Ibāḍīs no longer support much in the way of intellectual superstructure, whatever role they may play in the communal politics of the relevant parts of the Islamic world. Of the main sects and schools in terms of which the bulk of this book has been organised, only the Imāmī Shīʿites remain strongly differentiated from the broad spectrum of modern Islam.

This remaining division is, however, very real. It is not simply that the heritages of the Sunnīs and Imāmīs are in some ways very different in content and character. The contrast that will occupy us in this chapter relates rather to the dissimilar fates of the two scholastic traditions. That of the Sunnīs has become precisely a heritage (*turāth*): rather like a revered monument, it is cherished by people who no longer really inhabit it. The Imāmī scholastic tradition, by contrast, can still be described as a living one, owing its continuity and adaptation to scholars who operate within it. It may be that the difference is in some ways more apparent than real, and that in the long run it will disappear. But to date it remains a striking one. Accordingly this chapter is divided into two major sections. The first deals with the mainstream, overwhelmingly Sunnī, forms of modern Islamic thought, and the second with Imāmī Shīʿism. I shall return to the comparison between the two evolutions in the concluding section.

The chapter is subject to several limitations. First, in analysing recent Muslim discussions of forbidding wrong, I have deliberately concentrated on changes which have taken place in response to contemporary conditions of life and thought. Much space in the modern literature is devoted to repeating what was said by the medieval scholars; while this process is an essential part of the background to the developments described in this chapter, it would not be illuminating to investigate it in any detail. Secondly, I have not even tried to achieve a comprehensive coverage of the literature. The documentation for earlier centuries has been reduced to almost manageable proportions by the ravages of time; while much of value has doubtless been lost, it is surely also the case that a great deal of chaff has been winnowed out. This is emphatically not true of contemporary literature, for all that it is conventional for writers on forbidding wrong to lament that their topic is a neglected one.[1] I have made it my business to examine all modern discussions of the subject that have come my way, and in particular I have consulted all monographs on the duty that were available to me, if only in the manner of Ibn Sīnā (d. 428/1037).[2] But I have not, for example, made any attempt to cover systematically the large amount of relevant material that can be found scattered in Muslim journals and newspapers. Finally, the fact that we are dealing with the contemporary world opens up the possibility of escaping the confines of the literary record by recourse to field-work. I am all in favour of this; but I have not attempted it myself.

2. DEVELOPMENTS IN SUNNĪ ISLAM

For a long time the Western penetration of the Muslim world had little visible impact on the aspect of Islamic thought that concerns us. On the one hand, the religious scholars continued to write about forbidding wrong in the traditional way. This is true, for example, of the handling of Q3:104 in the Koran commentaries of Shawkānī (d. 1250/1834),[3] Maḥmūd al-Ālūsī (d. 1270/1854),[4] and Ṣiddīq Ḥasan Khān al-Qannawjī

[1] For a Sunnī example of this topos, so familiar in our own academic culture, see ʿAbd al-ʿAzīz ibn Aḥmad al-Masʿūd, *al-Amr biʾl-maʿrūf waʾl-nahy ʿan al-munkar wa-āthāruhumā fī ḥifẓ al-umma*, vol. 1, Riyāḍ 1414, 7.19; this author proceeds to make good by offering us a first volume of 571 pages (for a survey of what is yet to come, see *ibid.*, 26–32). For a Shīʿite example, see Sayyid Maḥmūd Madanī Bajistānī, *Amr bah maʿrūf wa nahy az munkar: do farīḍa-i bartar dar sīra-i maʿṣūmīn*, Qumm 1376 sh., 10.19.

[2] For Ibn Sīnā's reading habits, see R. Mottahedeh, *The mantle of the Prophet*, New York 1985, 88f. I am also aware of the existence of some dozen monographs on the duty to which I have not had access.

[3] Shawkānī (d. 1250/1834), *Fatḥ al-qadīr*, Cairo 1964, 1:369.15. In this context we can treat Shawkānī as in effect a Sunnī.

[4] Maḥmūd al-Ālūsī (d. 1270/1854), *Rūḥ al-maʿānī*, Cairo 1301–10, 1:643.9. An unusual feature in a Sunnī work is the reference to 'Shaykh Abū Jaʿfar [al-Ṭūsī] among the

(d. 1307/1890).[5] And on the other hand, few Muslims of this period whose thought was strongly influenced by the West seem to have shown much interest in forbidding wrong.[6]

Even when Western influence begins to affect the discussion of the duty, much remains essentially familiar. A good example of this is the salience of Ghazzālī (d. 505/1111). This, of course, is nothing new,[7] but my impression is that it becomes even more pronounced in modern times. Thus Qāsimī quotes Ghazzālī in his commentary to Q3:104,[8] as does Muḥammad ʿAbduh (d. 1323/1905).[9] Ḥaydarīzāde, as we have seen, based his Turkish account of the duty, written towards the end of the First World War, on that of Ghazzālī.[10] When ʿAbd al-Qādir ʿAwda (d. 1374/1954) wrote his treatise on Islamic criminal law some three decades later, he too drew most of the structure of his analysis of forbidding wrong from Ghazzālī.[11] More recent writers have followed suit.[12] Thus the Indian scholar Jalāl al-Dīn

Imāmiyya' as holding the view that *al-amr biʾl-maʿrūf* is an individual obligation (*ibid.*, 643.25; cf. above, ch. 11, note 156). This information doubtless derives from Ṭabrisī, *Majmaʿ*, 1:484.3; for the use Ālūsī made of Ṭabrisī's commentary, see M. ʿAbd al-Ḥamīd, *al-Ālūsī mufassiran*, Baghdad 1968, 205f.

5 Ṣiddīq Ḥasan Khān al-Qannawjī (d. 1307/1890), *Fatḥ al-bayān*, ed. ʿA. I. al-Anṣārī, Sidon and Beirut 1992, 2:304.4. The same is still true of Jamāl al-Dīn al-Qāsimī (d. 1332/1914) (*Maḥāsin al-taʾwīl*, ed. M. F. ʿAbd al-Bāqī, Beirut 1994, 2:107.10).

6 For two exceptions, see below, note 37.

7 See above, ch. 16, 450–5.

8 Qāsimī, *Maḥāsin*, 2:108.7, 108.18 (the latter a quotation of Ghazzālī's opening statement on *al-amr biʾl-maʿrūf*, a favourite with later generations). Qāsimī also wrote an epitome of the *Iḥyāʾ*, in which he naturally summarised Ghazzālī's doctrine of *al-amr biʾl-maʿrūf* (*Mawʿiẓat al-muʾminīn min Iḥyāʾ ʿulūm al-dīn*, ed. ʿA. B. al-Bayṭār, Beirut 1981, 243–50).

9 Rashīd Riḍā (d. 1354/1935), *Tafsīr al-Manār*, based on lectures of Muḥammad ʿAbduh, Cairo 1367–75, 4:30.13 (quoting ʿAbduh), and cf. 30.24, 31.4, 33.17; the set of this work that I used mixes volumes of various printings. For a discussion of the commentary on Q3:104 in the *Tafsīr al-Manār*, see Roest Crollius, 'Mission and morality', 275–82. Another author of this period who makes marked use of Ghazzālī in a brief account of *al-amr biʾl-maʿrūf* is Zammār (writing 1329/1911) (*al-Ḥukm waʾl-intiẓām*, Aleppo n.d., 26.6, 26.16, 29.8; he also quotes Ghazzālī's opening statement on *al-amr biʾl-maʿrūf*, *ibid.*, 5.4).

10 See above, ch. 12, 330–3, where the dependence of Osman Nuri on Ḥaydarīzāde is also noted. A later Turkish academic writer likewise cites Ḥaydarīzāde for the 'fundamental bases' (*temel esaslar*, sc. *arkān*) of the duty (E. Eşrefoğlu, 'İslâmiyetde ihtisâbın prensipleri', *Tarih Dergisi*, 25 (1971), 99).

11 ʿAbd al-Qādir ʿAwda (d. 1374/1954), *al-Tashrīʿ al-jināʾī al-Islāmī*, Cairo n.d., 1:489–513 §§340–50. The dependence is particularly clear – and acknowledged – at *ibid.*, 495–510 §§343–6. I owe this and several other references in this chapter to the kindness of Tufan Buzpınar of the İslâm Araştırmaları Merkezi, Üsküdar, who made available to me the relevant files of the Centre.

12 In addition to the examples given in the text, see Nashʾat al-Miṣrī, *al-Amr biʾl-maʿrūf waʾl-nahy ʿan al-munkar min Tafsīr Ibn Kathīr wa-shurūḥ Abī Ḥāmid al-Ghazzālī*, Cairo n.d., the title of which is self-explanatory (I am indebted to Maribel Fierro for sending me a copy of this work); Muḥammad Aḥmad al-Rāshid, *al-Munṭalaq*, Beirut 1976, 90.3, 151–4; Fārūq ʿAbd al-Majīd Ḥamūd al-Sāmarrāʾī, *Manāhij al-ʿulamāʾ fī ʾl-amr biʾl-maʿrūf waʾl-nahy ʿan al-munkar*, Jedda 1407, 9.2 (quoting Ghazzālī's opening statement), 54.14, 57.7,

ʿAmrī makes extensive use of Ghazzālī's account in a short but learned work devoted to the duty,[13] and the Syrian fundamentalist Saʿīd Ḥawwā (d. 1409/1989) likewise draws on it heavily.[14] Another Syrian, Aḥmad ʿIzz al-Dīn al-Bayānūnī, lifts most of the structure of his little book on forbidding wrong from Ghazzālī's account.[15] The well-known Algerian fundamentalist preacher ʿAlī ibn Ḥājj (Ali Belhadj) makes considerable use of Ghazzālī in a series of mosque talks on forbidding wrong; when a questioner asks for guidance on reading, he is strongly recommended to consult Ghazzālī.[16] Ghazzālī's account is equally the single most important source behind the structure of the exposition of forbidding wrong given by Khālid ibn ʿUthmān al-Sabt, a Saʿūdī writer in the Wahhābī tradition.[17] Thus he

Footnote 12 (*cont.*)
58.9, 188.8; ʿAbd al-Karīm Zaydān, *al-Mufaṣṣal fī aḥkām al-mar'a wa'l-bayt al-Muslim*, Beirut 1993, 4:354 §3,551 (quoting Ghazzālī's opening statement); 359–63 §§3,561–8; 364 §3,571 (I owe my knowledge of this work to Asma Sayeed); ʿAbd al-ʿAẓīm Ibrāhīm al-Maṭʿanī, *Taghyīr al-munkar fī madhhab ahl al-sunna wa'l-jamāʿa*, Cairo 1990, 76.19 (making tacit use of a schema of Ghazzālī), 77.16 (quoting him in the same connection), 109.10 (introducing a series of quotations on the question of the ruler's permission) (I owe my knowledge of the existence of this work to the files of the İslâm Araştırmaları Merkezi, and my copy to Margaret Larkin); Muḥammad Nuʿaym Yāsīn, *al-Jihād: mayādīnuhu wa-asālībuhu*, Amman 1978, 193–6 (adopting a schema of Ghazzālī).

[13] Jalāl al-Dīn al-ʿAmrī, *al-Amr bi'l-maʿrūf wa'l-nahy ʿan al-munkar*, translated from the Urdu by M. A. A. al-Iṣlāḥī, Kuwait 1984 (I am much indebted to Nurit Tsafrir for procuring me a copy of this work); note particularly his use of Ghazzālī's framework of conditions (*ibid.*, 231–48, cf. above, ch. 16, 429–33) and levels (*ibid.*, 291–3, cf. above, ch. 16, 438–41). The author, a member of the Jamāʿat-i Islāmī in India, was born around 1356/1937, and the preface is dated 1966; an English translation was also published in Kuwait in 1984, with the author's name given as 'Maulana Jalaluddin Ansar Umri' in the translator's note (xii). All references below are to the Arabic translation.

[14] Saʿīd Ḥawwā (d. 1409/1989), *Jund Allāh: thaqāfatan wa-akhlāqan*, n.p. n.d., 367.11–368.13, 384.4–386.8. It is striking that such an author should owe more in this regard to Ghazzālī than to Ibn Taymiyya (d. 728/1328), for all that the latter is the favourite authority of the fundamentalists and the author of a work on *al-amr bi'l-maʿrūf* (for which see above, ch. 7, 151f.).

[15] Aḥmad ʿIzz al-Dīn al-Bayānūnī, *al-Amr bi'l-maʿrūf wa'l-nahy ʿan al-munkar*, Aleppo 1973. Note, for example, the presentation of the conditions (*ibid.*, 35–48) and levels (here termed *marātib*) (*ibid.*, 48–51). Explicit quotations from Ghazzālī appear towards the end of the work (*ibid.*, 182.4, 183.2, 186.5). The book is clearly aimed at a wide audience.

[16] ʿAlī ibn Ḥājj, *al-Amr bi'l-maʿrūf wa'l-nahy ʿan al-munkar*, a set of seven cassettes distributed by the Librarie Islamique el-Badr, Paris, 7:1 (i.e. cassette 7, side 1). I am indebted to Emmanuel Sivan for lending me the first of the set in November 1992; I purchased cassettes 3, 4, 6 and 7 in Paris in March 1993, but have not had access to cassettes 2 and 5. They represent a series of talks (*durūs*) given in mosques (*ibid.*, 3:1, 7:1); there is no indication of the date at which they were given. The other reading suggestions offered by Ibn Ḥājj are the Ḥanbalites Ibn Taymiyya and Khallāl (d. 311/923), and a work by a certain Dr Fāris Barakāt. It is clear from cassettes 3:2 and 6:1 that Ibn Ḥājj adopts Ghazzālī's levels (*darajāt*), but his main discussion of them unfortunately falls in cassette 5. For further examples of his debt to Ghazzālī, see below, notes 168, 181. For a brief account of Ibn Ḥājj's career, see S. Labat, 'Islamism and Islamists: the emergence of new types of politico-religious militants', in J. Ruedy (ed.), *Islamism and secularism in North Africa*, New York 1994, 112. In Arabic his name is written indifferently as 'Ibn Ḥājj' or 'Balḥājj'.

[17] For this author see above, ch. 8, note 148.

adopts Ghazzālī's distinctive terminology,[18] and goes on to organise his account in terms of Ghazzālī's four components.[19] The popularity of Ghazzālī with modern authors is no surprise: the appeal of his systematic yet practical approach had always been one that crossed the boundaries of sects and schools. In this and other ways, we are still in a conceptual landscape that is eminently recognisable.

Yet at the same time, these writings contain numerous reminders, sometimes subtle and sometimes jarring, that the old concepts are being deployed in a new setting. At the very least, the influence of the West gave new vitality to the traditional repertoire of wrongdoing. For example, we are told that at a time of military misfortune the khedive Ismāʿīl (r. 1280–96/1863–79) was reproved by an unnamed scholar at the Azhar, the reproof consisting of a well-known Prophetic tradition on forbidding wrong.[20] Later, in private, the scholar elaborated: how could the khedive expect succour from heaven when the Mixed Courts operated under a law which allowed usury, when fornication was permitted, and the drinking of wine legal? The khedive's response was: 'What can we do now that foreigners live side by side with us, and this is their civilisation?'[21] Or as the Lebanese Shaykh Fayṣal Mawlawī put it in 1404/1984 to an audience of Muslims living in France, 'European countries are nothing but wrongs'.[22] (To the traditional wrongs he adds the cinema.[23]) Others are concerned with the duty of journalists to forbid wrong with the tongue,[24] the status of cafés where there is no backgammon, card-playing or liquor,[25] and the

[18] Sabt, *Amr*, 147.12.

[19] *Ibid.*, 148–367; see the table of contents. Ghazzālī is mentioned quite often in the work (see, for example, *ibid.*, 110.14, 147.1, 316.2), but the degree of dependence is partly obscured by the frequency with which Sabt acknowledges intermediate sources for material which they in turn derive from Ghazzālī. Thus he gives references for such material to Ibn al-Ukhuwwa (*ibid.*, 258.16, a story about a man and his cat which Ibn al-Ukhuwwa has from Ghazzālī, *Iḥyāʾ*, 2:306.4), Ibn al-Naḥḥās (Sabt, *Amr*, 275 n. 1, a point that Ibn al-Naḥḥās has from the *Iḥyāʾ*, see above, ch. 16, note 35) and Ṭāshköprīzāde (Sabt, *Amr*, 357.10, a purple passage from the *Iḥyāʾ* for which see above, ch. 16, note 124). On occasion he criticises Ghazzālī (Sabt, *Amr*, 316.6). Ghazzālī's account is also behind numerous points of detail, such as the terms *al-ʿajz al-ḥissī* (*ibid.*, 105.1, see above, ch. 16, note 38) and *taqlīl al-ʿalāʾiq* (*ibid.*, 258.8, see Ghazzālī, *Iḥyāʾ*, 2:306.4, and cf. above, ch. 16, note 97).

[20] Muḥammad Sulaymān, *Min akhlāq al-ʿulamāʾ*, Cairo 1353, 100–2 no. 218, with the tradition at 101.7 (quoted in Sāmarrāʾī, *Manāhij*, 138–40). The *isnād* prefixed to the story, while imposing, is not reassuring as to its historicity. The tradition is that discussed above, ch. 3, 36f.

[21] Sulaymān, *Min akhlāq al-ʿulamāʾ*, 102.2.

[22] Shaykh Fayṣal Mawlawī, *al-Amr biʾl-maʿrūf waʾl-nahy ʿan al-munkar*, cassette distributed by the Union des Organisations Islamiques en France, Section d'Information, side 2 (*bilād Uruppā kullhā munkarāt*); I am grateful to Emmanuel Sivan for lending me the cassette. This cassette seems to be the same as that described in G. Kepel, *Les banlieues de l'Islam*, Paris 1987, 259–62, whence I take the dating; for Mawlawī himself, see *ibid.*, 258. I am indebted to Bernard Lewis for bringing Kepel's study to my attention.

[23] *Ibid.*, 262.

[24] ʿAlī al-Ṭanṭāwī, *Fuṣūl Islāmiyya*, Damascus 1960, 176.4 (this work was brought to my attention by Yitzhak Nakash).

[25] *Ibid.*, 177.2.

ethics of car-parking – this latter an extension of Ghazzālī's discussion of the tethering of animals in the street.[26] Bayānūnī's worries range from the sale of photographs of women to physical contact between males and females in crowded buses, posters advertising dirty films, cafés, playing-cards, and music on the radio and television;[27] but his most insistent concern is the un-Islamic practice of shaving beards.[28]

The novelties also invade the realm of ideas. The formidable curriculum for Islamic missionaries which Muḥammad ʿAbduh, or perhaps rather Rashīd Riḍā (d. 1354/1935), proposed in commenting on Q3:104 is in large part a modern one;[29] it includes, for example, political science (*ʿilm al-siyāsa*), by which Riḍā assures us that ʿAbduh did not mean the kind of thing that Ibn Taymiyya (d. 728/1328) had written, but rather the study of modern states (*duwal al-ʿaṣr*).[30] Likewise Western influence presumably played a part in ʿAbduh's departure from a strictly revelationist view of right and wrong.[31] Ḥawwā implicitly acknowledges the seepage of Western thought when he lists among the insults that do not dispense one from performing the duty accusations of reactionariness (*rajʿiyya*) and backwardness (*taʾakhkhur*).[32] Other Western ideas which eventually make their appearance range from social control[33] to the unconscious.[34] Western ideas are also, of course, attacked. One writer on forbidding wrong finds it necessary to include in his work a

[26] Miṣrī, *Amr*, 72.7; cf. above, ch. 16, note 105.

[27] Bayānūnī, *Amr*, 135f. no. 6; 137 nos. 3 and 6; 138 no. 11; 139 no. 2. These items form part of an updated version of Ghazzālī's survey of wrongs (*ibid.*, 132–41).

[28] *Ibid.*, 63.10 (a first-hand anecdote); 91.5; 126.8; 136 no. 8; 189.11; 192.10.

[29] Riḍā, *Tafsīr al-Manār*, 4:38–44. The concern with Islamic missionary activity in the commentary to Q3:104 is discussed in J. Jomier, *Le commentaire coranique du Manâr*, Paris 1954, 333–7.

[30] Riḍā, *Tafsīr al-Manār*, 4:42 no. 8. ʿAbduh's personal confession of the difficulty he experienced in rebuking people (*ibid.*, 29.11) also has a modern ring to it.

[31] He stresses that what is needed in order to know them apart is common sense rather than erudition (*ibid.*, 27.10); compare the relativism that Rashīd Riḍā infuses into the concept of *maʿrūf* in his commentary to Q7:199 (*ibid.*, 9:536.15), and his exegesis of Q9:67 (*ibid.*, 10:618.19). By contrast, other Sunnīs who pronounce on the question tend to adhere to purely revelationist views of *maʿrūf* and *munkar* (ʿAwda, *Tashrīʿ*, 1:492.1, 492.8; ʿAmrī, *Amr*, 98.12; ʿAbd al-Karīm Zaydān, *Uṣūl al-daʿwa*, Baghdad 1968, 144.13; Sāmarrāʾī, *Manāhij*, 43.10, 46.4, 262f. no. 5). Two exceptions are Jamāl al-Dīn Muḥammad Maḥmūd (*Uṣūl al-mujtamaʿ al-Islāmī*, Cairo and Beirut 1992, 196.5, 199.13, a work brought to my attention by Kambiz Eslami) and Zaydān in a more recent work (*Mufaṣṣal*, 4:353f. §§3,547–50).

[32] Ḥawwā, *Jund Allāh*, 362.13.

[33] S. Ahmet Arvasî, *İlm-i hâl*, Istanbul 1990, 169. He categorises *al-amr biʾl-maʿrūf* as an important form of *içtimaî murakabe*, parenthetically glossed *sosyal kontrol* (he also glosses *nefs muhasebesi* as 'auto-critique'). Harun Nasution, an Indonesian neo-Muʿtazilite, likewise equates *al-amr biʾl-maʿrūf* with social control (Martin, *Defenders of reason in Islam*, 191, and cf. 151).

[34] ʿAmrī, *Amr*, 273.3. He is discussing the efficacy (*taʾthīr*) condition, his point being that a rebuke addressed to a fellow-Muslim may work on his subconscious mind.

refutation of the determinist fallacies (*aqwāl bāṭila*) of Schopenhauer and Spinoza.[35]

All this, however, is pretty much peripheral to the conception of the duty itself. What of the pull of Western ideas on this? One context in which forbidding wrong has played a part has been the enterprise of proving that all good things found in the West are Islamic.[36] Here the duty has been pressed into service in connection with a spectrum of Western political values ranging from constitutionalism to revolution. A prime example of the constitutionalist invocation of the duty is provided by Rashīd Riḍā: building on a hint of ʿAbduh's, he contrives to find in Q3:104 a basis for government by a representative assembly such as is found in republics and limited monarchies.[37] Writers linking forbidding wrong to revolution have more to appeal to in their heritage. ʿAmrī, in a careful discussion of the question,[38] enlists Ibn Ḥazm (d. 456/1064),[39] Jaṣṣāṣ (d. 370/981)[40] and Juwaynī (d. 478/1085);[41] his conclusion tends to support their views.[42] The Egyptian Muḥammad ʿUmāra finds in forbidding wrong a duty of political participation (*al-ishtighāl bi'l-shu'ūn al-ʿāmma*);[43] if non-violent participation is ineffective, then revolution becomes a duty.[44] ʿUmāra does not reveal his source of inspiration here, but to the extent that it is not simply modern, it is likely to be Zaydī and Muʿtazilite: he has a liking for these sectarians unusual in someone of Sunnī background.[45] An Ibāḍī

[35] Sāmarrāʾī, *Manāhij*, 32–8.

[36] There are in fact two distinct enterprises which may motivate this search for equivalences: the desire to legitimise the adoption of X from the West by finding an Islamic antecedent for it, and the desire to defend Islam against the charge of lacking X.

[37] Riḍā, *Tafsīr al-Manār*, 4:37.20, 38.2, 46.9. Likewise the Tunisian Khayr al-Dīn Pāshā (d. 1307/1890) sets up an analogy between, on the one hand, representative assemblies and freedom of the press in Europe, and, on the other, the duty of the *ʿulamāʾ* and notables of the Islamic world to engage in *taghyīr al-munkarāt*; in both cases the point is to check the arbitrary behaviour of rulers (*al-iḥtisāb ʿalā 'l-dawla*) (*Muqaddimat kitāb Aqwam al-masālik*, Istanbul 1293, 14.11). In a similar way ʿAbd al-Raḥmān al-Kawākibī (d. 1320/1902) sees representative assemblies as entirely in accordance with Q3:104 (*Ṭabāʾiʿ al-istibdād*, Cairo n.d., 82.11). Both are discussed in K. S. al-Husry, *Origins of modern Arab political thought*, Delmar 1980, 46–9, 66f., 138f.

[38] ʿAmrī, *Amr*, 175–83.

[39] *Ibid.*, 179–81, citing Ibn Ḥazm, *Fiṣal*, 4:171–6; cf. above, ch. 14, 390, and ch. 17, note 69. This passage is the most sustained statement of the revolutionary implications of *al-amr bi'l-maʿrūf* I have seen in pre-modern Sunnī literature.

[40] ʿAmrī, *Amr*, 182f.; cf. above, ch. 12, 336f.

[41] *Ibid.*, 183.3; cf. above, ch. 13, note 56.

[42] *Ibid.*, 183.10.

[43] Muḥammad ʿUmāra, *al-Islām wa-ḥuqūq al-insān*, Cairo and Beirut 1989, 82.15, 116.9, and cf. 84.1 (*farīḍat al-ishām al-ījābī fī shu'ūn al-mujtamaʿ wa'l-dawla*).

[44] *Ibid.*, 84.2, 94.9.

[45] He responds enthusiastically to the polemical equation of predestinationism and political quietism by the Zaydī imam al-Hādī (d. 298/911) (ʿUmāra, *Rasāʾil*, 2:12–14; cf. above, ch. 10, note 42). The catholicity of his tastes is indicated by the fact that he is also an admirer of Howard Fast's *Spartacus* (*ibid.*, 1:18); Fast wrote the book so that his readers 'may take strength for our own troubled future and that they may struggle against oppression and

author adds his own tradition to the revolutionary chorus.[46] In the recent efflorescence of literature on Islam and human rights,[47] forbidding wrong occasionally appears in yet another role: as a fundamental guarantee (*ḍamān*) of human rights in Islam.[48] Thus Shaukat Hussain considers that 'the greatest sanction for the practical implementation of Human Rights' is the duty of forbidding wrong.[49]

Alongside these rather sweeping invocations of the duty, we also find it linked with particular political rights from the Western liberal tradition. Occasionally it is used as a foundation for freedom of association. Thus the deputy postmaster-general of Peshawar quotes Q3:104 as his proof-text for freedom of association, commenting that God has thereby 'given the right to form association for pursuit of righteousness'.[50] (As in this case, political rights in their Islamic versions have a tendency to be rights to do or say good Islamic things, not bad un-Islamic things.)[51] But the standard equation, and it is an old one, is with freedom of speech (or expression, or opinion).

Footnote 45 (*cont.*)
wrong' (*Spartacus*, New York 1952, following the copyright page). A modern Zaydī document which identifies *al-amr bi'l-ma'rūf* with, among other things, opposing injustice (*muqāwamat al-ẓulm*) is the manifesto of the Ḥizb al-Ḥaqq, the main Zaydī political party in Yemen (*Bayān mashrū' Ḥizb al-Ḥaqq*, n.p. n.d., 8f. no. 2; I am indebted to Bernard Haykel for sending me a copy of this passage). For the Ḥizb al-Ḥaqq and *al-amr bi'l-ma'rūf*, see also S. Carapico, *Civil society in Yemen*, Cambridge 1998, 145; for a reformist appeal to *al-amr bi'l-ma'rūf* in 1360/1941, see J. L. Douglas, *The Free Yemeni Movement, 1935–1962*, Beirut 1987, 54 (I owe both references to Frank Stewart).

46 Bukayr ibn Sa'īd A'washt, *Dirāsāt Islāmiyya fī 'l-uṣūl al-Ibāḍiyya*, Cairo 1988, 107.19, 108.8.

47 For an uncharitable assessment of this literature see A. E. Mayer, *Islam and human rights: tradition and politics*, Boulder 1995. I owe such familiarity as I have with it to my participation in a conference held in November 1993 at Yale Law School on 'Law, culture and human rights: Islamic perspectives in the contemporary world'.

48 Muḥammad Fatḥī 'Uthmān, *Min uṣūl al-fikr al-siyāsī al-Islāmī*, Beirut 1979, 330.13. For a Zaydī author who adduces *al-amr bi'l-ma'rūf* in a discussion proving that Zaydism bestows on the individual the best that modern thought has to offer, see Faḍīl, *Man hum al-Zaydiyya?*, 58.5 (drawn to my attention by Bernard Haykel).

49 Shaukat Hussain, *Human rights in Islam*, New Delhi 1990, 104, and cf. 49f., 87. It is not far-fetched to see in some aspects of *al-amr bi'l-ma'rūf* a value that could in principle contribute to the creation of a culture supportive of human rights – or some tolerably exigent Islamic versions of some of them – in the states of the modern Islamic world.

50 Fakhruddin Malick, 'Islamic concept of human rights', in S. M. Haider (ed.), *Islamic concept of human rights*, Lahore 1978, 59; similarly Abul A'lā Mawdūdī (d. 1399/1979), *Human rights in Islam*, Delhi n.d., 29 no. 7. Mawdūdī has a piece devoted to *al-amr bi'l-ma'rūf* in his *Mafāhīm Islāmiyya* (Jedda and Dammām 1987, 111–21), but it is surprisingly uninteresting.

51 Thus Shaukat Hussain, who likewise links *al-amr bi'l-ma'rūf* and freedom of association, specifies that the right is to be used for the propagation of 'virtue and righteousness' (*Human rights in Islam*, 61). As Houchang Chehabi points out to me, this phenomenon has parallels in the history of Catholic thought in modern times. Thus Pope Leo XIII (1878–1903), discussing 'liberty of speech' in an encyclical of 1888, affirms that men have a right to propagate 'what things soever are true and honorable', but that 'lying opinions' and 'vices which corrupt the heart' should be 'diligently repressed by public authority' (J. J. Wynne (ed.), *The great encyclical letters of Pope Leo XIII*, New York 1903, 152).

Muwayliḥī (d. 1348/1930) adumbrates this in a jocular passage in which he identifies journalists as playing the part of 'those who command right and forbid wrong to whom Islamic law refers'.[52] A typical example of the linkage is found in a work of Saʿīd Muḥammad Aḥmad Bā Nāja.[53] He cites Article 19 of the Universal Declaration of Human Rights regarding freedom of opinion and expression, emphasising at the same time that governments – both Eastern and Western – have imposed serious restrictions on it. He then turns to Islam, and to the high status it confers on freedom of opinion as an individual right. Forbidding wrong, he points out, is among the most important duties of Islam, and its realisation necessarily requires freedom of opinion, as is apparent from many Koranic verses. He goes on to explain that this is not, of course, a right to propagate views contrary to Islamic beliefs or morals, and so forth. Thus Islam, he concludes, secures freedom of opinion and thought. Numerous authors associate forbidding wrong with freedom of speech in these or similar terms.[54] Some make separate reference to a right of protest or the like against rulers, and they have no problem in grounding this in forbidding wrong.[55]

[52] Muḥammad al-Muwayliḥī (d. 1348/1930), *Ḥadīth ʿĪsā ibn Hishām*, Cairo 1907, 41.9, translated in R. Allen, *A period of time*, Reading 1992, 137 (I am indebted to Roger Allen for drawing my attention to this passage). Cf. also above, notes 24, 37.

[53] Saʿīd Muḥammad Aḥmad Bā Nāja, *Dirāsa muqārina ḥawla 'l-Iʿlān al-ʿālamī li-ḥuqūq al-insān*, Beirut 1985, 49–51.

[54] See Hüseyin Kâzım Kadri (d. 1352/1934), *İnsan hakları beyannamesi'nin İslâm hukukuna göre izahı*, Istanbul 1949, 72.10, 73.3; ʿAbd al-Ḥamīd Mutawallī, *Mabādi' niẓām al-ḥukm fī 'l-Islām*, Alexandria 1974, 280.11; Muḥammad al-Mubārak, *Niẓām al-Islām: al-ḥukm wa'l-dawla*, Beirut and Cairo 1974, 121.1, 121.19 (I am indebted to Yitzhak Nakash for drawing this work to my attention); Muḥammad Maʿrūf al-Dawālībī, *al-Dawla wa'l-sulṭa fī 'l-Islām*, Beirut 1983, 56f., point 3 (also drawn to my attention by Yitzhak Nakash); Zaydān, *Uṣūl al-daʿwa*, 175–7 §§195f.; Ṣubḥī Maḥmaṣānī (d. 1407/1986), *Arkān ḥuqūq al-insān: baḥth muqārin fī 'l-sharīʿa al-Islāmiyya wa'l-qawānīn al-ḥadītha*, Beirut 1979, 143.16; Muḥammad Aḥmad Khiḍr, *al-Islām wa-ḥuqūq al-insān*, Beirut 1980, 32.6; al-Hay'a al-ʿĀmma lil-Istiʿlāmāt, *Ḥuqūq al-insān fī 'l-Islām*, n.p. n.d., 9.11; Aḥmad Bukayr, 'al-Ḍamīr al-dīnī wa-ḥuqūq al-insāniyya fī 'l-Islām', in Université de Tunis, Centre d'Etudes et de Recherches Economiques et Sociales, *IIIème Rencontre Islamo-Chrétienne: Droits de l'homme*, Tunis 1985, Arabic section, 152.12; Muḥammad Sayyid Muḥammad, 'Ḥaqq al-taʿlīm wa'l-iʿlām fī 'l-Islām', in *Ḥuqūq al-insān fī 'l-Islām: maqālāt al-Mu'tamar al-sādis lil-fikr al-Islāmī*, n.p. n.d. (conference held in Tehran in 1408/1988), 478.17 (speaking of a *ḥaqq al-iʿlām*); Malick, 'Islamic concept of human rights', 57–9; Hussain, *Human rights in Islam*, 51. As with Bā Nāja's exposition, a widespread feature of these accounts is the limitation of the freedom to good opinions. Thus Hussain in the passage just cited explains that 'this freedom of opinion must be used for propagation of virtue and truth and not for spreading evil or wickedness'; cf. Mayer, *Islam and human rights*, 76f., and J. Donnelly, *The concept of human rights*, New York 1985, 49f. (both commenting critically on this feature of Islamic human rights literature; Donnelly's work was drawn to my attention by Rhoda Howard).

[55] Bā Nāja, *Dirāsa*, 30.5, on *ḥaqq al-murāqaba*; Mubārak, *Niẓām*, 38–40, point 6; Khiḍr, *al-Islām wa-ḥuqūq al-insān*, 43.15; Jamāl al-Dīn ʿAṭiyya, 'Ḥuqūq al-insān fī 'l-Islām: al-naẓariyya al-ʿāmma', in *Ḥuqūq al-insān fī 'l-Islām: maqālāt al-Mu'tamar al-khāmis lil-fikr al-Islāmī*, Tehran 1987, 175 no. 3 (*raqābat taṣarrufāt al-wulāt*); Hussain, *Human rights in Islam*, 49f., 87.

The results of this syncretic activity are uneven. Sometimes they are quite plausible, as when forbidding wrong is linked to protest and revolution. But where the match is with liberal values, the effect can be jarring. The reason is not far to seek. Islam, within certain limits, tells people what to believe and how to live; liberalism, within certain limits, is about leaving them to work this out for themselves. It is this incompatibility that lies behind the unhappy notion of a right to freedom of opinion which protects only good opinions.[56] What makes the disparity so salient in the discussions that concern us is that forbidding wrong is precisely a practice for telling people what to believe and how to live – for imposing family values, not for enabling people to choose their lifestyles. This point has not been lost on modern Muslim writers, who have long been critical of excessive freedom in the West.[57] Sayyid Quṭb (d. 1386/1966) remarks that in the Jāhilī societies of the world today, debauchery and sin are considered to be 'personal matters' (*masāʾil shakhṣiyya*) in which no one has a right to interfere;[58] you tell people 'this is wrong!', and they respond: 'On the contrary, it's not wrong; it used to be wrong in the past, but the world "evolves", society "progresses", and attitudes vary.'[59] A more earthy writer contemporary with Quṭb opens his discussion of forbidding wrong with a characterisation of the modern, as opposed to the Islamic, fashion (*mōḍa*).[60] The modern fashion has it that people are free, nobody having any authority over anyone else, or any right to interfere in his affairs; if you see someone naked in a tram, or bad-mouthing religion, or drinking wine, or gambling, or kissing girls in the middle of the street, so what? The characterisation he then offers of the Islamic fashion stresses that the community is a single body; a public wrongdoer does harm not just to himself, but to you as well. He invokes a well-known Prophetic tradition about people in a boat who perish or survive together depending on their reaction to some of their number who set about making a hole in the keel – a clear indication that

[56] ʿAmrī, by contrast, simply dismisses the modern notion of freedom of thought where the well-being of the Muslim community is concerned, since it is a community united in its thought (*Amr*, 328.9).

[57] Already in a discussion of *al-amr biʾl-maʿrūf* as the basis of Islamic government, a religious scholar affiliated to the Cairo branch of the Committee of Union and Progress wrote that European states, while forbidding public wrongs, permit many personal vices in order to maximise freedom (*faḍla iṭlāq-i ḥürriyet bahānesiyle*) (Meḥmed Qadrī Nāṣiḥ (*fl.* early fourteenth/twentieth century), *Ẓulm ve ʿadl*, n.p. 1326, 168.7 (I am indebted to Şükrü Hanioğlu for supplying me with a copy of this text); for the author and his role in the Cairo branch of the Committee of Union and Progress, see M. Ş. Hanioğlu, *The Young Turks in opposition*, New York and Oxford 1995, 52, 248 n. 253; S. Balić, *Das unbekannte Bosnien*, Cologne 1992, 238, drawn to my attention by Şükrü Hanioğlu).

[58] Sayyid Quṭb (d. 1386/1966), *Fī ẓilāl al-Qurʾān*, Beirut 1973–4, 949.12 (to Q5:79).

[59] *Ibid.*, 950.10. [60] Ṭanṭāwī, *Fuṣūl*, 174.2.

the modern enemy is not just libertinism but also individualism.[61] Ibn Ḥājj attacks those who seek to emasculate the duty on the pretext that we live in a time of democracy and liberty, and that every individual is a free agent, as if democracy could abrogate this duty, which many today regard as interference in the lives of others and in itself a form of violence.[62] In the same article he invites the believers to sympathise with some upstanding young men who had gone to break up a dancing party, and were received by the police with a hail of tear-gas bombs.[63] Anonymous participants in a bottle-smashing incident which took place in B'rrāqī near Algiers in 1410/1989 give a vivid account of the affair, in the course of which they highlight the outrageous response of the vintner: 'Boumedienne permits taverns for wine and mosques for prayer; it's up to you to choose!'[64] It was with some foresight that Louis Gardet once wrote that forbidding wrong as moral reform ('réforme des moeurs'), though currently held in check by the modern state, was alive in the sentiments of the Muslim people, and could well reemerge in favourable circumstances.[65]

It is not surprising, then, that in the modern Islamic world forbidding wrong appears primarily as a praxis for the spreading of Islamic, not liberal, values. Conceived in this fashion, it is not in any flagrant discord with the old scholastic tradition; but we can nevertheless discern a significant shift of emphasis. The core of the old conception was a personal duty to right wrongs committed by fellow-believers as and when one encountered them; the core of the new conception is a systematic and organised propagation of Islamic values both within and outside the community. A couple of points may serve to illustrate the shift away from the old conception of the duty as primarily one of response by an individual to an immediate situation. One is the view of ʿAbd al-Karīm Zaydān that a Muslim has an obligation to be

61 *Ibid.*, 174.11; compare ʿAbd al-Muʿizz ʿAbd al-Sattār, *al-Amr biʾl-maʿrūf waʾl-nahy ʿan al-munkar*, Beirut and Damascus 1980, 10.14 (and cf. *ibid.*, 7.9, 16.8). For the boat tradition in classical sources, see, for example, Bukhārī, *Ṣaḥīḥ*, 2:111.19, 164.7; Ibn Ḥibbān, *Ṣaḥīḥ*, in the arrangement of Fārisī, 1:306–9 nos. 294f., 297. In Ibn Ḥibbān's first version, which is actually more apt than the versions of Bukhārī which modern Islamic authors cite, someone remarks: 'Leave him alone! He's only making a hole in his own place!' (*ibid.*, 306.13). Compare a version in an Ibāḍī source where the person making the hole says: 'It's my place, I can do what I like here!' (Abū Bakr al-Kindī, *Muṣannaf*, 12:11.7). The tradition is not usually made much of by pre-modern writers on forbidding wrong; but for an exception, see Ibn al-Naḥḥās, *Tanbīh*, 87.13–89.17.

62 ʿAlī Ibn Ḥājj, 'Man ṣāḥib al-ʿunf?', *al-Munqidh* (Algiers), 28 Jumādā II, 1410, 3d.49, translated in M. al-Ahnaf *et al.*, *L'Algérie par ses islamistes*, Paris 1991, 139. I owe all my material from *al-Munqidh* to Abdeslam Maghraoui, who kindly suppied me with copies.

63 Ibn Ḥājj, 'Man ṣāḥib al-ʿunf?', 2e.61, translated in Ahnaf, *Algérie*, 135.

64 *Ibid.*, 142 = anon., 'Hal atāka nabaʾ al-B'rrāqī?!', *al-Munqidh*, second half of Rabīʿ I, 1410, 2b.16. The article stresses that the action was taken only after less drastic measures had failed.

65 L. Gardet, *La cité musulmane*, Paris 1961, 187.

in a state of (psychological) readiness (*istiʿdād wa-tahayyuʾ*) to carry out the duty;[66] Zaydān, characteristically, is writing a work in a modern genre which might be called 'mission theory'. The other point is a tendency to emphasise long-term results. An example of this is ʿAmrī's argument, in the context of a discussion of the efficacy condition, that a reproof which goes unheeded in the short run may nevertheless work on the offender's subconscious mind.[67] But these are subtleties. By far the most obvious and widespread sign of the times is a new concern with organisation.

ʿAbduh's commentary on Q3:104 as developed by Riḍā is an early example of this concern, and it already places it in a context of mission theory. On the assumption that the 'community' who are to perform the duty are a subgroup of the community at large,[68] they proceed to discuss the nature of this subgroup. Sometimes, as we have seen, they appear to be talking about constitutional government.[69] But in one extended passage, they seem to be thinking primarily of missionaries,[70] whether their efforts be directed towards Muslims or non-Muslims.[71] This enterprise needs organisation: it should be in the hands of what these days is called an association (*jamʿiyya*), and it needs a leadership (*riyāsa*) to direct it.[72] The theme of organisation recurs in two anonymous – and somewhat vacuous – reformist letters published in a religious journal in 1333/1915[73] and 1334/1916.[74] Zaydān likewise stresses the need for the duty to be performed by organised groups,[75] and he is far from alone in this.[76] Thus

[66] Zaydān, *Uṣūl al-daʿwa*, 145.14. He is commenting on the 'three modes' tradition, from which he contrives to infer this obligation. [67] See above, note 34.

[68] See above, ch. 2, 17–20. We are not told whether or not this assumption is correct.

[69] See above, note 37. [70] See above, note 29.

[71] Cf. Riḍā, *Tafsīr al-Manār*, 4:27.18, 35.2 (non-Muslims); *ibid.*, 47.4 (both Muslims and non-Muslims). [72] *Ibid.*, 45.7, 47.1.

[73] Anon., 'Ḥāl al-Muslimīn al-yawm wa-Jamāʿat al-daʿwa wa'l-irshād', *al-Manār*, 18 (1333), 793.17, 794.16, 794.24 (calling for the establishment of such an association).

[74] Anon., 'Ḥāl al-Muslimīn al-ijtimāʿiyya wa-farīḍat al-amr bi'l-maʿrūf wa'l-nahy ʿan al-munkar', *al-Manār*, 19 (1334–5), 256.20. The reformist platform is clearly articulated in a passage denouncing indigenous tomb-cults and Western materialism (*ibid.*, 251.13).

[75] Zaydān, *Uṣūl al-daʿwa*, 271f. §351, esp. 272.6, 272.17.

[76] See Muḥammad ʿIzzat Darwaza (d. 1404/1984), *al-Tafsīr al-ḥadīth*, Cairo 1962–4, 5:14.12 (speaking of *al-jamāʿāt wa'l-munaẓẓamāt al-ijtimāʿiyya*, whose role he distinguishes from that of *man bi-yadihi 'l-sulṭān*); ʿUmāra, *al-Islām wa-ḥuqūq al-insān*, 116.12; ʿUthmān, *Min uṣūl al-fikr al-siyāsī al-Islāmī*, 261.25; Muḥammad ʿAlī Masʿūd, *al-Amr bi'l-maʿrūf wa'l-nahy ʿan al-munkar*, Cairo 1980, 58.4, 94.10; ʿAṭiyya, 'Ḥuqūq al-insān fī 'l-Islām', 147.27 (with the qualification that this should not limit the scope of individual activity); see also L. Gómez García, *Marxismo, islam e islamismo: el proyecto de Adil Husayn*, Madrid 1996, 338, 340 (this study was drawn to my attention by Maribel Fierro). The Basic Principles Committee of the Constituent Assembly of Pakistan recommended in 1952 that an organisation should be set up to make the teachings of Islam known to the people and to perform the duty (Basic Principles Committee, *Report*, Karachi 1952, 2, drawn to my attention by Yohanan Friedmann). The manifesto of the Zaydī Ḥizb al-Ḥaqq speaks of the

Ḥawwā explains that Muslims living in a corrupt Islamic state (*dawla Islāmiyya munḥarifa*) should organise performance of the duty 'with the hand'; this operation should avoid collision with the state, and should take as its target wrongs perpetrated by individuals (musical instruments, pictures of nudes, liquor, or the flaunting of female sexuality).[77] Sometimes it is hard to tell whether authors have in mind groups to be formed within the society or the official activity of the state.[78] The former is clearly envisaged in the Islamic human right of free association for the purposes of forbidding wrong.[79] Such societies for forbidding wrong have indeed been established from time to time; one was set up in Palestine in the time of the Mandate,[80] another is mentioned in Egypt.[81]

A sense of what has changed with this espousal of organisation can be obtained from a work in the mission theory genre by Muḥammad Aḥmad al-Rāshid.[82] His concern is to show that the great authorities of the past proclaimed the legality of collective action (*al-ʿamal al-jamāʿī*) in forbidding wrong, and thus to refute the claim that such action is an innovation alien to Islamic norms.[83] To this end, he collects some examples of traditional figures who are said to have performed the duty together with a group of associates.[84] Texts such as these, he remarks, are valuable discoveries which

need to develop a proper mode of performance of the duty 'on the part of individuals and groups (*jamāʿāt*)' (for this passage, see above, note 45).

77 Ḥawwā, *Jund Allāh*, 392 no. 6 (and see 391.1). He speaks here of *tanẓīm ʿamaliyyat al-jihād bi'l-yad*; but he has already defined his terms in such a fashion that *jihād* within the Islamic world is synonymous with *al-amr bi'l-maʿrūf*, *ibid.*, 364.8. For Ḥawwā's personal experience in this line of duty, see I. Weismann, 'Saʿid Hawwa: the making of a radical Muslim thinker in modern Syria', *Middle Eastern Studies*, 29 (1993), 613), and for his doctrine of *jihād*, see I. Weismann, 'Saʿid Hawwa and Islamic revivalism in Baʿthist Syria', *Studia Islamica*, 85 (1997), 149–53.

78 For passages where the term *tanẓīm* clearly refers to the latter, see ʿAwda, *Tashrīʿ*, 1:501.5; ʿAmrī, *Amr*, 244.2; Zaydān, *Mufaṣṣal*, 4:370 §3,584. Maḥmūd speaks of *tanẓīm* as desirable (*Uṣūl al-mujtamaʿ al-Islāmī*, 203.21), but is vague as to what he has in mind. A clear case where *tanẓīm* does not refer to the efforts of the state is the passage by Ḥawwā cited in the preceding note.

79 Hussain, *Human rights in Islam*, 114, art. XIV(a), and Mayer, *Islam and human rights*, 91 (both quoting the Universal Islamic Declaration of Human Rights, adopted by the Islamic Council of Europe in Paris in 1401/1981); cf. Munaẓẓamat al-Muʾtamar al-Islāmī, 'Wathīqat ḥuqūq al-insān fī 'l-Islām', in *Ḥuqūq al-insān fī 'l-Islām: maqālāt al-Muʾtamar al-khāmis lil-fikr al-Islāmī*, Tehran 1987, 559, art. 22(b).

80 See U. M. Kupferschmidt, *The Supreme Muslim Council: Islam under the British Mandate for Palestine*, Leiden 1987, 249f., on the *Jamʿiyyat al-amr bi'l-maʿrūf wa'l-nahy ʿan al-munkar al-markaziyya* of 1353/1935; note that the founders rendered the name of the society into English as 'Central Society for the Preservation of Public Morals'. I owe this reference to Mike Doran.

81 E. Sivan, *Radical Islam: medieval theology and modern politics*, New Haven and London 1985, 85. 82 Rāshid, *Munṭalaq*, 146–54. 83 *Ibid.*, 146.14, 148.6.

84 *Ibid.*, 149.12. The three examples given are the Companion Hishām ibn Ḥakīm ibn Ḥizām (see above, ch. 4, note 97), ʿAbd al-Raḥīm al-ʿAlthī (see above, ch. 6, note 103), and Abū Bakr al-Aqfālī (see above, ch. 17, note 204).

should take their place in the law of Islamic activism (***al-fiqh al-ḥarakī***).[85] He then quotes Ghazzālī's view that the permission of the ruler is not needed for the performance of forbidding wrong by armed bands.[86] This text, he adds, is one that should be written in letters of gold, and memorised by missionaries (***duʿāt***); it shows that the literature of the heritage (***kutub al-turāth***) abounds in sources for the law of activism.[87] Two things are noteworthy here. One is the gap between the precedents he invokes and the current practice he seeks to legitimise: the occasional examples of group action in the literature of the heritage never involve the kind of formal associations that have sprung up in the Islamic world under Western influence. The other is the sense of surprise that Rāshid displays.[88] He takes it for granted, not that his concerns and those of the heritage are identical, but that they come from different worlds; the relevance of the views of the medieval scholars to his own world is not an axiom but a discovery.

Who is it who is to engage in all this activity? One group that had traditionally been central to the performance of the duty gets remarkably little attention: the religious scholars. Two authors who still take them seriously are Sāmarrāʾī and Muḥammad ʿAlī Masʿūd. Much of what Sāmarrāʾī says about them is negative; but his high-flown rhetoric regarding the horrendous consequences of their silence in the face of wrongdoing does at least pay them the compliment of supposing that they matter.[89] In one of his rare expressions of personal opinion, he tells us that he feels it to be better for the duty to be undertaken by the scholars (***ʿulamāʾ***).[90] It may be that wrongdoing will become so rampant that they alone cannot handle it; in that case the individual members of the community are obligated to act – but under the leadership of their scholars.[91] Masʿūd seems to have in mind the old saying about the tripartite division of labour, though he does not quote it. The duty is to be performed in three modes (***marātib***). First, there is the mode of the rulers (***ḥukkām***),[92] who alone can use force. Second, there is that of the scholars, who are to perform the duty with their pens, tongues and ideas – but not with violence.[93] Finally, there are the common people (***ʿawāmm***), for whom he reserves a fairly energetic version of performance 'with the heart' – again without violence.[94] This ascribes a major

85 *Ibid.*, 151.9.
86 For this view see above, ch. 16, 441. Another figure who is very partial to this text is Ibn Ḥājj (see below, note 168). 87 Rāshid, *Munṭalaq*, 152.12.
88 See also *ibid.*, 147.5.
89 Sāmarrāʾī, *Manāhij*, 8–11. Ṣalāḥ al-Dīn al-Munajjid introduces a little anthology of encounters between *ʿulamāʾ* and rulers of the past with a similar lament (*al-Āmirūn biʾl-maʿrūf*, 5.3). 90 Sāmarrāʾī, *Manāhij*, 61.13. 91 *Ibid.*, 61.17.
92 Muḥammad ʿAlī Masʿūd, *Amr*, 24.2. 93 *Ibid.*, 27.1. 94 *Ibid.*, 30.15.

role to the scholars, though Masʿūd's concept of them is a broad and somewhat modernised one.[95]

A group that traditionally received rather little attention, and now gets significantly more, is women.[96] While no author actually denies their eligibility to perform the duty, ʿAmrī comes close to it: for although he is clearly composing his account with Ghazzālī's in front of him, he chooses to open his analysis of the conditions of obligation by stating that 'a man' (*al-rajul*) must be legally competent.[97] By contrast, an Egyptian academic writing on Zaydī thought reacts to the exclusion of women by the imam al-Muʾayyad Yaḥyā ibn Ḥamza (d. 749/1348f.) with the remark that he sees no ground for stipulating that the performer be male.[98] The Palestinian exegete Darwaza understands Q9:71 to establish the equality of women with men, in particular with regard to forbidding wrong.[99] The fact that he is alone in raising the question among the seventeen modern Sunnī exegetes whose commentaries I checked may suggest some reluctance to broach a sensitive issue.[100] Outside Koranic exegesis, however, the verse is quite often invoked to include women. Ibn Ḥājj takes it to say that the duty is incumbent on women as well as men – though he adds that women are a special case.[101] Muhammad Sharif Chaudhry interprets the verse to mean that Muslim men and women 'are severally and jointly responsible for enjoining the right and forbidding the wrong';[102] appropriately, his book has an introduction penned by his wife, Dr Nasreen Sharif of the Fatimah Jinnah Medical College. Faḍl Ilāhī, who teaches at a religious college in Riyāḍ, ends an otherwise somewhat arid work on the duty by calling on all male and female believers to concern themselves with forbidding wrong, and quoting the verse to

[95] He includes among them authors, school-teachers, preachers, spiritual guides, and whoever is learned in matters of religion (*ibid.*, 27.2).

[96] See above, ch. 17, 482–6.

[97] ʿAmrī, *Amr*, 246.11 (for his dependence on Ghazzālī, see above, note 13, and for the passage of the *Iḥyāʾ* that he is following at this point, see above, ch. 16, 429). Likewise in his comments on Q9:71, he does not take the opportunity to mention women (*ibid.*, 218.11). He does allow a wife to counsel her husband despite her subordination to him (*ibid.*, 344.1, citing Ghazzālī; cf. above, ch. 16, 431f.). An author who uses wording derived from Ghazzālī to include women is ʿAbd al-Wahhāb Rashīd Abū Ṣafiyya (*Sharḥ al-Arbaʿīn al-Nawawiyya fī thawb jadīd*, n.p. 1988, 399.15).

[98] Ṣubḥī, *Zaydiyya*, 310 n. 26; cf. above, ch. 10, notes 140f.

[99] Darwaza, *al-Tafsīr al-ḥadīth*, 12:186.8 (to Q9:71); and cf. *ibid.*, 9:71.21 (to Q4:34).

[100] Another plausible example of such reluctance is an article on forbidding wrong which appeared in an Egyptian women's journal, and yet never directly confronts the question (ʿAbd al-ʿAzīz al-Sharīf, 'al-Amr bi'l-maʿrūf wa'l-nahy ʿan al-munkar', *al-Nahḍa al-nisāʾiyya*, 9 (1931), 220–2, drawn to my attention by Beth Baron).

[101] Ibn Ḥājj, *Amr*, 1:2. There may be a fuller discussion of this verse on cassette 2.

[102] Muhammad Sharif Chaudhry, *Women's rights in Islam*, Delhi 1991, 148 no. 2.

make his point.[103] Fatḥī ʿUthmān cites the verse to show that in Islam women are not stripped of rights and duties, nor denied legal personality and social responsibility.[104]

A particularly strong proponent of female participation is ʿAbd al-Ḥalīm Muḥammad Abū Shuqqa, a pupil of Nāṣir al-Dīn al-Albānī. He adduces Q9:71 as a proof-text,[105] and finds examples in tradition (*ḥadīth*) of women performing the duty against men.[106] One of these is a story set among a tribal group which converted to Islam after the conquest of Mecca in the year 8/630. The best they could do for a prayer-leader was a boy of six or seven who happened to have learnt some of the Koran from travellers. Unfortunately his garment was so short that his bottom was exposed each time he prostrated himself. In response to this spectacle, a tribeswoman called out: 'Aren't you going to cover up your Koran-reciter's bottom from us?' (*a-lā tughaṭṭūn ʿannā ʾst qāriʾikum?*). The tribesmen thereupon made the boy's day by providing him with a shirt.[107] This is an original use of a tradition that plays no part in pre-modern discussions of forbidding wrong by women or anyone else.

What is less common is for these writers to face squarely the tensions between such views and the traditional subordination and seclusion of women. A generation ago Zaydān published a work in which he held that women should be involved in Muslim public affairs (though not in elections); he spoke of them performing the duty towards members of the family, neighbours, and other women[108] – but not, by implication, towards men in general. In a massive work on the legal status of women in Islam published a quarter of a century later, he is emphatic that women are obligated to perform the duty just as men are;[109] but again, he does not seem to think

[103] Faḍl Ilāhī, *al-Ḥisba: taʿrīfuhā wa-mashrūʿiyyatuhā wa-wujūbuhā*, Gujranwala 1993, 82.14. Ilāhī, whose work was drawn to my attention by Kambiz Eslami, uses the term *ḥisba* to cover both the official and individual duties.

[104] ʿUthmān, *Min uṣūl al-fikr al-siyāsī al-Islāmī*, 255.20.

[105] ʿAbd al-Ḥalīm Muḥammad Abū Shuqqa, *Taḥrīr al-marʾa fī ʿaṣr al-risāla*, Kuwait 1990–1, 1:89.6, and cf. 2:49.2, 223.2.

[106] *Ibid.*, 1:29.8, 2:49.16, 50.4, and cf. 226.9, 227.9.

[107] Bukhārī, *Ṣaḥīḥ*, 3:144.7. It is the boy, ʿAmr ibn Salima al-Jarmī (d. 85/704), who narrates the story in Baṣra in later life (see also Ibn Ḥanbal, *Musnad*, 5:30.1, 71.4; Abū Dāwūd, *Sunan*, 1:393f. no. 585; Ibn Saʿd, *Ṭabaqāt*, 7:1:63.16, 64.8, and cf. 64.12). This is not the only tradition of Bukhārī's that is manifestly intended to amuse us.

[108] Zaydān, *Uṣūl al-daʿwa*, 136.2, quoting Q9:71.

[109] Zaydān, *Mufaṣṣal*, 4:211f. §3,288, §3,291 (arguing that for this reason women too have freedom of opinion); 358 §3,557 (his key statement on the question). He inserts frequent references to women in rewriting the traditional rules (see, for example, *ibid.*, 356 §3,555 (*Muslim wa-Muslima*); 360 point *d* (*rajulan kāna aw imraʾa*); 363 §3,569 (*al-Muslim aw al-Muslima*)); he even does so in a text he takes from Qurṭubī (*ibid.*, 356 §3,554, citing Qurṭubī, *Jāmiʿ*, 4:47.11). He likewise extends Ghazzālī's remarks on boys who have not yet attained puberty to include girls in the same position (Zaydān, *Mufaṣṣal*, 4:360, point *a*; cf. above, ch. 16, 429). He states that some scholars had made no explicit

that they should do it to men, at least not outside the immediate family.[110] Instead, his earlier mention of women doing it to other women now reappears as a programme for endowing women with a parallel public space of their own. Thus where the state organises the duty officially, it may open a college to train female officers to perform it (*muḥtasibāt*).[111] Likewise Muslim women at the present day should undertake the duty as organised groups, forming female associations (*jamʿiyyāt nisāʾiyya*) for the purpose. These associations should operate among women, whether seeking them out in their homes or inviting them to their centres; they should publish weekly or monthly magazines, and arrange classes, lectures and discussions.[112] This, of course, is a rather progressive view. A more conservative attitude is represented by the Saʿūdī Khālid al-Sabt. Following Ghazzālī, he has no hesitation in taking the position that to be male is not a condition of obligation.[113] However, he goes on to make it very clear that we are talking about a woman in her own home; this is no licence for women to go outside their homes to practise the duty, involving themselves in religious and other affairs, as unfortunately happens so much these days.[114] Another conservative Saʿūdī author, ʿAbd al-ʿAzīz ibn Aḥmad al-Masʿūd, states that for women the normal mode of performance of the duty with respect to men is in the heart.[115] He does, however, take the view that they should do it to other women, and verbally to those males who are related to them.[116] This includes their husbands,[117] and, of course, their children; as he points out, they are well placed to perform the duty with regard to their children since, unlike men, they spend all their time at home.[118]

statement on the question of the performance of the duty by women because the answer was so obvious; he is at least able to invoke Ghazzālī's explicit statement on his side (*ibid.*, 358 §3,558; cf. above, ch. 16, note 15).

110 He repeats the old view that a wife may reprove her husband (*ibid.*, 362 §3,565; cf. above, ch. 16, 431f.); he adds a new twist by stating that a daughter may do it to her father (*ibid.*, 361 §3,564).

111 *Ibid.*, 370 §3,584.

112 *Ibid.*, 370 §3,585.

113 Sabt, *Amr*, 171.5; he quotes Q9:71 as a proof-text, *ibid.*, 172.6.

114 *Ibid.*, 172.11. He likewise disapproves of women showing their hands and faces (*ibid.*, 305.8), but he is by no means totally inflexible: in this age when the media have brought evil into every home, he is prepared to countenance Islamic summer centres for women on the principle of choosing the lesser evil (*ibid.*, 242.16). His general conservatism is indicated by the fact that he regards tobacco as a wrong on a par with drink, drugs, and the like (*ibid.*, 120.4, 217.11, 273.18, 353.11, and cf. 313.17).

115 ʿAbd al-ʿAzīz al-Masʿūd, *Amr*, 529.10.

116 *Ibid.*, 528.12.

117 *Ibid.*, 564.1.

118 *Ibid.*, 562.7. Comparable views are briefly set out by ʿAbd al-Ḥasīb Raḍwān: a woman is obligated, but her sphere is her home (including her husband) and her own sex (*Dirāsāt fī 'l-ḥisba*, Cairo 1990, 31.3, 32.20, 71.2; the author's name is vocalised 'Raḍwān' on the title-page). ʿAlī ibn Ḥasan al-Quranī says that a woman may forbid wrong within limits that do not lead her into anything legally perilous (*Ḥisba*, 111.8). Sāmarrāʾī remarks that some scholars have held that a woman may undertake the duty, but omits to name them (*Manāhij*, 68.5); he adduces traditions about ʿĀʾisha which would not support the idea of a woman reproving a man outside her immediate family.

What of the role of the state? This has always been a focus of tension, and it has become even more so with the rise of the modern state – under whatever ideological aegis – in the Islamic world. Thus Ḥawwā aptly remarks that the state in our epoch has come to hold sway over everything: education, instruction, the economy, the army, society, politics, intellectual life, culture.[119] In some Sunnī countries this has issued in forbidding wrong becoming a function of the state apparatus; this has long been the case in Saudi Arabia,[120] and more recently such a system has been established in Afghanistan.[121] The Saʿūdī model is not, however, widely discussed outside the kingdom, though it is occasionally mentioned.[122] Elsewhere there are broadly speaking two very different ways to react to the new salience of the state. One is to give ground and limit the performance of the duty to what modern conditions permit; the other is to capture the state for Islam, if necessary by revolution.[123]

[119] Ḥawwā, *Jund Allāh*, 396.10. Cf. also Maḥmūd, *Uṣūl al-mujtamaʿ al-Islāmī*, 207.10.

[120] See above, ch. 8, section 4.

[121] The Afghan system is known to me only from reports in the Western press, according to which the Ṭālibān established a 'Department for the Propagation of Virtue and the Prohibition of Vice' (or similar title) after their capture of Kabul in 1417/1996 (*New York Times*, 1 October 1996, 1; 29 August 1997, 4; 6 October 1997, 9; some of this material was sent to me by Robert Wisnovsky). According to the second of these reports, the rank and file of the religious police are called 'mohtasebs'. A photograph that appeared in a Madrid newspaper shows a member of the religious police armed with scissors good-humouredly cutting the fringe of a malefactor with curly hair at a crossroads in Kabul; he was apparently the fifty-seventh offender to get an involuntary haircut that day ('Flequillos satánicos en Afghanistán', *El País*, 5 November, 1997, 7, given to me by Maribel Fierro).

[122] When ʿAwda makes reference to a *hay'a* in connection with the organisation of *al-amr bi'l-maʿrūf* (*Tashrīʿ*, 1:500.12), it is likely enough that he has the Saʿūdī case in mind. The same is true when Muḥammad ʿAlī Masʿūd, a state-friendly author, calls for the formation of a *hay'a* of those involved in the *daʿwa* (*Amr*, 94.15). Ibn Ḥājj says that if the government of Algeria were Muslim, it could set up a special police force (*shurṭat al-amr bi'l-maʿrūf*) which would use force; such a police force does not, he continues, exist in any contemporary Muslim state – though by way of exception he makes a dismissive reference to the Ḥijāz (*Amr*, 3:2). It is, of course, no surprise that Abū Bakr Jābir al-Jazā'irī, who preaches in the Prophet's mosque in Medina, holds that Q3:104 requires the existence of committees (*hay'āt*) of *al-amr bi'l-maʿrūf* in all Muslim cities and villages (*Aysar al-tafāsīr*, Medina 1994, 1:358.16); in the same way Quranī extols the Saʿūdī system as a model for other Islamic countries (*Ḥisba*, 719.14, 831.7). But the enthusiastic endorsement of this system by the Egyptian ʿAbd al-Qādir Aḥmad ʿAṭā in the introduction to his edition of Khallāl (*Amr*, 67–9) is unusual in the literature I have consulted. Cf. also the view of the Jordanian Ibrāhīm al-Qaṭṭān (d. 1404/1984) that the special group performing the duty laid down in Q3:104 should be appointed by the ruler (*al-ḥākim*) so that anarchy can be avoided (*Taysīr al-tafsīr*, Amman 1982–, 1:286.15).

[123] I should perhaps also mention in passing the *ḥisba* procedure that has become notorious in the West through its recent use by Egyptian Islamists seeking to bring about the divorce of Naṣr Ḥāmid Abū Zayd from his Muslim wife on the ground that his views on the Koran constitute apostasy. This procedure is not, however, a form of *al-amr bi'l-maʿrūf* (nor of *ḥisba* in the sense of the role of the official censor). A *daʿwā ḥisba* is a suit which someone brings out of concern for God's rights – or in less theocentric language, the public inter-

We have already encountered the accommodationist reaction in the rewriting of Ghazzālī by the Ottoman Shaykh al-Islām Ḥaydarīzāde (d. 1349/1931).[124] But the characteristic expression of this tendency in the Arab world is the view that carrying out the duty 'with the hand' is reserved for those in authority. This idea is not new; but whereas it was rare outside Ḥanafī circles in traditional Islam,[125] it is significantly more common in modern writings. Perhaps surprisingly, it seems to owe its prominence to Ḥasan al-Bannā (d. 1368/1949). In the years immediately preceding the Second World War, the Muslim Brothers were divided by a dispute over the proper means of moral reform in Egypt; a group which in due course seceded from the movement believed in proceeding 'with the hand' in accordance with the 'three modes' tradition, whereas Bannā himself inclined rather to the 'good admonition' (*al-maw'iẓa al-ḥasana*) of Q16:125.[126] This origin has probably bestowed a certain prestige on an idea which might otherwise have seemed merely time-serving.

As could be expected, this notion is current in Egypt in quarters friendly to the state. Thus it is the main theme of an interview given by the Muftī

est – as opposed to one in which he has a personal stake (see Tyan, *Histoire de l'organisation judiciaire*, 618 no. 1; Gardet, *Cité*, 187 n. 2; Ḥ. al-Labīdī, *Daʿāwā 'l-ḥisba*, Asyūṭ 1983 (a monographic study); for the sense of *ḥisba* here, cf. above, ch. 16, note 135). The role of the individual in this procedure is essentially to lay testimony before the *qāḍī*, who is then responsible for any commanding or forbidding (cf. *ibid.*, 4.19, 165.14; for a classical use of the phrase *shahādat al-ḥisba*, see Ghazzālī, *Wajīz*, 2:163.15). What this has in common with *al-amr bi'l-maʿrūf* is the disinterested motivation of the individual who takes action. However, this feature does not make the procedure an aspect of *al-amr bi'l-maʿrūf*, and accounts of the duty of forbidding wrong do not treat it as such. Modern discussions of the procedure nevertheless make reference to *al-amr bi'l-maʿrūf*, perhaps by a kind of terminological osmosis (cf. Labīdī, *Daʿāwā 'l-ḥisba*, 44–8, 163.4). The Egyptian Court of Cassation (*Maḥkamat al-naqḍ*) in its decree (*ḥukm*) of 20 Rabīʿ I, 1417/5 August 1996 in the Abū Zayd case included in its discussion of the *daʿwā ḥisba* a paraphrase of the definition of *ḥisba* in terms of *al-amr bi'l-maʿrūf* with which Māwardī (d. 450/1058) opens his discussion of the censorship (the passage is at 9.10 of the typewritten decree, of which I owe my copy to Khaled Fahmy; for Māwardī's definition, see above, ch. 16, note 134; cf. Labīdī, *Daʿāwā 'l-ḥisba*, 2.6, 51.17). As in the Abū Zayd case, couples deemed not to be legally married are a longstanding target of the procedure (*ibid.*, 4.19, 132.9, 167.10, 201.16; Labīdī gives no extended discussion of this theme).

124 See above, ch. 12, 332. For the rewriting of Ghazzālī, see further below, 526f.

125 See above, ch. 17, notes 29f.

126 R. P. Mitchell, *The Society of the Muslim Brothers*, London 1969, 18, citing ʿAbd al-Khabīr al-Khūlī, *Qā'id al-daʿwa al-Islāmiyya Ḥasan al-Bannā*, Cairo 1952, 73.15. In one of his talks, Bannā remarks that righting wrongs 'with the hand' (*al-taghyīr bi'l-yad*) is the responsibility of the ruler (*al-ḥākim al-qādir*) (*Naẓarāt fī iṣlāḥ al-nafs wa'l-mujtamaʿ*, recorded by Aḥmad ʿĪsā ʿĀshūr, Cairo 1980, 42.9). This summary observation follows a lively discussion of the verbal performance of the duty (*ibid.*, 41.2), culminating in an anecdote about a Brother who was invited to a party in Ismāʿīliyya; foreigners were present, together with alcohol and other abominations, but the Brother was able to put things right with a relatively mild rebuke to his host (*ibid.*, 41.24). There is no discussion of the question in the talk devoted to *al-amr bi'l-maʿrūf* in Bannā's *Ḥadīth al-thulāthā'* (recorded by Aḥmad ʿĪsā ʿĀshūr, Cairo 1985, 119–28).

of the Republic, Muḥammad Sayyid Ṭanṭāwī, in an Egyptian magazine in 1408/1988.[127] He argues, among other things, that if everyone could right wrongs 'with the hand', the result would be anarchy.[128] (He is, of course, against anarchy: he brings up the awful example of Lebanon.)[129] It is not that he limits the requisite authority to the state; he himself, for example, has such authority over his children – but not over the children or wives of others.[130] Confronted with the view that Ibn Taymiyya had approved of performance of the duty 'with the hand',[131] the Muftī avers that great scholar to have been innocent of any such thing.[132] This interview should not be seen in isolation; it clearly reflects a period marked by vigorous polemical exchanges on the issue. Some of these are described by the Azhar scholar ʿAbd al-ʿAẓīm Ibrāhīm al-Maṭʿanī, himself a careful critic of the position represented by the Muftī;[133] he considers the view that performance 'with the hand' is restricted to the authorities to be a recent Egyptian heresy.[134]

The Muftī's views have also had less exalted adherents. One Aḥmad Ḥusayn tells a story about his youthful involvement in some activity 'with the hand' against liquor stores and his subsequent change of heart in prison; the setting is the schism among the Muslim Brothers.[135] ʿAlī al-Ṭanṭāwī, like his namesake, makes the point that for individuals to take to executing the duty 'with the hand' would lead to anarchy.[136] Other Egyptian writers in this camp are Muḥammad ʿAlī Masʿūd[137] and Yāsir Muḥammad al-ʿAdl.[138] Outside Egypt the same thinking can be found in

[127] Muḥammad Sayyid Ṭanṭāwī, interview in 'Ṣālūn Oktōbir wa-ḥiwār maʿa faḍīlat al-Muftī', *Oktōbir*, year 12, no. 601, 1 May 1988, 38–40. I am indebted to Emmanuel Sivan for drawing this interview to my attention.

[128] *Ibid.*, 38d.11. Compare the view of Ḥāfiẓ Wahba (above, ch. 8, note 115).

[129] *Ibid.*, 39d.6. [130] *Ibid.*, 38d.31, 39a.1. [131] Cf. above, ch. 7, note 60.

[132] *Ibid.*, 39d.24.

[133] Maṭʿanī, *Taghyīr al-munkar*, esp. 3–8; for his position at the Azhar, see *ibid.*, 80.3. His account makes it clear that the idea of the tripartite division of labour was in the air at the time (*ibid.*, 4.12, 15.11). See further F. Burgat, *L'Islamisme en face*, Paris 1995, 117 n. 8 (this book was drawn to my attention by Maribel Fierro).

[134] Maṭʿanī, *Taghyīr al-munkar*, 45.15; he uses the phrase *tafsīr bidʿī* in connection with this view, *ibid.*, 15.24.

[135] Aḥmad Ḥusayn, 'al-Amr biʾl-maʿrūf waʾl-nahy ʿan al-munkar yajib an yaẓall dāʾiman fī ḥudūd al-ḥikma waʾl-mawʿiẓa al-ḥasana', *Majallat al-Azhar*, 50 (1398), 742b.4. I owe this reference to the files of the İslâm Araştırmaları Merkezi.

[136] Ṭanṭāwī, *Fuṣūl*, 175.20.

[137] Muḥammad ʿAlī Masʿūd rejects unofficial violence (*Amr*, 20.4, 27.3, 31.7, 76.14; note his partiality for *mawʿiẓa ḥasana*). His book seems still to reflect the conditions of the period in which the Islamists were the allies of President Sādāt against the left.

[138] Righting wrongs 'with the hand' is for those in authority (Yāsir Muḥammad al-ʿAdl, *al-Fiqh al-ghāʾib*, Manṣūra 1993, 280.5). This includes you with respect to your own home, should you find your son in his cups; but as to tipplers over whom you do not have authority, you can only counsel them (cf. above, note 130). ʿAdl also quotes the saying about

Saudi Arabia,[139] as also in a European setting in the preaching of the Lebanese Shaykh Fayṣal Mawlawī.[140] Action against wrong 'with the hand', he says, is only for someone in authority within his proper sphere (*ṣāḥib al-sulṭān fī sulṭānihi*); and you are not such a person.[141] The Palestinian Darwaza is clearly thinking along the same lines: he ties the role of individuals to ethical and personal matters in which their activity will not lead to anarchy or the like.[142]

This view is both a flagrant divergence from the mainstream of traditional Islamic doctrine and an unmistakable assertion of political quietism. The combination guaranteed that it would not prove generally acceptable in a period of highly politicised Islamic resurgence. Writers with more respect for the heritage, or less respect for existing states, were naturally disinclined to go against the plain sense of the 'three modes' tradition. Thus ʿAwda, repeating the standard rejection of the view that the permission of the ruler is required, makes it clear that he believes that individuals have the right to perform the duty 'with their hands';[143] and ʿAmrī takes the position that ordinary people – or at least ordinary men – are entitled to perform the duty by force.[144] But those who reject the view that only the authorities may proceed 'with the hand' are not necessarily in favour of violence. Maṭʿanī, who considers the idea to be without foundation and

the tripartite division of labour (*ibid.*, 281.18), but offers no comment on it, and goes on to pile up further restrictions on action 'with the hand' (*ibid.*, 282f.). The book is a reaction to the fragmented violence of the Islamist movement in Egypt; ʿAdl has no tolerance for attacks on other Muslims with knives and machine-guns, or for the burning of churches and monasteries (*ibid.*, 271.14). To help the militants look bad, he presents them as a threat to the unity of Islam at the very time when the religion is the object of a world-wide conspiracy to destroy it (*ibid.*, 12.17, and cf. 289.16), and as a disruptive force in a context in which organisation is desperately needed to take action against such major wrongs as the fact that the *sharīʿa* is in abeyance (*ibid.*, 286.15). What a sad contrast the Muslims make to the Jews, every one of whom is fully involved in the Zionist movement, and knows his duty with regard to the state of Israel (*ibid.*, 290.1)! Despite his Muʿtazilite sympathies (see below, note 309, and cf. above, note 45), he quotes a Ḥanbalite condemnation of rebellion with implicit approval (*ibid.*, 269.1); the neo-Muʿtazilites are not the revolutionaries they were a generation ago. Cf. also Gómez García, *Marxismo*, 339.

139 ʿAbd al-Raḥmān Ḥasan al-Maydānī, who holds a professorship at the University of Umm al-Qurā in Mecca, expresses similar views (*Fiqh al-daʿwa ilā ʾllāh*, Damascus 1996, 2:237.15, 242.18, 243.2, with a broad definition of those in authority).

140 Kepel, *Banlieues*, 261f.

141 Mawlawī, *Amr*, side 2. Mawlawī doubtless derives this view from Ḥasan al-Bannā, to whom he makes frequent references on this cassette.

142 Darwaza, *al-Tafsīr al-ḥadīth*, 5:14.18.

143 ʿAwda, *Tashrīʿ*, 1:501.1.

144 ʿAmrī, *Amr*, 297.1, 303.2 (in the latter passage he speaks of *kull rajul*). He quotes, but does not endorse, the saying about the tripartite division of labour (*ibid.*, 296.5). Zaydān is in the same camp as ʿAwda and ʿAmrī in making no move to limit performance 'with the hand' to the authorities (*Mufaṣṣal*, 4:364 §3,570), and the same is true of Ilāhī (*Ḥisba*, 80.12).

has no difficulty in proving his point,[145] deplores the waves of terrorism and violence sweeping over Egypt.[146] He eventually makes it clear that, in his view, violence has no part in the performance 'with the hand' that is the province of individual subjects;[147] his key argument, or rather assumption, is that the use of violence constitutes punishment (*ʿuqūba*), and as such is reserved to the ruler and his subordinates.[148] Khālid al-Sabt shares with Maṭʿanī the formal rejection of the view that performance 'with the hand' is reserved for the authorities;[149] but in the next breath he speaks only of the action someone might take 'in his home or his market or the like'.[150] Others compromise in a less subtle way: they make the point that proceeding 'with the hand' is in the first instance a duty for the authorities, but do not exclude ordinary individuals from it.[151] They may also employ a very broad notion of who the authorities are. One such author, in a modern commentary on the forty traditions of Nawawī (d. 676/1277), includes those in charge of schools, factories and offices; someone in charge of a school is in a position to stamp out indecorous songs (*al-aghānī al-mājina*), while someone in charge of a factory or office can stop employees wasting time.[152] Looming behind this whole discussion of performance 'with the hand' is the appeal of the 'three modes' tradition to revolutionary fundamentalists.[153]

More direct indications of the attitudes of modern writers towards the use of violence in forbidding wrong can often be gleaned from their reactions to Ghazzālī's views on the subject. Several are clearly embarrassed.

145 Maṭʿanī, *Taghyīr al-munkar*, 15.8. Maṭʿanī returns to this battleground repeatedly in the rejoinders to a literary antagonist reprinted in the volume. 146 *Ibid.*, 9.2.

147 *Ibid.*, 112.5, and cf. 32.12, 107.16, 117.10.

148 *Ibid.*, 112.10, and cf. 116.7. Whatever its political merits, this assumption seems as ill-founded as the view he is attacking: obviously violence is sometimes used as a punishment, but why should this always be the case? The whole tract is an instructive example of an Azhar scholar attempting to position himself in the moral and political force-field of Mubārak's Egypt. 149 Sabt, *Amr*, 331.13. 150 *Ibid.*, 331.14.

151 Zaydān, *Uṣūl al-daʿwa*, 455 §587; Khālid al-Bayṭār, *al-Bayān fī sharḥ al-Arbaʿīn al-Nawawiyya*, Zarqāʾ 1987, 207.11; similarly Maḥmūd (*Uṣūl al-mujtamaʿ al-Islāmī*, 202.3, but contrast *ibid.*, 202.24). Cf. the view of Ibn Taymiyya, above, ch. 7, 155.

152 Bayṭār, *al-Bayān fī sharḥ al-Arbaʿīn*, 207.13. A comparable attitude towards such intermediate authorities is taken by Mawlawī in the context of the factory (see his remarks quoted in Kepel, *Banlieues*, 262; and cf. above, note 139, on Maydānī). Ibn Ḥājj, by contrast, is asked about a man who works in an agricultural market (*sūq al-fallāḥ*), where he seeks to right such wrongs as the mixing of men and women; the man in charge (*masʾūl*) tells him that this is not his job, and is on the point of punishing him. Ibn Ḥājj's response is that he should pay no attention to the manager (*mudīr*) and persist; it is God who provides the means of subsistence (*arzāq*) (*Amr*, 7:1).

153 Sivan, *Radical Islam*, 117, citing esp. S. E. Ibrahim, 'Islamic militancy as a social movement: the case of two groups in Egypt', in A. E. H. Dessouki (ed.), *Islamic resurgence in the Arab world*, New York 1982, 127; cf. also Burgat, *L'Islamisme en face*, 118, and ʿUmāra, *al-Islām wa-ḥuqūq al-insān*, 94.18.

Thus Jamāl al-Dīn al-Qāsimī in his epitome of Ghazzālī's *Revival of the religious sciences* omits the last three of Ghazzālī's levels of performance, and limits the fifth to officialdom when it involves the destruction of offending objects.[154] A similarly queasy response to Ghazzālī's attitude to armed conflict is that of a certain Ṣāliḥ Aḥmad al-Shāmī, who in his epitome of Ghazzālī's work discreetly omits to mention such conflict, not to speak of armed bands.[155] Khālid al-Sabt lists Ghazzālī's levels,[156] and gives a few pages each to the first two; but thereafter he tacitly forgets them, turning instead to the 'three modes'.[157] The many examples of performance 'with the hand' that he proceeds to give convey the message that it consists of violence directed against things (breaking and pouring) rather than people.[158] He has thus spared himself the awkwardness of confronting Ghazzālī's more aggressive levels of performance; and with regard to recourse to arms, he offers only the passing remark that more than one scholar has made this conditional on the ruler's permission.[159] A similar strategy is adopted by another Saʿūdī, ʿAbd al-ʿAzīz al-Masʿūd: his account of the levels simply drops those involving violence to the person,[160] and restricts performance 'with the hand' to objects;[161] he requires the permission of the ruler for recourse to arms.[162]

Others, within limits, are more comfortable with Ghazzālī's approach. Thus ʿAmrī approves the use of force,[163] but dislikes the idea of armed bands.[164] ʿAwda in his discussion of the use of violence follows Ghazzālī without flinching, even espousing his views of armed conflict and armed bands,[165] though he does adopt Ghazzālī's position that the subject may not use violence against the ruler.[166] Some recent figures lack even these inhibitions. Thus Ḥawwā strongly endorses Ghazzālī's views on

154 Qāsimī, *Mawʿiẓat al-muʾminīn*, 246.18. (Ghazzālī's fifth level is the fourth in Qāsimī's numbering.)

155 Ṣāliḥ Aḥmad al-Shāmī, *al-Muhadhdhab min Iḥyāʾ ʿulūm al-dīn*, Damascus and Beirut 1993, 1:474.10; similarly Bayānūnī, *Amr*, 50.6.

156 Sabt, *Amr*, 316.2 (he comes up with ten levels).

157 *Ibid.*, 323.4.

158 As *ibid.*, 328.5.

159 *Ibid.*, 332.9.

160 ʿAbd al-ʿAzīz al-Masʿūd, *Amr*, 519–26.

161 *Ibid.*, 511.12.

162 *Ibid.*, 205.7, claiming Ghazzālī's authority for this. In a discussion independent of Ghazzālī's, he makes it clear that the use of violence is excluded in normal circumstances where the ruler has set up an effective committee (*hayʾa*) to discharge the duty (*ibid.*, 104 no. 3). Quranī, who is well disposed towards the Saʿūdī state, takes Ghazzālī's series no further than blows, and in any case denies this option to the individual forbidder of wrong (*Ḥisba*, 256.10). For an author using Ḥanbalite sources, a good way to avoid confronting Ghazzālī's views on violence is to rely on the bowdlerised version of Ibn Qudāma's epitome of Ibn al-Jawzī's *Minhāj al-qāṣidīn* (cf. above, ch. 6, 139–41; for an example, see Raḍwān, *Dirāsāt fī ʾl-ḥisba*, 60.5).

163 See above, note 144.

164 ʿAmrī, *Amr*, 309.13; cf. above, ch. 16, 441.

165 ʿAwda, *Tashrīʿ*, 1:507.19, 508.15; cf. above, ch. 16, 441.

166 *Ibid.*, 509.22; cf. above, ch. 16, notes 33f.

violence.[167] Ibn Ḥājj quotes Ghazzālī's passage on armed bands with obvious relish, as also the denunciation of the quietist traditionists by Jaṣṣāṣ.[168]

Against this background, it must seem paradoxical that it is precisely one of the most radical of fundamentalist visions that has gone farthest in modern times towards voiding the duty of the individual to forbid wrong. When Sayyid Quṭb comments on Q3:104, he seems almost to deny the existence of this duty: 'commanding' and 'forbidding' are things only someone in authority (*dhū sulṭān*) can do, and accordingly we need an authority (*sulṭa*) to perform the duty.[169] This authority would seem to be the Muslim community;[170] there is no mention of the Muslims as individuals. But it is not until he comments on Q5:79 that we learn what has become of the duty of the individual. Here Quṭb remarks, promisingly, that the Muslim community is one in which no one who sees another act wrongly can say 'What's that to me?'[171] But there is a catch. A Muslim society is indeed one that enables a Muslim to devote himself to forbidding wrong, without his attempts being reduced to pointless gestures or made impossible altogether as is the case in the Jāhilī societies that exist today. The real task is thus to establish the good society as such, and this comes before the righting of small-scale, personal and individual wrongs (*iṣlāḥāt juz'iyya, shakhṣiyya wa-fardiyya*) by way of forbidding wrong; such efforts are vain when the whole society is corrupt.[172] All the sacred texts bearing on forbidding wrong, he argues, concern themselves with the duty of the Muslim in a Muslim society.[173] Thus in commenting on Q9:112, Quṭb invokes the early history of the Muslim community in

[167] Ḥawwā, *Jund Allāh*, 386.8; and cf. *ibid.*, 382.1, and above, note 77.

[168] Ibn Ḥājj, *Amr*, 6:2; cf. above, ch. 12, 336f. Unfortunately his views on performance 'with the hand' are on cassette 5 (see *ibid.*, 6:1). Cf. also above, notes 86f.

[169] Quṭb, *Fī ẓilāl al-Qur'ān*, 444.5, noted in O. Carré, *Mystique et politique: lecture révolutionnaire du Coran par Sayyid Quṭb, Frère musulman radical*, Paris 1984, 193.

[170] Quṭb, *Fī ẓilāl al-Qur'ān*, 444.24, 444.29, 445.10, 445.16; and cf. his *Ma'ālim fī 'l-ṭarīq*, n.p. n.d., 148.15 (quoting Q3:110). The language does not explicitly speak of an Islamic state, but it is doubtless what he has in mind.

[171] Quṭb, *Fī ẓilāl al-Qur'ān*, 949.3; cf. Carré, *Mystique et politique*, 211.

[172] Quṭb, *Fī ẓilāl al-Qur'ān*, 949.10. He repeats this message more than once in the next two pages, and again in commenting on Q9:112 (*ibid.*, 1720.1). Compare the deferral of the duty till the coming of the imam in the Sunnī caricature of the Imāmī view (see above, ch. 11, note 116).

[173] *Ibid.*, 949.28. He gives the example of the tradition on speaking out in the presence of an unjust ruler, here referred to as an imam: an imam is a ruler who accepts the authority of God and His law – otherwise he is simply an infidel ruler. Other writers, by contrast, invoke this or similar traditions in support of heroism ('Amrī, *Amr*, 260–4, quoting the tradition at 262.4; Rāshid, *Munṭalaq*, 229.10, quoting a *fatwā*; 'Abd al-Sattār, *Amr*, 25.9, in a discussion making it clear that this relates only to exceptional circumstances; and cf. 'Umāra, *al-Islām wa-ḥuqūq al-insān*, 95.4, and Ibn Ḥājj, *Amr*, 7:2).

support of his view: the followers of the Prophet first devoted their efforts to establishing the Muslim state and society, and only then turned to forbidding wrong in secondary matters.[174] It is noteworthy that this rationale of Quṭb for voiding forbidding wrong in the present is very much his own. Thus he does not invoke the authority of the eschatological traditions that foretell such a time.[175] He does at one point make use of the notion of performance in the heart,[176] but it plays no central role in his argument.

Although it is known to have been current among the followers of Quṭb, this renunciation has not become standard fundamentalist doctrine. Thus Rāshid, after quoting Quṭb's commentary to Q9:112, feels compelled to add that this does not mean that missionaries (*duʿāt*) should not instruct themselves and their followers in their Islamic duties, or that they should abstain from forbidding the kind of secondary wrongs that can in fact be stopped.[177] Mawlawī takes the view that in a non-Islamic society – particularly in Europe – it is utterly inappropriate for us to cut off relations with (Muslim) offenders, since all it does is to isolate us; instead we should persist, warning them once, twice, thrice, even ten times.[178] Ibn Ḥājj does not mention Quṭb, but he makes a point of identifying many of the Koranic verses he discusses as Meccan;[179] he asks rhetorically if the Prophet told his followers to be silent and abstain from performing the duty till they were established in Medina, and goes on to reject the idea that one can do away with forbidding wrong on the pretext that we do not live in an Islamic state (*dawla Islāmiyya*).[180] The activist tinge of this passage is likely to reflect his role as a populist leader in a revolutionary situation: he strongly endorses

174 Quṭb, *Fī ẓilāl al-Qurʾān*, 1720.7. 175 Cf. above, ch. 3, 39–42.

176 *Ibid.*, 951.18. He stresses that such performance is a positive, not a negative stance, because it creates the mental prerequisite for action when the time comes; but he seems not to conceive of it as having any outward behavioural manifestations. Some modern Sunnī writers, by contrast, tend to emphasise such manifestions (Jamāl al-Dīn al-Qāsimī (d. 1332/1914), *Iṣlāḥ al-masājid*, Beirut and Damascus 1983, 32.7 (this work was drawn to my attention by Maribel Fierro); ʿAwda, *Tashrīʿ*, 1:497.14; Ṭanṭāwī in 'Ṣālūn Oktōbir wa-ḥiwār maʿa faḍīlat al-Muftī', 39b.6; Muḥammad ʿAlī Masʿūd, *Amr*, 31.1; Sāmarrāʾī, *Manāhij*, 66.15); but others seem to have in mind a purely mental act (ʿAmrī, *Amr*, 284–7, esp. 286.12; Maḥmūd, *Uṣūl al-mujtamaʿ al-Islāmī*, 203.16; Zaydān, *Mufaṣṣal*, 4:364f. §3,572, 366 §3,576).

177 Rāshid, *Munṭalaq*, 202.14; similarly Yāsīn, *Jihād*, 182.18.

178 Mawlawī, *Amr*, side 2.

179 This is not a traditional concern of the scholars (for an exception, see above, ch. 4, note 12), but it has a modern precedent in Rashīd Riḍā (*Tafsīr al-Manār*, 9:534.18 (to Q7:199), 535.7 (regarding Q31.17)). Riḍā's motive in making the point is, however, quite different.

180 Ibn Ḥājj, *Amr*, 1:2; for *al-amr bi'l-maʿrūf* in Mecca, see also *ibid.*, 4:1. For an approving reference to Quṭb in a different context, see *ibid.*, 7:2. Compare also ʿAmrī, *Amr*, 127.1, 278.3, 282.9.

heroism,[181] and directs himself to a youth that is zealous in performing the duty and needs only to be instructed in its principles.[182] Even Ibn Ḥājj does not always speak with this voice.[183] But Khālid al-Sabt, who is not a radical,[184] reacts to Quṭb's position in much the same way;[185] lots of wrongs, he points out, can be dealt with perfectly well even in the absence of an Islamic state.[186]

3. DEVELOPMENTS IN IMĀMĪ SHĪʿISM

According to Ibn Ḥājj, some of the Shīʿa – he specifies the Imāmiyya – believe that forbidding wrong is not obligatory in the absence of an imam; he refutes them effortlessly by quoting Ghazzālī.[187] His Egyptian contemporary Aḥmad Ḥijāzī al-Saqqā is better informed. In the course of editing the commentary of a certain Abū Bakr ibn Maymūn on a work by Juwaynī (d. 478/1085), he comes upon a condemnation of the view of some of the Rawāfiḍ that the duty is suspended until the manifestation of the imam.[188] He begins his footnote to this by identifying the Rawāfiḍ as the Shīʿa, and goes on to observe that in our time the Shīʿa do not adhere to this position, but call people to forbid wrong. He explains that after the

[181] Ibn Ḥājj, *Amr*, 7:2, dwelling on appropriate quotations from Ibn al-ʿArabī (d. 543/1148) (see above, ch. 14, note 59) and Ghazzālī (see above, ch. 16, 433 case (4)).

[182] *Ibid.*, 4:1, 6:1, 7:1. Note in this connection his remarks to the effect that temporary marriage (*zawāj al-mutʿa*) is a matter on which there is disagreement, and cannot therefore be the target of the duty (*ibid.*, 4:2; for reports that this was permitted by Mālik ibn Anas (d. 179/795), see A. Gribetz, *Strange bedfellows: mutʿat al-nisāʾ and mutʿat al-ḥajj*, Berlin 1994, 111f.).

[183] In an article reflecting the changed atmosphere following the local elections held in Algeria in 1410/1990, Ibn Ḥājj strongly condemns hotheaded activism ('Ijādat al-taḥbīr fī bayān qawāʿid al-taghyīr', *al-Munqidh*, 5 Dhū 'l-Ḥijja, 1410, 9–11). That this marks a change of tune is confirmed by the reaction of a moderate Salafī a couple of numbers later, in effect welcoming Ibn Ḥājj back to the (politically marginalised) Islamist mainstream (Yaḥyā Muḥammad, 'Naẓarāt fī mawḍūʿ qawāʿid al-taghyīr lil-shaykh ʿAlī ibn Ḥājj', *al-Munqidh*, 4 Muḥarram, 1411, 20; I am grateful to Abdeslam Maghraoui for explaining the political background to me). However, most of the arguments deployed here by Ibn Ḥājj owe nothing to the eccentric ideas of Quṭb (nor to Bannā). He stresses the need for knowledge of the law, for a reckoning of costs and benefits, for experts to determine the priorities, for doing it nicely, and the like; and he is very explicit in noting the failings of Muslim youth ('Ijāda', cols. 9e.33, 11e.7, 11e.13). There is, nevertheless, a clear echo of Quṭb in his argument that most behavioural wrongs are manifestations of the more fundamental wrong of recognising norms other than God's, and that it is here that we should begin (*ibid.*, 10e.44; cf. above, note 172); he adds that Muslim youth who dissipate their energies on such behavioural wrongs are falling into a trap set by the political authorities.

[184] For his rejection of rebellion, on utilitarian grounds, see Sabt, *Amr*, 235.6; and see above, notes 156–9.

[185] *Ibid.*, 261.1 (stating Quṭb's position); *ibid.*, 261.17 (his reply). Like Ibn Ḥājj, he leaves Quṭb unnamed.

[186] *Ibid.*, 263.4.

[187] Ibn Ḥājj, *Amr*, 3:2; similarly Maṭʿanī, *Taghyīr al-munkar*, 113.22. Cf. above, ch. 11, note 116.

[188] Abū Bakr ibn Maymūn, *Sharḥ al-Irshād*, 605.17.

Shāh of Iran (Muḥammad Riḍā Pahlawī, ruled 1360–99/1941–79) sided with America, and spread corruption among the population by introducing American-style cinema and television, Khumaynī (d. 1409/1989) arose. He still prevails despite the war being waged on Iran by the Baʿthist secularists of Iraq; the Baʿthists are of course inspired by the Americans, who fear that Khumaynī may become the caliph of Shīʿites and Sunnīs alike.[189] This account may not have been a sophisticated piece of political analysis, but it correctly identifies two major features of the recent Imāmī development of forbidding wrong: enthusiasm for revolutionary politics and hostility to cultural pollution. Both are familiar from the Sunnī experience.

In the early decades of the Western impact on Iran, such an evolution might have seemed unlikely. What we find is rather the same lax syncretism that we saw on the Sunnī side. Initially this is the work of laymen. A fine early example is a brief account of freedom of expression given by Mīrzā Yūsuf Khān Mustashār al-Dawla (d. 1313/1895f.). He states that resistance to oppression (*mudāfaʿa-i ẓulm*) is a law (*qānūn*) in Europe (*Farangistān*), which explains European prosperity; this value is also enjoined in several passages of the Koran, of which the first he quotes is Q3:104.[190] One of the benefits of this law, he continues, is that freedom of expression (*ikhtiyār wa āzādī-i zabān wa qalam*) has become prevalent. This law too, he states, is in accordance with the law (*qānūn*) of Islam, and he proves his point by quoting one of the accounts of forbidding wrong given by Ṭūsī (d. 460/1067).[191] He then goes on to freedom of the press, and remarks that some aspects of this fall within the scope of forbidding wrong. He adds that in Paris there are a hundred presses and six hundred book shops.[192] The same idea appears in a discussion of 'freedom of speech and pen' by Mīrzā Malkum Khān (d. 1326/1908).[193] This very freedom,

[189] *Ibid.*, 605 n. 1 (the book was published in Egypt in 1407/1987). For Sunnī sympathy for the Iranian revolution and its limits, see E. Sivan, 'Sunni radicalism in the Middle East and the Iranian revolution', *International Journal of Middle East Studies*, 21 (1989); W. Buchta, *Die iranische Schia und die islamische Einheit 1979–1996*, Hamburg 1997, 227–34 (this study was drawn to my attention by Houchang Chehabi).

[190] Mīrzā Yūsuf Khān Mustashār al-Dawla (d. 1313/1895f.), *Yak kalima*, ed. Ṣ. Sajjādī, Tehran 1364 sh., 32.5, cited in A. Hairi, *Shīʿism and constitutionalism in Iran*, Leiden 1977, 34f. (and see *ibid.*, 30f., for the career of this reformist official); the work is dated 1287/1871 (*Yak kalima*, 61.6).

[191] Yūsuf Khān, *Yak kalima*, 33.4; cf. Ṭūsī, *Nihāya*, 299.8.

[192] Yūsuf Khān, *Yak kalima*, 34.1.

[193] Mīrzā Malkum Khān (d. 1326/1908), *Nidā-yi ʿadālat ba-majlis-i wuzarā-yi Īrān*, in *Majmūʿa-i āthār-i Mīrzā Malkum Khān*, collected by M. M. Ṭabāṭabāʾī, Tehran 1327 sh., 206–8 (cited in Hairi, *Shīʿism and constitutionalism*, 35 n. 97). The tract dates from 1323/1905 (see *Nidā-yi ʿadālat*, 194.2, and H. Algar, *Mīrzā Malkum Khān*, Berkeley 1973, 245–7), shortly before the Constitutional Revolution.

he says, which all civilised nations recognise as fundamental, is one which Muslims have established for the whole world in the two phrases 'commanding right' and 'forbidding wrong'. What positive law (*qānūn-i dawlatī*) has proclaimed this freedom more explicitly?[194] The Constitutional Revolution of 1324/1906 was likewise defended in terms of forbidding wrong.[195] Such thinking still continues. Recently the dissident cleric Ḥusayn-ʿAlī Muntaẓirī is reported to have issued a responsum calling for the formation of political parties in Iran as a modern way to apply the principle of forbidding wrong.[196] In all these cases the motivation of the syncretism is to render a Western idea acceptable in a Muslim context; but just as among the Sunnīs, we also find the same device used to defend Islam against the charge of deficiency. Thus when the Iraqi clergyman Muḥammad Bāqir al-Ḥakīm wishes to argue the superiority of Islam in providing guarantees (*ḍamānāt*) of human rights, he quotes Koranic verses on forbidding wrong.[197]

Among the Imāmīs, as among the Sunnīs, the resurgence of Islam as a political doctrine in a modern setting has been a development of the last two generations. But whereas in the Sunnī case the revival has throughout been primarily the work of laymen, this has not been so for the Imāmīs. There have certainly been laymen who have concerned themselves with such matters: ʿAlī Sharīʿatī (d. 1397/1977) is an obvious example.[198] At least one layman, Mahdī Bāzargān (d. 1415/1995), was involved in the rethinking of the duty of forbidding wrong at an early stage.[199] But the

194 Malkum Khān, *Nidā-yi ʿadālat*, 207.18.

195 Hairi summarises the views of a cleric who defends constitutionalism in this way (*Shīʿism and constitutionalism*, 100); and see Āghā Buzurg, *Nuqabāʾ al-bashar*, 568.14, for another instance.

196 This report appeared in the London newspaper *al-Ḥayāt*, 25 November 1997, 6c, in the last paragraph of the news item on Iran.

197 Muḥammad Bāqir al-Ḥakīm, 'Ḥuqūq al-insān min wijhat naẓar Islāmiyya', in *Ḥuqūq al-insān fī 'l-Islām: maqālāt al-Muʾtamar al-khāmis lil-fikr al-Islāmī*, Tehran 1987, 339.14. Cf. also Murtaḍā Muṭahharī (d. 1399/1979), *Jihād*, Qumm n.d., 42.12.

198 See S. Akhavi, 'Shariati's social thought', in N. R. Keddie (ed.), *Religion and politics in Iran*, New Haven and London 1983, 133f. Sharīʿatī's discussion of *al-amr biʾl-maʿrūf* in his *Shīʿa* (n.p. 1362 sh. (= *Majmūʿa-i āthār*, vol. 7), esp. 68–76) has themes also found on the clerical side (see below, notes 239, 329, 333).

199 Mahdī Bāzargān (d. 1415/1995), *Marz-i miyān-i dīn wa siyāsat*, Tehran 1341 sh., 39.5, 40.1, 40.9 (placing the duty in a context of modern oppositional politics); see H. E. Chehabi, *Iranian politics and religious modernism*, Ithaca 1990, 57 (this book provides extensive discussion of Bāzargān's ideas and politics). Akhavi suggests that it was laymen who rediscovered the political potential of *al-amr biʾl-maʿrūf* (S. Akhavi, *Religion and politics in contemporary Iran*, Albany 1980, 120). However, the chronological data available to me would not establish this. Bāzargān's *Marz* was published at the end of 1962 or the beginning of 1963 (Daymāh 1341 sh.). Two clerics had already given relevant talks devoted to *al-amr biʾl-maʿrūf* in 1960 (1339 sh.), later published in *Guftār-i māh* (for Muṭahharī's talk see above, ch. 11, note 298; for Āyatī's, see below, note 208; for this

events of the Islamic revolution of 1399/1979, and the subsequent consolidation of the clerical regime, have tended to eclipse lay thinkers. It is the role of the clerics, and the continuing vitality of their literary tradition, that distinguishes and dominates the Imāmī development.

The Imāmī clerics have reshaped their doctrine of forbidding wrong in two major respects. Roughly speaking, one concerns the process by which they eventually came to power, and the other the manner in which they now exercise it. We may consider each in turn.

The traditional Imāmī doctrine of forbidding wrong displayed a marked political quietism on two points. One was the danger condition, which in its Imāmī version voided not only the duty to proceed but also the virtue of doing so. The other was the requirement that the imam give permission for any serious recourse to violence. Recasting the Imāmī heritage as an ideology of political revolution was likely to put some strain on the traditional doctrine at both these points.

The best starting-point with regard to the danger condition is an account of forbidding wrong written by Khumaynī himself.[200] The framework of the account is provided by a set of brief and unremarkable general statements of doctrine; each such passage is followed by a string of specific points, most of them of no particular political significance. The presentation of the danger

series of talks, see Chehabi, *Iranian politics*, 170–2). And in the same month that Bāzargān published his *Marz*, Muḥammad Bihishtī (d. 1401/1981) briefly discussed *al-amr bi'l-ma'rūf* in an equally untraditional way in his 'Rūḥānīyat dar Islām wa dar miyān-i Muslimīn', in Muḥammad Ḥusayn Ṭabāṭabā'ī *et al.*, *Baḥthī dar bāra-i marja'īyat wa rūḥānīyat*, n.p. n.d., 160.9 (this second printing of the work notes that the first appeared in Daymāh 1341 sh.; for Bihishtī's contribution to the volume, see A. K. S. Lambton, 'A reconsideration of the position of the *marja' al-taqlīd* and the religious institution', *Studia Islamica*, 20 (1964), 129–31). Moreover, clerical writing about *al-amr bi'l-ma'rūf* in a modern vein seems to go back considerably before this period. While there is no hint of it in the treatment of *al-amr bi'l-ma'rūf* by the early Shī'ite modernist Khāraqānī (d. 1355/1936) (see his *Maḥw al-mawhūm*, n.p. 1379, 372–5), it is already apparent in the title of Luṭf Allāh Ṣāfī Gulpāyagānī's *Rāh-i iṣlāḥ yā amr bah ma'rūf wa nahy az munkar*, Qumm 1376 sh.; the work was mostly written at the beginning of 1369/1949, and completed in 1369/1950 (see *ibid.*, 108.5, and cf. 90.2). The theme of this short popular work is that *al-amr bi'l-ma'rūf* is the solution to the problem of the decline and backwardness of the Muslim world (see esp. *ibid.*, 6.17).

200 Khumaynī, *Taḥrīr*, 1:462–84 (cf. K.-H. Göbel, *Moderne Schiitische Politik und Staatsidee*, Opladen 1984, 188–92). The work is a commentary on the *Wasīlat al-najāt* of Abū 'l-Ḥasan al-Iṣfahānī (d. 1365/1946) (for which see Modarressi, *Introduction*, 58 no. (xi), 94); the *Wasīla*, however, contains no treatment of *al-amr bi'l-ma'rūf*, so that Khumaynī at this point is on his own. There is an article in Japanese on the modern development of the doctrine of *al-amr bi'l-ma'rūf* among the Imāmīs (K. Nakata, 'Shīa-ha hōgaku ni okeru "Zen no meirei to aku no soshi" riron no hatten to Homenī ni yoru sono kaikaku', *Annals of Japan Association for Middle East Studies*, 12 (1997)); from its references to primary sources, it appears to be well informed (I am indebted to Etan Kohlberg for bringing this article to my attention, and to Yasuko Makino for transcribing the title for me).

condition initially conforms to this pattern.[201] Much of what is said is fully compatible with the traditional doctrine. Thus one of the points made is that the prospect of any significant harm (*ḍarar*) to the performer or those associated with him voids the obligation,[202] while another is that if he fears for his life or honour, or those of other Muslims, it is forbidden to him to proceed.[203] But in the middle of this generally familiar scholastic material we come upon a jarring block of fourteen points which transparently relate to a contemporary political context, the confrontation between Khumaynī and the Shāh.[204] Many of these points do not in fact relate to forbidding wrong in any obvious way, but rather prescribe the boycotting of religious institutions controlled by the regime. The first six points are the ones that concern us. Taken together, they enunciate the doctrine that there is a category of wrongs of such relative weight (*ahammiyya*)[205] that the obligation to right them overrides the danger condition, particularly for the clergy (*ʿulamāʾ al-dīn wa-ruʾasāʾ al-madhhab*); typically such wrongs involve some threat to the very basis of Islam.[206] This new doctrine is inserted without any attempt to integrate it with the old.[207]

201 Khumaynī, *Taḥrīr*, 1:472–6. The term used by Khumaynī is *mafsada*.
202 *Ibid.*, 472 no. 1.
203 *Ibid.*, 472 no. 4. Khumaynī goes on to make distinctions regarding harm to property (cf. above, ch. 11, note 280).
204 *Ibid.*, 472–5 nos. 6–19 (there is more material of this kind in the discussion of the three modes, esp. *ibid.*, 477 nos. 3–6, but it lacks doctrinal interest). Khumaynī mentions in the preface to the *Taḥrīr* that he worked on the book after he was banished from Qumm in 1384/1964 and came to Bursa as a result of distressing events which history would perhaps record (*ibid.*, 4.5) – as indeed it did (see, for example, S. Bakhash, *The reign of the Ayatollahs*, New York 1990, 24–35). Already in the previous year he had enunciated a version of his new doctrine in the context of his struggle with the Shāh: given the way in which the regime was attacking the fundamentals of Islam, *taqiyya* was forbidden, whatever the consequences (*wa-law balagha mā balagha*) (Markaz-i Madārik-i Farhangī-i Inqilāb-i Islāmī, *Ṣaḥīfa-i nūr: majmūʿa-i rāhnamūd-hā-yi imām Khumaynī*, Tehran 1361–9 sh., 1:40.5).
205 Khumaynī uses this concept elsewhere in his discussion of the duty in contexts that are not politically loaded (see, for example, *Taḥrīr*, 1:464 nos. 9f., 467–9 nos. 4, 7, 16). It was of course no invention of his; see, for example, ʿAlī al-Mishkīnī al-Ardabīlī, *Muṣṭalaḥāt al-uṣūl*, Qumm 1383, 88.9 (on the role of *ahammiyya* in deciding which of two conflicting legal provisions overrides the other); Muḥammad Riḍā al-Muẓaffar, *Uṣūl al-fiqh*, Najaf 1959–62, 3:186.16 (the principle), 189.11 (listing some considerations that take precedence, including the safeguarding of Islamic territory and the preservation of life).
206 All but the first of these points also specify that this duty of the religious leaders to speak out overrides the efficacy condition (Khumaynī, *Taḥrīr*, 1:473 nos. 7–11). It is typical of the lack of systematic integration of the new doctrine into the old that no hint of this is given in the discussion of the efficacy condition itself (*ibid.*, 467–70).
207 This is likewise true of the account of *al-amr biʾl-maʿrūf* in the appendices to Khumaynī (d. 1409/1989), *Risāla-i tawḍīḥ al-masāʾil*, Tehran 1399, 573–81 (for the danger condition, see *ibid.*, 584.11; for the new doctrine, *ibid.*, 574f. nos. 2,792–6). An innovative, though secondary, feature of this work is its very inclusion of *al-amr biʾl-maʿrūf*; according to Āyatullāh Maḥfūẓī, it was the first work of this title to cover the topic, whence the

Khumaynī was not alone among the major scholars of his generation in qualifying the danger condition. Kāẓim Sharīʿatmadārī (d. 1406/1986) holds that what the condition excludes is suffering harm over and above the intrinsic inconveniences of performing the duty, and on a scale that outweighs the utility of the initiative; it is not every kind of harm that voids the duty.[208] Abū 'l-Qāsim al-Khūʾī (d. 1413/1992), after stating the danger condition in the usual way,[209] makes a rather clumsy addition in which he says that – provided the efficacy condition is satisfied – what has to be considered is the relative weight (*ahammiyya*) of the two considerations; forbidding wrong could thus be obligatory even with actual knowledge of consequent harm.[210] Khwānsārī (d. 1405/1985) remarks that it may be said that some wrongs are not such that they are not to be forbidden just because of bearable harm of whatever kind; that he means that there could be an actual obligation to forbid them despite such harm is indicated by the parallel he adduces from the duty of pilgrimage, which in the past was not voided by virtue of the protection money (*ukhuwwa*) that used to be levied on the pilgrims.[211] Muḥammad Ḥusaynī Shīrāzī in a short treatment of the duty states that the condition is overridden when Islam is in danger.[212] In a longer account, he adds a distinction between much and little harm. He takes the view that much harm voids the duty unless Islam is in danger; such a threat can be to the fundamental beliefs of the religion or to public morals.[213]

treatment of its possession as a crime by Savak (anon., 'Guzārishī az simīnār-i amr bah maʿrūf wa nahy az munkar dar Dānishgāh-i Tihrān', in *Risālat, pīsh shumāra* 3, 12 Abān, and *pīsh shumāra* 4, 23 Abān, 1364 sh., here 12 Abān, 4a.27). The work did not, however, originally include this section; it is not found in the printing of 1342 sh. Cf. also H. Dabashi, *Theology of discontent: the ideological foundations of the Islamic revolution in Iran*, New York and London 1993, 455, citing a brief responsum of Khumaynī's dated 1391/1971.

208 Ibrāhīm Sayyid ʿAlawī, *Niẓārat-i ʿumūmī-i Islāmī*, Tehran 1347 sh., 130.11, 131.7. The 'author' of this little work explains rather belatedly in a postscript that it is a record of lectures given by Sharīʿatmadārī in Qumm (*ibid.*, 143). For a rather similar view, see Muḥammad Ibrāhīm Āyatī (d. 1384/1964), 'Amr bah maʿrūf wa nahy az munkar', *Guftār-i māh*, 1 (1339–40 sh.), Tehran n.d., 53.10, 53.22 (in a talk given in 1339 sh./1960, see *ibid.*, 42.1). 209 Khūʾī, *Minhāj*, 7:150.5.

210 *Ibid.*, 151.2. Note that the identical text appears, but without the addition, in the work of the same title by Muḥsin al-Ṭabāṭabāʾī al-Ḥakīm (d. 1390/1970) (*Minhāj al-ṣāliḥīn, qism al-ʿibādāt*, Beirut 1976, 489.1). The problematic relationship in Khūʾī's text between the addition and the statement of the condition itself is pointed out in the commentary of Taqī al-Qummī (*Mabānī*, 7:152.9). The view put forward there is that there is no proof that danger voids the obligation (*ibid.*, 151.9, with the long activist tradition invoked in support); but the motivation is unlikely to be political (cf. above, ch. 11, 295f.).

211 Khwānsārī, *Jāmiʿ*, 5:406.5.

212 Muḥammad Ḥusaynī Shīrāzī, *Risāla-i tawḍīḥ al-masāʾil*, n.p. n.d., 388 no. 2,163; his statement of the condition itself is traditional (*ibid.*, 388.6). This work was drawn to my attention by Kambiz Eslami.

213 Muḥammad al-Ḥusaynī al-Shīrāzī, *Fiqh*, Qumm *c.* 1374–1408, 38:132–5 no. 6, esp. 134.18, 135.6.

Gulpāyagānī (d. 1414/1993) states uncompromisingly that we have no business modifying conditions we don't like, but then effectively compromises by saying that if what is at stake is the standing of a religious precept, that is another matter; the analogy would then be with holy war, and the issue would have no connection with forbidding wrong.[214] Even Muḥammad Amīn Zayn al-Dīn (d. 1419/1998), who as the head of the Akhbārī community in Baḥrayn might be expected to stand apart from developments among the Imāmī mainstream, adopts the principle of relative weight (*ahammiyya*) with regard to the danger condition.[215]

It is no surprise to find more recent scholars following Khumaynī. His pupil Murtaḍā Muṭahharī (d. 1399/1979), in a talk given in 1390/1970, expresses his regret that some Imāmī scholars of the past, from whom one would not have expected such a thing, had maintained the danger condition without qualification.[216] He accepts that the duty may be overridden when the result would be greater damage (*mafsada*) to Islam;[217] but, appealing to the example of Ḥusayn ibn ʿAlī (martyred in 61/680), he does not accept that mere personal harm (*ḍarar*) dispenses one from performing the duty.[218] It may be that what is at stake is something on which Islam sets a higher value (*ahammīyat*) than it does on life, property or dignity – as when the Koran is in danger.[219] ʿAlī Tihrānī, a cleric who was active in Mashhad, composed before the revolution a work on forbidding wrong in which he quietly adopts much material from Khumaynī;[220] in his

214 Muḥammad Riḍā Gulpāyagānī (d. 1414/1993), *Majmaʿ al-masāʾil* (in Persian), Qumm 1403–6, 1:419 no. 1,273; cf. his classical statement of the danger condition, *ibid.*, 418 no. 1,271, and 438.19. An authority who makes no modification to the danger condition is Shihāb al-Dīn Marʿashī Najafī (*Risāla-i tawḍīḥ al-masāʾil-i jadīd*, Qumm 1409, 500.13). Gulpāyagānī's point about holy war is also made by Ṭālib al-Rifāʿī in a rejoinder to an article by Fāḍil al-Ḥusaynī al-Mīlānī ('al-Amr bi'l-maʿrūf wa'l-nahy ʿan al-munkar', *al-Najaf*, 2 no. 2 (March 1968), 104.21; for Mīlānī's article, see below, note 219).

215 Muḥammad Amīn Zayn al-Dīn (d. 1419/1998), *Kalimat al-taqwā*, Qumm 1413–14, 2:308.9 no. 10. He assimilates cases involving serious harm to *jihād* in a manner reminiscent of Gulpāyagānī (*ibid.*, 308.17). He also invokes the principle of *ahammiyya* in an unrelated context (*ibid.*, 317.20, no. 35); he there observes that one has recourse to *al-faqīh al-jāmiʿ lil-sharāʾiṭ* in order to determine relative weight (*ibid.*, 318.2; cf. below, note 243).

216 Murtaḍā Muṭahharī (d. 1399/1979), *Ḥamāsa-i Ḥusaynī*, Tehran and Qumm 1364 sh., 2:128.6. For the date of the series of talks to which this one belongs, see *ibid.*, 7.3. It is noteworthy that there is no anticipation of this attack on the traditional danger condition in a talk by Muṭahharī on *al-amr bi'l-maʿrūf* which was given in 1380/1960 ('Amr bamaʿrūf wa nahy az munkar'; for this talk, see Akhavi, *Religion and politics*, 120).

217 Muṭahharī, *Ḥamāsa*, 2:131.12.

218 *Ibid.*, 132.1. Modern writers on *al-amr bi'l-maʿrūf* make frequent references to Ḥusayn, and like to quote the form of salutation used by pilgrims to his tomb (*ibid.*, 67.15, 179.11; Ḥusayn-ʿAlī Muntaẓirī, *Dirāsāt fī walāyat al-faqīh wa-fiqh al-dawla al-Islāmiyya*, Qumm 1408–11, 2:228.2 (this account was brought to my attention by Kambiz Eslami); and cf. Nūrī, *Amr*, 112.13; for the formula, see the references given above, ch. 11, note 50).

219 Muṭahharī, *Ḥamāsa*, 2:129.3. A similar position is taken by Fāḍil al-Ḥusaynī al-Mīlānī ('al-Amr bi'l-maʿrūf wa'l-nahy ʿan al-munkar', *al-Najaf*, 2 no. 1 (January 1968), 44.17).

220 ʿAlī Tihrānī, *Amr ba-maʿrūf wa nahy az munkar dar Islām*, Mashhad n.d. The work was

treatment of the danger condition, he integrates Khumaynī's new thinking more closely with the rest of this material.[221] Pupils of Khumaynī who have published legal handbooks for their followers tend to follow him closely, though again they may make changes to smooth over the intrusiveness of Khumaynī's innovation.[222] In a work free of the constrictions of this genre, Ḥusayn-ʿAlī Muntaẓirī – at one time Khumaynī's designated successor – takes the position that since the duty is one intended for the reform of society (*iṣlāḥ al-mujtamaʿ*) and the eradication of evil and corruption, one must weigh the prospective harm against the targeted wrong, and give precedence to the weightier (*ahamm*).[223] He goes on to speak of the kinds

written in 1393/1974 (*ibid.*, 188.15), and appears to have been published before the revolution – which may explain why Khumaynī is nowhere referred to by name (note the vague reference to views of 'major scholars' with which material deriving from Khumaynī's *Taḥrīr* is introduced, *ibid.*, 164.2; compare the similarly anonymous way in which another pre-revolutionary author, ʿAbbās-ʿAlī Islāmī, introduces the same material in his *Do az yād rafta: amr bah maʿrūf wa nahy az munkar*, Tehran 1354 sh., 121.9). For Tihrānī's involvement in opposition activities within a couple of years of the revolution, see Bakhash, *The reign of the Ayatollahs*, 134, 138–41.

221 He rewrites the condition itself to specify that the harm must be significant (*muʿtanā bihi*), and, more importantly, he incorporates the principle of *ahammīyat* (Tihrānī, *Amr*, 173.18, 173.21; cf. Khumaynī, *Taḥrīr*, 1:472.1). He likewise rewrites the efficacy condition to make a place for the category of issues of overriding religious importance (Tihrānī, *Amr*, 168.20, to be compared with Khumaynī, *Taḥrīr*, 1:467.9; and see Tihrānī, *Amr*, 175f. no. 44). He inserts references to this category at several other points (*ibid.*, 168 nos. 18, 21; 172 nos. 31f.; 175 no. 42; 180 no. 62; 183 no. 74). He also seeks to neutralise quietist traditions (*ibid.*, 153–62, esp. 157.7, 162.1).

222 Of the treatments of *al-amr biʾl-maʿrūf* in the various appropriations of Khumaynī's *Risāla-i tawḍīḥ al-masāʾil*, that of Ṣādiq Khalkhālī comes closest to being an example of *taqlīd* of a dead *mujtahid* (*Risāla-i tawḍīḥ al-masāʾil*, Qumm 1372 sh., 540–7). That of Ḥusayn-ʿAlī Muntaẓirī (*Risāla-i tawḍīḥ al-masāʾil*, Qumm 1362 sh., 363–70) is only slightly more adventurous in departing from the master's text (he adds an item which takes account of the existence of the Islamic Republic, *ibid.*, 367 no. 2,162); but unlike Khalkhālī, he revises the danger condition to incorporate the principle of *ahammīyat* (*ān-kih dar amr wa nahy, mafsadaʾī muhimmtar nabāshad*, *ibid.*, 364.16; contrast Khumaynī, *Risāla*, 574.11, and Khalkhālī, *Risāla*, 541.11, where the word *muhimmtar* does not appear). Nāṣir Makārim Shīrāzī gives only a brief account of *al-amr biʾl-maʿrūf* (*Risāla-i tawḍīḥ al-masāʾil*, Qumm n.d., 494f.), but most of what he does say is taken from Khumaynī; in his treatment of the danger condition, he begins with a classical formulation of it, but then appends the substance of Khumaynī's statement on *ahammīyat* (*ibid.*, 494.7; cf. Khumaynī, *Risāla*, 574f. no. 2,792). Muḥammad Ṣādiqī Tihrānī offers an account of *al-amr biʾl-maʿrūf* which is not a clone of Khumaynī's and does not really observe the conventions of the genre (*Risāla-i tawḍīḥ al-masāʾil*, Qumm n.d., 237–43); but he firmly endorses the principle of *ahammīyat* (*ibid.*, 239.20), saying that it makes no sense for the condition to hold without qualification (*ibid.*, 240.11; he also rejects the efficacy condition, *ibid.*, 240.16).

223 Muntaẓirī, *Dirāsāt*, 2:251.14, 255.20, 256.5. For other expressions of the idea that what counts is relative harm, see also Muḥammad Ṣādiqī, *al-Furqān fī tafsīr al-Qurʾān*, Tehran, Qumm and Beirut 1397–1410, 10–11:221.17 (to Q9:71) (again this author rejects the efficacy condition entirely, *ibid.*, 221.15); Muḥammad Jawād Maghniyya (d. 1400/1979), *al-Tafsīr al-kāshif*, Beirut 1968–70, 2:124.11 (to Q3:104); anon., 'Amr bah maʿrūf wa nahy az munkar yā ʿamal bah masʾūlīyat-hā-yi ijtimāʿī', a series of six articles which appeared in *Jumhūrī-i Islāmī*, 13, 14, 15, 17, 21 and 22 Urdībihisht, 1366 sh., on pages 9, 9, 7, 9, 9 and 7 respectively, here no. 6, col. f.32.

of evil where a modicum of harm could hardly be held to override the duty; these include contagious social ills and threats to the foundations of Islam.[224] Ḥusayn al-Nūrī al-Hamadānī in a rather noisy monograph on forbidding wrong gives a lengthy discussion of the danger condition,[225] mounting a sustained attack on the traditional Imāmī view. Like others he argues that, just as there can be no holy war without cost, so also there can be no forbidding wrong without cost.[226] He rehabilitates the long activist tradition with its contemptuous reference to those who perform the duty only 'when they are safe from harm'.[227] He greatly widens Khumaynī's view of the circumstances in which the condition is overridden: stopping a single act of fornication is worth a bloody nose.[228] And he strongly rejects any suggestion that martyrdom is tantamount to suicide[229] – indeed he suspects that the hidden hand of colonialism might have played a part in creating and spreading this misconception.[230] A more recent monograph on the duty is that of Muḥsin al-Kharrāzī.[231] His approach is dry and scholastic, and he avoids Nūrī's flights of rhetoric.[232] In his discussion of the danger condition, he makes no effort to conceal the weakness of the attestation of

[224] Muntaẓirī, *Dirāsāt*, 2:252.2.

[225] Nūrī, *Amr*, 99–135. According to my copy, Nūrī wrote the book in 1395/1975 (*ibid.*, 255.16), in other words a few years before the revolution. There was apparently a printing in Lahore for which I have seen the dates 1354 (sh.)/1975 (so in the bibliography of Ḥasan Islāmī Ardakānī, *Amr bah ma'rūf wa nahy az munkar*, Qumm 1375 sh., 207.15) and 1393/1973f. (*Turāthunā*, 12 (1417), nos. 45–6, 400b.6, drawn to my attention by Etan Kohlberg); these dates do not quite tally. The equation of Shī'ism (as opposed to Sunnism) with revolution is a prominent theme of the book (see *ibid.*, 182–90, 253f. point 3).

[226] *Ibid.*, 105.5, 117.9. This argument is also advanced by, for example, Shīrāzī (*Fiqh*, 38:134.11) and 'Alī-Akbar al-Sayfī (*Dalīl Taḥrīr al-Wasīla lil-Imām al-Khumaynī (s) fi 'l-amr bi'l-ma'rūf wa'l-nahy 'an al-munkar*, Qumm 1415, 163.3).

[227] Nūrī, *Amr*, 110.17, quoting and refuting the efforts of Najafī (d. 1266/1850) to explain the tradition away (cf. above, ch. 11, note 282). This tradition is a favourite of Nūrī: as well as quoting it at length (*ibid.*, 43.1), he repeatedly echoes its wording (*ibid.*, 16.3, 65.10, 65.21, 90.13, 106.20, 247.13), and never casts doubt on its reliability. This is in sharp contrast to his treatment of quietist traditions which get in his way (*ibid.*, 85.13, 86.16). Muntaẓirī, who might have been expected to be equally tendentious in his treatment of the long activist tradition, is too much of a scholar to attempt to conceal its defects (*Dirāsāt*, 2:218.6, 231.1).

[228] Nūrī, *Amr*, 118.18. What he says is comparable to Shīrāzī's view of cases where the prospective harm is small (see above, note 213).

[229] *Ibid.*, 119–35.

[230] *Ibid.*, 121.15. He is inhibited from pursuing this insight by the fact that he finds the misconception already present in the Koran commentary of Ṭabrisī (d. 548/1153).

[231] Muḥsin al-Kharrāzī, *al-Amr bi'l-ma'rūf wa'l-nahy 'an al-munkar*, Qumm 1415. The work is a commentary on the relevant part of the Muḥaqqiq's *Sharā'i'*, but it also addresses systematically specific points (*furū'*) often taken from Khumaynī's *Taḥrīr*.

[232] He makes only one reference to Nūrī, in connection with the latter's activist assault on the tradition about not confronting a man with a whip or sword (*ibid.*, 71.20, with reference to Nūrī, *Amr*, 85.14; for the tradition, see above, ch. 11, note 14). My impression is that he finds Nūrī's tone somewhat unprofessional.

the long activist tradition.[233] But he accepts the principle of relative weight where omission to perform the duty would have major untoward consequences.[234] He also quotes from Muḥsin al-Ṭabāṭabāʾī al-Ḥakīm (d. 1390/1970) a distinction between two kinds of wrong. On the one hand, there are extraordinary wrongs which threaten the foundations of the faith or the integrity of Islamic territory; the righting of these is not subject to the conditions of forbidding wrong. And on the other hand, there are commonplace wrongs – failing to pray, drinking wine – the righting of which is indeed subject to these conditions.[235] The Lebanese jurist Muḥammad Ḥusayn Faḍl Allāh likewise makes frequent use of the principle of relative weight in his account of forbidding wrong.[236]

An interesting figure who does not fit into the analysis given above is Aḥmad Ṭayyibī Shabistarī, who nevertheless provides the prototype for much of Nūrī's work. A cleric who had not passed the age of forty when he died in 1350 sh./1971, he wrote a rather hot-headed work on precautionary dissimulation (*taqiyya*) and forbidding wrong which was published soon after his death.[237] What is remarkable about it in the present connection is that Ṭayyibī, in his revolutionary enthusiasm,[238] was not content to qualify the danger condition more or less heavily; instead he rejected it outright,[239] just as he rejected the knowledge and efficacy conditions.[240] As we

[233] Kharrāzī, *Amr*, 100.15 (*daʿf sanadihi*); cf. also *ibid.*, 121.1, 130.1.

[234] *Ibid.*, 100.19; also *ibid.*, 104.15, 115.3.

[235] *Ibid.*, 102.11. He later picks up the distinction (*ibid.*, 114.13).

[236] Muḥammad Ḥusayn Faḍl Allāh, *al-Masāʾil al-fiqhiyya*, Beirut 1995–6, 2:305–13. He speaks of *ahammiyya* in nos. 761 (on the conditions under which the duty overrides such prohibitions as that of entering a home without leave), 763 (on the danger condition), 771 (on the duty of the *ʿulamāʾ al-dīn* in particular to speak out in the face of oppressive government), 774 (on the right of a wife to deny her husband sexual relations in order to induce him to reform); and cf. no. 770 (on *bidʿa*).

[237] Aḥmad Ṭayyibī Shabistarī (d. 1350 sh./1971), *Taqīya; amr bah maʿrūf wa nahy az munkar*, Tehran 1350 sh. He studied in Qumm and later at the University of Tehran (see the brief notice of his life, *ibid.*, 276f.). His picture (*ibid.*, 275) shows him as a cleric, and his editor, Ḥasan Tihrānī, dignifies him with the title Ḥujjat al-Islām (*ibid.*, 276.3). He was still engaged in writing the book a few days before his death (*ibid.*, 273.4). Ṭayyibī's views were well summarised by Hamid Enayat (*Modern Islamic political thought*, Austin 1982, 179f.); I am much indebted to Anna Enayat for lending me what had been his copy of the work.

[238] Ṭayyibī's work is typified by a fusion of Islam and modern revolution. He speaks of 'the revolution of Islam' (*inqilāb-i Islām*, see, for example, *Taqīya*, 202.13, 225.5), 'the black forces of reaction' (*quwā-yi siyāh-i irtijāʿ*, *ibid.*, 92.12), 'betraying the revolution' (*khiyānat bah inqilāb*, *ibid.*, 213.10) and the like. Words such as 'ideology', 'dynamic', 'revisionist' and 'opportunist' are shown in Latin characters (*ibid.*, 26.2, 53 n. 1, 58 nn. 1f., 213 nn. 1f.).

[239] *Ibid.*, 121–44. The absence of Khumaynī's principle of *ahammīyat* is striking (see particularly *ibid.*, 143.3); the most he concedes is to distinguish *al-amr bi'l-maʿrūf* from suicide (*intiḥār*) and the like (*ibid.*, 143.16). Ṭayyibī's rejection of the danger condition finds a parallel in the thought of Sharīʿatī (*Shīʿa*, 71.17).

[240] Ṭayyibī, *Taqīya*, 104.2, 114.2; and cf. 234.14.

have seen, not even Nūrī follows him so far, despite obvious similarities between them.[241]

The other quietist feature of the traditional doctrine was the requirement of the imam's permission for the performance of the duty in its more violent forms. Here one possibility would have been to reject the requirement altogether, a position that had distinguished representatives among the classical Imāmī jurists.[242] However, recent Imāmī scholars have shown no interest in so drastic a manoeuvre. Instead they have opted to render the necessary permission more accessible; this has been done most explicitly through the modification of a minority view of the early Ṣafawid period, according to which such action could be undertaken by a suitably qualified jurist.

Again, we can best begin with Khumaynī. He starts by telling us that, according to the stronger view, wounding and killing require the permission of the imam (*al-imām ʿalayhi ʾl-salām*); he then goes on to say that in our time the jurist who satisfies the relevant conditions (*al-faqīh al-jāmiʿ lil-sharāʾiṭ*) takes his place.[243] (The reference here is clearly to any suitably qualified jurist.[244]) Khumaynī's contemporaries are less explicit. Khwānsārī speaks only of the imam's permission.[245] Khūʾī does not mention permission at all, and restricts the higher levels of violent action to the imam or

[241] Ṭayyibī anticipates Nūrī's polemic against Najafī (see, for example, *ibid.*, 105.7, 134.10, 162.1), and his liking for the long activist tradition: he quotes and translates it (*ibid.*, 129–33), enthuses over its contemporary relevance (*ibid.*, 133.18), and uses it to trip up his opponents (*ibid.*, 134.7). Like Nūrī, he never impugns its transmission, though he is not above raising such an objection to a tradition he does not like (*ibid.*, 262.1). For all this, compare above, note 227. For another significant feature common to the two authors, see below, note 280. The two authors also agree in regarding *al-amr biʾl-maʿrūf* as having a grounding in reason (*ibid.*, 167.8, and see above, ch. 11, note 242), and in holding a mixed doctrine as to whether the duty is individual or collective (*ibid.*, 165.11, and see above, ch. 11, note 256).

[242] See above, ch. 11, 268, for the classical jurists, and cf. note 233 for the eclipse of this view in later centuries.

[243] Khumaynī, *Taḥrīr*, 1:481 no. 11 (and cf. nos. 10 and 12); similarly his *Risāla*, 580f. no. 2,824 (speaking of *mujtahid-i jāmiʿ al-sharāʾiṭ*; cf. also *ibid.*, nos. 2,823, 2,825). Khumaynī may owe this view to Burūjirdī (d. 1380/1961). In his book written in 1369/1949–50, Ṣāfī Gulpāyagānī devotes a few pages to points of legal doctrine according to the view (*muṭābiq-i fatwā*) of Burūjirdī (*Rāh-i iṣlāḥ*, 82–4), and he states there that killing and wounding require *idhn-i faqīh-i jāmiʿ al-sharāʾiṭ* (*ibid.*, 84.16). For the precedents for this view in the early Ṣafawid period, see above, ch. 11, note 234.

[244] See Khumaynī, *Taḥrīr*, 1:482 no. 2, where he equates the general deputies (*nuwwāb*) of the imam in his absence with the suitably qualified jurists (*al-fuqahāʾ al-jāmiʿūn li-sharāʾiṭ al-fatwā waʾl-qaḍāʾ*). Such is also the clear understanding of the English translation of the *Risāla* (Khomeini, *A clarification of questions*, trans. J. Borujerdi, Boulder and London 1984, 378f. nos. 2,823–5).

[245] Khwānsārī, *Jāmiʿ*, 5:410.9 (drawing heavily on Najafī). This goes well with his minimalist view of clerical authority (cf. *ibid.*, 3:98.17, 100.3; 5:411.8, 412.19).

his deputy (*nā'ib*).[246] However, Gulpāyagānī requires the permission of a jurist (*idhn az faqīh*),[247] and Shīrāzī requires the permission of the judicial authority (*ḥākim-i shar'*) where killing is involved.[248] Among more recent writers, Muntaẓirī and Makārim Shīrāzī are aligned with Shīrāzī's formulation,[249] while Nūrī echoes Khumaynī.[250] Kharrāzī comes to the conclusion that such action is reserved to the Supreme Guide to the exclusion of other jurists.[251] Thus where Khumaynī had originally allowed righteous violence to be unleashed by individual members of the clergy, for Kharrāzī it is a monopoly of the state.[252] Unsurprisingly, this latter view has the endorsement of the current Supreme Guide: Khāmina'ī declared in a speech of 1413/1992 that in an Islamic society the duty of ordinary people (*'āmma-i mardum*) is to command right and forbid wrong with the tongue; if the matter would lead to violence (*agar kār bah barkhwurd bikashad*), it is for the authorities (*mas'ūlīn*) to step in.[253]

246 Khū'ī, *Minhāj*, 7:159.2 (the mention of the imam's deputy is reminiscent of Najafī, see above, ch. 11, note 234). A view close to this is that of the Akhbārī Zayn al-Dīn (*Kalimat al-taqwā*, 2:311.13 no. 17). For similar views, in which the question of permission is likewise not raised, see Muṭahharī, 'Amr ba-ma'rūf', 81.12 (reserving violence to the *ḥākim-i shar'ī*), and Muḥammad Riḍā Āshtiyānī *et al.*, *Tafsīr-i numūna*, Tehran 1353–8 sh., 3:40f. no. 5 (to Q3:104) (excluding violence from the individual performance of the duty; otherwise the result would be mayhem); and cf. Bihishtī, 'Rūḥānīyat', 160.9. These views come close in substance to those of Sunnīs who deny to the individual the execution of the duty 'with the hand' (see above, 523–5); indeed the Lebanese Faḍl Allāh would seem to have been exposed to such thinking (*Masā'il*, 2:307 no. 759).

247 Gulpāyagānī, *Majma' al-masā'il*, 1:417 no. 1,268 (regarding blows that inflict wounds).

248 Shīrāzī, *Risāla*, 389 no. 2,168; and cf. his *Fiqh*, 38:143.19 (*ijāzat al-ḥākim al-shar'ī*). Cf. above, ch. 11, note 238, on Muḥsin al-Fayḍ.

249 Muntaẓirī, *Dirāsāt*, 2:219.18 (*idhn al-ḥākim*); Makārim Shīrāzī, *Risāla*, 495 no. 2,419 (*ijāza-i ḥākim-i shar'*); likewise Sayfī, *Dalīl*, 210.4 (*idhn al-ḥākim*).

250 Nūrī, *Amr*, 247.8, 255.5 (but cf. 248.20). In one passage he observes that the layman (*al-'ādī min al-nās*) may have difficulty figuring out the intricacies of the duty, and may be subject to inappropriate motivations where it leads to violence; the oversight of the jurist is therefore necessary, if only through the designation of a virtuous person or persons in each district to superintend the performance of the duty (*ibid.*, 247.22). Ṭayyibī does not discuss the question.

251 Kharrāzī, *Amr*, 152.13; and see *ibid.*, 146.11, 150.16, 155.17. He uses the term (*al-*)*walī al-faqīh*.

252 A similar tendency is apparent in Muntaẓirī's treatment of the duty. He makes violence and even, in some contexts, aspects of the verbal performance of the duty a matter for the ruling authority (*al-ḥākim al-mutasalliṭ*) (*Dirāsāt*, 2:225.3). Compare his similarly statist interpretations of Q3:104 (*ibid.*, 227.7), and of the long activist tradition, which makes no mention of the state (*ibid.*, 231.4, and cf. 228.19).

253 This speech is reported in 'Amr bah ma'rūf wa nahy az munkar bāyad hamānand-i namāz farāgīr shawad', in *Jumhūrī-i Islāmī*, 23 Tīr, 1371 sh., 14d.98; the passage is quoted in, for example, Muḥammad Isḥāq Mas'ūdī, *Pizhūhishī dar amr bah ma'rūf wa nahy az munkar az dīdgāh-i Qur'ān wa riwāyāt*, Tehran 1374 sh., 148 no. 3, 264.11. Mas'ūdī naturally adopts this view himself (*ibid.*, 264.5), as do Khusraw Taqaddusī Nīyā (*Dars-hāyī az amr bah ma'rūf wa nahy az munkar*, Qumm 1375 sh., 65.14) and Muḥammad Riḍā Akbarī (*Taḥlīlī naw wa 'amalī az amr bah ma'rūf wa nahy az munkar dar 'aṣr-i ḥāḍir*, Iṣfahān 1375 sh., 134.18).

The other major innovation in modern Imāmī thought on forbidding wrong parallels a development we have already documented on the Sunnī side: the increasing sense of the importance of being organised.[254] In a talk of 1380/1960, Muṭahharī observes that individual action is not very effective, particularly in the world as it is today; what is needed is cooperation.[255] Ten years later he simply equates forbidding wrong with fellow-feeling (*hamdardī*), solidarity (*hambastagī*), cooperation (*hamkārī*) and other such qualities.[256] Ṭayyibī speaks of the need for institutions and for an Islamic state.[257] Shīrāzī remarks that in this age commanding and forbidding require something like industrial planning (*taṣnīʿ wa-tansīq*).[258] Nūrī argues that in our time the forces of evil are well equipped (*mujahhaza bi-tajhīzāt*), and we have to respond in kind.[259] What is called for today is accordingly something much more concerted and systematic than the view of the duty enshrined in the old juristic tradition. It is not the business of the writers who concern us to tell us exactly what this revamping would consist of; but a couple of indications are given by Ṣādiqī, who infers from Q3:104 a duty to form a group of guardians (*pāsdārān*) of Islam,[260] and requires the Islamic state to establish a Ministry of Forbidding Wrong.[261]

In this new emphasis on organisation, the Imāmīs sound very much like the Sunnīs. Where they differ from them is that the Imāmīs have moved to provide a conceptual foundation for this emphasis through a development within their scholastic tradition. Specifically, what is involved is a new twist in the handling of three conditions of the classical four: the knowledge, efficacy and danger conditions.

254 We already find Ṣāfī Gulpāyagānī devoting a section to the need for cooperation in forbidding wrong (*Rāh-i iṣlāḥ*, 53–6). For the Sunnīs, see above, 516f.

255 Muṭahharī, 'Amr ba-maʿrūf', 89.5. The limited extent of the powers of individuals is also remarked on in Āshtiyānī, *Tafsīr-i numūna*, 3:36.7. Whether Muṭahharī would have liked the kind of cooperation that emerged in the Islamic Republic may be doubted. Expounding a proposal of Khumaynī in an interview that he gave two weeks before he was killed, he set aside the idea of a ministry for *al-amr biʾl-maʿrūf* on the ground that this would mean an undesirable clerical role in government (*Pīrāmūn-i Jumhūrī-i Islāmī*, Tehran and Qumm 1364 sh., 25.8); he called for organisation, training and central authority, but in the framework of an institution independent of the state (*ibid.*, 27.9). For the idea of a ministry for *al-amr biʾl-maʿrūf*, see also below, note 261.

256 Muṭahharī, *Ḥamāsa*, 2:160.4. 257 Ṭayyibī, *Taqīya*, 160.7, 165.11, 166.7, 253.9.

258 Shīrāzī, *Fiqh*, 38:145.13. His examples of ways in which it might be appropriate to perform the duty include opening a college, founding a club and creating a library (*ibid.*, 145.8). 259 Nūrī, *Amr*, 65.6.

260 Ṣādiqī, *Risāla*, 242.9. For the *Pāsdārān-i Inqilāb*, or Revolutionary Guard, as established during the revolution, see Bakhash, *The reign of the Ayatollahs*, 63f.

261 Ṣādiqī, *Risāla*, 243.5. For this idea, cf. also W. Floor, 'The office of muhtasib in Iran', *Iranian Studies*, 18 (1985), 53 (I owe this reference to Giorgio Vercellin); *al-Mūjaz ʿan Īrān*, 6 no. 3, November 1996, 7d.3; and above, note 255. Nūrī mentions that the jurist (sc. the Supreme Guide) should oversee the performance of the duty, if only by naming a good man or men in each locality (*ṣuqʿ wa-balad*) to superintend it (*Amr*, 248.2; cf. above, ch. 13, note 51).

It will be simplest to begin with Nūrī's account, since this presents the ideas in a fully developed form, and then to go back to trace their evolution. What Nūrī argues is more or less as follows. In a situation in which performance of the duty has been aborted because one of these conditions was not satisfied, we might be tempted to assume that we are thereby morally in the clear: we had no duty, and accordingly did nothing. But what such an outcome in fact suggests is that we were negligent in a prior duty to prepare ourselves for such eventualities. If the problem was that we did not know right from wrong, we should have been at pains to educate ourselves in advance.[262] If the problem was that we lacked the means to perform the duty effectively, we should have expended effort to prepare those means beforehand.[263] And if the problem was that we were in danger, that points to a weakness which again we should have had the foresight to remedy.[264]

This style of thought does have a root in the older Imāmī doctrine of forbidding wrong.[265] In discussing the knowledge condition, scholars of the early Ṣafawid period had suggested circumstances in which one might have a duty to get to know. It is a condition for valid prayer that one be in a state of ritual purity; but failure to put oneself into such a state does not mean that one is entitled to forget about prayer. In the same way, might it not be argued that in certain circumstances one has an obligation to inform oneself about right and wrong? The situation the jurists envisaged was that one knew (say from the testimony of two witnesses of good character) that what someone was doing was wrong, but that one did not oneself know just what was wrong about it. As this may suggest, the Ṣafawid jurists were not engaged in confronting a burning contemporary issue; in a style that was very typical of them, they were simply being clever. But the idea they put forward was one that could be applied to all three of the relevant conditions, and used to quite different effect.

262 Nūrī, *Amr*, 77–83, esp. 79.10, 83.5; cf. also *ibid.*, 94.17.

263 *Ibid.*, 89–95, esp. 95.9 (with analogy to the knowledge condition). He draws an analogy with *jihād* (*ibid.*, 89.14), defining the relation of *al-amr bi'l-ma'rūf* to *jihād* in a manner reminiscent of Sa'īd Ḥawwā (*ibid.*, 90.6; cf. above, note 77). He admits that the jurists have not explicitly addressed the issue of preparing the means of efficacy in advance, but finds a precedent in their argument that there is a duty to take office under an unjust ruler where one will thereby be enabled to forbid wrong (*ibid.*, 91.3; for an early statement of this view, see W. Madelung, 'A treatise of the Sharīf al-Murtaḍā on the legality of working for the government', *Bulletin of the School of Oriental and African Studies*, 43 (1980), 23.14 = 27). The power he is talking about may be cultural, social and financial (Nūrī, *Amr*, 92.15), or financial, economic and military (*ibid.*, 94.12). He speaks of *i'dād muqaddamāt al-ta'thīr* (*ibid.*, 89.16), or uses similar phrases.

264 *Ibid.*, 114.18.

265 See above, ch. 11, notes 288f. The underlying technical distinction is between a condition for being obligated (*sharṭ al-wujūb*) and a condition for valid performance of the duty (*sharṭ al-wājib*); the latter, unlike the former, imposes a duty to take action to fulfil the condition (see Sayyid 'Alawī, *Niẓārat*, 38.8).

To my knowledge, the first scholar to move significantly in this direction was Sharīʿatmadārī.[266] After raising the question with regard to the conditions in general,[267] he discusses the knowledge condition, and concludes that it is of the kind that one must take action to fulfil.[268] With regard to the efficacy condition, his position is more complicated. He has already introduced a typically modern distinction between a social (*ijtimāʿī*) and a personal (*fardī*) form of the duty; the former, unlike the latter, is performed by an organised group (*gurūh, jamʿīyat*) of suitably trained and qualified people.[269] He now says that in the case of the social and collective form of the duty – as opposed to the personal form – there is an obligation to satisfy the efficacy condition;[270] we must lay the foundations for the social duty so that its performance will be effective.[271] He does not discuss the question when he comes to the danger condition, though he remarks in his account of it that students of the Islamic sciences in particular need to be prepared to carry out the social duty.[272]

This style of thought does not seem to have been widespread in Sharīʿatmadārī's generation. Shīrāzī shared it, but only with respect to the knowledge condition;[273] Khumaynī was untouched by it, which helps to explain its rather unsteady progress. Two younger authors who took it up were Muṭahharī and Ṭayyibī. Muṭahharī showed no familiarity with it in his talk of 1380/1960, though his plea for logic (*manṭiq*) – by which he meant something like creativeness and ingenuity in social engineering[274] – could be construed as a concern to secure the means of efficacy.[275] In his

[266] The lectures written down by Sayyid ʿAlawī cannot have been given later than 1387/1967, the date that appears at the end of the book (*ibid.*, 137.13; cf. also the dating of the introduction, *ibid.*, 22.11). There is a rather vague anticipation (or echo?) of Sharīʿatmadārī's thinking in Bihishtī, 'Rūḥānīyat', 160.21. [267] *Ibid.*, 40.2.

[268] *Ibid.*, 44.7.

[269] *Ibid.*, 31.3, 31.13; and cf. *ibid.*, 17.7 in Sayyid ʿAlawī's introduction. Sharīʿatmadārī remarks that the social form of the duty brings into being a government which is one hundred per cent virtuous and Islamic (*ibid.*, 36.10). [270] *Ibid.*, 52.8.

[271] *Ibid.*, 53.4. [272] *Ibid.*, 130.8. [273] Shīrāzī, *Fiqh*, 38:127.6.

[274] Muṭahharī, 'Amr ba-maʿrūf', 89.14. For example, if we want to put a stop to vicious gossip among our traditional Iranian women, pious exhortations get us nowhere; we have to think up some other way for them to relax in their spare time (*ibid.*, 90.14).

[275] Cf. Muṭahharī, 'Amr ba-maʿrūf', 91.8. His insistence on logic goes with his emphasis on the fact that forbidding wrong, unlike praying or fasting, is an activity that turns on getting results (see Muṭahharī, ''Adālat az naẓar-i Islām', 45.9; his *Ḥamāsa*, 2:190.5; and his *Jādhiba wa dāfiʿa-i ʿAlī*, 124.18). One root of Muṭahharī's thinking here is the scholastic doctrine that the duty of forbidding wrong is *tawaṣṣulī* (that is, the duty is discharged if the purpose is achieved irrespective of the intention of the performer), not *taʿabbudī* (the duty is only discharged if the action is performed with the intention of obeying God) (for this distinction, see Mishkīnī Ardabīlī, *Muṣṭalaḥāt al-uṣūl*, 191.17; for its application to forbidding wrong, see Khumaynī, *Taḥrīr*, 1:465 no. 13, and Masʿūdī, *Pizhūhishī*, 254.2). It is, of course, good that the duty be performed with a pious intention; one medieval Imāmī jurist provides appropriate verbal formulae for such performance (Ibn Ṭayy, *Durr*, 104.5).

talk of 1390/1970 he continued to speak of logic.[276] But he also insisted on the duty to secure the power needed for efficacy. The response of Islam to the man who says he doesn't have the power to perform the duty is: 'Fine, but go and acquire the power!'[277] The other author who adopted the doctrine of prior duty, and with regard to all three conditions, was Ṭayyibī.[278] His doctrine is essentially Sharīʿatmadārī's, but extended to cover the danger condition, and expressed in a language suffused with political activism.[279] His call for the fulfilment of the prior duty of preparing the means of forbidding wrong is insistent.[280] Such views are by now widely known,[281] but they have not achieved the same recognition as the revision of the danger condition. The intellectually conservative Kharrāzī, in his recent monograph on forbidding wrong, does not pay much attention to them;[282] nevertheless, an equally recent commentator on one of Khumaynī's accounts adopts them.[283]

Alongside these doctrinal questions, the history of forbidding wrong as it has been established in the Islamic Republic over the last twenty years is a subject of considerable social, cultural and political interest. According to the Constitution, the duty is one that must be fulfilled 'by the people with respect to one another, by the government with respect to the people, and by the people with respect to the government'.[284] In practice, the first

[276] Muṭahharī, *Ḥamāsa*, 2:190.5.

[277] *Ibid.*, 193.22, and cf. 201.8 (speaking also of the knowledge condition). He gives the analogy of the traditional discussion of taking office under an unjust ruler (*ibid.*, 194.5; see above, note 263).

[278] This was already noted by Enayat (*Modern Islamic political thought*, 180).

[279] See esp. Ṭayyibī, *Taqīya*, 97–101; note the emphasis on extending the analysis of the knowledge condition to all three (*ibid.*, 101.10, 105.3). Ṭayyibī makes what is basically the same distinction as Sharīʿatmadārī between the personal and social forms of the duty (*ibid.*, 165.11), though in the context of the social duty he lays more emphasis on popular participation (*ibid.*, 166.7) and the role of the state (*ibid.*, 165.14, 253.12, 261.4); however for Ṭayyibī this distinction seems to have no special bearing on the efficacy condition.

[280] See, for example, *ibid.*, 144.4, 145.7, 165.3. He anticipates Nūrī's talk of *muqaddamāt* (see, for example, *ibid.*, 98.9, 146.15).

[281] An indication of this is the way in which authors who do not adopt the approach in any systematic way will nevertheless refer casually to the 'prerequisites' (*muqaddamāt*) of the duty. See Muntaẓirī, *Dirāsāt*, 2:256.1 (*iʿdād al-muqaddamāt*); Ṣādiqī, *Risāla*, 239.9 (*tahīya-i muqaddamātash nīz wājib ast*), and cf. 239.19; Kharrāzī, *Amr*, 155.15 (*wujūb taḥṣīl muqaddamātihi*); Ibrāhīm Amīnī in anon., 'Guzārishī az simīnār-i amr bah maʿrūf', 23 Abān, 4b.77 (*bāyad ān muqaddamāt farāham shawad*).

[282] For his casual use of the term *muqaddamāt*, see the preceding note. He accepts – with due qualification – the duty to get to know (Kharrāzī, *Amr*, 63.10), but that is as far as it goes. Contrast his endorsement of Khumaynī's qualification of the danger condition (see above, note 235).

[283] Sayfī, *Dalīl*, 101.4, 104.6 (on the knowledge condition); *ibid.*, 121.13 (on the efficacy condition). He emphasises the institutional aspect of the prior duty with regard to efficacy (*ibid.*, 121.16). He offers no comparable analysis of the danger condition, but this is because he more or less rejects the condition as such (*ibid.*, 167.3).

[284] Islamic Propagation Organization, *The Constitution of the Islamic Republic of Iran*, Tehran n.d., 21 article 8.

and third have been relatively muted by the din of the second.[285] Iran, like Saudi Arabia, has become a society in which forbidding wrong is overwhelmingly a function of the state apparatus, in this case involving a plurality of organs which do not always act in concert.[286] Because Iranian society is culturally richer than that of Saudi Arabia, and Iranian politics more open, there is a better story to be told here, and much more material with which to tell it.[287] 'It has been bad all morning,' as a pious Iranian confided to an American journalist regarding his task of forbidding wrongdoing by couples hiking in the mountains behind Tehran in the high summer. 'Girls in baseball caps, covered with makeup, coming up here without proper headscarves. And the boys use words I can't repeat and strip off their shirts. It is a dirty, lonely job. But we must be ready to die for God.'[288] Yet for all its considerable interest, this would not be a study which I am qualified to attempt; nor does it relate to the individual performance of the duty.

One source that does shed some light on the performance of the duty 'by the people with respect to one another' is a collection of responsa of Khumaynī which date mostly from the early years of the revolution.[289] The section on forbidding wrong contains twenty-three questions with

[285] I was told some years ago that the Supreme Guide issued a pronouncement stressing individual responsibility for *al-amr bi'l-maʿrūf* – this being a way to get the state off people's backs somewhat – and that discussion followed. I have no written record of this development.

[286] For a complaint about the lack of central coordination (*tansīq markazī*) between the various parts of the Iranian state apparatus whose activities bear on *al-amr bi'l-maʿrūf*, see ʿAbbās ʿAlī ʿAmīd Zanjānī, 'Ḥaqq al-mushāraka fī ṣiyāghat al-niẓām al-siyāsī wa'l-ijtimāʿī', in *Ḥuqūq al-insān fī 'l-Islām: maqālāt al-Muʾtamar al-khāmis lil-fikr al-Islāmī*, Tehran 1987, 75.21. A case in point is an incident in which the ʿAlī ibn Abī Ṭālib Foundation organised a competition to test the general public's knowledge of *al-amr bi'l-maʿrūf*. The Foundation ran into a storm of criticism because it had announced that one of the prizes would be a video – this at a time when traffic in videos had been declared illegal, and there were daily reports of clashes between the forces of order and the owners and distributors of videos (anon., 'Intiqād az iʿlām-i jāyiza-i "wīdīyo" barā-yi musābaqa-i ʿamr bah maʿrūf wa nahy az munkar', *Iran Times* (Washington), 2 October 1992; I am indebted to Shohreh Gholsorkhi for giving me a copy of this article).

[287] For two contrasting perspectives, see the lectures of Nabī Ṣādiqī published in Dādsarā-yi Inqilāb-i Islāmī-i Mubāraza bā Mawādd-i Mukhaddir wa Munkarāt-i Tihrān, *Shīwahā-yi ṣaḥīḥ-i amr bah maʿrūf wa nahy az munkar*, Tehran 1371 sh., and Geraldine Brooks, 'Teen-age infidels hanging out', *The New York Times Magazine*, 30 April 1995, 44–9. As Ṣādiqī sees it, the problems are not confined to teenage delinquents; he considers it intolerable that marriage-halls (*tālārhā-yi ʿarūsī*) in the Islamic Republic, though private, should not be under official supervision (*Shīwahā*, 228.11).

[288] Chris Hedges, 'With Mullahs' sleuths eluded, hijinks in the hills', *The New York Times*, 8 August 1994, 4. 'When we see couples go up the peaks, we must follow to make sure they are brothers and sisters or are married', the poor man explained. 'But all this climbing, all this walking, is hard. By the end of the day I collapse.'

[289] Khumaynī (d. 1409/1989), *Istiftāʾāt* (in Persian), Qumm 1366–72 sh. The introduction states that most of the questions were put to Khumaynī in 1360–2 sh. (i.e. 1981–3).

Khumaynī's answers.[290] Sometimes the questioner makes explicit reference to the duty,[291] but more often it is the answer that does so.[292] One question is about our obligation with regard to strangers 'under today's conditions';[293] but with few exceptions,[294] the common thread of the questions is a concern about our duty towards people with whom we have regular social relations. Can one, for example, be friends with an observant Muslim who lacks faith in the authority of the Supreme Guide (*wilāyat-i faqīh*) and has an eclectic (*iltiqāṭī*) style of thought?[295] Many of these problems concern family ties. Every Iranian family, it seems, is unhappy in the same way: one member or another remains mired in the immorality, irreligion or political allegiances of the fallen Ṭāghūtī regime. One questioner has four nephews and a niece who are not in the least religiously observant, make their living mostly from gambling and drug-peddling, and even now live in hope of a Ṭāghūtī restoration – may they never see it even in their dreams![296] A woman laments that her father does not believe in God, the Prophet, or the world to come, never prays, and is strongly opposed to the revolution – whereas her mother, sister and brothers are all believers. Talking to him nicely doesn't work, and things are getting worse by the day. At this point she mentions that she is married, and explains that matters have now reached a point where her husband refuses to visit her parents' house. What is she to do?[297] One husband of an impious wife complains that she never performs the dawn prayer.[298] Another has a wife who prays only once in a while, and then after much aggravation; he suffers mental anguish, and is worried as to whether he will be held responsible at the Resurrection.[299] In the years that

[290] *Ibid.*, 1:482–90. In what follows, I shall refer to the questions by their numbers within the section. [291] Nos. 1, 4, 8.

[292] Nos. 2, 10–12, 14–16, 18, 20, 22. In other cases the answer refers to counselling (*irshād*) (nos. 7, 9, 13, 19) or guidance (*hidāyat, rāhnumāʾī*) (nos. 21, 23). In some instances the reference to the duty is at most implicit (nos. 3, 5f., 17).

[293] No. 1. The point of the question seems to be that so many of our interactions under modern conditions are impersonal, and therefore unconducive to the performance of the duty.

[294] No. 5 is about the political stance to be adopted towards people with a lukewarm (but not overtly hostile) attitude to the struggle against 'World Ṭāghūt and Unbelief'; no. 6 poses the same question regarding pseudo-clerics who are openly pro-American; and no. 10 is about people who throw away food.

[295] No. 8. The answer is that one should counsel him.

[296] No. 13. Here, as in several other cases where ties of kinship are at issue, Khumaynī warns against severing such ties and enjoins counselling or reproving the offender (nos. 12f., 18, 21, and cf. nos. 17, 20). Where such ties are not at stake, cutting off relations, though not necessary in itself (no. 3, and cf. no. 8), may be a way to perform the duty (no. 2, and cf. no. 4). [297] No. 21. [298] No. 16.

[299] No. 15. Some of the same concerns occur in the responsa of Gulpāyagānī (see, for example, *Majmaʿ al-masāʾil*, 1:426 no. 1,298, 427 no. 1,301, 428 no. 1,304, 429 no. 1,309, 431 no. 1,315, 432 no. 1,317); but the presentation of the questions is rather dry, and the sharp political focus is absent.

have passed since Khumaynī pronounced on these questions, the tensions they reflect are likely to have diminished to the extent that sharp polarisation has given way to shared cynicism in the Iranian population.

We may end this survey by glancing at modern Imāmī attitudes towards the performance of the duty by women – an issue which the Imāmī scholars of the past had not thought to raise. Here those scholars who discuss the question – and many do not – usually quote Q9:71 and infer that women too are obligated.[300] Imāmī exegetes are significantly more likely than their Sunnī counterparts to highlight this aspect of the verse: of the fifteen modern Imāmī Koran commentaries I consulted, five did so.[301] But there is little discussion of how other aspects of the legal position of women might affect their performance of the duty. Ṭayyibī says that Muslim women must participate in the duty 'shoulder to shoulder' (*dūshādūsh*) with Muslim men, which certainly suggests that segregation should not be much of a barrier; and although his youthful enthusiasm is unlikely to represent settled clerical opinion, his phrase is echoed by two recent clerical writers of a more or less liberal bent.[302] Khumaynī himself was once consulted by a nurse (*parastār*) who was concerned about her duty with regard to war-wounded patients who failed to pray because of the inadequacy of their faith; he replied that it was her duty to forbid wrong.[303]

300 Ṭayyibī, *Taqīya*, 206.15 (a strong statement); Muntaẓirī, *Dirāsāt*, 2:225.11; Muḥammad Khāmina'ī, 'al-Ḥuqūq al-insāniyya lil-mar'a fī 'l-Islām wa-fī 'l-qawānīn al-waḍ'iyya', in *Ḥuqūq al-insān fī 'l-Islām: maqālāt al-Mu'tamar al-khāmis lil-fikr al-Islāmī*, Tehran 1987, 379.2 (explicitly putting men and women on an equal footing in this regard); Muhammad Jawad Bahonar, 'Islam and women's rights', in Muhammad Taqi Mesbah *et al.*, *Status of women in Islam*, New Delhi 1990, 38 (cited in Mayer, *Islam and human rights*, 121). In a seminar on the duty, Āyatullāhs Muḥammadī Gīlānī and Ibrāhīm Amīnī mention the inclusion of women, though without quoting the verse (anon., 'Guzārishī az simīnār-i amr bah ma'rūf', 23 Ābān, 4a.23, 4b.72), and Taqaddusī Nīyā relates a story in which a woman corrects the caliph 'Umar (r. 13–23/634–44) (*Dars-hāyī az amr bah ma'rūf*, 104f. no. 13). The Akhbārī Zayn al-Dīn, likewise without quoting the verse, remarks in a domestic context that a believing woman is obligated (*Kalimat al-taqwā*, 2:316.26 no. 32).

301 Muḥammad al-Karamī, *Tafsīr*, Qumm 1402, 4:102.11; Muḥammad Thaqafī Tihrānī (d. 1404/1983f.), *Rawān-i jadīd*, Tehran n.d., 2:600.9; 'Alī-Akbar Qurashī, *Tafsīr-i aḥsan al-ḥadīth*, Tehran 1366–71 sh., 4:269.23; Muḥammad Bāqir Ḥujjatī and 'Abd al-Karīm Bī-āzār Shīrāzī, *Tafsīr-i kāshif*, Tehran 1363– sh., 5:415.13; Akbar Hāshimī Rafsanjānī, *Tafsīr-i rāhnumā*, Qumm 1371– sh., 7:189 no. 8. A commentary that does not address the point is that of Bānū Mujtahida-i Amīn (d. 1403/1983), *Makhzan al-'irfān*, Iṣfahān n.d., 6:73. For Sunnī exegetes, cf. above, note 100.

302 Ṭayyibī, *Taqīya*, 208.5, and cf. 209.4. One of the authors who echo him is Abū 'Alī Khudākaramī (*Do aṣl-i ustuwār yā amr bah ma'rūf wa nahy az munkar*, Qumm 1375 sh., 137.13, and see 69.1; this author is in the tradition of Muṭahharī, see for example *ibid.*, 178.15). The other writer, and the more liberal, is Islāmī Ardakānī (*Amr*, 35.2). Women, he says, have the duty of commanding and forbidding men, who have to accept this from them (*ibid.*, 35.15). Ṭayyibī's work appears in Islāmī's select bibliography (*ibid.*, 206.13).

303 Khumaynī, *Istiftā'āt*, 1:489 no. 22 (it was well known at the time that such nurses were female). Khumaynī also says that, subject to the observance of Islamic norms, a girl may give guidance and assistance to a boy (*ibid.*, 490 no. 23). Gulpāyagānī tells a woman that

4. SUNNĪS AND IMĀMĪ SHĪʿITES COMPARED

So far I have presented the evolution of Sunnī and Imāmī attitudes towards forbidding wrong in modern times as two separate stories. It is now time to bring them together by considering the links between them and examining the major similarities and differences.

The links between the two camps have been notably asymmetrical – as might be expected from the disparity in size between the two communities. It is rare indeed for Sunnī authors to show awareness of Imāmī views, let alone a willingness to learn from them. As we have seen, the Egyptian Aḥmad Ḥijāzī al-Saqqā knows and approves of the fact that his Imāmī contemporaries are not following the doctrine attributed to them by the medieval Sunnī scholars.[304] The Jordanian Koran commentator Ibrāhīm al-Qaṭṭān (d. 1404/1984) quotes at length, and with implicit approval, a passage from a work of his Imāmī colleague Muḥammad Jawād Maghniyya (d. 1400/1979);[305] this is the only such case I have encountered. Egyptian writers sympathetic to the Muʿtazilites make occasional reference to Imāmī views in accordance with their catholic approach to the resources of the wider Islamic tradition.[306] A recent work in this vein by the leftist ʿĀdil al-Sukkarī is a case in point.[307] But for all his openness, he knows little about traditional Imāmī thought,[308] and nothing about modern developments;

if she can, she should forbid wrong to some improperly dressed women with whom she interacts socially (*Majmaʿ al-masāʾil*, 1:434 no. 1,324); but the question of her reproving men is not raised. Faḍl Allāh discusses the related question of pious young men admonishing women to whom they are not related, approving the practice with suitable qualifications (*Masāʾil*, 2:313 no. 775). [304] See above, 530f.

[305] Qaṭṭān, *Taysīr al-tafsīr*, 1:287.5 (to Q3:104), quoting Maghniyya, *al-Tafsīr al-kāshif*, 2:124.1. However, the passage from which Qaṭṭān is quoting includes a footnote citing the *Tafsīr al-Manār* (Maghniyya, *al-Tafsīr al-kāshif*, 2:125 n. 1) which Qaṭṭān discreetly omits (*Taysīr al-tafsīr*, 1:288.22): in it ʿAbduh compliments the Shīʿites on their proselytising zeal, and backs this up with a reminiscence about a proselytising Mutawālī wet-nurse whom he took into service in Beirut (Riḍā, *Tafsīr al-Manār*, 4:35.9). Cf. also above, note 4. [306] For this philo-Muʿtazilite trend, cf. above, note 45.

[307] ʿĀdil al-Sukkarī, *al-Amr biʾl-maʿrūf waʾl-nahy ʿan al-munkar ʿinda ʾl-uṣūliyyīn*, Cairo 1993. This author advertises his catholic approach (*ibid.*, 12.3), and makes frequent reference to Muʿtazilite sources and views (see, for example, *ibid.*, 21.5, 42.17, 69.6, 82.1), while Zaydīs, Ibāḍīs and Imāmīs are also represented in his footnotes (see, for example, *ibid.*, 56 n. 4 for the Zaydīs and Ibāḍīs, and *ibid.*, 31 n. 2, 39 nn. 2f., 47 n. 3 for the Imāmīs). Most strikingly, he shows no discomfort in lumping together Jaʿfar al-Ṣādiq (d. 148/765) and Ibn Ḥanbal (d. 241/855) as quietists (*ibid.*, 120.8). This gives him wide room to manoeuvre, which he uses to privilege a view intermediate between activism and quietism: we should maintain a truce (*hudna*) with unjust rule until such time as we are in a position to overthrow it (*ibid.*, 128.11, 131.15, 133.5). The elegance of this view is twofold. It enables him to distance himself from the current fundamentalist violence, which he dislikes (*ibid.*, 14.14, and cf. his unfavourable account of Ḥanbalite rampages in Baghdad in the time of Barbahārī (d. 329/941), *ibid.*, 122.15). And yet at the same time he is able to endorse the full range of Ghazzālī's levels (*ibid.*, 134–8), and to remain a revolutionary at heart. [308] See particularly *ibid.*, 37.9, 59.11, 110.9.

the traditional Imāmī doctrine of forbidding wrong has in any case little to offer a leftist. ʿAdl is another contemporary author with Muʿtazilite sympathies, though he keeps them more in check.[309] He knows enough to tell us that some Imāmī scholars consider forbidding wrong to be obligatory by reason, but spoils the effect by going on to say that they hold it not to be obligatory by revelation.[310]

Imāmī scholars, by contrast, are often prepared to make some use of the resources of Sunnī Islam. They like to draw on the first modern commentary on Q3:104, that of ʿAbduh and Riḍā. Thus ʿAbbās-ʿAlī Islāmī, a preacher,[311] takes a mass of material from it,[312] while Nūrī summarises its curriculum for prospective missionaries;[313] it is likewise cited in Koran commentaries,[314] and even finds its way into the newspapers of the Islamic Republic.[315] Imāmī authors also go back to older Sunnī sources. On occasion they quote Ghazzālī,[316] and they develop a liking for some Sunnī Prophetic traditions. One is the tradition about the people in the boat;[317] another states: 'Each of you is a shepherd, and each of you is responsible for his flock.'[318] As these examples suggest, the borrowing is not random:

309 For these sympathies, see, for example, ʿAdl, *al-Fiqh al-ghāʾib*, 252.7, 254.3.

310 *Ibid.*, 252.3; cf. above, ch. 11, notes 130f., 241f.

311 Islāmī, *Do az yād rafta*, 16.9 of the introduction.

312 *Ibid.*, 94–112. He also makes use of other Sunnī Koran commentaries, such as those of Fakhr al-Dīn al-Rāzī (d. 606/1210) (*ibid.*, 82.6) and Sayyid Quṭb (*ibid.*, 89.8), though not on the same scale. Cf. also Jaʿfar Mīr ʿAẓīmī, *Do farīḍa-i buzurg: amr bah maʿrūf wa nahy az munkar*, Qumm 1372 sh., 20.14.

313 Nūrī, *Amr*, 30.14; cf. above, note 29.

314 Maghniyya, *al-Tafsīr al-kāshif*, 2:125 n. 1; Āshtiyānī, *Tafsīr-i numūna*, 3:42.6 (to Q3:104).

315 Anon., 'Guzārishī az simīnār-i amr bah maʿrūf', 23 Abān, 4b.68; anon., 'Amr bah maʿrūf wa nahy az munkar yā ʿamal bah masʾūlīyat-hā-yi ijtimāʿī', no. 3, col. d.19. Cf. also Ṣādiqī, *Shīwahā*, 123.11.

316 Āyatī, 'Amr ba-maʿrūf', 48.2, 53.13 (from Ghazzālī, *Iḥyāʾ*, 2:306.4), 58.21, and cf. 66 nn. 2–4; Muṭahharī, *Ḥamāsa*, 2:44.18, 45.9; Ṣādiqī, *Shīwahā*, 138.9 (quoting the *Kīmiyā-yi saʿādat*). Both are rather eclectic authors: Muṭahharī quotes Sartre (*Ḥamāsa*, 2:107.19), while Ṣādiqī drops such names as Mendeleyev, Jung, Freud, Schopenhauer, Hammurabi, Samuel Smiles, Gustave Le Bon and Max Planck (*Shīwahā*, 18.11, 48.13, 48.16, 64.6, 67.4, 68.5, 113.1).

317 Ṣāfī Gulpāyagānī, *Rāh-i iṣlāḥ*, 14.13 (citing the *Ṣaḥīḥ* of Bukhārī (d. 256/870)); Sayyid ʿAlawī, *Niẓārat*, 81.4 (an unacknowledged paraphrase); Āshtiyānī, *Tafsīr-i numūna*, 3:37.20, whence Khumaynī (d. 1409/1989), *Risāla-i nawīn*, Tehran 1359–67 sh., vol. 4: *Masāʾil-i siyāsī wa ḥuqūqī*, collected by ʿAbd al-Karīm Bī-āzār Shīrāzī, 206.3; Abū ʾl-Qāsim ʿAlīzāda Ḥasanābādī, *Niẓārat-i millī yā amr bah maʿrūf wa nahy az munkar*, Qumm 1371 sh., 25.18; anon., 'Amr bah maʿrūf wa nahy az munkar yā ʿamal bah masʾūlīyat-hā-yi ijtimāʿī', no. 1, col. b.37; and cf. Masʿūdī, *Pizhūhishī*, 347.12; Muḥammad Taqī Miṣbāḥ Yazdī, 'Tashrīḥ-i falsafa wa angīza-i amr bah maʿrūf wa nahy az munkar', in *Niẓārat-i ṣāliḥān*, Tehran 1371 sh., 35.5; Taqaddusī Nīyā, *Dars-hāyī az amr bah maʿrūf*, 105f. no. 14. For the tradition, see above, note 61.

318 Ṣāfī Gulpāyagānī, *Rāh-i iṣlāḥ*, 45.12 (citing a Shīʿite source); Sayyid ʿAlawī, *Niẓārat*, 81.1 (saying that it is transmitted by Sunnīs and Shīʿites alike); Muṭahharī, *Ḥamāsa*, 2:155.4 (with a footnoted reference to a work of Suyūṭī (d. 911/1505); Islāmī, *Do az yād rafta*,

the theme, once again, is solidarity and organisation. It is in line with this that modern Imāmī writers show a marked interest in the classical Sunnī institution of the censorship (*ḥisba*) and its literature,[319] and even make occasional reference to the organisation of forbidding wrong in contemporary Islamic countries – by which they presumably intend Saudi Arabia.[320]

Turning to politics, Sunnīs and Imāmī Shīʿites have found themselves in rather different situations in recent decades. On the Imāmī side, the picture has been clear-cut. The fact that Iran is a major Islamic country, and also the only major Imāmī one, has given it an indisputable predominance in the Shīʿite world. This is fully reflected in its intellectual role; most of the Imāmī authors quoted in this chapter are Iranian, and it is the Iranian political scene to which their thinking is primarily related. Elsewhere, Imāmī communities usually find themselves within the borders of countries in which other communities predominate, often exercising outright hegemony – a situation that has not changed in the last few decades, and may well not do so in any foreseeable future. Meanwhile in Iran, the political context of Imāmī thought has changed sharply. Before the Islamic revolution, Imāmism faced a state that was at best inhospitable, and at worst inimical to its clergy; the choice was between putting up with the state and confronting it. Since the revolution, the state has been Islamic by definition, and revolution is now for export only; the choice has been between

11.8 (without a source); Mīr ʿAẓīmī, *Do farīḍa-i buzurg*, 7.12 (without a source); Ḥasanābādī, *Niẓārat-i millī*, 94.2 (with a reference to the *Ṣaḥīḥ* of Muslim (d. 261/875)); Masʿūdī, *Pizhūhishī*, 169.13 (citing both a Sunnī source and a rather recondite Shīʿite one). Khumaynī showed a liking for the tradition in the first year of the revolution (*Ṣaḥīfa-i nūr*, 7:34.9, 8:47.7, 9:194.13). It is mentioned once in Majlisī's *Biḥār* (75:38.23). Note also the pride of place given to the Sunnī 'three modes' tradition in Muḥammad Mahdī al-Āṣifī, 'Dirāsa fiqhiyya mūjaza ʿan ḥukm al-Islām fī mas'alat al-iʿtirāḍ ʿalā 'l-anẓima wa'l-ḥukm', *al-Nūr*, no. 44 (Shaʿbān 1415/January 1995), 37a.33, and cf. 37a.20 (I am indebted to Yitzhak Nakash for sending me a copy of this article). Other Sunnī traditions are quoted by Āyatī ('Amr ba-maʿrūf', 65.7, 65.19, 66.7).

319 Muṭahharī, 'Amr ba-maʿrūf', 78–82; Muṭahharī, *Ḥamāsa*, 2:197.21 (with a warm word for Orientalists, may God forgive their fathers, who publish such texts as the *Maʿālim al-qurba* of Ibn al-Ukhuwwa – the reference is to Reuben Levy, though he is not named); Mīlānī, 'al-Amr bi'l-maʿrūf', 46.12 (with reference to the *Maʿālim al-qurba*, *ibid.*, 47.4); Abū 'l-Faḍl Shakūrī, *Fiqh-i siyāsī-i Islām*, Qumm 1361 sh., 194.4 (with the suggestion that, with some revision of detail, the *Maʿālim al-qurba* could be adopted by the courts of the Islamic Republic in the struggle against wrongs, *ibid.*, 195.13); anon., 'Amr bah maʿrūf wa nahy az munkar yā ʿamal bah mas'ūlīyat-hā-yi ijtimāʿī', no. 2, col. f.49, and no. 3, col. a.1; Islāmī Ardakānī, *Amr*, 59–74 (with an account of the *Maʿālim al-qurba*, *ibid.*, 67.3); Khudākaramī, *Do aṣl-i ustuwār*, 77–106 (with many references to the *Maʿālim al-qurba*); Ramaḍān Fu'ādīyān, *Sayrī dar farīḍa-i amr bah maʿrūf wa nahy az munkar*, Qumm 1375 sh., 87–97 (with a long extract from Muṭahharī).

320 Tihrānī, *Amr*, 156.9; Ibrāhīm Amīnī in anon., 'Guzārishī az simīnār-i amr bah maʿrūf', 23 Abān, 4b.61; and cf. below, note 330.

identifying fully with the regime and pursuing a mildly dissident course within the limits of the system. This transition is readily apparent in the evolving doctrine of forbidding wrong, as it moved with considerable fanfare from quietist pessimism to revolutionary optimism, and then inconspicuously gave way to post-revolutionary concern for social order.[321]

By comparison with the Imāmī communities, the Sunnī world is enormously diverse and confusing. There is no one country whose politics set the pace, no single defining event, and in place of the stark contrast between the Shāh and Khumaynī there are many shades of grey. Few regimes are as adamantly secular as was that of the Shāh, while revolutionary Islamic regimes exist only in countries such as the Sudan and Afghanistan which are marginal to the intellectual life of the Muslim world; the one other self-consciously Islamic regime, that of Saudi Arabia, is deeply suspect in the eyes of many Islamic activists. Small wonder that the history of Sunnī political values as seen in modern Sunnī doctrines of forbidding wrong shows no clear and unequivocal evolution. Ironically, and in marked contrast to the Imāmī evolution, the most striking developments are in a quietist direction: the doctrine that performance of the duty 'with the hand' is for the state,[322] and the effective voiding of the duty by Sayyid Quṭb.[323]

The main concern that Sunnīs and Imāmīs have in common is solidarity and organisation.[324] It is in line with this that neither group shows much excitement about the humble traditional core of forbidding wrong: the duty of the individual to right wrongs as and when he comes across them, and to the best of his knowledge and abilities. The increased attention paid to the duty by modern Imāmī scholars[325] does not point to a revival of interest in this traditional core. Instead, the driving concerns of both Sunnīs and Imāmīs are at once more ambitious and characteristically modern, even when authentic features of the tradition can be adduced in support. Rāshid is excited to discover that the medieval scholars did on occasion touch on the law of Islamic activism.[326] Politically engaged Imāmīs were doubtless just as gratified to encounter in a work of the fourth/tenth-century author Ibn Shuʿba a speech of the martyr Ḥusayn in which forbidding wrong is the central term of a cascade of revolutionary rhetoric.[327] But it is precisely the rarity of such passages in the traditional

[321] See above, 533–41. [322] See above, 523–5. [323] See above, 528f.
[324] See above, 516–18, 542. [325] Cf. above, notes 200, 207. [326] See above, 517f.
[327] See the anthology of Maḥmūd Akbarzāda, *Ḥusayn pīshwā-yi insānhā*, Mashhad 1343 sh., 158.4; Khumaynī (d. 1409/1989), *al-Ḥukūma al-Islāmiyya*, n.p. n.d., 102.13 (the key passage, *ibid.*, 104.1, is repeated *ibid.*, 112.3); Khumaynī, *Wilāyat-i faqīh dar khuṣūṣ-i ḥukūmat-i Islāmī*, n.p. n.d., 124.14 (cf. Nagel, *Staat und Glaubensgemeinschaft*, 2:317f.);

sources that makes them finds, and by the same token the concern for organisation is very much a modern one. It is the result of living in a world in which the competitors for political power, whether states or parties, tend to be far more organised than ever before.

The countervailing tendency to marginalise what was previously central becomes explicit in some recent discussions. On the Sunnī side, we have seen how Quṭb downplays the individual aspect of the duty.[328] On the Imāmī side, such thinking abounds. Sharīʿatī denounces the reduction of the duty to a merely personal (*fardī*) one,[329] and the restriction of its scope to such trivialities as beards, hair and dress[330] – this at a time when the wrongs that really matter are such things as international imperialism, world Zionism, colonialism old and new, not to mention infatuation with the West (*Gharbzadagī*).[331] Ṭayyibī describes forbidding wrong as 'the most social of social questions';[332] he laments the fact that in recent centuries its 'social, progressive and revolutionary content' has been distorted, reducing the duty for the most part to a personal (*infirādī*) affair of little or no significance.[333] Muntaẓirī speaks of the performance of the duty by 'ordinary people in minor contexts' (*al-ashkhāṣ al-ʿādiyyīn fī ʾl-mawārid al-juzʾiyya*);[334] this petty form of the duty is clearly not much of a contribution to the grand objective of 'reforming society (*iṣlāḥ al-mujtamaʿ*) and extirpating corruption and wrong' – the purpose for which, he avers, the duty was created.[335] Nūrī formalises this attitude by distinguishing two circles.[336] In the first, our agenda is the total reform of society – moral, credal, economic and social – through the preparation and organisation of the means appropriate for the realisation of right in its broadest sense.[337] In the second, we are simply concerned with specific rights and wrongs that are actually happening or likely to do so.[338] God, as might be expected, is

Ṭayyibī, *Taqīya*, 158.11. For Ibn Shuʿba see above, ch. 11, note 49. Akbarzāda's anthology represents lay, not clerical activism; his immediate source for the speech is a work by Jawād Fāḍil which was published in 1334 sh./1955 (I am indebted to Azar Ashraf for obtaining this date for me).

328 See above, note 172. His dismissive reference to *iṣlāḥāt juzʾiyya* is echoed by Yāsīn (*Jihād*, 181.10, on not wasting all one's time on *ʿilāj al-juzʾiyyāt*), and he in turn is quoted by Ibn Ḥājj ('Ijāda', 10e.55). Ibrāhīm Dasūqī al-Shahāwī has a schema distinguishing three levels of *ḥisba*, of which the third is *al-daʿwa al-juzʾiyya* (*al-Ḥisba fī ʾl-Islām*, Cairo 1962, 26.5); while he does not actually disparage it, he passes over it very quickly (*ibid.*, 27.1). Cf. also Gómez García, *Marxismo*, 339.

329 Sharīʿatī, *Shīʿa*, 71.17, 74.11, 75.15.

330 *Ibid.*, 74.13, 75.5; cf. also the disparagement of the Saʿūdī practice of *al-amr biʾl-maʿrūf*, *ibid.*, 71.6.

331 *Ibid.*, 76.1, and cf. 75.8.

332 Ṭayyibī, *Taqīya*, 160.7.

333 *Ibid.*, 160.17. He concedes a little later that action on a personal basis (*iṣlāḥāt-i fardī*) is indeed part of the duty, but he does not want to see more important aspects of it sacrificed to this (*ibid.*, 163.17). See also *ibid.*, 254.1.

334 Muntaẓirī, *Dirāsāt*, 2:256.13.

335 *Ibid.*, 251.14.

336 See Nūrī, *Amr*, 66.23, where the distinction is introduced.

337 *Ibid.*, 69.12.

338 *Ibid.*, 67.5, and cf. 65.15, 66.16.

much more concerned with the first circle.[339] Other Imāmī scholars express similar attitudes.[340]

A Sunnī text that indirectly conveys a strong sense of the shift is found in a volume containing a separate printing of Ghazzālī's treatment of forbidding wrong.[341] In this format, this classic text becomes a little book of some 130 pages. It is not a scholarly edition, and was presumably aimed at a wide market. It is, however, accompanied by a short introduction by a scholar well known in the West, Riḍwān al-Sayyid. Sayyid's main concern in these pages is clearly to forestall the likely disappointment of the Muslim general reader. You might expect, he tells him, that Ghazzālī would take the opportunity of a discussion of forbidding wrong to set out the social and political problems confronting the Muslim world of his day, and propound solutions to them. And yet for whatever reason, Ghazzālī elected not to do this.[342] Sayyid's sense of what the contemporary reader might be looking for in a tract on forbidding wrong is doubtless accurate.[343] There are, of course, passages here and there in Ghazzālī's discussion that such a reader – like Rāshid – will find intensely rewarding, but all in all they are few and far between.[344] The core of Ghazzālī's message, however well articulated, is not one that speaks to the concerns of political Islam today.

While modern Sunnī and Imāmī thinkers show the same interest in getting organised, there is a significant divergence with regard to the identity of the organisers. On the Imāmī side the clergy has played the central role, whereas among the Sunnīs their position has been rather marginal. One might infer from this that Imāmī doctrine would be likely to differ sharply from that of the Sunnīs in conferring a much more prominent role in forbidding wrong on the clergy. But whatever the situation in real life, no such prominence is reflected in doctrine; as in the past, forbidding wrong is not a part of the law-book in which clerical authority is strongly entrenched.[345]

[339] *Ibid.*, 69.22.

[340] See Āshtiyānī, *Tafsīr-i numūna*, 3:36.2; and cf. Akbarī, *Taḥlīl*, 140.3, 142.2, and above, note 235.

[341] Ghazzālī (d. 505/1111), *Kitāb al-amr bi'l-ma'rūf wa'l-nahy 'an al-munkar min Iḥyā' 'ulūm al-dīn*, Beirut 1983. [342] See esp. *ibid.*, 5.16, 6.18, 8.1.

[343] Sayyid writes as if he himself were looking for it, but given his wide knowledge of medieval Islamic texts, he would hardly expect Ghazzālī's treatment of *al-amr bi'l-ma'rūf* to be a tract in the same genre as Lenin's *What is to be done?*

[344] For a particularly striking passage, see above, ch. 16, 445f.

[345] The main exception is, of course, Khumaynī's version of the doctrine of the imam's permission (see above, notes 243f.). Otherwise, authors may emphasise the special obligations of the clergy (see above, note 206, for Khumaynī), or state that the clergy have a special role in carrying out the duty (Nūrī, *Amr*, 28.9; Nūrī Ḥātim, *al-Amr bi'l-ma'rūf wa'l-nahy 'an al-munkar*, Qumm n.d., 220.10 (the most elaborate discussion I have seen;

Where the contrast does signify is in the relationship of modern to traditional scholastic thought. In the Sunnī world, the austerely traditionalist intellectual heritage of the scholars has combined with their marginalisation by social and political change to make it hard for their scholasticism to provide convincing Islamic solutions to modern problems. Maṭʿanī's literary polemics on righting wrongs 'with the hand'[346] provide a good example of their predicament. It is not just that neither the state nor 'religious youth' (*al-shabāb al-mutadayyin*), the two forces that define the political context of his thinking,[347] are likely to pay much attention to him. What he says is in itself problematic. When he attacks the view that action 'with the hand' is reserved to the authorities, the traditional Sunnī horror of doctrinal innovation is on his side. Like many a medieval scholar, he wins by rightly insisting that his position is not some innovation he thought up for himself (*lam abtadiʿhu min ʿindi nafsī*).[348] In the same vein, he describes the view he is rejecting as an unknown and innovatory interpretation (*tafsīr bidʿī ghayr maʿrūf*),[349] and as a recent opinion which not one of the scholars of the community had held in the past (*qawl muḥdath lam yaqul bihi aḥad min ʿulamāʾ al-umma*).[350] Having said all this in the manner of a medieval traditionalist, it is superfluous for him to argue that the position he is attacking is a bad idea. But when he puts forward his own idea – severely limiting the type of action 'with the hand' permitted to individuals – he is hoist with his own petard. We wait in vain for the roll-call of authoritative opinions from the past which alone could make his view respectable. Among the Sunnīs, therefore, new thinking – and in a new world there has to be some – cannot easily take place within the framework of the scholastic heritage; instead the locus of intellectual creativity of necessity shifts outside it. Among the Imāmīs, this does not have to be so. In their discussions of forbidding wrong, the modern Imāmī scholars have attacked and gone behind the traditional view of the conditions of obligation in a way that Maṭʿanī could never have done. Ṭayyibī, for example, invents a novel conception of a 'collective obligation'. He then considers the possibility that someone might object that it is new, and responds 'So be it!'[351] Other Imāmī scholars are not so brazen, but they are significantly less constricted than their Sunnī colleagues; witness the elaboration of the

the preface is dated 1416/1996); Islāmī Ardakānī, *Amr*, 34.11). But they do not go beyond this. [346] See above, notes 133f., 145–8.

[347] See, for example, Maṭʿanī, *Taghyīr al-munkar*, 3.8. [348] *Ibid.*, 4.8.

[349] *Ibid.*, 4.14, and cf. 15.24. [350] *Ibid.*, 45.11.

[351] Ṭayyibī, *Taqīya*, 166.13. He later proudly repeats the word 'new' in referring to his concept (*ibid.*, 253 n. 2, 261.7).

essentially novel doctrine of the prior duty to secure the prerequisites for forbidding wrong.[352]

The collective and political orientation of the Islamic revival also helps to explain another feature of contemporary writing on forbidding wrong in both communities: the fact that the traditional concern with rights of privacy[353] receives relatively little attention.

On the Sunnī side, the old material may be repeated, but it does not generate excitement.[354] Thus ʿAwda stipulates that a wrong must be manifest (*ẓāhir*) without spying or prying, among other things because God has said so (Q49:12), and because of the inviolability (*ḥurma*) of homes and persons until such time as sin is apparent.[355] To emphasise the point he relates the story of the three sins of the caliph ʿUmar (r. 13–23/634–44).[356] But when there is reliable evidence or good reason to believe that someone is engaging in covert wrongdoing in his home, these restrictions no longer apply.[357] The presentation is clear and balanced, but there is nothing electric about it. Likewise Khālid al-Sabt has some short discussions of aspects of privacy.[358] Thus the first sets out the conditions under which it may or may not be permissible to refrain from exposing sins (*satr*); but he says nothing here of any conditions under which one has an actual duty to refrain, or of any rights of sinners to privacy.

On the Imāmī side, where privacy was never a standard topic in the traditional discussion of the duty,[359] we usually hear even less of it. Imāmī authors attack Western individualism just as Sunnīs do,[360] and they frequently report and rebut the invocations of freedom and charges of meddlesomeness made by those subjected to forbidding wrong.[361] But this

[352] See above, 542–5. [353] See above, ch. 17, 479–82.

[354] See, in addition to the examples that follow, Bayānūnī, *Amr*, 44–7; Yāsīn, *Jihād*, 192f. no. 12; Muḥammad ʿAlī Masʿūd, *Amr*, 17.1; ʿAmrī, *Amr*, 320–4; Maḥmūd, *Uṣūl*, 204.10; Sukkarī, *Amr*, 82–6. For a recent Sunnī study of the law of privacy in Islam, see below, ch. 20, note 24; but the book is not concerned with forbidding wrong.

[355] ʿAwda, *Tashrīʿ*, 1:502.20.

[356] *Ibid.*, 503.8. For the story, see above, ch. 4, note 269, and ch. 17, note 85; it is also told by Bayānūnī (*Amr*, 45.1), ʿAmrī (*Amr*, 321.12) and Sukkarī (*Amr*, 83.5).

[357] ʿAwda, *Tashrīʿ*, 1:504.4. [358] Sabt, *Amr*, 296.13, 298.7, 316–19.

[359] It appears only, I think, in the accounts of authors who base themselves directly or indirectly on Ghazzālī (Fayḍ, *Mahajja*, 4:109.5; Muḥammad Mahdī al-Narāqī, *Jāmiʿ al-saʿādāt*, 2:242.14; Aḥmad Narāqī, *Miʿrāj al-saʿāda*, 516.3). For Ghazzālī's discussion, see above, ch. 16, 436.

[360] Miṣbāḥ Yazdī, 'Tashrīḥ', 34.1, and cf. Masʿūdī, *Pizhūhishī*, 169.16, 346.2. For the Sunnīs, see above, note 61.

[361] Akbarī gives a practical list of objections which those subjected to the duty come out with, together with apt replies for the pious forbidder of wrong. The first is 'I'm a free person!' (*āzād-am*); the second is 'This has nothing to do with you!', or, alternatively, 'Don't

does not lead them to a systematic discussion of the limits placed on intrusion by traditional Islamic values. Themes connected with privacy appear here and there in the modern Imāmī literature on the duty,[362] but there is no move to consolidate them into a bulwark against abuse, whether perpetrated by the state apparatus or by individual pietists.

To this there is one significant exception, though it is not entirely isolated inasmuch as the author in question owes some of his inspiration to Muṭahharī. One of many recent books on forbidding wrong by junior clerics is by Sayyid Ḥasan Islāmī Ardakānī. This one is skilfully written and nicely produced.[363] It opens with a graphic scene of a city asleep – we are

interfere!' (*Taḥlīl*, 204.3, 204.7). For a reasoned response to this challenge, which starts by taking seriously the value of individual freedom (*ḥurriyyat al-fard*) and the fact that *al-amr bi'l-ma'rūf* is a form of intrusion (*tadakhkhul*) which limits this right, see Ḥātim, *Amr*, 207–13. See also Gulpāyagānī, *Majma' al-masā'il*, 1:433 no. 1321 (on a man who both drinks and recites the Koran in his home, and claims that this is nobody else's business); 'Alī Kūrānī, *Amr bah ma'rūf wa nahy az munkar*, Tehran 1373 sh., 3.9, 7.12 (a much reprinted little work first published in 1359 sh.; the author says that of course *al-amr bi'l-ma'rūf* means interfering in other people's affairs, and naturally people with their heads stuffed full of Western ideas don't like it); Miṣbāḥ Yazdī, 'Tashrīḥ', 34.1 (complaining that as a result of Western influence, contemporary society regards forbidding wrong as meddlesomeness (*fuḍūlī*), and noting the characteristic response 'what's it to you?' (*bah to chih?*)), and cf. *ibid.*, 36.16; Mas'ūdī, *Pizhūhishī*, 169.16 (reporting the equation of forbidding wrong with improper interference (*dikhālat*) in the affairs of others), and cf. also *ibid.*, 346.2; Taqaddusī Nīyā, *Dars-hāyī az amr bah ma'rūf*, 84.4 (resolving the conflict in a few lines with the argument that human freedom does not consist in doing bad things), 105.12 (appealing to the tradition about the people in the boat); Muḥsin Qirā'atī, *Amr bah ma'rūf wa nahy az munkar*, Tehran 1375 sh., 76 no. 2 (describing freedom as a holy word in the shadow of which thousands of unholy deeds are done); and below, ch. 20, note 28.

362 For occasional brief mentions or discussions of the prohibition of spying, see Ṣāfī Gulpāyagānī, *Rāh-i iṣlāḥ*, 83.16, in the section reflecting the views of Burūjirdī; Qirā'atī, *Amr*, 141.14, 299.13; Khudākaramī, *Do aṣl-i ustuwār*, 94.2. Sometimes the category of hidden sin is mentioned (Qirā'atī, *Amr*, 153.15; 'Abd al-Ḥusayn Dastghayb, *Amr ba-ma'rūf wa nahy az munkar*, Tehran 1371 sh., 15.4, in the introduction by Muḥammad Hāshim Dastghayb; also, implicitly, Khumaynī, *Taḥrīr*, 1:468 no. 6). Bihishtī underlines the importance of the knowledge condition by contrasting it with unwitting intrusion into the affairs of others ('Rūḥānīyat', 160.16). For Muṭahharī's brief but pregnant remarks on privacy, see below, notes 373–6. For Khumaynī's emphasis on respect for privacy in his pronouncements in the winter of 1403/1982–3, see *Ṣaḥīfa-i nūr*, 17:106f. nos. 6f., 118.1, 145 no. 5; for the political context, see Bakhash, *Reign of the Ayatollahs*, 227–32.

363 The book was published in 1375 sh./1996 in Qumm, the centre of religious publishing in Iran; it is the fifth of a projected 110 volumes in a series entitled, with an obvious French resonance, 'What do we know about Islam?' (*Az Islām chih mīdānīm?*). The series is under the direction of Ḥujjat al-Islām Mahdī Karrūbī, who has been described by Douglas Jehl as 'a longtime anti-Western firebrand who has become a Khatami ally' ('New US–Iran dialogue', *The New York Times*, 6 June 1999, WK 4). The book is in Persian, the language in which clerics write for laymen. The author had already published a book on *al-amr bi'l-ma'rūf* with the Ministry of Culture and Guidance in 1373 sh./1994 (see Islāmī Ardakānī, *Amr*, 208.7), so he is not an outsider; I have not seen this earlier book.

not told when or where – and a man patrolling the streets.[364] He comes to a house, sniffs wrongdoing, finds the door closed, and enters by climbing over the wall and descending through the roof. He catches a man and a woman in their cups, and denounces the man as an enemy of God for his sin. The malefactor immediately responds by accusing the intruder of not one but three contraventions of divine law: spying on him, entering his home other than by the door, and doing so without asking his leave or greeting him. Thus someone who sought to expose the sin of another found that he himself had fallen into no less than three mortal sins. It is only now that the lay reader, who might at first have been under the disturbing misapprehension that the scene was set in our own dear Islamic Republic, gets to learn that the triple sinner was the second caliph, ʿUmar ibn al-Khaṭṭāb. Not being an old-fashioned bigot, Islāmī does not curse this traditional enemy of the Shīʿites; but neither does he find it necessary to bless him.[365] All told, this is not a story calculated to raise ʿUmar in the esteem of the Imāmī reader;[366] by the same token, and more to the point, it is well calculated to give intrusiveness a bad name among good Imāmīs today.

Later in the book, Islāmī uses another strategy to the same effect. In line with Muṭahharī and those who followed him, he gives considerable attention to the Sunnī institution of the censorship (*ḥisba*) as a mechanism for forbidding wrong.[367] By the time Islāmī was writing, of course, the novelty of Muṭahharī's discovery had long worn off. What excites Islāmī is not so much the institution itself as the reasons for its decay over the centuries.[368] Of these reasons, there is one he presents with particular eloquence: the abusive behaviour of those purportedly engaged in forbidding wrong. In this way the very institution that was supposed to be the solution itself became part of the problem.[369] Islāmī returns to the theme of abuse in the context of the question why the duty is in such a bad way in our own age, for all that we live at a time when Islam is being revived and an Islamic Republic has been established.[370] He reviews a number of factors, but one stands out: abuses which have given the duty a bad name.[371] There is, he

[364] *Ibid.*, 7.3. Islāmī is not the only modern Imāmī author on forbidding wrong to mention the anecdote, but he is alone in highlighting it in the way he does (cf. Fuʾādīyān, *Sayrī*, 254.21; Khudākaramī, *Do aṣl-i ustuwār*, 94.4). For modern Sunnī writers, see above, note 356.

[365] Islāmī Ardakānī, *Amr*, 8.7. He has the story from Ghazzālī (*ibid.*, 8.18). For current standards of political correctness in Iran with regard to the first three caliphs, see Buchta, *Die iranische Schia*, 71–4.

[366] This is why Muḥsin al-Fayḍ (d. 1091/1680) liked the story (see above, ch. 16, note 185).

[367] See above, note 319.

[368] Islāmī Ardakānī, *Amr*, 69–73.

[369] *Ibid.*, 71.4, and cf. 159.7.

[370] The question is posed *ibid.*, 77.7.

[371] *Ibid.*, 82–7. Islāmī is not alone in surveying the reasons why *al-amr biʾl-maʿrūf* is not doing as well as it should, or why people are reluctant to perform or submit to the duty;

says, no need to call witnesses; we have all encountered shamefully abusive conduct on the part of people supposedly engaged in forbidding wrong – people whose actions lead in fact to the ruin of the duty, and indeed of religion itself.[372] He then enlists in this protest an almost incontrovertible authority: the martyred Muṭahharī, a man who devoted his life to reviving the duty and died for the cause of establishing an Islamic government.[373] In his talk of 1380/1960, Muṭahharī had indeed shown strong antipathy to thuggery and intrusion. Referring to some recent activities carried out in the name of forbidding wrong, he commented that, if this was indeed what forbidding wrong amounted to, it was better that it should remain in oblivion.[374] We only have the right to intervene, he insisted, where wrongs are out in the public domain; we have no right to engage in spying (*tajassus*) and interference (*mudākhala*) in matters relating to people's private lives (*zindagī-i khuṣūṣī-i mardum*).[375] He had then told a searing story of over-zealous religious students who raided a wedding by scrambling across the rooftops, smashing musical instruments, and boxing the ears of the bride; later they were roundly rebuked by a senior cleric for their multiple sins.[376] Islāmī, of course, makes excellent use of this material.[377] All this is exciting, but also perhaps a trifle alarming: is the virtuous reader not in danger of being drawn into a profoundly subversive attack on the entire apparatus of religious enforcement in the Islamic Republic? Islāmī has thought of this, and slips in a timely reassurance. Fortunately, he tells us, the horrible activities to which Muṭahharī was alluding are quite unknown today, and it is devoutly to be hoped that such things will never again sully the purity of Islam.[378] The reader relaxes, albeit still slightly puzzled by the information that we have *all* witnessed abuses of this kind. Many of us can scarcely remember the bad old days before the revolution; and even if we do, over-zealous religious policing is not conventionally included among the crimes of the fallen regime.

When it comes to legal prescription, Islāmī again has a strategy. He proceeds by enlarging and enriching the category of the 'norms' (*ādāb*) of the duty which had originally been developed by Ghazzālī.[379] Happily, Islāmī

but other writers do not include such abuses among these reasons (Mas'ūdī, *Pizhūhishī*, 320–32; Ḥātim, *Amr*, 227–38; Akbarī, *Taḥlīl*, 144–53, 189–203; Qirā'atī, *Amr*, 101–7).

372 Islāmī Ardakānī, *Amr*, 83.5. 373 *Ibid.*, 83.13.

374 Muṭahharī, 'Amr ba-ma'rūf', 84.12. 375 *Ibid.*, 84.20. 376 *Ibid.*, 85.5.

377 For the story of the students on the rooftops, see Islāmī Ardakānī, *Amr*, 84.16.

378 *Ibid.*, 84.3.

379 *Ibid.*, 171–98. For Ghazzālī's norms, see above, ch. 16, 441f. That Islāmī is aware of this parentage is suggested by his observation that the norms have been discussed more by writers on ethics (*akhlāq*) than by jurists (*ibid.*, 173.1); a leading writer on ethics is none other than Ghazzālī (*ibid.*, 113.2).

is able to find an Imāmī precedent for the category; in any case, as he goes on to indicate, bringing a number of points together under this heading is to an extent just a matter of convenience.[380] Having justifed his use of the category, he goes on to present his set of ten norms. The first is that there must be no spying (*tajassus*).[381] Indeed the most important point there is to be made about forbidding wrong, he tells us, is that the forbidder should abstain from interference in the private lives of others (*dikhālat dar zindagī-i khuṣūṣī-i kasān*) and from prying into their wordly affairs.[382] What Islam requires is the elimination of manifest sin; secret sin is reserved for the jurisdiction of God.[383] The second, closely linked norm is that there should be no curtain-ripping (*parda-darī*), in other words no exposure of hidden sins.[384] In all this, Islāmī's leading quoted sources are Ghazzālī and Saʿdī (d. 691/1292); Imāmī authorities tend to take a back seat. Looming behind these Sunnīs, it does not take a very sharp eye to discern the ghostly presence of Western conceptions of rights. Sinners, Islāmī remarks, are human like us; they too have rights, and these are not to be trampled underfoot.[385]

Islāmī's ideas are certainly not representative of the prevailing religious culture in Iran. But they are likely to have considerable resonance for a significant part of the educated population. What this means for the future could perhaps be expressed in a highly conditional sentence. If civil society is fated to remain a globally relevant notion,[386] if Iran – and other Islamic countries – are to become recognisably civil societies, and if they are destined to do so under an Islamic aegis, then Islāmī's thinking about forbidding wrong can help us to imagine what such a development might look like.

[380] *Ibid.*, 172.8. The work he cites is not available to me.

[381] *Ibid.*, 173–7, esp. 173.16. See also *ibid.*, 9.14.

[382] *Ibid.*, 173.7.

[383] *Ibid.*, 173.9. See also *ibid.*, 9.12, 175.1, 175.5 (quoting Ghazzālī and the younger Narāqī (d. 1245/1829), who owes his Ghazzālian material to his father, see above, ch. 16, note 192), 176.12.

[384] *Ibid.*, 178–81. This is a vernacular rendering of *satr*, as is apparent from the Sunnī Prophetic traditions quoted.

[385] *Ibid.*, 159.8. See also *ibid.*, 182.5, 196.15.

[386] I choose the word 'notion' rather than 'concept' advisedly. I do not know anyone who knows exactly what civil society is, but most of us have some broad ideas about what it is not.

CHAPTER 19

ORIGINS AND COMPARISONS

1. INTRODUCTION

The expression 'to command right and forbid wrong', for all its salience in Islam, is not without parallels outside it. In England it was proposed in AD 1801 to establish a 'Society for the Suppression of Vice and the Encouragement of Religion and Virtue'.[1] A German legal document of AD 1616 offers the phrase 'recht gebieten und unrecht verbieten' with regard to the conduct incumbent on the judge of a certain court.[2] Blackstone (d. AD 1780) in his celebrated treatise on the laws of England defines municipal law as 'a rule of civil conduct prescribed by the supreme power in a state, commanding what is right and prohibiting what is wrong'.[3] His definition echoes one already adopted by the Stoics. Thus Chrysippus (d. 207 BC) opened his book on law with the statement that the law must, among other things, command what should be done and forbid what should not be done.[4] This in turn echoes Aristotle (d. 322 BC).[5] But it

[1] D. Thomas, *A long time burning: the history of literary censorship in England*, London 1969, 188f. (drawn to my attention by Frank Stewart). The society was indeed established, and proceeded to concern itself mainly with pornography.

[2] G. F. Führer, *Kurze Darstellung der Meyerrechtlichen Verfassung in der Grafschaft Lippe*, Lemgo 1804, 327 (cited in J. Grimm, *Deutsche Rechtsalterthümer*, Leipzig 1899, 1:38, which was drawn to my attention by Frank Stewart). I am indebted to the library of the Oberlandesgericht Celle for a copy of the relevant pages of Führer's work.

[3] William Blackstone (d. AD 1780), *Commentaries on the laws of England*, Oxford 1765–9, 1:44; and cf. his commentary, *ibid.*, 53–8 (drawn to my attention by Frank Stewart).

[4] H. von Arnim, *Stoicorum veterum fragmenta*, Stuttgart 1978–9, 3:77 no. 314 (I am indebted to Ruth Webb for help with this text). A similar formulation is already quoted from Zeno of Citium (d. 263 BC), the founder of the Stoic school (*ibid.*, 1:42 no. 162; and cf. *ibid.*, 3:158 nos. 613f.). The definition of Chrysippus is quoted near the beginning of the *Digest* of Justinian (r. AD 527–65) (ed. T. Mommsen and trans. A. Watson, Philadelphia 1985, 11), and Cicero (d. 43 BC) says something similar (*De republica*, III.xxii.33 (= ed. and trans. C. W. Keyes, London and Cambridge, Mass. 1951, 210.5 = 211)). I was put on the track of this material by Patricia Crone.

[5] Aristotle (d. 322 BC), *Nichomachean ethics*, V.ii.10 (= ed. H. Rackham, London and Cambridge, Mass. 1956, 264.21 = 265).

would be hard to argue that all occurrences of such phrases go back to a single origin. As will be seen later in this chapter, they also crop up among the Buddhists and Confucians,[6] and further parallels doubtless lurk elsewhere in the world's literatures.

If the phrase has such echoes in other cultures, should we think of the duty itself as a universal human value? Or is there in fact something peculiarly Islamic about it? The basic principle involved in the value is that if one encounters someone engaged in wrongdoing, one should do something to stop them. My guess is that this principle, or something like it, is to be found embedded (though not necessarily articulated) in just about all human cultures.[7] That is to say, I would expect that in almost any culture there will be occasions on which it makes sense to say something like: 'You can't just stand there and let him do that.' I have no idea how one might amass the empirical evidence that would put such a guess on a firmer foundation. The principle does not have a name either in common English or in the technical language of anthropologists; consequently ethnographers are not looking for the value, and if they happen to describe it, they are unlikely to signal this in a way that makes the information easy to locate in their ethnographies. In what follows, I shall simply assume that the value is pretty much universal.

The existence of this degree of uniformity would still leave room for a great deal of variation between cultures, not to mention the individuals who belong to them. Most obviously, there are extensive differences between cultures regarding what is considered right or wrong: witness the collision between West African and Islamic attitudes to female nudity.[8] But while such differences are clearly crucial for the practice of the value, they are not intrinsic to the way in which it is conceived.

More interestingly for our purposes, there are likely to be considerable variations regarding the extent to which our value is identified or emphasised in the moral vocabularies of different cultures. The same is true of the relative weight attached to it in relation to such antithetical principles as minding one's own business and keeping out of trouble. It would be a plausible guess that the vernacular subcultures of the Islamic world have tended to assign more weight to such antithetical principles than the mainstream religious tradition has done;[9] and it would not be surprising to find comparable differences obtaining between cultures at large. This would

[6] See below, notes 113, 121.

[7] Perhaps the Ik as described by Colin Turnbull lacked it; but this was a society that had lost its human values in general (C. M. Turnbull, *The mountain people*, New York 1972).

[8] See above, ch. 14, note 228. [9] Cf. above, ch. 17, 498f.

surely apply even within the set of the world's historic literary cultures. Here again, I do not know how one would go about making comparisons on a serious scale – neither the tables of contents nor the indices of ethnographies being of much assistance in this regard. I have accordingly made no serious attempt in this direction, except in one case of obvious historical relevance: pre-Islamic Arabia.

There is, however, a relevant difference between the literary heritages of high cultures which is relatively accessible to comparative exploration. This is the extent to which they subject our value to formal, systematic elaboration. I have consequently made it my business to ascertain which cultures make of our value what might be called scholastic doctrines. It is, for example, a striking and perhaps historically relevant fact that in the world of late antiquity, monks would rebuke the powerful with the same abrasiveness as ascetics in the Islamic world.[10] There was, moreover, an old Greek term for such outspokenness (*parrhēsia*).[11] But for all that the phenomenon was there, and possessed of a name, it does not seem to have given rise to any body of systematic thought in the Christian literature of the time; whereas some other cultures, as will be seen, have more to offer. Once we have collected some scholastic doctrines from different cultures, we can go on to make comparisons between them.

There are in fact two distinct projects that the existence of similar phenomena outside Islam can validly give rise to. One is genetic: here the question is whether the Islamic conception of 'commanding right and forbidding wrong' has identifiable pre-Islamic origins. The other is purely comparative: here the object is to learn what we can from the study of analogous, perhaps genetically unrelated, phenomena in different settings. In what follows, however, I have not formally separated the two exercises. What begins as a genetic inquiry into the origins of the Islamic value will end up as a comparative attempt to identify and explain what is distinctive about it.

2. THE JĀHILIYYA

There are two separate (though related) questions to be answered regarding the role of pre-Islamic Arabia in the origins of the Islamic conception

[10] P. Brown, *Power and persuasion in late antiquity*, Madison and London 1992, 106, 126, 135, 140. On the other hand, monks were not supposed to rebuke each other (C. White, *Christian friendship in the fourth century*, Cambridge 1992, 168f.).

[11] Brown, *Power and persuasion*, index *s.v.* The term is also well attested in relevant senses as a loan-word in Syriac (R. Payne Smith, *Thesaurus syriacus*, Oxford 1879–1901, 3242).

of forbidding wrong. The first concerns the terminology of the duty. Is the language used to describe it in Islam inherited – in whole or in part – from the Jāhiliyya? Or is it new to Arabic, perhaps derived from some extra-Arabian source? The second question concerns the idea of the duty. Did Jāhilī society give prominence to the notion that it is a man's business to right wrongs and seek to prevent their occurrence? Or was such activity highly valued only when it took place within the limits of specific social relationships that required it?[12]

Let us first examine two traditions relating to Mecca in the late pre-Islamic period, and then consider the evidence of Jāhilī poetry.

The first tradition concerns Ḥakīm ibn Umayya, a member of a Sulamī family well established in Mecca and a confederate (*ḥalīf*) of the Umayyad clan; he later converted to Islam.[13] It is reported that in pre-Islamic Mecca he exercised the role of restraining and disciplining the hot-blooded young men (*sufahāʾ*) of Quraysh, with the general consent of the tribe.[14] In this connection he is referred to in some sources as a 'censor' (*muḥtasib*); these sources then go on to describe him as '(commanding right and) forbidding wrong'.[15] Altogether their wording is so similar that their testimony must be treated as reflecting a single source. With regard to their terminology, are these authors then reporting actual Jāhilī usage, or are they merely retrojecting Islamic usage onto a Jāhilī phenomenon which happens to remind them of an Islamic one? Since they do not make any explicit claim to be reporting Jāhilī usage, the safest assumption is that they are retrojecting. With regard to the activity itself, what we have here is – as these authors indicate – a precedent for the official censorship (*ḥisba*), rather than for the duty of the individual believer. The account could further be held

[12] Cf. the remark of an ethnographer of the mountain tribesmen of the Yemen that it would be insulting for a man to presume to right some wrong done to another man's dependants or womenfolk (P. Dresch, *Tribes, government, and history in Yemen*, Oxford 1989, 61).

[13] One source has it that it was his great-great-grandfather who came to Mecca and became a confederate of ʿAbd Manāf himself (Ibn Saʿd, *Ṭabaqāt*, 8:113.4). For Ḥakīm's allegedly early conversion, see M. Lecker, *The Banū Sulaym*, Jerusalem 1989, 138 n. 151, citing Ibn Hishām, *Sīra*, 1–2:288.15, and other sources.

[14] See M. J. Kister, 'Some reports concerning Mecca from Jāhiliyya to Islam', *Journal of the Economic and Social History of the Orient*, 15 (1972), 83 (with the two addenda to this page, the first published *ibid.*, 93, and the second with the reprint of the article in M. J. Kister, *Studies in Jāhiliyya and early Islam*, London 1980, item II, 'Additional notes', 1); Chalmeta, *El 'señor del zoco'*, 350f.; Lecker, *The Banū Sulaym*, 120–2; ʿAmad, 'Nuṣūṣ turāthiyya'. The references to primary sources discussed below are taken from these studies.

[15] Ibn al-Kalbī (d. 204/819f.), *Jamharat al-nasab*, ed. N. Ḥasan, Beirut 1986, 407.4; Balādhurī (d. 279/892f.), *Ansāb al-ashrāf*, quoted from manuscript in Lecker, *The Banū Sulaym*, 122 n. 79; Ibn Ḥazm, *Jamhara*, 263.20.

to imply that disciplining wild young men across the board was not a normal activity of individuals, since it required a special arrangement to establish it and make it work;[16] but this implication is weak.

The case is somewhat different with a much more widely known institution of pre-Islamic Mecca, an alliance (known as the *ḥilf al-fuḍūl*) which was created for the purpose of righting wrongs.[17] A typical account of the formation of this alliance (*ḥilf*) is the following.[18] A member of the Yemeni tribe of the Banū Zubayd came to Mecca with commercial goods which he sold to a member of the Qurashī clan of the Banū Sahm. The latter, however, failed to pay for them. The public protest of the wronged merchant (in verse, of course) gave rise to such concern among Quraysh that four clans (other sources commonly list five) gathered and made a pact (*taḥālafū*) in the following terms: 'If anyone is wronged in Mecca, we will all take his part against the wrongdoer until we recover what is due to him from the one who has wronged him, whether he is noble or humble, one of us or not.'[19] As a result the Sahmī wrongdoer was prevailed upon to pay the Zubaydī merchant his due. Thereafter, if anyone wronged anyone else in Mecca, the members of the alliance were there to put matters right.[20] Again, we are in the generation before the rise of Islam; the Prophet himself is reported to have been present at the formation of the alliance.[21] To my knowledge, there are no other reports of such institutions in pre-Islamic Arabia, except that it is said by some that the alliance owed its name (*ḥilf al-fuḍūl*) to a similar alliance among Jurhum,[22] the somewhat shadowy possessors of the Meccan sanctuary in an earlier period.

Again, the story tends to suggest – but not very strongly – that righting wrongs in general was not the business of the individual: it required a

[16] Presumably we should understand that Ḥakīm's formal status as an outsider in Mecca was an asset in this context. But then why did his special relationship to the Banū Umayya not disrupt his role?

[17] See *EI*[2], art. 'Ḥilf al-fuḍūl' (C. Pellat), and P. Crone, *Meccan trade and the rise of Islam*, Princeton 1987, 143f., with references to a wide range of primary sources.

[18] Ibn Ḥabīb, *Munammaq*, 45–7.

[19] *Ibid.*, 46.6. The key terms are all forms of the root *ẓ-l-m*. I have not seen the term *munkar* in any account of the alliance other than those mentioned below, note 25.

[20] Ibn Ḥabīb goes on to report two such incidents, one involving the goods of a Thumālī (*ibid.*, 47.10), the other the daughter of a Khathʿamī merchant (*ibid.*, 48.9).

[21] *Ibid.*, 46.8. We are told here that this was five years before he began to receive revelation, which would take us to the first decade of the seventh century AD. Another version would place the event a decade earlier (Abū 'l-Faraj, *Aghānī*, 17:289.16, stating that the Prophet was aged twenty-five at the time).

[22] See, for example, *ibid.*, 288.14, 292.10, 293.3, 300.8. The point is that the Jurhumīs involved were all called Faḍl, or variants of the same root. This is one of a number of rival explanations of the puzzling term *fuḍūl*.

formal agreement to establish a group pledged to do this in a single locality.[23] This leaves us with the question of terminology. Ibn Abī ʾl-Ḥadīd (d. 656/1258) remarks of forbidding wrong (*al-nahy ʿan al-munkar*) that it was known to the pre-Islamic Arabs, and he establishes his point by adducing our alliance.[24] He does not here actually attribute such terminology to the pre-Islamic Arabs. However, a report transmitted by Zubayr ibn Bakkār (d. 256/870) does just this: it explicitly includes 'commanding right and forbidding wrong' in the terms of the agreement.[25] This is a clear-cut ascription of the phrase to the Jāhiliyya.[26] But the report is an isolated one among our many accounts of the agreement,[27] and this suggests that we would be right to regard it as anachronistic. Our sources, after all, are happy to impute statements about forbidding wrong to the Byzantines.[28]

The other source that calls for attention is poetry.[29] There are, of course, considerable problems regarding the authenticity of poetry ascribed to the

[23] Presumably the fact that a number of clans had come together to establish the arrangement was vital to its effective functioning. The omission of other clans might have been expected to be problematic in cases (such as that of the Sahmī) where the wrongdoer belonged to a clan outside the alliance, but we do not hear of this.

[24] Ibn Abī ʾl-Ḥadīd, *Sharḥ*, 19:305.13. Earlier in the work he gives accounts of the *ḥilf al-fuḍūl* quoted from Jāḥiẓ (d. 255/868f.) (*ibid.*, 15:203–6) and Zubayr ibn Bakkār (d. 256/870) (*ibid.*, 224–8).

[25] Abū ʾl-Faraj, *Aghānī*, 17:291.4 (for the ascription to Zubayr ibn Bakkār, see *ibid.*, 287.2); Ibn Abī ʾl-Ḥadīd, *Sharḥ*, 15:226.6. In Ibn Abī ʾl-Ḥadīd's version, Zubayr ibn Bakkār gives an *isnād* going back to the Medinese Muḥammad ibn Ibrāhīm ibn al-Ḥārith al-Taymī (d. 120/737f.); in that of the *Aghānī*, the same *isnād* appears but is combined with others into a composite *isnād*. The two versions have peculiarities in common over and above the reference to *al-amr biʾl-maʿrūf*, suggesting that they are indeed a single account.

[26] Likewise in a report which he transmits to the effect that the original Jurhumī participants had agreed that they would put right any wrong in the valley of Mecca, the word used is *ghayyarūhu* (Abū ʾl-Faraj, *Aghānī*, 17:288.14; the authorities for this report are vaguely referred to as 'others').

[27] See, for example, Ibn Hishām, *Sīra*, 1–2:133.8; Muṣʿab al-Zubayrī, *Nasab Quraysh*, 291.11; Ibn Ḥabīb, *Munammaq*, 46.6, 219.6, 341.1; Jāḥiẓ (d. 255/868f.), *Faḍl Hāshim ʿalā ʿAbd Shams*, in Ḥ. al-Sandūbī (ed.), *Rasāʾil al-Jāḥiẓ*, Cairo 1933, 71.23; Balādhurī, *Ansāb*, ed. Maḥmūdī, 12.15, 15.4; Abū ʾl-Faraj, *Aghānī*, 17:299.14. Abū ʾl-Faraj also gives several versions from Zubayr ibn Bakkār by *isnād*s other than that referred to above (note 25); none of these makes reference to *al-amr biʾl-maʿrūf* (*ibid.*, 288.8, 289.18, 290.9, 292.6, 292.13, 294.1).

[28] A Byzantine elder, explaining to the emperor Heraclius (r. AD 610–41) why the Muslims were winning, describes them as, among other things, commanding right and forbidding wrong (Dīnawarī, *Mujālasa*, 193.14, whence Ibn Kathīr, *Bidāya*, 7:15.22); likewise a Christian Arab spy speaks in the same way about the Muslims to a Byzantine general (Azdī (*fl. c.* 190/805), *Futūḥ al-Shām*, ed. W. N. Lees, Calcutta 1853–4, 189.6; I owe this reference to Larry Conrad). On the other hand van Ess, who cites the story of the formation of the *ḥilf al-fuḍūl* in the version of the *Aghānī*, treats the wording as authentic (*Theologie*, 2:387).

[29] My data derive almost entirely from the Concordance of Pre-Islamic and Umayyad Poetry of the Hebrew University of Jerusalem. They are unlikely to be complete, but they are certainly representative. I am much indebted to Albert Arazi for making this material available, to Nurit Tsafrir for copying the relevant cards for me, and to Andras Hamori for help with some of the texts.

pre-Islamic and early Islamic periods; but as will be seen, these problems are not of overriding significance in the present context. My main findings are as follows.

First, the words I have translated 'right' (*maʿrūf*, with its synonym *ʿurf*) and 'wrong' (*munkar*, with its synonym *nukr*) are widely attested in pre-Islamic poetry.[30] What is more, they are not infrequently used as antithetical terms. In their etymological senses of 'known' and 'unknown', they are already paired in a much-repeated hemistich of Muraqqish al-Akbar, who is perhaps our oldest Arab poet: speaking of dusty deserts, he tells of crossing the unknown wilderness to reach the known (*qaṭaʿtu ilā maʿrūfihā munkarātihā*).[31] In more evaluative senses, we find the words similarly paired by the Jāhilī poets Zuhayr ibn Abī Sulmā,[32] ʿUrwa ibn al-Ward,[33] Ḥātim al-Ṭāʾī,[34] and Nābigha

[30] For some examples, see the following notes.

[31] Mufaḍḍal al-Ḍabbī (d. 168/784f.), *Ikhtiyārāt* (= *Mufaḍḍaliyyāt*), ed. C. J. Lyall, Oxford and London 1918–24, 1:465 no. 47, line 7 (with translation, *ibid.*, 2:172). For Muraqqish al-Akbar, see Sezgin, *Geschichte*, 2:153f. The same hemistich is found in verses of the following: the Jāhilī Bishr ibn Abī Khāzim (*Dīwān*, ed. ʿI. Ḥasan, Damascus 1960, 114 no. 24, line 4; for this poet, see Sezgin, *Geschichte*, 2:211f.); the *mukhaḍram* Shammākh ibn Ḍirār (*Dīwān*, ed. Ṣ. al-Hādī, Cairo 1968, 84 no. 2, line 31; for this poet, see Sezgin, *Geschichte*, 2:239f.); the *mukhaḍram* Ḍābiʾ ibn al-Ḥārith (Aṣmaʿī (d. *c.* 216/831), *Aṣmaʿiyyāt*, ed. W. Ahlwardt, Berlin 1902, 56 no. 57, line 15; for this poet, see Sezgin, *Geschichte*, 2:205f.); the late first/seventh-century Ṭirimmāḥ (F. Krenkow (ed.), *The poems of Ṭufail ibn ʿAuf al-Ghanawī and aṭ-Ṭirimmāḥ ibn Ḥakīm aṭ-Ṭāʾyī*, London 1927, 76 no. 1, line 40; for this poet, see Sezgin, *Geschichte*, 2:351f.); and his contemporary Farazdaq (*Dīwān*, *apud* I. al-Ḥāwī, *Sharḥ Dīwān al-Farazdaq*, Beirut 1983, 1:210 no. 100, line 3; Ibn Qutayba (d. 276/889), *al-Shiʿr waʾl-shuʿarāʾ*, ed. M. J. de Goeje, Leiden 1904, 334.2; Marzubānī (d. 384/994), *Muwashshaḥ*, ed. ʿA. M. al-Bajāwī, Cairo 1965, 273.14; for this poet, see Sezgin, *Geschichte*, 2:359–63). Compare also the verse of the Jāhilī ʿUrwa ibn al-Ward (for whom see Sezgin, *Geschichte*, 2:141f.) in which he describes an owl (*hāma*) as complaining to whomever she sees, whether known or unknown to her (*tashtakī/ilā kulli maʿrūfin raʾat-hu wa-munkarī*, ʿUrwa ibn al-Ward, *Dīwān*, ed. ʿA. al-Mulūḥī, n.p. 1966, 67.1; see also Aṣmaʿī, *Aṣmaʿiyyāt*, 29 no. 31, line 4).

[32] He has a line speaking of a desert land in which his generosity is not held in low esteem (*maʿrūfī bihā ghayru munkarī*) (W. Ahlwardt (ed.), *The Divans of the six ancient Arabic poets*, London 1870, English section, 114 no. 30). The same line is quoted (with a variant) by Ibn Hishām, who ascribes it to a certain ʿUbayd ibn Wahb al-ʿAbsī (*Sīra*, 1–2:305.15). For Zuhayr, see Sezgin, *Geschichte*, 2:118–20.

[33] Here we find the hemistich *wa-abdhulu maʿrūfī lahū dūna munkarī* ('Am I to show him my kindness rather than my unkindness?', Abū Tammām (d. 231/846), *Ḥamāsa*, *apud* Abū ʾl-ʿAlāʾ al-Maʿarrī (d. 449/1057) (attrib.), *Sharḥ Dīwān Ḥamāsat Abī Tammām*, ed. Ḥ. M. Naqsha, Beirut 1991, 1047 no. 681, line 2). The same hemistich appears in a poem of the Jāhilī poet Ḥātim al-Ṭāʾī (*Dīwān*, 300 no. 113, line 2; for this poet, see Sezgin, *Geschichte*, 2:208f.); it is also found in one of the late first/seventh-century poet ʿUjayr al-Salūlī (Abū ʾl-Faraj, *Aghānī*, 13:66.15; for this poet, see Sezgin, *Geschichte*, 2:334f.).

[34] In one hemistich the poet, who claims to have turned a new leaf, says that he is no longer one who responds rudely to someone who behaves pleasantly to him (*wa-lā qāʾilin yawman li-dhī ʾl-ʿurfi munkarā*, Ḥātim al-Ṭāʾī, *Dīwān*, 267 no. 68, line 11). Two lines earlier in the same poem we have the hemistich *idhā qultu maʿrūfan lahū qāla munkarā* ('When I speak nicely to him, he responds rudely', *ibid.*, line 9, in the text of Zubayr ibn Bakkār, *Akhbār*, 419.2). See also the preceding note.

al-Dhubyānī.[35] We even find precedent for one of our Islamic phrases for taking action against a wrong (*ankara ʾl-munkar*).[36] This latter might be dismissed as retrojection, since it is not widely attested. But it would require a categorical rejection of the corpus of pre-Islamic poetry to dispose of the attestations of 'right' and 'wrong', and a high degree of scepticism to disallow the evidence for their pairing.

Second, the locutions 'commanding right' and 'forbidding wrong' are unknown to pre-Islamic poetry. They only begin to appear – and then sporadically – in poetry of the early Islamic period.[37] The most that can be said is that one of these early Islamic attestions purports to be describing a scene set in the pre-Islamic period.[38] In other words, it would require a high degree of credulity to find in poetry evidence that these phrases were used before Islam.

The situation is thus fairly clear-cut. Pre-Islamic Arabia knew well the terms 'right' and 'wrong', and seems to have paired them. But if we can judge from its poetry, it did not possess the notions of 'commanding' or 'forbidding' them. Nor, to my knowledge, is there evidence in poetry of

[35] Here we have the hemistich *fa-lā ʾl-nukru maʿrūfun wa-lā ʾl-ʿurfu ḍāʾiʿū* ('Neither is evil good, nor does a good deed perish', Nābigha al-Dhubyānī, *Dīwān*, ed. S. Fayṣal, Beirut 1968, 53 no. 3, line 35; also Khalīl ibn Aḥmad (d. 170/786f.), *Kitāb al-ʿayn*, ed. M. al-Makhzūmī and I. al-Sāmarrāʾī, Qumm 1405–10, 2:121.7). For this poet, see Sezgin, *Geschichte*, 2:110–13. The context of the hemistich is strongly religious, which renders its Jāhilī character somewhat suspect; compare the antithesis of *munkara* and *maʿrūfa* in an equally religious context in a hemistich from a suspect poem of Umayya ibn Abī ʾl-Ṣalt, who lived into Islamic times (*Dīwān*, ed. ʿA. al-Saṭlī, Damascus 1974, 354 no. 10, line 2; for this poet, see Sezgin, *Geschichte*, 2:298–300).

[36] The Jāhilī Qays ibn Zuhayr al-ʿAbsī (for whom see Sezgin, *Geschichte*, 2:216) has the line: *ulāqī min rijālin munkarātin/fa-unkiruhā wa-mā ana biʾl-ghashūmī* (*apud* Bevan, *Naḳāʾiḍ*, 97.6; also Mufaḍḍal ibn Salāma (*fl.* later third/ninth century), *Fākhir*, ed. ʿA. al-Ṭaḥāwī, Cairo 1960, 228.1, with *ẓalūm* for *ghashūm*). Cf. also the phrase *yunkirūna ʾl-munkarā* in a poem of the Jāhilī Abū Jundab al-Hudhalī (Sukkarī (d. 275/888f.), *Sharḥ Ashʿār al-Hudhaliyyīn*, ed. ʿA. A. Farrāj, Cairo 1965, 361 no. 9, in an isolated couplet; for this poet see Sezgin, *Geschichte*, 2:258).

[37] I have the following four attestations. (1) We find *amarta bi-maʿrūfin* in a poem of Ḥassān ibn Thābit (d. *c.* 54/674) (*Dīwān*, ed. W. N. ʿArafat, London 1971, 1:235 no. 111, line 3); for the context, see the following note. (2) A poem of ʿAmr ibn Maʿdī Karib has *amartuka bi . . . ʾl-maʿrūfi* (Ibn Hishām, *Sīra*, 3–4:583.22 (but contrast *ibid.*, 584.13); Ṭabarī, *Taʾrīkh*, series I, 1733.2, likewise from Ibn Isḥāq (d. 150/767f.)). ʿAmr had just returned from a visit to the Prophet during which he had converted to Islam, and was addressing a tribal chief who had ignored his advice to do likewise. (3) The phrase *alladhī yaʾmuru biʾl-ʿurfi* (cf. Q7:199) appears in a poem of Muḥammad ibn Iyās ibn al-Bukayr (Ibn Ḥabīb, *Munammaq*, 384.8). The context is the fatal wounding of Zayd ibn ʿUmar ibn al-Khaṭṭāb in an attempt to break up a fight, apparently during the reign of Muʿāwiya (r. 41–60/661–80). (4) The words *nāhīna . . . ʿani ʾl-nukrī* occur in a poem mourning the Ibāḍī rebels who perished in 130/747f. (see above, ch. 15, note 18).

[38] The context in attestation (1) in the preceding note is the death of Mālik ibn al-Najjār, who is being addressed by his sons. Mālik was an ancestor of Ḥassān, and lived eight generations before him (Ibn Ḥazm, *Jamhara*, 347.8).

such a value expressed in other terms. Protecting those who have been wronged is a familiar theme in pre-Islamic Arabia; but it is a protection extended to those who seek it, not to the wronged as such.[39]

From what has been said in this section, we can conclude that the Koran owes the terms 'right' and 'wrong' (*maʿrūf* and *munkar*) to pre-Islamic Arabia.[40] But what of 'commanding' and 'forbidding' them? We have no serious precedent for such a usage from within Arabia; nor, to my knowledge, do we have any from outside it that is likely to be historically relevant.[41] It is accordingly an obvious hypothesis, though not one we can hope to prove, that the usage which provides the Islamic duty with its name was a Koranic innovation. As far as terminology is concerned, there is little more to be said.

The religious recognition of the duty is another matter. As we have seen earlier in this book, it is by no means clear that the Koranic verses that speak of 'commanding right and forbidding wrong' are in fact talking about the duty we know from later Islamic thought, and this opacity is strongly reflected in early exegesis.[42] At the same time, an early usage which clearly does refer to our duty speaks not of 'forbidding' wrong but rather of 'righting' it.[43] We therefore have some reason to put the Koranic terminology to one side and to look elsewhere for the antecedents of the conception itself.

3. MONOTHEIST PARALLELS

Goldziher, in an extended discussion of the duty,[44] adduced two parallels from outside Islam. One was the institution of the censorship in Confucian China;[45] to this he might have added the more familiar censorship of Republican Rome.[46] Both were institutions maintained by the state, and as

39 Describing pre-Islamic Beduin society, Jacob remarks that when a man who has been wronged can get no help from his own tribe, he often turns to a more powerful tribe or prince; the latter is likely to see it as a point of honour to stand up for the weak, particularly when he can expect his deed to receive poetic recognition (G. Jacob, *Altarabisches Beduinenleben*, Berlin 1897, 217–18). Cf. also B. Farès, *L'honneur chez les Arabes avant l'Islam*, Paris 1932, 88–91, 151–3.

40 As suggested in R. Levy, *The social structure of Islam*, Cambridge 1957, 194.

41 Cf. above, 561f.

42 See above, ch. 2, section 1 and 22f.

43 See above, ch. 3, 34f.

44 Goldziher, *Livre*, 85–102.

45 *Ibid.*, 87. On this institution see C. O. Hucker, *The censorial system of Ming China*, Stanford 1966, esp. ch. 1 (drawn to my attention by Andy Plaks). Goldziher's parallel is not a good one: the traditional Chinese censorship was an official institution concerned with the monitoring of the state apparatus, not of society at large (see, for example, *ibid.*, 147); that its tone was moralistic and its operations involved frequent remonstrations is beside the point.

46 For a brief account of the Roman censorship and its *regimen morum*, see H. F. Jolowicz and B. Nicholas, *Historical introduction to the study of Roman law*, Cambridge 1972, 51–4.

such might bear comparison with the Islamic censorship (*ḥisba*) – itself a special case of forbidding wrong. But they are quite unlike the general Islamic conception of an executive power of individual believers existing outside any institutional framework. The other parallel adduced by Goldziher is from Rabbinic Judaism,[47] and this is considerably more to the point.[48]

In the first place, a comparable duty is already prescribed in scripture: 'you shall reprove your neighbour (*hokheaḥ tokhiaḥ et-ʿamitekha*), or you will incur guilt yourself' (Lev. 19:17). This is adduced by the rabbis, appropriately enough, to show that if a man sees something unseemly in his neighbour, it is his duty to rebuke him.[49] (Here and below, all Jewish sources adduced are pre-Islamic, unless otherwise indicated.) He also has the duty of repeating his rebuke if the offender does not take the point (*lo qibbel*).[50] How much come-back does he have to put up with in the performance of the duty? Here there is disagreement: till he is beaten? till he is cursed? till the offender becomes angry?[51] There is also dispute as to where one's duty lies if one's initiative will be of no avail. One rabbi declined to rebuke the members of the household of the exilarch on the grounds that they would not accept (*qabbel*) it from him; another held that he should rebuke them notwithstanding.[52] There should be no respect of persons: a disciple has the duty of rebuking a teacher.[53] Failure to perform

[47] Goldziher, *Livre*, 86 n. 1, quoting (or rather misquoting) Babylonian Talmud, Vilnius 1880–6, *Shabbat*, f. 54b.51, and noting in passing a certain 'parenté'. (I cite the Babylonian Talmud by the standard foliation, which appears also in the Soncino translation, ed. I. Epstein, London 1935–52.) Goldziher's rabbinic parallel has not received much attention from subsequent scholarship, but it has been noted by van Ess (*Theologie*, 2:387 n. 6), and independently rediscovered by H. Lazarus-Yafeh (*Intertwined worlds: medieval Islam and Bible criticism*, Princeton 1992, 145 and n. 9).

[48] For helpful surveys of the Jewish material, see *Encyclopaedia Judaica*, Jerusalem 1971–2, 13:1605f., art. 'Rebuke and reproof'; *Encyclopedia Talmudica*, Jerusalem 1969–, 2:616–18, art. 'Afroshe me-issura'; E. E. Urbach, *The Sages: their concepts and beliefs*, Cambridge, Mass. and London 1975, 563f. I am indebted to Mark Cohen and Menachem Lorberbaum for assistance with several of the references to primary sources in what follows.

[49] Babylonian Talmud, *ʿArakhin*, f. 16b.14. In another passage the duty is elicited from 1 Sam. 1:14, where Eli tells the apparently inebriated Hannah to put away her liquor (*ibid.*, *Berakhot*, f. 31a.61).

[50] *Ibid.*, *ʿArakhin*, f. 16b.16. Another passage states that one must repeat the rebuke even after four or five attempts (*Sifra*, Jerusalem 5743, second part, 4:8, f. 39a.10 = trans. J. Neusner, *Sifra: an analytical translation*, Atlanta 1988, 3:109 (to Lev. 19:17)); yet another that one should repeat the rebuke as much as a hundred times (Babylonian Talmud, *Baba Meṣiʿa*, f. 31a.43).

[51] *Ibid.*, *ʿArakhin*, f. 16b.31.

[52] *Ibid.*, *Shabbat*, f. 55a.11. The scriptural advice not to rebuke (*al-tokhaḥ*) a scoffer (Prov. 9:8) is quoted in support of the view that one should speak out only when one will be heard (*ibid.*, *Yebamot*, f. 65b.18).

[53] *Ibid.*, *Baba Meṣiʿa*, f. 31a.44.

the duty can lead to collective divine punishment: Jerusalem was destroyed because 'they did not rebuke one another'.[54] On the other hand, there is a preference for private rebuke: Jeroboam merited the kingship because he reproved Solomon, but was punished for reproving him in public (*ba-rabbim*).[55] Reproving people is not a way of making friends: if a young scholar is popular with his fellow-townsmen, it is because he does not rebuke them in religious matters.[56] As might be expected, the duty does not flourish in the present: no one in this generation is able to reprove, or able to accept (*le-qabbel*) reproof, or even knows how to reprove.[57]

In the second place, there is a duty (perhaps to be equated with the preceding) to protest (*le-maḥot*) at the misdeeds of others. This duty is aired in connection with the celebrated scandal of Rabbi Elʿazar ben ʿAzariah's cow. This cow would go out on the Sabbath with a strap between its horns, a practice on which the sages looked askance,[58] though Rabbi Elʿazar himself deemed it permissible.[59] So far, these commotions hardly concern us. In the Babylonian Talmud, however, a discussion takes place which puts a quite different complexion on the matter. Here it is suggested that the cow was not in fact Rabbi Elʿazar's at all, but rather the property of a female neighbour; it was accounted his because he failed to protest about it (*lo miḥah bah*).[60] The ensuing Talmudic discussion endorses the principle here suggested: that failure to protest when one is in a position to do so saddles one with responsibility for what one has failed to prevent.[61] In this way one can acquire an unwelcome responsibility for the sins of one's household, of one's fellow-townsmen, even of the world at large.[62] Elders are liable to divine punishment for failing to protest against the misdeeds of princes.[63] But what if

[54] *Ibid.*, *Shabbat*, f. 119b.42.

[55] *Ibid.*, *Sanhedrin*, f. 101b.43 (citing 1 Kings 11:27). Cf. the comment of Rashi (d. AD 1105) to Lev. 19:17 (*Perushe Rashi ʿal ha-Torah*, ed. H. D. Chavel, Jerusalem 1982, 373.21; I owe this reference to Simon Cook).

[56] Babylonian Talmud, *Ketubbot*, 105b.19.

[57] *Sifra*, second part, 4:9, f. 39a.11 (to Lev. 19:17), and cf. Babylonian Talmud, *ʿArakhin*, f. 16b.17.

[58] Mishnah, *Shabbat*, 5:4 = H. Danby (trans.), *The Mishnah*, Oxford 1933, 104. (I cite the Mishnah by the standard division of the text.)

[59] Mishnah, *Beṣah*, 2:8 (trans. Danby, 184); *ibid.*, *ʿEduyot*, 3:12 (trans. Danby, 428).

[60] Babylonian Talmud, *Shabbat*, f. 54b.49.

[61] This principle is stated explicitly in the Palestinian Talmud: whoever is able to protest (*le-maḥot*) and does not do so is himself guilty of the offence (Palestinian Talmud, *Shabbat*, 5:4 (Venice *c.* 1522, f. 7c.28 = trans. J. Neusner *et al.*, *The Talmud of the Land of Israel*, Chicago and London 1982–, 11:183); *ibid.*, *Ketubbot*, 13:1 (f. 35c.51 = trans. Neusner, 22:358f.); the first passage makes reference to the Babylonian discussion of the female neighbour and the cow).

[62] Babylonian Talmud, *Shabbat*, f. 54b.51.

[63] *Ibid.*, f. 55a.1, offered in explanation of Isa. 3:14.

protest would achieve nothing?[64] The issue is raised in a discussion between God and Justice regarding certain righteous men among the sinners of Jerusalem. Justice alleges against them that 'it was in their power to protest, but they did not do so'; God's retort is that it was already known that, had they protested, the sinners would not have accepted it from them.[65]

Finally, there is a duty to restrain others from forbidden actions (*le-afroshe me-issura*).[66] It is clear from the Talmudic passages in question that we have to do with a definite principle of law; it has a set phrasing, and in two instances is held to override other legal principles. Its performance, it emerges, may be by word (telling someone what to do, or shouting at them to restrain them from a violation), or by deed (stalking an unmarried couple with the intention of restraining them from performing a forbidden act). There is no reference to violence.

Here, then, we have the beginnings of a scholastic elaboration of a religious duty or duties similar in character to forbidding wrong, though relatively far less salient. So far as I know, there is nothing comparable in Syriac Christianity before Islamic times. A Jewish background to the Islamic duty is thus quite plausible. It is not, of course, proved by the general similarity, and I doubt if the case could be clinched. But this Jewish precedent would provide a starting-point for the development of the Muslim duty which is closer to the classical Islamic conception than are the vague Koranic verses that give the duty its name.[67]

It may be added in passing that the terminology of the Muslim duty was readily adopted by Jews writing in Arabic in Islamic times.[68] At the same

64 It is here that we find the discussion already cited on rebuking members of the exilarch's household (see above, note 52). This strongly suggests that the duties of 'rebuking' (*le-hokhiah*) and 'protesting' (*le-mahot*) are, as might be expected, one and the same. They are clearly taken to be so by Maimonides (d. AD 1204) in his discussion of the commandment to rebuke, see his *Mishneh Torah*, De'ot, 6:7 (Jerusalem and Tel Aviv 1965–7, 1:58b.26, 58b.32; for a translation of the chapter, see Maimonides, *The book of knowledge*, trans. H. M. Russell and J. Weinberg, Edinburgh 1981, 44–7).

65 Babylonian Talmud, *Shabbat*, f. 55a.23. Compare the principle stated in the Palestinian Talmud: when one is not in a position to protest (*le-mahot*) (effectively), one should not do so (*Soṭah*, 8:2 (f. 22b.41 = trans. Neusner, 27:201f.)).

66 Babylonian Talmud, *Shabbat*, f. 40b.36; *ibid.*, *'Erubin*, f. 63a.27; *ibid.*, *Sukkah*, f. 52a.53. Though the pre-Islamic material does not explicitly say so, one assumes that those to be restrained are other Jews.

67 For Muslim awareness of the Jewish precedent, cf. above, ch. 4, 47.

68 Sa'adya (d. AD 942) speaks of *al-amr bi'l-ma'rūf* in his work *al-Amānāt wa'l-i'tiqādāt* (ed. S. Landauer, Leiden 1880, 256.17, noted by Goldziher in his review in *Zeitschrift der Deutschen Morgenländischen Gesellschaft*, 35 (1881), 775 (drawn to my attention by Frank Stewart). The fourth/tenth-century Qaraite Qirqisānī adopts the terms *munkar* and *ghayyara*: *man ra'ā munkaran wa-kāna qādiran 'alā inkārihi* (Qirqisānī, *al-Anwār wa'l-marāqib*, ed. L. Nemoy, New York 1939–43, 416.9, and cf. 416.16); *idhā hum lam yunkirū wa-yughayyirū* (*ibid.*, 416.20). One fifth/eleventh-century Rabbanite document lists (*al-amr bi'l-ma'rūf*) *wa'l-nahy 'an al-munkar* among the prerogatives of the head of

time, some themes found on the Muslim side now make their first appearance in Jewish discussions of the duty of rebuke.[69] Christians seem to have been less receptive;[70] but we possess a Syriac account of forbidding wrong by Barhebraeus (d. AD 1286), derived as might be expected from that of Ghazzālī (d. 505/1111).[71]

While a Jewish point of departure for the scholastic elaboration of the duty in Islam is by no means implausible, there is a comparative observation which significantly weakens the case. Judaism and Islam are not the only cultures in which a duty of this kind receives formal scholastic development. Such a duty was also well known to the Latin West, where it was termed 'fraternal correction' (*correctio fraterna*). Rebuking others for their sins was, of course, a Christian habit of hoary antiquity and firm scriptural foundations.[72]

the yeshiva (*ra's al-mathība*) (in Jerusalem) (see S. D. Goitein, 'Arabic documents on the Palestinian Gaonate' (in Hebrew), *Eretz-Israel*, 10 (1971), 103 line 7, and see *ibid.*, 105, for Goitein's comments on the phrase, and *ibid.*, 100, for his dating of the document to the late 420s/1030s; I owe this reference to Gideon Libson). In another Rabbanite document from the same period, ten elders are to assist the head of the community in Old Cairo in, among other things, *al-amr bi'l-ma'rūf wa'l-nahy 'an al-munkar* (see S. D. Goitein, 'The local Jewish community in the light of the Cairo Geniza records', *The Journal of Jewish Studies*, 12 (1961), 156 line 9, and see *ibid.*, 144). As noted by Lazarus-Yafeh (*Intertwined worlds*, 145), Ibn Paquda (*fl.* later fifth/eleventh century) uses the phrase in several passages of a pietistic work (*al-Hidāya ilā farā'iḍ al-qulūb*, ed. A. S. Yahuda, Leiden 1912, 172.15, 196.11, 211.5, 248.20, 272.8, 330.18); in the latter two of these passages he makes mention of the three modes, and in the last (as noted by the editor in his introduction, 82 n. 2) he equates the duty with that of Lev. 19:17. Judah ha-Levi (d. AD 1141) uses the term of the philosophers in his *Khazarī* (*Kitāb al-radd wa'l-dalīl*, ed. D. H. Baneth, Jerusalem 1977, 170.11), as noted by Goldziher in his review of the first edition of the text (*Zeitschrift der Deutschen Morgenländischen Gesellschaft*, 41 (1887), 692, drawn to my attention by Frank Stewart).

69 In addition to the adoption of the three modes by Ibn Paquda (see the preceding note), there are two examples to be found in the chapter on the duty in the *Mishneh Torah* of Maimonides. First, he states that a man living among evildoers should emigrate (De'ot, 6:1 (1:58a.8)). Second, he stresses the importance of performing the duty gently (*ibid.*, 6:7 (1:58b.28)) and without initial harshness (*ibid.*, 6:8 (1:59a.3)). It is a pity that we have no account of the duty in the extant parts of the *Kifāyat al-'ābidīn* of his son Abraham Maimonides (d. AD 1237) (for this work, see S. D. Goitein, *A Mediterranean society*, Berkeley and Los Angeles 1967–93, 5:475–81).

70 The closest parallel I have seen to the Muslim terminology in Christian Arabic is in a work of Theodore Abū Qurra (*fl.* later second/eighth century) in which he quotes Muslims describing the mission of the Prophet: *wa-ya'muruka bi'l-ḥalāl wa-'amal al-khayr wa-yanhāka 'an al-ḥarām wa-'amal al-sū'* (*Mīmar fī wujūd al-khāliq wa'l-dīn al-qawīm*, ed. L. Cheikho, *al-Mashriq*, 15 (1912), 770.14, drawn to my attention by Robert Hoyland; this is presumably the passage to which van Ess refers, *Theologie*, 2:387).

71 See below, appendix 2.

72 See, for example, Lev. 19:17 and Matt. 18:15–17. The wording of Matt. 18:15 (*si autem peccaverit in te frater tuus, vade, et corripe eum inter te et ipsum solum*) can provide justification for the term *correptio fraterna*, 'fraternal rebuke'. For a study of the New Testament conception and its background, see A. Schenk-Ziegler, *Correctio fraterna im Neuen Testament: Die 'brüderliche Zurechtweisung' in biblischen, frühjüdischen und hellenistischen Schriften*, Würzburg 1997 (drawn to my attention by Sebastian Brock). The author, a Catholic, is interested in reviving the practice.

But to my knowledge, it was not the object of systematic doctrinal exposition until the thirteenth century AD. The tradition then established has remained a part, though not perhaps a very prominent one, of Catholic Christianity ever since.[73] The classic account is that of Thomas Aquinas (d. AD 1274),[74] and it will give us most of what we need.

Much of the detailed argumentation of Aquinas's account is naturally peculiar to the Christian tradition, and more particularly to its Latin form. Yet no reader who is familiar with the Islamic doctrine of forbidding wrong could fail to be struck by the broad similarities. Fraternal correction is a duty (*in praecepto*),[75] but not an absolute one: it is not to be carried out without regard for place and time,[76] and we are not to set ourselves up as investigators of the lives of others (*exploratores vitae aliorum*).[77] Correcting a sinner for his own sake by simple admonition (*admonitio*) is the business of everyone[78] who possesses charity, whether he be an inferior or a superior (*sive sit subditus sive praelatus*) – though the duty presses more heavily on superiors.[79] An inferior may thus correct a superior, provided this is done in private and in a gentle and respectful manner, without impudence and harshness (*non cum protervia et duritia,*

[73] For surveys, see the article 'Correction fraternelle' in the *Dictionnaire de théologie catholique*, Paris 1903–50 (G. Blanc), and J. A. Costello, *Moral obligation of fraternal correction*, Washington D.C. 1949. Both are written from within the tradition; Costello includes guidance on the proper response to some of the evils afflicting Catholic life in modern times (*ibid.*, 105–12). In general, the Catholic literature I have consulted on the duty lacks the wealth of anecdote and consideration of particular cases that we find on the Muslim side. To my surprise, I was unable to locate any systematic discussions in Protestant literature.

[74] Thomas Aquinas (d. AD 1274), *Summa theologiae*, 2a2ae. 33, 1–8. In what follows I cite the Blackfriars edition, with facing English translation (London and New York 1964–76, 34:274–305). Another account by Aquinas, this one using the term *correptio fraterna* (cf. above, note 72), is found in his *In quattuor libros Sententiarum*, IV, 19, 2, in his *Opera omnia*, ed. R. Busa, Stuttgart 1980, 1:549c–552c; I cite this only for some points not found in the *Summa theologiae*.

[75] Aquinas, *Summa*, 34:278f. (art. 2).

[76] *Ibid.*, 280f. (art. 2).

[77] *Ibid.*, 282f. (art. 2).

[78] On this point Aquinas quotes a passage from Gratian (writing *c.* AD 1140) to the effect that the rebuking (*redargutio*) of sinners is a duty not just of priests, but also of all the rest of the faithful (*reliqui fideles omnes*) (*ibid.*, 284 (art. 3), citing Gratian, *Decretum*, second part, XXIV, 3, 14 = Rome 1584, 1334). This citation is exceptional: fraternal correction is not a topic that is developed in canon law (cf. *Dictionnaire de droit canonique*, Paris 1935–65, art. 'Correptio' (H. Durand), 690).

[79] Aquinas, *Summa*, 34:284f. (art. 3). A *praelatus* is someone exercising public authority (see Aquinas, *In quattuor libros Sententiarum*, 550a ra6, and 551a co). In his handling of the relationship between fraternal correction and formally constituted authority, Aquinas is addressing an issue that was controversial in Latin Christendom both before and after his time. For a richly documented discussion, see P. Buc, *L'ambiguïté du Livre: prince, pouvoir, et peuple dans les commentaires de la Bible au Moyen Age*, Paris 1994, 352–6, 380–92, 394–8. Buc contrasts an egalitarian tendency with a hierarchic tendency (*ibid.*, 399); it is clear from his study that the hierarchic tendency was far more salient in Latin Christianity than its equivalent was in Islam (cf. above, ch. 17, notes 29f., 41, 158). Buc's study was drawn to my attention by Patricia Crone.

sed cum mansuetudine et reverentia);[80] however, if there is imminent danger to the faith, it must be done in public[81] (but not, it seems, harshly). Does a sinner have a duty to correct a wrongdoer?[82] He at least commits no sin if he reproves him with humility.[83] Do we have a duty to refrain from correction if we fear that it will merely make the sinner worse? In such a case, where it is judged probable (*probabiliter aestimatur*) that the offender will not accept the reproof (*admonitionem non recipiat*), fraternal correction is not to be attempted.[84] Does the duty require us to admonish the wrongdoer in secret before going on to public denunciation?[85] The answer, in general, is that it does.[86] What is more, we should continue to admonish him in private as long as there is hope that this will work (*quandiu spes probabiliter habetur de correctione*). But when we judge that private admonition is unlikely to succeed, we escalate (*procedendum est ulterius*).[87]

In later Catholic doctrine further resemblances appear. The duty is held to be established by both reason (*jure . . . naturali*) and revelation (*jure . . . divino positivo*),[88] a point Aquinas had not addressed. (This, of course, aligns Catholicism with an opinion held only by a minority of Muslim scholars.) The question whether it is obligatory to perform fraternal correction in the case of a venial sin is discussed.[89] Aquinas's treatment of the conditions of obligation is by Islamic standards unsystematic;[90] this is made good with the appearance of a schema of five conditions.[91]

80 Aquinas, *Summa*, 34:286f. (art. 4). 81 *Ibid.*, 288f. (art. 4).

82 *Ibid.*, 288f. (art. 5).

83 *Ibid.*, 290f. (art. 5). At one point the familiar argument is adduced that if sinners could not correct others, then no one could perform the duty (*ibid.*, 288f. (art. 5)).

84 *Ibid.*, 292–5 (art. 6). 85 *Ibid.*, 294f. (art. 7).

86 *Ibid.*, 298f. (art. 7). This applies to hidden sins without public implications.

87 *Ibid.*, 302f. (art. 8). He here takes issue with unnamed authorities who are against such escalation (*dicebant non esse ulterius procedendum*).

88 See Alphonsus Liguori (d. AD 1787), *Theologia moralis*, ed. L. Gaudé, Graz 1954, 1:331 §34; *Dictionnaire de théologie catholique*, art. 'Correction fraternelle', 1908. The work of Saint Alphonsus lies behind numerous Catholic treatises of moral theology written since his day, several of which are cited by Blanc (*ibid.*, 1911).

89 Alphonsus, *Theologia moralis*, 1:331 §34; *Dictionnaire de théologie catholique*, art. 'Correction fraternelle', 1909, reporting disagreement among the scholars.

90 Something more like a set of conditions is given by Albert the Great (d. AD 1280), a teacher of Aquinas. In responding to the question whether fraternal correction is to be performed by all against all, he answers that it is; according to the discretion of the wise, however, it is to be done with moderation, and with attention to four points: (1) the extent of the wrongdoer's guilt; (2) the expectation that he will reform (*spes emendationis*); (3) the status of the admonisher; and (4) his motivation. In his brief comments on these points, he says that if the guilt is slight and it is feared that the result would be worse disorder (*turbatio gravior*), there is no obligation (*Commentarii in quartum librum Sententiarum*, XIX, E, 20 = *Opera omnia*, ed. A. and E. Borgnet, Paris 1890–9, 29:825f.).

91 Alphonsus, *Theologia moralis*, 1:332f. §§38f. Such five-condition schemas appear in, for example, A. Lehmkuhl, *Theologia moralis*, Freiburg im Breisgau 1898, 1:365, and the *New Catholic Encyclopedia*, New York 1967, art. 'Correction, fraternal' (F. J. Connell), 349a.

What then of the major differences between fraternal correction and forbidding wrong? In the first place, two issues are treated at length which are alien to the Islamic doctrine of forbidding wrong. The first of the eight articles into which Aquinas divides his discussion is concerned with the question whether fraternal correction is an act of charity or of justice[92] – the answer being that it is the former.[93] The last of the eight articles likewise deals with an unfamiliar issue: whether witnesses should be brought in prior to public denunciation[94] – the answer being that in general they should.[95] This concern, which has no equivalent in Islam, is directly driven by Christian scripture (Matt. 18:16).

In the second place, there are two points worth noting where the issues are the same, but the answers somewhat different. First, Aquinas is by Islamic standards strikingly inflexible regarding the conditions that dispense one from performing the duty: it is a mortal sin to omit it out of fear (*propter timorem*). Thus fear would be no excuse in a case where one had reason to believe that one could persuade a sinner to pull back.[96] Later Catholic doctrine, however, is much more cautious on this point, voiding the obligation where it would involve serious harm (*grave damnum*) to oneself.[97] Second, Aquinas, as we have seen, does not envisage situations

Footnote 91 (*cont.*)
Noldin has four conditions (H. Noldin, *Summa theologiae moralis*, Innsbruck 1955–6, 2:90f. §96). Other authors adopt a schema of three conditions, as in the case of A. Koch and A. Preuss, *A handbook of moral theology*, St Louis, Mo. and London 1924, 5:31, and *Dictionnaire de théologie catholique*, art. 'Correction fraternelle', 1910. In this last source the three conditions are listed as follows: (1) the offender must definitely have committed the sin in question; (2) there must be good reason to expect success ('espoir fondé de réussite'); (3) the performer of the duty must not thereby place himself in serious danger ('aucun grave danger'). As will be seen below (notes 96f.), the third condition involves a substantive, though tacit, departure from the doctrine of Aquinas.

92 Aquinas, *Summa*, 34:274f. (art. 1). 93 *Ibid.*, 276f. (art. 1).

94 *Ibid.*, 300f. (art. 8). 95 *Ibid.*, 302f. (art. 8).

96 *Ibid.*, 280–3 (art. 2). Aquinas here yokes with fear the love of worldly things (*cupiditas*) as an unacceptable motive for failing to perform the duty. Presumably this would also rule out danger to one's property as an excuse. This whole discussion (including the term *cupiditas*) derives from an argument set out by Augustine (d. AD 430) in Book I, ch. 9 of the *City of God*: the Christians too deserved what they suffered in the sack of Rome because they had not done their duty in rebuking the sinners whose misdeeds provoked God's wrath (*De civitate Dei*, Turnhout 1955, 8–10 = *The City of God*, abridged translation, ed. V. J. Bourke, New York 1958, 46–9; cf. the Rabbinic discussion between God and Justice, above, note 65, and above, note 54). To make the argument work, Augustine naturally has to minimise excuses, and it is this residue of an ancient polemical context that probably lies behind Aquinas's inflexibility.

97 Alphonsus, *Theologia moralis*, 1:333 §39, condition 5; how this is to be squared with the view of Aquinas (cf. *ibid.*, 332 37) is not clear to me. Other authors follow this stipulation (so, for example, Lehmkuhl, *Theologia moralis*, 1:365; *New Catholic Encyclopedia*, art. 'Correction, fraternal', 349a; and see above, note 91). Noldin resolves the tension by specifying groundless fear (*vanus timor*) (*Summa*, 2:91 96, condition *a*, and cf. condition *c*).

in which it would be appropriate to speak harshly to a superior; the goldsmith of Marw has accordingly no place in his scheme of things.[98]

In the third place, there is a basic structural difference between the Christian and Islamic conceptions. What I did not make clear above is that Aquinas repeatedly distinguishes two kinds of correction. The first is the fraternal correction with which we are now familiar. This kind is done in the interests of the offender (whence it is an act of charity);[99] it is carried out by simple admonition, without any form of coercion (*non habens coactionem sed simplicem admonitionem*);[100] and it is the business of everyone.[101] The other kind of correction is carried out for the common good (*bonum commune*) (whence it is an act of justice);[102] it is marked by coercive force (*habet vim coactivam*), is reserved for superiors (*praelati*),[103] and may involve punishment (*punitio*).[104] Aquinas offers no term for this second type, but it passes under the name of 'juridical correction'.[105] How does this compare with Islamic conceptions? Fraternal correction has its equivalent in the verbal rebuke that any believer should administer to an offender. Juridical correction is part of the exercise of superior authority against wrongdoers.[106] What is missing on the Christian side is thus the entire domain of forbidding wrong as performed by the individual believer 'with the hand', whether or not this includes recourse to arms.

Finally, it is worth noting that later Catholic doctrine, unlike that of Aquinas, tends to minimise the extent to which private persons are obligated to perform 'fraternal correction'. One authority concludes his account of the conditions of obligation with the observation that it is clear that little or no blame attaches to private persons (*privati*) who fail to perform the duty.[107] Another stresses that it hardly ever extends to correcting a stranger, the reason being lack of good grounds to expect success in such a case; hence it is rare for private persons to be obligated to perform

[98] See above, notes 80f. The whole tone of the account suggests that illegitimate power was far less of a problem for Aquinas than it was in Islamic thought.

[99] Aquinas, *Summa*, 34:276f. (art. 1).

[100] *Ibid.*, 292f. (art. 6). Noldin says that the rebuke need not necessarily be verbal, but the alternative steps he mentions (e.g. putting on a sad face) are, in Islamic terms, in the nature of avoidance rather than action (*Summa*, 2:90 94(a)). Costello is unusual in stating that the duty can be performed by 'word or deed' (*Moral obligation*, 23); this goes beyond the authority he cites (*ibid.*, 21 n. 22), but he does not elaborate.

[101] Aquinas, *Summa*, 34:284f. (art. 3).

[102] *Ibid.*, 276f. (art. 1), 284f. (art. 3).

[103] *Ibid.*, 284f. (art. 3), 292f. (art. 6).

[104] *Ibid.*, 284f. (art. 3).

[105] *Dictionnaire de théologie catholique*, art. 'Correction fraternelle', 1907 ('correction juridique'). In his *In quattuor libros Sententiarum*, Aquinas makes the distinction by contrasting the terms *correctio* and *correptio*: 'while correction (*correctio*) is an act of justice, rebuke (*correptio*) is an act of charity' (*ibid.*, 550a ra6).

[106] This distinction would have appealed to ʿAbd al-Ghanī al-Nābulusī (d. 1143/1731) (see above, ch. 12, 326f.).

[107] Alphonsus, *Theologia moralis*, 1:333 §39.

the duty among themselves unless they know each other, and rarer still for an inferior to be obligated to correct a superior.[108]

Now it would be satisfying to argue that this Christian scholastic doctrine was in turn inspired by that of Islam. Latin Christendom and Islam were neighbours, and Aquinas lived in a period when a considerable volume of material had been translated from Arabic into Latin and received with great excitement. In this general historical context, an Islamic influence on the elaboration of the Christian doctrine of fraternal correction is eminently plausible. But again, clinching the argument is another matter. The process of translation from Arabic into Latin is reasonably well known, and the books translated were overwhelmingly works of science and philosophy; the limited corpus of specifically religious texts translated under the patronage of Peter the Venerable (d. AD 1156) offered no coverage of the scholastic tradition of Islam.[109] We thus have no knowledge of a translation that would have included a systematic account of forbidding wrong, and the likelihood that there ever was such a translation is probably small. At the same time, much that is reminiscent of Islamic doctrine in the account of Aquinas is missing from the slightly earlier discussion of William of Auxerre (d. AD 1231).[110] The systematic doctrine of fraternal correction could thus be seen as generated by the application of the new scholastic method to an old religious duty.[111] This in turn would tend to support the

[108] Lehmkuhl, *Theologia moralis*, 1:366; Noldin (*Summa*, 2:91 §96, condition *d*) and Koch and Preuss (*Handbook*, 5:31, 33) take a similar view. Compare the question put to Khumaynī (d. 1409/1989) (above, ch, 18. note 293). Another difference between later Catholic thought and that of the Muslim scholars is that among the Catholics a question arises about the scope of the duty of fraternal correction where the offence is a violation of a human law (Alphonsus, *Theologia moralis*, 1:331f. §36; *Dictionnaire de théologie catholique*, art. 'Correction fraternelle', 1909f., reporting considerable disagreement on the question and a shift of views).

[109] For this corpus, see J. Kritzeck, *Peter the Venerable and Islam*, Princeton 1964, ch. 3; and see also M.-T. d'Alverny, 'Deux traductions latines du Coran au Moyen Age', in her *La connaissance de l'Islam dans l'Occident médiéval*, Aldershot and Brookfield 1994, 125–7, and M.-T. d'Alverny and G. Vajda, 'Marc de Tolède, traducteur d'Ibn Tumart', in the same volume. For an unusual work of this period which draws on a wider range of Arabic material to produce a handbook of practical morality, see J. Jolivet, 'The Arabic inheritance', in P. Dronke (ed.), *A history of twelfth-century Western philosophy*, Cambridge 1988, 132f., on the *Disciplina clericalis* of the Spanish Jewish convert Petrus Alfonsi. But this work contains nothing relevant to forbidding wrong. I am indebted to Antony Black for bibliographical assistance in this field.

[110] William of Auxerre (d. AD 1231), *Summa aurea*, ed. J. Ribaillier, Paris and Rome 1980–7, 3:1034–44. His account deals only with three major questions. The first is whether all are obligated, to which he gives essentially the same answer as Aquinas (*ibid.*, 1037.89). The second is about escalation; here to an extent he seems to side with the unnamed scholars with whom Aquinas takes issue (*ibid.*, 1040.41, 1041.70; cf. above, note 87). The third is concerned with rebukes administered by superiors (*ibid.*, 1042.3); in other words, he does not yet distinguish this topic from fraternal correction proper.

[111] The question whether, or to what extent, the scholastic method as such had an Islamic

view that the Islamic doctrine originated independently of the Jewish conceptions considered above. In short, while we certainly should not rule out a monogenetic view of the incidence of the scholastic doctrines we have reviewed, the fact is that we have little chance of establishing such a hypothesis.

4. NON-MONOTHEIST PARALLELS

What then of the major non-monotheist traditions? I shall briefly consider here the belief-systems of ancient India and China, together with Zoroastrianism. To my knowledge, none of these traditions gives our duty a name, lays much emphasis on it, or elaborates it in a scholastic fashion.

To start with the Indians. I have not found anything of note in a sampling of the mainstream tradition deriving from the Vedas. Turning to the Buddhists, most of their literature is for monks, but there are exceptions; one of them (the *Sigālovādasutta*) is part of the Theravāda (Pāli) canon.[112] Here the Buddha (*c.* fifth century BC) includes among the virtues of the good friend who tells one what one needs to do that 'he restrains [one] from wrong; he establishes [one] in right' (***pāpā nivāreti: kalyāṇe niveseti***).[113] This has a formulaic ring, and indeed the phrase is shortly repeated: in one passage it is the parents who do this to their child, and in another the leaders in religious life who do it to the young layman of good family.[114] Yet the formula seems not to have achieved a wider currency in the canon.[115] Nor does the passage receive much attention in the exegetical literature,[116] or even in the one post-canonical Pāli work devoted to a systematic exposition of the proper conduct of the layman.[117] In short, the value

background does not concern us here (for the view that it did, see G. Makdisi, *The rise of colleges*, Edinburgh 1981, 245–60).

112 See K. R. Norman, *Pāli literature*, Wiesbaden 1983, 42.

113 *Dīgha nikāya*, ed. T. W. Rhys Davids and J. E. Carpenter, London 1947–60, 3:187 §24 = T. W. and C. A. F. Rhys Davids (trans.), *Dialogues of the Buddha*, London 1899–1921, 3:179 §24). For this work as a whole, see Norman, *Pāli literature*, 32–44.

114 *Dīgha nikāya*, 3:189 §28, and 191 §33 = Rhys Davids, *Dialogues*, 3:181 §28, and 183 §33.

115 See F. L. Woodward *et al.*, *Pāli Tipitakaṁ concordance*, London 1952–, 2:517f., entries for ***nivāreti*** and ***niveseti***.

116 There is a brief commentary on two of our texts in Buddhaghosa (fifth century AD), *Sumaṅgala-vilāsinī*, ed. T. W. Rhys Davids *et al.*, London 1886–1932, 3:950.22 §24, and 953.13 §28, and an equally brief supercommentary in the *Dīghanikāyaṭṭhakathāṭīkā līnatthavaṇṇanā*, ed. L. de Silva, London 1970, 3:175.16 §24, and 180.1 §28. For these works, see Norman, *Pāli literature*, 122, 149. I do not have a very clear idea what either of them has to say, but it does not seem to be of much interest to us.

117 *Upāsakajanālaṅkāra*, ed. H. Saddhatissa, London 1965, 269 §64, and 273 §82 (merely repeating the commentary of Buddhaghosa). The work probably dates from the twelfth century AD (Norman, *Pāli literature*, 170).

failed to catch the eye of Buddhist scholasticism. For the Jainas again I have nothing significant to report.[118]

The Chinese record, so far as it is known to me, is no richer. Confucius (d. 479 BC) has a saying to the effect that one should admonish friends, but give up if they fail to respond.[119] Mencius (fourth century BC) describes the admonition of the ruler by his ministers in similar terms: 'If repeated remonstrations fell on deaf ears, they would leave him.'[120] In the T'ang period (AD 618–907) it was reckoned one of the duties of the historian 'to encourage good and to reprove evil'.[121] Such stray parallels could doubtless be multiplied; but here again, there seems to be no single central value corresponding to ours, and no scholastic elaboration of such a duty.[122]

What this discussion of the Indian and Chinese cases might suggest is that there is something about the development of the duty in the Jewish, Christian and Islamic cases that has to do with the character of the monotheist tradition. The relevant features of this tradition might include the following: a sublimely ethical but personal conception of the divine (or

[118] There is a systematic presentation of the considerable Jaina scholastic literature on the duties of the layman in R. Williams, *Jaina yoga: a survey of the mediaeval śrāvakācāras*, London 1963. There are a few points at which a principle of preventing fellow-believers from acting wrongly might perhaps seem in place, but it does not actually appear (*ibid.*, 42, item (v); 67f., items (i), (ii) and (v); 272, item 4(iii)). I owe to K. R. Norman the information that the Jainas sometimes affirm the principle 'Do not permit (or consent to) the doing of evil'.

[119] Confucius (d. 479 BC), *Analects*, XII:23 = trans. D. C. Lau, Harmondsworth 1979, 117. Admonishing friends is a theme easily attested elsewhere; see, for example, the Pāli text cited above, note 113; Cicero (d. 43 BC), *Laelius de amicitia*, XXV:91 = ed. and trans. J. G. F. Powell, Warminster 1990, 68f. (*et monere et moneri proprium est verae amicitiae*); White, *Christian friendship*, 119, 193. Confucius also has a saying on remonstrating with one's parents which would not have displeased the Muslim scholars (*Analects*, IV:18 = trans. Lau, 74).

[120] Mencius (fourth century BC), *Mencius*, VB:9 = trans. D. C. Lau, Harmondsworth 1970, 159. It is ministers who are not of royal blood who merely retire in this way if not listened to; those who are of royal blood depose a ruler who has made a serious mistake and does not respond to remonstrations.

[121] See D. Twitchett, *The writing of official history under the T'ang*, Cambridge 1992, 71, 78, and D. McMullen, *State and scholars in T'ang China*, Cambridge 1988, 194. The phrase goes back to the *Tso chuan*, which uses it (with the two components in the opposite order) to praise the style of the *Spring and autumn* chronicle (*ch'eng o erh ch'üan shan*, see J. Legge (ed. and trans.), *The Chinese classics*, Hong Kong and London 1861–72, 5:384.12 = 385 par. 5; I am grateful to Andy Plaks for this reference). For the *Tso chuan*, a commentary on the *Spring and autumn* classic dating from between the fifth and first century BC, see M. Loewe (ed.), *Early Chinese texts: a bibliographical guide*, Berkeley 1993, 67–71.

[122] The Chinese milieu in which one might have expected to find our value most clearly articulated is Mohism, with its egalitarian and utilitarian ethic. But no such value is attested in what we know of Mohist ethics (see A. C. Graham, *Later Mohist logic, ethics and science*, Hong Kong and London 1978, esp. 44–52).

to put it less respectfully, a supremely self-righteous deity); a degree of active divine and human engagement in the affairs of this world (much posting o'er land and ocean without rest); and a tight sense of religious community (believers are their brothers' keepers). It could be argued that this combination is alien or peripheral to the central message of Buddhism, Jainism, the Vedic mainstream and Confucianism. But if this approach makes some sense, it does not in fact work out very neatly.

Consider the case of Zoroastrianism. Here we have a religion whose basic doctrines display relevant features of the monotheist tradition. It is true that Ahura Mazdā is not an overbearingly personal god in the style of Israelite monotheism. But what better sanction for moral activism here and now than a conception of individual moral life as part and parcel of the cosmic struggle between good and evil? 'Every person ought to know: "Where have I come from? For what purpose am I here? Where do I return?" I, for my part, know that I came from Ohrmazd the Lord, that I am here so as to make the demons powerless, and that I shall return to Ohrmazd.'[123] Yet in a characteristic text containing several hundred moral sayings,[124] we find no set phrase identifying the value of preventing others from doing wrong, and little of its substance. We do learn that it is a duty to prevail on someone 'to turn away from a sin through which he might become wicked'.[125] Likewise it is good to find a friend who will tell one one's faults so that one can correct them.[126] Yet in general it is a vice, not a virtue, to reproach a sinner for his sin;[127] rather, it seems, one should correct one's own faults and learn from the goodness of others.[128] In a couple of sayings the suggestive phrase 'the preservation of the good and the uprooting of the wicked' appears; but it seems to describe a function of rulers and magnates, not of the individual believer.[129]

The overall effect of the non-monotheist parallels is to confirm that there is some link between doctrines of forbidding wrong (to generalise the Islamic term) and the monotheist tradition. But these parallels do not give

123 S. Shaked (trans.), *The wisdom of the Sasanian sages (Dēnkard VI)*, Boulder 1979, 184f. no. D9. Ohrmazd is Ahura Mazdā. Compare also: 'At least three times a day one should reckon with oneself in the following manner: ". . . Have I been today an assistant of the gods or of the demons?"' (*ibid.*, 200f. no. E31e).

124 I.e. the sixth book of the *Dēnkard*, in the translation of Shaked cited in the previous note.

125 *Ibid.*, 128f. no. 322.

126 *Ibid.*, 46f. no. 115, and 204 = 207 no. E38a; cf. also 28f. no. 78.

127 *Ibid.*, 6–9 no. 14, and the parallels noted by Shaked, *ibid.*, 235, to no. 13.4.

128 *Ibid.*, 82f. no. 212, and cf. 110f. no. 284.

129 *Ibid.*, 44f. no. 113, and 48f. no. 118 (*dārishn ī wehān ud a-rōyishn ī wattarān*). I am grateful to Shaul Shaked for confirming my impression that the value that concerns us is not a prominent one in Zoroastrianism.

us much guidance as to how we should see the link. The Indian and Chinese material would fit the view that there is some elective affinity between forbidding wrong and monotheism; whereas the Zoroastrian comparison tends to restore the suspicion that there may be something monogenetic about the monotheist value. The result is to leave the question of origins undecided.

5. THE DISTINCTIVENESS OF THE ISLAMIC CASE

In his commentary to Q3:110, Fakhr al-Dīn al-Rāzī (d. 606/1210) asks why the fact that the Muslims command right, forbid wrong and believe in God should have made them the best religious community, given that other communities have shared these qualities.[130] In answer he quotes the Transoxanian Shāfiʿite exegete Qaffāl (d. 365/976).[131] According to this scholar, the difference between the Muslims and their predecessors is that the Muslims perform the duty in its most stringent form (*bi-ākad al-wujūh*): fighting (*qitāl*), which involves the risk of being killed. Though this view was not well received by Rashīd Riḍā (d. 1354/1935),[132] it is clear from the data on Judaism and Christianity presented above that Qaffāl cannot be faulted on his facts. Neither the Jewish nor the Christian accounts of the comparable duties provide any basis for recourse to violence by individual believers.[133] Nor, for that matter, do they incite them to confrontation with unjust rulers;[134] and the general tone of later Catholic doctrine is particularly tame.[135] All this is in striking contrast to the political salience and frequent abrasiveness of forbidding wrong in Islam. There are no Jewish or Christian parallels to the ways in which Muslim scholars link the duty to holy war[136] and Muslim rebels invoke it to grace insurrection.[137]

[130] Fakhr al-Dīn al-Rāzī, *Tafsīr*, 8:191.21. [131] For whom see above, ch. 13, 340f.

[132] Riḍā, *Tafsīr al-Manār*, 4:61.24, 62.11 (to Q3:110), noted in Roest Crollius, 'Mission and morality', 281.

[133] See above, 572, and note 100. As Gerald Hawting points out to me, it is striking that the Christian accounts discussed above make no mention of the New Testament story of the cleansing of the Temple by Jesus (Matt. 21:12f., etc.). This is a fine example of righting a wrong 'with the hand': Jesus drives out those engaged in buying and selling, and overturns the tables of the money-changers and the seats of the dove-sellers; in one account he uses a whip to drive sheep and cattle out of the Temple (John 2:15). Cf. below, appendix 2, notes 21f. [134] Cf. above, notes 52, 80, 98.

[135] See above, notes 107f. As pointed out to me by Alexander Nehamas, the fact that the Catholic church – unlike the scholars of Islam – is an organisation with executive authority must be part of the explanation for the relative tameness of the Catholic doctrine of fraternal correction. [136] See above, ch. 17, 490f.

[137] See above, ch. 17, 477f.

At the same time, the basic idea of the duty is antithetical to a hierarchic conception of society.[138] It is founded in the axiom that each and every legally competent Muslim possesses an executive power of the law of God.[139] And as elaborated in scholastic doctrine, the duty usually takes no account of differences of social standing. There are, as we have seen, some exceptions to this. In particular, there is the saying that allocates the 'three modes' to three groups in society: the rulers are to perform it with the hand, the scholars with the tongue, and the common people with the heart.[140] But it is uncommon to find a major scholar who commits himself to such notions in his formal account of the duty; perhaps the only significant example is the Shāfiʿite Ḥalīmī (d. 403/1012).[141] Since hierarchic conceptions of society were commonplace in the thought of medieval Muslims,[142] it is the relative absence of such notions in formal statements of the doctrine of forbidding wrong that is striking. Thus while parents are regularly presented as a special case, this is not so with social superiors in general.[143] It does not follow that the duty should be seen as actively subversive of all hierarchy. From this point of view, it is remarkable that its implications for some of the most fundamental inequalities are rarely explored: those between slaves and the free,[144] and between women and men.[145] Nevertheless, the egalitarian bias of the duty was by no means entirely neutralised in its exposure to a society that was in many ways saturated with hierarchic conceptions. Perhaps the everyday character of the duty and its individual locus rendered it fitter to survive the realities of medieval Islamic society than, for example, the contractual conception of political legitimacy.[146]

We have, then, a duty of an unusual character. It is an integral part of the mainstream scholastic tradition of Islamic societies; and yet it retains a marked potential for violence, subversion and egalitarianism.[147] In this combination lies the distinctive character of the Islamic conception of the duty.

[138] As Khumaynī puts it, commanding and forbidding are in the nature of an exercise of authority (*mawlawī*), even when undertaken by someone of humble station (*sāfil*), and are to be expressed accordingly (*Taḥrīr*, 1:465 no. 12).

[139] Compare the story of the ascetic who was challenged by the Sāmānid Naṣr ibn Aḥmad (r. 301–31/914–43) with the question who had charged him with *ḥisba*, and responded to the effect that God had done so (Yaʿqūb ibn Seyyid ʿAlī, *Sharḥ*, 497.24; for similar anecdotes, see above, ch. 16, notes 133, 226).

[140] See above, ch. 17, notes 29f., 158, and the cross-references given there; and cf. above, ch. 17, notes 159f. for similar trends.

[141] See above, ch. 13, 341f.

[142] L. Marlow, *Hierarchy and egalitarianism in Islamic thought*, Cambridge 1997, esp. 6–10.

[143] See, for example, Kāshif al-Ghiṭā', *Kashf*, 420.19.

[144] See above, ch. 17, 486.

[145] See above, ch. 17, 482–6.

[146] Cf. B. Lewis, *The political language of Islam*, Chicago and London 1988, 58.

[147] Or as Goldziher rather sourly put it, appeal to this exalted duty provided a ready occasion for all sorts of disturbances ('toutes les agitations') (*Livre*, 88, and cf. the examples given, *ibid.*, 88–96).

Here the question of origins is arguably more straightforward. Strothmann, who was much intrigued by what he called the 'democratic' character of the duty,[148] was inclined to see its origin in a combination of two elements: on the one hand the 'inclinations of a democratic Arabian ethos to a law of the jungle' (*faustrechtliche Neigungen eines demokratischen Arabertums*), and on the other an 'idea of a religious community' (*ein religiöser Gemeinschaftsgedanke*).[149] We have already touched on the relevance of a sense of religious community;[150] what concerns us here is Strothmann's invocation of the ethos of Jāhilī society.

Pre-Islamic Arabian society was tribal, and in considerable measure nomadic, inhabiting a land whose meagre resources favoured neither strong state authority nor elaborate social stratification. It was accordingly a society in which every man was an uncrowned king.[151] Or to put it in more prosaic terms, political and military participation were very widely spread, far more so than in the mainstream of human societies – whether those of the steppe nomads,[152] the later Islamic world, or the modern West. It was the fusion of this egalitarian and activist tribal ethos with the monotheist tradition that gave Islam its distinctive political character. In no other civilisation was rebellion for conscience sake so widespread as it was in the early centuries of Islamic history; no other major religious tradition has lent itself to revival as a political ideology – and not just a political identity – in the modern world.[153]

The uniqueness of the Islamic doctrine of forbidding wrong can be understood against this background. In Islam, of course, the sovereignty of God means that it is no longer admissible for every man to be a king. But as Ibn al-ʿArabī (d. 543/1148) put it, individuals (*āḥād al-nās*) act as God's deputies (*nuwwāb Allāh*) in forbidding wrong.[154]

[148] Strothmann, *Staatsrecht*, 92–4. Strothmann's remarks are aptly highlighted by van Ess (*Theologie*, 4:675 n. 15, 705 n. 14), who himself follows Strothmann in describing *al-amr bi'l-maʿrūf* as rooted in the egalitarian tribal ethos of pre-Islamic Arabia (*ibid.*, 707).

[149] Strothmann, *Staatsrecht*, 93. My translation of *Faustrecht* (literally 'fist-law') as 'law of the jungle' is perhaps misleading to the extent that it suggests the absence of any kind of law; Strothmann may rather have had in mind the practice of the late medieval German feud (see *Handwörterbuch zur deutschen Rechtsgeschichte*, Berlin 1971–97, 1:1079f., art. 'Faustrecht' (E. Kaufmann)).

[150] See above, 580f.

[151] 'Every man of us is a power unto himself' (*kull rajul minnā fī nafsihi ʿazīz*), as the Kutāma described their rather similar society to Abū ʿAbdallāh al-Shīʿī (d. 298/911) (Nuʿmān, *Iftitāḥ al-daʿwa*, 65.4).

[152] For the contrast with the richer, more stratified and politically more developed nomadic societies of the Eurasian steppes, see P. Crone, *Slaves on horses*, Cambridge 1980, ch. 2.

[153] P. Crone, 'The tribe and the state', in J. A. Hall (ed.), *States in history*, Oxford and New York 1986, 74–7.

[154] See above, ch. 14, note 53, and cf. Gardet, *Cité*, 185.

CHAPTER 20

CONCLUSION

1. INTRODUCTION

One culture which was conspicuously absent from the comparisons made in the previous chapter is our own. This culture may not have much standing *sub specie aeternitatis*, but here and now it has a certain call upon our attention, if only by virtue of being ours. I shall therefore conclude this book with an attempt to identify some key ways in which the attitudes bound up with forbidding wrong resemble or differ from those of the mainstream of contemporary Western culture.[1]

There is clearly no problem with the intelligibility, and indeed acceptability, of the basic idea of the value in Western culture. A contemporary Muslim writing in Arabic relates an anecdote about a Swede who told off a rich American tourist for speeding on a quiet Swedish country road; he comments that this is an instance of commanding right and forbidding wrong.[2] More than this, almost everything of substance that Muslim scholasticism has to say about the doctrine is intelligible to a Western reader who knows nothing about Islam; and a lot of it makes good sense. To see this, one has only to make the experiment of translating the doctrine of, say, the classical Imāmī scholars into plain English. It might go something like this:

'If you see someone doing something wrong, you ought to try to get them to stop. You should say something, or if that doesn't work, you

[1] All references to Western culture in this chapter are to its prevailing modern form – which I would describe as broadly secular and liberal. It is, of course, readily compatible with a non-fundamentalist allegiance to a variety of traditional religions, including Judaism, Christianity and Islam.

[2] 'Abd al-ʿAzīz Kāmil, 'Ḥuqūq al-insān fī 'l-Islām: naẓra fī 'l-mushkilāt al-nawʿiyya', in Université de Tunis, Centre d'Etudes et de Recherches Economiques et Sociales, IIIème Rencontre Islamo-Chrétienne, *Droits de l'homme*, Tunis 1985, 43–5. Kāmil's use of the anecdote trades on the moral solidarity of all civilised people (or at least, of Arabs and Europeans) against Americans. The American, of course, tells the Swede to mind his own business, but backs down in the face of the manifest solidarity of the Swedish bystanders with the author of the rebuke.

should do something. Failing that, well, you can just wish them to stop.[3] But don't get too violent – that's for the police. If somebody really ought to take a certain course of action, then you really ought to tell them to; but if it's just that it would be nice if they did, then maybe it's a nice idea to suggest it to them. If there's a lot of people there, and somebody else speaks out, you don't have to; but if nobody does, it's up to you. But don't think you ought to jump in just like that. There may be several good reasons for keeping out of it, such as: "Come on, what's wrong with what he's doing?"; "Look, they've stopped anyway"; "Forget it – those people just don't listen"; "Forget it – he's bigger than you"; "Last time somebody told them to stop they smashed up his car"; "Try that and you'll just end up making matters worse".'[4]

What then of the differences? One respect in which the Muslim doctrine of forbidding wrong immediately strikes us as alien is the scholastic manner of its presentation – whence my attempt to naturalise it by translating it into plain, rather than academic, English. In part, this reflects a widespread feature of the moral thinking of Western populations today. Whatever people may say about us, we have our moral values, and we think, talk and argue about them. But we do not do so in a technical language characterised by formal definitions and rules. We might like to describe our moral language as more spontaneous, more nuanced, more sensitive to the uniqueness of each individual case. Others might call it subjective, arbitrary and inconsistent – a primitive and untutored colloquial. Whether our way of handling moral questions is a good thing or a bad thing is beside the point;[5] what seems clear is that in this respect the Muslims have something we don't.

We do, of course, have moral philosophers in our universities. They are known to have a lot of sophisticated and inconclusive things to say about the foundations of morality, none of which they agree upon among themselves. But they have tended to provide us with relatively little direct assistance

[3] We may not have much use for this notion, but then neither did the Muʿtazilites. Of course if the idea is to scowl at the offender, that would make sense as a strategy.

[4] It would be harder to render into so plain an English the Imāmī discussion of the question whether the source of the obligation is revelation alone, or revelation and reason. But there are still a good many people in Western societies for whom this raises an intelligible issue.

[5] My opinion, for what it is worth, would be that the scholastic approach does not help much with the more intractable problems, such as assessing the relative costs of action and inaction. On this one might compare Walzer's observation on the indeterminacy of the 'proportionality maxim' with regard to the morality of war: 'We have no way that even mimics mathematics of comparing the costs of fighting to the costs of not fighting, since one set of costs is necessarily speculative, while the other comes in, as it were, over an indeterminate time span' (M. Walzer, *Just and unjust wars*, New York 1992, xvi). On the other hand, checklists can be very useful in everyday life. One cannot land a plane by mentally reciting a checklist, but even experienced pilots who fail to do so sometimes forget to put down the undercarriage.

when it comes to thinking through the moral problems that most of us actually face.[6] In any case, we are not in the habit of taking our moral dilemmas to moral philosophers, any more than a scientist would refer a research problem to a philosopher of science. Nor do they seem to expect us to consult them in this way.

This straightforward contrast between the scholastic moral thought of Islam and the vernacular thought of the West is not, however, quite right. For one thing, we can take it for granted that the overwhelming majority of Muslims down the ages did not think scholastically. For another, academic writers in the West have in fact produced a measure of systematic thought that is of interest to us. This thought is not precisely concerned with our duty, but it does grapple with a theme sufficiently close to be relevant. The theme in question is the duty – assuming it is one – of rescue.

2. RESCUE AND FORBIDDING WRONG

The difference between rescue and forbidding wrong can be set out as follows. The duty of rescue is by definition an obligation to come to the aid of people in trouble. Whether or not the trouble is an intentional consequence of human wrongdoing is to this extent irrelevant. Consider the case of rape at a local train station in Chicago with which we began this book. If the woman had been the victim, not of rape, but of falling masonry in an earthquake, then – other things being equal – the bystanders would still have been under an obligation to try to assist her. Forbidding wrong, by contrast, is not a duty to help people in trouble, but rather to stop people doing wrong. In this case what is irrelevant is whether or not the wrongdoing has a human (or animal) victim. If we assume for the sake of argument that consensual sex between an unmarried couple is wrong, then there would still have been a duty to stop the man having sex with the woman even if the two had been lovers. Each duty thus extends to an area which is foreign to the other. Where the woman is trapped by falling masonry, there is no wrong to be forbidden; where she is willingly having sex, there is no victim to be rescued.[7]

[6] They are likely to contribute more to our understanding of issues that are at once very new and frighteningly technical, as with the ethics of genetic engineering.

[7] There are ways in which one could seek to minimise the difference. On the one hand, the Muslim duty in respect of victimless wrongdoing could be seen in terms of rescuing a sinner who is in spiritual danger (a point I owe to Mark Johnston; cf. above, ch. 14, note 169). And on the other, there is a tendency for tort litigation in the United States to be based on the axiom that there is no such thing as bad luck (a formulation which I owe, I think, to the *Economist*).

But what of the intersection? When the man rapes the woman, we have both a wrongdoer and a victim. On this common ground, the two duties remain distinct in principle: one focuses on putting a stop to the wrongdoing, the other on coming to the aid of the victim. Yet in practice, things may not be so neatly compartmentalised. Real life is such that the two duties are easily conflated, not to say confused, and the results are apparent both in our thinking and in that of the medieval Muslims.[8]

On our side, the conflation is strikingly illustrated by the disparity between the words and deeds of Randy Kyles, the hero of the Chicago rape case. What he did was to ensure that a wrongdoer was brought to justice. Yet the reason he later gave for his conduct was that he 'had to do something to help that woman'.[9] This may be conceptually infelicitous, but it articulates a basic psychological reality: when we see one person maltreating another, our anger against the perpetrator and our sympathy for the victim are two sides of the same emotional coin. It would be untrue to the emotions we characteristically feel in such cases to say, for example: 'I have every sympathy with rapists, it's just that unfortunately their actions are harmful to their victims.'

A similar conflation is latent on the Muslim side. There is systematic thought in Islam about the duty of rescue, and in principle there should be no problem distinguishing this from the doctrine of forbidding wrong. But in fact, most of what I have learnt of Muslim views on rescue derives from material incorporated into accounts of forbidding wrong. A particularly striking example is found in a major Ibāḍī account of the duty. Here at one point we encounter a statement of one's duty in a situation in which a boy is stuck up a palm-tree and shouting for help.[10] This, clearly, is a case of rescue pure and simple: there is no question of any wrongdoing on the part of either the boy or the palm-tree, or of any right conduct that could be enjoined upon either. It is not, of course, that the Muslim scholars are unable to make the distinction between forbidding wrong and rescue when they

[8] It is noteworthy that such confusion is not in evidence in the aspects of Jewish and Catholic thought described above, ch. 19, section 3. The reason is perhaps that the duties analogous to forbidding wrong in these faiths are too low key to overlap with that of rescue.

[9] See above, preface, note 3. In other words, he presents himself as a good Samaritan; but what the Samaritan of the parable did was to attend to the needs of the victim, not to confront the long-departed robbers (Luke 10:29–37).

[10] Abū Bakr al-Kindī, *Muṣannaf*, 12:41.2, in a short chapter on coming to the help of those who cry out for it. Likewise the following statement forms part of an account of forbidding wrong: 'If he sees someone trying to kill another person, he is obligated to defend him as he would defend himself; for since he is obligated to save the life of another by giving him his food, and to save him from drowning, so likewise he is obligated to defend him' (Abū Yaʿlā, *Amr*, f. 109a.13).

want to,[11] but rather that the border tends not to be well demarcated. Again, this corresponds to the way things are. In real life, it would surely go against the natural flow of emotion for a Muslim engaged in forbidding wrong to be a zealous antagonist of rapists and yet at the same time more or less indifferent to the sufferings of their victims. In the reign of the caliph al-Muʿtaḍid (r. 279–89/892–902), the story goes, a tailor of Baghdad sought helpers to join him in confronting a high-ranking Turkish military officer who had abducted a beautiful young woman as she left the baths. He made his appeal in these terms: 'You know what this man has done. So come with me so that we can go and protest against him and save the woman from him' (*fa-qūmū maʿī ilayhi li-nunkir ʿalayhi wa-nukhalliṣ al-marʾa minhu*).[12] In the circumstances, Randy Kyles might have said the same.

This close affinity between rescue and forbidding wrong is perhaps linked to a character trait shared by those who habitually practise them. Modern Western study of rescuers suggests that, alongside their courage, they are characterised by what might be described as the lack of a faculty of social discrimination found in normal human beings. A Silesian countess who helped Jews in the Second World War explained that she did so because they were persecuted, not because they were Jews; their ethnicity, she emphasised, 'was not important to me at all', though it was clearly very salient to many Jews and non-Jews at the time.[13] But research suggests that it is not just ethnicity to which confirmed rescuers are blind: they fail to discriminate, in the way that the rest of us do, between their kith and kin on the one hand and strangers on the other.[14] This trait would probably have been immediately recognisable to many medieval Muslims who made a practice of forbidding wrong. At a certain level we greatly admire such

[11] See above, ch. 15, notes 183–5. One modern author makes a relevant distinction, including among his examples one that goes to the heart of the Chicago rape case: intervening to prevent illicit sex is an instance of forbidding wrong where the woman is willing, but not where she is unwilling (ʿAwda, *Tashrīʿ*, 1:511f. no. 349).

[12] Ibn Kathīr, *Bidāya*, 11:90.9. Likewise the tailor says of his initial attempt to act on his own: *fa-qumtu ilayhi fa-ankartu ʿalayhi wa-aradtu khalāṣ al-marʾa min yadayhi* (*ibid.*, 90.6). Later the caliph excoriates the Turk for his conduct, and denounces his violent treatment of the tailor, 'who commanded you right and forbade you wrong' (*ibid.*, 91.3). The whole story goes back to Tanūkhī (d. 384/994) (*al-Faraj baʿd al-shidda*, 218.20–221.9, and *Nishwār al-muḥāḍara*, 1:312–18); here the wording is different, but the concern for both the enormity of the sin and the well-being of the woman is just as clear in the narrative. A version also appears in Niẓām al-Mulk (d. 485/1092), *Siyar al-mulūk*, ed. H. Darke, Tehran 1372 sh., 66–78 (I owe this reference to Patricia Crone). The story is quoted from Ibn Kathīr in Sabt, *Amr*, 289–92.

[13] K. R. Monroe, *The heart of altruism: perceptions of a common humanity*, Princeton 1996, 148. She expressed her world-view as follows: 'You cannot just look at all this and do nothing. During my whole life, I've always been intervening in things I found unjust.' This is not how most of us think or act; if we intervene once in a while, it is likely to be in reaction to something that touches us much more closely than 'all this'.

[14] *Ibid.*, 19, 165.

indifference, and we are sometimes ready to emulate it at the level of ethnicity – which for an educated Westerner today is usually not too difficult. But even such Westerners are much less likely to maintain this indifference where their friends and relations are concerned. In other words, habitual rescuers and inveterate forbidders of wrong may have something in common that separates them from humanity at large. A pragmatic Yemeni ruler of the seventh/thirteenth century, refusing to take action against a pietist who had sabotaged plans for a party in Aden by pouring out large quantities of wine, remarked succinctly: 'Anyone who does that must be either a saint or a madman, and either way we have nothing to say to him.'[15] He could perhaps have said the same about outstanding rescuers.

Be this as it may, we can conclude that rescue and forbidding wrong, though conceptually distinct, overlap in a sufficiently intimate way to make them broadly comparable. With that much established, we can go on to ask about the relative salience of systematic thought about the two duties in the respective cultures. My overwhelming impression is that the scholastic doctrine of forbidding wrong is far more salient in Islamic culture than comparable discussion of rescue is in ours. The best evidence I can adduce for this is autobiographical: as I remarked at the outset, it was only as a by-product of my study of forbidding wrong in Islam that I became aware of the existence of a body of academic writing on the duty of rescue in my own culture.[16] This in turn tends to reinforce the finding of the previous chapter that there is something distinctly unusual about the development of the duty to forbid wrong in Islam.

3. RIGHT AND WRONG

Muslim and Western notions of the duty to stop wrongdoing also differ in another important area: the understanding of right and wrong. The differences are real, though not always as profound as they look.

[15] Yāfiʿī, *Mirʾāt*, 4:227.1. The ruler was the Rasūlid al-Malik al-Muẓaffar (r. 647–94/1250–95), and the pietist was a certain ʿAbdallāh ibn Abī Bakr al-Khaṭīb. I owe this reference to Tamer El-Leithy.

[16] See above, preface, xi. The recent Western attention to rescue has been driven partly by philosophical concerns, and partly by legal ones. For examples of the former, see E. Mack, 'Deontologism, negative causation, and the duty to rescue', in E. Regis Jr. (ed.), *Gewirth's ethical rationalism*, Chicago and London 1984 (and cf. A. Gewirth, 'Replies to my critics', *ibid.*, 233–41); T. Young, 'Analogical reasoning and easy rescue cases', *Journal of Philosophical Research*, 18 (1993). The legal concern is more immediately practical. Against the background of long-standing differences between legal systems, there has been a good deal of debate over the desirability or otherwise of laws imposing penalties for failure to rescue without good cause (see, for example, the references given above, preface, note 8, and Hunt, *The compassionate beast*, 150–2). Thanks to questions raised under a French law of this kind regarding the role of the paparazzi in the death of Princess Diana in a car-crash in Paris in 1997, this concern is now better known than it used to be in the English-speaking world.

Most obviously, there are significant differences as to which particular things are right and which are wrong. As we have seen repeatedly in this book, these differences are at their most colourful with regard to wine, women and song. Yet even here, Muslim norms are usually intelligible to us to the extent that they tend to be closely related to what we recognise as moral dangers. Mainstream Western culture has little use for an outright prohibition of alcohol; but we do not approve of drunken drivers or like to see people become alcoholics. Our ideas as to how women should be dressed and the degree to which they should be segregated, while puritanical by some West African standards, are a long way from traditional Islamic mores; yet we worry a great deal about the less desirable consequences of the interactions we permit between the sexes. It is perhaps only in the case of the stance of the Islamic scholars against music that cross-cultural intelligibility breaks down almost completely. It would be hard in the West to present the Saʿūdī campaign against the mouth organs of the street urchins of Jedda as anything but a comedy.[17] Yet even here, such attitudes to music can strike a chord in our past, not to mention the fringes of our present. There is, after all, nothing uniquely Islamic about puritans who do not like other people to have fun, and nothing exclusively Western or modern about anti-puritanism.[18] Nor should we forget one remarkable, if adventitious convergence: middle-class America has come to regard smoking with an intolerance verging on that of unreconstructed Wahhābism. But whether we dwell on the similarities or the differences, the fact remains that questions about the rightness or wrongness of particular activities have only an indirect bearing on the way in which the duty itself is conceived. They are merely the circumstances that trigger it.

There is, however, a contrast between the Muslim and Western views of rights and wrongs which takes us somewhat closer to the core of the value. This has to do with conceptions of public and private. We can best approach this contrast by going back to the moral – or amoral – principle that is so often pitted against forbidding wrong: minding one's own business.

As we have seen, telling a busybody to mind his own business was a stock response to unwelcome attempts to forbid wrong in the traditional Islamic world.[19] During his westward journey through North Africa, Ibn Tūmart

[17] See above, ch. 8, note 128.

[18] The late Qājār poet Īraj Mīrzā (d. 1344/1926) has a short poem ridiculing some pietists in Mashhad who rushed to a caravanserai to cover up a plaster image of a beautiful woman (*Dīwān-i kāmil*, ed. M. J. Maḥjūb, Van Nuys, Ca. 1989, 177f. no. 36, and see *ibid.*, 278 thereto). We can see this poem as the work of someone who had modern ideas and was at home in Russian and French (see J. Rypka *et al.*, *History of Iranian literature*, Dordrecht 1968, 384f.). But at the same time it is not out of place in an indigenous anti-puritan tradition going back to Ḥāfiẓ (d. 791/1389) (see above, ch. 17, notes 241–3).

[19] See above, ch. 17, 498f.

(d. 524/1130) found the people of Dashr Qallāl engaged in making music in mixed company. He sent two of his followers to forbid this wrong, but the response they met with was: 'This is how we do things.' When the disciples insisted to the offenders that Ibn Tūmart was commanding them right (*maʿrūf*), they received the retort: 'We go by our kind of right, and you go by yours; go away!'[20] The replies are laconic, but they clearly assert the moral sovereignty of the local community and the wider moral relativism this implies. In general, however, our sources give us little sense of the thinking behind the stock response. Is it the cynical irritation of the hardened wrongdoer who has no intention of mending his ways, or the moral outrage of someone confronting intrusion into what are properly his own affairs?

The idea of minding one's own business is doubtless more complex than it looks in either Muslim or Western culture. Perhaps the main point that needs to be made is that this value, though it may sound individualistic or parochial, is not necessarily so. What constitutes my business has as much to do with the social groups to which I belong as it does with the particular type of business in hand, and these groups may be large ones. For example, it was under the rubric of minding one's own business that, as a British child growing up in a Mediterranean country, I was counselled by fellow-nationals not to interfere when the locals were cruel to animals. The corollary, I take it, was that within the British moral community cruelty to animals would indeed have been my business. A national group of this kind falls well short of embracing the entire human race, but it goes considerably beyond the social groups we usually encounter in everyday life.

In modern Western thought, the demarcation of our business tends to be dominated by a pair of strongly articulated principles. The first is that where wrongdoing inflicts harm on others, it is everybody's business.[21] In accordance with this principle, we concern ourselves with violations of human rights in such culturally exotic regions as East Asia, the Middle East

[20] Lévi-Provençal, *Documents inédits*, 63.3 (*hākadhā ʾl-sīra ʿindanā*), 63.5 (*maʿrūfunā ʿindanā wa-maʿrūfukum ʿindakum, sīrā!*). I have departed from Lévi-Provençal's translation (*ibid.*, 98). For the context, see above, ch. 16, 458f.

[21] A few years ago a black Princeton undergraduate recounted how she was exposed to racial slurs in a local store. She stood up to her verbal assailants, and was subsequently complimented for this by white bystanders. But why, she asked, had the bystanders done nothing at the time? 'Obviously they felt it was right what I was saying, and maybe they felt scared or whatever or it wasn't any of their business. But it is their business, and it's everyone's business when something like that happens' (D. Vogl, 'The other side of Paradise: race relations and the minority community at Princeton', *The Princeton Eclectic*, Fall 1993, 6). The answer to her question is likely to have been the 'bystander effect' (see above, preface, note 5); but her observation about 'everyone's business' seems an entirely natural use of our moral language.

and Africa. Here our business is coterminous with that of the human race, and our censoriousness has no geographical or cultural bounds. The second principle is that wrongdoing that affects only the wrongdoer is nobody's business but his own;[22] indeed it may be argued that, for this very reason, there is no justification for calling it wrongdoing at all. In accordance with this second principle, we deny that moral puritans, social conservatives, missionaries and paternalists of all sorts have any business encroaching on our right to decide for ourselves how to live – and by extension, on the right of others to make the same decision for themselves. Here our business is transacted within the immunity of our castles, and would-be censors are contemptuously turned away. The two principles are in marked contrast to each other. But the combination is not illogical, and it makes very good sense – to us.

The situation in traditional Islamic thought is somewhat different, though once again not unrecognisably so. The distinction between wrongdoing that harms others and wrongdoing that affects only the wrongdoer is well established. The first is the business of a very large, though not in practice universal, group: the Muslim community.[23] If members of this community respond to fellow-Muslims who reprove them for this kind of wrongdoing by telling them to mind their own business, this riposte will sound more like cynical irritation than moral outrage.

With regard to wrongdoing that does no harm to others, the situation in traditional Islamic thought is more complicated. It is beyond question that in Islamic terms such wrongdoing is indeed wrongdoing. This is related to the fact that it is necessarily the business of at least one other person, namely God; in other words, it is sin. But the most significant point for our purposes is perhaps that such wrongdoing, while not in itself the business of other members of the community, can nevertheless become so. As we have seen, while Islam has definite notions of privacy and gives them

[22] Cf. the classic formulation of John Stuart Mill (d. AD 1873): 'the only purpose for which power can be rightfully exercised over any member of a civilized community, against his will, is to prevent harm to others'; whereas in the part of his conduct that merely concerns himself, 'his independence is, of right, absolute' (*On liberty*, London 1859, 22; note that in speaking of power he intends here not just legal sanctions, but also 'the moral coercion of public opinion', *ibid.*, 21). This suggests that the two principles are complementary, thus removing any basis for proceeding against a category of wrongs which, while they could not be said to do actual harm to others, nevertheless cause them great offence (see the highly imaginative list of such wrongs in Feinberg, *Moral limits*, 2:10–13).

[23] The believers are brothers (Q49:10). Compare the familial idiom in which Randy Kyles constructs a wider moral community: 'It could have been my mother, my aunt, one of my mother's friends' (see above, preface, note 3). Conversely, as pointed out to me by Alexander Nehamas, cases of failure to rescue trigger laments about 'the breakdown of community'.

strong articulation, there seems to be a difference between Islamic and Western thinking along the following lines.[24] In a Western perspective, certain kinds of behaviour tend to be thought of as an inherently private matter, whether or not they happen to become public knowledge.[25] In Islamic thought, by contrast, such behaviour may be only contingently private.[26] Wrongdoing that does not affect others will tend for that very reason to remain in the private domain; and by and large, it is urged, it should be allowed to remain there. But once it ceases to be private, the cat is out of the bag, and more drastic norms may properly come into play. Here the initial response to the censorious intruder that he should mind his own business does indeed bespeak a valid moral outrage;[27] but the Muslim's home may in the event prove to be something less than his castle.

These differences between modern Western and traditional Islamic views have clear consequences in the modern Islamic world. In consequence of the Western impact, the Muslim doctrine of forbidding wrong now confronts a theory of minding one's own business significantly different from its own. In the global setting in which we now live, there is a much stronger sense than before that the Muslim community is just one among others, and in consequence that it enjoys no monopoly of moral judgement. Its members are accordingly liable to be subjected to moral scrutiny and condemnation from outside their own community. At the same time the focus of this scrutiny is often precisely on the attempts of zealous Muslims to impose their own standards of virtue on their coreligionists. Such zealots may be materially assisted in this by the power of the modern state, which has a way of turning castles into sandcastles. But in the long run these states are not proving very successful in insulating the societies

[24] See above, ch. 17, 481f. For Muslim attitudes to privacy more generally, see above, ch. 17, section 3, and cf. above, ch. 18, 556–60. A brief but useful modern survey of the field is Muḥammad Rākān al-Dughmī, *Ḥimāyat al-ḥayāt al-khāṣṣa fī 'l-sharīʿa al-Islāmiyya*, Cairo 1985. The author represents a moderate Jordanian Islam.

[25] Writing in the United States in the last years of the millennium, I am compelled to make an exception with regard to the attitude of the local culture towards adultery among American politicians and military officers. But even here, Vernetha Grant of Harlem seemed in the event to speak for a considerable part of the American public when she summed up the scandal over President Clinton's affair with Monica Lewinsky in these words: 'This is a nation of busybodies. If he's guilty, let his wife handle it' (*The New York Times*, 27 January 1998, B1).

[26] The concept of 'private life' (*al-ḥayāt al-khāṣṣa*), which appears in Dughmī's title and shapes his work, is a Western one, without precedent in his Islamic sources (cf. the comment of ʿAbd al-ʿAzīz al-Khayyāṭ in his introduction to the book, *ibid.*, 3.19). The indigenous concepts (*satr*, *tajassus*) typically relate to the processes by which what is secret remains or ceases to be so.

[27] As in the story of ʿUmar's three sins (see above, ch. 4, note 269; ch. 17, note 85; and ch. 18, 557f.).

they rule against the influence of the West. A contemporary Iranian cleric complains that attempts to forbid wrong now meet with the following riposte: 'What's it to you? I'm free, it's a free country, it's a democracy, everybody does whatever he wants!'[28] The opening question is traditional, but the continuation is not. The prevalent Western values thus tell Muslims that it is *our* business how they treat other Muslims; and at the same time they tell them that it is not *their* business how other Muslims choose to live. Both messages involve sharp departures from the traditional – and modern – Islamic conception of forbidding wrong. It should not therefore be surprising that there has been considerable friction between Muslim and Western moral attitudes in such matters.

One example of this friction is a bruising exchange which took place between Āyatullāh Khumaynī (d. 1409/1989) and the Italian journalist Oriana Fallaci some months after the Iranian revolution.[29] With regard to the undemocractic direction in which the Islamic Republic was moving, Fallaci prompted Khumaynī to make these remarks: 'If you foreigners do not understand, too bad for you. It's none of your business, you have nothing to do with our choices. If some Iranians don't understand it, too bad for them. It means that they have not understood Islam.'[30] Later Fallaci raised the even more contentious topic of the segregation of women. She made pointed reference to Islamic norms governing behaviour on the beach, and mischievously posed the question: 'By the way, how do you swim in a chador?' To this, Khumaynī responded tetchily: 'This is none of your business. Our customs are none of your business.'[31] In claiming the standing to ask her impudent question, was Fallaci simply including herself in the brotherhood of all mankind? Or worse yet, was it her nefarious purpose to deny Khumaynī the standing to answer the question by excluding him from the sisterhood of all womankind? It is striking that in the face of this provocation, Khumaynī should have been reduced to talking like the people of Dashr Qallāl; as one commentator indicates,[32] an Āyatullāh might have been expected to appeal to a higher authority than local custom. Towards the end of the interview, Khumaynī's irritation increased perceptibly: 'And now that's enough. Go away. Go away.' Even at that point, however, Fallaci did not take the hint.[33]

[28] Miṣbāḥ Yazdī, 'Tashrīḥ', 34.3. Cf. above, ch. 18, note 361.
[29] Oriana Fallaci, 'An interview with Khomeini', *The New York Times Magazine*, 7 October 1979. This interview is cited in Feinberg, *Moral limits*, 4:39, and partly quoted *ibid.*, 342 n. 2. [30] Fallaci, 'Interview', 30c. [31] *Ibid.*, 31b.
[32] Feinberg, *Moral limits*, 4:39. [33] Fallaci, 'Interview', 31d.

In conclusion, it is worth noting that the two major differences between Muslim and Western ideas discussed in this chapter are closely linked. The reason why Western thought concentrates on rescue and neglects forbidding wrong is bound up with the fact that in Western thought the category of victimless wrong – pure sin, so to speak – has been stripped of most of its practical moral significance, if not denied to exist altogether. 'They're not doing any harm' is regularly given as a sufficient reason for leaving them alone. If all wrongs must have victims, then what is left of the moral ground is covered by rescue. This, of course, takes us back to a fundamental point of tension between the two world views: the standing, if any, of God in human affairs.

APPENDIX 1

KEY KORANIC VERSES AND TRADITIONS

Certain Koranic verses and traditions recur frequently in the preceding chapters. For the reader's convenience, I give here the text and translation of the more important verses, and a translation of the traditions most often referred to. Where relevant verses also contain material that does not bear significantly on forbidding wrong, I have omitted it. I have given traditions in a standard form without noting variants. For each verse or tradition, a cross-reference is given to the place where it is first discussed (not necessarily first cited).

A. KORANIC VERSES

(1) Q3:104: *wa-l-takun minkum ummatun yadʿūna ilā ʾl-khayri wa-yaʾmurūna biʾl-maʿrūfi wa-yanhawna ʿani ʾl-munkar* ('Let there be one community of you, calling to good, and commanding right and forbidding wrong'). See above, ch. 2, 13.

(2) Q3:110: *kuntum khayra ummatin ukhrijat lil-nāsi taʾmurūna biʾl-maʿrūfi wa-tanhawna ʿani ʾl-munkar* ('You were the best community ever brought forth to men, commanding right and forbidding wrong'). See above, ch. 2, note 5.

(3) Q5:78f.: *luʿina ʾlladhīna kafarū min Banī Isrāʾīla . . . kānū lā yatanāhawna ʿan munkarin faʿalūhu* ('Cursed were the unbelievers of the Children of Israel . . .; they forbade not one another wrong that they committed'). See above, ch. 2, 15f.

(4) Q5:105: *yā-ayyuhā ʾlladhīna āmanū ʿalaykum anfusakum lā yaḍurrukum man ḍalla idhā ʾhtadaytum* ('O believers, look after your own souls. He who is astray cannot hurt you, if you are rightly guided'). See above, ch. 2, 30f.

(5) Q7:164: *wa-idh qālat ummatun minhum: lima taʿiẓūna qawman illāhu muhlikuhum . . . qālū: maʿdhiratan ilā rabbikum wa-laʿallahum yattaqūn* ('And when a certain community of them said: "Why do you admonish a people God is about to destroy. . . ?", they said: "As an excuse to your Lord; and perhaps they will be godfearing."' This is the story of the Sabbath-breaking fishermen). See above, ch. 2, 16.

(6) Q9:67: *al-munāfiqūna wa'l-munāfiqātu baʿḍuhum min baʿḍin ya'murūna bi'l-munkari wa-yanhawna ʿani 'l-maʿrūf* ('The hypocrites, the men and the women, are as one another; they command wrong, and forbid right'). See above, ch. 2, note 2.

(7) Q9:71: *wa'l-mu'minūna wa'l-mu'minātu baʿḍuhum awliyā'u baʿḍin ya'murūna bi'l-maʿrūfi wa-yanhawna ʿani 'l-munkar* ('And the believers, the men and the women, are friends one of the other; they command right, and forbid wrong'). See above, ch. 2, note 20.

(8) Q22:41: *alladhīna in makkannāhum fī 'l-arḍi . . . amarū bi'l-maʿrūfi wa-nahaw ʿani 'l-munkar* ('Those who, if We establish them in the land . . ., command right and forbid wrong'). See above, ch. 2, 14.

(9) Q31:17: *yā-bunayya aqimi 'l-ṣalāta wa-'mur bi'l-maʿrūfi wa-'nha ʿani 'l-munkari wa-ṣbir ʿalā mā aṣābaka* ('O my son, perform the prayer, and command right and forbid wrong, and bear patiently whatever may befall thee.' The speaker is Luqmān). See above, ch. 2, 28f.

B. TRADITIONS

(1) The 'three modes' tradition

Marwān brought out the pulpit (*minbar*) on a feast-day, and started with the sermon (*khuṭba*) before the prayer.

So a man got up and said: 'Marwān, you've gone against the normative practice (*sunna*)! You've brought out the pulpit on a feast-day, when it used not to be; and you've started with the sermon before the prayer!'

Then Abū Saʿīd al-Khudrī said: 'Who's that?' They told him it was so-and-so son of so-and-so. He said: 'That man has done his duty. I heard the Prophet say: "Whoever sees a wrong (*munkar*), and is able to put it right with his hand (*an yughayyirahu bi-yadihi*), let him do so; if he can't, then with his tongue (*bi-lisānihi*); if he can't, then in his heart (*bi-qalbihi*), and that is the bare minimum of faith."' (Abū Dāwūd, *Sunan*, 1:677f no. 1140; see above, ch. 3, section 1.)

(2) *The 'three qualities' tradition*

It is not befitting for a man to command right and forbid wrong until he possesses three qualities (*khiṣāl*): [he must be] civil (*rafīq*) in what he commands and forbids, knowledgeable (*'ālim*) in what he commands and forbids, and a man of probity (*'adl*) in what he commands and forbids. (Daylamī, *Firdaws*, 5:137f. no. 7,741; see above, ch. 3, note 59. Daylamī has it from the Prophet, but this is unusual.)

(3) *The saying about the tripartite division of labour*

Putting things right with the hand (*al-taghyīr bi'l-yad*) is for the political authorities (*al-umarā'*), with the tongue (*bi'l-lisān*) for the scholars (*al-'ulamā'*), and in (or with) the heart (*bi'l-qalb*) for the common people (*al-'āmma*). (Abū 'l-Layth al-Samarqandī, *Tanbīh al-ghāfilīn*, 1:101.1; see above, ch. 6, note 166. As in this case, the saying is usually quoted anonymously.)

APPENDIX 2

BARHEBRAEUS ON FORBIDDING WRONG

Gregory Barhebraeus (d. AD 1286), though best known to Islamicists as a historian, contributed broadly to the Syriac literature of the Jacobite (West Syrian) church.[1] The work that concerns us here is his *Ethicon*.[2] A characteristic feature of this book is its extensive dependence on the *Iḥyāʾ ʿulūm al-dīn* of Ghazzālī (d. 505/1111).[3] Given this fact, it is no surprise to find that the chapter that Barhebraeus devotes to admonition (*martyānūtā*) and rebuke (*kuwwānā*)[4] is essentially a Christian recension of Ghazzālī's account of forbidding wrong.

This relationship is not in evidence in the first two of the five sections of the chapter, to which I will return for just that reason. But it is transparent in the last three. The third section is concerned with the 'elements' (*esṭūksē*) of rebuke. As in Ghazzālī's account, there are four: (1) the rebuker (*mkawwnānā*); (2) the rebuked (*metkawwnānā*); (3) the offence (*saklūtā*); and (4) the manner of rebuke (*znā d-kuwwānā*).[5] Within the latter, there are seven levels (*dargē*), which correspond to Ghazzālī's eight with some differences.[6] The fourth section offers a conspectus of sins classified into five kinds. The first kind (*gensā*) are those that occur in churches, the second in shops (*ḥānwātā*), the third in streets (*plāṭawwātā*), the fourth in baths and the fifth at banquets. These correspond well to Ghazzālī's categories of wrongs.[7] The final section is about reproving rulers, just as in Ghazzālī's

[1] See A. Baumstark, *Geschichte der syrischen Literatur*, Bonn 1922, 312–20 §51.

[2] Barhebraeus (d. AD 1286), *Ethicon*, ed. P. Bedjan, Paris and Leipzig 1898. The work is being edited anew and translated by H. G. B. Teule (Louvain 1993–).

[3] See Teule's remarks in his introduction to the first volume of his translation (xxx–xxxii), and the comparison of parallel passages in appendix I of the same volume.

[4] Barhebraeus, *Ethicon*, ed. Bedjan, 329–40. This chapter is still to come in Teule's edition and translation, but there is a helpful though brief summary of its contents in Teule's introduction to the first volume of his translation (xxvi). I am much indebted to Hubert Kaufhold for bringing this text to my attention, and to Sebastian Brock for responding to my queries.

[5] Compare above, ch. 16, 428f.

[6] Compare above, ch. 16, 438–41.

[7] See above, ch. 16, 443–5.

account.[8] At the same time, several specific points are carried over unchanged. Thus the offence must be out in the open (*metparsyā*).[9] Likewise someone using harsh words to a potentate must know that he alone is thereby endangered.[10] Barhebraeus ends his account, just as Ghazzālī does, by lamenting the fact that rulers are no longer rebuked as they were in the good old days.[11]

Naturally a great deal has changed in the process. Much material has been jettisoned; the chapter Barhebraeus has given us is shorter than Ghazzālī's *kitāb al-amr bi'l-ma'rūf* by an order of magnitude. At the same time, Barhebraeus has thoroughly stripped out all the Islamic elements in Ghazzālī's account and given it an appropriate Christian colouring. In place of Ghazzālī's Muslim authorities, Barhebraeus invokes the Old Testament, the New Testament, the Church Fathers of the fourth century AD, and some more parochial figures;[12] indeed the second section is devoted entirely to a collection of material of this kind which tends to discourage rebuke. In place of Ghazzālī's examples of legitimate differences between law-schools, he cites the differing practice of Syrians and Greeks with regard to the day of the week on which they break their fast: each group inherits its practice from its teachers and fathers, neither is in sin, and neither may rebuke the other.[13] In place of wrongs in mosques, we have sins committed in churches – though there is no lack of common ground. As to banquets, Barhebraeus has to limit his attack on liquor to excessive drinking, as opposed to the presence of wine as such.[14] But one of Ghazzālī's arguments is effortlessly adopted by Barhebraeus: the rebuker must be a believer, since rebuking is vindicating the faith, and how could one who is not a believer do that?[15] All that has changed here is the faith in which one has to believe.

There is nevertheless one difference between the two accounts that is of fundamental significance. Ghazzālī, like the Muslim scholars in general, is talking about a duty of believers as such. Barhebraeus, by contrast, limits

[8] See above, ch. 16, 446.

[9] Barhebraeus, *Ethicon*, ed. Bedjan, 333.19; compare above, ch. 16, 436. Likewise Barhebraeus tells us in his second level that one is not to investigate (*lā n'aqqeb*) a sin that has been committed in private (*ibid.*, 334.17; compare above, ch. 16, 438).

[10] *Ibid.*, 339.14; compare above, ch. 16, 446. Such harshness is exceptional; the duty in respect of rulers does not normally go beyond instruction and admonition (cf. above, ch. 16, notes 33f., 121).

[11] *Ibid.*, 340.12; compare above, ch. 16, 446. Barhebraeus uses the term *parr(h)ēsīyā* to refer to the lost outspokenness (cf. above, ch. 19, note 11).

[12] See, for example, *ibid.*, 330.4, 330.7, 330.12, 332.2.

[13] *Ibid.*, 333.20; compare above, ch. 16, 436f.

[14] *Ibid.*, 339.3; compare above, ch. 16, 444f. By contrast, there is no disagreement with regard to troupes of musicians.

[15] *Ibid.*, 333.7; compare above, ch. 16, 429f.

the duty of admonition and rebuke to those who wield ecclesiastical authority. He is, in other words, a clericalist of a kind we did not discover even among the Imāmī Shīʿites. This doctrine is formally inscribed in his account of the first of the four elements: the rebuker, he says, must be someone in authority (*rēshā*), such as a bishop, priest or deacon. The reason is that rebuke (*kuwwānā*) is a form of command (*puqdānā*), and orders are issued to an inferior, not to a superior or an equal.[16] This stipulation is doubtless linked to another noteworthy departure of Barhebraeus from Ghazzālī's account: the rebuker must be virtuous (*kēʾnā*) himself.[17] It also underlies the most significant divergence from Ghazzālī's pattern of levels. For Barhebraeus, the fifth level is threat, as in Ghazzālī's sixth level; but while Ghazzālī is talking about the threat of violence, for Barhebraeus what is threatened is exclusion from the Christian community.[18] His next level is harsh talk combined with the reality of such exclusion.[19] His seventh and last level is indeed violence, but he raises the possibility mainly to dismiss it. It is not for churchmen to act like the secular rulers of this world, who use punishment and force to rein in the wicked. And if a blow is occasionally needed, others should administer it.[20] At this point he considers an objection: if it is blameworthy to strike a sinner, how could Jesus have used a whip in cleansing the Temple?[21] The answer is that he used the whip only to drive out dumb animals, not to strike those who were selling them, who were rational beings; thus in the case of those who were selling doves, he used admonition, not violence.[22] Finally, in the discussion of rebuking rulers, Barhebraeus concerns himself exclusively with the role of the religious leader (*rēsh tawdītā*).[23]

This leaves one feature of the Christianisation of Ghazzālī's doctrine that is of some comparative interest. Barhebraeus opens his account with a section-heading announcing the point that the duty to rebuke others is not one of solitaries (*īḥīdāyē*) but rather of those who hold authority (*mdabbrānē*).[24] The correction (*turrāṣā*) of others, he explains, is the

[16] *Ibid.*, 333.4; contrast Ghazzālī's rejection of the idea that the ruler's permission is required for forbidding wrong (above, ch. 16, 430f.).
[17] *Ibid.*, 333.8; contrast above, ch. 16, 430.
[18] *Ibid.*, 335.16; contrast above, ch. 16, 440f.
[19] *Ibid.*, 335.19; cf. above, ch. 16, 439f.
[20] *Ibid.*, 336.7; contrast above, ch. 16, 441. Barhebraeus ignores Ghazzālī's armed bands.
[21] *Ibid.*, 336.16. The reference is to John 2:15 (cf. above, ch. 19, note 133).
[22] The reference is to John 2:16, where Jesus tells the dove-sellers to 'take these things hence'. [23] Barhebraeus, *Ethicon*, ed. Bedjan, 339.9.
[24] *Ibid.*, 329.18. I follow Teule in translating *īḥīdāyē* as 'solitaries' (see the introduction to the first volume of his translation, xxvi, xxxv no. 11); however, the term can also refer to monks – just as, etymologically speaking, a 'monk' is a solitary (*monachos*).

business of those whom God has appointed to proclaim His message: prophets, apostles, bishops, priests, deacons. By contrast, solitaries have only the duty of caring for their own persons, not for others.[25] In other words, they have dropped out of society, and can thus have no duty to rebuke those whom they have left behind. Thanks to the Ṣūfis, this idea is not totally unfamiliar to us.[26] But its centrality in the account of forbidding wrong that we owe to Barhebraeus highlights its marginality on the Islamic side of the fence. Ghazzālī himself, in a discussion of the advantages of the solitary life (*ʿuzla*), includes among them the fact that the solitary is not exposed to situations in which he would incur the duty of forbidding wrong.[27] It is an exigent and onerous duty: you fall into sin if you keep silent, and if you do not, you are likely to end up in the position of someone who tries to prop up a wall that is keeling over: when it falls on you, you wish you had left it alone.[28] But the Muslim solitary, on this view, merely avoids situations that would trigger the duty; his choice of lifestyle does nothing to exclude him from it in principle.

[25] Barhebraeus, *Ethicon*, ed. Bedjan, 330.5. Cf. above, ch. 19, note 10.
[26] See esp. above, ch. 16, note 288. [27] Ghazzālī, *Iḥyāʾ*, 2:208.26. [28] *Ibid.*, 208.35.

BIBLIOGRAPHY

Where a book has a Christian date of publication, I give it and ignore dates in other eras. If it bears no Christian date, but has a date in another era, I give that. The only era I mark is *hijrī shamsī*, distinguished from *hijrī qamarī* by the abbreviation 'sh.'

If a book bears more than two places of publication, I normally mention only the first.

Where possible, I give names of authors in minimal forms.

In the wording of titles, I usually follow the title-page of the book; the title that appears there may or may not have been chosen by the original author.

To save space, I have tended to be sparing in citing translations.

In addition to the material listed below, I have made limited use of archival sources. The main item here is British consular dispatches from Jedda preserved in the Public Record Office, London, which I have used in section 4 of ch. 8; there are also a few documents from the Başbakanlık Arşivi, Istanbul. With regard to newspapers and journals, apart from the numerous items listed below, I have occasionally cited reports from the *New York Times*, the *Chicago Tribune*, *al-Mūjaz 'an Īrān*, *al-Ḥayāt*, *Turāthunā*, and the 'Notizie varie' of *Oriente Moderno*; extensive use of the Meccan newspaper *Umm al-qurā* is made in section 4 of ch. 8.

My transcription of Arabic, here and in the body of the book, follows Anglo-Saxon conventions by *taqlīd*; were I to exercise *ijtihād* in this matter, I would adopt the system now used in Germany and France.

In transcribing Persian, my primary concern has been to minimise divergences between forms of names and terms that appear in both Persian and Arabic. My transcription is thus archaising and Arabising.

In transcribing Turkish, I have had the same concern, but I have also been pulled in the other direction by modern Turkish orthography. The result is a spectrum; what I have done in any given case has depended on such factors as whether an author is writing in Turkish or Arabic, whether a text dates from the high Ottoman, late Ottoman or Republican period, whether I am transcribing a whole passage or just a name or a title, and what I could and could not bring myself to write.

I specify the language of a book only where this is not apparent from the title (for example, if a book in Turkish or Persian has an Arabic title).

ʿAbbās, I., 'Maṣādir thawrat Abī Yazīd Makhlad ibn Kaydād', *al-Aṣāla*, 6 (1977)
Shiʿr al-Khawārij, Beirut 1974
ʿAbd al-Aḥad al-Nūrī (d. 1061/1651), *Mawʿiẓa ḥasana*, Istanbul 1263
ʿAbd al-Bāqī al-Mawāhibī (known as Ibn Faqīh Fiṣṣa) (d. 1071/1661), *al-ʿAyn wa'l-athar*, ed. ʿI. R. Qalʿajī, Damascus 1987
ʿAbd al-Ghanī al-Maqdisī (d. 600/1203), *al-Amr bi'l-maʿrūf wa'l-nahy ʿan al-munkar*, ed. S. A. al-Zuhayrī, Riyāḍ 1995
ʿAbd al-Ghanī al-Nābulusī (d. 1143/1731), *al-Ḥadīqa al-nadiyya*, Istanbul 1290
Murāsalāt, ed. B. ʿAlā' al-Dīn, Damascus 1996(?)
Taʿṭīr al-anām fī taʿbīr al-manām, Cairo n.d.
ʿAbd al-Ḥamīd, M., *al-Ālūsī mufassiran*, Baghdad 1968
ʿAbd ibn Ḥumayd (d. 249/863f.), *Musnad*, in the *Muntakhab* of Ibrāhīm ibn Khuzaym al-Shāshī, ed. Ṣ. al-Badrī al-Sāmarrā'ī and M. M. K. al-Ṣaʿīdī, Beirut 1988
ʿAbd al-Jabbār ibn Aḥmad (d. 415/1025), *Faḍl al-iʿtizāl wa-ṭabaqāt al-Muʿtazila*, ed. F. Sayyid, Tunis 1974
Mughnī, ed. Ṭ. Ḥusayn *et al.*, Cairo 1960–9
Mukhtaṣar fī uṣūl al-dīn, see: ʿUmāra, *Rasā'il*
Sharḥ al-Uṣūl al-khamsa, see: Mānkdīm, *Taʿlīq*
al-Uṣūl al-khamsa, see: Gimaret, 'Les *Uṣūl al-ḫamsa*'
ʿAbd al-Qādir al-Jazā'irī (d. 1300/1883), *al-Mawāqif fī 'l-taṣawwuf wa'l-waʿẓ wa'l-irshād*, Damascus 1966–7
ʿAbd al-Qādir al-Jīlī (d. 561/1166), *al-Ghunya li-ṭālibī ṭarīq al-ḥaqq*, Cairo 1322
ʿAbd al-Qāhir al-Baghdādī (d. 429/1037f.), *al-Milal wa'l-niḥal*, ed. A. N. Nādir, Beirut 1970
ʿAbd al-Raḥīm, ʿA. ʿA., *al-Dawla al-Suʿūdiyya al-ūlā*, Cairo 1975
ʿAbd al-Razzāq ibn Hammām al-Ṣanʿānī (d. 211/827), *Muṣannaf*, ed. Ḥ. al-Aʿẓamī, Beirut 1970–2
Tafsīr al-Qur'ān, ed. M. M. Muḥammad, Riyāḍ 1989
ʿAbd al-Sattār, ʿAbd al-Muʿizz, *al-Amr bi'l-maʿrūf wa'l-nahy ʿan al-munkar*, Beirut and Damascus 1980
ʿAbd al-Wāḥid al-Marrākushī (writing 621/1224), *Muʿjib*, ed. R. Dozy, Leiden 1881
ʿAbdallāh Afandī al-Iṣbahānī (d. 1130/1717f.), *Riyāḍ al-ʿulamā'*, ed. A. al-Ḥusaynī, Qumm 1401
ʿAbdallāh ibn Aḥmad ibn Ḥanbal (d. 290/903), *Masā'il al-imām Aḥmad ibn Ḥanbal*, ed. Z. al-Shāwīsh, Beirut and Damascus 1981
Sunna, ed. M. S. S. al-Qaḥṭānī, Dammām 1986

ʿAbdallāh ibn al-Ḥusayn ibn al-Qāsim (*fl.* later third/ninth century), *al-Nāsikh wa'l-mansūkh*, ms. Berlin, Glaser 128

Ābī, Ṣāliḥ ʿAbd al-Samīʿ al- (fourteenth/twentieth century), *Jawāhir al-iklīl*, Cairo n.d.

Abou El Fadl, K., 'The Islamic law of rebellion', Princeton Ph.D. 1999

Abrahamov, B., *al-Ḳāsim b. Ibrāhīm on the proof of God's existence*, Leiden 1990

Abū ʿAliyya, ʿA. Ḥ., *al-Dawla al-Suʿūdiyya al-thāniya*, Riyāḍ 1974

Abū ʿAmmār ʿAbd al-Kāfī (*fl.* mid-sixth/twelfth century), *Mūjaz*, *apud* ʿA. Ṭālibī, *Ārāʾ al-Khawārij al-kalāmiyya*, Algiers 1978

Abū 'l-ʿArab al-Tamīmī (d. 333/945), *Miḥan*, ed. ʿU. S. al-ʿUqaylī, Riyāḍ 1984

Ṭabaqāt ʿulamāʾ Ifrīqiya wa-Tūnis, ed. ʿA. al-Shābbī and N. Ḥ. al-Yāfī, Tunis 1968

Abū Bakr ibn Khayr (d. 575/1179), *Fahrasa*, ed. F. Codera and J. Ribera Tarrago, Beirut n.d.

Abū Bakr ibn Maymūn, *Sharḥ al-Irshād*, ed. A. Ḥ. A. al-Saqqā, Cairo 1987

Abū 'l-Barakāt al-Nasafī (d. 701/1301), *Madārik al-tanzīl*, Cairo 1936–42

Abū Dāwūd al-Sijistānī (d. 275/889), *Masāʾil al-imām Aḥmad*, Beirut n.d.

Sunan, ed. ʿI. ʿU al-Daʿʿās and ʿA. al-Sayyid, Ḥimṣ 1969–74

Abū Dāwūd al-Ṭayālisī (d. 204/819), *Musnad*, Hyderabad 1321

Abū 'l-Faraj al-Iṣbahānī (d. 356/967), *Aghānī*, Cairo 1927–74

Maqātil al-Ṭālibiyyīn, ed. A. Ṣaqr, Cairo 1949

Abū Ḥanīfa (d. 150/767f.) (attrib.), *al-Fiqh al-absaṭ*, ed. M. Z. al-Kawtharī in a collection of which the first item is Abū Ḥanīfa (attrib.), *al-ʿĀlim wa'l-mutaʿallim*, Cairo 1368

Musnad, Beirut 1985

Abū 'l-Ḥawārī Muḥammad ibn al-Ḥawārī (*fl. c.* 300/912), *Jāmiʿ*, Oman 1985 (default: vol. 1)

Abū Ḥayyān al-Gharnāṭī (d. 745/1344), *al-Baḥr al-muḥīṭ*, Cairo 1328

Abū Ḥayyān al-Tawḥīdī (d. 414/1023f.), *al-Baṣāʾir wa'l-dhakhāʾir*, ed. W. al-Qāḍī, Beirut 1988

Abū Hilāl al-ʿAskarī (writing 395/1005), *Awāʾil*, ed. W. Qaṣṣāb and M. al-Miṣrī, Riyāḍ 1981

Abū 'l-Ḥusayn al-Baṣrī (d. 436/1044), *al-Muʿtamad fī uṣūl al-fiqh*, ed. M. Hamidullah, Damascus 1964–5

Abū Isḥāq Ibrāhīm ibn Qays (fifth/eleventh century), *Dīwān al-sayf al-naqqād*, ed. Sulaymān al-Bārūnī, n.p. n.d.

Mukhtaṣar al-khiṣāl, Oman 1983

Abū Isḥāq al-Shīrāzī (d. 476/1083), *ʿAqīdat al-salaf*, *apud* his *al-Maʿūna fī 'l-jadal*, ed. ʿA. Turkī, Beirut 1988, and M. Bernand, *La Profession de foi d'Abū Isḥāq al-Šīrāzī*, Cairo 1987

Ṭabaqāt al-fuqahāʾ, Baghdad 1356

Abū 'l-Layth al-Samarqandī (d. 373/983), *Bustān al-ʿārifīn*, printed in the margin of his *Tanbīh al-ghāfilīn*, Cairo n.d.

Muḳaddima, see: Zajączkowski, *Traité*

Tafsīr, ed. ʿA. M. Muʿawwaḍ *et al.*, Beirut 1993 (default edition); ed. ʿA. A. al-Zaqqa, Baghdad 1985–6

Tanbīh al-ghāfilīn, ed. ʿA. M. al-Wakīl, Jedda 1980
Abū Mikhnaf (d. 157/773f.), *Maqtal al-Ḥusayn*, Qumm 1362 sh.
Abū ʾl-Muʾthir al-Ṣalt ibn Khamīs (third/ninth century), *al-Aḥdāth waʾl-ṣifāt*, see: Kāshif, *Siyar*
Sīra, see: Kāshif, *Siyar*
Abū Nuʿaym al-Iṣbahānī (d. 430/1038), *Dhikr akhbār Iṣbahān*, ed. S. Dedering, Leiden 1931–4
Ḥilyat al-awliyāʾ, ed. M. A. al-Khānjī, Cairo 1932–8
Abū ʾl-Qāsim Kāshānī (*fl.* early eighth/fourteenth century), *Zubdat al-tawārīkh*, section on the Ismāʿīlīs, ed. M. T. Dānishpazhūh, Tabrīz 1343 sh.
Abū Ṣafiyya, ʿAbd al-Wahhāb Rashīd, *Sharḥ al-Arbaʿīn al-Nawawiyya fī thawb jadīd*, n.p. 1988
Abū ʾl-Ṣalāḥ al-Ḥalabī (d. 447/1055), *al-Kāfī fī ʾl-fiqh*, ed. R. Ustādī, Iṣfahān 1403
Abū Shāma (d. 665/1267), *Tarājim rijāl al-qarnayn al-sādis waʾl-sābiʿ*, ed. ʿI. al-ʿAṭṭār al-Ḥusaynī, Cairo 1947
Abū ʾl-Shaykh (d. 369/979), *Ṭabaqāt al-muḥaddithīn bi-Iṣbahān*, ed. ʿA. ʿA. al-Balūshī, Beirut 1987–92
Abū Shuqqa, ʿAbd al-Ḥalīm Muḥammad, *Taḥrir al-marʾa fī ʿaṣr al-risāla*, Kuwait 1990–1
Abū ʾl-Suʿūd al-ʿImādī (d. 982/1574), *Irshād al-ʿaql al-salīm*, Riyāḍ n.d.
Abū Ṭālib al-Nāṭiq (d. 424/1032f.), *Amālī* (in the recension of Jaʿfar ibn Muḥammad ibn ʿAbd al-Salām (d. 573/1177f.), *Taysīr al-maṭālib fī Amālī al-imām Abī Ṭālib*), ed. Y. ʿA. al-Faḍīl, Beirut 1975
Mabādiʾ al-adilla fī uṣūl al-dīn, ms. Milan, Ambrosiana, Codex Griffini 27
Abū Tammām (d. 231/846), *Ḥamāsa*, *apud* Abū ʾl-ʿAlāʾ al-Maʿarrī (d. 449/1057) (attrib.), *Sharḥ Dīwān Ḥamāsat Abī Tammām*, ed. Ḥ. M. Naqsha, Beirut 1991
Abū Tammām (*fl.* first half of the fourth/tenth century), *Shajara*, *apud* W. Madelung and P. E. Walker, *An Ismaili heresiography*, Leiden 1998
Abū ʿUbayd al-Qāsim ibn Sallām (d. 224/838f.), *Amthāl*, ed. ʿA. Qaṭāmish, Damascus and Beirut 1980
Amwāl, ed. M. K. Harrās, Cairo 1981
al-Nāsikh waʾl-mansūkh, ed. J. Burton, Cambridge 1987
Abū Yaʿlā ibn al-Farrāʾ (d. 458/1066), *al-Aḥkām al-sulṭāniyya*, ed. M. Ḥ. al-Fiqī, Cairo 1966
al-Amr biʾl-maʿrūf waʾl-nahy ʿan al-munkar, ms. Damascus, Ẓāhiriyya, Majmūʿ no. 3,779
al-Muʿtamad fī uṣūl al-dīn, ed. W. Z. Haddad, Beirut 1974
Abū Yaʿlā al-Mawṣilī (d. 307/919), *Musnad*, ed. Ḥ. S. Asad, Damascus and Beirut 1984–8
Abū Yūsuf (d. 182/798), *Kharāj*, Cairo 1352
Abū Zakariyyāʾ al-Warjlānī (*fl.* late fifth/eleventh century), *Siyar al-aʾimma wa-akhbāruhum*, ed. I. al-ʿArabī, Algiers 1982
Abū Zayd al-ʿAlawī (*fl.* later third/ninth century), *Ishhād*, see: Modarressi, *Crisis and consolidation*
Abū Zayd al-Anṣārī (d. 215/830f.), *al-Nawādir fī ʾl-lugha*, ed. M. ʿA. Aḥmad, Beirut and Cairo 1981

Abū Zurʿa al-Dimashqī (d. 281/894), *Taʾrīkh*, ed. S. N. al-Qawjānī, Damascus n.d.

ʿAdawī (d. 1189/1775), *Ḥāshiya*, see: Kharashī, *Sharḥ*

ʿAdl, Yāsir Muḥammad al-, *al-Fiqh al-ghāʾib*, Manṣūra 1993

Āghā Buzurg al-Ṭihrānī (d. 1389/1970), *Nuqabāʾ al-bashar fī ʾl-qarn al-rābiʿ ʿashar* (in his *Ṭabaqāt aʿlām al-Shīʿa*), Najaf 1954–68

Aghbarī, *al-Naẓm al-maḥbūb*, Oman 1984

Aguadé, J., 'Abū Rakwa', *Actas del IV Coloquio Hispano-Tunecino*, Madrid 1983

Ahlwardt, W. (ed.), *The Divans of the six ancient Arabic poets*, London 1870

Verzeichniss der arabischen Handschriften der Königlichen Bibliothek zu Berlin, Berlin 1887–99

Ahmad, A., *Studies in Islamic culture in the Indian environment*, Oxford 1964

Aḥmad al-Karīm ibn al-Mukhtār ibn Ziyād (writing *c.* 1398/1978), *Naẓm fī ʾl-amr biʾl-maʿrūf waʾl-nahy ʿan al-munkar*, ms. Mauritania, Dār al-Barka

Risāla ṭawīla fī ʾl-ḥathth ʿalā ʾl-maʿrūf waʾl-nahy ʿan al-munkar, ms. Mauritania, Dār al-Barka

Aḥmad, Z. 'Abū Bakr al-Khallāl – the compiler of the teachings of Imām Aḥmad b. Ḥanbal', *Islamic Studies*, 9 (1970)

Ahnaf, M. al-, *et al.*, *L'Algérie par ses islamistes*, Paris 1991

Ājurrī (d. 360/970), *Sharīʿa*, ed. M. Ḥ. al-Fiqī, Riyāḍ 1992

Taḥrīm al-nard waʾl-shaṭranj waʾl-malāhī, ed. M. S. ʿU. Idrīs, n.p. 1984

Akbarī, Muḥammad Riḍā, *Taḥlīlī naw wa ʿamalī az amr bah maʿrūf wa nahy az munkar dar ʿaṣr-i ḥāḍir*, Iṣfahān 1375 sh.

Akbarzāda, Maḥmūd, *Ḥusayn pīshwā-yi insānhā*, Mashhad 1343 sh.

Akhavi, S., *Religion and politics in contemporary Iran*, Albany 1980

'Shariati's social thought', in N. R. Keddie (ed.), *Religion and politics in Iran*, New Haven and London 1983

Āl ʿAbd al-Qādir, Muḥammad ibn ʿAbdallāh, *Tuḥfat al-mustafīd bi-taʾrīkh al-Aḥsāʾ fī ʾl-qadīm waʾl-jadīd*, Riyāḍ and Damascus 1960–3

Āl al-Shaykh, ʿAbd al-Raḥmān ibn ʿAbd al-Laṭīf, *Mashāhīr ʿulamāʾ Najd wa-ghayrihim*, Riyāḍ 1394

Albānī, M. N. al-, *al-Muntakhab min makhṭūṭāt al-ḥadīth* (part of the *Fihris makhṭūṭāt Dār al-Kutub al-Ẓāhiriyya*), Damascus 1970

Albert the Great (d. AD 1280), *Commentarii in quartum librum Sententiarum*, in his *Opera omnia*, ed. A. and E. Borgnet, Paris 1890–9

Algar, H., *Mīrzā Malkum Khān*, Berkeley 1973

ʿAlī ibn ʿAbdallāh al-Khazrajī (d. 539/1145) (?), epitome of Ghazzālī (d. 505/1111), *Iḥyāʾ ʿulūm al-dīn*, ms. Madrid, Junta, no. 21

ʿAlī ibn al-Ḥusayn ibn al-Hādī (*fl.* early seventh/thirteenth century), *Lumaʿ*, ms. London, British Library, Or. 3,949

ʿAlī ibn Muḥammad al-ʿAlawī (*fl.* late third/ninth century), *Sīrat al-Hādī ilā ʾl-Ḥaqq Yaḥyā ibn al-Ḥusayn*, ed. S. Zakkār, Beirut 1972

ʿAlī al-Qārī (d. 1014/1606), *al-Mubīn al-muʿīn li-fahm al-Arbaʿīn*, Cairo 1910

Sharḥ ʿAyn al-ʿilm, Cairo 1351–3

ʿAlī Ṣadrī al-Qūnawī, commentary on Birgili's *Risāla*, ms. Princeton, Third Series 190

ʿĀlim ibn al-ʿAlāʾ al-Ḥanafī (compiling in 777/1375f.), *al-Fatāwā al-Tātārkhāniyya*, ed. S. Ḥusayn, Karachi 1990–
ʿAllāma al-Ḥillī, al- (d. 726/1325), *Ajwibat al-masāʾil al-Muhannāʾiyya*, Qumm 1401
al-Bāb al-ḥādī ʿashar, *apud* Miqdād al-Suyūrī (d. 826/1423), *al-Nāfiʿ yawm al-ḥashr*, Beirut 1988
Irshād al-adhhān, ed. F. al-Ḥassūn, Qumm 1410
Kashf al-murād, Beirut 1979
Mukhtalaf al-Shīʿa, Qumm 1412–
Muntahā ʾl-maṭlab, n.p. 1333
Nahj al-mustarshidīn, *apud* Miqdād al-Suyūrī (d. 826/1423), *Irshād al-ṭālibīn*, ed. M. al-Rajāʾī, Qumm 1405
Qawāʿid al-aḥkām, Qumm 1413–
Rijāl, ed. M. Ṣ. Baḥr al-ʿUlūm, Najaf 1961
Tabṣirat al-mutaʿallimīn, *apud* Ṣādiq al-Shīrāzī, *Sharḥ Tabṣirat al-mutaʿallimīn*, Qumm 1406
Tadhkirat al-fuqahāʾ, n.p. n.d.
Taḥrīr al-aḥkām, n.p. 1314
Alphonsus Liguori (d. AD 1787), *Theologia moralis*, ed. L. Gaudé, Graz 1954
Altunsu, A., *Osmanlı şeyhülislâmları*, Ankara 1972
Ālūsī, Maḥmūd al- (d. 1270/1854), *Rūḥ al-maʿānī*, Cairo 1301–10
Alverny, M. -T. d', 'Deux traductions latines du Coran au Moyen Age', in her *La connaissance de l'Islam dans l'Occident médiéval*, Aldershot and Brookfield 1994
Alverny, M.-T. d', and G. Vajda, 'Marc de Tolède, traducteur d'Ibn Tumart', in M.-T. d'Alverny, *La connaissance de l'Islam dans l'Occident médiéval*, Aldershot and Brookfield 1994
ʿAlwachī, ʿA. al-, *Muʾallafāt Ibn al-Jawzī*, Baghdad 1965
ʿAmad, I. Ṣ. al-, 'Nuṣūṣ turāthiyya ḥawla wujūd muḥtasib fī ʾl-mujtamaʿ al-Qurashī qabla ʾl-Islām', *Majallat Majmaʿ al-Lugha al-ʿArabiyya al-Urdunnī*, 41 (1991)
Amedroz, H. F., 'The Hisba jurisdiction in the Ahkam Sultaniyya of Mawardi', *Journal of the Royal Asiatic Society*, 1916
Āmidī (d. 631/1233), *Abkār al-afkār*, ms. Istanbul, Süleymaniye, Aya Sofya 2,166
Amīn, Bānū Mujtahida-i (d. 1403/1983), *Makhzan al-ʿirfān*, Iṣfahān n.d.
ʿAmri, H. ʿA. al-, *The Yemen in the 18th & 19th centuries*, London 1985
ʿAmrī, Jalāl al-Dīn al-, *al-Amr biʾl-maʿrūf waʾl-nahy ʿan al-munkar*, translated from the Urdu by M. A. A. al-Iṣlāḥī, Kuwait 1984 (default version); English translation, also Kuwait 1984
Anon., 'Amr bah maʿrūf wa nahy az munkar yā ʿamal bah masʾūlīyat-hā-yi ijtimāʿī', series of six articles in *Jumhūrī-i Islāmī*, 13, 14, 15, 17, 21 and 22 Urdībihisht 1366 sh., pages 9, 9, 7, 9, 9, and 7 respectively
Anon. (sixth/twelfth century), *Baḥr al-fawāʾid* (in Persian), ed. M. T. Dānish-pazhūh, Tehran 1345 sh.; trans. J. S. Meisami, *The sea of precious virtues*, Salt Lake City 1991

Anon., 'Fakhkh manṣūb wa-taṣfiya damawiyya qādima!', *al-Jazīra al-ʿArabiyya*, no. 13, February 1992

Anon., 'Flequillos satánicos en Afghanistán', *El País*, 5 November, 1997

Anon., 'Guzārishī az simīnār-i amr bah maʿrūf wa nahy az munkar dar Dānishgāh-i Tihrān', in *Risālat*, *pīsh shumāra* 3, 12 Abān, and *pīsh shumāra* 4, 23 Abān, 1364 sh.

Anon., 'Hal atāka naba' al-Bʿrrāqī?!', *al-Munqidh* (Algiers), second half of Rabīʿ I, 1410

Anon., 'Ḥāl al-Muslimīn al-yawm wa-Jamāʿat al-daʿwa wa'l-irshād', *al-Manār*, 18 (1333)

'Ḥāl al-Muslimīn al-ijtimāʿiyya wa-farīḍat al-amr bi'l-maʿrūf wa'l-nahy ʿan al-munkar', *al-Manār*, 19 (1334–5)

Anon., 'Intiqād az iʿlām-i jāyiza-i "wīdīyo" barā-yi musābaqa-i ʿamr bah maʿrūf wa nahy az munkar', *Iran Times* (Washington), 2 October 1992

Anon. (writing 425/1034), *al-Mabānī li-naẓm al-maʿānī*, in A. Jeffery (ed.), *Two Muqaddimas to the Qur'anic sciences*, Cairo 1954

Anon. (fourth/tenth century?), *Qur'ān-i Quds: kuhantarīn bargardān-i Qur'ān bah Fārsī?*, ed. ʿA. Riwāqī, Tehran 1364 sh.

Anon., *Risāla fī 'l-amr bi'l-maʿrūf wa'l-nahy ʿan al-munkar*, Institut Mauritanien de Recherche Scientifique, Nouakchott, ms. 2,764

Anon. (second half of fourth/tenth or first half of fifth/eleventh century), *Tafsīr-i Qur'ān-i majīd*, ed. J. Matīnī, n.p. 1349 sh.

Anon. (fourth/tenth or first half of fifth/eleventh century), *Tafsīrī bar ʿushrī az Qur'ān-i majīd*, ed. J. Matīnī, Tehran 1352 sh.

Anon. (third quarter of the fourth/tenth century), *Tarjuma-i Tafsīr-i Ṭabarī*, ed. Ḥ. Yaghmā'ī, Tehran 1339– sh.

Anṣārī, Khwāja ʿAbdallāh (d. 481/1089), *Ṭabaqāt al-ṣūfiyya* (in Persian), ed. M. S. Mawlā'ī, n.p. 1362 sh.

ʿAnsī, Qāḍī Aḥmad ibn Qāsim al-, *al-Tāj al-mudhhab li-aḥkām al-madhhab*, Ṣanʿā' n.d.

ʿAqīlī, M. A. 'I. al-, (*Min ta'rīkh*) *al-Mikhlāf al-Sulaymānī*, Riyāḍ 1958 and Cairo n.d.

Aquinas, Thomas (d. AD 1274), *In quattuor libros Sententiarum*, in his *Opera omnia*, ed. R. Busa, Stuttgart 1980

Summa theologiae, London and New York 1964–76

Arberry, A. J., *The Chester Beatty Library: a handlist of the Arabic manuscripts*, Dublin 1955–66

The Koran interpreted, London 1964

Arendonk, C. van, *Les débuts de l'imamat zaidite au Yémen*, Leiden 1960

ʿĀrif, A. ʿA., *al-Ṣila bayn al-Zaydiyya wa'l-Muʿtazila*, Beirut and Ṣanʿā' 1987

Aristotle (d. 322 BC), *Nichomachean ethics*, ed. H. Rackham, London and Cambridge, Mass. 1956

Arjomand, S. A., *The shadow of God and the hidden Imam*, Chicago and London 1984

Arnim, H. von, *Stoicorum veterum fragmenta*, Stuttgart 1978–9

Arvasî, S. Ahmet, *İlm-i hâl*, Istanbul 1990

Ashʿarī (d. 324/935f.), *Maqālāt al-islāmiyyīn*, ed. H. Ritter, Wiesbaden 1963

Āshtiyānī, Muḥammad Riḍā *et al.*, *Tafsīr-i numūna*, Tehran 1353–8 sh.

Āṣifī, Muḥammad Mahdī al-, 'Dirāsa fiqhiyya mūjaza ʿan ḥukm al-Islām fī mas'alat al-iʿtirāḍ ʿalā 'l-anẓima wa'l-ḥukm', *al-Nūr*, no. 44 (Shaʿbān 1415/January 1995)

Aṣmaʿī (d. *c.* 216/831), *Aṣmaʿiyyāt*, ed. W. Ahlwardt, Berlin 1902

Astarābādī, Sharaf al-Dīn al- (tenth/sixteenth century), *Ta'wīl al-āyāt al-ẓāhira*, Qumm 1407

ʿAṭā'ī, Nevʿīzāde (d. 1045/1635), *Ḥadā'iq al-ḥaqā'iq fī takmilat al-Shaqā'iq* (in Turkish), n.p. 1268

Aṭfayyish (d. 1332/1914), *Hīmyān al-zād*, ed. ʿA. Shalabī, Oman 1980–
Taysīr al-tafsīr, Cairo 1981–

Athamina, K., 'The early Murji'a: some notes', *Journal of Semitic Studies*, 35 (1990)
'ʿUqūbat al-nafy fī ṣadr al-Islām wa'l-dawla al-Umawiyya', *al-Karmil*, 5 (1984)

ʿAthāmina, K., see: Athamina, K.

ʿAṭiyya, Jamāl al-Dīn, 'Ḥuqūq al-insān fī 'l-Islām: al-naẓariyya al-ʿāmma', in *Ḥuqūq al-insān fī 'l-Islām: maqālāt al-Mu'tamar al-khāmis lil-fikr al-Islāmī*, Tehran 1987

Atsız, *İstanbul kütüphanelerine göre Birgili Mehmet Efendi (929–981 = 1523–1573) bibliografyası*, Istanbul 1966
'Kemalpaşa-oğlu'nun eserleri', *Şarkiyat Mecmuası*, 7 (1972)

Augustine (d. AD 430), *De civitate Dei*, Turnhout 1955; *The City of God*, abridged translation, ed. V. J. Bourke, New York 1958

Aʿwasht, Bukayr ibn Saʿīd, *Dirāsāt Islāmiyya fī 'l-uṣūl al-Ibāḍiyya*, Cairo 1988

ʿAwda, ʿAbd al-Qādir (d. 1374/1954), *al-Tashrīʿ al-jinā'ī al-Islāmī*, Cairo n.d.

Āyatī, Muḥammad Ibrāhīm (d. 1384/1964), 'Amr bah maʿrūf wa nahy az munkar', *Guftār-i māh*, 1 (1339–40 sh.), Tehran n.d.

ʿAyyāshī (early fourth/tenth century), *Tafsīr*, Qumm n.d.

Azdī (*fl. c.* 190/805), *Futūḥ al-Shām*, ed. W. N. Lees, Calcutta 1853–4

Azdī (d. *c.* 334/945), *Ta'rīkh al-Mawṣil*, ed. ʿA. Ḥabība, Cairo 1967

Azharī (d. 370/980), *Tahdhīb al-lugha*, ed. ʿA. M. Hārūn *et al.*, Cairo 1964–7

ʿAzīzī (d. 1070/1659f.), *al-Sirāj al-munīr*, Cairo 1357

Azraqī (d. *c.* 250/864), *Akhbār Makka*, ed. R. Ṣ. Malḥas, Madrid n.d.

Bā Nāja, Saʿīd Muḥammad Aḥmad, *Dirāsa muqārina ḥawla 'l-Iʿlān al-ʿālami li-ḥuqūq al-insān*, Beirut 1985

Babylonian Talmud, Vilnius 1880–6; Soncino translation, ed. I. Epstein, London 1935–52

Badawī, ʿA., *Mu'allafāt al-Ghazālī*, Cairo 1961

Badīʿ al-Zamān al-Hamadhānī (d. 398/1008), *Rasā'il*, *apud* Ibrāhīm Afandī al-Aḥdab al-Ṭarābulusī, *Kashf al-maʿānī wa'l-bayān ʿan Rasā'il Badīʿ al-Zamān*, Beirut 1890

Bādisī, ʿAbd al-Ḥaqq al- (writing 711/1311f.), *al-Maqṣad al-sharīf*, ed. S. Aʿrāb, Rabat 1982

Badr al-Rashīd (d. 768/1366f?), *Alfāẓ al-kufr*, published under the title *Tahdhīb risālat al-Badr al-Rashīd fī alfāẓ al-kufr*, Beirut 1991

Baghawī (d. 516/1122), *Maʿālim al-tanzīl*, ed. M. ʿA. al-Namir *et al.*, Riyāḍ 1993

Bahāʾ al-Dīn al-ʿĀmilī (d. 1030/1621), *Jāmiʿ-i ʿAbbāsī*, n.p. 1328

Kitāb al-arbaʿīn, Tabrīz 1378

Bahonar, Muhammad Jawad, 'Islam and women's rights', in Muhammad Taqi Mesbah *et al.*, *Status of women in Islam*, New Delhi 1990

Baḥrānī (d. 1107/1695f.), *al-Burhān fī tafsīr al-Qurʾān*, Tehran 1375 (also Tehran 1295–1302)

Bahrān al-Ṣaʿdī (d. 957/1550), *Jawāhir al-akhbār*, see: Ibn al-Murtaḍā, *Baḥr*

Baḥshal (d. 292/904f.), *Taʾrīkh Wāsiṭ*, ed. K. ʿAwwād, Baghdad 1967

Bājī (d. 474/1081), *Muntaqā*, Cairo 1332

Sunan al-ṣāliḥīn, ms. Leiden, Or. 506

Waṣiyya, see: Hilāl, 'Muqaddima'

Bajistānī, Sayyid Maḥmūd Madanī, *Amr bah maʿrūf wa nahy az munkar: do farīḍa-i bartar dar sīra-i maʿṣūmīn*, Qumm 1376 sh.

Bājūrī (d. 1276/1860), *Tuḥfat al-murīd*, *apud* Laqānī (d. 1041/1631), *Jawharat al-tawḥīd*, Cairo n.d.

Bakhash, S., *The reign of the Ayatollahs*, New York 1990

Bakhit, M. A., *The Ottoman province of Damascus in the sixteenth century*, Beirut 1982

Balādhurī (d. 279/892f.), *Ansāb al-ashrāf*, vol. 5, ed. S. D. F. Goitein, Jerusalem 1936; vol. 6, part 2, ed. K. Athamina, Jerusalem 1993; ed. M. B. al-Maḥmūdī, Beirut 1974; ms. Istanbul, Reisülküttap 598

Balić, S., *Das unbekannte Bosnien*, Cologne 1992

Balkhī, Muḥammad ibn ʿUthmān al- (d. 830/1426f.) (attrib.), *ʿAyn al-ʿilm*, see: ʿAlī al-Qārī, *Sharḥ ʿAyn al-ʿilm*

Bannā, Ḥasan al- (d. 1368/1949), *Ḥadīth al-thulāthāʾ*, recorded by Aḥmad ʿĪsā ʿĀshūr, Cairo 1985

Naẓarāt fī iṣlāḥ al-nafs waʾl-mujtamaʿ, recorded by Aḥmad ʿĪsā ʿĀshūr, Cairo 1980

Bannānī (d. 1163/1750), *Ḥāshiya*, see: Zurqānī, *Sharḥ*

Bar-Asher, M. M., 'Variant readings and additions of the Imāmī-Šīʿa to the Quran', *Israel Oriental Studies*, 13 (1993)

Bardakoğlu, A., 'Hüsn ve kubh konusunda aklın rolü ve İmam Mâturîdî', in *Ebû Mansur Semerkandî Mâturîdî*, Kayseri 1986

Barhebraeus (d. AD 1286), *Ethicon*, ed. P. Bedjan, Paris and Leipzig 1898; ed. and trans. H. G. B. Teule, Louvain 1993–

Barqī (d. 274/887f.) (attrib.), *Rijāl*, Tehran 1342 sh.

Barrādī (later eighth/fourteenth century), *Jawāhir*, Cairo 1302

Bassām, ʿAbdallāh ibn ʿAbd al-Raḥmān ibn Ṣāliḥ al-, *ʿUlamāʾ Najd khilāl sittat qurūn*, Mecca 1398

Baumstark, A., *Geschichte der syrischen Literatur*, Bonn 1922

Bayānūnī, Aḥmad ʿIzz al-Dīn al-, *al-Amr biʾl-maʿrūf waʾl-nahy ʿan al-munkar*, Aleppo 1973

Bayḍāwī (d. *c.* 710/1310), *Anwār al-tanzīl*, Cairo n.d.
Baydhaq (sixth/twelfth century), *Taʾrīkh al-Muwaḥḥidīn*, see: Lévi-Provençal, *Documents inédits*
Bayhaqī (d. 458/1066), *Dalāʾil al-nubuwwa*, ed. ʿA. Qalʿajī, Beirut 1985
Shuʿab al-īmān, ed. M. B. Zaghlūl, Beirut 1990
al-Sunan al-kubrā, Hyderabad 1344–55
Bayṭār, Khālid al-, *al-Bayān fī sharḥ al-Arbaʿīn al-Nawawiyya*, Zarqāʾ 1987
Bāzargān, Mahdī (d. 1415/1995), *Marz-i miyān-i dīn wa siyāsat*, Tehran 1341 sh.
Bazzār (d. 292/904f.), *al-Baḥr al-zakhkhār al-maʿrūf bi-Musnad al-Bazzār*, ed. M. Zayn Allāh, Medina and Beirut 1988–
Belhadj, Ali, see: Ibn Ḥājj, ʿAlī
Ben Cheneb, M., *Classes des savants de l'Ifrīqīya*, Beirut n.d.
Ben Hamadi, A., 'Y a-t-il une influence khāriǧite dans la pensée d'Ibn Tūmart?', in *Mélanges offerts à Mohamed Talbi*, Tunis 1993
Bercher, L., 'L'obligation d'ordonner le bien et d'interdire le mal selon Al-Ghazali', *IBLA* (= *Revue de l'Institut des belles lettres arabes*), 18 (1955), 20 (1957), 21 (1958), 23 (1960)
Bernand, M., 'Le *Kitāb al-radd ʿalā l-bidaʿ* d'Abū Muṭīʿ Makḥūl al-Nasafī', *Annales Islamologiques*, 16 (1980)
Bevan, A. A. (ed.), *The Naḳāʾiḍ of Jarīr and al-Farazdaḳ*, Leiden 1905–12
Bihishtī, Muḥammad (d. 1401/1981), 'Rūḥānīyat dar Islām wa dar miyān-i Muslimīn', in Muḥammad Ḥusayn Ṭabāṭabāʾī *et al.*, *Baḥthī dar bāra-i marjaʿīyat wa rūḥānīyat*, n.p. n.d.
Bilālī, Shams al-Dīn Muḥammad ibn ʿAlī al- (d. 820/1417), *Jannat al-maʿārif* (alternative title: *Iḥyāʾ al-Iḥyāʾ fī ʾl-taṣawwuf*), ms. Istanbul, Süleymaniye, Fatih 2,604
Biqāʿī (d. 885/1480), *Naẓm al-durar*, Hyderabad 1969–84
Birgili (d. 981/1573), *Risāla* (in Turkish), n.p. 1300
al-Ṭarīqa al-Muḥammadiyya, Cairo 1937
Bishr ibn Abī Khāzim (sixth century AD), *Dīwān*, ed. ʿI. Ḥasan, Damascus 1960
Bisyawī (fourth or fifth/tenth or eleventh century), *Jāmiʿ*, Ruwī 1984 (default: vol. 4)
Mukhtaṣar, Oman n.d.
Sīra, see: Kāshif, *Siyar*
Blackstone, William (d. AD 1780), *Commentaries on the laws of England*, Oxford 1765–9
Bonner, M., *Aristocratic violence and holy war: studies in the Jihad and the Arab–Byzantine frontier*, New Haven 1996
Bousquet, G.-H., *Ghazâlî, Ih'ya 'ouloûm ed-dîn ou Vivification des sciences de la foi: analyse et index*, Paris 1955
Bouyges, M., *Essai de chronologie des oeuvres de al-Ghazali*, Beirut 1959
Böwering, G., *The mystical vision of existence in classical Islam*, Berlin and New York 1980
Brockelmann, C., *Geschichte der Arabischen Litteratur*, first edition, Weimar and Berlin 1898–1902; supplementary volumes, Leiden 1937–42; second edition, Leiden 1943–9

Brooks, Geraldine, 'Teen-age infidels hanging out', *The New York Times Magazine*, 30 April 1995
Brown, P., *Power and persuasion in late antiquity*, Madison and London 1992
Brunschvig, R., *Deux récits de voyage inédits en Afrique du Nord au XVe siècle*, Paris 1936
'Métiers vils en Islam', *Studia Islamica*, 16 (1962)
Buc, P., *L'ambiguïté du Livre: prince, pouvoir, et peuple dans les commentaires de la Bible au Moyen Age*, Paris 1994
Buchta, W., *Die iranische Schia und die islamische Einheit 1979–1996*, Hamburg 1997
Buddhaghosa (fifth century AD), *Sumaṅgala-vilāsinī*, ed. T. W. Rhys Davids *et al.*, London 1886–1932
Bukayr, Aḥmad, 'al-Ḍamīr al-dīnī wa-ḥuqūq al-insāniyya fī 'l-Islām', in Université de Tunis, Centre d'Etudes et de Recherches Economiques et Sociales, *IIème Rencontre Islamo-Chrétienne: Droits de l'homme*, Tunis 1985
Bukhārī (d. 256/870), *Ṣaḥīḥ*, ed. L. Krehl, Leiden 1862–1908
al-Ta'rīkh al-kabīr, Hyderabad 1360–78
al-Ta'rīkh al-ṣaghīr, ed. M. I. Zāyid, Aleppo and Cairo 1976–7
Burckhardt, J. L., *Notes on the Bedouins and Wahábys*, London 1831
Burgat, F., *L'Islamisme en face*, Paris 1995
Calder, N., 'Judicial authority in Imāmī Shīʿī jurisprudence', *British Society for Middle Eastern Studies Bulletin*, 6 (1979)
'Legitimacy and accommodation in Safavid Iran: the juristic theory of Muḥammad Bāqir al-Sabzavārī (d. 1090/1679)', *Iran*, 25 (1987)
'Zakāt in Imāmī Shīʿī jurisprudence, from the tenth to the sixteenth century AD', *Bulletin of the School of Oriental and African Studies*, 44 (1981)
Carapico, S., *Civil society in Yemen*, Cambridge 1998
Carré, O., *Mystique et politique: lecture révolutionnaire du Coran par Sayyid Quṭb, Frère musulman radical*, Paris 1984
Caskel, W., *Ǧamharat an-nasab: Das genealogische Werk des Hišām ibn Muḥammad al-Kalbī*, Leiden 1966
Catalogue of the Arabic and Persian manuscripts in the Oriental Public Library at Bankipore, Calcutta and Patna 1908–46
Catalogus codicum manuscriptorum orientalium qui in Museo Britannico asservantur, Pars secunda, codices Arabicos amplectens, London 1846–52
Çavuşoğlu, S., 'The Ḳāḍīzādeli movement', Princeton Ph.D. 1990
Chabbi, J., 'Fuḍayl b. ʿIyāḍ, un précurseur du Hanbalisme', *Bulletin d'Etudes Orientales*, 30 (1978)
Chalmeta Gendron, P., *El 'señor del zoco' en España*, Madrid 1973
Chaudhry, Muhammad Sharif, *Women's rights in Islam*, Delhi 1991
Chāwīsh, ʿAbd al-ʿAzīz (d. 1347/1929), 'Tefsīr-i Qur'ān-i kerīm', *Sebīl ür-Reşād*, 14 (1331–4 *mālī*)
Chehabi, H. E., *Iranian politics and religious modernism*, Ithaca 1990
Cicero (d. 43 BC), *De republica*, ed. and trans. C. W. Keyes, London and Cambridge, Mass. 1951

Laelius de amicitia, ed. and trans. J. G. F. Powell, Warminster 1990
Cohen, M. R., *Under crescent and cross: the Jews in the Middle Ages*, Princeton 1994
Confucius (d. 479 BC), *Analects*, trans. D. C. Lau, Harmondsworth 1979
Cook, M., 'Activism and quietism in Islam: the case of the early Murji'a', in A. S. Cudsi and A. E. H. Dessouki (eds.), *Islam and power*, London 1981
'Early Islamic dietary law', *Jerusalem Studies in Arabic and Islam*, 7 (1986)
Early Muslim dogma: a source-critical study, Cambridge 1981
'The expansion of the first Saudi state: the case of Washm', in C. E. Bosworth *et al.* (eds.), *Essays in honor of Bernard Lewis: the Islamic world from classical to modern times*, Princeton 1989
'The historians of pre-Wahhābī Najd', *Studia Islamica*, 76 (1992)
'On the origins of Wahhābism', *Journal of the Royal Asiatic Society*, series 3, 2 (1992)
review of the first volume of van Ess's *Theologie* in *Bibliotheca Orientalis*, 50 (1993)
'Van Ess's second volume: testing a sample', *Bibliotheca Orientalis*, 51 (1994)
Costello, J. A., *Moral obligation of fraternal correction*, Washington, D. C. 1949
Crawford, M. J., 'Civil war, foreign intervention, and the question of political legitimacy: a nineteenth-century Sa'ūdī qāḍī's dilemma', *International Journal of Middle East Studies*, 14 (1982)
Creswell, K. A. C., *Early Muslim architecture: Umayyads*, Oxford 1969
Crone, P., *Meccan trade and the rise of Islam*, Princeton 1987
Slaves on horses, Cambridge 1980
'The tribe and the state', in J. A. Hall (ed.), *States in history*, Oxford and New York 1986
Crone, P., and M. Hinds, *God's caliph*, Cambridge 1986
Cuperly, P., 'L'Ibâḍisme au XIIème siècle: la 'Aqîda de Abû Sahl Yaḥyâ', *IBLA* (= *Revue de l'Institut des belles lettres arabes*), 42 (1979)
Introduction à l'étude de l'Ibāḍisme et de sa théologie, Algiers 1984
'Une profession de foi ibāḍite', *Bulletin d'Etudes Orientales*, 32–3 (1980–1)
Dabashi, H., *Theology of discontent: the ideological foundations of the Islamic revolution in Iran*, New York and London 1993
Dabbāgh, Abū Zayd al- (d. 696/1296f.), *Ma'ālim al-īmān fī ma'rifat ahl al-Qayrawān*, in the recension of Ibn Nājī (d. 839/1436), ed. I. Shabbūḥ *et al.*, Cairo and Tunis 1968–
Daftary, F., *The Ismā'īlīs: their history and doctrines*, Cambridge 1990
Daḥlān, Aḥmad ibn Zaynī (d. 1304/1886), *Khulāṣat al-kalām*, Cairo 1305
Daiber, H., *The Islamic concept of belief in the 4th/10th century*, Tokyo 1995
Dāmaghānī, Ḥusayn ibn Muḥammad al- (fifth/eleventh century?), *al-Wujūh wa'l-naẓā'ir*, ed. A. Bihrūz, Tabrīz 1366 sh.
Daniel, E. L., *The political and social history of Khurasan under Abbasid rule, 747–820*, Minneapolis and Chicago 1979
Dānishpazhūh, M. T., 'Dāwarī-i Fayḍ-i Kāshānī miyān-i pārsā wa dānishmand', *Nashriyya-i Dānishkada-i Adabiyyāt-i Tabrīz*, 9 (1336 sh.)
Danişmend, İ. H., *İzahlı Osmanlı tarihi kronolojisi*, Istanbul 1947–61

Dankoff, R., *Evliya Çelebi in Bitlis*, Leiden 1990

Dār al-Kutub al-Miṣriyya, *Fihrist al-kutub al-ʿArabiyya al-mawjūda biʾl-Dār li-ghāyat sanat 1921*, vol. 1, Cairo 1924

Dardīr (d. 1201/1786), *al-Sharḥ al-kabīr*, Cairo 1292

Darjīnī (seventh/thirteenth century), *Ṭabaqāt al-mashāyikh biʾl-maghrib*, ed. I. Ṭallāy, n.p. n.d.

Darwaza, Muḥammad ʿIzzat (d. 1404/1984), *al-Tafsīr al-ḥadīth*, Cairo 1962–4

Dastghayb, ʿAbd al-Ḥusayn, *Amr ba-maʿrūf wa nahy az munkar*, Tehran 1371 sh.

Dasūqī (d. 1230/1815), *Ḥāshiya* to Dardīr (d. 1201/1786), *al-Sharḥ al-kabīr*, Cairo n.d.

Dawālībī, Muḥammad Maʿrūf al-, *al-Dawla waʾl-sulṭa fī ʾl-Islām*, Beirut 1983

Dawānī (d. 908/1502), *Sharḥ ʿalā ʾl-ʿAqāʾid al-ʿAḍudiyya*, printed in the margin of the *Ḥāshiya*s thereto of Siyālkūtī (d. 1067/1657) and Muḥammad ʿAbduh (d. 1323/1905), Cairo 1322

Daylamī, al-Nāṣir Abū ʾl-Fatḥ al- (d. 444/1052f.), *al-Burhān fī tafsīr al-Qurʾān*, manuscript copied in 1046/1637, uncertain location

Daylamī, Shīrawayh ibn Shahradār al- (d. 509/1115), *al-Firdaws bi-maʾthūr al-khiṭāb*, Beirut 1986

Dhahabī (d. 748/1348), *ʿIbar*, ed. Ṣ. al-Munajjid and F. Sayyid, Kuwait 1960–6

Mīzān al-iʿtidāl, ed. ʿA. M. al-Bajāwī, Cairo 1963–5

Siyar aʿlām al-nubalāʾ, ed. S. al-Arnaʾūṭ *et al.*, Beirut 1981–8

Tadhkirat al-ḥuffāẓ, Hyderabad 1968–70

Taʾrīkh al-Islām, ed. ʿU. ʿA. Tadmurī, Beirut 1987–

Tarjamat al-imām Aḥmad (extracted from his *Taʾrīkh al-Islām*), ed. A. M. Shākir, n.p. 1946

Dickinson, E., ʻAḥmad b. al-Ṣalt and his biography of Abū Ḥanīfaʼ, *Journal of the American Oriental Society*, 116 (1996)

Dictionnaire de droit canonique, Paris 1935–65

Dictionnaire de théologie catholique, Paris 1903–50

Dīgha nikāya, ed. T. W. Rhys Davids and J. E. Carpenter, London 1947–60; trans. T. W. and C. A. F. Rhys Davids, *Dialogues of the Buddha*, London 1899–1921

Dīghanikāyaṭṭhakathāṭīkā līnatthavaṇṇanā, ed. L. de Silva, London 1970

Dīnawarī, Abū Bakr al- (d. 333/944f.), *al-Mujālasa wa-jawāhir al-ʿilm*, Frankfurt am Main 1986

Dīnawarī, Abū Ḥanīfa al- (d. 282/895), *al-Akhbār al-ṭiwāl*, ed. ʿA. ʿĀmir and J. al-Shayyāl, Cairo 1960

Donnelly, J., *The concept of human rights*, New York 1985

Douglas, J. L., *The Free Yemeni Movement, 1935–1962*, Beirut 1987

Dozy, R., *Supplément aux dictionnaires arabes*, Leiden 1881

Dresch, P., *Tribes, government, and history in Yemen*, Oxford 1989

Drory, J., ʻḤanbalīs of the Nablus region in the eleventh and twelfth centuriesʼ, *Asian and African Studies*, 22 (1988)

Dughmī, Muḥammad Rākān al-, *Ḥimāyat al-ḥayāt al-khāṣṣa fī ʾl-sharīʿa al-Islāmiyya*, Cairo 1985

Dūmī, A. ʿA. al-, *Aḥmad ibn Ḥanbal bayn miḥnat al-dīn wa-miḥnat al-dunyā*, Cairo 1961
Egypt, Court of Cassation (*Maḥkamat al-naqḍ*), decree of 20 Rabiʿ I, 1417/5 August 1996
*EI*², see: *Encyclopaedia of Islam*, second edition
Elisséeff, N., *Nūr ad-Dīn*, Damascus 1967
Enayat, H., *Modern Islamic political thought*, Austin 1982
Encyclopaedia Iranica, London 1982–
Encyclopaedia Judaica, Jerusalem 1971–2
Encyclopaedia of Islam, first edition, Leiden and London 1913–38; second edition, Leiden and London 1960–
Encyclopedia Talmudica, Jerusalem 1969–
Ennami, A. K., 'A description of new Ibadi manuscripts from North Africa', *Journal of Semitic Studies*, 15 (1970)
Studies in Ibāḍism, Beirut 1972
'Studies in Ibāḍism', Cambridge Ph.D. 1971
Ennāmi, ʿA. K., see: Ennami, A. K.
Ergin, see: Osman Nuri
Eşrefoğlu, E., 'İslâmiyetde ihtisâbın prensipleri', *Tarih Dergisi*, 25 (1971)
Ess, J. van, 'Biobibliographische Notizen zur islamischen Theologie', *Die Welt des Orients*, 11 (1980)
Frühe muʿtazilitische Häresiographie: Zwei Werke des Našiʾ al-Akbar (gest. 293 H.) herausgegeben und eingeleitet, Beirut 1971
'Kritisches zum *Fiqh akbar*', *Revue des Etudes Islamiques*, 54 (1986)
Une lecture à rebours de l'histoire du Muʿtazilisme, Paris 1984
Theologie und Gesellschaft im 2. und 3. Jahrhundert Hidschra, Berlin and New York 1991–7
Ungenützte Texte zur Karrāmīya, Heidelberg 1980
'Untersuchungen zu einigen ibāḍitischen Handschriften', *Zeitschrift der Deutschen Morgenländischen Gesellschaft*, 126 (1976)
Eygi, Mehmet Şevket, 'Kara para', *Millî Gazete*, 2 August 1999
Faath, S., *Die Banû Mîzâb: Eine religiöse Minderheit in Algerien zwischen Isolation und Integration*, Scheessel 1985
Faḍīl, Y. ʿA. al-, *Man hum al-Zaydiyya?*, Beirut 1975
Faḍl Allāh, Muḥammad Ḥusayn, *al-Masāʾil al-fiqhiyya*, Beirut 1995–6
Faḍl ibn al-Ḥawārī (d. 278/892), *Jāmiʿ*, Oman 1985 (default: vol. 3)
Fagnan, E. (trans.), *Extraits inédits relatifs au Maghreb*, Algiers 1924
Fakhr al-Muḥaqqiqīn (d. 771/1370), *Īḍāḥ al-fawāʾid*, n.p. 1387–9
Fākihānī, Tāj al-Dīn al- (d. 734/1234), *al-Manhaj al-mubīn*, ms. Princeton, Garrett 749H
Fallaci, Oriana, 'An interview with Khomeini', *The New York Times Magazine*, 7 October 1979
Farazdaq (d. *c.* 110/728), *Dīwān*, *apud* I. al-Ḥāwī, *Sharḥ Dīwān al-Farazdaq*, Beirut 1983
Farès, B., *L'honneur chez les Arabes avant l'Islam*, Paris 1932

Farrā' (d. 207/822f.), *Ma'ānī al-Qur'ān*, ed. A. Y. Najātī and M. 'A. al-Najjār, Cairo 1980–
Farrazādhī (*fl.* late fifth/eleventh century), *Ta'līq Sharḥ al-uṣūl al-khamsa*, ms. Ṣan'ā', Great Mosque, *kalām* 73
Fāryābī (d. 607/1210), *Khāliṣat al-ḥaqā'iq*, ms. Princeton, Garrett 1026H
Fasawī (d. 277/890), *al-Ma'rifa wa'l-ta'rīkh*, ed. A. Ḍ. al-'Umarī, Baghdad 1974–6
Fashnī (writing 978/1570), *al-Majālis al-saniyya*, Cairo 1278
Fast, Howard, *Spartacus*, New York 1952
Fayḍ, Muḥsin al- (d. 1091/1680), *Mafātīḥ al-sharā'i'*, ed. M. Rajā'ī, Qumm 1401
al-Maḥajja al-bayḍā' fī tahdhīb al-Iḥyā', ed. 'A. A. al-Ghaffārī, Tehran 1339–42 sh.
Nukhba, n.p. 1303
Tafsīr al-ṣāfī, Mashhad 1982
Wāfī, Tehran 1375
Feinberg, J., *The moral limits of the criminal law*, New York and Oxford 1984–8
Fierro, M. I., *La heterodoxia en al-Andalus durante el período omeya*, Madrid 1987
'Mu'āwiya b. Ṣāliḥ al-Ḥaḍramī al-Ḥimṣi: historia y leyenda', in M. Marín (ed.), *Estudios onomástico-biográficos de al-Andalus*, vol. 1, Madrid 1988
'El proceso contra Abū 'Umar al-Ṭalamankī a través de su vida y de su obra', *Sharq al-Andalus*, 9 (1992)
'El proceso contra Ibn Ḥātim al-Ṭulayṭulī', *Estudios onomástico-biográficos de al-Andalus*, vol. 6, Madrid 1994
'La religión', in M. J. Viguera Molíns (ed.), *Los reinos de taifas: al-Andalus en el siglo XI* (= *Historia de España Menéndez Pidal*, tomo VIII–I), Madrid 1994
'La religión', in M. J. Viguera Molíns (ed.), *El retroceso territorial de al-Andalus* (= *Historia de España Menéndez Pidal*, tomo VIII–II), Madrid 1997
translation of Ṭurṭūshī (d. 520/1126), *al-Ḥawādith wa'l-bida'*, Madrid 1993
'The treatises against innovations (*kutub al-bida'*)', *Der Islam*, 69 (1992)
Fierro Bello, M. I., see: Fierro, M. I.
Fığlalı, E. R., *İbâdiye'nin doğuşu ve görüşleri*, Ankara 1983
Fihrist al-kutub al-'Arabiyya al-maḥfūẓa bi'l-Kutubkhāna al-Khidīwiyya al-Miṣriyya, Cairo 1305–10
Firishte-oghlu, see: Ibn al-Malak
Fletcher, M., 'Ibn Tūmart's teachers: the relationship with al-Ghazālī', *Al-Qanṭara*, 18 (1997)
Floor, W. M., 'The office of muhtasib in Iran', *Iranian Studies*, 18 (1985)
'The political role of the Lutis in Iran', in M. E. Bonine and N. R. Keddie (eds.), *Modern Iran*, Albany 1981
Fórneas, J. M., 'De la transmisión de algunas obras de tendencia aš'arī en al-Andalus', *Awrāq*, 1 (1978)
Fouchécour, C.-H. de, *Moralia: les notions morales dans la littérature persane du 3e/9e au 7e/13e siècle*, Paris 1986
Frank, R. M., *al-Ghazālī and the Ash'arite school*, Durham and London 1994
Fu'ādīyān, Ramaḍān, *Sayrī dar farīḍa-i amr bah ma'rūf wa nahy az munkar*, Qumm 1375 sh.

Fück, J. W., 'Some hitherto unpublished texts on the Muʿtazilite movement from Ibn al-Nadīm's *Kitāb-al-Fihrist*', in S. M. Abdullah (ed.), *Professor Muḥammad Shafiʿ presentation volume*, Lahore 1955

Führer, G. F., *Kurze Darstellung der Meyerrechtlichen Verfassung in der Grafschaft Lippe*, Lemgo 1804

Furāt ibn Ibrāhīm al-Kūfī (*fl.* later third/ninth century), *Tafsīr*, Najaf n.d.

García-Arenal, M., 'La práctica del precepto de *al-amr bi-l-maʿrūf wa-l-nahy ʿan al-munkar* en la hagiografía magrebí', *Al-Qanṭara*, 13 (1992)

García Gómez, E., 'Unas "Ordenenzas del zoco" del siglo IX', *Al-Andalus*, 22 (1957)

Gardet, L., *La cité musulmane*, Paris 1961

Gause, F. G., *Oil monarchies*, New York 1994

Gewirth, A., 'Replies to my critics', in E. Regis Jr. (ed.), *Gewirth's ethical rationalism*, Chicago and London 1984

Geyer, R. (ed.), *Gedichte von ʾAbû Baṣîr Maimûn ibn Qais al-ʾAʿšâ nebst Sammlungen von Stücken anderer Dichter des gleichen Beinamens*, London 1928

Ghazzālī (d. 505/1111), *Iḥyāʾ ʿulūm al-dīn*, Beirut n.d. (default: this edition, vol. 2); Cairo 1967–8

Kīmiyā-yi saʿādat, ed. Ḥ. Khadīvjam, Tehran 1368 sh.

Kitāb al-amr biʾl-maʿrūf waʾl-nahy ʿan al-munkar min Iḥyāʾ ʿulūm al-dīn, Beirut 1983

Kitāb al-arbaʿīn fī uṣūl al-dīn, Cairo 1344

al-Maqṣad al-asnā, ed. F. A. Shehadi, Beirut 1971

Wajīz, Cairo 1317

Ghazzālī, Aḥmad al- (d. *c.* 520/1126), *Lubāb al-Iḥyāʾ*, ms. Princeton, Garrett 1079H

Ghazzī, Kamāl al-Dīn (d. 1214/1799), *al-Naʿt al-akmal li-aṣḥāb al-imām Aḥmad ibn Ḥanbal*, ed. M. M. al-Ḥāfiẓ and N. Abāẓa, Damascus 1982

Ghazzī, Najm al-Dīn al- (d. 1061/1651), *al-Kawākib al-sāʾira*, ed. J. S. Jabbūr, Beirut 1945–58

Ghubrīnī (d. 704/1304f.), *ʿUnwān al-dirāya*, ed. ʿA. Nuwayhiḍ, Beirut 1969

Ghurāb, S., 'Ḥawl iḥrāq al-Murābiṭīn li-*Iḥyāʾ* al-Ghazzālī', in *Actas del IV Coloquio Hispano-Tunecino*, Madrid 1983

Gilliot, C., *Exégèse, langue, et théologie en Islam: l'exégèse coranique de Tabari*, Paris 1990

'Islam et pouvoir: la commanderie du bien et l'interdiction du mal', *Communio*, 16 (1991)

'Textes arabes anciens édités en Egypte au cours des années 1994 à 1996', *MIDEO*, 23 (1997)

Gimaret, D., *Une lecture muʿtazilite du Coran: Le Tafsīr d'Abū ʿAlī al-Djubbāʾī (m. 303/915) partiellement reconstitué à partir de ses citateurs*, Louvain and Paris 1994

'Matériaux pour une bibliographie des Ǧubbāʾī', *Journal Asiatique*, 264 (1976)

'Matériaux pour une bibliographie des Jubba'i: note complémentaire', in M. E. Marmura (ed.), *Islamic theology and philosophy*, Albany 1984

Théories de l'acte humain en théologie musulmane, Paris 1980

'Les *Uṣūl al-ḫamsa* du Qāḍī ʿAbd al-Ǧabbār et leurs commentaires', *Annales Islamologiques*, 15 (1979)

Glassen, E., *Der mittlere Weg: Studien zur Religionspolitik und Religiosität der späteren Abbasiden-Zeit*, Wiesbaden 1981

Göbel, K.-H., *Moderne Schiitische Politik und Staatsidee*, Opladen 1984

Goitein, S. D., 'Arabic documents on the Palestinian Gaonate' (in Hebrew), *Eretz-Israel*, 10 (1971)

'The local Jewish community in the light of the Cairo Geniza records', *The Journal of Jewish Studies*, 12 (1961)

A Mediterranean society, Berkeley and Los Angeles 1967–93

Goldrup, L. P., 'Saudi Arabia: 1902–1932: the development of a Wahhabi society', University of California, Los Angeles, Ph.D. 1971

Goldziher, I., 'Zur Geschichte der ḥanbalitischen Bewegungen', *Zeitschrift der Deutschen Morgenländischen Gesellschaft*, 62 (1908)

Le livre de Mohammed ibn Toumert, Algiers 1903

'Matth. VII. 5 in der muhammedanischen Literatur', *Zeitschrift der Deutschen Morgenländischen Gesellschaft*, 31 (1877)

review of first edition of Judah ha-Levi's *Khazari*, *Zeitschrift der Deutschen Morgenländischen Gesellschaft*, 41 (1887)

review of Landauer's edition of Saʿadya's *Amānāt*, *Zeitschrift der Deutschen Morgenländischen Gesellschaft*, 35 (1881)

review of Patton, *Aḥmed ibn Ḥanbal and the Miḥna*, in *Zeitschrift der Deutschen Morgenländischen Gesellschaft*, 52 (1898)

Die Richtungen der islamischen Koranauslegung, Leiden 1920

Gómez García, L., *Marxismo, islam e islamismo: el proyecto de Adil Husayn*, Madrid 1996

Graham, A. C., *Later Mohist logic, ethics and science*, Hong Kong and London 1978

Gramlich, R., *Alte Vorbilder des Sufitums*, Wiesbaden 1995–6

Das Sendschreiben al-Qušayrīs über das Sufitum, Wiesbaden 1989

Gratian (writing *c.* AD 1140), *Decretum*, Rome 1584

Grey, T. C., *The legal enforcement of morality*, New York 1983

Gribetz, A., *Strange bedfellows: mutʿat al-nisāʾ and mutʿat al-ḥajj*, Berlin 1994

Griffini, E., 'Lista dei manoscritti Arabi Nuovo Fondo della Biblioteca Ambrosiana di Milano', *Rivista degli Studi Orientali*, 7 (1916–18)

Grimm, J., *Deutsche Rechtsalterthümer*, Leipzig 1899

Guidi, I., and D. Santillana (trans.), *Il 'Muḫtaṣar' o Sommario del diritto malechita di Ḫalīl ibn Isḥāq*, Milan 1919

Gulpāyagānī, Muḥammad Riḍā (d. 1414/1993), *Majmaʿ al-masāʾil* (in Persian), Qumm 1403–6

Gutas, D., review in *Journal of the American Oriental Society*, 117 (1997)

Habib, J. S., *Ibn Saʿud's warriors of Islam: the Ikhwan of Najd and their role in the creation of the Saʿudi kingdom, 1910–30*, Leiden 1978

Hādī ila 'l-Ḥaqq, al- (d. 298/911), *ʿAhd*, ms. London, British Library, Or. 3,798
al-Aḥkām fī 'l-ḥalāl wa'l-ḥarām, n.p. 1990
Daʿwa, ms. London, British Library, Or. 3,798
Kitāb fīhī maʿrifat Allāh, see: ʿUmāra, *Rasā'il*
al-Manzila bayn al-manzilatayn, ms. London, British Library, Or. 3,798
Uṣūl al-dīn, ms. London, British Library, Or. 3,798
Ḥāfiẓ-i Shīrāzī (d. 791/1389), *Dīwān*, ed. B. Khurramshāhī, Tehran 1373 sh.
Hairi, A., *Shīʿism and constitutionalism in Iran*, Leiden 1977
Ḥajjī, M., *al-Ḥaraka al-fikriyya bi'l-Maghrib fī ʿahd al-Saʿdiyyīn*, n.p. 1976–8
Ḥājjī Khalīfa (d. 1067/1657), *Kashf al-ẓunūn*, ed. Ş. Yaltkaya and R. Bilge, Istanbul 1941–3
Ḥājjī Khalīfa, see also: Kātib Chelebi
Ḥajjī Rejeb Efendi, see: Rajab ibn Aḥmad al-Āmidī
Ḥakīm, Muḥammad Bāqir al-, 'Ḥuqūq al-insān min wijhat naẓar Islāmiyya', in *Ḥuqūq al-insān fī 'l-Islām: maqālāt al-Mu'tamar al-khāmis lil-fikr al-Islāmī*, Tehran 1987
Ḥakīm, Muḥsin al-Ṭabāṭabā'ī al- (d. 1390/1970), *Minhāj al-ṣāliḥīn, qism al-ʿibādāt*, Beirut 1976
Ḥākim al-Naysābūrī, al- (d. 405/1014), *Mustadrak*, Hyderabad 1334–42
Ḥakīm al-Tirmidhī, al- (*fl.* late third/ninth century), *Nawādir al-uṣūl*, Beirut n.d.
Ḥalīmī (d. 403/1012), *al-Minhāj fī shuʿab al-īmān*, Damascus 1979
Halm, H., *Die Ausbreitung der šāfiʿitischen Rechtsschule von den Anfängen bis zum 8. /14. Jahrhundert*, Wiesbaden 1974
'Der Treuhänder Gottes: Die Edikte des Kalifen al-Ḥākim', *Der Islam*, 63 (1986)
Hamadānī, ʿAlī ibn Shihāb al-Dīn al- (d. 786/1385), *Dhakhīrat al-mulūk* (in Persian), Lahore 1905
Hamadhānī (d. 521/1127), *Takmilat Ta'rīkh al-Ṭabarī*, ed. A. Y. Kanʿān, Beirut 1959
Hamdani, A. 'The dāʿī Ḥātim ibn Ibrāhīm al-Ḥāmidī (d. 596 H/1199 AD) and his book *Tuḥfat al-qulūb*', *Oriens*, 23–4 (1974)
Ḥanbal ibn Isḥāq (d. 273/886), *Dhikr miḥnat al-imām Aḥmad ibn Ḥanbal*, Cairo 1977
Handwörterbuch zur deutschen Rechtsgeschichte, Berlin 1971–97
Hanioğlu, M. Ş., *The Young Turks in opposition*, New York and Oxford 1995
Ḥārith al-Muḥāsibī (d. 243/857f.), *Risālat al-mustarshidīn*, ed. ʿA. Abū Ghudda, Aleppo 1974
Harrāsī, Kiyā al- (d. 504/1110), *Aḥkām al-Qur'ān*, ed. M. M. ʿAlī and ʿI. ʿA. ʿI. ʿAṭiyya, Cairo 1974–5
Harrison, P. W., 'Al Riadh, the capital of Nejd', *The Moslem World*, 8 (1918)
Hartmann, A., 'Les ambivalences d'un sermonnaire ḥanbalite', *Annales Islamologiques*, 22 (1986)
an-Nāṣir li-Dīn Allāh, Berlin and New York 1975
Hartmann, R., 'Die Wahhābiten', *Zeitschrift der Deutschen Morgenländischen Gesellschaft*, 78 (1924)

Harvey, L. P., *Islamic Spain 1250–1500*, Chicago and London 1990
Ḥasanābādī, Abū ʾl-Qāsim ʿAlīzāda, *Niẓārat-i millī yā amr bah maʿrūf wa nahy az munkar*, Qumm 1371 sh.
Ḥasan al-Baṣrī (d. 110/728) (attrib.), *Arbaʿ wa-khamsūn farīḍa*, ms. Princeton, Arabic, Third Series, no. 288
Ḥasan, Ḥamza al-, *al-Shīʿa fī ʾl-Mamlaka al-ʿArabiyya al-Suʿūdiyya*, n.p. 1993
Ḥasanī, ʿA. al-, *Taʾrīkh al-wizārāt al-ʿIrāqiyya*, Sidon 1965–9
Ḥasanī, ʿAbd al-Ḥayy al- (d. 1341/1923), *Nuzhat al-khawāṭir*, Hyderabad 1947–70
Ḥassān ibn Thābit (d. *c.* 54/674), *Dīwān*, ed. W. N. ʿArafāt, London 1971
Ḥātim, Nūrī, *al-Amr biʾl-maʿrūf waʾl-nahy ʿan al-munkar*, Qumm n.d.
Ḥātim al-Ṭāʾī (sixth century AD), *Dīwān*, ed. ʿA. S. Jamāl, Cairo n.d.
Ḥawwā, Saʿīd (d. 1409/1989), *Jund Allāh: thaqāfatan wa-akhlāqan*, n.p. n.d.
Hayʾa al-ʿĀmma lil-Istiʿlāmāt, al-, *Ḥuqūq al-insān fī ʾl-Islām*, n.p. n.d.
Ḥaydarīzāde Ibrāhīm Efendi (d. 1349/1931), 'Amr biʾl-maʿrūf, nahy ʿan al-munkar' (in Turkish), *Sebīl ür-Reşād*, 15 (1334 *mālī*)
ʿ*Irāq ordusuna khıṭāb*, Istanbul 1335 *mālī*
Haykel, B. A., 'Order and righteousness: Muḥammad ʿAlī al-Shawkānī and the nature of the Islamic state in Yemen', Oxford D.Phil. 1997
'Al-Shawkānī and the jurisprudential unity of Yemen', *Revue du Monde Musulman et de la Méditerranée*, 67 (1994)
Haythamī (d. 807/1405), *Majmaʿ al-zawāʾid*, Cairo 1352–3
Hedges, Chris, 'Everywhere in Saudi Arabia, Islam is watching', *The New York Times*, 6 January 1993
'With Mullahs' sleuths eluded, hijinks in the hills', *The New York Times*, 8 August 1994
Hibatallāh ibn Salāma (d. 410/1019), *al-Nāsikh waʾl-mansūkh*, Cairo 1960
Ḥibshī, ʿA. M. al-, *Maṣādir al-fikr al-Islāmī fī ʾl-Yaman*, Sidon and Beirut 1988
Hilāl, J. ʿA., 'Muqaddimat waṣiyyat al-Qāḍī Abī ʾl-Walīd al-Bājī li-waladayhi', *Majallat al-Maʿhad al-Miṣrī*, 1 no. 3 (1955)
Ḥimmaṣī (d. early seventh/thirteenth century), *al-Munqidh min al-taqlīd*, Qumm 1412–14
Ḥimyarī (*fl.* later third/ninth century), *Qurb al-isnād*, Najaf 1950
Hitti, P. K., *et al.*, *Descriptive catalog of the Garrett Collection of Arabic manuscripts in the Princeton University Library*, Princeton and London 1938
Ḥizb al-Ḥaqq (Yemen), *Bayān mashrūʿ Ḥizb al-Ḥaqq*, n.p. n.d.
Hopkins, J. F. P., and N. Levtzion, *Corpus of early Arabic sources for West African history*, Cambridge 1981
Hucker, C. O., *The censorial system of Ming China*, Stanford 1966
Hūd ibn Muḥakkam al-Hawwārī (third/ninth century), *Tafsīr*, ed. B. S. Sharīfī, Beirut 1990
Ḥujjatī, Muḥammad Bāqir, and ʿAbd al-Karīm Bī-āzār Shīrāzī, *Tafsīr-i kāshif*, Tehran 1363– sh.
Ḥumaydī (d. 219/834f.), *Musnad*, ed. Ḥ. al-Aʿẓamī, Cairo and Beirut n.d.
Humphreys, R. S., *From Saladin to the Mongols: the Ayyubids of Damascus, 1193–1260*, Albany 1977

Hunt, M., *The compassionate beast: what science is discovering about the humane side of humankind*, New York 1990

Hunwick, J. O., 'Al-Ma[g]hîlî and the Jews of Tuwât: the demise of a community', *Studia Islamica*, 61 (1985)

The writings of central Sudanic Africa (= *Arabic literature of Africa*, vol. 2), Leiden 1995

Hunwick, J. O. (ed. and trans.), *Sharīʿa in Songhay: the replies of al-Maghīlī to the questions of Askia al-Ḥājj Muḥammad*, Oxford 1985

Ḥurr al-ʿĀmilī, al- (d. 1104/1693), *Bidāyat al-hidāya*, ed. M. ʿA. al-Anṣārī, n.p. n.d.

Wasāʾil al-Shīʿa, ed. ʿA. al-Rabbānī and M. al-Rāzī, Tehran 1376–89

Ḥusayn, Aḥmad, 'al-Amr biʾl-maʿrūf waʾl-nahy ʿan al-munkar yajib an yaẓall dāʾiman fī ḥudūd al-ḥikma waʾl-mawʿiẓa al-ḥasana', *Majallat al-Azhar*, 50 (1398)

Ḥusayn ibn Aḥmad ibn Yaʿqūb (*fl.* later fourth/tenth century), *Sīrat al-imām al-Manṣūr biʾllāh*, ms. London, British Library, Or. 3,816

Husry, K. S. al-, *Origins of modern Arab political thought*, Delmar 1980

Hussain, Shaukat, *Human rights in Islam*, New Delhi 1990

Ibn ʿAbbād al-Rundī (d. 792/1390), *al-Rasāʾil al-kubrā*, Fez 1320

Ibn ʿAbd al-Barr (d. 463/1071), *al-Istīʿāb fī maʿrifat al-aṣḥāb*, ed. ʿA. M. al-Bajāwī, Cairo n.d.

Istidhkār, Damascus and Beirut 1993

Jāmiʿ bayān al-ʿilm, ed. A. al-Zuhayrī, Dammām 1994 (default edition); Cairo n.d.

Kāfī, Riyāḍ 1980

Tamhīd, ed. M. A. al-ʿAlawī *et al.*, Rabat 1967–

Ibn ʿAbd al-Hādī, Shams al-Dīn (d. 744/1343), *al-ʿUqūd al-durriyya*, ed. M. Ḥ. al-Fiqī, Cairo 1938

Ibn ʿAbd al-Hādī, Yūsuf ibn al-Ḥasan (d. 909/1503), *al-Jawhar al-munaḍḍad fī ṭabaqāt mutaʾakhkhirī aṣḥāb Aḥmad*, ed. ʿA. S. al-ʿUthaymīn, Cairo 1987

Ibn ʿAbd al-Ḥakam (d. 257/871), *Futūḥ Miṣr wa-akhbāruhā*, ed. C. C. Torrey, New Haven 1922

Ibn ʿAbd al-Ḥakam, ʿAbdallāh (d. 214/829), *Sīrat ʿUmar ibn ʿAbd al-ʿAzīz*, ed. A. ʿUbayd, Damascus 1964

Ibn ʿAbd al-Wahhāb, Muḥammad (d. 1206/1792), *Muʾallafāt al-Shaykh al-imām Muḥammad ibn ʿAbd al-Wahhāb*, ed. ʿA. Z. al-Rūmī *et al.*, Riyāḍ 1398

Mukhtaṣar al-Inṣāf waʾl-Sharḥ al-kabīr, Cairo n.d.

Naṣīḥat al-muslimīn bi-aḥādīth khātam al-mursalīn, Cairo n.d.

Ibn Abī Dāwūd (d. 316/929), *Maṣāḥif*, see: Jeffery, *Materials*

Ibn Abī ʾl-Dunyā (d. 281/894), *al-Amr biʾl-maʿrūf waʾl-nahy ʿan al-munkar*, ed. Ṣ. ʿA. al-Shalāḥī, Medina 1997

Dhamm al-malāhī, in J. Robson (ed. and trans.), *Tracts on listening to music*, London 1938

ʿUqūbāt, ed. M. K. R. Yūsuf, Beirut 1996

Ibn Abī ʾl-Ḥadīd (d. 656/1258), *Sharḥ Nahj al-balāgha*, ed. M. A. Ibrāhīm, Cairo 1959–64

Ibn Abī Ḥātim al-Rāzī (d. 327/938), *Ādāb al-Shāfiʿī wa-manāqibuhu*, ed. ʿA. ʿAbd al-Khāliq, Cairo 1953

Tafsīr al-Qurʾān al-ʿaẓīm, ed. A. ʿA. al-ʿAmmārī al-Zahrānī and Ḥ. B. Yāsīn, Medina 1408

Taqdimat al-maʿrifa, ed. ʿA. al-Muʿallimī al-Yamānī, Hyderabad 1952

Ibn Abī Jumhūr al-Aḥsāʾī (*fl.* late ninth/fifteenth century), *ʿAwālī al-laʾālī*, ed. M. al-ʿArāqī, Qumm 1983–5

Ibn Abī ʾl-Majd (sixth/twelfth century?), *Ishārat al-sabq*, ed. I. Bahādurī, Qumm 1414

Ibn Abī Sharīf al-Maqdisī, Ibrāhīm (d. 923/1517), *al-ʿIqd al-naḍīd*, ms. Princeton, Yahuda 879

Ibn Abī Shayba (d. 235/849), *Muṣannaf*, ed. K. Y. al-Ḥūt, Beirut 1989

Ibn Abī ʾl-Wafāʾ (d. 775/1373), *al-Jawāhir al-muḍiyya fī ṭabaqāt al-Ḥanafiyya*, Hyderabad 1332

Ibn Abī Yaʿlā (d. 526/1131), *Ṭabaqāt al-Ḥanābila*, ed. M. Ḥ. al-Fiqī, Cairo 1952

al-Tamām li-mā ṣaḥḥa fī ʾl-riwāyatayn waʾl-thalāth waʾl-arbaʿ ʿan al-imām, ed. ʿA. M. A. al-Ṭayyār and ʿA. M. ʿA. al-Maddallāh, Riyāḍ 1414

Ibn Abī Zarʿ (*fl. c.* 700/1300), *Rawḍ al-qirṭās*, ed. C. J. Tornberg, Uppsala 1843–6

Ibn Abī Zayd al-Qayrawānī (d. 386/996), *al-Jāmiʿ fī ʾl-sunan waʾl-ādāb waʾl-maghāzī waʾl-taʾrīkh*, ed. M. Abū ʾl-Ajfān and ʿU. Baṭṭīkh, Beirut and Tunis 1982

Ibn ʿAdī (d. 365/976), *Kāmil*, Beirut 1984

Ibn al-ʿAdīm (d. 660/1262), *Bughyat al-ṭalab*, ed. S. Zakkār, Damascus 1988–9

Ibn ʿAfāliq al-Aḥsāʾī, Muḥammad ibn ʿAbd al-Raḥmān (d. 1163/1750), epistle to ʿUthmān ibn Muʿammar (1163/1750), ms. Berlin, Pm. 25

Ibn al-Aḥmar (d. 807/1404f.), *Buyūtāt Fās al-kubrā*, Rabat 1972

Ibn al-Amīr al-Ṣanʿānī (d. 1182/1768), *Subul al-salām*, Beirut 1960–71

Taṭhīr al-iʿtiqād ʿan adrān al-ilḥād, ed. M. ʿA. Khafājī, Cairo 1954

Ibn al-ʿArabī (d. 543/1148), *Aḥkām al-Qurʾān*, ed. ʿA. M. al-Bajāwī, Cairo 1957–8

ʿĀriḍat al-aḥwadhī bi-sharḥ Ṣaḥīḥ al-Tirmidhī, Cairo n.d.

al-ʿAwāṣim min al-qawāṣim, ed. ʿA. Ṭālibī, in his *Ārāʾ Abī Bakr ibn al-ʿArabī al-kalāmiyya*, Algiers n.d.

al-Nāsikh waʾl-mansūkh, ed. ʿA. al-ʿAlawī al-M'daghrī, Morocco 1988

al-Qabas fī sharḥ Muwaṭṭaʾ Mālik ibn Anas, ed. M. A. Walad Karīm, Beirut 1992

Ibn al-ʿArabī, Muḥyī ʾl-Dīn (d. 638/1240), *Tafsīr*, Beirut 1968

Ibn al-ʿArīf (d. 536/1141), *Miftāḥ al-saʿāda*, ed. ʿI. ʿA. Dandash, Beirut 1993

Ibn ʿAsākir (d. 571/1176), *Taʾrīkh madīnat Dimashq*, ed. ʿA. Shīrī, Beirut 1995–8 (default edition); *apud* Ibn Manẓūr (d. 711/1311f.), *Mukhtaṣar Taʾrīkh Dimashq li-Ibn ʿAsākir*, ed. R. al-Naḥḥās *et al.*, Damascus 1984–90

Ibn al-Ashʿath (*fl.* first half of fourth/tenth century), *al-Jaʿfariyyāt aw al-Ashʿathiyyāt*, published with Ḥimyarī's *Qurb al-isnād*, Tehran n.d.

Ibn ʿAskar (d. 986/1578), *Dawḥat al-nāshir*, ed. M. Ḥajjī, Rabat 1976

Ibn Aʿtham al-Kūfī (writing 204/819f.), *Futūḥ*, Hyderabad 1968–75

Ibn al-Athīr, ʿIzz al-Dīn (d. 630/1233), *Kāmil*, ed. C. J. Tornberg, Leiden 1851–76
Usd al-ghāba, Cairo 1280–6
Ibn al-Athīr, Majd al-Dīn (d. 606/1210), *Jāmiʿ al-uṣūl*, ed. ʿA. al-Arnāʾūṭ, Cairo 1969–73
Ibn ʿAṭiyya (d. 541/1146), *al-Muḥarrar al-wajīz*, Rabat 1975–
Ibn Bābawayh (d. 381/991f.), *Amālī*, Tehran 1404
Hidāya, printed with his *Muqniʿ*, Qumm and Tehran 1377
ʿIqāb al-aʿmāl, ed. ʿA. A. al-Ghaffārī with the *Thawāb al-aʿmāl*, Tehran 1391
Khiṣāl, Najaf 1971
ʿUyūn akhbār al-Riḍā, Najaf 1970
Ibn al-Bannāʾ (d. 471/1079), see: Makdisi, 'Autograph diary'
Ibn Baraka (fourth/tenth century), *Jāmiʿ*, ed. ʿI. Y. al-Bārūnī, Oman 1971–3 (default: vol. 1)
Ibn al-Barrāj (d. 481/1088), *Muhadhdhab*, Qumm 1406
Ibn Bashkuwāl (d. 578/1183), *Ṣila*, ed. ʿI. al-ʿAṭṭār, Cairo 1955
Ibn Bassām (seventh or eighth/thirteenth or fourteenth century?), *Nihāyat al-rutba*, ed. Ḥ. al-Sāmarrāʾī, Baghdad 1968
Ibn Baṭṭa (d. 387/997), *al-Sharḥ waʾl-ibāna ʿalā uṣūl al-sunna waʾl-diyāna*, see: Laoust, *La profession de foi d'Ibn Baṭṭa*
Ibn Baṭṭūṭa (d. 770/1368f.), *Riḥla*, ed. C. Defrémery and B. R. Sanguinetti, Paris 1853–8
Ibn Bishr (d. 1290/1873), *ʿUnwān al-majd fī taʾrīkh Najd*, Beirut n.d. (default edition); *al-Juzʾ al-awwal min kitāb ʿUnwān al-majd fī taʾrīkh Najd*, Baghdad 1328
Ibn Buluqqīn, ʿAbdallāh (writing *c.* 487/1094), *Tibyān*, ed. A. T. al-Ṭībī, Rabat 1995
Ibn Daqīq al-ʿĪd (d. 702/1302), *ʿAqīda*, in the commentary of Ibrāhīm ibn Abī Sharīf al-Maqdisī (d. 923/1517), *al-ʿIqd al-naḍīd*, ms. Princeton, Yahuda 879
Sharḥ al-Arbaʿīn ḥadīthan al-Nawawiyya, Cairo n.d.
Ibn Fahd al-Ḥillī (d. 841/1437f.), *al-Muhadhdhab al-bāriʿ*, ed. M. al-ʿArāqī, Qumm 1407–13
Ibn al-Faqīh (*fl.* late third/ninth century), *Buldān*, in *Baghdād: Madīnat al-Salām*, ed. Ṣ. A. al-ʿAlī, Baghdad and Paris n.d.
Ibn Faraḥ al-Ishbīlī (d. 699/1300), *Sharḥ al-Arbaʿīn*, ms. Princeton, Yahuda 4,161
Ibn al-Faras al-Gharnāṭī (d. 597/1201), *Aḥkām al-Qurʾān*, fragment edited by M. I. Yaḥyā under the title *Tafsīr sūratay Āl ʿImrān waʾl-Nisāʾ min kitāb Aḥkām al-Qurʾān*, Miṣrātā 1989
Ibn Farḥūn (d. 799/1397), *Tabṣirat al-ḥukkām*, ed. Ṭ. ʿA. Saʿd, Cairo 1986
Ibn al-Fuwaṭī (d. 723/1323) (attrib.), *al-Ḥawādith al-jāmiʿa*, Baghdad 1351
Ibn Ghannām (d. 1225/1810f.), *Rawḍat al-afkār*, Bombay 1337
Ibn Ḥabīb, ʿAbd al-Malik (d. 238/853), *Waṣf al-firdaws*, Beirut 1987
Ibn Ḥabīb, Muḥammad (d. 245/860), *Munammaq*, Hyderabad 1964
Ibn Ḥajar al-ʿAsqalānī (d. 852/1449), *al-Durar al-kāmina*, Hyderabad 1348–50

Inbā' al-ghumr, ed. Ḥ. Ḥabashī, Cairo 1969–72
al-Iṣāba fī tamyīz al-ṣaḥāba, ed. ʿA. M. al-Bajāwī, Cairo 1970–2
Lisān al-Mīzān, Hyderabad 1329–31
Tahdhīb al-Tahdhīb, Hyderabad 1325–7
Ibn Ḥajar al-Haytamī (d. 974/1567), *Fatḥ al-mubīn li-sharḥ al-Arbaʿīn*, Cairo 1352
al-Zawājir ʿan iqtirāf al-kabā'ir, Cairo 1980
Ibn Ḥājj, ʿAlī, *al-Amr bi'l-maʿrūf wal-nahy ʿan al-munkar*, a set of seven cassettes distributed by the Librarie Islamique el-Badr, Paris
'Ijādat al-taḥbīr fī bayān qawāʿid al-taghyīr', *al-Munqidh* (Algiers), 5 Dhū 'l-Ḥijja, 1410
'Man ṣāḥib al-ʿunf?', *al-Munqidh* (Algiers), 28 Jumādā II, 1410
Ibn al-Ḥājj (d. 737/1336f.), *Madkhal*, Cairo 1929
Ibn Ḥamdān (d. 695/1295), *Nihāyat al-mubtadi'īn*, ms. London, British Library, Or. 11,851
Ibn Ḥamdūn (d. 562/1166), *Tadhkira*, ed. I. and B. ʿAbbās, Beirut 1996
Ibn Ḥamza al-Ṭūsī (alive in 566/1171), *Wasīla*, ed. M. al-Ḥassūn, Qumm 1408
Ibn Ḥanbal (d. 241/855), *Aḥkām al-nisā'*, ed. ʿA. A. ʿAṭā, Beirut 1986
al-ʿIlal wa-maʿrifat al-rijāl, ed. W. M. ʿAbbās, Beirut and Riyāḍ 1988
Musnad, Būlāq 1313 (cited by page and line); ed. A. M. Shākir, Cairo 1949–58 (cited by page and number)
Waraʿ, ed. Z. I. al-Qārūṭ, Beirut 1983
Zuhd, Beirut n.d.
Ibn Ḥayyān (d. 469/1076), *Muqtabis*, ed. M. M. Antuña, Paris 1937
Ibn Ḥazm (d. 456/1064), *al-Akhlāq wa'l-siyar*, ed. and trans. N. Tomiche, Beirut 1961
Fiṣal, Cairo 1317–21
al-Iḥkām fī uṣūl al-aḥkām, ed. A. M. Shākir, Cairo 1345–7
Jamharat ansāb al-ʿArab, ed. ʿA. M. Hārūn, Cairo 1982
Muḥallā, ed. A. M. Shākir, Beirut n.d.
Risālat al-talkhīṣ, published with his *al-Radd ʿalā Ibn Naghrīla al-Yahūdī*, ed. I. ʿAbbās, Cairo 1960
Ibn Ḥibbān (d. 354/965), *Kitāb al-majrūḥīn*, ed. M. I. Zāyid, Aleppo 1395–6
Mashāhīr ʿulamā' al-amṣār, ed. M. Fleischhammer, Cairo 1959
Ṣaḥīḥ, in the arrangement of ʿAlā' al-Dīn al-Fārisī (d. 739/1339), ed. ʿA. M. ʿUthmān, Medina 1970–
Thiqāt, Hyderabad 1973–83
Ibn Hishām (d. 218/833), *al-Sīra al-nabawiyya*, ed. M. al-Saqqā *et al.*, Cairo 1955
Ibn al-Humām (d. 861/1457), *Fatḥ al-qadīr*, Cairo 1970
Ibn Ḥumayd (d. 1295/1878), *al-Suḥub al-wābila ʿalā ḍarā'iḥ al-Ḥanābila*, n.p. 1989
Ibn Idrīs (d. 598/1202), *Sarā'ir*, Qumm 1410–11
Ibn al-ʿImād (d. 887/1482), *Kashf al-sarā'ir*, ed. F. ʿA. Aḥmad and M. S. Dāwūd, Alexandria n.d.
Ibn al-ʿImād (d. 1089/1679), *Shadharāt al-dhahab*, ed. ʿA. and M. al-Arnā'ūṭ, Beirut 1986–93

Ibn ʿInaba (d. 828/1424), *ʿUmdat al-ṭālib*, ed. N. Riḍā, Beirut 1390
Ibn Isfandiyār (writing 613/1216f.), *Tārīkh-i Ṭabaristān*, ed. ʿA. Iqbāl, Tehran n.d.
Ibn al-Iskāfī (third/ninth century), *al-Miʿyār wa-ʾl-muwāzana*, ed. M. B. al-Maḥmūdī, Beirut 1981
Ibn ʿIyāḍ, Muḥammad (d. 575/1179f.), *al-Taʿrīf biʾl-Qāḍī ʿIyāḍ*, ed. M. Sharīfa, n.p. n.d.
Ibn Jamāʿa, ʿIzz al-Dīn Muḥammad (d. 819/1416), *al-Tabyīn fī sharḥ al-Arbaʿīn*, ms. Princeton, Yahuda 4,010
Ibn al-Jawzī (d. 597/1201), *Dafʿ shubah al-tashbīh*, ed. M. Z. al-Kawtharī, Cairo 1976
al-Ḥasan al-Baṣrī, ed. Ḥ. al-Sandūbī, Cairo 1931
al-ʿIlal al-mutanāhiya, Beirut 1983
Manāqib al-imām Aḥmad ibn Ḥanbal, ed. M. A. al-Khānjī, Cairo 1349
Minhāj al-qāṣidīn, see: Ibn Qudāma al-Maqdisī, *Mukhtaṣar*
al-Miṣbāḥ al-muḍīʾ, ed. N. ʿA. Ibrāhīm, Baghdad 1976–7
Muntaẓam, Hyderabad 1357–61 (for events from the year 257 on); ed. M. ʿA. and M. ʿA. ʿAṭā, Beirut 1992–3 (for events before the year 257)
Nuzhat al-aʿyun, ed. M. ʿA. K. al-Rāḍī, Beirut 1984
al-Radd ʿalā ʾl-mutaʿaṣṣib al-ʿanīd, ed. M. K. al-Maḥmūdī, n.p. 1983
Ṣayd al-khāṭir, ed. A. Abū Sunayna, Amman 1987
al-Shifāʾ fī mawāʿiẓ al-mulūk waʾl-khulafāʾ, ed. F. ʿA. Aḥmad, Alexandria 1978
Ṣifat al-ṣafwa, ed. M. Fākhūrī, Aleppo 1389–93
Talbīs Iblīs, Beirut n.d.
Zād al-masīr, Damascus and Beirut 1964–8
Ibn Jubayr (d. 614/1217), *Riḥla*, ed. W. Wright and M. J. de Goeje, Leiden and London 1907
Ibn Jumayʿ (eighth/fourteenth century), *ʿAqīda*, in Aḥmad ibn Saʿīd al-Shammākhī (d. 928/1522) and Dāwūd ibn Ibrāhīm al-Talātī (d. 967/1560), *Muqaddimat al-tawḥīd wa-shurūḥuhā*, ed. Ibrāhīm Aṭfayyish, Cairo 1353
Ibn al-Kalbī (d. 204/819f.), *Jamharat al-nasab*, ed. N. Ḥasan, Beirut 1986
Ibn Kathīr (d. 774/1373), *al-Bidāya waʾl-nihāya*, Cairo 1351–8
Ṭabaqāt al-fuqahāʾ al-Shāfiʿiyyīn, ed. A. ʿU. Hāshim and M. Z. M. ʿAzab, Cairo 1993
Tafsīr, Beirut 1966
Ibn Khaldūn (d. 808/1406), *ʿIbar*, Beirut 1956–9
Muqaddima, ed. E. M. Quatremère, Paris 1858
Ibn Khallikān (d. 681/1282), *Wafayāt al-aʿyān*, ed. I. ʿAbbās, Beirut 1971–2
Ibn Māja (d. 273/887), *Sunan*, ed. M. F. ʿAbd al-Bāqī, Cairo 1972
Ibn al-Malāḥimī (d. 536/1141), *al-Fāʾiq fī uṣūl al-dīn*, ms. Ṣanʿāʾ, Great Mosque, *kalām* no. 53
al-Muʿtamad fī uṣūl al-dīn, ed. M. McDermott and W. Madelung, London 1991
Ibn al-Malak (Firishte-oghlu) (*fl.* early eighth/fourteenth century), *Mabāriq al-azhār*, ed. A. ʿA. ʿAbd al-Raḥīm, Beirut 1995
Ibn Manẓūr (d. 711/1311f.), *Lisān al-ʿArab*, Beirut 1968

Ibn Miftāḥ (d. 877/1472), *Muntazaʿ*, Cairo 1332–58
Ibn al-Miʿmār (d. 642/1244), *Futuwwa*, ed. M. Jawād *et al.*, Baghdad 1958
Ibn Mufliḥ (d. 763/1362), *al-Ādāb al-sharʿiyya*, Cairo 1348–9
Ibn Mufliḥ, Burhān al-Dīn (d. 884/1479), *al-Maqṣad al-arshad fī dhikr aṣḥāb al-imām Aḥmad*, ed. ʿA. S. al-ʿUthaymīn, Riyāḍ 1990
Ibn al-Munāṣif (d. 620/1223), *Tanbīh al-ḥukkām*, ed. ʿA. Manṣūr, Tunis 1988
Ibn al-Murajjā, Musharraf (fifth/eleventh century), *Faḍāʾil Bayt al-Maqdis*, ed. O. Livne-Kafri, Shfaram 1995
Ibn al-Murtaḍā (d. 840/1437), *Azhār*, ed. Ṣ. Mūsā with the title *ʿUyūn al-Azhār*, Beirut 1975
al-Baḥr al-zakhkhār, ed. ʿA. M. Ṣadīq and ʿA. S. ʿAṭiyya, Cairo 1947–9
al-Durar al-farāʾid, in the abridgement of Ṣārim al-Dīn al-Ḥayyī, ms. Berlin, Glaser 202
al-Qalāʾid fī taṣḥīḥ al-ʿaqāʾid, ed. A. N. Nādir, Beirut 1985
Ṭabaqāt al-Muʿtazila, ed. S. Diwald-Wilzer, Wiesbaden 1961
Ibn al-Nadīm (d. 380/990), *Fihrist*, Beirut 1978
Ibn al-Naḥḥās (d. 814/1411), *Tanbīh al-ghāfilīn*, ed. ʿI. ʿA. Saʿīd, Beirut 1987
Ibn Nawbakht, Mūsā (*fl.* first half of the fourth/tenth century), *al-Kāmil fī asrār al-nujūm*, ed. and trans. A. Labarta, Madrid 1982
Ibn Paquda (*fl.* later fifth/eleventh century), *al-Hidāya ilā farāʾiḍ al-qulūb*, ed. A. S. Yahuda, Leiden 1912
Ibn Qāḍī ʿAljūn, Abū Bakr (d. 928/1522), *al-Kanz al-akbar fī ʾl-amr biʾl-maʿrūf waʾl-nahy ʿan al-munkar*, ms. Damascus, Ẓāhiriyya, Majmūʿ no. 3,745 *ʿāmm*
Ibn Qāḍī Shuhba (d. 851/1448), *Ṭabaqāt al-Shāfiʿiyya*, ed. ʿA. Khān, Hyderabad 1978–9
Taʾrīkh, ed. ʿA. Darwīsh, Damascus 1977–97
Ibn Qāniʿ (d. 351/962), *Muʿjam al-ṣaḥāba*, ed. Ṣ. S. al-Miṣrātī, Medina 1997
Ibn Qāsim al-ʿĀṣimī, ʿAbd al-Raḥmān (d. 1372/1953), *al-Durar al-saniyya fī ʾl-ajwiba al-Najdiyya*, Beirut 1978
Ibn al-Qaṭṭān (*fl.* mid-seventh/thirteenth century), *Naẓm al-jumān*, ed. M. ʿA. Makkī, Tetouan n.d.
Ibn Qayṣar (writing 1050/1640), *Sīrat al-imām Nāṣir ibn Murshid*, ed. ʿA. Ḥ. al-Qaysī, Oman 1983
Ibn Qayyim al-Jawziyya (d. 751/1350), *Aḥkām ahl al-dhimma*, ed. Ṣ. al-Ṣāliḥ, Beirut 1983
Asmāʾ muʾallafāt Ibn Taymiyya, ed. Ṣ. al-Munajjid, Damascus 1953
Ighāthat al-lahfān, ed. M. S. Kaylānī, Cairo 1961
Iʿlām al-muwaqqiʿīn, Beirut 1973
Miftāḥ dār al-saʿāda, ed. M. Ḥ. Rabīʿ, Cairo 1939
al-Ṭuruq al-ḥukmiyya fī ʾl-siyāsa al-sharʿiyya, ed. M. Ḥ. al-Fiqī, Cairo 1953
Ibn Qiba (d. not later than 319/931), *Naqḍ Kitāb al-ishhād*, see: Modarressi, *Crisis and consolidation*
Ibn Qudāma (d. 620/1223), *Mughnī*, Cairo 1367
Muqniʿ, Cairo n.d.
Rawḍat al-nāẓir, Cairo 1378

Ibn Qudāma al-Maqdisī, Aḥmad ibn ʿAbd al-Raḥmān (d. 689/1290), *Mukhtaṣar Minhāj al-qāṣidīn*, Damascus 1389

Ibn Qūlawayh (d. 368/978), *Kāmil al-ziyārāt*, ed. ʿA. al-Amīnī al-Tabrīzī, Najaf 1356

Ibn Qunfudh al-Qusanṭīnī (d. 810/1407f.), *Uns al-faqīr*, ed. M. al-Fāsī and A. Faure, Rabat 1965

Ibn Qutayba (d. 276/889), *Maʿārif*, ed. T. ʿUkāsha, Cairo 1981

al-Shiʿr waʾl-shuʿarāʾ, ed. M. J. de Goeje, Leiden 1904

Taʾwīl mushkil al-Qurʾān, ed. A. Ṣaqr, Cairo 1954

Ibn Rajab (d. 795/1393), *al-Dhayl ʿalā Ṭabaqāt al-Ḥanābila*, ed. H. Laoust and S. Dahan, Damascus 1951– (for death dates from 460 to 540); ed. M. Ḥ. al-Fiqī, Cairo 1952–3 (for death dates from 541)

al-Farq bayn al-naṣīḥa waʾl-taʿyīr, ed. N. A. Khalaf, Cairo n.d.

Jāmiʿ al-ʿulūm waʾl-ḥikam, Beirut 1987

Sharḥ wa-bayān li-ḥadīth Mā dhiʾbān jāʾiʿān, ed. M. Ṣ. Ḥ. Ḥallāq, Beirut 1992

Ibn Rushd (d. 520/1126), *al-Bayān waʾl-taḥṣīl*, ed. M. Ḥajjī *et al.*, Beirut 1984–91

Fatāwā, ed. M. Ṭ. al-Talīlī, Beirut 1987

al-Muqaddamāt al-mumahhadāt, ed. M. Ḥajjī and S. A. Aʿrāb, Beirut 1988

Ibn Rushd (d. 595/1126), *Bidāyat al-mujtahid*, Cairo 1970–4

Ibn Ruzayq (writing 1274/1857), *al-Fatḥ al-mubīn*, ed. ʿA. ʿĀmir and M. M. ʿAbdallāh, Oman 1977

al-Shuʿāʿ al-shāʾiʿ, ed. ʿA. ʿĀmir, Cairo 1978

Ibn Saʿd (d. 230/845), *al-Ṭabaqāt al-kabīr*, ed. E. Sachau *et al.*, Leiden 1904–21

al-Ṭabaqāt al-kubrā: al-qism al-mutammim li-tābiʿī ahl al-Madīna wa-man baʿdahum, ed. Z. M. Manṣūr, Medina 1983

Ibn Ṣaghīr (later third/ninth century), *Akhbār al-aʾimma al-Rustumiyyīn*, ed. Ḥ. ʿA. Ḥasan, Cairo 1984

Ibn Saḥmān, Sulaymān (d. 1349/1930), *Irshād al-ṭālib ilā ahamm al-maṭālib*, Cairo 1340

Ibn Saḥmān, Sulaymān (d. 1349/1930) (ed.), *al-Hadiyya al-sunniyya waʾl-tuḥfa al-Wahhābiyya al-Najdiyya*, Cairo 1344

Ibn Saʿīd al-Maghribī (d. *c.* 685/1286), *al-Nujūm al-zāhira*, ed. Ḥ. Naṣṣār, Cairo 1970

Ibn Sallām (third/ninth century), *Kitāb fīhi badʾ al-Islām wa-sharāʾiʿ al-dīn*, ed. W. Schwartz and Sālim ibn Yaʿqūb, Wiesbaden 1986

Ibn al-Samīn al-Ḥalabī (d. 756/1355), *al-Durr al-maṣūn*, ed. A. M. al-Kharrāṭ, Damascus 1986–7

Ibn Shuʿba (mid-fourth/tenth century), *Tuḥaf al-ʿuqūl*, ed. ʿA. A. al-Ghaffārī, Tehran 1376

Ibn Sīnā (d. 428/1037), *al-Ishārāt waʾl-tanbīhāt*, ed. J. Forget, Leiden 1892; with the commentary of Naṣīr al-Dīn al-Ṭūsī (d. 672/1274), Tehran 1377–9

Ibn Ṭāwūs (d. 664/1266), *Kashf al-maḥajja*, Najaf 1950

Ibn Taymiyya (d. 728/1328), *al-Amr biʾl-maʿrūf waʾl-nahy ʿan al-munkar*, ed. Ṣ. al-Munajjid, Beirut 1984 (default edition); ed. M. R. Sālim, Cairo 1997; Cairo n.d.

ʿAqīdat ahl al-sunna waʾl-firqa al-nājiya, Cairo 1358

al-ʿAqīda al-Wāsiṭiyya, in his *Majmūʿat al-rasāʾil al-kubrā*, Cairo 1966
Bayān al-dalīl ʿalā buṭlān al-taḥlīl, ed. F. S. ʿA. al-Muṭayrī, Damanhūr 1996
al-Ḥisba fī ʾl-Islām, Kuwait 1983
Iqtiḍāʾ al-ṣirāṭ al-mustaqīm, ed. M. Ḥ. al-Fiqī, Cairo 1950
Istiqāma, ed. M. R. Sālim, Riyāḍ 1983
Majmūʿ fatāwā Shaykh al-Islām Aḥmad ibn Taymiyya, collected and arranged by ʿA. Ibn Qāsim al-ʿĀṣimī, Riyāḍ 1381–6
Majmūʿat al-rasāʾil waʾl-masāʾil, ed. M. Rashīd Riḍā, Cairo 1341–9
Naqḍ al-manṭiq, ed. M. Ḥ. al-Fiqī, Cairo n.d.
Qāʿida fī ʾl-muʿjizāt waʾl-karāmāt, see: Ibn Taymiyya, *Majmūʿat al-rasāʾil waʾl-masāʾil*
al-Siyāsa al-sharʿiyya, Beirut n.d.; trans. Laoust, see: Laoust, *Traité*
ʿUbūdiyya, Damascus 1962
Ibn Taymiyya, Majd al-Dīn (d. 653/1255), *al-Muḥarrar fī ʾl-fiqh*, Cairo 1950
Ibn Ṭayy (d. 855/1451), *al-Durr al-manḍūd*, ed. M. Barakat, Shīrāz 1418
Ibn Tūmart (d. 524/1130), *Aʿazz ma yuṭlab*, see: Goldziher, *Livre*; also ed. ʿA. Ṭālibī, Algiers 1985
Ibn Ṭumlūs (d. 620/1223f.), *al-Madkhal li-ṣināʿat al-manṭiq*, ed. M. Asín, Madrid 1916
Ibn al-Ukhuwwa (d. 729/1329), *Maʿālim al-qurba fī aḥkām al-ḥisba*, ed. R. Levy, London 1938
Ibn Waḍḍāḥ, Muḥammad (d. 287/900), *Kitāb al-bidaʿ*, ed. and trans. M. I. Fierro, Madrid 1988
Ibn Wahb, ʿAbdallāh (d. 197/813), *Jāmiʿ*, fragment edited by M. Muranyi under the subtitle *Die Koranwissenschaften*, Wiesbaden 1992
Ibn al-Walīd, ʿAlī ibn Muḥammad (d. 612/1215), *Tāj al-ʿaqāʾid*, ed. ʿA. Tāmir, Beirut 1967
Ibn al-Wazīr (d. 840/1436), *al-Rawḍ al-bāsim fī ʾl-dhabb ʿan sunnat Abī ʾl-Qāsim*, Cairo n.d.
Ibn Zanjawayh (d. 251/865f.), *Amwāl*, ed. S. D. Fayyāḍ, Riyāḍ 1986
Ibn al-Zayyāt (d. *c.* 628/1230), *al-Tashawwuf ila rijāl al-taṣawwuf*, ed. A. al-Tawfīq, Rabat 1984
Ibrahim, S. E., 'Islamic militancy as a social movement: the case of two groups in Egypt', in A. E. H. Dessouki (ed.), *Islamic resurgence in the Arab world*, New York 1982
Idris, H. R., *La Berbérie orientale sous les Zīrīdes*, Paris 1962
'Essai sur la diffusion de l'ašʿarisme en Ifrîqiya', *Les Cahiers de Tunisie*, 1 (1953)
Ifrānī (d. *c.* 1155/1742), *Nuzhat al-ḥādī*, ed. O. Houdas, Paris 1888
Ījī (d. 756/1355), *al-ʿAqīda al-ʿAḍudiyya*, see: Dawānī, *Sharḥ*
Mawāqif, with the *Sharḥ* of al-Sayyid al-Sharīf al-Jurjānī (d. 816/1413), ed. T. Soerensen, Leipzig 1848
ʿIjlī (d. 261/874f.), *Taʾrīkh al-thiqāt*, in the rearrangement of Haythamī (d. 807/1405), ed. ʿA. Qalʿajī, Beirut 1984
Ilāhī, Faḍl, *al-Ḥisba: taʿrīfuhā wa-mashrūʿiyyatuhā wa-wujūbuhā*, Gujranwala 1993
Imām, M. K., *Uṣūl al-ḥisba fī ʾl-Islām: dirāsa taʾṣīliyya muqārina*, Cairo 1986

Imāmzāda (d. 573/1177f.), *Shirʿat al-Islām*, ms. Princeton, Garrett 836H; and see: Yaʿqūb ibn Seyyid ʿAlī, *Sharḥ*
ʿImrānī, see: Yaḥyā ibn Muḥammad
Īraj Mīrzā (d. 1344/1926), *Dīwān-i kāmil*, ed. M. J. Maḥjūb, Van Nuys, Ca. 1989
Isḥāq ibn Ibrāhīm ibn Hāniʾ al-Naysābūrī (d. 275/888f.), *Masāʾil al-imām Aḥmad ibn Ḥanbal*, ed. Z. al-Shāwīsh, Beirut and Damascus 1400
Isḥāq ibn Ibrāhīm ibn Sulaymān ibn Wahb al-Kātib (writing after 334/946), *al-Burhān fī wujūh al-bayān*, ed. A. Maṭlūb and K. al-Ḥadīthī, Baghdad 1967
Isḥāq ibn Wahb, see: Isḥāq ibn Ibrāhīm ibn Sulaymān ibn Wahb al-Kātib
Islāmī, ʿAbbās-ʿAlī, *Do az yād rafta: amr bah maʿrūf wa nahy az munkar*, Tehran 1354 sh.
Islāmī Ardakānī, Ḥasan, *Amr bah maʿrūf wa nahy az munkar*, Qumm 1375 sh.
Islamic Propagation Organization, *The Constitution of the Islamic Republic of Iran*, Tehran n.d.
Ismāʿīl Ḥaqqī Brūsevī (d. 1137/1725), *Rūḥ al-bayān*, Istanbul 1389
Sharḥ al-Arbaʿīn ḥadīthan (in Turkish), Istanbul 1253
Ismāʿīl Niyāzī (thirteenth/nineteenth century), *Sharḥ-i Niyāzī ʿalā ʾl-Qūnawī* (in Turkish), Istanbul 1264
Ismāʿīl Pāshā al-Baghdādī (d. 1339/1920), *Hadiyyat al-ʿārifīn*, Istanbul 1951–5
ʿIṣmat Allāh ibn Aʿẓam ibn ʿAbd al-Rasūl (d. 1133/1720f.), *Raqīb bāb al-maʿrūf waʾl-munkar*, ms. London, India Office, Delhi (Persian) 219
Isnawī (d. 772/1370), *Ṭabaqāt al-Shāfiʿiyya*, ed. ʿA. al-Jubūrī, Baghdad 1970–1
Iʿtimād al-Salṭana, Muḥammad Ḥasan Khān (d. 1313/1896), *Chihil sāl-i tārīkh-i Īrān*, ed. I. Afshār, Tehran 1363–8 sh.
Ivanow, W., *A creed of the Fatimids*, Bombay 1936
ʿIyāḍ, Qāḍī (d. 544/1149), *Ikmāl al-Muʿlim*, ms. Dublin, Chester Beatty, no. 3,836
Tartīb al-madārik, ed. A. B. Maḥmūd, Beirut n.d.
Izkawī (twelfth/eighteenth century), *Kashf al-ghumma*, ms. London, British Library, Or. 8,076; ed. A. ʿUbaydalī, Nicosia 1985
Izutsu, T., *Ethico-religious concepts in the Qurʾān*, Montreal 1966
ʿIzz al-Dīn ibn ʿAbd al-Salām (d. 660/1262), *Qawāʿid al-aḥkām*, Cairo n.d.
Izzi Dien, M., *The theory and the practice of market law in medieval Islam*, Warminster 1997
Jabartī (d. 1240/1824f.), *ʿAjāʾib al-āthār*, ed. Ḥ. M. Jawhar *et al.*, Cairo 1958–67; Beirut n.d.
Jabre, F., 'La biographie et l'oeuvre de Ghazālī reconsidérées à la lumière des *Ṭabaqāt* de Sobkī', in *MIDEO*, 1 (1954)
Jacob, G., *Altarabisches Beduinenleben*, Berlin 1897
Jadʿān, F., *al-Miḥna*, Amman 1989
Jaʿdī (*fl.* later sixth/twelfth century), *Ṭabaqāt fuqahāʾ al-Yaman*, ed. F. Sayyid, Cairo 1957
Jaʿfarīyān, R., 'Amr bah maʿrūf wa nahy az munkar dar dawra-i Ṣafawī', *Kayhān-i Andīsha*, 82 (1377 sh.)
Dīn wa siyāsat dar dawra-i Ṣafawī, Qumm 1370 sh.

Jaʿfar al-Ṣādiq (d. 148/765) (attrib.), *Miṣbāḥ al-sharīʿa*, Beirut 1961
Jāḥiẓ (d. 255/868f.), *Banū Umayya* (= *Nābita*), in his *Rasāʾil*, ed. Ḥ. al-Sandūbī, Cairo 1933
al-Bayān waʾl-tabyīn, ed. ʿA. M. Hārūn, Cairo 1948–50
Faḍl Hāshim ʿalā ʿAbd Shams, in Ḥ. al-Sandūbī (ed.), *Rasāʾil al-Jāḥiẓ*, Cairo 1933
Kitmān al-sirr wa-ḥifẓ al-lisān, in ʿA. M. Hārūn (ed.), *Rasāʾil al-Jāḥiẓ*, Cairo 1964–79
Risālat al-qiyān, ed. and trans. A. F. L. Beeston, Warminster 1980
Jakanī, Muḥammad al-Amīn ibn Aḥmad Zaydān al- (d. *c.* 1325/1907), *Sharḥ*, ed. H. ʿA. M. Aḥmad Zaydān, Beirut 1993
Jāmī (d. 898/1492), *Mathnawī-i haft awrang*, ed. M. Gīlānī, Tehran 1337 sh.
Janadī (d. 732/1331f.), *al-Sulūk fī ṭabaqāt al-ʿulamāʾ waʾl-mulūk*, ed. M. ʿA. Ḥ. al-Akwaʿ al-Ḥiwālī, Yemen 1983–
Jarrar, M., 'Bišr al-Ḥāfī und die Barfüssigkeit im Islam', *Der Islam*, 71 (1994)
Jāsir, Ḥ. al-, 'al-Ṣilāt bayn Ṣanʿāʾ waʾl-Dirʿiyya', *al-ʿArab*, 22 (1987)
Jaṣṣāṣ (d. 370/981), *Aḥkām al-Qurʾān*, Istanbul 1335–8
Jawād al-Kāẓimī (writing 1043/1633), *Masālik al-afhām*, ed. M. T. al-Kashfī and M. B. al-Bihbūdī, Tehran *c.* 1347 sh.
Jawharī (d. *c.* 398/1007), *Ṣiḥāḥ*, ed. A. ʿA. ʿAṭṭār, Cairo 1377
Jayṭālī (d. 750/1349f.), *Qanāṭir al-khayrāt*, Oman 1983
Jazāʾirī, ʿAbd al-Qādir al- (d. 1300/1883), *Mawāqif*, Damascus 1966–7
Jazāʾirī, Abū Bakr Jābir al-, *Aysar al-tafāsīr*, Medina 1994
Jazāʾirī, Aḥmad al- (d. 1151/1738f.), *Qalāʾid al-durar*, Najaf 1382–3
Jeffery, A., *Materials for the history of the text of the Qurʾān*, Leiden 1937
'The Qurʾān readings of Zaid b. ʿAlī', *Rivista degli Studi Orientali*, 16 (1937)
A reader on Islam, The Hague 1962
Jehl, Douglas, 'New US–Iran dialogue', *The New York Times*, 6 June 1999
Jishumī, al-Ḥākim al- (d. 494/1101), *Risālat Iblīs ilā ikhwānihi al-manāḥīs*, ed. Ḥ. al-Mudarrisī al-Ṭabāṭabāʾī, n.p. 1986
Sharḥ ʿUyūn al-masāʾil, ms. Leiden, Or. 2,584–B
al-Tahdhīb fī tafsīr al-Qurʾān, ms. Milan, Ambrosiana, F 184
al-ʿUyūn fī ʾl-radd ʿalā ahl al-bidaʿ, ms. Milan, Ambrosiana, B 66
Johansen, B., 'Commercial exchange and social order in Ḥanafite law', in C. Toll and J. Skovgaard-Petersen (eds.), *Law and the Islamic world past and present*, Copenhagen 1995
Jolivet, J., 'The Arabic inheritance', in P. Dronke (ed.), *A history of twelfth-century Western philosophy*, Cambridge 1988
Jolowicz, H. F., and B. Nicholas, *Historical introduction to the study of Roman law*, Cambridge 1972
Jomier, J., *Le commentaire coranique du Manâr*, Paris 1954
Judah ha-Levi (d. AD 1141), *Kitāb al-radd waʾl-dalīl*, ed. D. H. Baneth, Jerusalem 1977
Juhany, U. M. Al-, 'The history of Najd prior to the Wahhābīs', University of Washington Ph.D. 1983

Juhaymān al-ʿUtaybī (d. 1400/1980), *Rasāʾil Juhaymān al-ʿUtaybī qāʾid al-muqtaḥimīn lil-Masjid al-Ḥarām bi-Makka*, ed. R. S. Aḥmad, Cairo 1988
Jumayyil ibn Khamīs al-Saʿdī (*fl.* early thirteenth/nineteenth century), *Qāmūs al-sharīʿa*, Zanzibar 1297–9
Jurjānī, Abū ʾl-Fatḥ al- (d. 976/1568f.), *Tafsīr-i shāhī*, ed. W. al-Ishrāqī, Tabrīz 1380
Jurjānī, Abū ʾl-Maḥāsin (ninth or tenth/fifteenth or sixteenth century?), *Jilāʾ al-adhhān* (in Persian), n.p. 1378
Jurjānī, al-Sayyid al-Sharīf al- (d. 816/1413), *Taʿrīfāt*, ed. ʿA. ʿUmayra, Beirut 1987
Jurmūzī (d. 1077/1667), *al-Nubdha al-mushīra*, ms. London, British Library, Or. 3,329 (also published in facsimile, n.p. n.d.)
Jushamī, see: Jishumī
Justi, F., *Iranisches Namenbuch*, Marburg 1895
Justinian (r. AD 527–65), *Digest*, ed. T. Mommsen and trans. A. Watson, Philadelphia 1985
Juwaynī (d. 478/1085), *Ghiyāth al-umam*, ed. F. ʿA. Aḥmad and M. Ḥilmī, Alexandria 1979
al-Irshād ilā qawāṭiʿ al-adilla fī uṣūl al-iʿtiqād, ed. M. Y. Mūsā and ʿA. ʿA. ʿAbd al-Ḥamīd, Cairo 1950
Juwaynī (d. 681/1283), *Tārīkh-i jahān-gushā*, ed. Muḥammad Qazwīnī, Leiden and London 1912–37
Kadri, Hüseyin Kâzım (d. 1352/1934), *İnsan hakları beyannamesi'nin İslâm hukukuna göre izahı*, Istanbul 1949
Kaeuper, R. W., and E. Kennedy, *The Book of Chivalry of Geoffroi de Charny*, Philadelphia 1996
Kaḥḥāla, ʿU. R., *Muʿjam al-muʾallifīn*, Damascus 1957–61
al-Mustadrak ʿalā Muʿjam al-muʾallifīn, Beirut 1985
Kāmil, ʿAbd al-ʿAzīz, 'Ḥuqūq al-insān fī ʾl-Islām: naẓra fī ʾl-mushkilāt al-nawʿiyya', in Université de Tunis, Centre d'Etudes et de Recherches Economiques et Sociales, IIème Rencontre Islamo-Chrétienne, *Droits de l'homme*, Tunis 1985
Karakī (d. 940/1534), *Fawāʾid al-Sharāʾiʿ*, ms. Princeton, Arabic Manuscripts, New Series 695
Jāmiʿ al-maqāṣid, Qumm 1408–11
Karaman, H., 'İslâmda içtimaî terbiye ve kontrol', in H. Karaman, *İslâmın ışığında günün meseleleri*, Istanbul 1988
Karamī, Muḥammad al-, *Tafsīr*, Qumm 1402
Karamustafa, A. T., *God's unruly friends: dervish groups in the Islamic later middle period, 1200–1550*, Salt Lake City 1994
Kāsānī (d. 587/1191), *Badāʾiʿ al-ṣanāʾiʿ*, Cairo 1327–8
Kāshānī, Fatḥ Allāh (d. 988/1580f.), *Manhaj al-ṣādiqīn* (in Persian), Tehran 1336–7 sh.
Kāshif, S. I. (ed.), *al-Siyar waʾl-jawābāt li-ʿulamāʾ wa-aʾimmat ʿUmān*, Oman 1986–8
Kāshif al-Ghiṭāʾ (d. 1227/1812), *Kashf al-ghiṭāʾ*, Iṣfahān n.d.
Kāshifī, Ḥusayn Wāʿiẓ (d. 910/1504f.), *Mawāhib-i ʿaliyya*, Tehran 1317–29 sh.

Kashshī (*fl.* first half of the fourth/tenth century), *Rijāl*, ed. Ḥ. al-Muṣṭafawī, Mashhad 1348 sh.
Kātib Chelebi (d. 1067/1657), *Mīzān al-ḥaqq* (in Turkish), Istanbul 1306; trans. G. L. Lewis, *The balance of truth*, London 1957
Kātib Chelebi, see also: Ḥājjī Khalīfa
Kattānī (d. 1345/1927), *al-Risāla al-mustaṭrafa*, Damascus 1964
Kawākibī, ʿAbd al-Raḥmān al- (d. 1320/1902), *Ṭabāʾiʿ al-istibdād*, Cairo n.d.
Kemālpāshāzāde (d. 940/1534), *al-Risāla al-munīra*, n.p. 1296
Kepel, G., *Les banlieues de l'Islam*, Paris 1987
Kerr, M. H., *Islamic reform: the political and legal theories of Muḥammad ʿAbduh and Rashīd Riḍā*, Berkeley and Los Angeles 1966
Khādimī (d. 1176/1762f.), *Barīqa Maḥmūdiyya*, Cairo 1348
Khalīfa ibn Khayyāṭ (d. 240/854f.), *Ṭabaqāt*, ed. S. Zakkār, Beirut 1993
Taʾrīkh, ed. A. Ḍ. al-ʿUmarī, Najaf 1967
Khalīl ibn Aḥmad (d. 170/786f.), *Kitāb al-ʿayn*, ed. M. al-Makhzūmī and I. al-Sāmarrāʾī, Qumm 1405–10
Khalīl ibn Isḥāq (d. 767/1365), *Mukhtaṣar*, ed. Ṭ. A. al-Zāwī, Cairo n.d.
Khalīlī (d. 1287/1871) (attrib.), *al-Akhbār waʾl-āthār*, Oman 1984
Tamhīd qawāʿid al-īmān, Oman 1986–7 (default: vol. 7)
Khalkhālī, Ṣādiq, *Risāla-i tawḍīḥ al-masāʾil*, Qumm 1372 sh.
Khallāl, Abū Bakr al- (d. 311/923), *al-Amr biʾl-maʿrūf waʾl-nahy ʿan al-munkar*, ed. ʿA. A. ʿAṭā, Cairo 1975 (default edition); ed. I. al-Anṣārī, Cairo n.d.; ms. Hebrew University, MS AP AR° 158 (cited as J)
al-Musnad min masāʾil Abī ʿAbdillāh Aḥmad ibn Muḥammad ibn Ḥanbal, ed. Z. Ahmed, Dacca 1975
Khāminaʾī, ʿAlī, speech reported in 'Amr bah maʿrūf wa nahy az munkar bāyad hamānand-i namāz farāgīr shawad', in *Jumhūrī-i Islāmī*, 23 Tīr, 1371 sh.
Khāminaʾī, Muḥammad, 'al-Ḥuqūq al-insāniyya lil-marʾa fī ʾl-Islām wa-fī ʾl-qawānīn al-waḍʿiyya', in *Ḥuqūq al-insān fī ʾl-Islām: maqālāt al-Muʾtamar al-khāmis lil-fikr al-Islāmī*, Tehran 1987
Khāraqānī (d. 1355/1936), *Maḥw al-mawhūm*, n.p. 1379
Kharashī (d. 1101/1690), *Sharḥ* to the *Mukhtaṣar* of Khalīl (d. 767/1365), Būlāq 1317–18
Kharrāzī, Muḥsin al-, *al-Amr biʾl-maʿrūf waʾl-nahy ʿan al-munkar*, Qumm 1415
Khaṭīb, ʿA. al-, *Muḥammad Bahjat al-Bayṭār: ḥayātuhu wa-āthāruhu*, Damascus 1976
Khaṭīb al-Baghdādī, al- (d. 463/1071), *Mūḍiḥ awhām al-jamʿ waʾl-tafrīq*, Hyderabad 1959–60
Sharaf aṣḥāb al-ḥadīth, ed. M. S. Hatîboğlu, Ankara 1972
Taʾrīkh Baghdād, Cairo 1931
Khaṭṭābī (d. 388/998), *ʿUzla*, ed. Y. M. al-Sawwās, Damascus and Beirut 1987
Khayr al-Dīn Pāshā (d. 1307/1890), *Muqaddimat kitāb Aqwam al-masālik*, Istanbul 1293
Khayyāṭ (d. *c.* 300/912), *Intiṣār*, ed. and trans. A. N. Nader, Beirut 1957
Khāzin (d. 741/1341), *Lubāb al-taʾwīl*, Cairo 1328

Khiḍr, Muḥammad Aḥmad, *al-Islām wa-ḥuqūq al-insān*, Beirut 1980
Khiraqī (d. 334/945f.), *Mukhtaṣar*, ed. M. Z. al-Shāwīsh, Damascus 1378
Khomeini, see: Khumaynī
Khudākaramī, Abū ʿAlī, *Do aṣl-i ustuwār yā amr bah maʿrūf wa nahy az munkar*, Qumm 1375 sh.
Khūʾī (d. 1413/1992), *Minhāj al-ṣāliḥīn*, *apud* Taqī al-Ṭabāṭabāʾī al-Qummī, *Mabānī Minhāj al-ṣāliḥīn*, Qumm 1405–11
Khūlī, ʿAbd al-Khabīr al-, *Qāʾid al-daʿwa al-Islāmiyya Ḥasan al-Bannā*, Cairo 1952
Khumaynī (d. 1409/1989), *al-Ḥukūma al-Islāmiyya*, n.p. n.d.
Istiftāʾāt (in Persian), Qumm 1366–72 sh.
Risāla-i nawīn, Tehran 1359–67 sh., vol. 4: *Masāʾil-i siyāsī wa ḥuqūqī*, collected by ʿAbd al-Karīm Bī-āzār Shīrāzī
Risāla-i tawḍīḥ al-masāʾil, Tehran 1399 (default edition); n.p. 1342 sh.; trans. J. Borujerdi as Khomeini, *A clarification of questions*, Boulder and London 1984
Ṣaḥīfa-i nūr: majmūʿa-i rāhnamūd-hā-yi imām Khumaynī, compiled by the Markaz-i Madārik-i Farhangī-i Inqilāb-i Islāmī, Tehran 1361–9 sh.
Taḥrīr al-Wasīla, Beirut 1981
Wilāyat-i faqīh dar khuṣūṣ-i ḥukūmat-i Islāmī, n.p. n.d.
Khunjī (d. 927/1521), *Sulūk al-mulūk*, ed. M. ʿA. Muwaḥḥid, Tehran 1362 sh.
Khushanī (d. 361/971), *Akhbār al-fuqahāʾ waʾl-muḥaddithīn*, ed. M. L. Ávila and L. Molina, Madrid 1992
Quḍāt Qurṭuba, ed. ʿI. al-ʿAṭṭār al-Ḥusaynī, n.p. 1372
Khwājazāde al-Aqshehrī (eleventh/seventeenth century), *Ḥāshiya ʿalā ʾl-Ṭarīqa al-Muḥammadiyya*, ms. Istanbul, Süleymaniye, Fatih 2,607
Khwānsārī (d. 1313/1895), *Rawḍat al-jannāt*, Tehran and Qumm 1390–2
Khwānsārī (d. 1405/1985), *Jāmiʿ al-madārik*, Tehran 1383–92
Khwārazmī, Jamāl al-Dīn Muḥammad ibn ʿAbdallāh al-Shāfiʿī al- (d. 679/1280f?), *Dhukhr al-muntahī fī ʾl-ʿilm al-jalī waʾl-khafī*, ms. London, British Library, Add. 7,275
Kindī (d. 350/961), *Quḍāt*, in R. Guest (ed.), *The governors and judges of Egypt*, Leiden and London 1912
Wulāt, in R. Guest (ed.), *The governors and judges of Egypt*, Leiden and London 1912
Kindī, Abū ʿAbdallāh al- (d. towards 508/1114), *Bayān al-sharʿ*, Oman 1982–93 (default: vol. 29)
Kindī, Abū Bakr al- (d. *c.* 557/1161), *Muṣannaf*, Cairo and Maṭraḥ 1979–84 (default: vol. 12)
Kirmānī, Abū ʾl-Qāsim Khān (d. 1389/1969), *Fihrist*, Kirmān n.d.
Kirmānī, Muḥammad Karīm Khān (d. 1288/1871), *Faṣl al-khiṭāb*, Kirmān 1392
Risāla dar jawāb-i suʾālāt-i Niẓām al-ʿUlamāʾ, translated from the Arabic by Ḥusayn Āl-i Hāshimī, Kirmān n.d.
Sī faṣl, Kirmān 1368
Kisāʾī (uncertain date), *Qiṣaṣ al-anbiyāʾ*, ed. I. Eisenberg, Leiden 1922–3

Kister, M. J., 'Some reports concerning Mecca from Jāhiliyya to Islam', *Journal of the Economic and Social History of the Orient*, 15 (1972)

Studies in Jāhiliyya and early Islam, London 1980

Koch, A., and A. Preuss, *A handbook of moral theology*, St Louis, Mo. and London 1924

Kohlberg, E., 'Aspects of Akhbari thought in the seventeenth and eighteenth centuries', in N. Levtzion and J. O. Voll (eds.), *Eighteenth-century renewal and reform in Islam*, Syracuse 1987

'Authoritative scriptures in early Imāmī Shīʿism', in E. Patlagean and A. Le Boulluec (eds.), *Les retours aux écritures*, Louvain and Paris 1993

'The development of the Imāmī Shīʿī doctrine of *jihād*', *Zeitschrift der Deutschen Morgenländischen Gesellschaft*, 126 (1976)

A medieval Muslim scholar at work: Ibn Ṭāwūs and his library, Leiden 1992

'Medieval Muslim views on martyrdom', in Koninklijke Nederlandse Akademie van Wetenschappen, *Mededelingen*, Afdeling Letterkunde, 60 (1997)

'Some notes on the Imāmite attitude to the Qur'ān', in S. M. Stern *et al.* (eds.), *Islamic philosophy and the classical tradition: essays presented by his friends and pupils to Richard Walzer*, Oxford 1972

'*Al-uṣūl al-arbaʿumiʾa*', *Jerusalem Studies in Arabic and Islam*, 10 (1987)

Kraemer, J. L., *Humanism in the Renaissance of Islam: the cultural revival during the Buyid age*, Leiden 1986

Kraus, P., '*Kitāb al-akhlāq* li-Jālīnūs', *Majallat Kulliyyat al-ādāb biʾl-Jāmiʿa al-Miṣriyya*, 5 (1937)

Krenkow, F. (ed.), *The poems of Ṭufail ibn ʿAuf al-Ghanawī and aṭ-Ṭirimmāḥ ibn Ḥakīm aṭ-Ṭāʾyī*, London 1927

Kritzeck, J., *Peter the Venerable and Islam*, Princeton 1964

Kudamī (fourth/tenth century), *Muʿtabar*, Ruwī 1984

Kūfī, Muḥammad ibn Sulaymān al- (alive in 309/921), *Muntakhab*, Ṣanʿāʾ 1993

Kulaynī (d. 329/941), *Kāfī*, ed. ʿA. A. al-Ghaffārī, Tehran 1375–7

Kupferschmidt, U. M., *The Supreme Muslim Council: Islam under the British Mandate for Palestine*, Leiden 1987

Kūrānī, ʿAlī, *Amr bah maʿrūf wa nahy az munkar*, Tehran 1373 sh.

Labat, S., 'Islamism and Islamists: the emergence of new types of politico-religious militants', in J. Ruedy (ed.), *Islamism and secularism in North Africa*, New York 1994

Labīdī, Ḥ. al-, *Daʿāwā ʾl-ḥisba*, Asyūṭ 1983

Lagardère, V., 'Une théologie dogmatique de la frontière en al-Andalus aux XIe et XIIe siècles: l'ašʿarisme', in *Anaquel de Estudios Árabes*, 5 (1994)

Lambton, A. K. S., 'A reconsideration of the position of the *marjaʿ al-taqlīd* and the religious institution', *Studia Islamica*, 20 (1964)

State and government in medieval Islam, Oxford 1981

Landau-Tasseron, E., 'Zaydī imams as restorers of religion: *iḥyāʾ* and *tajdīd* in Zaydī literature', *Journal of Near Eastern Studies*, 49 (1990)

Landen, R. G., *Oman since 1856*, Princeton 1967

Lane, E. W., *An Arabic–English lexicon*, London 1863–93

Laoust, H., 'Les agitations religieuses à Baghdād aux IVe et Ve siècles de l'Hégire', in D. S. Richards (ed.), *Islamic civilisation 950–1150*, Oxford 1973

'La biographie d'Ibn Taimīya d'après Ibn Kaṯīr', *Bulletin d'Etudes Orientales*, 9 (1942–3)

Essai sur les doctrines sociales et politiques de Taḳī-d-Dīn Aḥmad b. Taimīya, Cairo 1939

'Le hanbalisme sous le califat de Bagdad', *Revue des Etudes Islamiques*, 27 (1959)

'Le hanbalisme sous les Mamlouks bahrides', *Revue des Etudes Islamiques*, 28 (1960)

'La pensée et l'action politiques d'al-Māwardī', *Revue des Etudes Islamiques*, 36 (1968)

La politique de Ġazālī, Paris 1970

'Les premières professions de foi hanbalites', in *Mélanges Louis Massignon*, Damascus 1956–7, vol. 3

La profession de foi d'Ibn Baṭṭa, Damascus 1958

La profession de foi d'Ibn Taymiyya, Paris 1986

'La survie de Ġazālī d'après Subkī', *Bulletin d'Etudes Orientales*, 25 (1972)

Le traité de droit public d'Ibn Taimīya, Beirut 1948

Lapidus, I. M., *Muslim cities in the later middle ages*, Cambridge, Mass. 1967

'The separation of state and religion in the development of early Islamic society', *International Journal of Middle East Studies*, 6 (1975)

Laqānī, ʿAbd al-Salām ibn Ibrāhīm al- (d. 1078/1668), *Itḥāf al-murīd*, Cairo 1955

Laqānī, Ibrāhīm al- (d. 1041/1631), *Hidāyat al-murīd*, ms. Princeton, Yahuda 504

Lārī, Muṣliḥ al-Dīn al- (d. 979/1572), *Sharḥ al-Arbaʿīn*, ms. Princeton, Yahuda 5,067

Layish, A., '*ʿUlamāʾ* and politics in Saudi Arabia', in M. Heper and R. Israeli (eds.), *Islam and politics in the modern Middle East*, New York 1984

Lazard, G., *La langue des plus anciens monuments de la prose persane*, Paris 1963

Lazarus-Yafeh, H., *Intertwined worlds: medieval Islam and Bible criticism*, Princeton 1992

Le Strange, G., *Baghdad during the Abbasid caliphate*, Oxford 1900

The lands of the eastern caliphate, Cambridge 1905

Le Tourneau, R., *The Almohad movement in North Africa in the twelfth and thirteenth centuries*, Princeton 1969

Lecker, M., *The Banū Sulaym*, Jerusalem 1989

Leder, S., *Ibn al-Ǧauzī und seine Kompilation wider die Leidenschaft*, Beirut 1984

Leemhuis, F., 'MS. 1075 Tafsīr of the Cairene Dār al-Kutub and Muǧāhid's *Tafsīr*', in R. Peters (ed.), *Proceedings of the Ninth Congress of the Union Européenne des Arabisants et Islamisants*, Leiden 1981

'Origins and early development of the *tafsīr* tradition', in A. Rippin (ed.), *Approaches to the history of the interpretation of the Qurʾān*, Oxford 1988

Legge, J. (ed. and trans.), *The Chinese classics*, Hong Kong and London 1861–72

Lehmkuhl, A., *Theologia moralis*, Freiburg im Breisgau 1898

Leo XIII, see: Wynne, J. J.

Lévi-Provençal, E., 'Un document sur la vie urbaine et les corps de métiers à Séville au début du XIIe siècle: le traité d'Ibn ʿAbdūn', *Journal Asiatique*, 224 (1934)
Lévi-Provençal, E. (ed.), *Documents inédits d'histoire almohade*, Paris 1928
Trois traités hispaniques de ḥisba, Cairo 1955
Levy, R., *The social structure of Islam*, Cambridge 1957
Lewicki, T., 'Les historiens, biographes et traditionnistes ibāḍites–wahbites de l'Afrique du Nord du VIIIe au XVIe siècle', *Folia Orientalia*, 3 (1961)
'Les subdivisions de l'Ibāḍiyya', *Studia Islamica*, 9 (1958)
Lewinstein, K., 'The Azāriqa in Islamic heresiography', *Bulletin of the School of Oriental and African Studies*, 54 (1991)
Lewis, B., *The political language of Islam*, Chicago and London 1988
Little, D. P., 'Did Ibn Taymiyya have a screw loose?', *Studia Islamica*, 41 (1975)
'The historical and historiographical significance of the detention of Ibn Taymiyya', *International Journal of Middle East Studies*, 4 (1973)
'Religion under the Mamluks', *The Muslim World*, 73 (1983)
Loewe, M. (ed.), *Early Chinese texts: a bibliographical guide*, Berkeley 1993
Löfgren, O., and R. Traini, *Catalogue of the Arabic manuscripts in the Biblioteca Ambrosiana*, Vicenza 1975–
Longrigg, S. H., *ʿIraq, 1900 to 1950*, London 1953
Lorimer, J. G., *Gazetteer of the Persian Gulf*, Calcutta 1908–15
Mach, R., *Catalogue of Arabic manuscripts (Yahuda Section) in the Garrett Collection, Princeton University Library*, Princeton 1977
Mach, R., and E. L. Ormsby, *Handlist of Arabic manuscripts (New Series) in the Princeton University Library*, Princeton 1987
Mack, E. 'Deontologism, negative causation, and the duty to rescue', in E. Regis Jr. (ed.), *Gewirth's ethical rationalism*, Chicago and London 1984
Madelung, W., 'Amr be maʿrūf', in *Encyclopaedia Iranica*, London 1982–
'The assumption of the title Shāhānshāh by the Būyids and "the reign of the Daylam" (*dawlat al-Daylam*)', *Journal of Near Eastern Studies*, 28 (1969)
'The early Murjiʾa in Khurāsān and Transoxania and the spread of Ḥanafism', *Der Islam*, 59 (1982)
'Zu einigen Werken des Imams Abū Ṭālib an-Nāṭiq bi l-Ḥaqq', *Der Islam*, 63 (1986)
'Frühe muʿtazilitische Häresiographie: das *Kitāb al-Uṣūl* des Ǧaʿfar b. Ḥarb?', *Der Islam*, 57 (1980)
Der Imam al-Qāsim ibn Ibrāhīm und die Glaubenslehre der Zaiditen, Berlin 1965
'Imam al-Qāsim ibn Ibrāhīm and Muʿtazilism', in *On both sides of al-Mandab: Ethiopian, South-Arabic and Islamic studies presented to Oscar Löfgren on his ninetieth birthday*, Swedish Research Institute in Istanbul, *Transactions*, 2 (1989)
'New documents concerning al-Maʾmūn, al-Faḍl b. Sahl and ʿAlī al-Riḍā', in W. al-Qāḍī (ed.), *Studia Arabica et Islamica: Festschrift for Iḥsān ʿAbbās*, Beirut 1981
Religious schools and sects in medieval Islam, London 1985

Religious trends in early Islamic Iran, Albany, 1988
review of Bernand, *La Profession de foi d'Abū Isḥāq al-Šīrāzī*, in *Journal of the Royal Asiatic Society*, 1989
review of Bernand's edition of Mutawallī, *Mughnī*, in *Journal of the Royal Asiatic Society*, 1988
'The Shiite and Khārijite contribution to pre-Ashʿarite *kalām*', in P. Morewedge (ed.), *Islamic philosophical theology*, Albany 1979
'Shiite discussions on the legality of the *kharāj*', in R. Peters (ed.), *Proceedings of the ninth Congress of the Union Européenne des Arabisants et Islamisants*, Leiden 1981
'The spread of Māturīdism and the Turks', in *Actas do IV congresso de estudos árabes e Islâmicos*, *Biblos*, 46 (1970)
'The theology of al-Zamakhsharī', in Union Européenne d'Arabisants et d'Islamisants, *Actas del XII Congreso*, Madrid 1986
'A treatise of the Sharīf al-Murtaḍā on the legality of working for the government', *Bulletin of the School of Oriental and African Studies*, 43 (1980)
'The vigilante movement of Sahl b. Salāma al-Khurāsānī and the origins of Ḥanbalism reconsidered', *Journal of Turkish Studies*, 14 (1990)
Madelung, W. (ed.), *Arabic texts concerning the history of the Zaydī Imāms of Ṭabaristān, Daylamān and Gīlān*, Beirut 1987
The Sīra of Imām Aḥmad b. Yaḥyā al-Nāṣir li-Dīn Allāh from Musallam al-Laḥjī's Kitāb Akhbār al-Zaydiyya bi l-Yaman, Exeter 1990
Maghniyya, Muḥammad Jawād (d. 1400/1979), *al-Tafsīr al-kāshif*, Beirut 1968–70
Maḥallī (d. 864/1459) and Suyūṭī (d. 911/1505), *Tafsīr al-Qur'ān al-karīm* (= *Tafsīr al-Jalālayn*), Cairo 1966
Mahdī, Aḥmad ibn al-Ḥusayn al- (d. 656/1258), *Mufīd*, ms. London, British Library, Or. 3,811
Maḥmaṣānī, Ṣubḥī (d. 1407/1986), *Arkān ḥuqūq al-insān: baḥth muqārin fī 'l-sharīʿa al-Islāmiyya wa'l-qawānīn al-ḥadītha*, Beirut 1979
Maḥmūd, Jamāl al-Dīn Muḥammad, *Uṣūl al-mujtamaʿ al-Islāmī*, Cairo and Beirut 1992
Maḥmūd ibn Abī 'l-Qāsim al-Iṣfahānī (d. 749/1349), *Tasdīd*, ms. Princeton, Yahuda 2,220
Maimonides (d. AD 1204), *Mishneh Torah*, Jerusalem and Tel Aviv 1965–7; *The book of knowledge*, trans. H. M. Russell and J. Weinberg, Edinburgh 1981
Majlisī (d. 1110/1699), *Biḥār al-anwār*, Tehran 1376–92
Malādh al-akhbār, ed. M. al-Rajā'ī, Qumm 1406–7
Mir'āt al-ʿuqūl, ed. H. al-Rasūlī *et al.*, Tehran 1404–11
Majmūʿa, see: *Majmūʿat al-rasā'il wa'l-masā'il al-Najdiyya*
Majmūʿat al-rasā'il wa'l-masā'il al-Najdiyya, Cairo 1344–9
Majmūʿat al-tawḥīd, Damascus 1962
Majmūʿat al-tawḥīd al-Najdiyya, ed. Y. ʿA. al-Nāfiʿ, Cairo 1375

Makārim Shīrāzī, Nāṣir, *Risāla-i tawḍīḥ al-masā'il*, Qumm n.d.

Makdisi, G., 'Ash'arī and the Ash'arites in Islamic religious history', *Studia Islamica*, 17 (1962)

'Autograph diary of an eleventh-century historian of Baghdād', *Bulletin of the School of Oriental and African Studies*, 18–19 (1956–7)

Ibn 'Aqīl et la résurgence de l'Islam traditionaliste au XIe siècle, Damascus 1963

Ibn 'Aqil: religion and culture in classical Islam, Edinburgh 1997

'The non-Ash'arite Shafi'ism of Abū Ḥāmid al-Ghazzālī', *Revue des Etudes Islamiques*, 54 (1986)

The rise of colleges, Edinburgh 1981

Malaṭī (d. 377/987f.), *Tanbīh*, ed. S. Dedering, Istanbul 1936

Malick, Fakhruddin, 'Islamic concept of human rights', in S. M. Haider (ed.), *Islamic concept of human rights*, Lahore 1978

Mālik (d. 179/795), *Muwaṭṭa'*, ed. M. F. 'Abd al-Bāqī, Cairo 1951

Risāla fī 'l-sunan wa'l-mawā'iẓ wa'l-ādāb, Cairo 1937

Mālikī, Abū Bakr al- (fifth/eleventh century), *Riyāḍ al-nufūs*, ed. H. Monés, Cairo 1951–

Malkum Khān, Mīrzā (d. 1326/1908), *Nidā-yi 'adālat ba-majlis-i wuzarā-yi Īrān*, in *Majmū'a-i āthār-i Mīrzā Malkum Khān*, collected by M. M. Ṭabāṭabā'ī, Tehran 1327 sh.

Mānkdīm (d. 425/1034), *Ta'līq Sharḥ al-Uṣūl al-khamsa*, ed. 'A. 'Uthmān, Cairo 1965 (published as 'Abd al-Jabbār ibn Aḥmad (d. 415/1025), *Sharḥ al-Uṣūl al-khamsa*)

Manṣūr, 'Abdallāh ibn Ḥamza al- (d. 614/1217), *al-Durra al-yatīma*, ms. London, British Library, Or. 3,976

al-'Iqd al-thamīn, ms. London, British Library, Or. 3,976

Manṣūr, al-Qāsim ibn Muḥammad al- (d. 1029/1620), *al-Asās li-'aqā'id al-akyās*, ed. A. N. Nādir, Beirut 1980

Manṣūr, Sharaf al-Dīn ibn Badr al-Dīn al- (d. 670/1271f.), *Anwār al-yaqīn*, ms. London, British Library, Or. 3,868

Manūnī, M. al-, '*Iḥyā' 'ulūm al-dīn* fī manẓūr al-gharb al-Islāmī ayyām al-Murābiṭīn wa'l-Muwaḥḥidīn', in *Abū Ḥāmid al-Ghazzālī: dirāsāt fī fikrihi wa-'aṣrihi wa-ta'thīrihi*, Rabat 1988

Maqbalī (d. 1108/1696f.), *al-Manār fī 'l-mukhtār*, Beirut and Ṣan'ā' 1988

Maqqarī (d. 1041/1631f.), *Nafḥ al-ṭīb*, ed. I. 'Abbās, Beirut 1968

Maqrīzī (d. 845/1442), *Itti'āẓ al-ḥunafā'*, ed. J. al-Shayyāl and M. Ḥ. M. Aḥmad, Cairo 1967–73

Khiṭaṭ, Būlāq 1270

Muqaffā, ed. M. Ya'lāwī, Beirut 1991

Mar'ashī, M., and A. Ḥusaynī, *Fihrist-i nuskhahā-yi khaṭṭī-i Kitābkhāna-i 'umūmī-i ḥaḍrat-i Āyatullāh al-'uẓmā Najafī Mar'ashī*, Qumm 1354– sh.

Mar'ashī Najafī, Shihāb al-Dīn, *Risāla-i tawḍīḥ al-masā'il-i jadīd*, Qumm 1409

Marcus, A., *The Middle East on the eve of modernity: Aleppo in the eighteenth century*, New York 1989

'Privacy in eighteenth-century Aleppo: the limits of cultural ideals', *International Journal of Middle East Studies*, 18 (1986)
Marghīnānī (d. 593/1197), *Hidāya*, Beirut 1990
al-Tajnīs wa'l-mazīd, ms. Istanbul, Süleymaniye, Yeni Cami 533
Mar'ī ibn Yūsuf (d. 1033/1623f.), *Ghāyat al-muntahā*, Riyāḍ 1981
Marín, M., 'Familias de ulemas en Toledo', *Estudios onomástico-biográficos de al-Andalus*, vol. 5, Madrid 1992
Markaz-i Madārik-i Farhangī-i Inqilāb-i Islāmī, see: Khumaynī, *Ṣaḥīfa-i nūr*
Marlow, L., *Hierarchy and egalitarianism in Islamic thought*, Cambridge 1997
Martin, R. C., *et al.*, *Defenders of reason in Islam*, Oxford 1997
Marwazī, Abū Bakr al- (d. 292/905), *Musnad Abī Bakr al-Ṣiddīq*, ed. S. al-Arnā'ūṭ, Beirut n.d.
Marzubānī (d. 384/994), *Muwashshaḥ*, ed. 'A. M. al-Bajāwī, Cairo 1965
Mason, H., *Two statesmen of mediaeval Islam*, The Hague and Paris 1972
Mas'ūd, 'Abd al-'Azīz ibn Aḥmad al-, *al-Amr bi'l-ma'rūf wa'l-nahy 'an al-munkar wa-āthāruhumā fī ḥifẓ al-umma*, vol. 1, Riyāḍ 1414
Mas'ūd, Muḥammad 'Alī, *al-Amr bi'l-ma'rūf wa'l-nahy 'an al-munkar*, Cairo 1980
Mas'ūdī (d. 345/956), *Murūj al-dhahab*, ed. C. Pellat, Beirut 1965–74
Mas'ūdī, Muḥammad Isḥāq, *Pizhūhishī dar amr bah ma'rūf wa nahy az munkar az dīdgāh-i Qur'ān wa riwāyāt*, Tehran 1374 sh.
Maṭ'anī, 'Abd al-'Aẓīm Ibrāhīm al-, *Taghyīr al-munkar fī madhhab ahl al-sunna wa'l-jamā'a*, Cairo 1990
Mattock, J. N., 'A translation of the Arabic epitome of Galen's book *Peri ēthōn*', in S. M. Stern *et al.* (eds.), *Islamic philosophy and the classical tradition*, Oxford 1972
Māturīdī (d. *c.* 333/944), *'Aqīda*, in Y. Z. Yörükân, *İslâm akaidine dair eski metinler*, Istanbul 1953
(attrib.), *Sharḥ al-fiqh al-akbar*, Hyderabad 1321 (default edition); ed. Daiber, *The Islamic concept of belief*; mss. Istanbul, Süleymaniye, Esat Efendi 1,581; Fatih 3,137, 3,139, 5,392; M. Arif M. Murad 177 (with various ascriptions)
Ta'wīlāt al-Qur'ān, ms. British Library, Or. 9,432
Māwardī (d. 450/1058), *Adab al-dunyā wa'l-dīn*, ed. M. al-Saqqā, Cairo 1973
al-Aḥkām al-sulṭāniyya, ed. A. M. al-Baghdādī, Kuwait 1989
al-Nukat wa'l-'uyūn, ed. S. 'A. 'Abd al-Raḥīm, Beirut 1992
Mawdūdī, Abū 'l-A'lā (d. 1399/1979), *Human rights in Islam*, Delhi n.d.
Mafāhīm Islāmiyya, Jedda and Dammām 1987
Mawdūdī, Abul A'lā, see: Mawdūdī, Abū 'l-A'lā
Mawlawī, Shaykh Fayṣal, *al-Amr bi'l-ma'rūf wa'l-nahy 'an al-munkar*, cassette distributed by the Union des Organisations Islamiques en France, Section d'Information
Mawṣilī, Sharaf al-Dīn al- (d. 622/1225), *Rūḥ al-Iḥyā' wa-rawḥ al-aḥyā'*, ms. Oxford, Bodleian, Pocock 240
Mawwāq (d. 897/1492), *al-Tāj wa'l-iklīl*, in the margin of Ḥaṭṭāb (d. 954/1547), *Mawāhib al-jalīl*, Cairo 1328–9

Maybudī (writing in 520/1126), *Kashf al-asrār*, Tehran 1331–9 sh.
Maydānī, ʿAbd al-Raḥmān Ḥasan al-, *Fiqh al-daʿwa ilā ʾllāh*, Damascus 1996
Mayer, A. E., *Islam and human rights: tradition and politics*, Boulder 1995
Maẓhar, ʿAbd al-Wahhāb, *Murshid al-ḥājj*, Cairo 1347
McDermott, M. J., *The theology of al-Shaikh al-Mufīd*, Beirut 1978
McMullen, D., *State and scholars in T'ang China*, Cambridge 1988
Melchert, C., *The formation of the Sunni schools of law, 9th–10th centuries* CE, Leiden 1997
'Religious policies of the caliphs from al-Mutawakkil to al-Muqtadir', *Islamic Law and Society*, 3 (1996)
Mencius (fourth century BC), *Mencius*, trans. D. C. Lau, Harmondsworth 1970
Mīlānī, Fāḍil al-Ḥusaynī al-, 'al-Amr bi'l-maʿrūf wa'l-nahy ʿan al-munkar', *al-Najaf*, 2 no. 1 (January 1968)
Mill, John Stuart (d. AD 1873), *On liberty*, London 1859
Miqdād al-Suyūrī (d. 826/1423), *Irshād al-ṭālibīn*, ed. M. al-Rajāʾī, Qumm 1405
Kanz al-ʿirfān, ed. M. B. al-Bihbūdī, Tehran 1384–5
Naḍd al-Qawāʿid al-fiqhiyya, ed. ʿA. al-Kūhkamarī, Qumm 1403
al-Nāfiʿ yawm al-ḥashr, Beirut 1988
al-Tanqīḥ al-rāʾiʿ, ed. ʿA. al-Kūhkamarī, Qumm 1404
Mīr ʿAẓīmī, Jaʿfar, *Do farīḍa-i buzurg: amr bah maʿrūf wa nahy az munkar*, Qumm 1372 sh.
Mīrghanī, ʿAbdallāh ibn Ibrāhīm al- (d. 1207/1792f.), *Baḥr al-ʿaqāʾid*, ms. Princeton, Yahuda 5,246
Mīrī, ʿUthmān ibn Yaḥyā ibn ʿAbd al-Wahhāb al-, *Mukhtaṣar Rawnaq al-majālis*, Damascus and Beirut 1985
Mīrzā-yi Qummī, see: Qummī, Mīrzā Abū ʾl-Qāsim
Miṣbāḥ Yazdī, Muḥammad Taqī, 'Tashrīḥ-i falsafa wa angīza-i amr bah maʿrūf wa nahy az munkar', in *Niẓārat-i ṣāliḥān*, Tehran 1371 sh.
Mishkīnī al-Ardabīlī, ʿAlī al-, *Muṣṭalaḥāt al-uṣūl*, Qumm 1383
Mishnah, cited by the standard division of the text; H. Danby (trans.), *The Mishnah*, Oxford 1933
Miskawayh (d. 421/1030), *Tajārib al-umam*, ed. H. F. Amedroz, Cairo 1914–16
Miṣrī, Nashʾat al-, *al-Amr biʾl-maʿrūf waʾl-nahy ʿan al-munkar min Tafsīr Ibn Kathīr wa-shurūḥ Abī Ḥāmid al-Ghazzālī*, Cairo n.d.
Mitchell, R. P., *The Society of the Muslim Brothers*, London 1969
Mizzī (d. 742/1341), *Tahdhīb al-Kamāl*, ed. B. ʿA. Maʿrūf, Beirut 1985–92
Modarressi, H., *Crisis and consolidation in the formative period of Shiʿite Islam*, Princeton 1993
An introduction to Shīʿī law, London 1984
Kharāj in Islamic law, London 1983
Zamīn dar fiqh-i Islāmī, Tehran 1362 sh.
Modarressi Tabātabāʾi, H., see: Modarressi, H.
Monroe, K. R., *The heart of altruism: perceptions of a common humanity*, Princeton 1996
Morabia, A., *Le ǧihâd dans l'Islam médiéval*, Paris 1993

Morton, A. H., '*Ḥisba* and glass stamps in eighth- and early ninth-century Egypt', in Y. Rāġib (ed.), *Documents de l'Islam médiéval*, Cairo 1991
Mottahedeh, R., *The mantle of the Prophet*, New York 1985
Mu'ayyad, Aḥmad ibn al-Ḥusayn al- (d. 411/1020), *Ifāda*, ms. London, British Library, Or. 4,031; also ms. Berlin, Glaser 188
Mu'ayyad, Yaḥyā ibn Ḥamza al-, see: Yaḥyā ibn Ḥamza
Mubārak, Muḥammad al-, *Niẓām al-Islām: al-ḥukm wa'l-dawla*, Beirut and Cairo 1974
Mubarrad (d. 286/900), *Kāmil*, ed. W. Wright, Leipzig 1864–92
Mudarrisī Ṭabāṭabā'ī, Ḥ., see: Modarressi, H.
Mufaḍḍal al-Ḍabbī (d. 168/784f.), *Ikhtiyārāt* (= *Mufaḍḍaliyyāt*), ed. C. J. Lyall, Oxford and London 1918–24
Mufaḍḍal ibn Salāma (*fl.* later third/ninth century), *Fākhir*, ed. ʿA. al-Ṭaḥāwī, Cairo 1960
Malāhī, ed. G. ʿA. Khashaba, Cairo 1984
Mufīd, al-Shaykh al- (d. 413/1022), *Awā'il al-maqālāt*, Tabrīz 1371
(attrib.), *Ikhtiṣāṣ*, ed. ʿA. A. al-Ghaffārī, Tehran 1379
Irshād, Tehran n.d.
Muqniʿa, Qumm 1410
al-Risāla al-thālitha fī 'l-ghayba, in his *ʿIddat rasā'il*, Qumm n.d.
Muḥallī (d. 652/1254f.), *al-Ḥadā'iq al-wardiyya*, ms. London, British Library, Or. 3,786
ʿUmdat al-mustarshidīn fī uṣūl al-dīn, ms. Princeton, Arabic, Third Series, no. 347
Muhammad, B. Y., and J. Hunwick, *Handlists of Islamic manuscripts: Nigeria*, section 1, *The Nigerian National Archives: Kaduna State*, vol. 1, London 1995
Muḥammad, Muḥammad Sayyid, 'Ḥaqq al-taʿlīm wa'l-iʿlām fī 'l-Islām', in *Ḥuqūq al-insān fī 'l-Islām: maqālāt al-Mu'tamar al-sādis lil-fikr al-Islāmī*, n.p. n.d.
Muḥammad, Yaḥyā, 'Naẓarāt fī mawḍūʿ qawāʿid al-taghyīr lil-shaykh ʿAlī ibn Ḥājj', *al-Munqidh* (Algiers), 4 Muḥarram, 1411
Muḥammad ibn Aḥmad al-Ḥanafī (writing 812/1410), *Sharḥ al-Arbaʿīn*, ms. London, British Library, Or. 12,543
Muḥammad ibn Maḥbūb ibn al-Raḥīl (d. 260/873), *Sīra*, see: Kāshif, *Siyar*
Muḥaqqiq al-Ḥillī, al- (d. 676/1277), *al-Mukhtaṣar al-nāfiʿ*, Tehran 1387
Sharā'iʿ al-Islām, ed. ʿA. M. ʿAlī, Najaf 1969
Muḥibbī (d. 1111/1699), *Khulāṣat al-athar*, Cairo 1284
Muḥsin al-Amīn (d. 1371/1952), *Sharḥ Tabṣirat al-mutaʿallimīn*, Damascus 1947
Muʿīn al-Dīn ibn Ṣafī al-Dīn al-Ījī (alive in 911/1506), *Sharḥ al-Arbaʿīn*, ms. Princeton, Garrett 117W
Mujāhid ibn Jabr (d. 104/722f.), *Tafsīr*, ed. ʿA. Ṭ. M. al-Sūratī, n.p. n.d.
Mullā al-Ḥanafī, Abū Bakr al- (d. 1270/1853), *Naẓm al-Jawāhir*, printed at the end of his *Qurrat al-ʿuyūn al-mubṣira*, Damascus n.d.
Munajjid, Ṣalāḥ al-Dīn al-, *al-Āmirūn bi'l-maʿrūf fī 'l-Islām*, Beirut 1979

Munāwī (d. 1031/1622), *Ta'līq*, ms. Princeton, Garrett 752H
Taysīr, Būlāq 1286
Munaẓẓamat al-Mu'tamar al-Islāmī, 'Wathīqat ḥuqūq al-insān fī 'l-Islām', in *Ḥuqūq al-insān fī 'l-Islām: maqālāt al-Mu'tamar al-khāmis lil-fikr al-Islāmī*, Tehran 1987
Mundhirī, 'Alī ibn Muḥammad al- (writing 1332/1914), *Mukhtaṣar al-Adyān li-ta'līm al-ṣibyān*, in I. Aṭfayyish (ed.), *al-Majmū'a al-qayyima*, Bahlā and Beirut 1989
Mu'nis, Ḥ., 'Nuṣūṣ siyāsiyya 'an fatrat al-intiqāl min al-Murābiṭīn ilā 'l-Muwaḥḥidīn', *Majallat al-Ma'had al-Miṣrī lil-dirāsāt al-Islāmiyya fī Madrīd*, 3 (1955)
Muntaẓirī, Ḥusayn-'Alī, *Dirāsāt fī walāyat al-faqīh wa-fiqh al-dawla al-Islāmiyya*, Qumm 1408–11
Risāla-i tawḍīḥ al-masā'il, Qumm 1362 sh.
Muqaddas al-Ardabīlī, al- (d. 993/1585), *Majma' al-fā'ida*, ed. M. al-'Arāqī *et al.*, Qumm 1402–
Zubdat al-bayān, ed. M. B. al-Bihbūdī, Tehran n.d.
Muqaddasī (*fl.* second half of the fourth/tenth century), *Aḥsan al-taqāsīm*, ed. M. J. de Goeje, Leiden 1906
Muqātil ibn Sulaymān (d. 150/767f.), *al-Ashbāh wa'l-naẓā'ir*, ed. 'A. M. Shiḥāta, Cairo 1975
Tafsīr, ed. 'A. M. Shiḥāta, Cairo 1979–89
Tafsīr al-khams mi'at āya, ed. I. Goldfeld, Shfaram 1980
Murādī (d. 1206/1791), *Silk al-durar*, Būlāq 1291–1301
Muranyi, M., 'Das *Kitāb al-Siyar* von Abū Isḥāq al-Fazārī', *Jerusalem Studies in Arabic and Islam*, 6 (1985)
Materialien zur mālikitischen Rechtsliteratur, Wiesbaden 1984
'Neue Materialien zur *tafsīr*-Forschung in der Moscheebibliothek von Qairawān', in S. Wild (ed.), *The Qur'an as text*, Leiden 1996
Murshad, Yaḥyā ibn al-Ḥusayn al- (d. 477/1084f.), *Amālī*, Cairo 1376
Murtaḍā (d. 436/1044), *Dhakhīra*, ed. A. al-Ḥusaynī, Qumm 1411
Jumal al-'ilm wa'l-'amal, ed. A. al-Ḥusaynī, Najaf 1387
Muqaddima fī 'l-uṣūl al-i'tiqādiyya, in M. Ḥ. Āl Yāsīn (ed.), *Nafā'is al-makhṭūṭāt*, Najaf and Baghdad 1952–6
Murtaḍā al-Zabīdī (d. 1205/1791), *Itḥāf al-sāda*, Cairo 1311
Tāj al-'arūs, ed. 'A. A. Farrāj *et al.*, Kuwait 1965–
Muṣ'ab al-Zubayrī (d. 236/851), *Nasab Quraysh*, ed. E. Lévi-Provençal, Cairo 1976
Muṣ'abī, see: Aṭfayyish, *Hīmyān*
Musallam, B., 'The ordering of Muslim societies', in F. Robinson (ed.), *The Cambridge illustrated history of the Islamic world*, Cambridge 1996
Muslim ibn al-Ḥajjāj (d. 261/875), *Ṣaḥīḥ*, ed. M. F. 'Abd al-Bāqī, Cairo 1955–6
Muṣṭafawī, Ḥ. al- (ed.), *al-Uṣūl al-sitta 'ashar*, Qumm 1405
Muṭahharī, Murtaḍā (d. 1399/1979), ''Adālat az naẓar-i Islām', in his *Bīst guftār*, n.p. 1357 sh.

'Amr ba-maʿrūf wa nahy az munkar', *Guftār-i māh*, 1 (1339–40 sh.), Tehran n.d.
Āshnāʾī bā ʿulūm-i Islāmī, Qumm n.d.
Ḥamāsa-i Ḥusaynī, Tehran and Qumm 1364 sh.
Jādhiba wa dāfiʿa-i ʿAlī ʿalayhi ʾl-salām, Tehran 1391
Jihād, Qumm n.d.
Pīrāmūn-i Jumhūrī-i Islāmī, Tehran and Qumm 1364 sh.
Sayrī dar sīra-i aʾimma-i aṭhār, Tehran and Qumm 1367 sh.
Mutawallī (d. 478/1086), *Mughnī*, ed. M. Bernand, Cairo 1986
Mutawallī, ʿAbd al-Ḥamīd, *Mabādiʾ niẓām al-ḥukm fī ʾl-Islām*, Alexandria 1974
Muttaqī al-Hindī, al- (d. 975/1567), *Kanz al-ʿummāl*, ed. Ṣ. al-Saqqā *et al.*, Aleppo 1969–77
Muwaffaq al-Shajarī, al- (first half of the fifth/eleventh century), *Iḥāṭa*, ms. Leiden, Or. 8,409
Muwaylihī, Muḥammad al- (d. 1348/1930), *Ḥadīth ʿĪsā ibn Hishām*, Cairo 1907; trans. R. Allen, *A period of time*, Reading 1992
Muẓaffar, Muḥammad Riḍā al-, *Uṣūl al-fiqh*, Najaf 1959–62
Nabarāwī (writing 1243/1828), *Sharḥ ʿalā ʾl-Arbaʿīn*, Cairo 1960
Nābigha al-Dhubyānī (sixth century AD), *Dīwān*, ed. S. Fayṣal, Beirut 1968
Nagel, T., *Staat und Glaubensgemeinschaft im Islam*, Zurich and Munich 1981
Naḥḥās (d. 338/950), *Maʿānī ʾl-Qurʾān al-karīm*, ed. M. ʿA. al-Ṣābūnī, Mecca 1988–
Naʿīmā (d. 1128/1716), *Tārīkh*, Istanbul 1283
Najafī (d. 1266/1850), *Jawāhir al-kalām*, Najaf and Tehran 1378–1404
Najarī (d. 877/1473), *Shāfī al-ʿalīl*, ed. A. ʿA. A. al-Shāmī, Ṣanʿāʾ and Beirut 1987–
Najjār, ʿA. al-, *al-Mahdī Ibn Tūmart*, n.p. 1983
Nakata, K., 'Shīa-ha hōgaku ni okeru "Zen no meirei to aku no soshi" riron no hatten to Homenī ni yoru sono kaikaku', *Annals of Japan Association for Middle East Studies*, 12 (1997)
Nallino, C. A., *L'Arabia Saʿūdiana (1938)*, in C. A. Nallino, *Raccolta di scritti editi e inediti*, Rome 1939–48
Narāqī, Aḥmad (d. 1245/1829), *Miʿrāj al-saʿāda* (in Persian), Qumm 1371 sh.
Narāqī, Muḥammad Mahdī al- (d. 1209/1794f.), *Jāmiʿ al-saʿādāt*, ed. M. Kalāntar, Najaf 1963
Nasafī, Najm al-Dīn al- (d. 537/1142), *al-Qand fī dhikr ʿulamāʾ Samarqand*, ed. N. M. al-Fāryābī, Saudi Arabia 1991
Tafsīr (in Persian), ed. ʿA. Juwaynī, n.p. 1353–4 sh.
Nasāʾī (d. 303/915), *Sunan*, ed. Ḥ. M. al-Masʿūdī, Cairo n.d.
Nawawī (d. 676/1277), *al-Adhkār al-muntakhaba min kalām Sayyid al-Abrār*, Cairo 1988
selection of forty traditions published as *Matn al-Arbaʿīn al-Nawawiyya*, Beirut 1977
commentary on his selection of forty traditions published as *Sharḥ matn al-Arbaʿīn al-Nawawiyya*, Damascus 1966
Sharḥ Ṣaḥīḥ Muslim, Beirut 1987

Nawbakhtī (alive in 300/912), *Firaq al-Shīʿa*, ed. H. Ritter, Istanbul 1931
Naysābūrī, Aḥmad ibn Ibrāhīm al- (*fl.* later fourth/tenth century), *Ithbāt al-imāma*, ed. M. Ghālib, Beirut 1984
al-Risāla al-mūjaza al-kāfiya fī adab al-duʿāt, *apud* V. Klemm, *Die Mission des fāṭimidischen Agenten al-Muʾayyad fī d-dīn in Šīrāz*, Frankfurt am Main 1989
New Catholic Encyclopedia, New York 1967
Newman, A. J., 'The nature of the Akhbārī/Uṣūlī dispute in late Ṣafawid Iran, Part 2: the conflict reassessed', *Bulletin of the School of Oriental and African Studies*, 55 (1992)
Nīshāpūrī, Muʿīn al-Dīn (sixth/twelfth century), *Tafsīr-i baṣāyir-i yamīnī*, n.p. 1359– sh.
Niẓām al-Dīn al-Naysābūrī (*fl.* early eighth/fourteenth century), *Gharāʾib al-Qurʾān*, ed. I. ʿA. ʿIwaḍ, Cairo 1962–71
Niẓām al-Mulk (d. 485/1092), *Siyar al-mulūk*, ed. H. Darke, Tehran 1372 sh.
Nöldeke, T., *et al.*, *Geschichte des Qorāns*, Leipzig 1909–39
Noldin, H., *Summa theologiae moralis*, Innsbruck 1955–6
Norman, K. R., *Pāli literature*, Wiesbaden 1983
Norris, H. T., 'Muslim Sanhāja scholars of Mauritania', in J. R. Willis (ed.), *Studies in West African Islamic history*, vol. 1, London 1979
Noth, A., and L. I. Conrad, *The early Arabic historical tradition*, Princeton 1994
Nuʿaym ibn Ḥammād (d. 228/843), *Fitan*, ed. S. Zakkār, Mecca n.d.
Nuʿaymī (d. 927/1521), *al-Dāris fī taʾrīkh al-madāris*, ed. J. al-Ḥasanī, Damascus 1948–51
Nuʿmān, Qāḍī (d. 363/974), *Daʿāʾim al-Islām*, ed. A. ʿA. A. Fayḍī, Beirut 1991
al-Himma fī ādāb atbāʿ al-aʾimma, ed. M. K. Ḥusayn, n.p. n.d.
al-Majālis waʾl-musāyarāt, ed. Ḥ. al-Faqī *et al.*, Tunis 1978
Risālat iftitāḥ al-daʿwa, ed. W. al-Qāḍī, Beirut 1970
Nūrī al-Hamadānī, Ḥusayn al-, *al-Amr biʾl-maʿrūf waʾl-nahy ʿan al-munkar*, Tehran 1990
Nūrī al-Ṭabarsī, al- (d. 1320/1902), *Mustadrak al-Wasāʾil*, Qumm 1407–8
Nwyia, P., *Ibn ʿAbbād de Ronda*, Beirut 1961
Ormsby, E. L., *Theodicy in Islamic thought: the dispute over al-Ghazālī's 'best of all possible worlds'*, Princeton 1984
Osman Nuri [Ergin] (d. 1381/1961), *Mejelle-i umūr-i belediye*, Istanbul 1330–8 *mālī*
ʿOthmān Nūrī, see: Osman Nuri
Pakistan, Basic Principles Committee, *Report*, Karachi 1952
Palestinian Talmud, Venice *c.* 1522; trans. J. Neusner *et al.*, *The Talmud of the Land of Israel*, Chicago and London 1982–
Palgrave, W. G., *Personal narrative of a year's journey through central and eastern Arabia*, London 1883
Patton, W. M., *Aḥmed ibn Ḥanbal and the Miḥna*, Leiden 1897
Payne Smith, R., *Thesaurus syriacus*, Oxford 1879–1901
Pazdawī, ʿAlī ibn Muḥammad al- (d. 482/1089), *Uṣūl*, *apud* ʿAbd al-ʿAzīz ibn Aḥmad al-Bukhārī (d. 730/1329f.), *Kashf al-asrār*, Istanbul 1308

Pelly, L., *Report on a journey to the Wahabee capital of Riyadh in central Arabia*, Bombay 1866
Peskes, E., *Muḥammad b. ʿAbdalwahhāb (1703–92) im Widerstreit*, Beirut 1993
Peters, J. R. T. M., *God's created speech*, Leiden 1976
Peters, R., 'The battered dervishes of Bab Zuwayla: a religious riot in eighteenth-century Cairo', in N. Levtzion and J. O. Voll (eds.), *Eighteenth-century renewal and reform in Islam*, Syracuse 1987
Philby, H. S. B., *The heart of Arabia: a record of travel & exploration*, London 1922
Saʿudi Arabia, London 1955
Poonawala, I. K., *Biobibliography of Ismāʿīlī literature*, Malibu 1977
Pouzet, L., *Damas au VIIe/XIIIe siècle*, Beirut 1988
Qāḍī Khān (d. 592/1196), *Fatāwā*, Cairo 1282
Qāḍī Ṣaʿda (d. 646/1248f.), *Durar al-aḥādīth*, ed. Y. ʿA. al-Faḍīl, Beirut 1979
Qāḍīzāde Aḥmed ibn Meḥmed Emīn (d. 1197/1783), *Jawhara-i bahiyya-i Aḥmadiyya* (in Turkish), Būlāq 1240
Qāḍīzāde Meḥmed Efendi (d. 1045/1635f.), *Risāla qāmiʿa lil-bidʿa*, ms. Istanbul, Süleymaniye, Serez 3,876
Tāj al-rasāʾil (in Turkish), ms. Istanbul, Süleymaniye, Hacı Mahmud 1,926
Qadrī Nāṣiḥ, Meḥmed (*fl.* early fourteenth/twentieth century), *Ẓulm ve ʿadl*, n.p. 1326
Qalqashandī (d. 821/1418), *Ṣubḥ al-aʿshā*, Cairo 1913–19
Qarabāghī, Maḥmūd ibn Muḥammad al- (tenth/sixteenth century?), *Muḥāḍarāt*, ms. Qumm, Marʿashī Library, no. 473
Qarāfī (d. 684/1285), *Furūq*, Cairo 1344–6
Qāsim ibn Ibrāhīm (d. 246/860f.) (attrib.), *al-ʿAdl waʾl-tawḥīd*, see: ʿUmāra, *Rasāʾil*
Masāʾil manthūra, ms. London, British Library, Or. 3,977
Qāsimī, Jamāl al-Dīn al- (d. 1332/1914), *Iṣlāḥ al-masājid*, Beirut and Damascus 1983
Maḥāsin al-taʾwīl, ed. M. F. ʿAbd al-Bāqī, Beirut 1994
Mawʿiẓat al-muʾminīn min Iḥyāʾ ʿulūm al-dīn, ed. ʿA. B. al-Bayṭār, Beirut 1981
Qaṭṭān, Ibrāhīm al- (d. 1404/1984), *Taysīr al-tafsīr*, Amman 1982–
Qazwīnī (d. 682/1283f.), *Āthār al-bilād*, ed. F. Wüstenfeld, Göttingen 1848
Qirāʾatī, Muḥsin, *Amr bah maʿrūf wa nahy az munkar*, Tehran 1375 sh.
Qirqisānī (fourth/tenth century), *al-Anwār waʾl-marāqib*, ed. L. Nemoy, New York 1939–43
Quḍāʿī (d. 454/1062), *Musnad al-shihāb*, ed. Ḥ. ʿA. al-Salafī, Beirut 1985
Qummī (alive in 307/919), *Tafsīr*, ed. Ṭ. M. al-Jazāʾirī, Najaf 1386–7
Qummī, Mīrzā Abū ʾl-Qāsim (d. 1231/1815f.), *Jāmiʿ al-shatāt* (in Persian), ed. M. Raḍawī, Tehran 1371– sh.
Qummī, Qāḍī Saʿīd al- (writing 1107/1696), *Sharḥ Tawḥīd al-Ṣadūq*, ed. N. Ḥabībī, Tehran 1415–16
Qummī, Taqī al-Ṭabāṭabāʾī al-, *Mabānī Minhāj al-ṣāliḥīn*, Qumm 1405–11
Quranī, ʿAlī ibn Ḥasan al-, *al-Ḥisba fī ʾl-māḍī waʾl-ḥāḍir*, Riyāḍ 1994

Qurashī, ʿAlī-Akbar, *Tafsīr-i aḥsan al-ḥadīth*, Tehran 1366–71 sh.

Qurṭubī (d. 671/1273), *al-Jāmiʿ li-aḥkām al-Qurʾān*, Cairo 1967

Qurṭubī, Aḥmad ibn ʿUmar al- (d. 656/1258), *Mufhim*, Damascus and Beirut 1996

Qushayrī (d. 334/945f.), *Taʾrīkh al-Raqqa*, ed. Ṭ. al-Naʿsānī, Ḥamāh 1959

Qushayrī (d. 465/1072), *Laṭāʾif al-ishārāt*, ed. I. Bisyūnī, Cairo n.d.–1971

Risāla, Cairo 1966

Quṭb, Sayyid (d. 1386/1966), *Fī ẓilāl al-Qurʾān*, Beirut 1973–4

Maʿālim fī ʾl-ṭarīq, n.p. n.d.

Rabīʿ ibn Ḥabīb (d. 170/786f?) (attrib.), *al-Jāmiʿ al-ṣaḥīḥ*, n.p. n.d.

Raḍī, al-Sharīf al- (d. 406/1015), *Nahj al-balāgha*, see: Ibn Abī ʾl-Ḥadīd, *Sharḥ*

Raḍwān, ʿAbd al-Ḥasīb, *Dirāsāt fī ʾl-ḥisba*, Cairo 1990

Rāfiʿī (d. 623/1226), *al-Tadwīn fī akhbār Qazwīn*, ed. ʿA. al-ʿUṭāridī, Beirut 1987

Rafsanjānī, Akbar Hāshimī, *Tafsīr-i rāhnumā*, Qumm 1371– sh.

Rāghib al-Iṣbahānī, al- (*fl.* later fourth/tenth century), *al-Mufradāt fī gharīb al-Qurʾān*, ed. M. A. Khalaf Allāh, n.p. 1970

Muḥāḍarāt al-udabāʾ, Beirut 1961

Rajab ibn Aḥmad al-Āmidī (Ḥājjī Rejeb Efendi) (writing 1087/1676), *al-Wasīla al-Aḥmadiyya*, Istanbul 1261

Rasāʾil Ikhwān al-Ṣafā, ed. K. al-Ziriklī, Cairo 1928

Rashi (d. AD 1105), *Perushe Rashi ʿal ha-Torah*, ed. H. D. Chavel, Jerusalem 1982

Rashid, I. al- (ed.), *Documents on the history of Saudi Arabia*, Salisbury, N.C. 1976

Rāshid, Muḥammad Aḥmad al-, *al-Munṭalaq*, Beirut 1976

Rashīd al-Dīn (d. 718/1318), *Jāmiʿ al-tawārīkh: qismat-i Ismāʿīlīyān wa Fāṭimīyān wa Nizārīyān wa dāʿīyān wa rafīqān*, ed. M. T. Dānishpazhūh and M. Mudarrisī Zanjānī, Tehran 1338 sh.

Rāwandī (d. 573/1177f.), *Fiqh al-Qurʾān*, ed. A. al-Ḥusaynī, Qumm 1397–9

Rāwandī (writing 599/1202f.), *Rāḥat al-ṣudūr* (in Persian), ed. M. Iqbàl, London 1921

Rāwandī, Abū ʾl-Riḍā al- (sixth/twelfth century), *Nawādir*, Beirut 1988

Raymond, A., *The great Arab cities in the 16th–18th centuries: an introduction*, New York and London 1984

Rāzī, Abū ʾl-Futūḥ (first half of sixth/twelfth century), *Rawḍ al-janān* (in Persian), ed. ʿA. A. Ghaffārī, Tehran 1382–7

Rāzī, Aḥmad ibn Sahl al- (*fl.* later third/ninth century), *Akhbār Fakhkh*, ed. M. Jarrar, Beirut 1995

Rāzī, ʿAlī ibn Muḥammad ibn Aḥmad al- (writing 689/1291), *al-Mustakhlaṣ min Iḥyāʾ ʿulūm al-dīn*, ms. Istanbul, Süleymaniye, Aya Sofya 2,097

Rāzī, Fakhr al-Dīn al- (d. 606/1210), *al-Tafsīr al-kabīr*, Cairo *c.* 1934–62

Rebstock, U., *Sammlung arabischer Handschriften aus Mauretanien*, Wiesbaden 1989

Reinhart, A. K., *Before revelation: the boundaries of Muslim moral thought*, Albany 1995

Reissner, J., 'Die Idrīsīden in ʿAsīr', *Die Welt des Islams*, 21 (1981)

Ribera, J. and M. Asín, *Manuscritos árabes y aljamiados de la Biblioteca de la Junta*, Madrid 1912

Richards, D. S., 'The Coptic bureaucracy under the Mamlūks', in *Colloque international sur l'histoire du Caire*, Cairo n.d.

'The *Rasā'il* of Badīʿ al-Zamān al-Hamadhānī', in A. Jones (ed.), *Arabicus Felix*, Reading 1991

Riḍā, Rashīd (d. 1354/1935), *Tafsīr al-Manār*, based on lectures of Muḥammad ʿAbduh (d. 1323/1905), Cairo 1367–73

Rieu, C., *Supplement to the catalogue of the Arabic manuscripts in the British Museum*, London 1894

Rifāʿī, Ṭālib al-, 'al-Amr bi'l-maʿrūf wa'l-nahy ʿan al-munkar', *al-Najaf*, 2 no. 2 (March 1968)

Rīḥānī, A. al-, see: Rihani, A.

Rihani, A., *Maker of modern Arabia*, Boston and New York 1928

Mulūk al-ʿArab, Beirut 1924–5

Ritter, H., 'Studien zur Geschichte des islamischen Frömmigkeit: I. Ḥasan al-Baṣrī', *Der Islam*, 21 (1933)

Robson, J., 'The transmission of Abū Dāwūd's *Sunan*', *Bulletin of the School of Oriental and African Studies*, 14 (1952)

Roest Crollius, A. A., 'Mission and morality', *Studia Missionalia*, 27 (1978)

Rosenthal, F., *General introduction*, in *The History of al-Ṭabarī*, vol. 1, Albany 1989

Rubinacci, R., 'Un antico documento di vita cenobitica musulmana', in Istituto Universitario Orientale di Napoli, *Annali*, new series, 10 (1960)

'La professione di fede di al-Ǧannāwunī', in Istituto Universitario Orientale di Napoli, *Annali*, new series, 14 (1964)

'La purità rituale secondo gli Ibāḍiti', in Istituto Universitario Orientale di Napoli, *Annali*, new series, 6 (1954–6)

Rudolf, U., *Al-Māturīdī und die sunnitische Theologie in Samarkand*, Leiden 1997

Rūmī, Jalāl al-Dīn (d. 672/1273), *Mathnawī*, ed. and trans. R. A. Nicholson, London 1925–40

Rummānī (d. 384/994), *Tafsīr al-Qur'ān*, ms. Paris, Bibliothèque Nationale, Arabe 6,523

Rypka, J., *et al.*, *History of Iranian literature*, Dordrecht 1968

Saʿadya (d. AD 942), *al-Amānāt wa'l-iʿtiqādāt*, ed. S. Landauer, Leiden 1880

Sabari, S., *Mouvements populaires à Bagdad à l'époque ʿabbasside*, Paris 1981

Sabt, Khālid ibn ʿUthmān al-, *al-Amr bi'l-maʿrūf wa'l-nahy ʿan al-munkar*, London 1995

Sabzawārī (d. 1090/1679f.), *Kifāyat al-aḥkām*, n.p. 1269

Sachau, E., 'Über die religiösen Anschauungen der Ibaditischen Muhammedaner in Oman und Ostafrika', *Mittheilungen des Seminars für Orientalische Sprachen*, 2 (1899)

Sachedina, A. A., *The just ruler (al-sultān al-ʿādil) in Shīʿite Islam*, New York and Oxford 1988

Ṣādiqī, Muḥammad, *al-Furqān fī tafsīr al-Qur'ān*, Tehran, Qumm and Beirut 1397–1410

Ṣādiqī, Nabī, lectures published in Dādsarā-yi Inqilāb-i Islāmī-i Mubāraza bā

Mawādd-i Mukhaddir wa Munkarāt-i Tihrān, *Shīwahā-yi ṣaḥīḥ-i amr bah maʿrūf wa nahy az munkar*, Tehran 1371 sh.
Ṣādiqī Tihrānī, Muḥammad, *Risāla-i tawḍīḥ al-masāʾil*, Qumm n.d.
Saffārīnī (d. 1188/1774f.), *al-Durra al-muḍiyya*, see: Saffārīnī, *Lawāmiʿ*
Ghidhāʾ al-albāb, ed. M. ʿA. al-Khālidī, Beirut 1996
Lawāmiʿ al-anwār al-bahiyya, Jedda 1380
Ṣāfī Gulpāyagānī, Luṭf Allāh, *Rāh-i iṣlāḥ yā amr bah maʿrūf wa nahy az munkar*, Qum 1376 sh.
Ṣāḥib ibn ʿAbbād, al- (d. 385/995), *al-Ibāna ʿan madhhab ahl al-ʿadl*, in M. Ḥ. Āl Yāsīn (ed.), *Nafāʾis al-makhṭūṭāt*, Najaf and Baghdad 1952–6
al-Tadhkira fī ʾl-uṣūl al-khamsa, in M. Ḥ. Āl Yāsīn (ed.), *Nafāʾis al-makhṭūṭāt*, Najaf and Baghdad 1952–6
Ṣaḥīfa-i nūr, see: Khumaynī
Sahl al-Tustarī (d. 283/896), *al-Muʿāraḍa waʾl-radd*, ed. M. K. Jaʿfar, Cairo 1980
Sahmī (d. 427/1035f.), *Taʾrīkh Jurjān*, Hyderabad 1950
Saḥnūn (d. 240/854), *Mudawwana*, Beirut n.d.
Sakhāwī (d. 902/1497), *al-Ḍawʾ al-lāmiʿ*, Cairo 1353–5
Tarjamat Shaykh al-Islām . . . Abī Zakariyyāʾ Muḥyī ʾl-Dīn al-Nawawī, ed. M. Ḥ. Rabīʿ, Cairo 1935
Salāmī (d. 774/1372), *Taʾrīkh ʿulamāʾ Baghdād*, ed. ʿA. al-ʿAzzāwī, Baghdad 1938
Ṣāliḥ ibn Aḥmad ibn Ḥanbal (d. 266/880), *Masāʾil al-imām Aḥmad ibn Ḥanbal*, ed. F. Dīn Muḥammad, Delhi 1988
Sīrat al-imām Aḥmad ibn Ḥanbal, ed. F. ʿA. Aḥmad, Alexandria 1981
Ṣāliḥī, Zayn al-Dīn al- (d. 856/1452), *al-Kanz al-akbar fī ʾl-amr biʾl-maʿrūf waʾl-nahy ʿan al-munkar*, Riyāḍ and Mecca 1997 (default edition); ed. M. ʿU. Ṣumayda, Beirut 1996 (vol. 1); ms. Istanbul, Süleymaniye, Fatih 1,136 (vol. 1); ms. Berlin, Landberg 167 (vol. 2)
Sālim ibn Dhakwān (*fl.* 70s/690s), *Sīra*, in Hinds Xerox
Sālimī (d. 1332/1914), *Jawhar al-Niẓām*, Cairo 1381
Madārij al-kamāl, Oman 1983
Tuḥfat al-aʿyān, Cairo 1961
Sālimī, Muḥammad ibn ʿAbdallāh al- (writing 1380/1961), *Nahḍat al-aʿyān*, Cairo n.d.
Sallār (d. 448/1056), *Marāsim*, ed. M. al-Bustānī, Beirut 1980
Samʿānī (d. 562/1166), *Ansāb*, ed. ʿA. al-Muʿallimī al-Yamānī, Hyderabad 1962–82 (default edition); British Library manuscript published in facsimile by D. S. Margoliouth, Leiden and London 1912
Samarqandī, Abū Ḥafṣ al- (second half of the fifth/eleventh century), *Rawnaq al-majālis*, ms. Istanbul, Süleymaniye, Aya Sofya 1,832
Samarqandī, Abū ʾl-Layth, see: Abū ʾl-Layth al-Samarqandī
Sāmarrāʾī, Fārūq ʿAbd al-Majīd Ḥamūd al-, *Manāhij al-ʿulamāʾ fī ʾl-amr biʾl-maʿrūf waʾl-nahy ʿan al-munkar*, Jedda 1407
Saqaṭī (late fifth/eleventh or first half of the sixth/twelfth century), *Ādāb al-ḥisba*, ed. G.-S. Colin and E. Lévi-Provençal, Paris 1931

Saudi Arabia, *al-Niẓām al-asāsī lil-ḥukm*, in *al-Sharq al-awsaṭ* (London), 2 March 1992
Ṣāwī (d. 1241/1825f.), *Bulghat al-sālik*, Cairo 1952
Sawwās, Y. M. al-, *Fihris Majāmīʿ al-Madrasa al-ʿUmariyya fī Dār al-Kutub al-Ẓāhiriyya bi-Dimashq*, Kuwait 1987
Sayfī, ʿAlī-Akbar al-, *Dalīl Taḥrīr al-Wasīla lil-Imām al-Khumaynī (s) fī ʾl-amr biʾl-maʿrūf waʾl-nahy ʿan al-munkar*, Qumm 1415
Sayyid, A. F., *Maṣādir taʾrīkh al-Yaman fī ʾl-ʿaṣr al-Islāmī*, Cairo 1974
Sayyid, R. al-, 'al-Dār waʾl-hijra wa-aḥkāmuhā ʿind Ibn al-Murtaḍā', *Ijtihād*, 3 (1991)
Sayyid ʿAlawī, Ibrāhīm, *Niẓārat-i ʿumūmī-i Islāmī*, Tehran 1347 sh.
Schaeder, H. H., 'Ḥasan al-Baṣrī: Studien zur Frühgeschichte des Islam', *Der Islam*, 14 (1925)
Schatkowski Schilcher, L., *Families in politics: Damascene factions and estates of the 18th and 19th centuries*, Stuttgart 1985
Schenk-Ziegler, A., *Correctio fraterna im Neuen Testament: Die 'brüderliche Zurechtweisung' in biblischen, frühjüdischen und hellenistischen Schriften*, Würzburg 1997
Schwartz, W., *Die Anfänge der Ibaditen in Nordafrika*, Wiesbaden 1983
Sebti, A., 'Hagiographie du voyage au Maroc médiéval', *Al-Qanṭara*, 13 (1992)
Sedgwick, M. J. R., 'Saudi Sufis: compromise in the Hijaz, 1925–40', *Die Welt des Islams*, 37 (1997)
Serjeant, R. B., 'A Zaidī manual of ḥisbah of the 3rd century (H)', *Rivista degli Studi Orientali*, 28 (1953)
Seyyid ʿAlīzāde Yaʿqūb, see: Yaʿqūb ibn Seyyid ʿAlī
Sezgin, F., *Geschichte des arabischen Schrifttums*, Leiden 1967–
Shabbūḥ, I., 'Sijill qadīm li-maktabat jāmiʿ al-Qayrawān', *Majallat Maʿhad al-Makhṭūṭāt al-ʿArabiyya*, 2 (1956)
Shabīb ibn ʿAṭiyya (*fl.* mid-second/eighth century), *Sīra*, see: Kāshif, *Siyar*
Shabrakhītī (d. 1106/1694f.), *al-Futūḥāt al-wahbiyya bi-sharḥ al-Arbaʿīn al-Nawawiyya*, Cairo 1280
Shabshīrī (d. *c.* 990/1582), *al-Jawāhir al-bahiyya*, ms. Princeton, Garrett 753H
Shahāwī, Ibrāhīm Dasūqī al-, *al-Ḥisba fī ʾl-Islām*, Cairo 1962
Shahīd al-Awwal, al- (d. 786/1384), *al-Durūs al-sharʿiyya*, Qumm 1412–14
Ghāyat al-murād, Qumm 1414–
al-Lumʿa al-Dimashqiyya, Tehran 1406
al-Qawāʿid waʾl-fawāʾid, ed. ʿA. al-Ḥakīm, Najaf 1980
Shahīd al-Thānī, al- (d. 965/1557f.), *Masālik al-afhām*, Qumm 1413–
al-Rawḍa al-bahiyya, ed. M. Kalāntar, Najaf 1386–90
Shaked, S. (trans.), *The wisdom of the Sasanian sages (Dēnkard VI)*, Boulder 1979
Shakūrī, Abū ʾl-Faḍl, *Fiqh-i siyāsī-i Islām*, Qumm 1361 sh.
Shāmī, Ṣāliḥ Aḥmad al-, *al-Muhadhdhab min Iḥyāʾ ʿulūm al-dīn*, Damascus and Beirut 1993
Shammākh ibn Ḍirār (d. *c.* 30/650), *Dīwān*, ed. Ṣ. al-Hādī, Cairo 1968

Shammākhī, Aḥmad ibn Saʿīd al- (d. 928/1522), *Siyar*, ed. A. S. al-Siyābī, Muscat 1987

Shammākhī, ʿĀmir ibn ʿAlī al- (d. 792/1389f.), *Diyānāt*, see: Cuperly, *Introduction*

Shaqṣī (*fl. c.* 1034/1625), *Manhaj al-ṭālibīn*, Cairo and Muscat *c.* 1979– (default: vol. 8)

Shaʿrānī (d. 973/1565), *Lawāqiḥ*, Cairo 1961

al-Ṭabaqāt al-kubrā, Cairo 1954

Sharīʿatī, ʿAlī (d. 1397/1977), *Shīʿa*, n.p. 1362 sh. (= *Majmūʿa-i āthār*, vol. 7)

Sharīʿatmadārī, Kāẓim, see: Sayyid ʿAlawī

Sharīf, ʿAbd al-ʿAzīz al-, ʻal-Amr bi'l-maʿrūf wa'l-nahy ʿan al-munkar', *al-Nahḍa al-nisāʾiyya*, 9 (1931)

Shāṭibī (d. 790/1388), *al-Muwāfaqāt fī uṣūl al-sharīʿa*, ed. ʿA. Darrāz, Cairo n.d.

Shaṭṭī, Ḥasan al- (d. 1274/1858), *Mukhtaṣar Lawāmiʿ al-anwār al-bahiyya*, Damascus 1931

Shaṭṭī, Jamīl al- (d. 1379/1959), *Mukhtaṣar Ṭabaqāt al-Ḥanābila*, Damascus 1339

Shaṭṭī, Muḥammad al- (d. 1307/1890), *Muqaddimat Tawfīq al-mawādd al-niẓāmiyya li-aḥkām al-sharīʿa al-Muḥammadiyya*, Cairo n.d.

Shawkānī (d. 1250/1834), *al-Badr al-ṭāliʿ*, Cairo 1348

al-Dawāʾ al-ʿājil, printed with his *Sharḥ al-ṣudūr bi-taḥrīm rafʿ al-qubūr*, ed. M. Ḥ. al-Fiqī, n.p. 1366

al-Durar al-bahiyya, in his *al-Darārī al-muḍiyya*, Cairo 1986

Fatḥ al-qadīr, Cairo 1964

Rafʿ al-rība, printed with his *Sharḥ al-ṣudūr bi-taḥrīm rafʿ al-qubūr*, ed. M. Ḥ. al-Fiqī, n.p. 1366

al-Sayl al-jarrār, ed. M. I. Zāyid, Beirut 1985

Shawkānī, Aḥmad al- (d. 1281/1864), *al-Sumūṭ al-dhahabiyya*, ed. I. B. ʿAbd al-Majīd, Beirut 1990

Shaybānī (d. 189/805), *Āthār*, ed. M. Tēgh Bahādur, Lucknow n.d.

Shayzarī (*fl.* later sixth/twelfth century), *Nihāyat al-rutba*, ed. S. B. al-ʿArīnī, Cairo 1946

Shboul, A. M. H., *al-Masʿūdī & his world*, London 1979

Shehadi, F., *Philosophies of music in medieval Islam*, Leiden 1995

Shiloah, A., *Music in the world of Islam*, Aldershot 1995

Shīrāzī, Muḥammad Ḥusaynī, see: Shīrāzī, Muḥammad al-Ḥusaynī al-

Shīrāzī, Muḥammad al-Ḥusaynī al-, *Fiqh*, Qumm *c.* 1374–1408

Risāla-i tawḍīḥ al-masāʾil, n.p. n.d.

Shīrāzī, Ṣādiq al-, *Sharḥ Tabṣirat al-mutaʿallimīn*, Qumm 1406

Shirbīnī (d. 977/1570), *Mughnī 'l-muḥtāj*, Cairo 1933

Shukrī, ʿA., *Baʿḍ malāmiḥ al-taghayyur al-ijtimāʿī al-thaqāfī fī 'l-waṭan al-ʿArabī*, Cairo 1979

Sibṭ ibn al-Jawzī (d. 654/1257), *Mirʾāt al-zamān*, vol. 8, Hyderabad 1951–2; ms. Paris, Bibliothèque Nationale, Arabe 1,506; ms. London, British Library, Add. 23,277

Ṣiddīq Ḥasan Khān al-Qannawjī (d. 1307/1890), *Abjad al-ʿulūm*, Bhopal 1295–6
Fatḥ al-bayān, ed. ʿA. I. al-Anṣārī, Sidon and Beirut 1992
Sifra, Jerusalem 5743; trans. J. Neusner, *Sifra: an analytical translation*, Atlanta 1988
Sindī, Muḥammad Ḥayāt al- (d. 1163/1750), *Sharḥ al-Arbaʿīn al-Nawawiyya*, ed. Ḥ. A. al-Ḥarīrī, Dammām 1995
Sivan, E., *Radical Islam: medieval theology and modern politics*, New Haven and London 1985
'Sunni radicalism in the Middle East and the Iranian revolution', *International Journal of Middle East Studies*, 21 (1989)
Sīvāsī, ʿAbd ül-Mejīd (d. 1049/1639), *Durar-i ʿaqāʾid* (in Turkish), ms. Istanbul, Süleymaniye, Mihrimah Sultan 300
Sīwāsī (d. 803/1400f.), *ʿUyūn al-tafsīr*, ms. Princeton, Yahuda 5,766
Sluglett, P., and M. Farouk-Sluglett, 'The precarious monarchy: Britain, Abd al-Aziz ibn Saud and the establishment of the Kingdom of Hijaz, Najd and its Dependencies, 1925–32', in T. Niblock (ed.), *State, society and economy in Saudi Arabia*, London 1982
Smith, G. R., 'The Omani manuscript collection at Muscat', *Arabian Studies*, 4 (1978)
Snouck Hurgronje, C., *Mekka*, The Hague 1888–9
Sourdel, D., *Le vizirat ʿabbāside*, Damascus 1959–60
Spectorsky, S. A., *Chapters on marriage and divorce: responses of Ibn Ḥanbal and Ibn Rāhwayh*, Austin 1993
Stern, S. M., *Studies in early Ismāʿīlism*, Jerusalem and Leiden 1983
Stewart, C., *et al.*, *General catalogue of Arabic manuscripts at the Institut Mauritanien de Recherche Scientifique*, Urbana and Nouakchott 1992
Storey, C. A., A. J. Arberry and R. Levy, *Catalogue of the Arabic manuscripts in the Library of the India Office*, vol. 2, London 1930–40
Strothmann, R., 'Die Literatur der Zaiditen', *Der Islam*, 2 (1911)
Das Staatsrecht der Zaiditen, Strasburg 1912
Stroumsa, S., 'The beginnings of the Muʿtazila reconsidered', *Jerusalem Studies in Arabic and Islam*, 13 (1990)
Ṣuʿaytirī (d. 815/1412), *Taʿlīq*, ms. Berlin, Glaser 145
Ṣubḥī, A. M., *Zaydiyya*, Cairo 1984
Subkī, Tāj al-Dīn (d. 771/1370), *Qāʿida fī ʾl-jarḥ waʾl-taʿdīl*, ed. A. Abū Ghudda, Aleppo 1968
al-Sayf al-mashhūr fī sharḥ ʿAqīdat Abī Manṣūr, ms. Istanbul, Süleymaniye, Hacı Mahmud 1,329
Ṭabaqāt al-Shāfiʿiyya al-kubrā, ed. M. M. al-Ṭanāḥī and ʿA. M. al-Ḥulw, Cairo 1964–76
Subkī, Taqī al-Dīn al- (d. 756/1355), *Fatāwā*, Cairo 1355–6
Sukkarī (d. 275/888f.), *Sharḥ Ashʿār al-Hudhaliyyīn*, ed. ʿA. A. Farrāj, Cairo 1965
Sukkarī, ʿĀdil al-, *al-Amr biʾl-maʿrūf waʾl-nahy ʿan al-munkar ʿinda ʾl-uṣūliyyīn*, Cairo 1993
Sulamī (d. 412/1021), *Ṭabaqāt al-Ṣūfiyya*, ed. N. Shurayba, Cairo 1969

'Uyūb al-nafs wa-mudāwātuhā, published with his *Jawāmi' ādāb al-Ṣūfiyya*, ed. E. Kohlberg, Jerusalem 1976

Sulaymān, Muḥammad, *Min akhlāq al-'ulamā'*, Cairo 1353

Sulaymān ibn Yakhlaf al-Mazātī (d. 471/1078f.), *Tuḥaf*, ms. Bārūnī, Kābāw, Jabal Nafūsa

Ṣūlī (d. 335/947), *Akhbār al-Rāḍī bi'llāh wa'l-Muttaqī lillāh*, ed. J. Heyworth Dunne, Cairo 1935; trans. M. Canard, Algiers 1946–50

Sunāmī (*fl.* early eighth/fourteenth century), *Niṣāb al-iḥtisāb*, ed. M. Y. 'Izz al-Dīn, Riyāḍ 1982; trans. Izzi Dien, see: Izzi Dien, *Theory*

Sūrābādī (494/1101), *Tafsīr-i Qur'ān-i karīm*, n.p. 1345 sh.

Suyūṭī (d. 911/1505), *al-Durr al-manthūr*, Cairo 1314

Jam' al-jawāmi', n.p. 1970–

al-Jāmi' al-ṣaghīr, Cairo 1954

Ṭabaqāt al-mufassirīn, ed. 'A. M. 'Umayr, Cairo 1976

Swartz, M. L. (ed. and trans.), *Ibn al-Jawzī's Kitāb al-quṣṣāṣ wa'l-mudhakkirīn*, Beirut 1971

'The rules of the popular preaching in twelfth-century Baghdad, according to Ibn al-Jawzî', in G. Makdisi *et al.*, *Prédication et propagande au Moyen Age: Islam, Byzance, Occident*, Paris 1983

Ṭabarānī (d. 360/971), *Du'ā'*, ed. M. 'A. 'Aṭā, Beirut 1993

al-Mu'jam al-kabīr, ed. Ḥ. 'A. al-Salafī, n.p. *c.* 1984–6

Ṭabarī (d. 310/923), *Jāmi' al-bayān*, Cairo 1323–9

Tafsīr, ed. M. M. and A. M. Shākir, Cairo n.d. (scholarly edition of the first part of the preceding work)

Tahdhīb al-āthār, ed. M. M. Shākir, Cairo 1982

Ta'rīkh al-rusul wa'l-mulūk, ed. M. J. de Goeje *et al.*, Leiden 1879–1901

Ṭabarī, 'Imād al-Dīn (?) (*fl.* second half of the seventh/thirteenth century), *Mu'taqad al-Imāmiyya* (in Persian), ed. M. T. Dānishpazhūh, Tehran 1961

Ṭabarsī, see: Ṭabrisī

Ṭabrisī (d. 548/1153), *Jawāmi' al-jāmi'*, Beirut 1985

Majma' al-bayān fi tafsīr al-Qur'ān, Qumm 1403

Ṭabrisī, Aḥmad ibn 'Alī al- (*fl.* early sixth/twelfth century), *Iḥtijāj*, Najaf 1966

Ṭabrisī, 'Alī ibn al-Ḥasan al- (*fl.* later sixth/twelfth century), *Mishkāt al-anwār*, Najaf 1965

Taeschner, F., *Zünfte und Bruderschaften im Islam: Texte zur Geschichte der Futuwwa*, Zurich and Munich 1979

Taftazānī (d. 793/1390), *Sharḥ ḥadīth al-Arba'īn al-Nawawī* (*sic*), Istanbul 1316

Sharḥ al-Maqāṣid, ed. 'A. 'Umayra, Beirut 1989

Ṭaḥāwī (d. 321/933) (attrib.), *Fuṣūl fi uṣūl al-dīn*, ms. Princeton, Arabic, Third Series, 288

Talbi, M., 'Kairouan et le malikisme espagnol', in *Etudes d'orientalisme dédiées à la mémoire de Lévi-Provençal*, Paris 1962

Talmon Heller, D., 'The shaykh and the community: popular Ḥanbalite Islam in 12th–13th century Jabal Nablus and Jabal Qasyūn, *Studia Islamica*, 79 (1994)

Tamīmī, Taqī al-Dīn al- (d. 1010/1601), *al-Ṭabaqāt al-saniyya fī tarājim al-Ḥanafiyya*, ed. ʿA. M. al-Ḥulw, Cairo 1970–
Ṭanṭāwī, ʿAlī al-, *Fuṣūl Islāmiyya*, Damascus 1960
Ṭanṭāwī, Muḥammad Sayyid, interview in 'Ṣālūn Oktōbir wa-ḥiwār maʿa faḍīlat al-Muftī', *Oktōbir*, year 12, no. 601, 1 May 1988
Tanūkhī (d. 384/994), *al-Faraj baʿd al-shidda*, Cairo 1955
Nishwār al-muḥāḍara, ed. ʿA. al-Shāljī, Beirut 1971–3
Taqaddusī Nīyā, Khusraw, *Dars-hāyī az amr bah maʿrūf wa nahy az munkar*, Qumm 1375 sh.
Ṭāshköprīzāde (d. 968/1561), *Miftāḥ al-saʿāda*, ed. K. K. Bakrī and ʿA. Abū 'l-Nūr, Cairo 1968
al-Shaqāʾiq al-Nuʿmāniyya, ed. A. S. Furat, Istanbul 1985
Ṭāshkubrīzāda, Taşköprüzade, see: Ṭāshköprīzāde
Ṭayyibī Shabistarī, Aḥmad (d. 1350 sh. /1971), *Taqīya; amr bah maʿrūf wa nahy az munkar*, Tehran 1350 sh.
Teufel, J. K., *Eine Lebensbeschreibung des Scheichs ʿAlī-i Hamadānī*, Leiden 1962
Thaʿālibī (d. 873/1468f.), *al-Jawāhir al-ḥisān*, ed. ʿA. al-Ṭālibī, Algiers 1985
Thaʿlabī (d. 427/1035), *al-Kashf wa'l-bayān fī tafsīr āy al-Qurʾān*, ms. British Library, Add. 19,926
Qiṣaṣ al-anbiyāʾ, Beirut n.d.
Thaqafī Tihrānī, Muḥammad (d. 1404/1983f.), *Rawān-i jadīd*, Tehran n.d.
Theodore Abū Qurra (*fl.* later second/eighth century), *Mīmar fī wujūd al-khāliq wa'l-dīn al-qawīm*, ed. L. Cheikho, *al-Mashriq*, 15 (1912)
Thomas, D., *A long time burning: the history of literary censorship in England*, London 1969
Tabghūrīn al-Malshūṭī (second half of the fifth/eleventh century), *Uṣūl al-dīn*, see: Ennami, 'Studies in Ibāḍism'
Tiflīsī, Ḥubaysh ibn Ibrāhīm al- (writing 558/1163), *Wujūh-i Qurʾān*, ed. M. Muḥaqqiq, Tehran 1340 sh.
Tihrānī, ʿAlī, *Amr ba-maʿrūf wa nahy az munkar dar Islām*, Mashhad n.d.
Tirmidhī (d. 279/892), *Ṣaḥīḥ*, ed. ʿI. ʿU. al-Daʿʿās, Ḥimṣ 1965–8
Töllner, H., *Die türkischen Garden am Kalifenhof von Samarra*, Walldorf-Hessen 1971
Tsafrir, N., 'The spread of the Ḥanafī school in the western regions of the ʿAbbāsid caliphate up to the end of the third century AH', Princeton Ph.D. 1993
Ṭūfī, Najm al-Dīn al- (d. 716/1316), *Sharḥ al-Arbaʿīn ḥadīthan al-Nawawiyya*, ms. Princeton, Yahuda 3,004
Sharḥ Mukhtaṣar al-Rawḍa, ed. ʿA. ʿA. al-Turkī, Beirut 1987–9
Tujībī (d. 419/1028), *Mukhtaṣar min Tafsīr al-imām al-Ṭabarī*, Cairo 1970–1
Ṭuʿma, S. H. al-, 'al-Makhṭūṭāt al-ʿArabiyya fī khizānat Āl al-Marʿashī fī Karbalāʾ', *al-Mawrid*, 3, no. 4 (1974)
Ṭurayḥī (d. 1085/1674f.), *Majmaʿ al-baḥrayn*, ed. A. al-Ḥusaynī, Najaf and Tehran 1381–95
Turnbull, C. M., *The mountain people*, New York 1972
Turner, R. L., *A comparative dictionary of the Indo-Aryan languages*, London 1966

Ṭurṭūshī (d. 520/1126), *al-Ḥawādith wa'l-bida'*, ed. ʿA. Turkī, Beirut 1990
Sirāj al-mulūk, Cairo 1935
Ṭūsī, Abū Jaʿfar al- (d. 460/1067), *Amālī*, Najaf 1964
Fihrist, ed. M. Ṣ. Āl Baḥr al-ʿUlūm, Najaf 1960
Iqtiṣād, Qumm 1400
al-Jumal wa'l-ʿuqūd, ed. M. W. Khurāsānī, Mashhad 1347 sh.
Nihāya, Beirut 1970
Rijāl, ed. M. Ṣ. Āl Baḥr al-ʿUlūm, Najaf 1961
Tahdhīb al-aḥkām, ed. Ḥ. M. al-Kharsān, Najaf 1958–62
Tamhīd al-uṣūl, ed. A. Mishkāt al-Dīnī, Tehran 1362 sh.
al-Tibyān fī tafsīr al-Qur'ān, Najaf 1957–63
Ṭūsī, Naṣīr al-Dīn al- (d. 672/1274), *Tajrīd al-iʿtiqād*, *apud* al-ʿAllāma al-Ḥillī (d. 726/1325), *Kashf al-murād*, Beirut 1979
Twitchett, D., *The writing of official history under the T'ang*, Cambridge 1992
Tyan, E., *Histoire de l'organisation judiciaire en pays d'Islam*, Leiden 1960
ʿUbādī, ʿAfīf al-Dīn al-Maṭarī al- (d. 765/1363f.), *Dhayl Ṭabaqāt al-fuqahā' al-Shāfiʿiyyīn*, see: Ibn Kathīr, *Ṭabaqāt*
Ubbī (d. 827/1423f.), *Ikmāl Ikmāl al-Muʿlim*, ed. M. S. Hāshim, Beirut 1994
Ujhūrī, ʿAbd al-Barr al- (later eleventh/seventeenth century), *Fatḥ al-qarīb*, ms. Princeton, Yahuda 5,504
ʿUlaymī, Mujīr al-Dīn al- (d. *c.* 927/1521), *al-Manhaj al-aḥmad fī tarājim aṣḥāb al-imām Aḥmad*, ed. ʿA. al-Arnā'ūṭ *et al.*, Beirut 1997
al-Uns al-jalīl bi-ta'rīkh al-Quds wa'l-Khalīl, Najaf 1968
ʿUmāra, Muḥammad, *al-Islām wa-ḥuqūq al-insān*, Cairo and Beirut 1989
ʿUmāra, Muḥammad (ed.), *Rasā'il al-ʿadl wa'l-tawḥīd*, Cairo 1971
ʿUmarī, ʿAlī ibn Abī 'l-Ghanā'im al- (fifth/eleventh century), *al-Majdī fī ansāb al-Ṭālibiyyīn*, ed. A. al-Mahdawī al-Dāmghānī, Qumm 1409
Umayya ibn Abī 'l-Ṣalt (d. *c.* 10/631), *Dīwān*, ed. ʿA. al-Saṭlī, Damascus 1974
Upāsakajanālaṅkāra, ed. H. Saddhatissa, London 1965
ʿUqbānī (d. 871/1467), *Tuḥfat al-nāẓir*, ed. A. Chenoufi, *Bulletin d'Etudes Orientales*, 19 (1965–6)
Urbach, E. E., *The Sages: their concepts and beliefs*, Cambridge, Mass. and London 1975
Uri, J., *Bibliothecae Bodleianae codicum manuscriptorum orientalium catalogus*, first part, Oxford 1787
Urvoy, D., 'La pensée d'Ibn Tūmart', *Bulletin d'Etudes Orientales*, 27 (1974)
ʿUrwa ibn al-Ward (sixth century AD), *Dīwān*, ed. ʿA. al-Mulūḥī, n.p. 1966
ʿUtbī (d. 255/869), *Mustakhraja*, see: Ibn Rushd, *Bayān*
ʿUthmān, Muḥammad Fatḥī, *Min uṣūl al-fikr al-siyāsī al-Islāmī*, Beirut 1979
Vānī Meḥmed Efendi (?) (d. 1096/1684f.), *Risāla-i durar-i ghawwāṣ* (in Arabic), ms. Istanbul, Süleymaniye, Kasidecizade 663
Vassie, R. (ed.), *A classified handlist of Arabic manuscripts acquired since 1912*, London 1995–
Veccia Vaglieri, L., and R. Rubinacci, *Scritti scelti di al-Ghazālī*, Turin 1970

Vehbī, Meḥmed (d. 1368–9/1949), *Khulāṣat al-bayān* (in Turkish), Istanbul 1341–3

Viguera Molins, M. J., 'La censura de costumbres en el *Tanbīh al-ḥukkām* de Ibn al-Munāṣif (1168–1223)', in Instituto Hispano-Árabe de Cultura, *Actas de las II Jornadas de Cultura Árabe e Islamica (1980)*, Madrid 1985

Vogl, D., 'The other side of Paradise: race relations and the minority community at Princeton', *The Princeton Eclectic*, Fall 1993

Voll, J., 'The non-Wahhābī Ḥanbalīs of eighteenth century Syria', *Der Islam*, 49 (1972)

Voorhoeve, P., *Handlist of Arabic manuscripts in the Library of the University of Leiden*, Leiden 1957

Wahba, Ḥ. (d. 1387/1967), *Jazīrat al-ʿArab fī 'l-qarn al-ʿishrīn*, fourth edition, Cairo 1961

Khamsūn ʿāman fī jazīrat al-ʿArab, Cairo 1960

Wāḥidī (d. 468/1076), *Asbāb nuzūl al-Qurʾān*, ed. A. Ṣaqr, Cairo 1969

Tafsīr al-basīṭ, ms. Istanbul, Nuru Osmaniye 240

al-Wajīz fī tafsīr al-kitāb al-ʿazīz, ed. Ṣ. ʿA. Dāwūdī, Damascus and Beirut 1995

al-Wasīṭ fī tafsīr al-Qurʾān al-majīd, ed. ʿA. A. ʿAbd al-Mawjūd *et al.*, Beirut 1994

Wāʾil ibn Ayyūb (second/eighth-century), *Nasab al-Islām*, see: Kāshif, *Siyar*

Wāʿiẓ-i Balkhī, Ṣafī al-Dīn (writing 610/1213f.), *Faḍāʾil-i Balkh*, ed. ʿA. Ḥabībī, Tehran 1350 sh.

Wakīʿ (d. 306/918), *Akhbār al-quḍāt*, ed. ʿA. M. al-Marāghī, Cairo 1947–50

Walzer, M., *Just and unjust wars*, New York 1992

Wansharīsī (d. 914/1508), *al-Miʿyār al-muʿrib*, ed. M. Ḥajjī *et al.*, Rabat 1981

Wāqidī (d. 207/823), *Maghāzī*, ed. M. Jones, London 1966

Ward, B. A. al-, *Aʿlām al-ʿIrāq al-ḥadīth*, Baghdad 1978–

Warjlānī (d. 570/1174f.), *Dalīl*, Cairo 1306

Watt, W. M., *The formative period of Islamic thought*, Edinburgh 1973

'Was Wāṣil a Khārijite?', in R. Gramlich (ed.), *Islamwissenschaftliche Abhandlungen: Fritz Meier zum sechzigsten Geburtstag*, Wiesbaden 1974

Weismann, I., 'Saʿid Hawwa: the making of a radical Muslim thinker in modern Syria', *Middle Eastern Studies*, 29 (1993)

'Saʿid Hawwa and Islamic revivalism in Baʿthist Syria', *Studia Islamica*, 85 (1997)

Wellhausen, J., *Die religiös-politischen Oppositionsparteien im alten Islam*, Berlin 1901

Wenner, M. W., *Modern Yemen 1918–1966*, Baltimore 1967

Wensinck, A. J., *The Muslim creed*, Cambridge 1932

'The refused dignity', in T. W. Arnold and R. A. Nicholson (eds.), *A volume of Oriental studies presented to Edward G. Browne*, Cambridge 1922

Wensinck, A. J., *et al.*, *Concordance et indices de la tradition musulmane*, Leiden 1936–88

White, C., *Christian friendship in the fourth century*, Cambridge 1992

Wieber, R., *Das Schachspiel in der arabischen Literatur von den Anfängen bis zur zweiten Hälfte des 16. Jahrhunderts*, Walldorf-Hessen 1972
Wilkinson, J. C., 'Bio-bibliographical background to the crisis period in the Ibāḍī Imāmate of Oman', *Arabian Studies*, 3 (1976)
'The Ibāḍī *imāma*', *Bulletin of the School of Oriental and African Studies*, 39 (1976)
The Imamate tradition of Oman, Cambridge 1987
'The Omani manuscript collection at Muscat', *Arabian Studies*, 4 (1978)
William of Auxerre (d. AD 1231), *Summa aurea*, ed. J. Ribaillier, Paris and Rome 1980–7
Williams, R., *Jaina yoga: a survey of the mediaeval śrāvakācāras*, London 1963
Winder, R. B., *Saudi Arabia in the nineteenth century*, London 1965
Woodward, F. L., *et al.*, *Pāli Tipitakaṁ concordance*, London 1952–
Wörterbuch der klassichen arabischen Sprache, Wiesbaden 1970–
Wynne, J. J. (ed.), *The great encyclical letters of Pope Leo XIII*, New York 1903
Yāfiʿī (d. 768/1367), *Mirʾāt al-janān*, Hyderabad 1337–9
Yaḥyā ibn Ḥamza, al-Muʾayyad (d. 749/1348f.), *al-Shāmil li-ḥaqāʾiq al-adilla*, ms. Leiden, Or. 2,587
Tasfiyat al-qulūb, Cairo 1985
Yaḥyā ibn Muḥammad ibn Mūsā, Muḥyī ʾl-Dīn Abū Zakariyyāʾ (= Yaḥyā ibn Abī ʾl-Khayr al-ʿImrānī (d. 558/1163)?), *Mukhtaṣar al-Iḥyāʾ*, ms. Bankipore, Arabic 841
Yaḥyā ibn Saʿīd (d. 689/1290), *al-Jāmiʿ lil-sharāʾiʿ*, *apud Silsilat al-yanābīʿ al-fiqhiyya*, Beirut 1990, vol. 9: *al-Jihād*
Yaḥyā ibn Sallām (d. 200/815), *Taṣārīf*, ed. H. Shalabī, Tunis 1979
Yaḥyā ibn ʿUmar (d. 289/902), *Aḥkām al-sūq*, in M. ʿA. Makkī, 'Kitāb aḥkām al-sūq li-Yaḥyā ibn ʿUmar al-Andalusī', *Revista del Instituto Egipcio de Estudios Islámicos en Madrid*, 4 (1956)
Yaʿqūb ibn Seyyid ʿAlī (Seyyid ʿAlīzāde Yaʿqūb) (d. 931/1524f.), *Sharḥ Shirʿat al-Islām*, Istanbul 1326
Yaʿqūbī (d. 284/897f.), *Taʾrīkh*, ed. M. T. Houtsma, Leiden 1883
Yāqūt (d. 626/1229), *Muʿjam al-buldān*, ed. F. Wüstenfeld, Leipzig 1866–73
Yāsīn, Muḥammad Nuʿaym, *al-Jihād: mayādīnuhu wa-asālībuhu*, Amman 1978
Yassini, A. Al-, *Religion and state in the Kingdom of Saudi Arabia*, Boulder and London 1985
Yçe de Chebir (writing AD 1462), 'Brebiario çunní', in *Memorial histórico español*, published by the Real Academia de la Historia, vol. 5, Madrid 1853
Young, T., 'Analogical reasoning and easy rescue cases', *Journal of Philosophical Research*, 18 (1993)
Yūsī (d. 1102/1691), *Muḥāḍarāt*, ed. M. Ḥajjī, Rabat 1976
Yūsuf Khān, Mīrzā, Mustashār al-Dawla (d. 1313/1895f.), *Yak kalima*, ed. Ṣ. Sajjādī, Tehran 1364 sh.
Ẓahīr al-Dīn Marʿashī (ninth/fifteenth century), *Tārīkh-i Gīlān wa-Daylamistān*, ed. M. Sutūda, Tehran 1347 sh.

Zajączkowski, A., *Le Traité arabe Mukaddima d'Abou-l-Lait as-Samarkandī en version mamelouk-kiptchak*, Warsaw 1962
Zajjāj (d. 311/923), *Maʿānī al-Qurʾān wa-iʿrābuhu*, ed. ʿA. ʿA. Shalabī, Beirut and Sidon 1973–4
Zamakhsharī (d. 538/1144), *Kashshāf*, Beirut 1947
al-Minhāj fī uṣūl al-dīn, ed. and trans. S. Schmidtke, *A Muʿtazilite creed of az-Zamaḫšarî*, Stuttgart 1997
Zaman, M. Q., *Religion and politics under the early ʿAbbāsids*, Leiden 1997
Zammār (writing 1329/1911), *al-Ḥukm wa'l-intiẓām*, Aleppo n.d.
Zanjānī, ʿAbbās ʿAlī ʿAmīd, 'Ḥaqq al-mushāraka fī ṣiyāghat al-niẓām al-siyāsī wa'l-ijtimāʿī', in *Ḥuqūq al-insān fī 'l-Islām: maqālāt al-Muʾtamar al-khāmis lil-fikr al-Islāmī*, Tehran 1987
Zarzūr, ʿA., *al-Ḥākim al-Jushamī wa-manhajuhu fī tafsīr al-Qurʾān*, n.p. n.d.
Zayd, ʿA. M., *Muʿtazilat al-Yaman*, Ṣanʿāʾ and Beirut 1981
Tayyārāt Muʿtazilat al-Yaman fī 'l-qarn al-sādis al-hijrī, Ṣanʿāʾ 1997
Zaydān, ʿAbd al-Karīm, *al-Mufaṣṣal fī aḥkām al-marʾa wa'l-bayt al-Muslim*, Beirut 1993
Uṣūl al-daʿwa, Baghdad 1968
Zayd ibn ʿAlī (d. 122/740) (attrib.), *Majmūʿ al-fiqh*, ed. E. Griffini, Milan 1919
Zayn al-Dīn, Muḥammad Amīn (d. 1419/1998), *Kalimat al-taqwā*, Qumm 1413–14
Zihdāzī (or Zihdārī) (early eighth/fourteenth century), *Īḍāḥ taraddudāt al-Sharāʾiʿ*, ed. M. al-Rajāʾī, Qumm 1408
Zilfi, M. C., *The politics of piety: the Ottoman ulema in the postclassical age (1600–1800)*, Minneapolis 1988
Ziriklī, K. al-, *Aʿlām*, Beirut 1979
Zubayr ibn Bakkār (d. 256/870), *al-Akhbār al-Muwaffaqiyyāt*, ed. S. M. al-ʿĀnī, Baghdad 1972
Jamharat nasab Quraysh wa-akhbārihā, ed. M. M. Shākir, Cairo 1381
Zurqānī, ʿAbd al-Bāqī al- (d. 1099/1688), *Sharḥ* to the *Mukhtaṣar* of Khalīl (d. 767/1365), Cairo 1307

POSTSCRIPT

To 236 note 69:
The work of Ḥusayn ibn Aḥmad ibn Yaʿqūb is published (ed. ʿA. M. al-Ḥibshī, Ṣanʿāʾ 1996).

To 396 note 19:
The forthcoming study mentioned here is P. Crone and F. Zimmermann, *The epistle of Sālim ibn Dhakwān*, Oxford 2001.

To 478 note 73:
A more striking example is found in the Turkish translation of a letter written by imam Yaḥyā to the Ottoman governor in 1324/1906. Here he swears that he is not seeking power (*riyāset dāʿiyesinde değilim*), and that he has no ambition beyond forbidding wrong (*emr-i maʿrūf ve nehy-i münkerden başka emelimiz yokdur*). See (Meḥmed) Memdūḥ (Pasha) (d. 1343/1925), *Yemen ıṣlāḥātı*, Istanbul 1325 (*mālī*), 104.4, drawn to my attention by Şükrü Hanioğlu.

INDEX

This index includes thematic entries, many of which will be found as sub-entries grouped together under "forbidding wrong" and "forbidding wrong, duty of." The former deals with what one is to forbid, how, and to whom. The latter treats questions of obligation. Wherever there is a doctrinal issue at stake, with divergent opinions, these entries are broken down by the various sects and schools in the manner used throughout the book. Note especially that, according to this arrangement, modern developments in Imāmī Shīʿism are listed under "modern developments," not under "Imāmīs."

holy war (*jihād*) and forbidding wrong, 476, 490f., 498, 582
biographical literature, 3, 6f., 11, 52 n. 39, 73
Ghazzālī, 433, 441
Ḥanafīs, 313, 325, 326
Ḥanbalites, 152, 166, 171, 174f., 179
Ibāḍīs, 401
Imāmīs, 252 n. 2, 301
Koran and exegesis, 14, 20f., 24 n. 45, 30
Mālikīs, 380, 385 n. 219
modern developments, 517 n. 77, 536, 538, 543 n. 263
Muʿtazilites, 198 n. 21
Shāfiʿites, 341
traditions, 38f., 228
Zaydīs, 228f., 233 n. 39, 234 n. 45, 237 n. 72
see also arms/armed conflict; martyrdom; violence
homes
entering private homes, 80–2, 94, 99f., 117, 139, 178 n. 90, 200, 230, 239, 245, 309 n. 14, 380, 381, 413 n. 147, 414, 417f., 436, 438, 454 n. 185, 480f., 539 n. 236, 556, 558
forbidding wrong in own home, 93f., 526, 548 n. 300
see also family; household; kin; privacy
honesty, *see* probity
hospitality, 372 n. 110, 444f.
household (forbidding members of household), 445, 529
see also family; homes; kin; slaves; tenants
Hūd ibn Muḥakkam (3rd/9th cent.), 23 n. 44, 402 n. 59
Ḥudhayfa ibn al-Yamān (d. 36/656f.), 52, 71, 102 n. 157, 104 n. 173
ḥudūd, *see* set punishments
Ḥujr ibn ʿAdī (d. 51/671f.), 477
human rights, 512f., 532, 592f.
hunting, *see* animals
Ḥuraymilāʾ, 167
Ḥurr al-ʿĀmilī (d. 1104/1693), 295 n. 282, 297 n. 303, 299 n. 312
Ḥusayn, Aḥmad, 524
Ḥusayn ibn ʿAlī (d. 61/680), 118, 171f., 209, 226 n. 175, 231, 259 n. 49, 260, 536, 552
Ḥusayn ibn ʿAlī (d. 169/786), 232
husbands (forbidding husbands), 95, 431f., 482, 519 n. 97, 521, 539 n. 236
see also family; wives
Ḥusn (slave-girl of Ibn Ḥanbal), 109, 110 n. 222
Hussain, Shaukat, 512, 513 n. 54
Ibāḍīs, 393–426, 568 n. 37
forbidding wrong, 19 n. 23, 28 n. 71, 47 n. 9, 48, 393–426, 470, 471, 478, 483, 484, 486, 487, 490 n. 173, 512, 549 n. 307, 588
non-Ibāḍī influence, 401 nn. 49 and 53, 419f.
traditions, 7 n. 18, 412, 413 n. 148, 416 n. 175, 420, 423 n. 230, 515 n. 61
see also Ghazzālī; Nukkārīs; Nukkāth; Yaʿrubī imams
Ibn ʿAbbād al-Rundī (d. 792/1390), 466
Ibn ʿAbbās (d. 68/687f.), 23 n. 43, 24 n. 47, 28, 30 n. 77, 43, 54, 55, 80, 487
Ibn ʿAbd al-Barr (d. 463/1071), 31 n. 85, 357 n. 1
Ibn ʿAbd al-Hādī (d. 744/1343), 159f.
Ibn ʿAbd al-Raʾūf (writer on *ḥisba*), 369 n. 78
Ibn ʿAbd al-Wahhāb, Muḥammad (d. 1206/1792), 166–70, 173f., 179
Ibn ʿAbdūn (later 5th/11th cent.), 369 n. 78
Ibn ʿAbdūs, Naṣrallāh (d. before 600/1204), 149 n. 33, 500
Ibn Abī ʿAqīl (4th/10th cent.), 270 n. 115
Ibn Abī Dhiʾb (d. 159/775f.), 56, 58 n. 80, 63, 80, 382
Ibn Abī ʾl-Ḥadīd (d. 656/1258), 218–23, 225 n. 165, 304, 393, 566
Ibn Abī Ḥassān al-Yaḥṣubī (d. 227/841f.), 385 n. 218
Ibn Abī Khālid (unidentified), 99 n. 126
Ibn Abī ʾl-Majd (6th/12th cent.?), 264, 268, 271, 272, 274, 277, 278 n. 189
Ibn Abī Sharīf al-Maqdisī, Burhān al-Dīn Ibrāhīm (d. 923/1517), 348 n. 72, 353 n. 111, 355 n. 138
Ibn Abī Shayba (d. 235/849), 39 n. 37
Ibn Abī ʿUmar al-Maqdisī (d. 682/1283), 148
Ibn ʿAfāliq al-Aḥsāʾī (d. 1163/1750), 167 n. 13
Ibn al-Amīr al-Ṣanʿānī (d. 1182/1768), 167, 249
Ibn al-Anbārī (d. 328/940), 124 n. 70
Ibn ʿAqīl (d. 513/1119), 87 n. 1, 123, 128, 493
Ibn al-ʿArabī, Abū Bakr (d. 543/1148), 26 n. 58, 30 n. 78, 365–7, 370, 378, 391f., 455 n. 194
Ibn al-ʿArabī, Muḥyī ʾl-Dīn (d. 638/1240), 460 n. 240, 465f.
Ibn ʿArafa (d. 803/1401), 376 n. 137
Ibn al-ʿArīf (d. 536/1141), 464f.

Lightning Source UK Ltd.
Milton Keynes UK
UKOW08f1034270417
300014UK00001B/140/P

9 780521 130936